Cor

An Anthology of Af [illegible] are

Cornerstones

An Anthology of African American Literature

edited by

Melvin Donalson

Pasadena City College/UCLA

St. Martin's Press

New York

Sponsoring editor: Nancy Lyman
Development associate: Susan Cottenden
Managing editor: Patricia Mansfield Phelan
Project editor: Diana M. Puglisi
Production supervisor: Joe Ford
Art director: Lucy Krikorian
Text design: Levavi & Levavi
Cover design: Patricia McFadden
Cover art: Courtesy of Jacob Lawrence and Francine Seders Gallery, Seattle WA

Library of Congress Catalog Card Number: 92-83973

Manufactured in the United States of America.

0 9 8 7 6
f e d c b a

For information, write:
St. Martin's Press, Inc.
175 Fifth Avenue
New York, NY 10010

ISBN: 0-312-09530-9

Acknowledgments

Samuel W. Allen. "Harriet Tubman," "Benin Bronze," and "About Poetry and South Africa." Samuel Allen © 1987. Reprinted with the permission of Samuel Allen.

Maya Angelou. Excerpts from *I Know Why the Caged Bird Sings* by Maya Angelou. Copyright © 1969 by Maya Angelou. Reprinted by permission of Random House, Inc.

Michael Awkward. "The Crookeds with the Straights" by Michael Awkward. Reprinted from *May All Your Fences Have Gates: Essays on the Drama of August Wilson,* edited by Alan Nadel by permission of the University of Iowa Press, copyright 1994 by University of Iowa Press.

Houston A. Baker, Jr. "There Is No More Beautiful Way: Theory and the Poetics of Afro-American Women's Writing." From Houston Baker and Patricia Redmond, eds., *Afro-American Literary Study in the 1990s,* pp. 135–155. Copyright © 1989 University of Chicago Press. Reprinted by permission of The University of Chicago Press and the author.

James Baldwin. "Previous Condition." "Previous Condition" was originally published in COMMENTARY collected in *Going to Meet the Man* © 1965 by James Baldwin. Copyright renewed. Reprinted with permission of the James Baldwin Estate.

Toni Cade Bambara. "A Tender Man" from *The Sea Birds Are Still Alive* by Toni Cade Bambara. Copyright © 1974, 1976, 1977 by Toni Cade Bambara. Reprinted by permission of Random House, Inc.

Acknowledgments and copyrights are continued at the back of the book on pages 990–994, which constitute an extension of the copyright page.

Through the years,
for all of those pre-dawn mornings
when he went to work to support me,
and for all of those late-night discussions
when she encouraged me,
I dedicate this book to my parents,
Wilbert and Dorothy Donalson

Contents

Preface

What Is African American Literature?

Generations of black scholars, critics, and writers have wrestled with the difficult task of defining the unique body of creative and factual writing that is broadly referred to as African American literature. Some have sought to assess the literature on the basis of various literary standards, but these efforts often generate new debates about which standards to apply—standards outside black culture, inside black culture, or somewhere in between. Others have pondered the value and meaning of various labels—such as *Negro, colored, Afro-American, Pan-African, black,* and *black American*—in defining the literature. These debates about standards and labels continue in the 1990s, particularly among academic and political leaders. While enlightening to some extent, they suggest that no single definition of African American literature can possibly satisfy everyone.

Thus, the question remains: *What is African American literature?* As far as this anthology is concerned, the answer is a broad one: African American literature is a body of written and oral works, created by writers who share both a black African heritage and a unique American experience, that defines and celebrates black history and culture. Although this definition of the literature does not clear away the clouds of debate, it will become obvious to readers of *Cornerstones* that African American literature not only reflects that unique American experience but also demands from its audience an intimate, subjective response. Possessing an extraordinary range of tones, topics, and styles, African American literature, whether it speaks gently or screams passionately, challenges and provokes response and action.

Distinguishing Features of the Literature

Among the most distinguishing features of African American literature is its inclusiveness. That is, the literature embraces a wide spectrum of authors and literary genres. In addition to the traditionally recognized genres of poetry, fiction, and drama, African American culture gives equal recognition to literature of the oral tradition and nonfiction prose. Indeed, in black literature, works of the oral tradition and nonfiction are regarded as having influenced the other literary genres.

The Oral Tradition

For nearly four centuries, the oral tradition has served as the creative core of black literature, providing black writers with a rich array of expression. Originating in the oral tradition are the vivid metaphors, sophisticated rhythms, witty double meanings, haunting symbols, resonant repetition, playful improvisation, and other features of African American literature. Similarly, black oral forms have inspired the content, tone, and structure of speeches, sermons, poetry, slave narratives, fiction, and drama, as have the multiple meanings of such black cultural activities as "playing the dozens" and "signifyin."

Black oral forms are especially noted for their representation of multiple meanings, as in the proverbs "The blacker the berry, the sweeter the juice" and "Every shut eye ain't sleep, and every good-bye ain't gone." Handed down over the centuries by generations of African Americans seeking to understand the world, these and other black oral expressions have merged with the written literature in such works as Wallace Thurman's novel *The Blacker the Berry* (1929), Shirlee Haizlip's autobiography *The Sweeter the Juice* (1994), Michael S. Harper and Anthony Walton's poetry anthology *Every Shut Eye Ain't Asleep* (1994), and Itabari Njeri's autobiography *Every Good-bye Ain't Gone* (1991).

The Collective Voice of Nonfiction

While the oral tradition has served as a major creative force in African American literature, it is in nonfiction that the African American experience has been most fully defined and explored by black writers. This genre provides a forum for issues and concerns to find public expression, and through it black writers have addressed the collective struggles of African Americans for centuries in slave narratives, autobiographies, and essays. Whether promoting racial separation (as in Marcus Garvey's "An Appeal to the Conscience of the Black Race to See Itself") or racial integration (Ralph Ellison's "What America Would Be Like without Blacks"), or advocating tolerance of sexual orientation (Ron Simmons's "Some Thoughts on the Challenges Facing Black Gay Intellectuals"), contemporary black nonfiction continues to define the black American experience as well as the dualities of the African American self and community.

The Importance of African American Literature

Perhaps most importantly, African American literature encompasses the breadth of the struggles, achievements, and roles of blacks in shaping American society. As black critic Valerie Smith acknowledges, "The political nature of [the] literature is especially pronounced, given . . . the larger fact that it is created by a people who represent a population that has historically been oppressed" (ix). However, as Smith and other black scholars also stress, despite the difficult or perilous circumstances in which it was created, African American literature goes beyond apology and protest to include an array of works that display their writers' talent, imagination, mastery of black verbal forms and Eurocentric language, and concern with themes both timely and timeless, personal and universal.

In addition, African American literature is important for its celebration of black culture and history, thereby helping to create a sense of racial cohesiveness and solidarity. Some examples from this anthology include Samuel W. Allen's "Harriet Tubman," Robert Hayden's "El-Hajj Malik El-Shabazz," and Jay Wright's "Benjamin Banneker Helps to Build a City"—poems that appraise African American leaders. Similarly, a striking sagacity emanates from the speeches of Frederick Douglass, "What to the Slave Is the Fourth of July?" and Mary McLeod Bethune, "A Century of Progress of Negro Women," as well as in the autobiography of Booker T. Washington, *Up from Slavery,* and the cultural essay by bell hooks, "Revolutionary Black Women." Some selections celebrate black heritage by linking African roots and a Caribbean background with the African American experience—as in Countee Cullen's poem "Heritage" and in Olaudah Equiano's "Interesting Narrative . . ."—while other selections celebrate black culture by showing its resilience under self-scrutiny—the anonymously written folktale "Why Negroes Are Black," Sonia Sanchez's poem "Summer Words of a Sistuh Addict," and Michael Eric Dyson's essay "The Culture of Hip-Hop." Together, the various literary forms of African American literature give us a fuller appreciation of a body of work that honors the social, political, intellectual, and cultural history of African Americans.

Features

The main objective of *Cornerstones*—to serve as a tribute to the scope, diversity, and importance of African American literature—is evident in the book's extensive collection of 161 writings by 99 authors. The book's title is symbolic of the contributions of numerous black writers to the foundation on which the black literary tradition has developed. *Cornerstones* aims, most of all, to be inclusive. To this end, readers will find the following features:

- **Diversity of writers.** The text includes selections from various genres by both recognized authors—such as Frederick Douglass, Charles W. Chesnutt, Langston Hughes, Richard Wright, and Ralph Ellison—and lesser known writers—such as Harriet Jacobs, Pauline Elizabeth Hopkins, Wallace Thurman, and Jess Mowry.

  This anthology also represents several authors of black African descent born outside of the United States whose writing, teaching, scholarship, and political activity have contributed to both the African American literary tradition and black literature worldwide. Coming from a west African or Caribbean background, authors Olaudah Equiano, Phillis Wheatley, Claude McKay, Derek Walcott, Kwame Toure, and Michael Thelwell discuss their experiences with race relations. These selections demonstrate the reciprocal influence of African American culture and other black cultures on the black literature of the world.
- **Variety of genres.** Along with the traditional genres of poetry, fiction, and drama, the text offers nonfiction prose and selections from the oral

tradition. The extensive collection of nonfiction writing—speeches, sermons, autobiographies, cultural and philosophical essays, and literary criticism—reflects a genre to which African American writers have so often turned to convey their experiences and ideas. In addition, *Cornerstones* recognizes the importance of the African American oral tradition, which for centuries has been a source of both creative expression and cultural identity within the black community. Of particular interest here is the role that song lyrics, orations, and folktales have served in popular culture.

- **Balance of gender.** The book acknowledges the importance of black women writers to the African American literary tradition. Despite the impressive output of black women authors, particularly within the past twenty-five years, most anthologies have not emphasized their contributions. *Cornerstones* affirms the creativity of both black women and black men, and thereby encourages an appreciation of both sexes in the development of the literature's various genres.
- **Authors in depth.** The text offers four Focused Studies of African American writers in various genres: Gwendolyn Brooks's poetry, Alice Walker's fiction, August Wilson's drama, and W. E. B. Du Bois's nonfiction prose. The poetry, fiction, and nonfiction sections are accompanied by a critical essay about the writer's work in order to expose students to extended reading and critical analysis of individual writers.

Finally, this anthology aims to demonstrate that, despite individual differences and the political connotations of various terms of description, people of black African descent have shared similar experiences, dilemmas, and aspirations in this country. Thus, the editorial writing in *Cornerstones* uses the terms *African American, black American,* and *black* interchangeably, while the selection authors use a variety of terms—including *Negro, colored,* and *Afro-American*—whose historical or thematic basis contributes to the integrity of their work.

In order to achieve these objectives, *Cornerstones* pursues an eclectic approach to the literature, encouraging students to juxtapose the various forms of the black literary tradition as they survey the selections and develop an awareness of their diversity. The book thus embraces a progressive approach as well, one that, like the literature itself, is not limited by formal literary theories or canonical boundaries. Its extensive representation of African American writers and genres is intended to meet the needs of student readers unfamiliar with the literature as well as those seeking to enhance an existing awareness.

Organization

Cornerstones consists of six parts organized by genre: the oral tradition, poetry, fiction, drama, nonfiction, and literary criticism. Structurally, each part includes an overview of the genre and the part's selections, an extensive collection of writings organized chronologically by the authors' birthdates, and a list of readings. In addition, each selection is preceded by a headnote that gives detailed information about the writer's life and work.

- *Part One, "The Oral Tradition,"* is divided into three sections. "Lyrics" explores the musical forms of the oral tradition, including spirituals, the blues, pop, and rap, whose potent lyrics send emotional, social, and political messages. "Orations: Speeches and Sermons" includes nine selections that show how black speakers of the nineteenth and twentieth centuries have inspired their audiences to reflect and take collective action on important issues. "Folktales" features seven oral works that merge fiction and facts to stimulate, educate, and entertain their audiences.
- *Part Two, "Poetry,"* begins with a Focused Study of Gwendolyn Brooks, including seven of her poems and an essay by noted scholar George Kent. The selections that follow survey the work of twenty-three other African American poets of the eighteenth to the twentieth centuries. A representative sampling of each poet's writings is included.
- *Part Three, "Fiction,"* features a Focused Study of Alice Walker, including three fiction selections and a critical essay by Barbara Christian, along with selections by twenty-seven other writers. The readings in this part include both short stories and excerpts from novels of the nineteenth and twentieth centuries.
- *Part Four, "Drama,"* contains two plays. In addition to the Focused Study of August Wilson's *Fences* and the critical essay by scholar Michael Awkward that accompanies it, Pearl Cleage's *Hospice: A Play in One Act* is included. The two plays offer contrasting perspectives on African American family structures, as well as distinctive uses of language by each playwright.
- *Part Five, "Nonfiction,"* begins with a Focused Study of W. E. B. Du Bois, including three prose pieces and a scholarly essay by critic Marcus Bruce. The part's nonfiction selections are divided into two sections, "Autobiography" and "Cultural and Philosophical Essays," each of which spans the writings of the eighteenth to the twentieth centuries. The six autobiographical pieces explore such issues as slavery, racial segregation, and sexism, while the fourteen essays about culture and philosophy cover a diverse range of interracial and intraracial issues.
- *Part Six, "Literary Criticism and Theory,"* focuses on this increasingly important and controversial area of African American writing. The eight selections by twentieth-century black critics cover developments in the field of literary criticism as well as the ongoing struggle to define and understand African American literature.

The genre-based organization of the book is designed to help students appreciate both the historical development of each genre and the creative diversity among works within each form. The history of various literary movements and themes, such as the Harlem Renaissance and the Black Arts movement, is emphasized in the part overviews, the selection headnotes, and the Focused Studies. In addition, the cultural essays in Part Five and the literary criticism pieces in Part Six help to foster a solid understanding of the important eras in the history of African American literature.

Finally, as the title of this anthology suggests, the ever-growing body of African American literature rests on a sturdy base of talented authors. Unfortunately, no one anthology can possibly include all of the authors and writings that make up that foundation. Nor can one volume accommodate all goals that an instructor or student might desire in a given course of study. However, *Cornerstones* offers an extensive collection of authors, forms, and works that demonstrate the vitality and diversity of African American literature. As such, the text serves as a comprehensive tool for guiding students through a rich and multifaceted body of literary expression.

Acknowledgments

In putting together such a comprehensive anthology as *Cornerstones,* I am indebted to the work of many other scholars who have compiled collections that honor the African American literary tradition. In addition, I am grateful for the invaluable support and encouragement of my friends and colleagues at UCLA, whose input inspired my organization and approach to this book: Bonnie Lisle, Randy Woodland, Rick Creese, Esha De, Joseph Giangello, Teshome Gabriel, Lisa Thompson, Reggie Waddell, Jami Jesek, and, especially, Perrin Reid. I also owe thanks to my friends and colleagues at Pasadena City College for their insightful critiques of the manuscript: Robert Foreman, Judith Branzburg, Roger Marheine, Mark McQueen, Ron Lanyi, and, especially, Phil Pastras. For providing suggestions for revisions that contributed to the book's final shape, I am indebted to Marcus Bruce, Michael Thelwell, Jess Mowry, Lupe Cadiz, and Saundra Shannon.

I wish to give special thanks to the many teachers and scholars who reviewed this manuscript; their incisive comments, criticisms, and suggestions have greatly improved this book: William L. Andrews, University of Kansas; Jeffry P. Berry, Adrian College; Owen E. Brady, Clarkson University; Lelia O. V. H. Crowders, Northern Virginia Community College; Donald J. Fay, Kennesaw State College; Ruth A. Hatcher, Washtenaw Community College; Robert Hemenway, University of Kentucky; Sue Houchins, Pitzer College; Sharon Howard, The Shomberg Center for Research in Black Culture; Geta LeSeur, University of Missouri–Columbia; Joyce Middleton, University of Rochester; Frank Moorer, Iowa State University; Philip Pastras, Pasadena City College; Phillip M. Richards, University of North Carolina at Chapel Hill; Joseph T. Skerrett Jr., University of Massachusetts at Amherst; C. Jan Swearingen, University of Texas at Arlington; and Kenneth W. Warren, University of Chicago.

My appreciation also goes to Carolyn Walthour, for her exceptional research and organizational skills and keen observations, and to Diane Kraut, for managing the challenging task of acquiring permissions. I am indebted to my development editor at St. Martin's Press, Diane Tasca, for her expertise in shaping the book's focus and coherence. I am also grateful to the many people at St. Martin's who worked tirelessly on this project—Susan Cottenden, Barbara Heinssen, Meg Spilleth, Erica Appel, and Diana Puglisi—for their energy, enthusiasm, and professionalism. To my wife, Beverly Tate, I owe special thanks; many difficult decisions about this project were made with her knowledgeable perspectives.

Finally, for their ongoing support of this endeavor and their faith in me, I am deeply indebted to Mike Rose, Cathy Pusateri, and Nancy Lyman.

Melvin Donalson

Work Cited

Smith, Valerie. *African American Writers.* New York: Collier, 1993.

Cornerstones

An Anthology of African American Literature

PART ONE

THE ORAL TRADITION

OVERVIEW

The Cradle of Literature

The African American oral tradition is like an endlessly rocking cradle. For centuries, it has shaped and reshaped the culture, keeping it in touch with the past while also renewing it. The oral tradition includes speech patterns, folktales, myths, legends, proverbs, anecdotes, riddles, songs, and orations, some of which predate written African American literature. It is also a prime source of black collective identity in this country—a matrix of expressions, motifs, and intonations that blacks, artists and nonartists alike, draw on to express themselves. Rocking in the cradle of the oral tradition, an ordinary black person could become an educator, entertainer, gossip, storyteller, and oracle—a self-appointed griot asserting an individual black voice yet participating in the collective black community.

Survival in the New World

Early on in the New World, the oral tradition became a survival strategy, allowing African Americans to maintain some control over their lives. Historically, an established oral tradition permeated west African cultures, where verbalization, vocal modulation, and spontaneity were integral factors in communication. When blacks reached American shores in the seventeenth century, they carried with them the oral forms that would be developed, modified, and merged within the new environment.

The west African origins of oral tradition bequeathed blacks a heritage of glory beyond the manacles of the New World. Connecting generations of African Americans, the oral tradition was validated and sustained on rural meeting grounds and in religious ceremonies, and later on urban street corners and in academic institutions. Vital among the masses of African Americans, the oral tradition touched the lives of the African American elite as well. Whether spontaneous or formalized, a philosophical grunt or a sentimental holler, the oral tradition has served as a carthartic declaration of self and an affirmation of community.

The Oral Tradition and Black Literature

It is not surprising that the African American oral tradition has survived across geographical, class, and educational lines, for it has been a unifying force among diverse black communities. Just as significantly, it has inspired the black literary imagination. The poetry of Langston Hughes, the fiction of Zora Neale Hurston, and the drama of Pearl Cleage are all rooted in black speech patterns as well as in blues and jazz. The autobiographical narratives of Olaudah Equiano, Malcolm X, and Itabari Njeri all proudly derive from the self-conscious storytelling of the folktale. Similarly, the essays of David

Walker, Martin Delany, Marcus Garvey, and Kwame Toure evoke the urgent tone of the orations delivered by black preachers testifying their faith.

Despite the inspirational and cultural value of the oral tradition, some African Americans have been restrained in their appreciation of it. As blacks of the 1870s to the 1920s struggled to integrate themselves into industrial America, some formally educated middle-class blacks viewed folkways as a negation of the refined self-image they desired to present to white society. Thus the folkways that appeared in the work of Zora Neale Hurston and Langston Hughes, for example, met with criticism from African Americans who condemned the depiction of uncultured and illiterate blacks. In an effort to gain approval by white society, they advocated leaving black folkways behind with the degradation of slavery. Some also sought to censor those vulgar elements in the oral tradition that suggested impropriety and low moral standards. But as black scholar Daryl Dance aptly notes in her folklore collection, "Humor is and always has been largely motivated by the enjoyment of forbidden themes. . . . And thus it is that excessive profanity, sex (especially sodomy, oral-genital sex, homosexuality, and zoophilia), and scatology are among the most popular and mirth-making subjects in Black folklore as well as in folklore generally" (263).

Furthermore, as African American literature confirms, the oral tradition, in all of its admirable and less admirable aspects, represents the distinct creative impulses of generations of black artists. In addition to shaping the literature for centuries, the oral tradition has stimulated black popular culture, and continues to do so today. The songs, art, dances, games, and other amusements that define black popular culture sprang from the oral tradition. By word-of-mouth, the meanings of new expressions and diversions in the popular culture have been passed along.

Mainstream Appropriations of Black Culture

Ironically, since the oral tradition had successfully disseminated the elements of black popular culture in the mainstream, they were easily borrowed by whites, Native Americans, and Spanish-speaking people. In the mid-1800s, for example, whites developed the minstrel show (see p. 462), a type of live entertainment that exploited and exaggerated black cultural forms and materials. In the twentieth century, whites continued to appropriate black cultural expressions for theater, motion pictures, radio, music, and television, often reducing the cultural significance of black idioms, dance, songs, and customs to racial stereotypes.

Fortunately, as late-twentieth-century technology and electronic media have made it easier to preserve and examine various kinds of expressions, African Americans are reclaiming their cultural identity, particularly the unique qualities of the oral tradition. Part One of this anthology considers three forms of the oral tradition within African American culture: song lyrics (including spirituals, the blues, pop lyrics, and rap lyrics), orations, and folktales. These forms of the African American oral tradition have functioned as part of an ethnic identity and have survived absorption by mainstream America. Existing separately but inextricably conjoined, they continue to fulfill various needs within African American culture.

Lyrics

Spirituals

From the seventeenth to the early nineteenth centuries, chants, work songs, and folksongs by anonymous composers offered black singers emotional release from their bondage. Often augmented by dance, foot tapping, and head bobbing, the song could be an individual fancy or a group meditation, an expression of joy or sadness. From these creative expressions sprang the *spirituals*. Mixing the promise of a divine reward with the duty to tolerate everyday injustices, the spirituals served as a bridge between the religious and secular worlds. Appealing to a wider American audience in the late nineteenth century, largely due to the traveling performances of the Fisk University Jubilee Singers, the spirituals revealed the human qualities and emotions of the black experience that were conspicuously absent from the minstrel show icons popular at the time.

Part One includes the lyrics of four anonymously composed spirituals: "Sometimes I Feel Like a Motherless Child," "Go Down Moses," "Steal Away to Jesus," and "Roll, Jordan, Roll." The selections exemplify the emotional range and religious allusions of the spiritual form. They also suggest the ambiguity of the spiritual form, often containing lyrics with overlapping religious and political messages.

The Blues

From the sorrow of the spirituals sprang the *blues*, the musical expression of the experiences of common black people. As Amiri Baraka (LeRoi Jones) observes in *Blues People* (1963), the "shouts" and "hollers" in the fields and the lamentations aboard the middle passage slave ships formed the core of the blues. In the early twentieth century, the blues were popularized through Tin Pan Alley publishers and Ragtime. But it was not until the classical blues appeared in the 1920s that the music was written down, urbanized, recorded as "race records," and appreciated beyond the "folk." Although some blues pieces simmered with sexual euphemisms and images, the blues' greatest potency flowed from its expression of the interplay of pain and ecstasy, of loss and hope.

Part One offers four blues pieces: "St. Louis Blues," by W. C. Handy; "Hard Times Blues," popularized by vocalist Ida Cox; "Mamie's Blues," credited to Jelly Roll Morton; and "Backwater Blues," styled by the legendary Bessie Smith.

Jazz and R & B

The so-called "race records" that captured blues performances were often condemned by the black and nonblack elite but enjoyed measurable popularity with the masses. At the same time, the popularity of *jazz* became infectious. In its infancy, jazz was an exclusively black musical form, but white musicians soon adapted it for their big-band arrangements. The blues and jazz, springing from black folk roots, best represented those African Americans migrating from the rural South to eastern and midwestern cities. The blues carried the memories, sorrow, and pain of the southern legacy, whereas jazz suggested hope and drive in its improvisational, upbeat rhythms.

In a similar way, religious music was transformed in the 1920s and 1930s. Shaking off the mournful veil of the spirituals, *gospel* music encouraged an emotional response bounded only by the singer's spiritual rapture. Nurtured in storefront urban churches and one-room rural meetinghouses by churchgoers, gospel music expressed their uninhibited declarations of joy through body movement, hand-clapping, tambourine playing, and "shouting."

In the late 1940s, "rhythm and blues" (R & B), a secular musical form, blended elements of the blues, jazz, and gospel and prompted listeners to physical and emotional responses outside the walls of the church. R & B acquired wide popularity via recordings, movies, radio, and, later, television. By the mid-1950s, R & B had influenced a new form of popular music—rock 'n' roll (rock). Although rock music became equated with white performers and producers, who collected most of its popular and financial rewards, black talents contributed significantly to the birth of rock.

Pop, Soul, Funk, Disco . . . and Rap

By the 1960s, when the term *pop music* had come to include R & B and rock, the racial chasm between black and white popular music expanded, a separation that was maintained through the "charts" and radio station programming. By the late 1960s, R & B gave birth to *soul music,* which was influenced by black activism and served as a new symbol for a distinct black culture within American society. Sustaining the raw, earthy attributes of soul music, *funk* stressed syncopated, explosive beats through bass and percussion instruments in the 1970s. At about the same time, in the mid-1970s, *disco* took the sexuality of funk and merged it with orchestral arrangements that encouraged dancing to a steady, seemingly unending bass beat. In the 1980s, reggae, Latin rhythms, heavy metal, and fusion expanded the realm of pop music. Emerging in the late 1970s as the most controversial pop music form, *rap music* brought popular music back full circle to the black oral tradition.

The Pop Lyrics section in Part One affords a glimpse of socially conscious writing by blacks from the 1970s to the 1980s. Marvin Gaye's "What's Going On" echoes the complex political problems of that turbulent time. Stevie Wonder's "Living for the City" gives musical form to the urban maze that serves as home for many African Americans. "Man in the Mirror," written by

Siedah Garrett for Michael Jackson, disputes the selfishness and indifference that seemed prevalent in the 1980s.

The Rap Lyrics section reflects the diverse styles and themes of that music form (see Michael Eric Dyson's essay in Part Five, p. 835). Early rap stylist Gil Scott-Heron criticizes blacks' passive acceptance of the status quo in "The Revolution Will Not Be Televised." "Fight the Power," Public Enemy's anthem of black determinism, condemns popular white images and declares the need for black pride. Finally, Queen Latifah's "U.N.I.T.Y." denounces the sexist language and behavior of men while urging black women to reclaim their self-esteem.

Orations: Speeches and Sermons

The Orations section focuses on the communicative power of speeches and sermons delivered to live audiences. Speeches and sermons have long provided a place for African American issues and the larger American agenda to intersect. Consequently, the familiar figure of the black speaker—whether in a clearing in the woods, on a pulpit, on a street corner, or on a dais at a national convention—has become a cultural icon, symbolizing racial identity, determination, spirituality, and survival.

These written texts fall short of conveying the complete experience of their original deliveries and settings, with passionate speakers exhorting live, often vocally responsive audiences. From spontaneous street corner diatribes to formal speeches delivered from a rostrum, the verbal creativity, intonations, phrasings, and physical nuances of black men and women speakers have enriched American oratory beyond measure. Chanting, repetition, pronounced rhythms, and antiphonal modes have heightened the eloquence of generations of African American speakers.

Arranged by the chronological birth year of the speakers, nine selections explore social, political, gender, cultural, philosophical, and religious themes significant to African Americans. Sojourner Truth's "Address to the First Annual Meeting of the American Equal Rights Association" (delivered in 1867) and Frederick Douglass's "What to the Slave Is the Fourth of July?" (1852) address the absence of equal rights for black women and men in America. In "Lynch Law in All Its Phases" (1893), Ida B. Wells-Barnett attacks the then-prevailing justifications for murdering blacks. Mary McLeod Bethune, a celebrated educator and black leader, assesses the status of African American women in "A Century of Progress of Negro Women" (1933).

The ideals that guided the leadership of Martin Luther King, Jr., are expressed in his "Love, Law, and Civil Disobedience" (1961). In a similar vein, two other ministers use the pulpit to stress political awareness: Reverend Dr. Cecil L. Murray probes the dynamics of the Los Angeles riots of 1992 in "Making an Offer You Can't Refuse" (1992), and Reverend Dr. Suzan D. Johnson Cook examines an Old Testament model of womanhood in "God's Woman" (1985).

Illuminating democratic and integrationist ideals, Barbara Jordan articulates the relevance of the Constitution to the average American in her keynote address for the 1976 Democratic Convention, entitled "Who Then Will Speak for the Common Good?", while optimism and self-motivation inspire Jesse Jackson's address to the 1988 Democratic Convention, "Common Ground and Common Sense."

Folktales

Part One concludes with a section on the African American legacy of the folktale. From their earliest presence in America, blacks spun and shared anonymous narratives. These folktales, marked by the union of imagination and untutored intellect, helped African Americans to survive in antagonistic surroundings. In the "Introduction to the Book of Negro Folklore," writer Arna Bontemps notes that slaves brought the practice of storytelling with them from Africa and that the form survived the institution of slavery. Bontemps concludes:

> While the masters of slaves went to some length to get rid of tribal languages and some tribal customs, like certain practices of sorcery, they accepted the animal stories as a harmless way to ease the time or entertain the master's children. That the folktales of these Negro slaves were actually projections of personal experiences and hopes and defeats in terms of symbols appears to have gone unnoticed. (30)

Folktales served a number of purposes for blacks suffering in the New World. As scholar Lawrence W. Levine points out, in *Black Culture, Black Consciousness* (1977), folktales were tools for entertainment, for keeping history, for educating, for pondering daily experiences, for explaining racial differences, and for celebrating black culture.

Existing orally among slaves and free blacks before the Civil War, African American folktales were popularized in the late nineteenth century through the writings of white authors, such as Joel Chandler Harris's *Uncle Remus: His Songs and His Sayings* (1880) and Charles C. Jones's *Negro Myths from the Georgia Court* (1888). Twentieth-century black authors have provided both a cultural context and a broader array of themes in their collections of folktales, including Zora Neale Hurston's *Mules and Men* (1935) and J. Mason Brewer's *Humorous Folk Tales of the South Carolina Negro* (1945). Richard Dorson, a white scholar, organized the extensively documented *American Negro Folktales* (1967), and Julius Lester, a black author, incorporated contemporary language into *Black Folktales* (1969) in order to reach adolescent readers. In *Shuckin' and Jivin': Folklore from Contemporary Black Americans* (1978), black scholar Daryl Dance presented stories she gathered from rural and urban Virginia that cross class, age, and educational lines.

Among the seven folktales included in Part One, the first four appear in Hurston's *Mules and Men*. "Why Negroes Are Black," "Why Women Always

Take Advantage of Men," and "What Smelled Worse" explore racial origin, gender conflict, and racial stereotyping, respectively. "Ole Massa and John Who Wanted to Go to Heaven" features a mythical survivor, John, who finds himself in a typical, self-induced predicament. "Who Ate Up the Butter?" and "The Bear and the Rabbit," both from Dorson's *American Negro Folktales*, provide examples of animal tales and tricksterism. Finally, "Tar Baby," a celebrated anonymous animal tale, contemplates community spirit, the pitfalls of selfishness and greed, and survival by mother-wit.

Works Cited

Bontemps, Arna. "Introduction to the Book of Negro Folklore." *Black Expressions*. Ed. Addison Gayle, Jr. New York: Weybright & Talley, 1969. 29–36.

Dance, Daryl Cumber. *Shuckin' and Jivin': Folklore from Contemporary Black Americans*. Bloomington: Indiana UP, 1978.

Jones, LeRoi (Amiri Baraka). *Blues People: Negro Music in White America*. New York: Morrow, 1963.

Levine, Lawrence W. *Black Culture and Black Consciousness*. New York: Oxford, 1977.

Suggested Readings

In addition to a generous number of articles in journals and other periodicals, a host of informative books on black music and musical idioms is available. These sources include *The Book of Negro Spirituals* (1925) by James Weldon Johnson; *Negro Workaday Songs* (1926) by Howard W. Odum and Gay B. Johnson; *The Negro and His Music* (1936) by Alain Locke; *Blues People* (1963) by Amiri Baraka; *The Book of Jazz: From Then Til Now* (1965) by Leonard Feather; *Black Song: The Forge and the Flame* (1972) by John Lovell, Jr.; *Rock Is Rhythm and Blues* (1974) by Lawrence N. Redd; *Sinful Tunes and Spirituals: Black Folk Music to the Civil War* (1977) by Dena J. Epstein; *The Roots of the Blues: An African Search* (1981) by Samuel Charters; *Roots of Black Music: The Vocal, Instrumental, and Dance Heritage of Africa and Black America* (1982) by Ashenafi Kedebe; *Black Popular Music in America* (1986) by Arnold Shaw; *Black Pearls: Black Queens of the 1920s* (1988) by Daphne Duval Harrison; *Rap: The Lyrics* (1992) by Lawrence A. Stanley; *Break It Down: The Inside Story from the New Leaders of Rap* (1992) by Michael Small; and *Rap: Black Studies and the Academy* (1994) by Houston A. Baker, Jr.

Many orations by African Americans have been anthologized in texts on American history and literature. In addition, the journal *Vital Speeches of the Day* carries numerous contemporary pieces. Collections of speeches by black orators include Alice Dunbar-Moore's *Masterpieces of Negro Eloquence* (1914); Marcus H. Boulware's *The Oratory of Negro Leaders, 1900–1968*

(1969); and Daniel J. Oneill's *Edited Speeches by Black Americans* (1971).

A number of sources, including religious organizations, have compiled sermons by black preachers over the decades. Two useful sources that examine and discuss sermons and preachings are William H. Pipes' *Say Amen, Brother! Old Time Negro Preaching: A Study in American Frustration* (1951), and Bruce A. Rosenberg's *The Art of the American Folk Preacher* (1970). Ella Pearson Mitchell's *Those Preachin' Women* (1985) is of particular interest because it reprints various sermons by black women.

For folktales and written folk literature, consider also *The Book of Negro Folklore* (1958) by Langston Hughes and Arna Bontemps; *Mother Wit from the Laughing Barrel: Readings in the Interpretation of Afro-American Folklore* (1973) by Alan Dundes; *A Treasury of Afro-American Folklore: The Oral Literature, Traditions, Recollections, Legends, Tales, Songs, Religious Beliefs, Customs, Sayings and Humor of Peoples of African Descent in the Americas* (1976) edited by Harold Courlander; and *Liberating Voices: Oral Tradition in African American Literature* (1991) by Gayl Jones.

On popular culture, see Robert C. Toll's *Blacking Up: The Minstrel Show in Nineteenth Century America* (1974); James Baldwin's *The Devil Finds Work* (1976); Donald Bogle's *Brown Sugar: Eighty Years of America's Black Female Superstars* (1980) and *Toms, Coons, Mommies, Mulattoes, and Bucks* (1992); and Gina Dent's *Black Popular Culture* (1992).

LYRICS

Spirituals

Sometimes I Feel Like a Motherless Child

Sometimes I feel like a motherless child,
Sometimes I feel like a motherless child,
Sometimes I feel like a motherless child,
A long ways from home;
A long ways from home.

True believer,
A long ways from home,
A long ways from home.

Sometimes I feel like I'm almos' gone,
Sometimes I feel like I'm almos' gone,
Sometimes I feel like I'm almos' gone;
Way up in de heab'nly lan'
Way up in de heab'nly lan'

True believer,
Way up in de heab'nly lan'
Way up in de heab'nly lan'

Sometimes I feel like a motherless child,
Sometimes I feel like a motherless child,
Sometimes I feel like a motherless child,
A long ways from home.

Go Down Moses

Go down, Moses
'Way down in Egypt land,
Tell ole—Pharaoh
To let my people go.

Go down, Moses
'Way down in Egypt land,
Tell ole—Pharaoh,
To let my people go.

When Israel was in Egypt land:
Let my people go,
Oppressed so hard they could not stand,
Let my people go.

Go down, Moses
'Way down in Egypt land,
Tell ole—Pharaoh,
To let my people go.

When spoke the Lord, bold Moses said:
Let my people go
If not I'll smite your first born dead,
Let my people go.

Go down, Moses
'Way down in Egypt land,
Tell ole—Pharaoh,
To let my people go.

Steal Away to Jesus

Steal away,
Steal away,
Steal away to Jesus!

Steal away,
Steal away home,
I ain't got long to stay here.

Steal away,
Steal away,
Steal away to Jesus!

Steal away,
Steal away home,
I ain't got long to stay here.

My Lord, He calls me,
He calls me by the thunder,
The trumpet sounds within a my soul,
I ain't got long to stay here.

Roll, Jordan, Roll

Roll Jordan, roll,
Roll Jordan, roll,
I want to go to heav'n when I die,
To hear ol' Jordan roll.

O, brethren,
Roll Jordan roll,
Roll Jordan roll,
Wanter go to heav'n when I die,
To hear ol' Jordan roll.

Oh, brothers you oughter been dere,
Yes, my Lord
A sittin' up in de kingdom,
To hear ol' Jordan roll.

Sing it ovah,
Oh, roll.
O, Roll Jordan, roll,
Roll Jordan, roll,
I wanter go to heav'n when I die,
To hear ol' Jordan roll.

Blues

St. Louis Blues

I hate to see de evenin' sun go down
I hate to see de evenin' sun go down
Cause mah baby, he done lef' dis town

Feelin' tomorrow lak I feel today
Feelin' tomorrow lak I feel today
I'll pack mah trunk, an' make mah getaway

St. Louis woman wid her diamon' rings
Pulls dat man aroun' by her apron strings
'Twant for powder an' for store-bought hair
De man I love would not gone nowhere

Got de St. Louis blues, jes as blue as I can be
Dat man got a heart lak a rock cast in de sea
Or else he wouldn't have gone so far from me

Been to de gypsy to get mah fortune tol'
To de gypsy, done got mah fortune tol'
Cause I'm most wild 'bout mah jelly roll

Gypsy done tol' me, "Don't you wear no black"
Yes, she done tol' me, "Don't you wear no black.
Go to St. Louis, you can win him back"

Help me to Cairo; make St. Louis by mahself
Git to Cairo, find mah ol' frien', Jeff
Gwine to pin mahself close to his side
If I flag his train, I sho can ride.

I loves dat man lak a schoolboy loves his pie
Lak a Kentucky Colonel loves his mint an' rye
I'll love mah baby till de day I die

You ought to see dat stovepipe brown o' mine
Lak he owns de Dimon' Joseph line
He'd make a cross-eyed 'oman go stone blind

Blacker than midnight, teeth lak flags of truce
Blackest man in de whole St. Louis
Blacker de berry, sweeter is de juice. . . .

Hard Times Blues

I never seen such real hard times befo'
Says, I never seen such real hard times befo'
De wolf keeps walkin' all aroun' mah do'

Dey howl all night long, an' dey moan till de break of day
Howl all night long, an' dey moan till de break of day
Dey seems to know mah good man gone away

I cain' go outside to mah grocery sto'
I cain' go outside to mah grocery sto'
I ain' got no money, an' mah credit doan go no mo'

Won't somebody please try an' find mah man fo' me
Won't somebody please try an' find mah man fo' me
Tell him I'm broke an' hongry, lonely as I can be. . . .

Mamie's Blues

De Two-Nineteen done took mah baby away
Two-Nineteen took mah babe away
Two-Seventeen bring her back some day

Stood on the corner with her feets soakin' wet
Stood on the corner with her feets soakin' wet
Beggin' each an' every man that she met

If you can't give me a dollar, give me a lousy dime
Can't give a dollar, give me a lousy dime
I wanna feed that hongry man of mine

Backwater Blues

When it rain five days an' de skies turned dark as night
When it rain five days an' de skies turned dark as night
Then trouble taken place in the lowland that night

I woke up this mornin', can't even get outa mah do'
I woke up this mornin', can't even get outa mah do'
That's enough trouble to make a po' girl wonder where she wanta go

They rowed a little boat about five miles 'cross the pond
Then they rowed a little boat about five miles 'cross the pond
I packed all mah clothes, th'owed 'em in, an' they rowed me along

When it thunder an' a-lightnin', an' the wind begin to blow
When it thunder an' a-lightnin', an' the wind begin to blow
An' thousan' people ain' got no place to go

Then I went an' stood up on some high ol' lonesome hill
I went an' stood up on some high ol' lonesome hill
An' looked down on the house where I used to live

Backwater blues done cause me to pack mah things an' go
Backwater blues done cause me to pack mah things an' go
Cause mah house fell down an' I cain' live there no mo'

O-o-o-oom, I cain' move no mo'
O-o-o-oom, I cain' move no mo'
There ain' no place fo' a po' ol' girl to go

Pop Lyrics

Marvin Gaye (1939–84)

Born a minister's son in Washington, D.C., Marvin Gaye (adding the "e" to professionalize his last name) began singing as a boy in the church choir, and, later, as a teenager, in a local secular group. He sang with several groups before making his way, in 1961, to Detroit and Motown. Initially at Motown he was used as a drummer, playing behind Smokey Robinson and the Miracles and Little Stevie Wonder. But in 1962, Gaye's singing career took root with the single "That Stubborn Kinda Fellow."

In the 1960s, his popularity increased as he recorded dance tunes, love songs, and bluesy-romance pieces, such as "Hitch Hike," "Can I Get a Witness," and "I Heard It through the Grapevine." He also strengthened his audience appeal by performing duets with Mary Wells, Kim Weston, and Tammi Terrell. Between 1967 and 1970, Gaye sang nine top-50 hits with Terrell, including "Your Pre-

cious Love," "You're All I Need to Get By," "Ain't Nothing Like the Real Thing Baby," and "Ain't No Mountain High Enough." When Terrell died of a brain tumor in 1970, Gaye's personal life and career reflected that loss.

With the release of his 1971 album, What's Going On, *Gaye began to approach the marketplace with songs expressing social and political thought, while also showcasing his talents as a songwriter and an instrumentalist. That album contains the songs "What's Going On," "Inner City Blues," and "Mercy, Mercy Me"—all confronting the declining standards in society and the natural environment. His 1973 song, "Let's Get It On," marked another shift, as the sexual suggestiveness of its contents merged with Gaye's traditional romantic flair.*

Over the next nine years, despite his release of eight albums, Gaye's professional life ebbed beneath his ongoing personal and financial difficulties. Moving from Motown to Columbia Records, Gaye released his final album, Midnight Love, *in 1982, one that brought him praise from the record industry and two Grammy Awards. In 1984, a tragic family conflict cost Gaye his life, as he was killed in a fight with his father. Since Gaye's death, a younger generation of artists has expressed a well-deserved admiration of his musical contributions by recording his songs and alluding to him in their own music.*

The expression "What's Going On?" was used as a casual greeting within inner-city neighborhoods during the 1960s and 1970s. However, on another level, as the song's lyrics suggest, the question served as a meditation on the seemingly overwhelming social maladies of the times.

What's Going On

Mother, mother
there's too many of you crying
brother, brother, brother
there's far too many of you dying
you know we've got to find a way
to bring some loving here today

Father, father
we don't need to escalate
you see, war is not the answer
for only love can conquer hate
you know we've got to find a way
to bring some loving here today

Picket lines (sister) and picket signs (sister)
don't punish me (sister) with brutality (sister)
talk to me (sister) so you can see (sister)
what's going on, what's going on, what's going on, what's going on

Mother, mother
everybody thinks we're wrong
but who are they to judge us

simply cause our hair is long
you know we've got to find a way
to bring some understanding here today

Picket lines (brother) and picket signs (brother)
don't punish me (brother) with brutality (brother)
talk to me (brother) so you can see (brother)
what's going on, what's going on, what's going on, what's going on

Stevie Wonder (1950–)

B*y the time he was forty, Stevie Wonder had recorded twenty-one albums, won sixteen Grammy Awards including three album-of-the-year honors, received an Academy Award for Best Song ("I Just Called to Say I Love You"), and been inducted into the Songwriters Hall of Fame. In addition, he had been a prime mover in a number of public service campaigns focusing on AIDS, cancer, the International Food Program, the crusade against drunk driving, and the efforts to honor Martin Luther King, Jr.'s birthday as a national holiday.*

Born in Saginaw, Michigan, as Steveland Morris, and blind since infancy, Stevie Wonder began his remarkable career at a very young age, when he was introduced by a member of the Miracles to Motown's Berry Gordy. In 1961, Gordy signed the exuberant youngster, who could make his harmonica sound as if several people were playing at once. Wonder's first album was titled Little Stevie Wonder: The 12 Year Old Genius *(1962). Wonder's career prospered under Motown with remakes of the songs "Blowing in the Wind" and "For Once in My Life," as well as with such original hits as "Uptight," "I Was Made to Love Her," "My Cherie Amour," and "Yester-Me, Yester-You, Yesterday."*

Although black audiences had known about Wonder throughout the 1960s, it was in 1972 that his popularity reached an even wider audience with the release of Music of My Mind, *his twelfth album. Wonder had complete creative control over the project, utilizing the MOOG synthesizer in his music. The album reached the number-two position on the pop music charts, and Wonder went on tour with the Rolling Stones.*

He followed the success of Music of My Mind *with* Talking Book *(1972), which includes the songs "Superstition" and "You Are the Sunshine of My Life," and* Innervisions *(1973), which includes "Living for the City" and "Mistra Know It All." At the age of twenty-three, Wonder had established himself as a soul legend and a pop superstar.*

Wonder's performances with other pop music stars, namely Michael Jackson, Gladys Knight, Elton John, and Paul McCartney, are noteworthy, but equally significant has been his support of other distinctive talents, specifically Syreeta Wright (Wonder's wife at one time), Deniece Williams, and Minnie Ripperton. In January 1995, Wonder gave a rare live performance at the Los Angeles Universal Amphitheater, promoting the release of his newest album, Conversation Peace *(1995).*

"Living for the City," taken from Wonder's 1973 album, tells of blacks' ongoing struggle with the day-to-day challenges and dangers of urban life.

Living for the City

A boy is born in hard time Mississippi
Surrounded by four walls that ain't so pretty
His parents give him love and affection
To keep him strong moving in the right direction
Living just enough, just enough for the city

His father works some days for fourteen hours
And you can bet he barely makes a dollar
His mother goes to scrub the floors for many
And you'd best believe she hardly gets a penny
Living just enough for the city

His sister's black but she is sho 'nuff pretty
Her skirt is short but Lord her legs are sturdy
To walk to school she's got to get up early
Her clothes are old but never are they dirty
Living just enough, just enough for the city

Her brother's smart he's got more sense than many
His patience's long but soon he won't have any
To find a job is like a haystack needle
Cause where he lives they don't use colored people
Living just enough, just enough for the city . . .

His hair is long, his feet are hard and gritty
He spends his life walking the streets of New York City
He's almost dead from breathing in air pollution
He tried to vote but to him there's no solution
Living just enough, just enough for the city

I hope you hear inside my voice of sorrow
And that it motivates you to make a better tomorrow
This place is cruel no where could be much colder
If we can't change, the world will soon be over
Living just enough, stop living just enough for the city!!!!

Siedah Garrett (b. ?)

Known as a vocalist and songwriter, Siedah Garrett has worked with numerous rhythm and blues talents and pop-jazz artists while also developing her solo career. As a singer, she has contributed background vocals to such performers as the Commodores, Sarah Vaughan, El DeBarge, Dennis Edwards, Quincy Jones, and Michael Jackson. As a songwriter, she has written successful lyrics for Natalie Cole ("As a Matter of Fact"), Aretha Franklin ("Mercy"), and Quincy Jones's Grammy Award-winning Back on the Block *("One Man Woman," "Wee B. Dooinit," and "The Secret Garden").*

Michael Jackson (1958–)

Michael Jackson's unparalleled career took flight in 1970 with the Jackson 5's debut album. Pre-teen Jackson's lead vocals carried him and his brothers from Gary, Indiana, to four consecutive number-one hits for Motown Records. Moving toward a solo career between 1972 and 1975, Jackson reached superstar status when he teamed with producer-composer Quincy Jones.

With Jones as his mentor, Jackson released Off the Wall *(1979), an album that features four top-10 hits, including "Don't Stop 'Til You Get Enough" and "Rock with You." Jackson and Jones collaborated again on* Thriller *(1982), an album with seven top-10 hits, including "Billie Jean," "Beat It," "Wanna Be Startin' Somethin'," and "Human Nature." Selling over forty million copies,* Thriller *became the best-selling record album ever and earned eight Grammy Awards.*

Bad *(1987) solidified Jackson's status as the top pop-crossover artist with several hit songs, including "Dirty Diana," "Smooth Criminal," "I Just Can't Stop Loving You" (a duet with Siedah Garrett), and "Man in the Mirror." In 1991, Jackson signed a multimillion-dollar contract with Sony Records, and his* Dangerous *(1992), a commercial success, includes the hit songs "Black and White," "Heal the World," "In the Closet," and "Remember the Time."*

During his career Jackson has performed duets with such artists as Diana Ross, Stevie Wonder, Paul McCartney, and Mick Jagger. In addition, he has served as the producer for other artists and has written successful songs, most notably "We Are the World," a collaboration with Lionel Ritchie for the African famine relief.

In 1994, Michael Jackson's unparalleled fame was tarnished by accusations of child molestation. After these accusations were dropped as a result of a financial settlement, Jackson shifted public attention back to his music. Despite the residue of personal scandal and eccentric behavior, Jackson has maintained his musical stature. With his history of popular hits and successful collaborations, Jackson has enjoyed international fame unequaled by any other performer.

In the song, "Man in the Mirror," Jackson's impassioned vocals give Siedah Garrett's lyrics sincerity and depth. The lyrics call for social awareness and change, while emphasizing the need for personal involvement and individual responsibility.

Man in the Mirror

I'm gonna make a change, for once in my life
It's gonna feel real good, gonna make a difference
Gonna make it right . . .

As I turn up the collar on my favorite winter coat
This wind is blowin' my mind
I see the kids in the street, with not enough to eat
Who am I, to be blind? Pretending not to see their needs
A summer's disregard, a broken bottle top

And a one man's soul
They follow each other on the wind ya' know
'Cause they got nowhere to go
That's why I want you to know

I'm starting with the man in the mirror
I'm asking him to change his ways
And no message could have been any clearer
If you wanna make the world a better place
(If you wanna make the world a better place)
Take a look at yourself, and then make a change
(Take a look at yourself, and then make a change)
(Na na na, na na na, na na, na nah)

I've been a victim of a selfish kind of love
It's time that I realize
That there are some with no home, not a nickel to loan
Could it be really me, pretending that they're not alone?

A willow deeply scarred, somebody's broken heart
And a washed-out dream
(Washed-out dream)
They follow the pattern of the wind, ya' see
Cause they got no place to be
That's why I'm starting with me
(Starting with me!)

I'm starting with the man in the mirror
(Ooh!)
I'm asking him to change his ways
(Ooh!)
And no message could have been any clearer
If you wanna make the world a better place
(If you wanna make the world a better place)
Take a look at yourself and then make a change
(Take a look at yourself and then make a change)

I'm starting with the man in the mirror
(Ooh!)
I'm asking him to change his ways
(Change his ways—ooh!)
And no message could've been any clearer
If you wanna make the world a better place
(If you wanna make the world a better place)
Take a look at yourself and then make that . . .
(Take a look at yourself and then make that . . .)
Change!

I'm starting with the man in the mirror,
(Man in the mirror—Oh yeah!)

I'm asking him to change his ways
(Better change!)
No message could have been any clearer
(If you wanna make the world a better place)
(Take a look at yourself and then make the change)
(You gotta get it right, while you got the time)
('Cause when you close your heart)
You can't close your . . . your mind!
(Then you close your . . . mind!)
That man, that man, that man, that man
With that man in the mirror
(Man in the mirror, oh yeah!)
That man, that man, that man
I'm asking him to change his ways
(Better change!)
You know . . . that man
No message could have been any clearer
If you wanna make the world a better place
(If you wanna make the world a better place)
Take a look at yourself and then make a change
(Take a look at yourself and then make a change)
Hoo! Hoo! Hoo! Hoo! Hoo!
Na na na, na na na, na na, na nah
(Oh yeah!)
Gonna feel real good now!
Yeah yeah! Yeah yeah! Yeah yeah!
Na na na, na na na, na na, na nah
(Ooooh . . .)
Oh no, no no . . .
I'm gonna make a change
It's gonna feel real good! Come on!
(Change . . .)
Just lift yourself
You know
You've got to stop it. Yourself!
(Yeah!—Make that change!)
I've got to make that change, today!
Hoo!
(Man in the mirror)
You got to
You got to not let yourself . . . brother . . .
Hoo!
(Yeah!—Make that change)
You know—I've got to get that man, that man . . .
(Man in the mirror)
You got to
You've got to move! Come on! Come on!
You got to . . .
Stand up! Stand up! Stand up!

(Yeah!—Make that change)
Stand up and lift yourself, now!
(Man in the mirror)
Hoo! Hoo! Hoo!
Aaow!
(Yeah!—Make that change)
Gonna make that change . . . come on!
You know it!
You know it!
You know it!
You know . . .
(Change . . .)
Make that change.

Rap Lyrics

Gil Scott-Heron (1949–)

Recognized primarily as a performer and musician, Gil Scott-Heron's academic background and literary creativity are not as widely known. Born in Chicago and raised in Tennessee, Scott-Heron began writing fiction as a teenager. As a student at Lincoln University, he wrote novels, and by the time he had earned an M.A. from Johns Hopkins University in 1972, he had published three books. His first, a book of poetry, Small Talk at 125th and Lenox *(1970), was followed by two novels:* The Vulture *(1970), which portrays a black revolutionary group's attempt to rebuild a neighborhood, and* The Nigger Factory *(1972), which focuses on students' struggle to change their small black college.*

In the early 1970s, collaborating with jazz musician Brian Jackson, Scott-Heron applied his gifts for storytelling and poetry to music. His influential blend of oral and musical forms meshes the spoken word and vocals with jazz, blues, and Latin rhythms.

Stylistically, Scott-Heron's narrative poetry, often spoken rhythmically, is layered over melodic blues or jazz riffs. At the same time, potent political, social, and cultural statements permeate his impassioned, resonant vocal phrasings. His approach to musical content and form reflected the progression of jazz, at the time while his command of language and intonation presaged the emergence of melodic rap tunes.

By the late 1980s, Scott-Heron had released sixteen albums and continued to perform at both jazz and pop music venues. One of his earliest and best-known pieces, "The Revolution Will Not Be Televised," written in 1971, parodies the inane aspects of commercial television. In it Scott-Heron's sarcasm punctuates his urgent appeal for black activism and new black leadership.

The Revolution Will Not Be Televised

You will not be able to stay home, brother.
You will not be able to plug in, turn on and cop out.
You will not be able to lose yourself on scag and

skip out for beer during commercials because
The revolution will not be televised.

The revolution will not be televised.
The revolution will not be brought to you by Xerox in four parts without commercial interruption.
The revolution will not show you pictures of Nixon blowing a bugle and leading a charge by John Mitchell, General Abramson and Spiro Agnew to eat hog maws confiscated from a Harlem sanctuary.
The revolution will not be televised.

The revolution will not be brought to you by
The Schaeffer Award Theatre and will not star
Natalie Wood and Steve McQueen or Bullwinkle and Julia.
The revolution will not give your mouth sex appeal.
The revolution will not get rid of the nubs.
The revolution will not make you look five pounds thinner.
The revolution will not be televised, brother.

There will be no pictures of you and Willie Mae
pushing that shopping cart down the block on the dead run
or trying to slide that color t.v. in a stolen ambulance.
NBC will not be able to predict the winner at 8:32 on reports from twenty-nine districts.
The revolution will not be televised.

There will be no pictures of pigs shooting down brothers
on the instant replay.
There will be no pictures of pigs shooting down brothers
on the instant replay.
There will be no slow motion or still lifes of Roy Wilkins strolling through Watts in a red, black and green liberation jumpsuit that he has been saving for just the proper occasion.

Green Acres, Beverly Hillbillies and Hooterville Junction
will no longer be so damned relevant
and women will not care if Dick finally got down with Jane
on Search for Tomorrow
because black people will be in the streets looking for
A Brighter Day.
The revolution will not be televised.

There will be no highlights on the Eleven O'Clock News
and no pictures of hairy armed women liberationists
and Jackie Onassis blowing her nose.
The theme song will not be written by Jim Webb or Francis Scott Key
nor sung by Glen Campbell, Tom Jones, Johnny Cash,
Englebert Humperdink or Rare Earth.
The revolution will not be televised.

The revolution will not be right back after a
message about a white tornado, white lightning or white people.
You will not have to worry about a dove in your bedroom,
the tiger in your tank or the giant in your toilet bowl.
The revolution will not get better with coke.
The revolution will not fight germs that may cause bad breath.
The revolution *will* put you in the driver's seat.
The revolution will not be televised
will not be televised
not be televised
be televised
The revolution will be no re-run, brothers.
The revolution will be LIVE.

Public Enemy (1988–)

Although Public Enemy's name, lyrics, and behavior underscore the group's nihilistic image, its two founding members come from middle-class, Long Island backgrounds. While attending Adelphi University in Garden City, New York, Carlton Ridenhour (who became Chuck D) and William Drayton (who became Flavor Flav) joined their creative interests and began writing and performing music for the college radio station. Chuck D and Flavor Flav also formed a rap group that included the disc jockey Terminator X and a coterie of dancer-bodyguards dressed in military gear and called S1W, or Security of the First World. S1W was led by Professor Griff, who also served as the "Minister of Information" for Public Enemy.

Emerging in 1988 with an apocalyptic and boastful cut, "Rebel without a Pause," Public Enemy's irreverent, confrontational lyrics focus on American society's racism, exploitation, and greed. By 1993, Public Enemy had released over a half-dozen albums and had found an audience of black and white fans. Despite its popular attraction across racial lines, the group was reproved for the anti-Semitic elements in its lyrics and for the black stereotyping antics of Flavor Flav. In a dispute over his anti-Semitic public comments, Griff left the group in 1989, but since then, the personal and legal problems of founding members Chuck D and Flavor Flav have kept the rappers in the news. Among rappers and rap fans, however, Public Enemy is regarded as the pioneering group in hard-core rap and the harbinger of the gangsta rap of the 1990s.

"Fight the Power," from Public Enemy's 1989 album Fear of a Black Planet, *was featured in Spike Lee's movie* Do the Right Thing *(1989). The lyrics address the ongoing racial oppression and exploitation by the American establishment, while exhorting blacks to rebel against the status quo.*

Fight the Power

K. Shocklee, E. Sadler, and C. Ridenhour

1989 the number another summer (get down)
Sound of the funky drummer

Music hittin' your heart cause I know you got soul
(Brothers and sisters, hey)
Listen if you're missin' y'all
Swingin' while I'm singin'
Givin' whatcha gettin'
Knowin' what I know
While the Black bands sweatin'
And the rhythm rhymes rollin'
Got to give us what we want
Gotta give us what we need
Our freedom of speech is freedom or death
Who got to fight the powers that be
Lemme hear you say
Fight the power

Chorus

As the rhythm designed to bounce
What counts is that the rhymes
Designed to fill your mind
Now that you've realized the prides arrived
We got to pump the stuff to make us tough
from the heart
It's a start, a work of art
To revolutionize make a change nothin's strange
People, people we are the same
No we're not the same
Cause we don't know the game
What we need is awareness, we can't get careless
You say what is this?
My beloved lets get down to business
Mental self-defensive fitness
(Yo) bum rush the show
You gotta go for what you know
Make everybody see, in order to fight the powers that be
Lemme hear you say . . .
Fight the power

Chorus

Elvis was a hero to most
But he never meant shit to me you see
Straight up racist that sucker was
Simple and plain
Mother fuck him and John Wayne
Cause I'm Black and I'm proud
I'm ready and hyped plus I'm amped
Most of my heroes don't appear on no stamps
Sample a look back you look and find

Nothing but rednecks for 400 years if you check
Don't worry be happy
Was a number one jam
Damn if I say if you can slap me right here
(Get it) let's get this party started right
Right on, c'mon
What we got to say
Power to the people no delay
To make everybody see
In order to fight the powers that be

(Fight the Power)

Queen Latifah (1970–)

B*orn Dana Owens and raised in Jersey City, New Jersey, Queen Latifah has built an impressive career at a young age, becoming the CEO of her own artist management company and record label, as well as a film and television actress. Her Flavor Unit Records and Management Company guides the careers of at least seventeen rap talents, including Naughty by Nature, Black Sheep, Nikki D, and Apache. In addition, she has acted in the films* Jungle Fever *(1991),* House Party 2 *(1991),* Juice *(1992), and* My Life *(1993), and since 1993 she has been a member of an ensemble cast of four black women in the situation comedy* Living Single.

Queen Latifah received her professional name when she was performing in high school in a rap group called Ladies Fresh; a Muslim cousin dubbed her "Latifah," which in Arabic means "feminine, nice, and kind." With the help of a local disc-jockey friend, she completed a demo tape that won her a contract with Tommy Boy Records.

Although Queen Latifah has released only three albums thus far, she has become, as her professional name suggests, royalty among women rappers. Her first album, All Hail the Queen *(1989), sold a million copies worldwide and, as critic Sherri McGee-Page notes, speaks "of racial pride and embrace[s] women all over the Diaspora. Her positive messages shatter . . . the rap nation's sexist stereotypes and replace . . . them with a black storm of womanist poetry."* Nature of a Sista *(1991), her second album, conveys a more pronounced sense of the artist's confidence as a rapper and a woman. With such tunes as "Bad as a Mutha," "Fly Girl," and "Nature of a Sista," Queen Latifah asserts the resilience, self-confidence, and wisdom of black women.*

Queen Latifah's third album, Black Reign *(1993), dedicated to her deceased brother, displays her usual musical diversity, showcasing both rap tunes and convincing vocals. "U.N.I.T.Y.," which comes from that album, addresses the exploitation of black women by black men through pejorative language and physical and emotional abuse. The lyrics reject both passivity on the part of black women and sexism by black men—two bankrupt attitudes that work against black unity.*

U.N.I.T.Y.

Instinct leads me to anotha flow
everytime I hear a brother call
a girl a bitch or a ho
trying to make a sista feel low
I know all of that gotsta go

Now everybody knows
there's exceptions to this rule
I don't be getting mad
When we playing its cool
But don't U be calling me out my name
I bring wreck to those who disrespect me like a dame

Thats why I'm talking
one day I was walkin down the block
I had my cut off shorts on right
cause it was crazy hot
I walked past these dudes when they passed me
One of them felt my booty, he was nasty

I turned around red, somebody was catchin the wrath,
then the little one said "Yeah Me Bitch" then laughed
Since he was with his boys he tried to break fly, hunh
I punched him dead in his eye and said
Who you callin a bitch

I hit the bottom there ain't no where
else to go but up
bad days at work give you an attitude
and you erupt
and take it out on me
but that's about enough
You put your hands on me again,
I'll put ya ass in handcuffs

I guess I fell so deep in love I grew dependency
I was too blind to see just how it was affecting me
All that I knew was U was all the man I had
And I was scared to let U go
Even though U treated me bad
but I don't wanna see my kids see me
getting beat down my daddy smacking
mommy all around

You say I'm nothing without ya
but I'm nothing witcha

Man don't really love ya if he hits ya
this is my notice, to the door
I'm not taking it no more,
I'm not your personal whore
thats not what I'm here for
Ain't nothing good gonna come to you
till U do right by me
brother you wait and see

Whats going on in your mind
Is what I ask ya,
But like Yo-Yo,
You don't hear me through

You wear a rag around ya head and
U call yourself a "Gangsta Bitch"
Now that you saw Apache's video
I saw you wilin actin like a fool
I peeped you out the window
jumpin girls after school
but where did all this come from
A minute ago U was a nerd and
nobody ever heard of ya

Now you a wanna be (hard)
You barely know your ABC's (please)
there's plenty of people out here with triggers
ready to pull it why you trying
to jump in front of the bullet
And real bad girls are the silent type

Ain't none of this worth getting your face sliced
cause that's what happened to ya
homegirl right? (barkin wit no bite)
She got to wear that for life

ORATIONS: SPEECHES AND SERMONS

Sojourner Truth (1797–1883)

Sojourner Truth, born into slavery in New York as Isabella Baumfree, was sold three times by the time she reached adolescence. She was raped by her second master and given to an older slave in marriage. From that marriage, she had five children, most of whom were sold to other masters. Emancipated by state law in 1827, Sojourner Truth took on domestic work, since she could not read or write.

She joined a religious order in New York City, but later became caught up in a scandal that implicated her in the murder of a fellow member. She sued for libel and was exonerated, but left the group.

Proclaiming herself the recipient of visions and voices, Sojourner Truth found a new name and undertook a mission of itinerant preaching about God and human rights. As she explained, "I went to the Lord and asked him to give me a new name. And the Lord gave me Sojourner because I was to travel up an' down the land showin' the people their sins an' bein' a sign unto them . . . and the Lord gave me Truth, because I was to declare the truth to the people."

A fervent dramatic speaker, Sojourner Truth pursued her mission throughout New England and New York, lecturing against slavery and for women's rights. Assisted financially by her friends, Truth supported herself by selling her autobiography, which she had dictated to a white friend. In 1851, she spoke at the Women's Rights Convention in Ohio, delivering her now-famous "Ain't I a Woman?" speech. In 1863, she was given a position as counselor to the Freedpersons of Arlington, Virginia, by the National Freedmen's Relief Association. This commitment to freed slaves inspired her to request that Congress provide public land in a western state for blacks to initiate new, independent lives. She continued to speak for that cause until she became ill in 1875. She settled during her last years in Battle Creek, Michigan, where she died in 1883.

Sojourner Truth delivered the speech presented here in 1867; it was recorded by Susan B. Anthony and her coeditors for publication in The History of Woman Suffrage *(1886).*

Address to the First Annual Meeting of the American Equal Rights Association

My friends, I am rejoiced that you are glad, but I don't know how you will feel when I get through. I come from another field—the country of the slave. They have got their liberty—so much good luck to have slavery partly destroyed; not entirely. I want it root and branch destroyed. Then we will all be free indeed. I feel that if I have to answer for the deeds done in my body just as much as a man, I have a right to have just as much as a man. There is a great stir about colored men getting their rights, but not a word about the colored women; and if colored men get their rights, and not colored women theirs, you see the colored men will be masters over the women, and it will be just as bad as it was before. So I am for keeping the thing going while things are stirring; because if we wait till it is still, it will take a great while to get it going again. White women are a great deal smarter, and know more than colored women, while colored women do not know scarcely anything. They go out washing, which is about as high as a colored woman gets, and their men go about idle, strutting up and down; and when the women come home, they ask for their money and take it all, and then scold because there is no food. I want you to consider on that, chil'n. I call you chil'n; you are somebody's chil'n, and I am old enough to be mother of all that is here. I want women to have their rights. In the courts women have no right, no voice; nobody speaks for them. I wish woman to have her voice there among the pettifoggers. If it is not a fit place for women, it is unfit for men to be there.

I am above eighty years old; it is about time for me to be going. I have been forty years a slave and forty years free, and would be here forty years more to have equal rights for all. I suppose I am kept here because something remains for me to do; I suppose I am yet to help to break the chain. I have done a great deal of work; as much as a man, but did not get so much pay. I used to work in the field and bind grain, keeping up with the cradler; but men doing no more, got twice as much pay; so with the German women. They work in the field and do as much work, but do not get the pay. We do as much, we eat as much, we want as much. I suppose I am about the only colored woman that goes about to speak for the rights of the colored women. I want to keep the thing stirring, now that the ice is cracked. What we want is a little money. You men know that you get as much again as women when you write, or for what you do. When we get our rights we shall not have to come to you for money, for then we shall have money enough in our own pockets; and may be you will ask us for money. But help us now until we get it. It is a good consolation to know that when we have got this battle once fought we shall not be coming to you any more. You have been having our rights so long, that you think, like a slave-holder, that you own us. I know that it is hard for one who has held the reins for so long to give up; it cuts like a knife. It will feel all the better when it closes up again. I have been in Washington about three years, seeing about these colored people. Now colored men have the right to vote. There ought to be equal rights now more than ever, since colored people have got their freedom. I am going to talk several times while I am here; so now I will do a little singing. I have not heard any singing since I came here.

We are going home. There, children, in heaven we shall rest from all our labors; first do all we have to do here. There I am determined to go, not to stop short of that beautiful place, and I do not mean to stop till I get there, and meet you there, too.

Frederick Douglass (1817–95)

I*n his* Narrative of the Life of Frederick Douglass, An American Slave *(1845), Douglass assessed the significance of a pivotal confrontation with a white overseer: "This battle with Mr. Covey was the turning point in my career as a slave. It rekindled the few expiring embers of freedom, and revived within me a sense of my own manhood. It recalled the departed self-confidence, and inspired me again with a determination to be free." This cataclysm propelled Douglass forward into the struggle for freedom and autonomy for himself and all black Americans.*

Born as Frederick Bailey in Maryland of a slave mother and an unknown white father, ten-year-old Douglass was sent from the plantation to work as a servant in Baltimore. Although while in the city he learned to read, his ongoing exploitation as a slave continued to define his life. In 1838, with the help of Anna Murray, a free black woman who would become his future wife, Douglass escaped slavery, going north to New York and then to Massachusetts. In 1841, after delivering a speech at the Nantucket antislavery convention, he began a lengthy acquaintanceship with the abolitionist white journalist, William Lloyd Garrison. As a result of that relationship, Douglass delivered speeches for the Massachusetts Anti-Slavery Society for four years.

After he published his autobiography in 1845, Douglass became concerned that widespread reading of his narrative would call attention to himself as a fugitive slave. And so he distanced himself from America by traveling to England. A year later, in 1846, friends raised money to purchase his freedom legally.

Douglass's return to the United States in 1847 marked a break from Garrison and his particular abolitionist strategies; specifically, Garrison's rejection of the Constitution and his belief that the northern states should secede from the Union. Douglass settled in Rochester, New York, and founded the North Star *newspaper, which served until 1860 as a forum for Douglass and other black writer-activists such as William Wells Brown and Martin Delany. Through his writings and speeches, Douglass maintained a vigilant abolitionism, though initially arguing against John Brown's assault on the Harpers Ferry arsenal.*

During the Civil War, Douglass campaigned with Sojourner Truth for the inclusion of black soldiers in the Union Ranks. President Abraham Lincoln finally acquiesced in 1862, and Douglass and Sojourner Truth actively recruited for the two Massachusetts black regiments. After the war, Douglass was appointed by President Ulysses Grant as the U.S. marshall for the District of Columbia, and, later, under President Chester Alan Arthur, Douglass assumed the responsibilities of the minister to Haiti.

During the 1880s, he aligned himself with the burgeoning women's rights movement. The early feminists, inspired by abolitionism and by various reform movements, often equated sexism with the oppressive elements of slavery. Douglass, however, was criticized by women suffragists for his support of the Fifteenth Amendment, which granted voting rights to black males but left women still disfranchised.

In addition to his numerous speeches and well-known autobiography, Douglass wrote My Bondage and My Freedom *(1855) and* The Life and Times of Frederick Douglass *(1881, revised 1892).*

The speech that follows, "What to the Slave Is the Fourth of July?" demonstrates well Douglass's powerful thematic focus and use of language. Delivered in Rochester, New York, on July 5, 1852—the day after Independence Day—Douglass underscores the hypocrisy of a nation that can celebrate its own independence while also sanctioning the institution of slavery.

What to the Slave Is the Fourth of July?

Fellow Citizens:

Pardon me, and allow me to ask, why am I called upon to speak here to-day? What have I or those I represent to do with your national independence? Are the great principles of political freedom and of natural justice, embodied in that Declaration of Independence, extended to us? and am I, therefore, called upon to bring our humble offering to the national altar, and to confess the benefits, and express devout gratitude for the blessings resulting from your independence to us?

Would to God, both for your sakes and ours, that an affirmative answer could be truthfully returned to these questions. Then would my task be light, and my burden easy and delightful. For who is there so cold that a nation's sympathy could not warm him? Why so obdurate and dead to the claims of gratitude, that would not thankfully acknowledge such priceless benefits? Who so stolid and selfish that would not give his voice to swell the halleluiahs of a nation's jubilee, when the chains of servitude had been torn from his limbs? I am not that man. In a case like that, the dumb might eloquently speak, and the "lame man leap like a hart."

But such is not the state of the case. I say it with a sad sense of disparity between us. I am not included within the pale of this glorious anniversary! Your high independence only reveals the immeasurable distance between us. The blessings in which you this day rejoice are not enjoyed in common. The rich inheritance of justice, liberty, prosperity, and independence bequeathed by your fathers is shared by you, not by me. The sunlight that brought life and healing to you has brought stripes and death to me. This Fourth of July is *yours*, not *mine*. *You* may rejoice, *I* must mourn. To drag a man in fetters into the grand illuminated temple of liberty, and call upon him to join you in joyous anthems, were inhuman mockery and sacrilegious irony. Do you mean, citizens, to mock me, by asking me to speak today? If so, there is a parallel to your conduct. And let me warn you, that it is dangerous to copy the example of a nation whose crimes, towering up to heaven, were thrown down by the breath of the Almighty, burying that nation in irrecoverable ruin. I can to-day take up the lament of a peeled and woe-smitten people.

"By the rivers of Babylon, there we sat down. Yes! We wept when we remembered Zion. We hanged our harps upon the willows in the midst thereof. For there they that carried us away captive, required of us a song; and they who wasted us, required of us mirth, saying, Sing us one of the songs of Zion. How can we sing the Lord's song in a strange land? If I forget thee, O Jerusalem, let my right hand forget her cunning. If I do not remember thee, let my tongue cleave to the roof of my mouth."

Fellow citizens, above your national, tumultuous joy, I hear the mournful wail of millions, whose chains, heavy and grievous yesterday, are to-day rendered more intolerable by the jubilant shouts that reach them. If I do forget, if I do not remember those bleeding children of sorrow this day, "may my right hand forget her cunning, and may my tongue cleave to the roof of my mouth!" To forget them, to pass lightly over their wrongs, and to chime in with the popular theme, would be treason most scandalous and shocking, and would make me a reproach before God and the world. My subject, then, fellow citizens, is "American Slavery." I shall see this day and its popular characteristics from the slave's point of view. Standing here, identified with the American bondman, making his wrongs mine, I do not hesitate to declare, with all my soul, that the character and conduct of this nation never looked blacker to me than on this Fourth of July. Whether we turn to the declarations of the past, or to the professions of the present, the conduct of the nation seems equally hideous and revolting. America is false to the past, false to the present, and solemnly binds herself to be false to the future. Standing with God and the crushed and bleeding slave on this occasion, I will, in the name of humanity, which is outraged, in the name of liberty, which is fettered, in the name of the Constitution and the Bible, which are disregarded and trampled upon, dare to call in question and to denounce, with all the emphasis I can command, everything that serves to perpetuate slavery—the great sin and shame of America! "I will not equivocate; I will not excuse;" I will use the severest language I can command, and yet not one word shall escape me that any man, whose judgment is not blinded by prejudice, or who is not at heart a slave-holder, shall not confess to be right and just.

But I fancy I hear some one of my audience say it is just in this circumstance that you and your brother abolitionists fail to make a favorable impression on the public mind. Would you argue more and denounce less, would you persuade more and rebuke less, your cause would be much more likely to succeed. But, I submit, where all is plain there is nothing to be argued. What point in the anti-slavery creed would you have me argue? On what branch of the subject do the people of this country need light? Must I undertake to prove that the slave is a man? That point is conceded already. Nobody doubts it. The slave-holders themselves acknowledge it in the enactment of laws for their government. They acknowledge it when they punish disobedience on the part of the slave. There are seventy-two crimes in the State of Virginia, which, if committed by a black man (no matter how ignorant he be), subject him to the punishment of death; while only two of these same crimes will subject a white man to like punishment. What is this but the acknowledgment that the slave is a moral, intellectual, and responsible being? The manhood of the slave is conceded. It is admitted in the fact that Southern statute-books are covered with enactments, forbidding, under severe fines and penalties, the teaching of the slave to read or write. When you can point to any such laws in reference to the beasts of the field, then I may consent to argue the manhood of the slave. When the dogs in your streets, when the fowls of the air, when the cattle on your hills, when the fish of the sea, and the reptiles that crawl, shall be unable to distinguish the slave from a brute, then will I argue with you that the slave is a man!

For the present it is enough to affirm the equal manhood of the Negro race. Is it not astonishing that, while we are plowing, planting, and reaping, using all kinds of mechanical tools, erecting houses, constructing bridges, building ships, working in metals of brass, iron, copper, silver, and gold; that while we are reading, writing, and cyphering, acting as clerks, merchants, and secretaries, having among us lawyers, doctors, ministers, poets, authors, editors, orators, and teachers; that while we are engaged in all manner of enterprises common to other men—digging gold in California, capturing the whale in the Pacific, feeding sheep and cattle on the hillside, living, moving, acting, thinking, planning, living in families as husbands, wives, and children, and above all, confessing and worshiping the Christian God, and looking hopefully for life and immortality beyond the grave—we are called upon to prove that we are men?

Would you have me argue that man is entitled to liberty? That he is the rightful owner of his own body? You have already declared it. Must I argue the wrongfulness of slavery? Is that a question for republicans? Is it to be settled by the rules of logic and argumentation, as a matter beset with great difficulty, involving a doubtful application of the principle of justice, hard to be understood? How should I look to-day in the presence of Americans, dividing and subdividing a discourse, to show that men have a natural right to freedom, speaking of it relatively and positively, negatively and affirmatively? To do so would be to make myself ridiculous, and to offer an insult to your understanding. There is not a man beneath the canopy of heaven who does not know that slavery is wrong *for him*.

What! Am I to argue that it is wrong to make men brutes, to rob them of their liberty, to work them without wages, to keep them ignorant of their relations to their fellow men, to beat them with sticks, to flay their flesh with the lash, to load their limbs with irons, to hunt them with dogs, to sell them at auction, to sunder their families, to knock out their teeth, to burn their flesh, to starve them into obedience and submission to their masters? Must I argue that a system thus marked with blood and stained with pollution is wrong? No; I will not. I have better employment for my time and strength that such arguments would imply.

What, then, remains to be argued? Is it that slavery is not divine; that God did not establish it; that our doctors of divinity are mistaken? There is blasphemy in the thought. That which is inhuman cannot be divine. Who can reason on such a proposition? They that can, may; I cannot. The time for such argument is past.

At a time like this, scorching irony, not convincing argument, is needed. Oh! had I the ability, and could I reach the nation's ear, I would to-day pour out a fiery streak of biting ridicule, blasting reproach, withering sarcasm, and stern rebuke. For it is not light that is needed, but fire; it is not the gentle shower, but thunder. We need the storm, the whirlwind, and the earthquake. The feeling of the nation must be quickened; the conscience of the nation must be roused; the propriety of the nation must be startled; the hypocrisy of the nation must be exposed; and its crimes against God and man must be denounced.

What to the American slave is your Fourth of July? I answer, a day that reveals to him, more than all other days of the year, the gross injustice and cruelty to which he is the constant victim. To him your celebration is a sham; your boasted liberty an unholy license; your national greatness, swelling vanity; your sounds of rejoicing are empty and heartless; your denunciations of tyrants, brass-fronted impudence; your shouts of liberty and equality, hollow mockery; your prayers and hymns, your sermons and thanksgivings, with all your religious parade and solemnity, are to him mere bombast, fraud, deception, impiety, and hypocrisy—a thin veil to cover up crimes which would disgrace a nation of savages. There is not a nation on the earth guilty of practices more shocking and bloody than are the people of these United States at this very hour.

Go where you may, search where you will, roam through all the monarchies and despotisms of the Old World, travel through South America, search out every abuse and when you have found the last, lay your facts by the side of the every-day practices of this nation, and you will say with me that, for revolting barbarity and shameless hypocrisy, America reigns without a rival.

Ida B. Wells-Barnett (1862–1931)

In Memphis, Tennessee, in 1892, three black businessmen were incarcerated and then lynched for allegedly starting a riot. Journalist Ida B. Wells investigated their murders and concluded that economics was at the root of the mob brutality that had taken their lives. Moreover, she argued that the lynching of black men was not related to rape, as was the popular notion, but was a direct result of the economic and political machinations of racism. In her Memphis newspaper, Free Speech, *Wells wrote: "Nobody in this section of the country believes the old threadbare lie that negro men rape white women. If Southern white men are not careful they will overreach themselves, and public sentiment will have a reaction. A conclusion will then be reached which will be very damaging to the moral reputation of their women." In response to Wells's words, her newspaper offices were destroyed; furthermore, threats of personal violence forced her out of the South. This 1892 confrontation was among many other tense episodes in the life of this political activist and journalist.*

Ida B. Wells grew up in Holly Springs, Mississippi, the oldest of eight children. When her parents and younger brother died in 1878 from yellow fever, sixteen-year-old Wells became the caretaker for her siblings. Having attended Rust College, a high school and industrial training school set up by the Freedmen's Bureau, Wells supported her family on a teacher's salary, moving to Memphis, where she taught until 1891. She became editor of the Evening Star *literary journal while still teaching in Memphis. After attending an 1889 meeting of the Colored Press Association in Washington, D.C., Wells was approached to become the editor of and a partner in the Memphis-based* Free Speech and Headlight *newspaper. Radical pieces similar to her attack on lynching became standard in the paper, and when she left the South after the 1892 editorial Wells obtained a position at* New York Age. *She augmented her journalistic writing by lecturing on lynching throughout the Northeast, as well as in Scotland and Wales. By 1893, Wells had ignited an international awareness of lynchings; throughout the United States, she had inspired black women's clubs to become involved with the issue.*

She went to Chicago in 1893 to write a protest piece—along with Frederick Douglass and black journalist Ferdinand Barnett—about racism at the Chicago's World Fair. Wells remained in that city, taking a job at Barnett's black newspaper, the Chicago Conservator. *She and Barnett married in 1895 and had four children.*

Marriage and motherhood did not slow Ida Wells-Barnett down, and she continued crusading on various fronts. She was involved with the formation of the NAACP in 1909, worked with the Negro Fellowship League in 1910 to secure lodging and employment for black migrant men, founded the black Alpha Suffrage Club in 1913, wrote critically of the violent urban riots in the late 1910s, and spoke at Universal Negro Improvement Association meetings in support of Marcus Garvey.

Wells-Barnett delivered the following speech, "Lynch Law in All Its Phases," in 1893 at Tremont Temple in Boston. In it she presents the details of the 1892 lynching that led to her personal crusade and examines the racist motivations behind the numerous lynchings in the South.

Lynch Law in All Its Phases

I am before the American people to-day through no inclination of my own, but because of a deep-seated conviction that the country at large does not know the extent to which lynch law prevails in parts of the Republic, nor the conditions which force into exile those who speak the truth. I cannot believe that the apathy and indifference which so largely obtains regarding mob rule is other than the result of ignorance of the true situation. And yet, the observing and thoughtful must know that in one section, at least, of our common country, a government of the people, by the people, and for the people, means a government by the mob; where the land of the free and home of the brave means a land of lawlessness, murder and outrage; and where liberty of speech means the license of might to destroy the business and drive from home those who exercise this privilege contrary to the will of the mob. Repeated attacks on the life, liberty and happiness of any citizen or class of citizens are attacks on distinctive American institutions; such attacks imperiling as they do the foundation of government, law and order, merit the thoughtful consideration of far-sighted Americans; not from a standpoint of sentiment, not even so much from a standpoint of justice to a weak race, as from a desire to preserve our institutions.

The race problem or negro question, as it has been called, has been omnipresent and all-pervading since long before the Afro-American was raised from the degradation of the slave to the dignity of the citizen. It has never been settled because the right methods have not been employed in the solution. It is the Banquo's ghost of politics, religion, and sociology which will not down at the bidding of those who are tormented with its ubiquitous appearance on every occasion. Times without number, since invested with citizenship, the race has been indicted for ignorance, immorality and general worthlessness—declared guilty and executed by its self-constituted judges. The operations of law do not dispose of negroes fast enough, and lynching bees have become the favorite pastime of the South. As excuse for the same, a new cry, as false as it is foul, is raised in an effort to blast race character, a cry which has proclaimed to the world that virtue and innocence are violated by Afro-Americans who must be killed like wild beasts to protect womanhood and childhood.

Born and reared in the South, I had never expected to live elsewhere. Until this past year I was one among those who believed the condition of the masses gave large excuse for the humiliations and proscriptions under which we labored; that when wealth, education and character became more general among us,—the cause being removed—the effect would cease, and justice be accorded to all alike. I shared the general belief that good newspapers entering regularly the homes of our people in every state could do more to bring about this result than any agency. Preaching the doctrine of self-help, thrift and economy every week, they would be the teachers to those who had been deprived of school advantages, yet were making history every day—and train to think for themselves our mental children of a larger growth. And so, three years ago last June, I became editor and part owner of the *Memphis Free Speech*. As editor, I had occasion to criticize the city School Board's employment of inefficient teachers and poor school-buildings for Afro-American children. I was in the employ of that board at the time, and at the close of that school-term one year ago, was not re-elected to a position I had held in the city schools for seven years. Accepting the decision of the Board of Education, I set out to make a race newspaper pay—a thing which older and wiser heads said could not be done. But there were enough of our people in Memphis and surrounding territory to support a paper, and I believed they would do so. With nine months' hard work the circulation increased from 1,500 to 3,500; in twelve months it was on a good paying basis. Throughout the Mississippi Valley in Arkansas, Tennessee and Mississippi—on plantations and in towns, the demand for and interest in the paper increased among the masses. The newsboys who would not sell it on the trains, voluntarily testified that they had never known colored people to demand a paper so eagerly.

To make the paper a paying business I became advertising agent, solicitor, as well as editor, and was continually on the go. Wherever I went among the people, I gave them in church, school, public gatherings, and home, the benefit of my honest conviction that maintenance of character, money getting and education would finally solve our problem and that it depended on us to say how soon this would be brought about. This sentiment bore good fruit in Memphis.

We had nice homes, representatives in almost every branch of business and profession, and refined society. We had learned that helping each other helped all, and every well-conducted business by Afro-Americans prospered. With all our proscription in theatres, hotels and on railroads, we had never had a lynching and did not believe we could have one. There had been lynchings and brutal outrages of all sorts in our own state and those adjoining us, but we had confidence and pride in our city and the majesty of its laws. So far in advance of other Southern cities was ours, we were content to endure the evils we had, to labor and to wait.

But there was a rude awakening. On the morning of March 9 [1892], the bodies of three of our best young men were found in an old field horribly shot to pieces. These young men had owned and operated the "People's Grocery," situated at what was known as the Curve—a suburb made up almost entirely of colored people—about a mile from city limits. Thomas Moss, one of the oldest letter-carriers in the city, was president of the company, Calvin McDowell was manager and Will Stewart was a clerk. There were about ten other stockholders, all colored men. The young men were well known and popular and their business flourished, and that of Barrett, a white grocer who kept store there before the "People's Grocery" was established, went down. One day an officer came to the "People's Grocery" and inquired for a colored man who lived in the neighborhood, and for whom the officer had a warrant. Barrett was with him and when McDowell said he knew nothing as to the whereabouts of the man for whom they were searching, Barrett, not the officer, then accused McDowell of harboring the man, and McDowell gave the lie. Barrett drew his pistol and struck McDowell with it; thereupon McDowell, who was a tall, fine-looking six-footer, took Barrett's pistol from him, knocked him down and gave him a good thrashing, while Will Stewart, the clerk, kept the special officer at bay. Barrett went to town, swore out a warrant for their arrest on a charge of assault and battery. McDowell went before the Criminal Court, immediately gave bond and returned to his store. Barrett then threatened (to use his own words) that he was going to clean out the whole store. Knowing how anxious he was to destroy their business, these young men consulted a lawyer who told them they were justified in defending themselves if attacked, as they were a mile beyond city limits and police protection. They accordingly armed several of their friends—not to assail, but to resist the threatened Saturday night attack.

When they saw Barrett enter the front door and a half dozen men at the rear door at 11 o'clock that night, they supposed the attack was on and immediately fired into the crowd, wounding three men. These men, dressed in citizen's clothes, turned out to be deputies who claimed to be hunting another man for whom they had a warrant, and whom any one of them could have arrested without trouble. When these men found they had fired upon officers of the law, they threw away their firearms and submitted to arrest, confident they should establish their innocence of intent to fire upon officers of the law. The daily papers in flaming headlines roused the evil passions of the whites, denounced these poor boys in unmeasured terms, nor permitted them a word in their own defense.

The neighborhood of the Curve was searched next day, and about thirty persons were thrown into jail, charged with conspiracy. No communication was to be had with friends any of the three days these men were in jail; bail was refused and Thomas Moss was not allowed to eat the food his wife prepared for him. The judge is reported to have said, "Any one can see them after three days." They were seen after three days, but they were no longer able to respond to the greetings of friends. On Tuesday following the shooting at the grocery, the papers which had made much of the sufferings of the wounded deputies, and promised it would go hard with those who did the shooting, if they died, announced that the officers were all out of danger, and would recover. The friends of the prisoners breathed more easily and relaxed their vigilance. They felt that as the officers would not die, there was no danger that in the heat of passion the prisoners would meet violent death at the hands of the mob. Besides, we had such confidence in the law. But the law did not provide capital punishment for shooting which did not kill. So the mob did what the law could not be made to do, as a lesson to the Afro-American that he must not shoot a white man,—no matter what the provocation. The same night after the announcement was made in the papers that the officers would get well, the mob, in obedience to a plan known to every prominent white man in the city, went to the jail between two and three o'clock in the morning, dragged out these young men, hatless and shoeless, put them on the yard engine of the railroad which was in waiting just behind the jail, carried them a mile north of city limits and horribly shot them to death while the locomotive at a given signal let off steam and blew the whistle to deaden the sound of the firing.

"It was done by unknown men," said the jury, yet the *Appeal-Avalanche*, which goes to press at 3 a.m., had a two-column account of the lynching. The papers also told how McDowell got hold of the guns of the mob, and as his grasp could not be loosened, his hand was shattered with a pistol ball and all the lower part of his face was torn away. There were four pools of blood found and only three bodies. It was whispered that he, McDowell, killed one of the lynchers with his gun, and it is well known that a policeman who was seen on the street a few days previous to the lynching, died very suddenly the next day after.

"It was done by unknown parties," said the jury, yet the papers told how Tom Moss begged for his life, for the sake of his wife, his little daughter and his unborn infant. They also told us that his last words were, "If you will kill us, turn our faces to the West."

All this we learned too late to save these men, even if the law had not been in the hands of their murderers. When the colored people realized that the flower of our young manhood had been stolen away at night and murdered, there was a rush for firearms to avenge the wrong, but no house would sell a colored man a gun; the armory of the Tennessee Rifles, our only colored military company, and of which McDowell was a member, was broken into by order of the Criminal Court judge, and its guns taken. One hundred men and irresponsible boys from fifteen years and up were armed by order of the authorities and rushed out to the Curve, where it was reported that the colored people were massing, and at point of the bayonet dispersed these men who could do nothing but talk. The cigars, wines, etc., of the grocery stock were freely used by the mob, who possessed the place on pretence of dispersing the conspiracy. The money drawer was broken into and contents taken. The trunk of Calvin McDowell, who had a room in the store, was broken open, and his clothing, which was not good enough to take away, was thrown out and trampled on the floor.

These men were murdered, their stock was attached by creditors and sold for less than one-eighth of its cost to that same man Barrett, who is to-day running his grocery in the same place. He had indeed kept his word, and by aid of the authorities destroyed the People's Grocery Company root and branch. The relatives of Will Stewart and Calvin McDowell are bereft of their protectors. The baby daughter of Tom Moss, too young to express how she misses her father, toddles to the wardrobe, seizes the legs of the trousers of his letter-carrier uniform, hugs and kisses them with evident delight and stretches up her little hands to be taken up into the arms which will nevermore clasp his daughter's form. His wife holds Thomas Moss, Jr., in her arms, upon whose unconscious baby face the tears fall thick and fast when she is thinking of the sad fate of the father he will never see, and of the two helpless children who cling to her for the support she cannot give. Although these men were peaceable, law-abiding citizens of this country, we are told there can be no punishment for their murderers nor indemnity for their relatives.

I have no power to describe the feeling of horror that possessed every member of the race in Memphis when the truth dawned upon us that the protection of the law which we had so long enjoyed was no longer ours; all this had been destroyed in a night, and the barriers of the law had been thrown down, and the guardians of the public peace and confidence scoffed away into the shadows, and all authority given into the hands of the mob, and innocent men cut down as if they were brutes—the first feeling was one of utter dismay, then intense indignation. Vengeance was whispered from ear to ear, but sober reflection brought the conviction that it would be extreme folly to seek vengeance when such action meant certain death for the men, and horrible slaughter for the women and children, as one of the evening papers took care to remind us. The power of the State, country and city, the civil authorities and the strong arm of the military power were all on the side of the mob and of lawlessness. Few of our men possessed firearms, our only company's guns were confiscated, and the only white man who would sell a colored man a gun, was himself jailed, and his store closed. We were helpless in our great strength. It was our first object lesson in the doctrine of white supremacy; an illustration of the South's cardinal principle that no matter what the attainments, character or standing of an Afro-American, the laws of the South will not protect him against a white man.

There was only one thing we could do, and a great determination seized upon the people to follow the advice of the martyred Moss, and "turn our faces to the West," whose laws protect all alike. The *Free Speech* supported by our ministers and leading business men advised the people to leave a community whose laws did not protect them. Hundreds left on foot to walk four hundred miles between Memphis and Oklahoma. A Baptist minister went to the territory, built a church, and took his entire congregation out in less than a month. Another minister sold his church and took his flock to California, and still another has settled in Kansas. In two months, six thousand persons had left the city and every branch of business began to feel this silent resentment of the outrage, and failure of the authorities to punish the lynchers. There were a number of business failures and blocks of houses were for rent. The superintendent and treasurer of the street railway company called at the office of the *Free Speech*, to have us urge the colored people to ride again on the street cars. A real estate dealer said to a colored man who returned some property he had been buying on the installment plan: "I don't see what you 'niggers' are cutting up about. You got off light. We first intended to kill every one of those thirty-one 'niggers' in jail, but concluded to let all go but the 'leaders.'" They did let all go to the penitentiary. These so-called rioters have since been tried in the Criminal Court for the conspiracy of defending their property, and are now serving terms of three, eight, and fifteen years each in the Tennessee State prison.

To restore the equilibrium and put a stop to the great financial loss, the next move was to get rid of the *Free Speech,*—the disturbing element which kept the waters troubled; which would not let the people forget, and in obedience to whose advice nearly six thousand persons had left the city. In casting about for an excuse, the mob found it in the following editorial which appeared in the Memphis *Free Speech,*—May 21, 1892: "Eight negroes lynched in one week. Since last issue of the *Free Speech* one was lynched at Little Rock, Ark., where the citizens broke into the penitentiary and got their man; three near Anniston, Ala., and one in New Orleans, all on the same charge, the new alarm of assaulting white women—and three near Clarksville, Ga., for killing a white man. The same program of hanging—then shooting bullets into the lifeless bodies—was carried out to the letter. Nobody in this section of the country believes the old threadbare lie that negro men rape white women. If Southern white men are not careful they will overreach themselves, and public sentiment will have a reaction. A conclusion will then be reached which will be very damaging to the moral reputation of their women." Commenting on this, *The Daily Commercial* of Wednesday following said: "Those negroes who are attempting to make lynching of individuals of their race a means for arousing the worst passions of their kind, are playing with a dangerous sentiment. The negroes may as well understand that there is no mercy for the negro rapist, and little patience with his defenders. A negro organ printed in this city in a recent issue published the following atrocious paragraph: 'Nobody in this section believes the old threadbare lie that negro men rape white women. If Southern white men are not careful they will overreach themselves and public sentiment will have a reaction. A conclusion will be reached which will be very damaging to the moral reputation of their women.' The fact that a black scoundrel is allowed to live and utter such loathsome and repulsive calumnies is a volume of evidence as to the wonderful patience of Southern whites. There are some things the Southern white man will not tolerate, and the obscene intimidation of the foregoing has brought the writer to the very uttermost limit of public patience. We hope we have said enough."

The Evening *Scimitar* of the same day copied this leading editorial and added this comment: "Patience under such circumstances is not a virtue. If the negroes themselves do not apply the remedy without delay, it will be the duty of those he has attacked, to tie the wretch who utters these calumnies to a stake at the intersection of Main and Madison streets, brand him in the forehead with a hot iron and—"

Such open suggestions by the leading daily papers of the progressive city of Memphis were acted upon by the leading citizens and a meeting was held at the Cotton Exchange that evening. *The Commercial* two days later had the following account of it:

ATROCIOUS BLACKGUARDISM

There will be no Lynching and no Repetition of the Offense.

> In its issue of Wednesday *The Commercial* reproduced and commented upon an editorial which appeared a day or two before in a negro organ known as the *Free Speech*. The article was so insufferably and indecently slanderous that the whole city awoke to a feeling of intense resentment which came within an ace of culminating in one of those occurrences whose details are so eagerly seized and so prominently published by Northern newspapers. Conservative counsels, however, prevailed, and no extreme measures were resorted to. On Wednesday afternoon a meeting of citizens was held. It was not an assemblage of hoodlums or irresponsible fire-eaters, but solid, substantial business men who knew exactly what they were doing and who were far more indignant at the villainous insult to the women of the South than they would have been at any injury done themselves. This meeting appointed a committee to seek the author of the infamous editorial and warn him quietly that upon repetition of the offense he would find some other part of the country a good deal safer and pleasanter place of residence than this. The committee called a negro preacher named Nightingale, but he disclaimed responsibility and convinced the gentlemen that he had really sold out his paper to a woman named Wells. This woman is not in Memphis at present. It was finally learned that one Fleming, a negro who was driven out of Crittenden Co. during the trouble there a few years ago, wrote the paragraph. He had, however, heard of the meeting, and fled from a fate which he feared was in store for him, and which he knew he deserved. His whereabouts could not be ascertained, and the committee so reported. Later on, a communication from Fleming to a prominent Republican politician, and that politician's reply were shown to one or two gentlemen. The former was an inquiry as to whether the writer might safely return to Memphis, the latter was an emphatic answer in the negative, and Fleming is still in hiding. Nothing further will be done in the matter. There will be no lynching, and it is very certain there will be no repetition of the outrage. If there should be—Friday, May 25 [sic].

The only reason there was no lynching of Mr. Fleming who was business manager and half owner of the *Free Speech*, and who did not write the editorial, was because this same white Republican told him the committee was coming, and warned him not to trust them, but get out of the way. The committee scoured the city hunting him, and had to be content with Mr. Nightingale who was dragged to the meeting, shamefully abused (although it was known he had sold out his interest in the paper six months before). He was struck in the face and forced at the pistol's point to sign a letter which was written by them, in which he denied all knowledge of the editorial, denounced and condemned it as slander on white women. I do not censure Mr. Nightingale for his action because, having never been at the pistol's point myself, I do not feel that I am competent to sit in judgment on him, or say what I would do under such circumstances.

I had written that editorial with other matter for the week's paper before leaving home the Friday previous for the General Conference of the A.M.E. Church in Philadelphia. Conference adjourned Tuesday, and Thursday, May 25

[sic], at 3 p.m., I landed in New York City for a few days' stay before returning home, and there learned from the papers that my business manager had been driven away and the paper suspended. Telegraphing for news, I received telegrams and letters in return informing me that the trains were being watched, that I was to be dumped into the river and beaten, if not killed; it had been learned that I wrote the editorial and I was to be hanged in front of the court-house and my face bled if I returned, and I was implored by my friends to remain away. The creditors attached the office in the meantime and the outfit was sold without more ado, thus destroying effectually that which it had taken years to build. One prominent insurance agent publicly declares he will make it his business to shoot me down on sight if I return to Memphis in twenty years, while a leading white lady had remarked that she was opposed to the lynching of those three men in March, but she did wish there was some way by which I could be gotten back and lynched.

I have been censured for writing that editorial, but when I think of the five men who were lynched that week for assault on white women and that not a week passes but some poor soul is violently ushered into eternity on this trumped-up charge, knowing the many things I do, and part of which I tried to tell in the *New York Age* of June 25 (and in the pamphlets I have with me) seeing that the whole race in the South was injured in the estimation of the world because of these false reports, I could no longer hold my peace, and I feel, yes, I am sure, that if it had to be done over again (provided no one else was the loser save myself) I would do and say the very same again.

The lawlessness here described is not confined to one locality. In the past ten years over a thousand colored men, women and children have been butchered, murdered and burnt in all parts of the South. The details of these horrible outrages seldom reach beyond the narrow world where they occur. Those who commit the murders write the reports, and hence these lasting blots upon the honor of a nation cause but a faint ripple on the outside world. They arouse no great indignation and call forth no adequate demand for justice. The victims were black, and the reports are so written as to make it appear that the helpless creatures deserved the fate which overtook them.

Not so with the Italian lynching of 1891. They were not black men, and three of them were not citizens of the Republic, but subjects of the King of Italy. The chief of police of New Orleans was shot and eleven Italians were arrested charged with the murder; they were tried and the jury disagreed; the good, law-abiding citizens of New Orleans thereupon took them from the jail and lynched them at high noon. A feeling of horror ran through the nation at this outrage. All Europe was amazed. The Italian government demanded thorough investigation and redress, and the Federal Government promised to give the matter the consideration which was its due. The diplomatic relations between the two countries became very much strained and for a while war talk was freely indulged. Here was a case where the power of the Federal Government to protect its own citizens and redeem its pledges to a friendly power was put to the test. When our State Department called upon the authorities of Louisiana for investigation of the crime and punishment of the criminals, the United States government was told that the crime was strictly within the authority of the State of Louisiana, and Louisiana would attend to it. After a farcical investigation, the usual verdict in such cases was rendered: "Death at the hand of parties unknown to the jury," the same verdict which has been pronounced over the bodies of over 1,000 colored persons! Our general government has thus admitted that it has no jurisdiction over the crimes committed at New Orleans upon citizens of the country, nor upon those citizens of a friendly power to whom the general government and not the State government has pledged protection. Not only has our general government made the confession that one of the states is greater than the Union, but the general government has paid $25,000 of the people's money to the King of Italy for the lynching of those three subjects, the evil-doing of one State, over which it has no control, but for whose lawlessness of the whole country must pay. The principle involved in the treaty power of the government has not yet been settled to the satisfaction of foreign powers; but the principle involved in the right of State jurisdiction in such matters, was settled long ago by the decision of the United States Supreme Court.

I beg your patience while we look at another phase of the lynching mania. We have turned heretofore to the pages of ancient and medieval history, to Roman tyranny, the Jesuitical Inquisition of Spain for the spectacle of a human being burnt to death. In the past ten years three instances, at least, have been furnished where men have literally been roasted to death to appease the fury of Southern mobs. The Texarkana instance of last year and the Paris, Texas, case of this month are the most recent as they are the most shocking and repulsive. Both were charged with crimes for which the laws provide adequate punishment. The Texarkana man, Ed Coy, was charged with assaulting a white woman. A mob pronounced him guilty, strapped him to a tree, chipped the flesh from his body, poured coal oil over him and the woman in the case set fire to him. The country looked on and in many cases applauded, because it was published that this man had violated the honor of the white woman, although he protested his innocence to the last. Judge Tourjee in the Chicago *Inter-Ocean* of recent date says investigation has shown that Ed Coy had supported this woman (who was known to be of bad character) and her drunken husband for over a year previous to the burning.

The Paris, Texas, burning of Henry Smith, February 1st, has exceeded all the others in its horrible details. The man was drawn through the streets on a float, as the Roman generals used to parade their trophies of war, while the scaffold ten feet high, was being built, and irons were heated in the fire. He was bound on it, and red-hot irons began at his feet and slowly branded his body, while the mob howled with delight at his shrieks. Red-hot irons were run down his throat and cooked his tongue; his eyes were burned out, and when he was at last unconscious, cotton seed hulls were placed under him, coal oil poured all over him, and a torch applied to the mass. When the flames burned away the ropes which bound Smith and scorched his flesh, he was brought back to sensibility—and burned and maimed and sightless as he was, he rolled off the platform and away from the fire. His half-cooked body was seized and trampled and thrown back into the flames while a mob of twenty thousand persons who came from all over the country howled with delight, and gathered up some buttons and ashes after all was over to preserve for relics. This man was charged with outraging and murdering a four-year-old white child, covering her body with brush, sleeping beside her through the night, then making his escape. If true, it was the deed of a madman, and should have been clearly proven so. The fact that no time for verification of the newspaper reports was given, is suspicious, especially when I remember that a negro was lynched in Indianola, Sharkey Co., Miss., last summer. The dispatches said it was because he had assaulted the sheriff's eight-year-old daughter. The girl was more than eighteen years old and was found by her father in this man's room, who was a servant on the place.

These incidents have been made the basis of this terrible story because they overshadow all others of a like nature in cruelty and represent the legal phases of the whole question. They could be multiplied without number—and each outrival the other in the fiendish cruelty exercised, and the frequent awful lawlessness exhibited. The following table shows the number of black men lynched from January 1, 1882, to January 1, 1892: In 1882, 52; 1883, 39; 1884, 53; 1885, 77; 1886, 73; 1887, 70; 1888, 72; 1889, 95; 1890, 100; 1891, 169. Of these 728 black men who were murdered, 269 were charged with rape, 253 with murder, 44 with robbery, 37 with incendiarism, 32 with reasons unstated (it was not necessary to have a reason), 27 with race prejudice, 13 with quarreling with white men, 10 with making threats, 7 with rioting, 5 with miscegenation, 4 with burglary. One of the men lynched in 1891 was Will Lewis, who was lynched because "he was drunk and saucy to white folks." A woman who was one of the 73 victims in 1886, was hung in Jackson, Tenn., because the white woman for whom she cooked, died suddenly of poisoning. An examination showed arsenical poisoning. A search in the cook's room found rat poison. She was thrown into jail, and when the mob had worked itself up to the lynching pitch, she was dragged out, every stitch of clothing torn from her body, and was hung in the public court house square in sight of everybody. That white woman's husband has since died, in the insane asylum, a raving maniac, and his ravings have led to the conclusion that he and not the cook, was the poisoner of his wife. A fifteen-year-old colored girl was lynched last spring, at Rayville, La., on the same charge of poisoning. A woman was also lynched at Hollendale, Miss., last spring, charged with being an accomplice in the murder of her white paramour who had abused her. These were only two of the 159 persons lynched in the South from January 1, 1892, to January 1, 1893. Over a dozen black men have been lynched already since this new year set in, and the year is not yet two months old.

It will thus be seen that neither age, sex nor decency are spared. Although the impression has gone abroad that most of the lynchings take place because of assaults on white women only one-third of the number lynched in the past ten years have been charged with that offense, to say nothing of those who were not guilty of the charge. And according to law none of them were guilty until proven so. But the unsupported word of any white person for any cause is sufficient to cause a lynching. So bold have the lynchers become, masks are laid aside, the temples of justice and strongholds of law are invaded in broad daylight and prisoners taken out and lynched, while governors of states and officers of law stand by and see the work well done.

And yet this Christian nation, the flower of the nineteenth century civilization, says it can do nothing to stop this inhuman slaughter. The general government is willingly powerless to send troops to protect the lives of its black citizens, but the state governments are free to use state troops to shoot them down like cattle, when in desperation the black men attempt to defend themselves, and then tell the world that it was necessary to put down a "race war."

Persons unfamiliar with the condition of affairs in the Southern States do not credit the truth when it is told them. They cannot conceive how such a condition of affairs prevails so near them with steam power, telegraph wires and printing presses in daily and hourly touch with the localities where such disorder reigns. In a former generation the ancestors of these same people refused to believe that slavery was the "league with death and the covenant with hell." Wm. Lloyd Garrison declared it to be, until he was thrown into a dungeon in Baltimore, until the signal lights of Nat Turner lit the dull skies of Northampton County, and until sturdy old John Brown made his attack on Harpers Ferry. When freedom of speech was martyred in the person of Elijah Lovejoy at Alton, when the liberty of free-discussion in Senate of the Nation's Congress was struck down in the person of the fearless Charles Sumner, the Nation was at last convinced that slavery was not only a monster but a tyrant. That same tyrant is at work under a new name and guise. The lawlessness which has been here described is like unto that which prevailed under slavery. *The very same forces are at work now as then.* The attempt is being made to subject to a condition of civil and industrial dependence, those whom the Constitution declares to be free men. The events which have led up to the present wide-spread lawlessness in the South can be traced to the very first year Lee's conquered veterans marched from Appomattox to their homes in the Southland. They were conquered in war, but not in spirit. They believed as firmly as ever that it was their right to rule black men and dictate to the National Government. The Knights of White Liners, and the Ku Klux Klans were composed of veterans of the Confederate army who were determined to destroy the effect of all the slave had gained by the war. They finally accomplished their purpose in 1876. The right of the Afro-American to vote and hold office remains in the Federal Constitution, but is destroyed in the constitution of the Southern states. Having destroyed the citizenship of the man, they are now trying to destroy the manhood of the citizen. All their laws are shaped to this end,—school laws, railroad car regulations, those governing labor liens on crops,—every device is adopted to make slaves of free men and rob them of their wages. Whenever a malicious law is violated in any of its parts, any farmer, any railroad conductor, or merchant can call together a posse of his neighbors and punish even with death the black man who resists and the legal authorities sanction what is done by failing to prosecute and punish the murders. The Repeal of the Civil Rights Law removed their last barrier and the black man's last bulwark and refuge. The rule of the mob is absolute.

Those who know this recital to be true, say there is nothing they can do—they cannot interfere and vainly hope by further concession to placate the imperious and dominating part of our country in which this lawlessness prevails. Because this country has been almost rent in twain by internal dissension, the other sections seem virtually to have agreed that the best way to heal the breach is to permit the taking away of civil, political, and even human rights, to stand by in silence and utter indifference while the South continues to wreak fiendish vengeance on the irresponsible cause. They pretend to believe that with all the machinery of law and government in its hands; with the jails and penitentiaries and convict farms filled with petty race criminals; with the well-known fact that no negro has ever been known to escape conviction and punishment for any crime in the South—still there are those who try to justify and condone the lynching of over a thousand black men in less than ten years—an average of one hundred a year. The public sentiment of the country, by its silence in press, pulpit and in public meetings has encouraged this state of affairs, and public sentiment is stronger than law. With all the country's disposition to condone and temporize with the South and its methods; with its many instances of sacrificing principle to prejudice for the sake of making friends and healing the breach made by the late war; of going into the lawless country with capital to build up its waste places and remaining silent in the presence of outrage and wrong—the South is as vindictive and bitter as ever. She is willing to make friends as long as she is permitted to pursue unmolested and uncensured, her course of proscription, injustice, outrage and vituperation. The malignant misrepresentation of General Butler, the uniformly indecent and abusive assault of this dead man whose only crime was a defence of his country, is a recent proof that the South has lost none of its bitterness. The *Nashville American*, one of the leading papers of one of the leading southern cities, gleefully announced editorially that " 'The Beast is dead.' Early yesterday morning, acting under the devil's orders, the angel of Death took Ben Butler and landed him in the lowest depths of hell, and we pity even the devil the possession he has secured." The men who wrote these editorials are without exception young men who know nothing of slavery and scarcely anything of the war. The bitterness and hatred have been instilled in and taught them by their parents, and they are men who make and reflect the sentiment of their section. The South spares nobody else's feelings, and it seems a queer logic that when it comes to a question of right, involving lives of citizens and the honor of the government, the South's feelings must be respected and spared.

Do you ask the remedy? A public sentiment strong against lawlessness must be aroused. Every individual can contribute to this awakening. When a sentiment against lynch law as strong, deep and mighty as that roused against slavery prevails, I have no fear of the result. It should be already established as a fact and not as a theory, that every human being must have a fair trial for his life and liberty, no matter what the charge against him. When a demand goes up from fearless and persistent reformers from press and pulpit, from industrial and moral associations that this shall be so from Maine to Texas and from ocean to ocean, a way will be found to make it so.

In deference to the few words of condemnation uttered at the M.E. General Conference last year, and by other organizations, Governors Hogg of Texas, Northern of Georgia, and Tillman of South Carolina, have issued proclamations offering rewards for the apprehension of lynchers. These rewards have never been claimed, and these governors knew they would not be when offered. In many cases they knew the ringleaders of the mobs. The prosecuting attorney of Shelby County, Tenn., wrote Governor Buchanan to offer a reward for the arrest of the lynchers of three young men murdered in Memphis. Everybody in that city and state knew well that the letter was written for the sake of effect and the governor did not even offer the reward. But the country at large deluded itself with the belief that the officials of the South and the leading citizens condemned lynching. The lynchings go on in spite of offered rewards, and in face of Governor Hogg's vigorous talk, the second man was burnt alive in his state with the utmost deliberation and publicity. Since he sent a message to the legislature the mob found and hung Henry Smith's stepson, because he refused to tell where Smith was when they were hunting for him. Public sentiment which shall denounce these crimes in season and out; public sentiment which turns capital and immigration from a section given over to lawlesness; public sentiment which insists on the punishment of criminals and lynchers by law must be aroused.

It is no wonder in my mind that the party which stood for thirty years as the champion of human liberty and human rights, the party of great moral ideas, should suffer overwhelming defeat when it has proven recreant to its professions and abandoned a position it created; when although its followers were being outraged in every sense, it was afraid to stand for the right, and appeal to the American people to sustain them in it. It put aside the question of a free ballot and fair count of every citizen and gave its voice and influence for the protection of the coat instead of the man who wore it, for the product of labor instead of the laborer; for the seal of citizenship rather than the citizen, and insisted upon the evils of free trade instead of the sacredness of free speech. I am no politician but I believe if the Republican party had met the issues squarely for human rights instead of the tariff it would have occupied a different position to-day. The voice of the people is the voice of God, and I long with all the intensity of my soul for the Garrison, Douglas, Sumner, Wittier, and Phillips who shall rouse this nation to a demand that from Greenland's icy mountains to the coral reefs of the Southern seas, mob rule shall be put down and equal and exact justice be accorded to every citizen of whatever race, who finds a home within the borders of the land of the free and the home of the brave.

Then no longer will our national hymn be sounding brass and a tinkling cymbal, but every member of this great composite nation will be a living, harmonious illustration of the words, and all can honestly and gladly join in singing:

> My country! 'tis of thee,
> Sweet land of liberty
> Of thee I sing.
> Land where our fathers died,
> Land of the Pilgrim's pride,
> From every mountain side
> Freedom does ring.

Mary McLeod Bethune (1875–1955)

A *persuasive advocate of Christian ideals and of an integrationist approach to race relations, Mary McLeod Bethune became the foremost black woman in American politics and education during the first half of the twentieth century. Born near Mayesville, South Carolina, the fifteenth child of former slaves, this great educator learned her first lessons in a school taught by a black missionary from the North. With this teacher's help, Bethune went on to study at a seminary in North Carolina before enrolling in what is now the Moody Bible Institute in Chicago.*

After completing her studies in 1895, Bethune was thwarted in her desire to serve as a missionary to Africa. And so she went back south to teach, first at the Haines Normal and Industrial Institute in Augusta, Georgia, and later at the Kendall Institute in Sumter, South Carolina, where she met her husband, a businessman. The couple moved to Savannah, Georgia, became parents, and then relocated to Florida, where she had accepted a teaching position.

By 1907, separated from her husband and living in Daytona Beach, Bethune had established her Daytona Educational and Industrial Institute. After more than a decade of careful economy and persistent public relations, the Institute granted diplomas to forty-seven women in 1920. It expanded in the 1920s, initiating a junior college program in 1924 and later merging with the Cookman Institute, a men's college from Jacksonville, to form Bethune-Cookman College. Bethune served full-time as college president from 1904 to 1942, and later as President Emeritus until the end of her life.

The impressive fortitude that marked Bethune's achievements in education led her to political activism as well. Her lifelong concern about the welfare of black women was reflected in her presidency of the Florida Federation of Colored Women's Clubs from 1917 to 1924. She became president of the National Association of Colored Women (NACW) in 1924, which claimed ten thousand members at the time. During the four years of her presidency, Bethune led efforts to press for black political action, children's welfare, and networking with national and international women's organizations.

In 1935, because she believed the NACW had become too locally focused, Bethune founded the National Council of Negro Women (NCNW), serving as its president until 1949. The NCNW worked to unite all black women's organizations to target racial segregation and published the Aframerican Women's Journal.

Working with other civil rights and educational associations at the time, Bethune developed an acquaintanceship with Eleanor Roosevelt and was appointed by President Franklin Roosevelt to the National Youth Administration (NYA), a 1935 New Deal program of youth employment. Bethune is credited with establishing weekly meetings of all blacks serving in the New Deal programs—Roosevelt's "Black Cabinet"—to solidify a push for civil rights in employment and government facilities. When the NYA was discontinued in 1943, Bethune became a special representative of the U.S. State Department at the conference in San Francisco that led to the 1945 founding of the United Nations.

In the following speech, "A Century of Progress of Negro Women," delivered to the Chicago Women's Federation in 1933, Bethune points out the distinctive history, contributions, and achievements of black women.

A Century of Progress of Negro Women

To Frederick Douglass is credited the plea that, "the Negro be not judged by the heights to which he is risen, but by the depths from which he has climbed." Judged on that basis, the Negro woman embodies one of the modern miracles of the New World.

One hundred years ago she was the most pathetic figure on the American continent. She was not a person, in the opinion of many, but a thing—a thing whose personality had no claim to the respect of mankind. She was a house-hold drudge,—a means for getting distasteful work done; she was an animated agricultural implement to augment the service of mules and plows in cultivating and harvesting the cotton crop. Then she was an automatic incubator, a producer of human live stock, beneath whose heart and lungs more potential laborers could be bred and nurtured and brought to the light of toilsome day.

Today she stands side by side with the finest manhood the race has been able to produce. Whatever the achievements of the Negro man in letters, business, art, pulpit, civic progress and moral reform, he cannot but share them with his sister of darker hue. Whatever glory belongs to the race for a development unprecedented in history for the given length of time, a full share belongs to the womanhood of the race. . . .

By the very force of circumstances, the part she has played in the progress of the race has been of necessity, to a certain extent, subtle and indirect. She has not always been permitted a place in the front ranks where she could show her face and make her voice heard with effect. . . . [But] she has been quick to seize every opportunity which presented itself to come more and more into the open and strive directly for the uplift of the race and nation. In that direction, her achievements have been amazing. . . .

Negro women have made outstanding contributions in the arts. Meta V. W. Fuller and May Howard Jackson are significant figures in Fine Arts development. Angelina Grimké, Georgia Douglass Johnson and Alice Dunbar Nelson are poets of note. Jessie Fausett has become famous as a novelist. In the field of Music Anita Patti Brown, Lillian Evanti, Elizabeth Greenfield, Florence Cole-Talbert, Marian Anderson and Marie Selika stand out pre-eminently.

Very early in the post-emancipation period women began to show signs of ability to contribute to the business progress of the Race. Maggie L. Walker, who is outstanding as the guiding spirit of the Order of Saint Luke . . . in 1902 . . . went before her Grand Council with a plan for a Saint Luke Penny Savings Bank. This organization started with a deposit of about eight thousand dollars and twenty-five thousand in paid-up capital, with Maggie L. Walker as the first Woman Bank President in America. For twenty-seven years she has held this place. Her bank has paid dividends to its stockholders; has served as a depository for gas and water accounts of the city of Richmond and has given employment to hundreds of Negro clerks, bookkeepers and office workers. . . .

With America's great emphasis on the physical appearance, a Negro woman left her wash-tub and ventured into the field of facial beautification. From a humble beginning Madame C. J. Walker built a substantial institution that is a credit to American business in every way.

Mrs. Annie M. Malone is another pioneer in this field of successful business. The C. J. Walker Manufacturing Company and the Poro College do not confine their activities in the field of beautification, to race. They serve both races and give employment to both. . . .

When the ballot was made available to the Womanhood of America, the sister of darker hue was not slow to seize the advantage. In sections where the Negro could gain access to the voting booth, the intelligent, forward-looking element of the Race's women have taken hold of political issues with an enthusiasm and mental acumen that might well set worthy examples for other groups. Oftimes she has led the struggle toward moral improvement and political record, and has compelled her reluctant brother to follow her determined lead. . . .

In time of war as in time of peace, the Negro woman has ever been ready to . . . [serve] . . . for her people's and the nation's good. . . . During the recent World War . . . she . . . pleaded to go in the uniform of the Red Cross nurse and was denied the opportunity only on the basis of racial distinction.

Addie W. Hunton and Kathryn M. Johnson gave yeoman service with the American Expeditionary Forces . . . with the YMCA group. . . .

Negro women have thrown themselves whole-heartedly into the organization of groups to direct the social uplift of their fellowmen . . . one of the greatest achievements of the race.

Perhaps the most outstanding individual social worker of our group today is Jane E. Hunter, founder and executive secretary of the Phillis Wheatley Association, Cleveland, Ohio.

In November, 1911, Miss Hunter, who had been a nurse in Cleveland for only a short time, recognizing the need for a Working Girls' Home, organized the Association and prepared to establish the work. Today the Association is housed in a magnificent structure of nine stories, containing one hundred thirty-five rooms, offices, parlours, a cafeteria and beauty parlour. It is not only a home for working girls but a recreational center and ideal hospice for the Young Negro woman who is living away from home. It maintains an employment department and a fine, up-to-date camp. Branches of the activities of the main Phillis Wheatley are located in other sections of Cleveland, special emphasis being given to the recreational facilities for children and young women of the vicinities in which the branches are located.

In no field of modern social relationship has the hand of service and the influence of the Negro woman been felt more distinctly than in the Negro orthodox church. . . . It may be safely said that the chief sustaining force in support of the pulpit and the various phases of missionary enterprise has been the feminine element of the membership. The development of the Negro church since the Civil War has been another of the modern miracles. Throughout its growth the untiring effort, the unflagging enthusiasm, the sacrificial contribution of time, effort and cash earnings of the black woman have been the most significant factors, without which the modern Negro church would have no history worth the writing. . . .

Both before and since emancipation, by some rare gift, she has been able . . . to hold onto the fibres of family unity and keep the home one unimpaired whole. In recent years it has become increasingly the case where in many instances, the mother is the sole dependence of the home, and single-handed, fights the wolf from the door, while the father submits unwillingly to enforced idleness and unavoidable unemployment. Yet in myriads of instances she controls home discipline with a tight rein and exerts a unifying influence that is the miracle of the century. . . .

The true worth of a race must be measured by the character of its womanhood. . . .

As the years have gone on the Negro woman has touched the most vital fields in the civilization of today. Wherever she has contributed she has left the mark of a strong character. The educational institutions she has established and directed have met the needs of her young people; her cultural development has concentrated itself into artistic presentation accepted and acclaimed by meritorious critics; she is successful as a poet and novelist; she is shrewd in business and capable in politics; she recognizes the importance of uplifting her people through social, civic and religious activities; starting at the time when as a "mammy" she nursed the infants of the other race and taught [them] her meagre store of truth, she has been a contributing factor of note to interracial relations. Finally, through the past century she has made and kept her home intact—humble though it may have been in many instances. She has made and is making history.

Martin Luther King, Jr. (1929–68)

I*n his 1958 book* Stride toward Freedom: The Montgomery Story, *Reverend Dr. Martin Luther King, Jr., concluded: "If the Negro is to achieve the goal of integration, he must organize himself into a militant and nonviolent mass movement. All three elements are indispensable. The movement for equality and justice can only be a success if it has both a mass and militant character; the barriers to be overcome require both. Nonviolence is an imperative in order* *to bring about ultimate community." For this 1964 Nobel Peace Prize recipient, civil disobedience, nonviolent resistance, and Christianity remained the dominant tenets of a public leadership whose influence has continued decades after his death.*

In his birthplace of Atlanta, Georgia, King graduated from Morehouse College in 1948, deciding to enter the ministry as his father and maternal grandfather had done. Spending three years at Crozer Theological Seminary in Chester, Pennsylvania, and receiving a bachelor of divinity degree in 1951, King immersed himself in graduate studies at Boston University, earning a Ph.D. in 1955 and a D.D. in 1959. King also received a doctor of divinity degree from the Chicago Theological Seminary in 1957.

While completing his graduate work, King made a propitious decision to return to the South and accept the pastorship at Dexter Avenue Baptist Church in 1954. In the following year, Rosa Parks refused to stand in the back of a Montgomery bus, and King was elected president of the Montgomery Improvement Association, which united blacks in their historic yearlong boycott of the Montgomery bus system. The legal result was the Supreme Court's validation of a federal court ruling against segregation on the city's bus lines. The personal result for King was his emergence as a civil rights leader of persuasive intelligence and impressive oratorical skills.

In 1957, King became president of the Southern Christian Leadership Conference (SCLC), the organization through which he maintained his national influence. Targeting segregation in education, public accommodations, public transportation, and voting, King's SCLC worked with other civil rights groups to win passage of the Civil Rights Act and the Voting Rights Act in 1964 and 1965, respectively. Once these fundamental rights became law, King guided the SCLC in its new campaign to tackle issues of urban poverty and institutional racism in the North, and to maintain black voter activism and political awareness in the South. By 1967, King had intensified his advocacy of human rights, merging public morality and private spirituality. He spoke against the Vietnam War, while his Poor People's Campaign underscored the economic oppression at the heart of the American system. It was his support of striking sanitation workers that brought him to Memphis in the spring of 1968, where he was assassinated. King's voice and message continue to challenge Americans to live by ideals higher than capitalism and imperialism.

In addition to Stride toward Freedom, *King's works include* The Measure of a Man *(1959),* Letter from Birmingham Jail *(1963),* Why We Can't Wait *(1964), and* Where Do We Go from Here: Class or Community? *(1967). His sermons have been organized in three volumes:* Strength of Love *(1963),* A Martin Luther King Treasury *(1964), and* Trumpet of Conscience *(1967).*

In the following oration, given in 1961 to the delegates of the Fellowship of the Concerned of the Southern Regional Council, King defines the moral connections among "Love, Law, and Civil Disobedience."

Love, Law, and Civil Disobedience

Members of the Fellowship of the Concerned of the Southern Regional Council, I need not pause to say how very delighted I am to be here today, and to have the opportunity to be a little part of this very significant gathering. I certainly want to express my personal appreciation to Mrs. Tilly and the members of the

Committee, for giving me this opportunity. I would also like to express just a personal word of thanks and appreciation for your vital witness in this period of transition which we are facing in our Southland, and in the nation, and I am sure that as a result of genuine concern, and your significant work in communities all across the South, we have a better South today and I am sure will have a better South tomorrow with your continued endeavor, and I do want to express my personal gratitude and appreciation to you of the Fellowship of the Concerned for your significant work and for your forthright witness.

Now, I have been asked to talk about the philosophy behind the student movement. There can be no gainsaying the fact that we confront a crisis in race relations in the United States. The crisis in 1954 outlawing segregation in the public schools has been precipitated on the one hand by the determined resistance of reactionary forces in the South to the Supreme Court's decision. And we know that at times this resistance has risen to ominous proportions. At times we find the legislative halls of the South ringing loud with such words as interposition and nullification. And all these forces have developed into massive resistance. But we must also say that the crisis has been precipitated on the other hand by the determination of hundreds and thousands and millions of Negro people to achieve freedom and human dignity. If the Negro stayed in his place and accepted discrimination and segregation, there would be no crisis. But the Negro has a new sense of dignity, a new self-respect and new determination. He has reevaluated his own intrinsic worth. Now this new sense of dignity on the part of the Negro grows out of the same longing for freedom and human dignity on the part of the oppressed people all over the world. Now we must say that this struggle for freedom will not come to an automatic halt, for history reveals to us that once oppressed people rise up against that oppression, there is no stopping-point short of full freedom. On the other hand, history reveals to us that those who oppose the movement for freedom are those who are in privileged positions who very seldom give up their privileges without strong resistance. And they seldom do it voluntarily. So the sense of struggle will continue. The question is how will the struggle be waged.

Now there are three ways that oppressed people have generally dealt with their oppression. One way is the method of acquiescence, the method of surrender; that is, the individuals will somehow adjust themselves to oppression, they adjust themselves to discrimination or to segregation or colonialism or what have you. The other method that has been used in history is that of rising up against the oppressor with corroding hatred and physical violence. Now, of course, we know about this method in western civilization, because in a sense it has been the hallmark of its grandeur, and the inseparable twin of western materialism. But there is a weakness in this method because it ends up creating many more social problems than it solves. And I am convinced that if the Negro succumbs to the temptation of using violence in his struggle for freedom and justice, unborn generations will be the recipients of a long and desolate night of bitterness. And our chief legacy to the future will be an endless reign of meaningless chaos.

But there is another way, namely the way of nonviolent resistance. This method was popularized in our generation by a little man from India, whose name was Mohandas K. Gandhi. He used this method in a magnificent way to free his people from the economic exploitation and the political domination inflicted upon them by a foreign power.

This has been the method used by the student movement in the South and all over the United States. And naturally whenever I talk about the student movement I cannot be totally objective. I have to be somewhat subjective because of my great admiration for what the students have done. For in a real sense they have taken our deep groans and passionate yearnings for freedom, and filtered them in their own tender souls, and fashioned them into a creative protest which is an epic known all over our nation. As a result of their disciplined, nonviolent, yet courageous struggle, they have been able to do wonders in the South, and in our nation. But this movement does have an underlying philosophy, it has certain ideas that are attached to it, it has certain philosophical precepts. These are the things that I would like to discuss for the few moments left.

I would say that the first point or the first principle in the movement is the idea that means must be as pure as the end. This movement is based on the philosophy that ends and means must cohere. Now this has been one of the long struggles in history, the whole idea of means and ends. Great philosophers have grappled with it, and sometimes they have emerged with the idea, from Machiavelli on down, that the end justifies the means. There is a great system of thought in our world today, known as Communism. And I think that with all of the weakness and tragedies of Communism, we find its greatest tragedy right there, that it goes under the philosophy that the end justifies the means that are used in the process. So we can read or we can hear the Leninists say that lying, deceit, or violence, that many of these things justify the ends of the classless society.

This is where the student movement and the nonviolent movement that is taking place in our nation would break with Communism and any other system that would argue that the end justifies the means. For in the long run, we must see that the end represents the means in process and the idea in the making. In other words, we cannot believe, or we cannot go with the idea that the end justifies the means because the end is preexistent in the means. So the idea of nonviolent resistance, the philosophy of nonviolent resistance, is the philosophy which says that in history, immoral destructive means cannot bring about moral and constructive ends.

There is another thing about this philosophy, this method of nonviolence which is followed by the student movement. It says that those who adhere to or follow this philosophy must follow a consistent principle of noninjury. They must consistently refuse to inflict injury upon another. Sometimes you will read the literature of the student movement, and see that, as they are getting ready for the sit-in or stand-in, they will read something like this, "If you are hit do not hit back, if you are cursed do not curse back." This is the whole idea, that the individual who is engaged in a nonviolent struggle must never inflict injury upon another. Now this has an external aspect and it has an internal one. From the external point of view it means that the individuals involved must avoid external physical violence. So they don't have guns, they don't retaliate with physical violence. If they are hit in the process, they avoid external physical violence at every point. But it also means that they avoid internal violence of spirit. This is why the love ethic stands so high in the student movement. We have a great deal of talk about love and nonviolence in this whole thrust.

Now when the students talk about love, certainly they are not talking about emotional bosh, they are not talking about merely a sentimental outpouring;

they're talking something much deeper, and I always have to stop and try to define the meaning of love in this context. The Greek language comes to our aid in trying to deal with this. There are three words in the Greek language for love, one is the word *eros*. This is a beautiful type of love, it is an aesthetic love. Plato talks about it a great deal in his Dialogue, the yearning of the soul for the realm of the divine. It has come to us to be a sort of romantic love, and so in a sense we have read about it and experienced it. We've read about it in all the beauties of literature. I guess in a sense Edgar Allan Poe was talking about eros when he talked about his beautiful Annabel Lee, with the love surrounded by the halo of eternity. In a sense Shakespeare was talking about eros when he said "Love is not love which alters when it alteration finds, or bends with the remover to remove: O, no! it is an ever-fixed mark that looks on tempests and is never shaken; it is the star to every wandering bark. . . ." (You know, I remember that because I used to quote it to this little lady when we were courting; that's eros.) The Greek language talks about *philia* which was another level of love. It is an intimate affection between personal friends, it is a reciprocal love. On this level you love because you are loved. It is friendship.

Then the Greek language comes out with another word which is called the *agape*. Agape is more than romantic love, agape is more than friendship. Agape is understanding, creative, redemptive, goodwill to all men. It is an overflowing love which seeks nothing in return. Theologians would say that it is the love of God operating in the human heart. So that when one rises to love on this level, he loves men not because he likes them, not because their ways appeal to him, but he loves every man because God loves him. And he rises to the point of loving the person who does an evil deed while hating the deed that the person does. I think this is what Jesus meant when he said "love your enemies." I'm very happy that he didn't say like your enemies, because it is very difficult to like someone bombing your home; it is pretty difficult to like somebody threatening your children; it is difficult to like congressmen who spend all of their time trying to defeat civil rights. But Jesus says love them, and love is greater than like. Love is understanding, redemptive, creative, goodwill for all men. And it is this whole ethic of love which is the idea standing at the basis of the student movement.

There is something else; that one seeks to defeat the unjust system, rather than individuals who are caught in that system. And that one goes on believing that somehow this is the important thing, to get rid of the evil system and not the individual who happens to be misled, who was taught wrong. The thing to do is to get rid of the system and thereby create a moral balance within society.

Another thing that stands at the center of this movement is another idea: that suffering can be a most creative and powerful social force. Suffering has certain moral attributes involved, but it can be a powerful and creative social force. Now, it is very interesting at this point to notice that both violence and nonviolence agree that suffering can be a very powerful social force. But there is this difference: violence says that suffering can be a powerful social force by inflicting suffering on somebody else; so this is what we do in war, this is what we do in the whole violent thrust of the violent movement. It believes that you achieve some end by inflicting suffering on another. The nonviolent say that suffering becomes a powerful social force when you willingly accept that violence on yourself, so that self-suffering stands at the center of the nonviolent movement and the individuals involved are able to suffer in a creative manner, feeling that unearned suffering is redemptive, and that suffering may serve to transform the social situation.

Another thing in this movement is the idea that there is within human nature an amazing potential for goodness. There is within human nature something that can respond to goodness. I know somebody's liable to say that this is an unrealistic movement if it goes on believing that all people are good. Well, I didn't say that. I think the students are realistic enough to believe that there is a strange dichotomy of disturbing dualism within human nature. Many of the great philosophers and thinkers through the ages have seen this. It caused Ovid, the Latin poet, to say, "I see and approve the better things of life, but the evil things I do." It caused even St. Augustine to say, "Lord, make me pure, but not yet." So that there is in human nature, Plato, centuries ago said that the human personality is like a charioteer with two headstrong horses, each wanting to go in different directions, so that within our own individual lives we see this conflict and certainly when we come to the collective life of man, we see a strange badness. But in spite of this there is something in human nature that can respond to goodness. So that man is neither innately good nor is he innately bad; he has potentialities for both. So in this sense, Carlyle was right when he said, that "there are depths in man which go down to the lowest hell, and heights which reach the highest heaven, for are not both heaven and hell made out of him, ever-lasting miracle and mystery that he is?" Man has the capacity to be good, man has the capacity to be evil.

And so the nonviolent resister never lets this idea go, that there is something within human nature that can respond to goodness. So that a Jesus of Nazareth or a Mohandas Gandhi can appeal to human beings and appeal to that element of evil within them, and a Hitler can appeal to the element of evil within them. But we must never forget that there is something within human nature that can respond to goodness, that man is not totally depraved; to put it in theological terms, the image of God is never totally done. And so the individuals who believe in this movement and who believe in nonviolence and our struggle in the South, somehow believe that even the worst segregationist can become an integrationist. Now sometimes it is hard to believe that this is what this movement says, and it believes it firmly, that there is something within human nature that can be changed, and this stands at the top of the whole philosophy of the student movement and the philosophy of nonviolence.

It says something else. It says that it is as much a moral obligation to refuse to cooperate with evil as it is to cooperate with good. Noncooperation with evil is as much a moral obligation as the cooperation with good. So that the student movement is willing to stand up courageously on the idea of evil disobedience. Now I think this is the part of the student movement that is probably misunderstood more than anything else. And it is a difficult aspect, because on the one hand the students would say, and I would say, and all the people who believe in civil rights would say: Obey the Supreme Court's decision of 1954 and at the same time, we would disobey certain laws that exist on the statutes of the South today.

This brings in the whole question of how can you be logically consistent when you advocate obeying some laws and disobeying other laws. Well, I think one would have to see the whole meaning of this movement at this point by seeing that the students recognize that there are two types of laws. There are just laws and there are unjust laws. And they would be the first to say obey the just laws, they would be the first to say that men and women have a moral obligation to obey just and right laws. And they would go on to say that we must see that there are unjust laws. Now the question comes into being, what is the difference, and who determines the difference, what is the difference between a just and an unjust law?

Well, a just law is a law that squares with a moral law. It is a law that squares with that which is right, so that any law that uplifts human personality is a just law. Whereas that law which is out of harmony with the moral is a law which does not square with the moral law of the universe. It does not square with the law of God, so for that reason it is unjust, and any law that degrades the human personality is an unjust law.

Well, somebody says that that does not mean anything to me; first, I don't believe in these abstract things called moral laws, and I'm not too religious, so I don't believe in the law of God; you have to get a little more concrete, and more practical. What do you mean when you say that a law is unjust, and a law is just? Well, I would go on to say in more concrete terms that an unjust law is a code that the majority inflicts on the minority that is not binding on itself. So that this becomes difference made legal. Another thing that we can say is that an unjust law is a code which the majority inflicts upon the minority, which that minority had no part in enacting or creating, because that minority had no right to vote in many instances, so that the legislative bodies that made these laws were not democratically elected. Who could ever say that the legislative body of Mississippi was democratically elected, or the legislative body of Alabama was democratically elected, or the legislative body even of Georgia has been democratically elected, when there are people in Terrell County and in other counties, because of the color of their skin, who cannot vote? They confront reprisals and threats and all of that; so that an unjust law is a law that individuals did not have a part in creating or enacting because they were denied the right to vote.

Now by the same token, a just law would be just the opposite. A just law becomes saneness made legal. It is a code that the majority, who happen to believe in that code, compel the minority, who don't believe in it, to follow, because they are willing to follow it themselves, so it is saneness made legal. Therefore the individuals who stand up on the basis of civil disobedience realize that they are following something that says that there are just laws and there are unjust laws. Now, they are not anarchists. They believe that there are laws which must be followed; they do not seek to defy the law, they do not seek to evade the law. For many individuals who would call themselves segregationists and who would hold on to segregation at any cost seek to defy the law, they seek to evade the law, and their process can lead on into anarchy. They seek in the final analysis to follow a way of uncivil disobedience, not civil disobedience. And I submit that the individual who disobeys the law, whose conscience tells him it is unjust and who is willing to accept the penalty by staying in jail until that law is altered, is expressing at the moment the very highest respect for law.

This is what the students have followed in their movement. Of course there is nothing new about this; they feel that they are in good company and rightly so. We go back and read the Apology and the Crito, and you see Socrates practicing civil disobedience. And to a degree academic freedom is a reality today because Socrates practiced civil disobedience. The early Christians practiced civil disobedience in a superb manner, to a point where they were willing to be thrown to the lions. They were willing to face all kinds of suffering in order to stand up for what they knew was right even though they knew it was against the laws of the Roman Empire.

We could come up to our own day and we see it in many instances. We must never forget that everything that Hitler did in Germany was "legal." It was illegal to aid and comfort a Jew, in the days of Hitler's Germany. But I believe that if I had the same attitude then as I have now I would publicly aid and comfort my Jewish brothers in Germany if Hitler were alive today calling this an illegal process. If I lived in South Africa today in the midst of the white supremacy law in South Africa, I would join Chief Luthuli and others in saying, break these unjust laws. And even let us come up to America. Our nation in a sense came into being through a massive act of civil disobedience, for the Boston Tea Party was nothing but a massive act of civil disobedience. Those who stood up against the slave laws, the abolitionists, by and large practiced civil disobedience. So I think these students are in good company, and they feel that by practicing civil disobedience they are in line with men and women through the ages who have stood up for something that is morally right.

Now there are one or two other things that I want to say about this student movement, moving out of the philosophy of nonviolence, something about what it is a revolt against. On the one hand it is a revolt against the negative peace that has encompassed the South for many years. I remember when I was in Montgomery, Alabama, one of the white citizens came to me one day and said—and I think he was very sincere about this—that in Montgomery for all of these years we have been such a peaceful community, we have had so much harmony in race relations and then you people have started this movement and boycott, and it has done so much to disturb race relations, and we just don't love the Negro like we used to love him, because you have destroyed the harmony and the peace that we once had in race relations. And I said to him, in the best way I could say and I tried to say it in nonviolent terms: We have never had peace in Montgomery, Alabama, we have never had peace in the South. We have had a negative peace, which is merely the absence of tension; we've had a negative peace in which the Negro patiently accepted his situation and his plight, but we've never had true peace, we've never had positive peace, and what we're seeking now is to develop this positive peace. For we must come to see that peace is not merely the absence of some negative force, it is the presence of a positive force. True peace is not merely the absence of tension, but it is the presence of justice and brotherhood. I think this is what Jesus meant when he said, "I come not to bring peace but a sword." Now Jesus didn't mean he came to start war, to bring a physical sword, and he didn't mean, I come not to bring positive peace. But I think what Jesus was saying in substance was this, that I come not to bring an old negative peace, which makes for stagnant passivity and deadening complacency, I come to bring something different, and whenever I come, a conflict is precipitated between the old and the new, whenever I come, a struggle takes place between justice and injustice, between the forces of light and the forces of darkness. I come not to bring a negative peace, but a positive peace, which is brotherhood, which is justice, which is the Kingdom of God.

And I think this is what we are seeking to do today, and this movement is a revolt against a negative peace and struggle to bring into being a positive peace, which makes for true brotherhood, true integration, true person-to-person relationships. This movement is also revolt against what is often called tokenism. Here again many people do not understand this, they feel that in this struggle the Negro will be satisfied with tokens of integration, just a few students and a few schools here and there and a few doors open here and there. But this isn't the meaning of the movement, and I think that honesty impels me to admit it everywhere I have an opportunity, that the Negro's aim is to bring about complete integration in American life. And he has come to see that token integration is little more than token democracy, which ends up with many new evasive schemes and it ends up with new discrimination, covered up with such niceties of complexity. It is very interesting to discover that the movement has thrived in many communities that had token integration. So this reveals that the movement is based on a principle that integration must become real and complete, not just token integration.

It is also a revolt against what I often call the myth of time. We hear this quite often, that only time can solve this problem. That if we will only be patient, and only pray—which we must do, we must be patient and we must pray—but there are those who say just do these things and wait for time, and time will solve this problem. Well, the people who argue this do not themselves realize that time is neutral, that it can be used constructively or destructively. At points the people of ill will, the segregationists, have used time more effectively than the people of goodwill. So individuals in the struggle must come to realize that it is necessary to aid time, that without this kind of aid, time itself will become an ally of the insurgent and primitive forces of social stagnation. Therefore, this movement is a revolt against the myth of time.

There is a final thing that I would like to say to you: This movement is a movement based on faith in the future. It is a movement based on a philosophy, the possibility of the future bringing into being something real and meaningful. It is a movement based on hope. I think this is very important. The students have developed a theme song for their movement, maybe you've heard it. It goes something like this: "We shall overcome, deep in my heart, I do believe, we shall overcome," and they go on to say another verse, "We are not afraid to day, deep in my heart, I do believe, we shall overcome." So it is out of this deep faith in the future that they are able to move out and adjourn the councils of despair, and to bring new light in the dark chambers of pessimism. I can remember the times that we've been together, I remember that night in Montgomery, Alabama, when we had stayed up all night, discussing the Freedom Rides, and that morning came to see that it was necessary to go on with the Freedom Rides, that we would not in all good conscience call an end to the Freedom Rides at that point. And I remember the first group got ready to leave, to take a bus for Jackson, Mississippi, we all joined hands and started singing together. "We shall overcome, we shall overcome." And something within me said, now how is it that these students can sing this, they are going down to Mississippi, they are going to face hostile and jeering mobs, and yet they could sing, "We shall overcome." They may even face physical death, and yet they could sing, "We shall overcome." Most of them realized that they would be thrown into jail, and yet they could sing, "We shall overcome, we are not afraid." Then something caused me to see at that moment the real meaning of the movement. That students had faith in the future. That the movement was based on hope, that this movement had something within it that says somehow even though the arc of the moral universe is long, it bends toward justice. And I think this should be a challenge to all others who are struggling to transform the dangling discords of our Southland into a beautiful symphony of brotherhood. There is something in this student movement which says to us, that we shall overcome. Before the victory is won, some will lose jobs, some will be called Communists and Reds, merely because they believe in brotherhood, some will be dismissed as dangerous rabble-rousers and agitators merely because they're standing up for what is right, but we shall overcome. That is the basis of this movement, and as I like to say, there is something in this universe that justifies Carlyle in saying no lie can live forever. We shall overcome because there is something in this universe which justifies William Cullen Bryant in saying truth crushed to earth shall rise again. We shall overcome because there is something in this universe that justifies James Russell Lowell in saying, truth forever on the scaffold, wrong forever on the throne. Yet that scaffold sways the future, and behind the dim unknown standeth God within the shadows, keeping watch above His own. With this faith in the future, with this determined struggle, we will be able to emerge from the bleak and the desolate midnight of man's inhumanity to man, into the bright and glittering daybreak of freedom and justice. Thank you.

Cecil L. Murray (1929–)

In 1977, Reverend Cecil L. Murray became minister of the oldest black congregation in Los Angeles, a church with only three hundred active members. Since that time, the congregation of the First African Methodist Episcopal church (FAME) has grown to 8,500 members, the majority of them aged twenty-five to forty-five years. With its goal to "Take the Church beyond Its Walls," FAME has conducted forty task force efforts in such areas as health, substance abuse, emergency food and clothing, homelessness, general and specialized housing, and tutoring, among others. Under Murray's leadership, the task forces have produced impressive results: a $4 million housing program for people with physical disabilities; winter housing for three hundred homeless persons; a pioneering twenty-four-hour "Lock-In" program for young people to discuss values; and an innovative bone-marrow donor program.

Born in Lakeland, Florida, and raised in West Palm Beach, Murray served ten years of active duty in the Air Force and was decorated with the Soldier's Medal in 1958. He completed his undergraduate work at Florida A & M University and later earned his doctorate of religion at the School of Theology at Claremont, California. Murray has lectured as an adjunct professor at Seattle University, the School of Theology at Claremont, Fuller Seminary, and Northwest Theological Seminary.

When violence and racial confrontation erupted in Los Angeles on April 29, 1992, after the first trial of the police officers involved in the Rodney King incident, Reverend Murray became a nationally recognized advocate for interracial peace and the process of rebuilding. Reprinted here is a shortened version of the sermon he delivered at FAME on the Sunday following the riot.

Making an Offer You Can't Refuse

. . . Our subject is going to be, "Making an Offer You Can't Refuse." The good shepherd always sentences you to life. The bad shepherd always sentences you to death. And the good sheep always know the difference. The good shepherd is the one with integrity. The good shepherd is the one who is genuine. What's our street language? "Straight up!" Jesus says to each and every one of you this morning, "Baby, I'm for real!" If I tell you I love you, I love you. If I tell you the truth, the truth will set you free. If I tell you, you are equal in the sight of God, red or yellow, black or white, all precious in his sight, I want you to believe that. "Baby, I'm for real!" Some here think that Coke is the real thing, both kinds of coke. That's because you haven't met Jesus yet. Ho, everyone who thirsts, come unto me and drink. Everyone, you don't need money, Jesus paid it all. If you are thirsty for righteousness, come unto me and drink. If you are thirsty for dignity, come unto me and drink. Jesus is the real thing. . . .

The bad shepherd loves all of the sheep, except the black sheep. You recall the four great heroes* of the west, who've been through training that said everyone is to be treated with dignity. You ought to love everyone within the environs of greater Los Angeles; and you have a club on your side and the National Guard at your back. You have the Army, Navy, and Marines waiting to come to your rescue. You don't have to be a bully force. And yet they [white policemen] crucified Little Rodney. . . . Surrounded by 20 armed police persons. Poor Little Rodney.† Prostrate, couldn't even help himself . . . but they [white policemen] love all citizens. They love all the sheep. Except for black sheep. And the jury charged . . . to lift up the dignity of the law, the law of our land, given to us by the law of God. The law that's so sacred, when it [is] taken away . . . we cannot live in peace with each other; we cannot live in fairness and equity with each other. Those twelve good people and true go into chambers, and they sit day after day, after day; and they come out and they say, we good twelve people and true love all of the sheep and we find these four sheep not guilty. We love all of the sheep, except the black sheep.

Then, there's the bad shepherd who wears the badge. The bad shepherd who says it's an aberration. The bad shepherd who gives a blanket of approval. "I want you to go out on the streets, and I want you to love all of the sheep." And then he waits in his gateway and says, "Except the black sheep." Then the sheep get together. . . . The white sheep get together over here. . . . And then the bad shepherd puts the black sheep over here. And the black sheep look at the white sheep and say, "Lord, what's going on? They outnumber us, 12 to 1." . . . And the white sheep put their heads together. "What we going to do about them black sheep?" And 50 percent of them say treat them fairly. And 50 percent of them say treat them poorly. Are we some aberration? No. Here's a poll conducted by a radio station represented here today. They polled 3,300 people about the outcome of the Rodney King verdict. And they just split almost down the middle. Fifty percent said, "We think it's a bad verdict. We think they brought in an inequity of justice. It was a bad verdict." And 50 percent . . . said, "We think it's a good verdict. They have done nothing wrong." So what we have is a good verdict from a good judge, sending it out in a change of venue . . . a good verdict coming down from a good jury. This good verdict that's good for nothing except creating chaos. . . . Causing us to hate one another. Good for nothing, good for nothing. . . .

---

* The four Los Angeles police officers accused of beating black motorist Rodney King in 1992 (editor's note).

† Rodney King, the black motorist whose beating by police officers in 1992 was captured on videotape by a witness (editor's note).

Jesus, I hope you can look at the alienation of black against white against Korean. Every man's hand is set against every other man. Every woman's hand is set against every other woman's because of this good verdict. Some shepherds create chaos. And some sheep capitalize on chaos. It's bad enough when the bad shepherd mistreats the black sheep, it's even worse when the black sheep mistreat each other. Black sheep, you didn't start all of those fires. Every four minutes a fire! My goodness, fires don't move on CPT! Our precious non-black brothers and sisters, CPT stands for Colored People's Time. The black sheep didn't start all of those fires. . . . When the record is clear maybe it will show we didn't set *most* of those fires. But we do have to confess we set *some* of those fires to our shame. . . . The truth of the matter, we have no excuse for going around setting fires. For now we have no place for mothers to buy milk for their children. It is in our communities that we have no means, and somebody is going to have to get a transfer, and a transfer, and go way up to another section of town, leaving our wealth in that section of town and coming back with nothing but a bag full of nothingness. We are not proud that we set those fires. But we'd like to make a distinction to America this morning. The difference between setting a fire and starting a fire. We set *some* of those fires, but we didn't start *any* of those fires. Those fires were started when some men of influence decided that this nation can indeed exist half-slave and half-free. Those fires were started when some men poured gasoline on the Constitution of the United States of America. Those fires were started when somebody decided that the very pioneers who started this city should not have freedom and justice under the law. Those fires were started when somebody poured gasoline on the criminal court and the civil court, when somebody took word and truth and poured gasoline on them and burned the whole structure down. But it is not to our credit that in the flicker of those fires we were found looting and robbing and pillaging and stealing. For that is not us, dear hearts. We are noble people. I know a mother can say, "I was stealing milk for my baby." I understand, baby, I understand. But why didn't you come to the church . . . ? I understand what you were doing, but I cannot condone it. Bah, bah, black sheep, have you any wool. Yes sir, yes sir, three bags full. Ham for my belly, booze for my brain, television for my entertainment just in case it rains. Oh, black sheep, black sheep, you must have wool on your head, and you are learning *that* wool is good wool cause God made it. But God put wool *on* your head, not *in* your head. You have to use your head. You ought to be able to say, "I'll go hungry before I'll go humiliated. . . ."

And you ask why the little black sheep are jumping on each other. Why? Oh, when I was a younger man they made a home brew called "Sneaky Pete." A lot of things go down smooth. Sneaky Pete went down as smooth as Dionne Warwick and Al Green. But once Sneaky Pete went into action, Sneaky Pete would blow the top of your head off. Sneaky Pete—150 of the men of the church standing on Western and Adams at three o'clock in the morning, having been up the night hours, standing between 50 police persons who want to do that . . . Kent State thing all over again.* You can look in some of their eyes

* "Western and Adams" were intersecting streets near Murray's FAME church, located in the center of a black neighborhood. At Kent State University in Ohio on May 4, 1970, four students were shot and killed by the National Guard during an antiwar demonstration on campus (editor's note).

and you see, "I ain't whipped on black sheep in a long time." Not all of them, but it only takes one idiot to make an "idiocracy"! And on the other hand, 150 young black men throwing rocks and stones and bottles, egged on from the alcohol they have consumed, provoking these police to move forward; and the men of the church saying, "No, no, no, no, don't throw that," and forming the line, presenting their bodies as living sacrifices. And what was edging the rock throwers on? Sneaky Pete! A little black sheep with a wooly mind, hollering out, "Throw the stone, throw the stone, throw the stone." And what does he have in his hand? Absolutely nothing. And where is he located? Way in the back. So that when the head whipping starts, he'll start. Sneaky Pete! But why would anybody follow Sneaky Pete? Whether he is Western-Adams Sneaky Pete, or Parker Center* Sneaky Pete. Why would anybody follow Sneaky Pete? Why would anybody endure an embarrassment to the City of the Angels, one of the most sophisticated cities in the world, having a little white sheep with a wooly mind talking for everybody? Why would we endure Sneaky Pete? . . .

The challenge comes to the good sheep. My good sheep, let me tell you this morning, we have to clean up the town. We've got to clean up the air. We've got to clean up the atmosphere. And as you clean up, smoke gets in your eyes. But don't you worry about that. Wait for a little bit and keep on walking. Smoke gets in your eyes, but blink a little bit because you cannot see through tear drops. You cannot see through . . . hatred and anger and violence. These cause you to lump all white folks together, you'll lump all Korean folks together, you'll lump all black folks together. Weep a little bit, but keep on walking. And when smoke gets too thick for you, sit down by the side of the road and have a little talk with Jesus. Tell him all about your troubles. Then remember, "Jesus, you brought me all the way. You're such a wonderful Savior. I've never known you to fail me. Jesus, you brought me all the way." Then you get up and keep on walking, walking up the King's highway. And when you know anything, there's a warm hand in your hand. There is your friend who brought you out of the Valley of the shadow of death. There is your friend who educated you when you couldn't educate yourself. There is your friend who defended you when you couldn't afford an attorney. There is your friend who helped you build a house when the bank red-lined your dreams. There is a friend, there is a friend. Go on with him, go on by faith . . . and you'll never walk alone. In the name of Jesus, Amen.

Barbara Jordan (1936–)

When Barbara Jordan retired from public office in 1978, she abruptly ended twelve years as a black juggernaut in American politics. She won national fame in 1974 as a member of the House Judiciary Committee that conducted hearings on the impeachment of President Richard Nixon. Delivering a televised speech about the Nixon administration, she became recognized as an eloquent defender of the Constitution and a forceful opponent of political corruption.

---

* Headquarters of the Los Angeles Police Department (editor's note).

Tracing her oratorical skills back to her birthplace of Houston, Texas, Jordan credits her parents and grandfather with instilling an early appreciation for education. During her high school years, she won awards for debating, an interest that she continued to pursue while attending Texas Southern University. She went on to earn her J.D. from Boston University Law School in 1959.

Returning to Houston, Jordan set up a legal practice. Politically, she became involved in the 1960 presidential campaign on behalf of the Democratic Kennedy-Johnson ticket, and in the early 1960s launched a personal effort to break into state government, finally succeeding in 1966. Jordan was the first black person since 1883 to win a seat in the Texas state senate, where she served for six years, presiding over crucial committees and councils. In 1972, she became the first black woman from the South to be elected to the U.S. Congress.

During the Nixon impeachment hearings of 1974, the American television audience grew familiar with Jordan's powerful presence and succinct articulation of her views. She remained a staunch defender of public morality, speaking at two Democratic National Conventions. Although illness forced her early retirement from elective office, Jordan continues to be honored for her contributions to American public discourse. She has been awarded over a dozen honorary doctorate degrees and in 1992 won the NAACP's Spingarn Medal.

As a result of Jordan's high visibility during the Nixon impeachment hearings, she was chosen to serve as the keynote speaker for the 1976 Democratic National Convention. Her speech "Who Then Will Speak for the Common Good?" is reprinted here.

Who Then Will Speak for the Common Good?

One hundred and forty-four years ago, members of the Democratic Party first met in convention to select a Presidential candidate. Since that time, Democrats have continued to convene once every four years and draft a party platform and nominate a Presidential candidate. And our meeting this week is a continuation of that tradition.

But there is something different about tonight. There is something special about tonight. What is different? What is special? I, Barbara Jordan, am a keynote speaker.

A lot of years passed since 1832, and during that time it would have been most unusual for any national political party to ask that a Barbara Jordan deliver a keynote address . . . but tonight here I am. And I feel that notwithstanding the past that my presence here is one additional bit of evidence that the American Dream need not forever be deferred.

Now that I have this grand distinction what in the world am I supposed to say?

I could easily spend this time praising the accomplishments of this party and attacking the Republicans but I don't choose to do that.

I could list the many problems which Americans have. I could list the problems which cause people to feel cynical, angry, frustrated: problems which include lack of integrity in government; the feeling that the individual no longer counts; the reality of material and spiritual poverty; the feeling that the grand

American experiment is failing or has failed. I could recite these problems and then I could sit down and offer no solutions. But I don't choose to do that either.

The citizens of America expect more. They deserve and they want more than a recital of problems.

We are a people in a quandry about the present. We are a people in search of our future. We are a people in search of a national community.

We are a people trying not only to solve the problems of the present: unemployment, inflation . . . but we are attempting on a larger scale to fulfill the promise of America. We are attempting to fulfill our national purpose; to create and sustain a society in which all of us are equal.

Throughout our history, when people have looked for new ways to solve their problems, and to uphold the principles of this nation, many times they have turned to political parties. They have often turned to the Democratic Party.

What is it, what is it about the Democratic Party that makes it the instrument that people use when they search for ways to shape their future? Well I believe the answer to that question lies in our concept of governing. Our concept of governing is derived from our view of people. It is a concept deeply rooted in a set of beliefs firmly etched in the national conscience, of all of us.

Now what are these beliefs?

First, we believe in equality for all and privileges for none. This is a belief that each American regardless of background has equal standing in the public forum, all of us. Because we believe this idea so firmly, we are an inclusive rather than an exclusive party. Let everybody come.

I think it no accident that most of those emigrating to America in the 19th century identified with the Democratic Party. We are a heterogeneous party made up of Americans of diverse backgrounds.

We believe that the people are the source of all governmental power; that the authority of the people is to be extended, not restricted. This can be accomplished only by providing each citizen with every opportunity to participate in the management of the government. They must have that.

We believe that the government which represents the authority of all the people, not just one interest group, but all the people, has an obligation to actively underscore, actively seek to remove those obstacles which would block individual achievement . . . obstacles emanating from race, sex, economic condition. The government must seek to remove them.

We are a party of innovation. We do not reject our traditions, but we are willing to adapt to changing circumstances, when change we must. We are willing to suffer the discomfort of change in order to achieve a better future.

We have a positive vision of the future founded on the belief that the gap between the promise and reality of America can one day be finally closed. We believe that.

This my friends, is the bedrock of our concept of governing. This is a part of the reason why Americans have turned to the Democratic Party. These are the foundations upon which a national community can be built.

Let's all understand that these guiding principles cannot be discarded for short-term political gains. They represent what this country is all about. They are indigenous to the American idea. And these are principles which are not negotiable.

In other times, I could stand here and give this kind of exposition on the beliefs of the Democratic Party and that would be enough. But today that is not enough. People want more. That is not sufficient reason for the majority of the people of this country to vote Democratic. We have made mistakes. In our haste to do all things for all people, we did not foresee the full consequences of our actions. And when the people raised their voices, we didn't hear. But our deafness was only a temporary condition, and not an irreversible condition.

Even as I stand here and admit that we have made mistakes I still believe that as the people of America sit in judgment on each party, they will recognize that our mistakes were mistakes of the heart. They'll recognize that.

And now we must look to the future. Let us heed the voice of the people and recognize their common sense. If we do not, we not only blaspheme our political heritage, we ignore the common ties that bind all Americans.

Many fear the future. Many are distrustful of their leaders, and believe that their voices are never heard. Many seek only to satisfy their private work wants. To satisfy private interests.

But this is the great danger America faces. That we will cease to be one nation and become instead a collection of interest groups: city against suburb, region against region, individual against individual. Each seeking to satisfy private wants.

If that happens, who then will speak for America?

Who then will speak for the common good?

This is the question which must be answered in 1976.

Are we to be one people bound together by common spirit sharing in a common endeavor or will we become a divided nation?

For all of its uncertainty, we cannot flee the future. We must not become the new puritans and reject our society. We must address and master the future together. It can be done if we restore the belief that we share a sense of national community, that we share a common national endeavor. It can be done.

There is no executive order; there is no law that can require the American people to form a national community. This we must do as individuals and if we do it as individuals, there is no President of the United States who can veto that decision.

As a first step, we must restore our belief in ourselves. We are a generous people so why can't we be generous with each other? We need to take to heart the words spoken by Thomas Jefferson:

"Let us restore to social intercourse that harmony and that affection without which liberty and even life are but dreary things."

A nation is formed by the willingness of each of us to share in the responsibility for upholding the common good.

A government is invigorated when each of us is willing to participate in shaping the future of this nation.

In this election year we must define the common good and begin again to shape a common good and begin again to shape a common future. Let each person do his or her part. If one citizen is unwilling to participate, all of us are going to suffer. For the American idea, though it is shared by all of us, is realized in each one of us.

And now, what are those of us who are elected public officials supposed to do? We call ourselves public servants but I'll tell you this: we as public servants must set an example for the rest of the nation. It is hypocritical for the public official to admonish and exhort the people to uphold the common good if we are derelict in upholding the common good. More is required of public officials than slogans and handshakes and press releases. More is required. We must hold ourselves strictly accountable. We must provide the people with a vision of the future.

If we promise as public officials, we must deliver. If we as public officials propose, we must produce. If we say to the American people it is time for you to be sacrificial, sacrifice. If the public official says that, we (public officials) must be the first to give. We must be. And again, if we make mistakes, we must be willing to admit them. We have to do that. What we have to do is strike a balance between the idea that government should do everything and the idea, the belief, that government ought to do nothing. Strike a balance.

Let there be no illusions about the difficulty of forming this kind of a national community. It's tough, difficult, not easy. But a spirit of harmony will survive in America only if each of us remembers that we share a common destiny. If each of us remembers when self-interest and bitterness seem to prevail, that we share a common destiny.

I have confidence that the Democratic Party can lead the way. I have that confidence. We cannot improve on the system of government handed down to us by the founders of the Republic, there is no way to improve upon that. But what we can do is to find new ways to implement that system and realize our destiny.

Now, I began this speech by commenting to you on the uniqueness of a Barbara Jordan making the keynote address. Well I am going to close my speech by quoting a Republican President and I ask you that as you listen to these words of Abraham Lincoln, relate them to the concept of a national community in which every last one of us participates. "As I would not be a slave, so I would not be a master. This expresses my idea of Democracy. Whatever differs from this, to the extent of the difference is no Democracy."

Jesse Jackson (1941–)

Born in Greenville, South Carolina, Jesse Jackson was an accomplished young man by the time he graduated from Sterling High School, where he had been president of his class, a member of the honor society and student council, and a three-letter athlete. His athletic skills helped him gain admittance into the University of Illinois in 1959, but a year later he transferred to North Carolina A & T, where he became a quarterback, an honor student, and the president of the student body. He also earned a B.A. in sociology. Jackson won a Rockefeller grant, which he used to study at the Chicago Theological Seminary. He was ordained as a Baptist minister in 1968.

In the 1960s, Jackson began to direct his energies into the civil rights movement, working as an organizer for the Congress of Racial Equality (CORE) and joining the Southern Christian Leadership Conference (SCLC) in 1965. In the SCLC, Jackson worked with Martin Luther King, Jr., using his familiarity with Chicago to assist the SCLC's Chicago Freedom Movement in 1966. The following year the organization made Jackson the national director of Operation Breadbasket, a program urging boycotts and strategic buying by black consumers to achieve economic advancement and equity for blacks.

Following the assassination of Martin Luther King, Jr., in 1968, Jackson came in conflict with certain SCLC leaders. By 1971, he had broken away from the SCLC to establish his own organization and economic and political agenda. Through his Chicago-based Operation PUSH (People United to Save Humanity), Jackson operated nationally for his proclaimed objectives. In the 1980s, Jackson began to augment his national leadership with international recognition, as he traveled, mediated, and politicked in South Africa, the Middle East, Cuba, Central America, Iraq, and Kuwait.

Jackson's remarkable success as a candidate for U.S. president secured his place in American political history. In 1984, Jackson entered his first presidential campaign as the first credible black candidate for president of the United States. He won enough support to gain access to the platform deliberations of the Democratic National Convention. And by the next presidential campaign Jackson was a formidable candidate, reaching out from the base of his Rainbow Coalition of various ethnic groups and social classes, feminists, and homosexuals to finish second among all candidates in the Democratic primary elections. After losing his bid for the 1988 Democratic presidential nominee, Jackson submerged himself in local politics in Washington, D.C. He was elected as a "statehood senator" to lobby Congress to award statehood to the District of Columbia.

In addition to writing A Time to Speak: The Autobiography of the Reverend Jesse Jackson *(1988), Jackson has hosted radio broadcasts from Chicago, as well as his syndicated television program,* Voices of America with Jesse Jackson, *since 1989.*

One of Jackson's most formidable talents is his spellbinding power as an orator. Reprinted here is the speech he delivered at the 1988 Democratic National Convention. Entitled "Common Ground and Common Sense," the speech earned a fifteen-minute ovation. In it Jackson details contemporary social dilemmas and urges all Americans to "keep hope alive."

Common Ground and Common Sense

Tonight we pause and give praise and honor to God for being good enough to allow us to be at this place at this time. When I look out at this convention, I see the face of America, red, yellow, brown, black and white, we're all precious in God's sight—the real rainbow coalition. All of us, all of us who are here and think that we are seated. But we're really standing on someone's shoulders. Ladies and gentlemen. Mrs. Rosa Parks.

The mother of the civil rights movement.

I want to express my deep love and appreciation for the support my family has given me over these past months.

They have endured pain, anxiety, threat and fear.

But they have been strengthened and made secure by a faith in God, in America and in you.

Your love has protected us and made us strong.

To my wife Jackie, the foundation of our family; to our five children whom you met tonight; to my mother Mrs. Helen Jackson, who is present tonight; and to my grandmother, Mrs. Matilda Burns; my brother Chuck and his family; my mother-in-law, Mrs. Gertrude Brown, who just last month at age 61 graduated from Hampton Institute, a marvelous achievement; I offer my appreciation to Mayor Andrew Young who has provided such gracious hospitality to all of us this week.

And a special salute to President Jimmy Carter.

President Carter restored honor to the White House after Watergate. He gave many of us a special opportunity to grow. For his kind words, for his unwavering commitment to peace in the world and the voters that came from his family, every member of his family, led by Billy and Amy, I offer him my special thanks, special thanks to the Carter family.

My right and my privilege to stand here before you has been won—in my lifetime—by the blood and the sweat of the innocent.

Twenty-four years ago, the late Fanny Lou Hamer and Aaron Henry—who sits here tonight from Mississippi—were locked out on the streets of Atlantic City, the head of the Mississippi Freedom Democratic Party.

But tonight, a black and white delegation from Mississippi is headed by Ed Cole, a black man, from Mississippi, 24 years later.

Many were lost in the struggle for the right to vote. Jimmy Lee Jackson, a young student, gave his life. Viola Luizzo, a white mother from Detroit, called nigger lover, and brains blown out at point blank range.

Schwerner, Goodman and Chaney—two Jews and a black—found in a common grave, bodies riddled with bullets in Mississippi. The four darling little girls in the church in Birmingham, Alabama. They died that we might have a right to live.

Dr. Martin Luther King, Jr. lies only a few miles from us tonight.

Tonight he must feel good as he looks down upon us. We sit here together, a rainbow, a coalition—the sons and daughters of slave masters and the sons and daughters of slaves sitting together around a common table, to decide the direction of our party and our country. His heart would be full tonight.

As a testament to the struggles of those who have gone before; as a legacy for those who will come after; as a tribute to the endurance, the patience, the courage of our forefathers and mothers; as an assurance that their prayers are being answered, their work has not been in vain, and hope is eternal; tomorrow night my name will go into nomination for the presidency of the United States of America.

We meet tonight at a crossroads, a point of decision.

Shall we expand, be inclusive, find unity and power; or suffer division and impotence.

We come to Atlanta, the cradle of the old south, the crucible of the new South.

Tonight there is a sense of celebration because we are moved, fundamentally moved, from racial battlegrounds by law, to economic common ground, tomorrow we will challenge to move to higher ground.

Common ground!

Think of Jerusalem—the intersection where many trails met. A small village that became the birthplace for three great religions—Judaism, Christianity and Islam.

Why was this village so blessed? Because it provided a crossroads where different people met, different cultures, and different civilizations could meet and find common ground.

When people come together, flowers always flourish and the air is rich with the aroma of a new spring.

Take New York, the dynamic metropolis. What makes New York so special?

It is the invitation of the Statue of Liberty—give me your tired, your poor, your huddled masses who yearn to breathe free.

Not restricted to English only.

Many people, many cultures, many languages—with one thing in common, the yearn to breathe free.

Common ground!

Tonight in Atlanta, for the first time in this century we convene in the South.

A state where governors once stood in school house doors. Where Julian Bond was denied his seat in the state legislature because of his conscientious objection to the Vietnam War.

A city that, through its five black universities, has graduated more black students than any city in the world.

Atlanta, now a modern intersection of the new South.

Common ground!

That is the challenge to our party tonight.

Left wing. Right wing. Progress will not come through boundless liberalism nor static conservatism, but at the critical mass of mutual survival. It takes two wings to fly.

Whether you're a hawk or a dove, you're just a bird living in the same environment, in the same world.

The Bible teaches that when lions and lambs lie down together, none will be afraid and there will be peace in the valley. It sounds impossible. Lions eat lambs. Lambs sensibly flee from lions. But even lions and lambs find common ground. Why?

Because neither lions nor lambs want the forest to catch on fire. Neither lions nor lambs want acid rain to fall. Neither lions nor lambs can survive nuclear war. If lions and lambs can find common ground, surely, we can as well, as civilized people.

The only time that we win is when we come together. In 1960, John Kennedy, the late John Kennedy, beat Richard Nixon by only 112,000 votes—less than one vote per precinct. He won by the margin of our hope. He brought us together. He reached out. He had the courage to defy his advisors and inquire about Dr. King's jailing in Albany, Georgia. We won by the margin of our hope, inspired by courageous leadership.

In 1964, Lyndon Johnson brought both wings together. The thesis, the antithesis and to create a synthesis and together we won.

In 1976, Jimmy Carter unified us again and we won. When we do not come together, we never win.

In 1968, division and despair in July led to our defeat in November.

In 1980, rancor in the spring and the summer led to Reagan in the fall. When we divide, we cannot win. We must find common ground as a basis for survival and development and change and growth.

Today when we debated, differed, deliberated, agreed to agree, agreed to disagree, when we had the good judgment to argue our case and then not self-destruct, George Bush was just a little further away from the White House and a little closer to private life.

Tonight, I salute Governor Michael Dukakis.

He has run a well-managed and a dignified campaign. No matter how tired or how tried, he always resisted the temptation to stoop to demagoguery.

I've watched a good mind fast at work, with steel nerves, guiding his campaign out of the crowded field without appeal to the worst in us. I've watched his perspective grow as his environment has expanded. I've seen his toughness and tenacity close up. I know his commitment to public service.

Mike Dukakis' parents were a doctor and a teacher; my parents, a maid, a beautician and a janitor.

There's a great gap between Brookline, Massachusetts, and Haney Street, the Fieldcrest Village housing projects in Greenville, South Carolina.

He studied law; I studied theology. There are differences of religion, region, and race; differences in experiences and perspectives. But the genius of America is that out of the many, we become one.

Providence has enabled our paths to intersect. His foreparents came to America on immigrant ships; my foreparents came to America on slave ships. But whatever the original ships, we're in the same boat tonight.

Our ships could pass in the night if we have a false sense of independence, or they could collide and crash. We would lose our passengers. But we can seek a higher reality and a greater good apart. We can drift on the broken pieces of Reaganomics, satisfy our baser instincts, and exploit the fears of our people. At our highest, we can call upon noble instincts and navigate this vessel to safety. The greater good is the common good.

As Jesus said, "Not my will, but thine be done." It was his way of saying there's a higher good beyond personal comfort or position.

The good of our nation is at stake—its commitment to working men and women, to the poor and the vulnerable, to the many in the world. With so many guided missiles, and so much misguided leadership, the stakes are exceedingly high. Our choice, full participation in a Democratic government, or more abandonment and neglect. And so this night, we choose not a false sense of independence, not our capacity to survive and endure.

Tonight we choose interdependency in our capacity to act and unite for the greater good. The common good is finding commitment to new priorities, to expansion and inclusion. A commitment to expanded participation in the Democratic Party at every level. A commitment to a shared national campaign strategy and involvement at every level. A commitment to new priorities that ensure that hope will be kept alive. A common ground commitment for a legislative agenda by empowerment for the John Conyers bill, universal, on-site, same-day registration everywhere—and commitment to D.C. statehood and empowerment—D.C. deserves statehood. A commitment to economic set-asides, a commitment to the Dellums bill for comprehensive sanctions against South Africa, a shared commitment to a common direction.

Common ground. Easier said than done. Where do you find common ground at the point of challenge? This campaign has shown that politics need not be marketed by politicians, packaged by pollsters and pundits. Politics can be a marvel arena where people come together, define common ground.

We find common ground at the plant gate that closes on workers without notice. We find common ground at the farm auction where a good farmer loses his or her land to bad loans or diminishing markets. Common ground at the schoolyard where teachers cannot get adequate pay, and students cannot get a scholarship and can't make a loan. Common ground, at the hospital admitting room where somebody tonight is dying because they cannot afford to go upstairs to a bed that's empty, waiting for someone with insurance to get sick. We are a better nation than that. We must do better.

Common ground. What is leadership if not present help in a time of crisis? And so I met you at the point of challenge in Jay, Maine, where paper workers were striking for fair wages; in Greenfield, Iowa, where family farmers struggle for a fair price; in Cleveland, Ohio, where working women seek comparable worth; in McFarland, California, where the children of Hispanic farm workers may be dying from poison land, dying in clusters with Cancer; in the AIDS hospice in Houston, Texas, where the sick support one another, 12 are rejected by their own parents and friends.

Common ground.

America's not a blanket woven from one thread, one color, one cloth. When I was a child growing up in Greenville, South Carolina, and grandmother could not afford a blanket, she didn't complain and we did not freeze. Instead, she took pieces of old cloth—patches, wool, silk, gabardine, crockersack on the patches—barely good enough to wipe off your shoes with.

But they didn't stay that way very long. With sturdy hands and a strong cord, she sewed them together into a quilt, a thing of beauty and power and culture.

Now, Democrats, we must build such a quilt. Farmers, you seek fair prices and you are right, but you cannot stand alone. Your patch is not big enough. Workers, you fight for fair wages. You are right. But your patch labor is not big enough. Women, you seek comparable worth and pay equity. You are right. But your patch is not big enough. Women, mothers, who seek Head Start and day care and pre-natal care on the front side of life, rather than jail care and welfare on the back side of life, you're right, but your patch is not big enough.

Students, you seek scholarships. You are right. But your patch is not big enough. Blacks and Hispanics, when we fight for civil rights, we are right, but our patch is not big enough. Gays and lesbians, when you fight against discrimination and a cure for AIDS, you are right, but your patch is not big enough. Conservatives and progressives, when you fight for what you believe, right-wing, left-wing, hawk, dove—you are right, from your point of view, but your point of view is not enough.

But don't despair. Be as wise as my grandmama. Pool the patches and the pieces together, bound by a common thread. When we form a great quilt of unity and common ground we'll have the power to bring about health care and housing and jobs and education and hope to our nation.

We the people can win. We stand at the end of a long dark night of reaction. We stand tonight united in a commitment to a new direction. For almost eight years, we've been led by those who view social good coming from private interest, who viewed public life as a means to increase private wealth. They have been prepared to sacrifice the common good of the many to satisfy the private interest and the wealth of a few. We believe in a government that's a tool of our democracy in service to the public, not an instrument of the aristocracy in search of private wealth.

We believe in government with the consent of the governed of, for, and by the people. We must not emerge into a new day with a new direction. Reaganomics, based on the belief that the rich had too much money—too little money, and the poor had too much.

That's classic Reaganomics. It believes that the poor had too much money and the rich had too little money.

So, they engaged in reverse Robin Hood—took from the poor, gave to the rich, paid for by the middle class. We cannot stand four more years of Reaganomics in any version, in any disguise.

How do I document that case? Seven years later, the richest 1 percent of our society pays 20 percent less in taxes; the poorest 10 percent pay 20 percent more. Reaganomics.

Reagan gave the rich and the powerful a multibillion-dollar party. Now, the party is over. He expects the people to pay for the damage. I take this principled position—convention, let us not raise taxes on the poor and the middle class, but those who had the party, the rich and the powerful, must pay for the party!

I just want to take common sense to high places. We're spending $150 billion a year defending Europe and Japan 43 years after the war is over. We have more troops in Europe tonight than we had seven years ago, yet the threat of war is ever more remote. Germany and Japan are now creditor nations—that means they've got a surplus. We are a debtor nation—it means we are in debt.

Let them share more of the burden of their own defense—use some of that money to build decent housing!

Use some of that money to educate our children!

Use some of that money for long-term health care!

Use some of that money to wipe out these slums and put America back to work!

I just want to take common sense to high places. If we can bail out Europe and Japan, if we can bail out Continental Bank and Chrysler—and Mr. Iacocca makes $8,000 an hour, we can bail out the family farmer.

I just want to make common sense. It does not make sense to close down 650,000 family farms in this country while importing food from abroad subsidized by the U.S. government.

Let's make sense. It does not make sense to be escorting oil tankers up and down the Persian Gulf paying $2.50 for every $1.00 worth of oil we bring out while oil wells are capped in Texas, Oklahoma and Louisiana. I just want to make sense.

Leadership must meet the moral challenge of its day. What's the moral challenge of our day? We have public accommodations. We have the right to vote. We have open housing.

What's the fundamental challenge of our day? It is to end economic violence. Plant closing without notice, economic violence. Even the greedy do not profit long from greed. Economic violence. Most poor people are not lazy. They're not black. They're not brown. They're mostly white, and female and young.

But whether white, black or brown, the hungry baby's belly turned inside out is the same color. Call it pain. Call it hurt. Call it agony. Most poor people are not on welfare.

Some of them are illiterate and can't read the want-ad sections. And when they can, they can't find a job that matches their address. They work hard every day, I know. I live amongst them. I'm one of them.

I know they work. I'm a witness. They catch the early bus. They work every day. They raise other people's children. They work every day. They clean the streets. They work every day. They drive vans with cabs. They work every day. They change the beds you slept in these hotels last night and can't get a union contract. They work every day.

No more. They're not lazy. Someone must defend them because it's right, and they cannot speak for themselves. They work in hospitals. I know they do. They wipe the bodies of those who are sick with fever and pain. They empty their bedpans. They clean out their commode. No job is beneath them, and yet when they get sick, they cannot lie in the bed they made up every day. America, that is not right. We are a better nation than that. We are a better nation than that.

We need a real war on drugs. You can't just say no. It's deeper than that. You can't just get a palm reader or an astrologer; it's more profound than that. We're spending $150 billion on drugs a year. We've gone from ignoring it to focusing on the children. Children cannot buy $150 billion worth of drugs a year. A few high profile athletes—athletes are not laundering $150 billion a year—bankers are.

I met the children in Watts who are unfortunate in their despair. Their grapes of hope have become raisins of despair, and they're turning to each other and they're self-destructing—but I stayed with them all night long. I wanted to hear their case. They said, "Jesse Jackson, as you challenge us to say no to drugs, you're right. And to not sell them, you're right. And to not use these guns, you're right."

And, by the way, the promise of CETA [Comprehensive Employment and Training Act]—they displaced CETA. They did not replace CETA. We have neither jobs nor houses nor services nor training—no way out. Some of us take drugs as anesthesia for our pain. Some take drugs as a way of pleasure—both short-term pleasure and long-term pain. Some sell drugs to make money. It's wrong, we know. But you need to know that we know. We can go and buy the drugs by the boxes at the port. If we can buy the drugs at the port, don't you believe the federal government can stop it if they want to?

They say, "We don't have Saturday night specials any more." They say, "We buy AK-47s and Uzis, the latest lethal weapons. We buy them across the counter on Long Beach Boulevard." You cannot fight a war on drugs unless and until you are going to challenge the bankers and the gun sellers and those who grow them. Don't just focus on the children, let's stop drugs at the level of supply and demand. We must end the scourge on the American culture.

Leadership. What difference will we make? Leadership cannot just go along to get along. We must do more than change presidents. We must change direction. Leadership must face the moral challenge of our day. The nuclear war build-up is irrational. Strong leadership cannot desire to look tough, and let that stand in the way of the pursuit of peace. Leadership must reverse the arms race.

At least we should pledge no first use. Why? Because first use begat first retaliation, and that's mutual annihilation. That's not a rational way out. No use at all—let's think it out, and not fight it out, because it's an unwinnable fight. Why hold a card that you can never drop? Let's give peace a chance.

Leadership—we now have this marvelous opportunity to have a breakthrough with the Soviets. Last year, 200,000 Americans visited the Soviet Union. There's a chance for joint ventures into space, not Star Wars and the war arms escalation, but a space defense initiative. Let's build in space together, and demilitarize the heavens. There's a way out.

America, let us expand. When Mr. Reagan and Mr. Gorbachev met, there was a big meeting. They represented together one-eighth of the human race. Seven-eighths of the human race was locked out of that room. Most people in the world tonight—half are Asian, one-half of them are Chinese. There are 22 nations in the Middle East. There's Europe; 40 million Latin Americans next door to us; the Caribbean; Africa—a half-billion people. Most people in the world today are yellow or brown or black, non-Christian, poor, female, young, and don't speak English—in the real world.

This generation must offer leadership to the real world. We're losing ground in Latin America, the Middle East, South Africa, because we're not focusing on the real world, that real world. We must use basic principles, support international law. We stand the most to gain from it. Support human rights; we believe in that. Support self-determination; we'll build on that. Support economic development; you know it's right. Be consistent, and gain our moral authority in the world.

I challenge you tonight, my friends, let's be bigger and better as a nation and as a party. We have basic challenges. Freedom in South Africa—we've already agreed as Democrats to declare South Africa to be a terrorist state. But don't just stop there. Get South Africa out of Angola. Free Namibia. Support the front-line states. We must now have a new, humane human rights assistance policy in Africa.

I'm often asked, "Jesse, why do you take on these tough issues? They're not very political. We can't win that way."

If an issue is morally right, it will eventually be political. It may be political and never be right. Fannie Lou Hamer didn't have the most votes in Atlantic City, but her principles have outlasted every delegate who voted to lock her out. Rosa Parks did not have the most votes, but she was morally right. Dr. King didn't have the most votes about the Vietnam War, but he was morally right. If we're principled first, our politics will fall in place.

Jesse, why did you take these big bold initiatives? A poem by an unknown author went something like this: We mastered the air, we've conquered the sea, and annihilated distance and prolonged life, we were not wise enough to live on this earth without war and without hate.

As for Jesse Jackson, I'm tired of sailing by little boat, far inside the harbor bar. I want to go out where the big ships float, out on the deep where the great ones are. And should my frail craft prove too slight, the waves that sweep those billows o'er, I'd rather go down in a stirring fight than drown to death in the sheltered shore.

We've got to go out, my friends, where the big boats are.

And then, for our children, young America, hold your head high now. We can win. We must not lose you to drugs and violence, premature pregnancy, suicide, cynicism, pessimism and despair. We can win.

Wherever you are tonight, I challenge you to hope and to dream. Don't submerge your dreams. Exercise above all else, even on drugs, dream of the day you're drug-free. Even in the gutter, dream of the day that you'll be up on your feet again. You must never stop dreaming. Face reality, yes. But don't stop with the way things are; dream of things as they ought to be. Dream. Face pain, but love, hope, faith, and dreams will help you rise above the pain.

Use hope and imagination as weapons of survival and progress, but you keep on dreaming, young America. Dream of peace. Peace is rational and reasonable. War is irrational in this age and unwinnable.

Dream of teachers who teach for life and not for living. Dream of doctors who are concerned more about public health than private wealth. Dream of lawyers more concerned about justice than a judgeship. Dream of preachers who are concerned more about prophecy than profiteering. Dream on the high road of sound values.

And in America, as we go forth to September, October and November and then beyond, America must never surrender to a high moral challenge.

Do not surrender to drugs. The best drug policy is a no first use. Don't surrender with needles and cynicism. Let's have no first use on the one hand, or clinics on the other. Never surrender, young America.

Go forward. America must never surrender to malnutrition. We can feed the hungry and clothe the naked. We must never surrender. We must go forward. We must never surrender to illiteracy. Invest in our children. Never surrender; and go forward.

We must never surrender to inequality. Women cannot compromise ERA or comparable worth. Women are making 60 cents on the dollar to what a man makes. Women cannot buy meat cheaper. Women cannot buy bread cheaper. Women cannot buy milk cheaper. Women deserve to get paid for the work that you do. It's right and it's fair.

Don't surrender, my friends. Those who have AIDS tonight, you deserve our compassion. Even with AIDS you must not surrender in your wheelchairs. I see you sitting here tonight in those wheelchairs. I've stayed with you. I've reached out to you across our nation. Don't you give up. I know it's tough sometimes. People look down on you. It took you a little more effort to get here tonight.

And no one should look down on you, but sometimes mean people do. The only justification we have for looking down on someone is that we're going to stop and pick them up. But even in your wheelchairs, don't you give up. We cannot forget 50 years ago when our backs were against the wall, Roosevelt was in a wheelchair. I would rather have Roosevelt in a wheelchair than Reagan and Bush on a horse. Don't you surrender and don't you give up.

Don't surrender and don't give up. Why can I challenge you this way? Jesse Jackson, you don't understand my situation. You be on television. You don't understand. I see you with the big people. You don't understand my situation. I understand. You're seeing me on TV but you don't know the me that makes me, me. They wonder why does Jesse run, because they see me running for the White House. They don't see the house I'm running from.

I have a story. I wasn't always on television. Writers were not always outside my door. When I was born late one afternoon, October 8th, in Greenville, S.C., no writers asked my mother her name. Nobody chose to write down our address. My mama was not supposed to make it. And I was not supposed to make it. You see, I was born to a teen-age mother who was born to a teen-age mother.

I understand. I know abandonment and people being mean to you, and saying you're nothing and nobody, and can never be anything. I understand. Jesse Jackson is my third name. I'm adopted. When I had no name, my grandmother gave me her name. My name was Jesse Burns until I was 12. So I wouldn't have a blank space, she gave me a name to hold me over. I understand when nobody knows your name. I understand when you have no name. I understand.

I wasn't born in the hospital. Mama didn't have insurance. I was born in the bed at home. I really do understand. Born in a three-room house, bathroom in the backyard, slop jar by the bed, no hot and cold running water. I understand. Wallpaper used for decoration? No. For a windbreaker. I understand. I'm a working person's person, that's why I understand you whether you're black or white.

I understand work. I was not born with a silver spoon in my mouth. I had a shovel programmed for my hand. My mother, a working woman. So many days she went to work early with runs in her stockings. She knew better, but she wore runs in her stockings so that my brother and I could have matching socks and not be laughed at at school.

I understand. At 3 o'clock on Thanksgiving Day we couldn't eat turkey because mama was preparing someone else's turkey at 3 o'clock. We had to play football to entertain ourselves and then around 6 o'clock she would get off the Alta Vista bus; then we would bring up the leftovers and eat our turkey—leftovers, the carcass, the cranberries around 8 o'clock at night. I really do understand.

Every one of these funny labels they put on you, those of you who are watching this broadcast tonight in the projects, on the corners, I understand. Call you outcast, low down, you can't make it, you're nothing, you're from nobody, subclass, underclass—when you see Jesse Jackson, when my name goes in nomination, your name goes in nomination.

I was born in the slum, but the slum was not born in me. And it wasn't born in you, and you can make it. Wherever you are tonight you can make it. Hold your head high, stick your chest out. You can make it. It gets dark sometimes, but the morning comes. Don't you surrender. Suffering breeds character. Character breeds faith. In the end faith will not disappoint.

You must not surrender. You may or may not get there, but just know that you're qualified and you hold on and hold out. We must never surrender. America will get better and better. Keep hope alive. Keep hope alive. Keep hope alive. On tomorrow night and beyond, keep hope alive.

I love you very much. I love you very much.

Suzan D. Johnson Cook (1957–)

Assessing her role as a contemporary minister, Reverend Suzan D. Johnson Cook states: "Today's pastor has to be a risk taker and pioneer. The church is still the strongest and most consistent institution in a community. . . . My role is to see life as it is and as it can be and help reach the goals people set that are realistic and achievable."

Born in Harlem and raised in the Bronx in New York City, Cook received her B.S. at age nineteen from Emerson College in Boston. She then earned her master of arts degree from Columbia University's Teacher's College in 1978 and her master of divinity degree from New York's Union Theological Seminary in 1983. She completed her doctoral studies in 1990 at the United Theological Seminary in Dayton, Ohio. Cook has published several books, including Wise Women Bearing Gifts: Joys and Struggles of Their Faith *(1988) and* Preaching in Two Voices *(1992), and has served as a visiting professor in Urban Studies and Homiletics at Harvard University's Divinity School.*

Although she has spoken in west Africa, Spain, Cuba, and Switzerland, Reverend Cook has been committed above all to church-related work in America's inner cities. After becoming the youngest elected senior pastor of an American Baptist congregation at age twenty-six, she led the Mariners' Temple Baptist church in New York City from an active membership of sixty to more than a thousand members. She has also spearheaded church programs focusing on interracial and interethnic cooperation, a weekly worship service for more than five hundred businesspeople, a media broadcast, a children's ministry, and an outreach project with the New York City Police Department.

In "God's Woman," first published in Those Preachin' Women, *an anthology edited by Ella P. Mitchell (1985), Cook highlights the Old Testament figure Esther to underscore the significance of women both to the community and to God.*

God's Woman

> I also and my maidens will fast likewise; and so will I go in unto the king, which is not according to the law: and if I perish, I perish.
>
> —Esther 4:16

Many preachers today wait until there is a special service for women, such as "Women's Day," before they'll preach a sermon about a woman of God. Unlike them, I like all the Scriptures all the time and find power in the word of God—in those stories about women *and* those about men, those about heroes and those about the defeated. Throughout the Scriptures we're able to see the mighty works of God, we're able to see God's limitless power. And so today, for just a little while, I'd like to focus attention on a mighty woman of God: Queen Esther.

Today's history books retell the stories told to many of us by our parents and grandparents about a scattered and an abused people—*our* people, Black people—who were brought to this strange land to live and work as slaves. We have had a disturbing history that is not very pleasant to remember or even speak about. It is the story of men and women, some of whom were once kings and queens in their homeland, who were freighted to this land like cattle, animals, or property. It is the sad story of a people dispersed through many different areas in an attempt totally to destroy their culture—*our* culture—and any reminder of who they—and we—were. But it is also the story of a people who, when at their lowest, found a Savior, a Liberator. How interesting—this painful yet joyful story of ours!

If you understand at all the depth of our African-American story, then you see that it would be a good background for this story of Queen Esther. For in her story we find that we were not the only people to be oppressed, and that as God delivered Esther and her people, God can and *will* deliver us if we only believe.

Esther was a Jewish woman living in Persia. She was in that land through the same circumstances that Black people came here: by enslavement. She was the second generation of those who had been enslaved, and so no one but an old cousin named Mordecai knew that she was a Jew. It was a secret, however. If the truth had been known, they would have been killed.

Have you ever felt that you had to hide your identity? Have you not been able to let yourself be known? I mean, you were not able to let folks know who you really were and what you really believed because you knew that there would be a great risk involved? It's hard when you want to be honest and truthful with folks and let them know all about you, but you really can't. It's terrible when you're in the midst of a multitude of people and can't find anyone around who's like you to whom you can talk. Many people go to church trying to find the "right" church where they can let things out. It's sad when even in the church of God, you feel all by yourself. Oh, it's a terrible feeling.

If you have felt this way, you can identify with Esther's predicament. Being a Jew and living in a Persian empire didn't really mix well, like oil and water. But Esther had to deal with life as it was presented to her, just as we must. The psalmist even spoke about this predicament when he wrote, "How shall we sing the LORD's song in a strange land?" We see that we are not the first to face displacement or to question why it happened to us.

Esther had no real support system with which to identify. She had no mother to "reach out and touch" and no sisters or brothers that she knew of; she had no one but her old cousin, Mordecai. This cousin helped to support her and take care of her. He worked in the king's court. He didn't have a big job; he was just a little civil servant who had to work each and every day to help make ends meet, just as you and I must do. But Mordecai loved his people and wanted the future generations to live in freedom and have a better life than he had had, just as many of us hope and pray that life will be easier for our children. I remember well how my parents had to work two and sometimes three jobs to help make ends meet. I would always ask them, "Why do you work so hard?" The answer would always be the same: "So that you can have it better than we've had it."

Now, in our story the Persian king was looking for a new wife to replace Queen Vashti, whom he had cut loose because she refused to dance nude in front of him and his friends. So he sent a search team to look throughout all the land for a new queen. I imagine that as all the women gathered, the scene was something like the Miss America pageant that we see today—the most "beautiful" women on parade. And of all the women that the king saw, the one he chose as his new wife was Esther, this Jew who was living in Persia. But, the king did not know that she was a Jew. She still could not let out the truth. (You know how we can keep things quiet that we don't want known.) All went well for a while. Then came a huge challenge for Esther, a chance to help her people. For the first time she was in a position to save someone else. Luke reminds us that "to whom much is given, of him will much be required" (Luke 12:48, RSV).

To fill you in on a few details of the story: Cousin Mordecai had refused to bow down to one of the king's princes, Haman. As a result, Haman arranged for a decree to be passed for all the Jewish people to be killed. Mordecai, knowing the situation, pleaded with Esther to save the Jewish people. He knew that Esther now had some influence with the king, for she was the queen. You know how some of us can get when we know people with power, or people we think have power. Usually, for selfish reasons, we begin to ask them to pull strings for us. But Mordecai knew that he was asking for help on behalf of a whole race of people. So he went straight to his cousin Esther—not to the chairman of the deacon board, not to his congressional representative, but straight to the source of salvation. He knew that if his people were going to survive, someone would have to intercede. Queen Esther would have to step in to halt a threat for which someone else was responsible.

Esther's story reminds me of some of us Black women and men who are trying to get it together, who want to do right. Yet our very existence is threatened for something completely beyond our control. We've been so scattered and dispersed for much of our lives that sometimes we feel that we have to disguise who we are and live a schizophrenic existence. It seems we can't tell folks who we really are. Many of us have an "identity crisis" and feel we can't tell people we're Black. We will go out of the way to tell them that we have every other kind of blood but Black blood. It's a sad story.

We can use many disguises. In the fifties women tried to disguise their blackness by using bleaching creams; in the sixties many tried to disguise their income levels by moving to the suburbs because they were embarrassed to say that they were poor. And now it's the eighties and folks are still trying to hide things.

Many of us feel that we can't even tell folks that we're Christian. Even right in God's house many of us are holding back. We hold back the Spirit when the Spirit comes. We don't want folks to know that we feel good and love the Lord. We can be so *cool* on God sometimes. We act cool when we don't say, "Amen," and know that the feeling has hit us, or when we don't shout even though the Spirit says to shout. And if we're out with non-Christian friends, many of us feel that we can't say a good word for the Lord and let them know that there's "something within me that holdeth the reign; something within me that I cannot explain." Disguises . . . because there's always a risk involved when you reveal who you are. And many of us, like Esther, do not find many people around to support us: no friends and few family members. We often feel all alone.

But God, being who he is, always places someone around us who will remind us of who we are, just as Mordecai reminded Esther of who she was. There's always someone around whom God will touch to reveal the responsibility that's attached to a position, whether it's that of a queen, or a deacon, or an usher. God is all-knowing and all-wise and so often touches the hand of a writer, like Paul, or the lips and heart of a preacher, like Martin Luther King, Jr., or the voice of a singer, like Mahalia Jackson bringing a message to us—a message not only of liberation but also of hope and of love.

So in the midst of this crisis in Persia, God spoke through a man—Mordecai—to remind a woman—Esther—that she was God's woman. And Esther realized that even though she was in a powerful position (in secular terms), she didn't have the real power that she needed. To be God's woman meant that she had to have a personal relationship with God. She had to get the power before she could go in to see the king. It's impossible to do things when you have the wrong kind of power. You can't use gas in an electric stove—it's the wrong kind of power.

But the joy came when Esther realized that she didn't need to do a whole lot of talking about getting this power; she didn't need to run to people to ask them their opinion. Once she realized that she needed the right kind of power, she went to the Source. She sought the right kind of power for herself, the kind of power she would need if she was going to be any help to her people or herself. And to go to God, she could take off all the masks and disguises that were hiding who she really was. She could be real with God, for there was no one else she could talk with as openly and honestly.

Esther sought power through fasting and through prayer. Prayer is good and it is powerful. It opens the door for God to come into our lives and work. Prayer takes our humanity and lets us make contact with divinity. There's power in prayer. It brings us closer to God.

I enjoy praying, for I realize that it's a source of my strength. But every now and then I also realize that I need to fast, just as Esther had to fast. Fasting means to abstain from physical food so that one can be strengthened with spiritual food. It allows the impure to go out so that the pure can come in: pure love, pure joy, pure hope, pure peace. For through prayer and fasting we can have perfect peace and keep our minds stayed on God (see Isaiah 26:3). There are no hidden dangers, toils, or snares when one fasts and prays to God.

For Esther the real power came when she invited others to join with her in fasting and prayer. This meant that not only would she get power but also others would get power. It meant that others trusted her enough to join with her, for they needed power too. When you unveil yourself and take off all the disguises so that you can be God's woman (or God's man), then you become a mirror for others so that they can also see the glory of God. Somebody wrote a song with the lyrics "Walk together, children, and don't you get weary." We can't run this race all by ourselves. We need others to walk and run with us.

I look forward with great anticipation to prayer meetings and Bible study on Wednesday nights at our church because I realize that none of us can keep the faith alone, but together we can lift one another up and then we can lift up the name of Jesus. When I begin to get weak, there is someone there who can lift me up, and when I am strong, I can help someone else. That's part of the process of my becoming God's woman. When we share the power, then the power grows in each of us.

Even Jesus, the Son of the living God, who came into this world as God in the flesh, had to be hidden for a little while because King Herod would have killed him if he had found him. Yet, in God's time Jesus was able to reveal who he really was—the Messiah—for the prophecy of his coming had been fulfilled. When God speaks, when God touches us, we can take off all of the disguises, for we know, as the hymn says, that it is well with our souls.

Even Jesus, God's Son, had to fast and pray for a closer walk with God. When times became too hard for him to bear alone, he would go into the garden or to a mountaintop and have a talk with God. When we remove ourselves from the physical, the carnal, then we grow stronger in the spiritual.

So Queen Esther, this woman of God, fasted. Esther prayed. And when she came forth, she knew that she had a *holy boldness*. She knew that she would not have to fight alone; she would have God to fight for her.

Jesus fasted and Jesus prayed. He prayed for us even when we could not pray for ourselves. But he also invited others to join with him in prayer so that they could draw closer to God. Jesus had a *holy boldness*. Yet Jesus perished, not because of anything that he had done, but because of what humanity had done. There at Calvary—oh, I can see it now—while his mother and followers watched, he perished. And because he perished for us, we should not perish if we believe on him. John 3:16 tells us "God so loved the world that he gave his only begotten Son, that whosoever believeth in him should not perish, but have everlasting life." On Calvary, he perished. As they pierced his side, he perished. As the blood came running down, he perished. Now you and I have the gift of God if only we believe.

Esther found a personal relationship with God, but she couldn't include Jesus Christ in her testimony, for he had not yet been born. You and I, though, can rejoice today because we have a story to tell. It's a story about Jesus and his love. It's a story about the Savior who came into our lives and healed us, liberated us, and saved us. You and I should be able to step out with the boldness that Jesus had and tell the world that the Savior has come. When we feel that our burdens are heavy or that the weight of our entire race or the entire world is upon us, remember the mighty woman of God, Esther, who took the weight to the Lord. But also remember a man who was the mighty man of God, Jesus the Christ, who has empowered us to go forth into the whole world telling the good news. Yes, our history has pain in it, yet our lives today can have everlasting joy. It's a joy that the world doesn't give to you. It's a joy that history can't take from you. It's a joy that no one can take away.

Who is God's woman? The woman who knows God for herself, who has a personal relationship with Jesus the Christ. Who is God's woman? One who takes off the disguises, owns all the things that have been hidden, and opens up to God. This is God's woman, the woman who gives her life to Jesus Christ. Amen.

FOLKTALES

Why Negroes Are Black

Long before they got thru makin' de Atlantic Ocean and haulin' de rocks for de mountains, God was makin' up de people. But He didn't finish 'em all at one time. Ah'm compelled to say dat some folks is walkin' 'round dis town right now ain't finished yet and never will be.

Well, He give out eyes one day. All de nations come up and got they eyes. Then He give out teeth and so on. Then He set a day to give out color. So seven o'clock dat mornin' everybody was due to git they color except de niggers. So God give everybody they color and they went on off. Then He set there for three hours and one-half and no niggers. It was gettin' hot and God wanted to git His work done and go set in de cool. So He sent de angels Rayfield and Gab'ull to go git 'em so He could 'tend some mo' business.

They hunted all over Heben till dey found de colored folks. All stretched out sleep on de grass under de tree of life. So Rayfield woke 'em up and tole 'em God wanted 'em.

They all jumped up and run on up to de th'one and they was so skeered they might miss sumpin' they begin to push and shove one 'nother, bumpin' against all de angels and turnin' over foot-stools. They even had de th'one all pushed one-sided.

So God hollered "Git back! Git back!" And they misunderstood Him and thought He said, "Git black," and they been black ever since.

Why Women Always Take Advantage of Men

You see in de very first days, God made a man and a woman and put 'em in a house together to live. 'Way back in them days de woman was just as strong as de man and both of 'em did de same things. They useter get to fussin' 'bout who gointer do this and that and sometime they'd fight, but they was even balanced and neither one could whip de other one.

One day de man said to hisself, "B'lieve Ah'm gointer go see God and ast Him for a li'l mo' strength so Ah kin whip dis 'oman and make her mind. Ah'm tired of de way things is." So he went on up to God.

"Good mawnin', Ole Father."

"Howdy man. Whut you doin' 'round my throne so soon dis mawnin'?"

"Ah'm troubled in mind, and nobody can't ease mah spirit 'ceptin' you."

God said: "Put yo' plea in de right form and Ah'll hear and answer."

"Ole Maker, wid de mawnin' stars glitterin' in yo' shinin' crown, wid de dust from yo' footsteps makin' worlds upon worlds, wid de blazin' bird we call de sun flyin' out of yo' right hand in de mawnin' and consumin' all day de flesh and blood of stump-black darkness, and comes flyin' home every evenin' to rest on yo' left hand, and never once in all yo' eternal years, mistood de left hand for de right, Ah ast you *please* to give me mo' strength than dat woman you give me, so Ah kin make her mind. Ah know you don't want to be always comin' down way past de moon and stars to be straightenin' her out and its got to be done. So give me a li'l mo' strength, Ole Maker and Ah'll do it."

"All right, Man, you got mo' strength than woman."

So de man run all de way down de stairs from Heben till he got home. He was so anxious to try his strength on de woman dat he couldn't take his time. Soon's he got in de house he hollered, "Woman! Here's yo' boss. God done tole me to handle you in which ever way Ah please. Ah'm yo' boss."

De woman flew to fightin' 'im right off. She fought 'im frightenin' but he beat her. She got her wind and tried 'im agin but he whipped her agin. She got herself together and made de third try on him vigorous but he beat her every time. He was so proud he could whip 'er at last, dat he just crowed over her and made her do a lot of things she didn't like. He told her, "Long as you obey me, Ah'll be good to yuh, but every time yuh rear up Ah'm gointer put plenty wood on yo' back and plenty water in yo' eyes."

De woman was so mad she went straight up to Heben and stood befo' de Lawd. She didn't waste no words. She said, "Lawd, Ah come befo' you mighty mad t'day. Ah want back my strength and power Ah useter have."

"Woman, you got de same power you had since de beginnin'."

"Why is it then, dat de man kin beat me now and he useter couldn't do it?"

"He got mo' strength than he useter have. He come and ast me for it and Ah give it to 'im. Ah gives to them that ast, and you ain't never ast me for no mo' power."

"Please suh, God, Ah'm astin' you for it now. Jus' gimme de same as you give him."

God shook his head. "It's too late now, woman. Whut Ah give, Ah never take back. Ah give him mo' strength than you and no matter how much Ah give you, he'll have mo'."

De woman was so mad she wheeled around and went on off. She went straight to de devil and told him what had happened.

He said, "Don't be dis-incouraged, woman. You listen to me and you'll come out mo' than conqueror. Take dem frowns out yo' face and turn round and go right back to Heben and ast God to give you dat bunch of keys hangin' by de mantel-piece. Then you bring 'em to me and Ah'll show you what to do wid 'em."

So de woman climbed back up to Heben agin. She was mighty tired but she was more out-done that she was tired so she climbed all night long and got back up to Heben agin. When she got befo' de throne, butter wouldn't melt in her mouf.

"O Lawd and Master of de rainbow, Ah know yo' power. You never make two mountains without you put a valley in between. Ah know you kin hit a straight lick wid a crooked stick."

"Ast for whut you want, woman."

"God, gimme dat bunch of keys hangin' by yo' mantel-piece."

"Take 'em."

So de woman took de keys and hurried on back to de devil wid 'em. There was three keys on de bunch. Devil say, "See dese three keys? They got mo' power in 'em than all de strength de man kin ever git if you handle 'em right. Now dis first big key is to de do' of de kitchen, and you know a man always favors his stomach. Dis second one is de key to de bedroom and he don't like to be shut out from dat neither and dis last key is de key to de cradle and he don't want to be cut off from his generations at all. So now you take dese keys and go lock up everything and wait till he come to you. Then don't you unlock nothin' until he use his strength for yo' benefit and yo' desires."

De woman thanked 'im and tole 'im, "If it wasn't for you, Lawd knows whut us po' women folks would do."

She started off but de devil halted her. "Jus' one mo' thing: don't go home braggin' 'bout yo' keys. Jus' lock up everything and say nothin' until you git asked. And then don't talk too much."

De woman went on home and did like de devil tole her. When de man come home from work she was settin' on de porch singin' some song 'bout "Peck on de wood make de bed go good."

When de man found de three doors fastened what useter stand wide open he swelled up like pine lumber after a rain. First thing he tried to break in cause he figgered his strength would overcome all obstacles. When he saw he couldn't do it, he ast de woman, "Who locked dis do'?"

She tole 'im, "Me."

"Where did you git de key from?"

"God give it to me."

He run up to God and said, "God, woman got me locked 'way from my vittles, my bed and my generations, and she say you give her the keys."

God said, "I did, Man, Ah give her de keys, but de devil showed her how to use 'em!"

"Well, Ole Maker, please gimme some keys jus' lak 'em so she can't git de full control."

"No, Man, what Ah give Ah give. Woman got de key."

"How kin Ah know 'bout my generations?"

"Ast de woman."

So de man come on back and submitted hisself to de woman and she opened de doors.

He wasn't satisfied but he had to give in. 'Way after while he said to de woman, "Le's us divide up. Ah'll give you half of my strength if you lemme hold de keys in my hands."

De woman thought dat over so de devil popped and tol her, "Tell 'im, naw. Let 'im keep his strength and you keep yo' keys."

So de woman wouldn't trade wid 'im and de man had to mortgage his strength to her to live. And dat's why de man makes and de woman takes. You men is still braggin' 'bout yo' strength and de women is sittin' on de keys and lettin' you blow off till she git ready to put de bridle on you.

Ole Massa and John Who Wanted to Go to Heaven

You know befo' surrender Ole Massa had a nigger name John and John always prayed every night befo' he went to bed and his prayer was for God to come git him and take him to Heaven right away. He didn't even want to take time to die. He wanted de Lawd to come git him just like he was—boot, sock and all. He'd git down on his knees and say: "O Lawd, it's once more and again yo' humble servant is knee-bent and body-bowed—my heart beneath my knees and my knees in some lonesome valley, crying for mercy while mercy kin be found. O Lawd, Ah'm astin' you in de humblest way I know how to be *so* pleased as to come in yo' fiery chariot and take me to yo' Heben and its immortal glory. Come Lawd, you know Ah have such a hard time. Old Massa works me *so* hard, and don't gimme no time to rest. So come, Lawd, wid peace in one hand and pardon in de other and take me away from this sin-sorrowing world. Ah'm tired and Ah want to go home."

So one night Ole Massa passed by John's shack and heard him beggin' de Lawd to come git him in his fiery chariot and take him away; so he made up his mind to find out if John meant dat thing. So he goes up to de big house and got hisself a bed sheet and come on back. He throwed de sheet over his head and knocked on de door.

John quit prayin' and ast: "Who dat?"

Ole Massa say: "It's me, John, de Lawd, done come wid my fiery chariot to take you away from this sin-sick world."

Right under de bed John had business. He told his wife: "Tell Him Ah ain't here, Liza."

At first Liza didn't say nothin' at all, but de Lawd kept right on callin' John: "Come on, John, and go to Heben wid me where you won't have to plough no mo' furrows and hoe no mo' corn. Come on, John."

Liza says: "John ain't here, Lawd, you hafta come back another time."

Lawd says: "Well, then Liza, you'll do."

Liza whispers and says: "John, come out from underneath dat bed and g'wan wid de Lawd. You been beggin' him to come git you. Now g'wan wid him."

John back under de bed not saying a mumblin' word. De Lawd out on de door step kept on callin'.

Liza says: "John, Ah thought you was so anxious to get to Heben. Come out and go on wid God."

John says: "Don't you hear him say 'You'll do'? Why don't you go wid him?"

"Ah ain't a goin' nowhere. Youse de one been whoopin' and hollerin' for him to come git you and if you don't come out from under dat bed Ah'm gointer tell God youse here."

Ole Massa makin' out he's God, says: "Come on, Liza, you'll do."

Liza says: "O, Lawd, John is right here underneath de bed."

"Come on John, and go to Heben wid me and its immortal glory."

John crept out from under de bed and went to de door and cracked it and when he seen all dat white standin' on de doorsteps he jumped back. He says: "O, Lawd, Ah can't go to Heben wid you in yo' fiery chariot in dese ole dirty britches; gimme time to put on my Sunday pants."

"All right, John, put on yo' Sunday pants."

John fooled around just as long as he could, changing them pants, but when he went back to de door, de big white glory was still standin' there. So he says agin: "O, Lawd, de Good Book says in Heben no filth is found and I got on dis dirty sweaty shirt. Ah can't go wid you in dis old nasty shirt. Gimme time to put on my Sunday shirt!"

"All right, John, go put on yo' Sunday shirt."

John took and fumbled around a long time changing his shirt, and den he went back to de door, but Ole Massa was still on de door step. John didn't had nothin' else to change so he opened de door a little piece and says:

"O, Lawd, Ah'm ready to go to Heben wid you in yo' fiery chariot, but de radiance of yo' countenance is *so* bright, Ah can't come out by you. Stand back jus' a li'l way please."

Ole Massa stepped back a li'l bit.

John looked out agin and says: "O, Lawd, you know dat po' humble me is less than de dust beneath yo' shoe soles. And de radiance of yo' countenance is so bright Ah can't come out by you. Please, please, Lawd, in yo' tender mercy, stand back a li'l bit further."

Ole Massa stepped back a li'l bit mo'.

John looked out agin and he says: "O, Lawd, Heben is so high and wese so low; youse so great and Ah'm so weak and yo' strength is too much for us poor sufferin' sinners. So once mo' and again yo' humber servant is knee-bent and body-bowed askin' you one mo' favor befo' Ah step into yo' fiery chariot to go to Heben wid you and wash in yo' glory—be so pleased in yo' tender mercy as to stand back jus' a li'l bit further."

Ole Massa stepped back a step or two mo' and out dat door John come like a streak of lightning. All across de punkin patch, thru de cotton over de pasture—John wid Ole Massa right behind him. By de time dey hit de cornfield John was way ahead of Ole Massa.

Back in de shack one of de children was cryin' and she ast Liza: "Mama, you reckon God's gointer ketch papa and carry him to Heben wid him?"

"Shet yo' mouf, talkin' foolishness!" Liza clashed at de chile. "You know de Lawd can't outrun yo' pappy—specially when he's barefooted at dat."

What Smelled Worse

Once they tried a colored man in Mobile for stealing a goat. He was so poorly dressed, and dirty—that de judge told him, "Six months on de county road, you stink so."

A white man was standing dere and he said, "Judge, he don't stink, Ah got a nigger who smells worser than a billy goat." De judge told de man to bring him on over so he could smell him. De next day de man took de billy goat and de nigger and went to de court and sent de judge word dat de nigger and de billy goat wuz out dere and which one did he want fust.

The judge told him to bring in de goat. When he carried de goat he smelled so bad dat de judge fainted. Dey got ice water and throwed it in de Judge's face 'til he come to. He told 'em to bring in de nigger and when dey brung in de nigger de goat fainted.

Who Ate Up the Butter?

All the animals was farming a crop together. And they bought a pound of butter—they was in a cahoots, all chipped in equally. So the next day they all goes to the field to work. All at once Brother Rabbit says, "Heya." All of them quits working, ask, "What is it, Brother Rabbit?"

"It's my wife, she's calling me, I ain't got time to fool with her." All of them together say, "Well you better go on, Brother Rabbit, and see what it is she wants." Off he goes to the house to see what his wife wants.

Twenty minutes he was back. They say, "What did your wife want, Brother Rabbit?" "Well she got a new baby up there." So they slapped Brother Rabbit on the back, said, "Good, good. You named him yet?" "Yes, I named him Quarter Gone."

So they begin to work again. About thirty minutes more Brother Rabbit begins to holler again, "What do you want?" They say, "What was that, who you talking to?" "That was my wife, didn't you hear her calling?" "Well, you better go see what she wants." The Rabbit said, "I'm working, I haven't got time to fool with her." They said, "You'd better go on, Brother Rabbit."

So he goes on to the house to see what she wants. In about twenty more minutes he was back again. "What's the trouble this time, Brother Rabbit, what did your wife want?" "Same thing, another baby." They all said, "Good, good, what was it?" Said, "It was a boy." "What did you name him?" Said, "Oh, Half Gone." Said, "That sure is a pretty name." So he goes back hard to work.

After a while he hollers again, "Oooh, I ain't studying about you." They said, "What you hollering about, what you studying about, we ain't seed no one. Who was it?" "It was my wife." (She'd been calling him all morning.) "Well, why don't you go on Brother Rabbit, and see what she wants." "No, we'll never get nothing done if I just keep running to the house; no, I'm not going." The animals said, "That's all right, Brother Rabbit, it's only a little time, we don't mind, go on."

So Brother Rabbit goes on to the house. Well, he was there about forty minutes this time. "Brother Rabbit, what was your trouble this time?" "My wife had twins." "Good, good, good." They just rejoiced over it. "You'll have to set 'em up when we go to town this time." He said, "Well, the reason I was gone so long I was studying what to name those two twins so it would sound nearly alike." They asked, "What did you name them, Brother Rabbit?" They'd never heard tell of twins before, or of the rabbit having four. "Three Quarters Gone and All Gone." They insist on "Let's go see 'em." He says, "Well, we'll just work on till noon, then we'll have plenty of time, no need to hurry."

So he sent Brother Terrapin into the house to get some water. Well, he drank the water. Then he wanted a match, he wanted a smoke bad. So he said to Brother Deer, "Brother Terrapin is too slow, you run up there and bring those matches." Told Brother Fox, "You run on and drive the horses to the barn, we think we're going to plow this evening. We'll be home 'gainst you get there." So he taken off to drive the horses. When Brother Fox got out of sight good, Brother Rabbit said, "Well, we'll go." So they had to go slow, 'cause Brother Terrapin poked along, and they all walked together with him. When they got to the house, Brother Fox was sitting on the front porch waiting for them. He said, "Mens, I sure is hungry, let's wash up and get in the kitchen."

In a few seconds, they was all washed up and in the kitchen they'd go. Brother Rabbit was the first one in there; he says, "Well, where's the butter? The butter's all gone!" (*Loud*) The first one they accused was Brother Rabbit. "Remember when he came by the house to see about his wife and them babies?"

He says, "No, I didn't even think about the butter. Now listen, you remember more than me come to the house, Brother Terrapin and Brother Deer and Brother Fox, and I'd be afraid to 'cuse them, for I know I didn't and I wouldn't say they did. But I got a plan and we can soon find out who done it, I or him or whom."

They all agreed to hear about Brother Rabbit's plan—they was confused and mad and forgot about being hungry, and said, "His plan always did work."

Now Brother Rabbit told them, "We'll make a big log heap and set fire to it, and run and jump, and the one that falls in it, he ate the butter." So they made the log heap and put the fire in it. The fire begins to burn and smoke, smoke and burn. "All right, we're ready to jump."

They were all lined up. Brother Deer taken the first jump. Brother Rabbit said, "Well, Brother Terrapin, guess I better take the next one." He done jump. Terrapin was waiting for the wind to turn. He was so short he knew he couldn't jump far. The wind started blowing the smoke down to the ground, on both sides of the log heap. So Brother Terrapin said, "Well, I guess it's my jump." He ran around the heap and turned somersault on the other side. Brother Rabbit and Brother Deer were looking way up in the smoke to see the others coming over; they weren't looking low, and thought he had jumped over. They said, "Well, Brother Terrapin he made it."

So all the rest of them they jumped it clear, Brother Fox, and Brother Bear, and that made everybody on the other side. "Well, Brother Deer, it's your jump again." So the three they jump over again, and only Brother Bear and Brother Terrapin is left. Brother Terrapin says, "Step here, Brother Bear, before you jump." Said, "I hear you can jump high across that fire, cross your legs and pull your teat out and show it to 'em (his back teat), stop in space, and then jump from there onto the other side. I don't know if you can, I only heard it." Brother Bear says, "O, yes I can." So Brother Terrapin was glad he was making that deal, for he didn't know if the smoke would be in his favor going back.

The Bear says, "Stand back, Mr. Terrapin, let me jump first this time, you can see this." (*Deep, gruff*) The Bear backed further, further than ever to get speed up to stop and cross his legs. He calls out, "Here goes Brother Bear," and takes off. In the middle he tries to cross his leg, and down he went, into the fire. Brother Rabbit said, "Push the fire on him, push the fire on him." (*Excited*) "He's the one that eat the butter." So all of them go to the end, and begin to shove the chunks on Brother Bear. They all give Brother Rabbit credit for being the smart one to find the guilty fellow what eat the butter.

None of them ever thought Brother Bear was the only one never went to the house. Just like in a law case many men are convicted from showing evidence against them where there isn't any. They get a smart lawyer to show you was there when you wasn't there at all, trap you with his questions, get you convicted and behind the bars. Then they say, "He's a smart lawyer."

The Bear and the Rabbit

Mr. Rabbit and Mr. Bear met one day, and got to discussin' 'bout different things in the world. Mr. Bear said he'd been all over the world. He'd seen everything but Man. "They tell me about Man, and I wants to see him." Brother Rabbit says, "Why I can show you a Man. Come on and go with me up here this side o' the road." They set down. After awhile along come a boy, about eight years old. Mr. Bear looks up. "Say, is that Man comin' yonder?" Brother Rabbit looks up, sees him. "Why no, that's going to be Man. But be patient, Man will be along directly." Brother Bear was so anxious to see them he kept his eyes on the road all the time. "Say Mr. Rabbit, that's Man comin' yonder." Brother Rabbit looked up, he seen an old man comin' on a stick, about eighty years old. Says, "No, no, that used to be Man. He's got a walkin' stick. But be patient. Man'll be along directly." Brother Bear keeps his eyes on the road. Brother Rabbit looks back the other way, the east end of the road. Says, "There comes Man, that's Man comin' down the road." Brother Bear straightens up and looks. "Now that's Man, go out and meet him." He's twenty-one years old and has a gun on his shoulder.

Off to the thicket Mr. Rabbit ran, down to the road and off to the woods. Mr. Bear walks down the road and stands up on his two legs, right in the middle of the road. Young man, off his shoulder come the gun, let the bear have both barrels, boom, boom. Down went Mr. Bear on all four'ses legs. Into the thicket he went, where Brother Rabbit was. "Say, I seen Man. He had a rail on his shoulder, he take it down and pointed at me, it lightened at one end, and it thundered at tother end. Look, it just filled me full of splinters all over." Said Mr. Rabbit, "Well you've met Man and you've seen what he is."

(You take a bad man, he beats up on a little boy or an old man, but when he meets a real man, he gets beat up.)

Tar Baby

Rabbit says to himself, "Gee, it's gittin' dry here; can't git any mo' water. Git a little in the mornin' but that ain't enough." So he goes along an' gits the gang to dig a well. So the Fox goes roun' an' calls all the animals together to dig this well. He gits Possum, Coon, Bear, an' all the animals an' they start to dig the well. So they come to Rabbit to help. Rabbit he sick. They say, "Come on, Brother Rabbit, help dig this well; we all need water." Rabbit say, "Oh the devil. I don't need no water; I kin drink dew." So he wouldn't go. So when the well was done Rabbit he was the first one to git some of the water. He went there at night an' git de water in jugs. The other animals see Rabbit's tracks from gittin' water in jugs. So all the animals git together an' see what they goin' to do about Brother Rabbit. So Bear say, "I tell you, I'll lay here an' watch for it. I'll ketch that Rabbit." So Bear watched but Rabbit was too fast for him. So Fox said, "I tell you, let's study a plan to git Brother Rabbit." So they all sit together an' study a plan. So they made a tar baby an' put it up by the well. So Brother Rabbit come along to git some water. He see the tar baby an' think it is Brother Bear. He say, "Can't git any water tonight; there's Brother Bear layin' for me." He looked some more, then he said, "No, that ain't Brother Bear, he's too little for Brother Bear." So he goes up to the tar baby an' say, "Whoo-oo-oo-oo." Tar Baby didn't move. So Rabbit got skeered. He sneaked up to it an' said, "Boo!" Tar Baby didn't move. Then Rabbit run all aroun' an' stood still to see did he move. But Tar Baby kept still. Then he moved his claw at him. Tar Baby stood still. Rabbit said, "That must be a chunk o'wood." He went up to see if it was a man. He said, "Hello, old man, hello, old man, what you doin' here?" The man didn't answer. He said again, "Hello, old man, hello, old man, what you doin' here?" The man didn't answer. Rabbit said, "Don't you hear me talkin' to you? I'll slap you in the face." The man ain't said nothin'. So Rabbit hauled off sure enough an' his paw stuck. Rabbit said, "Turn me loose, turn me loose or I'll hit you with the other paw." The man ain't said nothin'. So Rabbit hauled off with his other paw an' that one stuck too. Rabbit said, "You better turn me loose, I'll kick you if you don't turn me loose." Tar Baby didn't say anything. "Bup!" Rabbit kicked Tar Baby an' his paw stuck. So he hit him with the other an' that one got stuck. Rabbit said, "I know the things got blowed up now; I know if I butt you I'll kill you." So all the animals were hidin' in the grass watchin' all this. They all ran out an' hollered, "Aha, we knowed we was gonna ketch you, we knowed we was gonna ketch you." So Rabbit said, "Oh, I'm so sick." So the animals said, "Whut we gonna do?" So they has a great meetin' to see what they gonna do. So someone said, "Throw him in the fire." But the others said, "No, that's too good; can't let him off that easy." So Rabbit pleaded an' pleaded, "Oh, please, please throw me in the fire." So someone said, "Hang him." They all said, "He's too light, he wouldn't break his own neck." So a resolution was drawn up to burn him up. So they all went to Brother Rabbit an' said, "Well, today you die. We gonna set you on fire." So Rabbit said, "Aw, you couldn't give me anything better." So they all say, "We better throw him in the briar patch." Rabbit cry out right away, "Oh, for God's sake, don't do dat. They tear me feet all up; they tear me behind all up, they tear me eyes out." So they pick him up an' throw him in the briar patch. Rabbit run off an' cry, "Whup-pee, my God, you couldn't throw me in a better place! There where my mammy born me, in the briar patch."

PART TWO

POETRY

OVERVIEW

African American Poetry and the Oral Tradition

More than any other literary form, African American poetry has been inextricably bound to the spoken word. As a genre that expresses emotions and ideas through vivid, highly concentrated language, poetry has served as a bridge between the oral tradition and the written text in African American literature. Poems were the earliest literary efforts to be recognized within African American culture. As critic Calvin Hernton notes, "[b]ecause people talk and sing before they write, poetry is the protoplasm of all literature. . . . Black poetry originated in the fields with the slave songs. It went into the churches with the spirituals, and migrated with . . . blacks wherever they were scattered" (153).

The oral tradition is enriched with metaphorical language and the speaker's improvisational rhythms (see Part One). As such it has served as a basic model for written poetry by African Americans. Colloquialisms and ethnic speech patterns can be traced in decades of African American poetry, from the late nineteenth century in Paul Lawrence Dunbar's "When Malindy Sings" to the twentieth century in Gwendolyn Brooks's "Kitchenette Building" and Haki R. Madhubuti's "But He Was Cool." Later on, musical forms such as jazz and the blues, which themselves echo black verbal patterns, pervaded African American poetry. Langston Hughes's "Mother to Son" conveys the spontaneity of jazz in its free-verse structure, while Robert Hayden's "Night, Death, Mississippi" echoes the blues in its expression of loss and despair. Similarly, Nikki Giovanni's "The True Import of Present Dialogue, Black versus Negro" and Quincy Troupe's "South African Bloodstone" merge orality and jazz and demand to be read aloud.

Literary Bilingualism

Without losing touch with its oral matrix, African American poetry over the centuries has also exemplified an effective use of the language and conventions prevalent in traditional American literature. The writings of numerous poets, including Phillis Wheatley, Countee Cullen, Derek Walcott, and Rita Dove, among many others, have utilized standard English, Anglo-American forms, and European allusions.

As Michael S. Harper and Anthony Walton explain in their introduction to their anthology, *Every Shut Eye Ain't Asleep,* "There are many black voices, or more accurately, voices that can be described as 'black'. There has been a tendency by the academy to select a few" (3). The selections of African American poetry included within Part Two of this book demonstrate a respect for both the distinctive dynamics of black poetry and the spectrum of black authors who compose that poetry.

In the past, literary criticism focused on an apparent conflict between black poetry centered within black cultural expressions, on the one hand, and black poetry using standard elements from the larger American tradition, on the other. Decades of debate were spurred on by various political factors influencing the assessment of literature and the definition of art. However, some African American poets have comfortably moved between black and nonblack language and references. These poets display *literary bilingualism,* but they have not given up their ethnic roots, nor have they forfeited the value of their racial experiences. They have deliberately chosen the literary language that best suits each work. Poets who have exercised this choice have sometimes been condemned by both black and nonblack critics. However, since the late 1970s, particularly as black women have fashioned poetry from both a racial and a woman's perspective, literary bilingualism has met with increased acceptance from critics and readers alike.

An additional factor in the appraisal of African American poetry has been the inclination of many mainstream critics and readers to dismiss black poetry whenever it stresses cultural or political themes. This prejudice ignores the beauty and imaginative use of black vernacular and musical forms. After all, the structuring of syntax, mechanics, and figurative language that goes into re-creating black verbal forms—with complex diction, humor, cadences, multiple meanings, cultural references, and musical qualities—exemplifies the skills that black writers display in their work.

The First Words of Poetry in Print

African American poetry in written form began with Lucy Terry's "Bars Fight" (1746), but a New York slave named Jupiter Hammon has been noted as the first black poet to be published, with his poem "An Evening Thought: Salvation by Christ with Penetential Cries" (1760). The first published book by a black writer was Phillis Wheatley's *Poems on Various Subjects, Religious and Moral* (1773). Writing in the Neo-Classical format, using lofty language, didacticism, and a strict meter (as in the selection "On the Death of a Young Gentleman"), Wheatley demonstrated a formal mastery so impressive that whites questioned her authorship. Her work thus confirmed that blacks possessed the skills to produce poetry comparable to that of European poets of the time. Furthermore, recent criticism suggests that despite the absence of overt cultural themes, Wheatley's works indeed express "a keen awareness of [the poet's] African heritage" (Shields 354).

Although Wheatley avoided cultural as well as political themes, the black poets who followed her were more overt. In the first half of the nineteenth century, George Moses Horton, James Whitfield, and Frances E. W. Harper wrote poetry confronting racial oppression. Harper (who also wrote the first short fiction to be published by an African American author) composed works such as "Bury Me in a Free Land" which explores slavery's many aspects while imploring America to act upon its democratic principles. Harper's abolitionism inspired her feminism, shaping both her fiction and her poetry, as shown in the themes of her poem "A Double Standard."

Ethnic and Traditional Styles

During the latter half of the nineteenth century, black poets adopted the "Negro dialect" format in order to get their works into print. Paul Laurence Dunbar utilizes this style in "When Malindy Sings," in which words are given phonetic spellings to reflect the comic vernacular and speech patterns of common blacks. However, like other black dialect poets of the time, such as James Corrothers and James Edwin Campbell, Dunbar reaches beyond comic Negro speech to traditional English in such poems as "We Wear the Mask" and "Sympathy."

Black poets writing during the early years of the twentieth century sometimes focused on race and ethnicity, and sometimes did not. Georgia Douglas Johnson, Fenton Johnson, and James Weldon Johnson all published poetry early in the century, exploring themes involving relationships and religion, as well as black culture. As an example, Fenton Johnson's "The Ethiopian's Song" and "To an Afro-American Maiden" convey the poet's ethnic consciousness within the framework of traditional rhymes and diction.

The Harlem Renaissance

African American poetry flourished during the Harlem Renaissance of the 1920s, an artistic movement created by the intersection of several elements within black culture. (See David Levering Lewis's essay in Part Five, p. 762.) As black poet and critic Robert Hayden notes:

> [The] new Negro movement or Negro renaissance, resulting from the social, political, and artistic awakening of Negroes in the twenties brought into prominence poets whose work showed the influence of the poetic revolution. . . . Negro history and folklore were explored as new sources of inspiration. Spirituals, blues, and jazz suggested themes and verse patterns to young poets like Jean Toomer and Langston Hughes." (xxii).

The appreciation for black history and culture came together with the support of white patrons and the emerging American mass culture to create—most notably in Harlem in New York City—an atmosphere that fostered black literary creativity. The literature of the period reflected racial pride, social challenges, and political awareness within the black community. In this distinctive era in which African American literature served as a nexus joining the black masses, black intellectuals, black political philosophies, and black cultural expressions, poetry thrived and was enriched by a range of talents and thematic concerns. Anne Spencer, Claude McKay, Gwendolyn Bennett, Countee Cullen, Arna Bontemps, and Langston Hughes were the celebrated and revered poets of the Harlem Renaissance whose works displayed an assortment of tones and styles.

In particular, for the quality and quantity of his writing, Langston Hughes emerged as representative of the decade's enduring spirit. His poetry reflected the language of ordinary blacks, the free verse associated with jazz, and the rhymes and repetition borrowed from the blues. As in his fiction and drama, Hughes's poetry unashamedly utilized the cultural and artistic components of the oral tradition. Thematically, in such poems as "As I Grew Older," "Afro-American Fragment" and "Democracy," Hughes ponders the dual cultural identities of African Americans and their long, bitter wait for the realization of America's democratic ideals. In his character study "Mother to Son," Hughes renders the painful denial of interracial familial ties and the difficult lessons of black life and survival. The five poems by Hughes in Part Two, whether written during or after the Harlem Renaissance, demonstrate well the poet's sensitivity to musical rhythms and potent use of the free verse form.

Integration into the Mainstream

The poetry of the Great Depression and civil rights era augmented themes of cultural pride and integration with a conscious manipulation of form and language. Melvin Tolson, Sterling Brown, Margaret Walker, Robert Hayden, Owen Dodson, Samuel W. Allen, Mari Evans, and Derek Walcott exhibit impressive control of language, giving texture and layered meanings to their poetry. Schooled in black culture, as well as in European and Anglo history and literature, these authors produced a body of accomplished poetry that won admiration from their white contemporaries. These poets demonstrated their ability to unify standard English and European and Anglo references with erudition and control, ever conscious of connecting their styles and tones to mainstream sensibilities.

Still, numerous works by these same African American poets presented ethnic nuances and cultural concerns, demonstrating that black oriented poetry was commensurate with poetry inspired by European and Anglo sources. Sterling Brown's "Children of the Mississippi" raises a collective voice that speaks for the black folk who generated African American culture. Robert Hayden uses Mississippi as a symbol of southern mob violence in "Night, Death, Mississippi," which depicts the contradictions between white "Christian" behavior and black suffering. Enlarging on the racial exploitation treated in these poems, Derek Walcott dissects the irony of interethnic violence and exposes the politics of oppression in various historical and cultural settings. Like the other poets of the era, Walcott persuades the reader to accept both his experimental form and provocative content.

The Black Arts Movement

The poets who emerged in the late 1960s propelled African American poetry into new dimensions of racial consciousness. Informed by the Black Aesthetic and the Black Arts Movement, the poetry of this period venerated jazz and thereby encouraged oral delivery. (See Larry Neal's essay in Part Six, p. 925.)

Comparable to the outpouring of verse during the Harlem Renaissance four decades earlier, the poetry of the Black Arts Movement defined cultural identity through allusions rooted within the Black Power philosophy (see Kwame Toure's essay in Part Five, p. 782). As black critic Stephen Henderson notes, craftsmanship in poetry was crucial, but the "object of a Black Power poem [was] to raise Black People's consciousness" (195). The works of Sarah Webster Fabio, Henry Dumas, Carolyn Rodgers, Jay Wright, Mari Evans, June Jordan, and Quincy Troupe, to name some, emphasized cultural messages intended to shape the attitudes of young blacks, while the poets Etheridge Knight, Sonia Sanchez, Don L. Lee (Haki R. Madhubuti), and Nikki Giovanni gained the most attention as interpreters of the Black Arts Movement. These four poets' polemical verse advocated the revolutionary objectives of the times. Although some critics questioned the artistic merit of such politically charged poetry, the poets and theorists of the Black Aesthetic defended the need for and validity of such works.

Etheridge Knight's "Dark Prophecy: I Sing of Shine" honors the black oral tradition and presents a profane, urban language as representative of black discourse. Sonia Sanchez's "Blk/Rhetoric" and "Summer Words of a Sistuh Addict" typify her radical spelling of words and use of unconventional poetic structures to express themes of racial awareness and pride. Complementing these pieces, the didacticism of Haki R. Madhubuti's "But He Was Cool" and the incendiary tone of Nikki Giovanni's "The True Import of Present Dialogue: Black versus Negro" cry out for change and unity within the black community.

Like the poets of the Harlem Renaissance, the black revolutionary poets of the late 1960s and early 1970s found a distinctive and influential position within the continuum of African American poetry. However, in the late 1970s, some black poets moderated their language and tone as they continued to explore themes that stirred racial consciousness. Other poets, stepping outside of the Black Arts philosophy, confronted such issues as sexism, global politics, and environmentalism.

Contemporary Currents

African American poetry of the late 1970s to the 1990s has explored issues of gender, age, and class, in addition to racial themes. The extension of poetic content has been directly related to the increased number of black women poets during this time. As Audre Lorde has observed (see her essay in Part Five, p. 755), poetry is the most "economical" of the literary genres, requiring the least preparation, materials, and space; consequently, women regardless of class and background have found poetry the most accessible literary form (16). In the last two decades, African American women have published poems illuminating a broad array of purposes through vivid, diverse diction. Maya Angelou, Lucille Clifton, Jayne Cortez, Toi Derricotte,

Thulani Davis, Colleen J. McElroy, Cheryl Clarke, Wanda Coleman, and Rita Dove have produced an impressive body of poetry that proclaims commonalities of experiences as it highlights individual talents. The recognition of the black woman poet was particularly eminent at the 1993 Presidential Inauguration ceremonies, during which Maya Angelou read aloud to a national audience a poem she wrote for the occasion, "On the Pulse of Morning."

Wanda Coleman and Rita Dove, two of the most prolific African American poets since the 1980s, are represented in Part Two. Coleman's public readings and radio broadcasts have given her a wide popularity, especially on the West Coast. "Dear Mama" expresses a pronounced ethnicity, as a daughter recognizes her spiritual connection to her mother and grandmother, a connection that carries across society's racial stereotypes and gender barriers. "In This Waking" and "Shopping Bag Lady" treat the heavy burden that economics force upon the female–male relationship and on womanhood. Taking a different thematic direction, Dove's "Particulars" and "Your Death" present personas devoid of ethnic specificity who ponder moments of personal awareness; her "After Reading *Mickey in the Night Kitchen* for the Third Time before Bed" merges innocence and experience as a mother and daughter discuss genitalia and the stigmas attached to female sexuality.

Contemporary currents in poetry continue to push the possibilities of the genre. As the creative pendulum swings between black poetry and mainstream verse, African American poets affirm the value of composing both kinds of poems. Some black poets, as well as some playwrights and fiction writers, have balanced the dual "souls," the one black and the other white, so aptly described by W. E. B. DuBois at the turn of the century. Virtuosos in literary bilingualism, these contemporary black poets tell us that both souls are vital to and compatible within African American poetry.

In This Part

Part Two opens with a Focused Study of the poet Gwendolyn Brooks, whose extensive creativity and meticulous craftsmanship mark a convergence of artistic skills, political consciousness, and cultural awareness. The five poems by Brooks are followed by George Kent's critical essay, "Gwendolyn Brooks' Poetry Realism: A Developmental Survey." The poetry selections in Part Two, arranged chronologically by birth year, demonstrate the development and variety of African American verse across time and gender lines.

Works Cited

Harper, Michael S., and Athony Walton, eds. *Every Shut Eye Ain't Asleep: An Anthology of Poetry by African Americans since 1945*. Boston: Little, Brown, 1994.

Hayden, Robert. *Kaleidoscope: Poems by American Negro Poets*. New York: Harcourt, 1967.

Henderson, Stephen. "The Question of Form and Judgment in Contemporary Black American Poetry, 1962–1977." *The New Cavalcade*. Eds. Arthur P. Davis, J. Saunders Redding, and Joyce Ann Joyce. Vol. 2. Washington, DC: Howard UP, 1992. 177–97.

Hernton, Calvin. *The Sexual Mountain and Black Women Writers*. New York: Anchor, 1987.

Lorde, Audre. *Sister, Outsider*. Trumansburg, NY: Crossing, 1984. 114–23.

Shields, John C. "Phillis Wheatley." *African American Writers*. Ed. Valerie Smith. New York: Collier, 1993. 354–72.

Suggested Readings

Several texts contain selections of interest: Countee Cullen's *Caroling Dusk: An Anthology of Verse by Negro Poets* (1927); James Weldon Johnson's *The Book of American Negro Poetry* (1931); Robert T. Kerlin's *Negro Poets and Their Poems* (1935); Langston Hughes and Arna Bontemps's *The Poetry of the Negro* (1949); Clarence Major's *The New Black Poetry* (1969); William H. Robinson's *Early Black American Poets* (1969); Beatrice M. Murphy's *Today's Negro Voices: An Anthology by Young Negro Poets* (1970); Dudley Randall's *The Black Poets* (1971); Gwendolyn Brooks's *Jump Bad: A New Chicago Anthology* (1971); Bernard W. Bell's *Modern and Contemporary Afro-American Poetry* (1972); Ethelbert E. Miller's *Women Surviving Massacres and Men: Nine Women Poets, An Anthology* (1977); and Michael S. Harper and Anthony Walton's *Every Shut Eye Ain't Asleep: An Anthology of Poetry by African Americans since 1945* (1994).

Numerous works offer critical and historical perspectives on black poetry and poets: *The Negro Genius* (1937) by Benjamin Brawley; *The Black American Writer, Volume II: Poetry and Drama,* (1969) edited by C. W. E. Bigsby; *Understanding the New Black Poetry: Black Speech and Black Music as Poetic References* (1972) edited by Stephen Henderson; *The Folk Roots of Contemporary Afro-American Poetry* (1974) by Bernard W. Bell; *From a Dark Tower* (1974) by Arthur P. Davis; *Drumvoices: The Mission of Afro-American Poetry: A Critical History* (1976) by Eugene B. Redmond; *A Dark and Sudden Beauty: Two Essays in Black American Poetry by George Kent and Stephen Henderson* (1977) edited by Houston A. Baker, Jr.; *Black American Poets between Worlds, 1940–1960* (1986) edited by R. Baxter Miller; *Black Sister: Poetry by Black American Women, 1746–1980* (1981) by Erlene Stetson; and *A History of Afro-American Literature, Volume I: The Long Beginning, 1746–1895* (1989) by Blyden Jackson.

A FOCUSED STUDY: GWENDOLYN BROOKS (1917-)

As one critic aptly notes about the approach Gwendolyn Brooks takes to poetry, "she believes in the power of the ordinary to be both significant and beautiful, her motivation is not to mythologize or to romanticize her characters. She simply writes about black people as people, not as curios." Most critics recognize Brooks's commitment to an honest depiction of black life and praise the outstanding artistry she has demonstrated in her poetry for over fifty years.

Born in Topeka, Kansas, and raised in Chicago, Brooks began writing creatively at the early age of seven and published her first poems only three years later. She graduated from Wilson Junior College in 1936, and later taught creative writing at Chicago's Columbia College and the University of Wisconsin. In addition, she has lectured at the City College of New York and Northeastern Illinois University.

From the impressive achievements of Brooks's youth sprang a remarkable writing career. Her first volume of poetry, *A Street in Bronzeville* (1945), explores the commonplace lives of black city-dwellers. It won Brooks the Merit Award from *Mademoiselle* magazine, an American Academy of Arts and Letters award, and a two-year Guggenheim Fellowship. Her second volume, *Annie Allen* (1949), pursues similar themes but is written from the point of view of a black woman surviving the urban setting. It was awarded the Pulitzer Prize for Poetry in 1950, making Brooks the first black poet to receive that prestigious award. Brooks's other works include *Bronzeville: Boys and Girls* (1956) written for young readers, *The Bean Eaters* (1960), and *Selected Poems* (1963). In 1968, Brooks was honored as Illinois's Poet Laureate, succeeding Carl Sandburg.

Labeled an intellectual poet and a protest writer by various critics, Brooks rejects both designations. Instead, she views her work as the result of two distinctive periods in her creative life—pre-1967 and post-1967, or before and after her embrace of a new black consciousness. In her autobiography, *Report from Part One* (1972), Brooks reflects on that consciousness: "Until 1967 my own blackness did not confront me with a shrill spelling of itself. I knew that I was what most people were calling 'a Negro'; I called myself that, although always the word fell awkwardly on a poet's ear. . . . I had always felt that to be black was good. . . . " In her post-1967 period, Brooks published *In the Mecca* (1968), which one critic describes as "a long poem which uses the futile search for a murdered ghetto child as a vehicle for a compassionate portrayal of the people who live in a Chicago slum, and for a commentary to their lives" (Evans 483). Following the publication of *Riot* in 1969, Brooks went on to write several other books, including two children's books, *Aloneness* (1971) and *The Tiger Who Wore White Gloves* (1974); *Family Pictures* (1970); *Beckonings* (1975); and *A Capsule Course in Black Poetry Writing* (1975), a book of nonfiction prose coauthored with Keorapetse Kgositsile, Haki R. Madhubuti, and Dudley Randall.

A fountain of creativity, Brooks continued to pour forth works in her sixties and seventies. Her most recent books include *Primer for Blacks* (1980), *To Disembark* (1981), *The Near-Johannesburg Boy and Other Poems* (1987), *Blacks* (1987), and *Winnie* (1988). She also enjoyed the distinction of serving as consultant in poetry for the Library of Congress in 1985–86.

In addition to her only novel, *Maud Martha* (1953), Brooks has edited two important poetry anthologies—*A Broadside Treasury* and *Jump Bad,* both published in 1971.

The five selections reprinted here represent the thematic and stylistic range of Brooks's poetry from 1945 to 1975. As character studies, the poems "The Mother," "The Bean Eaters," "The Children of the Poor," and "The Boy Died in My Alley" pursue various themes with intricate, but subtle, rhyming schemes. While "The Children of the Poor" suggests a more traditional approach to rhythms and language, "The Mother," and "The Bean Eaters" begin in a conventional way but eventually break into the irregular rhythms and colloquial diction associated with free verse. "A Bronzeville Mother Loiters in Mississippi" maintains the free verse form as it depicts the attitudes that shaped racial stereotypes and led to the killing of blacks.

Works Cited

Evans, Mari, ed. *Afro-American Women Writers (1950–1980)*. Garden City, NY: Anchor/ Doubleday, 1984.

McLendon, Jacquelyn Y. "Gwen Brooks." *African American Writers.* Ed. Valerie Smith. New York: Collier, 1993. 29–40.

The Mother

Abortions will not let you forget.
You remember the children you got that you did not get,
The damp small pulps with a little or with no hair,
The singers and workers that never handled the air.
You will never neglect or beat
Them, or silence or buy with a sweet.
You will never wind up the sucking-thumb
Or scuttle off ghosts that come.
You will never leave them, controlling your luscious sigh,
Return for a snack of them, with gobbling mother-eye.

I have heard in the voices of the wind the voices of my dim killed children.
I have contracted. I have eased
My dim dears at the breasts they could never suck.
I have said, Sweets, if I sinned, if I seized
Your luck
And your lives from your unfinished reach,
If I stole your births and your names,
Your straight baby tears and your games,

Your stilted or lovely loves, your tumults, your marriages, aches, and your
deaths,
If I poisoned the beginnings of your breaths,
Believe that even in my deliberateness I was not deliberate.
Though why should I whine,
Whine that the crime was other than mine?—
Since anyhow you are dead.
Or rather, or instead,
You were never made.

But that too, I am afraid,
Is faulty: oh, what shall I say, how is the truth to be said?
You were born, you had body, you died.
It is just that you never giggled or planned or cried.

Believe me, I loved you all.
Believe me, I knew you, though faintly, and I loved, I loved you
All.

The Children of the Poor

1

People who have no children can be hard:
Attain a mail of ice and insolence:
Need not pause in the fire, and in no sense
Hesitate in the hurricane to guard.
And when wide world is bitten and bewarred
They perish purely, waving their spirits hence
Without a trace of grace or of offense
To laugh or fail, diffident, wonder-starred.
While through a throttling dark we others hear
The little lifting helplessness, the queer
Whimper-whine; whose unridiculous
Lost softness softly makes a trap for us.
And makes a curse. And makes a sugar of
The malocclusions, the inconditions of love.

2

What shall I give my children? who are poor,
Who are adjudged the leastwise of the land,
Who are my sweetest lepers, who demand
No velvet and no velvety velour;
But who have begged me for a brisk contour,
Crying that they are quasi, contraband
Because unfinished, graven by a hand
Less than angelic, admirable or sure.
My hand is stuffed with mode, design, device.
But I lack access to my proper stone.

And plentitude of plan shall not suffice
Nor grief nor love shall be enough alone
To ratify my little halves who bear
Across an autumn freezing everywhere.

3

And shall I prime my children, pray, to pray?
Mites, come invade most frugal vestibules
Spectered with crusts of penitents' renewals
And all hysterics arrogant for a day.
Instruct yourselves here is no devil to pay.
Children, confine your lights in jellied rules;
Resemble graves; be metaphysical mules;
Learn Lord will not distort nor leave the fray.
Behind the scurryings of your neat motif
I shall wait, if you wish: revise the psalm
If that should frighten you: sew up belief
If that should tear: turn, singularly calm
At forehead and at fingers rather wise,
Holding the bandage ready for your eyes.

4

First fight. Then fiddle. Ply the slipping string
With feathery sorcery; muzzle the note
With hurting love; the music that they wrote
Bewitch, bewilder. Qualify to sing
Threadwise. Devise no salt, no hempen thing
For the dear instrument to bear. Devote
The bow to silks and honey. Be remote
A while from malice and from murdering.
But first to arms, to armor. Carry hate
In front of you and harmony behind.
Be deaf to music and to beauty blind.
Win war. Rise bloody, maybe not too late
For having first to civilize a space
Wherein to play your violin with grace.

5

When my dears die, the festival-colored brightness
That is their motion and mild repartee
Enchanted, a macabre mockery
Charming the rainbow radiance into tightness
And into a remarkable politeness
That is not kind and does not want to be,
May not they in the crisp encounter see
Something to recognize and read as rightness?
I say they may, so granitely discreet,

The little crooked questionings inbound,
Concede themselves on most familiar ground,
Cold an old predicament of the breath:
Adroit, the shapely prefaces complete,
Accept the university of death.

The Bean Eaters

They eat beans mostly, this old yellow pair.
Dinner is a casual affair.
Plain chipware on a plain and creaking wood,
Tin flatware.

Two who are Mostly Good.
Two who have lived their day,
But keep on putting on their clothes
And putting things away.

And remembering . . .
Remembering, with twinklings and twinges,
As they lean over the beans in their rented back room that
 is full of beads and receipts and dolls and cloths,
 tobacco crumbs, vases and fringes.

A Bronzeville Mother Loiters in Mississippi. Meanwhile, A Mississippi Mother Burns Bacon.

From the first it had been like a
Ballad. It had the beat inevitable. It had the blood.
A wildness cut up, and tied in little bunches,
Like the four-line stanzas of the ballads she had never quite
Understood—the ballads they had set her to, in school.

Herself: the milk-white maid, the "maid mild"
Of the ballad. Pursued
By the Dark Villain. Rescued by the Fine Prince.
The Happiness-Ever-After.
That was worth anything.
It was good to be a "maid mild."
That made the breath go fast.

Her bacon burned. She
Hastened to hide it in the step-on can, and
Drew more strips from the meat case. The eggs and sour-milk biscuits
Did well. She set out a jar
Of her new quince preserve.

. . . But there was a something about the matter of the Dark Villain.
He should have been older, perhaps.
The hacking down of a villain was more fun to think about
When his menace possessed undisputed breadth, undisputed height,
And a harsh kind of vice.
And best of all, when his history was cluttered
With the bones of many eaten knights and princesses.

The fun was disturbed, then all but nullified
When the Dark Villain was a blackish child
Of fourteen, with eyes still too young to be dirty,
And a mouth too young to have lost every reminder
Of its infant softness.

That boy must have been surprised! For
These were grown-ups. Grown-ups were supposed to be wise.
And the Fine Prince—and that other—so tall, so broad, so
Grown! Perhaps the boy had never guessed
That the trouble with grown-ups was that under the magnificent shell of adulthood, just under,
Waited for the baby full of tantrums.
It occurred to her that there may have been something
Ridiculous in the picture of the Fine Prince
Rushing (rich with the breadth and height and
Mature solidness whose lack, in the Dark Villain, was impressing her,
Confronting her more and more as this first day after the trial
And acquittal wore on) rushing
With his heavy companion to hack down (unhorsed)
That little foe.
So much had happened, she could not remember now what that foe had done
Against her, or if anything had been done.
The one thing in the world that she did know and knew
With terrifying clarity was that her composition
Had disintegrated. That, although the pattern prevailed,
The breaks were everywhere. That she could think
Of no thread capable of the necessary
Sew-work.

She made the babies sit in their places at the table.
Then, before calling Him, she hurried
To the mirror with her comb and lipstick. It was necessary
To be more beautiful than ever.
The beautiful wife.
For sometimes she fancied he looked at her as though
Measuring her. As if he considered, Had she been worth it?
Had *she* been worth the blood, the cramped cries, the little stuttering bravado,
The gradual dulling of those Negro eyes,
The sudden, overwhelming *little-boyness* in that barn?

Whatever she might feel or half-feel, the lipstick necessity was something apart. He must never conclude
That she had not been worth It.

He sat down, the Fine Prince, and
Began buttering a biscuit. He looked at his hands.
He twisted in his chair, he scratched his nose.
He glanced again, almost secretly, at his hands.
More papers were in from the North, he mumbled. More meddling headlines.
With their pepper-words, "bestiality," and "barbarism," and
"Shocking."
The half-sneers he had mastered for the trial worked across
His sweet and pretty face.

What he'd like to do, he explained, was kill them all.
The time lost. The unwanted fame.
Still, it had been fun to show those intruders
A thing or two. To show that snappy-eyed mother,
That sassy, Northern, brown-black—

Nothing could stop Mississippi.
He knew that. Big Fella
Knew that.
And, what was so good, Mississippi knew that.
Nothing and nothing could stop Mississippi.
They could send in their petitions, and scar
Their newspapers with bleeding headlines. Their governors
Could appeal to Washington . . .

"What I want," the older baby said, "is 'lasses on my jam."
Whereupon the younger baby
Picked up the molasses pitcher and threw
The molasses in his brother's face. Instantly
The Fine Prince leaned across the table and slapped
The small and smiling criminal.

She did not speak. When the Hand
Came down and away, and she could look at her child,
At her baby-child,
She could think only of blood.
Surely her baby's cheek
Had disappeared, and in its place, surely,
Hung a heaviness, a lengthening red, a red that had no end.
She shook her head. It was not true, of course.
It was not true at all. The
Child's face was as always, the
Color of the paste in her paste-jar.

She left the table, to the tune of the children's lamentations, which were shriller

Than ever. She
Looked out of a window. She said not a word. *That*
Was one of the new Somethings—
The fear,
Tying her as with iron.

Suddenly she felt his hands upon her. He had followed her
To the window. The children were whimpering now.
Such bits of tots. And she, their mother,
Could not protect them. She looked at her shoulders, still
Gripped in the claim of his hands. She tried, but could not resist the idea
That a red ooze was seeping, spreading darkly, thickly, slowly,
Over her white shoulders, her own shoulders,
And over all of Earth and Mars.

He whispered something to her, did the Fine Prince, something
About love, something about love and night and intention.
She heard no hoof-beat of the horse and saw no flash of the shining steel.

He pulled her face around to meet
His, and there it was, close close,
For the first time in all those days and nights.
His mouth, wet and red,
So very, very, very red,
Closed over hers.

Then a sickness heaved within her. The courtroom Coca-Cola,
The courtroom beer and hate and sweat and drone,
Pushed like a wall against her. She wanted to bear it.
But his mouth would not go away and neither would the
Decapitated exclamation points in that Other Woman's eyes.

She did not scream.
She stood there.
But a hatred for him burst into glorious flower,
And its perfume enclasped them—big,
Bigger than all magnolias.

The last bleak news of the ballad.
The rest of the rugged music.
The last quatrain.

The Boy Died in My Alley

to Running Boy

The Boy died in my alley
without my Having Known.
Policeman said, next morning,
"Apparently died Alone."

"You heard a shot?" Policeman said.
Shots I hear and Shots I hear.
I never see the Dead.

The Shot that killed him yes I heard
as I heard the Thousand shots before;
careening tinnily down the nights
across my years and arteries.

Policeman pounded on my door.
"Who is it?" "POLICE!" Policeman yelled.
"A Boy was dying in your alley.
A Boy is dead, and in your alley.
And have you known this Boy before?"

I have known this Boy before.
I have known this Boy before, who
ornaments my alley.
I never saw his face at all.
I never saw his futurefall.
But I have known this Boy.

I have always heard him deal with death.
I have always heard the shout, the volley.
I have closed my heart-ears late and early.
And I have killed him ever.

I joined the Wild and killed him
with knowledgeable unknowing.
I saw where he was going.
I saw him Crossed. And seeing,
I did not take him down.

He cried not only "Father!"
but "Mother!
Sister!
Brother."
The cry climbed up the alley.
It went up to the wind.
It hung upon the heaven
for a long
stretch-strain of Moment.

The red floor of my alley
is a special speech to me.

A Critical Perspective: **George Kent** (1920–82)

Born in Columbus, Georgia, George Kent earned his B.A. from Savannah State College and his M.A. and Ph.D. from Boston University. Throughout the 1950s, he served as the chairperson of the Department of Languages and Literature at Delaware State College, later becoming chair of the English Department at that institution. In the mid-1960s, he relocated to New England, working as a professor and chairperson in the English Department at Quinnipiac College in Connecticut. In 1970, he became a tenured member of the English Department at the University of Chicago.

Recognized for his critical pieces on a number of black and nonblack authors, Kent has published two insightful books on African American literature: Blackness and the Adventure of Western Culture *(1972) and* A Life of Gwendolyn Brooks *(1990), issued after his death.*

The critical essay that follows was written for Black Women Writers *(1984) edited by Mari Evans. In the essay, Kent offers a detailed assessment of the work of Gwendolyn Brooks from 1945 to 1981.*

Gwendolyn Brooks' Poetic Realism: A Developmental Survey

Gwendolyn Brooks' style of poetic realism has undergone developments that conform its use to her changes in both general and racial outlook, and to the evolving state of her consciousness. Regarding her general outlook, Arthur P. Davis entitled an early article devoted to her "Gwendolyn Brooks: A Poet of the Unheroic" and assigned the source of her view of human stature to her responses to the dilemma of modern or contemporary society.[1] Perhaps two qualifications of Davis' conclusion can be made. In an unpublished poem entitled "After a Perusal of Ancient History," Brooks emphasized the encounter with "little people" with little minds engaged in minutiae as their "same little puzzled/ Helpless hands/Pull away at the Blinds," and ascribed the situation to human history, past, present, and future. The other qualification is that her outlook apparently allowed for powerful gestures amid much muddling and saw the fact of life itself as good. Thus a higher stature than that of the simple average is achieved by those with the courage to respond fully to the deepest sense of life they feel within themselves. On the grand level is the Negro hero in the poem so entitled, although he himself is from the ranks and acting from a tough realistic point of view. On a high level are those who insist upon living fully and exploring: Sadie of "Sadie and Maud," the desperate lovers of "A Lovely Love," the Naomi of the poem by that title, and others. Then there are those clearly below the level of usual versions of the heroic, who contribute value to existence by, as Mrs. Small does in the poem by that title, putting themselves fully into carrying out their part of the world's business.[2]

Nonetheless, an outlook which tests life by the responses of the average and the unsung calls for poetic realism, though one may note stylistic modifications along the way. This general outlook is tied to the racial outlook by its system of bonding the audience together and prevails until the late 1960s. In the general area, people are bonded together in recognition of their common challenges and humanity. In the racial area, the Black and white audiences, until the late 1960s, are invited to come together through the poetry's emphasis upon a common peoplehood and through avoidance of the faults which simply compound the problems of humanity's limited status within the universe: oppressiveness, delusion, timidity, fearfulness, vanity, stupidity, divisiveness, and others. From the late 1960s forward, the greater emphasis is upon bonding within the Black audience, increasing its power and cohesiveness. Major changes are thus racial in outlook and in consciousness and they produce changes in style.

II

The consciousness producing *A Street in Bronzeville* (1945) was one making its first compassionate outreach to the broad range of humanity. On the one hand, it represented the mastered past: the author's old neighborhood and youth. On the other hand, it represented an intense getting acquainted with the present which was pressurized by the raw currents of Chicago's racial practices, and by World War II. Optimism prevailed, however, since the war situation had produced both threatening violence and some evidence that a broadened democracy would be born from it. In the poet's early work, one result is a deceptively simple surface. Syntax is most often either in close correlation with the usual subject plus verb plus object or complement pattern of a familiar prose sentence or within calling distance. Wielding this syntax is a friendly observer giving one a tour of the neighborhood or quick views of situations. Thus abrupt beginnings sound pretty much the way they do in our communications with friends with whom we share clarifying reference points. The observer, in presenting "the old-marrieds," begins: "But in the crowding darkness not a word did they say." Joining the group in "kitchenette building," the observer-narrator pitches at us a long question but one so well ordered that it is painless: "But could a dream send up through onion fumes/Its white and violet, fight with fried potatoes/And yesterday's garbage ripening in the hall,/Flutter, or sing an aria down these rooms . . . ?" At the end of three more lines we complete the question, and are then given quick relief through a series of short declarative statements whose brevity drives home the drama and the pathos of the situation.

There are poems with much simpler syntax within this group and one sonnet with a far more complex syntax. The simplest derive from closeness to conversational patterns, from reproduction of speech tones, and from the already mentioned patterning upon simple prose statements. A form such as the ballad also has conventions which allow for great simplicity of syntactical structure. The more complex structure which probably puzzles on a first reading actually derives, in the following sonnet, from exploitation of one of the more complex rhetorical but conventional structures—the periodic sentence. The war sonnet "firstly inclined to take what it is told" begins with the following movement:

> Thee sacrosanct, Thee sweet, Thee crystalline,
> With the full jewel wile of mighty light—
> With the narcotic milk of peace for men
> Who find Thy beautiful center and relate
> Thy round command, Thy grand, Thy mystic good—
> Thee like the classic quality of a star:
> A little way from warmth, a little sad,

Delicately lovely to adore—
I had been brightly ready to believe.

The rest of the poem suggests that such a response to God was mere youthful innocence. Perhaps the additional parenthetical expression and the use of religious language and abstract terms also help to complicate matters; but no other poem in the book offers syntax with an equal degree of challenge.

In terms of the relationship to conversational language and actual speech tones one will find in the style a range running from "folk" speech (the Hattie Scott poems) to that which is more self-consciously literate and affected by formal traditions ("The Sundays of Satin Legs Smith" and the sonnets, for example). Brooks is also alert to the richness provided by bringing contrasting traditions into strategic conjunctions or, by movement, into a very formal eloquence; again, examples of both may be seen in "Satin Legs Smith." And finally there is the colloquial and hip level provided by such a poem as "Patent Leather": "That cool chick down on Calumet/Has got herself a brand new cat. . . ."

For the most part imagery goes beyond the simple functions of representing an object or pictorializing, activities characteristic of the most simple poems, and manages to do so quietly. "Pretty patent leather hair" obviously has its total effect in the literal picture it creates and the comment it makes upon the judgment of the cool chick. But Brooks expanded the range and function of the realistic image in several ways: attaching to it a striking descriptive term ("crowding darkness"), combining it with a figurative gesture ("could a dream send up through onion fumes/Its white and violet") contrasting realistic and symbolic functions (crooked and straight in "Hunchback Girl . . ."), presenting expressionistic description of a condition ("Mabbie on Mabbie with hush in the heart"), and emphasizing the figurative role of a basically realistic or pictorial expression ("wear the brave stockings of night-black lace," and "temperate holiness arranged/Ably on asking faces").

Perhaps the foregoing elements may be allowed to stand for other devices making up the total struggle with language meant by the word *style.* I have tried to suggest that the central trait of most of the language devices is that they convey the impression of actual simplicity and thus offer the appearance of easygoing accessibility. It is certainly not a total accessibility, in several cases. On one level people and their life stories appear in sharply outlined plots presenting easily recognized issues from the daily round of existence, and move to definite decisive conclusions. However, recognizing certain devices or reading at the tempo required not only by the story but by imagery and language changes will, at times, take us to another level. "Southeast corner," for example, seems interested in the artistry, as well as the vanity, of the deceased madam of the school of beauty, an interpretation suggested by the vivid image of shot silk shining over her tan "impassivity." "Satin Legs" has meanings which reveal themselves in the imagery, language shifts, and mixture of narrative attitudes, which go beyond the basic story, and so on.

But there is no question that in *A Street in Bronzeville* (and in individual poems over the body of her work) there is a general simplicity which seems easily to contain specific complexities. The fact makes Brooks a poet speaking still, not merely to critics and other poets, but to people.

It is probable that nearly all the stylistic developments of Brooks' subsequent works are embryonically present in *A Street in Bronzeville,* since, with its publication, she was emerging from a very long and earnest apprenticeship. Some clear foreshadowing of more complex stylistic developments is in the sonnets, and in "The Sundays of Satin Legs Smith." Whereas, for example, the full capacity of the narrator of the Hattie Scott poems may be shaded in the background, the sophistication and perception of the narrator of the sonnets and the life of Smith are clearly those of the narrator of *Annie Allen*. Yet it is understandable that people found the stylistic developments in this second work startling and complex.

If the opening poem of *A Street* makes things seem easy by providing a friendly narrator using language in seemingly customary ways, the opening poem of *Annie Allen,* "the birth in a narrow room," makes the reader feel that the narrator's assumption is that he is to the poetic manner born. The poem demands the reader's absolute commitment, an acceptance of the role of a tougher elliptical syntax, and a comprehension of imagery which functions both realistically and mythically. Actually, the syntax is difficult largely because for several lines the infant remains the *unnamed* subject of the poem. The sources for imagery are the fairy and timeless world and the "real" objects of the "real" world, both of which function to sustain temporarily complete freedom for the young child in an Edenic world. Thus the first poem warns the reader to expect to participate in complex struggles with language.

The style of *Annie Allen* emerges not only from the fact that the poet of the highly promising first book naturally expects to present greater mastery of the craft in the second but also from a changed focus in consciousness. In her first book Brooks' emphasis had been upon community consciousness. In her second her emphasis is upon self-consciousness—an attempt to give artistic structure to tensions arising from the artist's experience in moving from the Edenic environment of her parents' home into the fallen world of Chicago tenement life in the roles of young wife, mother, and artist. Her efforts, however, were not an attempt to be confessional but an attempt to take advantage of the poetic form to move experiences immediately into symbols broader than the person serving as subject. A thoroughgoing search of the territory and the aspiration for still greater mastery of craft called for a struggle with language, a fact which would require the reader to make also a creative struggle.

One device is to play conventional and unconventional structures against each other, and, sometimes, to work apparently conventional structures for very special effects. In "the parents: people like our marriage, Maxie and Andrew," the reader abruptly confronts the synecdochial opening lines: "Clogged and soft and sloppy eyes/Have lost the light that bites or terrifies." Afterward the poem gradually settles into the more conventional approach, though it demands that the reader absorb its realities from simple symbols instead of editorial statements. In such poems the reader's creative participation is sustained by other devices: unusual conjunctions of words, shifts in pace and rhythm, reproductions of speech tones at the point of the colloquial and at varying distances from it, figurative language, challenging twists in the diction, and others.

"Downtown vaudeville," a portrait of a white audience subjecting a Black stage clown to haughty ridicule, begins with conventional syntax, although the fact may be obscured by the startling locution "the hush that coughed." The more unconventional syntax makes itself strongly felt in the third and fourth stanzas.

What was not pleasant was the hush that coughed
When the Negro clown came on the stage and doffed
His broken hat. The hush, first. Then the soft

Concatenation of delight and lift,
The sugared hoot and hauteur. Then, the rift
Where is magnificent, heirloom, and deft

Leer at a Negro to the right, or left—
So joined to personal bleach, and so bereft:

Finding if that is locked, is bowed, or proud.
And what that is at all, spotting the crowd.

The strategy is to present the audience solely by its responses and its vain assumptions. Diction, the indirect reference system, shifts in the conventional grammatical roles of words, combine with the syntax to demand that the reader absorb the exact quality of the scene through absolute attention. Unusual conjunctions are a hallmark: decked dismissal, sugared hoot and hauteur, for example. But individual words bear up to heavy burdens also: "rift," in which the audience is beginning to assume a set of attitudes with which to be scornful to the Blacks within it; "magnificent," in which the audience is displaying its illusion of its own richness; "heirloom," in which the audience is adding other qualities to itself from tradition; "personal bleach," through which the suggestion seems to be that the audience is being, well, very white. "Locked," "bowed," "proud," are terms expressing the audience's concern that the Blacks be properly humiliated by the superiority of the whites and by their own supposed nothingness; unable to gain humanity from the white presence to which it is "joined." There can be little doubt that such terms as "magnificent" and "heirloom" are overburdened. But the achievement is a sharp break with earlier gestures from Black protest tradition. Gone is the protest rhetoric focused upon the figure of the suffering victim; the attack consists largely of a merciless description of the audience's behavior. Claude McKay, Black poet of 1920s fame, had tried to eliminate the subordinate stance and pleading tone of protest by creating the persona of a romantic rebel speaking in broad symbols and calling the reader to witness his endurance and his capacity to rise above his tormentors by using their torment to make of himself a superior person. But his little-modified acceptance of their standards and his Byronic rebel seemed to pay tribute to Caesar still. Though hampered by the amount of weight words were required to bear, Brooks' poem got beyond such limitations by holding before the audience a booby-trapped picture of itself.

In *Annie Allen* the imagery system pushes still further away from the simple representational into the symbolic, although the range of *A Street* is included within its broadening circle. In "Life for My Child Is Simple, and Is Good," she can take direct advantage of realism with such an expression as "And the water comes slooshing sloppily out across the floor." But in "Beverly Hills, Chicago," a poem rendering the complex response of the unaffluent to the graces money affords the rich, leaves become "The dry brown coughing beneath their feet" and *refuse* becomes "a neat brilliancy." The sonnet sequence "the children of the poor" succeeds by dint of numerous graces, but not least among them is the poet's skill in pushing imagery quickly into metaphoric operations and forcing abstract terms to describe concrete conditions. The first sonnet speaks of people without children attaining "a mail of ice and insolence" and of those with children struggling "through a throttling dark" and forced to make "a sugar of/The malocclusions, the inconditions of love."

A further range in the use of imagery stems from her exploration of romantic, expressionistic, and surreal categories, though the scale for exploring human nature and action remains realistic. The romantic is particularly noticeable in the ballad, but in "do not be afraid of no," a poem in which the self is sternly lectured regarding the path to integrity, the surreal creates Poelike patterns. The old pliable self is "like a street/That beats into a dead end and dies there," and like

> . . . a candle fixed
> Against dismay and countershine of mixed
> Wild moon and sun. And like
> A flying furniture, or bird with lattice wing; or gaunt thing,
>   a-stammer down a nightmare neon peopled with condor,
>   hawk and shrike.

However, the imagery seems to overdramatize the revulsion against the old self.

The long poem on young womanhood entitled "The Anniad" has the task of taking Annie into maturity by carrying her from the epic dreams of maidenhood into the prosaic and disillusioning realities provided by the married life. More concretely, having inherited the romance and love lore of Euro-Americans and disabilities imposed upon Black identity, she is, at once, the would-be heroine of song and story and the Black woman whom "the higher gods" forgot and the lower ones berate. The combination of the realistic and romantic portrays the flesh and blood person and the dreamer.

> Think of ripe and romp-about
> All her harvest buttoned in,
> All her ornaments untried;
> Waiting for the paladin
> Prosperous and ocean-eyed
> Who shall rub her secrets out
> And behold the hinted bride.

In contrast, awareness of how Black identity is challenged in such a universe brings the imagery back to the realism regarding the inadequate tickets she holds for admission: "unembroidered brown" imprinted with "bastard roses" and "black and boisterous hair."

To express the climax of accumulated problems, storms, and confusions of Annie's young life, Brooks turns completely to expressionistic imagery:

> In the indignant dark there ride
> Roughnesses and spiny things
> On infallible hundred heels.
> And a bodiless bee stings.

Cyclone concentration reels.
Harried sods dilate, divide,
Suck her sorrowfully inside.

The last stanzas return to the language of the realistic scale, although the language itself is not simply mimetic or pictorial. Annie is described as salvaging something of the more usual day-to-day fruits from her experiences: "Stroking swallows from the sweat./Fingering faint violet./Hugging gold and Sunday sun./ Kissing in her kitchenette/The minuets of memory."

In her 1969 interview with George Stavros (*Report from Part One*), the poet remembered warmly and affectionately the process of creating "The Anniad," a "labored" poem, "a poem that's very interested in the mysteries and magic of technique." Closely textured was "every stanza in that poem; every one was worked on and revised, tenderly cared for. More so than anything else I've written, and it is not a wild success; some of it just doesn't come off. But it was enjoyable."

On the level of telling the Annie Allen story, Brooks was thus able to experiment extensively with stylistic devices and license herself to move beyond realistic imagery. She did so by retaining realism as the base of conception and the norm for the behavior patterns the personalities must ultimately adopt. Thus the form includes devices for humor and pathos which register, in the world of the possible, Annie's excess of idealism, dreaminess, or self-absorption: intense pictures of imbalance, rhythms suggesting frenetic behavior, and a vocabulary suggesting the occupation of worlds which must prove incompatible. In short, the kindly satiric pat appears to halt unrealism, though the unrealism if it could be transformed into "reality" might make a richer world.

Annie Allen represents Brooks' most energetic reach for simply a great command of the devices of poetic style. Having developed this command, she could now wield the devices at will and make them relate more efficiently to form and intention. With this mastery of numerous devices came also the power to achieve originality by making variations in the contexts in which they were used and in the relationships one device makes with another. Then, too, a device which in the earlier stages of the artist's career could be completely summed up in the term *conventional* or *traditional* could, at times, now be put into innovative roles. In such a poem as "Beverly Hills, Chicago," for example, the very precision of a syntax based upon the simple declarative sentence drives home the tension of the rest of the structures: "It is only natural, however, that it should occur to us/How much more fortunate they [the rich] are than we are."

In *Bronzeville Boys and Girls* (1956), a volume for juveniles, Brooks' skills effectively work together to comprise a language of poetry that describes for the child his or her experiences. Poems with bouncy rhymes are intermixed with those of more subtle and varied sound patterns. Emphasis upon the monosyllabic word at the end of end-stopped lines and other places, varying lengths of lines, repetition, and other devices sustain an interesting poetics which unpatronizingly presents the childhood world. "Ella" reveals something of the magic maintained, even down to a simple use of paradox in the first two lines: "Beauty has a coldness/That keeps you very warm./'If I run out to see the clouds, That will be no harm!' "

In *The Bean Eaters* (1960) and certain of the new poems of *Selected Poems*

(1963), developments in style, for the most part, are responses to experimentations with loosened forms and the milage one can gain from very simple statements. In *Annie Allen* Brooks had loosened up the form of the sonnet in "The Rites for Cousin Vit," with the use of elliptical syntax, the pressures of colloquial speech, and the cumulative capacity of all the poetic devices to create the impact of hyperbole. Cousin Vit was simply too vital to have died; thus Brooks interjects into the language of the sonnet the idiomatic swing and sensuality of the street: that Vit continued to do "the snake-hips with a hiss. . . . " In *The Bean Eaters* she again loosened up sonnet form in "A Lovely Love" by adapting the Petrarchan rhyme scheme to the situation of the tenement lovers, intermingling short and long complete statements with elliptical ones, and managing a nervous rhythm which imposes the illusion of being a one-to-one imitation of the behavior of the lovers. The diction of the poem is a mixture of the romantic ("hyacinth darkness"), the realistic ("Let it be stairways, and a splintery box"), and the mythically religious ("birthright of our lovely love/In swaddling clothes. Not like that Other one"). Although the elliptical structures are more numerous and informal in "Cousin Vit," the rhythm of "A Lovely Love" seems to make that poem the more complex achievement.

Another technical development is the poet's bolder movement into a free verse appropriate to the situation which she sometimes dots with rhyme. The technique [is] more noticeable and surer in its achievement in the next volume, *In the Mecca*. But the poem "A Bronzeville Mother Loiters in Mississippi. Meanwhile, A Mississippi Mother Burns Bacon." gives the technique full rein, except for the rhyming. The lines frequently move in the rhythms of easygoing conversation or in the loose patterns of stream of consciousness, as the poet portrays the movement from romantic notions to reality in the consciousness of the young white woman over whom a young Black boy (reminiscent of the slain Emmett Till) has been lynched by her husband and his friend. The dramatic situation determines the length of lines, and the statements vary in form; short declarative sentences, simple sentences, phrase units understandable from their ties to preceding sentences, and long, complex structures. Additional sources of rhythm are repetition, parallel structures, and alliteration.

One of the more interesting techniques of the poem is that of playing romantic diction against the realistic. Thus a stanza containing such terms as "milk-white maid," "Dark Villain," "Fine Prince," and "Happiness-Ever-After" precedes one containing the following lines:

> Her bacon burned. She
> Hastened to hide it in the step-on can, and
> Drew more strips from the meat case. The eggs and sour-
> milk biscuits
> Did well.

Two . . . poems in *Selected Poems,* "To Be in Love" and "Big Bessie Throws Her Son into the Street," have lines and a use of rhyme closer to the method of the poems in *In The Mecca* in their tautness. "To Be in Love," a portrait of that state of being, leans as close as possible to direct statement. "To be in love/Is to touch things with a lighter hand." The next one-line stanza: "In yourself you stretch, you are well." Rhymes then dot several areas of the poem and, near the end, combine with more complex diction to provide the emotional climax. "Big Bessie," a portrait of a mother encouraging her son to seize his independence, has similar strategies, although it is less realistic and moves toward the impressionistic.

> A day of sunny face and temper
> The winter trees
> Are musical.

The next two lines begin the encouragement. "Bright lameness from my beautiful disease,/You have your destiny to chip and eat." Again rhymes dot other lines and their appearances increase near the end in preparation for the following command given in a one-line stanza: "Go down the street."

In the Mecca is comprised of the poem "In the Mecca" and several under the heading "After Mecca." The long poem "In the Mecca" has for setting a famous Chicago apartment building, half a block long, located between State and Dearborn streets, one block north of Thirty-fourth Street. The title poem in the company of the others marks Brooks' turn from Christianity and the hope of integration to that of nationalism. Obviously the situation means that motives different from those of the preceding works will place at the foreground the necessity for new stylistic developments. The language must emphasize Blacks developing common bonds with each other instead of the traditional "people are people" bonding. For a poet who has so intensively devoted herself to language, the situation means a turn to ways of touching deeply an audience not greatly initiated into the complexity of modern poetry and yet retaining a highly disciplined use of language. The challenge would seem all the greater since to acquire such brilliant command over so wide a range of poetic devices as Brooks had done over the years was also to build a set of reflexes in consciousness which, one would think, would weight the balance toward complex rendering.

Brooks had, nonetheless, certain assets with which to adjust her style. Although she had written complexly structured poems, she had also written numerous very simple ones, and she had kept in touch with the primordial roots of poetry and certain ways through which one avoided alienating people from poetry. The largest number of "simple" poems, some of which are deceptively simple, appeared in *A Street in Bronzeville,* and that volume today is still the favorite of a large number of readers. She had made many approaches to simple and to complex forms: the ballad, couplets, quatrains, the sonnet, etc. She had worked with a range of free verse and would continue to do so. But eventually the situation would require more radical changes, since the approach to people had now to turn from its emphasis upon *revelation* to a great emphasis upon *liberation*. (This is not to suggest that revelation is abandoned.)

In the Mecca thus represents, on the one hand, the poet at the very height of her command and utilization of complex renderings. On the other, it represents change of concern and expansion of the use of free verse. Actually, the poem "In the Mecca" required complex resources and rendering. Its unifying story line is simple. Mrs. Sallie, a domestic worker, returns from work to find that she has lost her courageous battle to support and rear nine "fatherless" children. Her missing child, Pepita, who seemed, at first, astray in the slum-blasted building, turns out to have been murdered and hidden under the bed of the mentally twisted murderer. However, the total story is complex: the renderings of the Mecca universe and what is happening to the holiness of the souls of nearly thirty people, if one counts only those characterized either by extended treatment or by the single incisive line or phrase. Obviously, all the resources the poet had accumulated over the years were needed.

The older stylistic resources seem, at times, to have received further growth. Mrs. Sallie leaves the repressive environment of her employer: "Infirm booms/ and suns that have not spoken die behind this/low-brown butterball." The imagery, strategic repetitions, ritualized and moralizing lines—some of which are rhymed for special emphasis—give further revelation of Mrs. Sallie's strength, complex responses, and dogged determination. Imagery and unusual conjunctions of words make each child memorable and his or her situation haunting. Yvonne of "bald innocence and gentle fright," the "undaunted," once "pushed her thumbs into the eyes of a thief." Though given a touch of irony, her love story has something of the direct style of the poem "To Be in Love."

> It is not necessary, says Yvonne,
> to have every day him whom
> to the end thereof you will love.
> Because it is tasty to remember
> he is alive, and laughs
> in somebody else's room,
> or is slicing a cold cucumber,
> or is buttoning his cuffs,
> or is signing with his pen
> and will plan
> to touch you again.

The language usage extends from the realistic to the expressionistic, from actual speech tones to formal eloquence. It is a language which must extend itself to engage the balked struggle and melancholy defeat of Mrs. Sallie; the embattled but tough innocence of the children; the vanities, frustrations, insanity, futility, and ruthlessness of certain characters—and the pathos of others; and, finally, the desperation, philosophies, and intellectual reaches of the young hero intellectuals seeking a way out. It also is a language which unites the disinherited of the Mecca Building with the disinherited across the universe. Here Brooks moves brilliantly into the language of biblical parody.

> Norton considers Belsen and Dachau,
> regrets all old unkindness and harms,
> . . . The Lord was their shepherd,
> Yet did they want.
> Joyfully would they have lain in jungles or pastures,
> Walked beside waters. Their gaunt
> souls were not restored, their souls were banished.
> In the shadow valley
> they feared the evil, whether with or without God.
> They were comforted by no Rod,
> no Staff, but flayed by, O besieged by, shot-a-plenty.

Beyond such formal and stylized eloquence are the speeches of Aunt Dill ("Little gal got/raped and choked to death last week . . .") and Great-Great Gram the ex-slave prompted by the Mecca situation to remember her slave childhood.

> Pern and me and all,
>
> we had no beds. Some slaves had beds of hay
> or straw, with cover-cloth. We-six-uns curled
> in corners of the dirt, and closed our eyes,
> and went to sleep—or listened to the rain
> fall inside, felt the drops
> big on our noses, bummies and tum-tums . . .

The quoted passages should also suggest something of the range of the free verse. The achievement is light-years beyond that cited in *The Bean Eaters* and *Selected Poems*. Here the language takes its contours and rhythms from a variety of voices and speech functions. The fact that each person seems to force the language into a distinctive pattern should be suggestive of the level of stylistic achievement.

This wide range of achievement in free verse is further tested by the varied functions it was required to serve in the remaining poems of the book. The function of "In the Mecca" was to continue deep definition, to lay bare, and to foreshadow. Though it contains rage, its central emotion is compassion, and Mrs. Sallie is bound within a traditional mode of responding and does not undergo a change of consciousness. Except for "To a Winter Squirrel," the succeeding poems are largely about new consciousness and the raw materials of the Black community. "The Chicago Picasso" is technically outside such a conclusion judged in its own right, but it is also present to highlight the communal celebration represented by "The Wall," since it represents individualism and conventional universalism.

The two sermons on the warpland represent the high point in the poet's struggle to move to the center of the Black struggle, with the first urging the building of solid bases for unity and communion and the second urging Blacks to bear up under the pains of the struggle and to "Live!/and have your blooming in the noise of the whirlwind." Parts I, III, and IV seem the more effective, since their style better combines the abstract and the concrete and their language moves more easily between the areas of formal eloquence and the colloquial. Effective poems addressing the communal concerns of Blacks are also in the pamphlet *Riot* (1969). The title poem's directness and, above all, its satire regarding the privileged John Cabot are effective when read to a Black audience. The satiric approach was both an older device of Brooks' and a feature of the new movement. The last poem, "An Aspect of Love, Alive in the Ice and Fire," reproduces the directness and simplicity of the earlier "To Be in Love."

Gwendolyn Brooks' subsequent poetry has seen the observer of the poems evidence more easily and casually membership in the group. As part of her mission to help inspire the bonding of Blacks to each other, she wished to write poetry which could be appreciated by the person in the tavern who ordinarily did not read poetry. This ambition required some additional emphasis upon simplicity. She had already had the experience of writing prose of poetic intensity in her novel *Maud Martha* (1953) and in the short story "The Life of Lincoln West," which first appeared in the Herbert Hill anthology *Soon One Morning:*

New Writing by American Negroes, 1940–1962 (1963). Making minor revisions she was able to rearrange "The Life of Lincoln West" in verse lines, and it became the lead-off poem in *Family Pictures* (1970), whose title signified the intimate relationship between the observer-writer and the community. It is the story of a little boy who is disliked because of his pronounced African features and who becomes reconciled to his situation when he learns that he "is the real thing." In style it creates an imagery, a syntax, and a diction which do not press greatly for meanings beyond the requirements of its narrative line and development. It moves close to what the poet would shortly be calling verse journalism in referring to her piece "In Montgomery" (*Ebony,* August 1971), in which she evoked the current situation and mood of the survivors and descendants of the Montgomery Bus Boycott. The following lines illustrate the simplicity of the approach in "The Life of Lincoln West."

> Even Christmases and Easters were spoiled.
> He would be sitting at the
> family feasting table, really
> delighting in the displays of mashed potatoes
> and the rich golden
> fat-crust of the ham or the festive
> fowl, when he would look up and find
> somebody feeling indignant about him.

The imagery remains realistic on a very simple level; diction and syntax approach the reader as old friends, and the narrator is an intimate chorus.

In the long poem "In Montgomery," the style has a similar realism but also ranges, extending from direct, prosy statement to a heightening produced by some of the older but simple approaches to diction in poetry.

> I came expecting
> the strong young—
> up of head, severe,
> not drowsy, not-in-bitten,
> not outwitted by the wiles of history.

The poet also clearly evidences the fact that she is visiting Montgomery as a concerned relative, a definite part of the family. In the opening passages she continuously announces her presence.

> My work: to cite in semi-song the
> meaning of Confederacy's Cradle.
> Well, it means to be rocking gently, rocking gently!
> In Montgomery is no Race Problem.
> There is the white decision, the white and pleasant
>   vow
> that the white foot shall not release the black neck.

In phrases which serve as structuring devices in parallel form, she continues to present the evidence of her presence, kinship, and role in the historical continuum: "I came expecting," "I came expecting," "I did not come expecting." Her references to Blackness and the Bible give the same kind of participatory testimony.

Such poems as those devoted to Lincoln West and to Montgomery display many qualities of post–*In the Mecca* style, and they should be added to from other poems in *Family Pictures, Beckonings,* and *Primer for Blacks* and from new poems as they arrive. Some stylistic qualities can be listed: use of various types of repetition, alliteration, neologisms (crit, creeple, makiteer), abstract terms gaining depth of meaning from reference to the group's shared experiences, epithets ("whip-stopper," "Tree-planting Man"), variations in expressional patterns usually associated with the simple ballad, ritualistic echoing of childhood-game rhythms and rhyme, gestural words, and simple words forced to yield new meanings from dramatic context. To these one might add the creation of sharp contrasts, and become inclusive by stating that the repertoire involves all the traditional resources provided for simplicity by free verse.

But such a list does not say as much as it seems to, since many of the above devices were already used in the more complex style, and the true distinguishing point is the new combination made of many of them in the later poetry. Under the caption Young Heroes in *Family Pictures* is a poem devoted to a young African poet, "To Keorapetse Kgositsile (Willie)," which illustrates the new simplicity and some carry-over of older devices in a somewhat simpler pattern.

> He sees
> hellishness among the half-men
> He sees
> pellmelling loneliness in the
> center of grouphood
> He sees
> lenient dignity. He
> sees pretty flowers under blood.

The poem is an introduction to Kgositsile's book *My Name Is Afrika!,* and concludes simply, " 'MY NAME IS AFRIKA/Well, every fella's a Foreign Country./ This Foreign Country speaks to You.' " Certainly, the use of capitals and lower-case expressions, unusual word conjunctions ("pellmelling loneliness," "lenient dignity"), and repetition can be found in the more complex style, but here, for the most part, the usage adapts to the creative capacity of an audience not drilled in poetic conventions.

In the same work, "To Don at Salaam" retains simplicity throughout and creates a warm portrait suggestive of disciplined intensity. The first stanza creates a symbolic picture of a person who poises himself easily amid forces that are usually overwhelming, and is notable for depending almost entirely upon monosyllabic words.

> I like to see you lean back in your chair
> so far you have to fall but do not—
> your arms back, your fine hands
> in your print pockets.

The third stanza notes his affectionateness, the fourth registers his definiteness in an indefinite world, the fifth brief stanza points to his harmoniousness and capable action, and the sixth, a one-line stanza, ends simply but dramatically: "I like to see you living in the world." Part of the style is the structuring of stanzas according to function and place in the dramatic whole.

Poems dealing with persons or fraternal situations within the family of Blacks tend to be the more successful, especially those dealing with specific persons. But the sermons and lectures contain effective passages and, frequently, longer and more complex movements. In *Beckonings,* "Boys, Black" admonishes the boys to develop health, proper Blackness, and sanity, in their approach to existence, and urges heroic struggle. The dramatic opening gives a sense of the positive direction suggested by the poem, and is noteworthy for drawing images and figures made simple by having been first validated by traditional usage.

> Boys. Black. Black Boys.
> Be brave to battle for your breath and bread.
> Your heads hold clocks that strike the new time of day.
> Your hearts are
> legislating Summer Weather now.
>   Cancel winter.

The poem also gives an example of a distinctive use of repetition in the first line, and, in the first and second lines, the creative use of alliteration. As it proceeds, it accumulates an in-group set of references. Aside from such expressions as the opening one and the second address ("boys, young brothers, young brothers"), there is the stanza offering caution:

> Beware
> the easy griefs.
> It is too easy to cry "ATTICA"
> and shock thy street,
> and purse thy mouth,
> and go home to "Gunsmoke." Boys,
> black boys,
> beware the easy griefs
> that fool and fuel nothing.

The ending is one of love and faith and admonition: "Make of my Faith an engine/Make of my Faith/a Black Star. I am Beckoning." Much revised and addressed to Blacks in general, "Boys, Black" appears in a collection of poems entitled *To Disembark,* published by Third World Press in 1981.

With the publishing of *To Disembark* it is apparent that Gwendolyn Brooks' change in outlook and consciousness has crystallized in an altered and distinctive style that offers the virtues of its own personality without denying its kinship with an earlier one. Most dramatic are the speaker's position in the center of her kinship group and the warmth and urgency of her speech. As indicated, the tendency of the language is toward a new simplicity. It can be seen in poems which, on the surface, remain very close to a traditional style of poetic realism but always evidence the fact that they proceed from an artist who is choosing from a wide range of resources. It can be seen in poems which will still, in particular passages, place language under great strain. Such patterns create also a recognizably new voice in the poetry. Thus the always-journeying poet sets the example of doing what she asks of others in the new poem *To the Diaspora.*

> Here is some sun. Some.
> Now off into the places rough to reach.
> Though dry, though drowsy, all unwillingly a-wobble,
> into the dissonant and dangerous crescendo.
> Your work, that was done, to be done to be done to be done.

NOTES

1. Arthur P. Davis, "Gwendolyn Brooks: A Poet of the Unheroic," *CLA Journal,* 7 (December 1963), 114–25.
2. Except where differently noted, citations are from the volume *The World of Gwendolyn Brooks* (New York: Harper & Row, 1971). The volume includes *A Street in Bronzeville* (1945), *Annie Allen* (1949), *Maud Martha* (1953), *The Bean Eaters* (1960), and *In the Mecca* (1968).

POETRY SELECTIONS

Phillis Wheatley (1753–84)

A*s black critic Benjamin Brawley has noted about Phillis Wheatley: "She not only had an unusual career and published the first book brought out by an American Negro, but for decades before other poets were heard of she was a shining example of Negro genius. . . . She thus has historical importance far beyond what the intrinsic merit of her verses might warrant."*

Certainly, Wheatley's historical value should not be underestimated, but neither should her creativity be overlooked. That her poetry avoided racial conflicts must be noted, but not at the expense of dismissing her success as a skillful poet who excelled in the Neo-Classical style of the era.

Born in Senegal in Africa, she was approximately eight years old when she was brought in a slave ship to Boston and purchased by John Wheatley, a tailor, as a personal attendant to his wife. The young Phillis Wheatley was raised in an environment where she was taught to read the Bible and Latin classics. Conditioned to be pious and racially accommodating, she began to compose elegies upon the deaths of friends of the Wheatley family. The precocious young woman's relationship with her white owners was described as an amiable one. When she became ill, the Wheatley family sent her to England in 1773, awarding the slave her freedom before she left.

It was in England that Wheatley won distinction for her writing. Although some whites doubted her abilities, her Boston acquaintances defended her authorship and talents. In London, she published her one volume of poetry, a historic work entitled Poems on Various Subjects, Religious and Moral *(1773). She was only twenty years old at the time.*

Sadly, Phillis Wheatley's brief life spiraled downward when she returned to

America in 1774. Three of the four members of the Wheatley family died between 1774 and 1778, leaving a void in the primary family relationships the poet had known since being brought to America. In 1778, she married John Peters, a free black man who held numerous jobs but had few financial resources. Wheatley lived in poverty, losing three children and eventually working as a domestic in a Boston boardinghouse. Finally succumbing to her chronically frail health, she died in 1784.

The two poems included here display the characteristic lofty language and strict form of Wheatley's poetry. "On the Death of a Young Gentleman" contains the praise typically found in her elegies, and "To S. M., A Young African Painter, on Seeing His Works," salutes the artistic talents of Scipio Moorhead, the black servant of a white minister.

On the Death of a Young Gentleman

Who taught thee conflict with the pow'rs of night,
To vanquish Satan in the fields of fight?
Who strung thy feeble arms with might unknown,
How great thy conquest, and how bright thy crown!
War with each princedom, throne, and pow'r is o'er,
The scene is ended to return no more.
O could my muse thy seat on high behold,
How deckt with laurel, how enrich'd with gold!
O could she hear what praise thine harp employs,
How sweet thine anthems, how divine thy joys!
What heav'nly grandeur should exalt her strain!
What holy raptures in her numbers reign!
To sooth the troubles of the mind to peace,
To still the tumult of life's tossing seas,
To ease the anguish of the parents heart,
What shall my sympathizing verse impart?
Where is the balm to heal so deep a wound?
Where shall a sov'reign remedy be found?
Look, gracious Spirit, from thine heav'nly bow'r,
And thy full joys into their bosoms pour;
The raging tempest of their grief control,
And spread the dawn of glory through the soul,
To eye the path the saint departed trod,
And trace him to the bosom of his God.

To S. M., A Young African Painter, on Seeing His Works

To show the lab'ring bosom's deep intent,
And thought in living characters to paint,
When first thy pencil did those beauties give,
And breathing figures learnt from thee to live,
How did those prospects give my soul delight,

A new creation rushing on my sight?
Still, wond'rous youth! each noble path pursue,
On deathless glories fix thine ardent view:
Still may the painter's and the poet's fire
To aid thy pencil, and thy verse conspire!
And may the charms of each seraphic theme
Conduct thy footsteps to immortal fame!
High to the blissful wonders of the skies
Elate thy soul, and raise thy wishful eyes.
Thrice happy, when exalted to survey
That splendid city, crown'd with endless day,
Whose twice six gates on radiant hinges ring:
Celestial *Salem* blooms in endless spring.
   Calm and serene thy moments glide along,
And may the muse inspire each future song!
Still, with the sweets of contemplation bless'd,
May peace with balmy wings your soul invest!
But when these shades of time are chas'd away,
And darkness ends in everlasting day,
On what seraphic pinions shall we move,
And view the landscapes in the realms above?
There shall thy tongue in heav'nly murmurs flow,
And there my muse with heav'nly transport glow:
No more to tell of *Damon's* tender sighs,
Or rising radiance of *Aurora's* eyes,
For nobler themes demand a nobler strain,
And purer language on th' ethereal plain.
Cease, gentle muse! the solemn gloom of night
Now seals the fair creation from my sight.

Frances E. W. Harper (1825–1911)

An abolitionist, feminist, lecturer, and author, Frances Ellen Watkins Harper possessed a host of talents that served her lifelong dedication to activism. Born free in Maryland, she was educated at a school organized by her uncle for free blacks. Education was essential to her development, and it led her to become an instructor at Union Seminary, an African Methodist-Episcopal school in Columbus, Ohio.

Harper's involvement in abolitionism began in 1852, when she became affiliated with the Anti-Slavery Society of Maine. In 1860, she married Fenton Harper, and the couple moved back to Columbus, Ohio, to maintain a farm. However, after the deaths of her only child and her husband, Harper rejoined the abolitionist movement. Her work for the cause of freedom continued until 1864; after the Civil War, her activism targeted the advancement of blacks and issues related to women's rights, including her efforts with the Women's Christian Temperance Union and the American Suffrage Association. Significantly, Harper was one of the founders of the National Association of Colored Women (see Mary Church Terrell in Part Five, p. 728).

Harper's writings reflect the cultural and political consciousness of her civic work. Poems on Miscellaneous Subjects *(1854), her first volume of poetry, reached a wide readership and went into an additional twenty editions by 1871. Her novel,* Iola Leroy, or Shadows Uplifted *(1892), centers on a woman from a racially mixed background who struggles to accept her racial identity.*

The two poems reprinted here exemplify the manner in which Harper's activist politics inspired her literary themes. "Bury Me in a Free Land" denounces the immorality of slavery, while "A Double Standard" contemplates the inequity in social and moral standards for women and men.

Bury Me in a Free Land

Make me a grave where'er you will,
In a lowly plain, or a lofty hill;
Make it among earth's humblest graves,
But not in a land where men are slaves.

I could not rest if around my grave
I heard the steps of a trembling slave;
His shadow above my silent tomb
Would make it a place of fearful gloom.

I could not rest if I heard the tread
Of a coffle gang to the shambles led,
And the mother's shriek of wild despair
Rise like a curse on the trembling air.

I could not sleep if I saw the lash
Drinking her blood at each fearful gash,
And I saw her babes torn from her breast,
Like trembling doves torn from their parent nest.

I'd shudder and start if I heard the bay
Of bloodhounds seizing their human prey,
And I heard the captive plead in vain
As they bound afresh his galling chain.

If I saw young girls from their mothers' arms
Bartered and sold for their youthful charms,
My eye would flash with a mournful flame,
My death-paled cheek grow red with shame.

I would sleep, dear friends, where bloated might
Can rob no man of his dearest right;
My rest shall be calm in any grave
Where none can call his brother a slave.

I ask no monument, proud and high,
To arrest the gaze of the passers-by;
All that my yearning spirit craves,
Is bury me not in a land of slaves.

A Double Standard

Do you blame me that I loved him?
  If when standing all alone
I cried for bread, a careless world
  Pressed to my lips a stone?

Do you blame me that I loved him,
  That my heart beat glad and free,
When he told me in the sweetest tones
  He loved but only me?

Can you blame me that I did not see,
  Beneath his burning kiss,
The serpent's wiles, nor even less hear
  The deadly adder hiss?

Can you blame me that my heart grew cold,
  That the tempted, tempter turned—
When he was feted and caressed
  And I was coldly spurned?

Would you blame him, when you drew from me
  Your dainty robes aside,
If he with gilded baits should claim
  Your fairest as his bride?

Would you blame the world if it should press
  On him a civic crown;
And see me struggling in the depth,
  Then harshly press me down?

Crime has no sex and yet today
  I wear the brand of shame;
Whilst he amid the gay and proud
  Still bears an honored name.

Can you blame me if I've learned to think
  Your hate of vice a sham,
When you so coldly crushed me down,
  And then excused the man?

Yes, blame me for my downward course,
  But oh! remember well,
Within your homes you press the hand
  That led me down to hell!

I'm glad God's ways are not your ways,
  He does not see as man;

Within his love I know there's room
For those whom others ban.

I think before His great white throne,
His theme of spotless light,
That whited sepulchres shall wear
The hue of endless night.

That I who fell, and he who sinned,
Shall reap as we have sown;
That each the burden of his loss
Must bear and bear alone.

No golden weights can turn the scale
Of justice in His sight;
And what is wrong in woman's life
In man's cannot be right.

Paul Laurence Dunbar (1872–1906)

Paul Laurence Dunbar published his first book at the young age of twenty-one and died only thirteen years later. In that brief time, his extensive writings included three volumes of poetry; four collections of short stories; and four novels. Perhaps his remarkable productivity was driven by the knowledge of his terminal tuberculosis, combined with his quest to win legitimacy as a mainstream writer.

Dunbar was born in Dayton, Ohio, of parents who were former slaves. At thirteen, he began reciting original poetry at church; at Central High School, where he was the only black student in his class, he was a member of a literary society and an editor of the High School Times. *Unable to finance a college education, Dunbar worked as an elevator operator until 1893, when he found a job as the assistant to Frederick Douglass, who was supervising the Haiti Exhibit at the World's Exposition in Chicago.*

In that same year, Dunbar privately published his first volume of poetry, Oak and Ivy, *followed by* Majors and Minors *in 1895. Dunbar marketed his books independently by reading and selling his poetry. After receiving a favorable review in* Harper's *by William Dean Howells, a prominent Caucasian writer, Dunbar gained the larger audience he desired. That audience was primarily made up of white readers familiar with the "Negro dialect" of literature depicting blacks through exaggerated, comical images. Although some of Dunbar's work follows the dialect form, as Richard Barksdale and Keneth Kinnamon suggest, "the general tone of . . . [Dunbar's] dialect poetry is quite different. . . . These poems radiate a warm humanity. . . ."*

Lyrics of Lowly Life *(1896), a selection of poems from his two earlier volumes, brought Dunbar national and international recognition and was praised for its dialect style. Yet Dunbar still hungered for an enthusiastic acceptance of his nondialect verse. Ironically, Dunbar wrote most of his poetry in standard English, using conventional symbols, rhythms, and rhyming patterns, but the pop-*

ularity of his dialect poetry overwhelmed the appreciation of his skill with mainstream language and forms.

Dunbar avoided direct attacks on American racism in his writing, which some critics have interpreted as a thematic weakness in his body of work. However, certain poems and stories serve as emblems of Dunbar's racial consciousness and pride, such as the poems "We Wear the Mask" and "Sympathy," which appear here.

Moving from poetry to fiction, Dunbar published several short story collections, including Folks from Dixie *(1898),* The Strength of Gideon and Other Stories *(1900),* In Old Plantation Days *(1903), and* The Heart of Happy Hollow *(1904).*

*For most critics, Dunbar's fiction possessed neither the mastery nor the impact of his poetry. Dismissed for an ineffective use of language and technique, all four of Dunbar's novels—*The Uncalled *(1898),* The Love of Landry *(1900),* The Fanatics *(1901), and* The Sports of the Gods *(1902)—suffered the common weaknesses of sentimental fiction, and in only one of them,* The Sports, *did he create significant black characters.*

Of the poems reprinted here, the lilting "When Malindy Sings" demonstrates Dunbar's skillful use of dialect, while "We Wear the Mask" and "Sympathy" both display his haunting artistry in using standard language and a serious tone.

When Malindy Sings

G'way an' quit dat noise, Miss Lucy—
  Put dat music book away;
What's de use to keep on tryin'?
  Ef you practise twell you're gray,
You cain't sta't no notes a-flyin'
  Lak de ones dat rants and rings
F'om de kitchen to de big woods
  When Malindy sings.

You ain't got de nachel o'gans
  Fu' to make de soun' come right,
You ain't got de tu'ns an' twistin's
  Fu' to make it sweet an' light,
Tell you one thing now, Miss Lucy,
  An' I'm tellin' you fu' true,
When hit comes to raal right singin',
  'T ain't no easy thing to do.

Easy 'nough fu' folks to hollah,
  Lookin' at de lines an' dots,
When dey ain't no one kin sence it,
  An' de chune comes in, in spots;
But fu' real melojous music,
  Dat jes' strikes yo' hea't and clings,
Jes' you stan' an' listen wif me
  When Malindy sings.

Ain't you nevah hyeahd Malindy?
  Blessed soul, tek up de cross!
Look hyeah, ain't you jokin', honey?
  Well, you don't know whut you los'.
Y'ought to hyeah dat gal a-wa'blin',
  Robins, la'ks, an' all dem things.
Heish dey moufs an' hides dey faces
  When Malindy sings.

We Wear the Mask

We wear the mask that grins and lies,
It hides our cheeks and shades our eyes,—
This debt we pay to human guile;
With torn and bleeding hearts we smile,
And mouth with myriad subtleties.

Why should the world be over-wise,
In counting all our tears and sighs?
Nay, let them only see us, while
    We wear the mask.

We smile, but, O great Christ, our cries
To thee from tortured souls arise.
We sing, but oh the clay is vile
Beneath our feet, and long the mile;
But let the world dream otherwise,
    We wear the mask.

Sympathy

I know what the caged bird feels, alas!
When the sun is bright on the upland slopes;
When the wind stirs soft through the springing grass
And the river flows like a stream of glass;
When the first bird sings and the first bud opes,
And the faint perfume from its chalice steals—
I know what the caged bird feels!

I know why the caged bird beats his wing
Till its blood is red on the cruel bars;
For he must fly back to his perch and cling
When he fain would be on the bough a-swing;
And a pain still throbs in the old, old scars
And they pulse again with a keener sting—
I know why he beats his wing!

I know why the caged bird sings, ah me,
When his wing is bruised or his bosom sore,—
When he beats his bars and would be free;
It is not a carol of joy or glee,
But a prayer that he sends from his heart's deep core,
But a plea, that upward to Heaven he flings—
I know why the caged bird sings!

Anne Spencer (1882–1975)

B*orn in Bramwell, West Virginia, and unable to read or write until the age of eleven, Anne Spencer graduated as valedictorian of her class from Virginia Seminary in Lynchburg. After teaching school briefly, she was able, with the support of her husband, to concentrate on her writing, reading, and gardening at home.*

Yet Spencer's cottage and garden were not just places of privilege and isolation. Her home also served as an intellectual and social meeting place for various Harlem Renaissance figures, such as James Weldon Johnson, Paul Robeson, Georgia Douglas Johnson, and Sterling Brown, among others. James Weldon Johnson is credited with discovering Spencer's poetry, urging her to submit "Before the Feast at Shusan," which was published in Crisis *in 1920. Although many of her poems have appeared in various literary journals and anthologies, Spencer never published a book of poetry. As critic Ann Allen Shockley points out, Spencer "published less than thirty of her poems, and her career lasted just over ten years. She scribbled thousands of her poems on pieces of paper, which were accidentally thrown out by house cleaners."*

Spencer's poetry is generally characterized as conventional verse devoid of ethnic themes. However, unlike the absence of overt racial concerns in her poetry, Spencer's public activities gave strong support to the civil rights movement. She founded the first permanent branch of the NAACP in Lynchburg and actively campaigned against segregation. For a 1955 anthology, Spencer expressed her awareness of the ambiguous and oppressive attitudes toward black women held by mainstream society: "I proudly love being a Negro woman—it's so involved and interesting. We are the problem—the great national game of Taboo."

In her later life, Spencer became the first librarian at Dunbar High School, a position she held for twenty-five years. She championed black youth, encouraging young people to read and to push themselves beyond the limitations of the local environment.

The two poems that follow were published in the early 1920s. "White Things" and "Black Man O' Mine" praise the physical and spiritual beauty of black men, employing end rhyme and allusions to the natural world to romanticize blackness.

White Things

Most things are colorful things—the sky, earth, and sea.
        Black men are most men; but the white are free!
White things are rare things; so rare, so rare

They stole from out a silvered world—somewhere.
Finding earth-plains fair plains, save greenly grassed,
They strewed white feathers of cowardice, as they passed;
        The golden stars with lances fine
        The hills all red and darkened pine,
They blanched with their wand of power;
And turned the blood in a ruby rose
To a poor white poppy-flower.

Black Man O' Mine

Black man o' mine,
If the world were your lover,
It could not give what I give to you,
Or the ocean would yield and you could discover
Its ages of treasure to hold and to view;
Could it fill half the measure of my heart's portion . . .
Just for you living, just for you giving all this devotion,
Black man o' mine.

Black man o' mine,
As I hush and caress you, close to my heart,
All your loving is just your needing what's true;
Then with your passing dark comes my darkest part,
For living without your loving is only rue.
Black man o' mine, if the world were your lover
It could not give what I give to you.

Fenton Johnson (1888–1958)

Fenton Johnson began writing poetry at the age of nine. Born and raised in Chicago, Johnson attended the University of Chicago, Northwestern University, and the Columbia University School of Journalism. After teaching for a year, he moved away from the classroom and into editing and publishing literary magazines, including Champion *and* Favorite *magazines, which he founded in 1916 and 1918, respectively.*

Throughout his career, Johnson wrote poetry, essays, drama, and short fiction. A number of his plays were produced in Chicago in the early 1900s, and some of his short stories appeared in the collection Tales of Darkest America *(1920). It was his poetry, however, that gained Johnson critical attention. He composed some poetry in dialect, but his most successful poems use standard English. While in his twenties, he explored the free verse form in poems that display "solid imagery, and actual speech rather than romantic bombast." His volumes of poetry include* A Little Dreaming *(1913),* Visions of the Dusk *(1915), and* Songs of the Soil *(1916).*

The two poems reprinted here, both from the 1913 volume, demonstrate Johnson's use of standard English. "The Ethiopian's Song" romanticizes black Af-

rica's refutation of white colonialism. Utilizing conventional language and end rhyme, "To an Afro-American Maiden" meditates on a symbolic black American woman who possesses the best of the cultural mix of black Africa, Greece, and America.

The Ethiopian's Song

I

Where I go the lily blooms,
Where I go the ivy climbs;
All the earth is slave to me,
All the orbs are merry chimes.
White man longs to rule the world;
I am happy where I am,—
I, the Lord of sweet content.

II

Where I go magnolias dance,
Where I go the jonquils prance;
Strength and might and power are mine,
Song and cheer my freedom's lance.
Let Ambition die her death;
I am happy where I am,—
I, the Lord of sweet content.

To an Afro-American Maiden

I

Sweet the perfume of an age bygone
When the gods breathed deep in every breeze,
Walked beside the sparkle of the sea,
Made their slumber haunt within the trees;
Now no censers swing along the groves
Of the land where swarthy men were brave,
Now the gods have faded as a dream
And dim yesterday lies in her grave.

II

But within the face of one whose race
Dwells exiled throughout this western land,
Comes in fancy all the days long dead
As tho' painted by a master hand;
Rich old Ethiop and Greece are there
In the swarthy skin and dreamy eye,
And the red man of the forest grants
Raven hair and figure tow'ring high.

III

Proud America to nurture one
Who has robbed the ages of their store,
Races three within her bosom strive,
Panting for the sweets of cant and lore;
All the world romantic lives in her
With the minstrels and the knights of mail
And the nymphs that dance within the shade,
Journeymen within the dreaming pale.

Claude McKay (1889–1948)

Claude McKay is regarded as one of the most important contributors to the Harlem Renaissance, and his book of verse, Harlem Shadows *(1922), has been proclaimed by Richard Barksdale and Keneth Kinnamon to be the "first great literary achievement" of that period. The work possesses a radical racial consciousness that gives McKay's verse a distinctive tone despite its traditional poetic forms, particularly the sonnet.*

Born in Jamaica as the youngest of eleven children, McKay's early education came from tutoring by an older brother and a white schoolmaster. Apprenticed as a cabinetmaker in his teens, McKay was even then turning to poetry. In his early twenties, he published two volumes of poetry that gained attention in Jamaica. Appearing in 1912, both volumes are written in the Jamaican dialect: Songs from Jamaica *explores the lives of the peasant people, while* Constab Ballads *depicts the harsh realities of the urban environment, emphasizing the clash between the law and the common people.*

After winning a scholarship with his poems, McKay traveled to the United States in 1912, attending Tuskegee Institute for only a few months and then Kansas State College for two years. However, academic life was secondary to the young poet's desire to achieve literary distinction. And so he moved to Harlem, where he worked at a series of menial jobs while following his creative urges.

McKay managed to publish numerous poems in several magazines in 1919 before leaving for London, where he published his volume Spring in New Hampshire and Other Poems *(1920). Because his second volume of Jamaican poetry,* Constab Ballads, *had already been published in London, McKay enjoyed some recognition from British writers and journalists. In England, he continued to write political essays, particularly for* Workers Dreadnought, *a Communist weekly.*

After returning to America in 1921, McKay expressed his political perspectives as assistant editor of the Liberator *and the* Masses. *A year later he journeyed to Russia to become a spokesman for the American Worker's Party, publishing a poem in* Pravda *and meeting Communist leaders Leon Trotsky and Nikolay Bukharin. Leaving Russia due to illness, McKay lived abroad for many years in various locales, including France, Spain, Germany, and Morocco.*

By the time he retraced his path back to the United States in the mid-1930s, McKay had published more poetry as well as novels and short stories that impressed many critics. His first novel, Home to Harlem *(1928), was followed by*

Banjo *(1929).* Gingertown *(1932), a short story collection, came out one year before his last novel,* Banana Bottom *(1933). His other works include an autobiography,* A Long Way from Home *(1937), and a book of critical prose,* Harlem: Negro Metropolis *(1940). However, McKay's poetry prevails as his greatest literary strength.* The Selected Poems of Claude McKay *(1953) was published five years after his death.*

The three poems reprinted here are notable for the striking contrast in their structures and tones. "If We Must Die" and "America" are from Harlem Shadows, *and "The White House" originally appeared in the early 1920s as well. Although the poems follow the traditional sonnet form, they forcibly express black anger and determination.*

If We Must Die

If we must die, let it not be like hogs
Hunted and penned in an inglorious spot,
While round us bark the mad and hungry dogs,
Making their mock at our accursèd lot.
If we must die, O let us nobly die,
So that our precious blood may not be shed
In vain; then even the monsters we defy
Shall be constrained to honor us though dead!
O kinsmen! we must meet the common foe!
Though far outnumbered let us show us brave,
And for their thousand blows deal one deathblow!
What though before us lies the open grave?
Like men we'll face the murderous, cowardly pack,
Pressed to the wall, dying, but fighting back!

The White House

Your door is shut against my tightened face,
And I am sharp as steel with discontent;
But I possess the courage and the grace
To bear my anger proudly and unbent.
The pavement slabs burn loose beneath my feet,
A chafing savage, down the decent street;
And passion rends my vitals as I pass,
Where boldly shines your shuttered door of glass.
Oh, I must search for wisdom every hour,
Deep in my wrathful bosom sore and raw,
And find in it the superhuman power
To hold me to the letter of your law!
Oh, I must keep my heart inviolate
Against the potent poison of your hate.

America

Although she feeds me bread of bitterness,
And sinks into my throat her tiger's tooth,
Stealing my breath of life, I will confess
I love this cultured hell that tests my youth!
Her vigor flows like tides into my blood,
Giving me strength against her hate.
Her bigness sweeps my being like a flood.
Yet as a rebel fronts a king in state,
I stand within her walls with not a shred
Of terror, malice, not a word of jeer.
Darkly I gaze into the days ahead,
And see her might and granite wonders there,
Beneath the touch of Time's unerring hand,
Like priceless treasures sinking in the sand.

Sterling Brown (1901–89)

Contemporary black poet Michael Harper describes Sterling Brown's poems as "deceptively literate; they move as images created and controlled or activated, as an agency of contact; in this sense he is a great poet of the community." Brown projects a genuine sense of folk language and attitude into much of his poetry. It resonates with the idioms and spirit of the men and women at the matrix of the African American community.

In significant ways, Brown's privileged personal background differed from the folk milieu he explored in his verse. Born in Washington, D.C., his father was a professor of theology at Howard University. Brown earned his bachelor's from Williams College in 1922 and his master's from Harvard University in 1924. In an extraordinary academic career, Brown taught at Virginia Seminary, Lincoln University (Missouri), Fisk University, and Howard University. He also served as a visiting professor at numerous academic institutions, including Atlanta University, New York University, Vassar College, and the University of Illinois at Chicago Circle. In 1969, he retired from teaching after forty years, having taught Amiri Baraka and Toni Morrison as just two among his thousands of students.

Brown's scholarship has played a fundamental role in the study and criticism of African American literature, music, folklore, and films. His scholarly works include Negro Poetry and Drama *(1937) and* The Negro in American Fiction *(1937). A pioneer in the study of African American literature, he coedited the extensive anthology,* The Negro Caravan *(1941). He also published numerous essays exploring literature, music, and popular culture, including "Negro Character as Seen by White Authors" (1933), "Athletes and Art" (1951), and "A Century of Negro Portraiture in American Literature" (1966).*

In addition, Brown wrote short stories, though his poetry earned him the most acclaim as a writer. As critic Arthur Davis notes, "The poetry of Sterling Brown deals mainly with the following general subjects: the endurance *of the Negro, the stark tragedy which is too often his lot, death as a means of release from his misery, the open road as another escape, and humor as a safety valve." Using a free verse style that echoes the blues and jazz, Brown's poetry, sometimes written in dialect, pays homage to the distinctive language of black culture. His first volume of poetry,* Southern Road, *was published in 1932. Decades later,* The Last Ride of Wild Bill and Eleven Narrative Poems *(1975) was issued, followed by* The Collected Poems of Sterling A. Brown *(1980), with selections chosen by editor Michael Harper.*

The three poems reprinted here were originally published in the 1930s. "Children of the Mississippi" (1932) expresses the collective voice of southern blacks who battled the dangers of the Mississippi River, both literally and figuratively. In comparison, "Return" (1932) depicts a persona who journeys back into a youthful reverie to find peace. In "Sharecroppers" (1939), peace comes only at death for a black victim terrorized by a mob.

Children of the Mississippi

These know fear; for all their singing
As the moon thrust her tip above dark woods,
Tuning their voices to the summer night,
These folk knew even then the hints of fear.
For all their loafing on the levee,
Unperturbedly spendthrift of time,
Greeting the big boat swinging the curve
"Do it, Mister Pilot! Do it, Big Boy!"
Beneath their dark laughter
Roaring like a flood roars, swung into a spillway,
There rolled even then a strong undertow
Of fear.

Now, intimately
These folk know fear.
They have seen
Blackwater creeping, slow-footed Fate,
Implacably, unceasingly
Over their bottomlands, over their cornstocks,
Past highwater marks, past wildest conjecture,
Black water creeping before their eyes,
Rolling while they toss in startled half sleep.

> *De Lord tole Norah*
> *Dat de flood was due,*
> *Norah listened to de Lord*
> *An' got his stock on board,*
> *Wish dat de Lord*
> *Had tole us too.*

These folk know grief.
They have seen
Black water gurgling, lapping, roaring,
Take their lives' earnings, roll off their paltry

Fixtures of home, things as dear as old hearthgods.
These have known death
Surprising, rapacious of cattle, of children,
Creeping with the black water
Secretly, unceasingly.

Death pick out new ways
Now fo' to come to us,
Black water creepin'
While folks is sleepin',
Death on de black water
Ugly an' treacherous.

These, for all their vaunted faith, know doubt.
These know no Ararat;
No arc of promise bedecking blue skies;
No dove, betokening calm;
No fondled favor towards new beginnings.
These know
Promise of baked lands, burnt as in brickkilns,
Cracked uglily, crinkled crust at the seedtime,
Rotten with stench, watched over by vultures.
Promise of winter, bleak and unpitying,
No buoyant hoping now, only dank memories
Bitter as the waters, bracken as the waters,
Black and unceasing as hostile waters.

Winter a-comin'
Leaner dan ever,
What we done done to you
Makes you do lak you do?
How we done harmed you
Black-hearted river?

These folk know fear, now, as a bosom crony;
Children, stepchildren
Of the Mississippi. . . .

Return

I have gone back in boyish wonderment
To things that I had foolishly put by. . . .
Have found an alien and unknown content
In seeing how some bits of cloud-filled sky
Are framed in bracken pools; through chuckling hours
Have watched the antic frogs, or curiously
Have numbered all the unnamed, vagrant flowers,
That fleck the unkempt meadows, lavishly.

Or where a headlong toppling stream has stayed
Its racing, lulled to quiet by the song
Bursting from out the thick-leaved oaken shade,
There I have lain while hours sauntered past—
I have found peacefulness somewhere at last,
Have found a quiet needed for so long.

Sharecroppers

When they rode up at first dark and called his name,
He came out like a man from his little shack.
He saw his landlord, and he saw the sheriff,
And some well-armed riff-raff in the pack.
When they fired questions about the meeting,
He stood like a man gone deaf and dumb,
But when the leaders left their saddles,
He knew then that his time had come.
In the light of the lanterns the long cuts fell,
And his wife's weak moans and the children's wails
Mixed with the sobs he could not hold.
But he wouldn't tell, he would not tell.
The Union was his friend, and he was Union,
And there was nothing a man could say.
So they trussed him up with stout ploughlines,
Hitched up a mule, dragged him far away
Into the dark woods that tell no tales,
Where he kept his secrets as well as they.

He would not give away the place,
Nor who they were, neither white nor black,
Nor tell what his brothers were about.
They lashed him, and they clubbed his head;
One time he parted his bloody lips
Out of great pain and greater pride,
One time, to laugh in his landlord's face;
Then his landlord shot him in the side.
He toppled, and the blood gushed out.
But he didn't mumble ever a word,
And cursing, they left him there for dead.
He lay waiting quiet, until he heard
The growls and the mutters dwindle away;
"Didn't tell a single thing," he said,
Then to the dark woods and the moon
He gave up one secret before he died:
"We gonna clean out dis brushwood round here soon,
Plant de white-oak and de black-oak side by side."

Langston Hughes (1902–67)

Langston Hughes's astonishing range and volume of work, published over a period of forty years, won the praise of the black audiences he wrote for as well as that of artists, critics, and readers beyond the African American community. Most scholars would concur with critic Arthur P. Davis's assessment: "Poet, fiction writer, dramatist, newspaper columnist, writer of autobiography, anthologist, compiler of children's works, and translator, Langston Hughes was by far the most experimental and versatile author of the [Harlem] Renaissance—and time may find him the greatest."

Hughes was born in Joplin, Missouri, but his early childhood mobility—he lived in seven different cities within only twelve years—was an indication of the restless life-style that would influence his writing throughout adulthood. While living in Lincoln, Illinois, with his divorced mother and stepfather, he was chosen as class poet in junior high school; he went on to become editor of his high school's yearbook, this time in Cleveland.

His restless spirit led to an unsatisfying family life for the young writer. In 1921, during an emotionally disturbing visit with his father in Mexico, Hughes taught English in Mexican schools and published his first poem, "The Negro Speaks of Rivers," which appeared in Crisis. *After attending Columbia University for only a year, Hughes set his sights on writing and traveling abroad. But by 1925, he had settled back in America, in Washington, D.C., and was working as a waiter. In that same year, several key events occurred: Hughes received recognition from established white writers, won a first prize for poetry from* Opportunity *magazine, and entered Lincoln University in Pennsylvania, where he won the Witter Bynner Prize for undergraduate poetry before earning his bachelor's in 1929.*

While still a student, and with his growing reputation as a poet, Hughes began to visit Harlem during holidays and school breaks. In 1926, he published his first volume of poetry, The Weary Blues, *and was hailed as one of the most promising artists of the Harlem Renaissance. In this and his other early work, Hughes displayed attributes that would distinguish his poetry for life—free verse forms, respect for black folkways and language, love of the blues and jazz, and themes of racial pride and survival. During the 1930s, Hughes went to Russia and Spain, but he continued to write about experiences relevant to African Americans. Much of his writing emphasizes the American aspect of being African American, particularly the right of all blacks to pursue their part of the American Dream.*

Hughes also taught courses at Atlanta University and the University of Chicago, and he traveled and lectured throughout the world, representing the U.S. Information Agency and attending the Dakar Arts Festival in 1966.

His poetry output was remarkable. Following The Weary Blues, *he published numerous other volumes of poetry:* Fine Clothes to the Jew *(1927),* The Dream Keeper *(1932),* Shakespeare in Harlem *(1942),* Fields of Wonder *(1947),* One Way Ticket *(1949),* Montage of a Dream Deferred *(1951),* Selected Poems of Langston Hughes *(1959),* Ask Your Mama: 12 Moods for Jazz *(1961), and* The Panther and the Lash *(1967). Hughes's prose, which ranges from fiction and drama to autobiographical editorial works, includes the novels* Not without Laughter *(1930),* Tambourines of Glory *(1959), and* The Sweet Flypaper of Life *(1955), a collaborative work. Many of his short stories are collected in* The Ways of White Folks *(1934),* Laughing to Keep from Crying *(1952), and* Something in Common *(1963). Unique among his fictional works is a series of sketches and stories that feature the fictional black everyman, Jesse B. Semple (known as "Simple"), who represents, according to Richard Barksdale and Keneth Kinnamon, "a coolly comic view of Black and white America." Through this character, Hughes asserts that "out of the complexities of modern urban living and the mountainous mass of human error, 'simple' men will emerge to pronounce 'simple' truths and provide 'simple' solutions." These pieces are collected in five volumes published between 1950 and 1965.*

In addition to writing two autobiographies, The Big Sea *(1940) and* I Wonder as I Wander *(1956), Hughes edited and collaborated on various books of African American literature and history, such as* The Best Short Stories by Negro Writers *(1967);* The Poetry of the Negro *(1949), co-edited with Arna Bontemps; and* Fight for Freedom: The Story of the NAACP *(1962). He also wrote full-length plays, one-act plays, and a musical. In 1963, he published the collection* Five Plays. *It contains his most acclaimed drama,* Mulatto *(1935), which had run on Broadway for a year.*

The six poems that appear here come from various collections published in the 1920s to the 1960s. The first four poems display Hughes's skill at employing the free verse form to create diverse tones and dilineate different themes. The last two poems are unified by discernible rhyming patterns and rhythm-shaping repetition.

As I Grew Older

It was a long time ago.
I have almost forgotten my dream.
But it was there then,
In front of me,
Bright like a sun—
My dream.

And then the wall rose,
Rose slowly,
Slowly,
Between me and my dream.
Rose slowly, slowly,
Dimming,
Hiding,
The light of my dream.
Rose until it touched the sky—
The wall.

Shadow.
I am black.

I lie down in the shadow.
No longer the light of my dream before me,

Above me.
Only the thick wall.
Only the shadow.

My hands!
My dark hands!
Break through the wall!
Find my dream!
Help me to shatter this darkness,
To smash this night,
To break this shadow
Into a thousand lights of sun,
Into a thousand whirling dreams
Of sun!

Afro-American Fragment

So long,
So far away
Is Africa.
Not even memories alive
Save those that history books create,
Save those that songs
Beat back into the blood—
Beat out of blood with words sad-sung
In strange un-Negro tongue—
So long,
So far away
Is Africa.

Subdued and time-lost
Are the drums—and yet
Through some vast mist of race
There comes this song
I do not understand,
This song of atavistic land,
Of bitter yearnings lost
Without a place—
So long,
So far away
Is Africa's
Dark face.
    Not ever.
    Niggers ain't my brother.

The Southern night is full of stars,
Great big yellow stars.
    O, sweet as earth,

Dusk dark bodies
Give sweet birth
To little yellow bastard boys.

Git on back there in the night,
You ain't white.

The bright stars scatter everywhere.
Pine wood scent in the evening air.
A nigger night,
A nigger joy.

I am your son, white man!

A little yellow
Bastard boy.

Mother to Son

Well, son, I'll tell you:
Life for me ain't been no crystal stair.
It's had tacks in it,
And splinters,
And boards torn up,
And places with no carpet on the floor—
Bare.
But all the time
I'se been a-climbin' on,
And reachin' landin's,
And turnin' corners,
And sometimes goin' in the dark
Where there ain't been no light.
So boy, don't you turn back.
Don't you set down on the steps
'Cause you finds it's kinder hard.
Don't you fall now—
For I'se still goin', honey,
I'se still climbin',
And life for me ain't been no crystal stair.

Georgia Dusk

Sometimes there's a wind in the Georgia dusk
That cries and cries and cries
Its lonely pity through the Georgia dusk
Veiling what the darkness hides.

Sometimes there's blood in the Georgia dusk,
Left by a streak of sun,
A crimson trickle in the Georgia dusk.
Whose blood? . . . Everyone's.

Sometimes a wind in the Georgia dusk
Scatters hate like seed
To sprout its bitter barriers
Where the sunsets bleed.

Democracy

Democracy will not come
Today, this year
    Nor ever
Through compromise and fear.

I have as much right
As the other fellow has
    To stand
On my two feet
And own the land.

I tire so of hearing people say,
Let things take their course.
Tomorrow is another day.
I do not need my freedom when I'm dead.
I cannot live on tomorrow's bread.

    Freedom
    Is a strong seed
    Planted
    In a great need.
    I live here, too.
    I want freedom
    Just as you.

Countee Cullen (1903–46)

A poet, novelist, playwright, editor, and teacher, Countee Cullen first became known as one of the outstanding talents of the Harlem Renaissance. His devotion to the traditional aesthetics of poetry shaped his verse without erasing his cultural consciousness from the content.

Born in New York City, Cullen was raised by his grandmother and adopted by Reverend Frederick A. Cullen, the pastor of the Salem African Methodist Episcopal church. After attending Dewitt Clinton High School, he went on to earn his bachelor's from New York University in 1925, and his master's from Harvard in 1926.

Cullen began writing poetry while in high school. During his sophomore year at college, he won the prestigious Witter Bynner Undergraduate Award for poetry. Cullen's productivity throughout the 1920s earned him an immutable position in the black cultural rebirth during that decade. His first book of poetry, Color *(1925), won the Harmon Foundation Award. It was followed by three more volumes of poetry:* Copper Sun *(1927),* The Ballad of the Brown Girl *(1927), and* The Black Christ *(1929).*

After the years of the Harlem Renaissance, Cullen continued his literary endeavors, but in more diverse areas. Having worked as an assistant editor at Opportunity *magazine, he edited* Caroling Dusk *(1927), an anthology of African American poetry. In 1932, he wrote his only novel,* One Way to Heaven, *which despite its satirical tone, according to Ruth Miller, presents a "realistic picture of the New Negro Renaissance Harlem." Three years later, in 1935, Cullen composed his translation of* Medea.

During the final six years of his life, Cullen developed two children's books— The Lost Zoo *(1940) and* My Lives and How I Lost Them! *(1942)—and worked with Arna Bontemps, the author of* God Sends Sunday *(1931), on adapting that novel as the musical* St. Louis Woman *(1946).* On These I Stand *(1947), a poetry collection, was published posthumously.*

The four poems that appear here, written in the 1920s, display the stylistic lyricism and racial sensitivity that mark Cullen's most memorable poetry.

Heritage

for Harold Jackman

What is Africa to me:
Copper sun or scarlet sea,
Jungle star or jungle track,
Strong bronzed men, or regal black
Women from whose loins I sprang
When the birds of Eden sang?
One three centuries removed
From the scenes his fathers loved,
Spicy grove, cinnamon tree,
What is Africa to me?

So I lie, who all day long
Want no sound except the song
Sung by wild barbaric birds
Goading massive jungle herds,
Juggernauts of flesh that pass
Trampling tall defiant grass
Where young forest lovers lie,
Plighting troth beneath the sky.
So I lie, who always hear,
Though I cram against my ear

Both my thumbs, and keep them there,
Great drums throbbing through the air.
So I lie, whose fount of pride,
Dear distress, and joy allied,
Is my somber flesh and skin,
With the dark blood dammed within
Like great pulsing tides of wine
That, I fear, must burst the fine
Channels of the chafing net
Where they surge and foam and fret.

Africa? A book one thumbs
Listlessly, till slumber comes.
Unremembered are her bats
Circling through the night, her cats
Crouching in the river reeds,
Stalking gentle flesh that feeds
By the river brink; no more
Does the bugle-throated roar
Cry that monarch claws have leapt
From the scabbards where they slept.
Silver snakes that once a year
Doff the lovely coats you wear,
Seek no covert in your fear
Lest a mortal eye should see;
What's your nakedness to me?
Here no leprous flowers rear
Fierce corollas in the air;
Here no bodies sleek and wet,
Dripping mingled rain and sweat,
Tread the savage measures of
Jungle boys and girls in love.
What is last year's snow to me,
Last year's anything? The tree
Budding yearly must forget
How its past arose or set—
Bough and blossom, flower, fruit,
Even what shy bird with mute
Wonder at her travail there,
Meekly labored in its hair.
One three centuries removed
From the scenes his fathers loved,
Spicy grove, cinnamon tree,
What is Africa to me?

So I lie, who find no peace
Night or day, no slight release
From the unremittant beat
Made by cruel padded feet

Walking through my body's street.
Up and down they go, and back.
Treading out a jungle track.
So I lie, who never quite
Safely sleep from rain at night—
I can never rest at all
When the rain begins to fall;
Like a soul gone mad with pain
I must match its weird refrain;
Ever must I twist and squirm,
Writhing like a baited worm,
While its primal measures drip
Through my body, crying, "Strip!
Doff this new exuberance.
Come and dance the Lover's Dance!"
In an old remembered way
Rain works on me night and day.

Quaint, outlandish heathen gods
Black men fashion out of rods,
Clay, and brittle bits of stone,
In a likeness like their own,
My conversion came high-priced;
I belong to Jesus Christ,
Preacher of humility,
Heathen gods are naught to me.

Father, Son, and Holy Ghost,
So I make an idle boast;
Jesus of the twice-turned cheek,
Lamb of God, although I speak
With my mouth thus, in my heart
Do I play a double part.
Ever at Thy glowing altar
Must my heart grow sick and falter,
Wishing He I served were black,
Thinking then it would not lack
Precedent of pain to guide it,
Let who would or might deride it;
Surely then this flesh would know
Yours had borne a kindred woe.
Lord, I fashion dark gods, too,
Daring even to give You
Dark despairing features where,
Crowned with dark rebellious hair,
Patience wavers just so much as
Mortal grief compels, while touches
Quick and hot, of anger, rise
To smitten cheek and weary eyes.

Lord, forgive me if my need
Sometimes shapes a human creed.
All day long and all night through,
One thing only must I do;
Quench my pride and cool my blood,
Lest I perish in the flood,
Lest a hidden ember set
Timber that I thought was wet
Burning like the dryest flax,
Melting like the merest wax,
Lest the grave restore its dead.
Not yet has my heart or head
In the least way realized
They and I are civilized.

The Wise

Dead men are wisest, for they know
How far the roots of flowers go,
How long a seed must rot to grow.

Dead men alone bear frost and rain
On throbless heart and heatless brain,
And feel no stir of joy or pain.

Dead men alone are satiate;
They sleep and dream and have no weight,
To curb their rest, of love or hate.

Strange, men should flee their company,
Or think me strange who long to be
Wrapped in their cool immunity.

Yet Do I Marvel

I doubt no God is good, well-meaning, kind,
And did He stoop to quibble could tell why
The little buried mole continues blind,
Why flesh that mirrors Him must someday die,
Make plain the reason tortured Tantalus
Is baited by the fickle fruit, declare
If merely brute caprice dooms Sisyphus
To struggle up a never-ending stair.
Inscrutable His ways are, and immune
To catechism by a mind too strewn
With petty cares to slightly understand
What awful brain compels His awful hand.

Yet do I marvel at this curious thing:
To make a poet black, and bid him sing!

From the Dark Tower

We shall not always plant while others reap
The golden increment of bursting fruit,
Not always countenance, abject and mute,
That lesser men should hold their brothers cheap;
Not everlastingly while others sleep
Shall we beguile their limbs with mellow flute,
Not always bend to some more subtle brute;
We were not made eternally to weep.

The night whose sable breast relieves the stark,
White stars is no less lovely being dark,
And there are buds that cannot bloom at all
In light, but crumple, piteous, and fall;
So in the dark we hide the heart that bleeds,
And wait, and tend our agonizing seeds.

Robert Hayden (1913–80)

Recognized as a poet whose assiduous work unites crafting of form and content, Robert Hayden pursued his personal standard of excellence through decades of social upheaval, overlapping the intellectual wartime voices of the 1940s and the polemical voices of the 1960s.

Born in Detroit as Asa Bundy Sheffey, Hayden completed his undergraduate studies at Wayne State University and earned a master's from the University of Michigan. Choosing an academic career, Hayden taught for two years at Michigan before taking a position in the English Department at Fisk University.

In Kaleidoscope *(1967), a collection of black American poetry edited by Hayden, he professes his view regarding the responsibility of the black writer, insisting that the shackle of restriction to speak only as a black artist undermines the writer's creative potential. Hayden's verse, though mainstream and traditional in its style, directly embraces themes and events relevant to African Americans.*

Hayden's numerous volumes of poetry include Heart-Shape in the Dust *(1940);* The Lion and the Archer *(1948), coauthored with Myron O'Higgins;* Figure of Time *(1955);* A Ballad of Remembrance *(1962);* Selected Poems *(1966);* Words in the Mourning Time *(1970);* The Night-Blooming Cereus *(1972);* Angle of Ascent: New and Selected Poems *(1975); and* American Journal *(1978). In addition, his collected poems appear in* The Collected Poems of Robert Hayden *(1985) edited by Frederick Glaysher.*

The two poems reprinted here were written in the 1960s. "Night, Death, Mississippi" contrasts an elderly man's fond memories of joining in a lynch mob with images of Christianity. "El-Hajj Malik El-Shabazz" tells about the history, religious journey, and political leadership of Malcolm X.

Night, Death, Mississippi

I

A quavering cry. Screech-owl?
Or one of them?
The old man in his reek
and gauntless laughs—

One of them, I bet—
and turns out the kitchen lamp,
limping to the porch to listen
in the windowless night.

Be there with Boy and the rest
if I was well again.
Time was. Time was.
White robes like moonlight

In the sweetgum dark.
Unbucked that one then
and him squealing bloody Jesus
as we cut it off.

Time was. A cry?
A cry all right.
He hawks and spits,
fevered as by groinfire.

Have us a bottle,
Boy and me—
he's earned him a bottle—
when he gets home.

II

Then we beat them, he said,
beat them till our arms was tired
and the big old chains
messy and red.

O Jesus burning on the lily cross

Christ, it was better
than hunting bear
which don't know why
you want him dead.

O night, rawhead and bloodybones night

You kids fetch Paw
some water now so's he

can wash that blood
off him, she said.

O night betrayed by darkness not its own

El-Hajj Malik El-Shabazz

(Malcolm X)

O masks and metamorphoses of Ahab, Native Son

I

The icy evil that struck his father down
and ravished his mother into madness
trapped him in violence of a punished self
struggling to break free.

As Home Boy, as Dee-troit Red,
he fled his name, became the quarry of
his own obsessed pursuit.

He conked his hair and Lindy-hopped,
zoot-suited jiver, swinging those chicks
in the hot rose and reefer glow.

His injured childhood bullied him.
He skirmished in the Upas trees
and cannibal flowers of the American Dream—

but could not hurt the enemy
powered against him there.

II

Sometimes the dark that gave his life
its cold satanic sheen would shift
a little, and he saw himself
floodlit and eloquent;

yet how could he, "Satan" in The Hole,
guess what the waking dream foretold?

Then false dawn of vision came;
he fell upon his face before
a racist Allah pledged to wrest him from
the hellward-thrusting hands of Calvin's Christ—

to free him and his kind
from Yakub's white-faced treachery.
He rose redeemed from all but prideful anger,

though adulterate attars could not cleanse
him of the odors of the pit.

III

Asalam alaikum!

He X'd his name, became his people's anger,
exhorted them to vengeance for their past;
rebuked, admonished them,

their scourger who
would shame them, drive them from
the lush ice gardens of their servitude.

Asalam alaikum!

Rejecting Ahab, he was of Ahab's tribe.
"Strike through the mask!"

IV

Time. "The martyr's time," he said.
Time and the karate killer,
knifer, gunman. Time that brought
ironic trophies as his faith

twined and sparked round the bole,
the fruit of neo-Islam.
"The martyr's time."

But first, the ebb time pilgrimage
toward revelation, hejira to
his final metamorphosis;

Labbayk! Labbayk!

He fell upon his face before
Allah the raceless in whose blazing Oneness all
were one. He rose renewed renamed, because
much more than there was time for him to be.

Samuel W. Allen (1917–)

Samuel W. Allen's poetry has been described as presenting an "enigmatic and fatalistic universe" for black people while also containing "a militant and revolutionary impulse that rejects passive acceptance of racism." Perhaps this mix of pessimism and radicalism emanated from Allen's profession as a lawyer. Or perhaps his living abroad—like other African American expatriates in the 1950s—contributed to the conflicting elements found in his creative work.

Born in Columbus, Ohio, Allen achieved great success in his studies at Fisk University, where he earned a bachelor's in 1938; at Harvard University Law School, where he received a doctor of laws in 1941; and at the Sorbonne. While studying in Paris, he met Richard Wright, whose support led to the publication of Allen's poetry in the French magazine, Présence Africaine, *in 1949. He published his first volume of poetry in 1956 in Germany, under the pseudonym Paul Vesey. It is a bilingual work by the title* Elfenbein Zähne, *or* Ivory Tusks.

Allen later became the English editor of Présence Africaine, *and in 1961, he served as a panelist on African literature at the conference of the United Nations Educational, Scientific, and Cultural Organization (UNESCO) in Boston. Allen has taught at Tuskegee and Wesleyan Universities, and has lectured and read poetry at various colleges. His publications include* Pan-Africanism Reconsidered *(1962), which he coedited,* Ivory Tusks and Other Poems *(1962), a reprint of his first volume;* Paul Vesey's Ledger *(1975); and* Every Round and Other Poems *(1987).*

Beyond his literary endeavors, Allen has worked in Africa and Latin America as assistant general counsel for the U.S. Information Agency. He has been a law professor, an attorney, and a deputy assistant district attorney. In 1964, he worked with the Community Relations Service of the Department of Justice.

The three poems that appear here, taken from his 1987 collection, display Allen's use of free verse. "Harriet Tubman" presents the courage and triumph of the legendary "Moses" of the underground railroad. "Benin Bronze" juxtaposes black American racial stereotypes with nobler black African images, while "About Poetry and South Africa" integrates nonfiction with poetry to ponder racism in South Africa.

Harriet Tubman

aka Moses

High in the darkening heavens
  the wind swift, the storm massing
the giant arrow rose, a crackling arch, a sign
  above the fleeing band of people,
toy figures in the canebrake
  below.

Far in the distance, moving quickly,
came the patterrollers
bloodhounds loping, silent.

Minutes before, one of the fleeing band had fallen,
the others for a moment waited
but he did not rise.
A small dark woman stood above him.
His words were slow to come and more a groan:

Can't make it, just can't make it
You all go ahead without me.

Moses pulled out her revolver and she quietly said:

Move or die.

You ain't stoppin now
You *can't* stop now
You gonna move
move or die.

If you won't go on
Gonna risk us all—
Ahma send your soul to glory, I said move!
Long time now, I got it figgered out
Ev'ry child a God got a double right, death
or liberty, Move, now
or you will die.

- - -

Listen to me

Way back yonder
down in bondage
on my knee
Th' moment that He gave his promise—
I was free
(Walk, children)

He said that when destruction rages
He *is* a rock—
the Rock of Ages
Declared that when the tempest ride
He just come mosey
straight—
to my side.
(Don't you get weary)

Promised me the desprit hour
be the signal for His power
Hounddogs closin on the track

Sunlight

and the thunderclap!
(How you get weary!)

Bloodhounds quickenin on the scent
Over my head, yesss
the heavens rent!

O He's a father He *is* a mother
A sister He will
   be your brother
Supplies the harvest, He raises up the grain
O don't you feel—it's fallin now
   the blessed rain.

Don't make no diffunce if you weary
Don't mean a hoot owl if you scared
He was with us in the six troubles
He won't desert you in the seventh.

Get on up now

That's it, no need a gettin weary
There is a glory there!

   There be a great rejoicin
      no more sorrow
      shout 'n *nev*vuh tire
      a great camp meetin
         in that land.

By fire in heaven she was guided
saved by stream
   and by water reed
By her terrible grimace of faith
   beautiful and defiant,
Till, for a moment
   in the long journey
   came the first faint glimpse
   of the stars   the everlasting stars   shining clear
   over the free
                  cold
                     land.

Benin Bronze

I gazed at Steppin Fetchit
   the West's poor clown
and, in the ship's hold of his eyes,
   saw the reddened torment of his father,

and his father's father
and his father's father's father
and beyond.

And beyond the do-rag
   and the slicked down hair

the click of dice
and Saturday night
beyond the fix of horse
the cry of rage
the flash of razor
and beyond,

from the shroud of a lost age
the depths of a long night

emerged

once again
the calm and cloudless features
of Benin.

About Poetry and South Africa

A Sequel

In 1928, Langston Hughes published in the *Crisis* an anti-poem:

In the Johannesburg mines
there are 240,000 natives working.
What kind of poem, he asked
would you make out of that?
In the Johannesburg mines
there are 240,000 natives working.

End of poem

it seemed.

- - -

In nineteen hundred and eighty, one half century later,
and Langston Hughes long dead,
the Sunday *Boston Globe* reported:

South African miners average less
than thirty five dollars a week,
laboring in a painful crouch
in waist high tunnels deep in the earth
with temperatures reaching 135 degrees
and more than 600 miners dying each year in rock slides.

What kind of poem would you make out of that?

- - -

The stooped and stunted years themselves
  must wonder
how long still
  still how long
    must Langston wonder
about poetry and South Africa.

Derek Walcott (1930–)

I*n 1992, Derek Walcott won a Nobel Prize for his epic poem* Omeros. *His distinctive story, which transplants Homer's* Odyssey *to the Caribbean, has been described by James P. Draper as "a complex work, both structurally and in its repeated examination of perennial themes in [the body of] Walcott's work—identity, exile, how history [was] suffered and survived, and the obligation of the artist."*

Born on the island of St. Lucia in the West Indies, Walcott was brought up to revere the arts, his parental inspiration complemented by his exposure to English literature in school. Although he originally planned to become a painter, at age eighteen he published his first book of poetry, Twenty-Five Poems *(1948). Since then, he has written some thirty other books of poetry and drama. Walcott's interest in these two literary genres can be traced to his childhood: to his mother's pursuit of teaching and the theater and to his deceased father's creation of poems and paintings.*

Receiving his bachelor's from St. Mary's College in St. Lucia in 1953, Walcott went on to attend the University of the West Indies in Kingston, Jamaica. He later taught at those two academic institutions as well as at various U.S. universities, including Columbia, Harvard, Rutgers, Yale, and Boston.

Walcott has received numerous awards for his writings. In addition to the Nobel Prize, he was awarded a Rockefeller Fellowship (1957); a Heinemann Award from the Royal Society of Literature (1966); a Eugene O'Neill Foundation–Wesleyan University Fellowship (1969); an Obie Award (1971); a MacArthur Foundation grant (1981); and a Los Angeles Times Book Review *Prize in Poetry (1986).*

Questioning the influence of colonial rule on his life, Walcott's dramas nevertheless display an acceptance of the two worlds of black folkways and British customs. His plays include Henri Christophe: A Chronicle in Seven Scenes *(1950),* The Sea at Dauphin: A Play in One Act *(1953),* Dream on Monkey Mountain *(1967),* The Charlatan *(1974), and* Three Plays *(1986).*

Walcott's poetry contains the same rich language and layered meanings found in his plays, though some critics argue that his verse is more effective than his drama in giving voice to intercultural themes. In addition to Twenty-Five Poems, *Walcott's other volumes of poetry include* In a Green Night: Poems, 1948–1960 *(1962),* Selected Poems *(1964),* The Castaway and Other Poems *(1965),* The Gulf and Other Poems *(1969),* Sea Grapes *(1976),* The Star-Apple Kingdom *(1979),* Fortune Traveller *(1981),* The Arkansas Testament *(1987),* Collected Poems, 1948–1984 *(1986),* Midsummer *(1984), and* Selected Poems *(1993).*

The three poems reprinted here exemplify Walcott's ease in weaving together language that elicits both an intellectual and an emotional response. In "Storm Figure" and "Elsewhere," which first appeared in The Arkansas Testament, *and "Blues," from* The Gulf and Other Poems, *Walcott's diction is provocative and enigmatic, requiring several readings to uncover his central themes and meanings.*

Storm Figure

The nineteenth century, like a hurricane lamp,
haloed, last night, the boards of the kitchen table.
With the lamp poles down, its wick smoke pined and flamed,
singeing the mind's ceiling like a Hardy novel.

Barefoot on the cold grass outside the beach house,
you see fresh channels furrowing the beach's dreck,
then a far, smoky figure where brown shallows
roll fallen trunks like bodies from a shipwreck.

The wrong time. The wrong ground. The Wessex coast
is in another century. The lamp's eye of flame
at its barred window, throughout the storm's harvest,
was once Fidelity. She has changed her name.

The shallow's mutterings suit her
thunder-gone waiting, clouds blowing in smoky scraps,
breakers that chuff; long, leaden swells of pewter,
the pier piles crumbling, mosses gripped by crabs.

Drop by slow drop each branch loses its pearls,
surf drags soiled petticoats through the beach's muck,
ice fetters her ankles fording the new rock pools,
sheet spray obscures her, but she is its watermark;

Current returns. Lights dot the wrecked roads.
To the morse of crickets this century takes shape.
The more you walk, the farther she recedes,
a figurehead fluttering without a ship.

Now sunshine with its mullioned mackerel dances
over lamp and novel by the double bed,
rippling the oval where her drowned face glances
till the circle of one century has settled.

On drying scarps, with loops of tidal grass,
her shadow fades into the clouding sand;
surf lifts its hem to let a low seagull pass
arrowing in silence, which is the soul's sound.

Elsewhere

for Stephen Spender

Somewhere a white horse gallops with its mane
plunging round a field whose sticks
are ringed with barbed wire, and men
break stones or bind straw into ricks.

Somewhere women tire of the shawled sea's
weeping, for the fishermen's dories
still go out. It is blue as peace.
Somewhere they're tired of torture stories.

That somewhere there was an arrest.
Somewhere there was a small harvest
of bodies in the truck. Soldiers rest
somewhere by a road, or smoke in a forest.

Somewhere there is the conference rage
at an outrage. Somewhere a page
is torn out, and somehow the foliage
no longer looks like leaves but camouflage.

Somewhere there is a comrade,
a writer lying with his eyes wide open
on mattress ticking, who will not read
this, or write. How to make a pen?

And here we are free for a while, but
elsewhere, in one-third, or one-seventh
of this planet, a summary rifle butt
breaks a skull into the idea of a heaven

where nothing is free, where blue air
is paper-frail, and whatever we write
will be stamped twice, a blue letter,
its throat slit by the paper knife of the state.

Through these black bars
hollowed faces stare. Fingers
grip the cross bars of these stanzas
and it is here, because of somewhere else

their stares fog into oblivion
thinly, like the faceless numbers
that bewilder you in your telephone
diary. Like last year's massacres.

The world is blameless. The darker crime
is to make a career of conscience,
to feel through our own nerves the silent scream
of winter branches, wonders read as signs.

Blues

Those five or six young guys
hunched on the stoop
that oven-hot summer night
whistled me over. Nice
and friendly. So, I stop.
MacDougal or Christopher
Street in chains of light.

A summer festival. Or some
saint's. I wasn't too far from
home, but not too bright
for a nigger, and not too dark.
I figured we were all
one, wop, nigger, jew,
besides, this wasn't Central Park.
I'm coming on too strong? You figure
right! They beat this yellow nigger
black and blue.

Yeah. During all this, scared
in case one used a knife,
I hung my olive-green, just bought
sports coat on a fire-plug.
I did nothing. They fought
each other, really. Life
gives them a few kicks,
that's all. The spades, the spicks.

My face smashed in, my bloody mug
pouring, my olive-branch jacket saved
from cuts and tears,
I crawled four flights upstairs.
Sprawled in the gutter, I
remember a few watchers waved
loudly, and one kid's mother shouting
like 'Jackie' or 'Terry'
'Now that's enough!'
It's nothing really.
They don't get enough love.

You know they wouldn't kill
you. Just playing rough,

like young America will.
Still, it taught me something
about love. If it's so tough,
forget it.

Etheridge Knight (1931–91)

B*orn in Corinth, Mississippi, Etheridge Knight managed to overcome failure and addiction to win both popular and critical admiration.*

Dropping out of school in the eighth grade, Knight obtained his education in bars, in poolrooms, and on street corners before entering the army at age sixteen. He received a shrapnel wound in the Korean War, and, tragically, the treatment for his wound sent him drifting into the use of narcotics. By 1960, Knight was a criminal supporting a demanding drug addiction. Found guilty of armed robbery, he served nine years in Indiana State Prison.

Knight's street education, his army experiences, his drug addiction, and his years behind bars came together to shape his writing, a pursuit he chose in prison as a survival strategy. But beyond self-preservation, Knight found that poetry gave him emotional release as well as a means to communicate with the outside world. In 1963, he began sending off his poetry for publication, while also keeping a prison notebook where he prophesied, "I will write. I will be a famous writer. . . . My voice will be heard and I will help my people."

Poems from Prison *(1968), Knight's first book of poetry, was published by Broadside Press while he was still in jail. Printed during the time of Black Power politics, Knight's book came to be viewed as one of the important literary works of the new Black Arts Movement.* *(See Larry Neal's essay on the movement in Part Six, p. 925.)*

Between 1969 and 1972, following his parole, Knight's literary career and personal life developed in promising directions, even while he continued to struggle against his drug addiction. He became writer-in-residence at the University of Pittsburgh, the University of Hartford, and Lincoln University. He received a National Endowment for the Arts grant in 1972 and a Guggenheim Fellowship in 1974. He married poet Sonia Sanchez, though that marriage eventually dissolved; he married a second time and had two children.

Knight's second book of poetry, Belly Song and Other Poems *(1973), was nominated for a Pulitzer Prize and a National Book Award.* Born of a Woman: New and Selected Poems *(1980), his third volume, was heralded as Knight's best artistic work. His final collection,* The Essential Etheridge Knight, *was published in 1986.*

Three poems are reprinted here. "For Freckled-Faced Gerald," originally written in 1968, appeared in the 1980 volume. "Dark Prophecy: I Sing of Shine" and "For Black Poets Who Think of Suicide" are from the 1973 volume. Significantly, "Dark Prophecy" is Knight's version of a street corner "toast," an oral narrative charged with sexuality, violence, and scatological language.

For Freckle-Faced Gerald

Now you take ol Rufus. He beat drums,
was free and funky under the arms,
fucked white girls, jumped off a bridge,

(and thought nothing of the sacrilege),
he copped out—and he was over twenty-one.

Take Gerald. Sixteen years hadn't even done
a good job on his voice. He didn't even know
how to talk tough, or how to hide a glow
of life before he was thrown in as "pigmeat"
for the buzzards to eat.

Gerald, who had no memory or hope of copper hot lips—
of firm upthrusting thighs
to reinforce his flow,
let tall walls and buzzards change the course
of his river from south to north.

(No safety in numbers, like back on the block:
two's aplenty. three? definitely not.
four? "you're all muslims."
five? "you were planning a race riot."
plus, Gerald could never quite win
with his precise speech and innocent grin
the trust and fists of the young black cats).

Gerald, sun-kissed ten thousand times on the nose
and cheeks, didn't stand a chance,
didn't even know that the loss of his balls
had been plotted years in advance
by wiser and bigger buzzards than those
who now hover above his track
and at night light upon his back.

Dark Prophecy: I Sing of Shine

And, yeah, brothers,
while white / america sings about the unsink-
able molly brown
(who was hustling the titanic
when it went down)
I sing to thee of Shine
the stoker who was hip enough to flee the fucking ship
and let the white folks drown
with screams on their lips
(jumped his black ass into the dark sea, Shine did,
broke free from the straining steel).
Yeah, I sing to thee of Shine
and how the millionaire banker stood on the deck
and pulled from his pockets a million dollar check
saying Shine Shine save poor me

and I'll give you all the money a black boy needs—
how Shine looked at the money and then at the sea
and said jump in mothafucka and swim like me—
And Shine swam on—Shine swam on—
and how the banker's daughter ran naked on the deck
with her pink tits trembling and her pants roun her neck
screaming Shine Shine save poor me
and I'll give you all the pussy a black boy needs—
how Shine said now pussy is good and that's no jive
but you got to swim not fuck to stay alive—
And Shine swam on Shine swam on—

How Shine swam past a preacher afloating on a board
crying save *me* nigger Shine in the name of the Lord—
and how the preacher grabbed Shine's arm and broke his stroke—
how Shine pulled his shank and cut the preacher's throat—
And Shine swam on—Shine swam on—
And when the news hit shore that the titanic had sunk
Shine was up in Harlem damn near drunk

For Black Poets Who Think of Suicide

Black Poets should live—not leap
From steel bridges (like the white boys do).
Black Poets should live—not lay
Their necks on railroad tracks (like the white boys do).
Black Poets should seek—but not search too much
In sweet dark caves, nor hunt for snipe
Down psychic trails (like the white boys do).

For Black Poets belong to Black People. Are
The Flutes of Black Lovers. Are
The Organs of Black Sorrows. Are
The Trumpets of Black Warriors.
Let All Black Poets die as Trumpets,
And be buried in the dust of marching feet.

Sonia Sanchez (1934–)

A *poet, activist, and professor, Sonia Sanchez has written thirteen books, has served as a contributing editor to* Black Scholar *and the* Journal of African Studies, *has lectured at over five hundred U.S. universities and colleges, and has given poetry readings to audiences across the world. She states, "I write to tell the truth about the Black condition as I see it. . . . The most fundamental truth to be told in any art form, as far as Blacks are concerned, is that America is killing us. But we continue to live and love and struggle and win."*

Born in Birmingham, Alabama, Sanchez received a bachelor's from Hunter College in 1955. She has taught at San Francisco State College, the University of Pittsburgh, Rutgers University, and Amherst College. The first presidential fellow at Temple University, she currently holds the Laura Carnell chair in English at that institution. During the 1970s, she was married to poet Etheridge Knight, a union that ended in divorce.

Sanchez came to prominence as a revolutionary black writer in the late 1960s, heightening the racial consciousness of fellow artists and black readers. Voicing the concerns, attitudes, and intentions of all African Americans but particularly women, Sanchez put the tenets of the Black Aesthetic into practice in her poetry, at the same time demonstrating her unique talent.

In addition to taking poetry and stage drama to a level where the polemical and artistic meet, Sanchez is recognized for her ongoing efforts in initiating black studies courses and programs. While stressing the needs of the black community, she pushes for recognition of the connections among curriculum, self-pride and liberation, and intercultural exchange.

Sanchez has received a host of awards, including the National Endowment for the Arts award, a Community Service Award from the National Black Caucus of State Legislators, a Peace and Freedom Award from the Women's International League for Peace and Freedom, and an American Book Award for homegirls and hand grenades *(1985). Her numerous other books of poetry include* Homecoming *(1969),* We a BaddDDD People *(1970),* It's a New Day *(1971),* Love Poems *(1973),* I've Been a Woman *(1981),* Under a Soprano Sky *(1987), and* Autumn Blues *(1992). The writer of a half-dozen plays as well as short fiction, Sanchez has edited two anthologies—*Three Hundred and Sixty Degrees of Blackness Comin' at You *(1971), a poetry collection, and* We Be Word Sorcerers: Twenty-Five Stories by Black Americans *(1973).*

The first two poems reprinted here, "Blk/Rhetoric" and "Summer Words of a Sistuh Addict," exhibit the themes and style characteristic of Sanchez's work in the late 1960s. The poem "elegy," from the 1987 volume, has more conventional spelling and syntax while maintaining the poet's ongoing political concerns.

Blk/Rhetoric

for Killebrew Keeby, Icewater, Baker, Gary Adams and Omar Shabazz

who's gonna make all
this beautiful blk/rhetoric
mean something.
like
i mean
who's gonna take
the words
blk/is/beautiful
and make more of it
than blk/capitalism.
u dig?
i mean
like who's gonna

take all the young/long/haired
natural/brothers and sisters
and let them
grow till
all that is
impt is them
selves
moving in straight/
revolutionary/lines
toward the enemy
(and we know who that is)
like. man.
who's gonna give our young
blk/people new heroes
(instead of catch/phrases)
(instead of cad/ill/acs)
(instead of pimps)
(instead of wite/whores)
(instead of drugs)
(instead of new dances)
(instead of chit/ter/lings)
(instead of a 35¢ bottle of ripple)
(instead of quick/fucks in the hall/way
of wite/america's mind)
like. this. is an SOS
me. calling . . .
calling . . .
some/one
pleasereplysoon.

Summer Words of a Sistuh Addict

the first day i shot dope
was on a sunday.
i had just come
home from church
got mad at my motha
cuz she got mad at me. u dig?
went out. shot up
behind a feelen against her.
it felt good.
gooder than dooing it. yeah.
it was nice.
i did it. uh huh. i did it. uh. huh.
i want to do it again. it felt so goooood.
and as the sistuh
sits in her silent/
remembered/high

someone leans for
ward gently asks her:
sistuh.
did u
finally
learn how to hold yo/mother?
and the music of the day
drifts in the room
to mingle with the sistuh's young tears.
and we all sing.

elegy

for MOVE and Philadelphia*

1.

philadelphia
a disguised southern city
squatting in the eastern pass of
colleges cathedrals and cowboys.
philadelphia. a phalanx of parsons
and auctioneers
modern gladiators
erasing the delirium of death from their shields
while houses burn out of control.

2.

c'mon girl hurry on down to osage st
they're roasting in the fire
smell the dreadlocks and blk/skins
roasting in the fire.

c'mon newsmen and tvmen
hurryondown to osage st and
when you have chloroformed the city
and after you have stitched up your words
hurry on downtown for sanctuary
in taverns and corporations

and the blood is not yet dry.

3.

how does one scream in thunder?

---

* MOVE: a Philadelphia based back to nature group whose headquarters was bombed by the police on May 13, 1985, killing men, women and children. An entire city block was destroyed by fire.

4.

they are combing the morning for shadows
and screams tongue-tied without faces
look. over there. one eye
escaping from its skin
and our heartbeats slowdown to a drawl
and the kingfisher calls out from his downtown capital
And the pinstriped general reenlists
his tongue for combat
and the police come like twin seasons of drought and flood.
they're combing the city for lifeliberty and
the pursuit of happiness.

5.

how does one city scream in thunder?

6.

hide us O lord
deliver us from our nakedness.
exile us from our laughter
give us this day our rest from seduction
peeling us down to our veins.

and the tower was like no other. amen.
and the streets escaped under the
cover of darkness amen.
and the voices called out from
their wounds amen.
and the fire circumsized the city amen.

7.

who anointeth this city with napalm? (i say)
who giveth this city in holy infanticide?

8.

beyond the mornings and afternoons
and deaths detonating the city.
beyond the tourist roadhouses
trading in lobotomies
there is a glimpse of earth
this prodigal earth.
beyond edicts and commandments
commissioned by puritans
there are people
navigating the breath of hurricanes.
beyond concerts and football

and mummers strutting their
sequined processionals.
there is this earth. this country. this city.
this people.
collecting skeletons from waiting rooms
lying in wait. for honor and peace.
one day.

Henry Dumas (1934–68)

A *poet and fiction writer, Henry Dumas was shot and killed by a police officer in 1968, in a case of mistaken identity on a Harlem train station platform. Dumas's short life gave him numerous experiences that fed his writing. Only thirty-four when he died, he left a legacy of posthumous works that are still being celebrated. His writings have been characterized by editor Linda Metzger as displaying "a rhythmic kind of language that [is] both basic and very complex. His rhythms [come] from gospel music, mystification, the Deep South and the streets, and his words [speak] pure truth."*

Dumas came to Harlem at age ten, from his birthplace of Sweet Home, Arkansas. Attending New York City public schools and entering City College, he truncated his studies to enter the air force in 1953, serving for four years. Dumas then attended Rutgers University, first full-time and later part-time, leaving in 1965 without completing his degree. As a part-time student, he supported himself as a printing machine operator for IBM, worked with the civil rights movement, and wrote during his free time. On occasion, he traveled to Mississippi and Tennessee to deliver clothing and goods to people living in the poverty of tent cities.

Dumas's primary literary activity during the 1950s and early 1960s involved editing "little" magazines such as Anthologist *and* Hiram Poetry Review. *Significantly, his positions as teacher/counselor and director of language workshops for the University of Illinois paved the way for the posthumous publication of his poetry and fiction. Dumas also taught at Southern Illinois University, where, following the urging and editing of fellow poet Eugene B. Redmond, the university press agreed to publish Dumas's works.*

His first volume of poetry, initially published as Poetry of My People *in 1970, was republished by Random House as* Play Ebony, Play Ivory *in 1974.* Knees of a Natural Man: The Selected Poetry of Henry Dumas *appeared in 1989. Dumas's short fiction is collected in two volumes:* Ark of Bones and Other Stories *(1970) and* Rope of Wind and Other Stories *(1979). His unfinished novel,* Jonoah and the Green Stone, *was released in 1976. These works were all edited by Redmond.*

As critic Carolyn Mitchell notes, "Dumas's poetry falls into roughly four categories: revolutionary poems . . . nature poetry . . . the blues . . . and poems that are akin to parables and aphorisms through which lessons are taught."

The two poems that follow are from Play Ebony, Play Ivory. *The first poem, in parable fashion, examines the tensions within the hyphenated identity of "Afro-American" through two metaphorical mothers, one black and the other white, who raise the same black child but toward different ends. With a revolutionary tone in "Black Star Line" whose title echoes the name of Marcus Garvey's back-*

to-Africa ships, Dumas meditates on the spiritual and historical connections between blacks in Africa and blacks in the new world.

Afro-American

my black mother birthed me
        my white mother girthed me
my black mother suckled me
        my white mother sucked me in
my black mother sang to me
        my white mother sanctified me
        she crucified me

my black mother is a fine beautiful thang
she bathed me and died for me
she stitched me together, took me into her
bosom and mixed her tears with mine
little black baby i was wretched
a shadow without a body, fatherless, sunless
my black mother shook sweet songs and sweat
all over me and her sugar and her salt saved me

        my white mother is a whore
        with the holy white plague
        a hollow cross between Martha and Mary
        she looked at me and screamed bastard!
        she left me light of body and of mind
        she took what my black mother gave me
        and left me half blind

bone is my black mother
ivory stone
strength is my black mother
my ancient skeletal home
force is my black mother
she maintains and transforms

my black mother is a long-limbed sensuous river
where the Kongo flows into the Mississippi she
is coming where my father's blood rises in jets
and like rain, glows, transformed red, tan, black
I am growing in the bosom and in the loins
of America
born and knitted in the soil, when I finish growing
you can pick me up as you would a rare and fabulous
seed and you can
blow Africa
on me as you would a holy reed.

Black Star Line

My black mothers I hear them singing.

Sons, my sons,
dip into this river with your ebony cups
A vessel of knowledge sails under power.
Study stars as well as currents.
Dip into this river with your ebony cups.

My black fathers I hear them chanting.

My Sons, my sons,
let ebony strike the blow that launches the ship!
Send cargoes and warriors back to sea.
Remember the pirates and their chains of nails.
Let ebony strike the blow that launches this ship.
Make your heads not idle sails, blown about
by any icy wind like a torn page from a book.
Bones of my bones,
all you golden-black children of the sun,
lift up! and read the sky
written in the tongue of your ancestors.
It is yours, claim it,
Make no idle sails, my sons,
make heavy-boned ships that break a wave and pass it.
Bring back sagas from Songhay, Kongo, Kaaba,
deeds and words of Malik, Toussaint, Marcus,
statues of Mahdi and a lance of lightning.
Make no idle ships.
Remember the pirates.
For it is the sea who owns the pirates,
not the pirates the sea.

My black mothers I hear them singing.

Children of my flesh,
dip into this river with your ebony cups.
A ship of knowledge sails unto wisdom.
Study what mars and what lifts up.
Dip into this river with your ebony cups.

Jay Wright (c. 1934–)

Jay Wright's poetry unites numerous ethnic visions, ideologies, and musical forms. As one critic Vera Kutzinski aptly notes, "the most distinctive feature of . . . Wright's poetry is what he himself calls 'a passion for what is hidden.' This passion for sounding the depths of varied histories and mythologies—West European, African, Caribbean, North and South American, and Asian—takes the poetic shape of a spiritual quest that is at once intensely personal and compellingly collective."

Born in Albuquerque, New Mexico, of Cherokee, Irish, and African heritage, Wright was raised by black guardians with a strong religious background. As an adolescent, he lived with his birth father in San Pedro, California, where his talent for baseball led to a few years as a minor league catcher.

During the mid-1950s, Wright served briefly overseas in the army, returning to California to earn a bachelor's in Comparative Literature at the University of California–Berkeley. He later received a Rockefeller grant to study religion at Union Theological Seminary in New York. Wright attended Rutgers University in 1962 as a graduate student in literature, left for two years to teach English and Medieval History in Guadalajara, Mexico, and then returned to Rutgers, receiving a master's degree in 1966. Rather than complete his doctoral studies, however, Wright opted to go to Harlem, where he could spend time with other black writers and intellectuals of the late 1960s, including Larry Neal, Amiri Baraka, and Henry Dumas. Since then he has traveled extensively, living abroad from time to time. Wright has been a writer-in-residence and taught at various institutions, including Texas Southern University, Princeton University, the University of North Carolina, Yale University, and Dartmouth College.

Wright's critical acclaim as a poet has eclipsed his popularity. He was awarded an Ingram Merrill Foundation Award (1974), a Guggenheim Fellowship (1974), an American Academy and Institute of Arts and Letters Literature Award (1981), a Derwood Writing Award (1985), and a MacArthur Fellowship (1986). His poetry appears in several collections published between the 1960s and 1990s: Death as History *(1967),* The Homecoming Singer *(1971),* Soothsayers and Omens *(1976),* Dimensions of History *(1976),* The Double Invention of Komo *(1980),* Explications *(1984),* Selected Poems of Jay Wright *(1987),* Elaine's Book *(1988), and* Boleros *(1991). He also wrote a one-act play,* Balloons, *published in 1968.*

The three poems reprinted here display Wright's poetic talents. In "The Appearance of a Lost Goddess," which originally appeared in Dimensions of History, *a persona travels to the water's edge to discover Eshu, an ancient goddess of black Africa who has been "neglected." "Journey to the Place of Ghosts," from* Elaine's Book, *explores the odyssey from the life of the flesh to the awakening of the soul after death, a natural communion of two worlds. In "Benjamin Banneker Helps to Build a City," also from* Dimensions, *Wright uses free verse extensively as he connects the historic black mathematician named in the title* *(see Benjamin Banneker in Part Five, page 706),* *to Amma and Nommo, ancient gods of the Dogon civilization of west Africa.*

The Appearance of a Lost Goddess

I have taken
this self-appointed priest
into my confidence.
Garbed like the very moon,
he leads me to the edge
of this water
where we cast for all
my lost connections.
Something, not my own.
has been riding me

without my consent.
But tonight, I am ready
to pay with my life
to see the shape of my own queens,
dancing here in the colors
of the moon and the water.
In the full light.
I see the first approach
—not the favorite,
but the mean one
who lies tangled at the bottom
of the water in her own hair.
Often now at night,
Eshu, capped like a sailor,
commandeers a boat,
and pushes out to stir the water.
The favored one,
in the garb of the moon herself,
grapples with the boat,
and the water foams
and disguises the rising
of the woman,
who comes raging from below,
until we cannot tell from which realm
she has appeared,
cannot tell if we should love,
or fear, her.
This one we cannot tell
may be the mother of all our gods,
casting off the weight of the water,
coming toward us with curses,
unable to forgive our neglect.
Here, at the water,
I have become the last initiate,
unable to put together the right form,
or to abide this goddess' curses.

Journey to the Place of Ghosts

Wölbe dich, Welt:
Wenn die Totenmuschel heranschwimmt,
will es hier läuten.

Vault over, world:
when the seashell of death washes up
there will be a knelling.

—Paul Celan, *Stimmen* (Voices)

Death knocks all night at my door.
The soul answers,

and runs from the water in my throat.
Water will sustain me when I climb
the steep hill
that leads to a now familiar place.
I began, even as a child, to learn water's order,
and, as I grew intact, the feel of its warmth
in a new sponge, of its weight in a virgin towel.
I have earned my wine in another's misery,
when rum bathed a sealed throat
and cast its seal on the ground.
I will be bound, to the one who leads me away,
by the ornaments on my wrists, the gold dust
in my ears, below my eye and tied to my
loin cloth in a leather pouch.
They dress me now in my best cloth,
and fold my hands, adorned with silk,
against my left cheek.
Gold lies with me on my left side.
Gold has become the color of distance,
and of your sorrow.

Sorrow lies, red clay on my brow.
Red pepper caresses my temples.
I am adorned in the russet-brown message
the soul brings from its coming-to-be.
There is a silken despair in my body
that grief shakes from it,
a cat's voice, controlled by palm-wine
and a widow's passion.
It is time to feed the soul
—a hen, eggs, mashed yams—
and encourage the thirst resting
near the right hand I see before me.
Always I think of death.
I cannot eat.
I walk in sadness, and I die.
Yet life is the invocation sealed in the coffin,
and will walk through our wall,
passing and passing and passing,
until it is set down,
to be lifted from this body's habitation.
I now assume the widow's pot,
the lamp that will lead me through solitude,
to the edge of my husband's journey.
I hold three stones upon my head,
darkness I will release when I run
from the dead,
with my eyes turned away
toward another light.

This is the day of rising.
A hut sits in the bush, sheltered by summe,
standing on four forked ends.
We have prepared for the soul's feast
with pestle, mortar, a strainer, three
hearthstones, a new pot and new spoon.
Someone has stripped the hut's body
and dressed it with the edowa.
Now, when the wine speaks
and the fire has lifted its voice,
the dead will be clothed in hair,
                        the signs of our grief.
Sun closes down on an intensity of ghosts.
It is time to close the path.
It is time for the snail's pace
of coming again into life,
                with the world swept clean,
                the crying done,
and our ordinary garments decent in the dead one's eyes.

Benjamin Banneker Helps to Build a City

In a morning coat,
hands locked behind your back,
you walk gravely along the lines in your head.
These others stand with you,
squinting the city into place,
yet cannot see what you see,
what you would see
—a vision of these paths,
laid out like a star,
or like a body,
the seed vibrating within itself,
breaking into the open,
dancing up to stop at the end of the universe.
I say your vision goes as far as this,
the egg of the world,
where everything remains, and moves,
holding what is most against it against itself,
moving as though it knew its end, against death.
In that order,
the smallest life, the small event take shape.
Yes, even here at this point,
Amma's plan consumes you,
the prefigured man, Nommo, the son of God.
I call you into this time,
back to that spot,
and read these prefigurations

into your mind,
and know it could not be strange to you
to stand in the dark and emptiness
of a city not your vision alone.

Now, I have searched the texts
and forms of cities that burned,
that decayed, or gave their children away,
have been picking at my skin,
watching my hand move,
feeling the weight and shuttle of my body,
listening with an ear as large as God's
to catch some familiar tone in my voice.
Now, I am here in your city,
trying to find that spot
where the vibration starts.
There must be some mistake.

Over the earth,
in an open space
you and I step to the time
of another ceremony.
These people, changed,
but still ours,
shake another myth
from that egg.
Some will tell you
that beginnings are only
possible here,
that only the clamor of these drums
could bring our God to earth.
A city, like a life,
must be made in purity.

So they call you,
knowing you are intimate with stars,
to create this city, this body.
So they call you,
knowing you must purge the ground.
"Sir, suffer me to recall to your mind that time,
in which the arms and tyranny of the British crown
were exerted, with every powerful effort, in order
to reduce you to a state of servitude: look back,
I entreat you, on the variety of dangers to which
you were exposed; reflect on that time, in which
every human aid appeared unavailable, and in which
even hope and fortitude wore the aspect of inability
to the conflict, and you cannot but be led to a serious
and grateful sense of your miraculous and providential

preservation; you cannot but acknowledge, that the present
freedom and tranquility which you enjoy you have mercifully
received, and that it is the peculiar blessing of Heaven."

"Reflect on that time."
The spirits move, even
in the events of men,
hidden in a language
that cannot hide it.
You were never lost
in the language of number alone:
you were never lost
to the seed vibrating alone,
holding all contradictions within it.
"Look back, I entreat you,"
over your own painful escapes.

The seed now vibrates into a city,
and a man now walks where you walked.
Wind and rain must assault him,
and a man must build against them.
We know now, too, that the house
must take the form of a man
—warmth at his head, movement at his feet,
his needs and his shrine at his hands.
Image of shelter, image of man,
pulled back into himself,
into the seed before the movement,
into the silence before the sound
of movement, into stillness,
which may be self-regard,
or only stillness.

Recall number.
Recall your calculations,
your sight, at night,
into the secrets of stars.
But still you must exorcise this ground.
"Here was a time, in which your tender feelings
for yourselves had engaged you thus to declare,
you were then impressed with proper ideas of the
great violation of liberty, and the free possession
of those blessings, to which you were entitled by nature;
but, Sir, how pitiable it is to reflect, that although
you were so fully convinced of the Father of Mankind,
and of his equal and impartial distribution of these
rights and privileges, which he hath conferred upon
them, that you should at the same time counteract his
mercies, in detaining by fraud and violence so numerous

a part of my brethren, under groaning captivity,
and cruel oppression, that you should at the same time
be found guilty of that most criminal act, which you
professedly detested in others, with respect to yourselves."
Can we say now
that it is the god
who chains us to this place?
Is it this god
who requires the movement,
the absence of movement,
the prefiguration of movement
only under his control?
If so,
what then is the reason
for these dancers,
these invocations,
the sight of these lesser gods
lining out the land?
How pitiable it is to reflect
upon that god, without grace,
without the sense of that small
beginning movement
where even the god
becomes another and not himself,
himself and not another.
So they must call you,
knowing you are intimate with stars;
so they must call you,
knowing different resolutions.
You sit in contemplation,
moving from line to line,
struggling for a city
free of that criminal act,
free of anything but the small,
imperceptible act, which itself becomes free.
Free. Free. How will the lines fall
into that configuration?
How will you clear this uneasiness,
posting your calculations and forecasts
into a world you yourself cannot enter?
Uneasy, at night,
you follow stars and lines to their limits,
sure of yourself, sure of the harmony
of everything, and yet you moan
for the lost harmony, the crack in the universe.
Your twin, I search it out,
and call you back:
your twin, I invoke
the descent of Nommo.

I say your vision goes as far as this.
And so you, Benjamin Banneker,
walk gravely along these lines,
the city a star, a body,
the seed vibrating within you,
and vibrating still,
beyond your power,
beyond mine.

Haki R. Madhubuti (1942–)

In 1973, Don L. Lee changed his birthname to Haki R. Madhubuti, a Swahili name that can be translated as "justice, awakening, strong." The name change marked the poet's assertion of his Afrocentric identity as he explains in the introduction to his first book of poems: "I was born into slavery in February of 1942. . . . Black. Poet. Black poet am I. This should leave little doubt in the minds of anyone as to which is first. Black art is created from black forces that live within the body. . . . Direct and meaningful contact with black people will act as [an] energizer for black forces. Black art will elevate and enlighten our people and lead them toward an awareness of self, i.e. their blackness."

Madhubuti's odyssey toward black awareness began in his birthplace of Little Rock, Arkansas, and then shifted to Detroit, where he assumed responsibility for an alcoholic mother, who died when he was sixteen. After finishing high school and living with an aunt in Chicago, he joined the army. While there he began to read extensively and found himself interacting closely with whites for the first time.

From the army, Madhubuti went on to Chicago City College in 1966 and Roosevelt University in Chicago, obtaining a masters of fine arts degree from the University of Iowa in 1984. During his college years, the poet took on an array of jobs to support himself while he wrote: he was employed as an apprentice curator at Chicago's Du Sable Museum of African History, a stock clerk for a department store, and a junior executive for Spiegel's. However, after his first two books of poetry brought him popular and critical attention in the late 1960s, he dedicated himself to writing, teaching, and publishing.

Madhubuti has been a writer-in-residence at Cornell University, the University of Illinois–Chicago, Morgan State College, Howard University, and Central State University in Ohio. Admired as a publisher and editor, he established Third World Press and was the founding editor of Black Books Bulletin, *an important source for critical evaluations of literary works by black authors. In 1969, he founded the Institute of Black American Culture, a collaborative effort by numerous African American writers to structure creative and intellectual settings that would promote black writing.*

Serving as a foundation for his academic and publishing endeavors, Madhubuti's writings include poetry as well as scholarly essays. In assessments of his poetry, some critics find fault with his insistent and unchanging theme of black assertiveness. Yet his intense commitment to that theme embodied in his verse, and his recitation of it, has garnered him a popularity that has been sustained in over a dozen books of poetry and essays.

His poetry is collected in several volumes: Think Black *(1967),* Black Pride

(1968), For Black People (and Negroes Too) *(1968),* Don't Cry, Scream *(1969),* We Walk the Way of the New World *(1970),* Directionscore: Selected and New Poems *(1971),* Kwanzaa *(1972),* Book of Life *(1973),* Earthquakes and Sunrise Missions: Poetry and Essays of Black Renewal, 1973–1983 *(1984), and* Killing Memory, Seeking Ancestors *(1987). Madhubuti's prose writings focus on literary and cultural criticism, exploring the political and psychological dynamics of various art forms, institutions, and issues. Among many other such writings, he has published* Dynamite Voices I: Black Poets of the 1960s *(1971),* Say That the River Turns: The Impact of Gwendolyn Brooks *(1987), and* Why L.A. Happened: Implications on the '92 Los Angeles Rebellion *(1993).*

Of the three poems that appear here, "But He Was Cool," belongs to the poet's Don L. Lee years, when staccato rhythms, street language, raw energy, and an exhorting tone were characteristic elements of his style. The other two poems, "Womenblack: We Begin with You" and "Black Manhood: Toward a Definition," both from Earthquakes and Sunrise Missions, *Madhubuti's language is more prosaic and textured and his tone more pensive.*

But He Was Cool

or: he even stopped for green lights

super-cool
ultrablack
a tan/purple
had a beautiful shade.

he had a double-natural
that wd put the sisters to shame.
his dashikis were tailor made
& his beads were imported sea shells
   (from some blk/country i never heard of)
he was triple-hip.

his tikis were hand carved
out of ivory
& came express from the motherland.
he would greet u in swahili
& say good-by in yoruba.
woooooooooooo-jim he bes so cool & ill tel li gent
                              cool-cool is so cool he was un-cooled by
                                 other niggers' cool
                              cool-cool ultracool was bop-cool/ice box
                                 cool so cool cold cool
                              his wine didn't have to be cooled, him was
                                 air conditioned cool
                              cool-cool/real cool made me cool—now
                                 ain't that cool
                              cool-cool so cool him nick-named refrigerator.

cool-cool so cool
he didn't know,
after detroit, newark, chicago &c.,
we had to hip
                cool-cool/ super-cool/ real cool
  that
to be black
is
to be
very-hot.

Womenblack: We Begin with You

for Safisha

our women we begin with you
black, beige, brown, yellowblack and
darkearth we dropped from your womb
in joyscreams lifegiver
you're worlds apart from the rest.

our women
imagine a warm breeze in any city
in the west that will not choke you,
be wife, be mother, a worker or professional
maker you still my lady.
our women
of fruits & vegetables
of greens & color   of sounds & pot holes
of mountains & earth clearing danger   from
doorways who did not ruin their teeth & bodies
with the blood of pigs & cattle or fried chicken
after stumppin at bob's place til five in the daylight.
partyin was almost like a job
in motion on the run we are the rhythm people.

womenblack
unusual maker you say,
fine as all getout you say,
finer than lemonade in the shade,
we are a part of you maker, woman of
the autumn earth mother of sunlight
& i seldom say "i love you"
love is not our word, love belongs to
soap operas & comic books, is the true
confessions of the pale people from
the winter's cold.
we are the people of motion, move on motion
dance on, summer, summer lady.

womenblack we care about you
a deep & uncontrollable penetrative
care as we listen to our own hearts,
whatever the weather.
you don't have to build a pyramid
in order to be one & you are still my
maker rhythm, rhythm lady.

our women we begin with you
black, beige, brown, yellowblack and
darkearth we dropped from your womb
in joyscreams lifegiver
you're worlds apart from the best.
you are in me & i in you
deep
deep and endless
forever
touch to touch,
end to beginning
until the stars kiss the earth
and
our music will be songs of liberation.

Black Manhood: Toward a Definition

your people first. a quiet strength. the positioning of oneself so that observation comes before reaction, where study is preferred to night life, where emotion is not seen as a weakness. love for self, family, children, and extentions of self is beyond the verbal.

Black manhood. making your life accessible to children in meaningful ways. able to recognize the war we are in & doing anything to take care of family so long as it doesn't harm or negatively affect other Black people. willing to share resources to the maximum, willing to struggle unrelentingly against the evils of this world especially evils that directly threaten the development of our people.

Black manhood. to seek and be that which is just, good and correct. properly positioning oneself in the context of our people. a listener, a student, a historian seeking hidden truths. one who develops leadership qualities and demands the same qualities of those who have been chosen to lead. see material rewards as means toward an end & not an end in themselves. clean-mentally, spiritually & physically.

protector of Black weak. one who respects elders.
practical idealist, questioner of the universe &
spiritually in tune with the best of the universe.
honest & trusting, your word is your connector.

Black manhood. direction giver, husband, sensitive to
Black women's needs and aspirations, realizing that it
is not necessary for them to completely absorb
themselves into us but that nothing separates the
communication between us. a seeker of truth. a
worker of the first order. teacher. example of what
is to be. fighter. a builder with vision. connects land
to liberation. a student of peace & war. statesman
and warrior. one who is able to provide as well as
receive. culturally sound. creative. a motivator &
stimulator of others.

Black manhood. a lover of life and all that is
beautiful. one who is constantly growing and who
learns from mistakes. a challenger of the known and
the unknown. the first to admit that he does not
know as he seeks to find out. able to solicit the
best out of self and others. soft. strong. not afraid
to take the lead. creative father. organized and
organizer. a brother to brothers. a brother to sisters.
understanding. patient. a winner. maintainer of the i
can, i must, i will attitude toward Black struggle
& life. a builder of the necessary. **always** & always in
a process of growth and without a doubt believes that
our values and traditions are not negotiable.

Nikki Giovanni (1943–)

Reflecting on her writing in the early 1980s, Nikki Giovanni said: "I like to think that if truth has any bearing on art, my poetry and prose is art because it's truthful. . . . We live now. As best we can. And we encourage others. We write, because we believe that the human spirit cannot be tamed and should not be trained." Giovanni merges her writing talents with her empathy with and respect for people unable to voice their own concerns and experiences. This poet who once wrote "What 'always is' is not the answer. What never will be must come" has fashioned a distinguished literary career, categorized early on as a black revolutionary poet and now accorded the mainstream accolade of an American writer.

Born in Knoxville, Tennessee, Giovanni graduated from Fisk University in 1967 before continuing her studies at the University of Pennsylvania and Columbia University. She has been awarded honorary doctorates from various academic institutions and has taught at Queens College, Livingston College of Rutgers University, and Virginia Polytechnic.

Early in her writing career, Giovanni was grouped with other young black writers who sought to interpret the radical attitudes of the post–civil rights period.

Claudia Tate assesses Giovanni's development over the years in this way: "Her later work also addresses contemporary issues, but the focus falls instead on human relationships rendered from the vantage point of a mother, a lover, and a woman. Giovanni's language remains startling, energetic, enraged, and loving."

Beginning with the publication of Black Feeling, Black Talk *in 1967, Giovanni went on to write nine other popular books of poetry:* Black Judgment *(1968),* Re:Creation *(1970),* Spin a Soft Black Song: Poems for Children *(1971),* Ego Tripping and Other Poems for Young People *(1973),* The Women and the Men *(1975),* Cotton Candy on a Rainy Day *(1978),* Vacation Time: Poems for Children *(1980),* Those Who Ride the Night Winds *(1983), and* Sacred Cows and Other Edibles *(1988). She has also edited a poetry anthology,* Night Comes Softly: Anthology of Black Female Voices *(1970) and written an autobiography,* Gemini: An Extended Autobiographical Statement on My First Twenty-Five Years of Being a Black Poet *(1971). Giovanni has also published illuminating discussions with two other notable authors,* A Dialogue: James Baldwin and Nikki Giovanni *(1973) and* A Poetic Equation: Conversations between Nikki Giovanni and Margaret Walker *(1974). Her most recent essay collection to date is* Racism 101 *(1994). Considered one of the most revered contemporary authors, her numerous writings and recordings of poetry readings, national awards, civic and community work, and lectures and poetry readings throughout the United States, Africa, and Europe have won Giovanni critical and popular acclaim.*

The four poems reprinted here demonstrate the breadth of Giovanni's tones, themes, and language. The "True Import of Present Dialogue, Black vs. Negro," originally published in Black Judgment, *displays radical, incendiary views of ethnic identity and political action. The more personally reflective "Age" and "Adulthood II," taken from* Cotton Candy, *exhibit the poet's characteristic use of unconventional poetic structure. In "Love: Is a Human Condition" (1983), Giovanni experiments with a prose-like structure and prosaic language to ponder the need for love.*

The True Import of Present Dialogue, Black vs. Negro

for Peppe, who will ultimately judge our efforts

Nigger
Can you kill
Can you kill
Can a nigger kill
Can a nigger kill a honkie
Can a nigger kill the Man
Can you kill nigger
Huh? nigger can you
kill
Do you know how to draw blood
Can you poison
Can you stab-a-Jew
Can you kill huh? nigger
Can you kill
Can you run a protestant down with your

'68 El Dorado
(that's all they're good for anyway)
Can you kill
Can you piss on a blond head
Can you cut it off
Can you kill
A nigger can die
We ain't got to prove we can die
We got to prove we can kill
They sent us to kill
Japan and Africa
We policed europe
Can you kill
Can you kill a white man
Can you kill the nigger
in you
Can you make your nigger mind
die
Can you kill your nigger mind
And free your black hands to
strangle
Can you kill
Can a nigger kill
Can you shoot straight and
Fire for good measure
Can you splatter their brains in the street
Can you kill them
Can you lure them to bed to kill them
We kill in Viet Nam
for them
We kill for UN & NATO & SEATO & US
And everywhere for all alphabet but
BLACK
Can we learn to kill WHITE for BLACK
Learn to kill niggers
Learn to be Black men

Age

we tend to fear old age
as some sort of disorder   that can be cured
with the proper brand of aspirin
or perhaps a bit of Ben Gay for the shoulders
it does   of course   pay to advertise

one hates the idea of the first gray hair
a shortness of breath
devastating blows to the ego

indications we are doing
what comes naturally

it's almost laughable
that we detest aging
when we first become aware
we want it
little girls of four or five push
with eyes shining brightly at gram or mommy
the lie that they are seven or eight
little girls at ten worry
that a friend has gotten her monthly
as she has not
little girls of twelve
can be socially crushed
by lack of nobs on their chests

little boys of fourteen want
to think they want
a woman
the little penis that simply won't erect
is shattering to their idea of manhood
if perhaps they get a little peach fuzz
on their faces they may survive
adolescence proving there may indeed be life
after high school
the children begin to play   older
without knowing the price is   weariness

age teaches us that our virtues
are neither virtuous nor our vices
foul
age doesn't matter   really
what frightens is mortality
it dawns upon us that we can die
at some point it occurs we surely shall

it is not death we fear
but the loss of youth
not the youth of our teens
where most of the thinking took place
somewhere between the navel and the knee
but the youth of our thirties where career
decisions were going well
and we were respected for our abilities
or the youth of our forties
where our decisions proved if not right
then not wrong either
and the house   after all   is half paid

it may simply be that work
is so indelibly tied
to age that the loss
of work brings the depression
of impending death
there are so many   too many
who have never worked
and therefore for whom death
is a constant companion

as lack of marriage
lowers divorce rates
lack of life
prevents death
the unwillingness to try
is worse than any failure

in youth our ignorance gives us courage
with age our courage gives us hope
with hope we learn that man is more
than the sum of what he does
we also are what we wish we did
and age teaches us
that even that doesn't matter

Adulthood II

There is always something
of the child
in us that wants
a strong hand to hold
through the hungry season
of growing up

when she was a child
summer lasted forever
and christmas seemed never
to come
now her bills from easter
usually are paid
by the 4th of july
in time to buy the ribs
and corn and extra bag of potatoes
for salad

the pit is cleaned
and labor day is near
time to tarpaulin
the above ground pool

thanksgiving turkey
is no sooner soup
than the children's shoes
wear thin saying
christmas is near again
bringing the february letters asking
"did you forget
us last month"

her life looks occasionally
as if it's owed to some
machine
and the only winning point
she musters is to tear
mutilate and twist
the cards demanding information
payment
and a review of her credit worthiness

Love: Is a Human Condition

An amoeba is lucky it's so small . . . else its narcissism would lead to war . . . since self-love seems so frequently to lead to self-righteousness . . .

I suppose a case could be made . . . that there are more amoebas than people . . . that they comprise the physical majority . . . and therefore the moral right . . . But luckily amoebas rarely make television appeals to higher Gods . . . and baser instincts . . . so one must ask if the ability to reproduce oneself efficiently has anything to do with love . . .

The night loves the stars as they play about the Darkness . . . the day loves the light caressing the sun . . . We love . . . those who do . . . because we live in a world requiring light and Darkness . . . partnership and solitude . . . sameness and difference . . . the familiar and the unknown . . . We love because it's the only true adventure . . .

I'm glad I'm not an amoeba . . . there must be more to all our lives than ourselves . . . and our ability to do more of the same . . .

Quincy Troupe (1943–)

The integration of musical forms, homages to legendary musicians, and politics have been a distinguishing feature of Quincy Troupe's poetry throughout his thirty years of writing. He expresses his poetic manifesto in this way: "American speech idioms—blues and jazz forms—[are] a viable poetic form. At the base of

American creativity is language . . . [and] what black people can do with the rhythms and the words, and musicians with the sounds coupled with the words is extraordinary. A modest goal is to continue the work of Dunbar, Sterling Brown, Hughes, and James Weldon Johnson and to meld the forms."

Born in New York City and raised in St. Louis, Troupe earned a bachelor's in history and political science from Grambling University in Louisiana in 1963, and an associate of arts in journalism from Los Angeles City College in 1967. Already a published poet by that time, Troupe became involved with creative and community-based organizations in the Los Angeles area, teaching creative writing for the Watts Writers Movement from 1966 to 1968 and functioning as the director of the Malcolm X Center during the summers of 1969 and 1970. He also served as the director of the John Coltrane Summer Festivals in Los Angeles.

Troupe's first collection of poetry, Embryo Poems, 1967–1971 *(1972), was followed by* Snake-Back Solos: Selected Poems, 1969–1977 *(1978), which won an American Book Award. According to the author, the title of that book referred to the Mississippi River* (Snake-Back) *and the "significance of the river in American history and music; and to the praise poems included in the volume for St. Louis poet Eugene Redmond, writer Steve Cannon, and Louis 'Satchmo' Armstrong." Troupe's use of the river as an inspirational symbol is also evident in his third book of poems,* Skulls along the River *(1984).*

*In addition to writing poetry, Troupe has edited two anthologies—*Watts Poets: A Book of New Poetry and Essays *(1968) and with Rainer Schulte* Giant Talk: An Anthology of Third World Writings *(1975). He coauthored, with David L. Wolper, a best-selling work of nonfiction,* The Inside Story of TV's "Roots" *(1978). In 1989, along with the legendary musician Miles Davis, Troupe cowrote* Miles, the Autobiography.

In addition to receiving a number of awards and fellowships for his writing, Troupe has taught creative writing and black literature courses at UCLA, the University of Southern California, Ohio University, the City University of New York, Columbia University, the University of Ghana at Legon, California State University, and the University of California at Berkeley.

The two poems reprinted here originally appeared in the 1975 anthology Giant Talk. *Through repetition, informal diction, and enjambment, "South African Bloodstone" honors a jazz musician and "After Hearing a Radio Announcement: A Comment on Some Conditions" depicts the declining social conditions of an urban setting.*

South African Bloodstone

For Hugh Masekela

South African bloodstone
drenched with the soil
drenched with the beauty
of the drum-drum beat of land

drenched with the beauty
of God's first creation of man

& sculpted into lean hawk look
eyes burning deep
bold diamonds of fire
dance sing music to the air

Conjureman/conjure up
the rhythm of voodoo walk
weave the spell/paint the trance
began the fire ritual

Hugh Masekela! homeboy
from the original home/going home
play your horn your trumpet horn
screech scream speak of ancestors

Conjureman/conjure up
the memory of ancestral lands
the easy walk the rhythmic walk
click click talk of trumpet genius

Hugh Masekela homeboy
from the original home going home

Speak South African bloodstone speak!

After Hearing a Radio Announcement: A Comment on Some Conditions

yesterday in new york city
the gravediggers went on strike
& today the undertakers went on strike
because they said of the overwhelming
amount of corpses
(unnessesarily they said because
of wars & stupid killings in the streets
& ecetera & ecetera)

sweating the world corpses
clogging up rivers jamming up freeways
stopping up elevators in the gutters corpses
everywhere you turn
(& the undertakers said that they were
being overworked with all this goddamned killing
going on said that they couldn't even enjoy
all the money they was making
said that this shit has got too stop)

& today eye just heard that
coffin-makers are waiting in the wings
for their chance too do the same thing
& tomorrow & if things keep going this way
eye expect to hear of the corpses
themselves boycotting death
until things get better

or at least getting themselves
together in some sort of union espousing
self-determination
for better funeral &
burial conditions
or something extroardinarily
heavy like that

Wanda Coleman (1946–)

R*aised in Los Angeles's Watts district, Wanda Coleman often draws on that city's settings, life-styles, and rhythms in her poetry and fiction. According to Joel Gersmann, "Coleman takes her inspiration from jazz and [the] oral tradition. Her poems are tough, brutal, street-smart, tender and lyrically ironic. . . . Her work is neither nasty, gratuitously mean-spirited, or bitter and is thoroughly informed with an earnest, gritty visual-verbal density."*

With hundreds of published poems and over five hundred poetry readings to her credit, Coleman is among the most popular contemporary poets. An essayist, fiction writer, and scriptwriter as well, this multitalented author is currently a contributing editor to Los Angeles Times Magazine. *She has received a National Endowment for the Arts Grant, a Guggenheim Fellowship, and a California Arts Council Fellowship Grant. Through her recordings and co-hosting of the Los Angeles radio program "The Poetry Connection," she has reached new audiences for poetry. Her recordings include* Twin Sisters *(1985),* Black Angeles *(1988),* High Priestess of Word *(1990),* Black and Blue News *(1991), and* Berserk on Hollywood Boulevard *(1992).*

Coleman has published several books of poetry and fiction, sometimes combining the two genres. Four volumes appeared in the 1980s: Imagoes *(1983), a book of verse;* Heavy Daughter Blues *(1987), a book of poems and short stories;* A War of Eyes and Other Stories *(1988); and* Dicksboro Hotel *(1989), a collection of poems. Her more recent collections are* African Sleeping Sickness *(1990), a group of poems and stories, and* Hand Dance *(1993), a volume of poetry.*

The three poems reprinted here are from Imagoes. *In each poem, Coleman uses the character study to examine the struggle of surviving in an urban milieu. "Dear Mama" presents a black woman who hopes to find in herself the same strength of character she recognizes in her mother. "In This Waking" tells the sad tale of a doomed relationship and a woman's tragic end. The street woman in "Shopping Bag Lady" dwells on feelings evoked by other people's discarded possessions.*

Dear Mama

she say that's what
mama's for

you don't know or maybe you do
time you couldn't buy us shoes and asked grandpa
for money. he sent you one dollar
i remember your eyes scanning the letter. the tears
you got us shoes somehow by the good grace of a friend
maybe you are hip in your old-fashioned oklahoma cornspun way

or the time we sat in the dark with no electricity
eating peaches and cold toast
wondering where you'd gone to get the money
for light

grandma named you lewana. it sounds hawaiian
not that bastard mix of white black and red you are
not that bitter cast of negro staged to play to
rowdy crowds on the off broadway of american poor

and she added mae—to make it sound *country*
like jemima or butterfly mc queen or bobbi jo
it's you. and you named us and fed us and
i can't love you enuff for it

you don't know or maybe you do
it hurts being a grown working black woman
branded strong
hurts being unable to get over
in this filthy white world
hurts to ask your parents for help
hurts to swallow those old beaten borrowed green backs
whole
hurts to know
it'll hurt worse if you don't

In This Waking

he walks the blistered boulevards for hours
hunting work
he goes in and out of restaurants
when he comes home he smells of smoke
and hot kitchens

she waits for the phone to sing/good news
if he gets the gig there'll be money for food dope rent
and the possibility of escape from hell

he smokes hemp. they smoke it together
and time and skin and rhythm merge
there is the drum and the hunger
a baby is made at his request

she finds work but doesn't have the strength
he thought would save them
and he doesn't have 400 years of patience

he's too good, she thinks. something is wrong
the walls tell her. and there is

he's developed an itch in his armpits

she walks the ledge
he has the choice of rescue
or taking her for the fall
one day she finds his goodbye
in the mailbox

and as she strikes cement she is certain
the shattered pieces of her sanity
will forever steal his sleep

Shopping Bag Lady

she winds her way down dark dingy avenues/alleys/mind
picks over discarded years looking for a good one
scavenging heartaches, pain, fear, disappointment
sparse nourishment for her toothless ever sucking mouth
rags, tatters and bits of courage to clothe
her fat lumpy black form or make patches or rejuvenate
for re-sale to some denizen of salvage
she keeps an eager eye out for love/rare as a lost diamond pendant
she rears and gags when the stench of hatred overcomes
leans against graffiti'd walls till nausea subsides
or cackles joy over the half emptied contents of romance/
a vintage wine tickles her ancient tongue
she seeks lost items for meager profit
swears rackish when she finds nothing
gloats and hums her way to the bus stop when
booty is plentiful and prospects for an evening meal improved

Rita Dove (1952–)

R*eflecting on the process of writing, Rita Dove observes, "There is some truth to the whole notion that something strikes the poet like a thunderbolt and she is then inspired. Inspiration is part of the writing process, and I think of it as being* *much more visceral than cerebral. . . . I try to engage all of my senses when I write. Absolutely and completely. . . . The mind, the soul, the heart, and the heartbeat try to get into sync. . . ."*

Born in Akron, Ohio, Dove began writing poetry at age ten, but she did not resolve to become a writer until later on as a college student. Chosen in 1970 as a Presidential Scholar—a distinction awarded to the most outstanding high school graduates in the United States—she was invited to visit the White House. In 1973, she received her bachelor's, graduating summa cum laude *from Miami University of Ohio. In 1977 she earned a master's in fine arts from the University of Iowa, where she had attended the Iowa Writers Workshop. Dove also studied at the University of Tubingen, Germany, on a Fulbright Scholarship and has taught creative writing at Arizona State University and the University of Virginia.*

Dove's poetry and fiction have received praise from both academic and popular audiences. In all of her writing, she remains conscious of the balance she must bring to being an artist and a black woman: "As a black woman writer, I recognize that there are powers that may choose not to consider me as part of the human family. This is no reason not to make the writing as honest as I possibly can. . . . It is difficult to show a character's faults when you know that there are people who already think of African-American women as lesser beings, but it is absolutely essential that you do."

In 1987, Dove was honored with a Pulitzer Prize for her third book of poetry, Thomas and Beulah, *which was inspired by the experiences of her grandparents' pilgrimage from the South into the North. In May 1993, Dove was named Poet Laureate of the year by the Library of Congress. Her other books of poetry include* The Yellow House on the Corner *and* The Only Dark Spot in the Sky (1980), Mandolin *(1982),* Museum *(1983),* The Other Side of the House *(1988),* Grace Notes *(1989), and* Selected Poems: Old and New *(1993). She also wrote a full-length verse drama,* The Darker Face of the Earth *(1994); a collection of short stories,* Fifth Sunday *(1985); and a novel,* Through the Ivory Gate *(1992).*

The three poems presented here, originally published in Grace Notes, *do not focus on specifically racial themes. The woman in "Particulars" comes to terms with the tears that have a permanent place in her daily life, while the grief and loss expressed in "Your Death" find their way into the mundane moments of the narrator's life. "After Reading* Mickey in the Night Kitchen *for the Third Time before Bed" strikes a lighter note than the other two selections, focusing on a mother's embarrassing but important discussion of anatomy with her young daughter.*

Particulars

She discovered she felt better
if the simplest motions
had their origin in agenda—
second coffee at nine or eating just
the top half of the muffin, no butter
with blueberry jam. She caught herself
crying every morning, ten sharp, as if
the weather front had swerved,

a titanic low pressure system
moving in as night steamed off
and left a day with nothing else
to fill it but moisture. She wept
steadily, and once
she recognized the pattern,
took care to be in one spot waiting
a few moments before. They weren't
tears of relief, and after a few weeks
not even a particular sorrow.
We never learn a secret until
it's useless, she thought, and perhaps
that was what she was weeping over:
the lack of conclusion,
the eternal *dénouement.*

After Reading *Mickey in the Night Kitchen* for the Third Time Before Bed

I'm in the milk and the milk's in me! . . . I'm Mickey!

My daughter spreads her legs
to find her vagina:
hairless, this mistaken
bit of nomenclature
is what a stranger cannot touch
without her yelling. She demands
to see mine and momentarily
we're a lopsided star
among the spilled toys,
my prodigious scallops
exposed to her neat cameo.

And yet the same glazed
tunnel, layered sequences.
She is three; that makes this
innocent. *We're pink!*
she shrieks, and bounds off.

Every month she wants
to know where it hurts
and what the wrinkled string means
between my legs. *This is good blood*
I say, but that's wrong, too.
How to tell her that it's what makes us—
black mother, cream child.
That we're in the pink
and the pink's in us.

Your Death

On the day that will always belong to you,
lunar clockwork had faltered
and I was certain. Walking
the streets of Manhattan I thought:
Remember this day. I felt already
like an urn, filling with wine.

To celebrate, your son and I
took a stroll through Bloomingdale's
where he developed a headache
among the copper skillets and
tiers of collapsible baskets.
Pain tracked us through
the china, driving us
finally to the subway
and home,

where the phone was ringing
with bad news. Even now,
my new daughter
asleep in her crib, I can't shake
the moment his headache stopped
and the day changed ownership.
I felt robbed. Even the first
bite of the tuna fish sandwich
I had bought at the corner
became yours.

PART THREE

FICTION

OVERVIEW

African American fiction has served as a forum for the meeting of imagination and ideological debate. The imagination of black fiction writers, particularly in recent years, has experimented with different techniques of expression and of entertaining readers. As a result, African American fiction has become a safe and open place to protest injustice, affirm cultural distinctions, discuss racial integration, advocate black nationalism and black feminism—in other words, to formulate the black experience in this country while hoping to transform that experience and the country.

Where the Folktale Meets the Slave Narrative

Although African American fiction is not alone in its impulse to enlighten, entertain, teach, and transform, its roots lie in the folktale and slave narrative. Like folktales, African American fiction springs from black legends, myths, proverbs, songs, and oral storytelling, which later black fiction writers have borrowed, developed, and expanded upon to create stories and novels that depict and commemorate black culture. In addition, the didactic voice, formulaic structure, and inspirational theme of the slave narrative influenced the direction of early African American fiction. Emphasizing content over aesthetics, the slave narrative found its way into print for propaganda purposes, while the black fiction published just before the Civil War emulated that didacticism. Olaudah Equiano's slave narrative (see Part Five) appeared some sixty years before William Wells Brown's novel, the first to be published by an African American.

First Novelists: Writers with an Agenda

Published in 1853, *Clotel, or, The President's Daughter* was written by an escaped slave and abolitionist. Brown's work was followed in 1859 by Harriet E. Wilson's *Our Nig: Or Sketches from the Life of a Free Black.* "Two Offers" by Frances E. W. Harper was the first short story published by a black author. The professional experiences of these authors dramatized the obstacles that plagued black writers then and continue to plague them now—the politics of publishing and distribution. Brown's novel was originally published in London, and Wilson's novel was published privately in America. Equally important, the two novels had a sociopolitical intention: to expose the black woman's plight under the oppressive conditions of slavery in the South and of servitude in the North.

Following the Civil War, black fiction writers continued to focus on racial issues while targeting a white audience. These writers understood that their readership would be composed primarily of Caucasians accustomed to the established techniques, language, and mores of the time. As a result, they wrote in a style likely to appeal to that audience, but they also brought African American concerns and culture to the attention of their white readers.

Local Colorists versus Experimenters

The African American writers of the late nineteenth and early twentieth centuries experimented with new ways of appealing to their audiences, such as by using combinations of black vernacular and standard English and by addressing a variety of themes in their fiction. Although such writers as Charles W. Chesnutt, Pauline Elizabeth Hopkins, Sutton E. Griggs, Paul Laurence Dunbar, and Alice Dunbar-Nelson met with varying degrees of success by mainstream standards, they contributed significantly to the development of African American fiction by exemplifying its range of tones, styles, and themes.

The most acclaimed black fiction writer of the period, Chesnutt's early fiction suited the then-popular trend of "local color" writing, which included the Negro dialect style. However, his more provocative work, including the selection reprinted here, "The Sheriff's Children," used standard English and black vernacular and addressed interracial and intraracial themes. Chesnutt respected the oral tradition; his short story collection, *The Conjure Woman* (1899), includes stories about slavery, African magic, and other issues, narrated by Uncle Julius, an ex-slave.

Offering a stylistic contrast to Chesnutt, two other selections appear here from that period. "A Dash for Liberty" exemplifies Pauline Hopkins's romantic and melodramatic language, while the excerpt from *Imperium In Imperio* reveals Sutton Grigg's political and verbose style.

The Harlem Renaissance

Early in the twentieth century, James Weldon Johnson, with his *Autobiography of an Ex-Colored Man* (1912), broke new ground in African American literature by telling the story of a light-skinned black man who decides to pass for white. The novel provided a male character's perspective on the popular theme of miscegenation—a theme usually developed through a woman character.

It would take another decade for black fiction to mature in scope and style. With its explosion of new voices, the Harlem Renaissance of the 1920s transformed African American literature, making it more known to both black and white cultures. Promoted by a number of factors (see David Levering Lewis's essay in Part Five, p. 762), the fiction of the Harlem Renaissance explored many issues of African American life: urban and rural experiences, working- and middle-class cultures, and racial and sexual conflict. During this time, creativity in fiction intersected with poetry, drama, and nonfiction prose to celebrate both the black American culture and the African heritage of African Americans.

The first impressive fictional work of the Harlem Renaissance, *Cane* (1923) by Jean Toomer, blended character studies, drama, and poetry to contrast blacks' experiences in the South and North and to comment on the spiritual roots of black culture. In the selection "Theater," which comes from *Cane,* the writer explores how an urban environment in the North, by fostering alienation, suspicion, and prejudice, prevents a black man and woman from communicating honestly with one another.

The Harlem Renaissance gave rise to many other memorable and influential writers—including Jessie Fauset (*There Is Confusion,* 1924), Eric Walrond (*Tropic Death,* 1926), Nella Larsen (*Quicksand,* 1928), Rudolph Fisher (*The Walls of Jericho,* 1928), Claude McKay (*Home to Harlem,* 1928), Wallace Thurman (*The Blacker the Berry,* 1929), and Zora Neale Hurston (*Jonah's Gourd Vine,* 1934)—some of whom are represented in Part Three. Together, the writers of the period conveyed varied black experiences through realistic and complex characters, thereby denying the earlier trend toward simplistic caricatures designed for white audiences.

In particular, the fiction writings of Zora Neale Hurston, like the poetry of Langston Hughes and Sterling Brown (see Part Two), cherished the folkways of the black community. In the selection reprinted here, titled "Sweat," as well as in her other short stories and novels (such as *Jonah's Gourd Vine,* 1934; and *Their Eyes Were Watching God,* 1937), Hurston confirms the complexity and dignity of working-class blacks through her characters. As a folklorist, she presented the vitality of black idioms, folk customs, hoodoo, and magic in such books as *Mules and Men* (1935) and *Tell My Horse* (1938).

The Quest for Integration

The creative spirit of the Harlem Renaissance lived on as the writers of the period continued to enlarge upon their cultural and social themes, and as new writers joined them in the social and political protest that dominated mainstream American fiction in the 1930s and 1940s. Most of the African American fiction published during these two decades was written by men who sought to protest racism, particularly as it applied to the black male. The most notable among this new wave of writers were Richard Wright (*Native Son,* 1940), William Attaway (*Blood on the Forge,* 1941), Chester Himes (*If He Hollers Let Him Go,* 1945), and Ann Petry (*The Street,* 1946).

The short stories by Wright, Himes, and Petry that appear in Part Three display a concern for the black male's struggle against racist attitudes and restrictions. Although the male protagonists in Wright's "The Man Who Killed a Shadow," Himes's "One More Way to Die," and Petry's "The Witness" inhabit different settings, they have all been physically or psychologically victimized because of stereotyped images of black masculinity. The most celebrated of these protest writers, Wright combined style, content, and political experimentation to depict the black artist as a defender of black culture and mainstream integration. His collection of stories, *Uncle Tom's Children* (1938), mixed elements of the slave narrative and oral tradition with the short story genre to indict southern racism. In a series of autobiographical vignettes that opened the book, Wright's personal experiences in the South gave added context and meaning to the stories that followed. Yet Wright's best-known novel, *Native Son* (1940), attacked urban racism in the North, where the black protagonist, Bigger Thomas, overwhelmed by the fear and shame caused by a racist system, became a killer and a fugitive within that system. The popular and critical success of *Native Son* can be credited to Wright's skill at rendering provocative characters and plot through vivid language.

African American fiction of the 1950s and 1960s persisted in the quest for mainstream integration. The two writers at the forefront of this group, Ralph Ellison and James Baldwin, reaped acclaim from within and outside the black community. Stressing a faith in the American democratic ideology, their works meticulously pointed out the ways in which that ideology neglected African Americans at that time. In their fiction as well as their essays, Ellison and Baldwin underscored the failure of the American system to respond to the needs of blacks, a failure that would eventually weaken the system as a whole. Both writers won eminence as literary and social critics for their appraisals of black cultural expressions within the larger American culture. Ellison's novel *Invisible Man* (1952), which exposed the complexities of ethnic identity in America in an integrationist age, is described by critic Eric J. Sundquist as "combin[ing] the self-reflexive techniques of autobiography, the vernacular resources of ethnography, and the nuanced harmonies of poetry" (2). Baldwin evoked the cadences of black sermons, black idioms, and poetic drama in *Go Tell It on the Mountain* (1953), a novel about familial conflicts. His plays, *The Amen Corner* (1957) and *Blues for Mister Charlie* (1964), demonstrated the interdependence of blacks and whites, who share Christian beliefs, a common American history, and similar class struggles. Baldwin's advocacy of tolerance extended to sexual orientation in such novels as *Giovanni's Room* (1956) and *Another Country* (1962), in which black and white homosexuals faced the same types of social discrimination. Although Ellison's work does not appear here, Baldwin's short story "Previous Condition" does illustrate an issue both authors treated in fiction—the psychological and emotional anxiety of blacks who struggle to fit into a social order that denigrates their ethnic identity and culture.

Other black writers of the 1950s and 1960s also stood as advocates of racial integration, and a growing number of them found a wider audience. Their works exhibited accomplished writing styles, celebrated African American humanity through various settings and themes, and affirmed civil rights and the potential of the American system. The most notable among the writers of this period included William Demby (*Battlecreek,* 1950), John Oliver Killens (*Youngblood,* 1954), Julian Mayfield (*The Hit,* 1957), Paule

Marshall (*Brown Girl, Brownstones,* 1959), John A. Williams (*Night Song,* 1961), William Melvin Kelley (*Different Drummer,* 1962), Kristin Hunter (*God Bless the Child,* 1964), Ernest Gaines (*Catherine Carmier,* 1964), Margaret Walker (*Jubilee,* 1966), and Rosa Guy (*Bird at My Window,* 1966).

Part Three includes short stories by John A. Williams and Toni Morrison. These selections, which address the possibilities and problems associated with interracial relationships in the 1950s and 1960s, demonstrate their authors' mastery of language, structure, and imagery.

Raising Consciousness: The Black Arts Movement

Concerns about mainstream critics and readers vanished with the surge of African American writers appearing during the Black Arts movement of the late 1960s and 1970s. Like the Harlem Renaissance, this later celebration of black culture provoked controversy and raised consciousness but was sustained by a political purpose and a growing pantheon of inspiring events and heroes, such as W. E. B. Du Bois, Ida Wells-Barnett, Mary McLeod Bethune, Martin Luther King, Jr., A. Phillip Randolph, Malcolm X, and Amiri Baraka.

The revolutionary writers of the time immersed their fiction in black culture and politics, driven forward by the Black Power movement, academic validation of the Black Aesthetic, and the burgeoning black presses. The heightened racial consciousness of the period was also evident in the works of Ronald Fair (*Hog Butcher,* 1966), John Edgar Wideman (*A Glance Away,* 1967), Ishmael Reed (*The Free-Lance Pallbearers,* 1967), Sam Greenlee (*The Spook Who Sat by the Door,* 1969), Alice Walker (*The Third Life of Grange Copeland,* 1970), Louise Meriwether (*Daddy Was a Numbers Runner,* 1970), Toni Morrison (*The Bluest Eye,* 1970), Toni Cade Bambara (*Gorilla, My Love,* 1972), Alice Childress (*A Hero Ain't Nothing but a Sandwich,* 1973), Charles Johnson (*Faith and the Good Thing,* 1974), Gayl Jones (*Corregidora,* 1975), and David Bradley (*South Street,* 1975).

The writers of the Black Arts movement became a barometer of the attitudinal changes blacks imposed on themselves at the time, as well as of the urgent demands blacks made on American society. Most important, however, was their call for African Americans to take positive action within the community, to affirm pride in black culture, and to strive toward black unity. In the selections included here by Reed, Wideman, Bambara, and Jones, one facet of the Black Aesthetic is evident: the call for blacks to explore and affirm their own perceptions about their ethnic identity. And Bambara and Jones emphasize an additional concern in their stories: the need to examine the dynamics of black female and black male relationships.

Raising Consciousness: Black Feminism

Many African American writers left both apology and protest behind in the 1970s, focusing instead on issues of gender and race. In tune with the rebirth of feminism in the late 1960s and early 1970s, black women writers raised the public's consciousness about male–female relationships within the African American community. In *The Bluest Eye* (1970), Toni Morrison portrayed the tragic impact of mainstream culture on black identity while also openly criticizing the treatment of black girls and women by their families, friends, and spouses. Alice Walker's *The Third Life of Grange Copeland* (1970) and later fiction conveyed a similar message (see Focused Study, p. 208).

In the 1980s, black women writers continued to explore relationships between women and men. Although some black male writers criticized feminist fiction and questioned white publishers' motives for promoting it, the black women authors maintained that their purpose was not to create division between the sexes, but to address the formidable problems facing men and women and thereby to strengthen the black community. In Part Three, Toni Cade Bambara's "A Tender Man" and Gayl Jones's "White Rat" consider how black men confront their responsibilities to a daughter and a girlfriend, respectively. Gloria Naylor's "Lucielia Louise Turner" (from *The Women of Brewster Place,* 1980) presents the tragic results of an emotionally abusive relationship between a black man and woman, while Terry McMillan's "Zora" (from *Disappearing Acts,* 1989) offers a black woman's assessment of the black men in her life.

An impressive number of other African American women published works of fiction in the 1980s that keenly dissected, evaluated, praised, and deplored various types of relationships, including romantic, familial, heterosexual, and homosexual ones. Among these authors were Sherley Anne Williams (*Dessa Rose,* 1986), Marita Golden (*A Woman's Place,* 1986), and Tina McElroy Ansa (*Baby in the Family,* 1989), who also wrote verse and personal and critical essays, bridging poetry, fiction, and nonfiction with detailed perspectives of black women within both the black community and American society. Williams's other work includes two volumes of poetry and an impressive book of literary criticism, *Give Birth to Brightness: A Thematic Study of Neo-Black Literature* (1972). Linking the progressivism of feminism to the black aesthetic, Williams asserts: "Feminist theory, like black aesthetics, offers us not only the possibility of changing one's reading of the world, but of changing the world itself. And like black aesthetics, it is far more egalitarian than the prevailing mode" (68–69). Golden has also written poetry and an autobiography, *Migrations of the Heart* (1983), and edited the anthology *Wild Women Don't Wear No Blues: Black Women Writers on Love, Men and Sex* (1993). Ansa contributed to that 1993 anthology an essay that demonstrated her skill with nonfiction prose.

In the 1990s, numerous works of fiction by black women writers have appeared, including works by Marsha Hunt (*Joy,* 1990), Jamaica Kincaid (*Lucy,* 1990), Xam Cartier (*Muse-Echo Blues,* 1991), Jewelle Gomez (*The Gilda Stories,* 1991), Carolivia Herron (*Thereafter Johnnie,* 1991), Pearl Cleage (*The Brass Bed and Other Stories,* 1991), Connie Porter (*All Bright Court,* 1991), Bebe Moore Campbell (*Your Blues Ain't Like Mine,* 1992), Barbara Neely (*Blanche on the Lam,* 1992), Rita Dove (*Through the Ivory*

Gate, 1992), Charlotte Watson Sherman (*One Dark Body,* 1993), and Gwendolyn M. Parker (*These Some Long Bones,* 1994). Many of these writers have also displayed creative versatility in several genres. For example, Cleage has published fiction, poetry, essays, and drama (see Part Four, p. 525); Campbell has written novels and an autobiography; Neely has been praised for her fiction and drama; and Dove has achieved critical acclaim for her fiction and volumes of poetry (see Part Two, p. 192).

Approaching the Twenty-First Century

This impressive collection of black woman writers does not mean that all African American fiction in the 1980s and 1990s has focused on feminist subject matter. On the contrary, recent African American fiction offers a tremendous variety of approaches to literature and some provocative renditions of black life. Specifically, Trey Ellis's satirical *Platitudes* (1987) contrasts strikingly with J. California Cooper's humorous *Homemade Love* (1987) and Jess Mowry's realistic *Six out Seven* (1993). These latter two authors, featured here, have demonstrated sharp differences in thematic focus, tone, and style. In contrast to Cooper's humorous reflection on interracial marriage in "Happiness Does Not Come in Colors," Mowry gives a stark glimpse into the urban street life that endangers black manhood in "Crusader Rabbit."

Alternative Fiction

Contributing to the diversity of African American literature are two distinctive forms of alternative fiction: works that do not focus on black culture and works of romance, science fiction, and mystery.

A number of works by notable black writers from various earlier periods as well as the present focus on characters, plots, and issues outside of African American culture. Frank Yerby (*Foxes of Harrow,* 1946), Willard Motley (*Knock on Any Door,* 1947), and William Gardner Smith (*Anger at Innocence,* 1950) explored fictional worlds peopled by major characters who were not black. And later, the award-winning fiction of James Alan McPherson (*Hue and Cry,* 1969) sprang from the author's personal philosophy that "color" belonged in the background of fiction.

The often unheralded but vital group of romance, science fiction, and mystery writings have seldom appeared on the reading lists of African American literature courses. However, collectively, these works represent a substantive part of the African American literary heritage.

Black romance fiction is characterized by episodic, melodramatic plots and sentimental language. It was given a strong foundation in the early twentieth-century work of Pauline Elizabeth Hopkins (*Contending Forces,* 1900) and in the later writings of Frank Yerby (*A Woman Called Fancy,* 1951; *The Devil's Daughter,* 1953; and *Captain Rebel,* 1956). In the 1990s, romance novels such as Beverly Jenkins's *Night Song* (1994), Monique Gilmore's *No Ordinary Love* (1994), Felicia Mason's *For the Love of You* (1994), and Angela Benson's *Bands of Gold* (1994) were published and marketed via independent bookstores as well as national bookstore chains.

In the area of science fiction, author and critic Samuel R. Delaney (*Babel-17,* 1967) has been notable for the success and popularity of his writing. Similarly, the immensely popular Octavia Butler, whose works include *Wild Seed* (1980) and *Kindred* (1979), has won a number of major science fiction awards. In the selection that appears in Part Three, excerpted from her novel *Kindred,* Butler uses time travel to take her protagonist, a contemporary black woman, back to an early 1800s plantation and a world of slavery.

Mystery writing, a particularly successful branch of African American literature, was pioneered by Chester Himes in his series of novels featuring the black detective team of Coffin Ed Johnson and Gravedigger Jones. First published in Paris and later in America, the series includes *The Real Cool Killers* (1959), *Cotton Comes to Harlem* (1965), and *A Rage in Harlem* (1965). More recently, three black mystery writers have found distinction within this field typically dominated by white males, infusing the traditional style of detective-crime writing with cultural nuances: Walter Mosley (*Devil in a Blue Dress,* 1990, with detective Easy Rawlins), Nikki Baker (*The Long Goodbyes,* 1993, with detective Virginia Kelly), and Gar Haywood (*You Can Die Trying,* 1993, with detective Aaron Gunner). Mosley, in particular, has gained international acclaim by both readers and critics for his mystery writings. In the selection reprinted in Part Three, excerpted from *Devil in a Blue Dress,* Mosley adds an interracial twist to a convention of the mystery novel—a detective hero in conflict with the police—thus redeeming an otherwise stock fictional device with layers of significance.

Alternative fiction has expanded the boundaries of African American literature, while also showcasing the imaginative power of black authors of romance, science fiction, and mystery. Earning serious attention by critics for the integrity and creativity of their work, Butler, Mosley, and other writers are also significant for injecting black culture into the various forms of alternative fiction.

In This Part

Part Three begins with a Focused Study of Alice Walker, a fiction writer whose remarkable literary output and tremendous success are mirrored by her immense popularity among multiethnic readers. The three selections by Walker are followed by Barbara Christian's critical essay, "Alice Walker: The Black Woman Artist as Wayward," which analyzes recurrent motifs in Walker's fiction and poetry.

An extensive collection of fictional works by black writers highlights the currents, themes, and styles of African American fiction from the late 1800s to the 1990s. Organized chronologically by the authors' birth years, the selections survey the continuum of African American fiction, provoking thought, challenging mainstream assumptions, and celebrating the depth and diversity of black culture.

Works Cited

Lundquist, Eric J. *Cultural Contexts for Ralph Ellison's* Invisible Man. Boston: Bedford, 1995.

Williams, Sherley Anne. "Some Implications of Womanist Theory." *Reading Black, Reading Feminist.* Ed. Henry Louis Gates, Jr. New York: Meridian, 1990. 68–75.

Suggested Readings

Anthologies of short stories and novel excerpts by African American writers include Henry Lee Faggett and Nick Aaron Ford's *Best Short Stories of Afro-American Writers, 1925–1950* (1950); John Henrik Clarke's *American Negro Short Stories* (1966); Langston Hughes's *The Best Short Stories of Negro Authors* (1967); William Robinson's *Early Black American Prose* (1971); Woodie King's *Black Short Story Anthology* (1972); Sonia Sanchez's *We Be Sorcerers: Twenty-Five Stories by Black Americans* (1973); Quandra P. Stadler's *Out of Our Lives: A Collection of Contemporary Black Fiction* (1975); Terry McMillan's *Breaking Ice: An Anthology of African American Fiction* (1990); and Clarence Major's *Calling the Wind: Twentieth Century African-American Short Stories* (1993).

Informative critical and historical perspectives on fiction writers and their works can be found in *The Negro in Literature and Art in the United States* (1930) by Benjamin Brawley; *Native Sons: A Critical Study of Twentieth-Century Negro African American Authors* (1969) by Edward Margolies; *The Black Novelist* (1970) edited by Robert Hemenway; *Give Birth to Brightness: A Thematic Study in Neo-Black Literature* (1972) by Sherley Ann Williams; *From the Dark Tower: Afro-American Writers, 1900–1960* (1974) by Arthur P. Davis; *The Way of the New World* (1975) by Addison Gayle, Jr.; *The Black American Short Story in the Twentieth Century: A Collection of Critical Essays* (1977) edited by Peter Bruck; *Sturdy Black Bridges: Visions of Black Women in Literature* (1979) edited by Roseann Pope Bell, Bettye J. Parker, and Beverly Guy-Sheftall; *Black Women Novelists: The Development of Tradition* (1980) by Barbara Christian; *Black Women Writers at Work* (1983) by Claudia Tate; *Black Women Writers, 1950–1980* (1984) edited by Mari Evans; *Conjuring: Black Women, Fiction, and Literary Tradition* (1985) edited by Marjorie Pryse and Hortense Spillers; and *Afro-American Women Writers, 1746–1933* (1988) by Ann Allen Shockley.

A FOCUSED STUDY: ALICE WALKER (1944-)

An internationally famous author of poetry, fiction, and nonfiction, Alice Walker has received both accolades and harsh criticisms for her diverse writings. Since 1968, she has published works that unashamedly explore sexism, racism, classism, and the commonalities among women.

Growing up in poverty in Eatonton, Georgia, Walker was the youngest of eight children. After a tragic childhood accident rendered her scarred and blind in one eye, she turned from her suicidal loneliness to reading and writing and her mother's strong support. In 1961, she won a scholarship to Spelman College, later transferring to Sarah Lawrence College, from which she graduated in 1965. Walker became active in the civil rights movement while at Spelman, and in the summer of 1965 she worked with the movement in Mississippi and Georgia, meeting the lawyer who would become her husband in 1967. Their marriage ended nine years later.

During the late 1960s and early 1970s, Walker taught at several colleges, including Jackson State University, Tougaloo College, Wellesley College, and the University of Massachusetts in Boston. By the mid-1970s, her publications and grants gave her the time she needed to concentrate on her writing.

Walker's first book, *Once* (1968), is a collection of poetry that she began writing while in college. With the help of a grant from the National Endowment for the Arts, she was able to complete her first novel, *The Third Life of Grand Copeland* (1970). That novel, which deals with conflicts between black women and black men within a destructive black family, raises some of the issues and controversies that would continue to be associated with Walker's fiction.

Revolutionary Petunias and Other Poems (1973), her second volume of poetry, won a William Smith Award and was nominated for a National Book Award. *In Love and Trouble: Stories of Black Women* (1973), won a Rosenthal Award from the National Institute of Arts and Letters.

Walker has also written *Langston Hughes, American Poet* (1974), a biography for young readers. Her collection of the writings of the influential author Zora Neale Hurston, *I Love Myself When I'm Laughing . . . and Then Again When I'm Mean and Impressive: A Zora Neale Hurston Reader,* published in 1979 by Feminist Press, encourages readers to discover Hurston's legacy of literary and intellectual pursuits.

Meridian (1976), Walker's second novel, focuses on a black woman protagonist who confronts a complex set of challenges: the work of the civil rights movement, cultural identity, interracial love, and sexual politics. Recognized with a Guggenheim Fellowship in 1979, Walker continued to explore different literary forms with *Good Night Willie Lee, I'll See You in the Morning* (1979), a poetry collection, and *You Can't Keep a Good Woman Down* (1981), a short story collection.

With *The Color Purple* (1982), Walker assumed international status, winning both a Pulitzer Prize and an American Book Award. The 1985 movie based on the novel increased public awareness of Walker and inflamed the controversy surrounding the book. Specifically, the presentation of uneducated black women characters and their confrontations with abusive black men characters provoked a negative response from several organizations and individuals within the black community. However, as Walker suggested, a complete reading of the novel illuminates the author's emphasis on redemption and wholeness as rewards for both black women and men.

In the eight years following the publication of *The Color Purple,* Walker's astounding literary output included five books: *In Search of Our Mothers' Gardens* (1983), a collection of essays; *Horses Make the Landscape Look More Beautiful* (1984), a book of poetry; *To Hell with Dying* (1987), a children's book; *Living by the Word: Selected Writings, 1973–1987* (1988), a collection of essays and journal entries; and *The Temple of My Familiar* (1990), a novel about cultural identity and its relationship to the spiritual interdependence between humans and other living creatures.

In the 1990s, Walker has continued to embrace controversy. Her novel *Possessing the Secret of Joy* (1992) tells the story of a black woman's emotional and psychological trauma stemming from the African ritual of female genital mutilation. Resurrecting characters from *The Color Purple,* the author presents female circumcision as an intolerable and pernicious practice. Again, voices from the black community denounced Walker's attack on a rite with historical and cultural significance for particular cultures. But adamantly opposed to the practice, Walker went on to publish *Warrior Marks: Female Genital Mutilation and the Sexual Blinding of Women* (1993), which functions as companion literature to a film she co-produced on female excising.

Walker has made a significant mark on African American literature, both with her creative output and her influential "womanist" perspective, defined in her 1983 book of essays as an assertion of women's rights, regardless of sexual orientation, ethnicity, class, or age. Undoubtedly, Walker's multifaceted body of work has enlarged the purpose and potential of black literature. Without apology, she aspires to encourage the black community to see itself whole: good and bad, ugly and beautiful.

The three selections reprinted here reflect Walker's characteristic focus on black women seeking to uncover truths in their lives; they also show the writer's stylistic progression through and experimentation with narrative structure. The story "Her Sweet Jerome," taken from *In Love and Trouble,* examines the tragic consequences of a black couple's failure to communicate honestly with each another. In "A Sudden Trip Home in the Spring," originally published in *You Can't Keep a Woman Down,* a black woman leaves her northern college to attend her father's funeral in Georgia, discovering that there's still much to learn about the black men in her family as well as about herself. An excerpt from *The Color Purple* illuminates the experiences of Celie and Shug, two black women characters in search of who they are and who they must become.

Her Sweet Jerome

Ties she had bought him hung on the closet door, which now swung open as she hurled herself again and again into the closet. Glorious ties, some with birds and dancing women in grass skirts painted on by hand, some with little polka dots with bigger dots dispersed among them. Some red, lots red and green, and one purple, with a golden star, through the center of which went his gold mustang stickpin, which she had also given him. She looked in the pockets of the black leather jacket he had reluctantly worn the night before. Three of his suits, a pair of blue twill work pants, an old gray sweater with a hood and pockets lay thrown across the bed. The jacket leather was sleazy and damply clinging to her hands. She had bought it for him, as well as the three suits: one light blue with side vents, one gold with green specks, and one reddish that had a silver imitation-silk vest. The pockets of the jacket came softly outward from the lining like skinny milktoast rats. Empty. Slowly she sank down on the bed and began to knead, with blunt anxious fingers, all the pockets in all the clothes piled around her. First the blue suit, then the gold with green, then the reddish one that he said he didn't like most of all, but which he would sometimes wear if she agreed to stay home, or if she promised not to touch him anywhere at all while he was getting dressed.

She was a big awkward woman, with big bones and hard rubbery flesh. Her short arms ended in ham hands, and her neck was a squat roll of fat that protruded behind her head as a big bump. Her skin was rough and puffy, with plump molelike freckles down her cheeks. Her eyes glowered from under the mountain of her brow and were circled with expensive mauve shadow. They were nervous and quick when she was flustered and darted about at nothing in particular while she was dressing hair or talking to people.

Her troubles started noticeably when she fell in love with a studiously quiet schoolteacher, Mr. Jerome Franklin Washington III, who was ten years younger than her. She told herself that she shouldn't want him, he was so little and cute and young, but when she took into account that he was a schoolteacher, well, she just couldn't seem to get any rest until, as she put it, "I were Mr. and Mrs. Jerome Franklin Washington the third, *and that's the truth!*"

She owned a small beauty shop at the back of her father's funeral home, and they were known as "colored folks with money." She made pretty good herself, though she didn't like standing on her feet so much, and her father let anybody know she wasn't getting any of his money while he was alive. She was proud to say she had never asked him for any. He started relenting kind of fast when he heard she planned to add a schoolteacher to the family, which consisted of funeral directors and bootleggers, but she cut him off quick and said she didn't want anybody to take care of her man but her. She had learned how to do hair from an old woman who ran a shop on the other side of town and was proud to say that she could make her own way. And much better than some. She was fond of telling schoolteachers (women schoolteachers) that she didn't miss her "eddicashion" as much as some did who had no learning and no money both together. She had a low opinion of women schoolteachers, because before and after her marriage to Jerome Franklin Washington III, they were the only females to whom he cared to talk.

The first time she saw him he was walking past the window of her shop with an armful of books and his coat thrown casually over his arm. Looking so neat and *cute.* What popped into her mind was that if he was hers the first thing she would get him was a sweet little red car to drive. And she worked and went into debt and got it for him, too—after she got him—but then she could tell he didn't like it much because it was only a Chevy. She had started right away to save up so she could make a down payment on a brand-new white Buick deluxe, with automatic drive and whitewall tires.

Jerome was dapper, every inch a gentleman, as anybody with half an eye could see. That's what she told everybody before they were married. He was beating her black and blue even then, so that every time you saw her she was sporting her "shades." She could not open her mouth without him wincing and pretending he couldn't stand it, so he would knock her out of the room to keep her from talking to him. She tried to be sexy and stylish, and was, in her fashion, with a predominant taste for pastel taffetas and orange shoes. In the summertime she paid twenty dollars for big umbrella hats with bows and flowers on them and when she wore black and white together she would liven it up with elbow-length gloves of red satin. She was genuinely undecided when she woke up in the morning whether she really outstripped the other girls in town for beauty, but could convince herself that she was equally good-looking by the time she had breakfast on the table. She was always talking with a lot of extra movement to her thick coarse mouth, with its hair tufts at the corners, and when she drank coffee she held the cup over the saucer with her little finger sticking out, while she crossed her short hairy legs at the knees.

If her husband laughed at her high heels as she teetered and minced off to church on Sunday mornings, with her hair greased and curled and her new dress bunching up at the top of her girdle, she pretended his eyes were approving. Other times, when he didn't bother to look up from his books and only muttered curses if she tried to kiss him good-bye, she did not know whether to laugh or cry. However, her public manner was serene.

"I just don't know how some womens can stand it, honey," she would say slowly, twisting her head to the side and upward in an elegant manner. "One thing my husband does not do," she would enunciate grandly, "he don't beat me!" And she would sit back and smile in her pleased oily fat way. Usually her listeners, captive women with wet hair, would simply smile and nod in sympathy and say, looking at one another or at her black eye, "You say he don't? Hummmm, well, hush your mouf." And she would continue curling or massaging or straightening their hair, fixing her face in a steamy dignified mask that encouraged snickers.

2

It was in her shop that she first heard the giggling and saw the smirks. It was at her job that gossip gave her to understand, as one woman told her, "Your cute little man is sticking his finger into somebody else's pie." And she was not and could not be surprised, as she looked into the amused and self-contented face, for she had long been aware that her own pie was going—and for the longest time had been going—strictly untouched.

From that first day of slyly whispered hints, "Your old man's puttin' something *over* on you, sweets," she started trying to find out who he was fooling around with. Her sources of gossip were malicious and mean, but she could think of nothing else to do but believe them. She searched high and she searched low.

She looked in taverns and she looked in churches. She looked in the school where he worked.

She went to whorehouses and to prayer meetings, through parks and outside the city limits, all the while buying axes and pistols and knives of all descriptions. Of course she said nothing to her sweet Jerome, who watched her maneuverings from behind the covers of his vast supply of paperback books. This hobby of his she heartily encouraged, relegating reading to the importance of scanning the funnies; and besides, it was something he could do at home, if she could convince him she should be completely silent for an evening, and, of course, if he would stay.

She turned the whole town upside down, looking at white girls, black women, brown beauties, ugly hags of all shades. She found nothing. And Jerome went on reading, smiling smugly as he shushed her with a carefully cleaned and lustered finger. "Don't interrupt me," he was always saying, and he would read some more while she stood glowering darkly behind him, muttering swears in her throaty voice, and then tramping flatfooted out of the house with her collection of weapons.

Some days she would get out of bed at four in the morning after not sleeping a wink all night, throw an old sweater around her shoulders, and begin the search. Her firm bulk became flabby. Her eyes were bloodshot and wild, her hair full of lint, nappy at the roots and greasy on the ends. She smelled bad from mouth and underarms and elsewhere. She could not sit still for a minute without jumping up in bitter vexation to run and search a house or street she thought she might have missed before.

"You been messin' with my Jerome?" she would ask whomever she caught in her quivering feverish grip. And before they had time to answer she would have them by the chin in a headlock with a long knife pressed against their necks below the ear. Such blood-chilling questioning of its residents terrified the town, especially since her madness was soon readily perceivable from her appearance. She had taken to grinding her teeth and tearing at her hair as she walked along. The townspeople, none of whom knew where she lived—or anything about her save the name of her man, "Jerome"—were waiting for her to attempt another attack on a woman openly, or, better for them because it implied less danger to a resident, they hoped she would complete her crack-up within the confines of her own home, preferably while alone; in that event anyone seeing or hearing her would be obliged to call the authorities.

She knew this in her deranged but cunning way. But she did not let it interfere with her search. The police would never catch her, she thought; she was too clever. She had a few disguises and a thousand places to hide. A final crack-up in her own home was impossible, she reasoned contemptuously, for she did not think her husband's lover bold enough to show herself on his wife's own turf.

Meanwhile, she stopped operating the beauty shop, and her patrons were glad, for before she left for good she had had the unnerving habit of questioning a woman sitting underneath her hot comb—"You the one ain't you?!"—and would end up burning her no matter what she said. When her father died he proudly left his money to "the schoolteacher" to share or not with his wife, as he had "learnin' enough to see fit." Jerome had "learnin' enough" not to give his wife one cent. The legacy pleased Jerome, though he never bought anything with the money that his wife could see. As long as the money lasted Jerome spoke of it as "insurance." If she asked insurance against what, he would say fire and theft. Or burglary and cyclones. When the money was gone, and it seemed to her it vanished overnight, she asked Jerome what he had bought. He said, Something very big. She said, Like what? He said, Like a tank. She did not ask any more questions after that. By that time she didn't care about the money anyhow, as long as he hadn't spent it on some woman.

As steadily as she careened downhill, Jerome advanced in the opposite direction. He was well known around town as a "shrewd joker" and a scholar. An "intellectual," some people called him, a word that meant nothing whatever to her. Everyone described Jerome in a different way. He had friends among the educated, whose talk she found unusually trying, not that she was ever invited to listen to any of it. His closest friend was the head of the school he taught in and had migrated south from some famous university in the North. He was a small slender man with a ferociously unruly beard and large mournful eyes. He called Jerome "brother." The women in Jerome's group wore short kinky hair and large hoop earrings. They stuck together, calling themselves by what they termed their "African" names, and never went to church. Along with the men, the women sometimes held "workshops" for the young toughs of the town. She had no idea what went on in these; however, she had long since stopped believing they had anything to do with cabinetmaking or any other kind of woodwork.

Among Jerome's group of friends, or "comrades," as he sometimes called them jokingly (or not jokingly, for all she knew), were two or three whites from the community's white college and university. Jerome didn't ordinarily like white people, and she could not understand where they fit into the group. The principal's house was the meeting place, and the whites arrived looking backward over their shoulders after nightfall. She knew, because she had watched this house night after anxious night, trying to rouse enough courage to go inside. One hot night, when a drink helped stiffen her backbone, she burst into the living room in the middle of the evening. The women, whom she had grimly "suspected," sat together in debative conversation in one corner of the room. Every once in a while a phrase she could understand touched her ear. She heard "slave trade" and "violent overthrow" and "off de pig," an expression she'd never heard before. One of the women, the only one of this group to acknowledge her, laughingly asked if she had come to "join the revolution." She had stood shaking by the door, trying so hard to understand she felt she was going to faint. Jerome rose from among the group of men, who sat in a circle on the other side of the room, and, without paying any attention to her, began reciting some of the nastiest-sounding poetry she'd ever heard. She left the room in shame and confusion, and no one bothered to ask why she'd stood so long staring at them, or whether she needed anyone to show her out. She trudged home heavily, with her head down, bewildered, astonished, and perplexed.

3

And now she hunted through her husband's clothes looking for a clue. Her hands were shaking as she emptied and shook, pawed and sometimes even lifted to her nose to smell. Each time she emptied a pocket, she felt there was something, *something,* some little thing that was escaping her.

Her heart pounding, she got down on her knees and looked under the bed. It was dusty and cobwebby, the way the inside of her head felt. The house was filthy, for she had neglected it totally since she began her search. Now it seemed that all the dust in the world had come to rest under her bed. She saw his shoes; she lifted them to her perspiring cheeks and kissed them. She ran her fingers inside them. Nothing.

Then, before she got up from her knees, she thought about the intense blackness underneath the headboard of the bed. She had not looked there. On her side of the bed on the floor beneath the pillow there was nothing. She hurried around to the other side. Kneeling, she struck something with her hand on the floor under his side of the bed. Quickly, down on her stomach, she raked it out. Then she raked and raked. She was panting and sweating, her ashen face slowly coloring with the belated rush of doomed comprehension. In a rush it came to her: "It ain't no woman." Just like that. It had never occurred to her there could be anything more serious. She stifled the cry that rose in her throat.

Coated with grit, with dust sticking to the pages, she held in her crude, indelicate hands, trembling now, a sizable pile of paperback books. Books that had fallen from his hands behind the bed over the months of their marriage. She dusted them carefully one by one and looked with frowning concentration at their covers. Fists and guns appeared everywhere. "Black" was the one word that appeared consistently on each cover. *Black Rage, Black Fire, Black Anger, Black Revenge, Black Vengeance, Black Hatred, Black Beauty, Black Revolution.* Then the word "revolution" took over. *Revolution in the Streets, Revolution from the Rooftops, Revolution in the Hills, Revolution and Rebellion, Revolution and Black People in the United States, Revolution and Death.* She looked with wonder at the books that were her husband's preoccupation, enraged that the obvious was what she had never guessed before.

How many times had she encouraged his light reading? How many times been ignorantly amused? How many times had he laughed at her when she went out looking for "his" women? With a sob she realized she didn't even know what the word "revolution" meant, unless it meant to go round and round, the way her head was going.

With quiet care she stacked the books neatly on his pillow. With the largest of her knives she ripped and stabbed them through. When the brazen and difficult words did not disappear with the books, she hastened with kerosene to set the marriage bed afire. Thirstily, in hopeless jubilation, she watched the room begin to burn. The bits of words transformed themselves into luscious figures of smoke, lazily arching toward the ceiling. "Trash!" she cried over and over, reaching through the flames to strike out the words, now raised from the dead in glorious colors. "I kill you! I kill you!" she screamed against the roaring fire, backing enraged and trembling into a darkened corner of the room, not near the open door. But the fire and the words rumbled against her together, overwhelming her with pain and enlightenment. And she hid her big wet face in her singed then sizzling arms and screamed and screamed.

A Sudden Trip Home in the Spring

for the Wellesley Class

Sarah walked slowly off the tennis court, fingering the back of her head, feeling the sturdy dark hair that grew there. She was popular. As she walked along the path toward Talfinger Hall her friends fell into place around her. They formed a warm jostling group of six. Sarah, because she was taller than the rest, saw the messenger first.

"Miss Davis," he said, standing still until the group came abreast of him, "I've got a telegram for ye." Brian was Irish and always quite respectful. He stood with his cap in his hand until Sarah took the telegram. Then he gave a nod that included all the young ladies before he turned away. He was young and good-looking, though annoyingly servile, and Sarah's friends twittered.

"Well, open it!" someone cried, for Sarah stood staring at the yellow envelope, turning it over and over in her hand.

"Look at her," said one of the girls, "isn't she beautiful! Such eyes, and hair, and *skin!*"

Sarah's tall, caplike hair framed a fact of soft brown angles, high cheekbones and large dark eyes. Her eyes enchanted her friends because they always seemed to know more, and to find more of life amusing, or sad, than Sarah cared to tell.

Her friends often teased Sarah about her beauty; they loved dragging her out of her room so that their boyfriends, naive and worldly young men from Princeton and Yale, could see her. They never guessed she found this distasteful. She was gentle with her friends, and her outrage at their tactlessness did not show. She was most often inclined to pity them, though embarrassment sometimes drove her to fraudulent expressions. Now she smiled and raised eyes and arms to heaven. She acknowledged their unearned curiosity as a mother endures the prying impatience of a child. Her friends beamed love and envy upon her as she tore open the telegram.

"He's dead," she said.

Her friends reached out for the telegram, their eyes on Sarah.

"It's her father," one of them said softly. "He died yesterday. Oh, Sarah," the girl whimpered, "I'm so sorry!"

"Me too." "So am I." "Is there anything we can do?"

But Sarah had walked away, head high and neck stiff.

"So graceful!" one of her friends said.

"Like a proud gazelle," said another. Then they all trooped to their dormitories to change for supper.

Talfinger Hall was a pleasant dorm. The common room just off the entrance had been made into a small modern art gallery with some very good original paintings, lithographs and collages. Pieces were constantly being stolen. Some of the girls could not resist an honest-to-God Chagall, signed (in the plate) by his own hand, though they could have afforded to purchase one from the gallery in town. Sarah Davis's room was next door to the gallery, but her walls were covered with inexpensive Gauguin reproductions, a Rubens ("The Head of a Negro"), a Modigliani and a Picasso. There was a full wall of her own drawings, all of black women. She found black men impossible to draw or to paint; she could not bear to trace defeat onto blank pages. Her women figures were matronly, massive of arm, with a weary victory showing in their eyes. Surrounded by Sarah's drawings was a red SNCC poster of a man holding a small girl whose face nestled in his shoulder. Sarah often felt she was the little girl whose face no one could see.

To leave Talfinger even for a few days filled Sarah with fear. Talfinger was her home now; it suited her better than any home she'd ever known. Perhaps she loved it because in winter there was a fragrant fireplace and snow outside her window. When hadn't she dreamed of fireplaces that really warmed, snow that almost pleasantly froze? Georgia seemed far away as she packed; she did not want to leave New York, where, her grandfather had liked to say, "the devil hung out and caught young girls by the front of their dresses." He had always believed the South the best place to live on earth (never mind that certain people invariably marred the landscape), and swore he expected to die no more than a few miles from where he had been born. There was tenacity even in the gray frame house he lived in, and in scrawny animals on his farm who regularly reproduced. He was the first person Sarah wanted to see when she got home.

There was a knock on the door of the adjoining bathroom, and Sarah's suite mate entered, a loud Bach concerto just finishing behind her. At first she stuck just her head into the room, but seeing Sarah fully dressed she trudged in and plopped down on the bed. She was a heavy blonde girl with large milk-white legs. Her eyes were small and her neck usually gray with grime.

"My, don't you look gorgeous," she said.

"Ah, Pam," said Sarah, waving her hand in disgust. In Georgia she knew that even to Pam she would be just another ordinarily attractive *colored* girl. In Georgia there were a million girls better looking. Pam wouldn't know that, of course; she'd never been to Georgia; she'd never even seen a black person to speak to, that is, before she met Sarah. One of her first poetic observations about Sarah was that she was "a poppy in a field of winter roses." She had found it weird that Sarah did not own more than one coat.

"Say listen, Sarah," said Pam, "I heard about your father. I'm sorry. I really am."

"Thanks," said Sarah.

"Is there anything we can do? I thought, well, maybe you'd want my father to get somebody to fly you down. He'd go himself but he's taking Mother to Madeira this week. You wouldn't have to worry about trains and things."

Pamela's father was one of the richest men in the world, though no one ever mentioned it. Pam only alluded to it at times of crisis, when a friend might benefit from the use of a private plane, train, or ship; or, if someone wanted to study the characteristics of a totally secluded village, island or mountain, she might offer one of theirs. Sarah could not comprehend such wealth, and was always annoyed because Pam didn't look more like a billionaire's daughter. A billionaire's daughter, Sarah thought, should really be less horsey and brush her teeth more often.

"Gonna tell me what you're brooding about?" asked Pam.

Sarah stood in front of the radiator, her fingers resting on the window seat. Down below girls were coming up the hill from supper.

"I'm thinking," she said, "of the child's duty to his parents after they are dead."

"Is that all?"

"Do you know," asked Sarah, "about Richard Wright and his father?"

Pam frowned. Sarah looked down at her.

"Oh, I forgot," she said with a sigh, "they don't teach Wright here. The poshest school in the U.S., and the girls come out ignorant." She looked at her watch, saw she had twenty minutes before her train. "Really," she said almost inaudibly, "why Tears Eliot, Ezratic Pound, and even Sara Teacake, and no Wright?" She and Pamela thought e. e. cummings very clever with his perceptive spelling of great literary names.

"Is he a poet then?" asked Pam. She adored poetry, all poetry. Half of America's poetry she had, of course, not read, for the simple reason that she had never heard of it.

"No," said Sarah, "he wasn't a poet." She felt weary. "He was a man who wrote, a man who had trouble with his father." She began to walk about the room, and came to stand below the picture of the old man and the little girl.

"When he was a child," she continued, "his father ran off with another woman, and one day when Richard and his mother went to ask him for money to buy food he laughingly rejected them. Richard, being very young, thought his father Godlike. Big, omnipotent, unpredictable, undependable and cruel. Entirely in control of his universe. Just like a god. But, many years later, after Wright had become a famous writer, he went down to Mississippi to visit his father. He found, instead of God, just an old watery-eyed field hand, bent from plowing, his teeth gone, smelling of manure. Richard realized that the most daring thing his 'God' had done was run off with that other woman."

"So?" asked Pam. "What 'duty' did he feel he owed the old man?"

"So," said Sarah, "that's what Wright wondered as he peered into that old shifty-eyed Mississippi Negro face. What was the duty of the son of a destroyed man? The son of a man whose vision had stopped at the edge of fields that weren't even his. Who was Wright without his father? Was he Wright the great writer? Wright the Communist? Wright the French farmer? Wright whose white wife could never accompany him to Mississippi? Was he, in fact, still his father's son? Or was he freed by his father's desertion to be nobody's son, to be his own father? Could he disavow his father and live? And if so, live as what? As whom? And for what purpose?"

"Well," said Pam, swinging her hair over her shoulders and squinting her small eyes, "if his father rejected him I don't see why Wright even bothered to go see him again. From what you've said, Wright earned the freedom to be whoever he wanted to be. To a strong man a father is not essential."

"Maybe not," said Sarah, "but Wright's father was one faulty door in a house of many ancient rooms. Was that one faulty door to shut him off forever from the rest of the house? That was the question. And though he answered this question eloquently in his work, where it really counted, one can only wonder if he was able to answer it satisfactorily—or at all—in his life."

"You're thinking of his father more as a symbol of something, aren't you?" asked Pam.

"I suppose," said Sarah, taking a last look around her room. "I see him as a door that refused to open, a hand that was always closed. A fist."

Pamela walked with her to one of the college limousines, and in a few minutes she was at the station. The train to the city was just arriving.

"Have a nice trip," said the middle-aged driver courteously, as she took her suitcase from him. But for about the thousandth time since she'd seen him, he winked at her.

Once away from her friends she did not miss them. The school was all they had in common. How could they ever know her if they were not allowed to know Wright, she wondered. She was interesting, "beautiful," only because they had no idea what made her, charming only because they had no idea from where she came. And where they came from, though she glimpsed it—in themselves and in F. Scott Fitzgerald—she was never to enter. She hadn't the inclination or the proper ticket.

2

Her father's body was in Sarah's old room. The bed had been taken down to make room for the flowers and chairs and casket. Sarah looked for a long time into the face, as if to find some answer to her questions written there. It was the same face, a dark Shakespearean head framed by gray, woolly hair and split almost in half by a short, gray mustache. It was a completely silent face, a shut face. But her father's face also looked fat, stuffed, and ready to burst. He wore a navy-blue suit, white shirt and black tie. Sarah bent and loosened the tie. Tears started behind her shoulder blades but did not reach her eyes.

"There's a rat here under the casket," she called to her brother, who apparently did not hear her, for he did not come in. She was alone with her father, as she had rarely been when he was alive. When he was alive she had avoided him.

"Where's that girl at?" her father would ask. "Done closed herself up in her room again," he would answer himself.

For Sarah's mother had died in her sleep one night. Just gone to bed tired and never got up. And Sarah had blamed her father.

Stare the rat down, thought Sarah, surely that will help. *Perhaps it doesn't matter whether I misunderstood or never understood.*

"We moved so much looking for crops, a place to *live,*" her father had moaned, accompanied by Sarah's stony silence. "The moving killed her. And now we have a real house, with *four* rooms, and a mailbox on the *porch,* and it's too late. She gone. *She* ain't here to see it." On very bad days her father would not eat at all. At night he did not sleep.

Whatever had made her think she knew what love was or was not?

Here she was, Sarah Davis, immersed in Camusian philosophy, versed in many languages, a poppy, of all things, among winter roses. But before she became a poppy she was a native Georgian sunflower, but still had not spoken the language they both knew. Not to him.

Stare the rat down, she thought, and did. The rascal dropped his bold eyes and slunk away. Sarah felt she had, at least, accomplished something.

Why did she have to see the picture of her mother, the one on the mantel among all the religious doodads, come to life? Her mother had stood stout against the years, clean gray braids shining across the top of her head, her eyes snapping, protective. Talking to her father.

"He called you out your name, we'll leave this place today. Not tomorrow. That be too late. Today!" Her mother was magnificent in her quick decisions.

"But what about your garden, the children, the change of schools?" Her father would be holding, most likely, the wide brim of his hat in nervously twisting fingers.

"He called out your name, we go!"

And go they would. Who knew exactly where, before they moved? Another soundless place, walls falling down, roofing gone; another face to please without leaving too much of her father's pride at his feet. But to Sarah then, no matter with what alacrity her father moved, foot-dragging alone was visible.

The moving killed her, her father had said, *but the moving was also love.*

Did it matter now that often he had threatened their lives with the rage of his despair? That once he had spanked the crying baby violently, who later died of something else altogether . . . and that the next day they moved?

"No," said Sarah aloud, "I don't think it does."

"Huh?" It was her brother, tall, wiry, black, deceptively calm. As a child he'd had an irrespressible temper. As a grown man he was tensely smooth, like a river that any day will overflow its bed.

He had chosen a dull gray casket. Sarah wished for red. Was it Dylan Thomas who had said something grand about the dead offering "deep, dark defiance"? It didn't matter; there were more ways to offer defiance than with a red casket.

"I was just thinking," said Sarah, "that with us Mama and Daddy were saying NO with capital letters."

"I don't follow you," said her brother. He had always been the activist in the family. He simply directed his calm rage against any obstacle that might exist, and awaited the consequences with the same serenity he awaited his sister's answer. Not for him the philosophical confusions and poetic observations that hung his sister up.

"That's because you're a radical preacher," said Sarah, smiling up at him. "You deliver your messages in person with your own body." It excited her that her brother had at last imbued their childhood Sunday sermons with the reality of fighting for change. And saddened her that no matter how she looked at it this seemed more important than Medieval Art, Course 201.

3

"Yes, Grandma," Sarah replied. "Cresselton is for girls only, and *no,* Grandma, I am not pregnant."

Her grandmother stood clutching the broad wooden handle of her black bag, which she held, with elbows bent, in front of her stomach. Her eyes glinted through round wire-framed glasses. She spat into the grass outside the privy. She had insisted that Sarah accompany her to the toilet while the body was being taken into the church. She had leaned heavily on Sarah's arm, her own arm thin and the flesh like crepe.

"I guess they teach you how to really handle the world," she said. "And who knows, the Lord is everywhere. I would like a whole lot to see a Great-Grand. You don't specially have to be married, you know. That's why I felt free to ask." She reached into her bag and took out a Three Sixes bottle, which she proceeded to drink from, taking deep swift swallows with her head thrown back.

"There are very few black boys near Cresselton," Sarah explained, watching the corn liquor leave the bottle in spurts and bubbles. "Besides, I'm really caught up now in my painting and sculpting. . . ." Should she mention how much she admired Giacometti's work? No, she decided. Even if her grandmother had heard of him, and Sarah was positive she had not, she would surely think his statues much too thin. This made Sarah smile and remember how difficult it had been to convince her grandmother that even if Cresselton had not given her a scholarship she would have managed to go there anyway. Why? Because she wanted somebody to teach her to paint and to sculpt, and Cresselton had the best teachers. Her grandmother's notion of a successful granddaughter was a married one, pregnant the first year.

"Well," said her grandmother, placing the bottle with dignity back into her purse and gazing pleadingly into Sarah's face, "I sure would 'preshate a Great-Grand." Seeing her granddaughter's smile, she heaved a great sigh, and, walking rather haughtily over the stones and grass, made her way to the church steps.

As they walked down the aisle, Sarah's eyes rested on the back of her grandfather's head. He was sitting on the front middle bench in front of the casket, his hair extravagantly long and white and softly kinked. When she sat down beside him, her grandmother sitting next to him on the other side, he turned toward her and gently took her hand in his. Sarah briefly leaned her cheek against his shoulder and felt like a child again.

4

They had come twenty miles from town, on a dirt road, and the hot spring sun had drawn a steady rich scent from the honeysuckle vines along the way. The church was a bare, weather-beaten ghost of a building with hollow windows and a sagging door. Arsonists had once burned it to the ground, lighting the dry wood of the walls with the flames from the crosses they carried. The tall spreading red oak tree under which Sarah had played as a child still dominated the churchyard, stretching its branches widely from the roof of the church to the other side of the road.

After a short and eminently dignified service, during which Sarah and her grandfather alone did not cry, her father's casket was slid into the waiting hearse and taken the short distance to the cemetery, an overgrown wilderness whose stark white stones appeared to be the small ruins of an ancient civilization. There Sarah watched her grandfather from the corner of her eye. He did not seem to bend under the grief of burying a son. His back was straight, his eyes dry and clear. He was simply and solemnly heroic; a man who kept with his pride his family's trust and his own grief. *It is strange,* Sarah thought, *that I never thought to paint him like this, simply as he stands; without anonymous meaningless people hovering beyond his profile; his face turned proud and brownly against the light.* The defeat that had frightened her in the faces of black men was the defeat of black forever defined by white. But that defeat was nowhere on her grandfather's face. He stood like a rock, outwardly calm, the comfort and support of the Davis family. The family alone defined him, and he was not about to let them down.

"One day I will paint you, Grandpa," she said, as they turned to go. "Just as you stand here now, with just"—she moved closer and touched his face with her hand—"just the right stubborn tenseness of your cheek. Just that look of Yes and No in your eyes."

"You wouldn't want to paint an old man like me," he said, looking deep into her eyes from wherever his mind had been. "If you want to make me, make me up in stone."

The completed grave was plump and red. The wreaths of flowers were arranged all on one side so that from the road there appeared to be only a large mass of flowers. But already the wind was tugging at the rose petals and the rain was making dabs of faded color all over the green foam frames. In a week the displaced honeysuckle vines, the wild roses, the grapevines, the grass, would be back. Nothing would seem to have changed.

5

"What do you mean, come *home?*" Her brother seemed genuinely amused. "We're all proud of you. How many black girls are at that school? Just *you?* Well, just one more besides you, and she's from the North. That's really something!"

"I'm glad you're pleased," said Sarah.

"Pleased! Why, it's what Mama would have wanted, a good education for little Sarah; and what Dad would have wanted too, if he could have wanted anything after Mama died. You were always smart. When you were two and I was five you showed me how to eat ice cream without getting it all over me. First, you said, nip off the bottom of the cone with your teeth, and suck the ice cream down. I never knew *how* you were supposed to eat the stuff once it began to melt."

"I don't know," she said, "sometimes you can want something a whole lot, only to find out later that it wasn't what you *needed* at all."

Sarah shook her head, a frown coming between her eyes. "I sometimes spend *weeks*," she said, "trying to sketch or paint a face that is unlike every other face around me, except, vaguely, for one. Can I help wonder if I'm in the right place?"

Her brother smiled. "You mean to tell me you spend *weeks* trying to draw one face, and you still wonder whether you're in the right place? You must be kidding!" He chucked her under the chin and laughed out loud. "You learn how to draw the face," he said, "then you learn how to paint me and how to make Grandpa up in stone. Then you can come home or go live in Paris, France. It'll be the same thing."

It was the unpreacherlike gaiety of his affection that made her cry. She leaned peacefully into her brother's arms. She wondered if Richard Wright had had a brother.

"You are my door to all the rooms," she said. "Don't ever close."

And he said, "I won't," as if he understood what she meant.

6

"When will we see you again, young woman?" he asked later, as he drove her to the bus stop.

"I'll sneak up one day and surprise you," she sad.

At the bus stop, in front of a tiny service station, Sarah hugged her brother with all her strength. The white station attendant stopped his work to leer at them, his eyes bold and careless.

"Did you ever think," said Sarah, "that we are a very old people in a very young place?"

She watched her brother from a window of the bus; her eyes did not leave his face until the little station was out of sight and the big Greyhound lurched on its way toward Atlanta. She would fly from there to New York.

7

She took the train to the campus.

"My," said one of her friends, "you look wonderful! Home sure must agree with you!"

"Sarah was home?" Someone who didn't know asked. "Oh, *great*, how was it?"

"Well, how was it?" went an echo in Sarah's head. The noise of the echo almost made her dizzy.

"How was it?" she asked aloud, searching for, and regaining, her balance. "How was it?" She watched her reflection in a pair of smiling hazel eyes.

"It was fine," she said slowly, returning the smile, thinking of her grandfather. "Just fine."

The girl's smile deepened. Sarah watched her swinging along toward the back tennis courts, hair blowing in the wind.

Stare the rat down, thought Sarah; *and whether it disappears or not, I am a woman in the world. I have buried my father, and shall soon know how to make my grandpa up in stone.*

from The Color Purple

Dear Nettie,

I don't write to God no more, I write to you.

What happen to God? ast Shug.

Who that? I say.

She look at me serious.

Big a devil as you is, I say, you not worried bout no God, surely.

She say, Wait a minute. Hold on just a minute here. Just because I don't harass it like some peoples us know don't mean I ain't got religion.

What God do for me? I ast.

She say, Celie! Like she shock. He gave you life, good health, and a good woman that love you to death.

Yeah, I say, and he give me a lynched daddy, a crazy mama, a lowdown dog of a step pa and a sister I probably won't ever see again. Anyhow, I say, the God I been praying and writing to is a man. And act just like all the other mens I know. Trifling, forgitful and lowdown.

She say, Miss Celie, You better hush. God might hear you.

Let 'im hear me, I say. If he ever listened to poor colored women the world would be a different place, I can tell you.

She talk and she talk, trying to budge me way from blasphemy. But I blaspheme much as I want to.

All my life I never care what people thought bout nothing I did, I say. But deep in my heart I care about God. What he going to think. And come to find out, he don't think. Just sit up there glorying in being deef, I reckon. But it ain't easy, trying to do without God. Even if you know he ain't there, trying to do without him is a strain.

I is a sinner, say Shug. Cause I was born. I don't deny it. But once you find out what's out there waiting for us, what else can you be?

Sinner's have more good times, I say.

You know why? she ast.

Cause you ain't all the time worrying bout God, I say.

Naw, that ain't it, she say. Us worry bout God a lot. But once us feel loved by God, us do the best us can to please him with what us like.

You telling me God love you, and you ain't never done nothing for him? I mean, not go to church, sing in the choir, feed the preacher and all like that?

But if God love me, Celie, I don't have to do all that. Unless I want to. There's a lot of other things I can do that I speck God likes.

Like what? I ast.

Oh, she say. I can lay back and just admire stuff. Be happy. Have a good time.

Well, this sound like blasphemy sure nuff.

She say, Celie, tell the truth, have you ever found God in church? I never did.

I just found a bunch of folks hoping for him to show. Any God I ever felt in church I brought in with me. And I think all the other folks did too. They come to church to *share* God, not find God.

Some folks don't have him to share, I said. They the ones didn't speak to me while I was there struggling with my big belly and Mr. ______ children.

Right, she say.

Then she say: Tell me what your God look like, Celie.

Aw naw, I say. I'm too shame. Nobody ever ast me this before, so I'm sort of took by surprise. Besides, when I think about it, it don't seem quite right. But it all I got. I decide to stick up from him, just to see what Shug say.

Okay, I say. He big and old and tall and graybearded and white. He wear white robes and go barefooted.

Blue eyes? she ast.

Sort of bluish-gray. Cool. Big though. White lashes, I say.

She laugh.

Why you laugh? I ast. I don't think it so funny. What you expect him to look like, Mr. ______?

That wouldn't be no improvement, she say. Then she tell me this old white man is the same God she used to see when she prayed. If you wait to find God in church, Celie, she say, that's who is bound to show up, cause that's where he live.

How come? I ast.

Cause that's the one that's in the white folks' white bible.

Shug! I say. God wrote the bible, white folks had nothing to do with it.

How come he look just like them, then? she say. Only bigger? And a heap more hair. How come the bible just like everything else they make, all about them doing one thing and another, and all the colored folks doing is gitting cursed?

I never thought bout that.

Nettie say somewhere in the bible it says Jesus' hair was like lamb's wool, I say.

Well, say Shug, if he came to any of these churches we talking bout he'd have to have it conked before anybody paid him any attention. The last thing niggers want to think about they God is that his hair kinky.

That's the truth, I say.

Ain't no way to read the bible and not think God white, she say. Then she sigh. When I found out I thought God was white, and a man, I lost interest! You mad cause he don't seem to listen to your prayers. Humph! Do the mayor listen to anything colored say? Ask Sofia, she say.

But I don't have to ast Sofia. I know white people never listen to colored, period. If they do, they only listen long enough to be able to tell you what to do.

Here's the thing, say Shug. The thing I believe. God is inside you and inside everybody else. You come into the world with God. But only them that search for it inside find it. And sometimes it just manifest itself even if you are not looking, or don't know what you looking for. Trouble do it for most folks, I think. Sorrow, lord. Feeling like shit.

It? I ast.

Yeah, It. God ain't a he or a she, but a It.

But what do it look like? I ast.

Don't look like nothing, she say. It ain't a picture show. It ain't something you can look at apart from anything else, including yourself. I believe God is everything, say Shug. Everything that is or ever was or ever will be. And when you can feel that, and be happy to feel that, you've found It.

Shug a beautiful something, let me tell you. She frown a little, look out cross the yard, lean back in her chair, look like a big rose.

She say, My first step from the old white man was trees. Then air. Then birds. Then other people. But one day when I was sitting quiet and feeling like a motherless child, which I was, it come to me: that feeling of being part of everything, not separate at all. I knew that if I cut a tree, my arm would bleed. And I laughed and I cried and I run all around the house. I knew just what it was. In fact, when it happen, you can't miss it. It sort of like you know what, she say, grinning and rubbing high up on my thing.

Shug! I say.

Oh, she say. God love all them feelings. That's some of the best stuff God did. And when you know God loves 'em you enjoys 'em a lot more. You can just relax, go with everything that's going, and praise God by liking what you like.

God don't think it dirty? I ast.

Naw, she say. God made it. Listen, God love everything you love—and a mess of stuff you don't. But more than anything else, God love admiration.

You saying God vain? I ast.

Naw, she say. Not vain, just wanting to share a good thing. I think it pisses God off if you walk by the color purple in a field somewhere and don't notice it.

What it do when it pissed off? I ast.

Oh, it makes something else. People think pleasing God is all God care about. But any fool living in the world can see it always trying to please us back.

Yeah? I say.

Yeah, she say. It always making little surprises and springing them on us when us least expect.

You mean it want to be loved, just like the bible say.

Yes, Celie, she say. Everything want to be loved. Us sing and dance, make faces and give flower bouquets, trying to be loved. You ever notice that trees do everything to git attention we do, except walk?

Well, us talk and talk bout God, but I'm still adrift. Trying to chase that old white man out of my head. I been so busy thinking bout him I never truly notice nothing God make. Not a blade of corn (how it do that?) not the color purple (where it come from?). Not the little wildflowers. Nothing.

Now that my eyes opening, I feels like a fool. Next to any little scrub of a bush in my yard, Mr. ______'s evil sort of shrink. But not altogether. Still, it is like Shug say, You have to git man off your eyeball, before you can see anything a'tall.

Man corrupt everything, say Shug. He on your box of grits, in your head, and all over the radio. He try to make you think he everywhere. Soon as you think he everywhere, you think he God. But he ain't. Whenever you trying to pray, and man plop himself on the other end of it, tell him to git lost, say Shug. Conjure up flowers, wind, water, a big rock.

But this hard work, let me tell you. He been there so long, he don't want to budge. He threaten lightening, floods and earthquakes. Us fight. I hardly pray at all. Every time I conjure up a rock, I throw it.

Amen

A Critical Perspective: **Barbara Christian** (1943–)

Barbara Christian, an eminent contemporary black scholar and professor, was born on St. Thomas in the U.S. Virgin Islands. After receiving a B.A. from Marquette University in 1963, Christian completed her M.A. and Ph.D. in Contemporary British and American Literature at Columbia University in 1964 and 1970, respectively.

Since 1963, the author has taught on numerous campuses, rooting herself at the University of California in Berkeley, where she has been a full professor since 1986. Over the years, her extensive college teaching of African American Studies and Women's Studies and Literature has taken her to such institutions as the University of Alaska, Anchorage; Amherst College; the University of Bologna, Italy; the University of Hawaii; the University of Michigan; the University of North Carolina; and Stanford University.

In addition to an extensive list of essays and reviews, Christian has published an impressive number of books, including Black Women Novelists: The Development of a Tradition, 1892–1976 *(1980),* Black Feminist Criticism: Perspectives on Black Women Writers *(1985), and* Alice Walker and The Color Purple *(1988). She has cowritten and coedited* In Search of Our Past: Six Units for the Teaching of Multiethnic Women's History *(1978),* Black Working Women: Debunking the Myth—A MultiDisciplinary Approach *(1983), and* The Feminist Companion to Literature in English: Women Writers from the Middle Ages to the Present *(1990). In 1993 and 1994, she edited three volumes:* Alice Walker's "Everyday Use": A Casebook, *the African American section of the* HarperCollins World Anthology, *and the contemporary section of the* Norton Anthology of African American Literature.

The following essay, "Alice Walker: The Black Woman Artist as Wayward," originally appeared in Black Women Writers *(1984) edited by Mari Evans. Assessing Walker's works from 1968 to 1983, the essay discusses themes and recurrent motifs in Walker's prose and poetry.*

Alice Walker: The Black Woman Artist as Wayward

I find my own
small person
a standing self
against the world
an equality of wills
I finally understand[1]

Alice Walker has produced a significant body of work since 1968, when *Once,* her first volume of poetry, was published. Prolific, albeit a young writer, she is already acclaimed by many to be one of America's finest novelists, having captured both the American Book Award and the coveted Pulitzer in 1983.

Her substantial body of writing, though it varies, is characterized by specific recurrent motifs. Most obvious is Walker's attention to the Black woman as creator, and to how her attempt to be whole relates to the health of her community.

This theme is certainly focal to Walker's two collections of short stories, *In Love and Trouble* and *You Can't Keep a Good Woman Down,* to her classic essay, *In Search of Our Mothers' Gardens,* and to *Meridian* and *The Color Purple,* her second and third novels. And it reverberates in her personal efforts to help rescue the works of Zora Neale Hurston from a threatening oblivion. Increasingly, as indicated by her last collection of poems, *Good Night Willie Lee,* Walker's work is Black women-centered.

Another recurrent motif in Walker's work is her insistence on probing the relationship between struggle and change, a probing that encompasses the pain of Black people's lives, against which the writer protests but which she will not ignore. Paradoxically such pain sometimes results in growth, precisely because of the nature of the struggle that must be borne, if there is to be change. Presented primarily through three generations of one family in Walker's first novel, *The Third Life of Grange Copeland,* the struggle to change takes on overt societal dimensions in *Meridian,* her second novel. Characteristically this theme is presented in her poetry, fiction, and essays, as a spiritual legacy of Black people in the South.

One might also characterize Walker's work as organically spare rather than elaborate, ascetic rather than lush, a process of stripping off layers, honing down to the core. This pattern, impressionistic in *Once,* is refined in her subsequent volumes of poetry and clearly marks the structure of her fiction and essays. There is a concentrated distillation of language which, ironically, allows her to expand rather than constrict. Few contemporary American writers have examined so many facets of sex and race, love and societal changes, as has Walker, without abandoning the personal grace that distinguishes her voice.

These elements—the focus on the struggle of Black people, especially Black women, to claim their own lives, and the contention that this struggle emanates from a deepening of self-knowledge and love—are characteristics of Walker's work. Yet it seems they are not really the essential quality that distinguishes her work, for these characteristics might be said to apply to any number of contemporary Black women writers—e.g., Toni Morrison, Paule Marshall, June Jordan. Walker's peculiar sound, the specific mode through which her deepening of self-knowledge and self-love comes, seems to have much to do with her contrariness, her willingness at all turns to challenge the fashionable belief of the day, to reexamine it in the light of her own experiences and of dearly won principles which she has previously challenged and absorbed. There is a sense in which the "forbidden" in the society is consistently approached by Walker as a possible route to truth. At the core of this contrariness is an unwavering honesty about what she sees. Thus in *Once,* her first volume of poems, the then twenty-three-year-old Walker wrote, during the heyday of Afro-Americans' romanticizing of their motherland, about her stay in Africa, in images that were not always complimentary. In her poem "Karamojans" Walker demystified Africa:

> A tall man
> Without clothes
> Beautiful
> Like a statue
> Up close
> His eyes
> Are running
> Sores[2]

Such a perception was, at that time, practically blasphemy among a progressive element of Black thinkers and activists. Yet, seemingly impervious to the risk of rebuke, the young Walker challenged the idealistic view of Africa as an image, a beautiful artifact to be used by Afro-Americans in their pursuit of racial pride. The poet does not flinch from what she sees—does not romanticize or inflate it ("His eyes/Are running/Sores.") Yet her words acknowledge that she knows the ideal African image as others project it: "Beautiful/Like a statue." It is the "Up close" that sets up the tension in the lines between appearance and reality, mystification and the real, and provides Walker's peculiar sound, her insistence on honesty as if there were no other way to be. The lines, then, do not scream at the reader or harp on the distinction between the image and the man she sees. The lines *are* that distinction. They embody the tension, stripping its dimensions down to the essentials. "Karamojans" ends:

> The Karamojans
> Never civilized
> A proud people
> I think there
> Are
> A hundred left.[3]

So much for the concept of pride without question.

At the cutting edge of much of Walker's early work is an intense examination of those ideas advocated by the most visible of recent Afro-American spokespersons. In 1970, at the height of cultural nationalism, the substance of most Black literary captivity was focused on the rebellious urban Black in confrontation with white society. In that year, Walker's first novel, *The Third Life of Grange Copeland,* was published. By tracing the history of the Copeland family through three generations, Walker demonstrated the relationship between the racist sharecropping system and the violence that the men, women, and children of that family inflict on each other. The novel is most emphatically located in the rural South, rather than the Northern urban ghetto; its characters are Southern peasants rather than Northern lumpen, reminding us that much of Afro-American population is still under the yoke of a feudal sharecropping system. And the novel is written more from the angle of the tentative survival of a Black family than from an overt confrontation between Black and white.

Also, Walker's first novel, like Marshall's *The Chosen Place, the Timeless People* (1969) and Morrison's *The Bluest Eye* (1970), seemed out of step with the end-of-the-decade work of such writers as Imamu Baraka, or Ishamel Reed—Black writers on opposing sides of the spectrum—in that the struggle her major characters wage against racism is located in, sometimes veiled by, a network of family and community. The impact of racism is felt primarily through the characters' mistaken definitions of themselves as men and women. Grange Copeland first hates himself because he is powerless, as opposed to powerful, the definition of maleness for him. His reaction is to prove his power by inflicting violence on the women around him. His brief sojourn in the North where he feels invisible, a step below powerlessness, causes him to hate whites as his oppressors. That, however, for Walker, does not precipitate meaningful struggle. It is only when he learns to love himself, through his commitment to his granddaughter, Ruth, that Grange Copeland is able to confront the white racist system. And in so doing, he must also destroy his son, the fruit of his initial self-hatred.

The Third Life of Grange Copeland, then, is based on the principle that societal change is invariably linked to personal change, that the struggle must be inner- as well as outer-directed. Walker's insistence on locating the motivation for struggle within the self led her to examine the definition of nigger, that oft-used word in the literature of the late sixties. Her definition, however, is not generalized but precise: a nigger is a Black person who believes he or she is incapable of being responsible for his or her actions, that the white folks are to blame for everything, including his or her behavior. As Grange says to his son, Brownfield, in their one meaningful exchange in the novel: " '. . . when they get you thinking they're to blame for everything they have you thinking they're some kind of gods. . . . Shit, nobody's as powerful as we make them out to be. We got our own souls, don't we?' "[4]

The question lingering at the end of this novel—whether the psychological impact of oppression is so great that it precludes one's overcoming of it—is also a major undercurrent of the literature of this period. There is a tension in the militant literature of the late sixties between a need to *assert* the love of Black people for Black people and an anger that Black people have somehow allowed themselves to be oppressed. The ambivalence caused by a desire for self-love and an expression of shame is seldom clearly articulated in the literature but implied in the militant Black writer's exhortation to their people to stop being niggers and start becoming Black men and women. What Walker did, in her first novel, was to give voice to his tension and to graph the development of one man in his journey toward its resolution.

Grange Copeland's journey toward this resolution is not, however, an idea that Walker imposes on the novel. A characteristic of hers is her attempt to use the essence of a complex dilemma organically in the composing of her work. So the structure of *The Third Life of Grange Copeland* is based on the dramatic tension between the pervasive racism of the society and the need for her characters, if they are to hold on to self-love, to accept responsibility for their own lives. The novel is divided into two parts, the first analyzing the degeneration of Grange's and then his son Brownfield's respective families, the second focusing on the regeneration of the Copelands, as Grange, against all odds, takes responsibility for Brownfield's daughter, Ruth. Within these two larger pieces, Walker created a quilt of recurring motifs which are arranged, examined, and rearranged so that the reader might understand the complex nature of the tension between the power of oppressive societal forces and the possibility for change. Walker's use of recurring economical patterns, much like a quilting process, gives the novel much of its force and uniqueness. Her insistence on critically examining the ideas of the time led her not only to analysis but also to a synthesis that increasingly marks her work.

Walker is drawn to the integral and economical process of quilt making as a model for her own craft. For through it, one can create out of seemingly disparate everyday materials patterns of clarity, imagination, and beauty. Two of her works especially emphasize the idea of this process: her classic essay *In Search of Our Mothers' Gardens* and her short story "Everyday Use." Each piece complements the other and articulates the precise meaning of the quilt as idea and process for this writer.

In *In Search of Our Mothers' Gardens,* Walker directly asks the question that every writer must: From whence do I, as a writer, come? What is my tradition? In pursuing the question she focuses most intensely on her female heritage, in itself a point of departure from the route most writers have taken. Walker traces the images of Black women in the literature as well as those few of them who were able to be writers. However, as significant as the tracing of that literary history is, Walker's major insight in the essay is her illumination of the creative legacy of "ordinary" Black women of the South, a focus which complements but finally transcends literary history. In her insistence on honesty, on examining the roots of *her own* creativity, she invokes not so much the literature of Black women, which was probably unknown to her as a budding child writer, but the creativity known to her of her mother, her grandmother, the women around her.

What did some slave women or Black women of this century do with the creativity that might have, in a less restrictive society, expressed itself in paint, words, clay? Walker reflects on a truth so obvious it is seldom acknowledged: they used the few media left them by a society that labeled them lowly, menial. Some, like Walker's mother, expressed it in the growing of magnificent gardens; some in cooking; others in quilts of imagination and passion like the one Walker saw at the Smithsonian Institution. Walker's description of that quilt's impact on her brings together essential elements of her more recent work: the theme of the Black woman's creativity—her transformation despite opposition of the bits and pieces allowed her by society into a work of functional beauty.

But Walker does not merely acknowledge quilts (or the art Black women created out of "low" media) as high art, a tendency now fostered by many women who have discovered the works of their maternal ancestors. She is also impressed by their *functional* beauty and by the process that produced them. Her short story "Everyday Use" is in some ways a conclusion in fiction to her essay. Just as she juxtaposed the history of Black women writers with the creative legacy of ordinary Black women, so she complemented her own essay, a search for the roots of her own creativity, with a story that embodies the idea itself.

In "Everyday Use," Walker again scrutinized a popular premise of the times. The story which is dedicated to "your grandmama" is about the use and misuse of the concept of heritage. The mother of two daughters, one selfish and stylish, the other scarred and caring, passes on to us its true definition. Dee, the sister who has always despised the backward ways of her Southern rural family comes back to visit her old home. She has returned to her Black roots because now they are fashionable. So she glibly delights in the artifacts of her heritage: the rough benches her father made, the handmade butter churn which she intends to use for a decorative centerpiece, the quilts made by her grandma Dee after whom she was named—the *things* that have been passed on. Ironically, in keeping with the times, Dee has changed her name to Wangero, denying the existence of her namesake, even as she covets the quilts she made.

On the other hand, her sister Maggie is not aware of the word *heritage.* But she loves her grandma and cherishes her memory in the quilts she made. Maggie has accepted the *spirit* that was passed on to her. The contrast between the two sisters is aptly summarized in Dee's focal line in the story: " 'Maggie can't appreciate these quilts!' she [Dee] said. 'She'd probably be backward enough to put them to everyday use.' "[5] Which her mother counters with: " 'She can always make some more. Maggie knows how to quilt.' "[6]

The mother affirms the functional nature of their heritage and insists that it must continually be renewed rather than fixed in the past. The mother's succinct phrasing of the meaning of *heritage* is underscored by Dee's lack of knowledge about the bits and pieces that make up these quilts, the process of quilting that Maggie knows. For Maggie appreciates the people who made them while Dee can only possess the "priceless" products. Dee's final words, ironically, exemplifies her misuse of the concept of heritage, of what is passed on:

" 'What don't I understand?' " I wanted to know.

" 'Your heritage,' she said. And then she turned to Maggie, kissed her and said. 'You ought to try to make something of yourself, too, Maggie. It's a new day for us. But from the way you and mama still live you'd never know it.' "[7]

In critically analyzing the uses of the concept of heritage, Walker arrived at important distinctions. As an abstraction rather than a living idea, its misuse can subordinate people to artifact, can elevate culture above the community. And because she used, as the artifact, quilts which were made by Southern Black women, she focused attention on those supposedly backward folk who never heard the word heritage but fashioned a functional tradition out of little matter and much spirit.

In "Everyday Use," the mother, seemingly in a fit of contrariness, snatches the beautiful quilts out of the hands of the "Black" Wangero and gives them to the "backward" Maggie. This story is one of eleven in Walker's first collection of short stories, *In Love and Trouble.* Though written over a period of some five years, the volume is unified by two of Walker's most persistent characteristics: her use of a Southern Black woman character as protagonist, and that character's insistence on challenging convention, on being herself, sometimes in spite of herself.

Walker sets the tone for this volume by introducing the stories with two excerpts, one from *The Concubine,* a novel by the contemporary West African writer Elechi Amadi, the other from *Letters to a Young Poet* by the early-twentieth-century German poet Rainer Maria Rilke. The first excerpt emphasizes the rigidity of West African convention in relation to women. Such convention results in a young girl's contrariness, which her society explains away by saying she is unduly influenced by *agwu,* her personal spirit. The second excerpt from Rilke summarizes a philosophy of life that permeates the work of Alice Walker:

> . . . People have (with the help of conventions) oriented all their solutions towards the easy and towards the easiest of the easy; but it is clear that we must hold to what is difficult; everything in nature grows and defines itself in its own way, and is characteristically and spontaneously itself, seeks at all costs to be so against all opposition.[8]

The protagonists in this volume embody this philosophy. They seek at all costs to be characteristically and spontaneously themselves. But because the conventions which gravely affect relationships between male and female, Black and white, young and old, are so rigid, the heroines of *In Love and Trouble* seem backward, contrary, mad. Depending on their degree of freedom within the society, they express their *agwu* in dream, word, or act.

Roselily, the poor mother of illegitimate children, can express her *agwu* only through dreaming, during her wedding to a Northern Black Muslim. Though her marriage is seen by most as a triumphant delivery from her poor backward condition, she sees that, as a woman, whether single or married, Christian or Muslim, she is confined. She can only dream that "She wants to live for once. But doesn't quite know what that means. Wonders if she ever has done it. If she ever will."[9]

In contrast to Roselily, Myrna, the protagonist of "Really, Doesn't Crime Pay" is the wife of a middle-class Southern Black man. Still, she too is trapped by her husband and society's view of woman, though her confinement is not within a black veil but in the decorative mythology of the Southern Lady. However, unlike Roselily, Myrna does more than dream, she writes. In a series of journal entries, she tells us how the restrictions imposed upon her creativity lead her to attempt to noisily murder her husband, an act certainly perceived by her society as madness.

Most of the young heroines in this volume struggle through dream or word, against age-old as well as new manifestations of societal conventions imposed upon them. In contrast, the older women act. Like the mother in "Everyday Use," the old woman in "The Welcome Table" totally ignores convention when she enters the white church from which she is barred. The contrary act of this backward woman challenges all the conventions—"God, mother, country, earth, church. It involved all that and well they knew it."[10]

Again, through juxtaposing the restrictions imposed on her protagonists with their subsequent responses, Walker illuminates the tension as she did in *The Third Life of Grange Copeland* between convention and the struggle to be whole. Only this time, the focus is very much on the unique vortex of restrictions imposed on Black women by their community and white society. Her protagonists' dreams, words, acts, often explained away by society as the expressions of a contrary nature, a troubled *agwu,* are the price all beings, against opposition, would pay to be spontaneously and characteristically themselves. In *In Love and Trouble,* Walker emphasized the impact of sexism as well as racism on Black communities. Her insistence on honesty, on the validity of her own experience as well as the experience of other Southern Black women, ran counter to the popular notion of the early seventies that racism was the only evil that affected Black women. Her first collection of short stories specifically demonstrated the interconnectedness of American sexism and racism, for they are both based on the notion of dominance and on unnatural hierarchical distinctions.

Walker does not choose Southern Black women to be her major protagonists only because she is one, but also, I believe, because she has discovered in the tradition and history they collectively experience an understanding of oppression which has elicited from them a willingness to reject convention and to hold to what is difficult. Meridian, her most developed character, is a person who allows "an idea—no matter where it came from—to penetrate her life." The idea that penetrates Meridian's life, the idea of nonviolent resistance, is really rooted in a question: when is it necessary, when is it right, to kill? And the intensity with which Meridian pursues that question is due to her view of herself as a mother, a creator rather than a destroyer of life. The source to which she goes for the answer to that question is her people, especially the heritage that has been passed on to her by her maternal ancestors. She is thrilled by the fact that Black women were "always imitating Harriet Tubman escaping to become something unheard of. Outrageous." And that "even in more conventional things black women struck out for the unknown."[11] Like Walker in *In Search of Our Mothers' Gardens,* Meridian seeks her identity through the legacy passed on to her by Southern Black women.

Yet Walker did not rest easy even with this idea, an idea which glorifies the Black woman. For in *Meridian* she scrutinized that tradition which is based on the monumental myth of Black motherhood, a myth based on the true stories of sacrifice Black mothers performed for their children. But the myth is also restrictive, for it imposes a stereotype of Black women, a stereotype of strength which denies them choice, and hardly admits of the many who were destroyed. In her characterization of Margaret and Mem Copeland in *The Third Life of Grange Copeland* Walker acknowledged the abused Black women who, unlike Faulkner's Dilsey, did not endure. She went a step further in *Meridian*. Meridian's quest for wholeness and her involvement in the Civil Rights Movement is initiated by her feelings of inadequacy in living up to the standards of Black motherhood. Meridian gives up her son because she believes she will poison his growth with the thorns of guilt and she has her tubes tied after a painful abortion. In this novel, then, Walker probed the idea of Black motherhood, as she developed a character who so elevates it that she at first believes she can not properly fulfill it. Again, Walker approaches the forbidden as a possible route to another truth.

Not only did Walker challenge the monument of Black motherhood in *Meridian,* she also entered the fray about the efficacy of motherhood in which American feminists were then, as they are now, engaged. As many radical feminists blamed motherhood for the waste in women's lives and saw it as a dead end for a woman, Walker insisted on a deeper analysis: she did not present motherhood in itself as restrictive. It is so because of the little value society places on children, especially Black children, on mothers, especially Black mothers, on life itself. In the novel, Walker acknowledged that a mother in this society is often "buried alive, walled away from her own life, brick by brick."[12] Yet the novel is based on Meridian's insistence on the sacredness of life. Throughout her quest she is surrounded by children whose lives she tries to preserve. In seeking the children she can no longer have she takes responsibility for the life of all the people. Her aborted motherhood yields to her a perspective on life—that of "expanding her mind with action." In keeping with this principle, Walker tells us in her essay "*One* Child of One's Own":

> It is not my child who has purged my face from history and herstory and left mystory just that, a mystery; my child loves my face and would have it on every page, if she could, as I have loved my own parents' faces above all others, and refused to let them be denied, or myself to let them go.[13]

In fact, *Meridian* is based on this idea, the sacredness and continuity of life—and on another, that it might be necessary to take life in order to preserve it and make it possible for future generations. Perhaps the most difficult paradox that Walker has examined to date is the relationship between violence and revolution, a relationship that so many take for granted that such scrutiny seems outlandish. Like her heroine, Meridian, who holds on to the idea of nonviolent resistance after it has been discarded as a viable means to change, Walker persists in struggling with this age-old dilemma—that of death giving life. What the novel *Meridian* suggests is that unless such a struggle is taken on by those who would change society, their revolution will not be integral. For they may destroy that which they abhor only to resurrect it in themselves. Meridian discovers, only through personal struggle in conjunction with her involvement with the everyday lives of her people,

> that the respect she owed her life was to continue, against whatever obstacles, to live it, and not to give up any particle of it without a fight to the death, preferably *not* her own. And that this existence extended beyond herself to those around her because, in fact, the years in America had created them One Life.[14]

But though the concept of One Life motivates Meridian in her quest toward physical and spiritual health, the societal evils which subordinate one class to another, one race to another, one sex to another, fragment and ultimately threaten life. So that the novel *Meridian,* like *The Third Life of Grange Copeland,* is built on the tension between the African concept of animism, "that spirit inhabits all life," and the societal forces that inhibit the growth of the living toward their natural state of freedom.

Because of her analysis of sexism in the novel as well as in *In Love and Trouble,* Walker is often labeled a feminist writer. Yet she also challenges this definition as it is formulated by most white American feminists. In "*One* Child of One's Own" (1978), Walker insisted on the twin "afflictions" of her life. That white feminists as well as some Black people deny the Black woman her womanhood—that they define issues in terms of Blacks on one hand, women (meaning white women) on the other. They miss the obvious fact—that Black people come in both sexes. Walker put it strongly:

> It occurred to me that perhaps white women feminists, no less than white women generally, cannot imagine that black women have vaginas. Or if they can, where imagination leads them is too far to go.
>
> Perhaps it is the black woman's children, whom the white woman—having more to offer her own children, and certainly not having to offer them slavery or a slave heritage or poverty or hatred, generally speaking: segregated schools, slum neighborhoods, the worst of everything—resents. For they must always make her feel guilty. She fears knowing that black women want the best for their children just as she does. But she also knows black children are to have less in this world so that her children, white children, will have more. (In some countries, all.)
>
> Better then to deny that the black woman has a vagina. Is capable of motherhood. Is a woman.[15]

And Walker *also* writes of the unwillingness of many Black women to acknowledge or address the problems of sexism that affect them because they feel they must protect Black men. To this she asserts that if Black women turn away from the women's movement, they turn away from women moving all over the world, not just in America. They betray their own tradition, which includes women such as Sojourner Truth and Ida B. Wells, and abandon their responsibility to their own people as well as to women everywhere.

In refusing to elevate sex above race, on insisting on the Black woman's responsibility to herself and to other women of color, Walker aligns herself neither with prevailing white feminist groups nor with Blacks who refuse to acknowledge male dominance in the world. Because her analysis does not yield to easy generalizations and nicely packaged clichés, she continues to resist the trends of the times without discarding the truths upon which they are based.

Walker's second collection of short stories, *You Can't Keep a Good Woman Down* (1981), delves even more emphatically into the "twin afflictions" of Black women's lives. Like *In Love and Trouble,* this book probes the extent to which Black women have the freedom to pursue their selfhood within the confines of a sexist and racist society. However, these two collections, published eight years apart, demonstrate a clear progression of theme. While the protagonists of *In Love and Trouble* wage their struggle in spite of themselves, the heroines of *You Can't Keep a Good Woman Down* consciously insist upon their right to challenge any societal chains that bind them. The titles of the two collections succinctly indicate the shift in tone, the first emphasizing trouble, the second the self-assertiveness of the Black woman so bodaciously celebrated in the blues tradition. The name of a famous blues song, "You Can't Keep a Good Woman Down," is dedicated to those who "*insist* on the value and beauty of the authentic."[16] Walker's intention in this volume is clearly a celebration of the Black woman's insistence on living. From whence does this insistence come, Walker asks? How does it fare in these contemporary times?

The stories in this collection are blatantly topical in their subject matter, as Walker focuses on societal attitudes and mores that women have, in the last decade, challenged—pornography and male sexual fantasies in "Porn," and "Coming Apart," abortion in "The Abortion," sadomasochism in "A Letter of the Times," interracial rape in "Advancing Luna." And the forms Walker invents to illuminate these issues are as unconventional as her subject matter. Many of the stories are process rather than product. Feminist thinkers of the seventies asserted a link between process (the unraveling of thought and feeling) and the way women have perceived the world. In keeping with this theory, Walker often gives us the story as it comes into being, rather than delivering the product, classic and clean. The author then not only breaks the rules by writing about "womanist" issues (Walker defines a womanist as a "black feminist"), she also employs a womanist process. For many of these stories reflect the present, when the process of confusion, resistance to the established order, and the discovery of a freeing order is, especially for women, a prerequisite for growth.

Such a story is "Advancing Luna," in which a young Southern Black woman's development is reflected through her growing understanding of the complexity of interracial rape. At the beginning of the story, practically everything she tells us is tinged with an air of taking things for granted. She lightly assumes that Black people are superior. This generalization, however, is tested when Luna, a white friend of hers, tells her that during the "movement," she was raped by a Black man they both know. Our narrator naturally is opposed to rape; yet she had not believed Black men actually raped white women. And she knows what happens if a Black man is even accused of such an act. Her earlier sense of clarity is shattered. Doubts, questions, push her to unravel her own feelings: "Who knows what the black woman thinks of rape? Who has asked her? Who *cares?*"[17]

Again Walker writes about a forbidden topic and again she resists an easy solution. For although she speaks from the point of view of sisterhood with all women she also insists, as she did in "*One* Child of One's Own," that all women must understand that sexism and racism in America are critically related. Like all her previous fiction, this blatantly contemporary story is rooted in and illuminated by history, in this instance, the work of the great antilynching crusader Ida B. Wells. The dialogue between our narrator and this nineteenth-century Black womanist focuses on the convoluted connection between rape and lynchings, sex and race, that continues to this day. As a result, "Advancing Luna" cannot end conclusively. There are two endings, Afterthoughts, Discarded Notes, and a Postscript as the narrator and writer mesh. Walker shows us her writing process, which cannot be neatly resolved since the questions she posed cannot be satisfactorily answered. The many endings prod the reader, insisting on the complexity of the issue and the characters.

> Dear God,
>
> Me and Sophie work on the quilt. Got it frame up on the porch. Shug Avery donate her old yellow dress for scrap, and I work in a piece every chance I get. It's a nice pattern call Sister's Choice.[18]

The form of *The Color Purple* (1982), Walker's most recent novel, is a further development in the womanist process she is evolving. The entire novel is written in a series of letters. Along with diaries, letters were the dominant mode of expression allowed women in the West. Feminist historians find letters to be a principal source of information, of facts about the everyday lives of women *and* their own perceptions about their lives, that is of both "objective" and "subjective" information. In using the epistolary style, Walker is able to have her major character Celie express the impact of oppression on her spirit as well as her growing internal strength and final victory.

Like Walker's other two novels, this work spans generations of one poor rural Southern Black family, interweaving the personal with the flow of history; and, like her essays and fiction, the image of quilting is central to its concept and form. But in *The Color Purple,* the emphases are the oppression Black women experience in their relationships with Black men (fathers, brothers, husbands, lovers) and the sisterhood they must share with each other in order to liberate themselves. As an image for these themes two sisters, Celie and Nettie, are the novel's focal characters. Their letters, Celie's to God, Nettie's to Celie, and finally Celie's to Nettie, are the novel's form.

Again, Walker approaches the forbidden in content as well as form. Just as the novel's form is radical, so are its themes, for she focuses on incest in a Black family and portrays a Black lesbian relationship as natural and freeing. The novel begins with Celie, a fourteen-year-old who is sexually abused by her presumed father and who manages to save her sister Nettie from the same fate. Celie is so cut off from everyone and her experience is so horrifying, even to herself, that she can only write it in letters to God. Her letters take us through her awful pregnancies, her children being taken away from her, and the abuses of a loveless marriage. She liberates herself, that is, she comes to value herself, through the sensuous love bond she shares with Shug, her husband's mistress, her appreciation of her sister-in-law Sophie's resistant spirit, and the letters from her sister Nettie which her husband had hidden from her for many years. We feel Celie's transformation intensely since she tells her story in her own rural idiomatic language, a discrete Black speech. Few writers since Zora Neale Hurston have so successfully expressed the essence of the folk's speech as Walker does in *The Color Purple.*

In contrast to Celie's letters, Nettie's letters to Celie from Africa, where she is a missionary, are written in standard English. These letters not only provide a contrast in style, they expand the novel's scope. The comparison-contrast between male-female relationships in Africa and the Black South suggest that sexism for Black women in America does not derive from racism, though it is qualitatively affected by it. And Nettie's community of missionaries graphically demonstrates Afro-Americans' knowledge of their ancestral link to Africa, which, contrary to American myth, predates the Black Power Movement of the 1960s.

Though different in form and language, *The Color Purple* is inextricably linked to Walker's previous works. In *In Search of Our Mothers' Gardens,* Walker speaks about three types of Black women: the physically and psychologically abused Black women (Mem and Margaret Copeland in *The Third Life of Grange Copeland*), the Black woman who is torn by contrary instincts (Meridian in her youth and college years), and the new Black woman who re-creates herself out of the creative legacy of her maternal ancestors. Meridian begins that journey of transformation. But it is Celie, even more than her predecessor, who completes Walker's cycle. For Celie is a "Mem" who survives and liberates herself through her sisters' strength and wisdom, qualities which are, like the color purple, derived from nature. To be free is the natural state of the living. And Celie's attainment of freedom affects not only others of her sisters, but her brothers as well.

Both Walker's prose and her poetry probe the continuum between the inner self and the outer world. Her volumes of poetry, like her fiction and essays, focus on the self as part of a community of changers, whether it is the Civil Rights Movement in *Once,* the struggle toward liberation in *Revolutionary Petunias,* the community of women who would be free in *Good Night Willie Lee.* Yet her poems are distinguished from her prose in that they are a graph of that self which is specifically Alice Walker. They are perhaps even more than her prose rooted in her desire to resist the easiest of the easy. In her poetry, Walker the wayward child challenges not only the world but herself. And in exposing herself, she challenges us to accept her as she is. Perhaps it is the stripping of bark from herself that enables us to feel that sound of the genuine in her scrutiny of easy positions advocated by progressive Blacks or women.

Her first volume, *Once,* includes a section, "Mornings/of an Impossible Love," in which Walker scrutinizes herself not through her reflections on the outer world as she does in the other sections, but through self-exposure. In the poem "Johann," Walker expresses feelings forbidden by the world of the 1960s.[19]

In "So We've Come at Last to Freud," she arrogantly insists on the validity of her own emotions as opposed to prescriptives:

> Don't label my love with slogans;
> My father can't be blamed
>   for my affection
>
> Or lack of it.
> Ask him
> He won't understand you.[20]

She resists her own attempt at self-pity in "Suicide":

> Thirdly if it is the thought
> of rest that

fascinates
laziness should be admitted
in the clearest terms[21]

Yet in "The Ballad of the Brown Girl," she acknowledges the pain of loss, the anguish of a forbidden love.[22]

As these excerpts show, Walker refuses to embellish or camouflage her emotions with erudite metaphor or phrase. Instead she communicates them through her emphasis on single-word lines, her selection of the essential word, not only for content but for cadence. The result is a graceful directness that is not easily arrived at.

The overriding theme of *Once,* its feel of unwavering honesty in evoking the forbidden, either in political stances or in love, persists in *Revolutionary Petunias.* Walker, however, expands from the almost quixotic texture of her first volume to philosophical though intensely personal probings in her second. For *Revolutionary Petunias* examines the relationship between the nature of love and that of revolution. In these poems she celebrates the openness to the genuine in people, an essential quality, for her, in those who would be revolutionaries. And she castigates the false conventions constructed by many so-called revolutionaries. As a result, those who are committed to more life rather than less are often outcasts and seem to walk forbidden paths.

The volume is arranged in five sections, each one evoking a particular stage in the movement forward. In the first section, "In These Dissenting Times," Walker asserts that while many label their ancestors as backward, true revolutionaries understand that the common folk who precede them are the source of their strength. She reminds us that we "are not the first to suffer, rebel fight love and die. The grace with which we embrace life, in spite of the pain, the sorrows, is always a measure of what has gone before."[23]

The second section, "Revolutionary Petunias, The Living Through," is about those who know that the need for beauty is essential to a desire for revolution, that the most rebellious of folk are those who feel so intensely the potential beauty of life that they would struggle to that end without ceasing. Yet because the narrow-minded scream that "poems of/love and flowers are/a luxury the Revolution/cannot afford," those so human as to be committed to beauty and love are often seen as "incorrect." Walker warns that in living through it one must "Expect nothing/Live frugally on surprise . . . wish for nothing larger/than your own small heart/Or greater than a star."[24] And in words that reverberate throughout her works, she exposes herself as one who must question, feel, pursue the mysteries of life. The title of the poem "Reassurance" affirms for us her need to sustain herself in her persistent questionings.

I must love the questions
themselves
as Rilke said
like locked rooms
full of treasure
to which my blind
and groping key
does not yet fit.[25]

Flowing out of the second section, the third, "Crucifixion," further underscores the sufferings of those who would see the urge to revolution as emanating from a love for people rather than empty proscriptive forms. In it the ideologues drive out the lovers, "forcing . . . the very sun/to mangled perfection/for your cause."[26] And many like the "girl who would not lie; and was not born 'correct,' " or those who "wove a life/of stunning contradiction" are driven mad or die.[27]

Yet some endured. The fourth section, "Mysteries . . . the Living Beyond," affirms the eventual triumph of those who would change the world because:

> . . . the purpose of being
> here, wherever we are, is to increase
> the durability and the occasions of
> love among and between peoples.[28]
> June Jordan

Love poems dominate this section, though always there is Walker's resistance to preordained form:

> In me there is a rage to defy
> the order of the stars
> despite their pretty patterns[29]

And in "New Face," Walker combines the philosophical urge to penetrate the mysteries of life with the personal renewal which for her is love. From this renewal comes her energy to dig deeper, push further.[30]

A single poem, "The Nature of This Flower Is to Bloom," is the last movement in this five-part collection, as Walker combines through capitalized short phrases ("Rebellious. Living./Against the Elemental crush")[31] the major elements of *Revolutionary Petunias*. In choosing a flower as the symbol for revolution, she suggests that beauty, love, and revolution exist in a necessary relationship. And in selecting the petunia as the specific flower, she emphasizes the qualities of color, exuberance, and commonness rather than blandness, rigidity, or delicacy.

In completing the volume with this succinct and graceful poem, Walker also reiterates her own stylistic tendencies. Most of her poems are so cohesive they can hardly be divided into parts. I have found it almost impossible to separate out a few lines from any of her poems without quoting it fully, so seamless are they in construction. This quality is even more pronounced in her most recent volume of poetry, *Good Night Willie Lee, I'll See You in the Morning*. As in Walker's collections, though there are a few long poems, most are compact. In general, the voice in her poem is so finely distilled that each line, each word is so necessary it cannot be omitted, replaced, or separated out.

Like *Revolutionary Petunias, Good Night Willie Lee* is concerned with the relationship between love and change, only now the emphasis is even more on personal change, on change in the nature of relationships between women and men. This volume is very much about the demystification of love itself; yet it is also about the past, especially the pain left over from the "Crucifixion" of *Revolutionary Petunias*.

Good Night Willie Lee, I'll See You in the Morning is a five-part journey from night into morning, the name of each movement being an indication of the route this writer takes in her urge to understand love, without its illusions or veils. In the first movement, "Confession," Walker focuses on a love that declines into suffering. In letting go of it, she must go through the process of "stripping bark from herself" and must go deeper into an understanding of her past in "Early Losses, a Requiem." Having finally let the past rest in peace, she can then move to "Facing the Way," and finally to a "Forgiveness" that frees her.

The first poem of "Confession" is entitled "Did This Happen to Your Mother? Did Your Sister Throw Up a Lot?," while the last poem of this section ends "Other/women have already done this/sort of suffering for you/or so I thought."[32] Between these two points, Walker confesses that "I Love a man who is not worth/my love" and that "Love has made me sick."[33] She sees that her lover is afraid, "he may fail me . . . it is this fear/that now devours/desire."[34] She is astute enough to understand that his fear of love caused him to hold "his soul/so tightly/it shrank/to fit his hand."[35] In tracing the decline of love she understands the pull of pain: "At first I did not fight it/I *loved* the suffering/It was being alive!" "I savored my grief like chilled wine."[36]

From this immersion in self-pity, she is saved by a woman, a friend who reminds her that other women have already done this for her and brings her back to herself. The steps of this first movement are particularly instructive for the rest of this volume, since Walker does not pretend, as so much feminist poetry does, that she is above passion, or the need or the desire for sharing love with a man. What she does is to communicate the peaks and pitfalls of such an experience, pointing always to the absolute necessity for self-love. Only through self-love can the self who can love be preserved. And for Walker, self-love comes from "Stripping Bark from Myself." In one of the finest poems of this volume, Walker chants her song of independence. Her wayward lines are a response to a worldwide challenge:

> because women are expected to keep silent about
> their close escapes I will not keep silent
>
> . . .
>
> No I am finished with living
> for what my mother believes
> for what my brother and father defend
> for what my lover elevates
> for what my sister, blushing, denies or rushes
> to embrace

for she has discovered some part of her self:

> Besides
> my struggle was always against
> an inner darkness: I carry with myself
> the only known keys
> to my death . . .

So she is

> . . . happy to fight
> all outside murderers
> as I see I must[37]

Such stripping of bark from herself enables her to face the way, to ask questions about her own commitment to revolution, whether she can give up the comforts of life especially "the art that transcends time," "whose sale would patch a roof/heat the cold rooms of children, replace an eye/feed a life."[38] And it is the stripping of bark from herself that helps her to understand that:

the healing
of all our wounds
is forgiveness
that permits a promise
of our return
at the end.[39]

It is telling, I believe, that Walker's discovery of the healing power of forgiveness comes from her mother's last greeting to her father at his burial. In this volume so permeated by the relationship of woman to man, her mother heads the list of a long line of women—some writers, like Zora Neale Hurston, others personal friends of Alice Walker—who pass unto her the knowledge they have garnered on the essence of love. Such knowledge helps Walker to demystify love and enables her to write about the tension between the giving of herself and the desire to remain herself.

In her dedication to the volume she edited of Zora Neale Hurston's work, Walker says of her literary ancestor: "Implicit in Hurston's determination to 'make it' in a career was her need to express 'the folk' and herself. Someone who knew her has said: 'Zora would have been Zora even if she'd been an Eskimo.' That is what it means to be yourself; it is surely what it means to be an artist."[40] These words, it seems to me, apply as well to Alice Walker.

NOTES

1. Alice Walker, "On Stripping Bark from Myself," *Good Night Willie Lee, I'll See You in the Morning,* Dial, 1979, p. 23.
2. Alice Walker, "Karamojans," *Once,* Harcourt Brace Jovanovich, 1978, p. 20.
3. Ibid., p. 22.
4. Alice Walker, *The Third Life of Grange Copeland,* Harcourt Brace Jovanovich, 1970, p. 207.
5. Alice Walker, "Everyday Use," *In Love and Trouble,* Harcourt Brace Jovanovich, 1973, p. 57.
6. Ibid., p. 58.
7. Ibid., p. 59.
8. Walker, *In Love and Trouble,* epigraph.
9. Walker, "Roselily," *In Love and Trouble,* p. 8.
10. Walker, "The Welcome Table," *In Love and Trouble,* p. 84.
11. Alice Walker, *Meridian,* Harcourt Brace Jovanovich, 1976, pp. 105–6.
12. Ibid., p. 41.
13. Alice Walker, "*One* Child of One's Own: A Meaningful Digression within the Work(s)," *The Writer on Her Work,* ed. Janet Sternburg, W. W. Norton, 1980, p. 139.
14. Walker, *Meridian,* p. 204.
15. Walker, "*One* Child of One's Own," pp. 131–32.
16. Alice Walker, *You Can't Keep a Good Woman Down,* Harcourt Brace Jovanovich, 1981, dedication.
17. Ibid., p. 71.
18. Alice Walker, *The Color Purple,* Harcourt Brace Jovanovich, 1982, p. 53.
19. Alice Walker, *Once,* p. 65.
20. Ibid., p. 61.
21. Ibid., p. 74.

22. Ibid., p. 73.
23. Alice Walker, "Fundamental Difference," *Revolutionary Petunias,* Harcourt Brace Jovanovich, 1973, p. 1.
24. Walker, "Expect Nothing," *Revolutionary Petunias,* p. 30.
25. Walker, "Reassurance," *Revolutionary Petunias,* p. 33.
26. Walker, "Lonely Particular," *Revolutionary Petunias,* p. 40.
27. Walker, "The Girl Who Died #2," *Revolutionary Petunias,* pp. 45–46.
28. Walker, "Mysteries" (June Jordan), *Revolutionary Petunias,* p. 51.
29. Walker, "Rage," *Revolutionary Petunias,* p. 61.
30. Walker, "New Face," *Revolutionary Petunias,* p. 66.
31. Walker, "The Nature of This Flower Is to Bloom," *Revolutionary Petunias,* p. 70.
32. Walker, "At First," *Good Night Willie Lee, I'll See You in the Morning,* p. 15.
33. Walker, "Did This Happen to Your Mother? Did Your Sister Throw Up a Lot?" *Good Night Willie Lee, I'll See You in the Morning,* p. 2.
34. Walker, "Threatened," *Good Night Willie Lee, I'll See You in the Morning,* p. 8.
35. Walker, "Gift," *Good Night Willie Lee, I'll See You in the Morning,* p. 5.
36. Walker, "At First," *Good Night Willie Lee, I'll See You in the Morning,* p. 15.
37. Walker, "On Stripping Bark from Myself," *Good Night Willie Lee, I'll See You in the Morning,* pp. 23–24.
38. Walker, "Facing the Way," *Good Night Willie Lee, I'll See You in the Morning,* pp. 44–45.
39. Walker, "Good Night Willie Lee, I'll See You in the Morning," *Good Night Willie Lee, I'll See You in the Morning,* p. 53.
40. Alice Walker, ed., *I Love Myself: A Zora Neale Hurston Reader . . . ,* Feminist Press, 1979, p. 3.

FICTION SELECTIONS

Harriet E. Wilson (1808–70)

Rediscovered and appreciated over a century after her death, Harriet E. Wilson has been hailed as an important figure in the literary history of African Americans. Although some facts about the author's life have been uncovered, much of her background still remains obscured by incomplete or contradictory information.

Wilson's only known novel, Our Nig: Or Sketches from the Life of a Free Black, *was privately published in the United States in 1859, making it the first novel written and published in this country by an African American.* Our Nig *also made Wilson the first black woman novelist, the literary ancestor of a distinguished line of writers. In her introduction to the novel, she confesses that financial strains and family health problems prompted her to compose the book. Additional bits of information suggest that the author lived in New Hampshire and Massachusetts, enduring an unsteady marriage, the loss of her child, and tenuous employment.*

Where autobiographical slave narratives focus on the miseries of plantation life, Our Nig *exposes the oppression of blacks as manifested in the North. The book's protagonist, Frado, who is the daughter of a black father and white mother, labors for her survival as a servant to a white household. According to black critic Henry Louis Gates, "Wilson's characterization of her protagonist . . . recalls the sort of complexity and abstention from moralistic simplification . . . which is not to be found in any other black novel published before the turn of the century. . . . We can cogently argue . . . without strain that Wilson is the most accomplished and subtle black novelist of the nineteenth century."*

In the chapter from Our Nig *reprinted here, "A Friend for Nig," Frado is abused by the white mother of the household in which she works but finds friendship with the children of the family.*

A Friend for Nig

Hours of my youth! when nurtured in my breast,
To love a stranger, friendship made me blest;—
Friendship, the dear peculiar bond of youth,
When every artless bosom throbs with truth;
Untaught by worldly wisdom how to feign;
And check each impulse with prudential reign;
When all we feel our honest souls disclose—
In love to friends, in open hate to foes;
No varnished tales the lips of youth repeat,
No dear-bought knowledge purchased by deceit.
—Byron

With what differing emotions have the denizens of earth awaited the approach of to-day. Some sufferer has counted the vibrations of the pendulum impatient for its dawn, who, now that it has arrived, is anxious for its close. The votary of pleasure, conscious of yesterday's void, wishes for power to arrest time's haste till a few more hours of mirth shall be enjoyed. The unfortunate are yet gazing in vain for golden-edged clouds they fancied would appear in their horizon. The good man feels that he has accomplished too little for the Master, and sighs that another day must so soon close. Innocent childhood, weary of its stay, longs for another morrow; busy manhood cries, hold! hold! and pursues it to another's dawn. All are dissatisfied. All crave some good not yet possessed, which time is expected to bring with all its morrows.

Was it strange that, to a disconsolate child, three years should seem a long, long time? During school time she had rest from Mrs. Bellmont's tyranny. She was now nine years old; time, her mistress said, such privileges should cease.

She could now read and spell, and knew the elementary steps in grammar, arithmetic, and writing. Her education completed, as *she* said, Mrs. Bellmont felt that her time and person belonged solely to her. She was under her in every sense of the word. What an opportunity to indulge her vixen nature! No matter what occurred to ruffle her, or from what source provocation came, real or fancied, a few blows on Nig seemed to relieve her of a portion of ill-will.

These were days when Fido was the entire confidant of Frado. She told him her griefs as though he were human; and he sat so still, and listened so attentively, she really believed he knew her sorrows. All the leisure moments she could gain were used in teaching him some feat of dog-agility, so that Jack pronounced him very knowing, and was truly gratified to know he had furnished her with a gift answering his intentions.

Fido was the constant attendant of Frado, when sent from the house on errands, going and returning with the cows, out in the fields, to the village. If ever she forgot her hardships it was in his company.

Spring was now retiring. James, one of the absent sons, was expected home on a visit. He had never seen the last acquisition to the family. Jack had written faithfully of all the merits of his colored *protégé,* and hinted plainly that mother did not always treat her just right. Many were the preparations to make the visit pleasant, and as the day approached when he was to arrive, great exertions were made to cook the favorite viands, to prepare the choicest tablefare.

The morning of the arrival day was a busy one. Frado knew not who would be of so much importance; her feet were speeding hither and thither so unsparingly. Mrs. Bellmont seemed a trifle fatigued, and her shoes which had, early in the morning, a methodic squeak, altered to an irregular, peevish snap.

"Get some little wood to make the fire burn," said Mrs. Bellmont, in a sharp tone. Frado obeyed, bringing the smallest she could find.

Mrs. Bellmont approached her, and, giving her a box on her ear, reiterated the command.

The first the child brought was the smallest to be found; of course, the second must be a trifle larger. She well knew it was, as she threw it into a box on the hearth. To Mrs. Bellmont it was a greater affront, as well as larger wood, so she "taught her" with the raw-hide, and sent her the third time for "little wood."

Nig, weeping, knew not what to do. She had carried the smallest; none left would suit her mistress; of course further punishment awaited her; so she gathered up whatever came first, and threw it down on the hearth. As she expected, Mrs. Bellmont, enraged, approached her, and kicked her so forcibly as to throw her upon the floor. Before she could rise, another foiled the attempt, and then followed kick after kick in quick succession and power, till she reached the door. Mr. Bellmont and Aunt Abby, hearing the noise, rushed in, just in time to see the last of the performance. Nig jumped up, and rushed from the house, out of sight.

Aunt Abby returned to her apartment, followed by John, who was muttering to himself.

"What were you saying?" asked Aunt Abby.

"I said I hoped the child never would come into the house again."

"What would become of her? You cannot mean *that,*" continued his sister.

"I do mean it. The child does as much work as a woman ought to; and just see how she is kicked about!"

"Why do you have it so, John?" asked his sister.

"How am I to help it? Women rule the earth, and all in it."

"I think I should rule my own house, John,"—

"And live in hell meantime," added Mr. Bellmont.

John now sauntered out to the barn to await the quieting of the storm.

Aunt Abby had a glimpse of Nig as she passed out of the yard; but to arrest her, or show her that *she* would shelter her, in Mrs. Bellmont's presence, would only bring reserved wrath on her defenceless head. Her sister-in-law had great prejudices against her. One cause of the alienation was that she did not give her right in the homestead to John, and leave it forever; another was that she was a professor of religion, (so was Mrs. Bellmont;) but Nab, as she called her, did not live according to her profession; another, that she *would* sometimes give Nig cake and pie, which she was never allowed to have at home. Mary had often noticed and spoken of her inconsistencies.

The dinner hour passed. Frado had not appeared. Mrs. B. made no inquiry or search. Aunt Abby looked long, and found her concealed in an outbuilding. "Come into the house with me," implored Aunt Abby.

"I ain't going in any more," sobbed the child.

"What will you do?" asked Aunt Abby.

"I've got to stay out here and die. I ha'n't got no mother, no home. I wish I was dead."

"Poor thing," muttered Aunt Abby; and slyly providing her with some dinner, left her to her grief.

Jane went to confer with her Aunt about the affair; and learned from her the retreat. She would gladly have concealed her in her own chamber, and ministered to her wants; but she was dependent on Mary and her mother for care, and any displeasure caused by attention to Nig, was seriously felt.

Toward night the coach brought James. A time of general greeting, inquiries for absent members of the family, a visit to Aunt Abby's room, undoing a few delicacies for Jane, brought them to the tea hour.

"Where's Frado?" asked Mr. Bellmont, observing she was not in her usual place, behind her mistress' chair.

"I don't know, and I don't care. If she makes her appearance again, I'll take the skin from her body," replied his wife.

James, a fine looking man, with a pleasant countenance, placid, and yet decidedly serious, yet not stern, looked up confounded. He was no stranger to his mother's nature; but years of absence had erased the occurrences once so familiar, and he asked, "Is that pretty little Nig, Jack writes to me about, that you are so severe upon, mother?"

"I'll not leave much of her beauty to be seen, if she comes in sight; and now, John," said Mrs. B, turning to her husband, "you need not think you are going to learn her to treat me in this way; just see how saucy she was this morning. She shall learn her place."

Mr. Bellmont raised his calm, determined eye full upon her, and said, in a decisive manner: "You shall not strike, or scald, or skin her, as you call it, if she comes back again. Remember!" and he brought his hand down upon the table. "I have searched an hour for her now, and she is not to be found on the premises. Do *you* know where she is? Is she *your* prisoner?"

"No! I have just told you I did not know where she was. Nab has her hid somewhere, I suppose. Oh, dear! I did not think it would come to this; that my own husband would treat me so." Then came fast flowing tears, which not one but Mary seemed to notice. Jane crept into Aunt Abby's room; Mr. Bellmont and James went out of doors, and Mary remained to condole with her parent.

"Do you know where Frado is?" asked Jane of her aunt.

"No," she replied. "I have hunted everywhere. She has left her first hiding-place. I cannot think what has become of her. There comes Jack and Fido; perhaps he knows;" and she walked to a window near, where James and his father were conversing together.

The two brothers exchanged a hearty greeting, and then Mr. Bellmont told Jack to eat his supper; afterward he wished to send him away. He immediately went in. Accustomed to all the phases of indoor storms, from a whine to thunder and lightning, he saw at a glance marks of disturbance. He had been absent through the day, with the hired men.

"What's the fuss?" asked he, rushing into Aunt Abby's.

"Eat your supper," said Jane; "go home, Jack."

Back again through the dining-room, and out to his father.

"What's the fuss?" again inquired he of his father.

"Eat your supper, Jack, and see if you can find Frado. She's not been seen since morning, and then she was kicked out of the house."

"I shan't eat my supper till I find her," said Jack, indignantly. "Come, James, and see the little creature mother treats so."

They started, calling, searching, coaxing, all their way along. No Frado. They returned to the house to consult. James and Jack declared they would not sleep till she was found.

Mrs. Bellmont attempted to dissuade them from the search. "It was a shame a little *nigger* should make so much trouble."

Just then Fido came running up, and Jack exclaimed, "Fido knows where she is, I'll bet."

"So I believe," said his father; "but we shall not be wiser unless we can outwit him. He will not do what his mistress forbids him."

"I know how to fix him," said Jack. Taking a plate from the table, which was still waiting, he called, "Fido! Fido! Frado wants some supper. Come!" Jack started, the dog followed, and soon capered on before, far, far into the fields, over walls and through fences, into a piece of swampy land. Jack followed close, and soon appeared to James, who was quite in the rear, coaxing and forcing Frado along with him.

A frail child, driven from shelter by the cruelty of his mother, was an object of interest to James. They persuaded her to go home with them, warmed her by the kitchen fire, gave her a good supper, and took her with them into the sitting-room.

"Take that nigger out of my sight," was Mrs. Bellmont's command, before they could be seated.

James led her into Aunt Abby's, where he knew they were welcome. They chatted awhile until Frado seemed cheerful; then James led her to her room, and waited until she retired.

"Are you glad I've come home?" asked James.

"Yes; if you won't let me be whipped tomorrow."

"You won't be whipped. You must try to be a good girl," counselled James.

"If I do, I get whipped;" sobbed the child. "They won't believe what I say. Oh, I wish I had my mother back; then I should not be kicked and whipped so. Who made me so?"

"God;" answered James.

"Did God make you?"

"Yes."

"Who made Aunt Abby?"

"God."

"Who made your mother?"

"God."

"Did the same God that made her make me?"

"Yes."

"Well, then, I don't like him."

"Why not?"

"Because he made her white, and me black. Why didn't he make us *both* white?"

"I don't know; try to go to sleep, and you will feel better in the morning," was all the reply he could make to her knotty queries. It was a long time before she fell asleep; and a number of days before James felt in a mood to visit and entertain old associates and friends.

William Wells Brown (1815–84)

A *remarkable man of the nineteenth century, William Wells Brown made several outstanding contributions to African American literature. Born a slave, he was the first black novelist to be published; he also wrote the first known play by an African American. His pioneering work as an autobiographer, poet, novelist, playwright, and abolitionist essayist and speechwriter helped lay the foundation for a national African American culture and won recognition for black literature even beyond American shores.*

Born in Lexington, Kentucky, to a slave mother and slaveholder father, Brown was relocated at age ten to St. Louis, Missouri, where he labored as a slave on steamboats. In 1834, he escaped to freedom, and his 1847 autobiography, Narrative, *was a testimony both to the demoralizing effects of slavery and to the potential for black achievement.*

In the 1840s, Brown worked for the cause of abolition. After publishing The Anti-Slavery Harp *(1848), a collection of poems, Brown traveled to Europe in 1849, speaking at the Paris Peace Congress at the invitation of Victor Hugo. He resided in England until 1854, and it was there that he published* Clotel, or, The President's Daughter *(1853), the first novel by an African American.*

Three Years in Europe *(1852), the first travel book written by an African American, chronicles Brown's experiences as he traveled the continent. He returned to America in 1854 on being granted his freedom and wrote* The Escape or a Leap for Freedom *(1858), the first play by an African American, based on his experiences as a slave. This work was followed by the study,* The Black Man: His Antecedents, His Genius, and His Achievements *(1863). Shortly after the Civil War, Brown completed* The Negro in the American Rebellion *(1867), which focuses on blacks and their participation in the military. Brown continued his cultural study of African Americans in* The Rising Son: Or the Antecedents and Advancements of the Colored Race *(1873), which served as a supplement to* The Black Man. *And with his final work,* My Southern Home *(1880), Brown composed his second autobiography, closing out an astounding career as a writer who not only wrote history but also made history.*

The following chapters are excerpted from Clotel, *a novel that exposes the horrors and hypocrisies of the institution of slavery. In the selection, the protagonist, Clotel, the daughter of "founding father" Thomas Jefferson, endures the loss of her child and undertakes a precarious escape from slavery.*

from Clotel, or, The President's Daughter

CHAPTER XV
To-day a Mistress; To-morrow a Slave

> I promised thee a sister tale
> Of man's perfidious cruelty;
> Come, then, and hear what cruel wrong
> Befel the dark ladie.
>
> —Coleridge

Let us return for a moment to the home of Clotel. While she was passing lonely and dreary hours with none but her darling child, Horatio Green was trying to find relief in that insidious enemy of man, the intoxicating cup. Defeated in politics, forsaken in love by his wife, he seemed to have lost all principle of honour, and was ready to nerve himself up to any deed, no matter how unprincipled. Clotel's existence was now well known to Horatio's wife, and both her and her father demanded that the beautiful quadroon and her child should be sold and sent out of the state. To this proposition he at first turned a deaf ear; but when he saw that his wife was about to return to her father's roof, he consented to leave the matter in the hands of his father-in-law. The result was, that Clotel was immediately sold to the slave-trader, Walker, who, a few years previous, had taken her mother and sister to the far South. But, as if to make her husband drink of the cup of humiliation to its very dregs, Mrs. Green resolved to take his child under her own roof for a servant. Mary was, therefore, put to the meanest work that could be found, and although only ten years of age, she was often compelled to perform labour, which, under ordinary circumstances, would have been thought too hard for one much older. One condition of the sale of Clotel to Walker was, that she should be taken out of the state, which was accordingly done. Most quadroon women who are taken to the lower countries to be sold are either purchased by gentlemen for their own use, or sold for waiting-maids; and Clotel, like her sister, was fortunate enough to be bought for the latter purpose. The town of Vicksburgh stands on the left bank of the Mississippi, and is noted for the severity with which slaves are treated. It was here that Clotel was sold to Mr. James French, a merchant.

Mrs. French was severe in the extreme to her servants. Well dressed, but scantily fed, and overworked were all who found a home with her. The quadroon had been in her new home but a short time ere she found that her situation was far different from what it was in Virginia. What social virtues are possible in a society of which injustice is the primary characteristic? in a society which is divided into two classes, masters and slaves? Every married woman in the far South looks upon her husband as unfaithful, and regards every quadroon servant as a rival. Clotel had been with her new mistress but a few days, when she was ordered to cut off her long hair. The negro, constitutionally, is fond of dress and outward appearance. He that has short, woolly hair, combs it and oils it to death. He that has long hair, would sooner have his teeth drawn than lose it. However painful it was to the quadroon, she was soon seen with her hair cut as short as any of the full-blooded negroes in the dwelling.

Even with her short hair, Clotel was handsome. Her life had been a secluded one, and though now nearly thirty years of age, she was still beautiful. At her short hair, the other servants laughed, "Miss Clo needn't strut round so big, she got short nappy har well as I," said Nell, with a broad grin that showed her teeth. "She tinks she white, when she come here wid dat long har of hers," replied Mill. "Yes," continued Nell; "missus make her take down her wool so she no put it up to-day."

The fairness of Clotel's complexion was regarded with envy as well by the other servants as by the mistress herself. This is one of the hard features of slavery. To-day this woman is mistress of her own cottage; to-morrow she is sold to one who aims to make her life as intolerable as possible. And be it remembered, that the house servant has the best situation which a slave can occupy. Some American writers have tried to make the world believe that the condition of the labouring classes of England is as bad as the slaves of the United States.

The English labourer may be oppressed, he may be cheated, defrauded, swindled, and even starved; but it is not slavery under which he groans. He cannot be sold; in point of law he is equal to the prime minister. "It is easy to captivate the unthinking and the prejudiced, by eloquent declamation about the oppression of English operatives being worse than that of American slave, and by exaggerating the wrongs on one side and hiding them on the other. But all informed and reflecting minds, knowing that bad as are the social evils of England, those of Slavery are immeasurably worse." But the degradation and harsh treatment that Clotel experienced in her new home was nothing compared with the grief she underwent at being separated from her dear child. Taken from her without scarcely a moment's warning, she knew not what had become of her. The deep and heartfelt grief of Clotel was soon perceived by her owners, and fearing that her refusal to take food would cause her death, they resolved to sell her. Mr. French found no difficulty in getting a purchaser for the quadroon woman, for such are usually the most marketable kind of property. Clotel was sold at private sale to a young man for a housekeeper; but even he had missed his aim. . . .

CHAPTER XVII
Retaliation

I had a dream, a happy dream;
  I thought that I was free:
That in my own bright land again
  A home there was for me.

With the deepest humiliation Horatio Green saw the daughter of Clotel, his own child, brought into his dwelling as a servant. His wife felt that she had been deceived, and determined to punish her deceiver. At first Mary was put to work in the kitchen, where she met with little or no sympathy from the other slaves, owing to the fairness of her complexion. The child was white, what should be done to make her look like other negroes, was the question Mrs. Green asked herself. At last she hit upon a plan: there was a garden at the back of the house over which Mrs. Green could look from her parlour window. Here the white slave girl was put to work, without either bonnet or handkerchief upon her head. A hot sun poured its broiling rays on the naked face and neck of the girl, until she sank down in the corner of the garden, and was actually broiled to sleep. "Dat little nigger ain't working a bit, missus," said Dinah to Mrs. Green, as she entered the kitchen.

"She's lying in the sun, seasoning; she will work better by and by," replied the mistress. "Dees white niggers always tink dey sef good as white folks," continued the cook. "Yes, but we will teach them better; won't we, Dinah?" "Yes, missus, I don't like dees mularter niggers, no how; dey always want to set dey sef up for something big." The cook was black, and was not without that prejudice which is to be found among the negroes, as well as among the whites of the Southern States. The sun had the desired effect, for in less than a fortnight Mary's fair complexion had disappeared, and she was but little whiter than any other mulatto children running about the yard. But the close resemblance between the father and child annoyed the mistress more than the mere whiteness of the child's complexion. Horatio made proposition after proposition to have the girl sent away, for every time he beheld her countenance it reminded him of the happy days he had spent with Clotel. But his wife had commenced, and determined to carry out her unfeeling and fiendish designs. This child was not only white, but she was the grand-daughter of Thomas Jefferson, the man who, when speaking against slavery in the legislature of Virginia, said,

> The whole commerce between master and slave is a perpetual exercise of the most boisterous passions; *the most unremitting despotism on the one part, and degrading submission on the other.* With what execration should the statesman be loaded who, permitting one half the citizens thus to trample on the rights of the other, transforms those into despots and these into enemies, destroys the morals of the one part, and the *amor patriae* of the other! For if the slave can have a country in this world, it must be any other in preference to that in which he is born to live and labour for another; in which he must lock up the faculties of his nature, contribute as far as depends on his individual endeavours to the evanishment of the human race, or entail his own miserable condition on the endless generations proceeding from him. And can the liberties of a nation be thought secure when we have removed their only firm basis, a conviction in the minds of the people that these liberties are the gift of God? that they are not to be violated but with his wrath? Indeed, I tremble for my country when I reflect that God is just; that his justice cannot sleep for ever; that, considering numbers, nature, and natural means only, a revolution of the wheel of fortune, an exchange of situation, is among possible events; that it may become probable by supernatural interference! The Almighty has no attribute which can take side with us in such a context. . . .
>
> What an incomprehensible machine is man! Who can endure toil, famine, stripes, imprisonment, and death itself, in vindication of his own liberty, and the next moment be deaf to all those motives, whose power supported him through his trial, and inflict on his fellow-men a bondage, *one hour of which is fraught with more misery than ages of that which he rose in rebellion to oppose!* But we must wait with patience the workings of an overruling Providence and hope that that is preparing the deliverance of these our suffering brethren. When the measure of their tears shall be full—when their tears shall have involved heaven itself in darkness—doubtless a God of justice will awaken to their distress, and by diffusing light and liberality among their oppressors, or at length by his exterminating thunder, manifest his attention to things of this world, and that they are not left to the guidance of blind fatality.

The same man, speaking of the probability that the slaves might some day attempt to gain their liberties by a revolution, said,

> I tremble for my country, when I recollect that God is just, and that His justice cannot sleep for ever. The Almighty has no attribute that can take sides with us in such a struggle.

But, sad to say, Jefferson is not the only American statesman who has spoken high-sounding words in favour of freedom and then left his own children to die slaves. . . .

CHAPTER XXV
Death Is Freedom

> I asked but freedom, and ye gave
> Chains, and the freedom of the grave.
> —Snelling

There are, in the district of Columbia, several slave prisons, or "negro pens," as they are termed. These prisons are mostly occupied by persons to keep their slaves in, when collecting their gangs together for the New Orleans market. Some of them belong to the government, and one, in particular, is noted for having been the place where a number of free coloured persons have been incarcerated from time to time. In this district is situated the capitol of the United States. Any free coloured persons visiting Washington, if not provided with papers asserting and proving their right to be free, may be arrested and placed in one of these dens. If they succeed in showing that they are free, they are set at liberty, provided they are able to pay the expenses of their arrest and imprisonment; if they cannot pay these expenses they are sold out. Through this unjust and oppressive law, many persons both in the Free States have been consigned to a life of slavery on the cotton, sugar, or rice plantations of the Southern States. By order of her master, Clotel was removed from Richmond and placed in one of these prisons, to await the sailing of a vessel for New Orleans. The prison in which she was put stands midway between the capitol at Washington and the president's house. Here the fugitive saw nothing but slaves brought in and taken out, to be placed in ships and sent away to the same part of the country to which she herself would soon be compelled to go. She had seen or heard nothing of her daughter while in Richmond, and all hope of seeing her now had fled. If she was carried back to New Orleans, she could expect no mercy from her master.

At the dusk of the evening previous to the day when she was to be sent off, as the old prison was being closed for the night, she suddenly darted past her keeper, and ran for her life. It is not a great distance from the prison to the Long Bridge, which passes from the lower part of the city across the Potomac, to the extensive forests and woodlands of the celebrated Arlington Place, occupied by that distinguished relative and descendant of the immortal Washington, Mr. George W. Curtis. Thither the poor fugitive directed her flight. So unexpected was her escape, that she had quite a number of rods the start before the keeper had secured the other prisoners, and rallied his assistants in pursuit. It was at an hour when, and in a part of the city where, horses could not be readily obtained for the chase; no bloodhounds were at hand to run down the flying woman; and for once it seemed as though there was to be a fair trial of speed and endurance between the slave and the slave-catchers. The keeper and his forces raised the hue and cry on her pathway close behind; but so rapid was the flight along the wide avenue, that the astonished citizens, as they poured forth from their dwellings to learn the cause of alarm, were only able to comprehend the nature of the case in time to fall in with the motley mass in pursuit, (as many a one did that night), to raise an anxious prayer to heaven, as they refused to join in the pursuit, that the panting fugitive might escape, and the merciless soul dealer for once be disappointed of his prey. And now with the speed of an arrow—having passed the avenue—with the distance between her and her pursuers constantly increasing, this poor hunted female gained the *"Long Bridge,"* as it is called, where interruption seemed improbable, and already did her heart begin to beat high with the hope of success. She had only to pass three-fourths of a mile across the bridge, and she could bury herself in a vast forest, just at the time when the curtain of night would close around her, and protect her from the pursuit of her enemies.

But God by his Providence had otherwise determined. He had determined that an appalling tragedy should be enacted that night, within plain sight of the President's house and the capital of the Union, which should be an evidence wherever it should be known, of the unconquerable love of liberty the heart may inherit; as well as a fresh admonition to the slave dealer, of the cruelty and enormity of his crimes. Just as the pursuers crossed the high draw for the passage of sloops, soon after entering upon the bridge, they beheld three men slowly approaching from the Virginia side. They immediately called to them to arrest the fugitive, whom they proclaimed a runaway slave. True to their Virginian instincts as she came near, they formed in line across the narrow bridge, and prepared to seize her. Seeing escape impossible in that quarter, she stopped suddenly, and turned upon her pursuers. On came the profane and ribald crew faster than ever, already exulting in her capture, and threatening punishment for her flight. For a moment she looked wildly and anxiously around to see if there was no hope of escape. On either hand, far down below, rolled the deep foamy waters of the Potomac, and before and behind the rapidly approaching step and noisy voices of pursuers, showing how vain would be any further effort for freedom. Her resolution was taken. She clasped her *hands* convulsively, and raised *them,* as she at the same time raised her *eyes* towards heaven, and begged for that mercy and compassion *there,* which had been denied her on earth; and then, with a single bound, she vaulted over the railings of the bridge, and sunk for ever beneath the waves of the river!

Thus died Clotel, the daughter of Thomas Jefferson, a president of the United States; a man distinguished as the author of the Declaration of American Independence, and one of the first statesmen of that country.

Had Clotel escaped from oppression in any other land, in the disguise in which she fled from the Mississippi to Richmond, and reached the United States, no honour within the gift of the American people would have been too good to have been heaped upon the heroic woman. But she was a slave, and therefore out of the pale of their sympathy. They have tears to shed over Greece and Poland; they have an abundance of sympathy for "poor Ireland;" they can furnish a ship of war to convey the Hungarian refugees from a Turkish prison to the "land of the free and home of the brave." They boast that America is the "cradle of liberty"; if it is, I fear they have rocked the child to death. The body of Clotel was picked up from the bank of the river, where it had been washed by the strong current, a hole dug in the sand, and there deposited, without either inquest being held over it, or religious service being performed. Such was the life and such the death of a woman whose virtues and goodness of heart would have done honour to me in a higher station of life, and who, if she had been born in any other land but that of slavery, would have been honoured and loved. . . .

Charles W. Chesnutt (1858–1932)

Born in Cleveland, Ohio, Charles W. Chesnutt spent most of his childhood and youth in Fayetteville, North Carolina. While still a teenaged student he began teaching, a profession he pursued for years in both North Carolina and South Carolina; he became the principal of the State Normal School in Fayetteville when he was only twenty-two. A few years later, Chesnutt journeyed to New York, where he worked as a court stenographer and journalist. But he soon moved back to Cleveland, where he became a legal stenographer and a lawyer. Most biographies of Chesnutt note that, although his fair complexion afforded him the choice to pass for white, his commitment to his black identity was firm. He honed his writing into a weapon against racism and color consciousness.

After having published numerous short stories in various periodicals, Chesnutt reached a national audience when two of his stories—"The Goophered Grapevine" (1887) and "Po Sandy" (1888)—appeared in the prestigious Atlantic Monthly. *Despite his use of Negro dialect in these stories, Chesnutt, unlike his white contemporaries, created black characters whose humanity and wisdom were evident.*

In 1899, two collections of short stories established Chesnutt as an outstanding black fiction writer of the late nineteenth century: The Conjure Woman, *a group of related stories set in the slaveholding South and featuring the remarkable tales and tactics of Uncle Julius, a crafty old black slave; and* The Wife of His Youth and Other Stories of the Color Line, *which explores racism against blacks as well as intraracial issues. The success of these two works enabled the author to publish his first novel,* The House behind the Cedars *(1900). It was followed by two more novels,* The Marrow of Tradition *(1901) and* The Colored's Dream *(1905).*

Chesnutt is also credited with writing essays, speeches, poetry, and six unpublished novels. But more than these other writings, it was his short fiction that elevated his literary reputation. In 1928, he was honored with an NAACP Spingarn Medal for his professional and civic work and his realistic literary depiction of African American life.

In "The Sheriff's Children," which appeared in The Wife of His Youth, *Chesnutt explores the tragic ways in which racism in America destroys familial bonds. It is interesting to note that the writer utilizes a dialect for both white and black characters, underscoring the shared interracial heritage that was too often denied.*

The Sheriff's Children

(*The first pages of this story describe the village of Troy, county seat of Branson County, North Carolina.*)

A murder was a rare event in Branson County. Every well-informed citizen could tell the number of homicides committed in the county for fifty years back, and whether the slayer in any given instance had escaped, either by flight or acquittal, or had suffered the penalty of the law. So when it became known in Troy early one Friday morning in summer, about ten years after the war, that old Captain Walker, who had served in Mexico under Scott and had left an arm on the field of Gettysburg, had been foully murdered during the night, there was intense excitement in the village. Business was practically suspended, and the citizens gathered in little groups to discuss the murder and speculate upon the identity of the murderer. It transpired from testimony at the coroner's inquest held during the morning, that a strange mulatto had been met going away from Troy early Friday morning by a farmer on his way to town. Other circumstances seemed to connect the stranger with the crime. The sheriff organized a posse to search for him, and early in the evening, when most of the citizens of Troy were at supper, the suspected man was brought in and lodged in the county jail.

By the following morning the news of the capture had spread to the farthest limits of the county. A much larger number of people than usual came to town that Saturday—bearded men in straw hats and blue homespun shirts, and butternut trousers of great amplitude of material and vagueness of outline; women in home-spun frocks and slat-bonnets, with faces as expressionless as the dreary sandhills which gave them a meager sustenance.

The murder was almost the sole topic of conversation. A steady stream of curious observers visited the home of mourning and gazed upon the rugged face of the old veteran, now stiff and cold in death; and more than one eye dropped a tear at the remembrance of the cheery smile, and the joke—sometimes superannuated, generally feeble, but always good-natured—with which the captain had been wont to greet his acquaintances. There was a growing sentiment of anger among these stern men toward the murderer who had thus cut down their friend, and a strong feeling that ordinary justice was too slight a punishment for such a crime.

Toward noon there was an informal gathering of citizens in Dan Ayson's store.

"I hear it 'lowed that Square Kyahtah's too sick ter hol' co'te this evenin'," said one, "an' that the purlim'nary hearin' 'll haf ter go over 'tel nex' week." A look of disappointment went round the crowd.

"Hit's the durndes', meanes' murder ever committed in this caounty," said another, with moody emphasis.

"I s'pose the nigger 'lowed the Cap'n had some greenbacks," observed a third speaker.

"The Cap'n," said another, with an air of superior information, "has left two bairls of Confedrit money, which he 'spected'd be good some day er nuther."

This statement gave rise to a discussion of the speculative value of Confederate money; but in a little while the conversation returned to the murder.

"Hangin' air too good fer the murderer," said one; "he oughter be burnt, stider bein' hung."

There was an impressive pause at this point, during which a jug of moonlight whisky went the round of the crowd.

"Well," said a round-shouldered farmer who, in spite of his peaceable expression and faded gray eye, was known to have been one of the most daring followers of a rebel guerrilla chieftain, "what air ye gwine ter do about it? Ef you fellers air gwine ter set down an' let a wuthless nigger kill the bes' white man in Branson, an' not say nuthin' ner do nuthin', *I'll* move outen the caounty."

This speech gave tone and direction to the rest of the conversation. Whether the fear of losing the round-shouldered farmer operated to bring about the result or not is immaterial to this narrative; but at all events the crowd decided to lynch the Negro. They agreed that this was the least that could be done to avenge the death of their murdered friend, and that it was a becoming way in which to honor his memory. They had some vague notions of the majesty of the law and the rights of the citizen, but in the passion of the moment these sunk into oblivion; a white man had been killed by a Negro.

"The Cap'n was an ole sodger," said one of his friends solemnly. "He'll sleep better when he knows that a co'te-martial has be'n hilt an' jestice done."

By agreement the lynchers were to meet at Tyson's store at five o'clock in the afternoon and proceed thence to the jail, which was situated down the Lumberton Dirt Road (as the old turnpike antedating the plank-road was called) about half a mile south of the court house. When the preliminaries of the lynching had been arranged and a committee appointed to manage the affair, the crowd dispersed, some to go to their dinners and some to secure recruits for the lynching party.

It was twenty minutes to five o'clock when an excited Negro, panting and perspiring, rushed up to the back door of Sheriff Campbell's dwelling, which stood at a little distance from the jail and somewhat farther than the latter building from the courthouse. A turbaned colored woman came to the door in response to the Negro's knock.

"Hoddy, Sis' Nance."

"Hoddy, Brer Sam."

"Is de shurff in?" inquired the Negro.

"Yas, Brer Sam, he's eatin' his dinner," was the answer.

"Will yer ax'im ter step ter de do' a minute, Sis' Nance?"

The woman went into the dining room, and a moment later the sheriff came to the door. He was a tall, muscular man, of a ruddier complexion than is usual among Southerners. A pair of keen, deep-set gray eyes looked out from under bushy eyebrows, and about his mouth was a masterful expression, which a full beard, once sandy in color but now profusely sprinkled with gray, could not entirely conceal. The day was hot; the sheriff had discarded his coat and vest, and had his white shirt open at the throat.

"What do you want, Sam?" he inquired of the Negro, who stood hat in hand, wiping the moisture from his face with a ragged shirt-sleeve.

"Shurff, dey gwine ter hang de pris'ner w'at lock' up in de jail. Dey're comin' dis a-way now. I wuz layin' down on a sack er corn down at de sto', behine a pile er flour-bairls, w'en I hearn Doc' Cain en Kunnel Wright talkin' erbout it. I slip' outen de back do', en run here as fas' as I could. I hearn you say down ter de sto' once't dat you wouldn't let nobody take a pris'ner 'way fum you widout walkin' over yo' dead body, en I thought I'd let you know 'fo' dey come, so yer could pertec' de pris'ner."

The sheriff listened calmly, but his face grew firmer, and a determined gleam lit up his gray eyes. His frame grew more erect, and he unconsciously assumed the attitude of a soldier who momentarily expects to meet the enemy face to face.

"Much obliged, Sam," he answered. "I'll protect the prisoner. Who's coming?"

"I dunno who-all *is* comin'," replied the Negro. "Dere's Mistah McSwayne, en Doc' Cain, en Maje' McDonal', and Kunnel Wright en a heap er yuthers. I wuz so skeered I done furgot mo' d'n half un em. I spec' dey mus' be mos' here by dis time, so I'll git outen de way, fer I don't want nobody fer ter think I wuz mix' up in dis business." The Negro glanced nervously down the road toward the town, and made a movement as if to go away.

"Won't you have some dinner first?" asked the sheriff.

The Negro looked longingly in at the open door, and sniffed the appetizing odor of boiled pork and collards.

"I ain't got no time fer ter tarry, Shurff," he said, "but Sis' Nance mought gin me sump'n I could kyar in my han' en eat on de way."

A moment later Nancy brought him a huge sandwich of split cornpone, with a thick slice of fat bacon inserted between the halves, and a couple of baked yams. The Negro hastily replaced his ragged hat on his head, dropped the yams in the pocket of his capacious trousers and, taking the sandwich in his hand, hurried across the road and disappeared in the woods beyond.

The sheriff reentered the house, and put on his coat and hat. He then took down a double-barreled shotgun and loaded it with buckshot. Filling the chambers of a revolver with fresh cartridges, he slipped it into the pocket of the sackcoat which he wore.

A comely young woman in a calico dress watched these proceedings with anxious surprises.

"Where are you going, Father?" she asked. She had not heard the conversation with the Negro.

"I'm goin' over to the jail," responded the sheriff. "There's a mob comin' this way to lynch the nigger we've got locked up. But they won't do it," he added, with emphasis.

"Oh, Father, don't go!" pleaded the girl, clinging to his arm. "They'll shoot you if you don't give him up."

"You never mind me, Polly," said her father reassuringly, as he gently unclasped her hands from his arm. "I'll take care of myself and the prisoner, too. There ain't a man in Branson County that would shoot me. Besides, I have faced fire too often to be scared away from my duty. You keep close in the house," he continued, "and if anyone disturbs you just use the old horse-pistol in the top bureau drawer. It's a little old-fashioned, but it did good work a few years ago."

The young girl shuddered at this sanguinary allusion, but made no further objection to her father's departure.

The sheriff of Branson was a man far above the average of the community in wealth, education, and social position. His had been one of the few families in the county that before the war had owned large estates and numerous slaves. He had graduated at the State University at Chapel Hill, and had kept up some acquaintance with current literature and advanced thought. He had traveled some in his youth, and was looked up to in the county as an authority on all subjects connected with the outer world. At first an ardent supporter of the Union, he had opposed the secession movement in his native state as long as opposition availed to stem the tide of public opinion. Yielding at last to the force of circumstances, he had entered the Confederate service rather late in the war and served with distinction through several campaigns, rising in time to the rank of colonel. After the war he had taken the oath of allegiance, and had been chosen by the people as the most available candidate for the office of sheriff, to which he had been elected without opposition. He had filled the office for several terms and was universally popular with his constituents.

Colonel or Sheriff Campbell, as he was indifferently called, as the military or civil title happened to be most important in the opinion of the person addressing him, had a high sense of the responsibility attached to his office. He had sworn to do his duty faithfully, and he knew what his duty was as sheriff perhaps more clearly than he had apprehended it in other passages of his life. It was therefore with no uncertainty in regard to his course that he prepared his weapons and went over to the jail. He had no fears for Polly's safety.

The sheriff had just locked the heavy front door of the jail behind him when a half dozen horsemen, followed by a crowd of men on foot, came round a bend in the road and drew near the jail. They halted in front of the picket fence that surrounded the building, while several of the committee of arrangements rode on a few rods farther to the sheriff's house. One of them dismounted and rapped on the door with his riding whip.

"Is the sheriff at home?" he inquired.

"No, he has just gone out," replied Polly, who had come to the door.

"We want the jail keys," he continued.

"They are not here," said Polly. "The sheriff has them himself." Then she added, with assumed indifference, "He is at the jail now."

The man turned away, and Polly went into the front room, from which she peered anxiously between the slats of the green blinds of a window that looked toward the jail. Meanwhile the messenger returned to his companions and announced his discovery. It looked as though the sheriff had learned of their design and was preparing to resist it.

One of them stepped forward and rapped on the jail door.

"Well, what is it?" said the sheriff, from within.

"We want to talk to you, Sheriff," replied the spokesman.

There was a little wicket in the door; this the sheriff opened, and answered through it.

"All right, boys, talk away. You are all strangers to me, and I don't know what business you can have." The sheriff did not think it necessary to recognize anybody in particular on such an occasion; the question of identity sometimes comes up in the investigation of these extrajudicial executions.

"We're a committee of citizens and we want to get into the jail."

"What for? It ain't much trouble to get into jail. Most people want to keep out."

The mob was in no humor to appreciate a joke, and the sheriff's witticism fell upon an unresponsive audience.

"We want to have a talk with the nigger that killed Cap'n Walker."

"You can talk to that nigger in the courthouse, when he's brought out for trial. Court will be in session here next week. I know what you fellows want, but you can't get my prisoner today. Do you want to take the bread out of a poor man's mouth? I get seventy-five cents a day for keeping this prisoner, and he's the only one in jail. I can't have my family suffer just to please you fellows."

One or two young men in the crowd laughed at the idea of Sheriff Campbell's suffering for want of seventy-five cents a day; but they were frowned into silence by those who stood near them.

"Ef yer don't let us in," cried a voice, "we'll bus' the do' open."

"Bust away," answered the sheriff, raising his voice so that all could hear. "But I give you fair warning. The first man that tries it will be filled with buckshot. I'm sheriff of this county; I know my duty, and I mean to do it."

"What's the use of kicking, Sheriff?" argued one of the leaders of the mob. "The nigger is sure to hang anyhow; he richly deserves it; and we've got to do something to teach the niggers their places or white people won't be able to live in the county."

"There's no use talking, boys," responded the sheriff. "I'm a white man outside, but in this jail I'm sheriff; and if this nigger's to be hung in this county, I propose to do the hanging. So you fellows might as well right-about-face, and march back to Troy. You've had a pleasant trip, and the exercise will be good for you. You know *me*. I've got powder and ball, and I've faced fire before now, with nothing between me and the enemy, and I don't mean to surrender this jail while I'm able to shoot." Having thus announced his determination, the sheriff closed and fastened the wicket and looked around for the best position from which to defend the building.

The crowd drew off a little, and the leaders conversed together in low tones.

The Branson County jail was a small, two-story brick building, strongly constructed, with no attempt at architectural ornamentation. Each story was divided into two large cells by a passage running from front to rear. A grated iron door gave entrance from the passage to each of the four cells. The jail seldom had many prisoners in it, and the lower windows had been boarded up. When the sheriff had closed the wicket, he ascended the steep wooden stairs to the upper floor. There was no window at the front of the upper passage, and the most available position from which to watch the movements of the crowd below was the front window of the cell occupied by the solitary prisoner.

The sheriff unlocked the door and entered the cell. The prisoner was crouched in a corner, his yellow face, blanched with terror, looking ghastly in the semi-darkness of the room. A cold perspiration had gathered on his forehead, and his teeth were chattering with affright.

"For God's sake, Sheriff," he murmured hoarsely, "don't let 'em lynch me; I didn't kill the old man."

The sheriff glanced at the cowering wretch with a look of mingled contempt and loathing.

"Get up," he said sharply. "You will probably be hung sooner or later, but it shall not be today if I can help it. I'll unlock your fetters, and if I can't hold the jail you'll have to make the best fight you can. If I'm shot, I'll consider my responsibility at an end."

There were iron fetters on the prisoner's ankles, and handcuffs on his wrists. These the sheriff unlocked, and they fell clanking to the floor.

"Keep back from the window," said the sheriff. "They might shoot if they saw you."

The sheriff drew toward the window a pine bench which formed a part of the scanty furniture of the cell, and laid his revolver upon it. Then he took his gun in hand, and took his stand at the side of the window where he could with least exposure of himself watch the movements of the crowd below.

The lynchers had not anticipated any determined resistance. Of course they had looked for a formal protest, and perhaps a sufficient show of opposition to excuse the sheriff in the eye of any stickler for legal formalities. They had not however come prepared to fight a battle, and no one of them seemed willing to lead an attack upon the jail. The leaders of the party conferred together with a good deal of animated gesticulation, which was visible to the sheriff from his outlook, though the distance was too great for him to hear what was said. At length one of them broke away from the group and rode back to the main body of the lynchers, who were restlessly awaiting orders.

"Well, boys," said the messenger, "we'll have to let it go for the present. The sheriff says he'll shoot, and he's got the drop on us this time. There ain't any of us that want to follow Cap'n Walker jest yet. Besides, the sheriff is a good fellow and we don't want to hurt 'im. But," he added, as if to reassure the crowd, which began to show signs of disappointment, "the nigger might as well say his prayers, for he ain't got long to live."

There was a murmur of dissent from the mob, and several voices insisted that an attack be made on the jail. But pacific counsels finally prevailed, and the mob sullenly withdrew.

The sheriff stood at the window until they had disappeared around the bend in the road. He did not relax his watchfulness when the last one was out of sight. Their withdrawal might be a mere feint, to be followed by a further attempt. So closely indeed was his attention drawn to the outside, that he neither saw nor heard the prisoner creep stealthily across the floor, reach out his hand and secure the revolver which lay on the bench behind the sheriff, and creep as noiselessly back to his place in the corner of the room.

A moment after the last of the lynching party had disappeared there was a shot fired from the woods across the road; a bullet whistled by the window and buried itself in the wooden casing a few inches from where the sheriff was standing. Quick as thought, with the instinct born of a semi-guerrilla army experience, he raised his gun and fired twice at the point from which a faint puff of smoke showed the hostile to have been sent. He stood a moment watching, and then rested his gun against the window and reached behind him mechanically for the other weapon. It was not on the bench. As the sheriff realized this fact, he turned his head and looked into the muzzle of the revolver

"Stay where you are, Sheriff," said the prisoner, his eyes glistening, his face almost ruddy with excitement.

The sheriff mentally cursed his own carelessness for allowing him to be caught in such a predicament. He had not expected anything of the kind. He had relied on the Negro's cowardice and subordination in the presence of an armed white man as a matter of course. The sheriff was a brave man, but realized that the prisoner had him at an immense disadvantage. The two men stood thus for a moment, fighting a harmless duel with their eyes.

"Well, what do you mean to do?" asked the sheriff with apparent calmness.

"To get away, of course," said the prisoner in a tone which caused the sheriff to look at him more closely, and with an involuntary feeling of apprehension; if the man was not mad, he was in a state of mind akin to madness, and quite as dangerous. The sheriff felt that he must speak to the prisoner fair and watch for a chance to turn the tables on him. The keen-eyed, desperate man before him was a different being altogether from the groveling wretch who had begged so piteously for life a few minutes before.

At length the sheriff spoke:—

"Is this your gratitude to me for saving your life at the risk of my own? If I had not done so, you would now be swinging from the limb of some neighboring tree."

"True," said the prisoner, "you saved my life, but for how long? When you came in, you said court would sit next week. When the crowd went away they said I had not long to live. It is merely a choice of two ropes."

"While there's life there's hope," replied the sheriff. He uttered this commonplace mechanically, while his brain was busy in trying to think out some way of escape. "If you are innocent you can prove it."

The mulatto kept his eye upon the sheriff. "I didn't kill the old man," he replied; "but I shall never be able to clear myself. I was at his house at nine o'clock. I stole from it the coat that was on my back when I was taken. I would be convicted even with a fair trial unless the real murderer were discovered beforehand."

The sheriff knew this only too well. While he was thinking what argument next to use, the prisoner continued:—

"Throw me the keys—no, unlock the door."

The sheriff stood a moment irresolute. The mulatto's eyes glittered ominously. The sheriff crossed the room and unlocked the door leading into the passage.

"Now go down and unlock the outside door."

The heart of the sheriff leaped within him. Perhaps he might make a dash for liberty and gain the outside. He descended the narrow stairs, the prisoner keeping close behind him.

The sheriff inserted the huge iron key into the lock. The rusty bolt yielded slowly. It still remained for him to pull the door open.

"Stop!" thundered the mulatto, who seemed to divine the sheriff's purpose. "Move a muscle, and I'll blow your brain out."

The sheriff obeyed; he realized that his chance had not yet come.

"Now keep on that side of the passage and go back upstairs."

Keeping the sheriff under cover of the revolver, the mulatto followed him up the stairs. The sheriff expected the prisoner to lock him into the cell and make his own escape. He had about come to the conclusion that the best thing he could do under the circumstances was to submit quietly and take his chances of recapturing the prisoner after the alarm had been given. The sheriff had faced death more than once upon the battlefield. A few minutes before, well armed, and with a brick wall between him and them, he had dared a hundred men to fight; but he felt instinctively that the desperate man confronting him was not to be trifled with, and he was too prudent a man to risk his life against such heavy odds. He had Polly to look after and there was a limit beyond which devotion to duty would be quixotic and even foolish.

"I want to get away," said the prisoner, "and I don't want to be captured; for if I am I know I will be hung on the spot. I am afraid," he added somewhat reflectively, "that in order to save myself I shall have to kill you."

"Good God!" exclaimed the sheriff in involuntary terror; "you would not kill the man to whom you owe your own life."

"You speak more truly than you know," replied the mulatto. "I indeed owe my life to you."

The sheriff started. He was capable of surprise, even in that moment of extreme peril. "Who are you?" he asked in amazement.

"Tom, Cicely's son," returned the other. He had closed the door and stood talking to the sheriff through the gated opening. "Don't you remember Cicely—Cicely whom you sold with her child to the speculator on his way to Alabama?"

The sheriff did remember. He had been sorry for it many a time since. It had been the old story of debts, mortgages, and bad crops. He had quarreled with the mother. The price offered for her and her child had been unusually large, and he had yielded to the combination of anger and pecuniary stress.

"Good God!" he gasped; "you would not murder your own father?"

"My father?" replied the mulatto. "It were well enough for me to claim the relationship, but it comes with poor grace from you to ask anything by reason of it. What father's duty have you ever performed for me? Did you give me your name, or even your protection? Other white men gave their colored sons freedom and money, and sent them to the free states. *You* sold *me* to the rice swamps."

"I at least gave you the life you cling to," murmured the sheriff.

"Life?" said the prisoner, with a sarcastic laugh. "What kind of a life? You gave me your own blood, your own feathers—no man need look at us together twice to see that—and you gave me a black mother. Poor wretch! She died under the lash, because she had enough spirit, and you made me a slave, and crushed it out."

"But you are free now," said the sheriff. He had not doubted, could not doubt, the mulatto's word. He knew whose passions coursed beneath that swarthy skin and burned in the black eyes opposite his own. He saw in this mulatto what he himself might have become had not the safeguards of parental restraint and public opinion been thrown around him.

"Free to do what?" replied the mulatto. "Free in name, but despised and scorned and set aside by the people to whose race I belong far more than to my mother's."

"There are schools," said the sheriff. "You have been to school." He had noticed the mulatto spoke more eloquently and used better language than most Branson County people.

"I have been to school, and dreamed when I went that it would work some marvelous change in my condition. But what did I learn? I learned to feel that no degree of learning or wisdom will change the color of my skin and that I shall always wear what in my own country is a badge of degradation. When I think about it seriously I do not care particularly for such a life. It is the animal in me, not the man, that flees the gallows. I owe you nothing," he went on, "and expect nothing of you; and it would be no more than justice if I should avenge upon you my mother's wrongs and my own. But still I have to shoot you; I have never yet taken human life—for I did *not* kill the old captain. Will you promise to give no alarm and make no attempt to capture me until morning, if I do not shoot?"

So absorbed were the two men in their colloquy and their own tumultuous thoughts that neither of them had heard the door below move upon its hinges. Neither of them had heard a light step come stealthily up the stairs, nor seen a slender form creep along the darkening passage toward the mulatto.

The sheriff hesitated. The struggle between his love of life and his sense of duty was a terrific one. It may seem strange that a man who could sell his own child into slavery should hesitate at such a moment, when his life was trembling in the balance. But the baleful influence of human slavery poisoned the very fountains of life, and created new standards of right. The sheriff was conscientious; his conscience had merely been warped by his environment. Let no one ask what his answer would have been; he was spared the necessity of a decision.

"Stop," said the mulatto, "you need not promise. I could not trust you if you did. It is your life for mine; there is but one safe way for me; you must die."

He raised his arm to fire, when there was a flash—a report from the passage behind him. His arm fell heavily at his side, and the pistol dropped at his feet.

The sheriff recovered first from his surprise, and throwing open the door secured the fallen weapon. Then seizing the prisoner he thrust him into the cell and locked the door upon him; after which he turned to Polly, who leaned half-fainting against the wall, her hands clasped over her heart.

"Oh, Father, I was just in time!" she cried hysterically and, wildly sobbing, threw herself into her father's arms.

"I watched until they went away," she said. "I heard the shot from the woods and I saw you shoot. Then when you did not come out I feared something had happened, that perhaps you had been wounded. I got out the other pistol and ran over here. When I found the door open I knew something was wrong, and when I heard voices I crept upstairs, and reached the top just in time to hear him say he would kill you. Oh, it was a narrow escape!"

When she had grown somewhat calmer, the sheriff left her standing there and went back into the cell. The prisoner's arm was bleeding from a flesh wound. His bravado had given place to a stony apathy. There was no sign in his face of fear or disappointment or feeling of any kind. The sheriff sent Polly to the house for cloth, and bound up the prisoner's wound with a rude skill acquired during his army life.

"I'll have a doctor come and dress the wound in the morning," he said to the prisoner. "It will do very well until then if you will keep quiet. If the doctor asks you how the wound was caused, you can say that you were struck by the bullet fired from the woods. It would do you no good to have it known that you were shot while attempting to escape."

The prisoner uttered no word of thanks or apology, but sat in sullen silence. When the wounded arm had been bandaged, Polly and her father returned to the house.

The sheriff was in an unusually thoughtful mood that evening. He put salt in his coffee at supper, and poured vinegar over his pancakes. To many of Polly's questions he returned random answers. When he had gone to bed he lay awake for several hours.

In the silent watches of the night, when he was alone with God, there came into his mind a flood of unaccustomed thoughts. An hour or two before, standing face to face with death, he had experienced a sensation similar to that which drowning men are said to feel—a kind of clarifying of the moral faculty, in which the veil of the flesh, with its obscuring passions and prejudices, is pushed aside for a moment, and all the acts of one's life stand out, in the clear light of truth, in their correct proportions and relations—a state of mind in which one sees himself as God may be supposed to see him. In the reaction following his rescue, this feeling had given place for a time to far different emotions. But now, in the silence of midnight, something of this clearness of spirit returned to the sheriff. He saw that he had owed some duty to this son of his—that neither law nor custom could destroy a responsibility inherent in the nature of mankind. He could not thus, in the eyes of God at least, shake off the consequences of his sin. Had he never sinned, this wayward spirit would never have come back from the vanished past to haunt him. As these thoughts came, his anger against the mulatto died away, and in its place there sprang up a great pity. The hand of parental authority might have restrained the passions he had seen burning in the prisoner's eyes when the desperate man spoke the words which had seemed to doom his father to death. The sheriff felt that he might have saved this fiery spirit from the sloth of slavery; that he might have sent him to the free North and given him there, or in some other land, an opportunity to turn to usefulness and honorable pursuits the talents that had run to crime, perhaps to madness; he might, still less, have given this son of his the poor simulacrum of liberty which men of his caste could possess in a slave-holding community; or least of all, but still something, he might have kept the boy on the plantation, where the burdens of slavery would have fallen lightly upon him.

The sheriff recalled his own youth. He had inherited an honored name to keep untarnished; he had had a future to make; the picture of a fair young bride had beckoned him on to happiness. The poor wretch now stretched upon a pallet of straw between the brick walls of the jail had had none of these things, no name, no father, no mother—in the true meaning of motherhood—and until the past few years no possible future, and that one vague and shadowy in its outline, and dependent for form and substance upon the slow solution of a problem in which there were many unknown quantities.

From what he might have done to what he might yet do was an easy transition for the awkward conscience of the sheriff. It occurred to him, purely as a hypothesis, that he might permit his prisoner to escape; but his oath of office, his duty as sheriff, stood in the way of such a course, and the sheriff dismissed the idea from his mind. He could, however, investigate the circumstances of the murder and move Heaven and earth to discover the real criminal, for he no longer doubted the prisoner's innocence; he could employ counsel for the accused, and perhaps influence public opinion in his favor. Acquittal once secured, some plan could be devised by which the sheriff might in some degree atone for his crime against this son of his—against society—against God.

When the sheriff had reached this conclusion he fell into an unquiet slumber, from which he awoke late the next morning.

He went over to the jail before breakfast and found the prisoner lying on his pallet, his face turned to the wall; he did not move when the sheriff rattled the door.

"Good morning," said the latter, in a tone intended to waken the prisoner.

There was no response. The sheriff looked more keenly at the recumbent figure; there was an unnatural rigidity about its attitude.

He hastily unlocked the door and, entering the cell, bent over the prostrate form. There was no sound of breathing; he turned the body over—it was cold and stiff. The prisoner had torn the bandage from his wound and bled to death during the night. He had evidently been dead several hours.

Pauline Elizabeth Hopkins (1859–1930)

In the preface of her novel Contending Forces *(1900), Pauline Elizabeth Hopkins reveals her pride in the accomplishments of blacks and her belief in the power of writing to mold interracial understanding and unity. She writes: "The colored race has historians, lecturers, ministers, poets, judges, and lawyers—men of brilliant intellects who have arrested the favorable attention of this busy, energetic nation. But after all, it is the simple, homely tale, unassumingly told, which cements the bond of brotherhood among all classes and all complexions."*

Born in Portland, Maine, and raised in Boston, Hopkins was a published author before she graduated from high school. At age fifteen, she wrote an essay, "Evils of Intemperance and Their Remedies," that won first prize in the William Wells Brown contest sponsored by the Congregational Publishing Society of Bos-

ton. The young Hopkins also appeared onstage with her mother and stepfather as a part of a large theatrical cast; she sang and acted the main role in the Hopkins's Colored Troubadours performance of Slaves Escape on the Underground Railroad, *an 1880 musical drama. Between 1880 and 1892, Hopkins toured with the show, revising its content and title on occasion, and wrote an unproduced play,* One Scene from the Drama of Early Days, *which presents the biblical story of Daniel in the lion's den.*

Supporting herself as a stenographer, Hopkins published her first novel in 1900: Contending Forces: A Romance Illustrative of Negro Life North and South. *She drew upon her performance and lecturing skills to conduct public readings to market the novel, which is described by one critic as presenting "a lovely young orphan with a hidden, violent past who must prove her virtue through additional suffering, eventually to be rewarded with an ideal husband." The book brought Hopkins enough attention to receive an invitation to contribute to the new* Colored American *magazine. For the initial issue in 1901, Hopkins wrote "The Mystery within Us," a short story. She also wrote numerous biographical essays for the magazine series on "Famous Women of the Negro Race" and "Famous Men of the Negro Race." However, fiction served as her creative field for exploring issues of interracial conflict and interracial mixing. From 1901 to 1903, Hopkins wrote three novels that were serialized in* Colored American: Hagar's Daughter: A Story of Southern Caste Prejudice; Winona: A Tale of Negro Life in the South and Southwest; *and* Of One Blood; or The Hidden Self.

In 1904, Hopkins continued to publish essays and fiction. Her novella, "Topsy Templeton" (1916), appeared in New Era. *Toward the end of her life, she returned to stenography for her livelihood. Hopkins died in a fire in 1930.*

"A Dash for Liberty," which appeared in a 1901 issue of Colored American, *is a good example of Hopkins's style, characterizations, and thematic concerns. The story focuses on Madison, an escaped male slave and "an unmixed African," who returns to Virginia to free his wife, a "beautiful octoroon," from slavery.*

A Dash for Liberty

Founded on an article written by
Col. T. W. Higginson,
for the Atlantic Monthly, *June 1861*

"So, Madison, you are bound to try it?"

"Yes, sir," was the respectful reply.

There was silence between the two men for a space, and Mr. Dickson drove his horse to the end of the furrow he was making and returned slowly to the starting point, and the sombre figure awaiting him.

"Do I not pay you enough, and treat you well?" asked the farmer as he halted.

"Yes, sir."

"Then why not stay here and let well enough alone?"

"Liberty is worth nothing to me while my wife is a slave."

"We will manage to get her to you in a year or two."

The man smiled and sadly shook his head. "A year or two would mean forever, situated as we are, Mr. Dickson. It is hard for you to understand; you white men are all alike where you are called upon to judge a Negro's heart," he continued bitterly. "Imagine yourself in my place; how would you feel? The relentless heel of oppression in the States will have ground my rights as a husband into the dust, and have driven Susan to despair in that time. A white man may take up arms to defend a bit of property; but a black man has no right to his wife, his liberty or his life against his master! This makes me low-spirited, Mr. Dickson, and I have determined to return to Virginia for my wife. My feelings are centred in the idea of liberty," and as he spoke he stretched his arms toward the deep blue of the Canadian sky in a magnificent gesture. Then with a deep-drawn breath that inflated his mighty chest, he repeated the word: "Liberty! I think of it by day and dream of it by night; and I shall only taste it in all its sweetness when Susan shares it with me."

Madison was an unmixed African, or grand physique, and one of the handsomest of his race. His dignified, calm and unaffected bearing marked him as a leader among his fellows. His features bore the stamp of genius. His firm step and piercing eye attracted the attention of all who met him. He had arrived in Canada along with many other fugitives during the year 1840, and being a strong, able-bodied man, and a willing worker, had sought and obtained employment on Mr. Dickson's farm.

After Madison's words, Mr. Dickson stood for some time in meditative silence.

"Madison," he said at length, "there's desperate blood in your veins, and if you get back there and are captured, you'll do desperate deeds."

"Well, put yourself in my place: I shall be there single-handed. I have a wife whom I love, and whom I will protect. I hate slavery, I hate the laws that make my country a nursery for it. Must I be denied the right of aggressive defense against those who would overpower and crush me by superior force?"

"I understand you fully, Madison; it is not your defense but your rashness that I fear. Promise me that you will be discreet, and not begin an attack." Madison hesitated. Such a promise seemed to him like surrendering a part of those individual rights for which he panted. Mr. Dickson waited. Presently the Negro said significantly: "I promise not to be indiscreet."

There were tears in the eyes of the kind-hearted farmer as he pressed Madison's hand.

"God speed and keep you and the wife you love; may she prove worthy."

In a few days, Madison received the wages due him, and armed with tiny saws and files to cut a way to liberty, if captured, turned his face toward the South.

It was late in the fall of 1840 when Madison found himself again at home in the fair Virginia State. The land was blossoming into ripe maturity, and the smiling fields lay waiting for the harvester.

The fugitive, unable to travel in the open day, had hidden himself for three weeks in the shadow of the friendly forest near his old home, filled with hope and fear, unable to obtain any information about the wife he hoped to rescue from slavery. After weary days and nights, he had reached the most perilous part of his mission. Tonight there would be no moon and the clouds threatened a storm; to his listening ears the rising wind bore the sound of laughter and singing. He drew back into the deepest shadow. The words came distinctly to his ears as the singers neared his hiding place.

All dem purty gals will be dar,
  Shuck dat corn before you eat.
Dey will fix it fer us rare,
  Shuck dat corn before you eat.
I know dat supper will be big,
  Shuck dat corn before you eat.
I think I smell a fine roast pig,
  Shuck dat corn before you eat.
Stuff dat coon an' bake him down,
I spec some niggers dar from town.
  Shuck dat corn before you eat.
Please cook dat turkey nice an' brown.
By de side of dat turkey I'll be foun',
  Shuck dat corn before you eat.

"Don't talk about dat turkey; he'll be gone before we git dar."

"He's talkin', ain't he?"

"Las' time I shucked corn, turkey was de toughes' meat I eat fer many a day; you's got to have teef sharp lak a saw to eat it."

"S'pose you ain't got no teef, den what you gwine ter do?"

"Why ef you ain't got no teef you muss gum it!"

"Ha, ha, ha!"

Madison glided in and out among the trees, listening until he was sure that it was a gang going to a corn-shucking, and he resolved to join it, and get, if possible some news of Susan. He came out upon the highway, and as the company reached his hiding place, he fell into the ranks and joined in the singing. The darkness hid his identity from the company while he learned from their conversation the important events of the day.

On they marched by the light of weird, flaring pine knots, singing their merry cadences, in which the noble minor strains habitual to Negro music, sounded the depths of sadness, glancing off in majestic harmony, that touched the very gates of paradise in suppliant prayer.

It was close to midnight; the stars had disappeared and a steady rain was falling when, by a circuitous route, Madison reached the mansion where he had learned that his wife was still living. There were lights in the windows. Mirth at the great house kept company with mirth at the quarters.

The fugitive stole noiselessly under the fragrant magnolia trees and paused, asking himself what he should do next. As he stood there he heard the hoof-beats of the mounted patrol, far in the distance, die into silence. Cautiously he drew near the house and crept around to the rear of the building directly beneath the window of his wife's sleeping closet. He swung himself up and tried it; it yielded to his touch. Softly he raised the sash, and softly he crept into the room. His foot struck against an object and swept it to the floor. It fell with a loud crash. In an instant the door opened. There was a rush of feet, and Madison stood at bay. The house was aroused; lights were brought.

"I knowed 'twas him!" cried the overseer in triumph. "I heern him a-gettin' in the window, but I kept dark till he knocked my gun down; then I grabbed him! I knowed this room'd trap him ef we was patient about it."

Madison shook his captor off and backed against the wall. His grasp tightened on the club in his hand; his nerves were like steel, his eyes flashed fire.

"Don't kill him," shouted Judge Johnson, as the overseer's pistol gleamed in the light. "Five hundred dollars for him alive!"

With a crash, Madison's club descended on the head of the nearest man; again, and yet again, he whirled it around, doing frightful execution each time it fell. Three of the men who had responded to the overseer's cry for help were on the ground, and he himself was sore from many wounds before, weakened by loss of blood, Madison finally succumbed.

The brig "Creole" lay at the Richmond dock taking on her cargo of tobacco, hemp, flax and slaves. The sky was cloudless, and the blue waters rippled but slightly under the faint breeze. There was on board the confusion incident to departure. In the hold and on deck men were hurrying to and fro, busy and excited, making the final preparations for the voyage. The slaves came aboard in two gangs: first the men, chained like cattle, were marched to their quarters in the hold; then came the women to whom more freedom was allowed.

In spite of the blue sky and the bright sunlight that silvered the water the scene was indescribably depressing and sad. The procession of gloomy-faced men and weeping women seemed to be descending into a living grave.

The captain and the first mate were standing together at the head of the gangway as the women stepped aboard. Most were very plain and bore the marks of servitude, a few were neat and attractive in appearances; but one was a woman whose great beauty immediately attracted attention; she was an octoroon. It was a tradition that her grandfather had served in the Revolutionary War, as well as in both Houses of Congress. That was nothing, however, at a time when the blood of the proudest F.F.V.'s* was freely mingled with that of the African slaves on their plantations. Who wonders that Virginia has produced great men of color from among the exbondmen, or, that illustrious black men proudly point to Virginia as a birthplace? Posterity rises to the plane that their ancestors bequeath, and the most refined, the wealthiest and the most intellectual whites of that proud State have not hesitated to amalgamate with the Negro.

"What a beauty!" exclaimed the captain as the line of women paused a moment opposite him.

"Yes," said the overseer in charge of the gang. "She's as fine a piece of flesh as I have had in trade for many a day."

"What's the price?" demanded the captain.

"Oh, way up. Two or three thousand. She's a lady's maid, well-educated, and can sing and dance. We'll get it in New Orleans. Like to buy?"

"You don't suit my pile," was the reply, as his eyes followed the retreating form of the handsome octoroon. "Give her a cabin to herself; she ought not to herd with the rest," he continued, turning to the mate.

He turned with a meaning laugh to execute the order.

The "Creole" proceeded slowly on her way towards New Orleans. In the

---

* First Families of Virginia, whites descended from colonists and early settlers.

men's cabin, Madison Monroe lay chained to the floor and heavily ironed. But from the first moment on board ship he had been busily engaged in selecting men who could be trusted in the dash for liberty that he was determined to make. The miniature files and saws which he still wore concealed in his clothing were faithfully used in the darkness of night. The man was at peace, although he had caught no glimpse of the dearly loved Susan. When the body suffers greatly, the strain upon the heart becomes less tense, and a welcome calmness had stolen over the prisoner's soul.

On the ninth day out the brig encountered a rough sea, and most of the slaves were sick, and therefore not watched with very great vigilance. This was the time for action, and it was planned that they should rise that night. Night came on; the first watch was summoned; the wind was blowing high. Along the narrow passageway that separated the men's quarters from the women's, a man was creeping.

The octoroon lay upon the floor of her cabin, apparently sleeping, when a shadow darkened the door, and the captain stepped into the room, casting bold glances at the reclining figure. Profound silence reigned. One might have fancied one's self on a deserted vessel, but for the sound of an occasional footstep on the deck above, and the murmur of voices in the opposite hold.

She lay stretched at full length with her head resting upon her arm, a position that displayed to the best advantage the perfect symmetry of her superb figure; the dim light of a lantern played upon the long black ringlets, finely-chiseled mouth and well-rounded chin, upon the marbled skin veined by her master's blood—representative of two races, to which did she belong?

For a moment the man gazed at her in silence; then casting a glance around him, he dropped upon one knee and kissed the sleeping woman full upon the mouth.

With a shriek the startled sleeper sprang to her feet. The woman's heart stood still with horror; she recognized the intruder as she dashed his face aside with both hands.

"None of that, my beauty," growled the man, as he reeled back with an oath, and then flung himself forward and threw his arm about her slender waist. "Why did you think you had a private cabin, and all the delicacies of the season? Not to behave like a young catamount, I warrant you."

The passion of terror and desperation lent the girl such strength that the man was forced to relax his hold slightly. Quick as a flash, she struck him a stinging blow across the eyes, and as he staggered back, she sprang out of the doorway, making for the deck with the evident intention of going overboard.

"God have mercy!" broke from her lips as she passed the men's cabin, closely followed by the captain.

"Hold on, girl; we'll protect you!" shouted Madison, and he stooped, seized the heavy black padlock which fastened the iron ring that encircled his ankle to the iron bar, and stiffening the muscles, wrenched the fastening apart, and hurled it with all his force straight at the captain's head.

His aim was correct. The padlock hit the captain not far from the left temple. The blow stunned him. In a moment Madison was upon him and had seized his weapons, another moment served to handcuff the unconscious man.

"If the fire of Heaven were in my hands, I would throw it at these cowardly whites. Follow me: it is liberty or death!" he shouted as he rushed for the quarter-deck. Eighteen others followed him, all of whom seized whatever they could wield as weapons.

The crew were all on deck; the three passengers were seated on the companion smoking. The appearance of the slaves all at once completely surprised the whites.

So swift were Madison's movements that at first the officers made no attempt to use their weapons; but this was only for an instant. One of the passengers drew his pistol, fired, and killed one of the blacks. The next moment he lay dead upon the deck from a blow with a piece of a capstan bar in Madison's hand. The fight then became general, passengers and crew taking part.

The first and second mates were stretched out upon the deck with a single blow each. The sailors ran up the rigging for safety, and in short time Madison was master of the "Creole."

After his accomplices had covered the slaver's deck, the intrepid leader forbade the shedding of more blood. The sailors came down to the deck, and their wounds were dressed. All the prisoners were heavily ironed and well guarded except the mate, who was to navigate the vessel; with a musket doubly charged pointed at his breast, he was made to swear to take the brig into a British port.

By one splendid and heroic stroke, the daring Madison had not only gained his own liberty, but that of one hundred and thirty-four others.

The next morning all slaves who were still fettered, were released, and the cook was ordered to prepare the best breakfast that the stores would permit; this was to be a fête in honor of the success of the revolt and as a surprise to the females, whom the men had not yet seen.

As the women filed into the captain's cabin, where the meal was served, weeping, singing and shouting their deliverance, the beautiful octoroon with one wild, half-frantic cry of joy sprang towards the gallant leader.

"Madison!"

"My God!, Susan! My wife!"

She was locked to his breast; she clung to him convulsively. Unnerved at last by the revulsion to more than relief and ecstasy, she broke into wild sobs, while the astonished company closed around them with loud hurrahs.

Madison's cup of joy was filled to the brim. He clasped her to him in silence, and humbly thanked Heaven for its blessing and mercy.

The next morning the "Creole" landed at Nassau, New Providence, where the slaves were offered protection and hospitality.

Every act of oppression is a weapon for the oppressed. Right is a dangerous instrument; woe to us if our enemy wields it.

Sutton E. Griggs (1872–1933)

Born in Chatfield, Texas, Sutton E. Griggs studied at Bishop College and Richmond Theological Seminary in Virginia, becoming an ordained Baptist minister. He headed a church in Virginia for two years before assuming a post as secretary of the Education Department of the National Baptist Convention in Nashville, Tennessee.

Credited with establishing his own publishing company, Griggs "solved the problem of distribution by selling his books in the black community and . . . was more widely read among African-Americans than his contemporaries," accord-

ing to Addison Gayle. More intent on the polemics and didacticism of his fiction than on its literary value, Griggs has been dismissed by some critics as a technically deficient writer. Although content overshadows form in his fiction, Griggs's work is nonetheless passionate and unequivocal in its presentation of racial themes.

Arguably, Griggs could be cited as the first African American to publish a black nationalist novel, Imperium in Imperio *(1899), translated as "an empire within an empire." A crucial element of the novel's plot is the secret black coalition that organizes itself economically and politically to challenge the American system. Griggs's second novel,* Overshadowed *(1901), was followed by* Unfettered *(1902) and* The Hindered Hand *(1905), which explores miscegenation, racial passing, and lynching, and defends blacks against the distorted images popularized by white author Thomas Dixon and other so-called plantation-genre writers of the time. In an essay at the end of the novel, Griggs attacks the racist propaganda of Dixon, labeling him a "misguided soul" who "ignored all of the good in the aspiring Negro; made every vicious offshoot that he pictured typical of the entire race; presented all mistakes independent of their environment and provocations; ignored or minimized all the evil in the more vicious elements of whites."*

In the chapters from Imperium in Imperio *reprinted here, two male characters present their contrasting philosophies for racial survival. Belton Piedmont, "poor and dark in complexion, represents the spirit of conservatism in the Negro race," whereas Bernard Belgrave, the "mulatto son of an interracial marriage, represents the spirit of intractable militancy."*

from Imperium in Imperio

CHAPTER XVI
Unwritten History

Belton, smiling, locked his arm in Bernard's and said: "Come with me. I will explain it all to you." They walked down the aisle together.

At the sight of these two most conspicuous representatives of all that was good and great in the race, moving down the aisle side by side, the audience began to cheer wildly and a band of musicians began playing "Hail to the Chief."

All of this was inexplicable to Bernard; but he was soon to learn what and how much it meant. Belton escorted him across the campus to the small but remarkably pretty white cottage with green vines clinging to trellis work all around it. Here they entered. The rooms were furnished with rare and antique furniture and were so tastefully arranged as to astonish and please even Bernard, who had been accustomed from childhood to choice, luxuriant magnificence.

They entered a side room, overlooking a beautiful lawn which could boast of lovely flowers and rose bushes scattered here and there. They sat down, facing each other. Bernard was a bundle of expectancy. He had passed through enough to make him so.

Belton said: "Bernard, I am now about to put the keeping of the property, the liberty, and the very lives of over seven million five hundred thousand people into your hands."

Bernard opened his eyes wide in astonishment and waited for Belton to further explain himself.

"Realize," said Belton, "that I am carefully weighing each remark I make and am fully conscious of how much my statement involves." Bernard bowed his head in solemn thought. Viola's recent death, the blood-curdling experiences of the day, and now Belton's impressive words all united to make that a sober moment with him; as sober as any that he had ever had in his life. He looked Belton in the face and said: "May revengeful lightning transfix me with her fiercest bolts; may hell's most fiery pillars roll in fury around me; may I be despised of man and forgotten of my God, if I ever knowingly, in the slightest way, do aught to betray this solemn, this most sacred trust."

Belton gazed fondly on the handsome features of his noble friend and sighed to think that only the coloring of his skin prevented him from being enrolled upon the scroll containing the names of the very noblest sons of earth. Arousing himself as from a reverie he drew near to Bernard and said: "I must begin. Another government, complete in every detail, exercising the sovereign right of life and death over its subjects, has been organized and maintained within the United States for many years. This government has a population of seven million two hundred and fifty thousand."

"Do you mean all that you say, Belton?" asked Bernard eagerly.

"I shall in a short time submit to you positive proofs of my assertion. You shall find that I have not overstated anything."

"But, Belton, how in the world can such a thing be when I, who am thoroughly conversant with every movement of any consequence, have not even dreamed of such a thing."

"All of that shall be made perfectly clear to you in the course of the narrative which I shall now relate."

Bernard leaned forward, anxious to hear what purported to be one of the most remarkable and at the same time one of the most important things connected with modern civilization.

Belton began: "You will remember, Bernard, that there lived, in the early days of the American Republic, a negro scientist who won an international reputation by his skill and erudition. In our school days, we spoke of him often. Because of his learning and consequent usefulness, this negro enjoyed the association of the moving spirits of the revolutionary period. By the publication of a book of science which outranked any other book of the day that treated of the same subject, this negro became a very wealthy man. Of course the book is now obsolete, science having made such great strides since his day. This wealthy negro secretly gathered other free negroes together and organized a society that had a two-fold object. The first object was to endeavor to secure for the free negroes all the rights and privileges of men, according to the teachings of Thomas Jefferson. Its other object was to secure the freedom of the enslaved negroes the world over. All work was done by this organization with the sole stipulation that it should be used for the furtherance of the two above named objects of the society, and for those objects alone.

"During slavery this organization confined its membership principally to free negroes, as those who were yet in physical bondage were supposed to have aspirations for nothing higher than being released from chains, and were, therefore, not prepared to eagerly aspire to the enjoyment of the highest privileges of freedom. When the War of Secession was over and all negroes were free, the society began to cautiously spread its membership among the emancipated.

They conducted a campaign of education, which in every case preceded an attempt at securing numbers. This campaign of education had for its object the instruction of the negro as to what real freedom was. He was taught that being released from chains was but the lowest form of liberty, and that he was no more than a common cur if he was satisfied with simply that. That much was all, they taught, that a dog howled for. They made use of Jefferson's writings, educating the negro to feel that he was not in the full enjoyment of his rights until he was on terms of equality with any other human being that was alive or had ever lived. This society used its influence secretly to have appointed over Southern schools of all kinds for negroes such teachers as would take especial pains to teach the negro to aspire for equality with all other races of men.

"They were instructed to pay especial attention to the history of the United States during the revolutionary period. Thus, the campaign of education moved forward. The negroes gained political ascendancy in many Southern states, but were soon hurled from power, by force in some quarters, and by fraud in others. The negroes turned their eyes to the federal government for redress and a guarantee of their rights. The federal government said: 'Take care of yourselves, we are powerless to help you.' The 'Civil Rights Bill,' was declared null and void by the Supreme Court. An 'honest election bill' was defeated in Congress by James G. Blaine and others. Separate coach laws were declared by the Supreme Court to be constitutional. State Constitutions were revised and so amended as to nullify the amendment of the Federal Constitution, giving the negro the right to vote. More than sixty thousand defenseless negroes were unlawfully slain. Governors would announce publicly that they favored lynching. The Federal Government would get elected to power by condemning these outrages, and when there, would confess its utter helplessness. One President plainly declared, what was already well known, 'that the only thing that they could do, would be to create a healthy sentiment.' This secret organization of which we have been speaking decided that some means must be found to do what the General Government could not do, because of a defect in the Constitution. They decided to organize a General Government that would protect the negro in his rights. This course of action decided upon, the question was as to how this could be done the most quickly and successfully. You well know that the negro has been a marvelous success since the war, as a builder of secret societies.

"One member of this patriotic secret society, of which we have been speaking, conceived the idea of making use of all of these secret orders already formed by negroes. The idea met with instant approval. A house was found already to hand. These secret orders were all approached and asked to add one more degree and let this added degree be the same in every negro society. This proposition was accepted, and the Government formed at once. Each order remained, save in this last degree where all were one. This last degree was nothing more nor less than a compact government exercising all the functions of a nation. The grand purpose of the government was so apparent, and so needful of attention, that men rushed into this last degree pledging their lives to the New Government.

"All differences between the race were to be settled by this Government, as it had a well organized judiciary. Negroes, members of this Government, were to be no longer seen fighting negroes before prejudiced white courts. An army was organized and every able-bodied citizen enlisted. After the adjournment of the lodge sessions, army drills were always executed. A Congress was duly elected, one member for every fifty thousand citizens. Branch legislatures were formed in each state. Except in a few, but important particulars, the constitution was modeled after that of the United States.

"There is only one branch to our Congress, the members of which are elected by a majority vote, for an indefinite length of time, and may be recalled at any time by a majority vote.

"This Congress passes laws relating to the general welfare of our people, and whenever a bill is introduced in the Congress of the United States affecting our race it is also introduced and debated here.

"Every race question submitted to the United States judiciary, is also submitted to our own. A record of our decisions is kept side by side with the decisions of the United States.

"The money which the scientist left was wisely invested, and at the conclusion of the civil war amounted to many millions. Good land at the South was offered after the war for twenty-five cents an acre. These millions were expended in the purchase of such lands, and our treasury is now good for $500,000,000. Our citizens own about $350,000,000. And all of this is pledged to our government in case it is needed.

"We have at our disposal, therefore, $850,000,000. This money can be used by the Government in any way that it sees fit, so long as it is used to secure the recognition of the rights of our people. They are determined to be free and will give their lives, as freely as they have given their property.

"This place is known as Jefferson College, but it is in reality the Capitol of our Government, and those whom you have just left are the Congressmen."

"But, Belton," broke in Bernard, "how does it happen that I have been excluded from all this?"

"That is explained in this way. The relation of your mother to the Anglo-Saxon race has not been clearly understood, and you and she have been under surveillance for many years.

"It was not until recently deemed advisable to let you in, your loyalty to the race never having fully been tested. I have been a member for years. While I was at Stowe University, though a young man, I was chairman of the bureau of education and had charge of the work of educating the race upon the doctrine of human liberty.

"While I was at Cadeville, Louisiana, that was my work. Though not attracting public attention, I was sowing seed broadcast. After my famous case I was elected to Congress here and soon thereafter chosen speaker, which position I now hold.

"I shall now come to matters that concern you. Our constitution expressly stipulates that the first President of our Government should be a man whom the people unanimously desired. Each Congressman had to be instructed to vote for the same man, else there would be no election. This was done because it was felt that the responsibility of the first President would be so great, and have such a formative influence that he should be the selection of the best judgment of the entire nation.

"In the second place, this would ensure his having a united nation at his back. Again, this forcing the people to be unanimous would have a tendency to heal dissensions within their ranks. In other words, we needed a George Washington.

"Various men have been put forward for this honor and vigorous campaigns have been waged in their behalf. But these all failed of the necessary unanimous vote. At last, one young man arose, who was brilliant and sound, genial and true, great and good. On every tongue was his name and in every heart his image. Unsolicited by him, unknown to him, the nation by its unanimous voice has chosen him the President of our beloved Government. This day he has unflinchingly met the test that our Congress decreed and has come out of the furnace, purer than gold. He feared death no more than the caress of his mother, when he felt that that death was to be suffered in behalf of his oppressed people. I have the great honor, on this the proudest occasion of my life, to announce that I am commissioned to inform you that the name of our President is Bernard Belgrave. You, sir, are President of the Imperium in Imperio, the name of our Government, and to you we devote our property, our lives, our all, promising to follow your banner into every post of danger until it is planted on freedom's hill. You are given three months in which to verify all of my claims, and give us answer as to whether you will serve us."

Bernard took three months to examine into the reality and stability of the Imperium. He found it well nigh perfect in every part and presented a form of government unexcelled by that of any other nation. . . .

CHAPTER XVIII
The Storm's Master

When Bernard ceased speaking and took his seat the house was as silent as a graveyard. All felt that the time for words had passed and the next and only thing in order was a deed.

Each man seemed determined to keep his seat and remain silent until he had some definite plan to suggest. At length one man, somewhat aged, arose and spoke as follows:

"Fellow citizens, our condition is indeed past enduring and we must find a remedy. I have spent the major portion of my life in close study of this subject, searching for a solution. My impression is that the negro will never leave this country. The day for the wholesale exodus of nations is past. We must, then, remain here. As long as we remain here as a separate and distinct race we shall continue to be oppressed. We must lose our identity. I, therefore, urge that we abandon the idea of becoming anything noteworthy as a separate and distinct race and send the word forth that we amalgamate."

When the word "amalgamate" escaped his lips a storm of hisses and jeers drowned further speech and he quickly crouched down in his seat. Another arose and advocated emigration to the African Congo Free State. He pointed out that this State, great in area and rich in resources, was in the hands of the weak kingdom of Belgium and could be wrested from Belgium with the greatest ease. In fact, it might be possible to purchase it, as it was the personal property of King Leopold.

He further stated that one of his chief reasons for suggesting emigration was that it would be a terrible blow to the South. The proud Southerner would then have his own forests to fell and fields to tend. He pictured the haughty Southern lady at last the queen of her own kitchen. He then called attention to the loss of influence and prestige which the South would sustain in the nation. By losing nearly one half of its population the South's representation in Congress would be reduced to such a point that the South would have no appreciable influence on legislation for one half a century to come. He called attention to the business depression that would ensue when the southern supply merchant lost such an extensive consumer as the negro.

He wound up by urging the Imperium to go where they would enjoy all the rights of freemen, and by picturing the demoralization and ruin of the South when they thus went forth. His suggestion met with much favor but he did not make clear the practicability of his scheme.

At length a bold speaker arose who was courageous enough to stick a match to the powder magazine which Bernard had left uncovered in all their bosoms. His first declaration was: "I am for war!" and it was cheered to the echo. It was many minutes before the applause died away. He then began an impassioned invective against the South and recited in detail horror after horror, for which the South was answerable. He described hangings, revolting in their brutality; he drew vivid word pictures of various burnings, mentioning one where a white woman struck the match and ignited the pile of wood that was to consume the trembling negro. He told of the Texas horror, when a colored man named Smith was tortured with a red hot poker, and his eyes gouged out; after which he slowly roasted to death. He then had Mrs. Cook arise and gather her children about her, and tell her sorrowful story. As she proceeded the entire assembly broke down in tears, and men fell on each other's necks and wept like babes. And oh! Their hearts swelled, their bosoms heaved, their breath came quick with choking passion, and there burst from all their throats the one hoarse cry: "War! war! war!"

Bernard turned his head away from this affecting sight and in his soul swore a terrible oath to avenge the wrongs of his people.

When quiet was sufficiently restored, the man with the match arose and offered the following resolutions:

"WHEREAS, the history of our treatment by the Anglo-Saxon race is but the history of oppression, and whereas, our patient endurance of evil has not served to decrease this cruelty, but seems rather to increase it; and whereas, the ballot box, the means of peaceful revolution is denied us, therefore;

"*Be it Resolved:* That the hour for wreaking vengeance for our multiplied wrongs has come.

"*Resolved* secondly: That we at once proceed to war for the purpose of accomplishing the end just named, and for the further purpose of obtaining all our rights due us as men.

"*Resolved* thirdly: That no soldier of the Imperium leave the field of battle until the ends for which this war was inaugurated are fully achieved."

A dozen men were on their feet at once to move the adoption of these resolutions. The motion was duly seconded and put before the house. The Chairman asked: "Are you ready to vote?" "Ready!" was the unanimous, vociferous response.

The chairman, Belton Piedmont, quietly said: "Not ready." All eyes were then pointed eagerly and inquiringly to him. He called the senior member of the house to the chair and came down upon the floor to speak.

We are now about to record one of the most remarkable feats of oratory known to history. Belton stood with his massive, intellectual head thrown back and a look of determined defiance shot forth from his eyes. His power in debate was well known and the members settled themselves back for a powerful onslaught of some kind; but exactly what to expect they did not know. . . .

Jessie Fauset (1882–1961)

Jessie Fauset was a charter member of the "talented tenth," a group of well-educated, middle-class African Americans who accounted for much of the writing put forth during the Harlem Renaissance. Born in Philadelphia of a well-established family, Fauset graduated phi beta kappa *from Cornell University, later receiving a master's degree from the University of Pennsylvania and studying at the Sorbonne in Paris. After teaching high school Latin and French in Washington, D.C., she moved in 1919 to New York City, where she served as literary editor and contributing editor of* The Crisis *magazine during the 1920s. Eventually, she returned to teaching and married businessman Herbert Harris.*

Fauset did most of her writing during the heyday of the Harlem Renaissance. A writer of short stories, essays, and poems, she is best known for her four novels: There Is Confusion *(1924),* Plum Bun *(1929),* The Chinaberry Tree *(1931), and* Comedy, American Style *(1933). Her "genteel"-style fiction examines blacks who enjoy high social standing, as Fauset did in her own life. Intent on portraying people and settings she felt had been ignored in earlier African American writing, Fauset set her works within the world of the black bourgeoisie, a group that Addison Gayle describes as "a class midway between white [people] and poor Blacks . . . differing little from its white counterparts."*

The following selection, "Mary Elizabeth," was originally published in The Crisis *in 1919. Fauset's concern with portraying class distinctions and diverse experiences among African Americans is evident in the story, which also reflects on the differences in attitude between men and women.*

Mary Elizabeth

Mary Elizabeth was late that morning. As a direct result, Roger left for work without telling me good-bye, and I spent most of the day fighting the headache which always comes if I cry.

For I cannot get a breakfast. I can manage a dinner—one just puts the roast in the oven and takes it out again. And I really excel in getting lunch. There is a good delicatessen near us, and with dainty service and flowers, I get along very nicely. But breakfast! In the first place, it's a meal I neither like nor need. And I never, if I live a thousand years, shall learn to like coffee. I suppose that is why I cannot make it.

"Roger," I faltered, when the awful truth burst upon me and I began to realize that Mary Elizabeth wasn't coming, "Roger, couldn't you get breakfast downtown this morning? You know last time you weren't so satisfied with my coffee."

Roger was hostile. I think he had just cut himself, shaving. Anyway, he was horrid.

"No, I can't get my breakfast downtown!" He actually snapped at me. "Really, Sally, I don't believe there's another woman in the world who would send her husband out on a morning like this on an empty stomach. I don't see how you can be so unfeeling."

Well, it wasn't "a morning like this," for it was just the beginning of November. And I had only proposed his doing what I knew he would have to do eventually.

I didn't say anything more, but started on that breakfast. I don't know why I thought I had to have hotcakes! The breakfast really was awful! The cakes were tough and gummy and got cold one second, exactly, after I took them off the stove. And the coffee boiled, or stewed, or scorched, or did whatever the particular thing is that coffee shouldn't do. Roger sawed at one cake, took one mouthful of the dreadful brew, and pushed away his cup.

"It seems to me you might learn to make a decent cup of coffee," he said icily. Then he picked up his hat and flung out of the house.

I think it is stupid of me, too, not to learn how to make coffee. But, really, I'm no worse than Roger is about lots of things. Take "Five Hundred." Roger knows I love cards, and with the Cheltons right around the corner from us and as fond of it as I am, we could spend many a pleasant evening. But Roger will not learn. Only the night before, after I had gone through a whole hand with him, with hearts as trumps, I dealt the cards around again to imaginary opponents and we started playing. Clubs were trumps, and spades led. Roger, having no spades, played triumphantly a Jack of Hearts and proceeded to take the trick.

"But, Roger," I protested, "you threw off."

"Well," he said, deeply injured, "didn't you say hearts were trumps when you were playing before?"

And when I tried to explain, he threw down the cards and wanted to know what difference it made; he'd rather play casino, anyway! I didn't go out and slam the door.

But I couldn't keep from crying this particular morning. I not only value Roger's good opinion, but I hate to be considered stupid.

Mary Elizabeth came in about eleven o'clock. She is a small, weazened woman, very dark, somewhat wrinkled, and a model of self-possession. I wish I could make you see her, or that I could reproduce her accent, not that it is especially colored—Roger's and mine are much more so—but her pronunciation, her way of drawing out her vowels, is so distinctively Mary Elizabethan!

I was ashamed of my red eyes and tried to cover up my embarrassment with sternness.

"Mary Elizabeth," said I, "you are late!" Just as though she didn't know it.

"Yas'm, Mis' Pierson," she said composedly, taking off her coat. She didn't remove her hat—she never does until she has been in the house some two or three hours. I can't imagine why. It is a small, black, dusty affair, trimmed with black ribbon, some dingy white roses, and a sheaf of wheat. I give Mary Elizabeth a dress and hat now and then, but, although I recognize the dress from time to time, I never see any change in the hat. I don't know what she does with my ex-millinery.

"Yas'm," she said again, and looked comprehensively at the untouched breakfast dishes and the awful viands, which were still where Roger had left them.

"Looks as though you'd had to git breakfast yoreself," she observed brightly. And went out in the kitchen and ate all those cakes and drank that unspeakable coffee! Really she did, and she didn't warm them up either.

I watched her miserably, unable to decide whether Roger was too finicky or Mary Elizabeth a natural-born diplomat.

"Mr. Gales led me an awful chase last night," she explained. "When I got home yistiddy evenin', my cousin whut keeps house fer me (!) tole me Mr. Gales went out in the mornin' en hadn't come back."

"Mr. Gales," let me explain, is Mary Elizabeth's second husband, an octogenarian, and the most original person, I am convinced, in existence.

"Yas'm," she went on, eating a final cold hotcake, "en I went to look fer 'im, en had the whole perlice station out all night huntin' 'im. Look like they wusn't never goin' to find 'im. But I ses, 'Jes' let me look fer enough en long enough en I'll find 'im,' I ses, en I did. Way out Georgy Avenue, with the hat on ole Mis' give 'im. Sent it to 'im all the way fum Chicaga. He's had it fifteen years—high silk beaver. I knowed he wusn't goin' too fer with that hat on.

"I went up to 'im, settin' by a fence all muddy, holdin' his hat on with both hands. En I ses, 'Look here, man, you come erlong home with me, en let me put you to bed.' En he come jest as meek! No-o-me, I knowed he wusn't goin' fer with ole Mis' hat on."

"Who was old 'Mis,' Mary Elizabeth?" I asked her.

"Lady I used to work fer in Noo York," she informed me. "Me en Rosy, the cook, lived with her fer years. Old Mis' was turrible fond of me, though her en Rosy used to querrel all the time. Jes' seemed like they couldn't git erlong. 'Member once Rosy run after her one Sunday with a knife, en I kep 'em apart. Reckon Rosy musta bin right put out with ole Mis' that day. By en by her en Rosy move to Chicaga, en when I married Mr. Gales, she sent 'im that hat. That old white woman shore did like me. It's so late, reckon I'd better put off sweepin' tel termorrer, ma'am."

I acquiesced, following her about from room to room. This was partly to get away from my own doleful thoughts—Roger really had hurt my feelings—but just as much to hear her talk. At first I used not to believe all she said, but after I investigated once and found her truthful in one amazing statement, I capitulated.

She had been telling me some remarkable tale of her first husband and I was listening with the stupefied attention to which she always reduced me. Remember she was speaking of her first husband.

"En I ses to 'im, I ses, 'Mr. Gale—' "

"Wait a moment, Mary Elizabeth," I interrupted, meanly delighted to have caught her for once. "You mean your first husband, don't you?"

"Yas'm," she replied. "En I ses to 'im, 'Mr. Gale, I ses—' "

"But, Mary Elizabeth," I persisted, "that's your second husband, isn't it—Mr. Gale?"

She gave me her long-drawn "No-o-me! My first husband was Mr. Gale and my second is Mr. *Gales*. He spells his name with a Z, I reckon. I ain't never see it writ. Ez I wus sayin', I ses to Mr. Gale—"

And it was true! Since then I have never doubted Mary Elizabeth.

She was loquacious that afternoon. She told me about her sister, "where's got a home in the country and where's got eight children." I used to read Lucy Pratt's stories about little Ephraim or Ezekiel, I forget his name, who always said "where's" instead of "who's," but I never believed it really till I heard Mary Elizabeth use it. For some reason or other she never mentions her sister without mentioning the home too. "My sister where's got a home in the country" is her unvarying phrase.

"Mary Elizabeth," I asked her once, "does your sister live in the country, or does she simply own a house there?"

"Yas'm," she told me.

She is fond of her sister. "If Mr. Gales wus to die," she told me complacently, "I'd go to live with her."

"If he should die," I asked her idly, "would you marry again?"

"Oh, no-o-me!" She was emphatic. "Though I don't know why I shouldn't, I'd come by it hones'. My father wus married four times."

That shocked me out of my headache. "Four times, Mary Elizabeth, and you had all those stepmothers!" My mind refused to take it in.

"Oh, no-o-me! I always lived with Mamma. She was his first wife."

I hadn't thought of people in the state in which I had instinctively placed Mary Elizabeth's father and mother as indulging in divorce, but as Roger says slangily, "I wouldn't know."

Mary Elizabeth took off the dingy hat. "You see, Papa and Mamma—" the ineffable pathos of hearing this woman of sixty-four, with a husband of eighty, use the old childish terms!

"Papa and Mamma wus slaves, you know, Mis' Pierson, and so of course they wusn't exackly married. White folks wouldn't let 'em. But they wus awf'ly in love with each other. Heard Mamma tell erbout it lots of times, and how Papa wus the han'somest man! Reckon she wus long erbout sixteen or seventeen then. So they jumped over a broomstick, en they wus jes as happy! But not long after I come erlong, they sold Papa down South, and Mamma never see him no mo' fer years and years. Thought he was dead. So she married again."

"And he came back to her, Mary Elizabeth?" I was overwhelmed with the woefulness of it.

"Yas'm. After twenty-six years. Me and my sister where's got a home in the country—she's really my half-sister, see, Mis' Pierson—her en Mamma en my stepfather en me wus all down in Bumpus, Virginia, workin' fer some white folks, and we used to live in a little cabin, had a front stoop to it. En one day an ole cullud man come by, had a lot o' whiskers. I'd saw him lots of times there in Bumpus, lookin' and peerin' into every cullud woman's face. En jes' then my sister she call out, 'Come here, you Ma'y Elizabeth,' en that old man stopped, en he looked at me en he looked at me, en he ses to me, 'Chile, is yo' name Ma'y Elizabeth?'

"You know, Mis' Pierson, I thought he wus jes' bein' fresh, en I ain't paid no 'tention to 'im. I ain't sed nuthin' ontel he spoke to me three or four times, en then I ses to 'im, 'Go 'way fum here, man, you ain't got no call to be fresh with me. I'm a decent woman. You'd oughta be ashamed of yoreself, an ole man like you.' "

Mary Elizabeth stopped and looked hard at the back of her poor wrinkled hands.

"En he says to me, 'Daughter,' he ses, jes' like that, 'daughter,' he ses, 'hones' I ain't bein' fresh. Is yo' name shore enough Ma'y Elizabeth?'

"En I tole him, 'Yas'r.'

" 'Chile,' he ses, 'whar is yo' daddy?'

" 'Ain't got no daddy,' I tole him peart-like. 'They done tuk 'im away fum me twenty-six years ago, I wusn't but a mite of a baby. Sol' 'im down the river. My mother often talks about it.' And, oh, Mis' Pierson, you shoulda see the glory come into his face!

" 'Yore mother!' he ses, kinda out of breath. 'Yore mother! Ma'y Elizabeth, whar is your mother?'

" 'Back thar on the stoop,' I tole 'im. 'Why, did you know my daddy?'

"But he didn't pay no 'tention to me, jes' turned and walked up the stoop whar Mamma wus settin'! She was feelin' sorta porely that day. En you oughta see me steppin' erlong after 'im.

"He walked right up to her and giv' her one look. 'Oh, Maggie,' he shout out, 'oh, Maggie! Ain't you know me? Maggie, ain't you know me?'

"Mamma look at 'im and riz up outa her cheer. 'Who're you,' she ses, kinda trimbly, 'callin' me Maggie thata way? Who're you?'

"He went up real close to her; then, 'Maggie,' he ses jes' like that, kinda sad 'n tender, 'Maggie!' And hel' out his arms.

"She walked right into them. 'Oh,' she ses, 'it's Cassius! It's Cassius! It's my husban' come back to me! It's Cassius!' They wus like two mad people.

"My sister Minnie and me, we jes' stood and gawped at 'em. There they wus, holding on to each other like two pitiful childrun, en he tuk her hands and kissed 'em.

" 'Maggie,' he ses, 'you'll come away with me, won't you? You gona take me back, Maggie? We'll go away, you en Ma'y Elizabeth en me. Won't we, Maggie?'

"Reckon my mother clean fergot my stepfather. 'Yes, Cassius,' she ses, 'we'll go away.' And then she sees Minnie, en it all comes back to her. 'Oh, Cassius,' she ses, 'I can't go with you, I'm married again, en this time fer real. This here gal's mine and three boys, too, and another chile comin' in November!' "

"But she went with him, Mary Elizabeth," I pleaded. "Surely she went with him after all those years. He really was her husband."

I don't know whether Mary Elizabeth meant to be sarcastic or not. "Oh, no-o-me, Mamma couldn't a done that. She wus a good woman. Her ole master, whut done sol' my father down river, brung her up too religious fer that, en anyways, Papa was married again, too. Had his fourth wife there in Bumpus with 'im."

The unspeakable tragedy of it!

I left her and went up to my room, and hunted out my dark-blue serge dress which I had meant to wear again that winter. But I had to give Mary Elizabeth something, so I took the dress down to her.

She was delighted with it. I could tell she was, because she used her rare and untranslatable expletive.

"Haytian!" she said. "My sister where's got a home in the country, got a dress looks somethin' like this, but it ain't as good. No-o-me. She got hers to wear at a friend's weddin'—gal she was riz up with. Thet gal married well, too, lemme tell you; her husband's a Sunday School sup'rintender."

I told her she needn't wait for Mr. Pierson, I would put dinner on the table. So off she went in the gathering dusk, trudging bravely back to her Mr. Gales and his high silk hat.

I watched her from the window till she was out of sight. It had been such a long time since I had thought of slavery. I was born in Pennsylvania, and neither my parents nor grandparents had been slaves; otherwise I might have had the same tale to tell as Mary Elizabeth, or, worse yet, Roger and I might have lived in those black days and loved and lost each other and futilely, damnably, met again like Cassius and Maggie.

Whereas it was now, and I had Roger and Roger had me.

How I loved him as I sat there in the hazy dusk. I thought of his dear, bronze perfection, his habit of swearing softly in excitement, his blessed stupidity. Just the same I didn't meet him at the door as usual, but pretended to be busy. He came rushing to me with the *Saturday Evening Post,* which is more to me than rubies. I thanked him warmly, but aloofly, if you can get that combination.

We ate dinner almost in silence for my part. But he praised everything—the cooking, the table, my appearance.

After dinner we went up to the little sitting-room. He hoped I wasn't tired—couldn't he fix the pillows for me? So!

I opened the magazine and the first thing I saw was a picture of a woman gazing in stony despair at the figure of a man disappearing around the bend of the road. It was too much. Suppose that were Roger and I! I'm afraid I sniffled. He was at my side in a moment.

"Dear loveliest! Don't cry. It was all my fault. You aren't any worse about coffee than I am about cards! And anyway, I needn't have slammed the door! Forgive me, Sally. I always told you I was hard to get along with. I've had a horrible day—don't stay cross with me, dearest."

I held him to me and sobbed outright on his shoulder. "It isn't you, Roger," I told him, "I'm crying about Mary Elizabeth."

I regret to say he let me go then, so great was his dismay. Roger will never be half the diplomat that Mary Elizabeth is.

"Holy smokes!" he groaned. "She isn't going to leave us for good, is she?"

So then I told him about Maggie and Cassius. "And oh, Roger," I ended futilely, "to think that they had to separate after all those years, when he had come back, old and with whiskers!" I didn't mean to be so banal, but I was crying too hard to be coherent.

Roger had got up and was walking the floor, but he stopped then aghast. "Whiskers!" he moaned. "My hat! Isn't that just like a woman?" He had to clear his throat once or twice before he could go on, and I think he wiped his eyes.

"Wasn't it the"—I really can't say what Roger said here—"wasn't it the darndest hard luck that when he did find her again, she should be married? She might have waited."

I stared at him astounded. "But, Roger," I reminded him, "he had married three other times; he didn't wait."

"Oh—!" said Roger, unquotably. "Married three fiddlesticks! He only did that to try to forget her."

Then he came over and knelt beside me again. "Darling, I do think it is a sensible thing for a poor woman to learn how to cook, but I don't care as long as you love me and we are together. Dear loveliest, if I had been Cassius"—he caught my hands so tight that he hurt them—"and I had married fifty times and had come back and found you married to someone else, I'd have killed you, killed you."

Well, he wasn't logical, but he was certainly convincing.

So thus, and not otherwise, Mary Elizabeth healed the breach.

Nella Larsen (1891–1963)

The overall framework of Nella Larsen's life seems to have furnished the core of the two novels she wrote. She was born in Chicago, her father a black man from the Virgin Islands and her mother a white woman with roots in Denmark. After her father's death, Larsen's mother married a Danish man, and Larsen and her white half-sister attended a small private school with students from European and Scandinavian backgrounds. At age sixteen, Larsen journeyed to Denmark and for three years stayed there with her mother's relatives. Returning to the United States to attend Fisk University, she retraced her way back to Denmark to attend the University of Copenhagen. (However, black scholar David Levering Lewis raises doubt that she studied in Copenhagen; see his essay in Part Five, p. 762.)

In 1911, when Larsen was about twenty, she traveled back to America, training as a nurse in New York and later working as superintendent of nurses at Tuskegee Hospital. Finally settling in New York in 1918, she was on the staff of the U.S. Department of Health. She then shifted her profession to the field of library science, becoming the children's librarian at the Harlem branch of the New York Public Library from 1921 to 1929. Larsen and her husband, an African American with a doctorate in physics, represented the educated, distinguished class that became highly visible during the Harlem Renaissance of the 1920s.

*Larsen's two novels—*Quicksand *(1928), which won a Harmon Foundation Award, and* Passing *(1929)—are described by one critic as "the quintessence of the tragic mulatto image." Often exploring the dilemmas facing black women characters of mixed parentage, Larsen, born of racially mixed parents herself, juxtaposes racial marginality with elements of the middle-class black life-style in her writings.*

Weathering charges of having plagiarized her short story "Sanctuary" (1930), Larsen became in 1930 the first African American woman to win a Guggenheim Award. Soon after, she retired into a private life in Greenwich Village and then Brooklyn until her death in 1963.

In the following excerpt from Passing, *Irene, the fair-complexioned protagonist, accidentally meets Clare, a fair-complexioned friend from her youth who has chosen to pass for white. In addition to the importance the characters place on racial identity, the speech patterns, diversions, and mannerisms of both women emphasize their class consciousness.*

from Passing

This is what Irene Redfield remembered.

Chicago. August. A brilliant day, hot, with a brutal staring sun pouring down rays that were like molten rain. A day on which the very outlines of the buildings shuddered as if in protest at the heat. Quivering lines sprang up from baked pavements and wriggled along the shining car-tracks. The automobiles parked at the kerbs were a dancing blaze, and the glass of the shop-windows threw out a blinding radiance. Sharp particles of dust rose from the burning sidewalks, stinging the seared or dripping skins of wilting pedestrians. What small breeze there was seemed like the breath of a flame fanned by slow bellows.

It was on that day of all others that Irene set out to shop for the things which she had promised to take home from Chicago to her two small sons, Brian junior and Theodore. Characteristically, she had put it off until only a few crowded days remained of her long visit. And only this sweltering one was free of engagements till the evening.

Without too much trouble she had got the mechanical aeroplane for Junior. But the drawing-book, for which Ted had so gravely and insistently given her precise directions, had sent her in and out of five shops without success.

It was while she was on her way to a sixth place that right before her smarting eyes a man toppled over and became an inert crumpled heap on the scorching cement. About the lifeless figure a little crowd gathered. Was the man dead, or only faint? someone asked her. But Irene didn't know and didn't try to discover. She edged her way out of the increasing crowd, feeling disagreeably damp and sticky and soiled from contact with so many sweating bodies.

For a moment she stood fanning herself and dabbing at her moist face with an inadequate scrap of handkerchief. Suddenly she was aware that the whole street had a wobbly look, and realized that she was about to faint. With a quick perception of the need for immediate safety, she lifted a wavering hand in the direction of a cab parked directly in front of her. The perspiring driver jumped out and guided her to his car. He helped, almost lifted her in. She sank down on the hot leather seat.

For a minute her thoughts were nebulous. They cleared.

"I guess," she told her Samaritan, "it's tea I need. On a roof somewhere."

"The Drayton, ma'am?" he suggested. "They do say as how it's always a breeze up there."

"Thank you. I think the Drayton'll do nicely," she told him.

There was that little grating sound of the clutch being slipped in as the man put the car in gear and slid deftly out into the boiling traffic. Reviving under the warm breeze stirred up by the moving cab, Irene made some small attempts to repair the damage that the heat and crowds had done to her appearance.

All too soon the rattling vehicle shot towards the sidewalk and stood still. The driver sprang out and opened the door before the hotel's decorated attendant could reach it. She got out, and thanking him smilingly as well as in a more substantial manner for his kind helpfulness and understanding, went in through the Drayton's wide doors.

Stepping out of the elevator that had brought her to the roof, she was led to a table just in front of a long window whose gently moving curtains suggested a cool breeze. It was, she thought, like being wafted upward on a magic carpet to another world, pleasant, quiet, and strangely remote from the sizzling one that she had left below.

The tea, when it came, was all that she had desired and expected. In fact, so much was it what she had desired and expected that after the first deep cooling drink she was able to forget it, only now and then sipping, a little absently, from the tall green glass, while she surveyed the room about her or looked out over some lower buildings at the bright unstirred blue of the lake reaching away to an undetected horizon.

She had been gazing down for some time at the specks of cars and people creeping about in streets, and thinking how silly they looked, when on taking up her glass she was surprised to find it empty at last. She asked for more tea and while she waited, began to recall the happenings of the day and to wonder what she was to do about Ted and his book. Why was it that almost invariably he wanted something that was difficult or impossible to get? Like his father. Forever wanting something that he couldn't have.

Presently there were voices, a man's booming one and a woman's slightly husky. A waiter passed her, followed by a sweetly scented woman in a fluttering dress of green chiffon whose mingled pattern of narcissuses, jonquils, and hyacinths was a reminder of pleasantly chill spring days. Behind her there was a man, very red in the face, who was mopping his neck and forehead with a big crumpled handkerchief.

"Oh dear!" Irene groaned, rasped by annoyance, for after a little discussion and commotion they had stopped at the very next table. She had been alone there at the window and it had been so satisfyingly quiet. Now, of course, they would chatter.

But no. Only the woman sat down. The man remained standing, abstractedly pinching the knot of his bright blue tie. Across the small space that separated the two tables his voice carried clearly.

"See you later, then," he declared, looking down at the woman. There was pleasure in his tones and a smile on his face.

His companion's lips parted in some answer, but her words were blurred by the little intervening distance and the medley of noises floating up from the streets below. They didn't reach Irene. But she noted the peculiar caressing smile that accompanied them.

The man said: "Well, I suppose I'd better," and smiled again, and said goodbye, and left.

An attractive-looking woman, was Irene's opinion, with those dark, almost black, eyes and that wide mouth like a scarlet flower against the ivory of her skin. Nice clothes too, just right for the weather, thin and cool without being mussy, as summer things were so apt to be.

A waiter was taking her order. Irene saw her smile up at him as she murmured something—thanks, maybe. It was an odd sort of smile. Irene couldn't quite define it, but she was sure that she would have classed it, coming from another woman, as being just a shade too provocative for a waiter. About this one, however, there was something that made her hesitate to name it that. A certain impression of assurance, perhaps.

The waiter came back with the order. Irene watched her spread out her napkin, saw the silver spoon in the white hand slit the dull gold of the melon. Then, conscious that she had been staring, she looked quickly away.

Her mind returned to her own affairs. She had settled, definitely, the problem of the proper one of two frocks for the bridge party that night, in rooms whose atmosphere would be so thick and hot that every breath would be like breathing soup. The dress decided, her thoughts had gone back to the snag of Ted's book, her unseeing eyes far away on the lake, when by some sixth sense she was acutely aware that someone was watching her.

Very slowly she looked around, and into the dark eyes of the woman in the green frock at the next table. But she evidently failed to realize that such intense interest as she was showing might be embarrassing, and continued to stare. Her demeanour was that of one who with utmost singleness of mind and purpose was determined to impress firmly and accurately each detail of Irene's features upon her memory for all time, nor showed the slightest trace of disconcertment at having been detected in her steady scrutiny.

Instead, it was Irene who was put out. Feeling her colour heighten under the continued inspection, she slid her eyes down. What, she wondered, could be the reason for such persistent attention? Had she, in her haste in the taxi, put her hat on backwards? Guardedly she felt at it. No. Perhaps there was a streak of powder somewhere on her face. She made a quick pass over it with her handkerchief. Something wrong with her dress? She shot a glance over it. Perfectly all right. *What* was it?

Again she looked up, and for a moment her brown eyes politely returned the stare of the other's black ones, which never for an instant fell or wavered. Irene made a little mental shrug. Oh well, let her look! She tried to treat the woman and her watching with indifference, but she couldn't. All her efforts to ignore her, it, were futile. She stole another glance. Still looking. What strange languorous eyes she had!

And gradually there rose in Irene a small inner disturbance, odious and hatefully familiar. She laughed softly, but her eyes flashed.

Did that woman, could that woman, somehow know that here before her very eyes on the roof of the Drayton sat a Negro?

Absurd! Impossible! White people were so stupid about such things for all that they usually asserted that they were able to tell; and by the most ridiculous means, finger-nails, palms of hands, shapes of ears, teeth, and other equally silly rot. They always took her for an Italian, a Spaniard, a Mexican, or a gipsy. Never, when she was alone, had they even remotely seemed to suspect that she was a Negro. No, the woman sitting there staring at her couldn't possibly know.

Nevertheless, Irene felt, in turn, anger, scorn, and fear slide over her. It wasn't that she was ashamed of being a Negro, or even of having it declared. It was the idea of being ejected from any place, even in the polite and tactful way in which the Drayton would probably do it, that disturbed her.

But she looked, boldly this time, back into the eyes still frankly intent upon her. They did not seem to her hostile or resentful. Rather, Irene had the feeling that they were ready to smile if she would. Nonsense, of course. The feeling passed, and she turned away with the firm intention of keeping her gaze on the lake, the roofs of the buildings across the way, the sky, anywhere but on that annoying woman. Almost immediately, however, her eyes were back again. In the midst of her fog of uneasiness she had been seized by a desire to outstare the rude observer. Suppose the woman did know or suspect her race. She couldn't prove it.

Suddenly her small fright increased. Her neighbour had risen and was coming towards her. What was going to happen now?

"Pardon me," the woman said pleasantly, "but I think I know you." Her slightly husky voice held a dubious note.

Looking up at her, Irene's suspicions and fears vanished. There was no mistaking the friendliness of that smile or resisting its charm. Instantly she surrendered to it and smiled too, as she said: "I'm afraid you're mistaken."

"Why, of course, I know you!" the other exclaimed. "Don't tell me you're not Irene Westover. Or do they still call you 'Rene?"

In the brief second before her answer, Irene tried vainly to recall where and when this woman could have known her. There, in Chicago. And before her marriage. That much was plain. High school? College? Y.W.C.A. committees? High school, most likely. What white girls had she known well enough to have been familiarly addressed as 'Rene by them? The woman before her didn't fit her memory of any of them. Who was she?

"Yes, I'm Irene Westover. And though nobody calls me 'Rene any more, it's good to hear the name again. And you—" She hesitated, ashamed that she could not remember, and hoping that the sentence would be finished for her.

"Don't you know me? Not really, 'Rene?"

"I'm sorry, but just at the minute I can't seem to place you."

Irene studied the lovely creature standing beside her for some clue to her identity. Who could she be? Where and when had they met? And through her perplexity there came the thought that the trick which her memory had played her was for some reason more gratifying than disappointing to her old acquaintance, that she didn't mind not being recognized.

And, too, Irene felt that she was just about to remember her. For about the woman was some quality, an intangible something, too vague to define, too remote to seize, but which was, to Irene Redfield, very familiar. And that voice. Surely she'd heard those husky tones somewhere before. Perhaps before time, contact, or something had been at them, making them into a voice remotely suggesting England. Ah! Could it have been in Europe that they had met? 'Rene. No.

"Perhaps," Irene began, "you—"

The woman laughed, a lovely laugh, a small sequence of notes that was like a trill and also like the ringing of a delicate bell fashioned of a precious metal, a tinkling.

Irene drew a quick sharp breath. "Clare!" she exclaimed, "not really Clare Kendry?"

So great was her astonishment that she had started to rise.

"No, no, don't get up," Clare Kendry commanded, and sat down herself. "You've simply got to stay and talk. We'll have something more. Tea? Fancy meeting you here! It's simply too, too lucky!"

"It's awfully surprising," Irene told her, and, seeing the change in Clare's smile, knew that she had revealed a corner of her own thoughts. But she only said: "I'd never in this world have known you if you hadn't laughed. You are changed, you know. And yet, in a way, you're just the same."

"Perhaps," Clare replied. "Oh, just a second."

She gave her attention to the waiter at her side. "M-mm let's see. Two teas. And bring some cigarettes. Y-es, they'll be all right. Thanks." Again that odd upward smile. Now, Irene was sure that it was too provocative for a waiter.

While Clare had been giving the order, Irene made a rapid mental calculation. It must be, she figured, all of twelve years since she, or anybody that she knew, had laid eyes on Clare Kendry.

After her father's death she'd gone to live with some relatives, aunts or cousins two or three times removed, over on the west side: relatives that nobody had known the Kendry's possessed until they had turned up at the funeral and taken Clare away with them.

For about a year or more afterwards she would appear occasionally among her old friends and acquaintances on the south side for short little visits that were, they understood, always stolen from the endless domestic tasks in her new home. With each succeeding one she was taller, shabbier, and more belligerently sensitive. And each time the look on her face was more resentful and brooding. "I'm worried about Clare, she seems so unhappy," Irene remembered her mother saying. The visits dwindled, becoming shorter, fewer, and further apart until at last they ceased.

Irene's father, who had been fond of Bob Kendry, made a special trip over to the west side about two months after the last time Clare had been to see them and returned with the bare information that he had seen the relatives and that Clare had disappeared. What else he had confided to her mother, in the privacy of their own room, Irene didn't know.

But she had had something more than a vague suspicion of its nature. For there had been rumours. Rumours that were, to girls of eighteen and nineteen years, interesting and exciting.

There was the one about Clare Kendry's having been seen at the dinner hour in a fashionable hotel in company with another woman and two men, all of them white. And *dressed!* And there was another which told of her driving in Lincoln Park with a man, unmistakably white, and evidently rich. Packard limousine, chauffeur in livery, and all that. There had been others whose context Irene could no longer recollect, but all pointing in the same glamorous direction.

And she could remember quite vividly how, when they used to repeat and discuss these tantalizing stories about Clare, the girls would always look knowingly at one another and then, with little excited giggles, drag away their eager shining eyes and say with lurking undertones of regret or disbelief some such thing as: "Oh, well, maybe she's got a job or something," or "After all, it mayn't have been Clare," or "You can't believe all you hear."

And always some girl, more matter-of-fact or more frankly malicious than the rest, would declare: "Of course it was Clare! Ruth said it was and so did Frank, and they certainly know her when they see her as well as we do." And someone else would say: "Yes, you can bet it was Clare all right." And then they would all join in asserting that there could be no mistake about it's having been Clare, and that such circumstances could mean only one thing. Working indeed! People didn't take their servants to the Shelby for dinner. Certainly not all dressed up like that. There would follow insincere regrets, and somebody would say: "Poor girl, I suppose it's true enough, but what can you expect. Look at her father. And her mother, they say, would have run away if she hadn't died. Besides, Clare always had a—a—having way with her."

Precisely that! The words came to Irene as she sat there on the Drayton roof, facing Clare Kendry. "A having way." Well, Irene acknowledged, judging from her appearance and manner, Clare seemed certainly to have succeeded in having a few of the things that she wanted.

It was, Irene repeated, after the interval of the waiter, a great surprise and a very pleasant one to see Clare again after all those years, twelve at least.

"Why, Clare, you're the last person in the world I'd have expected to run into. I guess that's why I didn't know you."

Clare answered gravely: "Yes. It is twelve years. But I'm not surprised to see you, 'Rene. That is, not so very. In fact, ever since I've been here, I've more or less hoped that I should, or someone. Preferably you, though. Still, I imagine that's because I've thought of you often and often, while you—I'll wager you've never given me a thought."

It was true, of course. After the first speculations and indictments, Clare had gone completely from Irene's thoughts. And from the thoughts of others too—if their conversation was any indication of their thoughts.

Besides, Clare had never been exactly one of the group, just as she'd never been merely the janitor's daughter, but the daughter of Mr. Bob Kendry, who, it was true, was a janitor, but who also, it seemed, had been in college with some of their fathers. Just how or why he happened to be a janitor, and a very inefficient one at that, they none of them quite knew. One of Irene's brothers, who had put the question to their father, had been told: "That's something that doesn't concern you," and given the advice to be careful not to end in the same manner as "poor Bob."

No, Irene hadn't thought of Clare Kendry. Her own life had been too crowded. So, she supposed, had the lives of other people. She defended her—their—forgetfulness. "You know how it is. Everybody's so busy. People leave, drop out, maybe for a little while there's talk about them, or questions; then, gradually they're forgotten."

"Yes, that's natural," Clare agreed. And what, she inquired, had they said of her for that little while at the beginning before they'd forgotten her altogether?

Irene looked away. She felt the telltale colour rising in her cheeks. "You can't," she evaded, "expect me to remember trifles like that over twelve years of marriages, births, deaths, and the war."

There followed that trill of notes that was Clare Kendry's laugh, small and clear and the very essence of mockery.

"Oh, 'Rene!" she cried, "of course you remember! But I won't make you tell me, because I know just as well as if I'd been there and heard every unkind word. Oh, I know, I know. Frank Danton saw me in the Shelby one night. Don't tell me he didn't broadcast that, and with embroidery. Others may have seen me at other times. I don't know. But once I met Margaret Hammer in Marshall Field's. I'd have spoken, was on the very point of doing it, but she cut me dead. My dear 'Rene, I assure you that from the way she looked through me, even I was uncertain whether I was actually there in the flesh or not. I remember it clearly, too clearly. It was that very thing which, in a way, finally decided me not to go out and see you one last time before I went away to stay. Somehow, good as all of you, the whole family, had always been to the poor forlorn child that was me, I felt I shouldn't be able to bear that. I mean if any of you, your mother or the boys or—Oh, well, I just felt I'd rather not know it if you did. And so I stayed away. Silly, I suppose. Sometimes I've been sorry I didn't go."

Irene wondered if it was tears that made Clare's eyes so luminous.

"And now 'Rene, I want to hear all about you and everybody and everything. You're married, I s'pose?"

Irene nodded.

"Yes," Clare said knowingly, "you would be. Tell me about it."

And so for an hour or more they had sat there smoking and drinking tea and filling in the gap of twelve years with talk. That is, Irene did. She told Clare about her marriage and removal to New York, about her husband, and about her two sons, who were having their first experience of being separated from their parents at a summer camp, about her mother's death, about the marriages of her two brothers. She told of the marriages, births and deaths in other families that Clare had known, opening up, for her, new vistas on the lives of old friends and acquaintances.

Clare drank it all in, these things which for so long she had wanted to know and hadn't been able to learn. She sat motionless, her bright lips slightly parted, her whole face lit by the radiance of her happy eyes. Now and then she put a question, but for the most part she was silent.

Somewhere outside, a clock struck. Brought back to the present, Irene looked down at her watch and exclaimed: "Oh, I must go, Clare!"

A moment passed during which she was the prey of uneasiness. It had suddenly occurred to her that she hadn't asked Clare anything about her own life and that she had a very definite unwillingness to do so. And she was quite well aware of the reason for that reluctance. But, she asked herself, wouldn't it, all things considered, be the kindest thing not to ask? If things with Clare were as she—as they all—had suspected, wouldn't it be more tactful to seem to forget to inquire how she had spent those twelve years?

If? It was that "if" which bothered her. It might be, it might just be, in spite of all gossip and even appearances to the contrary, that there was nothing, had been nothing, that couldn't be simply and innocently explained. Appearances, she knew now, had a way sometimes of not fitting facts, and if Clare hadn't—Well, if they had all been wrong, then certainly she ought to express some interest in what had happened to her. It would seem queer and rude if she didn't. But how was she to know? There was, she at last decided, no way; so she merely said again, "I must go, Clare."

"Please, not so soon, 'Rene," Clare begged, not moving.

Irene thought: "She's really almost too good-looking. It's hardly any wonder that she—"

"And now, 'Rene dear, that I've found you, I mean to see lots and lots of you. We're here for a month at least. Jack, that's my husband, is here on business. Poor dear! in this heat. Isn't it beastly? Come to dinner with us tonight, won't you?" And she gave Irene a curious little sidelong glance and a sly, ironical smile peeped out on her full red lips, as if she had been in the secret of the other's thoughts and was mocking her.

Irene was conscious of a sharp intake of breath, but whether it was relief or chagrin that she felt, she herself could not have told. She said hastily: "I'm afraid I can't, Clare. I'm filled up. Dinner and bridge. I'm so sorry."

"Come tomorrow instead, to tea," Clare insisted. "Then you'll see Margery—she's just ten—and Jack too, maybe, if he hasn't got an appointment or something."

From Irene came an uneasy little laugh. She had an engagement for tomorrow also and she was afraid that Clare would not believe it. Suddenly, now, that possibility disturbed her. Therefore it was with a half-vexed feeling at the sense of undeserved guilt that had come upon her that she explained that it wouldn't be possible because she wouldn't be free for tea, or for luncheon or dinner either. "And the next day's Friday when I'll be going away for the week-end, Idlewild, you know. It's quite the thing now." And then she had an inspiration.

"Clare!" she exclaimed, "why don't you come up with me? Our place is probably full up—Jim's wife has a way of collecting most of the most impossible people—but we can always manage to find room for one more. And you'll see absolutely everybody."

In the very moment of giving the invitation she regretted it. What a foolish, what an idiotic impulse to have given way to! She groaned inwardly as she thought of the endless explanations in which it would involve her, of the curiosity and the talk and the lifted eyebrows. It wasn't, she assured herself, that she was a snob, that she cared greatly for the petty restrictions and distinctions with which what called itself Negro society chose to hedge itself about; but that she had a natural and deeply rooted aversion to the kind of front-page notoriety that Clare Kendry's presence in Idlewild, as her guest, would expose her to. And here she was, perversely and against all reason, inviting her.

But Clare shook her head. "Really, I'd love to, 'Rene," she said, a little mournfully. "There's nothing I'd like better. But I couldn't. I mustn't, you see. It wouldn't do at all. I'm sure you understand. I'm simply crazy to go, but I can't." The dark eyes glistened and there was a suspicion of a quaver in the husky voice. "And believe me, 'Rene, I do thank you for asking me. Don't think I've entirely forgotten just what it would mean for you if I went. That is, if you still care about such things."

All indications of tears had gone from her eyes and voice, and Irene Redfield, searching her face, had an offended feeling that behind what was now only an ivory mask lurked a scornful amusement. She looked away, at the wall far beyond Clare. Well, she deserved it, for, as she acknowledged to herself, she *was* relieved. And for the very reason at which Clare had hinted. The fact that Clare had guessed her perturbation did not, however, in any degree lessen that relief. She was annoyed at having been detected in what might seem to be an insincerity; but that was all.

The waiter came with Clare's change. Irene reminded herself that she ought immediately to go. But she didn't move.

The truth was, she was curious. There were things that she wanted to ask Clare Kendry. She wished to find out about this hazardous business of "passing," this breaking away from all that was familiar and friendly to take one's chance in another environment, not entirely strange, perhaps, but certainly not entirely friendly. What, for example, one did about background, how one accounted for oneself. And how one felt when one came into contact with other Negroes. But she couldn't. She was unable to think of a single question that in its context or its phrasing was not too frankly curious, if not actually impertinent.

As if aware of her desire and her hesitation, Clare remarked, thoughtfully: "You know, 'Rene, I've often wondered why more coloured girls, girls like you and Margaret Hammer and Esther Dawson and—oh, lots of others—never 'passed' over. It's such a frightfully easy thing to do. If one's the type, all that's needed is a little nerve."

"What about background? Family, I mean. Surely you can't just drop down on people from nowhere and expect them to receive you with open arms, can you?"

"Almost," Clare asserted. "You'd be surprised, 'Rene, how much easier that is with white people than with us. Maybe because there are so many more of them, or maybe because they are secure and so don't have to bother. I've never quite decided."

Irene was inclined to be incredulous. "You mean that you didn't have to explain where you came from? It seems impossible."

Clare cast a glance of repressed amusement across the table at her. "As a matter of fact, I didn't. Though I suppose under any other circumstances I might have had to provide some plausible tale to account for myself. I've a good imagination, so I'm sure I could have done it quite creditably, and credibly. But it wasn't necessary. There were my aunts, you see, respectable and authentic enough for anything or anybody."

"I see. They were 'passing' too."

"No. They weren't. They were white."

"Oh!" And in the next instant it came back to Irene that she had heard this mentioned before; by her father, or, more likely, her mother. They were Bob Kendry's aunts. He had been a son of their brother's, on the left hand. A wild oat.

"They were nice old ladies," Clare explained, "very religious and as poor as church mice. That adored brother of theirs, my grandfather, got through every penny they had after he'd finished his own little bit."

Clare paused in her narrative to light another cigarette. Her smile, her expression, Irene noticed, was faintly resentful.

"Being good Christians," she continued, "when dad came to his tipsy end, they did their duty and gave me a home of sorts. I was, it was true, expected to earn my keep by doing all the housework and most of the washing. But do you realize, 'Rene, that if it hadn't been for them, I shouldn't have had a home in the world?"

Irene's nod and little murmur were comprehensive, understanding.

Clare made a small mischievous grimace and proceeded. "Besides, to their notion, hard labour was good for me. I had Negro blood and they belonged to the generation that had written and read long articles headed: 'Will the Blacks Work?' Too, they weren't quite sure that the good God hadn't intended the sons and daughters of Ham to sweat because he had poked fun at old man Noah once when he had taken a drop too much. I remember the aunts telling me that that old drunkard had cursed Ham and his sons for all time."

Irene laughed. But Clare remained quite serious.

"It was more than a joke, I assure you, 'Rene. It was a hard life for a girl of sixteen. Still, I had a roof over my head, and food, and clothes—such as they were. And there were the Scriptures, and talks on morals and thrift and industry and the loving-kindness of the good Lord."

"Have you ever stopped to think, Clare," Irene demanded, "how much unhappiness and downright cruelty are laid to the loving-kindness of the Lord? And always by His most ardent followers, it seems."

"Have I?" Clare exclaimed. "It, they, made me what I am today. For, of course, I was determined to get away, to be a person and not a charity or a problem, or even a daughter of the indiscreet Ham. Then, too, I wanted things. I knew I wasn't bad-looking and that I could 'pass.' You can't know, 'Rene, how, when I used to go over to the south side, I used almost to hate all of you. You had all the things I wanted and never had had. It made me all the more determined to get them, and others. Do you, can you understand what I felt?"

She looked up with a pointed and appealing effect, and, evidently finding the sympathetic expression on Irene's face sufficient answer, went on. "The aunts were queer. For all their Bibles and praying and ranting about honesty, they didn't want anyone to know that their darling brother had seduced—ruined, they called it—a Negro girl. They could excuse the ruin, but they couldn't forgive the tar-brush. They forbade me to mention Negroes to the neighbours, or even to mention the south side. You may be sure that I didn't. I'll bet they were good and sorry afterwards."

She laughed and the ringing bells in her laugh had a hard metallic sound.

"When the chance to get away came, that omission was of great value to me. When Jack, a schoolboy acquaintance of some people in the neighbourhood, turned up from South America with untold gold, there was no one to tell him that I was coloured, and many to tell him about the severity and the religiousness of Aunt Grace and Aunt Edna. You can guess the rest. After he came, I stopped slipping off to the south side and slipped off to meet him instead. I couldn't manage both. In the end I had no great difficulty in convincing him that it was useless to talk marriage to the aunts. So on the day that I was eighteen, we went off and were married. So that's that. Nothing could have been easier."

"Yes, I do see that for you it was easy enough. By the way! I wonder why they didn't tell father that you were married. He went over to find out about you when you stopped coming over to see us. I'm sure they didn't tell him. Not that you were married."

Clare Kendry's eyes were bright with tears that didn't fall. "Oh, how lovely! To have cared enough about me to do that. The dear sweet man! Well, they couldn't tell him because they didn't know it. I took care of that, for I couldn't be sure that those consciences of theirs wouldn't begin to work on them afterwards and make them let the cat out of the bag. The old things probably thought I was living in sin, wherever I was. And it would be about what they expected."

An amused smile lit the lovely face for the smallest fraction of a second. After a little silence she said soberly: "But I'm sorry if they told your father so. That was something I hadn't counted on."

"I'm not sure that they did," Irene told her. "He didn't say so, anyway."

"He wouldn't, 'Rene dear. Not your father."

"Thanks. I'm sure he wouldn't."

"But you've never answered my question. Tell me, honestly, haven't you ever thought of 'passing'?"

Irene answered promptly: "No. Why should I?" And so disdainful was her voice and manner that Clare's face flushed and her eyes glinted. Irene hastened to add: "You see, Clare, I've everything I want. Except, perhaps, a little more money."

At that Clare laughed, her spark of anger vanished as quickly as it had appeared. "Of course," she declared, "that's what everybody wants, just a little more money, even the people who have it. And I must say I don't blame them. Money's awfully nice to have. In fact, all things considered, I think, 'Rene, that it's even worth the price."

Irene could only shrug her shoulders. Her reason partly agreed, her instinct wholly rebelled. And she could not say why. And though conscious that if she didn't hurry away, she was going to be late to dinner, she still lingered. It was as if the woman sitting on the other side of the table, a girl that she had known, who had done this rather dangerous and, to Irene Redfield, abhorrent thing successfully and had announced herself well satisfied, had for her a fascination, strange and compelling.

Clare Kendry was still leaning back in the tall chair, her sloping shoulders against the carved top. She sat with an air of indifferent assurance, as if arranged for, desired. About her clung that dim suggestion of polite insolence with which a few women are born and which some acquire with the coming of riches or importance.

Clare, it gave Irene a little prick of satisfaction to recall, hadn't got that by passing herself off as white. She herself had always had it.

Just as she'd always had that pale gold hair, which, unsheared still, was drawn loosely back from a broad brow, partly hidden by the small close hat. Her lips, painted a brilliant geranium-red, were sweet and sensitive and a little obstinate. A tempting mouth. The face across the forehead and cheeks was a trifle too wide, but the ivory skin had a peculiar soft lustre. And the eyes were magnificent! dark, sometimes absolutely black, always luminous, and set in long, black lashes. Arresting eyes, slow and mesmeric, and with, for all their warmth, something withdrawn and secret about them.

Ah! Surely! They were Negro eyes! mysterious and concealing. And set in that ivory face under that bright hair, there was about them something exotic.

Yes, Clare Kendry's loveliness was absolute, beyond challenge, thanks to those eyes which her grandmother and later her mother and father had given her.

Into those eyes there came a smile and over Irene the sense of being petted and caressed. She smiled back.

"Maybe," Clare suggested, "you can come Monday, if you're back. Or, if you're not, then Tuesday."

With a small regretful sigh, Irene informed Clare that she was afraid she wouldn't be back by Monday and that she was sure she had dozens of things for Tuesday, and that she was leaving Wednesday. It might be, however, that she could get out of something Tuesday.

"Oh, do try. Do put somebody else off. The others can see you any time, while I—Why, I may never see you again! Think of that, 'Rene! You'll have to come. You'll simply have to! I'll never forgive you if you don't."

At that moment it seemed a dreadful thing to think of never seeing Clare Kendry again. Standing there under the appeal, the caress, of her eyes, Irene had the desire, the hope, that this parting wouldn't be the last.

"I'll try, Clare," she promised gently. "I'll call you—or will you call me?"

"I think, perhaps, I'd better call you. Your father's in the book, I know, and the address is the same. Sixty-four eighteen. Some memory, what? Now remember, I'm going to expect you. You've got to be able to come."

Again that peculiar mellowing smile.

"I'll do my best, Clare."

Irene gathered up her gloves and bag. They stood up. She put out her hand. Clare took and held it.

"It has been nice seeing you again, Clare. How pleased and glad father'll be to hear about you!"

"Until Tuesday, then," Clare Kendry replied. "I'll spend every minute of the time from now on looking forward to seeing you again. Good-bye, 'Rene dear. My love to your father, and this kiss for him."

The sun had gone from overhead, but the streets were still like fiery furnaces. The languid breeze was still hot. And the scurrying people looked even more wilted than before Irene had fled from their contact.

Crossing the avenue in the heat, far from the coolness of the Drayton's roof, away from the seduction of Clare Kendry's smile, she was aware of a sense of irritation with herself because she had been pleased and a little flattered at the other's obvious gladness at their meeting.

With her perspiring progress homeward this irritation grew, and she began to wonder just what had possessed her to make her promise to find time, in the crowded days that remained of her visit, to spend another afternoon with a woman whose life had so definitely and deliberately diverged from hers; and whom, as had been pointed out, she might never see again.

Why in the world had she made such a promise?

As she went up the steps to her father's house, thinking with what interest and amazement he would listen to her story of the afternoon's encounter, it came to her that Clare had omitted to mention her marriage name. She had referred to her husband as Jack. That was all. Had that, Irene asked herself, been intentional?

Clare had only to pick up the telephone to communicate with her, or to drop her a card, or to jump into a taxi. But she couldn't reach Clare in any way. Nor could anyone else to whom she might speak of their meeting.

"As if I should!"

Her key turned in the lock. She went in. Her father, it seemed, hadn't come in yet.

Irene decided that she wouldn't, after all, say anything to him about Clare Kendry. She had, she told herself, no inclination to speak of a person who held so low an opinion of her loyalty, or her discretion. And certainly she had no desire or intention of making the slightest effort about Tuesday. Nor any other day for that matter.

She was through with Clare Kendry.

Jean Toomer (1894–1967)

*A fascinating figure for both his creative writing and his personal pursuits, Jean Toomer (born Nathan Eugene Toomer) was a distinctive participant in the Harlem Renaissance. His accolades resulted from the one major book of his literary career—*Cane *(1923), a mixture of poetry and fiction.*

A racial maverick with a restless spirit, Toomer was born in Washington, D.C., and raised in a white community. His fair complexion came from the mixed heritage of both his parents; his mother's father, Pinckney Pinchback, had been a noted Reconstruction politician in Louisiana. After his father died, Toomer moved first to Brooklyn and then to New Rochelle, New York, with his mother and his new white stepfather. When Toomer was fifteen, his mother died, and he returned to Washington, D.C., to live with his grandparents in a middle-class interracial neighborhood.

He studied agriculture in Wisconsin and Massachusetts before enrolling in a physical training class in Chicago. Rejected for duty in the First World War, Toomer drifted through employment as a salesperson, a teacher, and a shipyard worker. While serving temporarily as the superintendent of a Negro school in Georgia in 1921, Toomer entered a compelling black environment, an experience that inspired his writing of Cane. *Although the book brought Toomer much critical acclaim as a writer, he turned his attention to studying spiritual philosophy in France at the Gurdjieff Institute, which taught a blend of psychology and mysticism. Although unable to successfully disseminate this philosophy to the Harlem masses, Toomer reached a number of notable intellectuals, both black and white. In the 1940s, he went on another spiritual journey, pouring his energies into the Quaker religion. A light-skinned man who married two Cau-*

casian women, Toomer maintained his black identity while in his later writings affirming his belief in the possibility of a raceless society in the future.

Cane *has been hailed as a work of African American racial pride, modernism, mysticism, impressionism, naturalism, and sensualism. "Theater," taken from the second section of* Cane, *is a brief vignette that displays Toomer's experimentation with narrative voice and structure. Set in Washington, D.C., the selection provokes reflections on class consciousness, on the influence of the urban environment on individual behavior, and on the gender games played by women and men.*

Theater

Life of nigger alleys, of pool rooms and restaurants and near-beer saloons soaks into the walls of Howard Theater and sets them throbbing jazz songs. Black-skinned, they dance and shout above the tick and trill of white-walled buildings. At night, they open doors to people who come in to stamp their feet and shout. At night, road-shows volley songs into the mass-heart of black people. Songs soak the walls and seep out to the nigger life of alleys and near-beer saloons, of the Poodle Dog and Black Bear cabarets. Afternoons, the house is dark, and the walls are sleeping singers until rehearsal begins. Or until John comes within them. Then they start throbbing to a subtle syncopation. And the space-dark air grows softly luminous.

John is the manager's brother. He is seated at the center of the theater, just before rehearsal. Light streaks down upon him from a window high above. One half his face is orange in it. One half his face is in shadow. The soft glow of the house rushes to, and compacts about, the shaft of light. John's mind coincides with the shaft of light. Thoughts rush to, and compact about it. Life of the house and of the slowly awakening stage swirls to the body of John, and thrills it. John's body is separate from the thoughts that pack his mind.

Stage-lights, soft, as if they shine through clear pink fingers. Beneath them, hid by the shadow of a set, Dorris. Other chorus girls drift in. John feels them in the mass. And as if his own body were the mass-heart of a black audience listening to them singing, he wants to stamp his feet and shout. His mind, contained above desires of his body, singles the girls out, and tries to trace origins and plot destinies.

A pianist slips into the pit and improvises jazz. The walls awake. Arms of the girls, and their limbs, which . . . jazz, jazz . . . by lifting up their tight street skirts they set free, jab the air and clog the floor in rhythm to the music. (Lift your skirts, Baby, and talk t papa!) Crude, individualized, and yet . . . monotonous. . . .

John: Soon the director will herd you, my full-lipped, distant beauties, and tame you, and blunt your sharp thrusts in loosely suggestive movements, appropriate to Broadway. (O dance!) Soon the audience will paint your dusk faces white, and call you beautiful. (O dance!) Soon I. . . . (O dance!) I'd like. . . .

Girls laugh and shout. Sing discordant snatches of other jazz songs. Whirl with loose passion into the arms of passing show-men.

John: Too thick. Too easy. Too monotonous. Her whom I'd love I'd leave before she knew that I was with her. Her? Which? (O dance!) I'd like to. . . .

Girls dance and sing. Men clap. The walls sing and press inward. They press the men and girls, they press John towards a center of physical ecstasy. Go to it,

Baby! Fan yourself, and feed your papa! Put . . . nobody lied . . . and take . . . when they said I cried over you. No lie! The glitter and color of stacked scenes, the gilt and brass and crimson of the house, converge towards a center of physical ecstasy. John's feet and torso and his blood press in. He wills thought to rid his mind of passion.

"All right, girls. Alaska. Miss Reynolds, please."

The director wants to get the rehearsal through with.

The girls line up. John sees the front row: dancing ponies. The rest are in shadow. The leading lady fits loosely in the front. Lack-life, monotonous. "One, two, three—" Music starts. The song is somewhere where it will not strain the leading lady's throat. The dance is somewhere where it will not strain the girls. Above the staleness, one dancer throws herself into it. Dorris. John sees her. Her hair, crisp-curled, is bobbed. Bushy, black hair bobbing about her lemon-colored face. Her lips are curiously full, and very red. Her limbs in silk purple stockings are lovely. John feels them. Desires her. Holds off.

John: Stage-door johnny; chorus-girl. No, that would be all right. Dictie,* educated, stuck-up; show-girl. Yep. Her suspicion would be stronger than her passion. It wouldn't work. Keep her loveliness. Let her go.

Dorris sees John and knows that he is looking at her. Her own glowing is too rich a thing to let her feel the slimness of his diluted passion.

"Who's that?" she asks her dancing partner.

"Th manager's brother. Dictie. Nothin doin, hon."

Dorris tosses her head and dances for him until she feels she has him. Then, withdrawing disdainfully, she flirts with the director.

Dorris: Nothin doin? How come? Aint I as good as him? Couldnt I have got an education if I'd wanted one? Dont I know respectable folks, lots of em, in Philadelphia and New York and Chicago? Aint I had men as good as him? Better. Doctors an lawyers. Whats a manager's brother, anyhow?

Two steps back, and two steps front.

"Say, Mame, where do you get that stuff?"

"Whatshmean, Dorris?"

"If you two girls cant listen to what I'm telling you, I know where I can get some who can. Now listen."

Mame: Go to hell, you black bastard.

Dorris: Whats eatin at him, anyway?

"Now follow me in this, you girls. Its three counts to the right, three counts to the left, and then you shimmy—"

John: —and then you shimmy. I'll bet she can. Some good cabaret, with rooms upstairs. And what in hell do you think you'd get from it? Youre going wrong. Here's right: get her to herself—(Christ, but how she'd bore you after the first five minutes)—not if you get her right she wouldnt. Touch her, I mean. To herself—in some room perhaps. Some cheap, dingy bedroom. Hell no. Cant be done. But the point is, brother John, it can be done. Get her to herself somewhere, anywhere. Go down in yourself—and she'd be calling you all sorts of asses while you were in the process of going down. Hold em, bud. Cant be done. Let her go. (Dance and I'll love you!) And keep her loveliness.

---

* Black slang for a middle-class, educated black person who affects a superior attitude toward other blacks.

"All right now, Chicken Chaser.* Dorris and girls. Where's Dorris? I told you to stay on the stage, didnt I? Well? Now thats enough. All right. All right there, Professor?** All right. One, two, three—"

Dorris swings to the front. The line of girls, four deep, blurs within the shadow of suspended scenes. Dorris wants to dance. The director feels that and steps to one side. He smiles, and picks her for a leading lady, one of these days. Odd ends of stage-men emerge from the wings, and stare and clap. A crap game in the alley suddenly ends. Black faces crowd the rear stage doors. The girls, catching joy from Dorris, whip up within the footlights' glow. They forget set steps; they find their own. The director forgets to bawl them out. Dorris dances.

John: Her head bobs to Broadway. Dance from yourself. Dance! O just a little more.

Dorris' eyes burn across the space of seats to him.

Dorris: I bet he can love. Hell, he cant love. He's too skinny. His lips are too skinny. He wouldnt love me anyway, only for that. But I'd get a pair of silk stockings out of it. Red silk. I got purple. Cut it, kid. You cant win him to respect you that away. He wouldnt anyway. Maybe he would. Maybe he'd love. I've heard em say that men who look like him (what does he look like?) will marry if they love. O will you love me? And give me kids, and a home, and everything? (I'd like to make your nest, and honest, hon, I wouldnt run out on you.) You will if I make you. Just watch me.

Dorris dances. She forgets her tricks. She dances.

Glorious songs are the muscles of her limbs.

And her singing is of canebrake loves and mangrove feastings.

The walls press in, singing. Flesh of a throbbing body, they press close to John and Dorris. They close them in. John's heart beats tensely against her dancing body. Walls press his mind within his heart. And then, the shaft of light goes out the window high above him. John's mind sweeps up to follow it. Mind pulls him upward into dream. Dorris dances. . . .

John dreams:

> Dorris is dressed in a loose black gown splashed with lemon ribbons. Her feet taper long and slim from trim ankles. She waits for him just inside the stage door. John, collar and tie colorful and flaring, walks towards the stage door. There are no trees in the alley. But his feet feel as though they step on autumn leaves whose rustle has been pressed out of them by the passing of a million satin slippers. The air is sweet with roasting chestnuts, sweet with bonfires of old leaves. John's melancholy is a deep thing that seals all senses but his eyes, and makes him whole.
>
> Dorris knows that he is coming. Just at the right moment she steps from the door, as if there were no door. Her face is tinted like the autumn alley. Of old flowers, or of a southern canefield, her perfume. "Glorious Dorris." So his eyes speak. And their sadness is too deep for sweet untruth. She barely touches his arms. They glide off with footfalls softened on the leaves, the old leaves powdered by a million satin slippers.
>
> They are in a room. John knows nothing of it. Only, that the flesh and blood

* A popular dance.
** Nickname for a pianist.

of Dorris are its walls. Singing walls. Lights, soft, as if they shine through clear pink fingers. Soft lights, and warm.

John reaches for a manuscript of his, and reads. Dorris, who has no eyes, has eyes to understand him. He comes to a dancing scene. The scene is Dorris. She dances. Dorris dances. Glorious Dorris. Dorris whirls, whirls, dances. . . .

Dorris dances.

The pianist crashes a bumper chord. The whole stage claps. Dorris, flushed, looks quick at John. His whole face is in shadow. She seeks for her dance in it. She finds it a dead thing in the shadow which is his dream. She rushes from the stage. Falls down the steps into her dressing-room. Pulls her hair. Her eyes, over a floor of tears, stare at the whitewashed ceiling. (Smell of dry paste, and paint, and soiled clothing.) Her pal comes in. Dorris flings herself into the old safe arms, and cries bitterly.

"I told you nothin doin," is what Mame says to comfort her.

Zora Neale Hurston (1901–60)

Speaking about Zora Neale Hurston in an interview, Alice Walker said, "Hurston was never afraid to let her characters be themselves, funny talk and all. She was incapable of being embarrassed by anything black people did, and so was able to write about everything with freedom and fluency. My feeling is that Zora Neale Hurston is probably one of the most misunderstood, least appreciated writers of this century. Which is a pity. She is great. A writer of courage, and incredible humor, with poetry in every line." Embraced by black women writers and critics for her artistic and pioneering work in fiction, Hurston only recently received much of the acclaim that eluded her when she died penniless in Florida in 1960.

Emerging from that Florida background to move north as a teenager, Hurston brought her sharp awareness of and pride in southern black culture with her. She left home to escape family conflict. After attending high school in Baltimore, she went on to Howard University in Washington, D.C. She graduated in 1927 from Barnard College in New York, where she studied with the great anthropologist Franz Boas. Hurston—with her mix of folkways, academic pursuits, and literary interests—became one of the major talents of the Harlem Renaissance. Some literary critics vacillate on the extent of Hurston's artistic acceptance by her Renaissance contemporaries, suggesting that they may have appreciated her more for her upbeat spirit than for her literary talent. However, other critics praise Hurston's work for celebrating grassroots black folk and for bringing the experiences of black women into literary focus.

After publishing a number of short stories and the award-winning play Color Struck *(1925), Hurston completed her first novel,* Jonah's Gourd Vine, *in 1934. Her interest in anthropology continued from her college days; she received a Rosennald Fellowship in anthropology in 1935, and a Guggenheim Fellowship in 1936 to study West Indian and Haitian folklore.*

Her second novel, Their Eyes Were Watching God *(1937), continues to captivate a wide spectrum of readers, scholars, and authors. The novel follows its independent protagonist, Janie, through an odyssey of painful relationships to self-realization. According to scholar Barbara Christian,* "Their Eyes Were Watching God *invokes not our class but the total community—its language, images, mores, and prejudices—as its context. In so doing, it articulates the Afro-American experience not only as a condition but as a culture."*

Hurston's other works persistently blend her cultural interests, anthropological research, and independent viewpoints. Mules and Men *(1935) is a book of folkways and folktales compiled from the Florida environment (see Part One, pp. 81–86);* Tell My Horse *(1938) is another book of folklore.* Moses, Man of the Mountain *(1939), a novel, explores the biblical figure of Moses;* Dust Tracks on a Road *(1942) is her autobiography; and* Seraph on the Swanee *(1948), Hurston's final novel, centers on poor white characters.*

The following selection, "Sweat," originally appeared in 1926 in the anthology Fire *edited by Wallace Thurman. The story, set in the South, presents the consequences of an abusive marriage. In it Hurston uses dialogue, allusions to nature, songs, and characterizations to render the grassroots environment that she so passionately studied in much of her other writings as well.*

Sweat

It was eleven o'clock of a Spring night in Florida. It was Sunday. Any other night, Delia Jones would have been in bed for two hours by this time. But she was a washwoman, and Monday morning meant a great deal to her. So she collected the soiled clothes on Saturday when she returned the clean things. Sunday night after church, she sorted them and put the white things to soak. It saved her almost a half day's start. A great hamper in the bedroom held the clothes that she brought home. It was so much neater than a number of bundles lying around.

She squatted in the kitchen floor beside the great pile of clothes, sorting them into small heaps according to color, and humming a song in a mournful key, but wondering through it all where Sykes, her husband, had gone with her horse and buckboard.

Just then something long, round, limp and black fell upon her shoulders and slithered to the floor beside her. A great terror took hold of her. It softened her knees and dried her mouth so that it was a full minute before she could cry out or move. Then she saw that it was the big bull whip her husband liked to carry when he drove.

She lifted her eyes to the door and saw him standing there bent over with laughter at her fright. She screamed at him.

"Sykes, what you throw dat whip on me like dat? You know it would skeer me—looks just like a snake, an' you knows how skeered Ah is of snakes."

"Course Ah knowed it! That's how come Ah done it." He slapped his leg with his hand and almost rolled on the ground in his mirth. "If you such a big fool dat you got to have a fit over a earth worm or a string, Ah don't keer how bad Ah skeer you."

"You aint got no business doing it. Gawd knows it's a sin. Some day Ah'm gointuh drop dead from some of yo' foolishness. 'Nother thing, where you been wid mah rig? Ah feeds dat pony. He aint fuh you to be drivin' wid no bull whip."

"Yo sho is one aggravatin' nigger woman!" he declared and stepped into the room. She resumed her work and did not answer him at once. "Ah done tole you time and again to keep them white folks' clothes outa dis house."

He picked up the whip and glared down at her. Delia went on with her work. She went out into the yard and returned with a galvanized tub and set it on the washbench. She saw that Sykes had kicked all of the clothes together again, and now stood in her way truculently, his whole manner hoping, *praying,* for an argument. But she walked calmly around him and commenced to re-sort the things.

"Next time, Ah'm gointer to kick 'em outdoors," he threatened as he struck a match along the leg of his corduroy breeches.

Delia never looked up from her work, and her thin, stooped shoulders sagged further.

"Ah aint for no fuss t'night Sykes. Ah just come from taking sacrament at the church house."

He snorted scornfully. "Yeah, you just come from de church house on a Sunday night, but heah you is gone to work on them clothes. You ain't nothing but a hypocrite. One of them amen-corner Christians—sing, whoop, shout, then come home and wash white folks clothes on the Sabbath."

He stepped roughly upon the whitest pile of things, kicking them helter-skelter as he crossed the room. His wife gave a little scream of dismay, and quickly gathered them together again.

"Sykes, you quit grindin' dirt into these clothes! How can Ah git through by Sat'day if Ah don't start on Sunday?"

"Ah don't keer if you never git through. Anyhow, Ah done promised Gawd and a couple of other men, Ah aint gointer have it in mah house. Don't gimme no lip neither, else Ah'll throw 'em out and put mah fist up side yo' head to boot."

Delia's habitual meekness seemed to slip from her shoulders like a blown scarf. She was on her feet; her poor little body, her bare knuckly hands bravely defying the strapping hulk before her.

"Looka heah, Sykes, you done gone too far. Ah been married to you fur fifteen years, and Ah been takin' in washin' for fifteen years. Sweat, sweat, sweat! Work and sweat, cry and sweat, pray and sweat!"

"What's that got to do with me?" he asked brutally.

"What's it got to do with you, Sykes? Mah tub of suds is filled yo' belly with vittles more times than yo' hands is filled it. Mah sweat is done paid for this house and Ah reckon Ah kin keep on sweatin' in it."

She seized the iron skillet from the stove and struck a defensive pose, which act surprised him greatly, coming from her. It cowed him and he did not strike her as he usually did.

"Naw you won't," she panted, "that ole snaggle-toothed black woman you runnin' with aint comin' heah to pile up on *mah* sweat and blood. You aint paid for nothin' on this place, and Ah'm gointer stay right heah till Ah'm toted out foot foremost."

"Well, you better quit gittin' me filed up, else they'll be totin' you out sooner than you expect. Ah'm so tired of you Ah don't know whut to do. Gawd! how Ah hates skinny wimmen!"

A little awed by this new Delia, he sidled out of the door and slammed the back gate after him. He did not say where he had gone, but she knew too well. She knew very well that he would not return until nearly daybreak also. Her work over, she went on to bed but not to sleep at once. Things had come to a pretty pass!

She lay awake, gazing upon the debris that cluttered their matrimonial trail. Not an image left standing along the way. Anything like flowers had long ago been drowned in the salty stream that had been pressed from her heart. Her tears, her sweat, her blood. She had brought love to the union and he had brought a longing for the flesh. Two months after the wedding, he had given her the first brutal beating. She had the memory of numerous trips to Orlando with all of his wages when he had returned to her penniless, even before the first year had passed. She was young and soft then, but now she thought of her knotty, muscled limbs, her harsh knuckly hands, and drew herself up into an unhappy little ball in the middle of the big feather bed. Too late now to hope for love, even if it were not Bertha it would be someone else. This case differed from the others only in that she was bolder than the others. Too late for everything except her little home. She had built it for her old days, and planted one by one the trees and flowers there. It was lovely to her, lovely.

Somehow before sleep came, she found herself saying aloud: "Oh well, whatever goes over the Devil's back, is got to come under his belly. Sometime or ruther, Sykes, like everybody else, is gointer reap his sowing." After that she was able to build a spiritual earthworks against her husband. His shells could no longer reach her. *Amen.* She went to sleep and slept until he announced his presence in bed by kicking her feet and rudely snatching the cover away.

"Gimme some kivah heah, an' git yo' damn foots over on yo' own side! Ah oughter mash you in yo' mouf fuh drawing dat skillet on me."

Delia went clear to the rail without answering him. A triumphant indifference to all that he was or did.

The week was as full of work for Delia as all other weeks, and Saturday found her behind her little pony, collecting and delivering clothes.

It was a hot, hot day near the end of July. The village men on Joe Clarke's porch even chewed cane listlessly. They did not hurl the caneknots as usual. They let them dribble over the edge of the porch. Even conversation had collapsed under the heat.

"Heah comes Delia Jones," Jim Merchant said, as the shaggy pony came 'round the bend of the road toward them. The rusty buckboard was heaped with baskets of crisp, clean laundry.

"Yep," Joe Lindsay agreed. "Hot or col', rain or shine, jes ez reg'lar ez de weeks roll roun' Delia carries 'em an' fetches 'em on Sat'day."

"She better if she wanter eat," said Moss. "Syke Jones aint wuth de shot an' powder hit would tek tuh kill 'em. Not to *huh* he aint."

"He sho' aint," Walter Thomas chimed in. "It's too bad, too, cause she wuz a right pritty lil trick when he got huh. Ah'd uh mah'ied huh mahseff if he hadnter beat me to it."

Delia nodded briefly at the men as she drove past.

"Too much knockin' will ruin *any* 'oman. He done beat huh 'nough tuh kill three women, let 'lone change they looks," said Elijah Mosely. "How Syke kin stommuck dat big black greasy Mogul he's layin' roun' wid, gets me. Ah swear dat eight-rock couldn't kiss a sardine can Ah done thowed out de back do' 'way las' yeah."

"Aw, she's fat, thass how come. He's allus been crazy 'bout fat women," put in Merchant. "He'd a'been tied up wid one long time ago if he could a' found one tuh have him. Did Ah tell yuh 'bout him come sidlin' round *mah* wife—bringin' her a basket uh pee-cans outa his yard fuh a present? Yes-sir, mah wife! She tol' him tuh take 'em right straight back home, cause Delia works so hard ovah dat washtub she reckon everything on de place taste lak sweat an' soapsuds. Ah jus' wisht Ah'd a' caught 'im 'roun' dere! Ah'd a' made his hips ketch on fiah down dat shell road."

"Ah know he done it, too. Ah sees 'im grinnin' at every 'oman dat passes," Walter Thomas said. "But even so, he useter eat some mighty big hunks uh humble pie tuh git dat lil' 'oman he got. She wuz ez pritty ez a speckled pup! Dat wuz fifteen years ago. He useter be so skeered uh losin' huh, she could make him do some parts of a husband's duty. Dey never wuz de same in de mind."

"There oughter be a law about him," said Lindsay. "He aint fit tuh carry guts tuh a bear."

Clarke spoke for the first time. "Taint no law on earth dat kin make a man be decent if it aint in 'im. There's plenty men dat takes a wife lak dey do a joint uh sugar-cane. It's round, juicy an' sweet when dey gits it. But dey squeeze an' grind, squeeze an' grind an' wring tell dey wring every drop uh pleasure dat's in 'em out. When dey's satisfied dat dey is wrung dry, dey treats 'em jes lak dey do a cane-chew. Dey throws 'em away. Dey knows whut dey is doin' while dey is at it, an' hates theirselves fuh it but they keeps on hangin' after huh tell she's empty. Den dey hates huh fuh bein' a cane-chew an' in de way."

"We oughter take Syke an' dat stray 'oman uh his'n down in Lake Howell swamp an' lay on de rawhide till they cain't say 'Lawd a' mussy.' He allus wuz uh ovahbearin' niggah, but since dat white 'oman from up north done teached 'im how to run a automobile, he done got too biggety to live—an' we oughter kill 'im," Old Man Anderson advised.

A grunt of approval went around the porch. But the heat was melting their civic virtue and Elijah Moseley began to bait Joe Clarke.

"Come on, Joe, git a melon outa dere an' slice it up for yo' customers. We'se all sufferin' wid de heat. De bear's done got *me*!"

"Thass right, Joe, a watermelon is jes' whut Ah needs tuh cure de eppizudicks," Walter Thomas joined forces with Moseley. "Come on dere, Joe. We all is steady customers an' you aint set us up in a long time. Ah chooses dat long, bowlegged Floridy favorite."

"A god, an' be dough. You all gimme twenty cents and slice away," Clarke retorted. "Ah needs a col' slice m'self. Heah, everybody chip in. Ah'll lend y'll mah meat knife."

The money was quickly subscribed and the huge melon brought forth. At that moment, Sykes and Bertha arrived. A determined silence fell on the porch and the melon was put away again.

Merchant snapped down the blade of his jackknife and moved toward the store door.

"Come on in, Joe, an' gimme a slab uh sow belly an' uh pound uh coffee—almost fuhgot 'twas Sat'day. Got to git on home." Most of the men left also.

Just then Delia drove past on her way home, as Sykes was ordering magnificently for Bertha. It pleased him for Delia to see.

"Git whutsoever yo' heart desires, Honey. Wait a minute, Joe. Give huh two botles uh strawberry soda-water, uh quart uh parched ground-peas, an' a block uh chewin' gum."

With all this they left the store, with Sykes reminding Bertha that this was his town and she could have it if she wanted it.

The men returned soon after they left, and held their watermelon feast. "Where did Syke Jones git dat 'oman from nohow?" Lindsay asked.

"Ova Apopka. Guess dey musta been cleanin' out de town when she lef'. She don't look lak a thing but a hunk uh liver wid hair on it."

"Well, she sho' kin squall," Dave Carter contributed. "When she gits ready tuh laff, she jes' opens huh mouf an' latches it back tuh de las' notch. No ole grandpa alligator down in Lake Bell ain't got nothin' on huh."

Bertha had been in town three months now. Sykes was still paying her room rent at Della Lewis'—the only house in town that would have taken her in. Sykes took her frequently to Winter Park to "stomps." He still assured her that he was the swellest man in the state.

"Sho' you kin have dat lil' ole house soon's Ah kin git dat 'oman outa dere. Everything b'longs tuh me an' you sho' kin have it. Ah sho' 'bominates uh skinny 'oman. Lawdy, you sho' is got one portly shape on you! You kin git *anything* you wants. Dis is *mah* town an' you sho' kin have it."

Delia's work-worn knees crawled over the earth in Gethsemane and up the rocks of Calvary many, many times during these months. She avoided the villagers and meeting places in her efforts to be blind and deaf. But Bertha nullified this to a degree, by coming to Delia's house to call Sykes out to her at the gate.

Delia and Sykes fought all the time now with no peaceful interludes. They slept and ate in silence. Two or three times Delia had attempted a timid friendliness, but she was repulsed each time. It was plain that the breaches must remain agape.

The sun had burned July to August. The heat streamed down like a million hot arrows, smiting all things living upon the earth. Grass withered, leaves browned, snakes went blind in shedding and men and dogs went mad. Dog days!

Delia came home one day and found Sykes there before her. She wondered, but started to go on into the house without speaking, even though he was standing in the kitchen door and she must either stoop under his arm or ask him to move. He made no room for her. She noticed a soap box beside the steps, but paid no particular attention to it, knowing that he must have brought it there. As she was stooping to pass under his outstretched arm, he suddenly pushed her backward, laughingly.

"Look in de box dere Delia, Ah done brung yuh somethin'!"

She nearly fell upon the box in her stumbling, and when she saw what it held, she all but fainted outright.

"Syke! Syke, mah Gawd! You take dat rattlesnake 'way from heah! You *gottuh*. Oh, Jesus, have mussy!"

"Ah aint gut tuh do nothin' uh de kin'—fact is Ah aint got tuh do nothin' but die. Taint no use uh you puttin' on airs makin' out lak you skeered uh dat snake—he's gointer stay right heah tell he die. He wouldn't bite me cause Ah knows how tuh handle 'im. Nohow he wouldn't risk breakin' out his fangs 'gin *yo'* skinny laigs."

"Naw, now Syke, don't keep dat thing 'roun' heah tuh skeer me tuh death.

You knows Ah'm even feared uh earth worms. Thass de biggest snake Ah evah did see. Kill 'im Syke, please."

"Doan ast me tuh do nothin' fuh yuh. Goin' 'roun' tryin' to be so damn asterperious. Naw, Ah aint gonna kill it. Ah think uh damn sight mo' uh him dan you! Dat's a nice snake an' anybody doan lak 'im kin jes' hit de grit."

The village soon heard that Sykes had the snake, and came to see and ask questions.

"How de hen-fire did you ketch dat six-root rattler, Syke?" Thomas asked.

"He's full uh frogs so he caint hardly move, thass how Ah eased up on 'm. But Ah'm a snake charmer an' knows how tuh handle 'em. Shux, dat aint nothin'. Ah could ketch on eve'y day if Ah so wanted tuh."

"Whut he needs is a heavy hick'ry club leaned real heavy on his head. Dat's de bes 'way tuh charm a rattlesnake."

"Naw, Walt, y'll jes' don't understand dese diamon' backs lak Ah do," said Syke in a superior tone of voice.

The village agreed with Walter, but the snake stayed on. His box remained by the kitchen door with its screen wire covering. Two or three days later it had digested its meal of frogs and literally came to life. It rattled at every movement in the kitchen or the yard. One day as Delia came down the kitchen steps she saw his chalky-white fangs curved like scimitars hung in the wire meshes. This time she did not run away with averted eyes as usual. She stood for a long time in the doorway in a red fury that grew bloodier for every second that she regarded the creature that was her torment.

That night she broached the subject as soon as Sykes sat down to the table.

"Syke, Ah wants you tuh take dat snake 'way fum heah. You done starved me an' Ah put up widcher, you done beat me an Ah took dat, but you done kilt all mah insides bringin' dat varmint heah."

Sykes poured out a saucer full of coffee and drank it deliberately before he answered her.

"A whole lot Ah keer 'bout how you feels inside uh out. Dat snake aint goin' no damn wheah till Ah gits ready fuh 'im tuh go. So fur as beatin' is concerned, yuh aint took near all dat you gointer take ef yuh stay 'roun' *me*."

Delia pushed back her plate and got up from the table. "Ah hates you, Sykes," she said calmly. "Ah hates you tuh de same degree dat Ah useter love yuh. Ah done took an' took till mah belly is full up tuh mah neck. Dat's de reason Ah got mah letter fum de church an' moved mah membership tuh Woodbridge—so Ah don't haftuh take no sacrament wid yuh. Ah don't wantuh see yuh 'round' me atall. Lay 'round' wid dat 'oman all yuh wants tuh, but gwan 'way fum me an' mah house. Ah hates yuh lak uh suck-egg dog."

Sykes almost let the huge wad of corn bread and collard greens he was chewing fall out of his mouth in amazement. He had a hard time whipping himself to the proper fury to try to answer Delia.

"Well, Ah'm glad you does hate me. Ah'm sho' tiahed uh you hangin' ontuh me. Ah don't want yuh. Look at yuh stringey ole neck! Yo' raw-bony laigs an' arms is enough tuh cut uh man tuh death. You looks jes' lak de devvul's doll-baby tuh *me*. You caint hate me no worse dan Ah hates you. Ah been hatin' *you* fuh years.

"Yo' ole black hide don't look lak nothin' tuh me, but uh passle uh wrinkled up rubber, wid yo' big ole yeahs flappin' on each side lak up paih uh buzzard wings. Don't think Ah'm gointuh be run 'way fum mah house neither. Ah'm goin' tuh de white folks about *you,* mah young man, de very nex' time yo lay yo' hand's on me. Mah cup is done run ovah." Delia said this with no signs of fear and Sykes departed from the house, threatening her, but made not the slightest move to carry out any of them.

That night he did not return at all, and the next day being Sunday, Delia was glad that she did not have to quarrel before she hitched up her pony and drove the four miles to Woodbridge.

She stayed to the night service—"love feast"—which was very warm and full of spirit. In the emotional winds her domestic trials were borne far and wide so that she sang as she drove homeward,

> *"Jurden water, black an' col'*
> *Chills de body, not de soul*
> *An' Ah wantah cross Jurden in uh calm time."*

She came from the barn to the kitchen door and stopped.

"Whut's de mattah, ol' satan, you aint kickin' up yo' racket?" She addressed the snake's box. Complete silence. She went on into the house with a new hope in its birth struggles. Perhaps her threat to go to the white folks had frightened Sykes! Perhaps he was sorry! Fifteen years of misery and suppression had brought Delia to the place where she would hope *anything* that looked towards a way over or through her wall of inhibitions.

She felt in the match safe behind the stove at once for a match. There was only one there.

"Dat niggah wouldn't fetch nothin' heah tuh save his rotten neck, but he kin run thew whut Ah brings quick enough. Now he done toted off nigh on tuh haff uh box uh matches. He done had dat 'oman heah in mah house, too."

Nobody but a woman could tell how she knew this even before she struck the match. But she did and it put her into a new fury.

Presently she brought in the tubs to put the white things to soak. This time she decided she need not bring the hamper out of the bedroom; she would go in there and do the sorting. She picked up the pot-bellied lamp and went in. The room was small and the hamper stood hard by the foot of the white iron bed. She could sit and reach through the bedposts—resting as she worked.

"Ah wantah cross Jurden in uh calm time." She was singing again. The mood of the "love feast" had returned. She threw back the lid of the basket almost gaily. Then, moved by both horror and terror, she sprang back toward the door. *There lay the snake in the basket!* He moved sluggishly at first, but even as she turned round and round, jumped up and down in an insanity of fear, he began to stir vigorously. She saw him pouring his awful beauty from the basket upon the bed, then she seized the lamp and ran as fast as she could to the kitchen. The wind from the open door blew out the light and the darkness added to her terror. She sped to the darkness of the yard, slamming the door after her before she thought to set down the lamp. She did not feel safe even on the ground, so she climbed up in the hay barn.

There for an hour or more she lay sprawled upon the hay a gibbering wreck.

Finally she grew quiet, and after that, coherent thought. With this, stalked through her a cold, blood rage. Hours of this. A period of introspection, a space of retrospection, then a mixture of both. Out of this an awful calm.

"Well, Ah done de bes' Ah could. If things aint right, Gawd knows taint mah fault."

She went to sleep—a twitchy sleep—and woke up to a faint gray sky. There was a loud hollow sound below. She peered out. Sykes was at the wood-pile, demolishing a wire-covered box.

He hurried to the kitchen door, but hung outside there some minutes before he entered, and stood some minutes more inside before he closed it after him.

The gray in the sky was spreading. Delia descended without fear now, and crouched beneath the low bedroom window. The drawn shade shut out the dawn, shut in the night. But the thin walls held back no sound.

"Dat ol' scratch is woke up now!" She mused at the tremendous whirr inside, which every woodsman knows, is one of the sound illusions. The rattler is a ventriloquist. His whirr sounds to the right, to the left, straight ahead, behind, close under foot—everywhere but where it is. Woe to him who guesses wrong unless he is prepared to hold up his end of the argument! Sometimes he strikes without rattling at all.

Inside, Sykes heard nothing until he knocked a pot lid off the stove while trying to reach the match safe in the dark. He had emptied his pockets at Bertha's.

The snake seemed to wake up under the stove and Sykes made a quick leap into the bedroom. In spite of the gin he had had, his head was clearing now.

"Mah Gawd!" he chattered, "ef Ah could on'y strack uh light!"

The rattling ceased for a moment as he stood paralyzed. He waited. It seemed that the snake waited also.

"Oh, fuh de light! Ah thought he'd be too sick"—Sykes was muttering to himself when the whirr began again, closer, right underfoot this time. Long before this, Sykes' ability to think had been flattened down to primitive instinct and he leaped—onto the bed.

Outside Delia heard a cry that might have come from a maddened chimpanzee, a stricken gorilla. All the terror, all the horror, all the rage that man possibly could express, without a recognizable human sound.

A tremendous stir inside there, another series of animal screams, the intermittent whirr of the reptile. The shade torn violently down from the window, letting in the red dawn, a huge brown hand seizing the window stick, great dull blows upon the wooden floor punctuating the gibberish of sound long after the rattle of the snake had abruptly subsided. All this Delia could see and hear from her place beneath the window, and it made her ill. She crept over to the four-o'clocks and stretched herself on the cool earth to recover.

She lay there. "Delia, Delia!" She could hear Sykes calling in a most despairing tone as one who expected no answer. The sun crept on up, and he called. Delia could not move—her legs were gone flabby. She never moved, he called, and the sun kept rising.

"Mah Gawd!" She heard him moan, "Mah Gawd fum Heben!" She heard him stumbling about and got up from her flower-bed. The sun was growing warm. As she approached the door she heard him call out hopefully, "Delia, is dat you Ah heah?"

She saw him on his hands and knees as soon as she reached the door. He crept an inch or two toward her—all that he was able, and she saw his horribly swollen neck and his one open eye shining with hope. A surge of pity too strong to support bore her away from that eye that must, could not, fail to see the tubs. He would see the lamp. Orlando with its doctors was too far. She could scarcely reach the Chinaberry tree, where she waited in the growing heat while inside she knew the cold river was creeping up and up to extinguish that eye which must know by now that she knew.

Wallace Thurman (1902–34)

In his short life of thirty-two years, the multitalented Wallace Thurman was a novelist, short story writer, essayist, editor, ghost writer, playwright, and screenwright. Referred to as "one of the true Renaissance intellectuals," Thurman was unique in his ability to function in the dual worlds of black Renaissance artists and white publishing figures.

Born in Salt Lake City, Utah, Thurman studied at the University of Utah and later transferred to the University of Southern California, where he completed his undergraduate degree in 1925. He finally settled on the East Coast, living in New York City, and in 1926 became an editor of The Messenger. *He also joined forces with other artists to establish* Fire, *a "Negro quarterly of the arts." When that publication failed two years later, he went on to put together* Harlem, *another magazine to showcase black authors, though that project failed as well. In 1929, he became the only black reader at Macaulay's Publishing Company, ultimately becoming a writer for* True Story *magazine under various pseudonyms.*

Thurman first gained attention as a playwright for his successful drama Harlem *(1929), coauthored with the white writer William Jourdan Rapp. He also collaborated on his fourth novel,* The Interne *(1932), with Abraham L. Furman. However, two of his earlier novels—*The Blacker the Berry *(1929) and* Infants of the Spring *(1932)—were the works that secured his central status with his Harlem Renaissance contemporaries. Thurman's personal residence in Harlem, referred to as "Niggerati manor," became a central meetingplace for a number of Renaissance authors and friends, including Gwendolyn Bennett, Langston Hughes, Zora Neale Hurston, and Dorothy West. According to West, Thurman held a prominent role among his contemporary writers: "We called him our leader. . . . I always say the Harlem Renaissance ended when Wallie [Thurman] died because then we could see that we could die."*

The Blacker the Berry *focuses on the character Emma Lou Morgan, a dark-skinned African American woman whose negative feelings about her skin color generate self-destructive elements in her nature. In the excerpt reprinted here, "Emma Lou," the young woman journeys from her small hometown to Los Angeles to begin college, carrying with her the baggage of color consciousness.*

Emma Lou

More acutely than ever before Emma Lou began to feel that her luscious black complexion was somewhat of a liability, and that her marked color variation from the other people in her environment was a decided curse. Not that she minded being black, being a Negro necessitated having a colored skin, but she did mind being too black. She couldn't understand why such should be the case, couldn't comprehend the cruelty of the natal attenders who had allowed her to be dipped, as it were, in indigo ink when there were so many more pleasing colors on nature's palette. Biologically, it wasn't necessary either; her mother was quite fair, so was her mother's mother, and her mother's brother, and her mother's brother's son; but then none of them had had a black man for a father. Why *had* her mother married a black man? Surely there had been some eligible brown-skin men around. She didn't particularly desire to have had a "high yaller" father, but for her sake certainly some more happy medium could have been found.

She wasn't the only person who regretted her darkness either. It was an acquired family characteristic, this moaning and grieving over the color of her skin. Everything possible had been done to alleviate the unhappy condition, every suggested agent had been employed, but her skin, despite bleachings, scourgings, and powderings, had remained black—fast black—as nature had planned and effected.

She should have been born a boy, then color of skin wouldn't have mattered so much, for wasn't her mother always saying that a black boy could get along, but that a black girl would never know anything but sorrow and disappointment? But she wasn't a boy; she was a girl, and color did matter, mattered so much that she would rather have missed receiving her high school diploma than have to sit as she now sat, the only odd and conspicuous figure on the auditorium platform of the Boise high school. Why had she allowed them to place her in the center of the first row, and why had they insisted upon her dressing entirely in white so that surrounded as she was by similarly attired pale-faced fellow graduates she resembled, not at all remotely, that comic picture her Uncle Joe had hung in his bedroom? The picture wherein the black, kinky head of a little red-lipped pickaninny lay like a fly in a pan of milk amid a white expanse of bedclothes.

But of course she couldn't have worn blue or black when the call was for the wearing of white, even if white was not complementary to her complexion. She would have been odd-looking anyway no matter what she wore and she would also have been conspicuous, for not only was she the only dark-skinned person on the platform, she was also the only Negro pupil in the entire school, and had been for the past four years. Well, thank goodness, the principal would soon be through with his monotonous farewell address, and she and the other members of her class would advance to the platform center as their names were called and receive the documents which would signify their unconditional release from public school.

As she thought of these things, Emma Lou glanced at those who sat to the right and to the left of her. She envied them their obvious elation, yet felt a strange sense of superiority because of her immunity for the moment from an ephemeral mob emotion. Get a diploma?—What did it mean to her? College?—Perhaps. A job?—Perhaps again. She was going to have a high school diploma, but it would mean nothing to her whatsoever. The tragedy of her life was that she was too black. Her face and not a slender roll of ribbon-bound parchment was to be her future identification tag in society. High school diploma indeed! What she needed was an efficient bleaching agent, a magic cream that would remove this unwelcome black mask from her face and make her more like her fellow men.

"Emma Lou Morgan."

She came to with a start. The principal had called her name and stood smiling down at her benevolently. Some one—she knew it was her Cousin Buddie, stupid imp—applauded, very faintly, very provokingly. Some one else snickered.

"Emma Lou Morgan."

The principal had called her name again, more sharply than before and his smile was less benevolent. The girl who sat to the left of her nudged her. There was nothing else for her to do but to get out of that anchoring chair and march forward to receive her diploma. But why did the people in the audience have to stare so? Didn't they all know that Emma Lou Morgan was Boise high school's only nigger student? Didn't they all know—but what was the use. She had to go get that diploma, so summoning her most insouciant manner, she advanced to the platform center, brought every muscle of her lithe limbs into play, haughtily extended her shiny black arm to receive the proffered diploma, bowed a chilly thanks, then holding her arms stiffly at her sides, insolently returned to her seat in that forboding white line, insolently returned once more to splotch its pale purity and to mock it with her dark, outlandish difference.

Emma Lou had been born in a semi-white world, totally surrounded by an all-white one, and those few dark elements that had forced their way in had either been shooed away or else greeted with derisive laughter. It was the custom always of those with whom she came into most frequent contact to ridicule or revile any black person or object. A black cat was a harbinger of bad luck, black crape was the insignia of mourning, and black people were either evil niggers with poisonous blue gums or else typical vaudeville darkies. It seemed as if the people in her world never went half-way in their recognition or reception of things black, for these things seemed always to call forth only the most extreme emotional reactions. They never provoked mere smiles or mere melancholy, rather they were the signal either for boisterous guffaws or pain-induced and tear-attended grief.

Emma Lou had been becoming increasingly aware of this for a long time, but her immature mind had never completely grasped its full, and to her, tragic significance. First there had been the case of her father, old black Jim Morgan they called him, and Emma Lou had often wondered why it was that he of all the people she heard discussed by her family should always be referred to as if his very blackness condemned him to receive no respect from his fellow men.

She had also begun to wonder if it was because of his blackness that he had never been in evidence as far as she knew. Inquiries netted very unsatisfactory answers. "Your father is no good." "He left your mother, deserted her shortly after you were born." And these statements were always prefixed or followed by some epithet such as "dirty black no-gooder" or "durn his onery black hide." There was in fact only one member of the family who did not speak of her father in this manner, and it was her Uncle Joe, who was also the only person in the family to whom she really felt akin, because he alone never seemed to regret, to bemoan, or to ridicule her blackness of skin. It was her grandmother who did all the regretting, her mother who did the bemoaning, her Cousin Buddie and her playmates, both white and colored, who did the ridiculing.

Emma Lou's maternal grandparents, Samuel and Maria Lightfoot, were both mulatto products of slave-day promiscuity between male masters and female chattel. Neither had been slaves, their own parents having been granted their freedom because of their rather close connections with the white branch of the family tree. These freedmen had migrated into Kansas with their children, and when these children had grown up they in turn had joined the westward-ho parade of that current era, and finally settled in Boise, Idaho. . . .

Summer vacation was nearly over and it had not yet been decided what to do with Emma Lou now that she had graduated from high school. She herself gave no help nor offered any suggestions. As it was, she really did not care what became of her. After all it didn't seem to matter. There was no place in the world for a girl as black as she anyway. Her grandmother had assured her that she would never find a husband worth a dime, and her mother had said again and again, "Oh, if you had only been a boy!" until Emma Lou had often wondered why it was that people were not able to effect a change of sex or at least a change of complexion.

It was her Uncle Joe who finally prevailed upon her mother to send her to the University of Southern California in Los Angeles. There, he reasoned, she would find a larger and more intelligent social circle. In a city the size of Los Angeles there were Negroes of every class, color, and social position. Let Emma Lou go there where she would not be as far away from home as if she were to go to some eastern college.

Jane and Maria, while not agreeing entirely with what Joe said, were nevertheless glad that at last something which seemed adequate and sensible could be done for Emma Lou. She was to take the four year college course, receive a bachelor degree in education, then go South to teach. That, they thought, was a promising future, and for once in the eighteen years of Emma Lou's life every one was satisfied in some measure. Even Emma Lou grew elated over the prospects of the trip. Her Uncle Joe's insistence upon the differences of social contacts in larger cities intrigued her. Perhaps he was right after all in continually reasserting to them that as long as one was a Negro, one's specific color had little to do with one's life. Salvation depended upon the individual. And he also told Emma Lou, during one of their usual private talks, that it was only in small cities one encountered stupid color prejudice such as she had encountered among the blue vein circle in her home town.

"People in large cities," he had said, "are broad. They do not have time to think of petty things. The people in Boise are fifty years behind the times, but you will find that Los Angeles is one of the world's greatest and most modern cities, and you will be happy there."

On arriving in Los Angeles, Emma Lou was so busy observing the colored inhabitants that she had little time to pay attention to other things. Palm trees and wild geraniums were pleasant to behold, and such strange phenomena as pepper trees and century plants had to be admired. They were very obvious and they were also strange and beautiful, but they impinged upon only a small corner of Emma Lou's consciousness. She was minutely aware of them, necessarily took them in while passing, viewing the totality without pondering over or lingering to praise their stylistic details. They were, in this instance, exquisite theatrical props, rendered insignificant by a more strange and a more beautiful human pageant. For to Emma Lou, who, in all her life, had never seen over five hundred Negroes, the spectacle presented by a community containing over fifty thousand, was sufficient to make relatively commonplace many more important and charming things than the far famed natural scenery of Southern California.

She had arrived in Los Angeles a week before registration day at the university, and had spent her time in being shown and seeing the city. But whenever these sightseeing excursions took her away from the sections where Negroes lived, she immediately lost all interest in what she was being shown. The Pacific Ocean in itself did not cause her heart beat to quicken, nor did the roaring of its waves find an emotional echo within her. But on coming upon Bruce's Beach for colored people near Redondo, or the little strip of sandied shore they had appropriated for themselves at Santa Monica, the Pacific Ocean became an intriguing something to contemplate as a background for their activities. Everything was interesting as it was patronized, reflected through, or acquired by Negroes.

Her Uncle Joe had been right. Here, in the colored social circles of Los Angeles, Emma Lou was certain that she would find many suitable companions, intelligent, broad-minded people of all complexions, intermixing and being too occupied otherwise to worry about either their own skin color or the skin color of those around them. Her Uncle Joe had said that Negroes were Negroes whether they happened to be yellow, brown, or black, and a conscious effort to eliminate the darker elements would neither prove nor solve anything. There was nothing quite so silly as the creed of the blue veins: "Whiter and whiter, every generation. The nearer white you are the more white people will respect you. Therefore all light Negroes marry light Negroes. Continue to do so generation after generation, and eventually white people will accept this racially, bastard aristocracy, thus enabling those Negroes who really matter to escape the social and economic inferiority of the American Negro."

Such had been the credo of her grandmother and of her mother and of their small circle of friends in Boise. But Boise was a provincial town, given to the molding of provincial people with provincial minds. Boise was a backwoods town out of the main stream of modern thought and progress. Its people were cramped and narrow, their intellectual concepts stereotyped and static. Los Angeles was a happy contrast in all respects.

On registration day, Emma Lou rushed out to the campus of the University of Southern California one hour before the registrar's office was scheduled to open. She spent the time roaming around, familiarizing herself with the layout of the campus and learning the names of the various buildings, some old and vineclad, others new and shiny in the sun, and watching the crowds of laughing students, rushing to and fro, greeting one another and talking over their plans for the coming school year. But her main reason for such an early arrival on the campus had been to find some of her fellow Negro students. She had heard that there were to be quite a number enrolled, but in all her hour's stroll she saw not one, and finally somewhat disheartened she got into the line stretched out in front of the registrar's office, and, for the moment, became engrossed in becoming a college freshman.

All the while, though, she kept searching for a colored face, but it was not until she had been duly signed up as a student and sent in search of her advisor that she saw one. Then three colored girls had sauntered into the room where she was having a conference with her advisor, sauntered in, arms interlocked, greeted her advisor, then sauntered out again. Emma Lou had wanted to rush after them—to introduce herself, but of course it had been impossible under the circumstances. She had immediately taken a liking to all three, each of whom was what is known in the parlance of the black belt as high brown, with modishly-shingled bobbed hair and well formed bodies, fashionably attired in flashy sport garments. From then on Emma Lou paid little attention to the business of choosing subjects and class hours, so little attention in fact that the advisor thought her exceptionally tractable and somewhat dumb. But she liked students to come that way. It made the task of being advisor easy. One just made out the program to suit oneself, and had no tedious explanations to make as to why the student could not have such and such a subject at such and such an hour, and why such and such a professor's class was already full.

After her program had been made out, Emma Lou was directed to the bursar's office to pay her fees. While going down the stairs she almost bumped into two dark-brown-skinned boys, obviously brothers if not twins, arguing as to where they should go next. One insisted that they should go back to the registrar's office. The other was being equally insistent that they should go to the gymnasium and make an appointment for their required physical examination. Emma Lou boldly stopped when she saw them, hoping they would speak, but they merely glanced up at her and continued their argument, bringing cards and pamphlets out of their pockets for reference and guidance. Emma Lou wanted to introduce herself to them, but she was too bashful to do so. She wasn't yet used to going to school with other Negro students, and she wasn't exactly certain how one went about becoming acquainted. But she finally decided that she had better let the advances come from the others, especially if they were men. There was nothing forward about her, and since she was a stranger it was no more than right that the old-timers should make her welcome. Still, if these had been girls . . . , but they weren't, so she continued her way down the stairs.

In the bursar's office, she was somewhat overjoyed at first to find that she had fallen into line behind another colored girl who turned around immediately, and, after saying hello, announced in a loud, harsh voice:

"My feet are sure some tired!"

Emma Lou was so taken aback that she couldn't answer. People in college didn't talk that way. But meanwhile the girl was continuing:

"Ain't this registration a mess?"

Two white girls who had fallen into line behind Emma Lou snickered. Emma Lou answered by shaking her head. The girl continued:

"I've been standin' in line and climbin' stairs and talkin' and a-signin' till I'm just 'bout done for."

"It is tiresome," Emma Lou returned softly, hoping the girl would take a hint and lower her own strident voice. But she didn't.

"Tiresome ain't no name for it," she declared more loudly than ever before, then, "Is you a new student?"

"I am," answered Emma Lou, putting much emphasis on the "I am."

She wanted the white people who were listening to know that she knew her grammar if this other person didn't. "Is you," indeed! If this girl was a specimen of the Negro students with whom she was to associate, she most certainly did not want to meet another one. But it couldn't be possible that all of them—those three girls and those two boys for instance—were like this girl. Emma Lou was unable to imagine how such a person had ever gotten out of high school. Where on earth could she have gone to high school? Surely not in the North. Then she must be a southerner. That's what she was, a southerner—Emma Lou curled her lips a little—no wonder the colored people in Boise spoke as they did about southern Negroes and wished that they would stay South. Imagine any one preparing to enter college saying "Is you," and, to make it worse, right before all these white people, these staring white people, so eager and ready to laugh. Emma Lou's face burned.

"Two mo', then I goes in my sock."

Emma Lou was almost at the place where she was ready to take even this statement literally, and was on the verge of leaving the line. Supposing this creature did "go in her sock!" God forbid!

"Wonder where all the spades keep themselves? I ain't seen but two 'sides you."

"I really do not know," Emma Lou returned precisely and chillily. She had no intentions of becoming friendly with this sort of person. Why she would be ashamed even to be seen on the street with her, dressed as she was in a red-striped sport suit, a white hat, and white shoes and stockings. Didn't she know that black people had to be careful about the colors they affected?

The girl had finally reached the bursar's window and was paying her fees, and loudly differing with the cashier about the total amount due.

"I tell you it ain't that much," she shouted through the window bars. "I figured it up myself before I left home."

The cashier obligingly turned to her adding machine and once more obtained the same total. When shown this, the girl merely grinned, examined the list closely, and said:

"I'm gonna' pay it, but I still think you're wrong."

Finally she moved away from the window, but not before she had turned to Emma Lou and said,

"You're next," and then proceeded to wait until Emma Lou had finished.

Emma Lou vainly sought some way to escape, but was unable to do so, and had no choice but to walk with the girl to the registrar's office where they had their cards stamped in return for the bursar's receipt. This done, they went onto the campus together. Hazel Mason was the girl's name. Emma Lou had fully expected it to be either Hyacinth or Geranium. Hazel was from Texas, Prairie Valley, Texas, and she told Emma Lou that her father, having become quite wealthy when oil had been found on his farm lands, had been enabled to realize two life ambitions—obtain a Packard touring car and send his only daughter to a "fust-class" white school.

Emma Lou had planned to loiter around the campus. She was still eager to become acquainted with the colored members of the student body, and this encounter with the crass and vulgar Hazel Mason had only made her the more eager. She resented being approached by any one so flagrantly inferior, any one so noticeably a typical southern darky, who had no business obtruding into the more refined scheme of things. Emma Lou planned to lose her unwelcome companion somewhere on the campus so that she could continue unhindered her quest for agreeable acquaintances.

But Hazel was as anxious to meet some one as was Emma Lou, and having found her was not going to let her get away without a struggle. She, too, was new to this environment and in a way was more lonely and eager for the companionship of her own kind than Emma Lou, for never before had she come into such close contact with so many whites. Her life had been spent only among Negroes. Her fellow pupils and teachers in school had always been colored, and as she confessed to Emma Lou, she couldn't get used "to all these white folks."

"Honey, I was just achin' to see a black face," she had said, and, though Emma Lou was experiencing the same ache, she found herself unable to sympathize with the other girl, for Emma Lou classified Hazel as a barbarian who had most certainly not come from a family of best people. No doubt her mother had been a washerwoman. No doubt she had innumerable relatives and friends all as ignorant and as ugly as she. There was no sense in any one having a face as ugly as Hazel's, and Emma Lou thanked her stars that though she was black, her skin was not rough and pimply, nor was her hair kinky, nor were her nostrils completely flattened out until they seemed to spread all over her face. No wonder people were prejudiced against dark skinned people when they were so ugly, so haphazard in their dress, and so boisterously mannered as was this present specimen. She herself was black, but nevertheless she had come from a good family, and she could easily take her place in a society of the right sort of people.

The two strolled along the lawn-bordered gravel path which led to a vine-covered building at the end of the campus. Hazel never ceased talking. She kept shouting at Emma Lou, shouting all sorts of personal intimacies as if she were desirous of the whole world hearing them. There was no necessity for her to talk so loudly, no necessity for her to afford every one on the crowded campus the chance to stare and laugh at them as they passed. Emma Lou had never before been so humiliated and so embarrassed. She felt that she must get away from her offensive companion. What did she care if she had to hurt her feelings to do so. The more insulting she could be now, the less friendly she would have to be in the future.

"Good-by," she said abruptly, "I must go home." With which she turned away and walked rapidly in the opposite direction. She had only gone a few steps when she was aware of the fact that the girl was following her. She quickened her pace, but the girl caught up with her and grabbing hold of Emma Lou's arm, shouted,

"Whoa there, Sally."

It seemed to Emma Lou as if every one on the campus was viewing and enjoying this minstrel-like performance. Angrily she tried to jerk away, but the girl held fast.

"Gal, you sure walk fast. I'm going your way. Come on, let me drive you home in my buggy."

And still holding on to Emma Lou's arm, she led the way to the side street where the students parked their cars. Emma Lou was powerless to resist. The girl didn't give her a chance, for she held tight, then immediately resumed the monologue which Emma Lou's attempted leave-taking had interrupted. They reached the street, Hazel still talking loudly, and making elaborate gestures with her free hand.

"Here we are," she shouted, and releasing Emma Lou's arm, salaamed before a sport model Stutz roadster. "Oscar," she continued, "meet the new girl friend. Pleased to meetcha, says he. Climb aboard."

And Emma Lou had climbed aboard, perplexed, chagrined, thoroughly angry, and disgusted. What was this little black fool doing with a Stutz roadster? And of course, it would be painted red—Negroes always bedecked themselves and their belongings in ridiculously unbecoming colors and ornaments. It seemed to be a part of their primitive heritage which they did not seem to have sense enough to forget and deny. Black girl—white hat—red and white striped sport suit—white shoes and stockings—red roadster. The picture was complete. All Hazel needed to complete her circus-like appearance, thought Emma Lou, was to have some purple feathers stuck in her hat.

Still talking, the girl unlocked and proceeded to start the car. As she was backing it out of the narrow parking space, Emma Lou heard a chorus of semi-suppressed giggles from a neighboring automobile. In her anger she had failed to notice that there were people in the car parked next to the Stutz. But as Hazel expertly swung her machine around, Emma Lou caught a glimpse of them. They were all colored and they were all staring at her and at Hazel. She thought she recognized one of the girls as being one of the group she had seen earlier that morning, and she did recognize the two brothers she had passed on the stairs. And as the roadster sped away, their laughter echoed in her ears, although she hadn't actually heard it. But she had seen the strain in their faces, and she knew that as soon as she and Hazel were out of sight, they would give free rein to their suppressed mirth.

Although Emma Lou had finished registering, she returned to the university campus on the following morning in order to continue her quest for collegiate companions without the alarming and unwelcome presence of Hazel Mason. She didn't know whether to be sorry for the girl and try to help her or to be disgusted and avoid her. She didn't want to be intimately associated with any such vulgar person. It would damage her own position, cause her to be classified with some one who was in a class by herself, for Emma Lou was certain that there was not, and could not be, any one else in the university just like Hazel. But despite her vulgarity, the girl was not all bad. Her good nature was infectious, and Emma Lou had surmised from her monologue on the day before how utterly unselfish a person she could be and was. All of her store of the world's goods were at hand to be used and enjoyed by her friends. There was not, as she had said, "a selfish bone in her body." But even that did not alter the disgusting fact that she was not one who would be welcome by the "right sort of people." Her flamboyant style of dress, her loud voice, her raucous laughter, and her flagrant disregard or ignorance of English grammar seemed inexcusable to Emma Lou, who was unable to understand how such a person could stray so far from the environment in which she rightfully belonged to enter a first class university. Now Hazel, according to Emma Lou, was the type of Negro who should go to a Negro college. There were plenty of them in the South whose standard of scholarship was not beyond her ability. And then, in one of those schools, her darky-like clownishness would not have to be paraded in front of white people, thereby causing discomfort and embarrassment to others of her race, more civilized and circumspect than she.

The problem irritated Emma Lou. She didn't see why it had to be. She had looked forward so anxiously, and so happily to her introductory days on the campus, and now her first experience with one of her fellow colored students had been an unpleasant one. But she didn't intend to let that make her unhappy. She was determined to return to the campus alone, seek out other companions, see whether they accepted or ignored the offending Hazel, and govern herself accordingly.

It was early and there were few people on the campus. The grass was still wet from a heavy overnight dew, and the sun had not yet dispelled the coolness of the early morning. Emma Lou's dress was of thin material and she shivered as she walked or stood in the shade. She had no school business to attend to; there was nothing for her to do but to walk aimlessly about the campus.

In another hour, Emma Lou was pleased to see that the campus walks were becoming crowded, and that the side streets surrounding the campus were now heavy with student traffic. Things were beginning to awaken. Emma Lou became jubilant and walked with jaunty step from path to path, from building to building. It then occurred to her that she had been told that there were more Negro students enrolled in the School of Pharmacy than in any other department of the university, so finding the Pharmacy building she began to wander through its crowded hallways.

Almost immediately, she saw a group of five Negro students, three boys and two girls, standing near a water fountain. She was both excited and perplexed, excited over the fact that she was so close to those she wished to find, and perplexed because she did not know how to approach them. Had there been only one person standing there, the matter would have been comparatively easy. She could have approached with a smile and said, "Good morning." The person would have returned her greeting and it would then have been a simple matter to get acquainted.

But five people in one bunch, all known to one another and all chatting intimately together!—it would seem too much like an intrusion to go bursting into their gathering—too forward and too vulgar. Then, there was nothing she could say after having said "good morning." One just didn't break into a group of five and say, "I'm Emma Lou Morgan, a new student, and I want to make friends with you." No, she couldn't do that. She would just smile as she passed, smile graciously and friendly. They would know that she was a stranger, and her smile would assure them that she was anxious to make friends, anxious to become a welcome addition to their group.

One of the group of five had sighted Emma Lou as soon as she had sighted them:

"Who's this?" queried Helen Wheaton, a senior in the College of Law.

"Some new 'pick,' I guess," answered Bob Armstrong, who was Helen's fiancé and a senior in the School of Architecture.

"I bet she's going to take Pharmacy," whispered Amos Blaine.

"She's hottentot enough to take something," mumbled Tommy Brown. "Thank God, she won't be in any of our classes, eh Amos?"

Emma Lou was almost abreast of them now. They lowered their voices, and made a pretense of mumbled conversation among themselves. Only Verne Davis looked directly at her and it was she alone who returned Emma Lou's smile.

"Whatcha grinnin' at?" Bob chided Verne as Emma Lou passed out of earshot.

"At the little frosh, of course. She grinned at me. I couldn't stare at her without returning it."

"I don't see how anybody could even look at her without grinning."

"Oh, she's not so bad," said Verne.

"Well, she's bad enough."

"That makes two of them."

"Two of what, Amos?"

"Hottentots, Bob."

"Good grief," exclaimed Tommy, "why don't you recruit some good-looking co-eds out here?"

"We don't choose them," Helen returned.

"I'm going out to the Southern Branch where the sight of my fellow female students won't give me dyspepsia."

"Ta-ta, Amos," said Verne, "and you needn't bother to sit in my car any more if you think us so terrible." She and Helen walked away, leaving the boys to discuss the sad days which had fallen upon the campus.

Emma Lou, of course, knew nothing of all this. She had gone her way rejoicing. One of the students had noticed her, had returned her smile. This getting acquainted was going to be an easy matter after all. It was just necessary that she exercise a little patience. One couldn't expect people to fall all over one without some preliminary advances. True, she was a stranger, but she would show them in good time that she was worthy of their attention, that she was a good fellow and a well-bred individual quite prepared to be accepted by the best people.

She strolled out on to campus again trying to find more prospective acquaintances. The sun was warm now, the grass dry, and the campus overcrowded. There was an infectious germ of youth and gladness abroad to which Emma Lou could not remain immune. Already she was certain that she felt the presence of that vague something known as "college spirit." It seemed to enter into her, to make her jubilant and set her every nerve tingling. This was no time for sobriety. It was the time for youth's blood to run hot, the time for love and sport and wholesome fun.

Then Emma Lou saw a solitary Negro girl seated on a stone bench. It did not take her a second to decide what to do. Here was her chance. She would make friends with this girl and should she happen to be a new student, they could become friends and together find their way into the inner circle of those colored students who really mattered.

Emma Lou was essentially a snob. She had absorbed this trait from the very people who had sought to exclude her from their presence. All of her life she had heard talk of "right sort of people," and of "the people who really mattered," and from these phrases she had formed a mental image of those to whom they applied. Hazel Mason most certainly could not be included in either of these categories. Hazel was just a vulgar little nigger from down South. It was her kind, who, when they came North, made it hard for the colored people already resident there. It was her kind who knew nothing of the social niceties or the polite conventions. In their own home they had been used only to coarse work and coarser manners. And they had been forbidden the chance to have intimate contact in schools and in public with white people from whom they might absorb some semblance of culture. When they did come North and get a chance to go to white schools, white theaters, and white libraries, they were too unused to them to appreciate what they were getting, and could be expected to continue their old way of life in an environment where such a way was decidedly out of place.

Emma Lou was determined to become associated only with those people who really mattered, northerners like herself or superior southerners, if there were any, who were different from whites only in so far as skin color was concerned. . . .

Richard Wright (1908–60)

Few writers have had Richard Wright's impact on twentieth-century American literature. In a literary career spanning several decades and genres, including fiction, autobiography, poetry, and essays, Wright forced American society to recognize the extent to which racism permeated its core. In addition, throughout his adult life, he searched for viable political and philosophical beliefs that he hoped could achieve peace for individuals and racial equality for society. Labeled a protest writer by many, Wright's fiction has been classified as a mix of naturalism, expressionism, and sensationalism.

Born in Natchez, Mississippi, Wright lived in the Deep South for the first nineteen years of his life. Those years were bitter ones for Wright because of the racial oppression of the Jim Crow system and the stern restrictions of his grandmother's religious doctrines. Uncle Tom's Children *(1938), a collection of short stories, reflects those violent and painful experiences, as does* Black Boy *(1945), an intriguing autobiography.*

Moving to Chicago in 1927, Wright confronted northern discrimination, and in the ensuing years he affiliated himself with Marxist organizations. In the 1930s, he wrote poetry for Left Front *and other magazines with an anticapitalist political stance. His political beliefs and experiences culminated in his major novel,* Native Son *(1940), which blends northern urban experiences and Communist perspectives in its presentation of black man's life in America. Through the book's protagonist, Bigger Thomas, Wright reveals the tragic psychological and social effects of racial oppression. He explains in the introduction to* Native Son *"How 'Bigger' Was Born": "I had written a book of short stories which was published under the title of* Uncle Tom's Children. *When the reviews of that book began to appear, I realized that I had made an awfully naive mistake. I found that I had written a book which even bankers' daughters could read and weep over and feel good about. I swore to myself that if I ever wrote another book, no one would weep over it; that it would be so hard and deep that they would have to face it without the consolation of tears."*

By the mid-1940s, Wright had turned away from the Communist Party and left the United States to reside in France. Much has been written of his exposure to French writers and philosophers and of their influence on his provocative novel The Outsider *(1953). The story focuses on the black protagonist, Cross Damon, whose life is overwrought with emotional and financial complications. The novel is thick with philosophy, violence, and symbolism; African American critic Nathan Scott, Jr., offers this mixed assessment of the work: "It may appear to be only a rather lurid sort of potboiler; and, to be sure, there is no minimizing the harshness of its violence. Yet, for all of its melodramatic sensationalism, it is an impressive book. Indeed, it is one of the very few American novels of our time that, in admitting into itself a large body of systematic ideas, makes us think that it wants seriously to compete with the major philosophic intelligence in the contemporary period."*

Wright's later fiction includes the novels Savage Holiday *(1954),* The Long Dream *(1958), and* Lawd Today *(published posthumously in 1963); and a mosaic of fiction and autobiography,* Eight Men *(1961), also published after his death. Augmenting Wright's fiction are other works that explore the nature of culture and society around the world.* Black Power *(1954) examines African culture and politics;* The Color Curtain *(1956) focuses on Asia; and* Pagan Spain *(1957) contains critical commentary on that country.* White Man, Listen! *(1957) is a collection of Wright's lectures on culture and race.*

The following selection, "The Man Who Killed a Shadow," was originally published in Eight Men. *The story centers on Saul Saunders, a black man who struggles with the psychological and social forces that dictate his behavior. Like his literary ancestor Bigger Thomas in* Native Son, *Saul is trapped by racist proscriptions that leave him little control over his life.*

The Man Who Killed a Shadow

It all began long ago when he was a tiny boy who was already used, in a fearful sort of way, to living with shadows. But what were the shadows that made him afraid? Surely they were not those beautiful silhouettes of objects cast upon the earth by the sun. Shadows of that kind are innocent and he loved trying to catch them as he ran along sunlit paths in summer. But there were subtler shadows which he saw and which others could not see: the shadows of his fears. And this boy had such shadows and he lived to kill one of them.

Saul Saunders was born black in a little Southern town, not many miles from Washington, the nation's capital, which means that he came into a world that was split in two, a white world and a black one, the white one being separated from the black by a million psychological miles. So, from the very beginning, Saul looking timidly out from his black world, saw the shadowy outlines of a white world that was unreal to him and not his own.

It so happened that even Saul's mother was but a vague, shadowy thing to him, for she died long before his memory could form an image of her. And the same thing happened to Saul's father, who died before the boy could retain a clear picture of him in his mind.

People really never became personalities to Saul, for hardly had he ever got to know them before they vanished. So people became for Saul symbols of uneasiness, of a deprivation that evoked in him a sense of the transitory quality of life, which always made him feel that some invisible, unexplainable event was about to descend upon him.

He had five brothers and two sisters who remained strangers to him. There was, of course, no adult in his family with enough money to support them all, and the children were rationed out to various cousins, uncles, aunts, and grandparents.

It fell to Saul to live with his grandmother who moved constantly from one small Southern town to another, and even physical landscapes grew to have but little emotional meaning for the boy. Towns were places you lived in for a while, and then you moved on. When he had reached the age of twelve, all reality seemed to him to be akin to his mother and father, like the white world that surrounded the black island of his life, like the parade of dirty little towns that passed forever before his eyes, things that had names but not substance, things that happened and then retreated into an incomprehensible nothingness.

Saul was not dumb or lazy, but it took him seven years to reach the third grade in school. None of the people who came and went in Saul's life had ever prized learning and Saul did likewise. It was quite normal in his environment to reach the age of fourteen and still be in the third grade, and Saul liked being normal, liked being like other people.

Then the one person—his grandmother—who Saul had thought would endure forever, passed suddenly from his life, and from that moment on Saul did not ever quite know what to do. He went to work for the white people of the South and the shadow-like quality of his world became terribly manifest, continuously present. He understood nothing of this white world into which he had been thrown; it was just there, a faint and fearful shadow cast by some object that stood between him and a hidden and powerful sun.

He quickly learned that the strange white people for whom he worked considered him inferior; he did not feel inferior and he did not think that he was. But when he looked about him he saw other black people accepting this definition of themselves, and who was he to challenge it? Outwardly he grew to accept it as part of the vast shadow-world that came and went, pulled by forces which he nor nobody he knew understood.

Soon all of Saul's anxieties, fears, and irritations became focused upon this white shadow-world which gave him his daily bread in exchange for his labor. Feeling unhappy and not knowing why, he projected his misery out from himself and upon the one thing that made him most constantly anxious. If this had not happened, if Saul had not found a way of putting his burden upon others, he would have early thought of suicide. He finally did, in the end, think of killing himself, but then it was too late . . .

At the age of fifteen Saul knew that the life he was then living was to be his lot, that there was no way to rid himself of his plaguing sense of unreality, no way to relax and forget. He was most self-forgetful when he was with black people, and that made things a little easier for him. But as he grew older, he became more afraid, yet none of his friends noticed it. Indeed, many of Saul's friends liked him very much. Saul was always kind, attentive; but no one suspected that his kindness, his quiet, waiting loyalty came from his being afraid.

Then Saul changed. Maybe it was luck or misfortune; it is hard to tell. When he took a drink of whisky, he found that it helped to banish the shadows, lessened his tensions, made the world more reasonably three-dimensional, and he grew to like drinking. When he was paid off on a Saturday night, he would drink with his friends and he would feel better. He felt that whisky made life complete, that it stimulated him. But, of course, it did not. Whisky really depressed him, numbed him somewhat, reduced the force and number of the shadows that made him tight inside.

When Saul was sober, he almost never laughed in the presence of the white shadow-world, but when he had a drink or two he found that he could. Even when he was told about the hard lives that all Negroes lived, it did not worry him, for he would take a drink and not feel too badly. It did not even bother him when he heard that if you were alone with a white woman and she screamed, it was as good as hearing your death sentence, for, though you had done nothing, you would be killed. Saul got used to hearing the siren of the police car screaming in the Black Belt, got used to seeing white cops dragging Negroes off to jail. Once he grew wildly angry about it, felt that the shadows would some day claim him as he had seen them claim others, but his friends warned him that it was dangerous to feel that way, that always the black man lost, and the best thing to do was to take a drink. He did, and in a little while they were all laughing.

One night when he was mildly drunk—he was thirty years old and living in Washington at the time—he got married. The girl was good for Saul, for she too liked to drink and she was pretty and they got along together. Saul now felt that things were not so bad; as long as he could stifle the feeling of being hemmed in, as long as he could conquer the anxiety about the unexpected happening, life was bearable.

Saul's jobs had been many and simple. First he had worked on a farm. When he was fourteen he had gone to Washington, after his grandmother had died, where he did all kinds of odd jobs. Finally he was hired by an old white army colonel as chauffeur and butler and he averaged about twenty dollars every two weeks. He lived in and got his meals and uniform and remained with the colonel for five years. The colonel too liked to drink, and sometimes they would both get drunk. But Saul never forgot that the colonel, though drunk and feeling fine, was still a shadow, unreal, and might suddenly change toward him.

One day, when whisky was making him feel good, Saul asked the colonel for a raise in salary, told him that he did not have enough to live on, and that prices were rising. But the colonel was sober and hard that day and said no. Saul was so stunned that he quit the job that instant. While under the spell of whisky he had for a quick moment felt that the world of shadows was over, but when he had asked for more money and had been refused, he knew that he had been wrong. He should not have asked for money; he should have known that the colonel was a no-good guy, a shadow.

Saul was next hired as an exterminator by a big chemical company and he found that there was something in his nature that made him like going from house to house and putting down poison for rats and mice and roaches. He liked seeing concrete evidence of his work and the dead bodies of rats were no shadows. They were real. He never felt better in his life than when he was killing with the sanction of society. And his boss even increased his salary when he asked for it. And he drank as much as he liked and no one cared.

But one morning, after a hard night of drinking which had made him irritable and high-strung, his boss said something that he did not like and he spoke up, defending himself against what he thought was a slighting remark. There was an argument and Saul left.

Two weeks of job hunting got him the position of janitor in the National Cathedral, a church and religious institution. It was the solitary kind of work he liked; he reported for duty each morning at seven o'clock and at eleven he was through. He first cleaned the Christmas card shop, next he cleaned the library; and his final chore was to clean the choir room.

But cleaning the library, with its rows and rows of books, was what caught Saul's attention, for there was a strange little shadow woman there who stared at him all the time in a most peculiar way. The library was housed in a separate building and, whenever he came to clean it, he and the white woman would be there alone. She was tiny, blonde, blue-eyed, weighing about 110 pounds, and standing about five feet three inches. Saul's boss had warned him never to quarrel with the lady in charge of the library. "She's a crackpot," he had told Saul. And naturally Saul never wanted any trouble, in fact, he did not even know the woman's name. Many times, however, he would pause in his work, feeling that his eyes were being drawn to her and he would turn around and find her staring at him. Then she would look away quickly, as though ashamed. "What in hell does she want from me?" he wondered uneasily. The woman never spoke to him except to say good morning and she even said that as though she did not want to say it. Saul thought that maybe she was afraid of him; but how could that be? He could not recall when anybody had ever been afraid of him, and he had never been in any trouble in his life.

One morning while sweeping the floor he felt his eyes being drawn toward her and he paused and turned and saw her staring at him. He did not move, neither did she. They stared at each other for about ten seconds, then she went out of the room, walking with quick steps, as though angry or afraid. He was frightened, but forgot it quickly. "What the hell's wrong with that woman?" he asked himself.

Next morning Saul's boss called him and told him, in a nice quiet tone—but it made him scared and mad just the same—that the woman in the library had complained about him, had said that he never cleaned under her desk.

"Under her desk?" Saul asked, amazed.

"Yes," his boss said, amused at Saul's astonishment.

"But I clean under her desk every morning," Saul said.

"Well, Saul, remember, I told you she was a crackpot," his boss said soothingly. "Don't argue with her. Just do your work."

"Yes, sir," Saul said.

He wanted to tell his boss how the woman always stared at him, but he could not find courage enough to do so. If he had been talking with his black friends, he would have done so quite naturally. But why talk to one shadow about another queer shadow?

That day being payday, he got his weekly wages and that night he had a hell of a good time. He drank until he was drunk, until he blotted out almost everything from his consciousness. He was getting regularly drunk now whenever he had the money. He liked it and he bothered nobody and he was happy while doing it. But dawn found him broke, exhausted, and terribly depressed, full of shadows and uneasiness, a way he never liked it. The thought of going to his job made him angry. He longed for deep, heavy sleep. But, no, he had a good job and he had to keep it. Yes, he would go.

After cleaning the Christmas card shop—he was weak and he sweated a lot—he went to the library. No one was there. He swept the floor and was about to dust the books when he heard the footsteps of the woman coming into the room. He was tired, nervous, half asleep; his hands trembled and his reflexes were overquick. "So you're the bitch who snitched on me, hunh?" he said irritably to himself. He continued dusting and all at once he had the queer feeling that she was staring at him. He fought against the impulse to look at her, but he could not resist it. He turned slowly and saw that she was sitting in her chair at her desk, staring at him with unblinking eyes. He had the impression that she was about to speak. He could not help staring back at her, waiting.

"Why don't you clean under my desk?" she asked him in a tense but controlled voice.

"Why, ma'am," he said slowly, "I just did."

"Come here and look," she said, pointing downward.

He replaced the book on the shelf. She had never spoken so many words to him before. He went and stood before her and his mind protested against what his eyes saw, and then his senses leaped in wonder. She was sitting with her knees sprawled apart and her dress was drawn halfway up her legs. He looked from her round blue eyes to her white legs whose thighs thickened as they went to a V clothed in tight, sheer, pink panties; then he looked quickly again into her eyes. Her face was a beet red, but she sat very still, rigid, as though she was being impelled into an act which she did not want to perform but was being driven to perform. Saul was so startled that he could not move.

"I just cleaned under your desk this morning," he mumbled, sensing that he was not talking about what she meant.

"There's dust there now," she said sternly, her legs still so wide apart that he felt that she was naked.

He did not know what to do; he was so baffled, humiliated, and frightened that he grew angry. But he was afraid to express his anger openly.

"Look, ma'am," he said in a tone of suppressed rage and hate, "you're making trouble for me!"

"Why don't you do your work?" she blazed at him. "That's what you're being paid to do, you black nigger!" Her legs were still spread wide and she was sitting as though about to spring upon him and throw her naked thighs about his body.

For a moment he was still and silent. Never before in his life had he been called a "black nigger." He had heard that white people used that phrase as their supreme humiliation of black people, but he had never been treated so. As the insult sank in, as he stared at her gaping thighs, he felt overwhelmed by a sense of wild danger.

"I don't like that," he said and before he knew it he had slapped her flat across her face.

She sucked in her breath, sprang up, and stepped away from him. Then she screamed sharply, and her voice was like a lash cutting into his chest. She screamed again and he backed away from her. He felt helpless, strange; he knew what he had done, knew its meaning for him; but he knew that he could not have helped it. It seemed that some part of him was there in that room watching him do things that he should not do. He drew in his breath and for a moment he felt that he could not stand upon his legs. His world was now full of all the shadows he had ever feared. He was in the worst trouble that a black man could imagine.

The woman was screaming continuously now and he was running toward the stairs. Just as he put his foot on the bottom step, he paused and looked over his shoulder. She was backing away from him, toward an open window at the far end of the room, still screaming. Oh God! In her scream he heard the sirens of the police cars that hunted down black men in the Black Belts and he heard the shrill whistles of white cops running after black men and he felt again in one rush of emotion all the wild and bitter tales he had heard of how whites always got the black who did a crime and this woman was screaming as though he had raped her.

He ran on up the steps, but her screams were coming so loud that when he neared the top of the steps he slowed. Those screams would not let him run any more, they weakened him, tugged and pulled him. His chest felt as though it would burst. He reached the top landing and looked round aimlessly. He saw a fireplace and before it was a neat pile of wood and while he was looking at that pile of wood the screams tore at him, unnerved him. With a shaking hand he reached down and seized in his left hand—for he was lefthanded—a heavy piece of oaken firewood that had jagged, sharp edges where it had been cut with an ax. He turned and ran back down the steps to where the woman stood screaming. He lifted the stick of wood as he confronted her, then paused. He wanted her to stop screaming. If she had stopped, he would have fled, but while she screamed all he could feel was a hotness bubbling in him and urging him to do something. She would fill her lungs quickly and deeply and her breath would come out at full blast. He swung down his left arm and hit her a swinging blow on the side of her head, not to hurt her, not to kill her, but to stop that awful noise, to stop that shadow from screaming a scream that meant death . . . He felt her skull crack and give as she sank to the floor, but she still screamed. He trembled from head to feet. Goddamn that woman . . . Why didn't she stop that yelling? He lifted his arm and gave her another blow, feeling the oaken stick driving its way into her skull. But still she screamed. He was about to hit her again when he became aware that the stick he held was light. He looked at it and found that half of it had broken off, was lying on the floor. But she screamed on, with blood running down her dress, he legs sprawled nakedly out from under her. He dropped the remainder of the stick and grabbed her throat and choked her to stop her screams. That seemed to quiet her; she looked as though she had fainted. He choked her for a long time, not trying to kill her, but just to make sure that she would not scream again and make him wild and hot inside. He was not reacting to the woman, but to the feelings that her screams evoked in him.

The woman was limp and silent now and slowly he took his hands from her throat. She was quiet. He waited. He was not certain. Yes, take her downstairs into the bathroom and if she screamed again no one would hear her . . . He took her hands in his and started dragging her away from the window. His hands were wet with sweat and her hands were so tiny and soft that time and again her little fingers slipped out of his palms. He tried holding her hands tighter and only succeeded in scratching her. Her ring slid off into his hand while he was dragging her and he stood still for a moment, staring in a daze at the thin band of shimmering gold, then mechanically he put it into his pocket. Finally he dragged her down the steps to the bathroom door.

He was about to take her in when he saw that the floor was spotted with drippings of blood. That was bad . . . He had been trained to keep floors clean, just as he had been trained to fear shadows. He propped her clumsily against a wall and went into the bathroom, and took wads of toilet paper and mopped up the red splashes. He even went back upstairs where he had first struck her and found blood spots and wiped them up carefully. He stiffened; she was hollering again. He ran downstairs and this time he recalled that he had a knife in his pocket. He took it out, opened it, and plunged it deep into her throat; he was frantic to stop her from hollering . . . He pulled the knife from her throat and she was quiet.

He stood, his eyes roving. He noticed a door leading down to a recess in a wall through which steam pipes ran. Yes, it would be better to put her there; then if she started yelling no one would hear her. He was not trying to hide her; he merely wanted to make sure that she would not be heard. He dragged her again and her dress came up over her knees to her chest and again he saw her pink panties. It was too hard dragging her and he lifted her in his arms and while carrying her down the short flight of steps he thought that the pink panties, if he would wet them, would make a good mop to clean up the blood. Once more he sat her against the wall, stripped her of her pink panties—and not once did he so much as glance at her groin—wetted them and swabbed up the spots, then pushed her into the recess under the pipes. She was in full view, easily seen. He tossed the wet ball of panties in after her.

He sighed and looked around. The floor seemed clean. He went back upstairs. That stick of broken wood . . . He picked up the two shattered ends of wood and several splinters; he carefully joined the ends together and then fitted the splinters into place. He laid the mended stick back upon the pile before the fireplace. He stood listening, wondering if she would yell again, but there was no sound. It never occurred to him that he could help her, that she might be in pain; he never wondered even if she were dead. He got his coat and hat and went home.

He was nervously tired. It seemed that he had just finished doing an old and familiar job of dodging the shadows that were forever around him, shadows that he could not understand. He undressed, but paid no attention to the blood on his trousers and shirt; he was alone in the room; his wife was at work. When he pulled out his billfold, he saw the ring. He put it in the drawer of his night table, more to keep his wife from seeing it than to hide it. He climbed wearily into bed and at once fell into a deep, sound sleep from which he did not awaken until late afternoon. He lay blinking bloodshot eyes and he could not remember what he had done. Then the vague, shadowlike picture of it came before his eyes. He was puzzled, and for a moment he wondered if it had happened or had someone told him a story of it. He could not be sure. There was no fear or regret in him.

When at last the conviction of what he had done was real in him, it came only in terms of flat memory, devoid of all emotion, as though he were looking when very tired and sleepy at a scene being flashed upon the screen of a movie house. Not knowing what to do, he remained in bed. He had drifted off to sleep again when his wife came home late that night from her cooking job.

Next morning he ate breakfast his wife prepared, rose from the table and kissed her, and started off toward the Cathedral as though nothing had happened. It was not until he actually got up to the Cathedral steps that he became shaky and nervous. He stood before the door for two or three minutes, and then he realized that he could not go back in there this morning. Yet it was not danger that made him feel this way, but a queer kind of repugnance. Whether the woman was alive or not did not enter his mind. He still did not know what to do. Then he remembered that his wife, before she had left for her job, had asked him to buy some groceries. Yes, he would do that. He wanted to do that because he did not know what else on earth to do.

He bought the groceries and took them home, then spent the rest of the day wandering from bar to bar. Not once did he think of fleeing. He would go home, sit, turn on the radio, then go out into the streets and walk. Finally he would end up at a bar, drinking. On one of his many trips into the house, he changed his clothes, rolled up his bloody shirt and trousers, put the blood-stained knife inside the bundle, and pushed it into a far corner of a closet. He got his gun and put it into his pocket, for he was nervously depressed.

But he still did not know what to do. Suddenly he recalled that some months ago he had bought a cheap car which was now in a garage for repairs. He went to the garage and persuaded the owner to take it back for twenty-five dollars; the thought that he could use the car for escape never came to his mind. During that afternoon and early evening he sat in bars and drank. What he felt now was no different from what he had felt all his life.

Toward eight o'clock that night he met two friends of his and invited them for a drink. He was quite drunk now. Before him on the table was a sandwich and a small glass of whisky. He leaned forward, listening sleepily to one of his friends tell a story about a girl, and then he heard:

"Aren't you Saul Saunders?"

He looked up into the faces of two white shadows.

"Yes," he admitted readily. "What do you want?"

"You'd better come along with us. We want to ask you some questions," one of the shadows said.

"What's this all about?" Saul asked.

They grabbed his shoulders and he stood up. Then he reached down and picked up the glass of whisky and drank it. He walked steadily out of the bar to a waiting auto, a policeman to each side of him, his mind a benign blank. It was not until they were about to put him into the car that something happened and whipped his numbed senses to an apprehension of danger. The policeman patted his waist for arms; they found nothing because his gun was strapped to his chest. Yes, he ought to kill himself . . . The thought leaped into his mind with such gladness that he shivered. It was the answer to everything. Why had he not thought of it before?

Slowly he took off his hat and held it over his chest to hide the movement of his left hand, then he reached inside of his shirt and pulled out the gun. One of the policemen pounced on him and snatched the gun.

"So, you're trying to kill us too, hunh?" one asked.

"Naw. I was trying to kill myself," he answered simply.

"Like hell you were!"

A fist came onto his jaw and he sank back limp.

Two hours later, at the police station, he told them everything speaking in a low, listless voice without a trace of emotion, vividly describing every detail, yet feeling that it was utterly hopeless for him to try to make them understand how horrible it was for him to hear that woman screaming. His narrative sounded so brutal that the policemen's faces were chalky.

Weeks later a voice droned in a court room and he sat staring dully.

". . . The Grand Jurors of the United States of America, in and for the District of Columbia aforesaid, upon their oath, do present:

"That one Saul Saunders, on, to wit, the first day of March, 19—, and at and within the District of Columbia aforesaid, contriving and intending to kill one Maybelle Eva Houseman . . ."

"So *that's* her name," he said to himself in amazement.

". . . Feloniously, wilfully, purposefully, and of his deliberate and premeditated malice did strike, beat, and wound the said Maybelle Eva Houseman, in and upon the front of the head and in and upon the right side of the head of her, the said Maybelle Eva Houseman, two certain mortal wounds and fractures; and did fix and fasten about the neck and throat of her, the said Maybelle Eva Houseman, his hand or hands—but whether it was one of his hands or both of his hands is to the Grand Jury aforesaid unknown—and that he, the said Saul Saunders, with his hand or hands as aforesaid fixed and fastened about the throat of her, did choke and strangle the said Maybelle Eva Houseman, of which said choking and strangling the said Maybelle Eva Houseman, on, to wit, the said first day of March, 19—, and at and within the said District of Columbia, did die."

He longed for a drink, but that was impossible now. Then he took a deep breath and surrendered to the world of shadows about him, the world he had feared so long; and at once the tension went from him and he felt better than he had felt in a long time. He was amazed at how relaxed and peaceful it was when he stopped fighting the world of shadows.

". . . By force and violence and against resistance and by putting in fear, did steal, take, and carry away, from and off the person and from the immediate, actual possession of one Maybelle Eva Houseman, then and there being, a certain finger ring, of the value of, to wit, ten dollars."

He listened now with more attention but no anxiety:

"And in and while perpetrating robbery aforesaid did kill and murder the said Maybelle Eva Houseman; against the form of the statute in such case made and provided, and against the peace and government of the United States of America."

P.S. Thereupon Dr. Herman Stein was called as a witness and being first duly sworn testified as follows:

". . . On examination of the genital organs there was no evidence of contusion, abrasion, or trauma, and the decedent's hymen ring was intact. This decedent had not been criminally assaulted or attempted to be entered. It has been ascertained that the decedent's age was 40."

Chester Himes (1909–84)

A *literary defender of black manhood against a host of belittling forces, Chester Himes spent a portion of his literary career lost within the shadow of his friend Richard Wright. And though there are similarities in tone and theme between the two authors, Himes's work is no mere imitation of Wright's.*

Born in Jefferson City, Missouri, Himes grew up in Mississippi and Ohio. Although he entered Ohio State University in the late 1920s, he did not complete a degree for reasons that remain unclear. He became involved with gambling, and in 1928 he was sentenced to the Ohio State Penitentiary for robbery. While incarcerated, Himes began publishing short stories. As black critic Arthur P. Davis points out, "After his release [from prison] in 1936, Himes began a bizarre life, doing many things, living in many places—Chicago, San Francisco, Los Angeles, and New York. Although he followed other pursuits temporarily, he always came back to his writing."

Himes's novels include If He Hollers Let Him Go *(1945),* Lonely Crusade *(1947),* Cast the First Stone *(1952),* Third Generation *(1954),* The Primitive *(1955), and* Pinktoes *(1965).*

Relocating to Europe in the mid-1950s, Himes won acclaim in France for a series of detective novels, which are set in America and feature two black detectives—Coffin Ed Smith and Gravedigger Jones. Published later in America, these novels include The Real Cool Killers *(1959),* The Crazy Kill *(1959),* All

Shot Up (1960), The Big Gold Dream *(1960),* A Rage in Harlem *(1965),* Cotton Comes to Harlem *(1965),* Run Man Run *(1966), and* Blind Man with a Pistol *(1969). When two of them—*Cotton Comes to Harlem *and* A Rage in Harlem*—were made into movies, in 1970 and 1992, respectively, Himes gained the attention of a wider, younger audience. His personal story,* The Quality of Hurt, *was published in 1972.*

The following selection, "One More Way to Die," originally appeared in 1946. Capturing the violent world of its narrator, William Brown, the story emphasizes the racist victimization wielded by the system's authority figures.

One More Way to Die

When I got off work at the cannery, I went home and washed the slop off my hands and face and washed under my arms then changed from my overalls to a slack suit. I got my money out of the tin can back of the stove where I kept it hid and counted it. I had eighteen bucks and some change. I went out and walked up Long Beach to José's at the corner of 40th and bought a quart of beer.

José wiped the bar with a dirty rag, then wiped the sweat off his face with the same rag and said, "You owe me thirty-five cents from yesterday."

"Pay you munanner," I said.

"Always mañana, mañana!" he beefed and spit in the sink.

"Hey, don't spit in the sink where you wash the glasses," some paddy down the bar said.

José shrugged. "All the same," he said.

I beat at the flies and drank my beer. It made me sweat like a son of a gun.

"The Spanish kid," another paddy took it up. "Spit where you please, Spanish."

José wiped his face with the dirty rag and gave the paddy a side-wise look.

There was three paddies and a coupla Mexes and two other spooks scattered along the bar. Some pachuco kids were ganged about the juke box, talking in Mex and blowing weed; and a coupla beat-up colored mamas sat in the window booth waiting for chumps. In the next booth a big snuff-dipping mama had her two slaving studs in overalls; and the booth in back had a coupla Mexes from old Mexico drinking "Mus-I-Tell."

When I finished my second quart, I had to go. I went out in the alley at the side. Then I went back and said, "Gimme another quart, les fill 'er up again."

Two old beat-up high-yellow biddies came in with a big yellow stud called "Sweet Wine" who went for bad. They sat down beside me and Sweet Wine leaned on my shoulder and said, "Buy us some beer, Tar Baby."

I didn't like the stud, and I didn't like to be called "Tar Baby"—Brown is my name—but I didn't have my blade so I just said, "Here, you can have some of what I got," shoving him the bottle.

He picked it up and drank it dry and set it down.

"Now ain't dat sompin'," one of the old biddies said to the other. "Ain't offered you or me a drap." She turned to me, "You'll buy us a lil beer, won'tcha, mister?"

Sweet Wine said, "Sure, this nigger'll buy us a drink; he got everything, working at the cannery, making all that gold. Come on, Tar Baby, set us up."

I knew he was looking for trouble. "Four wines," I said to José.

I had to break a five to pay him. The biddy next to me leaned over and said, "Come on, les you'n me have some fun."

The other old biddy giggled.

I said, "What's the matter with the fun you already got?"

"That nigger done gone," she said.

The other old biddy giggled again.

I looked around and sure 'nough, Sweet Wine had slipped out. I oughta know that old yellow hag didn't want nobody black as me, but I said anyway, "Come on down to my pad."

We hadn't no more than got outside by the alley, when she grabbed me from behind and Sweet Wine came out the alley and cold-cocked me. When I come to, the pachucos had me halfway up the alley, rolling me. I turned over, braced my hands against the ground, pushed to my knees. Then I got to my feet. My jaw felt numb. I fingered it lightly, moved it from side to side to see if it was broken.

Then I said to the pachucos, "Gimme back my dough."

One of them laughed. "Sweet Wine cleaned you 'fore he turned you loose."

"He sure clipped you," another said.

I fanned myself anyway, just to be sure, but I was bare. "Which-away they go?" I asked.

The pachucos shrugged. I started home to get my blade to look for 'em and run into a police cruiser down at Vernon.

"Hey!" I called. "Wait a minute; I been robbed."

The young cop driving backed over to the curb and said, "Cummere, boy."

I came over by the car, and he and the other cop, an older man with gray hair and a sergeant's stripes, looked me up and down.

"Who robbed you?" the young cop asked.

"A fellow they call Sweet Wine," I said. "He and some woman who was with him."

"Where'd they rob you?"

"Down by the alley right next to José's."

He sniffed my breath. "Drunk, eh? They rolled you, eh?"

"No sir. I was in José's drinking beer and wasn't bothering nobody when they come in and want me to buy 'em a drink. I bought 'em the drink just to keep from having no trouble, then Sweet Wine, he left. Then after a while me and the woman come out and—"

"Oh, you were with the woman?" he cut in.

"No sir. I just come out with her. Sweet Wine, he was *with* her. I just come out on the street with her. Then she grabbed me, and he cold-cocked me. When I come to—"

"What's your name, boy?" he cut in again.

"Brown," I said. "William Brown."

"What do they call you?"

"Well, some calls me Tar Baby, but most just calls me Brown by my name."

"You ain't the Tar Baby what stabbed that sailor up here a coupla nights ago, are you?" he asked.

"No sir. I ain't been up here a couple nights ago. I work at the cannery," I told him.

The sergeant said, "I knew a dinge in Kansas City called Ruckus Fuckus."

"We picked up a boy the other night called White Baby," the young cop said. "He was black as my shoe."

They laughed a little. Then the young cop jumped out the car and shook me down. When he didn't find anything, he said, "Where's that knife, boy?"

"I don't carry no knife," I said.

He got back in the car and started the motor. The sergeant said, "Better go home, boy. We'll find Sweet Wine and get your money. How much was it you said he took?"

" 'Bout fifteen dollars."

I went home and got my knife and put it in my pocket and went back to José's. Sweet Wine and the woman hadn't come back. I walked down Long Beach to the Cove at 36th. They weren't there either. I cut across to Ascot, stopped in two or three joints along the way, then turned back out toward Vernon.

It was about eleven o'clock when I found them out at the new Dew Drop Inn at 51st and Hooper. I saw the old hag sitting at the bar guzzling juice, but I didn't see Sweet Wine. Next to her a guy was drinking a quart of beer. The bar was filled, and all the booths along the wall was filled. There was a lot of people standing around.

I went in and picked up the quart bottle the guy had next to her and broke it across her head. She staggered up, snapped open a switchblade knife and slashed at me. I jumped back and popped open my blade and cut her on the arm. Sweet Wine come from somewhere behind me and hit me across the head with a chair.

I fell forward into her, butting her back into the Juke Box. I went down on my hands and knees but I turned and crawled between somebody's legs before she got herself set. People was running all around trying to get out the way so neither of us could get to the other. Sweet Wine got over to one side of me and reached around behind a guy and hit me with the chair again. Somebody kicked me on the side of the face trying to get out the way. I got between somebody's legs and cut Sweet Wine on the leg. I just reached around the fat part of his leg and pulled my shiv forward like I was chopping down sugar cane. He kicked me in the mouth, and I stabbed him in the thigh.

People was all running out into the street, screaming and cussing. The old hag run up and stabbed me in the back. I jumped to my feet and began slashing out right and left, cutting at everybody. What people was left, run over each other trying to get out of the way. I moved around, getting both her and Sweet Wine in front of me, then I jumped at 'em and slashed as fast as I could move my arm. I didn't cut neither one of 'em. The old hag ran toward me, slashing back and forth like I was. She didn't cut me, neither, but she made me back up. I kept on backing up until I backed into something, and I looked around and saw cases of pop bottles stacked against the wall.

I slashed at her real fast until she backed up a little; then I stuck my knife in my pocket and started chunking bottles. The first one popped Sweet Wine square in the forehead and bust the skin wide open; the next one caught him in the mouth and bust his lips. The woman was running around trying to get behind the bar to chunk some wine bottles and the bartender was trying to stop her. Her arm was bloody where I had cut her and she bled all over the floor. Sweet Wine turned and tried to run, but his leg was cut so bad all he could do was hobble.

I bust him a couple of times in the back, but I was chunking bottles so fast I couldn't see where they was going.

Then all of a sudden I heard somebody scream, "He hit me with a bottle!" and I looked up and saw an old white woman standing in the door with blood coming out of her head.

Everybody knew her. She was an old wino used to come there every night and get juiced up. Lived somewhere close by.

But when we saw her standing there with the blood coming out her head everybody stopped and just gaped at her. We quit fighting and just stood there. I was scared maybe I had killed her and she a white woman, too.

She started cussing everybody out and then the police came. They were two young guys this time. They held all four of us there waiting for the ambulance and the paddy wagon and they kept gritting their teeth and looking at me.

"This the nigger what hit you, mam?" one of 'em asked the old white lady, grabbing me by the collar.

"That's the dirty black bastard!" she screamed. "Hitting me with a pop bottle!"

"I didn't go to hit you, lady," I said. I was scared as hell. "I wasn't chunking at you, lady. I was chunking at these people what rob—"

The cop drew back and hit me in the mouth. "Shut up, you black son of a bitch," he said. "Goddamn you, we kill niggers for hitting white women in Texas."

People was coming back into the joint and they was crowding all about looking at us but wasn't nobody saying nothing. They just stood there looking black and evil and wondering what the cops was going to do to me.

"I didn't go to hit her, cap," I said. "Hones' to God—"

"Well, goddamn you, you black bastard, what'd you hit her for?" the other cop asked.

"She just happen to come in, cap; you know I wasn't chunking at no white—"

"Goddamn you, don't you say nothing when you talk back to me!" he said.

"Yes sir."

"If I had you in Texas—" the first cop began.

About that time the ambulance drove up. They put the white woman in on the stretchers, and the other woman sat there in the back on a chair. Then they looked at me and Sweet Wine. They wrapped a string of something around Sweet Wine's leg and drew it tight and said it'd be all right to bring him down in the paddy wagon. When they started to look at me, one of the cops said, "We'll bring this nigger in, he ain't hurt!"

The other cop said, "Yet!"

"I'se stabbed in the back—" I began. The first cop hit me in the mouth again.

When the paddy wagon came they put Sweet Wine in it and drove off, then they took me out to the cruiser and put me in the back seat with one of the cops sitting beside me.

"Where y'll taking me, cap?" I asked. "Y'll ain't gonna beat me, are you, cap?"

"Shut up, you black son of a bitch!" the cop said, and hit me across the mouth with his pistol butt.

I didn't say no more. They turned up Vernon to Long Beach and kept downtown 'til they came to where the railroad tracks split off. Then they drove up a dark alley beside a scrap iron foundry and the cop told me to get out.

"Cap'n, you oughtn'ta whip me," I began. "I'se hurt, cap, I'se been—"

He grabbed me by the collar and jerked me out on the ground. I lay there just like I fell, scared to move. The other cop got out and came around the car. One of them shot me. My stomach went hollow and my chest seemed to cave in. I was so scared I couldn't hardly breathe. "Y'all ain't gonna shoot me, are you cap?" I begged.

One of the cops laughed. "What's he think we're doing now."

"This is what we do with niggers in Texas," the other one said, and shot me square through the stomach.

"Cap'n, y'all ain't gonna kill me!" I cried.

They stood there looking down at me, grinning. One of them spit at me. Then the whole sky began to spin around and around and the telegraph poles along Long Beach began shimmying like they were alive and then everything began to go away. I kept looking at the two cops, looking at their faces until they was just blurred and white, and I couldn't hardly make 'em out at all.

I was begging 'em over and over again, "Cap'n, please don't kill me. Please cap'n. I swear I'll never hit another white woman as long as I live, not even by mistake." I knew my lips were moving, but I couldn't even hear my own voice.

I heard the first cop says, "Let's get it over with."

Then I heard the sound of the shot and felt the bullet go right through my chest. I couldn't even see nothing at all. I felt myself leaking all inside. It was just like a kettle on the stove and begin running over. But I didn't hurt much. I was just going on away.

The last thing I heard was a whole lot of shots real fast and I could feel all the bullets going through me. But they didn't hurt at all. It was just like a guy sticking a fork in soft butter. Like a guy jabbing an icepick into a piece of fresh killed meat.

The last thing I thought as I lay there on the goddamned ground and died was, "It's just ain't no goddamned sense in you white folks killing me."

Ann Petry (1911–)

Coming from a New England background in Old Saybrook, Connecticut, Ann Petry initially followed her family's tradition by becoming a pharmacist, receiving her degree in that field from the University of Connecticut. However, in 1938, she moved to Harlem to begin a new life and career as a journalist, writing for the Amsterdam News *and later the* People's Voice.

Petry began publishing short stories in the early 1940s, but it was her first novel, The Street *(1946), that gained her a wide audience. The novel, which concentrates on an African American mother and her son as they face the challenges of Harlem's tough environment, won a Houghton Mifflin Fellowship. Addison Gayle describes Petry as "a master of the metaphor and the image, proficient in the creation of suggestive art. Her style varies, ranging from the sharp, crisp idiom of the black community in her first novel . . . to the stilted language of the English romantics . . . in* The Narrows."

The Street *was followed by two other novels:* Country Place *(1947), which centers on white characters living in a small, conservative town; and* The Narrows *(1953), an interracial love story set in a New England town. In addition, Petry wrote a number of books for young readers, including* The Drug Store Cat

(1949), Harriet Tubman: Conductor of the Underground Railroad *(1955),* Tituba of Salem Village *(1964), and* Legends of the Saints *(1970).*

The following selection "The Witness," originally appeared in Petry's short story collection, Miss Muriel and Other Stories *(1971). The story portrays the dilemma of black intellectual and teacher, Charles Woodruff, who finds himself caught between the racist trap and hideous crime of a group of troubled boys.*

The Witness

It had been snowing for twenty-four hours, and as soon as it stopped, the town plows began clearing the roads and sprinkling them with a mixture of sand and salt. By nightfall the main roads were what the roadmaster called clean as a whistle. But the little winding side roads and the store parking lots and the private walkways lay under a thick blanket of snow.

Because of the deep snow, Charles Woodruff parked his station wagon, brand-new, expensive, in the road in front of the Congregational church rather than risk getting stuck in the lot behind the church. He was early for the minister's class so he sat still, deliberately savoring the new-car smell of the station wagon. He found himself sniffing audibly and thought the sound rather a greedy one and so got out of the car and stood on the snow-covered walk, studying the church. A full moon lay low on the horizon. It gave a wonderful luminous quality to the snow, to the church, and to the branches of the great elms dark against the winter sky.

He ducked his head down because the wind was coming in gusts straight from the north, blowing the snow so it swirled around him, stinging his face. It was so cold that his toes felt as though they were freezing and he began to stamp his feet. Fortunately his coat insulated his body against the cold. He hadn't really planned to buy a new coat but during the Christmas vacation he had been in New York City and he had gone into one of those thickly carpeted, faintly perfumed, crystal-chandeliered stores that sell men's clothing and he had seen the coat hanging on a rack—a dark gray cashmere coat, lined with nutria and adorned by a collar of black Persian lamb. A tall, thin salesman who smelled of heather saw him looking at the coat and said: "Try it on, sir—it's toast-warm, cloud-light, guaranteed to make you feel like a prince—do try it on, here let me hold your coat, sir." The man's voice sounded as though he were purring and he kept brushing against Woodruff like a cat, and managed to sell him the coat, a narrow-brimmed felt hat, and a pair of fur-lined gloves.

If Addie had been alive and learned he had paid five hundred dollars for an overcoat, she would have argued with him fiercely, nostrils flaring, thin arched eyebrows lifted. Standing there alone in the snow, in front of the church, he permitted himself a small indulgence. He pretended Addie was standing beside him. He spoke to her, aloud: "You always said I had to dress more elegantly than my students so they would respect my clothes even if they didn't respect my learning. You said—"

He stopped abruptly, thinking he must look like a lunatic, standing in the snow, stamping his feet and talking to himself. If he kept it up long enough, someone would call the state police and a bulletin about him would go clattering out over the teletype: "Attention all cruisers, attention all cruisers, a black man, repeat, a black man is standing in front of the Congregational church in

Wheeling, New York; description follows, description follows, thinnish, tallish black man, clipped moustache, expensive (extravagantly expensive, outrageously expensive, unjustifiably expensive) overcoat, felt hat like a Homburg, eyeglasses glittering in the moonlight, feet stamping in the moonlight, mouth muttering in the moonlight. Light of the moon we danced. Glimpses of the moon revisited . . ."

There was no one in sight, no cars passing. It was so still it would be easy to believe that the entire population of the town had died and lay buried under the snow and that he was the sole survivor, and that would be ironic because he did not really belong in this all-white community.

The thought of his alien presence here evoked an image of Addie—dark-skinned, intense, beautiful. He was sixty-five when she died. He had just retired as professor of English at Virginia College for Negroes. He had spent all of his working life there. He had planned to write a grammar to be used in first-year English classes, to perfect his herb garden, catalogue his library, tidy up his files, and organize his clippings—a wealth of material in those clippings. But without Addie these projects seemed inconsequential—like the busy work that grade school teachers devise to keep children out of mischief. When he was offered a job teaching in a high school in a small town in New York, he accepted it quickly.

Everybody was integrating and so this little frozen Northern town was integrating, too. Someone probably asked why there were no black teachers in the school system and the school board and the Superintendent of Schools said they were searching for "one"—and the search yielded the brand-new black widower, Charles Woodruff (nigger in the woodpile, he thought, and then, why that word, a word he despised and never used so why did it pop up like that, does a full moon really affect the human mind) and he was eager to escape from his old environment and so for the past year he had taught English to academic seniors in Wheeling High School.

No problems. No hoodlums. All of his students were being herded toward college like so many cattle. He referred to them (mentally) as the Willing Workers of America. He thought that what was being done to them was a crime against nature. They were hard-working, courteous, pathetic. He introduced a new textbook, discarded a huge anthology that was filled with mutilated poetry, mutilated essays, mutilated short stories. His students liked him and told him so. Other members of the faculty said he was lucky but just wait until another year—the freshmen and the sophomores were "a bunch of hoodlums"—"a whole new ball game—"

Because of his success with his English classes, Dr. Shipley, the Congregational minister, had asked him if he would assist (Shipley used words like "assist" instead of "help") him with a class of delinquent boys—the class met on Sunday nights. Woodruff felt he should make some kind of contribution to the life of this small town which had treated him with genuine friendliness so he had said yes.

But when he first saw those seven boys assembled in the minister's study, he knew that he could neither help nor assist the minister with them—they were beyond his reach, beyond the minister's reach. They sat silent, motionless, their shoulders hunched as though against some chill they found in the air of that small book-lined room. Their eyelids were like shutters drawn over their eyes. Their long hair covered their foreheads, obscuring their eyebrows, reaching to the collars of their jackets. Their legs, stretched out straight in front of them, were encased in pants that fit as tightly as the leotards of a ballet dancer.

He kept looking at them, studying them. Suddenly, as though at a signal, they all looked at him. This collective stare was so hostile that he felt himself stiffen and sweat broke out on his forehead. He assumed that the same thing had happened to Dr. Shipley because Shipley's eyeglasses kept fogging up, though the room was not overly warm.

Shipley had talked for an hour. He began to get hoarse. Though he paused now and then to ask a question and waited hopefully for a reply, there was none. The boys sat mute and motionless.

After they left, filing out, one behind the other, Woodruff had asked Shipley about them—who they were and why they attended this class in religion.

Shipley said, "They come here under duress. The Juvenile Court requires their attendance at this class."

"How old are they?"

"About sixteen. Very bright. Still in high school. They're all sophomores—that's why you don't know them. Rambler, the tall thin boy, the ringleader, has an IQ in the genius bracket. As a matter of fact, if they weren't so bright, they'd be in reform school. This class is part of an effort to—well—to turn them into God-fearing responsible young citizens."

"Are their families poor?"

"No, indeed. The parents of these boys are—well, they're the backbone of the great middle class in this town."

After the third meeting of the class where the same hostile silence prevailed, Woodruff said, "Dr. Shipley, do you think we are accomplishing anything?" He had said "we" though he was well aware that these new young outlaws spawned by the white middle class were, praise God, Shipley's problem—the white man's problem. This crippling tight shoe was usually on the black man's foot. He found it rather pleasant to have the position reversed.

Shipley ran his fingers through his hair. It was very short hair, stiff-looking, crew-cut.

"I don't know," he said frowning. "I really don't know. They don't even respond to a greeting or a direct question. It is a terribly frustrating business, an exhausting business. When the class if over, I feel as though I had spent the entire evening lying prone under the unrelieved weight of all their bodies."

Woodruff, standing outside the church, stamping his feet, jumped and then winced because he heard a sound like a gunshot. It was born on the wind so that it seemed close at hand. He stood still, listening. Then he started moving quickly toward the religious education building which housed the minister's study.

He recognized the sound—it was made by the car the boys drove. It had no muffler and the snorting, back-firing sounds made by the spent motor were like a series of gunshots. He wanted to be out of sight when the boys drove up in their rusted car. Their lithe young bodies were a shocking contrast to the abused and ancient vehicle in which they traveled. The age of the car, its dreadful condition, was like a snarled message aimed at the adult world: All we've got is the crumbs, the leftovers, whatever the fat cats don't want and can't use; the turnpikes and the throughways and the seventy-mile-an-hour speedways are filled with long, low, shiny cars built for speed, driven by bald-headed, big-bellied rat finks and we're left with the junk, the worn-out beat-up chassis, the thin tires, the brakes that don't hold, the transmission that's shot to hell. He had seen them push the car out of the parking lot behind the church. It wouldn't go in reverse.

Bent over, peering down, picking his way through the deep snow lest he stumble and fall, Woodruff tried to hurry and the explosive sound of that terrible engine kept getting closer and closer. He envisioned himself as a black beetle in a fur-collared coat silhouetted against the snow trying to scuttle out of danger. Danger: Why should he think he was in danger? Perhaps some sixth sense was trying to warn him and his beetle's antenna (did beetles have antennae, did they have five senses and some of them an additional sense, extrasensory—) picked it up—by pricking of my thumbs, something wicked this way comes.

Once inside the building he drew a deep breath. He greeted Dr. Shipley, hung his hat and coat on the brass hat rack, and then sat down beside Shipley behind the old fumed oak desk. He braced himself for the entrance of the boys.

There was the sound of the front door opening followed by the click-clack sound of their heavy boots, in the hall. Suddenly they were all there in the minister's study. They brought cold air in with them. They sat down with their jackets on—great quilted dark jackets that had been designed for European ski slopes. At the first meeting of the class, Dr. Shipley had suggested they remove their jackets and they simply sat and stared at him until he fidgeted and looked away obviously embarrassed. He never again made a suggestion that was direct and personal.

Woodruff glanced at the boys and then directed his gaze away from them, thinking, if a bit of gilt braid and a touch of velvet were added to their clothing, they could pass for the seven dark bastard sons of some old and evil twelfth-century king. Of course they weren't all dark. Three of them were blond, two had brown hair, one had red hair, only one had black hair. All of them were white. But there was about them an aura of something so evil, so dark, so suggestive of the far reaches of the night, of the black horror of nightmares, that he shivered deep inside himself whenever he saw them. Though he thought of them as being black, this was not the blackness of human flesh, warm, soft to the touch, it was the blackness and the coldness of the hole from which D. H. Lawrence's snake emerged.

The hour was almost up when to Woodruff's surprise, Rambler, the tall boy, the one who drove the ramshackle car, the one Shipley said was the leader of the group, began asking questions about cannibalism. His voice was husky, low in pitch, and he almost whispered when he spoke. Woodruff found himself leaning forward in an effort to hear what the boy was saying. Dr. Shipley leaned forward, too.

Rambler said, "Is it a crime to eat human flesh?"

Dr. Shipley said, surprised, "Yes. It's cannibalism. It is a sin and it is also a crime." He spoke slowly, gently, as though he were wooing a timid, wild animal that had ventured out of the woods and would turn tail and scamper back if he spoke in his normal voice.

"Well, if the cats who go for this human flesh bit don't think it's a sin and if they eat it because they haven't any other food, it isn't a sin for them, is it?" The boy spoke quickly, not pausing for breath, running his words together.

"There are many practices and acts that are acceptable to non-Christians which are sinful. Christians condemn such acts no matter what the circumstances."

Woodruff thought uncomfortably, why does Shipley have to sound so pompous, so righteous, so from-off-the-top-of-Olympus? The boys were all staring at him, bright-eyed, mouths slightly open, long hair obscuring their foreheads. Then Rambler said, in his husky whispering voice, "What about you, Doc?"

Dr. Shipley said, "Me?" and repeated it, his voice losing its coaxing tone, rising in pitch, increasing in volume. "Me? What do you mean?"

"Well, man, you're eatin' human flesh, ain't you?"

Woodruff had no idea what the boy was talking about. But Dr. Shipley was looking down at his own hands with a curious self-conscious expression and Woodruff saw that Shipley's nails were bitten all the way down to the quick.

The boy said, "It's self-cannibalism, ain't it, Doc?"

Shipley put his hands on the desk, braced himself, preparatory to standing up. His thin, bony face had reddened. Before he could move, or speak, the boys stood up and began to file out of the room. Rambler leaned over and ran his hand through the minister's short-cut, bristly hair and said, "Don't sweat it, Doc."

Woodruff usually stayed a half-hour or more after the class ended. Dr. Shipley liked to talk and Woodruff listened to him patiently, though he thought Shipley had a second-rate mind and rambled when he talked. But Shipley sat with his head bowed, a pose not conducive to conversation and Woodruff left almost immediately after the boys, carrying in his mind's eye a picture of all those straight, narrow backs with the pants so tight they were like elastic bandages on their thighs, and the oversized bulky jackets and the long, frowsy hair. He thought they looked like paper dolls, cut all at once, exactly alike with a few swift slashes of scissors wielded by a skilled hand. Addie could do that—take paper and fold it and go snip, snip, snip with the scissors and she'd have a string of paper dolls, all fat, or all thin, or all bent over, or all wearing top hats, or all bearded Santas or all Cheshire cats. She had taught arts and crafts in the teacher-training courses for elementary-school teachers at Virginia College and so was skilled in the use of crayon and scissors.

He walked toward his car, head down, picking his way through the snow and then he stopped, surprised. The boys were standing in the road. They had surrounded a girl. He didn't think she was a high school girl though she was young. She had long blond hair that spilled over the quilted black jacket she was wearing. At first he couldn't tell what the boys were doing but as he got closer to them, he saw that they were moving toward their ancient car and forcing the girl to move with them though she was resisting. They were talking to each other and to her, their voices companionable, half-playful.

"So we all got one in the oven."

"So it's all right if it's all of us."

The girl said, "No."

"Aw, come on, Nellie, hurry up."

"It's colder'n hell, Nellie. Move!"

They kept pushing her toward the car and she turned on them and said, "Quit it."

"Aw, get in."

One of them gave her a hard shove, sent her closer to the car and she screamed and Rambler clapped his hand over her mouth and she must have bitten his hand because he snatched it away and then she screamed again because he slapped her and then two of them picked her up and threw her on the front seat and one of them stayed there, holding her.

Woodruff thought, There are seven of them, young, strong, satanic. He ought to go home where it was quiet and safe, mind his own business—black man's business; leave this white man's problem for a white man, leave it alone, not his, don't interfere, go home to the bungalow he rented—ridiculous type of architecture in this cold climate, developed for India, a hot climate, and that open porch business—

He said, "What are you doing?" He spoke with the voice of authority, the male schoolteacher's voice and thought, Wait, slow down, cool it, you're a black man speaking with a white man's voice.

They turned and stared at him; as they turned, they all assumed what he called the stance of the new young outlaw: the shoulders hunched, the hands in the pockets. In the moonlight he thought they looked as though they belonged in a frieze around a building—the hunched-shoulder posture repeated again and again, made permanent in stone. Classic.

"What are you doing?" he said again, voice louder, deeper.

"We're standin' here."

"You can see us, can't you?"

"Why did you force that girl into your car?"

"You're dreamin'."

"I saw what happened. And that boy is holding her in there."

"You been readin' too much."

They kept moving in, closing in on him. Even on this cold, windy night he could smell them and he loathed the smell—cigarettes, clothes washed in detergents and not rinsed enough and dried in automatic driers. They all smelled like that these days, even those pathetic college-bound drudges, the Willing Workers of America, stank so that he was always airing out his classroom. He rarely ever encountered the fresh clean smell of clothes that had been washed in soap and water, rinsed in boiling water, dried in the sun—a smell that he associated with new-mown hay and flower gardens and—Addie.

There was a subtle change in the tone of the voice of the next speaker. It was more contemptuous and louder.

"What girl, ho-daddy, what girl?"

One of them suddenly reached out and knocked his hat off his head, another one snatched his glasses off and threw them in the road and there was the tinkling sound of glass shattering. It made him shudder. He was half-blind without his glasses, peering about, uncertain of the shape of objects—like the woman in the Thurber cartoon, oh, yes, of course, three balloons and an H or three cats and a dog—only it was one of those scrambled alphabet charts.

They unbuttoned his overcoat, went through the pockets of his pants, of his jacket. One of them took his wallet, another took his car keys, picked up his hat, and then was actually behind the wheel of his station wagon and was moving off in it.

He shouted, "My car. Damn you, you're stealing my car—" his brand-new station wagon; he kept it immaculate, swept it out every morning, washed the windows. He tried to break out of that confining circle of boys and they simply pushed him back toward their car.

"Don't sweat it, man. You goin' ride with us and this little chick-chick."

"You goin' be our pro-tec-shun, ho-daddy. You goin' be our pro-tec-shun."

They took his coat off and put it around him backward without putting his arms in the sleeves and then buttoned it up. The expensive coat was just like a strait jacket—it pinioned his arms to his sides. He tried to work his way out of it by flexing his muscles, hoping that the buttons would pop off or a seam would give, and thought, enraged, They must have stitched the goddamn coat to last for a thousand years and put the goddamn buttons on the same way. The fur collar pressed against his throat, choking him.

Woodruff was forced into the back seat, two boys on each side of him. They were sitting half on him and half on each other. The one holding his wallet examined its contents. He whistled. "Hey!" he said, "Ho-daddy's got one hundred and forty-four bucks. We got us a rich ho-daddy—"

Rambler held out his hand and the boy handed the money over without a protest, not even a sigh. Then Rambler got into the front seat behind the wheel. The girl was quiet only because the boy beside her had his hand around her throat and from the way he was holding his arm, Woodruff knew he was exerting a certain amount of pressure.

"Give the man a hat," Rambler said.

One of the boys felt around until he found a cap. They were so close to each other that each of his movements slightly disrupted their seating arrangement. When the boy shifted his weight, the rest of them were forced to shift theirs.

"Here you go," the boy said. He pulled a black wool cap down on Woodruff's head, over his eyes, over his nose.

He couldn't see anything. He couldn't breathe through his nose. He had to breathe through his mouth or suffocate. The freezing cold air actually hurt the inside of his mouth. The overcoat immobilized him and the steady pressure of the fur collar against his windpipe was beginning to interfere with his normal rate of breathing. He knew that his whole circulatory system would gradually begin to slow down. He frowned, thinking what a simple and easily executed method of rendering a person helpless—just an overcoat and a knit cap. Then he thought, alarmed, If they should leave me out in the woods like this, I would be dead by morning. What do they want of me anyway?

He cleared his throat preparatory to questioning them but Rambler started the car and he could not make himself heard above the sound of the engine. He thought the noise would shatter his eardrums and he wondered how these boys could bear it—the terrible cannon fire sound of the engine and the rattling of the doors and the windows. Then they were off and it was like riding in a jeep—only worse because the seat was broken and they were jounced up out of the seat and then back down into a hollowed-out place, all of them on top of each other. He tried to keep track of the turns the car made but he couldn't, there were too many of them. He assumed that whenever they stopped it was because of a traffic light or a stop sign.

It seemed to him they had ridden for miles and miles when the car began to jounce up and down more violently than ever and he decided that they had turned onto a rough, rutted road. Suddenly they stopped. The car doors were opened and the boys pushed him out of the car. He couldn't keep his balance and he stumbled and fell flat on his face in the snow and they all laughed. They had to haul him to his feet for his movements were so constricted by the overcoat that he couldn't get up without help.

The cap had worked up a little so that he could breathe more freely and he could see anything that was in his immediate vicinity. Either they did not notice that the cap had been pushed out of place or they didn't care. As they guided him along he saw that they were in a cemetery that was filled with very old tombstones. They were approaching a small building and his station wagon was parked to one side. The boy who had driven it opened the door of the building and Woodruff saw that it was lighted inside by a big bulb that dangled from the ceiling. There were shovels and rakes inside and a grease-encrusted riding mower, bags of grass seed, and a bundle of material that looked like the artificial grass used around new graves.

Rambler said, "Put the witness here."

They stood him against the back wall, facing the wall.

"He's here and yet he ain't here."

"Ho-daddy's here—and yet—he ain't here."

"He's our witness."

And then Rambler's voice again, "If he moves, ice him with a shovel."

The girl screamed and then the sound was muffled, only a kind of far-off moaning sound coming through something. They must have gagged her. All the sounds were muffled—it was like trying to see something in a fog or hear something when other sounds overlay the one thing you're listening for. What had they brought him here for? They would go away and leave him with the girl but the girl would know that he hadn't—

How would she know? They had probably blindfolded her, too. What were they doing? He could see shadows on the wall. Sometimes they moved, sometimes they were still, and then the shadows moved again and then there would be laughter. Silence after that and then thuds, thumps, silence again. Terrible sounds behind him. He started to turn around and someone poked him in the back, sharply, with the handle of a shovel or a rake. He began to sweat despite the terrible cold.

He tried to relax by breathing deeply and he began to feel as though he were going to faint. His hands and feet were numb. His head ached. He had strained so to hear what was going on behind him that he was afraid he had impaired his own hearing.

When Rambler said, "Come on, ho-daddy, it's your turn," he was beginning to lose all feeling in his arms and legs.

Someone unbuttoned his coat, plucked the cap off his head. He let his breath out in a long drawn-out sigh. He doubted that he could have survived much longer with that pressure on his throat. The boys looked at him curiously. They threw his coat on the hard-packed dirt floor and tossed the cap on top of it. He thought that the black knit cap they'd used, like a sailor's watch cap, was as effective a blindfold as could be found—providing, of course, the person couldn't use his hands to remove it.

The girl was lying on the floor, half-naked. They had put some burlap bags under her. She looked as though she were dead.

They pushed him toward her saying, "It's your turn."

He balked, refusing to move.

"You don't want none?"

They laughed. "Ho-daddy don't want none."

They pushed him closer to the girl and someone grabbed one of his hands and placed it on the girl's thigh, on her breasts, and then they laughed again. They handed him his coat, pulled the cap down on his head.

"Let's go, ho-daddy. Let's go."

Before he could put his coat back on they hustled him outdoors. One of them threw his empty wallet at him and another aimed his car keys straight at his head. The metal stung as it hit his cheek. Before he could catch them the keys disappeared in the snow. The boys went back inside the building and emerged carrying the girl, half-naked, head hanging down limply the way the head of a corpse would dangle.

"The girl—" Woodruff said.

"You're our witness, ho-daddy. You're our big fat witness."

They propped the girl up in the back seat of their car. "You're the only witness we got," they repeated it, laughing. "Take good care of yourself."

"She'll freeze to death like that," he protested.

"Not Nellie."

"She likes it."

"Come on, man, let's go, let's go, let's go," Rambler said impatiently.

Woodruff's arms and hands were numb that he had trouble getting his coat on. He had to take his gloves off and poke around in the snow with his bare hands before he could retrieve his wallet and the car keys. The pain in his hands was as sharp and intense as if they had been burned.

Getting into his car he began to shake with fury. Once he got out of this wretched cemetery he would call the state police. Young animals. He had called them outlaws; they weren't outlaws, they were animals. In his haste he dropped the keys and had to feel around on the floor of the car for them.

When he finally got the car started he was shivering and shaking and his stomach was quivering so that he didn't dare try to drive. He turned on the heater and watched the tiny taillight on Rambler's car disappear—an old car and the taillight was like the end of a pencil glowing red in the dark. The loud explosive sound of the engine gradually receded. When he could no longer hear it, he flicked on the light in his car and looked at his watch. It was quarter past three. Wouldn't the parents of those godforsaken boys wonder where they were at that hour? Perhaps they didn't care—perhaps they were afraid of them—just as he was.

Though he wanted to get home as quickly as possible, so he could get warm, so he could think, he had to drive slowly, peering out at the narrow rutted road because he was half blind without his glasses. When he reached the cemetery gates he stopped, not knowing whether to turn right or left for he had no idea where he was. He took a chance and turned right and followed the macadam road, still going slowly, saw a church on a hill and recognized it as the Congregational church in Brooksville, the next town, and knew he was about five miles from home.

By the time he reached his own driveway, sweat was pouring from his body just like water coming out of a showerhead—even his eyelashes were wet; it ran down his ears, dripped off his nose, his lips, even the palms of his hands.

In the house he turned on the lights, in the living room, in the hall, in his bedroom. He went to his desk, opened a drawer and fished out an old pair of glasses. He had had them for years. They looked rather like Peter Cooper's glasses—he'd seen them once in the Cooper Union Museum in New York—small-lensed, with narrow, silvery-looking frames. They evoked an image of a careful scholarly man. When he had started wearing glasses, he had selected frames like Peter Cooper's. Addie had made him stop wearing them. She said they gave him the look of another era, made it easy for his students to caricature him—the tall, slender figure, slightly stooped, the steel-rimmed glasses. She said that his dark, gentle eyes looked as though they were trapped behind those little glasses.

Having put on the glasses, he went to the telephone and stood with one hand resting on it, sweating again, trembling again. He turned away, took off his overcoat and hung it on a hanger and placed it in the hall closet.

He began to pace up and down the living room—a pleasant spacious room, simply furnished. It had a southern exposure and there were big windows on that side of the room. The windows faced a meadow. The thought crossed his mind, lightly, like the silken delicate strand of a cobweb, that he would have to leave here and he brushed it away—not quite away, a trace remained.

He wasn't going to call the police. Chicken. That was the word his students used. Fink was another one. He was going to chicken out. He was going to fink out.

Why wasn't he going to call the police? Well, what would he tell them? That he'd been robbed? Well, that was true. That he'd been kidnapped? Well, that was true, too, but it seemed like a harsh way of putting it. He'd have to think about that one. That he'd been witness to a rape? He wasn't even certain that they had raped the girl. No? Who was he trying to kid? Himself? Himself.

So why wasn't he going to the police? He hadn't touched the girl. But those horrible little hoods, toads rather, why toads, toe of frog ingredient of witches' brew, poisonous substance in the skin—bufotenine, a hallucinogen found in the skin of the frog, of the toad. Those horrible toadlike hoods would say he had touched her. Well, he had. Hadn't he? They had made sure of that. Would the police believe him? The school board? The PTA? "Where there's smoke there must be fire." "I'm not going to let my daughter stay in his class."

He started shivering again and made himself a cup of tea and sat down on the window seat in the living room to drink it and then got up and turned off the lights and looked out at the snow. The moonlight was so bright that he could see wisps of tall grass in the meadow—yellow against the snow. Immediately he thought of the long blond hair of that starvation-thin young girl. Bleached hair? Perhaps. It didn't lessen the outrage. She was dressed just like the boys—big quilted jacket, skin-tight pants, even her hair worn like theirs, obscuring the forehead, the sides of the face.

There was a sudden movement outside the window and he frowned and leaned forward, wondering what was moving about at this hour. He saw a pair of rabbits, leaping, running, literally playing games with each other. He had never before seen such free joyous movement, not even children at play exhibited it. There was always something unrelaxed about the eyes of children, about the way they held their mouths, wrinkled their foreheads—they looked as though they had been cornered and were impelled to defend themselves or that they were impelled to pursue some object that forever eluded them.

Watching the joyous heel-kicking play of the rabbits, he found himself thinking, I cannot continue to live in the same small town with that girl and those seven boys. The boys knew, before he did, that he wasn't going to report this—this incident—these crimes. They were bright enough to know that he would quickly realize how neatly they had boxed him in and thus would keep quiet. If he dared enter a complaint against them they would accuse him of raping the girl, would say they found him in the cemetery with her. Whose story would be believed? "Where there's smoke there's fire."

Right after that he started packing. He put his clothes into a foot locker. He stacked his books on the floor of the station wagon. He was surprised to find among the books a medical textbook that had belonged to John—Addie's brother.

He sat down and read all the material on angina pectoris. At eight o'clock he called the school and said he wasn't feeling well (which was true) and that he would not be in. Then he called the office of the local doctor and made an appointment for that afternoon.

When he talked to the doctor he described the violent pain in his chest that went from the shoulder down to his finger tips on the left side, causing a squeezing, crushing sensation that left him feeling faint, dizzy.

The doctor, a fat man in an old tweed jacket and a limp white shirt, said after he examined him, "Angina. You'll have to take three or four months off until we can get this thing under control."

"I will resign immediately."

"Oh, no. That isn't necessary. Besides I've been told you're the best English teacher we've ever had. It would be a great pity to lose you."

"No," Woodruff said, "it is better to resign." Come back here and look at that violated little girl? Come back here? Ever?

He scarcely listened to the detailed instructions he was to follow, did not even glance at the three prescriptions he was handed, for he was eager to be on his way. He composed a letter of resignation in his mind. When he went back to the bungalow he wrote it quickly and then put it on the front seat of the station wagon to be mailed en route.

Then he went back into the house and stayed there just long enough to call his landlord. He said he'd had a heart attack and was going back to Virginia to convalesce, that he had turned the thermostat down to sixty-five and he would return the house keys by mail. The landlord said, My goodness, you just paid a month in advance, I'll mail you a refund, what's your new address, so sorry, ideal tenant.

Woodruff hung up the receiver and said, "Peace be with you, brother—" There was already an echo in the room though it wasn't empty—all he'd removed were his books and his clothes.

He put on his elegant overcoat. When he got back to Virginia, he would give the coat away, his pleasure in it destroyed now for he would always remember the horrid feel of the collar tight across his throat, even the feel of the fabric under his finger tips would evoke an image of the cemetery, the tool shed, and the girl.

He drove down the road rather slowly. There were curves in the road and he couldn't go fast, besides he liked to look at this landscape. It was high rolling land. Snow lay over it—blue-white where there were shadows cast by the birch trees and the hemlocks, yellow-white and sparkling in the great meadow where he had watched the heel-kicking freedom of the rabbits at play.

At the entrance to the highway he brought the car to a halt. As he sat there waiting for an opportunity to get into the stream of traffic, he heard close at hand the loud explosive sound of an engine—a familiar sound. He was so alarmed that he momentarily experienced all the symptoms of a heart attack, the sudden terrible inability to breathe and the feeling that something was squeezing his chest, kneading it so that pain ran through him as though it were following the course of his circulatory system.

He knew from the sound that the car turning off the highway, entering the same road that he was now leaving, was Rambler's car. In the sunlight, silhouetted against the snow, it looked like a junkyard on wheels, fenders dented, sides dented, chassis rusted. All the boys were in the car. Rambler was driving. The thin blond girl was in the front seat—a terrible bruise under one eye. For a fraction of a second Woodruff looked straight into Rambler's eyes, just visible under the long, untidy hair. The expression was cold, impersonal, analytical.

After he got on the highway, he kept looking in the rearview mirror. There was no sign of pursuit. Evidently Rambler had not noticed that the car was loaded for flight—books and cartons on the seats, foot locker on the floor, all this was out of his range of vision. He wondered what they were doing. Wrecking the interior of the bungalow? No. They were probably waiting for him to return so they could blackmail him. Blackmail a black male.

On the turnpike he kept going faster and faster—eighty-five miles an hour, ninety, ninety-five, one hundred. He felt exhilarated by this tremendous speed. It was clearing his mind, heartening him, taking him out of himself.

He began to rationalize about what had happened. He decided that Rambler and his friends didn't give a damn that he, Woodruff, was a black man. They couldn't care less. They were very bright boys, bright enough to recognize him for what he was: a black man in his sixties, conditioned all his life by the knowledge that "White woman taboo for you" (as one of his African students used to say). The moment he attempted to intervene there in front of the church, they decided to take him with them. They knew he wasn't going to the police about any matter which involved sex and a white girl, especially where there was the certainty that all seven of them would accuse him of having relations with the girl. They had used his presence in that tool shed to give an extra exquisite fillip to their dreadful game.

He turned on the radio and waited impatiently for music, any kind of music, thinking it would distract him. He got one of those stations that play what he called thump-and-blare music. A husky-voiced woman was shouting a song—not singing, shouting:

> I'm gonna turn on the big heat
> I'm gonna turn up the high heat
> For my ho-daddy, ho-daddy,
> For my ho-daddy, ho-daddy.

He flipped the switch, cutting off the sound and he gradually diminished the speed of the car, slowing, slowing, slowing. "We got us a rich ho-daddy." That's what one of the boys had said there in front of the church when he plucked the money out of Woodruff's wallet. A rich ho-daddy? A black ho-daddy. A witness. Another poor scared black bastard who was a witness.

James Baldwin (1924–87)

In his collection of essays Notes of a Native Son *(1955), James Baldwin wrote: "The most crucial time in my own development came when I was forced to recognize that I was a kind of bastard of the West; when I followed the lives of my past I did not find myself in Europe but in Africa." Like other African American writers of the 1950s, James Baldwin searched outside of the United States for a sense of "home," for a place that would accept him as a black man and writer.*

Harlem-born, Baldwin's troubled youth—his father's death, his family poverty, and a stormy relationship with his stepfather—led him to seek refuge in religion. Between the ages of fourteen and seventeen, he discovered a haven as a preacher in the church. But at eighteen, having developed a love for reading, Baldwin moved from the church toward writing as a sanctuary, serving as editor of his high school literary magazine. After graduating from high school in 1942, Baldwin trekked from Harlem to New Jersey to bohemian Greenwich Village to live the life of a writer. In 1945, he met Richard Wright (see page 317), who encouraged Baldwin's writing and helped him with a Eugene F. Saxton Memorial Trust Award for his first novel, Go Tell It on the Mountain *(eventually published in 1953).*

In the late 1940s, Baldwin published articles and short stories and won several other awards and fellowships for his writing. However, as he gained prominence as an author, Baldwin also reached a breaking point with America's racial injustices. In 1948, he left the United States to live in Paris. Once again he faced poverty, but he found both professional and personal satisfaction: the first, in the publication of Go Tell It on the Mountain, *and the second, in his relationship with a Swiss lover.*

During the civil rights era of the 1950s and early 1960s, Baldwin lived a nomadic life. But his creative and critical works consistently targeted racism in America, and the writer came to be regarded by many as an eminent literary voice of African American protest.

A prolific writer, Baldwin's other fiction includes Giovanni's Room *(1956),* Another Country *(1962),* Going to Meet the Man: A Short Story Collection *(1965),* Tell Me How Long the Train's Been Gone *(1968),* If Beale Street Could Talk *(1974), and* Just above My Head *(1979). In addition he wrote four plays:* The Amen Corner *(1957),* Giovanni's Room *(1957),* Blues for Mister Charlie *(1964); and* A Deed from the King of Spain *(1974).*

Baldwin's nonfiction has brought him as much prestige as his fiction. His critical works and collections of essays include Notes of a Native Son *(1955),* Nobody Knows My Name *(1961),* The Fire Next Time *(1963),* Nothing Personal *(1964),* A Rap on Race *(1971),* No Name in the Street *(1972),* The Devil Finds Work *(1976), and* The Price of a Ticket: Collected Nonfiction, 1948–1985 *(1985).*

Although some African American critics and writers of the late 1960s and 1970s questioned Baldwin's racial pride and cultural identity, his works and literary stature continue to inspire many literary voices, both black and non-

black. Along with his brilliant writing, his personal courage in fighting racism and in asserting his homosexuality provides an invaluable legacy for African American culture.

The following selection, "Previous Condition," is from Baldwin's early writings, first published in 1948. In chronicling an ugly day in the life of a young black actor, the story expresses Baldwin's sensitivity to both racial intolerance and the emotional currents among people of different races.

Previous Condition

I woke up shaking alone in my room. I was clammy cold with sweat; under me the sheet and the mattress were soaked. The sheet was gray and twisted like a rope. I breathed like I had been running.

I couldn't move for the longest while. I just lay on my back, spread-eagled, looking up at the ceiling, listening to the sounds of people getting up in other parts of the house, alarm clocks ringing and water splashing and doors opening and shutting and feet on the stairs. I could tell when people left for work: the hall doorway downstairs whined and shuffled as it opened and gave a funny kind of double slam as it closed. One thud and then a louder thud and then a little final click. While the door was open I could hear the street sounds too, horses' hoofs and delivery wagons and people in the streets and big trucks and motor cars screaming on the asphalt.

I had been dreaming. At night I dreamt and woke up in the morning trembling, but not remembering the dream, except that in the dream I had been running. I could not remember when the dream—or dreams—had started; it had been long ago. For long periods maybe, I would have no dreams at all. And then they would come back, every night, I would try not to go to bed, I would go to sleep frightened and wake up frightened and have another day to get through with the nightmare at my shoulder. Now I was back from Chicago, busted, living off my friends in a dirty furnished room downtown. The show I had been with had folded in Chicago. It hadn't been much of a part—or much of a show either, to tell the truth. I played a kind of intellectual Uncle Tom, a young college student working for his race. The playwright had wanted to prove he was a liberal, I guess. But, as I say, the show had folded and here I was, back in New York and hating it. I knew that I should be getting another job, making the rounds, pounding the pavement. But I didn't. I couldn't face it. It was summer. I seemed to be fagged out. And every day I hated myself more. Acting's a rough life, even if you're white. I'm not tall and I'm not good looking and I can't sing or dance and I'm not white; so even at the best of times I wasn't in much demand.

The room I lived in was heavy ceilinged, perfectly square, with walls the color of chipped dry blood. Jules Weissman, a Jewboy, had got the room for me. It's a room to sleep in, he said, or maybe to die in but God knows it wasn't meant to live in. Perhaps because the room was so hideous it had a fantastic array of light fixtures: one on the ceiling, one on the left wall, two on the right wall, and a lamp on the table beside my bed. My bed was in front of the window through which nothing ever blew but dust. It was a furnished room and they'd thrown enough stuff in it to furnish three rooms its size. Two easy chairs and a desk, the bed, the table, a straight-backed chair, a bookcase, a cardboard wardrobe; and my books and my suitcase, both unpacked; and my dirty clothes flung in a corner. It was the kind of room that defeated you. It had a fireplace, too, and a heavy marble mantelpiece and a great gray mirror above the mantelpiece. It was hard to see anything in the mirror very clearly—which was perhaps just as well—and it would have been worth your life to have started a fire in the fireplace.

"Well, you won't have to stay here long," Jules told me the night I came. Jules smuggled me in, sort of, after dark, when everyone had gone to bed.

"Christ, I hope not."

"I'll be moving to a big place soon," Jules said. "You can move in with me." He turned all the lights on. "Think it'll be all right for a while?" He sounded apologetic, as though he had designed the room himself.

"Oh, sure. D'you think I'll have any trouble?"

"I don't think so. The rent's paid. She can't put you out."

I didn't say anything to that.

"Sort of stay undercover," Jules said. "You know."

"Roger," I said.

I had been living there for three days, timing it so I left after everyone else had gone, coming back late at night when everyone else was asleep. But I knew it wouldn't work. A couple of the tenants had seen me on the stairs, a woman had surprised me coming out of the john. Every morning I waited for the landlady to come banging on the door. I didn't know what would happen. It might be all right. It might not be. But the waiting was getting me.

The sweat on my body was turning cold. Downstairs a radio was tuned in to the Breakfast Symphony. They were playing Beethoven. I sat up and lit a cigarette. "Peter," I said, "don't let them scare you to death. You're a man, too." I listened to Ludwig and I watched the smoke rise to the dirty ceiling. Under Ludwig's drums and horns I listened to hear footsteps on the stairs.

I'd done a lot of traveling in my time. I'd knocked about through St. Louis, Frisco, Seattle, Detroit, New Orleans, worked at just about everything. I'd run away from my old lady when I was about sixteen. She'd never been able to handle me. You'll never be nothin' *but* a bum, she'd say. He lived in an old shack in a town in New Jersey in the nigger part of town, the kind of houses colored people live in all over the U.S. I hated my mother for living there. I hated all the people in my neighborhood. They went to church and they got drunk. They were nice to the white people. When the landlord came around they paid him and took his crap.

The first time I was ever called nigger I was seven years old. It was a little white girl with long black curls. I used to leave the front of my house and go wandering by myself through town. This little girl was playing ball alone and as I passed her the ball rolled out of her hands into the gutter.

I threw it back to her.

"Let's play catch," I said.

But she held the ball and made a face at me.

"My mother don't let me play with niggers," she told me.

I did not know what the word meant. But my skin grew warm. I stuck my tongue out at her.

"I don't care. Keep your old ball." I started down the street.

She screamed after me: "Nigger, nigger, nigger!"

I screamed back: "Your mother was a nigger!"

I asked my mother what a nigger was.

"Who called you that?"

"I heard somebody say it."

"Who?"

"Just somebody."

"Go wash your face," she said. "You dirty as sin. Your supper's on the table."

I went to the bathroom and splashed water on my face and wiped my face and hands on the towel.

"You call that clean?" my mother cried. "Come here, boy!"

She dragged me back to the bathroom and began to soap my face and neck.

"You run around dirty like you do all the time, everybody'll call you a little nigger, you hear?" She rinsed my face and looked at my hands and dried me. "Now, go on and eat your supper."

I didn't say anything. I went to the kitchen and sat down at the table. I remember I wanted to cry. My mother sat down across from me.

"Mama," I said. She looked at me. I started to cry.

She came around to my side of the table and took me in her arms.

"Baby, don't fret. Next time somebody calls you nigger you tell them you'd rather be your color than be lowdown and nasty like some white folks is."

We formed gangs when I was older, my friends and I. We met white boys and their friends on the opposite sides of fences and we threw rocks and tin cans at each other.

I'd come home bleeding. My mother would slap me and scold me and cry.

"Boy, you wanna get killed? You wanna end up like your father?"

My father was a bum and I had never seen him. I was named for him: Peter.

I was always in trouble: truant officers, welfare workers, everybody else in town.

"You ain't never gonna be nothin' *but* a bum," my mother said.

By and by older kids I knew finished school and got jobs and got married and settled down. They were going to settle down and bring more black babies into the world and pay the same rents for the same old shacks and it would go on and on—

When I was sixteen I ran away. I left a note and told Mama not to worry, I'd come back one day and I'd be all right. But when I was twenty-two she died. I came back and put my mother in the ground. Everything was like it had been. Our house had not been painted and the porch floor sagged and there was somebody's raincoat stuffed in the broken window. Another family was moving in.

Their furniture was stacked along the walls and their children were running through the house and laughing and somebody was frying pork chops in the kitchen. The oldest boy was tacking up a mirror.

Last year Ida took me driving in her big car and we passed through a couple of towns upstate. We passed some crumbling houses on the left. The clothes on the line were flying in the wind.

"Are people living there?" asked Ida.

"Just darkies," I said.

Ida passed the car ahead, banging angrily on the horn. "D'you know you're becoming paranoiac, Peter?"

"All right. All right. I know a lot of white people are starving too."

"You're damn right they are. I know a little about poverty myself."

Ida had come from the kind of family called shanty Irish. She was raised in Boston. She's a very beautiful woman who married young and married for money—so now I can afford to support attractive young men, she'd giggle. Her husband was a ballet dancer who was forever on the road. Ida suspected that he went with boys. Not that I give a damn, she said, as long as he leaves me alone. When we met last year she was thirty and I was twenty-five. We had a pretty stormy relationship but we stuck. Whenever I got to town I called her; whenever I was stranded out of town I'd let her know. We never let it get too serious. She went her way and I went mine.

In all this running around I'd learned a few things. Like a prizefighter learns to take a blow or a dancer learns to fall, I'd learned how to get by. I'd learned never to be belligerent with policemen, for instance. No matter who was right, I was certain to be wrong. What might be accepted as just good old American independence in someone else would be insufferable arrogance in me. After the first few times I realized that I had to play smart, to act out the role as I was expected to play. I only had one head and it was too easy to get it broken. When I faced a policeman I acted like I didn't know a thing. I let my jaw drop and I let my eyes get big. I didn't give him any smart answers, none of the crap about my rights. I figured out what answers he wanted and I gave them to him. I never let him think he wasn't king. If it was more than routine, if I was picked up on suspicion of robbery or murder in the neighborhood, I looked as humble as I could and kept my mouth shut and prayed. I took a couple of beatings but I stayed out of prison and I stayed off chain gangs. That was also due to luck, Ida pointed out once. "Maybe it would've been better for you if you'd been a little less lucky. Worse things have happened than chain gangs. Some of them have happened to you."

There was something in her voice. "What are you talking about?" I asked.

"Don't lose your temper. I said maybe."

"You mean you think I'm a coward?"

"I didn't say that, Peter."

"But you meant that. Didn't you?"

"No. I didn't mean that. I didn't mean anything. Let's not fight."

There are times and places when a Negro can use his color like a shield. He can trade on the subterranean Anglo-Saxon guilt and get what he wants that way; or some of what he wants. He can trade on his nuisance value, his value as forbidden fruit; he can use it like a knife, he can twist it and get his vengeance that way. I knew these things long before I realized that I knew them and in the beginning I used them, not knowing what I was doing. Then when I began to see it, I felt betrayed. I felt beaten as a person. I had no honest place to stand.

This was the year before I met Ida. I'd been acting in stock companies and little theaters; sometimes fairly good parts. People were nice to me. They told me I had talent. They said it sadly, as though they were thinking, What a pity, he'll never get anywhere. I had got to the point where I resented praise and I resented pity and I wondered what people were thinking when they shook my hand. In New York I met some pretty fine people; easygoing, hard-drinking, flotsam and jetsam; and they liked me; and I wondered if I trusted them; if I was able any longer to trust anybody. Not on top, where all the world could see, but underneath where everybody lives.

Soon I would have to get up. I listened to Ludwig. He shook the little room like the footsteps of a giant marching miles away. On summer evenings (and maybe we would go this summer) Jules and Ida and I would go up to the Stadium and sit beneath the pillars on the cold stone steps. There it seemed to me the sky was far away; and I was not myself, I was high and lifted up. We never talked, the three of us. We sat and watched the blue smoke curl in the air and watched the orange tips of cigarettes. Every once in a while the boys who sold popcorn and soda pop and ice cream climbed the steep steps chattering; and Ida shifted slightly and touched her blue-black hair; and Jules scowled. I sat with my knee up, watching the lighted half-moon below, the black-coated, straining conductor, the faceless men beneath him moving together in a rhythm like the sea. There were pauses in the music for the rushing, calling, halting piano. Everything would stop except the climbing soloist; he would reach a height and everything would join him, the violins first and then the horns; and then the deep blue bass and the flute and the bitter trampling drums; beating, beating, and mounting together and stopping with a crash like daybreak. When I first heard the *Messiah* I was alone; my blood bubbled like fire and wine; I cried; like an infant crying for its mother's milk; or a sinner running to meet Jesus.

Now below the music I heard footsteps on the stairs. I put out my cigarette. My heart was beating so hard I thought it would tear my chest apart. Someone knocked on the door.

I thought: Don't answer. Maybe she'll go away.

But the knocking came again, harder this time.

Just a minute, I said. I sat on the edge of the bed and put on my bathrobe. I was trembling like a fool. For Christ's sake, Peter, you've been through this before. What's the worst thing that can happen? You won't have a room. The world's full of rooms.

When I opened the door the landlady stood there, red-and-whitefaced and hysterical.

"Who are you? I didn't rent this room to you."

My mouth was dry. I started to say something.

"I can't have no colored people here," she said. "All my tenants are complainin'. Women afraid to come home nights."

"They ain't gotta be afraid of me," I said. I couldn't get my voice up; it rasped and rattled in my throat; and I began to be angry. I wanted to kill her. "My friend rented this room for me," I said.

"Well, I'm sorry, he didn't have no right to do that, I don't have nothin' against you, but you gotta get out."

Her glasses blinked, opaque in the light on the landing. She was frightened to death. She was afraid of me but she was more afraid of losing her tenants. Her face was mottled with rage and fear, her breath came rushed and little bits of spittle gathered at the edges of her mouth; her breath smelled bad, like rotting hamburger on a July day.

"You can't put me out," I said. "This room was rented in my name." I started to close the door, as though the matter was finished: "I live here, see, this is my room, you can't put me out."

"You get outa my house!" she screamed. "I got the right to know who's in my house! This is a white neighborhood. I don't rent to colored people. Why don't you go on uptown, like you belong?"

"I can't stand niggers," I told her. I started to close the door again but she moved and stuck her foot in the way. I wanted to kill her, I watched her stupid, wrinkled frightened white face and I wanted to take a club, a hatchet, and bring it down with all my weight, splitting her skull down the middle where she parted her iron-grey hair.

"Get out of the door," I said. "I want to get dressed."

But I knew that she had won, that I was already on my way. We stared at each other. Neither of us moved. From her came an emanation of fear and fury and something else. You maggot-eaten bitch, I thought. I said evilly, "You wanna come in and watch me?" Her face didn't change, she didn't take her foot away. My skin prickled, tiny hot needles punctured my flesh. I was aware of my body under the bathrobe; and it was as though I had done something wrong, something monstrous, years ago, which no one had forgotten and for which I would be killed.

"If you don't get out," she said, "I'll get a policeman to put you out."

I grabbed the door to keep from touching her. "All right. All right. You can have the goddamn room. Now get out and let me dress."

She turned away. I slammed the door. I heard her going down the stairs, I threw stuff into my suitcase. I tried to take as long as possible but I cut myself while shaving because I was afraid she would come back upstairs with a policeman.

Jules was making coffee when I walked in.

"Good morning, good morning! What happened to you?"

"No room at the inn," I said. "Pour a cup of coffee for the notorious son of man." I sat down and dropped my suitcase on the floor.

Jules looked at me. "Oh. Well. Coffee coming up."

He got out the coffee cups. I lit a cigarette and sat there. I couldn't think of anything to say. I knew that Jules felt bad and I wanted to tell him that it wasn't his fault.

He pushed coffee in front of me and sugar and cream.

"Cheer up, baby. The world's wide and life—life, she is very long."

"Shut up. I don't want to hear any of your bad philosophy."

"Sorry."

"I mean, let's not talk about the good, the true, and the beautiful."

"All right. But don't sit there holding onto your table manners. Scream if you want to."

"Screaming won't do any good. Besides I'm a big boy now."

I stirred my coffee. "Did you give her a fight?" Jules asked.

I shook my head. "No."

"Why the hell not?"

I shrugged; a little ashamed now. I couldn't have won it. What the hell.

"You might have won it. You might have given her a couple of bad moments."

"Goddamit to hell, I'm sick of it. Can't I get a place to sleep without dragging it through the courts? I'm goddamn tired of battling every Tom, Dick, and Harry for what everybody else takes for granted. I'm tired, man, tired! Have you ever been sick to death of something? Well, I'm sick to death. And I'm scared. I've been fighting so goddamn long I'm not a person any more. I'm not Booker T. Washington. I've got no vision of emancipating anybody. I want to emancipate myself. If this goes on much longer, they'll send me to Bellevue, I'll blow my top, I'll break somebody's head. I'm not worried about that miserable little room. I'm worried about what's happening to me, *to me,* inside. I don't walk the streets, I crawl. I've never been like this before. Now when I go to a strange place I wonder what will happen, will I be accepted, if I'm accepted, can I accept?—"

"Take it easy," Jules said.

"Jules, I'm beaten."

"I don't think you are. Drink your coffee."

"Oh," I cried, "I know you think I'm making it dramatic, that I'm paranoiac and just inventing trouble! Maybe I think so sometimes, how can I tell? You get so used to being hit you find you're always waiting for it. Oh, I know, you're Jewish, you get kicked around, too, but you can walk into a bar and nobody *knows* you're Jewish and if you go looking for a job you'll get a better job than mine! How can I say what it feels like? I don't know. I know everybody's in trouble and nothing is easy, but how can I explain to you what it feels like to be black when I don't understand it and don't want to and spend all my time trying to forget it? I don't want to hate anybody—but now maybe, I can't love anybody either—are we friends? Can we be really friends?"

"We're friends," Jules said, "don't worry about it." He scowled. "If I wasn't Jewish I'd ask you why you don't live in Harlem." I looked at him. He raised his hand and smiled—"But I'm Jewish, so I didn't ask you. Ah Peter," he said, "I can't help you—take a walk, get drunk, we're all in this together."

I stood up. "I'll be around later. I'm sorry."

"Don't be sorry. I'll leave my door open. Bunk here for awhile."

"Thanks," I said.

I felt that I was drowning; that hatred had corrupted me like cancer in the bone.

I saw Ida for dinner. We met in a restaurant in the Village, an Italian place in a gloomy cellar with candles on the tables.

It was not a busy night, for which I was grateful. When I came in there were only two other couples on the other side of the room. No one looked at me. I sat down in a corner booth and ordered a Scotch old-fashioned. Ida was late and I had three of them before she came.

She was very fine in black, a high-necked dress with a pearl choker; and her hair was combed page-boy style, falling just below her ears.

"You look real sweet, baby."

"Thank you. It took fifteen extra minutes but I hoped it would be worth it."

"It was worth it. What're you drinking?"

"Oh—what're you drinking?"

"Old-fashioneds."

She sniffed and looked at me. "How many?"

I laughed. "Three."

"Well," she said, "I suppose you had to do something." The waiter came over. We decided on one Manhattan and one lasagna and one spaghetti with clam sauce and another old-fashioned for me.

"Did you have a constructive day, sweetheart? Find a job?"

"Not today," I said. I lit her cigarette. "Metro offered me a fortune to come to the coast and do the lead in *Native Son* but I turned it down. Type casting, you know. It's so difficult to find a decent part."

"Well, if they don't come up with a decent offer soon tell them you'll go back to Selznick. *He'll* find you a part with guts—the very *idea* of offering you *Native Son!* I wouldn't stand for it."

"You ain't gotta tell me. I told them if they didn't find me a decent script in two weeks I was through, that's all."

"Now that's talking, Peter my lad."

The drinks came and we sat in silence for a minute or two. I finished half of my drink at a swallow and played with the toothpicks on the table. I felt Ida watching me.

"Peter, you're going to be awfully drunk."

"Honeychile, the first thing a southern gentleman learns is how to hold his liquor."

"That myth is older than the rock of ages. And anyway you come from Jersey."

I finished my drink and snarled at her: "That's just as good as the South."

Across the table from me I could see that she was readying herself for trouble; her mouth tightened slightly, setting her chin so that the faint cleft showed: "What happened to you today?"

I resented her concern; I resented my need. "Nothing worth talking about," I muttered, "just a mood."

And I tried to smile at her, to wipe away the bitterness.

"Now I know something's the matter. Please tell me."

It sounded trivial as hell: "You know the room Jules found for me? Well, the landlady kicked me out of it today."

"God save the American republic," Ida said. "D'you want to waste some of my husband's money? We can sue her."

"Forget it. I'll end up with lawsuits in every state in the union."

"Still, as a gesture—"

"The devil with the gesture. I'll get by."

The food came. I didn't want to eat. The first mouthful hit my belly like a gong. Ida began cutting up lasagna.

"Peter," she said, "try not to feel so badly. We're all in this together the whole world. Don't let it throw you. What can't be helped you have to learn to live with."

"That's easy for you to say," I told her.

She looked at me quickly and looked away. "I'm not pretending that it's easy to do," she said.

I didn't believe that she could really understand it; and there was nothing I could say. I sat like a child being scolded, looking down at my plate, not eating, not saying anything. I wanted her to stop talking, to stop being intelligent about it, to stop being calm and grown-up about it; good Lord, none of us has ever grown up, we never will.

"It's no better anywhere else," she was saying. "In all of Europe there's famine and disease, in France and England they hate the Jews—nothing's going to change, baby, people are too empty-headed, too empty-hearted—it's always been like that, people always try to destroy what they don't understand—and they hate almost everything because they understand so little—"

I began to sweat in my side of the booth. I wanted to stop her voice. I wanted her to eat and be quiet and leave me alone. I looked around for the waiter so I could order another drink. But he was on the far side of the restaurant, waiting on some people who had just come in; a lot of people had come in since we had been sitting there.

"Peter," Ida said, "Peter please don't look like that."

I grinned: the painted grin of the professional clown. "Don't worry, baby, I'm all right. I know what I'm going to do. I'm gonna go back to my people where I belong and find me a nice, black nigger wench and raise me a flock of babies."

Ida had an old maternal trick; the grin tricked her into using it now. She raised her fork and rapped me with it across the knuckles. "Now, stop that. You're too old for that."

I screamed and stood up screaming and knocked the candle over: "Don't *do* that, you bitch, don't *ever* do that!"

She grabbed the candle and set it up and glared at me. Her face had turned perfectly white: "Sit down! Sit *down!*"

I fell back into my seat. My stomach felt like water. Everyone was looking at us. I turned cold, seeing what they were seeing: a black boy and a white woman, alone together. I knew it would take nothing to have them at my throat.

"I'm sorry," I muttered. "I'm sorry, I'm sorry."

The waiter was at my elbow. "Is everything all right, miss?"

"Yes, quite, thank you." She sounded like a princess dismissing a slave. I didn't look up. The shadow of the waiter moved away from me.

"Baby," Ida said, "forgive me, please forgive me."

I stared at the tablecloth. She put her hand on mine, brightness and blackness.

"Let's go," I said, "I'm terribly sorry."

She motioned for the check. When it came she handed the waiter a ten dollar bill without looking. She picked up her bag.

"Shall we go to a nightclub or a movie or something?"

"No, honey, not tonight." I looked at her. "I'm tired, I think I'll go on over to Jules's place. I'm gonna sleep on his floor for a while. Don't worry about me. I'm all right."

She looked at me steadily. She said: "I'll come see you tomorrow?"

"Yes, baby, please."

The waiter brought the change and she tipped him. We stood up; as we passed the table (not looking at the people) the ground under me seemed falling, the doorway seemed impossibly far away. All my muscles tensed; I seemed ready to spring; I was waiting for the blow.

I put my hands in my pockets and we walked to the end of the block. The lights were green and red, the lights from the theater across the street exploded blue and yellow, off and on.

"Peter?"

"Yes?"

"I'll see you tomorrow?"

"Yeah. Come by Jules's. I'll wait for you."

"Goodnight, darling."

"Goodnight."

I started to walk away. I felt her eyes on my back. I kicked a bottle-top on the sidewalk.

God save the American republic.

I dropped into the subway and got on an uptown train, not knowing where it was going and not caring. Anonymous, islanded people surrounded me, behind newspapers, behind make-up, fat, fleshy masks and flat eyes. I watched the empty faces. (No one looked at me.) I looked at the ads, unreal women and pink-cheeked men selling cigarettes, candy, shaving cream, nightgowns, chewing gum, movies, sex; sex without organs, drier than sand and more secret than death. The train stopped. A white boy and a white girl got on. She was nice, short, svelte. Nice legs. She was hanging on his arm. He was the football type, blond, ruddy. They were dressed in summer clothes. The wind from the doors blew her print dress. She squealed, holding the dress at the knees and giggled and looked at him. He said something I didn't catch and she looked at me and the smile died. She stood so that she faced him and had her back to me. I looked back at the ads. Then I hated them. I wanted to do something to make them hurt, something that would crack the pink-cheeked mask. The white boy and I did not look at each other again. They got off at the next stop.

I wanted to keep on drinking. I got off in Harlem and went to a rundown bar on Seventh Avenue. My people, my people. Sharpies stood on the corner, waiting. Women in summer dresses pranced by on wavering heels. Click clack. Click clack. There were white mounted policemen in the streets. On every block there was another policeman on foot. I saw a black cop.

God save the American republic.

The juke box was letting loose with "Hamps' Boogie." The place was jumping, I walked over to the man.

"Rye," I said.

I was standing next to somebody's grandmother. "Hello, papa. What you puttin' down?"

"Baby, you can't pick it up," I told her. My rye came and I drank.

"Nigger," she said, "you must think you's somebody."

I didn't answer. She turned away, back to her beer, keeping time to the juke box, her face sullen and heavy and aggrieved. I watched her out of the side of my eye. She had been good looking once, pretty even, before she hit the bottle and started crawling into too many beds. She was flabby now, flesh heaved all over in her thin dress. I wondered what she'd be like in bed; then I realized that I was a little excited by her; I laughed and set my glass down.

"The same," I said. "And a beer chaser."

The juke box was playing something else now, something brassy and commercial which I didn't like. I kept on drinking, listening to the voices of my people, watching the faces of my people. (God pity us, the terrified republic.) Now I was sorry to have angered the woman who still sat next to me, now deep in conversation with another, younger woman. I longed for some opening, some sign, something to make me a part of the life around me. But there was nothing except my color. A white outsider coming in would have seen a young Negro drinking in a Negro bar, perfectly in his element, in his place, as the saying goes. But the people here knew differently, as I did. I didn't seem to have a place.

So I kept on drinking by myself, saying to myself after each drink, Now I'll go. But I was afraid; I didn't want to sleep on Jules's floor; I didn't want to go to sleep. I kept on drinking and listening to the juke box. They were playing Ella Fitzgerald, "Cow-Cow Boogie."

"Let me buy you a drink," I said to the woman.

She looked at me, startled, suspicious, ready to blow her top.

"On the level," I said. I tried to smile. "Both of you."

"I'll take a beer," the young one said.

I was shaking like a baby. I finished my drink.

"Fine," I said. I turned to the bar.

"Baby," said the old one, "what's your story?"

The man put three beers on the counter.

"I got no story, Ma," I said.

John A. Williams (1925–)

John A. Williams has described himself as "a realistic writer. I've been called a melodramatic writer, but I think that's only because I think the ending of a novel should be at the ending of a book. . . . What I try to do with novels is to deal in forms that are not standard, to improvise as jazz musicians do with their music, so that a standard theme comes out looking brand new. . . . I am trying to do things with form that are not always immediately perceptible to most people."

Born in Jackson, Mississippi, Williams grew up in Syracuse, New York. After serving in the navy during the Second World War, he entered Syracuse University, but he left school before receiving his degree and worked at a number of diverse jobs.

Although he began publishing short stories in 1957, The Angry Ones *(1960) was Williams's first novel. He wrote four more novels in the 1960s:* Night Song *(1961),* Sissie *(1963),* The Man Who Cried I Am *(1967), and* Sons of Darkness, Sons of Light *(1969). His later novels include* Captain Blackman *(1972),* Mothersill and the Foxes *(1975),* The Junior Bachelor Society *(1976),* !Click Song *(1982),* The Berhama Account *(1985), and* Jacob's Ladder *(1987).*

Williams was a scholar at the Breadloaf Conference in 1960, and while writing his first five novels, he traveled extensively throughout the United States, Africa, France, and Spain. He has taught at a number of American colleges, including City College of New York, the University of California at Santa Barbara, and Boston University. Presently, he serves as the Paul Robeson professor of English at Rutgers University.

In addition to his fiction, Williams has published poetry and essays and written television scripts. His series of articles on the United States became the foundation of This Is My Country, Too *(1965). He published* Africa: Her History, Lands, and People *in 1962, and edited two anthologies of black literature—*The Angry Black *(1962) and* Beyond the Angry Black *(1966). His two studies of African American cultural icons appeared in 1970:* The Most Native of Sons: A Biography of Richard Wright *and* The King God Didn't Save, *a critical commentary on the philosophies of Martin Luther King, Jr. In 1991, he and Dennis A. Williams, his son, collaborated on a biographical study of Richard Pryor,* If I

Stop I'll Die: The Comedy and the Tragedy of Richard Pryor. *Most recently, he coedited with Gilbert H. Muller* Bridges: Literature across Cultures *(1994), a college reader and anthology.*

The following selection, "Son in the Afternoon," originally appeared in The Angry Black. *The story focuses on a black Los Angeles writer who soothes his bitter feelings by exposing a white mother's hypocrisy.*

Son in the Afternoon

It was hot. I tend to be a bitch when it's hot. I goosed the little Ford over Sepulveda Boulevard toward Santa Monica until I got stuck in the traffic that pours from L.A. into the surrounding towns. I'd had a very lousy day at the studio.

I was—still am—a writer and this studio had hired me to check scripts and films with Negroes in them to make sure the Negro moviegoer wouldn't be offended. The signs were already clear one day the whole of American industry would be racing pell-mell to get a Negro, showcase a spade. I was kind of a pioneer. I'm a *Negro* writer, you see. The day had been tough because of a couple of verbs—slink and walk. One of those Hollywood hippies had done a script calling for a Negro waiter to slink away from the table where a dinner party was glaring at him. I said the waiter should walk, not slink, because later on he becomes a hero. The Hollywood hippie, who understood it all because he had some colored friends, said that it was essential to the plot that the waiter slink. I said you don't slink one minute and become a hero the next; there has to be some consistency. The Negro actor I was standing up for said nothing either way. He had played Uncle Tom roles so long that he had become Uncle Tom. But the director agreed with me.

Anyway . . . hear me out now. I was on my way to Santa Monica to pick up my mother, Nora. It was a long haul for such a hot day. I had planned a quiet evening: a nice shower, fresh clothes, and then I would have dinner at the Watkins and talk with some of the musicians on the scene for a quick taste before they cut to their gigs. After, I was going to the Pigalle down on Figueroa and catch Earl Grant at the organ, and still later, if nothing exciting happened, I'd pick up Scottie and make it to the Lighthouse on the Beach or to the Strollers and listen to some of the white boys play. I liked the long drive, especially while listening to Sleepy Stein's show on the radio. Later, much later of course, it would be home, back to Watts.

So you see, this picking up Nora was a little inconvenient. My mother was a maid for the Couchmans. Ronald Couchman was an architect, a good one I understood from Nora who has a fine sense for this sort of thing; you don't work in some hundred-odd houses during your life without getting some idea of the way a house should be laid out. Couchman's wife, Kay, was a playgirl who drove a white Jaguar from one party to another. My mother didn't like her too much; she didn't seem to care much for her son, Ronald, junior. There's something wrong with a parent who can't really love her own child, Nora thought. The Couchmans lived in a real fine residential section, of course. A number of actors lived nearby, character actors, not really big stars.

Somehow it is very funny. I mean that the maids and butlers knew everything about these people, and these people knew nothing at all about the help. Through Nora and her friends I knew who was laying whose wife; who had money and who *really* had money; I knew about the wild parties hours before the police, and who smoked marijuana, when, and where they got it.

To get to Couchman's driveway I had to go three blocks up one side of a palm-planted center strip and back down the other. The driveway bent gently, then swept back out of sight of the main road. The house, sheltered by slim palms, looked like a transplanted New England Colonial. I parked and walked to the kitchen door, skirting the growling Great Dane who was tied to a tree. That was the route to the kitchen door.

I don't like kitchen doors. Entering people's houses by them, I mean. I 'd done this thing most of my life when I called at places where Nora worked to pick up the patched or worn sheets or the half-eaten roasts, the battered, tarnished silver—the fringe benefits of a housemaid. As a teen-ager I'd told Nora I was through with that crap; I was not going through anyone's kitchen door. She only laughed and said I'd learn. One day soon after, I called for her and without knocking walked right through the front door of this house and right on through the living room. I was almost out of the room when I saw feet behind the couch. I leaned over and there was Mr. Jorgensen and his wife making out like crazy. I guess they thought Nora had gone and it must have hit them sort of suddenly and they went at it like the hell-bomb was due to drop any minute. I've been that way too, mostly in the spring. Of course, when Mr. Jorgensen looked over his shoulder and saw me, you know what happened. I was thrown out and Nora right behind me. It was the middle of winter, the old man was sick and the coal bill three months overdue. Nora was right about those kitchen doors: I learned.

My mother saw me before I could ring the bell. She opened the door. "Hello," she said. She was breathing hard, like she'd been running or something. "Come in and sit down. I don't know *where* that Kay is. Little Ronald is sick and she's probably out gettin' drunk again." She left me then and trotted back through the house, I guess to be with Ronnie. I hated the combination of her white nylon uniform, her dark brown face and the wide streaks of gray in her hair. Nora had married this guy from Texas a few years after the old man had died. He was all right. He made out okay. Nora didn't have to work, but she just couldn't be still; she always had to be doing something. I suggested she quit work, but I had as much luck as her husband. I used to tease her about liking to be around those white folks. It would have been good for her to take an extended trip around the country visiting my brothers and sisters. Once she got to Philadelphia, she could go right out to the cemetery and sit awhile with the old man.

I walked through the Couchman home. I liked the library. I thought if I knew Couchman I'd like him. The room made me feel like that. I left it and went into the big living room. You could tell that Couchman had let his wife do that. Everything in it was fast, dart-like, with no sense of ease. But on the walls were several of Couchman's conceptions of buildings and homes. I guess he was a disciple of Wright.* My mother walked rapidly through the room without looking at me and said, "Just be patient, Wendell. She should be here real soon."

"Yeah," I said, "with a snootful." I had turned back to the drawings when Ronnie scampered into the room, his face twisted with rage.

"Nora!" he tried to roar, perhaps the way he'd seen the parents of some of his

* Frank Lloyd Wright (1867–1959), American architect noted for his contributions to modern designs during his seventy-year career.

friends roar at their maids. I'm quite sure Kay didn't shout at Nora, and I don't think Couchman would. But then no one shouts at Nora. "Nora, you come right back here this minute!" the little bastard shouted and stamped and pointed to a spot on the floor where Nora was supposed to come to roost. I have a nasty temper. Sometimes it lies dormant for ages and at other times, like when the weather is hot and nothing seems to be going right, it's bubbling and ready to explode. "Don't talk to *my* mother like that, you little—!" I said sharply, breaking off just before I cursed. I wanted him to be large enough for me to strike. "How'd you like for me to talk to *your* mother like that?"

The nine-year-old looked up at me in surprise and confusion. He hadn't expected me to say anything. I was just another piece of furniture. Tears rose in his eyes and spilled out onto his pale cheeks. He put his hands behind him, twisted them. He moved backwards, away from me. He looked at my mother with a "Nora, come help me" look. And sure enough, there was Nora, speeding back across the room, gathering the kid in her arms, tucking his robe together. I was too angry to feel hatred for myself.

Ronnie was the Couchman's only kid. Nora loved him. I suppose that was the trouble. Couchman was gone ten, twelve hours a day. Kay didn't stay around the house any longer than she had to. So Ronnie had only my mother. I think kids should have someone to love, and Nora wasn't a bad sort. But somehow when the six of us, her own children, were growing up we never had her. She was gone, out scuffling to get those crumbs to put into our mouths and shoes for our feet and praying for something to happen so that all the space in between would be taken care of. Nora's affection for us took the form of rushing out into the morning's five o'clock blackness to wake some silly bitch and get her coffee; took form in her trudging five miles home every night instead of taking the streetcar to save money to buy tablets for us, to use at school, we said. But the truth was that all of us liked to draw and we went through a writing tablet in a couple of hours every day. Can you imagine? There's not a goddamn artist among us. We never had the physical affection, the pat on the head, the quick, smiling kiss, the "gimmee a hug" routine. All of this Ronnie was getting.

Now he buried his little blond head in Nora's breast and sobbed. "There, there now," Nora said. "Don't you cry, Ronnie. Ol' Wendell is just jealous, and he hasn't much sense either. He didn't mean nuthin'."

I left the room. Nora had hit it of course, hit it and passed on. I looked back. It didn't look so incongruous, the white and black together, I mean. Ronnie was still sobbing. His head bobbed gently on Nora's shoulder. The only time I ever got that close to her was when she trapped me with a bearhug so she could whale the daylights out of me after I put a snowball through Mrs. Grant's window. I walked outside and lit a cigarette. When Ronnie was in the hospital the month before, Nora got me to run her way over to Hollywood every night to see him. I didn't like that worth a damn. All right, I'll admit it: it did upset me. All that affection I didn't get nor my brothers and sisters going to that little white boy who, without a doubt, when away from her called her the names he'd learned from adults. Can you imagine a nine-year-old kid calling Nora a "girl," "our girl"? I spat at the Great Dane. He snarled and then I bounced a rock off his fanny. "Lay down, you bastard," I muttered. It was a good thing he was tied up.

I heard the low cough of the Jaguar slapping against the road. The car was throttled down, and with a muted roar it swung into the driveway. The woman aimed it for me. I was evil enough not to move. I was tired of playing with these people. At the last moment, grinning, she swung the wheel over and braked. She bounded out of the car like a tennis player vaulting over a net.

"Hi," she said, tugging at her shorts.

"Hello."

"You're Nora's boy?"

"I'm Nora's son." Hell, I was as old as she was; besides, I can't stand "boy."

"Nora tells us you're working in Hollywood. Like it?"

"It's all right."

"You must be pretty talented."

We stood looking at each other while the dog whined for her attention. Kay had a nice body and it was well tanned. She was high, boy, was she high. Looking at her, I could feel myself going into my sexy bastard routine; sometimes I can swing it great. Maybe it all had to do with the business inside. Kay took off her sunglasses and took a good look at me. "Do you have a cigarette?"

I gave her one and lit it. "Nice tan," I said. Most white people I know think it's a great big deal if a Negro compliments them on their tans. It's a large laugh. You have all this volleyball about color and come summer you can't hold the white folks back from the beaches, anyplace where they can get some sun. And of course the blacker they get, the more pleased they are. Crazy. If there is ever a Negro revolt, it will come during the summer and Negroes will descend upon the beaches around the nation and paralyze the country. You can't conceal cattle prods and bombs and pistols and police dogs when you're showing your birthday suit to the sun.

"You like it?" she asked. She was pleased. She placed her arm next to mine. "Almost the same color," she said.

"Ronnie isn't feeling well," I said.

"Oh, the poor kid. I'm so glad we have Nora. She's such a charm. I'll run right in and look at him. Do have a drink in the bar. Fix me one too, will you?" Kay skipped inside and I went to the bar and poured out two strong drinks. I made hers stronger than mine. She was back soon. "Nora was trying to put him to sleep and she made me stay out." She giggled. She quickly tossed off her drink. "Another, please?" While I was fixing her drink she was saying how amazing it was for Nora to have such a talented son. What she was really saying was that it was amazing for a servant to have a son who was not also a servant. "Anything can happen in a democracy," I said. "Servants' sons drink with madames and so on."

"Oh, Nora isn't a servant," Kay said. "She's part of the family."

Yeah, I thought. Where and how many times had I heard *that* before?

In the ensuing silence, she started to admire her tan again. "You think it's pretty good, do you? You don't know how hard I worked to get it." I moved closer to her and held her arm. I placed my other arm around her. She pretended not to see or feel it, but she wasn't trying to get away either. In fact she was pressing closer and the register in my brain that tells me at the precise moment when I'm in, went off. Kay was very high. I put both arms around her and she put both hers around me. When I kissed her, she responded completely.

"Mom!"

"Ronnie, come back to bed," I heard Nora shout from the other room. We could hear Ronnie running over the rug in the outer room. Kay tried to get away from me, push me to one side, because we could tell that Ronnie knew where to look for his Mom: he was running right for the bar, where we were. "Oh, please," she said, "don't let him see us." I wouldn't let her push me away. "Stop!" she hissed. "He'll *see* us!" We stopped struggling just for an instant, and we listened to the echoes of the word *see*. She gritted her teeth and renewed her efforts to get away.

Me? I had the scene laid right out. The kid breaks into the room, see, and sees his mother in this real wriggly clinch with this colored guy who's just shouted at him, see, and no matter how his mother explains it away, the kid has the image—the colored guy and his mother—for the rest of his life, see?

That's the way it happened. The kid's mother hissed under her breath, *"You're crazy!"* and she looked at me as though she were seeing me or something about me for the very first time. I'd released her as soon as Ronnie, romping into the bar, saw us and came to a full, open-mouthed halt. Kay went to him. He looked first at me, then at his mother. Kay turned to me, but she couldn't speak.

Outside the living room my mother called, "Wendell, where are you? We can go now."

I started to move past Kay and Ronnie. I felt many things, but I made myself think mostly, *There you little bastard, there.*

My mother thrust her face inside the door and said, "Good-bye, Mrs. Couchman. See you tomorrow. 'Bye, Ronnie."

"Yes," Kay said, sort of stunned. "Tomorrow." She was reaching for Ronnie's hand as we left, but the kid was slapping her hand away. I hurried quickly after Nora, hating the long drive back to Watts.

Toni Morrison (1931–)

About the art of writing novels Toni Morrison has said, "It seems to me that the best art is political and you ought to be able to make it unquestionably political and irrevocably beautiful at the same time." Among only a few authors who successfully blend art and politics, Morrison's fiction is a chronicle of African American culture, connecting historical events to contemporary issues.

She was born Chloe Anthony Wofford during the Depression in Lorain, Ohio, a steel town. Her father worked at a steel mill and other available jobs, while her mother maintained the house for her husband and four children. The second oldest child, Morrison received her bachelor's from Howard University in 1953 and her master's from Cornell University in 1955. She has taught English and creative writing at Texas Southern University, Howard University, Yale University, the State University of New York-Purchase, and Princeton University. While teaching at Howard University, she married and had two sons. But after spending years in a disappointing marriage, Morrison divorced her Jamaican husband, keeping his surname and the manuscripts she had written and relocating to Syracuse, New York. Morrison's new environment brought her a job as an editor at Random House, where she helped several noted black women writers to gain publication, including Angela Davis, Toni Cade Bambara, and Gayle Jones.

Morrison described her writing in this way: "There are things that I try to incorporate into my fiction that are directly and deliberately related to what I regard as the major characteristics of Black art. . . . One of which is the ability to be both print and oral literature. . . . [African American literature] should try deliberately to make you stand up and make you feel something profoundly in the same way that a Black preacher requires his congregation to speak, to join him . . . to weep and to cry and to accede to change and to modify. . . ." Succeeding in these aspects, Morrison's works echo the voices of narrators seen and unseen, living in the present of the story while also rooted in the past. Readers are pulled into that world both emotionally and intellectually through language that demands an active response.

Her novels include The Bluest Eye *(1970);* Sula *(1973);* Song of Solomon *(1977), winner of a National Book Critics Award;* Tar Baby *(1981);* Beloved *(1987), winner of a Pulitzer Prize; and* Jazz *(1992). Her play,* Dreaming Emmett, *was produced in 1986, and her nonfiction includes two books of essays:* Playing in the Dark: Whiteness and the Literary Imagination *(1992) and* Racing Justice, En-Gendering Power: Essays on Anita Hill, Clarence Thomas, and the Others on the Constructing of Social Reality *(1992).*

In 1993, Morrison became the first African American woman to win the Nobel Prize for literature, an award that honored the body of her writing.

"Recitatif" was originally published in Confirmation: An Anthology of African-American Women *(1983) edited by Amiri and Amini Baraka. The story looks at two women—one black and one white—who for over twenty years have shared intersecting lives as well as guilt about a childhood experience.*

Recitatif

My mother danced all night and Roberta's was sick. That's why we were taken to St. Bonny's. People want to put their arms around you when you tell them you were in a shelter, but it really wasn't bad. No big long room with one hundred beds like Bellevue. There were four to a room, and when Roberta and me came, there was a shortage of state kids, so we were the only ones assigned to 406 and could go from bed to bed if we wanted to. And we wanted to, too. We changed beds every night and for the whole four months we were there we never picked one out as our own permanent bed.

It didn't start out that way. The minute I walked in and the Big Bozo introduced us, I got sick to my stomach. It was one thing to be taken out of your own bed early in the morning—it was something else to be stuck in a strange place with a girl from a whole other race. And Mary, that's my mother, she was right. Every now and then she would stop dancing long enough to tell me something important and one of the things she said was that they never washed their hair and they smelled funny. Roberta sure did. Smell funny, I mean. So when the Big Bozo (nobody ever called her Mrs. Itkin, just like nobody ever said St. Bonaventure)—when she said, "Twyla, this is Roberta. Roberta, this is Twyla. Make each other welcome," I said, "My mother won't like you putting me in here."

"Good," said Bozo. "Maybe then she'll come and take you home."

How's that for mean? If Roberta had laughed I would have killed her, but she didn't. She just walked over to the window and stood with her back to us.

"Turn around," said the Bozo. "Don't be rude. Now Twyla. Roberta. When you hear a loud buzzer, that's the call for dinner. Come down to the first floor. Any fights and no movie." And then, just to make sure we knew what we would be missing, *"The Wizard of Oz."*

Roberta must have thought I meant that my mother would be mad about my being put in the shelter. Not about rooming with her, because as soon as Bozo left she came over to me and said, "Is your mother sick too?"

"No," I said. "She just likes to dance all night."

"Oh." She nodded her head and I liked the way she understood things so fast. So for the moment it didn't matter that we looked like salt and pepper standing there and that's what the other kids called us sometimes. We were eight years old and got F's all the time. Me because I couldn't remember what I read or what the teacher said. And Roberta because she couldn't read at all and didn't even listen to the teacher. She wasn't good at anything except jacks, at which she was a killer: pow scoop pow scoop pow scoop.

We didn't like each other all that much at first, but nobody else wanted to play with us because we weren't real orphans with beautiful dead parents in the sky. We were dumped. Even the New York City Puerto Ricans and the upstate Indians ignored us. All kinds of kids were in there, black ones, white ones, even two Koreans. The food was good, though. At least I thought so. Roberta hated it and left whole pieces of things on her plate. Spam, Salisbury steak—even Jell-O with fruit cocktail in it, and she didn't care if I ate what she wouldn't. Mary's idea of supper was popcorn and a can of Yoo-Hoo. Hot mashed potatoes and two weenies was like Thanksgiving for me.

It really wasn't bad, St. Bonny's. The big girls on the second floor pushed us around now and then. But that was all. They wore lipstick and eyebrow pencil and wobbled their knees while they watched TV. Fifteen, sixteen, even, some of them were. They were put-out girls, scared runaways most of them. Poor little girls who fought their uncles off but looked tough to us, and mean. God, did they look mean. The staff tried to keep them separate from the younger children, but sometimes they caught us watching them in the orchard where they played radios and danced with each other. They'd light out after us and pull our hair or twist our arms. We were scared of them, Roberta and me, but neither of us wanted the other one to know it. So we got a good list of dirty names we could shout back when we ran from them through the orchard. I used to dream a lot and almost always the orchard was there. Two acres, four maybe, of these little apple trees. Hundreds of them. Empty and crooked like beggar women when I first came to St. Bonny's but fat with flowers when I left. I don't know why I dreamt about that orchard so much. Nothing really happened there. Nothing all that important, I mean. Just the big girls dancing and playing the radio. Roberta and me watching. Maggie fell down there once. The kitchen woman with legs like parentheses. And the big girls laughed at her. We should have helped her up, I know, but we were scared of those girls with lipstick and eyebrow pencil. Maggie couldn't talk. The kids said she had her tongue cut out, but I think she was just born that way: mute. She was old and sandy-colored and she worked in the kitchen. I don't know if she was nice or not. I just remember her legs like parentheses and how she rocked when she walked. She worked from early in the morning till two o'clock, and if she was late, if she had too much cleaning and didn't get out till two-fifteen or so, she'd cut through the orchard so she wouldn't miss her bus and have to wait another hour. She wore this really stupid little hat—a kid's hat with ear flaps—and she wasn't much taller than we were. A really awful little hat. Even for a mute, it was dumb—dressing like a kid and never saying anything at all.

"But what about if somebody tries to kill her?" I used to wonder about that. "Or what if she wants to cry? Can she cry?"

"Sure," Roberta said. "But just tears. No sounds come out."

"She can't scream?"

"Nope. Nothing."

"Can she hear?"

"I guess."

"Let's call her," I said. And we did.

"Dummy! Dummy!" She never turned her head.

"Bow legs! Bow legs!" Nothing. She just rocked on, the chin straps of her baby-boy hat swaying from side to side. I think we were wrong. I think she could hear and didn't let on. And it shames me even now to think there was somebody in there after all who heard us call her those names and couldn't tell on us.

We got along all right, Roberta and me. Changed beds every night, got F's in civics and communication skills and gym. The Bozo was disappointed in us, she said. Out of 130 of us state cases, 90 were under twelve. Almost all were real orphans with beautiful dead parents in the sky. We were the only ones dumped and the only ones with F's in three classes including gym. So we got along—what with her leaving whole pieces of things on her plate and being nice about not asking questions.

I think it was the day before Maggie fell down that we found out our mothers were coming to visit us on the same Sunday. We had been at the shelter twenty-eight days (Roberta twenty-eight and a half) and this was their first visit with us. Our mothers would come at ten o'clock in time for chapel, then lunch with us in the teachers' lounge. I thought if my dancing mother met her sick mother it might be good for her. And Roberta thought her sick mother would get a big bang out of a dancing one. We got excited about it and curled each other's hair. After breakfast we sat on the bed watching the road from the window. Roberta's socks were still wet. She washed them the night before and put them on the radiator to dry. They hadn't, but she put them on anyway because their tops were so pretty—scalloped in pink. Each of us had a purple construction-paper basket that we had made in craft class. Mine had a yellow crayon rabbit on it. Roberta's had eggs with wiggly lines of color. Inside were cellophane grass and just the jelly beans because I'd eaten the two marshmallow eggs they gave us. The Big Bozo came herself to get us. Smiling she told us we looked very nice and to come downstairs. We were so surprised by the smile we'd never seen before, neither of us moved.

"Don't you want to see your mommies?"

I stood up first and spilled the jelly beans all over the floor. Bozo's smile disappeared while we scrambled to get the candy up off the floor and put it back in the grass.

She escorted us downstairs to the first floor, where the other girls were lining up to file into the chapel. A bunch of grown-ups stood to one side. Viewers mostly. The old biddies who wanted servants and the fags who wanted company looking for children they might want to adopt. Once in a while a grandmother. Almost never anybody young or anybody whose face wouldn't scare you in the night. Because if any of the real orphans had young relatives they wouldn't be real orphans. I saw Mary right away. She had on those green slacks I hated and hated even more now because didn't she know we were going to chapel? And that fur jacket with the pocket linings so ripped she had to pull to get her hands out of them. But her face was pretty—like always—and she smiled and waved like she was the little girl looking for her mother, not me.

I walked slowly, trying not to drop the jelly beans and hoping the paper handle would hold. I had to use my last Chiclet because by the time I finished cutting everything out, all the Elmer's was gone. I am left-handed and the scissors never worked for me. It didn't matter, though; I might just as well have chewed the gum. Mary dropped to her knees and grabbed me, mashing the basket, the jelly beans, and the grass into her ratty fur jacket.

"Twyla, baby. Twyla, baby!"

I could have killed her. Already I heard the big girls in the orchard the next time saying,"Twyyyyyla, baby!" But I couldn't stay mad at Mary while she was smiling and hugging me and smelling of Lady Esther dusting powder. I wanted to stay buried in her fur all day.

To tell the truth I forgot about Roberta. Mary and I got in line for the traipse into chapel and I was feeling proud because she looked so beautiful even in those ugly green slacks that made her behind stick out. A pretty mother on earth is better than a beautiful dead one in the sky even if she did leave you all alone to go dancing.

I felt a tap on my shoulder, turned, and saw Roberta smiling. I smiled back, but not too much lest somebody think this visit was the biggest thing that ever happened in my life. Then Roberta said, "Mother, I want you to meet my roommate, Twyla. And that's Twyla's mother."

I looked up it seemed for miles. She was big. Bigger than any man and on her chest was the biggest cross I'd ever seen. I swear it was six inches long each way. And in the crook of her arm was the biggest Bible ever made.

Mary, simpleminded as ever, grinned and tried to yank her hand out of the pocket with the raggedy lining—to shake hands, I guess. Roberta's mother looked down at me and then looked down at Mary too. She didn't say anything, just grabbed Roberta with her Bible-free hand and stepped out of line, walking quickly to the rear of it. Mary was still grinning because she's not too swift when it comes to what's really going on. Then this light bulb goes off in her head and she says "That bitch!" really loud and us almost in the chapel now. Organ music whining; the Bonny Angels singing sweetly. Everybody in the world turned around to look. And Mary would have kept it up—kept calling names if I hadn't squeezed her hands as hard as I could. That helped a little, but she still twitched and crossed and uncrossed her legs all through service. Even groaned a couple of times. Why did I think she would come there and act right? Slacks. No hat like the grandmothers and viewers, and groaning all the while. When we stood for hymns she kept her mouth shut. Wouldn't even look at the words on the page. She actually reached in her purse for a mirror to check her lipstick. All I could think of was that she really needed to be killed. The sermon lasted a year, and I knew the real orphans were looking smug again.

We were supposed to have lunch in the teacher's lounge, but Mary didn't bring anything, so we picked fur and cellophane grass off the mashed jelly beans and ate them. I could have killed her. I sneaked a look at Roberta. Her mother had brought chicken legs and ham sandwiches and oranges and a whole box of chocolate-covered grahams. Roberta drank milk from a thermos while her mother read the Bible to her.

Things are not right. The wrong food is always with the wrong people. Maybe that's why I got into waitress work later—to match up the right people with the right food. Roberta just let those chicken legs sit there, but she did bring a stack of grahams up to me later when the visit was over. I think she was sorry that her mother would not shake my mother's hand. And I liked that and I liked the fact that she didn't say a word about Mary groaning all the way through the service and not bringing any lunch.

Roberta left in May when the apple trees were heavy and white. On her last day we went to the orchard to watch the big girls smoke and dance by the radio. It didn't matter that they said, "Twyyyyyla, baby." We sat on the ground and breathed. Lady Esther. Apple blossoms. I still go soft when I smell one or the other. Roberta was going home. The big cross and the big Bible was coming to get her and she seemed sort of glad and sort of not. I thought I would die in that room of four beds without her and I knew Bozo had plans to move some other dumped kid in there with me. Roberta promised to write every day, which was really sweet of her because she couldn't read a lick so how could she write anybody? I would have drawn pictures and sent them to her but she never gave me her address. Little by little she faded. Her wet socks with the pink scalloped tops and her big serious-looking eyes—that's all I could catch when I tried to bring her to mind.

I was working behind the counter at the Howard Johnson's on the Thruway just before the Kingston exit. Not a bad job. Kind of a long ride from Newburgh, but okay once I got there. Mine was the second night shift, eleven to seven. Very light until a Greyhound checked in for breakfast around six-thirty. At that hour the sun was all the way clear of the hills behind the restaurant. The place looked better at night—more like shelter—but I loved it when the sun broke in, even if it did show all the cracks in the vinyl and the speckled floor looked dirty no matter what the mop boy did.

It was August and a bus crowd was just unloading. They would stand around a long while: going to the john, and looking at gifts and junk-for-sale machines, reluctant to sit down so soon. Even to eat. I was trying to fill the coffeepots and get them all situated on the electric burners when I saw her. She was sitting in a booth smoking a cigarette with two guys smothered in head and facial hair. Her own hair was so big and wild I could hardly see her face. But the eyes. I would know them anywhere. She had on a powder-blue halter and shorts outfit and earrings the size of bracelets. Talk about lipstick and eyebrow pencil. She made the big girls look like nuns. I couldn't get off the counter until seven o'clock, but I kept watching the booth in case they got up to leave before that. My replacement was on time for a change, so I counted and stacked my receipts as fast as I could and signed off. I walked over to the booth, smiling and wondering if she would remember me. Or even if she wanted to remember me. Maybe she didn't want to be reminded of St. Bonny's or to have anybody know she was ever there. I know I never talked about it to anybody.

I put my hands in my apron pockets and leaned against the back of the booth facing them.

"Roberta? Roberta Fisk?"

She looked up. "Yeah?"

"Twyla."

She squinted for a second and then said, "Wow."

"Remember me?"

"Sure. Hey. Wow."

"It's been awhile," I said, and gave a smile to the two hairy guys.

"Yeah. Wow. You work here?"

"Yeah," I said. "I live in Newburgh."

"Newburgh? No kidding?" She laughed then, a private laugh that included the guys but only the guys, and they laughed with her. What could I do but laugh too and wonder why I was standing there with my knees showing out from under that uniform. Without looking I could see the blue-and-white triangle on my head, my hair shapeless in a net, my ankles thick in white oxfords. Nothing could have been less sheer than my stockings. There was this silence that came down right after I laughed. A silence it was her turn to fill up. With introductions, maybe, to her boyfriends or an invitation to sit down and have a Coke. Instead she lit a cigarette off the one she'd just finished and said, "We're on our way to the Coast. He's got an appointment with Hendrix." She gestured casually toward the boy next to her.

"Hendrix? Fantastic," I said. "Really fantastic. What's she doing now?"

Roberta coughed on her cigarette and the two guys rolled their eyes up at the ceiling.

"Hendrix. Jimi Hendrix, asshole. He's only the biggest—Oh, wow. Forget it."

I was dismissed without anyone saying good-bye, so I thought I would do it for her.

"How's your mother?" I asked. Her grin cracked her whole face. She swallowed. "Fine," she said. "How's yours?"

"Pretty as a picture," I said and turned away. The backs of my knees were damp. Howard Johnson's really was a dump in the sunlight.

James is as comfortable as a house slipper. He liked my cooking and I liked his big loud family. They have lived in Newburgh all of their lives and talk about it the way people do who have always known a home. His grandmother has a porch swing older than his father and when they talk about streets and avenues and buildings they call them names they no longer have. They still call the A&P Rico's because it stands on property once a mom-and-pop store owned by Mr. Rico. And they call the new community college Town Hall because it once was. My mother-in-law puts up jelly and cucumbers and buys butter wrapped in cloth from a dairy. James and his father talk about fishing and baseball and I can see them all together on the Hudson in a raggedy skiff. Half the population of Newburgh is on welfare now, but to my husband's family it was still some upstate paradise of a time long past. A time of ice houses and vegetable wagons, coal furnaces and children weeding gardens. When our son was born my mother-in-law gave me the crib blanket that had been hers.

But the town they remembered had changed. Something quick was in the air. Magnificent old houses, so ruined they had become shelter for squatters and rent risks, were bought and renovated. Smart IBM people moved out of their suburbs back into the city and put shutters up and herb gardens in their backyards. A brochure came in the mail announcing the opening of a Food Emporium. Gourmet food, it said—and listed items the rich IBM crowd would want. It was located in a new mall at the edge of town and I drove out to shop there one day—just to see. It was late in June. After the tulips were gone and the Queen Elizabeth roses were open everywhere. I trailed my cart along the aisle tossing in smoked oysters and Robert's sauce and things I knew would sit in my cupboard for years. Only when I found some Klondike ice cream bars did I feel less guilty about spending James's fireman's salary so foolishly. My father-in-law ate them with the same gusto little Joseph did.

Waiting in the checkout line I heard a voice say, "Twyla!"

The classical music piped over the aisles had affected me and the woman leaning toward me as dressed to kill. Diamonds on her hand, a smart white summer dress. "I'm Mrs. Benson," I said.

"Ho. Ho. The Big Bozo," she sang.

For a split second I didn't know what she was talking about. She had a bunch of asparagus and two cartons of fancy water.

"Roberta!"

"Right."

"For heaven's sake. Roberta."

"You look great," she said.

"So do you. Where are you? Here? In Newburgh?"

"Yes. Over in Annandale."

I was opening my mouth to say more when the cashier called my attention to her empty counter.

"Meet you outside." Roberta pointed her finger and went into the express line.

I placed the groceries and kept myself from glancing around to check Roberta's progress. I remembered Howard Johnson's and looking for a chance to speak only to be greeted with a stingy "wow." But she was waiting for me and her huge hair was sleek now, smooth around a small, nicely shaped head. Shoes, dress, everything lovely and summery and rich. I was dying to know what happened to her, how she got from Jimi Hendrix to Annandale, a neighborhood full of doctors and IBM executives. Easy, I thought. Everything is so easy for them. They think they own the world.

"How long," I asked her. "How long have you been here?"

"A year. I got married to a man who lives here. And you, you're married too, right? Benson, you said."

"Yeah. James Benson."

"And is he nice?"

"Oh, is he nice?"

"Well, is he?" Roberta's eyes were steady as though she really meant the question and wanted an answer.

"He's wonderful, Roberta. Wonderful."

"So you're happy."

"Very."

"That's good," she said and nodded her head. "I always hoped you'd be happy. Any kids? I know you have kids."

"One. A boy. How about you?"

"Four."

"Four?"

She laughed. "Step kids. He's a widower."

"Oh."

"Got a minute? Let's have a coffee."

I thought about the Klondikes melting and the inconvenience of going all the way to my car and putting the bags in the trunk. Served me right for buying all that stuff I didn't need. Roberta was ahead of me.

"Put them in my car. It's right here."

And then I saw the dark blue limousine.

"You married a Chinaman?"

"No." She laughed. "He's the driver."

"Oh, my. If the Big Bozo could see you now."

We both giggled. Really giggled. Suddenly, in just a pulse beat, twenty years disappeared and all of it came rushing back. The big girls (whom we called gar girls—Roberta's misheard word for the evil stone faces described in a civics class) there dancing in the orchard, the ploppy mashed potatoes, the double weenies, the Spam with pineapple. We went into the coffee shop holding on to one another and I tried to think why we were glad to see each other this time and not before. Once, twelve years ago, we passed like strangers. A black girl and a white girl meeting in a Howard Johnson's on the road and having nothing to say. One in a blue-and-white triangle waitress hat, the other on her way to see Hendrix. Now we were behaving like sisters separated for much too long. Those four short months were nothing in time. Maybe it was the thing itself. Just being there, together. Two little girls who knew what nobody else in the world knew—how not to ask questions. How to believe what had to be believed. There was politeness in that reluctance and generosity as well. Is your mother sick too? No, she dances all night. Oh—and an understanding nod.

We sat in a booth by the window and fell into recollection like veterans.

"Did you ever learn to read?"

"Watch." She picked up the menu. "Special of the day. Cream of corn soup. Entrées. Two dots and a wriggly line. Quiche. Chef salad, scallops. . . ."

I was laughing and applauding when the waitress came up.

"Remember the Easter baskets?"

"And how we tried to *introduce* them?"

"Your mother with that cross like two telephone poles."

"And yours with those tight slacks."

We laughed so loudly heads turned and made the laughter hard to suppress.

"What happened to the Jimi Hendrix date?"

Roberta made a blow-out sound with her lips.

"When he died I thought about you."

"Oh, you heard about him finally?"

"Finally. Come on, I was a small-town country waitress."

"And I was a small-town country dropout. God, were we wild. I still don't know how I got out of there alive."

"But you did."

"I did. I really did. Now I'm Mrs. Kenneth Norton."

"Sounds like a mouthful."

"It is."

"Servants and all?"

Roberta held up two fingers.

"Ow! What does he do?"

"Computers and stuff. What do I know?"

"I don't remember a hell of lot from those days, but Lord, St. Bonny's is as clear as daylight. Remember Maggie? The days she fell down and those gar girls laughed at her?"

Roberta looked up from her salad and stared at me. "Maggie didn't fall," she said.

"Yes, she did. You remember."

"No, Twyla. They knocked her down. Those girls pushed her down and tore her clothes. In the orchard."

"I don't—that's not what happened."

"Sure it is. In the orchard. Remember how scared we were?"

"Wait a minute. I don't remember any of that."

"And Bozo was fired."

"You're crazy. She was there when I left. You left before me."

"I went back. You weren't there when they fired Bozo."

"What?"

"Twice. Once for a year when I was about ten, another for two months when I was fourteen. That's when I ran away."

"You ran away from St. Bonny's?"

"I had to. What do you want? Me dancing in that orchard?"

"Are you sure about Maggie?"

"Of course I'm sure. You've blocked it, Twyla. It happened. Those girls had behavior problems, you know."

"Didn't they, though. But why can't I remember the Maggie thing?"

"Believe me. It happened. And we were there."

"Who did you room with when you went back?" I asked her as if I would know her. The Maggie thing was troubling me.

"Creeps. They tickled themselves in the night."

My ears were itching and I wanted to go home suddenly. This was all very well but she couldn't just comb her hair, wash her face, and pretend everything was hunky-dory. After the Howard Johnson's snub. And no apology. Nothing.

"Were you on dope or what that time at Howard Johnson's?" I tried to make my voice sound friendlier than I felt.

"Maybe, a little. I never did drugs much. Why?"

"I don't know, you acted sort of like you didn't want to know me then."

"Oh, Twyla, you know how it was in those days: black—white. You know how everything was."

But I didn't know. I thought it was just the opposite. Busloads of blacks and whites came into Howard Johnson's together. They roamed together then: students, musicians, lovers, protesters. You got to see everything at Howard Johnson's, and blacks were very friendly with whites in those days. But sitting there with nothing on my plate but two hard tomato wedges wondering about the melting Klondikes it seemed childish remembering the slight. We went to her car and, with the help of the driver, got my stuff into my station wagon.

"We'll keep in touch this time," she said.

"Sure," I said. "Sure. Give me a call."

"I will," she said, and then, just as I was sliding behind the wheel, she leaned into the window. "By the way. Your mother. Did she ever stop dancing?"

I shook my head. "No. Never."

Roberta nodded.

"And yours? Did she ever get well?"

She smiled a tiny sad smile. "No. She never did. Look, call me, okay?"

"Okay," I said, but I knew I wouldn't. Roberta had messed up my past somehow with that business about Maggie. I wouldn't forget a thing like that. Would I?

Strife came to us that fall. At least that's what the paper called it. Strife. Racial strife. The word made me think of a bird—a big shrieking bird out of 1,000,000,000 B.C. Flapping its wings and cawing. Its eye with no lid always bearing down on you. All day it screeched and at night it slept on the rooftops. It woke up in the morning, and from the *Today* show to the eleven o'clock news it kept you an awful company. I couldn't figure it out from one day to the next. I knew I was supposed to feel something strong, but I didn't know what, and James wasn't any help. Joseph was on the list of kids to be transferred from the junior high school to another one at some far-out-of-the-way place and I thought it was a good thing until I heard it was a bad thing. I mean I didn't know. All the schools seemed dumps to me, and the fact that one was nicer looking didn't hold much weight. But the papers were full of it and then the kids began to get jumpy. In August, mind you. Schools weren't even open yet. I thought Joseph might be frightened to go over there, but he didn't seem scared so I forgot about it, until I found myself driving along Hudson Street out there by the school they were trying to integrate and saw a line of women marching. And who do you suppose was in line, big as life, holding a sign in front of her bigger than her mother's cross? MOTHERS HAVE RIGHTS TOO! it said.

I drove on and then changed my mind. I circled the block, slowed down, and honked my horn.

Roberta looked over and when she saw me she waved. I didn't wave back, but I didn't move either. She handed her sign to another woman and came over to where I was parked.

"Hi."

"What are you doing?"

"Picketing. What's it look like?"

"What for?"

"What do you mean, 'What for?' They want to take my kids and send them out of the neighborhood. They don't want to go."

"So what if they go to another school? My boy's being bussed too, and I don't mind. Why should you?"

"It's not about us, Twyla. Me and you. It's about our kids."

"What's more *us* than that?"

"Well, it is a free country."

"Not yet, but it will be."

"What the hell does that mean? I'm not doing anything to you."

"You really think that?"

"I know it."

"I wonder what made me think you were different."

"I wonder what made me think you were different."

"Look at them," I said. "Just look. Who do they think they are? Swarming all over the place like they own it? And now they think they can decide where my child goes to school. Look at them, Roberta. They're Bozos."

Roberta turned around and looked at the women. Almost all of them were standing still now, waiting. Some were even edging toward us. Roberta looked at me out of some refrigerator behind her eyes. "No, they're not. They're just mothers."

"And what am I? Swiss cheese?"

"I used to curl your hair."

"I hated your hands in my hair."

The women were moving. Our faces looked mean to them of course and they looked as though they could not wait to throw themselves in front of a police car or, better yet, into my car and drag me away by my ankles. Now they surrounded my car and gently, gently began to rock it. I swayed back and forth like a sideways yo-yo. Automatically I reached for Roberta, like the old days in the orchard when they saw us watching them and we had to get out of there, and if one of us fell the other pulled her up and if one of us was caught the other stayed to kick and scratch, and neither would leave the other behind. My arm shot out of the car window but no receiving hand was there. Roberta was looking at me sway from side to side in the car and her face was still. My purse slid from the car seat down under the dashboard. The four policemen who had been drinking Tab in their car finally got the message and strolled over, forcing their way through the women. Quietly, firmly they spoke. "Okay, ladies. Back in line or off the streets."

Some of them went away willingly; others had to be urged away from the car doors and the hood. Roberta didn't move. She was looking steadily at me. I was fumbling to turn on the ignition, which wouldn't catch because the gearshift was still in drive. The seats of the car were a mess because the swaying had thrown my grocery coupons all over and my purse was sprawled on the floor.

"Maybe I am different now, Twyla. But you're not. You're the same little state kid who kicked a poor old black lady when she was down on the ground. You kicked a black lady and you have the nerve to call me a bigot."

The coupons were everywhere and the guts of my purse were bunched under the dashboard. What was she saying? Black? Maggie wasn't black.

"She wasn't black," I said.

"Like hell she wasn't, and you kicked her. We both did. You kicked a black lady who couldn't even scream."

"Liar!"

"You're the liar! Why don't you just go home and leave us alone, huh?"

She turned away and I skidded away from the curb.

The next morning I went into the garage and cut the side out of the carton our portable TV had come in. It wasn't nearly big enough, but after a while I had a decent sign: red spray-painted letters on a white background—AND SO DO CHILDREN****. I meant just to go down to the school and tack it up somewhere so those cows on the picket line across the street could see it, but when I got there, some ten or so others had already assembled—protesting the cows across the street. Police permits and everything. I got in line and we strutted in time on our side while Roberta's group strutted on theirs. That first day we were all dignified, pretending the other side didn't exist. The second day there was name calling and finger gestures. But that was about all. People changed signs from time to time, but Roberta never did and neither did I. Actually my sign didn't make sense without Roberta's. "And so do children what?" one of the women on my side asked me. Have rights, I said, as though it was obvious.

Roberta didn't acknowledge my presence in any way, and I got to thinking maybe she didn't know I was there. I began to pace myself in the line, jostling people one minute and lagging behind the next, so Roberta and I could reach the end of our respective lines at the same time and there would be a moment in our turn when we would face each other. Still, I couldn't tell whether she saw me and knew my sign was for her. The next day I went early before we were scheduled to assemble. I waited until she got there before I exposed my new creation. As soon as she hoisted her MOTHERS HAVE RIGHTS TOO I began to wave my new one, which said, HOW WOULD YOU KNOW? I know she saw that one, but I had gotten addicted now. My signs got crazier each day, and the women on my side decided that I was a kook. They couldn't made heads or tails out of my brilliant screaming posters.

I brought a painted sign in queenly red with huge black letters that said, IS YOUR MOTHER WELL? Roberta took her lunch break and didn't come back for the rest of the day or any day after. Two days later I stopped going too and couldn't have been missed because nobody understood my signs anyway.

It was a nasty six weeks. Classes were suspended and Joseph didn't go to anybody's school until October. The children—everybody's children—soon got bored with that extended vacation they thought was going to be so great. They looked at TV until their eyes flattened. I spent a couple of mornings tutoring my son, as the other mothers said we should. Twice I opened a text from last year that he had never turned in. Twice he yawned in my face. Other mothers organized living room sessions so the kids would keep up. None of the kids could concentrate, so they drifted back to *The Price Is Right* and *The Brady Bunch*. When the school finally opened there were fights once or twice and some sirens roared through the streets every once in a while. There were a lot of photographers from Albany. And just when ABC was about to send up a news crew, the kids settled down like nothing in the world had happened. Joseph hung my HOW WOULD YOU KNOW? sign in his bedroom. I don't know what became of AND SO DO CHILDREN****. I think my father-in-law cleaned some fish on it. He was always puttering around in our garage. Each of his five children lived in Newburgh, and he acted as though he had five extra homes.

I couldn't help looking for Roberta when Joseph graduated from high school, but I didn't see her. It didn't trouble me much what she had said to me in the car. I mean the kicking part. I know I didn't do that, I couldn't do that. But I was puzzled by her telling me Maggie was black. When I thought about it I actually couldn't be certain. She wasn't pitch-black, I knew, or I would have remembered that. What I remember was the kiddie hat and the semicircle legs. I tried to reassure myself about the race thing for a long time until it dawned on me that the truth was already there, and Roberta knew it. I didn't kick her; I didn't join in with the gar girls and kick that lady, but I sure did want to. We watched and never tried to help her and never called for help. Maggie was my dancing mother. Deaf, I thought, and dumb. Nobody inside. Nobody who would hear you if you cried in the night. Nobody who could tell you anything important that you could use. Rocking, dancing, swaying as she walked. And when the gar girls pushed her down and started roughhousing, I knew she wouldn't scream, couldn't—just like me—and I was glad about that.

We decided not to have a tree, because Christmas would be at my mother-in-law's house, so why have a tree at both places? Joseph was at SUNY New Paltz and we had to economize, we said. But at the last minute, I changed my mind. Nothing could be that true. So I rushed around town looking for a tree, something small but wide. By the time I found a place, it was snowing and very late. I dawdled like it was the most important purchase in the world and the tree man was fed up with me. Finally I chose one and had it tied onto the trunk of the car. I drove away slowly because the sand trucks were not out yet and the streets could be murder at the beginning of a snowfall. Downtown the streets were wide and rather empty except for a cluster of people coming out of the Newburgh Hotel. The one hotel in town that wasn't built out of cardboard and Plexiglas. A party, probably. The men huddled in the snow were dressed in tails and the women had furs. Shiny things glittered from underneath their coats. It made me tired to look at them. Tired, tired, tired. On the next corner was a small diner with loops and loops of paper bells in the window. I stopped the car and went in. Just for a cup of coffee and twenty minutes of peace before I went home and tried to finish everything before Christmas Eve.

"Twyla?"

There she was. In a silvery evening gown and dark fur coat. A man and another woman were with her, the man fumbling for change to put in the cigarette machine. The woman was humming and tapping on the counter with her fingernails. They all looked a little bit drunk.

"Well. It's you."

"How are you?"

I shrugged. "Pretty good. Frazzled. Christmas and all."

"Regular?" called the woman from the counter.

"Fine," Roberta called back and then, "Wait for me in the car."

She slipped into the booth beside me. "I have to tell you something, Twyla. I made up my mind if I ever saw you again, I'd tell you."

"I'd just as soon not hear anything, Roberta. It doesn't matter now, anyway."

"No," she said. "Not about that."

"Don't be long," said the woman. She carried two regulars to go and the man peeled his cigarette pack as they left.

"It's about St. Bonny's and Maggie."

"Oh, please."

"Listen to me. I really did think she was black. I didn't make that up. I really thought so. But now I can't be sure. I just remembered her as old, so old. And because she couldn't talk—well, you know, I thought she was crazy. She'd been brought up in an institution like my mother was and like I thought I would be too. And you were right. We didn't kick her. It was the gar girls. Only them. But, well, I wanted to. I really wanted them to hurt her. I said we did it, too. You and me, but that's not true. And I don't want you to carry that around. It was just that I wanted to do it so bad that day—wanting to is doing it."

Her eyes were watery from the drinks she'd had, I guess. I know it's that way with me. One glass of wine and I start bawling over the littlest thing.

"We were kids, Roberta."

"Yeah. Yeah. I know, just kids."

"Eight."

"Eight."

"And lonely."

"Scared, too."

She wiped her cheeks with the heel of her hand and smiled. "Well, that's all I wanted to say."

I nodded and couldn't think of any way to fill the silence that went from the diner past the paper bells on out into the snow. It was heavy now. I thought I'd better wait for the sand trucks before starting home.

"Thanks, Roberta."

"Sure."

"Did I tell you? My mother, she never did stop dancing."

"Yes. You told me. And mine, she never got well." Roberta lifted her hands from the tabletop and covered her face with her palms. When she took them away she really was crying. "Oh, shit, Twyla. Shit, shit, shit. What the hell happened to Maggie?"

Ishmael Reed (1938–)

A *poet, novelist, dramatist, essayist, and editor, the multitalented Ishmael Reed is best known for his fiction writing. John O'Brien describes Reed's novels as "mov[ing] across an unexplored landscape composed of fantasy, and vaudevillian humor, phantasmagoric colors, voodoo rituals, and surrealistic imagery. His novels generally discard plot and resemble more a dream whose revelations are made through piecing together image and episode."*

Born in Chattanooga, Tennessee, Reed grew up in Buffalo, New York. He attended the University of Buffalo, where he majored in American studies, but he left school in his junior year "to continue experimenting" and avoid becoming "a slave to what somebody else was going to use as a career and a way of gaining tenure." Although Reed later regretted leaving college, he brought his interest in literature and history to various writing workshops, arts festivals, and newspaper positions in the New York City and Newark areas. This background, along with his fascination with Africa and the Caribbean, is apparent in the mix of myths and symbols found in his fiction.

In the late 1960s, Reed traveled to northern California, where he taught at the University of California at Berkeley. Forming coalitions with other writers of color, Reed established several resources and publications, such as the Before Columbus Foundation, the anthology The Yardbird Reader, *and the journal* Quilt.

Reed's first novel, The Free-Lance PallBearers *(1967), was applauded by critics for its humor and originality. His subsequent novels continue in an experimental, satirical mode:* Yellow Back Radio Broke-Down *(1969),* Mumbo-Jumbo *(1973),* The Last Days of Louisiana Red *(1974),* Flight to Canada *(1976),* The Terrible Twos *(1982),* Reckless Eyeballing *(1986),* The Terrible Threes *(1989), and* Japanese by Spring *(1993), from which the following selection is taken. Reed's versatility as a writer is evident in his other works as well, including five books of poems and four plays. He edited four anthologies and four collections of essays:* Shrovetide in Old New Orleans *(1978),* God Made Alaska for the Indians *(1982),* Writing Is Fighting *(1988), and* Airing Dirty Laundry *(1993). Most recently, he edited a series of multicultural literature anthologies published in 1995.*

The following selection includes several chapters from Japanese by Spring, *Reed's quiltwork of literature, factual events and people, pop culture, language, and myth. In that novel, the black professor Benjamin Puttbutt, who will do whatever is politically expedient to gain tenure at a predominantly white college, finds himself elevated to a position of power when the college is purchased by a Japanese organization.*

from Japanese by Spring

CHAPTER ONE

When Benjamin "Chappie" Puttbutt's mom and dad said Off to the Wars, they really meant it. George Eliott Puttbutt was a two-star Air Force general, cited and decorated for distinguishing himself in two of the three great yellow wars, the wars against Japan, Korea and Vietnam, and Ruby Puttbutt's star was on the rise as a member of the United States Intelligence community. As a military brat Benjamin knew the techniques of survival and so, after reading that Japan would become a future world power, Puttbutt began to study Japanese while enrolled at the Air Force Academy during the middle sixties. It was the end of an upbringing characterized by regimen and discipline. George and Ruby Puttbutt's idea of education was similar to John Milton's. In his "Of Education," he recommends that "two hours before supper [students] . . . be called out to their military motions, under sky or covert according to the season, as was the Roman wont; first on foot, then, as their age permits, on horseback, to all the art of cavalry . . . in all the skill of embattling . . . fortifying, besieging, and battering, with all of the helps of ancient and modern stratagems, tactics, and warlike maxims." . . .

That's not the only attitude they shared with Milton. With their continuous need for enemies, their motto could have been taken from Milton's panegyric for Cromwell: "New Foes Arise." Their favorite blues singer was "Little Milton." Their favorite comedian: Milton Berle.

Chappie had disappointed his family by being expelled from the Air Force Academy. The academy regarded him as a troublemaker, because he had tried to organize a Black Panther chapter among the few black cadets who were enrolled there, in the middle 1960s. At least that's what everybody thought. In those days he wore a big Afro. It was so big that once some blackbirds tried to make a nest in it. He'd finally received his M.A. from a small college in Utah, and after years of one- to two-year stands at different schools he'd settled at the English department at Jack London College. The deal was, that after three years of commuting between the African-American Studies department, between those who believed Europe to be the center of all culture and those who said that the center of culture was Africa, he'd receive tenure in the Humanity department. Those were the terms of the agreement he'd made with Jack London during his job interview at the MLA. He'd preferred that his tenure be in the Humanity department. He'd be on the winning side, or so he thought. He remembered the rich baritone laughter of his father when he had informed him that he had gotten a job teaching English and literature.

Breaking a tradition going back to the revolutionary war, when the first Puttbutt volunteered for service. Not exactly. In the photos of his ancestors in their military garb, which lined the wall of his father's Maryland den, one was missing. No Puttbutt served in World War II. His grandfather was missing. Didn't serve. Both his mother and father, when they were angry with him, would say, "You're just like your grandfather." Other than that, they never mentioned the man. His expulsion from the Air Force Academy prevented him from finishing Japanese. He got as far as the fifteenth lesson.

Benjamin "Chappie" Puttbutt III was now going to give Japanese another go. He had read one of those ads in the newspaper, "Japanese by Spring," and had signed up with a private tutor at the beginning of the spring semester, 1990, hoping that by spring of 1991 he would know enough to take advantage of the new global realities. He was talking that way now. Sounding like a graduate student in political science. All about global realities. Geopolitical this. Realpolitik that. Weltanschauung this. He was sounding like an edition of *Foreign Affairs*.

CHAPTER TWO

The ambulance carrying one injured black student was pulling away and heading toward the gate. Another student could be seen inside another ambulance. He was being administered oxygen by paramedics. Two others were being chased by a mob of white students led by the Bass boy. One tried to climb a fence, but he was pulled down by some members of the mob and pummeled. He screamed. There was blood everywhere. Robert Bass, Jr., president of the Amerikaner Student Society and the American Student Chapter of the Order of the Boer Nation, a nationwide organization of right-wing students, who were being bankrolled by old man Only and his friends, lifted the student from the pavement and punched him one more time. Flecks of blood flew from his face before he passed out. The other student had disappeared beneath a group of whites, who were attacking him with a baseball bat. The baseball bat and the nightstick had become the favorite weapons in the domestic war. Sometimes those using the nightstick recited baseball metaphors when punishing some poor "suspect." The Los Angeles police who beat Rodney King boasted of having hit "quite a few home runs" on his head. "I haven't had a good game of hardball like this in a long time," one said. (The films of the King beating were similar to the scenes in nature films where hyenas circle and attack a prey while other scavengers approach and retreat.)

There was a television crew processing the scene. Nowadays, the TV crew was an essential body part of the mob. Seeing Benjamin Puttbutt, who had achieved notoriety for his magazine article in the *New York Exegesis,* denouncing affirmative action, the television crew headed in his direction. The reporters were shouting over each other, competing for his attention.

"Mr. Puttbutt, another black student has been beaten. What is your reaction to yet another attack on black students by white students?" Puttbutt walked briskly toward his office, the reporters following him, waiting for the answers to their questions. He didn't disappoint them. The reporters began scribbling in their notebooks and the TV cameras closed in on him.

"The black students bring this on themselves," he said, sucking on a menthol cigarette. Frowning to indicate gravity. Being careful not to leak any of the ashes on his blue blazer or gray slacks. "With their separatism, their inability to fit in, their denial of mainstream values, they get the white students angry. The white students want them to join in, to participate in this generous pie called the United States of America. To end their disaffiliation from the common culture. Black students, and indeed black faculty, should stop their confrontational tactics. They should start to negotiate. They should stop worrying these poor whites with their excessive demands. The white students become upset with these demands. Affirmative action. Quotas. They get themselves worked up. And so it's understandable that they go about assaulting the black students. The white students are merely giving vent to their rage. This is a healthy exercise. It's perfectly understandable. After all, the whites are the real oppressed minority. I can't think of anybody who has as much difficulty on this campus as blondes."

"But one student, the one they sent to the hospital, suffered a fractured skull," a reporter said.

"Was he wearing one of those Malcolm X caps?" A white reporter volunteered that, yes, he indeed was wearing a Malcolm X cap.

"There. So you see. I was correct. He was confronting instead of negotiating. Why, this black separatism is tempting such reactions from the white students. These black students must cease their intellectually tawdry practice of playing to white guilt. They should do more to improve and develop themselves. That way, whites will respect them."

"But this has been the thirteenth black student to have been beaten over the last three weeks." Puttbutt didn't answer the last question. The reporters and camera crews dropped off and headed toward some other interviews.

He walked past the bronze statue of Jack London that stood in the middle of the campus. He paused for a moment to look up. London had his hands in the pockets of a navy pea jacket. The sculptor had captured what was called Jack London's boyish good looks . . . pompadour, racoonlike shaded eyes. The apostle of the blond beast, the Nietzschean üabermensch was a brunet just as his fellow blond beast admirer, Adolph Hitler. In the sculpture, a wolflike dog seemed attached to London's pants leg. London's solution to the Yellow Peril was outlined in a strange fiction entitled "The Unparalleled Invasion" (1910) in which Jacobus Laningdale, "a professor employed in the laboratories of the health office of New York City," works on a plan that will relieve the world of "the Chinese problem."

In 1975, President Moyer meets with Jacobus Laningdale for three hours. They discuss the increase in the Chinese population—by 1975, one billion and growing. With its industrial awakening generated by the Japanese invasion, China is a threat to the white world and does not heed its requirement that it reduce its population, and indeed scoffs at the West's concerns. Li Tang Fwung, described in the London story as "the power behind the Dragon Throne," replies to a convention of 1975 called in Philadelphia and including all Western nations to appeal to and threaten China about its soaring birthrate. He says, "What does

China care for the community of nations? We have our own destiny to accomplish. It is unpleasant that our destiny does not jibe with the destiny of the rest of the world, but what would you do? You have talked windily about the royal races and the heritage of the earth, and we can only reply that, that remains to be seen. You cannot invade us. Never mind about your navies. . . . Our strength is in our population, which will soon be a billion. Thanks to you, we are equipped with all modern war machinery." After his speech London writes, "The world was nonplused, helpless, terrified." (In 1991, the U.S. is so obsessed with the forty-billion-dollar trade deficit with Japan, which means that Japan is selling forty billion dollars more in the U.S. than the U.S. is selling in Japan, that the twenty-billion deficit with China is virtually ignored.) What does the world do? It adopts the plan concocted by Jacobus Laningdale. In a scene reminiscent of the B-52 dropping the atom bomb on Hiroshima, Jack London places an airship above the streets of Peking. "From the airship, as it curved its flight back and forth over the city, fell missiles . . . tubes of fragile glass that shattered into thousands of fragments on streets and house-tops." In this story, Jack London, Oakland's most prominent novelist, candidate for mayor in 1912, the man for whom Oakland's tourist draw, Jack London Square, is named, recommended the extermination of the Chinese: "every virulent form of infectious death stalked the land, wrought from bacteria, and germs and microbes and bacilli, cultured in the laboratories of the West that had come down upon China in the rain of glass."

After the Chinese are wiped out, a multicultural civilization is raised on its remains. "It was a vast and happy intermingling of nations that settled down in China in 1982 and in the years that followed a tremendous and successful experiment in cross-fertilization." Jack London College of Oakland was named for the apostle of Anglo-Saxon superiority. He swallowed the doctrine of development which has polluted the earth and is destroying the ozone, posing a greater threat to those whose lack of pigmentation makes them vulnerable to ultraviolet rays than all of the Yellow Perils, Black Studies programs and Rap musicians combined. "There was no way to communicate Western ideas to the Chinese mind. China remained asleep. The material achievement and progress of the West was a closed book to her; nor could the West open the book." But even with his faith in Anglo destiny, London was as miserable as most superracists are. A bad husband and father. Given to petty outbursts. Paranoid. He thought that the third world was mocking him. London thought that the yellows, blacks and reds were laughing at him. Laughing at Jack London, whose final solution for the Chinese was written in a book called *The Strength of the Strong* penned by a man who hung out at the Piedmont baths among "beautiful" men. In the story "The Unparalleled Invasion," China laughs at the West and, by implication, Jack London. On page 88 of the story, "China laughs." On page 91, "China smiled." On page 92, "China smiled," and on page 92, "China smiled." On the same page, "China smiled," again. In 1911, Jack London pined for a white man who would "wipe that golden smile" off heavyweight champion Jack Johnson's face. Jack London thought that "third world people" were laughing at him. Laughing at the blond beast admirer's brunet hair. Laughing at his addiction to heroin.

Another demonstration passed by. A more J. C. campus organization known as Faith of our Fathers, or the FF, was marching through the campus and shouting their slogan, "We are Wiggers. We are Wiggers," to indicate their status as white niggers. Everybody was a nigger these days. Women, gays, always comparing their situations with blacks.

Puttbutt was a member of the growing anti–affirmative action industry. A black pathology merchant. Throw together a three-hundred-page book with graphs and articles about illegitimacy, welfare dependency, single-family households, drugs and violence; paint the inner cities as the circles of hell in the American paradise—the suburban and rural Americas which were, in the media's imagination, wonderlands with sets by Disney—and you could write your way to the top of the best-sellers list. Get on C-SPAN. It was the biggest literary hustle going and Puttbutt decided that he was going to get his. He had written a dozen or so articles about affirmative action. About how your white colleagues don't respect you. About how you feel stigmatized. About how you feel inferior. You know, the usual. All of these speeches, op-eds and lectures, he felt, would get him where he wanted to be. Would get him tenure. Hadn't his colleagues come up to him after every printed interview he'd given to congratulate him? To tell him that he said what many of them could only whisper? To congratulate him for broaching a subject that was painful to discuss? Being a military brat, a survivor and a loner, he was thinking of the only person in his life who counted. He was thinking of himself. About how his ordeal from semester to semester would end. He would have an opportunity to end his arrangement with African-American Studies. Though its chairman, Charles Obi, was cordial to him, the others made it clear that they didn't want him. He was regarded as an Uncle Ben. Being in the English department was a cup of tea in comparison to the muje that he suffered in the Department of African-American Studies. To say that they weren't comfortable with him would be an understatement. They made it clear to him that they wanted a "club member," which was the code phrase for those of similar ideology, and the ideology kept shifting.

Though there were a few guys still wearing those nationalist pillbox hats, and "Black is Back," or "Black is the Future," sweaters, dreadlocks, the defining ideology of the eighties was feminism. Puttbutt was still a feminist. Memorized every mediocre line by Zora Neale Hurston. Could recite Sylvia Plath from memory. Could toss around terms like phallocentricity. Struggled to make sense of Catharine A. MacKinnon. But now their power was waning—the few black women who had joined the white feminist cause had walked out and formed their own organizations, and the California white men, like Rhett Butler, were deserting the Scarlett O'Haras, were leaving white women for Asian women. Some of those in the Department of Humanity who were to vote on his tenure were feminists and so he still had to be friends with them in case he needed their vote. They'd been trying to attract April Jokujoku, a firebrand radical lesbian ecologist activist to the campus. They were going to pay her three times his salary. Her poetry collected causes the way some people collect stray cats. His informant, Effie Singleton, who worked in African-American Studies and who knew just about everything that was happening on campus, told him that some of those women wanted to replace Puttbutt with her. But he had asked Marsha

Marx, chairperson of Women's Studies, about these rumors and she had assured him that they had no basis in fact.

CHAPTER THREE

An African professor named Kwaku Ladzekpo said that, when teaching, he had picked up from some white students that they felt more intelligent than him.

"Here I am, standing in front of a college class talking about my own culture, and some students would contradict me and say that they knew more about Africa than I did. I was dealing with a lot of eighteen-year-olds who were the products of the TV society and who basically believed that America was the greatest country to ever be on the face of the earth." Professor Ladzekpo was right. And like Professor Ladzekpo, Chappie never knew when he'd be tested. Other black professors, no matter how many credentials they had, or how much rank, would constantly complain about the racism they encountered in white classrooms and the lack of respect in the classrooms that were largely black. Not Chappie, as he was called. While he constantly criticized black students, their study habits, their lack of discipline, he, in the manner of other black neocons, never criticized whites, and indeed blamed blacks for his rude treatment from whites. (Though Chappie was called a neoconservative, neither the Neolithic Conservatives nor the Paleolithic Conservatives would accept him. A speech he had made before the neocon think tank, the Woodwork Foundation, had fallen flat. A reporter recounted that after Chappie Puttbutt had retold the story of how he was once part of the Black Power movement, but left after they discarded his "white comrades in the struggle," nobody applauded.) If only African Americans—a phrase he hated—would shape up, then the white students would be prepared for a man of his depth, Chappie thought.

While the white students called their other professors Professor this, or Mr. that, they called him Chappie. It took them about a month to recognize him as a member of the human species. Chappie was always writing op-eds about how whites were confusing him with members of the "underclass," which is what the media were calling black nowadays. If the underclass worked hard and achieved what he had, the white students would know better, he felt. Wouldn't confuse him with them. Because they would all be like Chappie. So this too was the underclass's fault. For not trying to belong. For being marooned. For still hanging on to "blackness."

Chappie's black days were behind him. He no longer suffered from the double consciousness that Du Bois spoke of. The black part of him had been completely annihilated. His photo could appear on a box of Wheaties and nobody would know the difference.

Toni Cade Bambara (1939–)

***B**orn and raised in New York City, Toni Cade Bambara studied theater arts and English literature at Queens College, receiving a bachelor's in 1959. While earning her master's in American literature from the City College of New York, she* *performed social work. Later, she studied at the University of Florence and the École de Mime Étienne Decroux in Paris. She has taught at Rutgers University, City College of New York, Duke University, Livingston College, and Spelman College.*

Bambara began to publish her short stories in the late 1960s, at a time when she was active in civil rights and community organizations. For one such organization, the SEEK project, a social, educational, and literary program for black women run by the City College of New York, she advised and assisted high school dropouts.

It was the publication of her first collection of short stories, Gorilla, My Love, *(1972), that brought Bambara critical attention. She followed it with another book of stories,* The Sea Birds Are Still Alive *(1977), and a novel,* The Salt Eaters *(1980), which won an American Book Award. Bambara has also edited two anthologies:* The Black Woman: An Anthology *(1970) and* Tales and Stories for Black Folks *(1971).*

"A Tender Man" is taken from Bambara's 1977 collection of stories. In it, a woman friend forces a black man to confront his unfulfilled responsibilities to a daughter from a former interracial marriage. Both dialogue and narrative voice root the characters within a black milieu.

A Tender Man

The girl was sitting in the booth, one leg wrapped around the other cartoon-like. Knee socks drooping, panties peeping from her handbag, ears straining from her head for the soft crepe footfalls, straining less Aisha silent and sudden catch her unawares with the dirty news.

She hadn't caught Cliff's attention. His eyes were simply at rest in that direction. And nothing better to do, he had designed a drama of her. His eyes resting on that booth, on that swivel chair, waiting for Aisha to return and fill it. When the chatty woman in the raincoat had been sitting where the nervous girl sat now, Aisha had flashed him a five-minute sign. That was fifteen minutes ago.

He hadn't known he'd mind the waiting. But he'd been feeling preoccupied of late, off-center, anxious even. Thought he could shrug it off, whatever it was. But sitting on the narrow folding chair waiting, nothing to arrest his attention and focus him, he felt crowded by something too heavy to shrug off. He decided he was simply nervous about the impending student takeover.

He flipped through a tattered *Ebony,* pausing at pictures of children, mothers and children, couples and children, grandparents and children. But no father and child. It was a conspiracy, he chuckled to himself, to keep fathers—he searched for a word—outside. He flipped through the eligible bachelors of the year, halting for a long time at the photo of Carl Davis, his ole army mate who'd nearly deserted in the spring of '61. He was now with RCA making $20,000 a year. Cliff wondered doing what.

The girl was picking her face, now close to panic. In a moment she would bolt for the door. He could imagine heads lifting, swiveling, perfect strangers providing each other with hairy explanations. He could hear the woman tsk-tsking, certain that their daughters would never. Aisha came through the swinging doors and he relaxed, not realizing till that moment how far he had slipped into the girl's drama. Aisha shot three fingers in his direction and he nodded. The girl was curled up tight now, Cliff felt her tension, staring at the glass slide Aisha slid onto the table. She leaned over the manila folder Aisha opened, hand screening the side of her face as though to block the people out. She was crying. The sobbing audible, though muffled now that the screening hand was doubled up in her mouth. Cliff was uncomfortable amongst so many women and this young one crying. Cliff got up to look for the water fountain.

Up and down the corridors folks walked distractedly, clutching slips of colored papers. A few looked terror-struck, like models for the covers of the books he often found his students buried in. Glancing at the slips of green or white, checking them against the signs on the doors, each had a particular style with the entrance, he noted. Knocking timidly, shivering, Judgment Day. Turning knobs stealthily and looking about, second-story types. Brisk entrances with caps yanked low, yawl deal with me, shit. Cliff moved in and out among the paper-slip clutchers, doorway handlers, teen-agers pulling younger brothers and sisters along, older folks pausing to read the posters. The walls were lined with posters urging VD tests, Pap smears, examinations painless and confidential. In less strident Technicolor, others argued the joys of planned parenthood.

Cliff approached the information desk, for the sister on the switchboard seemed to be wearing two wigs at once and he had to see that. The guard leaned way back before considering his question about the water fountain, stepped away from a woman leaning over the desk inquiring after a clinic, gave wide berth to all the folk who entered and headed in that direction, then pointed out the water fountain, backed up against the desk in a dramatic recoil. Cliff smiled at first and considered fucking with the dude, touching him, maybe drooling a bit on his uniform. But he moved off, feeling unclean.

At the water fountain a young father hoisted his daughter too far into the spout. Cliff held the button down and the brother smiled relief, a two-handed grip centering now the little girl, who gurgled and horsed around in the water, then held a jaw full even after she was put down on the floor again.

"This place is a bitch, ain't it?" The brother nodding vigorous agreement to his own remark.

"My wife's visiting her folks and I'm about to lose my mind with these kids." He smiled proudly, though, jutting his chin in the direction of the rest of his family. Two husky boys around eight and ten were doing base slides in the upper corridor.

"Man, if I had the clap, I sure as hell wouldn't come here for no treatments." His frown made Cliff look around. In that moment the lights seem to dim, the paint job age, the posters slump. A young girl played hopscotch in the litter, her mother pushing her along impatiently.

Yeh, a bitch, Cliff had meant to say, but all that came out was a wheezy mumble.

"My ole lady says to me 'go to the clinic and pick up my pills.' Even calls me long distance to remind me she's running out. 'Don't forget to get the pills, B. J.' So I come to get the damn pills, right?" He ran his hand through his bush, gripping a fistful and tossing his head back and forth. "Man oh man," he groaned, shaking his head by the hair. The gesture had started out as a simple self-caress, had moved swiftly into an I-don't-believe-this-shit nod, and before Cliff knew it, the brother'd become some precinct victim, his head bam-bam against the walls. "Man oh man, this crazy-ass place! Can't even get a word in for the 'What's your clinic number?' 'Where's your card?' 'Have you seen the cashier?' 'Have you got insurance?' 'Are you on the welfare?' 'Do you have a yellow slip?' 'Where's your card?' 'Who's ya mama?' Phwweeoo! I'm goin straight to the drugstore and get me a crate of rubbers right on. I ain't puttin my woman through this shit."

"Daddy." The little girl was yanking on his pants leg for attention. When she got it, she made a big X in the air.

"Oh, right. I forgot. Sorry, baby." He turned to Cliff and shrugged in mock sheepishness. "Gotta watch ya mouth round these kids these days, they get on ya. Stay on my case bout the smoking, can't even bring a poke chop in the house, gotta sneak a can of beer and step out on the fire escape to smoke the dope. Man, these kids sompthin!" He was starting that vigorous nodding again, watching his sons approach. Cliff couldn't keep his eyes off the brother's bobbing head. It reminded him of Granddaddy Mobley so long ago, playing horsy, whinnying down the hallway of Miss Hazel's boardinghouse, that head going a mile a minute and his sister Alma riding high, whipping her horse around the head and shoulders and laughing so hard Miss Hazel threatened to put them out.

"Yeh," he was sighing, nudging Cliff less he miss the chance to dig on the two young dudes coming, punching invisible catcher's mitts, diddyboppin like their daddy must've done it years before. "Later for them pills, anyway. It's back to good ole reliable Trojans."

"Pills dangerous," Cliff said.

"Man, just living is a danger. And every day. Every day, man."

"We going to the poolroom now?" the older brother was asking, nodding first to Cliff.

"I want some Chinese food." The younger seemed to be addressing this to Cliff, shifting his gaze to his father long after he'd finished speaking.

"Hold it, youngbloods. Hold on a damn minute. I gotta catch me some sleep and get to work in a coupla hours. Yawl bout to wear my ass out."

"Daddy."

"Oh damn, I'm sorry. Sorry." The brother made two huge X's in the air and dropped his head shamefaced till his daughter laughed.

"Man, you got kids?"

"Yeah" was all Cliff said, not sure what else he could offer. It had been pleasant up to then, the brother easy to be easy with. But now he seemed to be waiting for Cliff to share what Cliff wasn't sure he had to share. He bent to take a drink. "Daughter," he offered, trying to calculate her age. He'd always used the Bay of Pigs invasion as a guide.

"They sompthin, ain't they?" the brother broke in, his children dragging him off to the door. "Take it slow, my man."

Cliff nodded and bent for another drink. Bay of Pigs was the spring of '61. His daughter had been born that summer. He bit his lip. Hell, how many fathers could just tick off the ages of their children, right off the bat? Not many. But then if the brother had put the question to him, as Aisha had the day before—What sort of person is your daughter?—Cliff would not have known how to answer. He let the water bubble up against closed lips for a while, not sure what that fact said about the man he was, or at least had thought he was, hoped he was, had planned to be for so long, was convinced when still a boy he could be once he got out of that house of worrisome women.

Aisha had come quietly up behind him and linked arms. "Hey, mister," she cooed, "how bout taking a po' colored gal to dinner." She pulled him away from the water fountain. "I'm starving."

Starving. Cliff looked at her quickly, but she did not react. Starving. He stared at her, but she was checking the buttons on her blouse, then stepping back for him to catch the door. She moved out swiftly and down the stairs ahead of him, not so much eager to get away, for she'd said how much she liked her job at the clinic. But eager to be done with it for the day and be with him. She waited at the foot of the stairs and linked arms again.

Cliff smiled. He dug her. Had known her less than a week, but felt he knew her. A chick who dealt straight up. No funny changes to go through. He liked the way she made it clear that she dug him.

"Whatcha grinnin about?" she asked, adjusting her pace to his. She was a brisk walker—he had remarked on it the day before—Northern urban brisk. I bet you like to lead too when you dance, he had teased her.

"Thinking about the first time I called you," he said.

"Oh? Oh." She nodded and was done, as though in that split second she had retrieved the tape from storage, played it, analyzed his version of what went down, and knew exactly what he had grinned about and that was that. He had kidded her about that habit too. "You mean the way I push for clarity, honesty?"

That was what he had meant, but he didn't like the cocky way she said it with the phony question mark on the end. She was a chick who'd been told she was too hard, too sure, too swift, and had made adjustments here and there, softening the edges. He wasn't sure that was honest of her, though he'd never liked women with hard edges.

"No," he half-lied. "Your sensitivity. I like the way you said, after turning me down for a drink, 'Hey, Brother—' "

"I called you Cliff. I'm not interested in being your sister."

He hugged her arm. "Okay, 'Hey, Cliff,' you said, 'I ain't rejecting you, but I don't drink, plus I got to get up at the crack of dawn tomorrow to prepare for a workshop. How about dinner instead?' "

"And that tickles you?"

"It refreshes me," he said, laughing, feeling good. It wasn't so easy being a dude, always putting yourself out there to be rejected. He'd never much cared for aggressive women; on the other hand, he appreciated those who met him halfway. He slowed her down some more. "Hey, city girl," he drawled. "This here a country boy you walkin wid, ain't used to shoes yet. The restaurant'll be there. Don't close till late."

"I'm starving, fool. Come on and feed me. You can take off them shoes. I'll carry em."

He hugged her arm again and picked up his pace. It was silly, he told himself, these endless control games he liked to play with assertive types. He was feeling too good. But then he wasn't. Starving. She had raised that question: Can you swear no child of yours is starving to death? Not confronting him or even asking him, softening the edges, but addressing the workshop, reading off a list of questions that might get the discussion started. The brother next to him had slapped his knees with his cap and muttered, "Here we go again with some women lib shit." But a sister across the aisle had been more vocal, jumping up to say, "Run it down to the brothers. Let's just put them other questions on hold and stay with this one a while," she demanded. "Yeah, can you swear?" Her hot eyes sweeping the room. "Can you deal with that, you men in here? Can you deal with that one?"

The discussion got sidetracked, it'd seemed to Cliff at the time. Everybody talking at once, all up in each other's face. Paternity, birth control, genocide, responsibility, fathering, mothering, children, child support, warrants, the courts, prison. One brother had maintained with much heat that half the bloods behind the walls were put there by some vengeful bitch. Warriors for the revolution wasting away in the joint for nonsupport or some other domestic bullshit. "Well, that should point something out!" a sister in the rear had yelled, trying to be heard over a bunch of brothers who stood up to say big-mouth sisters like herself were responsible for Black misery.

Starving. Cliff had spaced on much of the discussion, thinking about his daughter Rhea. Going over in his mind what he might have said had he been there to hear Donna murmur, "Hey, Cliff, I think I missed my period." But he had been in the army. And later when the pregnancy was a certainty, he was in Norfolk, Virginia, on his way overseas, he thought. And all the way out of port he lay in his bunk, Donna's letter under his head, crinkly in the pillowcase, gassing with Carl Davis about that ever-breathtaking announcement that could wreck a perfectly fine relationship—Hey, baby, I think I'm pregnant.

He had not quite kept track of the workshop debate the night before, for he was thinking about parenthood, thinking too of his own parents, his mother ever on the move to someplace else his father'd been rumored to be but never was, dragging him and his little sister Alma over the South till the relatives in Charlotte said whoa, sister, park em here. And he had grown up in a household of women only, women always. Crowded, fussed over, intruded upon, continually compared to and warned not to turn out like the dirty dog who'd abandoned Aunt Mavis or that no-good nigger who'd done Cousin Dorcas dirty or some other low-down bastard that didn't mean no woman no good.

"You're unusually preoccupied, Cliff," Aisha was saying gently, as if reluctant to intrude, but hesitant about leaving him alone to wrassle with the pain he was sure was readable in his face. "Not that I know you well enough to know what's usual." He followed her gaze toward the park. "You feel like walking a while? Talking? Or maybe just being quiet?"

"Thought you were starving?" He heard an edge to his voice, but she didn't seem to notice.

"I am. I am." She waited at the curb, ready to cross over to the park or straight ahead to the Indian restaurant. Cliff disengaged his arm and fished out a cigarette, letting the light change. Had he been alone, he would have crossed over to the park. He had put off taking inventory for too long, his life was in a drift, unmonitored. Just that morning shaving, trying to fix in his mind what role he'd been called on to play in the impending student takeover, he'd scanned the calendar over the sink. The student demands would hit the campus paper on the anniversary of the Bay of Pigs.

He'd made certain promises that day, that spring day in '61 when the boat shipped out for Vietnam they'd thought, but headed directly for the Caribbean. He'd made certain promises about what his life would be like in five years, ten years, ever after if he lived. Had made certain promises to himself, to the unborn child, to God, he couldn't remember to whom, as the ship of Puerto Ricans,

Chicanos and Bloods were cold-bloodedly transported without their knowing from Norfolk to Cuba to kill for all the wrong reasons. Then the knowledge of where they were and what they were expected to do, reminded of the penalty for disobeying orders, he'd made promises through clenched teeth, not that he was any clearer about the Cuban Revolution than he was about the Vietnamese struggle, but he knew enough about Afro-Cuban music to make some connections and conclude that the secret mission was low-down. Knew too that if they died, no one at home'd be told the truth. Missing in action overseas. Taken by the Vietcong. Killed in Nam in the service of God and country.

"Worries?" Aisha asked, "or just reminiscing?"

He put his arm around her shoulders and hugged her close. His life was not at all the way he'd promised. "I was just thinking," he said slowly, crossing them toward the restaurant, "about the first time I came North as a kid." He wasn't sure that was a lie. The early days came crowding in on him every time he thought of his daughter and the future. And his daughter filled his mind on every mention of starving.

He hadn't even known as a boy that he was or for what, till that Sunday his aunts had hustled him and Alma to the train depot. But Granddaddy Mobley didn't even get off the train when it slowed. Just leaned down and hauled them up by the wrists, first Alma, then him.

"Hop aboard, son," he'd said, bouncing the cigar to the back of his jaw. "This what you call a rescue job."

Son. He had been sugar dumpling, sweetie pie, honey darling for so long, as though the horror of Southern living in general, the bitterness of being in particular some poor fatherless child could be sweetened with a sugar tit, and if large enough could fill him up, fill up those drafty places somewhere inside. So long hugged and honey-bunched, he didn't know he was starving or for what till "son" was offered him and the grip on his wrist became a handshake man to man.

Dumfounded, the women were trotting along after the still-moving train, cousin Dorcas calling his name, Aunt Evelyn calling Granddaddy Mobley a bunch of names.

"Train, iz you crazy?!" Aunt Mavis had demanded when she realized that was all the train intended to do, slow up for hopping off or kidnapping. "Have you lost your mind?" Cliff could never figure to whom this last remark was said. But he remembered he laughed like hell.

Granddaddy Mobley chuckled too, watching Cousin Dorcas through the gritty windows, trotting along the landing, shaking her fist, dodging the puffs of steam and the chunks of gravel thrown up by the wheels, the ribbons of her hat flying in and out of her shouting mouth.

Leaning out of an open window over his sister's head, Cliff could make out the women on the landing getting smaller, staring pop-eyed and pop-mouthed too. And when he glanced down, li'l Alma was looking straight up into his face the way she did from the bunk beds when the sun came up, the look asking was everything okay and could the day begin. He grinned back out the window, and grinned too at his sister cause yeah, everything would be all right. He couldn't blame the women, though, for carrying on like that, having taken all morning to get the chicken fried and the rugs swept and the sheets boiled and dough beat up. Then come to find ole Mobley, highstepping, fun-loving, outrageous, drinking, rambler, gambler and everything else necessary to thoroughly scandalize the family name, upset the household with his annual visits, giving them something to talk about as the lamps glowed at night till next visiting time, ole Mobley wasn't even thinking about a visit at all this time. Wasn't even stopping long enough to say hello to his daughter, not that she was there. Just came to snatch the darling little girl and the once perfect little gentleman now grown rusty and hardheaded just like his daddy for the world.

"We going North with you?" Alma had asked, not believing she could go anywhere without her flouncy dresses, her ribbons, and their mother's silver hairbrush from the world's fair.

"That's right."

"We going to live with you?" young Cliff had pressed, eager to get things straight. "To live with you till we grown or just for summer or what?"

Instead of answering, the old man whipped out a wad of large, white handkerchiefs and began to unfold them with very large gestures. The children settled in their seats waiting for the magic show to commence. But the old man just spread them out on the seats, three for sitting on and one for his hat. Cliff and Alma exchanged a look, lost for words. And in that moment, the old man leaned forward, snatched Alma's little yellow-haired doll and pitched it out the window.

"And you better not cry," he said.

"No, ma'am."

Cliff laughed and the old man frowned. "Unless you in training to take care of white folks' babies when you grown."

"No, ma'am."

Cliff had smiled smugly, certain that Alma had no idea what this rescue man was saying. He did. And he looked forward to growing up with a man like this. Alma slid her small hand into his and Cliff squeezed it. And not once did she look back after her doll, or he at the town.

"I met your wife in the bus terminal—"

"Ex-wife," Cliff said, jolted out of his reverie.

Aisha poured the tea. "Ex-wife. Met her last Monday and—"

"You told me."

"I didn't tell you the whole thing."

Cliff looked up from his plate of meat patties. He wasn't sure he wanted to hear about it. Every time he had tried to think of his daughter, he discovered he couldn't detach her from the woman he'd married. Thinking about Donna made him mad. Thinking about his daughter Rhea just made him breathless. Rising, he jingled change in his pocket and stalled for time at the jukebox. That was the first thing Aisha had said to him when they were introduced just four days ago on campus. "Hemphill? I think I know your wife, Donna Hemphill. Ran into her at the bus terminal less than an hour ago."

After his one class of the day and a quick meeting with the Black student union, he'd sought her out in the faculty dining room, convinced his chairman would at least give her the semi-deluxe treatment, particularly considering his taste for black meat (or so the rumor went, though he rarely did more toward orienting new faculty members than pointing out their cubicle, shoving a faculty handbook at them, and warning them about the "Mau Mau," his not-so-affectionate name for the Black student union). She had pursued the topic the minute Cliff had seated himself next to her, remarking quietly that his wife had seemed on the verge of collapse. He welcomed the mention of Donna only for the opportunity it offered to point out that one, she was very much an ex, two he was single, three he found her, Aisha, attractive. Beyond that, he could care less about Donna or her mental state. Aisha had remarked then—too sarcastically for his taste—that this very ex-wife with the mental state was the woman who was raising his daughter. He had eaten the dry roast beef sullenly, grateful for the appearance of his colleague Robinson, who swung the conversation toward the students and the massive coronaries they were causing in administrative circles.

Some Indian movie music blared out at Cliff's back as he picked out one of the umpteen rhythms to stroll back to the table doing, slapping out the beat on his thigh.

"I didn't say this before"—Aisha was reaching for the drumming hand—"cause you cut me short last Tuesday. I'm sorry I didn't press it then on campus, cause it's harder now . . . that I know you . . . and all."

"Then forget it."

She slid her hand back to her side of the table and busied herself with the meat patties. He drummed on the table with both hands, trying to read her mood. He felt he owed her some explanation, wanted even to talk this thing out, his feelings about his daughter. Then resented Aisha for that. He drummed away. The last thing he would have wanted for this evening, the first time they'd been together with no other appointments to cut into their time, the last thing he wanted, feeling already a little off-center, crowded, was a return to that part of his history that seemed so other, over with, some dim drama starring a Cliff long since discarded. Cliff the soldier, Cliff the young father, Cliff the sociology instructor—there was clarity if not continuity. But Cliff the husband . . . blank.

He had pronounced the marriage null and void in the spring of '61. On the troop ship speeding to who knew where, or at least none of the dudes in that battalion knew yet, but to die most probably. He'd read the letter over and over, and was convinced Donna was lying about being pregnant and so far advanced. He was due home for good soon, and this was her way to have him postpone thinking of a split. He and Carl Davis had gassed the whole time out of port about what they were going to do with their lives if they still had them in five months' time. Then some of the soldiers were saying the fleet was in the Caribbean. And all hell broke loose, the men mistakenly assuming—assuming, then readying up for shore leave in Trinidad. The CO told them different, though not much. First there was a sheaf of papers that had to be signed, or court-martial, papers saying they never would divulge to press, to family, to friends, even to each other anything at all regarding the secret mission they were about to embark upon. Then they got their duties. Most work detail the same—painting over the ship's numbers, masking all U.S. identification, readying up the equipment for the gunners, checking their packs and getting new issues of ammunition.

"We're headed for Cuba," Carl Davis had said.

"That's crazy. The action's in Vietnam."

"Mate, I'm telling you, we're off to Cuba. T. J. was upside and got the word.

The first invasionary battalions are Cuban exiles. They'll hook up with the forces there on the island to overthrow Fidel Castro."

"You got to be kidding."

Carl had sneered at Cliff's naïveté. "Mate, they got air coverage that'd made the Luftwaffe look silly. We rendezvous with a carrier and a whole fleet of marines moving in from Nicaragua. I'm telling you, this is it."

T. J. had skidded down the stair rail and whispered. "They got Kennedy on a direct line. Kennedy! Jim, this operation is being directed from the top."

"Holy shit." Cliff had collapsed on his bunk, back pack and all, the letter crumpling under his ear. A child was being born soon, the letter said. He was going to be a father. And if he died, what would happen to his child? His marriage had been in shreds before he'd left, a mere patchwork job on the last leave, and she'd been talking of going back home. His child. Her parents. That world. Those people.

"I never knew Donna well," Aisha was saying. "We worked at Family Services and I used to see her around, jazz concerts, the clubs. I pretty much wrote her off as a type. One of those gray girls who liked to follow behind Black musicians, hang out and act funky."

Cliff looked at Aisha quickly. Was she the type to go for blood? He'd had enough of the white girl–brother thing. Had been sick of it all, of hearing, of reading about it, of arguing, of defending himself, even back then on the tail end of the Bohemian era, much less in the Black and Proud times since.

"Use to run into her a lot when I lived downtown. The baby didn't surprise me—hell, half of Chelsea traffic was white girls pushing mulatto babies in strollers. We used to chat. You two seemed to be always on the verge of breakup, and she was forever going down in flames. I got the impression the baby was something of . . . a hostage?" She seemed to wait for his response. He blanked his face out. "A hostage," she continued, seeming to relish the word, "as per usual."

The waiter slid a dish of chutney at Cliff's elbow, then leaned in to replace the teapot with a larger, steamier one. Cliff leaned back as the plates and bowls were taken from the tray in some definite, mysterious order and placed just so on the table. Cliff rearranged the plate of roti and the cabbage. The waiter looked at him and placed them in their original spots. Cliff sneaked a look at Aisha and they shared a stone-faced grin.

"Cliff?" She seemed to call to him, the him behind his poker face. He leaned forward. Whatever she had to say, it'd be over with soon and they could get on with the Friday evening he had in mind.

"I asked Donna on Tuesday to give up the child. To give your daughter to me. I'm prepared to raise—"

Cliff stared, not sure he heard that right.

"Look. She's standing in the bus terminal having a crying jag, listing fifty-leven different brands of humiliations and bump-offs from the Black community. She's been trying to enroll your daughter in an independent Black school, at a Yoruba cultural center, at the Bedford-Stuyvesant—"

"Bedford-Stuyvesant?"

"Yeah, your wife lives in Brooklyn."

"Ex-wife."

Aisha spread her napkin and asked very pointedly, "You were not aware that your daughter's been living in Brooklyn for two years?" Cliff tried to remember the last address he had sent money to, recalled he had always given it to Alma. But then Alma had moved to the coast last spring. . . .

"Hey, look, Cliff, I've noticed the way you keep leaning on this 'ex' business. I'm sure you're sick to death of people jumping on you, especially sisters, about the white-woman thing. Quite frankly I don't give a shit who you married or who you are . . . not now . . . I only thought I did," she said, spacing her words out in a deliberate challenge. "What does interest me is the kid. I'll tell you just what I told her, I'm prepared to take the girl—"

"Hold it. Hold it." Cliff shoved his plate away and tried to sort out what he was hearing. If only he could have a tape of this, he was thinking, to play at his leisure, not have to respond or be read. "Back up, you're moving too fast for me. I'm just a country boy." He smiled, not surprised that she did smile back. She looked tired.

"Okay. She's been trying to move your daughter into cultural activities and whatnot. Very concerned about the kid's racial identity. For years she's always been asking me to suggest places to take her and how to handle things and so forth. So I'm standing in the bus terminal while this white woman falls apart on me, asking to be forgiven her incompetence, her racism, her hysteria. And I'm pissed. So I ask her—"

"Where's the nigger daddy who should be taking the weight."

Aisha studied her fork and resumed eating. Cliff clenched his jaws. She was eating now as though she'd been concentrating on that chicken curry for hours, had not even spoken, did not even know he was there. Was that the point of it all, to trigger that outburst? And it had been an outburst, his face was still burning. Was she out for blood? It was a drag. Cliff reached for the chutney and sensed her tense up. She looked coiled on her side of the table, mouth full of poisonous fangs. She was a type, he decided, a type he didn't like. She had seemed a groovy woman, but she was just another bitch. She had looked good to him less than half an hour ago, bouncing around in the white space shoes. Had looked good in that slippery white uniform wrinkling at her hips. And all he thought he wanted to do was take her to his place and tell her so, show her. He thought he still might like to take her home to make love to her—no, to fuck her. The atmosphere kept changing, the tone, the whole quality of his feelings for her kept shifting. She kept him off balance. Yeh, he'd like to fuck her, but not cause she looked good. Cliff tore off a piece of roti, then decided he didn't want it. Looked at her and decided he was being absurd. What had she said she was pissed about? Donna, an unhinged white woman raising a Black child. Why had he been so defensive?

"This was a bad time to meet," he heard himself saying. "I wish we had met at some other time when—"

"Look, sugar," she spat out with a malice that didn't match the words, "no matter when or where or how we met, the father question would've come up. And I'd have had to judge what kind of man you are behind your whole sense of what it means to bring a child into the world. I'm funny that way, mister."

"What I was thinking was," he pressed on, shoving aside the anger brewing, clamping down hard on the urge to bust her in the jaw, not sure the urge to hold her close wasn't just as strong, "in a year or so you might have met me with my daughter. I've been considering for a long time fighting for custody of Rhea."

"How long?"

"Off and on for years. But here lately, last few weeks . . ." It occurred to him that that was exactly what he'd been trying to pull together in his mind, a plan. That was what had been crowding him.

"Donna said she'd talk to you about it, Cliff, then get back to me. It was a serious proposal I was making."

"She hasn't called me. Matter of fact, we haven't talked in years."

"Uh-hunh." She delivered this with the jauntiness of a gum-cracking sister from Lenox Avenue. Cliff read on her face total disbelief of all he'd said, as though he couldn't have been really considering it and not talk with the child's mother. He was pissed off. How did it get to be her business, any of it?

"Anyway, Brother," she said, shifting into still another tone, "I'm prepared to take the child. I've got this job at the clinic, it'll hold me till summer when the teaching thing comes through. My aunt runs a school up on Edgecombe. She's not the most progressive sister in the world, but the curriculum's strong academically. And there're several couples on my block who get together and take the kids around. I'm good with children. Raised my nephews and my sisters, I'd do right by the little girl, Cliff. What do you want to ask me?"

Her voice had faded away to a whisper. She sipped her tea now, and for a minute he thought she was about to cry. He wasn't sure for what, but felt he was being unjustly blamed for something. She hadn't believed him. That made him feel unsure about himself. He watched her, drifting in and out among the fragments of sensations, questions that wouldn't stay formed long enough for him to get a hold of. He studied her until his food got cold.

She wasn't going to sleep with him, that was clear. He knew from past experiences that the moment had passed, that moment when women resolved the tension by deciding yes they would, then relaxed one way, or no they wouldn't, and eased into another rhythm. Often at the critical point, especially with younger women, he'd step into their timing and with one remark or a caress of the neck could turn the moment in his favor. He hadn't even considered it with Aisha. There had seemed time enough to move leisurely, no rush. They'd had dinner that first night, then he'd had a Black faculty meeting. He'd picked her up last night to get to the workshop, and after they'd had coffee with Acoli and Essa and talked way into the night about the students' demands. He hadn't even considered that this evening, which just a half-hour ago seemed stretched out so casual and unrushed, would turn out as anything but right.

Hell, they weren't children. They had established right from the jump that this would be a relationship, a relationship of meaning. And he'd looked forward to it, had even thought of calling Alma long distance and working Aisha somehow into the conversation. He knew it would please his sister, for he knew well how it pained her whenever he launched into his dissertation on Black women, the bitterness for those Black women who had raised him surfacing always, and for the others so much like them—though Alma argued it wasn't so—who'd stepped into his life with such explosions, leaving ashes in their wake. And Alma argued that wasn't so either, just his own blindness contracted from poisons he should have pumped out somehow long ago cause they weren't reasonably come by either. He was sick of his dissertation, the arguing, the venom, even thinking about it.

"You can imagine, Cliff . . . well, the irony of it all, meeting you right after seeing Donna after all these years of running into her, hearing about you. . . . Look, it's very complicated—my feelings about . . . the whole thing."

"How so?" He poured the last of the hot tea into her cup and waited. She seemed to study the cup for a long time as though considering whether to reject it, wait for it to cool, drink it, or maybe fling it in his face. He couldn't imagine why that last seemed such a possibility. His sister Alma would have argued that he simply expected the worst always and usually got it, provoked it.

"On the one hand, I'm very attracted to you, Cliff. You care about the students. I mean . . . well, you have a reputation on campus for being—" She was blushing and that surprised the hell out of him. He decided he didn't know women at all. They were too weird, all of them. "Well, for being one of the good guys. Plus you so sharp, ya know, and a great sense of humor. Not to mention you fine." She was looking suddenly girlish. He wanted to laugh, but he didn't want to interrupt her. He was liking this. "And I dig being with you. You're comfortable, even when you're drifting off, you're comfortable to be with." He bowed in his seat. They were smiling again.

"On the other hand"—she cocked her head to signal she hoped to get through this part with the same chumminess—"well. . . ." She drank the tea now, two fingers pressed on each side of the Oriental cup, her face moving into the steam, lips pursing to blow. If they ever got around to the pillow talk, he'd ask her about her gesture and whether or not it had been designed to get him. He found all this blowing and sipping very arousing, for no reason he could think of.

"On the other hand," she said again, "while you seem to be a principled person. . . . I mean, clearly you're not a bastard or a coward . . . not handling the shit on campus like you been doing . . . but—" She put the cup down.

"Hey look. It's like this, Cliff. I don't understand brothers who marry white girls, I really don't. And I really don't see how you can just walk away from the kid, let your child just. . . . Well, damn, what is your daughter, a souvenir?" It was clear to Cliff that his reaction was undisguised and that she was having no trouble reading his face. "Perhaps"—she was looking hopeful now, his cue to rise to the occasion—"perhaps you really have been trying to figure out how to do it, how to get custody?"

"I considered it long before we even broke up. When I first heard that the child was an actual fact, was about to be born, I was in the army. As a matter of fact, I was up to my neck in the Bay of Pigs shit." He had never discussed it before, was amazed he could do it now, could relate it all in five or six quick sentences, when times earlier he hadn't even been able to pull it together coherently in a whole night, staring at the ceiling, wondering how many brothers had been rerouted to the Philippines to put down the resistance to Marcos and the corporate bosses, how many to Ethiopia to vamp on the Eritrean Front, and how many would wind up in southern Africa all too soon, thinking they were going who knew where. How many more caught in the trick bag of colored on colored death if all who knew remained silent on the score, chumps afraid of change?

Cliff had always maintained he despised people who saw and heard but would not move on what they knew. His colleagues who could wax lyric analyzing the hidden agenda of SEEK and other OEO* circuses engineered to fail,

* Office of Economic Opportunity.

but did nothing about it. Bloods in his department grooming the students for caretaker positions, all the while screaming on the system, the oppression, hawking revolution, but carefully cultivating caretakers to negotiate a separate peace for a separate piece of the corrupt pie, claiming the next generation would surely do it. And even Cousin Dorcas and Aunt Mavis years before, going through a pan of biscuits and a pot of coffee laying out with crystal clarity the madness of his mother's life, chronically on hold till she could just get to that one more place to find the man never where folks said he'd be. But never once wrassling the woman, their sister, their kin, to the floor, demanding she at least put the children on her agenda, if not herself. And Cliff himself, heroic in spots, impotent in others, he had postponed for too long an inventory of his self, his life.

"The Cuban people were ready. They kicked our ass. That first landing troop ran smack into an alligator farm in Playa Girón and got wiped out. The second got wasted fore they even got off the beach. And all the while our ship was getting hit. Cannonballs sailing right between the smoke stacks of the ship. And Kennedy on the line saying, 'Pull back,' realizing them balls were a warning, a reminder of what could happen in the world if the U.S. persisted."

Aisha poured him a glass of ginger beer and waited for him to continue. Cliff felt opened up like he hadn't been in years.

"The idea that I might be killed, that my wife Donna would move back to her parents, my child growing up in an all-white environment. . . . I used to run the my-wife-is-an-individual-white-person number. . . . I dunno . . . it all scared the shit out of me," he was saying, not able to find the bridge, the connection, the transition from those thoughts, those promises made in Cuban waters and what in fact he lived out later and called his life.

"When we broke up, I turned my back, I guess," he said, finding his place again, but not the bridge. "I use to see my daughter a lot when my sister Alma lived in the city. And if I could just figure out how to manage it all, have time for my work and —"

"Your work?" she said, clutching the tablecloth. "Your work?" she sneered. "You one of those dudes who thinks his 'real' work is always outside of—separate from—oh, shit."

He felt her withdraw. He would make an effort to draw her out again, even if she came out blazing in a hot tirade about "women's work," and "men's work" and "what a load of horseshit." He would do it for himself. Later for the them that might have been.

"We were discussing all this recently in class—'The Black Family in the Twentieth Century,' my new course."

"Yeah, I know," she said.

"You know?"

"My niece is in your class. She tapes your lectures. Big fan of yours, my niece."

"Oh." Cliff couldn't remember now just what he had wanted to say, had lost the thread. Aisha had motioned the waiter over and was scanning the dessert list. He shook his head. Dessert was not what he wanted at this point.

He had handed back the students' research papers on their own families when the vet who sat in the back got up to say how odd it was that their generation, meaning the sophomores or juniors, despite the persistent tradition in their own families of folks raising children not their own, odd that this younger generation felt exempt. How many here, someone in the front of the room had asked then, can see themselves adopting children or taking in a kid from the streets, or from a strung-out neighbor, as their own? Cliff had expected a split down the middle, the brothers opting for pure lineage, the sisters charging ego and making a case for "the children" rather than "my child." But it didn't go down that way. The discussion never got off the ground. And after class, the vet had criticized Cliff for short-circuiting the discussion. Cliff hadn't seen his point then. But now, watching Aisha coax the recipe for some dessert or other from the waiter, he could admit that he had probably spaced.

Naturally he'd been thinking of his daughter Rhea, wondering how many others in the class had children and whether it would be fruitful to ask that first. The problem was, he could never think of Rhea without also thinking of Donna. Even after he refused to visit the child on his wife's turf, preferring the serenity of Alma's home for the visits, Rhea was still daughter to the woman who'd been his wife. And he was outside.

He'd been so proud when as a baby she had learned to say "Daddy" first. That had knocked him out. His sister had offered some psycholinguistic-somethinorother explanation, completely unsolicited and halfway unheard, about a baby's physical capacity to produce *d* sounds long before *m* sounds. Cliff paid Alma no mind.

But as the baby grew more independent, more exploratory of the world beyond her skin, he realized why she could say "Daddy" so much sooner. Cause Mommy was not separate, Mommy was part of the baby's world, attached to her own ego. He was distinctly different. Outside. It was some time before Mommy was seen as other. And still later that Rhea could step back from herself and manage "Rhea," then "me." Meanwhile he was outside. Way before that even he was outside—pregnancy, labor, delivery, breastfeeding. Women and babies, mothers and children, mother and child. Him outside. If only she had looked more like him, though in fact she resembled Alma more than Donna. But still there was distance. He knew no terms for negotiating a relationship with her that did not also include her mother. How had Donna managed that? Hostage, Aisha had said.

He chuckled to himself and stared at Aisha. He started up a nutty film in his head. All over the country, sisters crouching behind bushes with croaker sacks ready to pounce and spirit away little mulatto babies. Mulatto babies were dearer, prizer. Or sisters shouting from the podiums, the rooftops, the bedrooms, telling warriors dirty diapers was revolutionary work. Sisters coiled in red leather booths mesmerizing fathers into a package deal. He clamped down hard on fantasies leaching poisons into his brain. Package deal—me and the kid.

"Were you proposing to me by any chance?" he asked just for the hell of it.

"Say what?" She first looked bewildered, then angry, then amazed. She burst out laughing, catching him off-guard when she asked in icy tones, "Is that basically your attitude? Big joke?"

He shrugged in innocence and decided to leave it alone. She was bristly. Let her eat her pastry and drink her mint tea, he instructed himself. Put her in a cab and send her home. He wanted time to himself, time to take a good look at the yellow chair Alma had bequeathed to him when she moved to the coast. Its unfolding capacity never failed to amaze him. It would make a better bed than the Disney pen he'd spied in a children's store that morning. He was feeling good again.

He leaned forward and Aisha slid a forkful of crumbly pastry into his mouth. She was looking good to him once more. He grinned. She jerked her chin as if to ask what was he about to say. He wasn't about to say anything. But he was thinking that no, they hadn't met at the wrong time. It'd been the right time for him. The wrong time for them maybe. But what the hell.

"What did you want to be when you grew up?" she asked. He leaned in for another forkful of pastry. "Just don't be like your daddy" rang in his ears. "A tender man," he said and watched her lashes flutter lower.

The question he would put to himself when he got home and stretched out in that yellow chair was what had he promised his daughter in the spring of '61. He smiled at Aisha and leaned up out of his chair to kiss her on the forehead. She blushed. He was sure he could come true for the Cliff he'd been.

J. California Cooper (c. 1940–)

J. *California Cooper expresses her views on writing in this way: "What I like about myself as a writer is not that I write, or that I am a black woman writer, but that I don't lie. . . . I think that we as black women writers should be proud of who we are, but not be controlled by what we are. Because before we are black, and before we are woman, we are human. So as writers, we need to write from the human experience."*

Born Joan Cooper in Berkeley, California, the writer added "California" to her name after someone compared her writing to that of playwright Tennessee Williams, who also had chosen a state as part of his professional writing name. At the age of five, Cooper was already writing plays and performing them for captive audiences of family members and friends. In the 1970s, she and her plays came to the Berkeley Black Repertory Theatre, and by the end of the decade, she had written a dozen plays that had been produced in the San Francisco area. She was honored as Black Playwright of the Year for her play Strangers *in 1978.*

When Cooper turned to fiction writing in the 1980s, her stories won her a national readership. Critics consistently marvel at the writer's adept rendering of language and characters, laced with subtle humor. Her four collections of short stories focus on African Americans who confront diverse personal challenges and survive with admirable and inspiring resilience.

Her first collection, A Piece of Mine *(1984), was also the first book to be published by Alice Walker's Wild Tree Press. Walker has assessed Cooper's writing in these terms: "In its strong folk flavor, Cooper's work reminds us of Langston Hughes and Zora Neale Hurston. Like theirs, her style is deceptively simple and direct, and the vale of tears in which some of her characters reside is never so deep that a rich chuckle at a foolish person's foolishness can not be heard. It is a delight to read her stories."*

A second book of stories, Homemade Love, *appeared in 1986 and won an American Book Award. It contains thirteen stories featuring narrators who "speak of the common wisdom of everyday life."* Some Soul to Keep *(1987) includes five long stories with characters "choosing love over security, revenge, or dependence."* The Matter Is Life *(1991), Cooper's fourth collection of stories, was followed by two novels,* Family *(1991) and* In Search of Satisfaction *(1994).*

The following selection, "Happiness Does Not Come in Colors," is from Homemade Love. *Narrated by a young African American woman, the story traces her changing ideas about love as she observes an older friend's interracial relationship and eventual marriage.*

Happiness Does Not Come in Colors

My mama always said I was the busiest, talkinest child she ever did see! But it's so much to talk about! It's a big, big world at the same time it's a small one. And it's so much goin on! I'm very smart too, so sometime I notice things like . . . love seem to make everything the same. Just like sometime hate makes everything the same. It just all depend on what you feel that makes up what you see.

I don't really have no right to talk cause I ain't really never been nowhere and done nothing. I got to be thirty years old and hadn't even been married and had no children.

It wasn't all my fault tho, cause where I live is a small town up here bout seventy-five miles from New York. But who needs a city if New York is so close? New York got everything so we didn't need everything here. It's a few black families here, but everybody mostly stays to themselves til something like a wedding or a funeral comes up. Once or twice a year maybe we have a dance and everybody comes, even some of the white folks.

Now I want to make it clear that I like some white folks. Some of them are really nice, human people. Not greedy and full of hate. The rest of em I can't stand! Cause of history and some other things happening today that will be history next week!

It's mostly farming done around here, livestock and things. I don't like that kind of work! Something I must have inherited from some old great-grandmother was a slave or something! I blive that stuff comes down to younguns. And I'm mighty careful to stay away from things even look like they close to slavery.

I remember during them times when they was having freedom marches and sit-ins and stand-ins, ever what all they was, we was tryin to get *in*! I saw it on TV and my mama and daddy read it in the papers. Me and my best friend, she's a Indian, use to sit on her porch eatin some of that good bread her mama baked and talk about how we wish we could go somewhere and march. Her mama talked Indian language so I asked her, "How come your mama don't talk American?" She told me, "She *does* talk American! We're speaking the first American language!"

I told her, "Maybe if you spoke that white man's talk you woulda known better when one of em was lyin to you!" She was my best friend but she didn't like to talk about that, so we went back to talkin bout marches and freedom! That was the day her mama went to the store to get some beans and when old Mr. White who owns the store gave her less than the two pounds she paid for, she asked him to weigh them again. He wouldn't! He told her to leave em or go! Well, they got mad at him but couldn't decide what to do, how to fight it. Who was they going to tell that it happened all the time? The white sheriff who leaned on Mr. White's counter drinking pop spiked with liquor? No! So I decided to watch him.

One day my mama gave me 50¢ for two pounds of beans. Mr. White weighed em so fast, snatchin em off the scale, that I asked him to weigh them again. He said, "You kids get outta here!" He started to put the beans back so I said, "My mama wants them beans! Give me my beans!" He growled, "Pay for em and get on out!" So I did. But I walked to the small department store, went to the scale department and weighed em. They weighed one and three-quarter pound, bout! I told my mama and she went to the store. Mr. White told her I musta spilled some cause his weights was right, then he showed her, gave her a new bag and said don't send me in there no more!

My chest was poked way out in front bout my mama! And she pat me on my back for lookin out for her money. I thought about it while I went to sleep that night and the next day I got my best friend and we made up two signs. One said, SOMETHING AIN'T RIGHT—I THINK IT'S MR. WHITE! The other one said, MR. WHITE CHEATS! Then we went back and marched in front of Mr. White's store!

First, and soon, Mr. White ran us away. We went back. Then the sheriff ran us away. She had to go home, my friend, but I went across the street and marched. When they ran me away from there, I went up to the corner and marched, carrying both signs! Then the sheriff went and got my mama, brought her down here and she got me. When we got home I waited to see was she going to whip me for standin up for my rights. She said, "Have a piece of cake and a glass of milk and rest." I smiled and loved her. Then she said the best of all. "I bet Mr. White will think twice before he cheats anybody again!" Well, that's what I wanted to hear—that I had made something right! Even the white ladies that shopped there started checking the scales! But that got old and there wasn't that much cheatin you could find round here, so time passed and I grew up a little more while I was waitin for something to come along.

I was so happy when this black lady named Joyce moved here and rented that veterinary man's house. He had moved to the top floor of his office after his wife died, leavin his house empty for a long time. Joyce rented it and I went over to meet her and ended up with a little job of helpin her settle in. It wasn't real bad, just dusty and spider webs, mice, and a few snakes trying to keep warm.

I was glad cause jobs and friends are hard to find in a little place like this. We got two groceries, two gas stations, the post office, one little department store, one bar that's always full, one hamburger shop with hot dogs, and, see, that's all! Mostly family-owned. If you need a job you got to go in business or leave town, one or the other!

Joyce came in like the wind. She kept me busy. I ain't never seen a Black woman with all her gumption! And all that stuff she had! Books, piano, records, thinkin games, fishin stuff. Oh, she had plenty more things! And running round the country all by herself! She is something! Bout in her forties and a real nice-looking woman wearing that natural hair, real soft and pretty and neat. She was not skinny and not fat, just in the middle. Now, what I liked best, she had all kinds of books and pamphlets and things talkin bout freedom and fight for your rights! Black power, Black economy, and stuff like that. She said she had gone all over the country fightin for equal rights for all! Not communist, just tired of not being treated right by white folks who she say run everything in sight and some out of sight too! Her husband had got killed in some march and she was right beside him! Ain't no sense in tryin to say by who. They never did catch em. But if he was black and fightin for his rights, we know who killed him! They even kill other white folks who are tryin to fight for equal rights for everybody. She was alone now and from what all she say, she planned to stay that way. I told her she came to the right place to stay that way cause I'm bout thirty and ain't never been no way but single! Sides, it's mostly white men here and she couldn't stand white people no kinda way, she said.

We use to sit and talk a lot.

She say, "I'm never going to find the kind of man I want nowhere, noway in this world! I don't even think of bein married. I'm tired. I need a rest. Besides, my last husband would be too hard to beat! When my man died, the fire in my house went out!"

I say, "Well you safe here, honey."

She say, "I'd be safe anywhere."

So I say, "What kind of man would you want?"

And she say, "The kind I want ain't been born or he's already dead."

But since I want to know somethin about men, I keep on. "Yes, but if you did want one, what kind would he be?"

She thought a minute then said, "He'd have to be an honest man. That would take me a hundred years to find right there!" We laughed and she got up to pull down some curtains.

I said, "Okay, honest and what else?" I got up and started folding the old draperies, tryin to keep workin so she will keep talkin. I was trying to see what kind of man I should look for.

She smiled as she moved a piece of furniture, then got serious. "And kind. He would have to be kind. And clean. Like to laugh a lot. He's got to love animals. Like to go fishin. Love music. Like at-home games . . . and good food, even cook a little! And just so I don't never marry on a mistake, he has got to build me a home . . . all my own! Now, there! Oh, yes, and have a little money left over!"

I laughed. "Wow! You sure fixed it so he be hard to find!"

She puffed a pillow. "Above all, he has got to be Black!" She looked sad a minute. "Oh, I never will meet him. I'm sure he's somewhere I'm not. Or done been killed . . . dead."

Now, Mr. Brady the vet was white. All that spring and summer he was coming by to see how she was doing and all, with the house, of course. She use to get mad when she would see him coming up the drive. "He ain't doing nothing but tryin to see if this Black is tearing down his house. What he need to keep coming around here for? I pay my rent on time! Shit!"

But I didn't think he was coming round for that. Even tho I ain't been around much as she has, I know bout some things. He was always stopping in the living room where the piano was, looking through her records when she let him. Her music was always playing, you see. Sometimes Billie Holiday, Erroll Garner, or sometimes somebody named Motzart! Mr. Brady would talk about his flute he played. She would just stand with her arms folded looking at him and patting her foot softly. If he was in the kitchen, he would look at her seasoning shelf or something and talk about how he used certain spices in such 'n' such a thing. I know he wanted to look in them pots what was smelling so good with the steam coming up in the air. But he knew better cause she would say, "Vet man, don't you put your fingers on my pots! I'm the tenant, not the cook!" He would laugh a little lonely smile, wave his hand and walk slowly out the back door. She wouldn't let him use the front door even in his own house! Said, "I pay the rent til he take it back, its my front door! Somebody see that white man going out my front door might get the wrong idea!"

Flower, that's my Indian friend, liked Joyce too. She gave us so much good advice. About living and growing up being something and doing something with our lives. We thought we was too old. Bout to be thirty and all. She told Flower she ought to study law cause, she said, "That's what white folks mess with you with! They make the ones they need as they need them. Their friends pass them, specially if they against some other race and then they can do what they want to you. Cause you been made against the law!" She said Indians really need some lawyers so they could fight that shit! I ask her what I needed and she said, "Learn something that will make you independent. Like for going into business or something. Learn about money! They got classes for that! Save 10¢ out of every dollar you ever get for the rest of your life and learn what to do with it. Cause you gonna need some money! Forever!"

Out of some of her books she helped us find places for grants and also what schools and colleges to apply to. I looked up one day and Flower and I was going off to learn some knowledge. Flower left her daughter with her mama. Said they was all staring misery in the face anyway, so why not try for something better? We, me and Joyce, took her to the station. She had a purse full of addresses and things Joyce had given her and a suitcase full of all we could get together to add to her own. Then we were waving goodbye. I was lonely for her, but not for long cause my date was set to leave and I was going to stay closer to home by going to New York to junior college. Junior college but still a college!

In the meantime Joyce said she had to find a job or move back to New York. Well, I surely didn't want her to go! She had only been here bout two years and my life was changing for the better because of her. So one day I mentioned it to Mr. Vet what she had said. The next time I went by Joyce's house she said Mr. Vet, out the clear blue sky, had said he would like to set up some kennels for certain animals he needed to keep awhile, and some for people who left pets while they was on vacation, and if she would feed them in exchange for her rent and a few dollars he would get somebody else to clean em up. She told him she would clean them up with help, so they had a bargain! He started building them kennels right away. I could see he liked to be around that house that he had rushed away from before. And she stopped patting her foot when he came around. I never told her what I told him. She was happy again cause she was still independent. After a while she even stopped folding her arms when she talked to him!

When it was time for me to leave, I was so happy I was silly. I was only going to be gone about two years. Flower ended up staying away five years all together, coming home in between. I was all set up to stay in a nice rooming house with a friend of Joyce's and had a part-time job lined up except for the interview. I'm tellin you, Joyce was a good friend. There ain't many would take their time to help somebody. Sometime your own family won't do it! And here she was, a stranger! She was very careful bout her time too. Said all of it belonged to her at last! Still, she helped me and Flower change our lives.

I got the job, cause I meant to! I started college and it wasn't no snap! I'm thirty and had forgot how to study and think in this new way. So many new things were coming at me. Oh, I loved it! Pretty soon, in six months or so, I caught myself *thinking* even when I wasn't trying! Lord, Lord!

I was looking better, much better, cause I made my own money to buy things and I could sew, naturally. I was learning about money and its magic. How you can work magic with it, if you just understand it! I was saving not 10¢ but 25¢ out of most every dollar I made. Well, I had the grants too and my rent was low. Chile, I just didn't see no end to how far I could go!

I met a man about my age going to college also. He liked me, but I didn't even like his name . . . Jason, much less him. He was so square to me. Dressed so dumblike. I knew he was poor and trying to save his money for a better college. We took a lot of the same classes. I found he had a few dreams about what he wanted to do and I kinda started liking him. But I thought his squareness would rub off on me to the other students so I avoided him most of the time. That man would sometime walk about seven miles from where he lived to where I lived and I would hide and tell them to tell that old square I wasn't home. He even gave me a picture he spent some of his dear money for and I threw it in the back of a dresser drawer, slammed that drawer shut and forgot it. I also had forgotten all those years when I was just longing for somebody, anybody, to pay me some attention. I was Ms. Hot Stuff studying in college now, on a campus full of boys and men, who, I got to tell the truth, didn't hardly pay me no mind. Well, sometimes when they needed help with some homework!

I went home for Xmas vacation to show my mama and Joyce how good I was turning out. Flower had come home a week earlier and you know what that woman had done? She was new at this law stuff but she had done some learning cause the landlord was fixing up that house she and her mama rented! Another thing, the agency who was handling her mama's money? Found out they had been giving her less than she had coming, for years! That was on its way . . . soon! She ended up talking to Joyce about what to do with it. Joyce told her, "Buy some land with your own house on it. That will be some land nobody can take back when they see something they like on it." Flower did just that. Bought a piece of land with a house on it and bought her mama a new stove, refrigerator, washer and dryer. Her mama liked to sleep on the hard floor so Flower bought her a Japanese bed, king-size! Laws were changing their lives now that Flower was beginning to understand them. I was checking myself out with the newspaper, making penny investments, trying to see how good I was at it. Sometimes following Jason's advice, which was always good it seemed.

Jason didn't have anywhere to go for Xmas vacation. No family except a mother who was in a hospital somewhere and they never expected her to come home again . . . too poor . . . no home. I didn't want to be bothered with him so I left without telling him. After he walked that seven miles, they told him.

I went to see my friend Joyce, of course. Joyce, who was still hating white folks, was going fishing at least twice a week with Mr. Vet, who was still white. I mentioned it to Joyce that she was changing. She said with a grin, "He may be white, but he is fair and honest and that's all I need to know. They must not all be the same after all." She was packing a lunch at the time, for another fishing trip. He was too! They took off and stayed out there all day! Just them two! I said, "Well!" Soon I was heading back to college.

I decided to move nearer the campus to increase my chances of meeting more people and getting a husband to take me away from my little country town forever. I moved in with a girlfriend I had who was always surrounded by men.

Very popular. We had a nice little place, fixed up nice and breezy. We had plenty company. I was having a natural ball! I didn't tell Jason where I was living.

I really was having a ball, only they drank a little too much for me and missed a lot of classes. A fellow that always came with the group started paying me attention. He never had before. I was thrilled. One day we all played music, dancing. He danced me right on in my room. I was laughing and being witty just like a fool. When I looked up I had been screwed and almost didn't realize it, he moved so fast! It was over and he was gone! Now, I'm going to tell you two things. One, I didn't plan on making sex with him. I'm after love and a husband. Two, everything that looks good, ain't! Don't have to turn out to be nothing! A lots of girls were after him and there wasn't really nothing to be after . . . if you know what I mean.

I felt pretty cheap for some reason, thinking, "Lord, how can I look that boy in the face after he been under my dress?! All in my business!!" But I didn't have to worry. He hardly waved at me. His eye was on somebody new for the next night! My ego hurt a quick minute, but see, I knew I wasn't missing nothing! Hear me if you can! That evening when I got to my room and was putting things away, Jason's picture fell faceup and I looked at him a little different. He had respected me, really liked me. I let his picture sit on the dresser faceup this time.

I studied a little harder, played around less, but still joined in sometime. I watched that liquor tho, cause I wasn't going to have everybody on the campus saying they passed through me!

One night my roommate asked me if I wanted to go see a gambling joint and a after-hour place. Of course I wanted to go! I had heard about them and I wanted to see everything! I knew I wasn't going to drink too much so if there was a raid I could get out without staggering into some wall. I dressed and I knew I looked good. We went with a group of fellows, of course, cause we were ladies!

Well, honey, it wasn't nothin but a den, a joint, a dump! But the people inside made it look pretty . . . in the dark! They were dressed to kill! These cooks and domestics were sharp, all mixed in with the hustlers, prostitutes and pimps. Only big diamonds could tell you who the pimps were and not always then! Some had diamonds they only wore on Saturday night. Little pieces of furs and great long pieces of fur around thin and fat necks, sweating in the smoke and heat of all that talking, laughing. Music blasting out hitting the walls, running down ears and throats. Faces with eyes open big but still not big enough to see everything! They must have been reading lips cause you could hardly hear a word . . . til you went into the crap-shooting rooms. Just a little cussing now and then cause they were concentrating in there.

I watched awhile in the gambling room, looking at all the men with all that money! Thinking of what they could do on the stock exchange. I asked could I play 50¢ and they hardly looked up, just went on playing. I asked again and a very good-looking man, who was holding the dice, handed them to me and said, "I will even put up your 50¢!" I laughed, taking the dice . . . threw them out and got a six. Somebody said, "Six is the point!" I threw them again and got seven. Somebody scooped up the 50¢ like a whiz. Handsome, smiling at me, said, "Now, you know little girls should do little-girl things." I smiled back, but I was disappointed! I didn't know then, but I know now, those dice did me a favor, the biggest, by helping me lose. Lord, I've seen, now, some women gamble and lose everything they had, just like a fool, then stand around the table and beg, or run off and turn a quick trick or something, bring that money back . . . and lose that too!

Good-looking took my hand and held it a minute then dropped it like a hot rock when they handed him the dice. I wandered on away after a while. You know when you aren't drinking too much, people who do tends to look stupid to you. I was not enjoying myself. The excitement was gone. Then good-looking came out of the back room and caught my eye, came over and offered me a drink. I was so anxious not to run him away, I took one. To tell the truth, I ended up taking about eight! We talked and talked, just silly fun, but the more I drank the more sense he made. You know what? When I woke up the next morning in my bed, he was laying right there beside me! I don't even know how we got home! My home!

I woke him up to ask him how and why. Chile, that man didn't pay me no mind, just went on along his business with me! I soon forgot my own question and couldn't feel nothing but glad he was there with me. Honey that man knew more about lovin then gambling! It's some things I thought I never would say cause I'm a lady, but he made me say em! It's some things I thought I never would do, but he made me do em! Not all of em tho!

Later, I asked him didn't he have to get up for work, cause I had a class and a job. He told me, "When I hang up my pajamas I have hung up my working clothes!" Show you how you can hear and not understand, cause I laughed. I have to admit, however he graduated, it was a summa cum lawdy, chile!

I didn't mean to see him again, but do you know how it is? He didn't call me and I didn't have no number for him so I went over to the gambling joint by myself. He was there. Seem like that's where he always was, when he wasn't performing his "job"! We ended up at my place, again, with me wondering why he never took me anywhere else with some of his money!

Soon he was taking me out once or twice a week. I was even cutting some classes to cook for him, wash his silk underwear, give him a massage, whatever he wanted! Now, college was very important to me and here I was . . . letting it drop behind, all for this man! Cause he made me feel good.

I am not a loose woman, contrary to what you might think. He was the second person since that handsome mess I stumbled into the time I got high. I guess I was a square. But the truth is I really liked this man, even thought I loved him.

Time passed and I was happy to see him whenever I could. He had told me he had other women, that he didn't love but who helped him, so he couldn't let them go for me until he had made it big and had enough money to go off with me and live happy ever after. I'm so smart, I believed him!

One evening he came over to take me to dinner. I was excited about it cause usually he just came over to go to bed, about three or four in the morning. I said to myself, "Huh! I'm getting to this man!" I even got a little smart with him about things I thought he ought to be doing til he slapped hell out of me! I didn't like that! My mama hadn't ever slapped me in my face! I wanted to tell him to get out! but was scared he really would so I just cried and fell out cross the bed. He lay down and made love to me better than ever, then told me as I lay in his arms, "Baby, I need some money, bad."

I really wanted to ask him bout them women of his, but one slap is enough. I asked instead, "Why? What for?"

He answered, "I got to take care my bisness and my women done worked and got together all they can and it ain't enough!" He smiled that beautiful smile directly on me. "If they was half the woman I know you are, I wouldn't have this problem!"

I said, "I am?!" And it wasn't no happy "I am?" either! He just went on talking and holding me. I wanted to move away from this conversation but decided I better stay and get it all. I knew what was coming! My mama had already warned me when I left for New York!

He was saying, "I want to leave them alone anyway. Don't want nobody but you!"

My throat was tight, I had to whisper, "Nobody but me?" All of a sudden I didn't feel like I was thirty years old. Didn't feel so grown-up.

He licked my cheek. "Nobody but you." He kissed me. "I wish we could . . . I want us to make our own money! Not depend on nobody but ourselves!"

I said to myself, "I do make my own money, cause you ain't never helped me!" Funny how he looked different, not so good, when I knew he was getting ready to ask me for my money. Or, Lord forbid, ask me to hustle for him!

He went on hugging and kissing, telling me he needed $2,000 right away and he knew where I could get it (while he waited for it) and how I could be showing my love for him! How I would never regret it. How we could be together . . . forever. (Forever seemed too long all of a sudden!)

I thought of those women of his who thought he was going to be with THEM forever . . . and had already been using up their bodies for him. Done sold the most precious thing they would *ever* have . . . for him. I knew if I was very rich and wanted him, he would leave and never look back at them or what they had given up for him! I said one thing, cause I am proud of being Black and trying to go to college to better myself. I asked, "Why you want me to do that? Can't you appreciate a Black woman trying to live decent? . . . Go to college? Better the race?"

He leaned back, looking into my eyes, laughing. "College is for squares! Ain't no money in college! We get the money them college people make! They are tricks! Who you think supports them women out there on them streets?! All them people who done been to college! That's who!"

I wanted to shut up but had to ask him, "Was Ms. Cadillac a prostitute? Ms. Ford? Ms. Lord and Ms. Taylor? Ms. M. L. King? Ms. Johnson? Ms. Tubman? Prostitutes don't make this world go round! They got to wait out there on that street til some square bring them some money." I wanted to duck but was in his arms, so just tightened up.

Laughter all gone, he said, "Don't talk that dumb college shit to me!" He said some more things but you already know what they were. He made love again and I let him cause I liked him and the feelings he gave me. I knew I had to let him go tho, so I wanted all I could get before he wasn't in my life anymore.

We got up, bathed, ate breakfast while he told me what to do, how to act. Even told me what to wear, where he would meet me and what to say. I listened and watched him, with dying love cause I knew he didn't love me . . . might not even like me! One thing I remember my mama teaching me, and even from my own good sense. "Don't nobody who love you want to see you, or even hear of you, being in nobody else's arms making love!" She also said, "If you ever find a old whore who's happy, you done found the needle in the hay!" And she said if I did turn out to be that way, I look just as good in my own Cadillac as anybody else! Don't nothing but a fool give such hard-earned money away! I was thinking all these things as I watched him leave. Huh! He wanted me to pay him, to let me kill myself!

I kissed him goodbye, watched him as he strutted away, smiling. Then I packed my clothes. Heading home!

I wrote a note to my roommate giving notice. Called the college with an emergency, made a few calls for a new place to live when I came back. Then I went home to my mama. This time I carried Jason's picture with me.

I enjoyed being home around people I knew loved me! I was soon heading over to Joyce's house. Mr. Vet was there and they were playing a duet. She was on the piano, he was on the flute and the records were playing to accompany them. I said, "Uh-huh!" Later when I asked her about him, being white and all that stuff, she said, "He is peaceful and he is kind. He is fair and these are things I like. Besides, he likes to go fishing, he likes animals, and he can cook. He is sweet and he says he loves me. He likes music and can play it. What can I say?"

I said, "But he is white!"

She said a little angrily, "I didn't plan on loving no white man! I used to wish he would stay away from here. But he didn't! I got to know him and . . . one thing led to another."

I said, "Love sure must be something if it makes you change your whole mind about life! You really use to hate them white folks!"

She looked at me a long time, thinking, before she answered, "I don't hate white skin. It's some Black people that have whiter skin than some white people! That's what's wrong with white people, some of them, they hate skin, black skin, red skin, yellow skin, no matter what's inside it! I just hate what most white people, white exploiters, have done to this earth and to so many people on it for thousands of years. I didn't really know any white men like Mr. Vet. But he is all the things I like in my man. So I am not going to be a fool!"

I smiled. "Plus, he ain't poor!"

She laughed. "Plus, he isn't poor!"

I laughed too. "You sure changed! All the way from Black to white!"

She pointed her finger at me. "Happiness does not come in colors! It comes from what's inside people, not what's outside! I wish sometimes. . . ." She looked off into space. "I wish he might be Black . . . but I rather he be kind, honest, loving and loyal . . . in any color at all."

I laughed with her about other things, then I left to walk home. She had put something on my mind . . . Jason! Talking about kindness, loving and loyal!

When I got back to New York, I took Jason's picture out and bought a frame for it, putting it on top of my nightstand. I called him and we started going out again. I began to see different things about him. He was still square, but so was I, and I liked him that way now.

My mama had put $100 down on an old car with a $350 balance so I would come home more often. We split the payments. Jason kept it running. He knew how to do so many things! We went to see his mother too. She wasn't too sick, just old with no home to go to and couldn't get any money for herself til she had one. That worried Jason. He studied and worked hard trying to get to where he could do something for her. I liked her. She still laughed a lot and I found Jason did too, rusty unused laughter.

Of course I took Jason home to meet my mama. She really liked him cause of the way he was about his mama. He liked her and the small town too! He worked in the yard, trimmed the trees, and went fishing with Joyce and Vet.

Joyce was Mrs. Vet now and he was building her a house! Over near the lake. She could almost fish out her windows now!

I told her, laughing, "That's what you said you wanted!"

She answered, not laughing, "Life's too short for lying!"

It was on that trip we made love for the first time. He hadn't rushed me. Don't nobody need to think a good square is a boring lover! I had heard that in school. It ain't true! He made love . . . with love. It don't get no better! We left there, exhausted and happy.

One day not too long after that trip, I was sitting in class and I thought, "What am I doing here? There are no stock exchanges in my little hometown! I sure don't want to stay in New York!" I called home, checked on a few things, then went to see Jason. We talked. Mostly about what we want out of life. Not to get rich. But a home, children, love, peace and happiness. All the things we need and some of the things we want. I told him my plan and he liked it. We included his mother. Oh, I loved him! Thank God nobody else got him while I was being foolish, growing up.

Now, I had heard from Flower. She was still in law college and doing a lot of things to help Indians all over America, but she was also getting married. He was a lawyer already. And he was white. I asked, "What you doing? I thought you were going to college to learn how to fight them!?"

She told me, "I found one who fights for me, with me! He loves me and my people. His family is so different. What can you do when you meet someone who is so kind and good? I love him." She was even moving her mama to her new home. That hit me.

You know, I had heard that old song when I was growing up, something bout, "The lovebug will get you if you don't watch out!" Them lovebugs are somethin!

Within two months, saving all we could, taking care of his mama's business, we all moved to my little hometown. We were married and moving into Flower's house cause it had more land and she was going to let us buy it someday when we could afford it. We did income taxes and paid rent for the whole year from that. Jason kept books for people and even drove out a ways getting new accounts we worked on together. The rest of the time we had for working in our garden, fishing . . . and making love. I really like that lovemaking, specially out here in the middle of nowhere, when it's raining and it's like nobody else in the world but us.

One day, looking up through the trees at the sky with my fishing pole between my legs, I thought about my closest friends being married to white men now and how happy they were. It was all so different from what it was in the beginning! There didn't seem to be any logic to this love stuff. Just happiness seemed to be what mattered the most. I thought about my happiness with Jason. Even with his mama who wanted a grandchild before she died. We did have enough happiness to share!

I turned to Jason who was casting for the hundredth time cause men don't know how to rest when they go fishin. I said, "Jason, let's start on us a family. Let's make us a baby fore you get too old."

Jason was trying to get his line untangled. If he had sat down and left it alone it wouldn't be tangled. He said, "Did you come out here to fish or . . ."

Then I remembered his logical mind, them accountants, you know! I said, "It's just logical. We got love, let's make a baby with it. Let's make twins. That's balanced!"

He threw that ole wooden pole out in the lake. Said, "Now . . . or when we get home?" Laughing.

I said as I fixed my pole in a tree, "Now! The logic of love is that you make it when you feel it!"

My logical little baby will be born some time next month in my little hometown, in our little warm house, to a mother and father who already love it. Two grandmas too. To happiness, I hope.

I'm going to try to teach it all I know to help it find its happiness someday. Cause it's hard to put your finger on just what it takes sometimes. But looking round me at my friends, I know one thing for sure. Happiness, love either, does not come in colors. . . . You may have different kinds . . . but the heart must not have eyes cause it ain't lookin at the color of nothing! The lovebug is blind!

John Edgar Wideman (1941–)

A *recognized scholar, John Edgar Wideman spent the early stages of his professional and academic life in the fields of psychology and English. He describes the shift in disciplines that he made in the late 1960s while teaching at the University of Pennsylvania: "I was one of the few black faculty members at Penn; they [black students] came to me [to teach a black literature course]. . . . I gave them the stock academic reply. . . . But I felt so ashamed that I agreed to teach the course and began my second education."*

Wideman's "first" education began in Pittsburgh, Pennsylvania. While still a youngster, he moved there with his family from his birthplace of Washington, D.C., to a black neighborhood called Homewood. By the time he had become a basketball star, senior class president, and valedictorian at Peabody High, his family moved again, this time to Pittsburgh's white, middle-class section called Shadyside. Wideman went on to attend the University of Pennsylvania, where his outstanding academic achievements won him a Rhodes Scholarship to Oxford University. The first African American Rhodes Scholar since scholar Alain Locke in 1905, Wideman studied eighteenth-century novelists and earned a bachelor of philosophy from Oxford in 1966.

Returning to the University of Pennsylvania to teach, Wideman thus began his "second education." The urging of his black students for an African American literature course encouraged him to discover the breadth and legacy of black writers. From 1972 to 1973, Wideman chaired the university's first Afro-American studies program. This new direction in his academic life was mirrored in his creative pursuits, as he sought to integrate "black cultural material, history, archetypes, myths, the language itself" into "the so-called mainstream."

His first novel, A Glance Away *(1967), was followed by* Hurry Home *(1969). According to one critic, Wideman's "first two novels . . . reflect . . . [his] formal training as well as his own experiments with narrative technique. These works involve a search for self by protagonists who are confused and dominated by their pasts."*

Although in the 1970s Wideman published only the one novel The Lynchers *(1973), in the following decade he would write three novels,* Hiding Place *(1981),* Sent for You Yesterday *(1983), and* Reuben *(1987); two short fiction collections,* Damballah *(1981) and* Fever: Twelve Stories *(1989); as well as a work of nonfiction,* Brothers and Keepers *(1984), an extended essay about his relationship with his brother, who is currently serving a life sentence in prison. Consistently productive in the 1990s, Wideman has completed four books:* Philadelphia Fire *(1990), a novel;* The Stories of John Edgar Wideman *(1992);* All Stories Are True *(1993); and* Fatheralong: A Meditation on Fathers and Sons, Race and Society *(1994).*

In "Doc's Story," which originally appeared in Fever, *Wideman depicts a young black man brooding over a crumbling relationship and finding inspiration in the tale of a basketball legend.*

Doc's Story

He thinks of her small, white hands, blue veined, gaunt, awkwardly knuckled. He'd teased her about the smallness of her hands, hers lost in the shadow of his when they pressed them together palm to palm to measure. The heavy drops of color on her nails barely reached the middle joints of his fingers. He'd teased her about her dwarf's hands but he'd also said to her one night when the wind was rattling the windows of the apartment on Cedar and they lay listening and shivering though it was summer on the brass bed she'd found in a junk store on Haverford Avenue, near the Woolworth's five-and-dime they'd picketed for two years, that God made little things closer to perfect than he ever made big things. Small, compact women like her could be perfectly formed, proportioned, and he'd smiled out loud running his hand up and down the just-right fine lines of her body, celebrating how good she felt to him.

She'd left him in May, when the shadows and green of the park had started to deepen. Hanging out, becoming a regular at the basketball court across the street in Regent Park was how he'd coped. No questions asked. Just the circle of stories. If you didn't want to miss anything good you came early and stayed late. He learned to wait, be patient. Long hours waiting were not time lost but time doing nothing because there was nothing better to do. Basking in sunshine on a stone bench, too beat to play any longer, nowhere to go but an empty apartment, he'd watch the afternoon traffic in Regent Park, dog strollers, baby carriages, winos, kids, gays, students with blankets they'd spread out on the grassy banks of the hollow and books they'd pretend to read, the black men from the neighborhood who'd search the park for braless young mothers and white girls on blankets who didn't care or didn't know any better than to sit with their crotches exposed. When he'd sit for hours like that, cooking like that, he'd feel himself empty out, see himself seep away and hover in the air, a fine mist, a little, flattened-out gray cloud of something wavering in the heat, a presence as visible as the steam on the window as he stares for hours at winter.

He's waiting for summer. For the guys to begin gathering on the court again. They'll sit in the shade with their backs against the Cyclone fencing or lean on cars parked at the roller-coaster curb or lounge in the sun on low, stone benches catty-corner from the basketball court. Some older ones still drink wine, but most everybody cools out on reefer, when there's reefer passed along, while they bullshit and wait for winners. He collects the stories they tell. He needs a story now. The right one now to get him through this long winter because she's gone and won't leave him alone.

In summer fine grit hangs in the air. Five minutes on the court and you're coughing. City dirt and park dust blowing off bald patches from which green is long gone, and deadly ash blowing over from New Jersey. You can taste it some days, bitter in your spit. Chunks pepper your skin, burn your eyes. Early fall while it's still warm enough to run outdoors the worst time of all. Leaves pile up against the fence, higher and higher, piles that explode and jitterbug across the court in the middle of a game, then sweep up again, slamming back where they blew from. After a while the leaves are ground into coarse, choking powder. You eat leaf trying to get in a little hoop before the weather turns, before those days when nobody's home from work yet but it's dark already and too cold to run again till spring. Fall's the only time sweet syrupy wine beats reefer. Ripple, Manischewitz, Taylor's Tawny Port coat your throat. He takes a hit when the jug comes round. He licks the sweetness from his lips, listens for his favorite stories one more time before everybody gives it up till next season.

His favorite stories made him giggle and laugh and hug the others, like they hugged him when a story got so good nobody's legs could hold them up. Some stories got under his skin in peculiar ways. Some he liked to hear because they made the one performing them do crazy stuff with his voice and body. He learned to be patient, learned his favorites would be repeated, get a turn just like he got a turn on the joints and wine bottles circulating the edges of the court.

Of all the stories, the one about Doc had bothered him most. Its orbit was unpredictable. Twice in one week, then only once more last summer. He'd only heard Doc's story three times, but that was enough to establish Doc behind and between the words of all the other stories. In a strange way Doc presided over the court. You didn't need to mention him. He was just there. Regent Park stories began with Doc and ended with Doc and everything in between was preparation, proof the circle was unbroken.

They say Doc lived on Regent Square, one of the streets like Cedar, dead-ending at the park. On the hottest afternoons the guys from the court would head for Doc's stoop. Jars of ice water, the good feeling and good talk they'd share in the shade of Doc's little front yard was what drew them. Sometimes they'd spray Doc's hose on one another. Get drenched like when they were kids and the city used to turn on fire hydrants in the summer. Some of Doc's neighbors would give them dirty looks. Didn't like a whole bunch of loud, sweaty, half-naked niggers backed up in their nice street where Doc was the only colored on the block. They say Doc didn't care. He was just out there like everybody else having a good time.

Doc had played at the University. Same one where Doc taught for a while. They say Doc used to laugh when white people asked him if he was in the Athletic Department. No reason for niggers to be at the University if they weren't playing ball or coaching ball. At least that's what white people thought, and since they thought that way, that's the way it was. Never more than a sprinkle of black faces in the white sea of the University. Doc used to laugh till the joke got old. People freedom-marching and freedom-dying, Doc said, but some dumb stuff never changed.

He first heard Doc's story late one day, after the yellow streetlights had popped on. Pooner was finishing the one about gang warring in North Philly: Yeah. They sure nuff lynched this dude they caught on their turf. Hung him up on the goddamn poles behind the backboard. Little kids found the sucker in the morning with his tongue all black and shit down his legs, and the cops had to come cut him down. Worst part is them little kids finding a dead body swinging up there. Kids don't be needing to find nothing like that. But those North Philly gangs don't play. They don't even let the dead rest in peace. Run in a funeral parlor and fuck up the funeral. Dumping over the casket and tearing up the flowers. Scaring people and turning the joint out. It's some mean shit. But them gangs don't play. They kill you they ain't finished yet. Mess with your people, your house, your sorry-ass dead body to get even. Pooner finished telling it and he looked round at the fellows and people were shaking their heads and then there was a chorus of You got that right, man. It's a bitch out there, man. Them niggers crazy, boy, and Pooner holds out his hand and somebody passes the joint. Pooner pinches it in two fingers and takes a deep drag. Everybody knows he's finished, it's somebody else's turn.

One of the fellows says, I wonder what happened to old Doc. I always be thinking about Doc, wondering where the cat is, what he be doing now . . .

Don't nobody know why Doc's eyes start to going bad. It just happen. Doc never even wore glasses. Eyes good as anybody's far as anybody knew till one day he come round he got goggles on. Like Kareem. And people kinda joking, you know. Doc got him some goggles. Watch out, youall. Doc be skyhooking youall to death today. Funning, you know. Cause Doc like to joke and play. Doc one the fellas like I said, so when he come round in goggles he subject to some teasing and one another thing like that cause nobody thought nothing serious wrong. Doc's eyes just as good as yours or mine, far as anybody knew.

Doc been playing all his life. That's why you could stand him on the foul line and point him at the hoop and more times than not, Doc could sink it. See he be remembering. His muscles know just what to do. You get his feet aimed right, line him up so he's on target, and Doc would swish one for you. Was a game kinda. Sometimes you get a sucker and Doc win you some money. Swish. Then the cat lost the dough start crying. He ain't blind. Can't no blind man shoot no pill. Is you really blind, brother? You niggers trying to steal my money, trying to play me for a fool. When a dude start crying the blues like that Doc wouldn't like it. He'd walk away. Wouldn't answer.

Leave the man lone. You lost fair and square. Doc made the basket so shut up and pay up, chump.

Doc practiced. Remember how you'd hear him out here at night when people sleeping. It's dark but what dark mean to Doc? Blacker than the rentman's heart but don't make no nevermind to Doc, he be steady shooting fouls. Always be somebody out there to chase the ball and throw it back. But shit, man. When Doc into his rhythm, didn't need nobody chase the ball. Ball be swishing with that good backspin, that good arch bring it back blip, blip, blip, three bounces and it's coming right back to Doc's hands like he got a string on the pill. Spooky if you didn't know Doc or know about foul shooting and understand when you got your shit together don't matter if you blindfolded. You put the motherfucker up and you know it's spozed to come running back just like a dog with a stick in his mouth.

Doc always be hanging at the court. Blind as wood but you couldn't fool Doc.

Eyes in his ears. Know you by your walk. He could tell if you wearing new sneaks, tell you if your old ones is laced or not. Know you by your breath. The holes you make in the air when you jump. Doc was hip to who fucking who and who was getting fucked. Who could play ball and who was jiving. Doc use to be out here every weekend, steady rapping with the fellows and doing his foul-shot thing between games. Every once in a while somebody tease him, Hey, Doc. You want to run winners next go? Doc laugh and say, No, Dupree . . . I'm tired today, Dupree. Besides which you ain't been on a winning team in a week have you, Du? And everybody laugh. You know, just funning cause Doc one the fellas.

But one Sunday the shit got stone serious. Sunday I'm telling youall about, the action was real nice. If you wasn't ready, get back cause the brothers was cooking. Sixteen points, rise and fly. Next. Who got next? . . . Come on out here and take your ass kicking. One them good days when it's hot and everybody's juices is high and you feel you could play till next week. One them kind of days and a run's just over. Doc gets up and he goes with Billy Moon to the foul line. Fellas hanging under the basket for the rebound. Ain't hardly gon be a rebound Doc get hisself lined up right. But see, when the ball drop through the net you want to be the one grab it and throw it back to Billy. You want to be out there part of Doc shooting fouls just like you want to run when the running's good.

Doc bounce the ball, one, two, three times like he does. Then he raise it. Sift it in his fingers. You know he's a ballplayer, a shooter already way the ball spin in them long fingers way he raises it and cocks his wrist. You know Doc can't see a damn thing through his sunglasses but swear to God you'd think he was looking at the hoop way he study and measure. Then he shoots and ain't a sound in whole Johnson. Seems like everybody's heart stops. Everybody's breath behind that ball pushing it and steadying it so it drops through clean as new money.

But that Sunday something went wrong. Couldna been wind cause wasn't no wind. I was there. I know. Maybe Doc had playing on his mind. Couldn't help have playing on his mind cause it was one those days wasn't nothing better to do in the world than play. Whatever it was, soon as the ball left his hands, you could see Doc was missing, missing real bad. Way short and way off to the left. Might hit the backboard if everybody blew on it real hard.

A young boy, one them skinny, jumping-jack young boys got pogo sticks for legs, one them kids go up and don't come back down till they ready, he was standing on the left side the lane and leap up all the sudden catch the pill out the air and jams it through. Blam. A monster dunk and everybody break out in Goddamn. Do it, Sky, and Did you see that nigger get up? People slapping five and all that mess. Then Sky, the young boy they call Sky, grinning like a Chessy cat and strutting out with the ball squeezed in one hand to give it to Doc. In his glory. Grinning and strutting.

Gave you a little help, Doc.

Didn't ask for no help, Sky. Why'd you fuck with my shot, Sky?

Well, up jumped the Devil. The joint gets real quiet again real quick. Doc ain't cracked smile the first. He ain't playing.

Sorry, Doc. Didn't mean no harm, Doc.

You must think I'm some kind of chump fucking with my shot that way.

People start to feeling bad. Doc is steady getting on Sky's case. Sky just a young, light-in-the-ass kid. Jump to the moon but he's just a silly kid. Don't mean no harm. He just out there like everybody else trying to do his thing. No harm in Sky but Doc ain't playing and nobody else says shit. It's quiet like when Doc's shooting. Quiet as death and Sky don't know what to to. Can't wipe that lame look off his face and can't back off and can't hand the pill to Doc neither. He just stands there with his arm stretched out and his rusty fingers wrapped round the ball. Can't hold it much longer, can't let it go.

Seems like I coulda strolled over to Doc's stoop for a drinka water and strolled back and those two still be standing there. Doc and Sky. Billy Moon off to one side so it's just Doc and Sky.

Everybody holding they breath. Everybody want it over with and finally Doc says, Forget it, Sky. Just don't play with my shots anymore. And then Doc say, Who has next winners?

If Doc was joking nobody took it for no joke. His voice still hard. Doc ain't kidding around.

Who's next? I want to run.

Now Doc knows who's next. Leroy get next winners and Doc knows Leroy always saves a spot so he can pick up a big man from the losers. Leroy tell you to your face, I got my five, man, but everybody know Leroy saving a place so he can build him a winner and stay on the court. Leroy's a cold dude that way, been that way since he first started coming round and ain't never gon change and Doc knows that, everybody knows that but even Leroy ain't cold enough to say no to Doc.

I got it, Doc.

You got your five yet?

You know you got a spot with me, Doc. Always did.

Then I'ma run.

Say to myself, Shit . . . Good God Almighty. Great Googa-Mooga. What is happening here? Doc can't see shit. Doc blind as this bench I'm sitting on. What Doc gon do out there?

Well, it ain't my game. If it was, I'd a lied and said I had five. Or maybe not. Don't know what I'da done, to tell the truth. But Leroy didn't have no choice. Doc caught him good. Course Doc knew all that before he asked.

Did Doc play? What kinda question is that? What you think I been talking about all this time, man? Course he played. Why the fuck he be asking for winners less he was gon play? Helluva run as I remember. Overtime and shit. Don't remember who won. Somebody did, sure nuff. Leroy had him a strong unit. You know how he is. And Doc? Doc ain't been out on the court for a while but Doc is Doc, you know. Held his own . . .

If he had tried to tell her about Doc, would it have made a difference? Would the idea of a blind man playing basketball get her attention or would she have listened the way she listened when he told her stories he'd read about slavery days when Africans could fly, change themselves to cats and hummingbirds, when black hoodoo priests and conjure queens were feared by powerful whites even though ordinary black lives weren't worth a penny. To her it was folklore, superstition. Interesting because it revealed the psychology, the pathology of the oppressed. She listened intently, not because she thought she'd hear truth. For her, belief in magic was like belief in God. Nice work if you could get it. Her skepticism, her hardheaded practicality, like the smallness of her hands, appealed to him. Opposites attracting. But more and more as the years went by, he'd wanted her with him, wanted them to be together . . .

They were walking in Regent Park. It was clear to both of them that things weren't going to work out. He'd never seen her so beautiful, perfect.

There should have been stars. Stars at least, and perhaps a sickle moon. Instead the edge of the world was on fire. They were walking in Regent Park and dusk had turned the tree trunks black. Beyond them in the distance, below the fading blue of sky, the colors of sunset were pinched into a narrow, radiant band. Perhaps he had listened too long. Perhaps he had listened too intently for his own voice to fill the emptiness. When he turned back to her, his eyes were glazed, stinging. Grit, chemicals, whatever it was coloring, poisoning the sky, blurred his vision. Before he could blink her into focus, before he could speak, she was gone.

If he'd known Doc's story he would have said: *There's still a chance. There's always a chance. I mean this guy, Doc. Christ. He was stone blind. But he got out on the court and played. Over there. Right over there. On that very court across the hollow from us. It happened. I've talked to people about it many times. If Doc could do that, then anything's possible. We're possible . . .*

If a blind man could play basketball, surely we . . . If he had known Doc's story, would it have saved them? He hears himself saying the words. The ball arches from Doc's fingertips, the miracle of it sinking. Would she have believed any of it?

Octavia Butler (1947–)

Octavia Butler has been writing fantasy and science fiction most of her adult life because she says, "these seemed to be the genres in which I could be freest, most creative."

Born and educated in Pasadena, California, Butler began writing at the age of ten as a way of dealing with loneliness and boredom. After graduating from California State University in 1969, she attended the Clarion Science Fiction Writers' Workshop in 1970 and soon after began selling her stories to science fiction publications. Finding a literary home in the science fiction genre, Butler won three of the field's most prestigious awards in 1985: a Nebula Award, a Hugo Award, and a Locus Award.

The only black woman writer to receive such accolades for her field of writing, Butler explains: "I remember that when I began reading science fiction . . . I was disappointed at how little this creativity and freedom was used to portray the many racial, ethnic, and class variations. Also, I could not help noticing how few significant women characters there were in science fiction. Fortunately, all of this has been changing over the past few years. I intend my writing to contribute to the change." Indeed, her intentions have been endorsed by both critics and readers.

*Four of Butler's novels—*Patternmaster *(1976),* Mind of My Mind *(1977),* Survivor *(1978), and* Wild Seed *(1980)—belong to an interrelated saga called the Patternist Series. The connecting thread in the series is a "group of mentally superior beings who are telepathically connected to one another." Spanning time and space from seventeenth-century Africa to a futuristic world, Butler's fiction infuses racism and sexism into the power struggles and social relationships of her imaginary worlds.*

Butler's other works include the novels Kindred *(1979),* Clay's Ark *(1984),* Dawn: Xenogenesis *(1987), and* Parable of the Sower *(1993).*

In the excerpt from Kindred *reprinted here, the novel's protagonist, a modern-day black woman named Dana, finds herself mysteriously pulled back in time to an 1815 southern plantation.*

from Kindred

The River

The trouble began long before June 9, 1976, when I became aware of it, but June 9 is the day I remember. It was my twenty-sixth birthday. It was also the day I met Rufus—the day he called me to him for the first time.

Kevin and I had not planned to do anything to celebrate my birthday. We were both too tired for that. On the day before, we had moved from our apartment in Los Angeles to a house of our own a few miles away in Altadena. The moving was celebration enough for me. We were still unpacking—or rather, I was still unpacking. Kevin had stopped when he got his office in order. Now he was closeted there either loafing or thinking because I didn't hear his typewriter. Finally, he came out to the living room where I was sorting books into one of the big bookcases. Fiction only. We had so many books, we had to try to keep them in some kind of order.

"What's the matter?" I asked him.

"Nothing." He sat down on the floor near where I was working. "Just struggling with my own perversity. You know, I had half-a-dozen ideas for that Christmas story yesterday during the moving."

"And none now when there's time to write them down."

"Not a one." He picked up a book, opened it, and turned a few pages. I picked up another book and tapped him on the shoulder with it. When he looked up, surprised, I put a stack of nonfiction down in front of him. He stared at it unhappily.

"Hell, why'd I come out here?"

"To get more ideas. After all, they come to you when you're busy."

He gave me a look that I knew wasn't as malevolent as it seemed. He had the kind of pale, almost colorless eyes that made him seem distant and angry whether he was or not. He used them to intimidate people. Strangers. I grinned at him and went back to work. After a moment, he took the nonfiction to another bookcase and began shelving it.

I bent to push him another box full, then straightened quickly as I began to feel dizzy, nauseated. The room seemed to blur and darken around me. I stayed on my feet for a moment holding on to a bookcase and wondering what was wrong, then finally, I collapsed to my knees. I heard Kevin make a wordless sound of surprise, heard him ask, "What happened?"

I raised my head and discovered that I could not focus on him. "Something is wrong with me," I gasped.

I heard him move toward me, saw a blur of gray pants and blue shirt. Then, just before he would have touched me, he vanished.

The house, the books, everything vanished. Suddenly, I was outdoors kneeling on the ground beneath trees. I was in a green place. I was at the edge of a woods. Before me was a wide tranquil river, and near the middle of that river was a child splashing, screaming . . .

Drowning!

I reacted to the child in trouble. Later I could ask questions, try to find out where I was, what had happened. Now I went to help the child.

I ran down to the river, waded into the water fully clothed, and swam quickly to the child. He was unconscious by the time I reached him—a small red-haired boy floating, face down. I turned him over, got a good hold on him so that his head was above water, and towed him in. There was a red-haired woman waiting for us on the shore now. Or rather, she was running back and forth crying on the shore. The moment she saw that I was wading, she ran out, took the boy from me and carried him the rest of the way, feeling and examining him as she did.

"He's not breathing!" she screamed.

Artificial respiration. I had seen it done, been told about it, but I had never done it. Now was the time to try. The woman was in no condition to do anything useful, and there was no one else in sight. As we reached shore, I snatched the child from her. He was no more than four or five years old, and not very big.

I put him down on his back, tilted his head back, and began mouth-to-mouth resuscitation. I saw his chest move as I breathed into him. Then, suddenly, the woman began beating me.

"You killed my baby!" she screamed. "You killed him!"

I turned and managed to catch her pounding fists. "Stop it!" I shouted, putting all the authority I could into my voice. "He's alive!" Was he? I couldn't tell. Please God, let him be alive. "The boy's alive. Now let me help him." I pushed her away, glad she was a little smaller than I was, and turned my attention back to her son. Between breaths, I saw her staring at me blankly. Then she dropped to her knees beside me, crying.

Moments later, the boy began breathing on his own—breathing and coughing and choking and throwing up and crying for his mother. If he could do all that, he was all right. I sat back from him, feeling light-headed, relieved. I had done it!

"He's alive!" cried the woman. She grabbed him and nearly smothered him. "Oh, Rufus, baby . . ."

Rufus. Ugly name to inflict on a reasonably nice-looking little kid.

When Rufus saw that it was his mother who held him, he clung to her, screaming as loudly as he could. There was nothing wrong with his voice, anyway. Then, suddenly, there was another voice.

"What the devil's going on here?" A man's voice, angry and demanding.

I turned, startled, and found myself looking down the barrel of the longest rifle I had ever seen. I heard a metallic click, and I froze, thinking I was going to be shot for saving the boy's life. I was going to die.

I tried to speak, but my voice was suddenly gone. I felt sick and dizzy. My vision blurred so badly I could not distinguish the gun or the face of the man behind it. I heard the woman speak sharply, but I was too far gone into sickness and panic to understand what she said.

Then the man, the woman, the boy, the gun all vanished.

I was kneeling in the living room of my own house again several feet from where I had fallen minutes before. I was back at home—wet and muddy, but intact. Across the room, Kevin stood frozen, staring at the spot where I had been. How long had he been there?

"Kevin?"

He spun around to face me. "What the hell . . . how did you get over there?" he whispered.

"I don't know."

"Dana, you . . ." He came over to me, touched me tentatively as though he wasn't sure I was real. Then he grabbed me by the shoulders and held me tightly. "What happened?"

I reached up to loosen his grip, but he wouldn't let go. He dropped to his knees beside me.

"Tell me!" he demanded.

"I would if I knew what to tell you. Stop hurting me."

He let me go, finally, stared at me as though he'd just recognized me, "Are you all right?"

"No." I lowered my head and closed my eyes for a moment. I was shaking with fear, with residual terror that took all the strength out of me. I folded forward, hugging myself, trying to be still. The threat was gone, but it was all I could do to keep my teeth from chattering.

Kevin got up and went away for a moment. He came back with a large towel and wrapped it around my shoulders. It comforted me somehow, and I pulled it tighter. There was an ache in my back and shoulders where Rufus's mother had pounded with her fists. She had hit harder than I'd realized, and Kevin hadn't helped.

We sat there together on the floor, me wrapped in the towel and Kevin with his arm around me calming me just by being there. After a while, I stopped shaking.

"Tell me now," said Kevin.

"What?"

"Everything. What happened to you? How did you . . . how did you move like that?"

I sat mute, trying to gather my thoughts, seeing the rifle again leveled at my head. I had never in my life panicked that way—never felt so close to death.

"Dana." He spoke softly. The sound of his voice seemed to put distance between me and the memory. But still . . .

"I don't know what to tell you," I said. "It's all crazy."

"Tell me how you got wet," he said. "Start with that."

I nodded. "There was a river," I said. "Woods with a river running through. And there was a boy drowning. I saved him. That's how I got wet." I hesitated, trying to think, to make sense. Not that what had happend to me made sense, but at least I could tell it coherently.

I looked at Kevin, saw that he held his expression carefully neutral. He waited. More composed, I went back to the beginning, to the first dizziness, and remembered it all for him—relived it all in detail. I even recalled things that I hadn't realized I'd noticed. The trees I'd been near, for instance, were pine trees, tall and straight with branches and needles mostly at the top. I had noticed that much somehow in the instant before I had seen Rufus. And I remembered something extra about Rufus's mother. Her clothing. She had worn a long dark dress that covered her from neck to feet. A silly thing to be wearing on a muddy riverbank. And she had spoken with an accent—a southern accent. Then there was the unforgettable gun, long and deadly.

Kevin listened without interrupting. When I was finished, he took the edge of the towel and wiped a little of the mud from my leg. "This stuff had to come from somewhere," he said.

"You don't believe me?"

He stared at the mud for a moment, then faced me. "You know how long you were gone?"

"A few minutes. Not long."

"A few seconds. There were no more than ten or fifteen seconds between the time you went and the time you called my name."

"Oh, no . . ." I shook my head slowly. "All that couldn't have happened in just seconds."

He said nothing.

"But it was real! I was there!" I caught myself, took a deep breath, and slowed down. "All right. If you told me a story like this, I probably wouldn't believe it either, but like you said, this mud came from somewhere."

"Yes."

"Look, what did you see? What do you think happened?"

He frowned a little, shook his head. "You vanished." He seemed to have to force the words out. "You were here until my hand was just a couple of inches from you. Then, suddenly, you were gone. I couldn't believe it. I just stood there. Then you were back again and on the other side of the room."

"Do you believe it yet?"

He shrugged. "It happened. I saw it. You vanished and you reappeared. Facts."

"I reappeared wet, muddy, and scared to death."

"Yes."

"And I know what I saw, and what I did—my facts. They're no crazier than yours."

"I don't know what to think."

"I'm not sure it matters what we think."

"What do you mean?"

"Well . . . it happened once. What if it happens again?"

"No. No, I don't think . . ."

"You don't know!" I was starting to shake again. "Whatever it was, I've had enough of it! It almost killed me!"

"Take it easy," he said. "Whatever happens, it's not going to do you any good to panic yourself again."

I moved uncomfortably, looked around. "I feel like it could happen again—like it could happen anytime. I don't feel secure here."

"You're just scaring yourself."

"No!" I turned to glare at him, and he looked so worried I turned away again. I wondered bitterly whether he was worried about my vanishing again or worried about my sanity. I still didn't think he believed my story. "Maybe you're right," I said. "I hope you are. Maybe I'm just like a victim of robbery or rape or something—a victim who survives, but who doesn't feel safe any more." I shrugged. "I don't have a name for the thing that happened to me, but I don't feel safe any more."

He made his voice very gentle. "If it happens again, and if it's real, the boy's father will know he owes you thanks. He won't hurt you."

"You don't know that. You don't know what could happen." I stood up unsteadily. "Hell, I don't blame you for humoring me." I paused to give him a chance to deny it, but he didn't. "I'm beginning to feel as though I'm humoring myself."

"What do you mean?"

"I don't know. As real as the whole episode was, as real as I know it was, it's beginning to recede from me somehow. It's becoming like something I saw on television or read about—like something I got second hand."

"Or like a . . . a dream?"

I looked down at him. "You mean a hallucination."

"All right."

"No! I know what I'm doing. I can see. I'm pulling away from it because it scares me so. But it was real."

"Let yourself pull away from it." He got up and took the muddy towel from me. "That sounds like the best thing you can do, whether it was real or not. Let go of it."

The Fire

1

I tried.

I showered, washed away the mud and the brackish water, put on clean clothes, combed my hair . . .

"That's a lot better," said Kevin when he saw me.

But it wasn't.

Rufus and his parents had still not quite settled back and become the "dream" Kevin wanted them to be. They stayed with me, shadowy and threatening. They made their own limbo and held me in it. I had been afraid that the dizziness might come back while I was in the shower, afraid that I would fall and crack my skull against the tile or that I would go back to that river, wherever it was, and find myself standing naked among strangers. Or would I appear somewhere else naked and totally vulnerable?

I washed very quickly.

Then I went back to the books in the living room, but Kevin had almost finished shelving them.

"Forget about any more unpacking today," he told me. "Let's go get something to eat."

"Go?"

"Yes, where would you like to eat? Someplace nice for your birthday.

"Here."

"But . . ."

"Here, really. I don't want to go anywhere."

"Why not?"

I took a deep breath. "Tomorrow," I said. "Let's go tomorrow." Somehow, tomorrow would be better. I would have a night's sleep between me and whatever had happened. And if nothing else happened, I would be able to relax a little.

"It would be good for you to get out of here for a while," he said.

"No."

"Listen . . ."

"No!" Nothing was going to get me out of the house that night if I could help it.

Kevin looked at me for a moment—I probably looked as scared as I was—then he went to the phone and called out for chicken and shrimp.

But staying home did no good. When the food had arrived, when we were eating and I was calmer, the kitchen began to blur around me.

Again the light seemed to dim and I felt the sick dizziness. I pushed back from the table, but didn't try to get up. I couldn't have gotten up.

"Dana?"

I didn't answer.

"Is it happening again?"

"I think so." I sat very still, trying not to fall off my chair. The floor seemed farther away than it should have. I reached out for the table to steady myself, but before I could touch it, it was gone. And the distant floor seemed to darken and change. The linoleum tile became wood, partially carpeted. And the chair beneath me vanished.

2

When my dizziness cleared away, I found myself sitting on a small bed sheltered by a kind of abbreviated dark green canopy. Beside me was a little wooden stand containing a battered old pocket knife, several marbles, and a lighted candle in a metal holder. Before me was a red-haired boy. Rufus?

The boy had his back to me and hadn't noticed me yet. He held a stick of wood in one hand and the end of the stick was charred and smoking. Its fire had apparently been transferred to the draperies at the window. Now the boy stood watching as the flames ate their way up the heavy cloth.

For a moment, I watched too. Then I woke up, pushed the boy aside, caught the unburned upper part of the draperies and pulled them down. As they fell, they smothered some of the flames within themselves, and they exposed a half-open window. I picked them up quickly and threw them out the window.

The boy looked at me, then ran to the window and looked out. I looked out too, hoping I hadn't thrown the burning cloth onto a porch roof or too near a wall. There was a fireplace in the room; I saw it now, too late. I could have safely thrown the draperies into it and let them burn.

It was dark outside. The sun had not set at home when I was snatched away, but here it was dark. I could see the draperies a story below, burning, lighting the night only enough for us to see that they were on the ground and some distance from the nearest wall. My hasty act had done no harm. I could go home knowing that I had averted trouble for the second time.

I waited to go home.

My first trip had ended as soon as the boy was safe—had ended just in time to keep me safe. Now, though, as I waited, I realized that I wasn't going to be that lucky again.

I didn't feel dizzy. The room remained unblurred, undeniably real. I looked around, not knowing what to do. The fear that had followed me from home flared now. What would happen to me if I didn't go back automatically this time?

What if I was stranded here—wherever here was? I had no money, no idea how to get home.

I stared out into the darkness fighting to calm myself. It was not calming, though, that there were no city lights out there. No lights at all. But still, I was in no immediate danger. And wherever I was, there was a child with me—and a child might answer my questions more readily than an adult.

I looked at him. He looked back, curious and unafraid. He was not Rufus. I could see that now. He had the same red hair and slight build, but he was taller, clearly three or four years older. Old enough, I thought, to know better than to play with fire. If he hadn't set fire to his draperies, I might still be at home.

I stepped over to him, took the stick from his hand, and threw it into the fireplace. "Someone should use one like that on you," I said, "before you burn the house down."

I regretted the words the moment they were out. I needed this boy's help. But still, who knew what trouble he had gotten me into!

The boy stumbled back from me, alarmed. "You lay a hand on me, and I'll tell my daddy!" His accent was unmistakably southern, and before I could shut out the thought, I began wondering whether I might be somewhere in the South. Somewhere two or three thousand miles from home.

If I was in the South, the two- or three-hour time difference would explain the darkness outside. But wherever I was, the last thing I wanted to do was meet this boy's father. The man could have me jailed for breaking into his house—or he could shoot me for breaking in. There was something specific for me to worry about. No doubt the boy could tell me about other things.

And he would. If I was going to be stranded here, I had to find out all I could while I could. As dangerous as it could be for me to stay where I was, in the house of a man who might shoot me, it seemed even more dangerous for me to go wandering into the night totally ignorant. The boy and I would keep our voices down, and we would talk.

"Don't you worry about your father," I told him softly. "You'll have plenty to say to him when he sees those burned draperies."

The boy seemed to deflate. His shoulders sagged and he turned to stare into the fireplace. "Who are you anyway?" he asked. "What are you doing here?"

So he didn't know either—not that I had really expected him to. But he did seem surprisingly at ease with me—much calmer than I would have been at his age about the sudden appearance of a stranger in my bedroom. I wouldn't even have still been in the bedroom. If he had been as timid a child as I was, he would probably have gotten me killed.

"What's your name?" I asked him.

"Rufus."

For a moment, I just stared at him. "Rufus?"

"Yeah. What's the matter?"

I wished I knew what was the matter—what was going on! "I'm all right," I said. "Look . . . Rufus, look at me. Have you ever seen me before?"

"No."

That was the right answer, the reasonable answer. I tried to make myself accept it in spite of his name, his too-familiar face. But the child I had pulled from the river could so easily have grown into this child—in three or four years.

"Can you remember a time when you nearly drowned?" I asked, feeling foolish.

He frowned, looked at me more carefully.

"You were younger," I said. "About five years old, maybe. Do you remember?"

"The river?" The words came out low and tentative as though he didn't quite believe them himself.

"You do remember then. It was you."

"Drowning . . . I remember that. And you . . . ?"

"I'm not sure you ever got a look at me. And I guess it must have been a long time ago . . . for you."

"No, I remember you now. I saw you."

I said nothing. I didn't quite believe him. I wondered whether he was just telling me what he thought I wanted to hear—though there was no reason for him to lie. He was clearly not afraid of me.

"That's why it seemed like I knew you," he said. "I couldn't remember—maybe because of the way I saw you. I told Mama, and she said I couldn't have really seen you that way."

"What way?"

"Well . . . with my eyes closed."

"With your—" I stopped. The boy wasn't lying; he was dreaming.

"It's true!" he insisted loudly. Then he caught himself, whispered, "That's the way I saw you just as I stepped in the hole."

"Hole?"

"In the river. I was walking in the water and there was a hole. I fell, and then I couldn't find the bottom any more. I saw you inside a room. I could see part of the room, and there were books all around—more than in Daddy's library. You were wearing pants like a man—the way you are now. I thought you were a man."

"Thanks a lot."

"But this time you just look like a woman wearing pants."

I sighed. "All right, never mind that. As long as you recognize me as the one who pulled you out of the river . . ."

"Did you? I thought you must have been the one."

I stopped, confused. "I thought you remembered."

"I remember seeing you. It was like I stopped drowning for a while and saw you, and then started to drown again. After that Mama was there, and Daddy."

"And Daddy's gun," I said bitterly. "Your father almost shot me."

"He thought you were a man too—and that you were trying to hurt Mama and me. Mama says she was telling him not to shoot you, and then you were gone."

"Yes." I had probably vanished before the woman's eyes. What had she thought of that?

"I asked her where you went," said Rufus, "and she got mad and said she didn't know. I asked her again later, and she hit me. And she never hits me."

I waited, expecting him to ask me the same question, but he said no more. Only his eyes questioned. I hunted through my own thoughts for a way to answer him.

"Where do you think I went, Rufe?"

He sighed, said disappointedly, "You're not going to tell me either."

"Yes I am—as best I can. But answer me first. Tell me where you think I went."

He seemed to have to decide whether to do that or not. "Back to the room," he said finally. "The room with the books."

"Is that a guess, or did you see me again?"

"I didn't see you. Am I right? Did you go back there?"

"Yes. Back home to scare my husband almost as much as I must have scared your parents."

"But how did you get there? How did you get here?"

"Like that." I snapped my fingers.

"That's no answer."

"It's the only answer I've got. I was at home; then suddenly, I was here helping you. I don't know how it happens—how I move that way—or when it's going to happen. I can't control it."

"Who can?"

"I don't know. No one." I didn't want him to get the idea that he could control it. Especially if it turned out that he really could.

"But . . . what's it like? What did Mama see that she won't tell me about?"

"Probably the same thing my husband saw. He said when I came to you, I vanished. Just disappeared. And then reappeared later."

He thought about that. "Disappeared? You mean like smoke?" Fear crept into his expression. "Like a ghost?"

"Like smoke, maybe. But don't go getting the idea that I'm a ghost. There are no ghosts."

"That's what Daddy says."

"He's right."

"But Mama says she saw one once."

I managed to hold back my opinion of that. His mother, after all . . . Besides, I was probably her ghost. She had had to find some explanation for my vanishing. I wondered how her more realistic husband had explained it. But that wasn't important. What I cared about now was keeping the boy calm.

"You needed help," I told him. "I came to help you. Twice. Does that make me someone to be afraid of?"

"I guess not." He gave me a long look, then came over to me, reached out hesitantly, and touched me with a sooty hand.

"You see," I said, "I'm as real as you are."

He nodded. "I thought you were. All the things you did . . . you had to be. And Mama said she touched you too."

"She sure did." I rubbed my shoulder where the woman had bruised it with her desperate blows. For a moment, the soreness confused me, forced me to recall that for me, the woman's attack had come only hours ago. Yet the boy was years older. Fact then: Somehow, my travels crossed time as well as distance. Another fact: The boy was the focus of my travels—perhaps the cause of them. He had seen me in my living room before I was drawn to him; he couldn't have made that up. But I had seen nothing at all, felt nothing but sickness and disorientation.

"Mama said what you did after you got me out of the water was like the Second Book of Kings," said the boy.

"The what?"

"Where Elisha breathed into the dead boy's mouth, and the boy came back to life. Mama said she tried to stop you when she saw you doing that to me because you were just some nigger she had never seen before. Then she remembered Second Kings."

I sat down on the bed and looked over at him, but I could read nothing other than interest and remembered excitement in his eyes. "She said I was what?" I asked.

"Just a strange nigger. She and Daddy both knew they hadn't seen you before."

"That was a hell of a thing for her to say right after she saw me save her son's life."

Rufus frowned. "Why?"

I stared at him.

"What's wrong?" he asked. "Why are you mad?"

"Your mother always call black people niggers, Rufe?"

"Sure, except when she has company. Why not?"

His air of innocent questioning confused me. Either he really didn't know what he was saying, or he had a career waiting in Hollywood. Whichever it was, he wasn't going to go on saying it to me.

"I'm a black woman, Rufe. If you have to call me something other than my name, that's it."

"But . . ."

"Look, I helped you, I put the fire out, didn't I?"

"Yeah."

"All right then, you do me the courtesy of calling me what I want to be called."

He just stared at me.

"Now," I spoke more gently, "tell me, did you see me again when the draperies started to burn? I mean, did you see me the way you did when you were drowning?"

It took him a moment to shift gears. Then he said, "I didn't see anything but fire." He sat down in the old ladder-back chair near the fireplace and looked at me. "I didn't see you until you got here. But I was so scared . . . it was kind of like when I was drowning . . . but not like anything else I can remember. I thought the house would burn down and it would be my fault. I thought I would die."

I nodded. "You probably wouldn't have died because you would have been able to get out in time. But if your parents are asleep here, the fire might have reached them before they woke up."

The boy stared into the fireplace. "I burned the stable once," he said. "I wanted Daddy to give me Nero—a horse I liked. But he sold him to Reverend Wyndham just because Reverend Wyndham offered a lot of money. Daddy already has a lot of money. Anyway, I got mad and burned down the stable."

I shook my head wonderingly. The boy already knew more about revenge than I did. What kind of man was he going to grow up into? "Why did you set this fire?" I asked. "To get even with your father for something else?"

"For hitting me. See?" He turned and pulled up his shirt so that I could see the crisscross of long red welts. And I could see old marks, ugly scars of at least one much worse beating.

"For Godsake . . . !"

"He said I took money from his desk, and I said I didn't." Rufus shrugged. "He said I was calling him a liar, and he hit me."

"Several times."

"All I took was a dollar." He put his shirt down and faced me.

I didn't know what to say to that. The boy would be lucky to stay out of prison when he grew up—if he grew up. He went on,

"I started thinking that if I burned the house, he would lose all his money. He ought to lose it. It's all he ever thinks about." Rufus shuddered. "But then I remembered the stable, and the whip he hit me with after I set that fire. Mama said if she had not stopped him, he would have killed me. I was afraid this time he would kill me, so I wanted to put the fire out. But I couldn't. I didn't know what to do."

So he had called me. I was certain now. The boy drew me to him somehow when he got himself into more trouble than he could handle. How he did it, I didn't know. He apparently didn't even know he was doing it. If he had, and if he had been able to call me voluntarily, I might have found myself standing between father and son during one of Rufus's beatings. What would have happened then, I couldn't imagine. One meeting with Rufus's father had been enough for me. Not that the boy sounded like that much of a bargain either. But, "Did you say he used a whip on you, Rufe?"

"Yeah. The kind he whips niggers and horses with."

That stopped me for a moment. "The kind he whips . . . who?"

He looked at me warily. "I wasn't talking about you."

I brushed that aside. "Say blacks anyway. But . . . your father whips black people?"

"When they need it. But Mama said it was cruel and disgraceful for him to hit me like that no matter what I did. She took me to Baltimore City to Aunt May's house after that, but he came and got me and brought me home. After a while, she came home too."

For a moment, I forgot about the whip and the "niggers." Baltimore City. Baltimore, Maryland? "Are we far from Baltimore now, Rufe?"

"Across the bay."

"But . . . we're still in Maryland, aren't we?" I had relatives in Maryland—people who would help me if I needed them, and if I could reach them. I was beginning to wonder, though, whether I would be able to reach anyone I knew. I had a new, slowly growing fear.

"Sure we're in Maryland," said Rufus. "How could you not know that."

"What's the date?"

"I don't know."

"The year! Just tell me the year!"

He glanced across the room toward the door, then quickly back at me. I realized I was making him nervous with my ignorance and my sudden intensity. I forced myself to speak calmly. "Come on, Rufe, you know what year it is, don't you?"

"It's . . . eighteen fifteen."

"When?"

"Eighteen fifteen."

I sat still, breathed deeply, calming myself, believing him. I did believe him.

I wasn't even as surprised as I should have been. I had already accepted the fact that I had moved through time. Now I knew I was farther from home than I had thought. And now I knew why Rufus's father used his whip on "niggers" as well as horses.

I looked up and saw that the boy had left his chair and come closer to me.

"What's the matter with you?" he demanded. "You keep acting sick."

"It's nothing, Rufe. I'm all right." No, I was sick. What was I going to do? Why hadn't I gone home? This could turn out to be such a deadly place for me if I had to stay in it much longer. "Is this a plantation?" I asked.

"The Weylin plantation. My daddy's Tom Weylin."

"Weylin . . ." The name triggered a memory, something I hadn't thought of for years. "Rufus, do you spell your last name, W-e-y-l-i-n?"

"Yeah, I think that's right."

I frowned at him impatiently. A boy his age should certainly be sure of the spelling of his own name—even a name like this with an unusual spelling.

"It's right," he said quickly.

"And . . . is there a black girl, maybe a slave girl, named Alice living around here somewhere?" I wasn't sure of the girl's last name. The memory was coming back to me in fragments.

"Sure. Alice is my friend."

"Is she?" I was staring at my hands, trying to think. Every time I got used to one impossibility, I ran into another.

"She's no slave, either," said Rufus. "She's free, born free like her mother."

"Oh? Then maybe somehow . . ." I let my voice trail away as my thoughts raced ahead of it fitting things together. The state was right, and the time, the unusual name, the girl, Alice . . .

"Maybe what?" prompted Rufus.

Yes, maybe what? Well, maybe, if I wasn't completely out of my mind, if I wasn't in the middle of the most perfect hallucination I'd ever heard of, if the child before me was real and was telling the truth, maybe he was one of my ancestors. . . .

Gayl Jones (1949–)

According to literary critic Claudia Tate, intense psychological realism is the single most powerful element in Gayl Jones's fiction: "All of Jones's works are carefully wrought narratives developed from her determination to relay a story entirely in terms of the mental processes of the main character, without any authorial intrusion. . . . Her style and method reflect her mastery in combining improvisational storytelling and sophisticated formal techniques, so that the stories do not appear contrived or to be relying on obtrusive narrative devices."

Jones was born in Lexington, Kentucky. After receiving a bachelor's in English from Connecticut College in 1971, she attended Brown University in Rhode Island, where she studied with African American poet Michael Harper. Jones earned a master's and a doctorate in creative writing from Brown, in 1973 and 1975, respectively, and she published her first novel, Corregidora *(1975), while a graduate student. From 1975 to 1983, she was an English professor at the University of Michigan; currently, she teaches Afro-American literature and creative writing at that institution.*

In her novels and short stories, Jones often focuses on black women characters who struggle with painful conflicts and difficult personal histories. She followed Corregidora *with another novel,* Eva's Man *(1976), and a book of short stories,* White Rat *(1977). Although her fiction has received the most critical attention, Jones has also won awards for her poetry and drama. She has published three volumes of poetry*—Song for Anninho *(1981),* The Hermit-Woman *(1983), and* Xargue and Other Poems *(1985)—and one play,* Chile Woman *(1973), which won an American College Theatre Festival Award. Her most recent publication is a critical study,* Liberating Voices: Oral Tradition in African American Literature *(1991).*

In "White Rat," the title story from Jones's 1977 collection, the main character recounts his experiences as a fair-complexioned black man while weighing his responsibilities to an estranged girlfriend.

White Rat

I learned where she was when Cousin Willie come down home and said Maggie sent for her but told her not to tell nobody where she was, especially me, but Cousin Willie come and told me anyway cause she said I was the lessen two evils and she didn't like to see Maggie stuck up in the room up there like she was. I asked her what she mean like she was. Willie said that she was pregnant by J. T. J. T. the man she run off with because she said I treat her like dirt. And now Willie say J. T. run off and left her after he got her knocked up. I asked Willie where she was. Willie said she was up in that room over Babe Lawson's. She told me not to be surprised when I saw her looking real bad. I said I wouldn't be least surprised. I asked Willie she think Maggie come back. Willie say she better.

The room was dirty and Maggie looked worser than Willie say she going to look. I knocked on the door but there weren't no answer so I just opened the door and went in and saw Maggie laying on the bed turned up against the wall. She turnt around when I come in but she didn't say nothing. I said Maggie we getting out a here. So I got the bag she brung when she run away and put all her loose things in it and just took her by the arm and brung her on home. You couldn't tell nothing was in her belly though.

I been taking care of little Henry since she been gone but he three and a half years old and ain't no trouble since he can play hisself and know what it mean when you hit him on the ass when he do something wrong.

Maggie don't say nothing when we get in the house. She just go over to little Henry. He sleeping in the front room on the couch. She go over to little Henry and bend down and kiss him on the cheek and then she ask me have I had supper and when I say naw she go back in the kitchen and start fixing it. We sitting at the table and nobody saying nothing but I feel I got to say something.

"You can go head and have the baby," I say. "I give him my name."

I say it meaner than I want to. She just look up at me and don't say nothing. Then she say, "He ain't yours."

I say, "I know he ain't mine. But don't nobody else have to know. Even the baby. He don't even never have to know."

She just keep looking at me with her big eyes that don't say nothing, and then she say, "You know. I know."

She look down at her plate and go on eating. We don't say nothing no more and then when she got through she clear up the dishes and I just go round front and sit out on the front porch. She don't come out like she used to before she start saying I treat her like dirt, and then when I go on in the house to go to bed, she hunched up on her side, with her back to me, so I just take my clothes off and get on in the bed on my side.

Maggie a light yeller woman with chicken-scratch hair. That what my mama used to call it, chicken-scratch hair, cause she say there weren't enough hair for a chicken to scratch around in. If it weren't for her hair she look like she was a white woman, a light yeller white woman though. Anyway, when we was coming up somebody say, "Woman cover you hair if you ain't go'n straightin' it. Look like chicken scratch." Sometime they say look like chicken shit, but they don't tell them to cover it no more, so they wear it like it is. Maggie wears hers like it is.

Me, I come from a family of white-looking niggers, some of 'em, my mama, my daddy musta been; my half daddy he weren't. Come down from the hills round Hazard, Kentucky, most of them and claimed nigger cause somebody grandmammy way back there was. First people I know ever claim nigger, 'cept my mama say my daddy hate hoogies (up north I hear they call em honkies) worser than anybody. She say cause he look like he one hisself and then she laugh. I laugh too but I didn't know why she laugh. She say when I come, I look just like a little white rat, so tha's why some a the people I hang aroun with call me "White Rat." When little Henry come he look just like a little white rabbit, but don't nobody call him "White Rabbit," they just call him little Henry. I guess the other jus' ain't took. I tried to get them to call him little White Rabbit, but Maggie say naw, cause she say when he grow up he develop a complex, what with the problem he got already. I say what you come at me for with this a complex and then she say, Nothin, jus' something I heard on the radio on one of them edgecation morning shows. And then I say Aw. And then she say, Anyway by the time he get seven or eight he probably get the pigment and be dark, cause some of her family was. So I say where I heard somewhere where the chil'ren couldn't be no darker'n the darkest of the two parent and bout the best he could do would be high yeller like she was. And then she say how her sister Lucky got the pigment when she was bout seven and come out real dark. I tell her, Well y'all's daddy was dark. And she say, "Yeah." Anyway, I guess she still think little Henry gonna get the pigment when he get to be seven or eight, and told me about all these people come out lighter'n I was and got the pigment fore they growed up.

Like I told you my relatives come down out of the hills and claimed nigger, but only people that believe 'em is people that got to know 'em and people that know 'em, so I usually just stay around with people I know and go in some joint over to Versailles or up to Lexington or down over in Midway where they know me cause I don't like to walk in no place where they say, "What's that white man doing in here?" They probably say "yap"—that the Kentucky word for honky. Or "What that yap doing in here with that nigger woman?" So I jus' keep to the places where they know me. I member when I was young me and the other niggers used to ride around in these cars, and when we go to some town where they don't know "White Rat" everybody look at me like I'm some hoogie, but I don't pay them no mind. 'Cept sometime it hard not to pay em no mind cause I hate the hoogie much as they do, much as my daddy did. I drove up to this filling station one time and these other niggers drove up at the same time, they mighta even drove up a little ahead a me, but this filling station man come up to me first and bent down and said, "I wait on you first, 'fore I wait on them niggers," and then he laugh. And then I laugh and say,"You can wait on them first. I'm a nigger too." He don't say nothing. He just look at me like he thought I was crazy. I don't remember who he wait on first. But I guess he be careful next time who he say nigger to, even somebody got blond hair like me, most which done passed over anyhow. That, or the way things been go'n, go'n be trying to pass back. I member once all us was riding around one Saturday night, I must a been bout twenty-five then, close to forty now, but we was driving around, all us drunk cause it was Saturday, and Shotgun, he was driving and probably drunker'n a skunk and drunken the rest of us hit up on this police car and the police got out and by that time Shotgun done stop, and the police come over and told all us to get out the car, and he looked us over, he didn't have to do much looking because he probably smell it before he got there, but he looked us all over and say he gonna haul us all in for being drunk and disord'ly. He say, "I'm gone haul all y'all in." And I say, "Haul y'all all." Everybody laugh, but he don't hear me cause he over to his car ringing up the police station to have them send the wagon out. He turn his back to us cause he know we wasn goin nowhere. Didn't have to call but one man cause the only people in the whole Midway police station is Fat Dick and Skinny Dick, Buster Crab and Mr. Willie. Sometime we call Buster, Crab Face too, and Mr. Willie is John Willie, but everybody call him Mr. Willie cause the name just took. So Skinny Dick come out with the wagon and hauled us all in. So they didn't know me well as I knew them. Thought I was some hoogie jus' run around with the niggers instead of be one of them. So they put my cousin Covington, cause he dark, in the cell with Shotgun and the other niggers and they put me in the cell with the white men. So I'm drunker'n a skunk and I'm yellin' Let me outa here I'm a nigger too. And Crab Face say, "If you a nigger I'm a Chinee." And I keep rattling the bars and saying "Cov, they got me in here with the white men. Tell 'em I'm a nigger too," and Cov yell back, "He a nigger too," and then they all laugh, all the niggers laugh, the hoogies they laugh too, but for a different reason, and Cov say, "Tha's what you get for being drunk and orderly." And I say, "Put me in there with the niggers too, I'm a nigger too." And then one of the white men, he's sitting over in his corner say, "I ain't never heard of a white man want to be a nigger. 'Cept maybe for the nigger women." So I look around at him and haul off cause I'm goin hit him and then some man grab me and say, "He keep a blade," but that don't make me no difrent and I say, "A spade don't need a blade." But then he get his friend to help hole me and then he call Crab Face to come get me out a the cage. So Crab Face come and get me out a the cage and put me in a cage by myself and say, "When you get out a here you can run around with the niggers all you want, but while you in here you ain't getting no niggers." By now I'm more sober so I jus' say, "My cousin's a nigger." And he say, "My cousin a monkey's uncle."

By that time Grandy come. Cause Cov took his free call but didn't nobody else. Grandy's Cov's grandmama. She my grandmama too on my stepdaddy's side. Anyway, Grandy come and she say, "I want my *two* sons." And he take her over to the nigger cage and say, "Which two?" and she say, "There one of them," and points to Cov'ton. "But I don't see t'other one." And Crab Face say, "Well, if you don't see him I don't see him." Cov'ton just standing there grinning and don't say nothing. I don't say nothing. I'm just waiting. Grandy ask, "Cov, where Rat?" Sometime she just call me Rat and leave the "White" off. Cov say, "They put him in the cage with the white men." Crab Face standing there looking funny now. His back to me, but I figure he looking funny now. Grandy says,"Take me to my other boy, I want to see my other boy." I don't think Crab Face want her to know he thought I was white so he don't say nothing. She just standing there looking up at him cause he tall and fat and she short and fat. Crab Face finally say, "I put him in a cell by hisself cause he started a ruckus." He point over to me, and she turn and see me and frown. I'm just sitting there. She look back at Crab Face and say, "I want them both out." "That be about five dollars apiece for the both of them for disturbing the peace." That what Crab Face say. I'm sitting there thinking he a poet and don't know it. He a bad poet and don't know it. Grandy say she pay it if it take all her money, which it probably did. So the police let Cov and me out. And Shotgun waving. Some of the others already settled. Didn't care if they got out the next day. I wouldn't a cared neither, but Grandy say she didn like to see nobody in a cage, specially her own. I say I pay her back. Cov say he pay her back too. She say we can both pay her back if we just stay out a trouble. So we got together and pay her next week's grocery bill.

Well, that was one 'sperience. I had others, but like I said, now I jus' about keep to the people I know and that know me. The only other big 'sperience was when me and Maggie tried to get married. We went down to the courthouse and fore I even said a word, the man behind the glass cage look up at us and say, "Round here nigger don't marry white." I don't say nothing, just standing up there looking at him and he looking like a white toad, and I'm wondering if they call him "white toad," more likely "white turd." But I just keep looking at him. Then he the one get tired a looking first and he say, "Next." I'm thinking I want to reach in that little winder and pull him right out of that little glass cage. But I don't. He say again, "Around here nigger don't marry white." I say, "I'm a nigger. Nigger marry nigger, don't they?" He just look at me like he think I'm crazy. I say,"I got rel'tives blacker'n your shit. Ain't you never heard a niggers what look like they white?" He just look at me like I'm a nigger too, and tell me where to sign.

Then we get married and I bring her over here to live in this house in Huntertown ain't got but three rooms and a outhouse, that's where we always lived, seems like to me, all us Hawks, cept the ones come down from the mountains way back yonder, cept they don't count no more anyway. I keep telling Maggie it get harder and harder to be a white nigger now specially since it don't count no more how much white blood you got in you, in fact, it make you worser for it. I said nowadays sted a walking around like you something special people look at you, after they find out what you are if you like me, like you some kind a bad news that you had something to do with. I tell em I ain't had nothing to do with the way I come out. They ack like they like you better if you go on ahead and try to pass, cause least then they know how to feel about you. Cept nowadays everybody want to be a nigger, or it getting that way. I tell Maggie she got it made, cause at least she got that chicken-shit hair, but all she answer is, "That why you treat me like chicken shit." But tha's only since we been having our troubles.

Little Henry the cause a our troubles. I tell Maggie I ain't changed since he was borned, but she say I have. I always say I been a hard man, kind of quick-tempered. A hard man to crack like one of them walnuts. She say all it take to crack a walnut is your teeth. She say she put a walnut between her teeth and it crack not even need a hammer. So I say I'm a nigger-toe nut then. I ask her if she ever seen one of them nigger-toe nuts they the toughest nuts to crack. She say, "A nigger-toe nut is black. A white nigger-toe nut be easy to crack." Then I don't say nothing and she keep saying I changed cause I took to drink. I tell her I drink before I married her. She say then I start up again. She say she don't like it when I drink cause I'm quicker tempered than when I ain't drunk. She say I come home drunk and say things and then go sleep and then the next morning forget what I say. She won't tell me what I say. I say, "You a woman scart of words. Won't do nothing." She say she ain't scart of words. She say one of these times I might not jus' say something. I might *do* something. Short time after she say that was when she run off with J. T.

Reason I took to drink again was because little Henry was borned club-footed. I tell the truth in the beginning I blamed Maggie, cause I herited all those hill man's superstitions and nigger superstitions too, and I said she didn't do something right when she was carrying him or she did something she shouldn't oughta did or looked at something she shouldn't oughta looked at like some cows fucking or something. I'm serious. I blamed her. Little Henry come out looking like a little club-footed rabbit. Or some rabbits being birthed or something. I said there weren't never nothing like that in my family ever since we been living on this earth. And they must have come from her side. And then I said cause she had more of whatever it was in her than I had in me. And then she said that brought it all out. All that stuff I been hiding up inside me cause she said I didn't hated them hoogies like my daddy did and I just been feeling I had to live up to something he set and the onliest reason I married her was because she was the lightest and brightest nigger woman I could get and still be nigger. Once that nigger start to lay it on me she jus' kept it up till I didn't feel nothing but start to feeling what she say, and then I even told her I was leaving and she say, "What about little Henry?" And I say, "He's your nigger." And then it was like I didn't know no other word but nigger when I was going out that door.

I found some joint and went in it and just start pouring the stuff down. It weren't no nigger joint neither, it was a hoogie joint. First time in my life I ever been in a hoogie joint too, and I kept thinking a nigger woman did it. I wasn't drunk enough *not* to know what I was saying neither. I was sitting up to the bar talking to the tender. He just standing up there, wasn nothing special to him, he probably weren't even lisen cept but with one ear. I say, "I know this nigger. You know I know the niggers. (He just nod but don't say nothing.) Know them close. You know what I mean. Know them like they was my own. Know them where you s'pose to know them." I grinned at him like he was s'pose to know them too. "You know my family came down out of the hills, like they was some kind of rain gods, you know, miss'ology. What they teached you bout the Juicifer. Anyway, I knew this nigger what made hisself a priest, you know turned his white color I mean turned his white collar backwards and dressed up in a monkey suit—you get it?" He didn't get it. "Well, he made hisself a priest, but after a while he didn't want to be no priest, so he pronounced hisself." The bartender said, "Renounced." "So he 'nounced hisself and took off his turned-back collar and went back to just being a plain old every day chi'lins and downhome and hamhocks and corn pone nigger. And you know what else he did? He got married. Yeah the nigger what once was a priest got married. Once took all them vows of cel'bacy come and got married. Got married so he could come." I laugh. He don't. I got evil. "Well, he come awright. He come and she come too. She come and had a baby. And you know what else? The baby come too. Ha. No ha? The baby come out club-footed. So you know what he did? He didn't blame his wife he blamed hisself. The nigger blamed hisself cause he said the God put a curse on him for goin' agin his vows. He said the God put a curse on him cause he took his vows of cel'bacy, which mean no fuckin', cept everybody know what *they* do, and went agin his vows of cel'bacy and married a nigger woman so he could do what every ord'narry onery person was doing and the Lord didn't just put a curse on him. He said he could a stood that. But the Lord carried the curse clear over to the next gen'ration and put a curse on his little baby boy who didn do nothing in his whole life . . . cept come." I laugh and laugh. Then when I quit laughing I drink some more, and then when I quit drinking I talk some more. "And you know something else?" I say. This time he say, "No." I say, "I knew another priest what took the vows, only this priest was white. You wanta know what happen to him. He broke his vows same as the nigger and got married same as the nigger. And they had a baby too. Want to know what happen to him?" "What?" "He come out a nigger."

Then I get so drunk I can't go no place but home. I'm thinking it's the Hawks' house, not hers. If anybody get throwed out it's her. She the nigger. I'm goin' fool her. Throw her right *out* the bed if she in it. But then when I get home I'm the one that's fool. Cause she gone *and* little Henry gone. So I guess I just bad-mouthed the walls like the devil till I jus' layed down and went to sleep. The next morning little Henry come back with a neighbor woman but Maggie don't come. The woman hand over little Henry, and I ask her, "Where Maggie?" She looked at me like she think I'm the devil and say,"I don't know, but she lef' me this note to give to you." So she jus' give me the note and went. I open the note and read. She write like a chicken too, I'm thinking, chicken scratch. I read: "I run off with J. T. cause he been wanting me to run off with him and I ain't been wanting to tell now. I'm send little Henry back cause I just took him away last night cause I didn't want you to be doing nothing you regrit in the morning." So I figured she figured I got to stay sober if I got to take care of myself and little Henry. Little Henry didn't say nothing and I didn't say nothing. I just put him on in the house and let him play with hisself.

That was two months ago. I ain't take a drop since. But last night Cousin Willie come and say where Maggie was and now she moving around in the kitchen and feeding little Henry and I guess when I get up she feed me. I get up and get dressed and go in the kitchen. She say when the new baby come we see whose fault it was. J. T. blacker'n a lump of coal.

Maggie keep saying, "When the baby come we see who fault it was." It's two more months now that I been look at her, but I still don't see no belly change.

Gloria Naylor (1950–)

G*loria Naylor has confessed, "Growing up in the North in integrated schools, I wasn't taught anything about Black history or literature. . . . When I discovered that there was this whole long literary tradition of Black folk in this country, I felt*

I had been cheated out of something. I wanted to sit down and write about something that I hadn't read about, and that was all about me—the Black woman in America."

Born and raised in New York City in a working-class family, Naylor was motivated in her early life by a strong religious zeal. She worked as a Jehovah's Witness missionary, between 1968 and 1975, in New York, North Carolina, and Florida. Following her missionary work, she studied nursing for a while, but settled into studying English at Brooklyn College, receiving her bachelor's in 1981.

Inspired by Toni Morrison's work The Bluest Eye *(1970), Naylor began writing her first novel during her sophomore year, supporting herself as a hotel switchboard operator. That novel—the award-winning* Women of Brewster Place *(1982)—was published by the time Naylor earned her master's in African American studies from Yale University in 1983. Since then, she has lectured and led workshops at various campuses, including New York University, Cornell University, Brandeis University, Princeton University, the University of Pennsylvania, Boston University, and George Washington University. She has also written three other novels:* Linden Hills *(1985),* Mama Day *(1988), and* Bailey's Cafe *(1992).*

One of the primary voices in twentieth-century African American fiction, Naylor's fiction encourages black women to contemplate their own identities. According to the writer, her four novels are "all meant to be loosely connected," creative worlds in which she explores racism, sexism, classism, and intraracial conflicts.

Naylor received a National Endowment for the Arts Fellowship in 1985, a Candace Award from the National Coalition of One Hundred Black Women in 1986, and a Guggenheim Fellowship in 1988. The Women of Brewster Place *won Naylor an American Book Award for first fiction in 1983, as well as a wider audience when it was made into a television movie starring Oprah Winfrey in 1989.*

In the following excerpt from The Women of Brewster Place, *Lucielia Louise Turner is one of the seven black women characters whose intersecting lives on Brewster Place are the focus of the novel. Having been abandoned by her parents and raised by her grandmother as a youngster, the adult Lucielia now patiently and painfully works at saving a doomed relationship with the father of her child.*

Lucielia Louise Turner

Lucielia had just run water into the tea kettle and was putting it on the burner when she heard the cylinder turn. He didn't have to knock on the door; his key still fit the lock. Her thin knuckles gripped the handle of the kettle, but she didn't turn around. She knew. The last eleven months of her life hung compressed in the air between the click of the lock and his "Yo, baby."

The vibrations from those words rode like parasites on the air waves and came rushing into her kitchen, smashing the compression into indistinguishable days and hours that swirled dizzily before her. It was all there: the frustration of being left alone, sick, with a month-old baby; her humiliation reflected in the caseworker's blue eyes for the unanswerable "you can find him to have it, but can't find him to take care of it" smile; the raw urges that crept, uninvited, between her thighs on countless nights; the eternal whys all meshed with the explainable hate and unexplainable love. They kept circling in such a confusing pattern before her that she couldn't seem to grab even one to answer with him. So there was nothing in Lucielia's face when she turned it toward Eugene, standing in her kitchen door holding a ridiculously pink Easter bunny, nothing but sheer relief. . . .

"So he's back." Mattie sat at Lucielia's kitchen table, playing with Serena. It was rare that Mattie ever spoke more than two sentences to anybody about anything. She didn't have to. She chose her words with the grinding precision of a diamond cutter's drill.

"You think I'm a fool, don't you?"

"I ain't said that."

"You didn't have to," Ciel snapped.

"Why you mad at me, Ciel? It's your life, honey."

"Oh, Mattie, you don't understand. He's really straightened up this time. He's got a new job on the docks that pays real good, and he was just so depressed before with the new baby and no work. You'll see. He's even gone out now to buy paint and stuff to fix up the apartment. And, and Serena needs a daddy."

"You ain't gotta convince me, Ciel."

No, she wasn't talking to Mattie, she was talking to herself. She was convincing herself it was the new job and the paint and Serena that let him back into her life. Yet, the real truth went beyond her scope of understanding. When she laid her head in the hollow of his neck there was a deep musky scent to his body that brought back the ghosts of the Tennessee soil of her childhood. It reached up and lined the inside of her nostrils so that she inhaled his presence almost every minute of her life. The feel of his sooty flesh penetrated the skin of her fingers and coursed through her blood and became one, somewhere, wherever it was, with her actual being. But how do you tell yourself, let alone this practical old woman who loves you, that he was back because of that. So you don't.

You get up and fix you both another cup of coffee, calm the fretting baby on your lap with her pacifier, and you pray silently—very silently—behind veiled eyes that the man will stay.

Ciel was trying to remember exactly when it had started to go wrong again. Her mind sought for the slender threads of a clue that she could trace back to—perhaps—something she had said or done. Her brow was set tightly in concentration as she folded towels and smoothed the wrinkles over and over, as if the answer lay concealed in the stubborn creases of the terry cloth.

The months since Eugene's return began to tick off slowly before her, and she examined each one to pinpoint when the nagging whispers of trouble had begun in her brain. The friction on the towels increased when she came to the month that she had gotten pregnant again, but it couldn't be that. Things were different now. She wasn't sick as she had been with Serena, he was still working—so it wasn't the baby. It's not the baby, it's not the baby—the rhythm of those words sped up the motion of her hands, and she had almost yanked and folded and pressed them into a reality when, bewildered, she realized that she had run out of towels.

Ciel jumped when the front door slammed shut. She waited tensely for the metallic bang of his keys on the coffee table and the blast of the stereo. Lately that was how Eugene announced his presence home. Ciel walked into the living room with the motion of a swimmer entering a cold lake.

"Eugene, you're home early, huh?"

"You see anybody else sittin' here?" He spoke without looking at her and rose to turn up the stereo.

He wants to pick a fight, she thought, confused and hurt. He knows Serena's taking her nap, and now I'm supposed to say, Eugene, the baby's asleep, please cut the music down. Then he's going to say, you mean a man can't even relax in his own home without being picked on? I'm not picking on you, but you're going to wake up the baby. Which is always supposed to lead to: You don't give a damn about me. Everybody's more important than me—that kid, your friends, everybody. I'm just chickenshit around here, huh?

All this went through Ciel's head as she watched him leave the stereo and drop defiantly back down on the couch. Without saying a word, she turned and went into the bedroom. She looked down on the peaceful face of her daughter and softly caressed her small cheek. Her heart became full as she realized, this is the only thing I have ever loved without pain. She pulled the sheet gently over the tiny shoulders and firmly closed the door, protecting her from the music. She then went into the kitchen and began washing the rice for their dinner.

Eugene, seeing that he had been left alone, turned off the stereo and came and stood in the kitchen door.

"I lost my job today," he shot at her, as if she had been the cause.

The water was turning cloudy in the rice pot, and the force of the stream from the faucet caused scummy bubbles to rise to the surface. These broke and sprayed tiny starchy particles onto the dirty surface. Each bubble that broke seemed to increase the volume of the dogged whispers she had been ignoring for the last few months. She poured the dirty water off the rice to destroy and silence them, then watched with a malicious joy as they disappeared down the drain.

"So now, how in the hell I'm gonna make it with no money, huh? And another brat comin' here, huh?"

The second change of the water was slightly clearer, but the starch-speckled bubbles were still there, and this time there was no way to pretend deafness to their message. She had stood at that sink countless times before, washing rice, and she knew the water was never going to be totally clear. She couldn't stand there forever—her fingers were getting cold, and the rest of the dinner had to be fixed, and Serena would be waking up soon and wanting attention. Feverishly she poured the water off and tried again.

"I'm fuckin' sick of never getting ahead. Babies and bills, that's all you good for."

The bubbles were almost transparent now, but when they broke they left light trails of starch on top of the water that curled around her fingers. She knew it would be useless to try again. Defeated, Ciel placed the wet pot on the burner, and the flames leaped up bright red and orange, turning the water droplets clinging on the outside into steam.

Turning to him, she silently acquiesced. "All right, Eugene, what do you want me to do?"

He wasn't going to let her off so easily. "Hey, baby, look, I don't care what you do. I just can't have all these hassles on me right now, ya know?"

"I'll get a job. I don't mind, but I've got no one to keep Serena, and you don't want Mattie watching her."

"Mattie—no way. That fat bitch'll turn the kid against me. She hates my ass, and you know it."

"No, she doesn't, Eugene." Ciel remembered throwing that at Mattie once. "You hate him, don't you?" "Naw, honey," and she had cupped both hands on Ciel's face. "Maybe I just loves you too much."

"I don't give a damn what you say—she ain't minding my kid."

"Well, look, after the baby comes, they can tie my tubes—I don't care." She swallowed hard to keep down the lie.

"And what the hell we gonna feed it when it gets here, huh—air? With two kids and you on my back, I ain't never gonna have nothin'." He came and grabbed her by the shoulders and was shouting into her face. "Nothin', do you hear me, nothin'!"

"Nothing to it, Mrs. Turner." The face over hers was as calm and antiseptic as the room she lay in. "Please, relax. I'm going to give you a local anesthetic and then perform a simple D&C, or what you'd call a scraping to clean out the uterus. Then you'll rest here for about an hour and be on your way. There won't even be much bleeding." The voice droned on in its practiced monologue, peppered with sterile kindness.

Ciel was not listening. It was important that she keep herself completely isolated from these surroundings. All the activities of the past week of her life were balled up and jammed on the right side of her brain, as if belonging to some other woman. And when she had endured this one last thing for her, she would push it up there, too, and then one day give it all to her—Ciel wanted no part of it.

The next few days Ciel found it difficult to connect herself up again with her own world. Everything seemed to have taken on new textures and colors. When she washed the dishes, the plates felt peculiar in her hands, and she was more conscious of their smoothness and the heat of the water. There was a disturbing split second between someone talking to her and words penetrating sufficiently to elicit a response. Her neighbors left her presence with slight frowns of puzzlement, and Eugene could be heard mumbling, "Moody bitch."

She became terribly possessive of Serena. She refused to leave her alone, even with Eugene. The little girl went everywhere with Ciel, toddling along on plump uncertain legs. When someone asked to hold or play with her, Ciel sat nearby, watching every move. She found herself walking into the bedroom several times when the child napped to see if she was still breathing. Each time she chided herself for this unreasonable foolishness, but within the next few minutes some strange force still drove her back.

Spring was slowly beginning to announce itself at Brewster Place. The arthritic cold was seeping out of the worn gray bricks, and the tenants with apartment windows facing the street were awakened by six o'clock sunlight. The music no longer blasted inside of 3C, and Ciel grew strong with the peacefulness of her household. The playful laughter of her daughter, heard more often now, brought a sort of redemption with it.

"Isn't she marvelous, Mattie? You know she's even trying to make whole sentences. Come on, baby, talk for Auntie Mattie."

Serena, totally uninterested in living up to her mother's proud claims, was trying to tear a gold-toned button off the bosom of Mattie's dress.

"It's so cute. She even knows her father's name. She says, my da da is Gene."

"Better teach her your name," Mattie said, while playing with the baby's hand. "She'll be using it more."

Ciel's mouth flew open to ask her what she meant by that, but she checked herself. It was useless to argue with Mattie. You could take her words however you wanted. The burden of their truth lay with you, not her.

Eugene came through the front door and stopped short when he saw Mattie. He avoided being around her as much as possible. She was always polite to him, but he sensed a silent condemnation behind even her most innocent words. He constantly felt the need to prove himself in front of her. These frustrations often took the form of unwarranted rudeness on his part.

Serena struggled out of Mattie's lap and went toward her father and tugged on his legs to be picked up. Ignoring the child and cutting short the greetings of the two women, he said coldly, "Ciel, I wanna talk to you."

Sensing trouble, Mattie rose to go. "Ciel, why don't you let me take Serena downstairs for a while. I got some ice cream for her."

"She can stay right here," Eugene broke in. "If she needs ice cream, I can buy it for her."

Hastening to soften his abruptness, Ciel said, "That's okay, Mattie, it's almost time for her nap. I'll bring her later—after dinner."

"All right. Now you all keep good." Her voice was warm. "You too, Eugene," she called back from the front door.

The click of the lock restored his balance to him. "Why in the hell is she always up here?"

"You just had your chance—why didn't you ask her yourself? If you don't want her here, tell her to stay out," Ciel snapped back confidently, knowing he never would.

"Look, I ain't got time to argue with you about that old hag. I got big doings in the making, and I need you to help me pack." Without waiting for a response, he hurried into the bedroom and pulled his old leather suitcase from under the bed.

A tight, icy knot formed in the center of Ciel's stomach and began to melt rapidly, watering the blood in her legs so that they almost refused to support her weight. She pulled Serena back from following Eugene and sat her in the middle of the living room floor.

"Here, honey, play with the blocks for Mommy—she has to talk to Daddy." She piled a few plastic alphabet blocks in front of the child, and on her way out of the room, she glanced around quickly and removed the glass ashtrays off the coffee table and put them on a shelf over the stereo.

Then, taking a deep breath to calm her racing heart, she started toward the bedroom.

Serena loved the light colorful cubes and would sometimes sit for an entire half-hour, repeatedly stacking them up and kicking them over with her feet. The hollow sound of their falling fascinated her, and she would often bang two of them together to re-create the magical noise. She was sitting, contentedly engaged in this particular activity, when a slow dark movement along the baseboard caught her eye.

A round black roach was making its way from behind the couch toward the kitchen. Serena threw one of her blocks at the insect, and, feeling the vibrations of the wall above it, the roach sped around the door into the kitchen. Finding a totally new game to amuse herself, Serena took off behind the insect with a block in each hand. Seeing her moving toy trying to bury itself under the linoleum by the garbage pail she threw another block, and the frantic roach now raced along the wall and found security in the electric wall socket under the kitchen table.

Angry at losing her plaything, she banged the block against the socket, attempting to get it to come back out. When that failed, she unsuccessfully tried to poke her chubby finger into the thin horizontal slit. Frustrated, tiring of the game, she sat under the table and realized she had found an entirely new place in the house to play. The shiny chrome of the table and chair legs drew her attention, and she experimented with the sound of the block against their smooth surfaces.

This would have entertained her until Ciel came, but the roach, thinking itself safe, ventured outside of the socket. Serena gave a cry of delight and attempted to catch her lost playmate, but it was too quick and darted back into the wall. She tried once again to poke her finger into the slit. Then a bright slender object, lying dropped and forgotten, came into her view. Picking up the fork, Serena finally managed to fit the thin flattened prongs into the electric socket.

Eugene was avoiding Ciel's eyes as he packed. "You know, baby, this is really a good deal after me bein' out of work for so long." He moved around her still figure to open the drawer that held his T-shirts and shorts. "And hell, Maine ain't far. Once I get settled on the docks up there, I'll be able to come home all the time."

"Why can't you take us with you?" She followed each of his movements with her eyes and saw herself being buried in the case under the growing pile of clothes.

" 'Cause I gotta check out what's happening before I drag you and the kid up there."

"I don't mind. We'll make do. I've learned to live on very little."

"No, it just won't work right now. I gotta see my way clear first."

"Eugene, please." She listened with growing horror to herself quietly begging.

"No, and that's it!" He flung his shoes into the suitcase.

"Well, how far is it? Where did you say you were going?" She moved toward the suitcase.

"I told ya—the docks in Newport."

"That's not in Maine. You said you were going to Maine."

"Well, I made a mistake."

"How could you know about a place so far up? Who got you the job?"

"A friend."

"Who?"

"None of your damned business!" His eyes were flashing with the anger of a caged animal. He slammed down the top of the suitcase and yanked it off the bed.

"You're lying, aren't you? You don't have a job, do you? Do you?"

"Look, Ciel, believe whatever the fuck you want to. I gotta go." He tried to push past her.

She grabbed the handle of the case. "No, you can't go."

"Why?"

Her eyes widened slowly. She realized that to answer that would require that she uncurl that week of her life, pushed safely up into her head, when she had done all those terrible things for that other woman who had wanted an abortion. She and she alone would have to take responsibility for them now. He must understand what those actions had meant to her, but somehow, he had meant even more. She sought desperately for the right words, but it all came out as—

"Because I love you."

"Well, that ain't good enough."

Ciel had let the suitcase go before he jerked it away. She looked at Eugene, and the poison of reality began to spread through her body like gangrene. It drew his scent out of her nostrils and scraped the veil from her eyes, and he stood before her just as he really was—a tall, skinny black man with arrogance and selfishness twisting his mouth into a strange shape. And, she thought, I don't feel anything now. But soon, very soon, I will start to hate you. I promise—I will hate you. And I'll never forgive myself for not having done it sooner—soon enough to have saved my baby. Oh, dear God, my baby.

Eugene thought the tears that began to crowd into her eyes were for him. But she was allowing herself this one last luxury of brief mourning for the loss of something denied to her. It troubled her that she wasn't sure exactly what that something was, or which one of them was to blame for taking it away. Ciel began to feel the overpowering need to be near someone who loved her. I'll get Serena and we'll go visit Mattie now, she thought in a daze.

Then they heard the scream from the kitchen.

The church was small and dark. The air hung about them like a stale blanket. Ciel looked straight ahead, oblivious to the seats filling up behind her. She didn't feel the damp pressure of Mattie's heavy arm or the doubt that invaded the air over Eugene's absence. The plaintive Merciful Jesuses, lightly sprinkled with sobs, were lost on her ears. Her dry eyes were locked on the tiny pearl-gray casket, flanked with oversized arrangements of red-carnationed bleeding hearts and white-lilied eternal circles. The sagging chords that came loping out of the huge organ and mixed with the droning voice of the black-robed old man behind the coffin were also unable to penetrate her.

Ciel's whole universe existed in the seven feet of space between herself and her child's narrow coffin. There was not even room for this comforting God whose melodious virtues floated around her sphere, attempting to get in. Obviously, He had deserted or damned her, it didn't matter which. All Ciel knew was that her prayers had gone unheeded—that afternoon she had lifted her daughter's body off the kitchen floor, those black days in the hospital, and now. So she was left to do what God had chosen not to.

People had mistaken it for shock when she refused to cry. They thought it some special sort of grief when she stopped eating and even drinking water unless forced to; her hair went uncombed and her body unbathed. But Ciel was not grieving for Serena. She was simply tired of hurting. And she was forced to slowly give up the life that God had refused to take from her.

After the funeral the well-meaning came to console and offer their dog-eared faith in the form of coconut cakes, potato pies, fried chicken, and tears. Ciel sat in the bed with her back resting against the headboard; her long thin fingers, still as midnight frost on a frozen pond, lay on the covers. She acknowledged their kindnesses with nods of her head and slight lip movements, but no sound. It was as if her voice was too tired to make the journey from the diaphragm through the larynx to the mouth.

Her visitors' impotent words flew against the steel edge of her pain, bled slowly, and returned to die in the senders' throats. No one came too near. They stood around the door and the dressing table, or sat on the edges of the two worn chairs that needed upholstering, but they unconsciously pushed themselves back against the wall as if her hurt was contagious.

A neighbor woman entered in studied certainty and stood in the middle of the room. "Child, I know how you feel, but don't do this to yourself. I lost one, too. The Lord will . . ." And she choked, because the words were jammed down into her throat by the naked force of Ciel's eyes. Ciel had opened them fully now to look at the woman, but raw fires had eaten them worse than lifeless—worse than death. The woman saw in that mute appeal for silence the ragings of a personal hell flowing through Ciel's eyes. And just as she went to reach for the girl's hand, she stopped as if a muscle spasm had overtaken her body and, cowardly, shrank back. Reminiscences of old, dried-over pains were no consolation in the face of this. They had the effect of cold beads of water on a hot iron—they danced and fizzled up while the room stank from their steam.

Mattie stood in the doorway, and an involuntary shudder went through her when she saw Ciel's eyes. Dear God, she thought, she's dying, and right in front of our faces.

"Merciful Father, no!" she bellowed. There was no prayer, no bended knee or sackcloth supplication in those words, but a blasphemous fireball that shot forth and went smashing against the gates of heaven, raging and kicking, demanding to be heard.

"No! No! No!" Like a black Brahman cow, desperate to protect her young, she surged into the room, pushing the neighbor woman and the others out of her way. She approached the bed with her lips clamped shut in such force that the muscles in her jaw and the back of her neck began to ache.

She sat on the edge of the bed and enfolded the tissue-thin body in her huge ebony arms. And she rocked. Ciel's body was so hot it burned Mattie when she first touched her, but she held on and rocked. Back and forth, back and forth—she held Ciel so tightly she could feel her young breasts flatten against the buttons of her dress. The black mammoth gripped so firmly that the slightest increase of pressure would have cracked the girl's spine. But she rocked.

And somewhere from the bowels of her being came a moan from Ciel, so high at first it couldn't be heard by anyone there, but the yard dogs began an unholy howling. And Mattie rocked. And then, agonizingly slow, it broke its way through the parched lips in a spaghetti-thin column of air that could be faintly heard in the frozen room.

Ciel moaned. Mattie rocked. Propelled by the sound, Mattie rocked her out of that bed, out of that room, into a blue vastness just underneath the sun and above time. She rocked her over Aegean seas so clean they shone like crystal, so clear the fresh blood of sacrificed babies torn from their mother's arms and given to Neptune could be seen like pink froth on the water. She rocked her on and on, past Dachau, where soul-gutted Jewish mothers swept their children's entrails off laboratory floors. They flew past the spilled brains of Senegalese infants whose mothers had dashed them on the wooden sides of slave ships. And she rocked on.

She rocked her into her childhood and let her see murdered dreams. And she rocked her back, back into the womb, to the nadir of her hurt, and they found it—a slight silver splinter, embedded just below the surface of the skin. And Mattie rocked and pulled—and the splinter gave way, but its roots were deep, gigantic, ragged, and they tore up flesh with bits of fat and muscle tissue clinging to them. They left a huge hole, which was already starting to pus over, but Mattie was satisfied. It would heal.

The bile that had formed a tight knot in Ciel's stomach began to rise and gagged her just as it passed her throat. Mattie put her hand over the girl's mouth and rushed her out the now-empty room to the toilet. Ciel retched yellowish-green phlegm, and she brought up white lumps of slime that hit the seat of the toilet and rolled off, splattering onto the tiles. After a while she heaved only air, but the body did not seem to want to stop. It was exorcising the evilness of pain.

Mattie cupped her hands under the faucet and motioned for Ciel to drink and clean her mouth. When the water left Ciel's mouth, it tasted as if she had been rinsing with a mild acid. Mattie drew a tub of hot water and undressed Ciel. She let the nightgown fall off the narrow shoulders, over the pitifully thin breasts and jutting hipbones. She slowly helped her into the water, and it was like a dried brown autumn leaf hitting the surface of a puddle.

And slowly she bathed her. She took the soap, and, using only her hands, she washed Ciel's hair and the back of her neck. She raised her arms and cleaned the armpits, soaping well the downy brown hair there. She let the soap slip between the girl's breasts, and she washed each one separately, cupping it in her hands. She took each leg and even cleaned under the toenails. Making Ciel rise and kneel in the tub, she cleaned the crack in her behind, soaped her pubic hair, and gently washed the creases in her vagina—slowly, reverently, as if handling a newborn.

She took her from the tub and toweled her in the same manner she had been bathed—as if too much friction would break the skin tissue. All of this had been done without either woman saying a word. Ciel stood there, naked, and felt the cool air play against the clean surface of her skin. She had the sensation of fresh mint coursing through her pores. She closed her eyes and the fire was gone. Her tears no longer fried within her, killing her internal organs with their steam. So Ciel began to cry—there, naked, in the center of the bathroom floor.

Mattie emptied the tub and rinsed it. She led the still-naked Ciel to a chair in the bedroom. The tears were flowing so freely now Ciel couldn't see, and she allowed herself to be led as if blind. She sat on the chair and cried—head erect. Since she made no effort to wipe them away, the tears dripped down her chin and landed on her chest and rolled down to her stomach and onto her dark pubic hair. Ignoring Ciel, Mattie took away the crumpled linen and made the bed, stretching the sheets tight and fresh. She beat the pillows into a virgin plumpness and dressed them in white cases.

And Ciel sat. And cried. The unmolested tears had rolled down her parted thighs and were beginning to wet the chair. But they were cold and good. She put out her tongue and began to drink in their saltiness, feeding on them. The first tears were gone. Her thin shoulders began to quiver, and spasms circled her body as new tears came—this time, hot and stinging. And she sobbed, the first sound she'd made since the moaning.

Mattie took the edges of the dirty sheet she'd pulled off the bed and wiped the mucus that had been running out of Ciel's nose. She then led her freshly wet, glistening body, baptized now, to the bed. She covered her with one sheet and laid a towel across the pillow—it would help for a while.

And Ciel lay down and cried. But Mattie knew the tears would end. And she would sleep. And morning would come.

Terry McMillan (1951–)

Millions of readers identify with Terry McMillan's novels and stories of love and conflict, the realistic language of her characters, and the truth of the themes she addresses. McMillan has accomplished an impressive feat in contemporary African American fiction: she's made intimacy between black women and black men realistic, honest, and complex for a multiethnic audience. Also, by taking relationships that were previously underrepresented in fiction and throwing a spotlight on them, she has singled them out as an immediate priority in the emotional health of the African American community.

Born in Port Huron, Michigan, northeast of Detroit, McMillan grew up in a working-class family. She received her bachelor's in journalism from the University of California at Berkeley in 1978 and attended the program in film at Columbia University, where she earned her master's degree. McMillan has since taught at the University of Wyoming in Laramie and the University of Arizona at Tucson.

Absent from the young McMillan's working-class home was an emphasis on reading, generally, and on black literature in particular. Her ignorance of African American literature as a teen led her to reject the significance of such writers as James Baldwin. She explains: "I . . . did not read his book because I was too afraid. I couldn't imagine that he'd have anything better or different to say than Thomas Mann, Henry Thoreau, Ralph Waldo Emerson. . . . Needless to say, I was not just naive, but had not yet acquired an ounce of black pride."

Her awareness of African American literature grew in her early college years. While still an undergraduate at UC-Berkeley, McMillan published her first short story, in 1976. After attending the Harlem Writer's Guild, her two stays at the MacDonell Artist Colony and Yaddo Artist Retreat allowed her to complete her first novel, Mama *(1987), which grew out of one of her short works of fiction. Taking the initiative to promote the novel independently, McMillan sent over three thousand letters to bookstores, academic institutions, and other booksellers. Her effort was rewarded by good critical reviews, over thirty public readings, and, after only six weeks of publication, a third printing of* Mama.

McMillan solidified her reputation as a novelist with Disappearing Acts *(1989), from which the following selection is taken. The novel focuses on a black woman and black man who struggle to overcome personal differences and past failures in order to build a positive love relationship.* Waiting to Exhale *(1992), her most recent novel, is considered a milestone in terms of popularity, for both the writer and for contemporary African American literature. Entering marketing doors that had already been opened by Alice Walker, Toni Morrison, and Gloria Naylor, the novel made McMillan a media star in a publicity campaign marked by book tours and appearances on major television programs. In addition to fiction writing, McMillan has edited* Breaking Ice: An Anthology of African-American Fiction *(1990); it is her response to the salient omission of black fiction from most previous literature anthologies.*

"Zora" is the opening passage of Disappearing Acts. *In this excerpt, the black woman narrator ponders her needs in life, particularly as they relate to men.*

Zora

I've got two major weaknesses: tall black men and food. But not necessarily in that order.

When I'm lonely, I eat. When I'm bored, I eat. When I'm horny (and can't resolve it), I eat. When I get excited, I eat. When I'm depressed, I eat. When I just feel like it, I eat. When I smoked, I didn't eat as much, but smoking wasn't half as satisfying as eating, so I made a choice. I chose food. I had migrated up to a size sixteen, and that's when I looked at myself in the mirror and couldn't stand it. I said, "Just wait one damn minute here, Zora!" *and, along with some of the other flabby teachers at the junior high school where I teach, joined Weight Watchers. I lasted about a year and am now down to a slender size twelve—well, it's slender enough, considering I'm almost five foot eight. Of course I've still got this damn cellulite, which drives me crazy. I can feel the ripples other people can't see. Which is precisely why I went out and bought Jane Fonda. Now, when I wake up, before I have my coffee, I work out with Jane. I've been doing it with her for a few weeks now, but so far I can't see a bit of difference.*

Weight Watchers turned out to be a drag. It was just like going to the fit doctor, aka neurologist. One thing I can't stand is people telling me what to do—after all the years I'd been told what not to eat, drink, and think—so I quit when I thought I looked halfway decent in my favorite Betsey Johnson dress.

Yes, I used to have fits. And not the kind kids have when they can't get their way. Real fits. Seizures. When I was little, I fell off a sliding board and hit my head on the cement, and I guess that's what did it. But it's been almost four years since I've had one. The neurologist calls it a remission, but that's not true. I stopped taking those stupid pills is what I did, and started picturing myself fit-free. No one really believes in the power of this stuff, but I don't care, it's worked for me—so far. As a matter of fact, when I started visualizing myself less abundant, and desirable again, that's how I think I was able to get here—to 139 pounds. And no, I am not from California. I just taught myself how to say no.

I cannot lie. There are times when I have to say yes to chocolate, but I try to minimize my intake. And Lord knows I make the best peach cobbler and sweet potato pie in the world, but I've not only learned to share, but also to freeze things that beg to be consumed in one sitting.

Except when it comes to men. I've got a history of jumping right into the fire, mistaking desire for love, lust for love, and, the records show, on occasion, a good lay for love. But those days are over. I mean it. Shit, I'm almost thirty years

---

This passage was set in italics in the original; hence, the italics have been retained here. –Ed.

old, and every time I look up, I'm back at the starting gate. So yes. I would *like a man to become a permanent fixture in my life for once. But don't get me wrong. I'm not out here cruising with lasers and aiming it at hopefuls. My Daddy always said, "Sometimes you can't see for looking," so what I'm saying is that from now on, no more hunting, no more rushing to discos with Portia on a Saturday night, standing around, trying to look necessary. I made up my mind that the next time I'm "out here"—which just so happens to be right now—it'll have to start with dinner (which won't be me) and at least one or two movies and quite a few hand-holding walks before I slide under the covers and scream out his name like I've known him all my life. Some flowers wouldn't hurt either.*

And just why do I feel like this? Because some of 'em don't last as long as a Duracell, no matter how much you keep recharging 'em. And I've been tricked too many times. Maybe misled would be a better word. No, maybe falsely impressed would be even more accurate. Then again, I'm really too damn gullible. I believe what I want to believe. One of my best girlfriends, Claudette, told me that my biggest problem was that I didn't do my homework. "Find out the most vital things first," she said.

"Like what?" I asked, even though I knew exactly what she meant.

"Has he been to college? Does he have a drug problem? Interested in personal hygiene? Does he believe in God, and if so, when was the last time he set foot inside a church? Does he know that respect is a verb? Does he love his mother and father? What's his family like? His friends? How does he feel about children and marriage? Has he ever been married? Does he have any idea what he'll be doing ten or twenty years from now? Is it remotely close to what he's doing now? That kind of shit."

But I'm not into interrogation. I prefer to wait and see if the image he projects lives up to the man. And vice versa. Let's face it: All men are not husband material. Some of 'em are only worth a few nights of pleasure. But some of 'em make you get on your knees at night and pray that they choose Door Number One, which is the one you happen to be standing behind. And it's not that I haven't been picked before. Because I have. They turned out to be a major disappointment. Said one thing and did another. Couldn't back up half of what they'd led me to believe. Then begged me to be patient. And like a fool, I tried it, until I got tired of idling, and the needle fell on empty. Some of 'em just weren't ready. They wanted to play house. Or The Dating Game. Or Guess Where I'm Coming From? or Show Me How Much You Love Me Then I'll Show You. And then there're the ones who got scared when they realized I wasn't playing. "You're too intense," one said. "Too serious," said another one. "You take them lyrics you write to heart, don't you, Miss Z?" I told them that this wasn't high school or college, but the grown-up edition of life. They were still more comfortable not having a care in the world, so I let 'em run and hide, especially the ones that needed professional help. So now I'm taking off the blindfolds and doing the bidding myself. After a while, even a fool would get tired of bringing home the TV and finding out it only gets two or three channels.

None of this is to say I'm perfect. I just know what I've got to offer—and it's worth millions. Hell, I'm a strong, smart, sexy, good-hearted black woman, and one day I want to make some man so happy he'll think he hit the lottery. I don't care what anybody says—love is a two-way street. So yes, I want my heart oiled. I don't want to participate in any more of these transient romances—I'm inter-

ested in longevity. Let's face it: Some men take more interest in their pets than they do in their women. And even though I wish loving a man could be as easy for me as it was for Cinderella, I know it's not that simple. But it can be. And it should be. All you need is two people who are willing to expend the energy so that their hearts don't rust.

Which is one reason why I envy Claudette. She is so normal. She's a lawyer, married, has a daughter, and she's happy. She loves her husband. Her husband loves her. They are buying their house. They have lawn furniture. They ski in the winter and spend weeks in the Caribbean. He brushes her hair at night. She rubs his feet. And after seven years of marriage, they still unplug their phone.

On the other hand, Portia, who Claudette can't stand but I love, has an entirely different set of standards. "He's gotta have hair on his chest and no skinny legs. And he's gotta have some money. I don't care what color he is, but ain't no getting around no empty bank account."

"Money isn't everything," I said.

"Since when?"

Portia thinks her pussy is gold. She's not all that educated—she got as far as court reporting school—but I don't care. I refuse to discriminate when it comes to my friends. I'm more interested in the quality of their character than I am with credentials. Besides, I know plenty of folks with degrees that are stupid. They lack the one essential thing you need to get by in this world: common sense.

I can't lie: Sometimes I fall into that category myself. Because I still don't know what it is about deep-black skin and long legs that turns me on, but some things aren't worth analyzing. It's taken me years to realize what I like and what I don't like. For instance, short men simply do not appeal to me, at least none have so far. And men who could stand a few trips to the dentist will never kiss me. Men who are afraid of deodorant knock me out. Men who roll over, stick it in, and think they've done something miraculous make me want to slap 'em instead of shudder. I can't stand vulgar men. Dumb men. Lazy men. Men who think the word respect means expect. Men who are so pretty they spend more time in the mirror than I do. Men whose brains can be measured by the size of their dicks. Selfish men. Men who don't vote. Who think all the news that's fit to print is on the sports page. Liars. Men who think that the world owes them something. Men who care more about the cushion between my legs than they do about the rest of me. Men who don't stand for anything in particular. Who think passion is synonymous only with fucking. And men who don't take chances—who are too afraid to stick their damn necks out for fear that they're going to drown.

So I guess you could say that the kind of man I like is just the opposite of these. Which means I like a clean, tall, smart, honest, sensuous, spontaneous, energetic, aggressive man with white teeth who smells good and reads a good book every now and then, who votes and wants to make a contribution to the world instead of holding his hands out. A man who stands for something. Who feels passion for more than just women. And a man who appreciates that my pussy is good but also respects the fact that I have a working brain. And last but not least, a man who knows how to make love.

I have not run into him lately.

Every man I've ever loved—and there've been three and a half—or that I've cared substantially about, brought me to these conclusions in a haphazard way, but I'm grateful to all of 'em, because had I not experienced them, *I wouldn't have had any.*

When I was sixteen, there was Bookie Cooper, whose skin shone like india ink and whose fingernails were yellow. He had muscles. He fixed the chain on my bike when it broke, then walked me home through the woods the long way and gave me my first kiss. Bookie used to whisper in my ear. He had such a soft voice that I often had to stare at his lips in order to figure out what he was saying. He was the first boy that made me tingle. And he taught me the power of kissing—just how serious it can be. But Bookie got killed. He was crossing the street on his bicycle when an ambulance hit him. For months, I couldn't believe it. I slept with that orange elephant he'd won for me at the state fair, so I would still feel close to him. I even walked by his house and waited for him to come out, but another family had moved in, and this white woman with pink sponge rollers in her hair kept peeking through the curtains suspiciously. It took a long time for it to register that Bookie's absence was permanent. But I can't lie: I had to teach myself to forget him.

There was Champagne, the college basketball star who held my hand and stroked my hair while he talked, and forever smelled like British Sterling. Even though I was just a junior in high school, he made me feel like a woman. After my senior prom, with my very first glass of rum and Coke exaggerating everything, he talked me into giving up my virginity, and I did it because I was tired of saying no and figured if I got pregnant at least I'd be out of high school by the time it was born. And it hurt. I was grateful when it was finally over, and couldn't understand why everybody had made such a big deal about sex if this was supposed to be the thrill of a lifetime. I never did feel electric. But I didn't care; I still wanted Champagne. Being wrapped inside his strong arms was warm enough for me. As a matter of fact, I used to lie beside him and dream about him. Play every sad, slow song by Aretha and Smokey Robinson I could get my hands on and dig my face in the pillow and cry. Which is how I knew I was in love. We agreed to get married once we both finished college and he was playing in the pros. But what happened? I won a music scholarship to Ohio State, and he went to a Big Ten university in Indiana and never wrote so much as a word, not to mention the fact that his fingers must've been stricken with arthritis, because he never called either.

"To hell with Champagne," is what I said when I met David, who was bowlegged, walked like Clint Eastwood, drove a Harley-Davidson, and boxed. He was so black he was purple, and I swear I could've eaten him alive. Especially after he lifted me up on top of him and let me move any way I wanted to, as long as I wanted to. And I liked it. Loved it, really. He taught me that there were no limits to passion if you didn't impose any. So every time I felt like doing it I would dial his number. Tell him I needed to see him. David's body was my very first addiction. It was so cooperative. And he would take me for long motorcycle rides—in the rain, at night, in freezing weather, it didn't matter. This was the first time I experienced real adventure and understood what freedom felt like. But we hardly ever talked. So by the time David asked me to marry him, I realized two things: that he was boring except in bed and that there was a big difference between wanting to spend the rest of your life with someone and wanting to experience continuous moments of ecstasy. I said no and told him I was moving to New York City to launch my singing career. I told him I wanted

to live a bold and daring life, not a safe little cozy one in Toledo. He said he would make it exciting, but I told him I'd rather not try.

By the time I got here, I decided to take a short sabbatical from men. But not all that short. It lasted about four months. Sometimes men can be more of a distraction than anything. Marie—she's my comedienne friend—says that I not only take them too seriously but I put too much emphasis on their worth. But I can't help it. As corny as it may sound—considering this is the eighties and everything—there's nothing better than feeling loved and needed. And until God comes up with a better substitute, I'll just keep my fingers crossed that one day I'll meet someone with my name stamped on his back.

So I met Percy, the plumber. He was a smart, handsome plumber, but he wanted a wife too badly. He had put the clamps on me in less than a month. He was from Louisiana and gave the best head I ever had in my life. As a matter of fact, he was the first man who made me come that way. All the others had always gnawed and chewed so much that it got to the point that when one offered, I refused the invitation. Percy changed all that. Of course I was already strung out by the time he asked me to quit my job, marry him, and move to some little off-the-wall town in Louisiana that I'd never even heard of and run a farm and have babies. And he was serious. I told him he was out of his mind, which is why when I found out I was carrying his baby, I rushed down to the Women's Center and did not tell him. I blacked out his name in my address book and changed my number to unlisted.

And Dillon. He was a DJ who claimed he wanted to be a record producer. I thought we had something in common. Hah! He was—I later found out the correct term—a premature ejaculator. He would give me ten or twelve minutes of pleasure, and poof! it was over. He just kept telling me that I was so good I should be grateful I could make him come so fast. If he hadn't favored Billy Dee Williams so much, or listened to me sing, I'd have given up on him sooner. But Dillon had a ton of energy in other areas. He was the first black man I knew who skied. By the time I heard about a concert I wanted to see, he already had the tickets. And he talked me to death. His dreams were as loud as mine, and I liked that. As I later found out, cocaine had a whole lot to do with it. When I first met him, Dillon told me he had sinus problems, so I was used to him sniffling all the time. He also loved me fat, and actually got nervous when I started shedding the pounds. "You looked good big," he said, and swore he'd give up coke if I would just stop losing weight. Naturally, he was crazy as hell, and our goodbye was so ugly that when I missed my period again, there was no way I could bring myself to tell him. So I did it again, but swore I would never hop up on one of those tables and count backward from a hundred unless whatever came out was going home with me and my husband.

There have been others, but they're not worth mentioning because none of them made me fall from grace or feel the earth move, for lack of a better cliché.

I know I may sound fickle, but I'm not. I was taught to give all human beings a chance to prove their worth before I dismissed them. I assumed that meant men too. And even though I get so lonely sometimes it feels like I'm dying, or my heart and head get mixed up and the only thing I can do to fill the emptiness or stop the ache of nothingness is to take a Tylenol, I do not stand in front of the mirror anymore, holding these 36C's in my palms and praying that someone was there kissing them. I have learned how to satisfy myself, although I can't lie and say

I make myself feel as good as a real man could. But like my Daddy always said, "Work with what you've got."

What I've got is a good set of lungs and vocal cords.

Mount Olive Baptist used to be standing room only when word got out that I was doing a solo. I used to make people cry and speak in tongues, and those fans would be swaying so fast you couldn't even see the name of the funeral parlor on 'em. There is no greater feeling than singing a song that makes people feel glad to be alive.

Marguerite—that's my stepmother—has always accused me of being too idealistic. "You always reaching for what you can't see, chile." My real Mama died in a car accident when I was three years old, which is how I got stuck with Marguerite as a replacement. Not that she hasn't been a nice stepmother, but I've never had anyone to compare her to. She did teach me how to cook, how to shave my armpits and legs, and told me when to douche. Daddy married her when I was thirteen. She's taller than him, flat-chested, with an ever-growing behind and hazel eyes. Every six weeks she dyes her gray hair black, because she says, "I ain't got no time to be looking old."

My Daddy looks old, but I guess if you'd worked for the railroad for thirty-six years and married someone who insisted you take all the overtime you could get, then snatched your paycheck every Friday and lived at Sears, gave you an allowance, and only closed the bedroom door on Saturday nights, you'd look old too.

When I told my Daddy I was moving to New York City to sing, he just blew a cloud of smoke out of his cigar, tapped off an inch of ashes, grinned—that gold tooth sparkling—and said, "You go 'head, baby. Life ain't nothin' to be scared of. 'Sides, the Lord'll follow you wherever you go."

I've had my doubts.

The problem is I've been influenced by so many folks that I sound like a whole lot of singers all rolled up. This has bothered me for too long, because I don't know what my real *voice is. Sure, every now and then I hear myself with such clarity, with such precision, that I get surprised—even a bit scared—because what I hear sounds like someone I could envy. But it's not consistent. I can imitate just about anybody I admire. Joan Armatrading. Chaka Khan. Joni Mitchell. Laura Nyro. Aretha and Gladys too.*

Sometimes I stay after school—since my piano's in layaway and I still owe three hundred dollars on it—and compose. I sit there with my eye closed, and when my fingers press against the keys and I start to sing, the room often moves. My heart opens up and lets in light. Writing songs allows me to fix what's wrong. And when I'm singing, I'm not lonely, just overwhelmed by desire. I'm not looking for a man; I've found one. Folks aren't starving; I'm giving 'em food from my plate. I invent jobs. Get rid of torment and racism and hatred, and spin a world so rich with righteousness that usually, by the time I finish, I'm perspiring something awful, and I don't even realize how much time has passed until I walk outside and see that it's dark.

As it stands now, I do most of my singing in the shower. I get clean and let out pain at the same time—watch it go down the drain. And not just my pain but everybody else's that I've known who's ever felt or known hurt. And there are millions of us. To tell the truth, sometimes I get scared when I think of myself being in a world where I don't make a bit of difference. Where I could die and the only people who would ever know I was here would be friends, lovers, and relatives. I want to affect people in a positive way, which is one reason why I teach music. But it's not enough. I want to sing songs that'll make people float.

That's why I'm looking for a coach. I need to learn how to control my voice. Find my center. Learn to pay attention to what I feel in my heart so that it comes out of my pen, then my mouth, instead of screaming inside my head. I don't care if I'm never as famous as Diana or Aretha or Liza or Barbra. I don't have to make Billboard*'s Top 40 either. I'd be just as content squeezing a microphone in my hands in some smoky club, with an audience who came to hear me sing. The only way I'll ever be able to afford a voice coach is by moving out of this expensive-ass apartment, which is precisely why you can have Manhattan and its Upper West Side. I'm going to Brooklyn, where they say you can at least get your money's worth. My Daddy always said, "You gotta give up somethin' to get somethin'." I'm giving up roaches, water bugs, mice, $622 a month, and a view of a brick wall.*

Right now I'm staring at the ceiling and can hear birds chirping. This is a good sign. But I can't lie: I am lonely, and it has *been almost six months since I've been touched by a man. I'll live, though. Instead of wasting my time wishing and hoping, sleeping with self-pity and falling in love over and over again with ghosts, I'm going to stop concentrating so hard on what's missing in my life and be grateful for what I've got. For instance, this organ inside my chest. God gave me a gift, and I'd be a fool not to use it. And if there's a man out there who's willing to ride or walk or run or even fly with me, he'll show up. Probably out of nowhere. I'm just not going to hold my breath.*

Walter Mosley (1952–)

Commenting on his goals in writing mystery novels, Walter Mosley states: "A good novel comes out into the world and grows as people read it. . . . I want black people to read the book and say, 'That's my language, that's my life, that's my history.' But I want white people to say, 'Boy, you know, I feel just like that!"

Mosley was born and raised in Los Angeles, but by the end of his high school years he was eager to sever himself from a city that he felt held too many limitations for personal growth. He thus enrolled at Goddard College in Vermont, but that school's radical curriculum and small setting did not provide the fulfillment he sought. After drifting across several other campuses, Mosley settled at Johnson State College in Vermont, receiving his bachelor's in 1977.

He decided to become a writer while working on a doctorate at the University of Massachusetts in Amherst and supporting himself as a computer programmer. Fighting boredom at work one day, he typed several creative lines that, he says, inspired him to pursue writing as a career. In 1985, he enrolled in a graduate-level creative writing program at the City College of New York and won the college's Du Jur Award for his fiction. With the assistance of his writing professor, Mosley obtained an agent and began publishing.

Devil in a Blue Dress *(1990)—the first novel in Mosley's highly acclaimed series of mysteries featuring the black detective Easy Rawlins—was honored with a Shamus Award and an Edward Award nomination for best new mystery. Mosley's rendering of Easy Rawlins's life continues in* A Red Death *(1991), nominated for a Golden Dagger Award;* White Butterfly *(1992), winner of a*

Golden Dagger Award; and Black Betty *(1994). One critic describes the character Easy Rawlins "as the sort of black male figure that so much of popular culture has collectively erased from public consciousness or has yet to find a place for at the dinner table. There is a familiarity about him, a human softness. . . ." Mosley planned to write five additional novels featuring detective Easy Rawlins, but in 1995, Mosley ventured in a different direction, writing* RL's Dream, *a contemporary novel focusing on an elderly black blues musician living in New York City.*

Mosley's popularity has soared among avid readers of detective stories as well as among those new to the genre. Having been named as President Bill Clinton's favorite mystery writer, and having seen his first three novels translated into seventeen languages, Mosley has established an impressive literary position, recently enhanced by the 1995 movie version of Devil in a Blue Dress.

In the following chapter from Devil in a Blue Dress, *a confrontation unfolds between Easy Rawlins and a group of white police officers. Set in Los Angeles in 1948, the novel centers on Easy's efforts to pay his bills by hiring out to find an attractive blond woman who dares to socialize in the black area of the city.*

from Devil in a Blue Dress

I was home by noon. The street was empty and the neighborhood was quiet. There was a dark Ford parked across the street from my house. I remember thinking that a bill collector was making his rounds. Then I laughed to myself because all my bills were paid well in advance. I was a proud man that day; my fall wasn't far behind.

As I was closing the gate to the front yard I saw the two white men getting out of the Ford. One was tall and skinny and he was wearing a dark blue suit. The other one was my height and three times my girth. He had on a wrinkled tan suit that had greasy spots here and there.

The men strode quickly in my direction but I just turned slowly and walked toward my door.

"Mr. Rawlins!" one of them called from behind.

I turned. "Yeah?"

They were approaching fast but cautiously. The fat one had a hand in his pocket.

"Mr. Rawlins, I'm Miller and this is my partner Mason." They both held out badges.

"Yeah?"

"We want you to come with us."

"Where?"

"You'll see," fat Mason said as he took me by the arm.

"Are you arresting me?"

"You'll see," Mason said again. He was pulling me toward the gate.

"I've got the right to know why you're taking me."

"You got a right to fall down and break your face, nigger. You got a right to die," he said. Then he hit me in the diaphragm. When I doubled over he slipped the handcuffs on behind my back and together they dragged me to the car. They tossed me in the back seat where I lay gagging.

"You vomit on my carpet and I'll feed it to ya," Mason called back.

They drove me to the Seventy-seventh Street station and carried me in the front door.

"You got'im, huh, Miller?" somebody said. They were holding me by my arms and I was sagging with my head down. I had recovered from the punch but I didn't want them to know it.

"Yeah, we got him coming home. Nothing on'im."

They opened the door to a small room that smelled faintly of urine. The walls were unpainted plaster and there was only a bare wooden chair for furniture. They didn't offer me the chair though, they just dropped me on my knees and walked out, closing the door behind them.

The door had a tiny peephole in it.

I pushed my shoulder against the wall until I was standing. The room didn't look any better. There were a few bare pipes along the ceiling that dripped now and then. The edge of the linoleum floor was corroded and chalky from the moisture. There was only one window. It didn't have glass but only a crisscross of two two-inch bars down and two bars across. Very little light came in through the window due to the branches and leaves that had pushed their way in. It was a small room, maybe twelve by twenty, and I had some fear that it was to be the last room I ever inhabited.

I was worried because they didn't follow the routine. I had played the game of "cops and nigger" before. The cops pick you up, take your name and fingerprints, then they throw you into a holding tank with other "suspects" and drunks. After you were sick from the vomit and foul language they'd take you to another room and ask why you robbed that liquor store or what did you do with the money?

I would try to look innocent while I denied what they said. It's hard acting innocent when you are but the cops know that you aren't. They figure that you did something because that's just the way cops think, and you telling them that you're innocent just proves to them that you have something to hide. But that wasn't the game that we were playing that day. They knew my name and they didn't need to scare me with any holding tank; they didn't need to take my fingerprints. I didn't know why they had me, but I did know that it didn't matter as long as they thought they were right.

I sat down in the chair and looked up at the leaves coming in through the window. I counted thirty-two bright green oleander leaves. Also coming in through the window was a line of black ants that ran down the side of the wall and around to the other side of the room where the tiny corpse of a mouse was crushed into a corner. I speculated that another prisoner had killed the mouse by stamping it. He probably had tried in the middle of the floor at first but the quick rodent had swerved away two, maybe even three times. But finally the mouse made the deadly mistake of looking for a crevice in the wall and the inmate was able to block off his escape by using both feet. The mouse looked papery and dry so I supposed that the death had occurred at the beginning of the week; about the time I was getting fired.

While I was thinking about the mouse the door opened again and the officers stepped in. I was angry at myself because I hadn't tried to see if the door was locked. Those cops had me where they wanted me.

"Ezekiel Rawlins," Miller said.

"Yes, sir."

"We have a few questions to ask. We can take off those cuffs if you want to start cooperating."

"I am cooperating."

"Told ya, Bill," fat Mason said. "He's a smart nigger."

"Take off the cuffs, Charlie," Miller said and the fat man obliged.

"Where were you yesterday morning at about 5 A.M.?"

"What morning is that?" I stalled.

"He means," fat Mason said as he planted his foot in my chest and pushed me over backwards, "Thursday morning."

"Get up," Miller said.

I got to my feet and righted the chair.

"That's hard to say." I sat down again. "I was out drinking and then I helped carry a drunk friend home. I could'a been on my way home or maybe I was already in bed. I didn't look at a clock."

"What friend is that?"

"Pete. My friend Pete."

"Pete, huh?" Mason chuckled. He wandered over to my left and before I could turn toward him I felt the hard knot of his fist explode against the side of my head.

I was on the ground again.

"Get up," Miller said.

I got up again.

"So where was you and your peter drinkin'?" Mason sneered.

"Down at a friend's on Eighty-nine."

Mason moved again but this time I turned. He just looked at me with an innocent face and his palms turned upward.

"Would that be an illegal nightclub called John's?" Miller asked.

I was quiet.

"You got bigger problems than busting your friend's bar, Ezekiel. You got bigger troubles than that."

"What kinds troubles?"

"Big troubles."

"What's that mean?"

"Means we can take your black ass out behind the station and put a bullet in your head," Mason said.

"Where were you at five o'clock on Thursday morning, Mr. Rawlins?" Miller asked.

"I don't know exactly."

Mason had taken off his shoe and started swatting the heel against his fat palm.

"Five o'clock," Miller said.

We played that game a little while longer. Finally I said, "Look, you don't have to beat up your hand on my account; I'm happy to tell you what you wanna know."

"You ready to cooperate?" Miller asked.

"Yes, sir."

"Where did you go when you left Coretta James' house on Thursday morning?"

"I went home."

Mason tried to kick the chair out from under me but I was on my feet before he could.

"I had enough'a this shit, man!" I yelled, but neither cop seemed very impressed. "I told you I went home, and that's all."

"Have a seat, Mr. Rawlins," Miller said calmly.

"Why'm I gonna sit and you keep tryin' to knock me down?" I cried. But I sat down anyway.

"I told ya he was crazy, Bill," Mason said. "I told ya this was a section eight."

"Mr. Rawlins," Miller said. "Where did you go after you left Miss James' house?"

"I went home."

No one hit me that time; no one tried to kick the chair.

"Did you see Miss James later that day?"

"No, sir."

"Did you have an altercation with Mr. Bouchard?"

I understood him but I said, "Huh?"

"Did you and Dupree Bouchard have words over Miss James?"

"You know," Mason chimed in. "Pete."

"That's what I call him sometimes," I said.

"Did you," Miller repeated, "have an altercation with Mr. Bouchard?"

"I didn't have nuthin' with Dupree. He was asleep."

"So where did you go on Thursday?"

"I went home with a hangover. I stayed there all day and night and then I went to work today. Well"—I wanted to keep them talking so that Mason wouldn't lose his temper with the furniture again—"not to work really because I got fired Monday. But I went to get my job back."

"Where did you go on Thursday?"

"I went home with a hangover . . ."

"Nigger!" Mason tore into me with his fists. He knocked me to the floor but I grabbed onto his wrists. I swung around and twisted so that I was straddling his back, sitting on his fat ass. I could have killed him the way I'd killed other white men in uniforms, but I could feel Miller behind me so I stood straight up and moved to the corner.

Miller had a police special in his hand.

Mason made like he was going to come after me again but the belly-flop had winded him. From his knees Mason said, "Lemme have'im alone fer a minute."

Miller weighed the request. He kept looking back and forth between me and the fat man. Maybe he was afraid that I'd kill his partner or maybe he didn't want the paperwork; it could have been that Miller was a secret humanitarian who didn't want bloodshed and ruin on his hands. Finally he whispered, "No."

"But . . . ," Mason started.

"I said no. Let's move."

Miller hooked his free hand under the fat man's armpit and helped him to his feet. Then he holstered his pistol and straightened his coat. Mason sneered at me and then followed Miller out of the cell door. He was starting to remind me of a trained mutt. The lock snapped behind him.

I got back in the chair and counted the leaves again. I followed the ants to the dead mouse again. This time, though, I imagined that I was the convict and that mouse was officer Mason. I crushed him so that his whole suit was soiled and shapeless in the corner; his eyes came out of his head.

There was a light bulb hanging from a wire at the ceiling but there was no way to turn it on. Slowly the little sun that filtered in through the leaves faded and the room became twilight. I sat in the chair pressing my bruises now and then to see if the pain was lessening.

I didn't think a thing. I didn't wonder about Coretta or Dupree or how the police knew so much about my Wednesday night. All I did was sit in darkness, trying to become the darkness. I was awake but my thinking was like a dream. I dreamed in my wakefulness that I could become the darkness and slip out between the eroded cracks of that cell. If I was nighttime nobody could find me; no one would even know I was missing.

I saw faces in the darkness; beautiful women and feasts of ham and pie. It's only now that I realize how lonely and hungry I was then. . . .

It was fully black in that cell when the light snapped on. I was still trying to blink away the glare when Miller and Mason came in. Miller closed the door.

"You think of anything else to say?" Miller asked me.

I just looked at him.

"You can go," Miller said.

"You heard him, nigger!" Mason shouted while he was fumbling around to check that his fly was zipped up. "Get outta here!"

They led me into the open room and past the desk watch. Everywhere people turned to stare at me. Some laughed, some were shocked.

They took me to the desk sergeant, who handed me my wallet and pocket-knife.

"We might be in touch with you later, Mr. Rawlins," Miller said. "If we have any questions we know where you live."

"Questions about what?" I asked, trying to sound like an honest man asking an honest question.

"That's police business."

"Ain't it my business if you drag me outta my own yard an' bring me down here an' throw me around?"

"You want a complaint form?" Miller's thin, gray face didn't change expression. He looked like a man I once knew, Orrin Clay. Orrin had a peptic ulcer and always held his mouth like he was just about to spit.

"I wanna know what's goin' on." I said.

"We'll be coming 'round if we need you."

"How am I supposed to get home from way out here? The buses stop after six."

Miller turned away from me. Mason was already gone.

Jess Mowry (1960–)

In his short stories and novels, Jess Mowry aims to reach a specific audience—inner-city black adolescents, who suffer the greatest risk of loss yet possess the greatest potential within the African American community. Mowry's fiction explores their world of seductive temptations and the possibilities of survival.

Mowry knows the urban jungle through personal experience. When he was an infant, his father brought him to Oakland from his birthplace near Starkville, Mississippi. Mowry's boredom with school was balanced by his growing interest in reading fiction at home, but by the eighth grade he had left school to pursue a street life in his Oakland neighborhood. By age thirteen, he was surviving in the city through illegal activities; by seventeen, he was a father attempting to support his family by recycling empty containers.

It was in the late 1980s when Mowry first turned to a used typewriter to deal with the world he knew and to reach out to the street kids he understood. He explains: "My main message is stop killin' each other, you stupid little suckers, because there's a race war goin' on in the ghetto, and it's on you."

Mowry's writing is straightforward and stark, rendered in the language and graphic details of the urban milieu that most other writers avoid. His first published work, the short story collection Rats in the Trees *(1990), won a PEN Oakland Award. He followed it with three novels:* Children of the Night *(1991);* Way Past Cool *(1992), which gained national notice; and* Six Out Seven *(1993), which reached an even wider audience and subjected Mowry to the public attention he prefers to avoid.*

Still living in Oakland, Mowry continues to help inner-city youths by donating time and money to churches, civic organizations, alternative schools, and other sources of support in the community. He thus tries to keep his mission and message consistent despite the intrusions of fame into his life.

"Crusader Rabbit," originally published in 1991, explores the realities of an urban environment for its young protagonist. At the same time, the story functions as social commentary on the dynamics of manhood as it relates to race, class, and social responsibility.

Crusader Rabbit

"You could be my dad."

Jeremy stood, waist-deep in the dumpster, arms slimed to the elbows from burrowing, and dropped three beer cans to the buckled asphalt.

Raglan lined them up, pop-tops down, and crushed them to crinkled discs under his tattered Nike, then added them to the half-full gunny sack. Finally, he straightened and studied the boy in the dumpster. It wasn't the first time. "Yeah. I could be."

Jeremy made no move to climb out, even though the stink of what he stood in seemed to surround him like a bronze-green cloud, wavering upward like the heat-ghosts from other dumpster lids along the narrow alley. The boy wore only ragged jeans, the Airwalks on his bare feet buried somewhere below, and his wiry dusk-colored body glistened with sweat.

Not for the first time, Raglan thought that Jeremy was a beautiful kid; 13, small muscles standing out under tight skin, big hands and feet like puppy paws, and hair like an ebony dandelion puff. A ring glinted gold and fierce in his left ear, and a red bandana, sodden with sweat, hung loosely around his neck. His eyes were bright obsidian, but closed now, the bruise-like marks beneath them were fading, and his teeth flashed strong and white as he panted.

Raglan could have been a larger copy of the boy, twice his age but looking it only in size, and without the earring. There was an old knife slash on his chest; a deep one, with a high ridge of scar.

The Oakland morning fog had burned off hours ago, leaving the alley to bake in tar and rot-smell, yet Raglan neither panted nor sweated. There were three more dumpsters to check out, and the recycle place across town would be closing soon, but Raglan asked, "Want a smoke?"

Jeremy watched through lowered lashes as Raglan's eyes changed . . . not so much softening as going light-years away somewhere. Jeremy hesitated, long fingers clenching and unclenching on the dumpster's rusty rim. "Yeah . . . no. I think it's time."

Jeremy's movements were stiff and awkward as he tried to climb out. Garbage sucked wetly at his feet. Raglan took the boy, slippery as a seal, under the arms and lifted him over the edge. The boy stank, but that was mostly from a long day digging. Together, they walked back to the truck.

It was a '55 GMC one-ton, as rusted and battered as the dumpsters. There were splintery plywood sideboards on the bed. The cab was crammed with things, as self-contained as a Land Rover on safari. Even after two months, it still surprised Jeremy sometimes what Raglan could pull out from beneath the seat or the piled mess on the dash . . . toilet paper, comic books, or a .45 automatic.

Raglan emptied the gunny sack into an almost-full garbage can in the back of the truck, then leaned against the sideboard and started to roll a cigarette from Top tobacco while Jeremy opened the driver's door and slipped a scarred-up Sesame Street Band-Aids box from under the floormat. The boy's hands shook slightly. He tried not to hurry as he spread out his things on the seat: a little rock-bottle with gray-brown powder in the bottom instead of crack crystals; a puff of cotton; candle stub; flame-tarnished spoon, and needle, its point protected by a chunk of Styrofoam. On the cab floor by the shift lever was a gallon plastic jug from Pay-Less Drugs that used to hold "fresh spring water from clear mountain streams." Raglan filled it from gas station hoses, and the water always tasted like rubber. Jeremy got it out, too.

Raglan finished making his cigarete, fired it with a Bic, handed the lighter to the boy, then started making another as he smoked. His eyes were still far away.

Jeremy looked up as he worked. "Yo. I know your ole name. I seen it on your driver license. Why's your street name Raglan?"

Smoke drifted from Raglan's nostrils. He came close to smiling. "My dad started callin' me that. Spose to be from some old time cartoon, when he was just a little kid. *Crusader Rabbit.* But I never seen it. The rabbit's homey was a tiger. Raglan T. Tiger. Maybe they was somethin' like the Ninja Turtles. Had adventures an shit. It was a long time ago."

"Oh." Jeremy sat on the cab floor. He wrapped a strip of inner-tube around his arm. It was hard to get it right, one-handed. He looked up again. "Um . . ."

"Yeah." Raglan knelt and pulled the strip tighter. His eyes were distant again, neither watching nor looking away as the boy put the needle in. "You got good veins. Your muscles make 'em stand out."

The boy's eyes shifted from the needle, lowering, and his chest hardened a little. "I do got some muscles, huh?"

"Yeah. But don't let 'em go to your head."

Jeremy chewed his lip. "I used to miss 'em . . . my veins, I mean. A long time ago. An sometimes I poked right through."

"Yeah. I done that too. A long time ago."

The boy's slender body tensed a moment, then he relaxed with a sigh, his face almost peaceful and his eyes closed. But a few seconds later they opened again and searched out Raglan's. "It only makes me normal now."

Raglan nodded. "Yeah. On two a day, that's all." He handed Jeremy the other cigarette and fired the lighter.

The boy pulled in smoke, holding it a long time, then puffing out perfect rings and watching them hover in the hot, dead air. "Next week, it's only gonna be one." He held Raglan's eyes. "It gonna hurt some more, huh?"

"Yeah."

"Um, when do you stop wanting it?"

Raglan stood, snagging the jug and taking a few swallows. Traffic rumbled past the alley. Exhaust fumes drifted in from the street. Flies buzzed in clouds over the dumpsters, and a rat scuttled past in no particular hurry. "When you decide there's somethin else you want more."

Jeremy began putting his things away. The little bottle was empty. It would take most of today's cans to score another for tomorrow. "Yo. You must be my dad, man. Why else would you give a shit?"

"I don't know. You figure it out." Raglan could have added that. When he'd first found Jeremy, the boy wouldn't have lived another week. But dudes Jeremy's age would think that was bad . . . almost cool. Why? Who in hell knew. Raglan didn't remember a lot about being 13, but he remembered that.

He dropped his cigarette on the pavement, slipped the sack off the sideboard, and started toward the other dumpsters. There really wasn't much use in checking these last dumpsters; this was the worst part of Oakland, and poor people's garbage was pitiful, everything already scraped bone-bare, rusted or rotted or beaten beyond redemption, and nothing left of any value at all. Jeremy followed, his moves flowing smooth like a black kid's once more.

A few paces ahead of the boy, Raglan flipped back a lid so that it clanged against the sooty brick wall. Flies scattered in swarms. For a second or two he just looked at what lay on top of the trash. He'd seen this before, too many times, but it was about the only thing he wouldn't accept as just what it was. His hand clamped on Jeremy's shoulder, holding the boy back. But Jeremy saw the baby anyhow.

"Oh . . . God." It came out of sigh. Jeremy pressed close to Raglan, and Raglan's arm went around him.

"I heard bout them," the boy whispered. "But I never figured it happened for real."

"Best take a good look, then."

But the boy's eyes lifted to Raglan's. "Why do people do that?"

But Raglan's gaze was distant once more, seeing but not seeing the little honey-brown body, the tiny and perfect fingers and toes. "I don't know."

Jeremy swallowed once. His lean chest expanded to pull in air. "What should we do?"

Raglan's eyes turned hard. He was thinking of cops and their questions, then of a call from some pay phone. There was one at the recycle place. Time was running short. The truck's tank was almost full, but there was food to buy after Jeremy's need, and the cans were the only money. Still he said, "What do you want to do?"

The boy looked back at the baby. Automatically he waved flies away. "What do they . . . do with 'em?" He turned to Raglan. "I mean . . . is there some little coffin . . . an flowers?"

Raglan took his arm off the boy. "They burn 'em."

"No!"

"The ones they find. Other times they just get hauled to the dump an the bulldozers bury 'em with the rest of the garbage. You been to the dump."

Almost, the boy clamped his hands to his ears, but then his fists clenched. "No! Goddamn you! Shup up, sucker!" Jeremy's fists clenched, then a hand darted to the pocket where he carried the blade.

The boy's chest heaved, muscles standing out stark. His hand poised. Raglan was quiet a minute. Finally he gripped Jeremy's shoulder once more. "Okay." Raglan walked back to the truck while Jeremy watched from beside the dumpster, waving away flies.

Raglan stopped around back. There was a ragged canvas tarp folded behind the cab. On foggy or rainy nights he spread it over the sideboards to make a roof. A piece of that would do. Salty sweat burned Raglan's eyes, and he blinked in the sunlight stabbing down between buildings. The canvas was oily, and stank. Going around to the cab, he pulled his black T-shirt from behind the seat.

The old GMC was a city truck, an inner-city truck, that measured its moves in blocks, not miles. It burned oil, the radiator leaked, and its tires were almost bald. There were two bullet holes in the right front fender. But it managed to maintain a grudging 55, rattling first across the Bay Bridge into San Francisco, and then over the Golden Gate, headed north. It had a radio/tape-deck, ancient and minus knobs, but Jeremy didn't turn on KSOL or play the old *Dangerous* tape he'd scored in a dumpster and patiently rewound with a pencil. He stayed silent, just rolling cigarettes for Raglan and himself, and looking once in awhile through the grimy back window at the little black bundle in the bed. Even when they turned off 101 near Novato onto a narrow two-lane road leading west Jeremy just stared through the windshield glass, his eyes a lot like Raglan's even though an open countryside of gentle green hills spread out around them.

It was early evening, with the sunlight slanting gold when Raglan slowed the truck and searched the roadside ahead. The air was fresh and clean, scented with things that lived and grew, and tasting of the ocean somewhere close at hand. There was a dirt road that Raglan almost missed, hardly more than twin tracks with a strip of yellow dandelions between. It led away toward more low hills, through fields of tall grass and wild mustard flowers of wild mustard. Raglan swung the truck off the pavement and they rolled slowly to the hills in third gear. Jeremy began to watch the flowered fields passing by, then turned to Raglan. "Yo. You ever been here before?"

"A long time ago."

"I never knew there was places like this, pretty an without no people an cars an shit. Not for real."

"It's real."

The road entered a cleft between the hills, and a little stream ran down to meet it, sparkling over rocks. For awhile the road followed the splashing water, then turned and wound upward. The truck took the grade growling in second. The road got fainter as it climbed, then finally just ended at the top of the hill. Raglan cut the engine. A hundred feet ahead a cliff dropped off shear to the sea.

Big waves boomed and echoed on rocks below, sending up silver streamers of spray.

Jeremy seemed to forget why they'd come. He jumped from the truck and ran to the cliff's edge, stopping as close as possible like any boy might. Then he just stood gazing out over the water.

Raglan leaned on the fender and watched.

The boy spread his arms wide for a moment, his head thrown back. Then he looked down at his dirty jeans. Raglan watched a little longer as the boy stripped to stand naked before the sea and the sun. Then Raglan went to the rear of the truck. There was an old square-nosed cement shovel and an Army trenching tool he used when he cleaned up yards.

Jeremy joined him, solemn, though his eyes sparkled. Raglan said nothing, though he smiled a moment, before taking up the shovel and the little bundle. Jeremy put his jeans back on and followed with the trenching tool.

The ground rose again, nearby, to a final hillock that looked out over the sea. They climbed to the top. Raglan cut the thick sweet-smelling sod into blocks with his shovel, then they both dug. The sun was almost gone when they finished, and though the air was cooling, Jeremy was sheened in sweat once more. But he picked some of the wild mustard and dandelion flowers and laid them on the little mound.

Far out on the water, the sun grew huge and ruddy red as it sank. Raglan made a fire near the truck, and Jeremy got the blankets, surprised again when Raglan produced two dusty cans of Campbell soup and a pint of Jack Daniels from somewhere in the cab. A little later, when it was dark and still and the food was warm inside them, they sat side by side near the fire, smoking, and sipping the whiskey. The sea boomed softly below.

"Is this campin' out?" asked Jeremy.

"Yeah. I guess it is."

Jeremy passed the bottle back to Raglan, then glanced toward the truck. "We don't got enough gas to get back, huh?"

Raglan gazed into the flames. "Uh uh. But maybe there's a place somewhere around here that buys cans."

"Um, so you never seen that Crusader Rabbit . . . don't know what he looked like?"

"I think he carried a sword, an' fought dragons."

Jeremy stared at the fire too. "It's gonna hurt a lot, huh?"

"Yeah."

"You are my dad, huh?"

Raglan put his arm around the boy and pulled him close.

PART FOUR

DRAMA

OVERVIEW

African American drama combines ritual, mythology, poetic language, polemics, and histrionics to bring black experiences and culture to vivid life before multiethnic audiences. As it weaves together elements of the oral tradition, poetry, and fiction to entertain audiences, it also communicates with them on a visceral level. Most African American dramatists are highly sensitive to black speech patterns and oratory, the blues and jazz, and other cultural factors that serve as sources of structure, tone, and subject matter. Similarly, black drama absorbs the imagery, allusions, and figurative language of poetry and the narrative style and other storytelling conventions of fiction.

A Late-Blooming Art

Of all the traditional literary forms, drama is the last in which significant writing by blacks has been recognized in America, finally coming into its own in the late twentieth century. It took centuries for the portrayal of blacks onstage to move beyond grotesque clichés. As black critic Darwin T. Turner notes, until World War II, a menagerie of stereotypes distorted the dramatic representation of the black experience; in the earliest known American dramas of the 1700s, black characters were created solely by white playwrights and performers (1–7). And even in the early twentieth century, when black performers were permitted to act in theaters owned by whites, the stereotypes persisted in plays as well as in movies and on radio.

Nineteenth-Century Drama

Pioneers: The African Grove Theater and Ira Aldridge

Despite its late recognition, African American drama was not without black talents during its long period of rejection and ridicule by American theatergoers. In the early 1800s, two pioneers inspired its development: the African Grove Theater in New York City and black actor Ira Aldridge.

The African Grove Theater sought to entertain free blacks and interested whites. In 1823, however, events surrounding the theater foreshadowed the plight of future black dramatists. A competing white theater owner used racial politics to criticize the production of *The Drama of King Shotaway* and to bring about a public denouncement of the theater. As black playwright-critic William B. Branch notes, whites rejected black talents performing Shakespearean roles and reviled the theater artists for having "the nerve to fashion a play of their own . . . in which they called upon their enslaved brethren [in the United States to] . . . revolt against their masters" (xii). Probably the first known African American dramatic work, no known copies of the play exist. All that is known of the play is its basic plot, whose call for revolt presaged the abolitionist texts of the nineteenth century (see, for example, David Walker's *Appeal* on p. 709 and Martin Delany's *The Condition* on p. 715).

In addition, achievement in black theater during the early 1800s came in the work of black actor Ira Aldridge (1804–67), who performed in Shakespearean productions in Europe and England. Aldridge's success abroad not only affirmed early on the potential of black talent; given the praise he received from white audiences overseas, it also underscored the hypocrisy of the American situation that denied black performers access to serious drama.

Polemical Plays and Jokesters in Blackface

Beginning in the mid-1800s, just before the Civil War, black writers began to win some recognition in drama. The earliest surviving play by a black writer was the abolitionist work *The Escape: Or a Leap to Freedom* (1858) by William Wells Brown (who was also the first African American to publish a novel, *Clotel*—see Part Three). Based on Brown's experiences as a slave, the play proclaimed the evils of slavery and the need for liberation. In allying itself with the abolitionist political movement, *The Escape* also foretold the connections between politics and art in African American drama.

But it would take almost a half-century for another play to appear: Joseph S. Cotter's drama *Caleb the Degenerate* (1903), which, according to black critic Arthur P. Davis, explored the merits of an industrial versus a liberal education (11). Even by the turn of the century, white playwrights were unwilling to write serious dramas involving black characters, and black dramatists found little opportunity to write or showcase their material.

From the 1840s to the 1890s, the immensely popular minstrel show projected stereotyped images of blacks onstage that defamed African American life and culture. The typical minstrel show included about fifteen white performers who darkened their skin with burnt cork, exaggerated the size of their lips with a white cosmetic, wore white gloves, and spoke in thick dialect to mimic singing, dancing, and joking black folks. Even when African Americans themselves were allowed to perform in minstrel shows, beginning in the 1860s, they were obliged to follow the convention of blackface makeup. Although it may be argued that black artists gained some useful experience in minstrel shows, the format was not representative of the African American experience and was demeaning to blacks.

In addition, from the 1890s to the 1920s, vaudeville did little to improve the image of African Americans onstage. The vaudeville show was made up of numerous specialty acts, including black comedians.

The 1920s to 1940s: First Black Productions and the Harlem Renaissance

Despite the well-intentioned efforts of some white playwrights, such as Eugene O'Neill (*The Emperor Jones*, 1920) and Marc Connelly (*The Green*

Pastures, 1930), pejorative black stereotypes typically peopled the works of most other white playwrights until the 1940s. However, following World War I some black playwrights began—occasionally—to see their plays produced and published. The first play by an African American writer to be professionally produced onstage, Angelina Grimké's *Rachel*, was written in 1916 and published in 1920. The first successful African American Broadway production was the musical comedy *Shuffle Along* (1921), written by black writers Flournoy Miller and Aubrey Lyles and black composers Noble Sissle and Eubie Blake, and featuring an all-black cast, a romantic plot, and the hit song "I'm Just Wild about Harry."

With its Broadway success, *Shuffle Along* offered a tentative entree into American theater for the more serious African American drama that came out of the Harlem Renaissance of the 1920s (see David Levering Lewis's essay in Part Five, p. 762). Willis Richardson's *The Chip Woman's Fortune* (1923) was the first serious drama by a black playwright to be produced on Broadway. By portraying a struggling but cohesive black family, reinforced by unselfish behavior on the part of supporting black characters, this one-act play departed from the long-held racial stereotypes associated with African Americans onstage.

Two years later, Garland Anderson's *Appearances* (1925) tackled the taboo of miscegenation by focusing on a black bellhop accused of raping a white woman. The production thus moved African American drama into sensitive areas of race relations, reflecting the provocative realities of sexual phobia and latent violence. Similarly, the collaboration of black writer Wallace Thurman and white author William Jordan Rapp on the play *Harlem* (1928) reflected the interracial nature of the Harlem Renaissance. That play examined the dilemmas of an African American family relocating from the South to the urban setting of Harlem.

Before the emergence of the civil rights movement, however, serious works by black dramatists were scarce. Still, Langston Hughes's *Mulatto* (1935) became the longest-running play by an African American at that time. Treating the subject of miscegenation in new ways, the play focused on a young black male of mixed racial heritage who confronts his Caucasian father. Theodore Ward's *The Big White Fog* (1940) explored the financial and social pressures on an urban black family and the resilient dream of a "Marcus Garveyite," and Ward's *Our Lan'* (1947) centered on the unfulfilled promises of the post–Civil War Reconstruction period.

The Drama of the Civil Rights Era

Following the Second World War, which made racial discrimination and genocide international concerns, the civil rights movement emerged to work toward racial integration in America. Black dramatists in increasing numbers thus gave that cause a special platform, exposing multiethnic audiences to African American culture, historical events, contemporary conflicts, and family and community issues onstage.

During the 1950s, a number of notable plays by African Americans were produced, including *A Medal for Willie* (1951) by William B. Branch, *Trouble in Mind* (1955) by Alice Childress, *Land beyond the River* (1956) by Loften Mitchell, and *Simply Heavenly* (1957) by Langston Hughes. Two other productions are especially noteworthy for their emphasis on the link between economics and the African American family structure: *Take a Giant Step* (1953) by Louis Peterson, which portrayed a young black male from a middle-class family in search of his racial identity amid a white neighborhood and white friends, and Lorraine Hansberry's *A Raisin in the Sun* (1959), which memorably dramatized the experiences of an African American family living in an inner-city environment. The longest-running African American play on Broadway up to that time, Hansberry's work presented a multigenerational household whose family members clashed over their individual and collective dreams and whose beliefs in religion and the American system both hindered and sustained the family.

The 1900s to 1950s: Black Women Playwrights

African American women playwrights received little recognition before Lorraine Hansberry's success with *A Raisin in the Sun* in 1959 and *The Sign in Sidney Brustein's Window* in 1964. As early twentieth-century black male playwrights still struggled for respect in an area dominated by white males, the obstacles facing black women playwrights were even greater. And some critics argue that African American women writers continue to be held back by racial and gender barriers. In a 1982 survey, "Black Women Playwrights from Grimké to Shange," Jeanne-Marie A. Miller targeted racism and sexism as significant obstacles facing black women playwrights. Similarly, critic Sydne Mahone perceives the issue in this way: "The very act of a black woman telling her story, speaking her truth, can be perceived as an act of resistance to oppression: the real power in her exercise of artistic freedom is the casting of her own image by her own hand" (xviii). That is, in choosing to be a playwright, the African American woman must also engage in a political fight against well-established racial and gender limitations in order to gain recognition as a writer.

Still, the dramatic works of black women—and one-act and full-length plays, dramas and comedies, contemporary and historical pieces—have been staged and published since the early twentieth century. Angelina Grimké's *Rachel* (1916) and Alice Dunbar-Nelson's *Mine Eyes Have Seen* (1918) led the way for a number of other plays by black women in the ensuing decades. Among them were Dorothy C. Guinn's *Out of the Dark* (1924), Georgia Douglass Johnson's *A Sunday Morning in the South* (1925), Myrtle Smith Livingston's *For Unborn Children* (1926), Marita Bonner's *The Purple Flower* (1928), Frances Gunner's *The Light of the Women* (1930), May Miller's *Christophe's Daughters* (1935), and Alice Childress's *Florence* (1950). But it was not until 1959 and Hansberry's groundbreaking *A Raisin in the Sun* that a black woman playwright gained serious critical attention. Her remarkable success inspired the emergence of other black women playwrights in the latter half of the twentieth century.

The 1960s: Drama of the Black Arts Movement

The African American playwrights of the 1960s experimented with a diverse range of structures and tones in their plays. For example, Ossie Davis's *Purlie Victorious* (1961) took a humorous look at racial stereotypes, and Adrienne Kennedy's *Funnyhouse of the Negro* (1963) was a surrealistic exploration of racial identity. Similarly, whereas James Baldwin's *Blues for Mister Charlie* (1964) realistically portrayed the racial hatred of a southern lynching, Douglas Turner Ward's *Day of Absence* (1965) satirized the helplessness of whites in a world without blacks, and Sonia Sanchez's *The Bronx Is Next* (1968) explored black militancy and male–female relationships. In Charles Gordone's Pulitzer Prize-winning *No Place to Be Somebody* (1969), black and nonblack urban-dwellers strived for respect, identity, and power.

In addition, African American drama's most polemical playwright, Amiri Baraka, appeared in the mid-1960s; his works would influence the revolutionary playwrights of the following decade. Also a poet, essayist, critic, and fiction writer, Baraka's electrifying and provocative dramas combined artistic expression, cultural distinctiveness, racial cohesiveness, and revolutionary ideology. They also represented a marked transition in African American drama, magnetizing established theatrical conventions with a racial and political agenda. As cofounder of the Black Arts Repertory Theater School and organizer of Newark's Spirit House, a black cultural center, Baraka was a professed black nationalist who believed that art, politics, and culture were inextricably united. Four of his most intriguing works, all one-act plays, appeared in 1964: *The Baptism, The Toilet, Dutchman,* and *The Slave.* Baraka's nationalist politics and writings have been criticized as sexist and homophobic by some black critics, including Itabari Njeri (p. 689) and Charles I. Nero (p. 971). However, other critics have acknowledged Baraka's artistry and activism; William J. Harris notes that "Baraka's entire career has been devoted to bringing the revolution to the word. . . . He is more than the most brilliant writer of the black arts movement . . . he is simply a great twentieth-century American writer" (27).

As Baraka's dramas advanced the flourishing Black Arts Movement (see Larry Neal's essay in Part Six, p. 925) other black playwrights also contributed to the field. Ron Milner (*Who's Got His Own,* 1966), Lonnie Elder (*Ceremonies in Dark Old Men,* 1968), Ed Bullins (*Clara's Old Man,* 1969), Ben Caldwell (*Prayer Meeting, or the First Militant Minister,* 1969), and Joseph A. Walker (*The River Niger,* 1972) were among the playwrights of the period.

Various production groups, including the Negro Ensemble Company, the New Lafayette Theater, the New Federal Theater, the American Place Theater, and Joseph Papp's Public Theater, helped sustain the growth of black theater by sponsoring emerging black playwrights. In 1975, such efforts led to the production of a unique and creative drama, *For Colored Girls Who Have Considered Suicide When the Rainbow Is Enuf,* written by Ntozake Shange and produced by Papp's Public Theater. In development for two years before its actual production, the play combined dramatic monologues and dance in its focus on the pride, tragedies, and victories of black women. The characters were introspective, independent, bewildered, and assertive, encouraging an appreciation for the particular experiences of African American women.

The 1970s to 1990s: Continued Diversity and Experimentation

The 1970s and 1980s witnessed renewed interest in black musicals, some of which were written by African Americans. Several of these plays followed coherent storylines; others used the revue format to celebrate the interplay of music, choreography, and singing. The most popular musicals of the period included *Timbuktu* (1975), *The Wiz* (1975), and *Dream Girls* (1981). Other successful revues and pageants were *Don't Bother Me, I Can't Cope* (1972), *Bubbling Brown Sugar* (1976), *Ain't Misbehavin'* (1978), *Eubie!* (1978, which celebrated the work of Eubie Blake, one of the creators of the first black Broadway production, *Shuffle Along*), and *Sophisticated Ladies* (1981). In the 1970s and 1980s black playwrights demonstrated diverse writing styles, while multiethnic audiences came to appreciate a broader array of African American characterizations, themes, and tones.

In the late 1980s and early 1990s, the Pultizer Prize-winning playwright August Wilson, whose play *Fences* (1987) appears in the Focused Study section of Part Four, found unprecedented success with multiethnic audiences and critics. His other works include *Ma Rainey's Black Bottom* (1984), *The Piano Lesson* (1990), and *Two Trains Running* (1992).

In addition, several black women playwrights gained critical acclaim and popularity with audiences in the 1990s. Velina Houston's pronounced interethnic background is evident in her dramas, which confront such issues as racial heritage, marginality, and ethnic identity in a decade marked by debates over the significance of multiculturalism. Four of her plays—*The Chairman's Wife, Wakako Yamauchi, Bitter Cane,* and *Genny Lin*—appear in the volume *The Politics of Life: Four Plays* (1993). Anna Deavere Smith, the multitalented actress, playwright, and professor, personified contemporary racism and interethnic hostilities in her award-winning play, *Fires in the Mirror* (1993). In this one-person project, inspired by a confrontation between African Americans and Jews in Brooklyn's Crown Heights neighborhood, Smith conceived and acted out dozens of characters of various ages, gender, races, and classes. In her next play, *Twilight* (1994), she created and performed sixteen different characters, expressing their reactions to the 1992 Los Angeles riots. Pearl Cleage, an accomplished writer in various literary genres, has been selected as the featured dramatist in this part because of her skillful rendering of language and the major focus of most of her plays: the courage and survival of African American women. *Hospice,* which appears here, demonstrates Cleage's deft handling of characters and dialogue that examine the specific challenges of being black and female in America.

The diversity of contemporary drama offers various options for African American playwrights to express themselves—their realities, fantasies, and aspirations. In addition, the genre continues to attract an expanded multiethnic audience. However, unlike other literary genres, drama, to be fully realized in its intended format, requires a specific location, a variety of materials, and a cast of actors and others. As a result, the playwright's ability to get a play onstage is often contingent on the availability of financial backing, and the black patron's ability to attend a performance is often dependent on the price of tickets. Still, African American drama thrives in urban theaters, as well as in school auditoriums, church basements, and civic building conference halls. Moreover, its importance is not assessed merely on the basis of ticket sales or the number of scripts published. As with poetry and fiction, the significance of black drama rests in its vital role in interpreting African American life.

In This Part

Part Four begins with a Focused Study of playwright August Wilson and his Pulitzer Prize-winning *Fences.* Set in Pittsburgh in the 1950s, the play portrays a troubled African American family, particularly the complex and dynamic relationship between a father and his teenage son. A critical essay by Michael Awkward, " 'The Crookeds with the Straights': *Fences,* Race, and the Politics of Adaptation," astutely examines the cost exacted by the "literal and figurative fences" erected by the play's characters.

The featured drama selection in Part Four, Pearl Cleage's *Hospice,* offers a marked contrast to Wilson's *Fences. Hospice,* a one-act play with two characters, takes an insightful look at a black mother and daughter struggling emotionally to reach each other through barriers of personal choices and regrets.

Works Cited

Branch, William B., ed. *Black Thunder: An Anthology of Contemporary African American Drama.* New York: Penguin, 1992.

Davis, Arthur P. *From a Dark Tower.* Washington, DC: Howard UP, 1974.

Harris, William J. "Amiri Baraka." *African American Writers.* Ed. Valerie Smith, Lea Baechler, and A. Walton Litz. New York: Scribner's, 1993. 15–27.

Mahone, Sydne, ed. *Moon Marked and Touched by Sun: Plays by African American Women.* New York: Theater Communications, 1994.

Miller, Jeanne-Marie A. "Black Women Playwrights from Grimké to Shange."

All the Women Are White, All the Blacks Are Men, but Some of Us Are Brave. Ed. Gloria T. Hull, Patricia Bell Scott, and Barbara Smith. Old Westbury, NY: Feminist P, 1982. 280–296.

Turner, Darwin T., ed. *Black Drama in America: An Anthology*. New York: Fawcett, 1971.

Suggested Readings

Several bibliographies and collections offer information on African American playwrights and their works: *Negro Playwrights in the American Theater: 1925–1959* (1969) by Dorothy Abramson; *Black Drama: An Anthology* (1970) by William Brasmer; *New Black Playwrights: An Anthology* (1970) edited by William Couch, Jr.; *Black Drama Anthology* (1971) by Woodie King and Ron Milner; *Black Theater: A Twentieth-Century Collection of the Work of Its Best Playwrights* (1971) by Lindsay Patterson; *Black Theater, U.S.A.: Forty-Five Plays by Black Americans, 1847–1974* (1974) edited by James Hatch and Ted Shine; *Black American Playwrights, 1800–Present: A Bibliography* (1976) by Esther S. Arata and Nicholas J. Rotoli; *Dictionary of the Black Theater: Broadway, Off-Broadway, and Selected Harlem Theaters* (1983) by Allen Woll; *Black Thunder: An Anthology of Contemporary African American Drama* (1992); and *Moon Marked and Touched by Sun: Plays by African-American Women* (1994) edited by Sydne Mahone.

For informative overviews of historical and critical viewpoints on African American drama, see Loften Mitchell's *Black Drama: The Story of the American Negro in the Theater* (1967), Lindsay Patterson's *Anthology of the American Negro in the Theater: A Critical Approach* (1967), C. W. E. Bigsby's *Poetry and Drama,* vol. 2 of *The Black American Writer* (1969), Darwin T. Turner's *Black Drama in America: An Anthology* (1971), Kimberly Benston's *Baraka: The Renegade and the Mask* (1976), and Femi Euba's *Archetypes, Imprecations, and Victims of Fate: Origins and Developments of Satire in Black Drama* (1989).

A FOCUSED STUDY: AUGUST WILSON (1945-)

In a 1991 interview, August Wilson talked about the influence of poetry on his drama: "[Poetry is] the bedrock of my writing . . . not so much in the language as in the approach and the thinking. . . . The idea of metaphor is a very large idea in my plays and something that I find lacking in most contemporary plays. I think I write the kinds of plays that I do because I have twenty-six years of writing poetry underneath all of that."

Praised for his incorporation of African American history, metaphorical language, and the blues into his plays, Wilson has succeeded as an author despite the hard times of his youth. He was born and raised, along with his five siblings, in a two-room residence in a Pittsburgh ghetto known as the Hill. When his white father left the family, Wilson's mother, an African American, guided her children through the economic difficulties and racism of the inner city. Leaving school in the ninth grade after an accusation of plagiarism, Wilson educated himself by reading library books, especially books on black literature and culture.

While earning a living as a stock clerk and cook, Wilson began to write poetry about the people and events in his neighborhood. What he witnessed there was violence, desperation, and intraracial conflict, but he also discerned ethnic pride and a determination to survive. During his twenties, Wilson gravitated toward the black nationalist ideas that he discovered in literature on the Black Arts Movement of the 1960s. In particular, Wilson admired and was influenced by the philosophies of Amiri Baraka and Malcolm X.

With a friend, Wilson co-established Black Horizon, a theater for reading and performing black drama. In the late 1970s, he went to St. Paul, Minnesota, to write plays for a theater established by a director he had known from Pittsburgh. At the same time, he became involved with the Playwrights' Center in Minneapolis and wrote short scripts for live historical skits performed at exhibitions at the Science Museum of Minnesota.

Although Wilson's first two plays, *Black Bart and the Sacred Hills* (1981) and *Jitney* (1982), did not win the playwright a wide audience, his third play, *Ma Rainey's Black Bottom* (1984), gained the attention of the National Playwrights Conference and, subsequently, of Lloyd Richards, artistic director of the Yale Repertory Theater and dean of the Yale Drama School. Richards directed *Ma Rainey's Black Bottom* at Yale in 1984 and later on Broadway. A series of critically acclaimed and popular plays by Wilson followed over the next eight years: the Pulitzer Prize-winning *Fences* (1987), which is reprinted here; *Joe Turner's Come and Gone* (1988); *The Piano Lesson* (1990), which also won a Pulitzer Prize; *Two Trains Running* (1992); and *Seven Guitars* (1995). Wilson has received a host of drama awards, fellowships, and grants, enabling him to support himself entirely by writing plays and lecturing, a singular accomplishment among African American playwrights.

Citing as his main influences the collagist painter Romare Bearden, the writers Amiri Baraka and Jorge Luis Borges, and the blues, Wilson seeks to create with his dramatic works an African American saga: a series of plays, each set within a decade of the twentieth century, that explores the progression of African American life in U.S. society. Having already composed seven plays in this saga—*Jitney* through *Seven Guitars*—Wilson plans to complete the series. Most recently, however, he has begun writing a novel.

Wilson's plays have been compared by some critics to the works of white playwrights Eugene O'Neill and Arthur Miller. Other critics single out Wilson's skillful delineation of black cultural elements, particularly the blues and jazz forms, language, history, and mythology. His ability to fulfill a multiethnic audience's theatrical expectations and to validate a black audience's heritage contributes to Wilson's remarkable success. Wilson is the only African American playwright since Lorraine Hansberry to enjoy such immense critical and popular appeal.

The following selection, *Fences,* centers on an African American family living in an urban neighborhood between 1957 and 1965. The play focuses in particular on the relationships among Troy Maxson, his wife, Rose, and Cory, their teenage son. Troy's past failures return to weaken his connection with his son, as well as his relationships with other family members and friends; similarly, his extramarital intimacies erode his marriage. *Fences* underscores the impact of racism on blacks, while also examining the individual characters' dreams and disappointments—metaphorical fences that border their lives.

Fences

Characters

TROY MAXSON
JIM BONO, Troy's friend
ROSE, Troy's wife
LYONS, Troy's oldest son by previous marriage
GABRIEL, Troy's brother
CORY, Troy and Rose's son
RAYNELL, Troy's daughter

SETTING: *The setting is the yard which fronts the only entrance to the Maxson household, an ancient two-story brick house set back off a small alley in a big-city neighborhood. The entrance to the house is gained by two or three steps leading to a wooden porch badly in need of paint.*

A relatively recent addition to the house and running its full width, the porch lacks congruence. It is a sturdy porch with a flat roof. One or two chairs of dubious value sit at one end where the kitchen window opens onto the porch. An old-fashioned icebox stands silent guard at the opposite end.

The yard is a small dirt yard, partially fenced, except for the last scene, with a wooden sawhorse, a pile of lumber, and other fence-building equipment set off to the side. Opposite is a tree from which hangs a ball made of rags. A baseball bat leans against the tree. Two oil drums serve as garbage receptacles and sit near the house at right to complete the setting.

THE PLAY: *Near the turn of the century, the destitute of Europe sprang on the city with tenacious claws and an honest and solid dream. The city devoured them. They swelled its belly until it burst into a thousand furnaces and sewing machines, a thousand butcher shops and bakers' ovens, a thousand churches and hospitals and funeral parlors and money-lenders. The city grew. It nourished itself and offered each man a partnership limited only by his talent, his guile, and his willingness and capacity for hard work. For the immigrants of Europe, a dream dared and won true.*

The descendants of African slaves were offered no such welcome or participation. They came from places called the Carolinas and the Virginias, Georgia, Alabama, Mississippi, and Tennessee. They came strong, eager, searching. The city rejected them and they fled and settled along the riverbanks and under bridges in shallow, ramshackle houses made of sticks and tarpaper. They collected rags and wood. They sold the use of their muscles and their bodies. They cleaned houses and washed clothes, they shined shoes, and in quiet desperation and vengeful pride, they stole, and lived in pursuit of their own dream. That they could breathe free, finally, and stand to meet life with the force of dignity and whatever eloquence the heart could call upon.

By 1957, the hard-won victories of the European immigrants had solidified the industrial might of America. War had been confronted and won with new energies that used loyalty and patriotism as its fuel. Life was rich, full, and flourishing. The Milwaukee Braves won the World Series, and the hot winds of change that would make the sixties a turbulent, racing, dangerous, and provocative decade had not yet begun to blow full.

ACT I

Scene I

It is 1957. Troy and Bono enter the yard, engaged in conversation. Troy is fifty-three years old, a large man with thick, heavy hands; it is this largeness that he strives to fill out and make an accommodation with. Together with his blackness, his largeness informs his sensibilities and the choices he has made in his life.

Of the two men, Bono is obviously the follower. His commitment to their friendship of thirty-odd years is rooted in his admiration of Troy's honesty, capacity for hard work, and his strength, which Bono seeks to emulate.

It is Friday night, payday, and the one night of the week the two men engage in a ritual of talk and drink. Troy is usually the most talkative and at times he can be crude and almost vulgar, though he is capable of rising to profound heights of expression. The men carry lunch buckets and wear or carry burlap aprons and are dressed in clothes suitable to their jobs as garbage collectors.

BONO: Troy, you ought to stop that lying!

TROY: I ain't lying! The nigger had a watermelon this big. *(He indicates with his hands.)* Talking about . . . "What watermelon, Mr. Rand?" I liked to fell out! "What watermelon, Mr. Rand?" . . . And it sitting there big as life.

BONO: What did Mr. Rand say?

TROY: Ain't said nothing. Figure if the nigger too dumb to know he carrying a watermelon, he wasn't gonna get much sense out of him. Trying to hide that great big old watermelon under his coat. Afraid to let the white man see him carry it home.

BONO: I'm like you . . . I ain't got no time for them kind of people.

TROY: Now what he look like getting mad cause he see the man from the union talking to Mr. Rand?

BONO: He come to me talking about . . . "Maxson gonna get us fired." I told him to get away from me with that. He walked away from me calling you a troublemaker. What Mr. Rand say?

TROY: Ain't said nothing. He told me to go down the Commissioner's office next Friday. They called me down there to see them.

BONO: Well, as long as you got your complaint filed, they can't fire you. That's what one of them white fellows tell me.

TROY: I ain't worried about them firing me. They gonna fire me cause I asked a question? That's all I did. I went to Mr. Rand and asked him, "Why? Why you got the white mens driving and the colored lifting?" Told him, "what's the matter, don't I count? You think only white fellows got sense enough to drive a truck. That ain't no paper job! Hell, anybody can drive a truck. How come you got all whites driving and the colored lifting?" He told me "take it to the union." Well, hell, that's what I done! Now they wanna come up with this pack of lies.

BONO: I told Brownie if the man come and ask him any questions . . . just tell the truth! It ain't nothing but something they done trumped up on you cause you filed a complaint on them.

TROY: Brownie don't understand nothing. All I want them to do is change the job description. Give everybody a chance to drive the truck. Brownie can't see that. He ain't got that much sense.

BONO: How you figure he be making out with that gal be up at Taylors' all the time . . . that Alberta gal?

TROY: Same as you and me. Getting just as much as we is. Which is to say nothing.

BONO: It is, huh? I figure you doing a little better than me . . . and I ain't saying what I'm doing.

TROY: Aw, nigger, look here . . . I know you. If you had got anywhere near that gal, twenty minutes later you be looking to tell somebody. And the first one you gonna tell . . . that you gonna want to brag to . . . is me.

BONO: I ain't saying that. I see where you be eyeing her.

TROY: I eye all the women. I don't miss nothing. Don't never let nobody tell you Troy Maxson don't eye the women.

BONO: You been doing more than eyeing her. You done bought her a drink or two.

TROY: Hell yeah, I bought her a drink! What that mean? I bought you one, too. What that mean cause I buy her a drink? I'm just being polite.

BONO: It's all right to buy her one drink. That's what you call being polite. But when you wanna be buying two or three . . . that's what you call eyeing her.

TROY: Look here, as long as you known me . . . you ever known me to chase after women?

BONO: Hell yeah! Long as I done known you. You forgetting I knew you when.

TROY: Naw, I'm talking about since I been married to Rose?

BONO: Oh, not since you been married to Rose. Now, that's the truth, there. I can say that.

TROY: All right then! Case closed.

BONO: I see you be walking up around Alberta's house. You supposed to be at Taylors' and you be walking up around there.

TROY: What you watching where I'm walking for? I ain't watching after you.

BONO: I seen you walking around there more than once.

TROY: Hell, you liable to see me walking anywhere! That don't mean nothing cause you see me walking around there.

BONO: Where she come from anyway? She just kinda showed up one day.

TROY: Tallahassee. You can look at her and tell she one of them Florida gals. They got some big healthy women down there. Grow them right up out the ground. Got a little bit of Indian in her. Most of them niggers down in Florida got some Indian in them.

BONO: I don't know about that Indian part. But she damn sure big and healthy. Woman wear some big stockings. Got them great big old legs and hips as wide as the Mississippi River.

TROY: Legs don't mean nothing. You don't do nothing but push them out of the way. But them hips cushion the ride!

BONO: Troy, you ain't got no sense.

TROY: It's the truth! Like you riding on Goodyears!

Rose enters from the house. She is ten years younger than Troy, her devotion to him stems from her recognition of the possibilities of her life without him: a succession of abusive men and their babies, a life of partying and running the streets, the Church, or aloneness with its attendant pain and frustration. She recognizes Troy's spirit as a fine and illuminating one and she either ignores or forgives his faults, only some of which she recognizes. Though she doesn't drink, her presence is an integral part of the Friday night rituals. She alternates between the porch and the kitchen, where supper preparations are under way.

ROSE: What you all out here getting into?

TROY: What you worried about what we getting into for? This is men talk, woman.

ROSE: What I care what you all taking about? Bono, you gonna stay for supper?

BONO: No, I thank you, Rose. But Lucille say she cooking up a pot of pigfeet.

TROY: Pigfeet! Hell, I'm going home with you! Might even stay the night if you got some pigfeet. You got something in there to top them pigfeet, Rose?

ROSE: I'm cooking up some chicken. I got some chicken and collard greens.

TROY: Well, go on back in the house and let me and Bono finish what we was talking about. This is men talk. I got some talk for you later. You know what kind of talk I mean. You go on and powder it up.

ROSE: Troy Maxson, don't you start that now!

TROY *(puts his arm around her):* Aw, woman . . . come here. Look here, Bono . . . when I met this woman . . . I got out that place, say, "Hitch up my pony, saddle up my mare . . . there's a woman out there for me somewhere. I looked here. Looked there. Saw Rose and latched on to her." I latched on to her and told her—I'm gonna tell you the truth—I told her, "Baby, I don't wanna marry, I just wanna be your man." Rose told me . . . tell him what you told me, Rose.

ROSE: I told him if he wasn't the marrying kind, then move out the way so the marrying kind could find me.

TROY: That's what she told me. "Nigger, you in my way. You blocking the view! Move out the way so I can find me a husband." I thought it over two or three days. Come back—

ROSE: Ain't no two or three days nothing. You was back the same night.

TROY: Come back, told her . . . "Okay, baby . . . but I'm gonna buy me a banty rooster and put him out there in the backyard . . . and when he see a stranger come, he'll flap his wings and crow . . ." Look here, Bono, I could watch the front door by myself . . . it was that back door I was worried about.

ROSE: Troy, you ought not talk like that. Troy ain't doing nothing but telling a lie.

TROY: Only thing is . . . when we first got married . . . forget the rooster . . . we ain't had no yard!

BONO: I hear you tell it. Me and Lucille was staying down there on Logan Street. Had two rooms with the outhouse in the back. I ain't mind the outhouse none. But when that goddamn wind blow through there in the winter . . . that's what I'm talking about! To this day I wonder why in hell I ever stayed down there for six long years. But see, I didn't know I could do no better. I thought only white folks had inside toilets and things.

ROSE: There's a lot of people don't know they can do no better than they doing now. That's just something you got to learn. A lot of folks still shop at Bella's.

TROY: Ain't nothing wrong with shopping at Bella's. She got fresh food.

ROSE: I ain't said nothing about if she got fresh food. I'm talking about what she charge. She charge ten cents more than the A&P.

TROY: The A&P ain't never done nothing for me. I spends my money where I'm treated right. I go down to Bella, say, "I need a loaf of bread, I'll pay you Friday." She give it to me. What sense that make when I got money to go and spend it somewhere else and ignore the person who done right by me? That ain't in the Bible.

ROSE: We ain't talking about what's in the Bible. What sense it make to shop there when she overcharge?

TROY: You shop where you want to. I'll do my shopping where the people been good to me.

ROSE: Well, I don't think it's right for her to overcharge. That's all I was saying.

BONO: Look here . . . I got to get on. Lucille going be raising all kind of hell.

TROY: Where you going, nigger? We ain't finished this pint. Come here, finish this pint.

BONO: Well, hell, I am . . . if you ever turn the bottle loose.

TROY *(hands him the bottle):* The only thing I say about the A&P is I'm glad Cory got that job down there. Help him take care of his school clothes and things. Gabe done moved out and things getting tight around here. He got that job. . . . He can start to look out for himself.

ROSE: Cory done went and got recruited by a college football team.

TROY: I told that boy about that football stuff. The white man ain't gonna let him get nowhere with that football. I told him when he first come to me with it. Now you come telling me he done went and got more tied up in it. He ought to go and get recruited in how to fix cars or something where he can make a living.

ROSE: He ain't talking about making no living playing football. It's just something the boys in school do. They gonna send a recruiter by to talk to you. He'll tell you he ain't talking about making no living playing football. It's a honor to be recruited.

TROY: It ain't gonna get him nowhere. Bono'll tell you that.

BONO: If he be like you in the sports . . . he's gonna be all right. Ain't but two men ever played baseball as good as you. That's Babe Ruth and Josh Gibson. Them's the only two men ever hit more home runs than you.

TROY: What it ever get me? Ain't got a pot to piss in or a window to throw it out of.

ROSE: Times have changed since you was playing baseball, Troy. That was before the war. Times have changed a lot since then.

TROY: How in hell they done changed?

ROSE: They got lots of colored boys playing ball now. Baseball and football.

BONO: You right about that, Rose. Times have changed, Troy. You just come along too early.

TROY: There ought not never have been no time called too early! Now you take that fellow . . . what's that fellow they had playing right field for the Yankees back then? You know who I'm talking about, Bono. Used to play right field for the Yankees.

ROSE: Selkirk?

TROY: Selkirk! That's it! Man batting .269, understand? .269. What kind of sense that make? I was hitting .432 with thirty-seven home runs! Man batting .269 and playing right field for the Yankees! I saw Josh Gibson's daughter yesterday. She walking around with raggedy shoes on her feet. Now I bet you Selkirk's daughter ain't walking around with raggedy shoes on her feet! I bet you that!

ROSE: They got a lot of colored baseball players now. Jackie Robinson was the first. Folks had to wait for Jackie Robinson.

TROY: I done seen a hundred niggers play baseball better than Jackie Robinson. Hell, I know some teams Jackie Robinson couldn't even make! What you talking about Jackie Robinson. Jackie Robinson wasn't nobody. I'm talking about if you could play ball then they ought to have let you play. Don't care what color you were. Come telling me I come along too early. If you could play . . . then they ought to have let you play.

Troy takes a long drink from the bottle.

ROSE: You gonna drink yourself to death. You don't need to be drinking like that.

TROY: Death ain't nothing. I done seen him. Done wrassled with him. You can't tell me nothing about death. Death ain't nothing but a fastball on the outside corner. And you know what I'll do to that! Lookee here, Bono . . . am I lying? You get one of them fastballs, about waist high, over the outside corner of the plate where you can get the meat of the bat on it . . . and good god! You can kiss it goodbye. Now, am I lying?

BONO: Naw, you telling the truth there. I seen you do it.

TROY: If I'm lying . . . that 450 feet worth of lying! *(Pause.)* That's all death is to me. A fastball on the outside corner.

ROSE: I don't know why you want to get on talking about death.

TROY: Ain't nothing wrong with talking about death. That's part of life. Everybody gonna die. You gonna die, I'm gonna die. Bono's gonna die. Hell, we all gonna die.

ROSE: But you ain't got to talk about it. I don't like to talk about it.

TROY: You the one brought it up. Me and Bono was talking about baseball . . . you tell me I'm gonna drink myself to death. Ain't that right, Bono? You know I don't drink this but one night out of the week. That's Friday night. I'm gonna drink just enough to where I can handle it. Then I cuts it loose. I leave it alone. So don't you worry about me drinking myself to death. 'Cause I ain't worried about Death. I done seen him. I done wrestled with him.

Look here, Bono . . . I looked up one day and Death was marching straight at me. Like Soldiers on Parade! The Army of Death was marching straight at me. The middle of July, 1941. It got real cold just like it be winter. It seem like Death himself reached out and touched me on the shoulder. He touch me just like I touch you. I got cold as ice and Death standing there grinning at me.

ROSE: Troy, why don't you hush that talk.

TROY: I say . . . what you want, Mr. Death? You be wanting me? You done brought your army to be getting me? I looked him dead in the eye. I wasn't fearing nothing. I was ready to tangle. Just like I'm ready to tangle now. The Bible say be ever vigilant. That's why I don't get but so drunk. I got to keep watch.

ROSE: Troy was right down there in Mercy Hospital. You remember he had pneumonia? Laying there with a fever talking plumb out of his head.

TROY: Death standing there staring at me . . . carrying that sickle in his hand. Finally he say, "You want bound over for another year?" See, just like that . . . "You want bound over for another year?" I told him, "Bound over hell! Let's settle this now!"

It seem like he kinda fell back when I said that, and all the cold went out of me. I reached down and grabbed that sickle and threw it just as far as I could throw it . . . and me and him commenced to wrestling.

We wrestled for three days and nights. I can't say where I found the strength from. Every time it seemed like he was gonna get the best of me, I'd reach way down deep inside myself and find the strength to do him one better.

ROSE: Every time Troy tell that story he find different ways to tell it. Different things to make up about it.

TROY: I ain't making up nothing. I'm telling you the facts of what happened. I wrestled with Death for three days and three nights and I'm standing here to tell you about it. *(Pause.)* All right. At the end of the third night we done weakened each other to where we can't hardly move. Death stood up, throwed on his robe . . . had him a white robe with a hood on it. He throwed on that robe and went off to look for his sickle. Say, "I'll be back." Just like that. "I'll be back." I told him, say, "Yeah, but . . . you gonna have to find me!" I wasn't no fool. I wan't going looking for him. Death ain't nothing to play with. And I know he's gonna get me. I know I got to join his army . . . his camp followers. But as long as I keep my strength and see him coming . . . as long as I keep up my vigilance . . . he's gonna have to fight to get me. I ain't going easy.

BONO: Well, look here, since you got to keep up your vigilance . . . let me have the bottle.

TROY: Aw hell, I shouldn't have told you that part. I should have left out that part.

ROSE: Troy be talking that stuff and half the time don't even know what he be talking about.

TROY: Bono know me better than that.

BONO: That's right. I know you. I know you got some Uncle Remus in your blood. You got more stories than the devil got sinners.

TROY: Aw hell, I done seen him too! Done talked with the devil.

ROSE: Troy, don't nobody wanna be hearing all that stuff.

Lyons enters the yard from the street. Thirty-four years old, Troy's son by a previous marriage, he sports a neatly trimmed goatee, sport coat, white shirt, tieless and buttoned at the collar. Though he fancies himself a musician, he is more caught up in the rituals and idea of being a musician than in the actual practice of the music. He has come to borrow money from Troy, and while he knows he will be successful, he is uncertain as to what extent his lifestyle will be held up to scrutiny and ridicule.

LYONS: Hey, Pop.

TROY: What you come "Hey, Popping" me for?

LYONS: How you doing, Rose? *(He kisses her.)* Mr. Bono. How you doing?

BONO: Hey, Lyons . . . how you been?

TROY: He must have been doing all right. I ain't seen him around here last week.

ROSE: Troy, leave your boy alone. He come by to see you and you wanna start all that nonsense.

TROY: I ain't bothering Lyons. *(Offers him the bottle.)* Here . . . get you a drink. We got an understanding. I know why he come by to see me and he know I know.

LYONS: Come on, Pop . . . I just stopped by to say hi . . . see how you was doing.

TROY: You ain't stopped by yesterday.

ROSE: You gonna stay for supper, Lyons? I got some chicken cooking in the oven.

LYONS: No, Rose . . . thanks. I was just in the neighborhood and thought I'd stop by for a minute.

TROY: You was in the neighborhood all right, nigger. You telling the truth there. You was in the neighborhood cause it's my payday.

LYONS: Well, hell, since you mentioned it . . . let me have ten dollars.

TROY: I'll be damned! I'll die and go to hell and play blackjack with the devil before I give you ten dollars.

BONO: That's what I wanna know about . . . that devil you done seen.

LYONS: What . . . Pop done seen the devil? You too much, Pops.

TROY: Yeah, I done seen him. Talked to him too!

ROSE: You ain't seen no devil. I done told you that man ain't had nothing to do with the devil. Anything you can't understand, you want to call it the devil.

TROY: Look here, Bono . . . I went down to see Hertzberger about some furniture. Got three rooms for two-ninety-eight. That what it say on the radio. "Three rooms . . . two-ninety-eight." Even made up a little song about it. Go down there . . . man tell me I can't get no credit. I'm working every day and can't get no credit. What to do? I got an empty house with some raggedy furniture in it. Cory ain't got no bed. He's sleeping on a pile of rags on the floor. Working every day and can't get no credit. Come back here—Rose'll tell you—madder than hell. Sit down . . . try to figure what I'm gonna do. Come a knock on the door. Ain't been living here but three days. Who know I'm here? Open the door . . . devil standing there bigger than life. White fellow . . . white fellow . . . got on good clothes and everything. Standing there with a clipboard in his hand. I ain't had to say nothing. First words come out of his mouth was . . . "I understand you need some furniture and can't get no credit." I liked to fell over. He say, "I'll give you all the credit you want, but you got to pay the interest on it." I told him, "Give me three rooms worth and charge whatever you want." Next day a truck pulled up here and two men unloaded them three rooms. Man what drove the truck give me a book. Say send ten dollars, first of every month to the address in the book and everything will be all right. Say if I miss a payment the devil was coming back and it'll be hell to pay. That was fifteen years ago. To this day . . . the first of the month I send my ten dollars, Rose'll tell you.

ROSE: Troy lying.

TROY: I ain't never seen that man since. Now you tell me who else that could have been but the devil? I ain't sold my soul or nothing like that, you understand. Naw, I wouldn't have truck with the devil about nothing like that. I got my furniture and pays my ten dollars the first of the month just like clockwork.

BONO: How long you say you been paying this ten dollars a month?

TROY: Fifteen years!

BONO: Hell, ain't you finished paying for it yet? How much the man done charged you?

TROY: Ah hell, I done paid for it. I done paid for it ten times over! The fact is I'm scared to stop paying it.

ROSE: Troy lying. We got that furniture from Mr. Glickman. He ain't paying no ten dollars a month to nobody.

TROY: Aw hell, woman. Bono know I ain't that big a fool.

LYONS: I was just getting ready to say . . . I know where there's a bridge for sale.

TROY: Look here, I'll tell you this . . . it don't matter to me if he was the devil. It don't matter if the devil give credit. Somebody has got to give it.

ROSE: It ought to matter. You going around talking about having truck with the devil . . . God's the one you gonna have to answer to. He's the one gonna be at the Judgment.

LYONS: Yeah, well, look here, Pop . . . let me have that ten dollars. I'll give it back to you. Bonnie got a job working at the hospital.

TROY: What I tell you, Bono? The only time I see this nigger is when he wants something. That's the only time I see him.

LYONS: Come on, Pop, Mr. Bono don't want to hear all that. Let me have the ten dollars. I told you Bonnie working.

TROY: What that mean to me? "Bonnie working." I don't care if she working. Go ask her for the ten dollars if she working. Talking about "Bonnie working." Why ain't you working?

LYONS: Aw, Pop, you know I can't find no decent job. Where am I gonna get a job at? You know I can't get no job.

TROY: I told you I know some people down there. I can get you on the rubbish if you want to work. I told you that the last time you came by here asking me for something.

LYONS: Naw, Pop . . . thanks. That ain't for me. I don't wanna be carrying nobody's rubbish. I don't wanna be punching nobody's time clock.

TROY: What's the matter, you too good to carry people's rubbish? Where you think that ten dollars you talking about come from? I'm just supposed to haul people's rubbish and give my money to you cause you too lazy to work. You too lazy to work and wanna know why you ain't got what I got.

ROSE: What hospital Bonnie working at? Mercy?

LYONS: She's down at Passavant working in the laundry.

TROY: I ain't got nothing as it is. I give you that ten dollars and I got to eat beans the rest of the week. Naw . . . you ain't getting no ten dollars here.

LYONS: You ain't got to be eating no beans. I don't know why you wanna say that.

TROY: I ain't got no extra money. Gabe done moved over to Miss Pearl's paying her the rent and things done got tight around here. I can't afford to be giving you every payday.

LYONS: I ain't asked you to give me nothing. I asked you to loan me ten dollars. I know you got ten dollars.

TROY: Yeah, I got it. You know why I got it? Cause I don't throw my money away out there in the streets. You living the fast life . . . wanna be a musician . . . running around in them clubs and things . . . then, you learn to take care of yourself. You ain't gonna find me going and asking nobody for nothing. I done spent too many years without.

LYONS: You and me is two different people, Pop.

TROY: I done learned my mistake and learned to do what's right by it. You still trying to get something for nothing. Life don't owe you nothing. You owe it to yourself. Ask Bono. He'll tell you I'm right.

LYONS: You got your way of dealing with the world . . . I got mine. The only thing that matters to me is the music.

TROY: Yeah, I can see that! It don't matter how you gonna eat . . . where your next dollar is coming from. You telling the truth there.

LYONS: I know I got to eat. But I got to live too. I need something that gonna help me to get out of the bed in the morning. Make me feel like I belong in the world. I don't bother nobody. I just stay with the music cause that's the only way I can find to live in the world. Otherwise there ain't no telling what I might do. Now I don't come criticizing you and how you live. I just come by to ask you for ten dollars. I don't wanna hear all that about how I live.

TROY: Boy, your mamma did a hell of a job raising you.

LYONS: You can't change me, Pop. I'm thirty-four years old. If you wanted to change me, you should have been there when I was growing up. I come by to see you . . . ask for ten dollars and you want to talk about how I was raised. You don't know nothing about how I was raised.

ROSE: Let the boy have ten dollars, Troy.

TROY *(to Lyons):* What the hell you looking at me for? I ain't got no ten dollars. You know what I do with my money. *(To Rose.)* Give him ten dollars if you want him to have it.

ROSE: I will. Just as soon as you turn it loose.

TROY *(handing Rose the money):* There it is. Seventy-six dollars and forty-two cents. You see this, Bono? Now, I ain't gonna get but six of that back.

ROSE: You ought to stop telling that lie. Here, Lyons. *(She hands him the money.)*

LYONS: Thanks, Rose. Look . . . I got to run . . . I'll see you later.

TROY: Wait a minute. You gonna say, "thanks, Rose" and ain't gonna look to see where she got that ten dollars from? See how they do me, Bono?

LYONS: I know she got it from you, Pop. Thanks. I'll give it back to you.

TROY: There he go telling another lie. Time I see that ten dollars . . . he'll be owing me thirty more.

LYONS: See you, Mr. Bono.

BONO: Take care, Lyons!

LYONS: Thanks, Pop. I'll see you again.

Lyons exits the yard.

TROY: I don't know why he don't go and get him a decent job and take care of that woman he got.

BONO: He'll be all right, Troy. The boy is still young.

TROY: The *boy* is thirty-four years old.

ROSE: Let's not get off into all that.

BONO: Look here . . . I got to be going. I got to be getting on. Lucille gonna be waiting.

TROY *(puts his arm around Rose):* See this woman, Bono? I love this woman. I love this woman so much it hurts. I love her so much . . . I done run out of ways of loving her. So I got to go back to basics. Don't you come by my house Monday morning talking about time to go to work . . . 'cause I'm still gonna be stroking!

ROSE: Troy! Stop it now!

BONO: I ain't paying him no mind, Rose. That ain't nothing but gin-talk. Go on, Troy. I'll see you Monday.

TROY: Don't you come by my house, nigger! I done told you what I'm gonna be doing.

The lights go down to black.

Scene II

The lights come up on Rose hanging up clothes. She hums and sings softly to herself. It is the following morning.

ROSE *(sings):* Jesus, be a fence all around me every day
Jesus, I want you to protect me as I travel on my way.
Jesus, be a fence all around me every day.

Troy enters from the house.

Jesus, I want you to protect me
As I travel on my way.
(To Troy.) 'Morning, You ready for breakfast? I can fix it soon as I finish hanging up these clothes?

TROY: I got the coffee on. That'll be all right. I'll just drink some of that this morning.

ROSE: That 651 hit yesterday. That's the second time this month. Miss Pearl hit for a dollar . . . seem like those that need the least always get lucky. Poor folks can't get nothing.

TROY: Them numbers don't know nobody. I don't know why you fool with them. You and Lyons both.

ROSE: It's something to do.

TROY: You ain't doing nothing but throwing your money away.

ROSE: Troy, you know I don't play foolishly. I just play a nickel here and a nickel there.

TROY: That's two nickels you done thrown away.

ROSE: Now I hit sometimes . . . that makes up for it. It always comes in handy when I do hit. I don't hear you complaining then.

TROY: I ain't complaining now. I just say it's foolish. Trying to guess out of six hundred ways which way the number gonna come. If I had all the money niggers, these Negroes, throw away on numbers for one week—just one week—I'd be a rich man.

ROSE: Well, you wishing and calling it foolish ain't gonna stop folks from playing numbers. That's one thing for sure. Besides . . . some good things come from playing numbers. Look where Pope done bought him that restaurant off of numbers.

TROY: I can't stand niggers like that. Man ain't had two dimes to rub together. He walking around with his shoes all run over bumming money for cigarettes. All right. Got lucky there and hit the numbers . . .

ROSE: Troy, I know all about it.

TROY: Had good sense, I'll say that for him. He ain't throwed his money away. I seen niggers hit the numbers and go through two thousand dollars in four days. Man bought him that restaurant down there . . . fixed it up real nice . . . and then didn't want nobody to come in it! A Negro go in there and can't get no kind of service. I seen a white fellow come in there and order a bowl of stew. Pope picked all the meat out the pot for him. Man ain't had nothing but a bowl of meat! Negro come behind him and ain't got nothing but the potatoes and carrots. Talking about what numbers do for people, you picked a wrong example. Ain't done nothing but make a worser fool out of him than he was before.

ROSE: Troy, you ought to stop worrying about what happened at work yesterday.

TROY: I ain't worried. Just told me to be down there at the Commissioner's office on Friday. Everybody think they gonna fire me. I ain't worried about them firing me. You ain't got to worry about that. *(Pause.)* Where's Cory? Cory in the house? *(Calls.)* Cory?

ROSE: He gone out.

TROY: Out, huh? He gone out 'cause he know I want him to help me with this fence. I know how he is. That boy scared of work.

Gabriel enters. He comes halfway down the alley and, hearing Troy's voice, stops.

TROY *(continues):* He ain't done a lick of work in his life.

ROSE: He had to go to football practice. Coach wanted them to get in a little extra practice before the season start.

TROY: I got his practice . . . running out of here before he get his chores done.

ROSE: Troy, what is wrong with you this morning? Don't nothing set right with you. Go on back in there and go to bed . . . get up on the other side.

TROY: Why something got to be wrong with me? I ain't said nothing wrong with me.

ROSE: You got something to say about everything. First it's the numbers . . . then it's the way the man runs his restaurant . . . then you done got on Cory. What's it gonna be next? Take a look up there and see if the weather suits you . . . or is it gonna be how you gonna put up the fence with the clothes hanging in the yard.

TROY: You hit the nail on the head then.

ROSE: I know you like I know the back of my hand. Go on in there and get you some coffee . . . see if that straighten you up. 'Cause you ain't right this morning.

Troy starts into the house and sees Gabriel. Gabriel starts singing. Troy's brother, he is seven years younger than Troy. Injured in World War II, he has a metal plate in his head. He carries an old trumpet tied around his waist and believes with every fiber of his being that he is the Archangel Gabriel. He carries a chipped basket with an assortment of discarded fruits and vegetables he has picked up in the strip district and which he attempts to sell.

GABRIEL *(singing):* Yes, ma'am, I got plums
You ask me how I sell them
Oh ten cents apiece
Three for a quarter
Come and buy now
'Cause I'm here today
And tomorrow I'll be gone

Gabriel enters.

Hey, Rose!

ROSE: How you doing, Gabe?

GABRIEL: There's Troy . . . Hey, Troy!

TROY: Hey, Gabe.

Exit into kitchen.

ROSE *(to Gabriel):* What you got there?

GABRIEL: You know what I got, Rose. I got fruits and vegetables.

ROSE *(looking in basket):* Where's all these plums you talking about?

GABRIEL: I ain't got no plums today, Rose. I was just singing that. Have some tomorrow. Put me in a big order for plums. Have enough plums tomorrow for St. Peter and everybody.

Troy reenters from kitchen, crosses to steps.

(To Rose.) Troy's mad at me.

TROY: I ain't mad at you. What I got to be mad at you about? You ain't done nothing to me.

GABRIEL: I just moved over to Miss Pearl's to keep out from in your way. I ain't mean no harm by it.

TROY: Who said anything about that? I ain't said anything about that.

GABRIEL: You ain't mad at me, is you?

TROY: Naw . . . I ain't mad at you, Gabe. If I was mad at you I'd tell you about it.

GABRIEL: Got me two rooms. In the basement. Got my own door too. Wanna see my key? *(He holds up a key.)* That's my own key! Ain't nobody else got a key like that. That's my key! My two rooms!

TROY: Well, that's good, Gabe. You got your own key . . . that's good.

ROSE: You hungry, Gabe? I was just fixing to cook Troy his breakfast.

GABRIEL: I'll take some biscuits. You got some biscuits? Did you know when I was in heaven . . . every morning me and St. Peter would sit down by the gate and eat some big fat biscuits? Oh, yeah! We had us a good time. We'd sit there and eat us them biscuits and then St. Peter would go off to sleep and tell me to wake him up when it's time to open the gates for the judgment.

ROSE: Well, come on . . . I'll make up a batch of biscuits.

Rose exits into the house.

GABRIEL: Troy . . . St. Peter got your name in the book. I seen it. It say . . . Troy Maxson. I say . . . I know him! He got the same name like what I got. That's my brother!

TROY: How many times you gonna tell me that, Gabe?

GABRIEL: Ain't got my name in the book. Don't have to have my name. I done died and went to heaven. He got your name though. One morning St. Peter was looking at his book . . . marking it up for the judgment . . . and he let me see your name. Got it in there under M. Got Rose's name . . . I ain't seen it like I seen yours . . . but I know it's in there. He got a great big book. Got everybody's name what was ever been born. That's what he told me. But I seen your name. Seen it with my own eyes.

TROY: Go on in the house there. Rose going to fix you something to eat.

GABRIEL: Oh, I ain't hungry. I done had breakfast with Aunt Jemimah. She come by and cooked me up a whole mess of flapjacks. Remember how we used to eat them flapjacks?

TROY: Go on in the house and get you something to eat now.

GABRIEL: I got to sell my plums. I done sold some tomatoes. Got me two quarters. Wanna see? *(He shows Troy his quarters.)* I'm gonna save them and buy me a new horn so St. Peter can hear me when it's time to open the gates. *(Gabriel stops suddenly. Listens.)* Hear that? That's the hellhounds. I got to chase them out of here. Go on get out of here! Get out!

Gabriel exits singing.

Better get ready for the judgment
Better get ready for the judgment
My Lord is coming down

Rose enters from the house.

TROY: He's gone off somewhere.

GABRIEL *(offstage):* Better get ready for the judgment
Better get ready for the judgment morning
Better get ready for the judgment
My God is coming down

ROSE: He ain't eating right. Miss Pearl say she can't get him to eat nothing.

TROY: What you want me to do about it, Rose? I done did everything I can for the man. I can't make him get well. Man got half his head blown away . . . what you expect?

ROSE: Seem like something ought to be done to help him.

TROY: Man don't bother nobody. He just mixed up from that metal plate he got in his head. Ain't no sense for him to go back into the hospital.

ROSE: Least he be eating right. They can help him take care of himself.

TROY: Don't nobody wanna be locked up, Rose. What you wanna lock him up for? Man go over there and fight the war . . . messin' around with them Japs, get half his head blown off . . . and they give him a lousy three thousand dollars. And I had to swoop down on that.

ROSE: Is you fixing to go into that again?

TROY: That's the only way I got a roof over my head . . . cause of that metal plate.

ROSE: Ain't no sense you blaming yourself for nothing. Gabe wasn't in no condition to manage that money. You done what was right by him. Can't nobody say you ain't done what was right by him. Look how long you took care of him . . . till he wanted to have his own place and moved over there with Miss Pearl.

TROY: That ain't what I'm saying, woman! I'm just stating the facts. If my brother didn't have that metal plate in his head . . . I wouldn't have a pot to piss in or a window to throw it out of. And I'm fifty-three years old. Now see if you can understand that!

Troy gets up from the porch and starts to exit the yard.

ROSE: Where you going off to? You been running out of here every Saturday for weeks. I thought you was gonna work on this fence?

TROY: I'm gonna walk down to Taylors'. Listen to the ball game. I'll be back in a bit. I'll work on it when I get back.

He exits the yard. The lights go to black.

Scene III

The lights come up on the yard. It is four hours later. Rose is taking down the clothes from the line. Cory enters carrying his football equipment.

ROSE: Your daddy like to had a fit with you running out of here this morning without doing your chores.

CORY: I told you I had to go to practice.

ROSE: He say you were supposed to help him with this fence.

CORY: He been saying that the last four or five Saturdays, and then he don't never do nothing, but go down to Taylors. Did you tell him about the recruiter?

ROSE: Yeah, I told him.

CORY: What he say?

ROSE: He ain't said nothing too much. You get in there and get started on your chores before he gets back. Go on and scrub down them steps before he gets back here hollering and carrying on.

CORY: I'm hungry. What you got to eat, Mama?

ROSE: Go on and get started on your chores. I got some meat loaf in there. Go on and make you a sandwich . . . and don't leave no mess in there.

Cory exits into the house. Rose continues to take down the clothes. Troy enters the yard and sneaks up and grabs her from behind.

Troy! Go on, now. You liked to scared me to death. What was the score of the game? Lucille had me on the phone and I couldn't keep up with it.

TROY: What I care about the game? Come here, woman. *(He tries to kiss her.)*
ROSE: I thought you went down Taylors' to listen to the game. Go on, Troy! You supposed to be putting up this fence.
TROY *(attempting to kiss her again):* I'll put it up when I finish with what is at hand.
ROSE: Go on, Troy. I ain't studying you.
TROY *(chasing after her):* I'm studying you . . . fixing to do my homework!
ROSE: Troy, you better leave me alone.
TROY: Where's Cory? That boy brought his butt home yet?
ROSE: He's in the house doing his chores.
TROY *(calling):* Cory! Get your butt out here, boy!

Rose exits into the house with the laundry. Troy goes over to the pile of wood, picks up a board, and starts sawing. Cory enters from the house.

TROY: You just now coming in here from leaving this morning?
CORY: Yeah, I had to go to football practice.
TROY: Yeah, what?
CORY: Yessir.
TROY: I ain't but two seconds off you noway. The garbage sitting in there overflowing . . . you ain't done none of your chores . . . and you come in here talking about "Yeah."
CORY: I was just getting ready to do my chores now, Pop . . .
TROY: Your first chore is to help me with this fence on Saturday. Everything else come after that. Now get that saw and cut them boards.

Cory takes the saw and begins cutting the boards. Troy continues working. There is a long pause.

CORY: Hey, Pop . . . why don't you buy a TV?
TROY: What I want with a TV? What I want one of them for?
CORY: Everybody got one. Earl, Ba Bra . . . Jesse!
TROY: I ain't asked you who had one. I say what I want with one?
CORY: So you can watch it. They got lots of things on TV. Baseball games and everything. We could watch the World Series.
TROY: Yeah . . . and how much this TV cost?
CORY: I don't know. They got them on sale for around two hundred dollars.
TROY: Two hundred dollars, huh?
CORY: That ain't that much, Pop.
TROY: Naw, it's just two hundred dollars. See that roof you got over your head at night? Let me tell you something about that roof. It's been over ten years since that roof was last tarred. See now . . . the snow come this winter and sit up there on that roof like it is . . . and it's gonna seep inside. It's just gonna be a little bit . . . ain't gonna hardly notice it. Then the next thing you know, it's gonna be leaking all over the house. Then the wood rot from all that water and you gonna need a whole new roof. Now, how much you think it cost to get that roof tarred?
CORY: I don't know.
TROY: Two hundred and sixty-four dollars . . . cash money. While you thinking about a TV, I got to be thinking about the roof . . . and whatever else go wrong here. Now if you had two hundred dollars, what would you do . . . fix the roof or buy a TV?

CORY: I'd buy a TV. Then when the roof started to leak . . . when it needed fixing . . . I'd fix it.

TROY: Where you gonna get the money from? You done spent it for a TV. You gonna sit up and watch the water run all over your brand new TV.

CORY: Aw, Pop. You got money. I know you do.

TROY: Where I got it at, huh?

CORY: You got it in the bank.

TROY: You wanna see my bankbook? You wanna see that seventy-three dollars and twenty-two cents I got sitting up in there.

CORY: You ain't got to pay for it all at one time. You can put a down payment on it and carry it on home with you.

TROY: Not me. I ain't gonna owe nobody nothing if I can help it. Miss a payment and they come and snatch it right out your house. Then what you got? Now, soon as I get two hundred dollars clear, then I'll buy a TV. Right now, as soon as I get two hundred and sixty-four dollars, I'm gonna have this roof tarred.

CORY: Aw . . . Pop!

TROY: You go on and get you two hundred dollars and buy one if ya want it. I got better things to do with my money.

CORY: I can't get no two hundred dollars. I ain't never seen two hundred dollars.

TROY: I'll tell you what . . . you get you a hundred dollars and I'll put the other hundred with it.

CORY: All right, I'm gonna show you.

TROY: You gonna show me how you can cut them boards right now.

Cory begins to cut the boards. There is a long pause.

CORY: The Pirates won today. That makes five in a row.

TROY: I ain't thinking about the Pirates. Got an all-white team. Got that boy . . . that Puerto Rican boy . . . Clemente. Don't even half-play him. That boy could be something if they give him a chance. Play him one day and sit him on the bench the next.

CORY: He gets a lot of chances to play.

TROY: I'm talking about playing regular. Playing every day so you can get your timing. That's what I'm talking about.

CORY: They got some white guys on the team that don't play every day. You can't play everybody at the same time.

TROY: If they got a white fellow sitting on the bench . . . you can bet your last dollar he can't play! The colored guy got to be twice as good before he get on the team. That's why I don't want you to get all tied up in them sports. Man on the team and what it get him? They got colored on the team and don't use them. Same as not having them. All them teams the same.

CORY: The Braves got Hank Aaron and Wes Covington. Hank Aaron hit two home runs today. That makes forty-three.

TROY: Hank Aaron ain't nobody. That what you supposed to do. That's how you supposed to play the game. Ain't nothing to it. It's just a matter of timing . . . getting the right follow-through. Hell, I can hit forty-three home runs right now!

CORY: Not off no major-league pitching, you couldn't.

TROY: We had better pitching in the Negro leagues. I hit seven home runs off of Satchel Paige. You can't get no better than that!

CORY: Sandy Koufax. He's leading the league in strikeouts.

TROY: I ain't thinking of no Sandy Koufax.

CORY: You got Warren Spahn and Lew Burdette. I bet you couldn't hit no home runs off of Warren Spahn.

TROY: I'm through with it now. You go on and cut them boards. *(Pause.)* Your mama tell me you done got recruited by a college football team? Is that right?

CORY: Yeah. Coach Zellman say the recruiter gonna be coming by to talk to you. Get you to sign the permission papers.

TROY: I thought you supposed to be working down there at the A&P. Ain't you suppose to be working down there after school?

CORY: Mr. Stawicki say he gonna hold my job for me until after the football season. Say starting next week I can work weekends.

TROY: I thought we had an understanding about this football stuff? You suppose to keep up with your chores and hold that job down at the A&P. Ain't been around here all day on a Saturday. Ain't none of your chores done . . . and now you telling me you done quit your job.

CORY: I'm going to be working weekends.

TROY: You damn right you are! And ain't no need for nobody coming around here to talk to me about signing nothing.

CROY: Hey, Pop . . . you can't do that. He's coming all the way from North Carolina.

TROY: I don't care where he coming from. The white man ain't gonna let you get nowhere with that football noway. You go on and get your book-learning so you can work yourself up in that A&P or learn how to fix cars or build houses or something, get you a trade. That way you have something can't nobody take away from you. You go on and learn how to put your hands to some good use. Besides hauling people's garbage.

CORY: I get good grades, Pop. That's why the recruiter wants to talk with you. You got to keep up your grades to get recruited. This way I'll be going to college. I'll get a chance . . .

TROY: First you gonna get your butt down there to the A&P and get your job back.

CORY: Mr. Stawicki done already hired somebody else 'cause I told him I was playing football.

TROY: You a bigger fool than I thought . . . to let somebody take away your job so you can play some football. Where you gonna get your money to take out your girlfriend and whatnot? What kind of foolishness is that to let somebody take away your job?

CORY: I'm still gonna be working weekends.

TROY: Naw . . . naw. You getting your butt out of here and finding you another job.

CORY: Come on, Pop! I got to practice. I can't work after school and play football too. The team needs me. That's what Coach Zellman say . . .

TROY: I don't care what nobody else say. I'm the boss . . . you understand? I'm the boss around here. I do the only saying what counts.

CORY: Come on, Pop!

TROY: I asked you . . . did you understand?

CORY: Yeah . . .

TROY: What?!

CORY: Yessir.

TROY: You go on down there to that A&P and see if you can get your job back. If you can't do both . . . then you quit the football team. You've got to take the crookeds with the straights.

CORY: Yessir. *(Pause.)* Can I ask you a question?

TROY: What the hell you wanna ask me? Mr. Stawicki the one you got the questions for.

CORY: How come you ain't never liked me?

TROY: Liked you? Who the hell say I got to like you? What law is there say I got to like you? Wanna stand up in my face and ask a damn fool-ass question like that. Talking about liking somebody. Come here, boy, when I talk to you.

Cory comes over to where Troy is working. He stands slouched over and Troy shoves him on his shoulder.

Straighten up, goddammit! I asked you a question . . . what law is there say I got to like you?

CORY: None.

TROY: Well, all right then! Don't you eat every day? *(Pause.)* Answer me when I talk to you! Don't you eat every day?

CORY: Yeah.

TROY: Nigger, as long as you in my house, you put that sir on the end of it when you talk to me!

CORY: Yes . . . sir.

TROY: You eat every day.

CORY: Yessir!

TROY: Got a roof over your head.

CORY: Yessir!

TROY: Got clothes on your back.

CORY: Yessir.

TROY: Why you think that is?

CORY: Cause of you.

TROY: Ah, hell I know it's cause of me . . . but why do think that is?

CORY *(hesitant)*: Cause you like me.

TROY: Like you? I go out of here every morning . . . bust my butt . . . putting up with them crackers every day . . . cause I like you? You are the biggest fool I ever saw. *(Pause.)* It's my job. It's my responsibility! You understand that? A man got to take care of his family. You live in my house . . . sleep you behind on my bedclothes . . . fill you belly up with my food . . . cause you my son. You my flesh and blood. Not cause I like you! Cause it's my duty to take care of you. I owe a responsibility to you! Let's get this straight right here . . . before it go along any further . . . I ain't got to like you. Mr. Rand don't give me my money come payday cause he likes me. He give me cause he owe me. I done give you everything I had to give you. I gave you your life! Me and your mama worked that out between us. And liking your black ass wasn't part of the bargain. Don't you try and go through life worrying about if somebody like you or not. You best be making sure they doing right by you. You understand what I'm saying, boy?

CORY: Yessir.

TROY: Then get the hell out of my face, and get on down to that A&P.

Rose has been standing behind the screen door for much of the scene. She enters as Cory exits.

ROSE: Why don't you let the boy go ahead and play football, Troy? Ain't no harm in that. He's just trying to be like you with the sports.

TROY: I don't want him to be like me! I want him to move as far away from my life as he can get. You the only decent thing that ever happened to me. I wish him that. But I don't wish him a thing else from my life. I decided seventeen years ago that boy wasn't getting involved in no sports. Not after what they did to me in the sports.

ROSE: Troy, why don't you admit you was too old to play in the major leagues? For once . . . why don't you admit that?

TROY: What do you mean too old? Don't come telling me I was too old. I just wasn't the right color. Hell, I'm fifty-three years old and can do better than Selkirk's .269 right now!

ROSE: How's was you gonna play ball when you were over forty? Sometimes I can't get no sense out of you.

TROY: I got good sense, woman. I got sense enough not to let my boy get hurt over playing no sports. You been mothering that boy too much. Worried about if people like him.

ROSE: Everything that boy do . . . he do for you. He wants you to say "Good job, son." That's all.

TROY: Rose, I ain't got time for that. He's alive. He's healthy. He's got to make his own way. I made mine. Ain't nobody gonna hold his hand when he get out there in that world.

ROSE: Times have changed from when you was young, Troy. People change. The world's changing around you and you can't even see it.

TROY *(slow, methodical):* Woman . . . I do the best I can do. I come in here every Friday. I carry a sack of potatoes and a bucket of lard. You all line up at the door with your hands out. I give you the lint from my pockets. I give you my sweat and my blood. I ain't got no tears. I done spent them. We go upstairs in that room at night . . . and I fall down on you and try to blast a hole into forever. I get up Monday morning . . . find my lunch on the table. I go out. Make my way. Find my strength to carry me through to the next Friday. *(Pause.)* That's all I got, Rose. That's all I got to give. I can't give nothing else.

Troy exits into the house. The lights go down to black.

Scene IV

It is Friday. Two weeks later. Cory starts out of the house with his football equipment. The phone rings.

CORY *(calling):* I got it! *(He answers the phone and stands in the screen door talking.)* Hello? Hey, Jesse. Naw . . . I was just getting ready to leave now.

ROSE *(calling):* Cory!

CORY: I told you, man, them spikes is all tore up. You can use them if you want, but they ain't no good. Earl got some spikes.

ROSE *(calling):* Cory!

CORY *(calling to Rose):* Mam? I'm talking to Jesse. *(Into phone.)* When she say that? *(Pause.)* Aw, you lying, man. I'm gonna tell her you said that.

ROSE *(calling):* Cory, don't you go nowhere!

CORY: I got to go to the game, Ma! *(Into the phone.)* Yeah, hey, look, I'll talk to you later. Yeah, I'll meet you over Earl's house. Later. Bye, Ma.

Cory exits the house and starts out the yard.

ROSE: Cory, where you going off to? You got that stuff all pulled out and thrown all over your room.

CORY *(in the yard):* I was looking for my spikes. Jesse wanted to borrow my spikes.

ROSE: Get up there and get that cleaned up before your daddy get back in here.

CORY: I got to go to the game! I'll clean it up *when I get back.*

Cory exits.

ROSE: That's all he need to do is see that room all messed up.

Rose exits into the house. Troy and Bono enter the yard. Troy is dressed in clothes other than his work clothes.

BONO: He told him the same thing he told you. Take it to the union.

TROY: Brownie ain't got that much sense. Man wasn't thinking about nothing. He wait until I confront them on it . . . then he wanna come crying seniority. *(Calls.)* Hey, Rose!

BONO: I wish I could have seen Mr. Rand's face when he told you.

TROY: He couldn't get it out of his mouth! Liked to bit his tongue! When they called me down there to the Commissioner's office . . . he thought they was gonna fire me. Like everybody else.

BONO: I didn't think they was gonna fire you. I thought they was gonna put you on the warning paper.

TROY: Hey, Rose! *(To Bono.)* Yeah, Mr. Rand like to bit his tongue.

Troy breaks the seal on the bottle, takes a drink, and hands it to Bono.

BONO: I see you run right down to Taylors' and told that Alberta gal.

TROY *(calling):* Hey Rose! *(To Bono.)* I told everybody. Hey, Rose! I went down there to cash my check.

ROSE *(entering from the house):* Hush all that hollering, man! I know you out here. What they say down there at the Commissioner's office?

TROY: You supposed to come when I call you, woman. Bono'll tell you that. *(To Bono.)* Don't Lucille come when you call her?

ROSE: Man, hush your mouth. I ain't no dog . . . talk about "come when you call me."

TROY *(puts his arm around Rose):* You hear this, Bono? I had me an old dog used to get uppity like that. You say, "C'mere, Blue!" . . . and he just lay there and look at you. End up getting a stick and chasing him away trying to make him come.

ROSE: I ain't studying you and your dog. I remember you used to sing that old song.

TROY *(he sings):* Hear it ring! Hear it ring! I had a dog his name was Blue.

ROSE: Don't nobody wanna hear you sing that old song.

TROY *(sings):* You know Blue was mighty true.

ROSE: Used to have Cory running around here singing that song.

BONO: Hell, I remember that song myself.

TROY *(sings)*: You know Blue was a good old dog.
Blue treed a possum in a hollow log.
That was my daddy's song. My daddy made up that song.

ROSE: I don't care who made it up. Don't nobody wanna hear you sing it.

TROY *(makes a song like calling a dog)*: Come here, woman.

ROSE: You come in here carrying on, I reckon they ain't fired you. What they say down there at the Commissioner's office?

TROY: Look here, Rose . . . Mr. Rand called me into his office today when I got back from talking to them people down there . . . it come from up top . . . he called me in and told me they was making me a driver.

ROSE: Troy, you kidding!

TROY: No I ain't. Ask Bono.

ROSE: Well, that's great, Troy. Now you don't have to hassle them people no more.

Lyons enters from the street.

TROY: Aw hell, I wasn't looking to see you today. I thought you was in jail. Got it all over the front page of the *Courier* about them raiding Sefus's place . . . where you be hanging out with all them thugs.

LYONS: Hey, Pop . . . that ain't got nothing to do with me. I don't go down there gambling. I go down there to sit in with the band. I ain't got nothing to do with the gambling part. They got some good music down there.

TROY: They got some rogues . . . is what they got.

LYONS: How you been, Mr. Bono? Hi, Rose.

BONO: I see where you playing down at the Crawford Grill tonight.

ROSE: How come you ain't brought Bonnie like I told you? You should have brought Bonnie with you, she ain't been over in a month of Sundays.

LYONS: I was just in the neighborhood . . . thought I'd stop by.

TROY: Here he come . . .

BONO: Your daddy got a promotion on the rubbish. He's gonna be the first colored driver. Ain't got to do nothing but sit up there and read the paper like them white fellows.

LYONS: Hey, Pop . . . if you knew how to read you'd be all right.

BONO: Naw . . . naw . . . you mean if the nigger knew how to *drive* he'd be all right. Been fighting with them people about driving and ain't even got a license. Mr. Rand know you ain't got no driver's license?

TROY: Driving ain't nothing. All you do is point the truck where you want it to go. Driving ain't nothing.

BONO: Do Mr. Rand know you ain't got no driver's license? That's what I'm talking about. I ain't asked if driving was easy. I asked if Mr. Rand know you ain't got no driver's license.

TROY: He ain't got to know. The man ain't got to know my business. Time he find out, I have two or three driver's licenses.

LYONS *(going into his pocket)*: Say, look here, Pop . . .

TROY: I knew it was coming. Didn't I tell you, Bono? I know what kind of "Look here, Pop" that was. The nigger fixing to ask me for some money. It's Friday night. It's my payday. All them rogues down there on the avenue . . . the ones that ain't in jail . . . and Lyons is hopping in his shoes to get down there with them.

LYONS: See, Pop . . . if you give somebody else a chance to talk sometimes, you'd see that I was fixing to pay you back your ten dollars like I told you. Here . . . I told you I'd pay you when Bonnie got paid.

TROY: Naw . . . you go ahead and keep that ten dollars. Put it in the bank. The next time you feel like you wanna come by here and ask me for something . . . you go on down there and get that.

LYONS: Here's your ten dollars, Pop. I told you I don't want you to give me nothing. I just wanted to borrow ten dollars.

TROY: Naw . . . you go on and keep that for the next time you want to ask me.

LYONS: Come on, Pop . . . here go your ten dollars.

ROSE: Why don't you go on and let the boy pay you back, Troy?

LYONS: Here you go, Rose. If you don't take it I'm gonna have to hear about it for the next six months. *(He hands her the money.)*

ROSE: You can hand yours over here too, Troy.

TROY: You see this, Bono. You see how they do me.

BONO: Yeah, Lucille do me the same way.

Gabriel is heard singing offstage. He enters.

GABRIEL: Better get ready for the Judgment! Better get ready for . . . Hey! . . . Hey! . . . There's Troy's boy!

LYONS: How are you doing, Uncle Gabe?

GABRIEL: Lyons . . . The King of the Jungle! Rose . . . hey, Rose. Got a flower for you. *(He takes a rose from his pocket.)* Picked it myself. That's the same rose like you is!

ROSE: That's right nice of you, Gabe.

LYONS: What you been doing, Uncle Gabe?

GABRIEL: Oh, I been chasing hellhounds and waiting on the time to tell St. Peter to open the gates.

LYONS: You been chasing hellhounds, huh? Well . . . you doing the right thing, Uncle Gabe. Somebody got to chase them.

GABRIEL: Oh, yeah . . . I know it. The devil's strong. The devil ain't no pushover. Hellhounds snipping at everybody's heels. But I got my trumpet waiting on the judgment time.

LYONS: Waiting on the Battle of Armageddon, huh?

GABRIEL: Ain't gonna be too much of a battle when God get to waving that Judgment sword. But the people's gonna have a hell of a time trying to get into heaven if them gates ain't open.

LYONS *(putting his arm around Gabriel):* You hear this, Pop. Uncle Gabe, you all right!

GABRIEL *(laughing with Lyons):* Lyons! King of the Jungle.

ROSE: You gonna stay for supper, Gabe? Want me to fix you a plate?

GABRIEL: I'll take a sandwich, Rose. Don't want no plate. Just wanna eat with my hands. I'll take a sandwich.

ROSE: How about you, Lyons? You staying? Got some short ribs cooking.

LYONS: Naw, I won't eat nothing till after we finished playing. *(Pause.)* You ought to come down and listen to me play, Pop.

TROY: I don't like that Chinese music. All that noise.

ROSE: Go on in the house and wash up, Gabe . . . I'll fix you a sandwich.

GABRIEL *(to Lyons, as he exits):* Troy's mad at me.

LYONS: What you mad at Uncle Gabe for, Pop?

ROSE: He thinks Troy's mad at him cause he moved over to Miss Pearl's.

TROY: I ain't mad at the man. He can live where he want to live at.

LYONS: What he move over there for? Miss Pearl don't like nobody.

ROSE: She don't mind him none. She treats him real nice. She just don't allow all that singing.

TROY: She don't mind that rent he be paying . . . that's what she don't mind.

ROSE: Troy, I ain't going through that with you no more. He's over there cause he want to have his own place. He can come and go as he please.

TROY: Hell, he could come and go as he pleases here. I wasn't stopping him. I ain't put no rules on him.

ROSE: It ain't the same thing, Troy. And you know it.

Gabriel comes to the door.

Now, that's the last I wanna hear about that. I don't wanna hear nothing else about Gabe and Miss Pearl. And next week . . .

GABRIEL: I'm ready for my sandwich, Rose.

ROSE: And next week . . . when that recruiter come from that school . . . I want you to sign that paper and go on and let Cory play football. Then that'll be the last I have to hear about that.

TROY *(to Rose as she exits into the house):* I ain't thinking about Cory nothing.

LYONS: What . . . Cory got recruited? What school he going to?

TROY: That boy walking around here smelling his piss . . . thinking he's grown. Thinking he's gonna do what he want, irrespective of what I say. Look here, Bono . . . I left the Commissioner's office and went down to the A&P . . . that boy ain't working down there. He lying to me. Telling me he got his job back . . . telling me he working weekends . . . telling me he working after school . . . Mr. Stawicki tell me he ain't working down there at all!

LYONS: Cory just growing up. He's just busting at the seams trying to fill out your shoes.

TROY: I don't care what he's doing. When he get to the point where he wanna disobey me . . . then it's time for him to move on. Bono'll tell you that. I bet he ain't never disobeyed his daddy without paying the consequences.

BONO: I ain't never had a chance. My daddy came on through . . . but I ain't never knew him to see him . . . or what he had on his mind or where he went. Just moving on through. Searching out the New Land. That's what the old folks used to call it. See a fellow moving around from place to place . . . woman to woman . . . called it searching out the New Land. I can't say if he ever found it. I come along, didn't want no kids. Didn't know if I was gonna be in one place long enough to fix on them right as their daddy. I figured I was going searching too. As it turned out I been hooked up with Lucille near about as long as your daddy been with Rose. Going on sixteen years.

TROY: Sometimes I wish I hadn't known my daddy. He ain't cared nothing about no kids. A kid to him wasn't nothing. All he wanted was for you to learn how to walk so he could start you to working. When it come time for eating . . . he ate first. If there was anything left over, that's what you got. Man would sit down and eat two chickens and give you the wing.

LYONS: You ought to stop that, Pop. Everybody feed their kids. No matter how hard times is . . . everybody care about their kids. Make sure they have something to eat.

TROY: The only thing my daddy cared about was getting them bales of cotton in to Mr. Lubin. That's the only thing that mattered to him. Sometimes I used to wonder why he was living. Wonder why the devil hadn't come and got him. "Get them bales of cotton in to Mr. Lubin" and find out he owe him money . . .

LYONS: He should have just went on and left when he saw he couldn't get nowhere. That's what I would have done.

TROY: How he gonna leave with eleven kids? And where he gonna go? He ain't knew how to do nothing but farm. No, he was trapped and I think he knew it. But I'll say this for him . . . he felt a responsibility toward us. Maybe he ain't treated us the way I felt he should have . . . but without that responsibility he could have walked off and left us . . . made his own way.

BONO: A lot of them did. Back in those days what you talking about . . . they walk out their front door and just take on down one road or another and keep on walking.

LYONS: There you go! That's what I'm talking about.

BONO: Just keep on walking till you come to something else. Ain't you never heard of nobody having the walking blues? Well, that's what you call it when you just take off like that.

TROY: My daddy ain't had them walking blues! What you talking about? He stayed right there with his family. But he was just as evil as he could be. My mama couldn't stand him. Couldn't stand that evilness. She run off when I was about eight. She sneaked off one night after he had gone to sleep. Told me she was coming back for me. I ain't never seen her no more. All his women run off and left him. He wasn't good for nobody.

When my turn come to head out, I was fourteen and got to sniffing around Joe Canewell's daughter. Had us an old mule we called Greyboy. My daddy sent me out to do some plowing and I tied up Greyboy and went to fooling around with Joe Canewell's daughter. We done found us a nice little spot, got real cozy with each other. She about thirteen and we done figured we was grown anyway . . . so we down there enjoying ourselves . . . ain't thinking about nothing. We didn't know Greyboy had got loose and wandered back to the house and my daddy was looking for me. We down there by the creek enjoying ourselves when my daddy come up on us. Surprised us. He had them leather straps off the mule and commenced to whupping me like there was no tomorrow. I jumped up, mad and embarrassed. I was scared of my daddy. When he commenced to whupping on me . . . quite naturally I run to get out of the way. *(Pause.)* Now I thought he was mad cause I ain't done my work. But I see where he was chasing me off so he could have the gal for himself. When I see what the matter of it was, I lost all fear of my daddy. Right there is where I become a man . . . at fourteen years of age. *(Pause.)* Now it was my turn to run him off. I picked up them same reins that he had used on me. I picked up them reins and commenced to whupping on him. The gal jumped up and run off . . . and when my daddy turned to face me, I could see why the devil had never come to get him . . . cause he was the devil himself. I don't know what happened. When I woke up, I was laying right there by the creek, and Blue . . . this old dog we had . . . was licking my face. I thought I was blind. I couldn't see nothing. Both my eyes were swollen shut. I laid there and cried. I didn't know what I was gonna do. The only thing I knew was the time had come for me to leave my daddy's house. And right there the world suddenly got big. And it was a long time before I could cut it down to where I could handle it.

Part of that cutting down was when I got to the place where I could feel him kicking in my blood and knew that the only thing that separated us was the matter of a few years.

Gabriel enters from the house with a sandwich.

LYONS: What you got there, Uncle Gabe?

GABRIEL: Got me a ham sandwich. Rose gave me a ham sandwich.

TROY: I don't know what happened to him. I done lost touch with everybody except Gabriel. But I hope he's dead. I hope he found some peace.

LYONS: That's a heavy story, Pop. I didn't know you left home when you was fourteen.

TROY: And didn't know nothing. The only part of the world I knew was the forty-two acres of Mr. Lubin's land. That's all I knew about life.

LYONS: Fourteen's kinda young to be out on your own. *(Phone rings.)* I don't even think I was ready to be out on my own at fourteen. I don't know what I would have done.

TROY: I got up from the creek and walked on down to Mobile. I was through with farming. Figured I could do better in the city. So I walked the two hundred miles to Mobile.

LYONS: Wait a minute . . . you ain't walked no two hundred miles, Pop. Ain't nobody gonna walk no two hundred miles. You talking about some walking there.

BONO: That's the only way you got anywhere back in them days.

LYONS: Shhh. Damn if I wouldn't have hitched a ride with somebody!

TROY: Who you gonna hitch it with? They ain't had no cars and things like they got now. We talking about 1918.

ROSE *(entering):* What you all out here getting into?

TROY *(to Rose):* I'm telling Lyons how good he got it. He don't know nothing about this I'm talking.

ROSE: Lyons, that was Bonnie on the phone. She say you supposed to pick her up.

LYONS: Yeah, okay, Rose.

TROY: I walked on down to Mobile and hitched up with some of them fellows that was heading this way. Got up here and found out . . . not only couldn't you get a job . . . you couldn't find no place to live. I thought I was in freedom. Shhh. Colored folks living down there on the riverbanks in whatever kind of shelter they could find for themselves. Right down there under the Brady Street Bridge. Living in shacks made of sticks and tarpaper. Messed around there and went from bad to worse. Started stealing. First it was food. Then I figured, hell, if I steal money I can buy me some food. Buy me some shoes too! One thing led to another. Met your mama. I was young and anxious to be a man. Met your mama and had you. What I do that for? Now I got to worry about feeding you and her. Got to steal three times as much. Went out one day looking for somebody to rob . . . that's what I was, a robber. I'll tell you the truth. I'm ashamed of it today. But it's the truth. Went to rob this fellow . . . pulled out my knife . . . and he pulled out a gun. Shot me in the chest. I felt just like somebody had taken a hot branding iron and laid it on me. When he shot me I jumped at him with my knife. They told me I killed him and they put me in the penitentiary and locked me up for fifteen years. That's where I met Bono. That's where I learned how to play baseball. Got out that place and your mama had taken you and went on to make life without me. Fifteen years was a long time for her to wait. But that fifteen years cured me of that robbing stuff. Rose'll tell you. She asked me when I met her if I had gotten all that foolishness out of my system. And I told her, "Baby, it's you and baseball all what count with me." You hear me, Bono? I meant it too. She say, "Which one comes first?" I told her, "Baby, ain't no doubt it's baseball . . . but you stick and get old with me and we'll both outlive this baseball." Am I right, Rose? And it's true.

ROSE: Man, hush your mouth. You ain't said no such thing. Talking about, "Baby, you know you'll always be number one with me." That's what you was talking.

TROY: You hear that, Bono. That's why I love her.

BONO: Rose'll keep you straight. You get off the track, she'll straighten you up.

ROSE: Lyons, you better get on up and get Bonnie. She waiting on you.

LYONS *(gets up to go):* Hey, Pop, why don't you come on down to the Grill and hear me play?

TROY: I ain't going down there. I'm too old to be sitting around in them clubs.

BONO: You got to be good to play at the Grill.

LYONS: Come on, Pop . . .

TROY: I got to get up in the morning.

LYONS: You ain't got to stay long.

TROY: Naw, I'm gonna get my supper and go on to bed.

LYONS: Well, I got to go. I'll see you again.

TROY: Don't you come around my house on my payday.

ROSE: Pick up the phone and let somebody know you coming. And bring Bonnie with you. You know I'm always glad to see her.

LYONS: Yeah, I'll do that, Rose. You take care now. See you, Pop. See you, Mr. Bono. See you, Uncle Gabe.

GABRIEL: Lyons! King of the Jungle!

Lyons exits.

TROY: Is supper ready, woman? Me and you got some business to take care of. I'm gonna tear it up too.

ROSE: Troy, I done told you now!

TROY *(puts his arm around Bono):* Aw hell, woman . . . this is Bono. Bono like family. I done known this nigger since . . . how long I done know you?

BONO: It's been a long time.

TROY: I done know this nigger since Skippy was a pup. Me and him done been through some times.

BONO: You sure right about that.

TROY: Hell, I done know him longer than I known you. And we still standing shoulder to shoulder. Hey, look here, Bono . . . a man can't ask for no more than that. *(Drinks to him.)* I love you, nigger.

BONO: Hell, I love you too . . . I got to get home see my woman. You got yours in hand. I got to go get mine.

Bono starts to exit as Cory enters the yard, dressed in his football uniform. He gives Troy a hard, uncompromising look.

CORY: What you do that for, Pop?

He throws his helmet down in the direction of Troy.

ROSE: What's the matter? Cory . . . what's the matter?

CORY: Papa done went up to the school and told Coach Zellman I can't play football no more. Wouldn't even let me play the game. Told him to tell the recruiter not to come.

ROSE: Troy . . .

TROY: What you Troying me for. Yeah, I did it. And the boy know why I did it.

CORY: Why you wanna do that to me? That was the one chance I had.

ROSE: Ain't nothing wrong with Cory playing football, Troy.

TROY: The boy lied to me. I told the nigger if he wanna play football . . . to keep up his chores and hold down that job at the A&P. That was the conditions. Stopped down there to see Mr. Stawicki . . .

CORY: I can't work after school during the football season, Pop! I tried to tell you that Mr. Stawicki's holding my job for me. You don't never want to listen to nobody. And then you wanna go and do this to me!

TROY: I ain't done nothing to you. You done it to yourself.

CORY: Just cause you didn't have a chance! You just scared I'm gonna be better than you, that's all.

TROY: Come here.

ROSE: Troy . . .

Cory reluctantly crosses over to Troy.

TROY: All right! See. You done made a mistake.

CORY: I didn't even do nothing!

TROY: I'm gonna tell you what your mistake was. See . . . you swung at the ball and didn't hit it. That's strike one. See, you in the batter's box now. You swung and you missed. That's strike one. Don't you strike out!

Lights fade to black.

ACT II

Scene I

The following morning Cory is at the tree hitting the ball with the bat. He tries to mimic Troy, but his swing is awkward, less sure. Rose enters from the house.

ROSE: Cory, I want you to help me with this cupboard.

CORY: I ain't quitting the team. I don't care what Poppa say.

ROSE: I'll talk to him when he gets back. He had to go see about your Uncle Gabe. The police done arrested him. Say he was disturbing the peace. He'll be back directly. Come on in here and help me clean out the top of this cupboard.

Cory exits into the house. Rose sees Troy and Bono coming down the alley.

Troy . . . what they say down there?

TROY: Ain't said nothing. I give them fifty dollars and they let him go. I'll talk to you about it. Where's Cory?

ROSE: He's in there helping me clean out these cupboards.

TROY: Tell him to get his butt out here.

Troy and Bono go over to the pile of wood. Bono picks up the saw and begins sawing.

TROY *(to Bono):* All they want is the money. That makes six or seven times I done went down there and got him. See me coming they stick out their hands.

BONO: Yeah. I know what you mean. That's all they care about . . . that money. They don't care about what's right. *(Pause.)* Nigger, why you got to go and get some hard wood? You ain't doing nothing but building a little old fence. Get you some soft pine wood. That's all you need.

TROY: I know what I'm doing. This is outside wood. You put pine wood inside the house. Pine wood is inside wood. This here is outside wood. Now you tell me where the fence is gonna be?

BONO: You don't need this wood. You can put it up with pine wood and it'll stand as long as you gonna be here looking at it.

TROY: How you know how long I'm gonna be here, nigger? Hell, I might just live forever. Live longer than old man Horsely.

BONO: That's what Magee used to say.

TROY: Magee's a damn fool. Now you tell me who you ever heard of gonna pull their own teeth with a pair of rusty pliers.

BONO: The old folks . . . my granddaddy used to pull his teeth with pliers. They ain't had no dentists for the colored folks back then.

TROY: Get clean pliers! You understand? Clean pliers! Sterilize them! Besides we ain't living back then. All Magee had to do was walk over to Doc Goldblum's.

BONO: I see where you and that Tallahassee gal . . . that Alberta . . . I see where you all done got tight.

TROY: What you mean "got tight"?

BONO: I see where you be laughing and joking with her all the time.

TROY: I laughs and jokes with all of them, Bono. You know me.

BONO: That ain't the kind of laughing and joking I'm talking about.

Cory enters from the house.

CORY: How you doing, Mr. Bono?

TROY: Cory? Get that saw from Bono and cut some wood. He talking about the wood's too hard to cut. Stand back there, Jim, and let that young boy show you how it's done.

BONO: He's sure welcome to it.

Cory takes the saw and begins to cut the wood.

Whew-e-e! Look at that. Big old strong boy. Look like Joe Louis. Hell, must be getting old the way I'm watching that boy whip through that wood.

CORY: I don't see why Mama want a fence around the yard noways.

TROY: Damn if I know either. What the hell she keeping out with it? She ain't got nothing nobody want.

BONO: Some people build fences to keep people out . . . and other people build fences to keep people in. Rose wants to hold on to you all. She loves you.

TROY: Hell, nigger, I don't need nobody to tell me my wife loves me. Cory . . . go on in the house and see if you can find that other saw.

CORY: Where's it at?

TROY: I said find it! Look for it till you find it!

Cory exits into the house.

What's that supposed to mean? Wanna keep us in?

BONO: Troy . . . I done known you seem like damn near my whole life. You and Rose both. I done know both of you all for a long time. I remember when you met Rose. When you was hitting them baseball out the park. A lot of them old gals was after you then. You had the pick of the litter. When you picked Rose, I was happy for you. That was the first time I knew you had any sense. I said . . . My man Troy knows what he's doing . . . I'm gonna follow this nigger . . . he might take me somewhere. I been following you too. I done learned a whole heap of things about life watching you. I done learned how to tell where the shit lies. How to tell it from the alfalfa. You done learned me a lot of things. You showed me how to not make the same mistakes . . . to take life as it comes along and keep putting one foot in front of the other. *(Pause.)* Rose a good woman, Troy.

TROY: Hell, nigger, I know she a good woman. I been married to her for eighteen years. What you got on your mind, Bono?

BONO: I just say she a good woman. Just like I say anything. I ain't got to have nothing on my mind.

TROY: You just gonna say she a good woman and leave it hanging out there like that? Why you telling me she a good woman?

BONO: She loves you, Troy. Rose loves you.

TROY: You saying I don't measure up. That's what you trying to say. I don't measure up cause I'm seeing this other gal. I know what you trying to say.

BONO: I know what Rose means to you, Troy. I'm just trying to say I don't want to see you mess up.

TROY: Yeah, I appreciate that, Bono. If you was messing around on Lucille I'd be telling you the same thing.

BONO: Well, that's all I got to say. I just say that because I love you both.

TROY: Hell, you know me . . . I wasn't out there looking for nothing. You can't find a better woman than Rose. I know that. But seems like this woman just stuck onto me where I can't shake her loose. I done wrestled with it, tried to throw her off me . . . but she just stuck on tighter. Now she's stuck on for good.

BONO: You's in control . . . that's what you tell me all the time. You responsible for what you do.

TROY: I ain't ducking the responsibility of it. As long as it sets right in my heart . . . then I'm okay. Cause that's all I listen to. It'll tell me right from wrong every time. And I ain't talking about doing Rose no bad turn. I love Rose. She done carried me a long ways and I love and respect her for that.

BONO: I know you do. That's why I don't want to see you hurt her. But what you gonna do when she find out? What you got then? If you try and juggle both of them . . . sooner or later you gonna drop one of them. That's common sense.

TROY: Yeah, I hear what you saying, Bono. I been trying to figure a way to work it out.

BONO: Work it out right, Troy. I don't want to be getting all up between you and Rose's business . . . but work it so it come out right.

TROY: Ah hell, I get all up between you and Lucille's business. When you gonna get that woman that refrigerator she been wanting? Don't tell me you ain't got no money now. I know who your banker is. Mellon don't need that money bad as Lucille want that refrigerator. I'll tell you that.

BONO: Tell you what I'll do . . . when you finish building this fence for Rose . . . I'll buy Lucille that refrigerator.

TROY: You done stuck your foot in your mouth now!

Troy grabs up a board and begins to saw. Bono starts to walk out the yard.

Hey, nigger . . . where you going?

BONO: I'm going home. I know you don't expect me to help you now. I'm protecting my money. I wanna see you put that fence up by yourself. That's what I want to see. You'll be here another six months without me.

TROY: Nigger, you ain't right.

BONO: When it comes to my money . . . I'm right as fireworks on the Fourth of July.

TROY: All right, we gonna see now. You better get out your bankbook.

Bono exits, and Troy continues to work. Rose enters from the house.

ROSE: What they say down there? What's happening with Gabe?

TROY: I went down there and got him out. Cost me fifty dollars. Say he was disturbing the peace. Judge set up a hearing for him in three weeks. Say to show cause why he shouldn't be recommitted.

ROSE: What was he doing that cause them to arrest him?

TROY: Some kids was teasing him and he run them off home. Say he was howling and carrying on. Some folks seen him and called the police. That's all it was.

ROSE: Well, what's you say? What'd you tell the judge?

TROY: Told him I'd look after him. It didn't make no sense to recommit the man. He stuck out his big greasy palm and told me to give him fifty dollars and take him on home.

ROSE: Where's he at now? Where'd he go off to?

TROY: He's gone about his business. He don't need nobody to hold his hand.

ROSE: Well, I don't know. Seem like that would be the best place for him if they did put him into the hospital. I know what you're gonna say. But that's what I think would be best.

TROY: The man done had his life ruined fighting for what? And they wanna take and lock him up. Let him be free. He don't bother nobody.

ROSE: Well, everybody got their own way of looking at it I guess. Come on and get your lunch. I got a bowl of lima beans and some cornbread in the oven. Come and get something to eat. Ain't no sense you fretting over Gabe.

Rose turns to go into the house.

TROY: Rose . . . got something to tell you.
ROSE: Well, come on . . . wait till I get this food on the table.
TROY: Rose!

She stops and turns around.

I don't know how to say this. *(Pause.)* I can't explain it none. It just sort of grows on you till it gets out of hand. It starts out like a little bush . . . and the next thing you know it's a whole forest.

ROSE: Troy . . . what is you talking about?

TROY: I'm talking, woman, let me talk. I'm trying to find a way to tell you . . . I'm gonna be a daddy. I'm gonna be somebody's daddy.

ROSE: Troy . . . you're not telling me this? You're gonna be . . . what?

TROY: Rose . . . now . . . see . . .

ROSE: You telling me you gonna be somebody's daddy? You telling your *wife* this?

Gabriel enters from the street. He carries a rose in his hand.

GABRIEL: Hey, Troy! Hey, Rose!

ROSE: I have to wait eighteen years to hear something like this.

GABRIEL: Hey, Rose . . . I got a flower for you. *(He hands it to her.)* That's a rose. Same rose like you is.

ROSE: Thanks, Gabe.

GABRIEL: Troy, you ain't mad at me is you? Them bad mens come and put me away. You ain't mad at me is you?

TROY: Naw, Gabe, I ain't mad at you.

ROSE: Eighteen years and you wanna come with this.

GABRIEL *(take a quarter out of his pocket)*: See what I got? Got a brand new quarter.

TROY: Rose . . . it's just . . .

ROSE: Ain't nothing you can say, Troy. Ain't no way of explaining that.

GABRIEL: Fellow that give me this quarter had a whole mess of them. I'm gonna keep this quarter till it stop shining.

ROSE: Gabe, go on in the house there. I got some watermelon in the Frigidaire. Go on and get you a piece.

GABRIEL: Say, Rose . . . you know I was chasing hellhounds and them bad mens come and get me and take me away. Troy helped me. He come down there and told them they better let me go before he beat them up. Yeah, he did!

ROSE: You go on and get you a piece of watermelon, Gabe. Them bad mens is gone now.

GABRIEL: Okay, Rose . . . gonna get me some watermelon. The kind with the stripes on it.

Gabriel exits into the house.

ROSE: Why, Troy? Why? After all these years to come dragging this in to me now. It don't make no sense at your age. I could have expected this ten or fifteen years ago, but not now.

TROY: Age ain't got nothing to do with it, Rose.

ROSE: I done tried to be everything a wife should be. Everything a wife could be. Been married eighteen years and I got to live to see the day you tell me you been seeing another woman and done fathered a child by her. And you know I ain't never wanted no half nothing in my family. My whole family is half. Everybody got different fathers and mothers . . . my two sisters and my brother. Can't hardly tell who's who. Can't never sit down and talk about Papa and Mama. It's your papa and your mama and my papa and my mama . . .

TROY: Rose . . . stop it now.

ROSE: I ain't never wanted that for none of my children. And now you wanna drag your behind in here and tell me something like this.

TROY: You ought to know. It's time for you to know.

ROSE: Well, I don't want to know, goddamn it!

TROY: I can't just make it go away. It's done now. I can't wish the circumstance of the thing away.

ROSE: And you don't want to either. Maybe you want to wish me and my boy away. Maybe that's what you want? Well, you can't wish us away. I've got eighteen years of my life invested in you. You ought to have stayed upstairs in my bed where you belong.

TROY: Rose . . . now listen to me . . . we can get a handle on this thing. We can talk this out . . . come to an understanding.

ROSE: All of a sudden it's "we." Where was "we" at when you was down there rolling around with some godforsaken woman? "We" should have come to an understanding before you started making a damn fool of yourself. You're a day late and a dollar short when it comes to an understanding with me.

TROY: It's just . . . She gives me a different idea . . . a different understanding about myself. I can step out of this house and get away from the pressures and problems . . . be a different man. I ain't got to wonder how I'm gonna pay the bills or get the roof fixed. I can just be a part of myself that I ain't never been.

ROSE: What I want to know . . . is do you plan to continue seeing her. That's all you can say to me.

TROY: I can sit up in her house and laugh. Do you understand what I'm saying. I can laugh out loud . . . and it feels good. It reaches all the way down to the bottom of my shoes. *(Pause.)* Rose, I can't give that up.

ROSE: Maybe you ought to go on and stay down there with her . . . if she's a better woman than me.

TROY: It ain't about nobody being a better woman or nothing. Rose, you ain't the blame. A man couldn't ask for no woman to be a better wife than you've been. I'm responsible for it. I done locked myself into a pattern trying to take care of you all that I forgot about myself.

ROSE: What the hell was I there for? That was my job, not somebody else's.

TROY: Rose, I done tried all my life to live decent . . . to live a clean . . . hard . . . useful life. I tried to be a good husband to you. In every way I knew how. Maybe I come into the world backwards, I don't know. But . . . you born with two strikes on you before you come to the plate. You got to guard it closely . . . always looking for the curve ball on the inside corner. You can't afford to let none get past you. You can't afford a call strike. If you going down . . . you going down swinging. Everything lined up against you. What you gonna do. I fooled them, Rose. I bunted. When I found you and Cory and a halfway decent job . . . I was safe. Couldn't nothing touch me. I wasn't gonna strike out no more. I wasn't going back to the penitentiary. I wasn't gonna lay in the streets with a bottle of wine. I was safe. I had me a family. A job. I wasn't gonna get that last strike. I was on first looking for one of them boys to knock me in. To get me home.

ROSE: You should have stayed in my bed, Troy.

TROY: Then when I saw that gal . . . she firmed up my backbone. And I got to thinking that if I tried . . . I just might be able to steal second. Do you understand after eighteen years I wanted to steal second.

ROSE: You should have held me tight. You should have grabbed me and held on.

TROY: I stood on first base for eighteen years and I thought . . . well, goddamn it . . . go on for it!

ROSE: We're not talking about baseball! We're talking about you going off to lay in bed with another woman . . . and then bring it home to me. That's what we're talking about. We ain't talking about no baseball.

TROY: Rose, you're not listening to me. I'm trying the best I can to explain it to you. It's not easy for me to admit that I been standing in the same place for eighteen years.

ROSE: I been standing with you! I been right here with you, Troy. I got a life too. I gave eighteen years of my life to stand in the same spot with you. Don't you think I ever wanted other things? Don't you think I had dreams and hopes? What about my life? What about me. Don't you think it ever crossed my mind to want to know other men? That I wanted to lay up somewhere and forget about my responsibilities? That I wanted someone to make me laugh so I could feel good? You not the only one who's got wants and needs. But I held on to you, Troy. I took all my feelings, my wants and needs, my dreams . . . and I buried them inside you. I planted a seed and watched and prayed over it. I planted myself inside you and waited to bloom. And it didn't take me no eighteen years to find out the soil was hard and rocky and it wasn't never gonna bloom.

But I held on to you, Troy. I held you tighter. You was my husband. I owed you everything I had. Every part of me I could find to give you. And upstairs in that room . . . with the darkness falling in on me . . . I gave everything I had to try and erase the doubt that you wasn't the finest man in the world. And wherever you was going . . . I wanted to be there with you. Cause you was my husband. Cause that's the only way I was gonna survive as your wife. You always talking about what you give . . . and what you don't have to give. But you take too. You take . . . and don't even know nobody's giving!

Rose turns to exit into the house; Troy grabs her arm.

TROY: You say I take and don't give!

ROSE: Troy! You're hurting me!

TROY: You say I take and don't give!

ROSE: Troy . . . you're hurting my arm! Let go!

TROY: I done give you everything I got. Don't you tell that lie on me.

ROSE: Troy!

TROY: Don't you tell that lie on me!

Cory enters from the house.

CORY: Mama!

ROSE: Troy. You're hurting me.

TROY: Don't you tell me about no taking and giving.

Cory comes up behind Troy and grabs him. Troy, surprised, is thrown off balance just as Cory throws a glancing blow that catches him on the chest and knocks him down. Troy is stunned, as is Cory.

ROSE: Troy. Troy. No!

Troy gets to his feet and starts at Cory.

Troy . . . no. Please! Troy!

Rose pulls on Troy to hold him back. Troy stops himself.

TROY *(to Cory):* All right. That's strike two. You stay away from around me, boy. Don't you strike out. You living with a full count. Don't you strike out.

Troy exits out the yard as the lights go down.

Scene II

It is six months later, early afternoon. Troy enters from the house and starts to exit the yard. Rose enters from the house.

ROSE: Troy, I want to talk to you.

TROY: All of a sudden, after all this time, you want to talk to me, huh? You ain't wanted to talk to me for months. You ain't wanted to talk to me last night. You ain't wanted no part of me then. What you wanna talk to me about now?

ROSE: Tomorrow's Friday.

TROY: I know what day tomorrow is. You think I don't know tomorrow's Friday? My whole life I ain't done nothing but look to see Friday coming and you got to tell me it's Friday.

ROSE: I want to know if you're coming home.

TROY: I always come home, Rose. You know that. There ain't never been a night I ain't come home.

ROSE: That ain't what I mean . . . and you know it. I want to know if you're coming straight home after work.

TROY: I figure I'd cash my check . . . hang out at Taylors' with the boys . . . maybe play a game of checkers.

ROSE: Troy, I can't live like this. I won't live like this. You livin' on borrowed time with me. It's been going on six months now you ain't been coming home.

TROY: I be here every night. Every night of the year. That's 365 days.

ROSE: I want you to come home tomorrow after work.

TROY: Rose . . . I don't mess up my pay. You know that now. I take my pay and I give it to you. I don't have no money but what you give me back. I just want to have a little time to myself . . . a little time to enjoy life.

ROSE: What about me? When's my time to enjoy life?

TROY: I don't know what to tell you, Rose. I'm doing the best I can.

ROSE: You ain't been home from work but time enough to change your clothes and run out . . . and you wanna call that the best you can do?

TROY: I'm going over to the hospital to see Alberta. She went into the hospital this afternoon. Look like she might have the baby early. I won't be gone long.

ROSE: Well, you ought to know. They went over to Miss Pearl's and got Gabe today. She said you told them to go ahead and lock him up.

TROY: I ain't said no such thing. Whoever told you that is telling a lie. Pearl ain't doing nothing but telling a big fat lie.

ROSE: She ain't had to tell me. I read it on the papers.

TROY: I ain't told them nothing of the kind.

ROSE: I saw it right there on the papers.

TROY: What it say, huh?

ROSE: It said you told them to take him.

TROY: Then they screwed that up, just the way they screw up everything. I ain't worried about what they got on the paper.

ROSE: Say the government send part of his check to the hospital and the other part to you.

TROY: I ain't got nothing to do with that if that's the way it works. I ain't made up the rules about how it work.

ROSE: You did Gabe just like you did Cory. You wouldn't sign the paper for Cory . . . but you signed for Gabe. You signed that paper.

The telephone is heard ringing inside the house.

TROY: I told you I ain't signed nothing, woman! The only thing I signed was the release form. Hell, I can't read, I don't know what they had on that paper! I ain't signed nothing about sending Gabe away.

ROSE: I said send him to the hospital . . . you said let him be free . . . now you done went down there and signed him to the hospital for half his money. You went back on yourself, Troy. You gonna have to answer for that.

TROY: See now . . . you been over there talking to Miss Pearl. She done got mad cause she ain't getting Gabe's rent money. That's all it is. She's liable to say anything.

ROSE: Troy, I seen where you signed the paper.

TROY: You ain't seen nothing I signed. What she doing got papers on my brother anyway? Miss Pearl telling a big fat lie. And I'm gonna tell her about it too! You ain't seen nothing I signed. Say . . . you ain't seen nothing I signed.

Rose exits into the house to answer the telephone. Presently she returns.

ROSE: Troy . . . that was the hospital. Alberta had the baby.

TROY: What she have? What is it?

ROSE: It's a girl.

TROY: I better get on down to the hospital to see her.

ROSE: Troy . . .

TROY: Rose . . . I got to see her now. That's only right . . . what's the matter . . . the baby's all right, ain't it?

ROSE: Alberta died having the baby.

TROY: Died . . . you say she's dead? Alberta's dead?

ROSE: They said they done all they could. They couldn't do nothing for her.

TROY: The baby? How's the baby?

ROSE: They say it's healthy. I wonder who's gonna bury her.

TROY: She had family, Rose. She wasn't living in the world by herself.

ROSE: I know she wasn't living in the world by herself.

TROY: Next thing you gonna want to know if she had any insurance.

ROSE: Troy, you ain't got to talk like that.

TROY: That's the first thing that jumped out your mouth. "Who's gonna bury her?" Like I'm fixing to take on that task for myself.

ROSE: I am your wife. Don't push me away.

TROY: I ain't pushing nobody away. Just give me some space. That's all. Just give me some room to breathe.

Rose exits into the house. Troy walks about the yard.

TROY *(with a quiet rage that threatens to consume him):* All right . . . Mr. Death. See now . . . I'm gonna tell you what I'm gonna do. I'm gonna take and build me a fence around this yard. See? I'm gonna build me a fence around what belongs to me. And then I want you to stay on the other side. See? You stay over there until you're ready for me. Then you come on. Bring your army. Bring your sickle. Bring your wrestling clothes. I ain't gonna fall down on my vigilance this time. You ain't gonna sneak up on me no more. When you ready for me . . . when the top of your list say Troy Maxson . . . that's when you come around here. You come up and knock on the front door. Ain't nobody else got nothing to do with this. This is between you and me. Man to man. You stay on the other side of that fence until you ready for me. Then you come up and knock on the front door. Anytime you want. I'll be ready for you.

The lights go down to black.

Scene III

The lights come up on the porch. It is late evening three days later. Rose sits listening to the ball game waiting for Troy. The final out of the game is made and Rose switches off the radio. Troy enters the yard carrying an infant wrapped in blankets. He stands back from the house and calls.

Rose enters and stands on the porch. There is a long, awkward silence, the weight of which grows heavier with each passing second.

TROY: Rose . . . I'm standing here with my daughter in my arms. She ain't but a wee bittie little old thing. She don't know nothing about grownups' business. She innocent . . . and she ain't got no mama.

ROSE: What you telling me for, Troy?

She turns and exits into the house.

TROY: Well . . . I guess we'll just sit out here on the porch.

He sits down on the porch. There is an awkward indelicateness about the way he handles the baby. His largeness engulfs and seems to swallow it. He speaks loud enough for Rose to hear.

A man's got to do what's right for him. I ain't sorry for nothing I done. It felt right in my heart. *(To the baby.)* What you smiling at? Your daddy's a big man. Got these great big old hands. But sometimes he's scared. And right now your daddy's scared cause we sitting out here and ain't got no home. Oh, I been homeless before. I ain't had no little baby with me. But I been homeless. You just be out on the road by your lonesome and you see one of them trains coming and you just kinda go like this . . .

He sings a lullaby.

Please, Mr. Engineer let a man ride the line
Please, Mr. Engineer let a man ride the line
I ain't got no ticket please let me ride the blinds

Rose enters from the house. Troy, hearing her steps behind him, stands and faces her.

She's my daughter, Rose. My own flesh and blood. I can't deny her no more than I can deny them boys. *(Pause.)* You and them boys is my family. You and them and this child is all I got in the world. So I guess what I'm saying is . . . I'd appreciate it if you'd help me take care of her.

ROSE: Okay, Troy . . . you're right. I'll take care of your baby for you . . . cause . . . like you say . . . she's innocent . . . and you can't visit the sins of the father upon the child. A motherless child has got a hard time. *(She takes the baby from him.)* From right now . . . this child got a mother. But you a womanless man.

Rose turns and exits into the house with the baby. Lights go down to black.

Scene IV

It is two months later. Lyons enters from the street. He knocks on the door and calls.

LYONS: Hey, Rose! *(Pause.)* Rose!

ROSE *(from inside the house):* Stop that yelling. You gonna wake up Raynell. I just got her to sleep.

LYONS: I just stopped by to pay Papa this twenty dollars I owe him. Where's Papa at?

ROSE: He should be here in a minute. I'm getting ready to go down to the church. Sit down and wait on him.

LYONS: I got to go pick up Bonnie over her mother's house.

ROSE: Well, sit it down there on the table. He'll get it.

LYONS *(enters the house and sets the money on the table):* Tell Papa I said thanks. I'll see you again.

ROSE: All right, Lyons. We'll see you.

Lyons starts to exit as Cory enters.

CORY: Hey, Lyons.

LYONS: What's happening, Cory? Say man, I'm sorry I missed your graduation. You know I had a gig and couldn't get away. Otherwise, I would have been there, man. So what you doing?

CORY: I'm trying to find a job.

LYONS: Yeah I know how that go, man. It's rough out here. Jobs are scarce.

CORY: Yeah, I know.

LYONS: Look here, I got to run. Talk to Papa . . . he know some people. He'll be able to help get you a job. Talk to him . . . see what he say.

CORY: Yeah . . . all right, Lyons.

LYONS: You take care. I'll talk to you soon. We'll find some time to talk.

Lyons exits the yard. Cory wanders over to the tree, picks up the bat, and assumes a batting stance. He studies an imaginary pitcher and swings. Dissatisfied with the result, he tries again. Troy enters. They eye each other for a beat. Cory puts the bat down and exits the yard. Troy starts into the house as Rose exits with Raynell. She is carrying a cake.

TROY: I'm coming in and everybody's going out.

ROSE: I'm taking this cake down to the church for the bake sale. Lyons was by to see you. He stopped by to pay you your twenty dollars. It's laying in there on the table.

TROY *(going into his pocket):* Well . . . here go this money.

ROSE: Put it in there on the table, Troy. I'll get it.

TROY: What time you coming back?

ROSE: Ain't no use in you studying me. It don't matter what time I come back.

TROY: I just asked you a question, woman. What's the matter . . . can't I ask you a question?

ROSE: Troy, I don't want to go into it. Your dinner's in there on the stove. All you got to do is heat it up. And don't you be eating the rest of them cakes in there. I'm coming back for them. We having a bake sale at the church tomorrow.

Rose exits the yard. Troy sits down on the steps, takes a pint bottle from his pocket, opens it, and drinks. He begins to sing.

TROY: Hear it ring! Hear it ring!
Had an old dog his name was Blue
You know Blue was mighty true
You know Blue was a good old dog
Blue trees a possum in a hollow log
You know from that he was a good old dog

Bono enters the yard.

BONO: Hey, Troy.

TROY: Hey, what's happening, Bono?

BONO: I just thought I'd stop by to see you.

TROY: What you stop by and see me for? You ain't stopped by in a month of Sundays. Hell, I must owe you money or something.

BONO: Since you got your promotion I can't keep up with you. Used to see you every day. Now I don't even know what route you working.

TROY: They keep switching me around. Got me out in Greentree now . . . hauling white folks' garbage.

BONO: Greentree, huh? You lucky, at least you ain't got to be lifting them barrels. Damn if they ain't getting heavier. I'm gonna put in my two years and call it quits.

TROY: I'm thinking about retiring myself.

BONO: You got it easy. You can *drive* for another five years.

TROY: It ain't the same, Bono. It ain't like working the back of the truck. Ain't got nobody to talk to . . . feel like you working by yourself. Naw, I'm thinking about retiring. How's Lucille?

BONO: She all right. Her arthritis get to acting up on her sometime. Saw Rose on my way in. She going down to the church, huh?

TROY: Yeah, she took up going down there. All them preachers looking for somebody to fatten their pockets. *(Pause.)* Got some gin here.

BONO: Naw, thanks. I just stopped by to say hello.

TROY: Hell, nigger . . . you can take a drink. I ain't never known you to say no to a drink. You ain't got to work tomorrow.

BONO: I just stopped by. I'm fixing to go over to Skinner's. We got us a domino game going over his house every Friday.

TROY: Nigger, you can't play no dominoes. I used to whup you four games out of five.

BONO: Well, that learned me. I'm getting better.

TROY: Yeah? Well, that's all right.

BONO: Look here . . . I got to be getting on. Stop by sometime, huh?

TROY: Yeah, I'll do that, Bono. Lucille told Rose you bought her a new refrigerator.

BONO: Yeah, Rose told Lucille you had finally built your fence . . . so I figured we'd call it even.

TROY: I knew you would.

BONO: Yeah . . . okay. I'll be talking to you.

TROY: Yeah, take care, Bono. Good to see you. I'm gonna stop over.

BONO: Yeah. Okay, Troy.

Bono exits. Troy drinks from the bottle.

TROY: Old Blue died and I dig his grave
Let him down with a golden chain
Every night when I hear old Blue bark
I know Blue treed a possum in Noah's Ark.
Hear it ring! Hear it ring!

Cory enters the yard. They eye each other for a beat. Troy is sitting in the middle of the steps. Cory walks over.

CORY: I got to get by.

TROY: Say what? What's you say?

CORY: You in my way. I got to get by.

TROY: You got to get by where? This is my house. Bought and paid for. In full. Took me fifteen years. And if you wanna go in my house and I'm sitting on the steps . . . you say excuse me. Like your mama taught you.

CORY: Come on, Pop . . . I got to get by.

Cory starts to maneuver his way past Troy. Troy grabs his leg and shoves him back.

TROY: You just gonna walk over top of me?

CORY: I live here too!

TROY *(advancing toward him):* You just gonna walk over top of me in my own house?

CORY: I ain't scared of you.

TROY: I ain't asked if you was scared of me. I asked if you was fixing to walk over top of me in my own house? That's the question. You ain't gonna say excuse me? You just gonna walk over top of me?

CORY: If you wanna put it like that.

TROY: How else am I gonna put it?

CORY: I was walking by you to go into the house cause you sitting on the steps drunk, singing to yourself. You can put it like that.

TROY: Without saying excuse me???

Cory doesn't respond.

I asked you a question. Without saying excuse me???

CORY: I ain't got to say excuse me to you. You don't count around here no more.

TROY: Oh, I see . . . I don't count around here no more. You ain't got to say excuse me to your daddy. All of a sudden you done got so grown that your daddy don't count around here no more . . . Around here in his own house and yard that he done paid for with the sweat of his brow. You done got so grown to where you gonna take over. You gonna take over my house. Is that right? You gonna wear my pants. You gonna go in there and stretch out on my bed. You ain't got to say excuse me cause I don't count around here no more. Is that right?

CORY: That's right. You always talking this dumb stuff. Now, why don't you just get out of my way?

TROY: I guess you got someplace to sleep and something to put in your belly. You got that, huh? You got that? That's what you need. You got that, huh?

CORY: You don't know what I got. You ain't got to worry about what I got.

TROY: You right! You one hundred percent right! I done spent the last seventeen years worrying about what you got. Now it's your turn, see? I'll tell you what to do. You grown . . . we done established that. You a man. Now, let's see you act like one. Turn your behind around and walk out this yard. And when you get out there in the alley . . . you can forget about this house. See? Cause this is my house. You go on and be a man and get your own house. You can forget about this. Cause this is mine. You go on and get yours cause I'm through with doing for you.

CORY: You talking about what you did for me . . . what'd you ever give me?

TORY: Them feet and bones! That pumping heart, nigger! I give you more than anybody else is ever gonna give you.

CORY: You ain't never gave me nothing! You ain't never done nothing but hold me back. Afraid I was gonna be better than you. All you ever did was try and make me scared of you. I used to tremble every time you called my name. Every time I heard your footsteps in the house. Wondering all the time . . . what's Papa gonna say if I do this? . . . What's he gonna say if I do that? . . . What's Papa gonna say if I turn on the radio? And Mama, too . . . she tries . . . but she's scared of you.

TROY: You leave your mama out of this. She ain't got nothing to do with this.

CORY: I don't know how she stand you . . . after what you did to her.

TROY: I told you to leave your mama out of this!

He advances toward Cory.

CORY: What you gonna do . . . give me a whupping? You can't whup me no more. You're too old. You just an old man.

TROY *(shoves him on his shoulder):* Nigger! That's what you are. You just another nigger on the street to me!

CORY: You crazy! You know that?

TROY: Go on now! You got the devil in you. Get on away from me!

CORY: You just a crazy old man . . . talking about I got the devil in me.

TROY: Yeah, I'm crazy! If you don't get on the other side of that yard . . . I'm gonna show you how crazy I am! Go on . . . get the hell out of my yard.

CORY: It ain't your yard. You took Uncle Gabe's money he got from the army to buy this house and then you put him out.

TROY *(advances on Cory):* Get your black ass out of my yard!

Troy's advance backs Cory up against the tree. Cory grabs up the bat.

CORY: I ain't going nowhere! Come on . . . put me out! I ain't scared of you.

TROY: That's my bat!

CORY: Come on!

TROY: Put my bat down!

CORY: Come on, put me out.

Cory swings at Troy, who backs across the yard.

What's the matter? You so bad . . . put me out!

Troy advances toward Cory.

CORY *(backing up):* Come on! Come on!

TROY: You're gonna have to use it! You wanna draw that bat back on me . . . you're gonna have to use it.

CORY: Come on! . . . Come on!

Cory swings the bat at Troy a second time. He misses. Troy continues to advance toward him.

TROY: You're gonna have to kill me! You wanna draw that bat back on me. You're gonna have to kill me.

Cory, backed up against the tree, can go no farther. Troy taunts him. He sticks out his head and offers him a target.

Come on! Come on!

Cory is unable to swing the bat. Troy grabs it.

TROY: Then I'll show you.

Cory and Troy struggle over the bat. The struggle is fierce and fully engaged. Troy ultimately is the stronger and takes the bat from Cory and stands over him ready to swing. He stops himself.

Go on and get away from around my house.

Cory, stung by his defeat, picks himself up, walks slowly out of the yard and up the alley.

CORY: Tell Mama I'll be back for my things.
TROY: They'll be on the other side of that fence.

Cory exits.

TROY: I can't taste nothing. Helluljah! I can't taste nothing no more. *(Troy assumes a batting posture and begins to taunt Death, the fastball on the outside corner.)* Come on! It's between you and me now! Come on! Anytime you want! Come on! I be ready for you . . . but I ain't gonna be easy.

The lights go down on the scene.

Scene V

The time is 1965. The lights come up in the yard. It is the morning of Troy's funeral. A funeral plaque with a light hangs beside the door. There is a small garden plot off to the side. There is noise and activity in the house as Rose, Gabriel, and Bono have gathered. The door opens and Raynell, seven years old, enters dressed in a flannel nightgown. She crosses to the garden and pokes around with a stick. Rose calls from the house.

ROSE: Raynell!
RAYNELL: Mam?
ROSE: What you doing out there?
RAYNELL: Nothing.

Rose comes to the door.

ROSE: Girl, get in here and get dressed. What you doing?
RAYNELL: Seeing if my garden growed.
ROSE: I told you it ain't gonna grow overnight. You got to wait.
RAYNELL: It don't look like it never gonna grow. Dag!
ROSE: I told you a watched pot never boils. Get in here and get dressed.
RAYNELL: This ain't even no pot, Mama.
ROSE: You just have to give it a chance. It'll grow. Now you come on and do what I told you. We got to be getting ready. This ain't no morning to be playing around. You hear me?
RAYNELL: Yes, mam.

Rose exits into the house. Raynell continues to poke at her garden with a stick. Cory enters. He is dressed in a Marine corporal's uniform, and carries a duffel bag. His posture is that of a military man, and his speech has a clipped sternness.

CORY *(to Raynell):* Hi. *(Pause.)* I bet your name is Raynell.
RAYNELL: Uh huh.
CORY: Is your mama home?

Raynell runs up on the porch and calls through the screen door.

RAYNELL: Mama . . . there's some man out here. Mama?

Rose comes to the door.

ROSE: Cory? Lord have mercy! Look here, you all!

Rose and Cory embrace in a tearful reunion as Bono and Lyons enter from the house dressed in funeral clothes.

BONO: Aw, looka here . . .
ROSE: Done got all grown up!
CORY: Don't cry, Mama. What you crying about?
ROSE: I'm just so glad you made it.
CORY: Hey Lyons. How you doing, Mr. Bono.

Lyons goes to embrace Cory.

LYONS: Look at you, man. Look at you. Don't he look good, Rose. Got them Corporal stripes.
ROSE: What took you so long?
CORY: You know how the Marines are, Mama. They got to get all their paperwork straight before they let you do anything.
ROSE: Well, I'm sure glad you made it. They let Lyons come. Your Uncle Gabe's still in the hospital. They don't know if they gonna let him out or not. I just talked to them a little while ago.
LYONS: A Corporal in the United States Marines.
BONO: Your daddy knew you had it in you. He used to tell me all the time.
LYONS: Don't he look good, Mr. Bono?
BONO: Yeah, he remind me of Troy when I first met him. *(Pause.)* Say, Rose, Lucille's down at the church with the choir. I'm gonna go down and get the pallbearers lined up. I'll be back to get you all.
ROSE: Thanks, Jim.
CORY: See you, Mr. Bono.
LYONS *(with his arm around Raynell):* Cory . . . look at Raynell. Ain't she precious? She gonna break a whole lot of hearts.
ROSE: Raynell, come and say hello to your brother. This is your brother, Cory. You remember Cory.
RAYNELL: No, Mam.
CORY: She don't remember me, Mama.
ROSE: Well, we talk about you. She heard us talk about you. *(To Raynell.)* This is your brother, Cory. Come on and say hello.
RAYNELL: Hi.
CORY: Hi. So you're Raynell! Mama told me a lot about you.
ROSE: You all come on into the house and let me fix you some breakfast. Keep up your strength.
CORY: I ain't hungry, Mama.
LYONS: You can fix me something, Rose. I'll be in there in a minute.
ROSE: Cory, you sure you don't want nothing? I know they ain't feeding you right.
CORY: No, Mama . . . thanks. I don't feel like eating. I'll get something later.
ROSE: Raynell . . . get on upstairs and get that dress on like I told you.

Rose and Raynell exit into the house.

LYONS: So . . . I hear you thinking about getting married.
CORY: Yeah, I done found the right one, Lyons. It's about time.
LYONS: Me and Bonnie been split up about four years now. About the time Papa retired. I guess she just got tired of all them changes I was putting her through.

(Pause.) I always knew you was gonna make something out yourself. Your head was always in the right direction. So . . . you gonna stay in . . . make it a career . . . put in your twenty years?

CORY: I don't know. I got six already, I think that's enough.

LYONS: Stick with Uncle Sam and retire early. Ain't nothing out here. I guess Rose told you what happened with me. They got me down the workhouse. I thought I was being slick cashing other people's checks.

CORY: How much time you doing?

LYONS: They give me three years. I got that beat now. I ain't got but nine more months. It ain't so bad. You learn to deal with it like anything else. You got to take the crookeds with the straights. That's what Papa used to say. He used to say that when he struck out. I seen him strike out three times in a row . . . and the next time up he hit the ball over the grandstand. Right out there in Homestead Field. He wasn't satisfied hitting in the seats . . . he want to hit it over everything! After the game he had two hundred people standing around waiting to shake his hand. You got to take the crookeds with the straights. Yeah, Papa was something else.

CORY: You still playing?

LYONS: Cory . . . you know I'm gonna do that. There's some fellows down there we got us a band . . . we gonna try and stay together when we get out . . . but yeah, I'm still playing. It still helps me to get out of bed in the morning. As long as it do that I'm gonna be right there playing and trying to make some sense out of it.

ROSE *(calling):* Lyons, I got these eggs in the pan.

LYONS: Let me go on and get these eggs, man. Get ready to go bury Papa. *(Pause.)* How you doing? You doing all right?

Cory nods. Lyons touches him on the shoulder and they share a moment of silent grief. Lyons exits into the house. Cory wanders about the yard. Raynell enters.

RAYNELL: Hi.

CORY: Hi.

RAYNELL: Did you used to sleep in my room?

CORY: Yeah . . . that used to be my room.

RAYNELL: That's what Papa call it. "Cory's room." It got your football in the closet.

Rose comes to the door.

ROSE: Raynell, get in there and get them good shoes on.

RAYNELL: Mama, can't I wear these? Them other one hurt my feet.

ROSE: Well, they just gonna have to hurt your feet for a while. You ain't said they hurt your feet when you went down to the store and got them.

RAYNELL: They didn't hurt then. My feet done got bigger.

ROSE: Don't you give me no backtalk now. You get in there and get them shoes on.

Raynell exits into the house.

Ain't too much changed. He still got that piece of rag tied to that tree. He was out here swinging that bat. I was just ready to go back in the house. He swung that bat and then he just fell over. Seem like he swung it and stood there with this grin on his face . . . and then he just fell over. They carried him on down to the hospital, but I knew there wasn't no need . . . why don't you come on in the house?

CORY: Mama . . . I got something to tell you. I don't know how to tell you this . . . but I've got to tell you . . . I'm not going to Papa's funeral.

ROSE: Boy, hush your mouth. That's your daddy you talking about. I don't want hear that kind of talk this morning. I done raised you to come to this? You standing there all healthy and grown talking about you ain't going to your daddy's funeral?

CORY: Mama . . . listen . . .

ROSE: I don't want to hear it, Cory. You just get that thought out of your head.

CORY: I can't drag Papa with me everywhere I go. I've got to say no to him. One time in my life I've got to say no.

ROSE: Don't nobody have to listen to nothing like that. I know you and your daddy ain't seen eye to eye, but I ain't got to listen to that kind of talk this morning. Whatever was between you and your daddy . . . the time has come to put it aside. Just take it and set it over there on the shelf and forget about it. Disrespecting your daddy ain't gonna make you a man, Cory. You got to find a way to come to that on your own. Not going to your daddy's funeral ain't gonna make you a man.

CORY: The whole time I was growing up . . . living in his house . . . Papa was like a shadow that followed you everywhere. It weighed on you and sunk into your flesh. It would wrap around you and lay there until you couldn't tell which one was you anymore. That shadow digging in your flesh. Trying to crawl in. Trying to live through you. Everywhere I looked, Troy Maxson was staring back at me . . . hiding under the bed . . . in the closet. I'm just saying I've got to find a way to get rid of that shadow, Mama.

ROSE: You just like him. You got him in you good.

CORY: Don't tell me that, Mama.

ROSE: You Troy Maxson all over again.

CORY: I don't want to be Troy Maxson. I want to be me.

ROSE: You can't be nobody but who you are, Cory. That shadow wasn't nothing but you growing into yourself. You either got to grow into it or cut it down to fit you. But that's all you got to make life with. That's all you got to measure yourself against that world out there. Your daddy wanted you to be everything he wasn't . . . and at the same time he tried to make you into everything he was. I don't know if he was right or wrong . . . but I do know he meant to do more good than he meant to do harm. He wasn't always right. Sometimes when he touched he bruised. And sometimes when he took me in his arms he cut.

When I first met your daddy I thought . . . Here is a man I can lay down with and make a baby. That's the first thing I thought when I seen him. I was thirty years old and had done seen my share of men. But when he walked up to me and said, "I can dance a waltz that'll make you dizzy," I thought, Rose Lee, here is a man that you can open yourself up to and be filled to bursting. Here is a man that can fill all them empty spaces you been tipping around the edges of. One of them empty spaces was being somebody's mother.

I married your daddy and settled down to cooking his supper and keeping clean sheets on the bed. When your daddy walked through the house he was so big he filled it up. That was my first mistake. Not to make him leave some room for me. For my part in the matter. But at that time I wanted that. I wanted a house that I could sing in. And that's what your daddy gave me. I didn't know to keep up his strength I had to give up little pieces of mine. I did that. I took on his life as mine and mixed up the pieces so that you couldn't hardly tell which was which anymore. It was my choice. It was my life and I didn't have to live it like that. But that's what life offered me in the way of being a woman and I took it. I grabbed hold of it with both hands.

By the time Raynell came into the house, me and your daddy had done lost touch with one another. I didn't want to make my blessing off of nobody's misfortune . . . but I took on to Raynell like she was all them babies I had wanted and never had.

The phone rings.

Like I'd been blessed to relive a part of my life. And if the Lord see fit to keep up my strength . . . I'm gonna do her just like your daddy did you . . . I'm gonna give her the best of what's in me.

RAYNELL *(entering, still with her old shoes):* Mama . . . Reverend Tollivier on the phone.

Rose exits into the house.

RAYNELL: Hi.
CORY: Hi.
RAYNELL: You in the Army or the Marines?
CORY: Marines.
RAYNELL: Papa said it was the Army. Did you know Blue?
CORY: Blue? Who's Blue?
RAYNELL: Papa's dog what he sing about all the time.
CORY *(singing):* Hear it ring! Hear it ring!
I had a dog his name was Blue
You know Blue was mighty true
You know Blue was a good old dog
Blue treed a possum in a hollow log
You know from that he was a good old dog.
Hear it ring! Hear it ring!

Raynell joins in singing.

CORY AND RAYNELL: Blue treed a possum out on a limb
Blue looked at me and I looked at him
Grabbed that possum and put him in a sack
Blue stayed there till I came back
Old Blue's feets was big and round
Never allowed a possum to touch the ground.

Old Blue died and I dug his grave
I dug his grave with a silver spade
Let him down with a golden chain
And every night I call his name
Go on Blue, you good dog you
Go on Blue, you good dog you

RAYNELL: Blue laid down and died like a man
Blue laid down and died . . .
BOTH: Blue laid down and died like a man
Now he's treeing possums in the Promised Land
I'm gonna tell you this to let you know
Blue's gone where the good dogs go
When I hear old Blue bark
When I hear old Blue bark
Blue treed a possum in Noah's Ark
Blue treed a possum in Noah's Ark.

Rose comes to the screen door.

ROSE: Cory, we gonna be ready to go in a minute.
CORY *(to Raynell):* You go on in the house and change them shoes like Mama told you so we can to go Papa's funeral.
RAYNELL: Okay, I'll be back.

Raynell exits into the house. Cory gets up and crosses over to the tree. Rose stands in the screen door watching him. Gabriel enters from the alley.

GABRIEL *(calling):* Hey, Rose!
ROSE: Gabe?
GABRIEL: I'm here, Rose. Hey Rose, I'm here!

Rose enters from the house.

ROSE: Lord . . . Look here, Lyons!
LYONS: See, I told you Rose . . . I told you they'd let him come.
CORY: How you doing, Uncle Gabe?
LYONS: How you doing, Uncle Gabe?
GABRIEL: Hey, Rose. It's time. It's time to tell St. Peter to open the gates. Troy, you ready? You ready, Troy. I'm gonna tell St. Peter to open the gates. You get ready now.

Gabriel, with great fanfare, braces himself to blow. The trumpet is without a mouthpiece. He puts the end of it into his mouth and blows with great force, like a man who has been waiting some twenty-odd years for this single moment. No sound comes out of the trumpet. He braces himself and blows again with the same result. A third time he blows. There is a weight of impossible description that falls away and leaves him bare and exposed to a frightful realization. It is a trauma that a sane and normal mind would be unable to withstand. He begins to dance. A slow, strange dance, eerie and life-giving. A dance of atavistic signature and ritual. Lyons attempts to embrace him. Gabriel pushes Lyons away. He begins to howl in what is an attempt at song, or perhaps a song turning back into itself in an attempt at speech. He finishes his dance and the gates of heaven stand open as wide as God's closet.

That's the way that go!

A Critical Perspective: **Michael Awkward** (1959–)

Literary critic Michael Awkward teaches English and Afro-American Studies at the University of Michigan, where he is also director of the Center for Afro-American and African Studies. He has written two books of literary criticism— Inspiriting Influences: Tradition, Revision, and Afro-American Women's Novels *(1989) and* Negotiating Difference: Race, Gender, and the Politics of Positionality (1995)*—and edited* New Essays on Their Eyes Were Watching God (1990).

The following essay, " 'The Crookeds with the Straights': Fences, *Race, and the Politics of Adaptation," appeared in an anthology of critical essays on August Wilson titled* May All Your Fences Have Gates *(1994) edited by Alan Nadel. In the essay (appearing here in a truncated version), Awkward provides an illuminating analysis of the symbolic motifs that permeate the play and Wilson's skillful development of characters, themes, and dramatic structure.*

"The Crookeds with the Straights": *Fences,* Race, and the Politics of Adaptation

I want to turn now to Wilson's *Fences* itself, a text which we might consider one of the "strong and effective vehicles that have become the flag-bearers for [Afro-American] self-determination and self-identity." The play, which explores, among other matters, male intergenerational conflict and the motivations for and repercussions of the protragonist's extramarital affair, is peopled with characters who attempt to erect domestic and social boundaries—literal and figurative fences, if you will—as a means of marking both domestic space itself and its inhabitants as "property and possession" in order to shield them from the corruptive and/or murderous forces of the outside world while at the same time protecting the marking subject from the threat of abandonment. Ultimately, I want to investigate the play's examination of the possibilities of erecting protective fences around black familial space in terms of the quite different trajectory of Wilson's efforts to find a black film director in order to protect his creation from potentially contaminating caucacentric forces. While the playwright orchestrates the search primarily for what are ideologically justifiable reasons, its perspectives appear on the surface at least to be at odds with *Fences'* inquiry into the advisability of protectionist imperatives.

An interrogation of boundaries commences in the play's first act, which offers a series of pointed delineations of the social and personal restrictions placed on racial and gendered interaction which the play's protagonist, Troy Maxson, seeks to negotiate. *Fences* begins with Troy and Jim Bono entering the former's partially fenced yard on "Friday night, payday, and the one night of the week the two men engage in a ritual of talk and drink" [471].* This ritualistic space is filled immediately with discussion of contrasting means of responding to racially motivated socioeconomic inequality. In the first instance, Troy describes one such type of negotiation whose rejection serves as a means by which to introduce both Troy's subversive act and Wilson's own afrocentric thematics.

* Bracketed numbers refer to page number in *Fences*.

> *Troy:* I ain't lying. The nigger had a watermelon this big. Talking about . . . "What watermelon, Mr. Rand?" I liked to fell out! "What watermelon, Mr. Rand?" . . . And it sitting there big as life.
>
> *Bono:* What did Mr. Rand say?
>
> *Troy:* Ain't said nothing. Figure if the nigger too dumb to know he carrying a watermelon, he wasn't gonna get much sense out of him. Trying to hide that great big old watermelon under his coat. Afraid to let the white man see him carry it home. [471–472]

In its reference to watermelons, apparent black simpletons, and white male authority figures involved in a comic interchange about petty larceny, Troy's language recalls—and rejects vehemently as a mode of interracial interchange—a tradition of minstrelsy which, according to Houston Baker, is characterized by "nonsense, misappropriation, or mis-hearing."[1] At one time a popular theatrical behavior which operated as a dramatic formalizing of hegemonically enforced manners of black behavior, minstrelsy was a "device," according to Baker designed to remind white consciousness that black men and women are mis-speakers bereft of humanity—carefree devils strumming and humming all day—unless, in a gaslight misidentification, they are violent devils fit for lynching, a final exorcism that will leave whites alone.[2]

Wilson sets the stage, as it were, for a different style of black dramatic representation by offering, in the play's first words, discursive structures which both recall and forcefully repudiate this comically inflected modality whose social practice had previously constituted a means by which to contain both white and black violent impulses. In other words, the play's opening scene attempts to bracket or set containing boundaries around traditional notions of black theatrical representation, thereby insisting that what follows will not conform to the nonsense syllables and actions characteristic of black participation in the theater of America historically. After relegating this manner of negotiating social difference to the realm of the antiquated—Bono says pointedly, "I'm like you . . . I ain't got no time for them kind of people" [472]—the men then begin to discuss Troy's enactment of other, newer strategies of black behavior whose purpose is to effect social change.

> *Troy:* I ain't worried about them firing me. They gonna fire me cause I asked a question? That's all I did. I went to Mr. Rand and asked him, "Why? Why you got the white mens driving and the colored lifting?" Told him, "what's the matter, don't I count? You think only white fellows got sense enough to drive a truck. That ain't no paper job! Hell, anybody can drive a truck. How come you got all whites driving and the colored lifting?" He told me "take it to the union." Well, hell, that's what I done! Now they wanna come up with this pack of lies. [472]

If minstrel performances such as those of the watermelon-stealing "nigger" (and scores of other Afro-Americans in their interactions with representatives of a white hegemonic structure) might be effectively characterized in terms of the serious play with pejorative racist stereotypes and other extant cultural forms which Baker calls "the mastery of form," then Troy's insurgent act, which insists on white confirmation of its responsibilities to ensuring constitutionally guaranteed Afro-American rights, might be viewed as an instance of a black "deformation of mastery." For Baker, "deformation is a go(uer)rilla action in the face of acknowledged adversaries."[3] While watermelon theft seeks as its end the temporary satisfaction of black desire, deformation—a formal challenge to the racially hierarchical status quo—attempts to delegitimize permanently the hegemonic structures which have sought historically to contain and control that desire.

Troy and Bono move directly from the subject of negotiating interracial relations to an investigation of (hetero)sexual politics and dynamics. Specifically, they begin discussing "that Alberta gal" and the relative success of the efforts of males in their community—themselves included—in attracting her attention. Again they speak in terms of respecting (or rejecting) boundaries:

> *Bono:* . . . I see where you be eyeing her.
>
> *Troy:* I eye all the women. I don't miss nothing. Don't never let nobody tell you Troy Maxson don't eye the women.
>
> *Bono:* You been doing more than eyeing her. You done bought her a drink or two.
>
> *Troy:* Hell yeah, I bought her a drink! What that mean? I bought you one, too. What that mean cause I buy her a drink? I'm just being polite. [472]

What concerns Bono is that his friend, who Wilson's stage directions indicate is admirable to Bono because of his "honesty, capacity for hard work, and his strength" [471], is not cognizant of the potentially disruptive nature of his interest in Alberta to others' and Troy's own sense of his character and integrity. Indeed, as Bono later suggests, the threat of disruption, of dissolution of a lifestyle that she has come to see as normative, motivates Rose's desire to have a fence built around the Maxson home. As he tells Troy, "some people build fences to keep people out . . . and other people build fences to keep people in. Rose wants to hold on to you all. She loves you" [499]. Specifically, Bono is worried that Troy's attention to Alberta, which he is aware includes not only the polite purchase of "a drink or two" but also frequent visits to her apartment, suggests that his best friend may overstep the boundaries of acceptable marital behavior, that his actions may compromise his sense of self and his relationship with Rose, whom both men describe as "a good woman" [499]. Troy's extramarital desires trouble Bono not merely because of his concern for Troy's well-being but also because of his status as role model for Bono himself. As he tells Troy later in the play when he more directly confronts him with his suspicions:

> When you picked Rose, I was happy for you. That was the first time I knew you had any sense. I said . . . My man Troy knows what he's doing . . . I'm gonna follow this nigger . . . he might take me somewhere. I been following you too. I done learned a whole heap of things about life watching you. I done learned how to tell where the shit lies. How to tell it from the alfalfa. You done learned me a lot of things. You showed me how to not make the same mistakes . . . to take life as it comes along and keep putting one foot in front of the other. [499]

When Troy commences a more public relationship with Alberta, the affair eventuates in the dissolution of the rituals of friendship with Bono in part because the grounds upon which the intensity of the latter's admiration of the protagonist is based—evidence of Troy's clear-sightedness, his ability to understand and not be tempted to overstep the boundaries with which his life presents him—have been undercut.

One of *Fences'* most resonant examinations of boundaries appears in Troy's discussion with Lyons about the material and psychological benefits of gainful employment.

> *Troy:* I done learned my mistake and learned to do what's right by it. You still trying to get something for nothing. Life don't owe you nothing. You owe it to yourself . . .
>
> *Lyons:* You got your way of dealing with the world . . . I got mine. The only thing that matters to me is the music.
>
> *Troy:* Yeah, I can see that! It don't matter how you gonna eat . . . where your next dollar is coming from. You telling the truth there.
>
> *Lyons:* I know I got to eat. But I got to live too. I need something that gonna help me to get out of bed in the morning. Make me feel like I belong in the world. I don't bother nobody. I just stay with the music cause that's the only way I can find to live in the world. Otherwise there ain't no telling what I might do. [479]

Here we are presented with a contrast between what the play presents as two poles of available male behavior: Troy's hypermasculine sense of self-sacrifice and economic responsibility and Lyons's self-indulgent search for personal fulfillment. What is particularly striking about this scene is its principals' energetic articulation of positions which, at this moment in the history of their weekly ritual of filial money borrowing and paternal castigation, they preach much more energetically than practice. For Lyons is only minimally dedicated to his art (the stage directions which proceed his appearance describe him as "more caught up in the rituals and 'idea' of being a musician than in the actual practice of the music" [477]), and Troy has slipped from the lofty position from which he has somewhat self-righteously critiqued others. (Moreover, as we will see, Lyons's discourse of self-fulfillment and irresponsibility is later echoed in his father's description to Rose of the motivations for his infidelity.)

While in his talks with Lyons and, later, Cory about financial responsibility he demonstrates—though not without some authorial irony—some of the more admirable aspects of his character, in his discussion with his younger son about paternal displays of affection (both his own demonstration and those of his father) Troy most poignantly displays both his most positive and most negative dimensions. After Troy asserts that his son's continued participation in football depends on a near-impossible commitment to both housework and store employment, Cory asks whether his father's generally harsh treatment of him is motivated by a lack of paternal affection. Troy responds:

> Liked you? Who the hell say I got to like you? What law is there say I got to like you? Wanna stand up in my face and ask a damn fool-ass question like that. Talking about liking somebody. . . . I go out of here every morning . . . bust my butt . . . putting up with them crackers everyday . . . cause I like you? You about the biggest fool I ever saw . . . It's my job. It's my responsibility! You understand that? A man got to take care of his family. You live in my house . . . sleep you behind on my bedclothes . . . fill you belly up with my food . . . cause you my son. You

my flesh and blood. Not cause I like you! Cause it's my duty to take care of you. I owe a responsibility to you! . . . Mr. Rand don't give me my money come payday cause he likes me. He give me cause he owe me. . . . Don't you try and go through life worrying about if somebody like you or not. You best be making sure they doing right by you. You understand what I'm saying, boy? [488]

In Troy's estimation, Cory's question demonstrates that he is unaware of the boundaries of interpersonal responsibility, of the central role an economics of duty plays in profitable human interactions. While this perspective may encourage appropriate responses to a society characterized by deceit and institutionalized inequality, clearly it lacks the ability to foster an appreciation of the potential tenderness of intimate human relations. Put another way, Troy's economics of duty—learned from an abusive father so embittered by his parental "responsibility" to "eleven children" that "all his women run off and left him" [494]—leaves him poorly equipped to deal with the emotional demands of intimate personal relations. "[D]oing right," in such relations, is not merely providing clean sheets and nourishing foods, but also demonstrating an intense concern about the psychic welfare of those for whom one has assumed responsibility. Troy's discussion of familial duty, then, reflects inherent flaws in his worldview caused, it would appear, by his failure to attend to important aspects of intimacy.

I am suggesting, then, that at the point at which we meet him, Troy's code of living is defective because it leaves no space for a pursuit of self-fulfillment. While this self-protective mechanism of boundary maintenance serves effectively to check the impulse toward familial abandonment which Troy terms the "walking blues" [494], a condition manifested in the form of "a fellow moving around from place to place . . . woman to woman . . . searching out the New Land" [493], it is limited as a means of responding to the full range of human emotional possibilities.

Apparently, as his discussions with both Bono and Rose about his affair attest, he recognizes that the absence of joy in his own life renders him unable to reconcile his words and actions to the philosophical views by which he had been governed. When Troy states, for example, "I can't shake her loose," Bono insists that he remain true to his oft-stated perspectives on individual culpability and responsibility:

Bono: You's in control . . . that's what you tell me all the time. You responsible for what you do.

Troy: I ain't ducking the responsibility of it. As long as it sets right in my heart . . . then I'm okay. Cause that's all I listen to. It'll tell me right from wrong every time. And I ain't talking about doing Rose no bad turn. I love Rose. She done carried me a long ways and I love and respect her for that. [499]

His intentions not to do Rose a "bad turn" and his faith in his "heart" notwithstanding, his manner of constructing his motives for infidelity makes it clear that the pursuit of self-fulfillment has served effectively to block his limited capacity to attend to his wife's feelings:

It's just . . . She gives me a different idea . . . a different understanding about myself. I can step out of this house and get away from the pressures and problems . . .

be a different man. I ain't got to wonder how I'm gonna pay the bills or get the roof fixed. I can just be a part of myself that I ain't never been. . . . I can sit up in her house and laugh . . . I can laugh out loud . . . and it feels good. It reaches all the way down to the bottom of my shoes. *(Pause.)* Rose, I can't give that up. [502]

After an interchange most notable, in my view, for its evidence of the participants' communicative gaps or discursive boundaries (he employs baseball metaphors, a mode of discourse which Rose considers inappropriate, telling him, "We're not talking about baseball! We're talking about you going off to lay in bed with another woman . . . and then bring it home to me"), Troy seeks to win his wife's sympathy by turning his attention to the difficulty he has encountered in being confronted with evidence of his inadequacy.

Troy: Rose, you're not listening to me. I'm trying the best I can to explain it to you. It's not easy for me to admit that I been standing in the same place for eighteen years.

Rose: I been standing with you! I been right here with you, Troy. I got a life too. I gave eighteen years of my life to stand in the same spot with you. Don't you think I ever wanted other things? . . . What about my life? What about me. Don't you think it ever crossed my mind to want to know other men. That I wanted to lay up somewhere and forget about my responsibilities? That I wanted someone to make me laugh so I could feel good? You not the only one who's got wants and needs. But I held on to you, Troy. I took all my feelings, my wants and needs, my dreams . . . and I buried them inside you. I planted a seed and watched and prayed over it. I planted myself inside you and waited to bloom. And it didn't take me no eighteen years to find out the soil was hard and rocky and it wasn't never gonna bloom. [503]

Rose shifts the discursive ground from a masculinist metaphorics of individually determined psychic and socioeconomic advancement to a nature-centered figuration of the growth of the un(der)developed. In figuring the interior spaces of the self-protective male as potential uterine site of her own development, Rose defies—and, in fact, denies—the limitations of both the biological and Troy's economics of duty. Just as Troy believes that imparting to Cory his philosophy of financial self-support will allow him to discharge his parental responsibilities in a sufficient manner, so, too, does he feel that by sleeping every night with and turning over his weekly pay to Rose he is meeting his marital duties. The costs of accommodating herself to this worldview by containing and thereby ignoring her own desires are extremely high for Rose, as she tells Cory upon his return to the house from which he had been banished for his father's funeral:

I married your daddy and settled down to cooking his supper and keeping clean sheets on the bed. When your daddy walked through the house he was so big he filled it up. That was my first mistake. Not to make him leave some room for me. For my part in the matter. But at that time I wanted that. I wanted a house that I could sing in. And that's what your daddy gave me. I didn't know to keep up his strength I had to give up little pieces of mine. I did that. . . . It was my choice. It was my life and I didn't have to live it like that. But that's what life offered me

> in the way of being a woman and I took it. I grabbed hold of it with both hands. [515]

Rose describes here the consequences of her efforts to achieve her dèsire for material space, which include, most importantly, her failure to pursue her own desires in order to direct her attentions to satisfying the wishes of her forceful husband. Given the gender politics of the period and the direct correlation between Rose's self-sacrifice and Troy's fairly stable and positive self-image—as she says, "to keep up his strength I had to give up little pieces of mine"—her immolation apparently was necessary in order to stave off the onset of a masculinist "walking blues." To put the matter somewhat differently, the cost of the maintenance of material space for even a restricted articulation of female song is the loss of verbal strength and the possibility of self-actualization within a domicile dominated by Troy's pragmatic economics of duty. The fences that Troy and Rose place around their marriage, their feelings, and their unarticulated desires for a more fulfilling existence are effective while these characters exclude intense self-investigation from their rituals of living. The price both pay for self-protection—for the protective barriers of "fences"—includes stagnation and the repression of cognition of intense dissatisfaction. . . .

Until more-comprehensive changes are made to the basic structure of American society where the questions of racial and cultural differences are concerned—changes that will affect the grammar of motives upon which significant aspects of our shared culture is constructed—seemingly important transformations such as Troy's improved employment status, August Wilson's own success as a dramatist, and Hollywood's recent interest in sophisticated representations of Afro-American life such as *Fences* will constitute merely local, individual victories. Wilson seems cognizant of one of American hegemony's strategies of operation vis-à-vis the oppressed wherein it presents impressive gifts to individual members of disenfranchised groups as a substitute for a wider redistribution of its socioeconomic and cultural assets, and he is apparently less concerned with personal profit from the returns for a film version of his play than in employing the cultural capital he has earned in order to assist efforts to ensure the continued alteration of racist American discourse that always already questions Afro-American qualifications.

Despite his insistence at some points in "I Want a Black Director" to the contrary, whether or not whites can understand and disseminate the culturally specific aspects of *Fences* is not the most central issue in Wilson's formulation of his position. Of preeminent importance to the playwright, I believe, is whether, given the persistence of caucacentric discourse and actions in our nation, Afro-Americans can afford to allow patterns of expressive cultural distribution to continue wherein blacks remain pawns to the whims and racialist will of white entrepreneurial forces interested primarily in economic bottom lines rather than in working to destroy the still-evident barriers to social, economic, and cultural power for a large portion of the black population. . . .

NOTES

1. Houston A. Baker, Jr., *Modernism and the Harlem Renaissance*. Chicago: University of Chicago Press, 1987, p. 18.
2. Ibid., p. 21.
3. Ibid., p. 50.

DRAMA SELECTION

Pearl Cleage (1948–)

A*n eminent poet, fiction writer, essayist, and playwright, Pearl Cleage says she writes "with a specific audience in mind. I know that my experiences as a black woman connect me in a very real way to contemporary African American women. . . . I'm always trying to get black women to show a nod of recognition—to say, 'Yeah! That's true!' If black men also have that feeling, if white women have it, or white men, if Native Americans have it—that's wonderful, but my main concern is . . . to truthfully convey what it is like to be a black woman here in America, at this moment."*

Born in Springfield, Massachusetts, her father, a minister, and her mother, a teacher, provided Cleage with a background filled with books and black liberation activism. After receiving a bachelor's degree from Spelman College in Atlanta in 1971, Cleage went on to do graduate study at Atlanta University, though she did not complete that degree.

Her professional career has included a mix of writing, broadcasting, and teaching. She worked at the Martin Luther King, Jr., Archival Library in Atlanta (1969–70) and served as an interviewer for Black Viewpoints, *a television show produced by WETV at Clark College (1970–71). After serving as director of communications for the City of Atlanta from 1974 to 1976, Cleage became an instructor at Emory University in 1978. Currently, she is the artistic director of Just Us Theater Company in Atlanta, a playwright-in-residence at the Spelman College Department of Theater and Drama, and the editor of* Catalyst *magazine.*

In addition to contributing to numerous periodicals, such as Afro-American Review, Essence, Atlanta Magazine, *and* New York Times Book Review, *Cleage has published several collections of her work in various genres. Her first book,* We Don't Need No Music *(1971) is a collection of poems. It was followed by two short story collections,* One for the Brothers *(1983) and* The Brass Bed and Other Stories *(1991); a book of nonfiction prose,* Mad at Miles: A Blackwoman's Guide to Truth *(1990); and a collection of personal essays,* Deals with the Devil *(1993).*

However, Cleage is best known for her prolific work as a playwright. In addition to numerous other performance pieces written for the stage, Cleage has seen ten of her plays produced: Hymn for the Rebels *(1968),* Duet for Three Voices *(1969),* The Sale *(1972),* puppetplay *(1983),* Hospice *(1983),* Good News *(1984),* Essentials *(1985),* Chain *(1991),* Last Bus to Mecca *(1991), and* Flyin' West *(1992).*

Hospice, *the one-act play that appears here, won a 1983 Audelco Recognition Award for outstanding achievement as an off-Broadway play. In this drama about the strained relationship of a terminally ill mother and her pregnant daughter, Cleage also examines middle-class ethics, black expatriatism, and the black writer's responsibilities to the black community.*

Hospice

A Play in One Act

Cast

ALICE ANDERSON, a black woman, age 47
JENNY ANDERSON, her daughter, age 30

(*The time is early morning. The set is a small house with upstairs and downstairs. The downstairs area is the main playing space, but the upstairs must be large enough to accommodate the bed, dresser with mirror, etc. This is* ALICE*'s bedroom.* JENNY *sleeps downstairs, but her bed is not visible. The house is small and crowded with the accumulated paraphernalia of a lifetime. The walls are full of framed photos of dead family. There is a couch with a comforter or soft, warm coverlet of some sort thrown across the back. A coffee table in front is piled high with newspapers, books, mail, papers and medicine bottles. On the table also is a vase holding a dozen beautiful, long-stemmed red roses. In the corner of the room is a small table piled almost as high as the coffee table with papers of various kinds. Somewhere in the middle is a typewriter. This is the area where* JENNY *writes. Tucked next to the table is a small suitcase. There is also a record player surrounded by record albums in and out of their covers. It is not an expensive, modern stereo, but has surprisingly good quality sound for its age and size. There are several brimming bookcases, some potted plants in various states of well-being, etc. The feeling of the room is cluttered, but not claustrophobic.*

An elaborately carved wooden cane sits against the record player. It is morning. Early. The light is that thin early morning kind that lets you know the sun is still undecided. As the lights come up, we hear the sound of a typewriter clicking away. The daughter, JENNY, *is hunched over her work. There is a floor lamp burning over her, creating a small pool of light in the eerie morning gloom.* JENNY *is thirty years old and very pregnant. She is frowning at the page which is still dangling from her typewriter. Re-reading over what she has just typed, she rips the page out and adds it to the small pile of crumpled balls at her feet. She shifts uncomfortably in her straight-back chair, and placing both hands behind her, arches her back, massaging the kinks out of her spine. She has been up for awhile. She shakes her head, and resumes her typing. Upstairs, her mother stirs and turns over in her bed restlessly with a soft moan. Hearing the noise,* JENNY *stops typing suddenly, listening. There is no immediate movement upstairs. She leans back to her work and is suddenly irritated by the fact that her very pregnant belly keeps her from getting as close to the table as she wants to. It is awkward. She tries turning sideways which means she has to type across her stomach. This is even more awkward. She tries several more approaches, but nothing works. During this process, the mother,* ALICE, *sits up slowly. She is in obvious pain. The upstairs light is always blue and dim. The impression is of silhouette and shadow.* ALICE *almost doubles over when she sits up, but straightens slowly and with great effort. She is thin and very frail. She is dying of cancer and her head is bald or very lightly fuzzed over with hair from chemotherapy. Her head should not be covered during the course of the play. Slowly and painfully her back straightens, her shoulders are square, and she finds the strength to push the covers off and slowly swing her legs over the side of the bed. She is wearing a long cotton nightgown with sleeves. The effort of sitting up has been very great. She remains motionless, seated on the edge of the bed.)*

JENNY (*loudly*): Well, damn! (*She has spoken more loudly than she meant to and looks guiltily upstairs.* ALICE*'s head looks up in the direction of the curse. When there is no follow-up sound, she droops again.* JENNY *rises and goes to the bottom of the stairs, listening. No sound from* ALICE. JENNY *seems obviously relieved and crosses back to sit down at her typewriter. She pours herself a cup of tea from the pot near her. She sips the tea slowly, reading over the page that is in the typewriter and absentmindedly stroking her belly. Suddenly,* JENNY *drops the pages and begins to pant rapidly. She is having a contraction. When it ends, she checks her watch and crosses slowly to the phone. She is excited, but trying to contain it. She dials quietly.*) Alexis? I'm sorry! I know it's early, but I think it's happening! Yes! Since early this morning . . . No. I'm okay . . . Yes . . . Alright . . . I'll call you later.

(*Upstairs,* ALICE *stands quietly and walks to the dresser. It is an old-fashioned wardrobe with a full-length mirror on the door. She slowly takes off her nightgown and looks at herself naked in the mirror. We see her in shadow, but it is clear that she is gazing at her body. She folds the nightgown and lays it on the bed. Downstairs,* JENNY *finishes her tea and resumes typing.* ALICE *dresses slowly. Underwear, long socks, long skirt, sweater buttoned over it all. She slips on her shoes and makes her slow, painful, laborious way down the stairs. Holding the bannister tightly, she manages it, but the effort to do it with such a straight back and measured gait is immense.* JENNY *is typing loudly, continuously, and is thoroughly absorbed in her work. She does not look up when* ALICE *reaches the bottom of the stairs and stops to catch her breath. After a moment,* ALICE *turns to look at* JENNY. JENNY, *typing furiously, is oblivious.* ALICE *walks slowly over to the record player and puts the needle down on the record already on the turntable. It is not the first cut on the album, but she goes right to the spot as if she'd done it a thousand times before. With sudden and unexpected richness, the strains of Leontyne Price singing Puccini's "Madame Butterfly" fill the room. It is "Un Bel Di."* JENNY *jumps, startled out of her reverie by the blast of music.* ALICE *moves slowly but with determination over to the couch and sits down slowly, eyes closed, listening to the music and trying not to give in to the pain.*)

JENNY: God! You scared me! (*She moves to turn down the record. No word from* ALICE.) I thought I heard you get up. (JENNY *moves to her desk and carefully takes her work out of the typewriter and puts it face down on her desk. No response from* ALICE. *Her eyes are closed. She is listening intently.*) Are you okay? (ALICE *looks at her, and* JENNY *looks a little guilty at what could be a loaded question.*)

ALICE (*sarcastic*): Never been better. What were you cussing about?

JENNY: What? Oh. I'm sorry. I got stuck in the middle of something. You know . . .

ALICE: I didn't mean to startle you. I wasn't ready to wake up yet.

JENNY: Did you sleep much?

ALICE: No.

JENNY: Me neither. I try to lie on my back, but after awhile, she gets so heavy, I feel like I'm smothering.

ALICE: Well, it won't be long now, as they say.

JENNY: As they say. You want some tea? I just made it a few minutes ago. (ALICE *nods but doesn't answer. She is listening. Eyes closed.* JENNY *goes for the tea.*)

ALICE: Turn it up a little, will you? (JENNY *stops at the record player and turns it up. The rest of "Un Bel Di" is sung by Leontyne Price as* JENNY *gets the tea and* ALICE *leans back, eyes closed, while she listens.* JENNY *brings the tea, standing quietly until the song finishes and then turns off the record.* ALICE *sits motionless for a few moments as if in a trance, then comes back to reality and sits fully erect, eyes open, back in touch with the world around her.* JENNY *hands* ALICE *her tea and goes back to her work.*) Deadline?

JENNY: Not really. I told them I wasn't going home to work. I was going home to have a baby! (*Laughs at her own determination.*) I knew I could get away with it. They've never had a black film critic before. (*Evasively.*) I'm working on a couple of things, but it's hard when the only deadlines are self-imposed.

ALICE: I've always found those to be the hardest ones to miss. Well, I hope you're not blaming this lack of discipline on me. This is your choice, you know. Just keep that in mind.

JENNY: Don't worry. I accept full responsibility.

ALICE: You should.

JENNY: I have.

ALICE (*a beat*): I envy your confidence, but I wish it didn't make you start typing quite so early in the morning.

JENNY (*very controlled*): I think you completed your bad night by getting up on the wrong side of the bed this morning. I said I'm sorry I woke you. I'll say it again, only because I really mean it. I'm sorry.

ALICE: Me too.

(JENNY *rises, stretches, and sits down Indian style on the floor. She has the soles of her feet together and is bouncing her knees toward the floor, pushing them down closer with every bounce. She continues as she speaks, trying to make "neutral conversation."*)

JENNY: Daddy laughed when I first started doing movie reviews. He thought it was the perfect job for me. We used to go to the movies all the time. It gave us something neutral to talk about. No matter how many demonstrators the police locked up, Katherine Hepburn was going to marry Cary Grant; Norma Shearer was going to smile that sweet, sad smile; and Natalie Wood was gonna do Juliet all over Spanish Harlem.

ALICE (*putting her cup down with a smash, irritated by* JENNY*'s chatter and her bouncing knees*): Do you have to talk about that now? (JENNY *stops abruptly and sits perfectly still.* ALICE *winces, recovers quickly, and looks fully into* JENNY*'s face.*)

JENNY (*softly*): You ought to take something.

ALICE: Like what?

JENNY: Like something for the pain. There's no shame in that.

ALICE: Shame? (*She laughs and shakes her head.*) You've been watching too many of those Hollywood movies. No real sick person gives a damn about shame.

JENNY (*reaching for the medicine*): Then take something. (ALICE*'s hand on hers stops her abruptly and with finality.*)

ALICE: I'm not myself when I take something.

JENNY: Then, by all means, take two.

ALICE: Touche, Sister. Touche! (JENNY *extends a pill and pours a small glass of water from a pitcher on the table.* ALICE *relents and swallows the pill and several more. She leans back again, waiting for the medication to take effect.* JENNY *lays down on her back near the couch and takes a long, deep Lamaze cleansing breath. She sucks in as much air as she can, holds it, then lets it out with an extended "whoosh!"* ALICE *opens her eyes and watches her.* JENNY *places her hands very lightly on either side of her stomach and breathes in and out, using the Lamaze method.*) What is that supposed to do?

(JENNY *holds up a finger to indicate that she has to complete the cycle before breaking the breathing to respond. She accelerates her breathing until she is panting rapidly and loudly. She stops after a minute, takes another deep cleansing breath, and lets it out.*)

JENNY: I've tried to explain all of this to you before. Why do you always wait until I'm in the middle of it to decide you want to listen?

ALICE: I'm easily distracted.

JENNY: It's supposed to minimize the pain during labor. Redirect your energy or something.

ALICE: It's not your energy you're going to be concerned about. Trust me.

JENNY: No horror stories please! I can't stand it when people tell a pregnant woman horror stories, especially when I'm the pregnant woman!

ALICE: You've already heard all the horror stories I know. You've probably written them all down, too.

JENNY: You're very closemouthed with your stories, now that you mention it. Horror or otherwise.

ALICE: But the few gems I've let slip have not escaped your attention. You've probably made a few notes, just in case.

JENNY: I probably have. Would you mind?

ALICE: I'm not sure. I guess not. It's not like I'm going to use them for anything. You're not, are you?

JENNY: Going to write about you? (ALICE *waits but does not answer.*) Probably.

ALICE (*laughs*): God! That isn't really fair, is it? Why write about me now? Another dreary tale of a cancer-ridden mother attended by her long lost, but dutiful, daughter. The last days of Acid Alice. (*Laughs bitterly.*) Not the stuff best sellers are made of, Sister. Not this year. Not this color.

JENNY: I'll risk it.

ALICE: Don't fool yourself. You're not risking anything. It would probably be great therapy at the very least. (*A beat.*) I'm sorry. I'll be better in a minute. Soon as this pill decides which pain to concentrate on first. Is there any more of that sweet wine we had around here the other day?

JENNY: I stuck it away someplace.

ALICE: What are you writing about that makes you start cussin' so early in the morning?

JENNY (*hedging; sheepishly*): I'm trying to create a portrait of "the new woman."

ALICE: Is there such a creature?

JENNY (*laughingly*): That's the problem. I've read endless magazine articles about her. I've gone to conferences dedicated to her and read novels supposedly written by her about herself. But . . .

ALICE: Different costumes, Sister, same character.

JENNY: Voila!

ALICE: I can't stand the taste of sweet wine. I've never liked it, but it's the only kind that doesn't upset my stomach. Probably just another part of the penance. It's true, you know.

JENNY: What's true?

ALICE: About your not risking anything. It's true. I don't want you to fool yourself about that.

JENNY: I'll try not to. (JENNY *hands* ALICE *her wine and drinks some herself.*) Cheers! Getting pretty decadent around here, aren't we? It's not even nine o'clock in the morning, and we're already drinking wine.

ALICE (*draining her glass*): I'm your mother. It's okay.

JENNY (*suddenly concerned*): Is this okay for you to be drinking that with your medicine? (*She looks on the bottle label for possible warning label.*)

ALICE: Probably not. But what's the worst that can happen? It might kill me.

JENNY: I don't want all of our conversations to be about dying!

ALICE (*very quietly*): Then get out.

(JENNY *looks stunned as if* ALICE *had struck her.*)

JENNY (*looking for a neutral subject*): What happened to all of those old Billie Holiday records you used to have?

ALICE (*still calm and quiet*): I don't think you should be here, Jenny. I don't want you here.

JENNY: Your timing is lousy, mother. I'm having a baby any minute now, remember?

ALICE: I'm not asking you to go to the moon, Sister. It is my understanding that Prince Charming resides just across town.

JENNY: That's not open for discussion! And what difference does it make? I had a man and I don't have him anymore.

ALICE: I'm old-fashioned. I believe that if you ever have them, you always have them.

JENNY (*wearily*): We're not all as lucky as you are.

ALICE: Alright, Sister. Let's get the ground rules straight. This is my house. It was left to me, not to you, by my mother, not yours! I own it. Lock, stock and mothballs, and I came a very long way to get here in time enough to die in it.

JENNY: I wouldn't have moved in here if I had known you would be coming. It never occurred to me. It's not like you have a history of dropping in.

ALICE: It's not like I have a history at all as far as you're concerned, so why not just go wherever it was you would have gone if it had occurred to you that I might drop in.

JENNY: I want to stay.

ALICE: No, you don't. You think you ought to stay. Nobody wants to bring a new baby home to a death house!

JENNY: This is not a death house! I'm here, and I'm very much alive!

ALICE: I'm looking for a hospice, Sister. A place to die in peace, not in pieces. (*A beat. Wearily.*) It's just that I get so tired . . .

JENNY (*very gently*): I want to help you.

ALICE (*angered at her own vulnerability*): Why are you alone?

JENNY: Because I choose to be.

ALICE: Nobody chooses to be alone. You might choose your sanity, or your freedom, or some other wild thing that results in your being alone, but that's the fallout. The unavoidable consequences. Not the choice.

JENNY: Why can't you let me help you?

ALICE: You're not here to help. You're here to hide.

JENNY: I haven't got any reason to hide. I'm not ashamed of anything.

ALICE: Well, that's something we have in common. Shamelessness.

JENNY: I want to make the best of it.

ALICE: The best of *this?*

JENNY: The best of the time we have together.

ALICE: That's not one of my strong points, making the best of it.

JENNY: It's my specialty . . .

ALICE: You want to make a fairy tale out of it! You want me to tell you the secret of life and give you my motherly blessing. You want me to make up for twenty years of silence in two weeks. You want the two of us to play mother and daughter.

JENNY (*hurt and angry*): We *are* mother and daughter! (*Frustrated and confused.*) This is crazy! This doesn't make any sense!

ALICE: Is it supposed to make sense?

JENNY: Isn't it? I'm not a child anymore! We are two grown women!

ALICE: My mother used to tell me that once she was sure I understood what being grown meant, she'd never have to worry about me again.

JENNY: Is that why you came here? To see if I was grown?

ALICE: No. To see if I was. (*A beat.*) I'm dying, Sister. I'm only forty-seven years old, and I'm dying. I don't have the energy to figure out what you need to know and tell it to you.

JENNY: What are you talking about?

ALICE: You've been sitting around with that hopeful look on your face ever since I got here. You want too much, Sister.

JENNY: I don't want anything from you! You're my mother, and I'm your daughter. Isn't that enough?

ALICE: Yes, you are my daughter. (*A beat. The medication and the wine make her a little drowsy.*) My very own baby daughter. (*A beat.*) I'd like to have been better at this, Sister. But I just don't have any energy left for it now. I need all my energy for myself. I have to pay very close attention to what's happening up here. (*Taps her temple lightly.*)

JENNY: I understand . . .

ALICE (*sarcastic*): Do you?

JENNY: I think I do. (*She resumes her Lamaze exercises quietly.*)

ALICE: Well, then, you don't need any advice from me. You've got everything under control here, Sister. You've got it all organized. You've found a way to redirect your energies and feel no pain. You've even taken the guessing out of boys and girls.

JENNY: It's safer, that's all. I just wanted to be careful since she's my first one.

ALICE: It's a violation.

JENNY: No, mother. Nothing so dramatic as that. It's a simple test that lets you know in advance if your baby is going to have two heads and by the way reveals the gender. It just gives Alexis a little more information to work with. There's a certain amount of risk in having a baby when you're as old as I am.

ALICE: I can't tell you anything about that. You and my eighteenth birthday arrived neck and neck. Is thirty late? Women used to have babies from nine to ninety.

JENNY: It's late for a first one. What are you talking about anyway? (*Laughs.*) You sound like a pioneer woman. "Nine to ninety."

ALICE: It's all different now. Your doctor doesn't even sound like a doctor.

JENNY: Alexis?

ALICE: How can you call your doctor Alexis?

JENNY: That's her name, mother. Don't act so shocked. You're not so old that ought to shock you.

ALICE: No, I guess not. (*A beat.*) I don't even know if the doctor who delivered you had a first name. Dr. Stewart. I never heard anybody call him anything else. Young Dr. Stewart. That was it.

JENNY: "Young Dr. Stewart" . . . sounds like a soap opera doctor.

ALICE: He only delivered babies at the Catholic hospital. The whole time I was in labor with you I had to look at all these bleeding crucifixes. Nails in the palms, a sword in the side, and a great big bleeding valentine right in the middle of his chest.

JENNY: Want some more wine?

ALICE: No. Yes, I guess so. I'm on to you, Sister. You think I'll get high and reveal those secrets you think I'm guarding so closely.

JENNY: No, I don't. I'm hoping you'll get a little high and remember where you put those Billie Holiday records.

ALICE (*irritated*): They're down there with the rest of the records, or they should be. Where else would I put them? Upstairs in my room? It's been awhile since I was in any condition to be playing Billie Holiday in my bedroom!

(JENNY *rummages through the records looking for Billie Holiday.*)

JENNY: I told someone once that the music of Billie Holiday ran through my early life like a leitmotiv.

ALICE: What did he say?

JENNY: Why do you assume I was talking to a man?

ALICE: It's a seduction line, Sister. I'm not that sick. What did he say?

JENNY: He said, "What's a leitmotiv?"

(*They both laugh.*)

ALICE: You know what your father said when you were born?

JENNY: What?

ALICE: I thought he might be disappointed because you weren't a boy, so I said I'd heard that sometimes kings divorce their wives if the firstborn is female. And he laughed and shook his head. "Not in my tribe," he said. "Not in my tribe."

JENNY (*delighted*): He never told me that!

ALICE: It's not a man's story. That's a story women tell each other. (*A beat.*) You see how you're looking at me? You're doing it again! I shouldn't have told you anything! It's only going to make you think you were right about those secrets. Forget it, Sister! It's only the way this medicine (*holding up the wine*) and this medicine (*taps medication bottle*) make my mind wander. There are no secrets. (*A beat.*) Well, maybe one.

JENNY: And what's that?

ALICE: That there are no secrets! (*A beat.* ALICE *is exhausted. She closes her eyes.*) How was it . . . for your grandmother?

JENNY: I think the memory loss was the worst part, for her and for me. She thought the nurse's aides were her daughters. Once when I went to visit, two of them were helping her pick out the earrings she was going to wear that day. She had about five pairs spread out on the sheet, and they were talking as seriously as if she had been getting ready for a night at the opera. (*A beat.*) Sometimes she would make me sit right in front of her and hold my face in her hands and look real hard. (*A beat.*) Sometimes she would remember that I was her granddaughter. Sometimes she could remember my name, but all of that went after awhile.

ALICE: What did they decide?

JENNY: Decide about what?

ALICE: The earrings.

JENNY: A pair of carved gold hoops with ram's heads. They were so heavy they pulled her earlobes down long. Stretched them out like a Watusi woman. She laughed when they held up a mirror so she could see herself. "There now," she said. "That's better."

ALICE: I gave her those.

JENNY: I wondered what she was doing with earrings like that.

ALICE: She used to tell me that the only women who wore big gold hoops in their ears were gypsies or prostitutes.

JENNY: She kept tossing her head so they would bump against her neck. They were very beautiful.

ALICE: When I sent them, I wrote and told her she was too prim ever to be mistaken for a gypsy and too old to be mistaken for a prostitute, so I thought it was safe for her to wear them. She wrote me back and said she was still my mother, and some things didn't change.

JENNY: God! I wish I knew what those things were!

ALICE (*sarcastic, but gently*): Oh, you know, Sister. The right way and the wrong way of doing things. What makes a "lady" and what does not.

JENNY (*finds the record*): Well, here's the only Lady that matters . . . in full gardenia!

ALICE: Don't play that now!

JENNY: Why not? (ALICE *does not respond. A beat.*) When she died, the paper said it was a drug overdose, and you were furious. You told me it wasn't the drugs that killed her. She died because she had to feel everything. Every time. You said nobody could live that way. Not for long.

ALICE: I was wrong, Sister. It's the only way you can tell you're still alive. (*A beat.*) Your father never liked Billie Holiday.

JENNY: I know. He said she made him feel lonesome.

ALICE: He wasn't the only one. You know she had a song that they made them stop playing on the radio because every time they did, the suicide rate in the city would go through the ceiling.

JENNY: Which one was that?

ALICE: "Gloomy Monday." Is it on there?

JENNY (*checks the label*): Yep.

ALICE: Well, don't play it! Lord knows we don't need any additional depression around here.

JENNY: What do you want to hear?

ALICE: How about a poem or two?

JENNY (*startled, covering*): I'm a journalist. You're the poet, remember?

ALICE: There's no journalist in the world who gets up at six in the morning to work. Journalists work late at night. Poets work at dawn. Don't fool yourself.

JENNY: That's the second time you've said that this morning.

ALICE: If I say it three times, believe me. That probably means it's good advice.

JENNY (*hesitantly*): Well, I have been working on something new.

ALICE (*raising eyebrow*): You're writing poems now?

JENNY (*nervously, fingering the pages*): Well . . . sometime . . . I hardly ever show them to anybody though. They can't help comparing mine to yours. (*She laughs ruefully.*) You're a hard act to follow.

ALICE: Then don't try it. And on second thought, don't read anything to me either. If I'm a tough act, I'm probably an impossible audience. Where's Butterfly?

JENNY (*disappointed*): Again?

ALICE: Indulge me. If you're going to stay and keep watch at my death bed, the least you can do is indulge me.

JENNY: I should have told that kid Puccini ran through my life like a leitmotiv.

ALICE: No. That would only have added insult to injury.

JENNY: I used to be so embarrassed when you played this stuff.

ALICE: You have no shame about being the unwed mother of a fatherless child, and you were embarrassed at lovely Leontyne singing "Un Bel Di?"

JENNY: She has a father. Besides, you have to admit that Puccini was not exactly the dominant musical influence in our neighborhood. Our driveway was the only place where you had to be careful or you might get hit by a blast of "La Boheme" in the middle of a serious handball game. Everybody else was playing The Supremes! (*Laughing at the memory.*) I remember one day I was trying to get you to at least turn it down a little, and you made me listen to "Un Bel Di" all the way through. You told me to see if I could hear the same thing in it that made me love Smokey Robinson. You said forget about Italians and operas and just try to hear the passion.

ALICE: You looked at me like I was crazy, but you closed your eyes and listened. (*A beat.*) Ten years old . . . trying to hear the passion.

JENNY: I used your analogy a couple of weeks later when Dwan Johnson asked me what was playing at our house. I told him it was "Un Bel Di," and when he asked what it meant, I said, "one fine day." And he said, oh yeah? Just like the Chiffons!

ALICE (*laughs gingerly*): You know I hate the idea of taking these damn pills, but they do help.

JENNY (*a beat*): You know, when I got to college half the girls in my dorm had your books. It was a weird feeling. I had never seen them before, and they would come up to me and ask me about you. It was like some of them knew more about you than I did!

ALICE (*a beat*): I guess I should eat something.

JENNY: What would you like?

ALICE: There's some jello in there, I think. (*She shudders at the thought.*)

JENNY: How about some soup?

ALICE: I don't think so.

JENNY: It's just broth. I don't think it will upset your stomach.

ALICE: Maybe later. It's bad enough to be babbling like this without being nauseated too!

JENNY: There should be something in there that will appeal to you. Let me take a look. I'll put this on to entertain you while I'm gone.

ALICE: I don't want to be entertained. That's what I've been trying to tell you!

JENNY: Alright, alright. I stand corrected.

ALICE: Oh, hell. What's the difference? (JENNY *sets the record on and exits to the kitchen. It is "In My Solitude."* ALICE *winces a little in pain now that she is alone, but she quickly straightens and takes several more pills rapidly.*)

JENNY (*calling from the kitchen*): I've got some plain yogurt too. What do you think? (ALICE *leans back listening, eyes closed. She reaches out to touch the beautiful roses.* JENNY *enters with a small tray. She has to balance it precariously on the pile of stuff already on the coffee table. She fusses over the food until the song ends.*) If I thought taking heroin could make me sing like that, I'd be a junkie with no regrets.

ALICE: You can't sing like that without some regrets, Sister. Don't you know that yet? You better put some sugar in those roses.

JENNY: Sugar? Why?

ALICE: Flowers always live longer if you put some sugar in the water.

JENNY: I guess everything does better with a little sweetening.

ALICE: The woman who told me that was a fiend for roses. She was beautiful, and her boyfriends always sent her roses. Red only! Her apartment was full of them. The scent would choke you when you went to see her. She had so many roses she used to float their petals on her bath water.

JENNY: I tried that once. It sounds beautiful, but it feels like a tub full of hot, sticky rose petals.

ALICE: You know, this place looks very different.

JENNY: It needed a lot of work. Renovations, repairs. I did most of it myself. It took longer than I thought it would. I made a lot of mistakes. Do you like it?

ALICE: I'm not sure yet. (*A beat.*) I sure went the long way around to end up sleeping in the house I was born in.

JENNY (*a beat*): I can't believe you're really here.

ALICE: That makes two of us, Sister. (*A beat.*) The quiet in this house used to be so strong it was a part of the conversation. Mother and Daddy were so calm about everything. They never raised their voices. (*A beat.*) I used to wonder if I was their natural child. I used to study them, looking for clues. They were so damn certain! (ALICE *closes her eyes and leans back.* JENNY *watches her and then suddenly has a contraction. She handles it calmly, blowing out for a few seconds Lamaze style.* ALICE *speaks without opening her eyes.*)

ALICE: You're not going to start that again, are you?

JENNY (*out of breath*): No. I'm going to pack. (*She begins putting things in the large suitcase near her desk.* ALICE *opens her eyes and watches.*)

ALICE: What all are you taking to the hospital, Sister?

JENNY (*laughing*): Not much. This is the only bag I have.

ALICE: I've got a carpetbag. Very bohemian. I guarantee there'll be nothing like it on the ward.

JENNY: Sounds wonderful. Where is it?

ALICE: Look upstairs.

(JENNY *goes upstairs and rummages around to find the carpetbag, still talking.*)

JENNY: I wish I had a bed jacket to take with me. I love those scenes in the movies where the new mother is always propped up on lace pillows in a pink satin bed jacket. (*As* JENNY *rummages and talks,* ALICE *rises stiffly and wanders rather aimlessly around the room. She stops to touch a picture frame here, a piece of furniture, but all very absently. She is not looking for anything. She is simply moving around restlessly. She moves to* JENNY*'s desk and sees the two pages* JENNY *was working on this morning. She picks up the pages slowly and reads a little. Upstairs,* JENNY *finds the carpetbag and opens it to look inside.*) They don't hardly make bed jackets like that anymore. I guess they . . . (*She seems to be surprised by what she sees and reaches in to withdraw a cheap wig. She realizes that* ALICE *may have worn it as a concession to vanity when her hair started to fall out.* JENNY *is embarrassed to have found it.* ALICE *is aware that* JENNY *has stopped in mid-sentence. She breaks off her reading and looks upstairs.* JENNY *puts the wig back in the closet and starts talking again nervously, coming downstairs.*) I always like that scene in "The Women" where Joan Crawford and Norma Shearer are getting ready to have it out and the store lingerie model keeps sweeping through saying "Try our new one-piece foundation. Zips up the back and no bones."

ALICE (*watches* JENNY *with irritation as she crosses to sit down again, wincing slightly*): I don't care, you know?

JENNY: About what?

ALICE: About what you think. About your crude efforts to capture my madcap phase in your schoolgirl poetry. Hardly a fitting memorial. (*A beat.*) It just doesn't matter, Sister. Can't you see that?

JENNY (*stung and hurt*): What does matter to you?

ALICE: My own heartbeat. The way my blood feels rushing through my veins. The parts of my body that are going to start hurting again in a few minutes. All of that matters. (ALICE *winces, and* JENNY *moves toward her.*)

JENNY: Are you okay?

ALICE: Stop asking me that! I'm not anywhere in the vicinity of okay, and I'm not going to be for the rest of the time you know me. (ALICE *leans back and takes a pill wearily.* JENNY *has retreated and started transferring her things from her big bag to the carpetbag. She realizes there is still something in it. She withdraws a small packet of things: papers, photographs, etc., bound up with string.*)

JENNY (*cautiously, but curious*): What's this?

ALICE (*wearily*): What?

JENNY: All this "stuff"? (JENNY *hands the packet to* ALICE *who holds it delicately in her hands.*)

ALICE: Some old photographs. A poem or two. Your father's letters.

JENNY (*startled*): He wrote you?

ALICE: Yes.

JENNY (*surprised*): When?

ALICE: For years.

JENNY: He never showed me your letters!

ALICE: I didn't say that I wrote to him. I said he wrote to me.

JENNY: You never wrote back?

ALICE: No.

JENNY: Not once?

ALICE: Not once. If I had had anything left to say to your father, I wouldn't have been in Paris.

JENNY: How long did he write to you?

ALICE: I told you for years.

JENNY: But how many? How many years?

ALICE: Until he died.

JENNY: Where are the rest of them?

ALICE: I burned them.

JENNY: You burned them? God! Don't you ever think about anybody but yourself? You could have given them to me!

ALICE: He asked me to burn them! Besides, they were my letters. Nobody else's.

(JENNY, *knowing this is true, but still hurt by the secret, turns away.*)

JENNY: What did he say about me?

ALICE: He never wrote about you. When I left he told me he wanted to write to me. I told him he could, but not to expect answers to his letters and that if he ever referred to you in any way, I would never open another letter that he sent to me.

JENNY: And he believed you?

ALICE: That's a child's question, Sister. Children can never imagine that their parents could sustain exchanges of over five seconds without discussing them. (JENNY *turns away, and* ALICE *begins to talk almost to herself.*) He wrote about almost everything. Books and politics. Gossip about people we knew and what they were doing. What he was thinking; ideas.

JENNY: He used to talk to me like that, too. Sometimes I felt like listening to Daddy talking was as close as words could ever hope to get to being music. He could start off with Langston Hughes, move to Stokely Carmichael, swoop down long enough to touch on whoever I fancied myself to be in love with at the time and finish up with Duke Ellington without ever taking a breath.

ALICE: He wrote me when Malcolm was shot down. He must have sensed how hard it was to be in Paris then. When something like that happens, you want to be around your own. It seemed like we all heard the news at the same time. We ended up gathering at the cafe where we spent half our lives, crying in our Pernod and trying not to feel so black and helpless and far away from home. But then we looked up the street and here comes this young brother who we know works at the American Embassy. That's all we knew about him because he never hung around with us, but here he comes in his dark blue, pin-striped suit with a step ladder under his arm.

JENNY: A step ladder?

ALICE: He walked right up in front of the cafe, opened the thing up and cleared his throat. Speaking the most perfect, diplomatic corps French, he invited us to express ourselves on the death of "our shining black prince." Then he stepped about halfway up that ladder, left the flawless French behind, and told us in good old Southside Chicago English how his heart was broken by what he had heard happened in the Audobon Ballroom. When he got done, somebody else got up and talked about hearing Malcolm at the Temple in Detroit, way back when, and I told about another meeting where he brought us all to our feet. Everybody had a memory of the man. (*A beat.*) We must have been there a couple of hours. When everybody had had their say, the young brother from the Embassy thanked us, folded up his ladder, and went on up the street.

JENNY: What was his name?

ALICE: I don't remember. I don't think I ever knew, really. He killed himself . . .

JENNY (*distracting* ALICE *from death*): What about pictures?

ALICE (*bemused*): Just some ancient snaps of the ex-patriot colored poetess in her prime. (*She hands the photos to* JENNY *who looks through them eagerly.*)

JENNY: Look at that dress! You look wonderful! Where were you going?

ALICE: Who knows? We are always . . . (*She catches herself suddenly, suspicious of being so unguarded.*) When are you planning to have this baby anyway?

JENNY: Any minute now!

ALICE: I want you to make other arrangements for after she is born.

JENNY: What?

ALICE: I don't want you to bring her back here. I don't want to see her.

JENNY: Not at all?

ALICE: No. Not at all.

JENNY: She's your granddaughter!

ALICE: We've been all through this, Sister. Why don't you just go home?

JENNY: This is home!

ALICE: Why don't you go to where home was before this was home?

JENNY: Because I can't.

ALICE: There's a big difference between can't and won't.

JENNY: Yes. I know. (*Picking up the snapshots again, hoping to resume the conversation.*) Who were you playing here?

ALICE: Probably a cross between Josephine Baker and Anais Nin. I had a lover who loved my "leetle 'ead." He had a lot of money, and it amused him to keep a black American poet. Poetess! That was the phase when I started calling myself Simone and wrapping my head round and around with silver ribbons. (*A beat. She looks at the photo.*) They told me my hair was going to fall out when they started the chemotherapy. They explain everything to sick people, you know, so we won't be surprised when the awful things that are going to happen actually start happening. They explain everything as they take you into those little dark rooms and sit you down. Then they ask you if you've got any more questions, and since they've just described the horrors of hell to you, you probably don't want to hear any more, so you say no, thank you. Then they ease the needles into your arm so that the poison can drip into you for an hour or so, and that's it. Sometimes you feel okay. A little weak, but pretty good. You might even eat something, which is usually a mistake because then you start throwing up. And your hair starts falling out, and pretty soon they tell you it didn't work, and you've still got the cancer, and they're real sorry about . . . your . . . hair. (*A beat.*) He used to love to rub my head, this European fool. I told him that in the United States, black folks didn't tolerate white folks rubbing their heads because we knew they thought it gave them good luck and we needed all our good luck for our damn selves. He just laughed. He didn't know what I was talking about. "You have such a perfectly shaped leetle 'ead," he used to tell me. "Such a leetle 'ead."

JENNY: I shaved my head once.

ALICE: Bald?

JENNY: Completely.

ALICE: If there isn't a good story associated with that kind of madness, there is no excuse for it.

JENNY: It's not much of a story at all really. It was during a time when all the white girls at school were ironing their hair, morning, noon and night. You couldn't walk into the laundry room without bumping into Mary Jo or Susie Q. in their drawers with their hair thrown over the ironing boards.

ALICE: Why didn't you tell them about Madame Walker and her straightening comb?

JENNY: They weren't interested. I think in some weird way they thought the ironing board thing was some kind of ethnic beauty secret.

ALICE: Ethnic, maybe. But not black. There aren't enough of us with hair long enough to throw across an ironing board.

JENNY: After a couple of months, things moved from fad to fetish. All anybody talked about was ironing hair. The best temperatures to use. The advantage of steam over no steam. Techniques to do it yourself and tips on doing it with a friend. It was silly, but it started to get on my nerves. One day at dinner, I told them all I thought hair—ironed or otherwise—was the most boring subject in the world and to prove it I was going upstairs and shave all of mine off. And I did.

ALICE: How did you like it?

JENNY: The look or the feeling?

ALICE: Both.

JENNY: It felt great. Cool and strange. Sensual. The look took some getting used to, though.

ALICE: My Frenchman would have loved you! "Such a lovely leetle 'ead!"

JENNY: I liked what it did to those girls though. It made them keep their distance. They were intimidated by whatever it was that made me do it.

ALICE: Ordinary people often mistake courage for insanity. It frightens them. (*A beat.*) What did your father say?

JENNY: He never saw it completely bald. It had grown in some before I went home. It was still too short to suit him though. He looked at me real hard and then he said, "I don't think you've got the face for it."

ALICE: Your father never was one for the avant garde.

JENNY (*pulls some other papers from the packet*): What are these?

ALICE: Poems, Sister. Those are the poems. (*A beat.*) You recognize a poem when you see one, don't you?

JENNY: Can I read them?

ALICE: I should have burned them, too.

JENNY: Why?

ALICE: Because some things are better left unsaid.

JENNY: Are they about Daddy?

ALICE: Yes.

JENNY: All of them?

ALICE: Yes, Sister. They are all about Daddy. (*A beat.*) I was so young when I met your father that he was not just the only man I'd ever slept with, he was the only man I'd ever fantasized about. He was very gentle with me. Very tender. He knew I was a very young girl. He had been a man out in the world longer than I had been alive!

JENNY: "A man out in the world . . ." Listen to how old-fashioned that sounds!

ALICE: Those were different times. Black folks were a little more prim in the fifties just like white folks. Besides, I was only seventeen. I graduated from high school on Wednesday and married your father in the sanctuary of Plymouth Church on Friday night.

JENNY: Daddy said you looked so young to him when he looked into your face to say his vows that he was afraid you had lied and he was marrying a child.

ALICE: When we first got married, I used to write two or three serious love poems everyday. I used to write them on little tiny pieces of paper and put them under his pillow. Whenever he reached under there and found one, I'd read it to him. One night, I told him I wanted to send one of them to a magazine and he ate it!

JENNY: He did what?

ALICE: He ate it. Rolled it up in a little ball, popped it in his mouth, chewed a couple of times, and swallowed it right down.

JENNY: Was it your only copy?

ALICE: That's hardly the point, Sister. He told me those poems were a gift from me to him. He said my words went all down inside him and made him stronger. So I said, that's all very fine, but why did you eat my poem? And he just laughed and said, so the white folks wouldn't get it.

JENNY: Is that when you stopped writing them?

ALICE: No. I wrote them for awhile after that. I just had to memorize them, too. I didn't stop writing them until you were born. Then I didn't have . . . time. (*A beat.*) You want to know what I learned in Paris? Almost twenty years abroad and you know what I learned, Sister? (*She does not give* JENNY *a chance to respond.*) I learned that my name is Alice and not Simone and that the Left Bank is not as far from the West Side of Detroit as I was hoping it would be.

JENNY: It was as far away as another planet to me.

ALICE (*a beat*): I just don't have the energy to figure out what you need to know and tell it to you, Sister. I don't have enough time, and I won't pretend that I do.

JENNY: You never would pretend. Even when it hurt to tell the truth.

ALICE: It hurt you. It hurt me to lie.

JENNY: To lie about *what?*

ALICE: There was a voice screaming inside my head, Sister. After awhile, the only thing that mattered was to make her stop shouting.

JENNY: Did she tell you to go to Paris?

ALICE: She told me to go!

JENNY: Did she tell you not to take me with you?

ALICE: She never considered you at all.

JENNY (*recoils from this statement, but is silent for a moment. She stares at* ALICE): Is it such a crime? To want to know the things your mother knows?

ALICE: And what if I tell you that I don't know anything at all? What if I tell you that running around Europe playing the exotic . . . playing god knows what . . . What if I told you it didn't teach me a damn thing?

JENNY: I wouldn't believe you.

ALICE: Now you do sound like your father. Confront the man directly with an unassailable truth—a provable reality—and he would look calmly into your face and say, "I don't believe you."

JENNY: There's more than one reality.

ALICE: Multiple truths? No. Multiple fantasy, but only one truth.

JENNY: You're making this so hard on me.

ALICE: Join the Club. Membership is absolutely voluntary.

JENNY: Even now, you just can't let it go, can you?

ALICE: Let what go? You're talking movie-speak again. Hollywood alone has created the myth of a secret guilt that torments the dying. Forget it, Sister. I let it go. I let it all go. Your father . . . the poems . . .

JENNY: Well, that's nothing new, is it?

ALICE: That's what I've been trying to tell you.

JENNY: I just . . .

ALICE (*interrupting angrily*): . . . you just decided to leave your husband or your lover or your friend and move into your grandmother's house to have a baby, and you liked the whole idea so much you couldn't drag yourself away even when your long lost decaying mother arrived at the door? Give up, Sister! That sepia-tone photograph you've been carrying around in your head for twenty years hasn't got anything to do with me. I wasn't that way then, and I'm not that way now.

JENNY: You don't want to know anything about me at all. You've already drawn your own conclusions.

ALICE: I have drawn no conclusions. I have made no judgments. You are free to do whatever you please.

JENNY: At what price?

ALICE: We all have to pay for something.

JENNY: Why can't you just be my mother for once and not some world-weary, wisecracking, black caricature of a cynical ex-patriot?

ALICE: I am being your mother. This is what your mother is, Sister. A world-weary, wisecracking, black caricature of a cynical ex-patriot.

JENNY (*quietly*): That is not the answer.

ALICE: Don't try for answers, Sister. You don't even understand the questions.

JENNY: That's where you're wrong!

ALICE: Am I?

JENNY: Yes, you are. I understand all the questions. Every single one. (*A beat.*) Right after you left, Daddy sent me away to boarding school. He thought I needed . . . I don't know . . . stability, safety. There had been bombings, threats on his life. So he sent me off to Massachusetts where I'd be safe. I knew he was doing the best he could, so I didn't tell him how much I hated it. I thought that if he really loved me, he would know. Somehow, he would feel it and come and get me. (*A beat.*) But he never did. (*A beat.*) That's one of the questions, isn't it? How come people that love you can't read your mind?

ALICE: Why should they?

JENNY: So that they can love you better!

ALICE: There is no better or worse, Sister. You either do or you don't.

JENNY: You make choices.

ALICE (*outraged*): Choices? Okay, Sister. Take a look! My parting gift to you is a close-up look at the end result of all those choices you're talking about with such enthusiasm. Choices? Take a good, long look at me, and save your reaction to this terrible truth for the labor room. You can scream about the injustice of it all in there, and nobody will pay you the slightest bit of mind. All the ladies do it. They'll never know that your screaming is different. That yours isn't about the pain of your bones separating to let your daughter out. That yours is about the presence of injustice in the world! They'll never suspect a thing. And it doesn't really matter anyway. In spite of their feigned interest, nobody else really gives a damn if you do your birthing and your living and your dying well, or if you shriek and holler and cling to the nurse's arm.

JENNY: You left me?

ALICE: I did not see my future as the dedicated wife of the charismatic leader, dabbling in a little poetry, being indulged at cultural conferences and urged to read that one about the beautiful brothers and sisters in Soweto, or Watts, or Montgomery, Alabama. I just couldn't be that. The world is bigger than that. The world inside my head is bigger than that. Even now . . . I used to watch your father at rallies and in church on Sunday morning, and he'd be so strong and beautiful, it was all I could do to sit still and look prim in my pew. But he was committed to "the movement." He didn't have time anymore to lay in bed with me and improvise. I'd been a wife since I was seventeen, and here I was almost thirty, with a ten-year-old daughter, trying to convince your father to let me publish some love poems! But he couldn't. Or he wouldn't. The kind of love he had to give me now didn't allow for that. And I couldn't do without it. So I left. Not much of a story is it?

JENNY: I could have gone with you. I was old enough.

ALICE: I can tell you the day, the hour, the minute you were conceived. (*A beat.*) I couldn't stand to look at you. (*Changes her tone.*) And I'm selfish! You said it yourself. What was I going to do in Paris with a ten-year-old child? Besides, you were always more your father's child than you ever were mine.

JENNY: I didn't have much choice, did I?

ALICE: Neither did I, Sister. Neither did I. I've spent my life trying to heal a hurt I'm not supposed to have. I got so tired of being trapped inside that tiny little black box. No air, Sister. I couldn't get any air. Everybody was mad at somebody, or about something. (*A beat.*) My mother spent her life catching the bus downtown to the Anis Fur Company. Sitting there in that hot little back room sewing purple silk linings in rich white ladies' sable coats. I went there with her once when I was little. There must have been thirty black women in a room smaller than this one. It was hot and dusty and close. I felt like I was smothering. (*A beat.*) No air, Sister. No goddamn air.

JENNY: Daddy never wanted that.

ALICE: No. He wanted exactly what I was looking for. A way out of that black box. It's just that I was prepared to admit defeat and let the white folks have this particular piece of ground since they wanted it so bad. But your father was different. He was not prepared to give an inch. He was always talking about survival, and I was always talking about love.

JENNY: You were happy once.

ALICE: But the moment passes, Sister.

JENNY: Does that mean it never happened?

ALICE: It means most of the time nobody's even listening.

JENNY: I was listening.

ALICE (*angry*): For what? So you could make up schoolgirl fairy tales about my exotic existence? So you could record my tragic demise for posterity? (*She picks up the poetry and waves it at* JENNY.) Read it to me, why don't you? No? Okay! I'll read it to you then. I used to be good at this. "Pretend it's Paris." (*Her voice is totally sarcastic.*) "For mother . . ."

JENNY: Don't! (JENNY *grabs the poem away and crumples it in her hand.* ALICE *smiles cruelly.*)

ALICE: You're not a poet, Sister. You're a runner. Don't you even understand that? There are people who are runners, Sister. Runners who spend their whole life in flight. Sometimes the speed may have a kind of flash to it—a certain style—but in the end, it's nothing but a hard, scared run, and you end up somewhere panting and hurting and babbling over your shoulder into the dark. (ALICE *turns her back to* JENNY. *She is spent.* JENNY *speaks slowly but with confidence. Something in her tone makes* ALICE *turn as she speaks.*)

JENNY: "you ration yourself out
like there was a war on.
In Paris, the soldiers threw
chocolate bars and silk stockings.
some people saved the sweets
and hid the stockings in a bureau drawer.
safe and sound.
not me. i was the one
in my stocking feet
with chocolate smeared
across my smile
dancin' and grinnin'
unsafe/unsound/undone.
there's more i can give
if there's more you can take.
the only thing
i wanna do
is make love
and drink champagne
in the middle of the day
and in the middle of the night
and sometimes in the morning
i am the one
in my stocking feet
with chocolate smeared
across my smile
dancin' and grinnin'
i am the one.
oh, yes, i am the one.
close your eyes.
take a deep breath.
pretend it's Paris.
pretend it's Paris.
pretend it's Paris. . .

(*They look at each other for a long moment.*)

ALICE (*quietly*): It's too late to be sorry, Sister, but I . . .

JENNY (*stops her*): Sometimes the love is enough. When it's all you've got. Sometimes just the possibility is enough. And we don't have to explain it. We just have to be here together and try. We only have to try! (*A beat.*) All I ever wanted to tell you was that I understood. I think I always understood.

(JENNY *and* ALICE *look straight at each other in silence.* JENNY *moves to* ALICE, *but then stops and winces slightly. She puts her hands to her stomach lightly, breathing through her mouth.*)

ALICE: What is it?

JENNY (*panting a little*): Contractions! I'd better call Alexis. (JENNY *goes to the phone and dials quickly.* ALICE *slowly picks up the crumpled pages of the poem, smoothing them carefully as* JENNY *speaks.*) Alexis? I think it's . . . Yes. Pretty strong . . . Okay. I'll be ready. (*She hangs up.*) She's going to come by and pick me up.

(*They look at each other.* ALICE *touches* JENNY*'s cheek lightly.*)

ALICE: I think when I married your father so young, my mother was afraid she wouldn't have time to get all the women lessons in before I was gone.

JENNY: Did she?

ALICE: She told me what she knew. I guess that's the best anybody can do. (*Suddenly.*) Forgive me, Sister. I did what I could.

(*They embrace each other very gently. Alexis' car horn blows outside.*)

ALICE (*breaking the embrace and urging* JENNY *to the door*): Don't try to be brave now, Sister. Scream as loud as you want.

JENNY (*stops at the door and looks back at* ALICE): I love you, Mamma.

ALICE: And I was always some place loving you, Baby. I was always some place loving you. (JENNY *exits.* ALICE *sits down slowly in the rocking chair. She looks down slowly at the poem in her hand and all the energy seems to leave her body. She drops the pages to the floor.*) Don't fool yourself, Miss Alice. Just don't fool yourself.

(*Lights go down slowly.* ALICE *remains in a blue spot in the dark and then it also fades.* BLACK.)

PART FIVE

NONFICTION

OVERVIEW

Nonfiction is traditionally the genre in which ideas, experiences, and issues are presented more directly and more openly than in other literary modes. As such, nonfiction has provided a forum for African Americans to address matters of race and identity and to forge a community of shared ideas and experiences. It thus contains a plethora of written expressions—autobiographies, speeches, essays, letters, diaries, pamphlets, and journalistic pieces—written by former slaves, scholars, poets, preachers, and politicians, among others. While nonfiction is driven by a clear purpose and speaks to a distinct audience, often it is also influenced by other literary forms. This influence is especially evident here in the essay selections by writers whose other works include fiction or poetry. For example, factual content intersects with imaginative language in Martin R. Delany's "The Condition, Elevation, and Destiny of the Colored People," Audre Lorde's "Age, Race, Class, and Sex: Women Defining Difference," Ralph Ellison's "What America Would Be Like without Blacks," and Maya Angelou's *I Know Why the Caged Bird Sings*. These and many other African American writers have drawn on their imaginative impulses in nonfiction prose, employing metaphorical language, black colloquialisms, double meanings, allusions, and symbols to express their ideas. Ultimately, however, nonfiction is not judged for its similarity to other literary genres but for its success in persuading readers to accept the author's ideas.

The Personal and Collective Voice

Perhaps it is the clear-cut, direct nature of nonfiction as a mode of communication that has led many literary anthologies to neglect this type of writing as less imaginative than fiction and poetry. But African American nonfiction deserves special attention as a body of literature not only for its detailed portrait of African American life, history, and culture but also for its role in representing the personal and collective voices of African Americans. Sharing common experiences in this country, African Americans have sought to maintain a collective identity while also professing the self; as black writer-critic Gerald Early notes, the African American is black in a generic sense but is also a black individual (xvi). For over two hundred years, the nonfiction genre has allowed African American writers the greatest freedom to express their "generic" and "individual" identities.

Part Five focuses on the two dominant modes of African American nonfiction: the autobiography and the essay. Two other forms of nonfiction—orations and literary criticism—are covered in Parts One and Six, respectively.

Through autobiographical accounts and cultural and philosophical essays in particular, African American writers have since the sixteenth century expressed the personal and collective voices of black Americans.

Autobiography

The earliest autobiographies by blacks came in the form of the slave narrative in the mid-1700s. Dominating black nonfiction until the mid-nineteenth century, slave narratives gave way to autobiographies that detailed the diverse accomplishments of African Americans. And in the twentieth century, as blacks entered diverse and celebrated arenas within American society, the autobiography developed into a popular form of expression that reached a national readership of blacks and nonblacks.

Until the Civil War, black writers used the slave narratives to describe the various dimensions of slavery, as well as to convey personal experiences and political viewpoints. Most often written by men who had escaped slavery, the slave narrative became an essential tool of the abolitionist seeking to expose cruelties of slavery; to give testimony to the moral, religious, and other defining qualities of black culture; and to emphasize the unfulfilled educational and social potential of African Americans.

The first known African American autobiographical work, written by Briton Hammon in 1760, was the pamphlet *A Narrative of the Uncommon Sufferings and Surprising Deliverance of Briton Hammon, a Negro Man*. About three decades later, the more extensive autobiography of Olaudah Equiano was published. Two chapters of his *Interesting Narrative of the Life of Olaudah Equiano, or Gustavus Vassa, the African* (1789) are reprinted in Part Five. In addition, Harriet Jacobs's "The Perils of a Slave Woman's Life," excerpted from her *Incidents in the Life of a Slave Girl* (1860), provides an example of a nineteenth-century slave narrative by a black woman writer. These two autobiographical works provide contrasting accounts of life in slavery: Equiano documents his experiences as a black man who spent most of his life outside of America, while Jacobs depicts her life as a black woman who endured the hard labor and sexual exploitation of slavery.

Many other slave narratives, by such writers as Henry Bibb, Moses Roper, William and Ellen Craft, Solomon Northrup, Josiah Henson, William Wells Brown, and Frederick Douglass, helped complete the portrait of the institution of slavery in America in all its intrinsic malevolence. The most outstanding work in the slave narrative form, *Narrative of the Life of Frederick Douglass, an American Slave* (1845), was revised and updated by the writer several times between 1845 and 1881. In it Douglass contrasted his former life as a slave with his impressive accomplishments as a free man to underscore the significance of his experiences. His *Narrative* also provided insight into how African American families survived the threats posed by slavery and offered informative descriptions of urban slavery in contrast to the southern plantation variety.

Scholars have long debated the veracity of some slave narratives, questioning in particular the methods by which the works made their way into print. For example, some narratives were dictated by African Americans to white writers or supportive abolitionists for recording; other narratives were set down by black writers and then edited by white publishers. Some scholars have also criticized what they perceive as the sensational content, vague details, and didactic tone of certain slave narratives, arguing that the works were more like fiction than nonfiction. However, other critics have argued that the fictional elements of some slave narratives were rooted in the oral tradition (see Part One). That is, like the African American folktale, the slave narrative sought to entertain and teach its audience, and like the sermon, the slave narrative used an urgent tone to convey the promise of everlasting redemption to blacks who escaped slavery and to whites who opposed it.

Autobiographical Accounts of Upward Mobility

Post–Civil War autobiographical writings by African Americans maintained the prewar focus on slavery until the late nineteenth or early twentieth century, when accounts of upward mobility began to appear in the autobiographies of black educators, authors, and leaders, most of whom were men. These accounts, such as Kelly Miller's *Out of the House of Bondage* (1914) and James Corrothers's *In Spite of Handicap* (1916), served as a forum for discussing the dilemmas of and barriers to racial equality in post-Reconstruction America.

An especially important autobiographical work, Booker T. Washington's *Up from Slavery* (1901), bridged the tragedies of slavery and the triumphs of freedom. In the excerpt included in this part, we see why Washington's public persona offered evidence of the African American's ability to attain social status. Restrained in his attacks on the American system, Washington was a capitalist who, despite his exploitation by the system, was able to achieve eminence within it.

Autobiography in an Age of Literary Freedom

The number of autobiographies published by African American men and women increased as the twentieth century wore on. Most of these works emphasized the triumphs and achievements of their authors through inspirational prose aimed at confirming the values of perseverance and self-motivation as well as exposing defects in American society. In this period of great literary freedom and experimentation, black autobiographers have expressed their individuality while helping also to define the collective black identity.

One of the most outstanding black authors of autobiography in recent years, Maya Angelou is also a poet and an educator. She has made a literary career out of serializing her life, publishing five installments of her autobiography between 1970 and 1986. Caught in the web of rural–urban conflict, class challenges, gender exploitation, and social obstacles, Angelou has shared an intimate view of her experiences, giving a personal voice to decades of cultural, national, and international events. The excerpt from *I Know Why the Caged Bird Sings* (1970) in this part highlights Angelou's youth, particularly the traumatic circumstances of her adolescence.

The Autobiography of Malcolm X (1965) was a gripping account of this twentieth-century African American's life and his conflict with the American system of government. Malcolm X's inspirational story revealed how his religious faith, self-education, and political views combined to form his personal vision and philosophical commitment. In the excerpt appearing here, Malcolm X documents the remarkable process by which he became one of black culture's most enduring heroes and one of America's most influential leaders.

The life of a contemporary black woman who challenges assumptions inside and outside the African American community is chronicled in Itabari Njeri's *Every Good-bye Ain't Gone* (1990). Addressing the conflict within her family and her struggle as a young woman to formulate an identity inside her culture, her autobiography also uncovered two myths: the supposed resilience of the family structure and the presumed progressivism of the late 1960s' revolutionaries. In the chapter included here, "Has-beens Who Never Were," Njeri reflects on her high school and college years, a period of growth that took her from adolescent dreams of singing to an adulthood of journalism and black activism.

Cultural and Philosophical Essays

Early Arguments against Racism and Slavery

Black cultural and philosophical essayists of the eighteenth and nineteenth centuries used prose as a didactic instrument. Responding to the events and attitudes of their day, these writers addressed social injustice and ways of ending the oppression of African Americans.

Benjamin Banneker's eloquent "Letter to Thomas Jefferson" (1792) confronted the degrading views about blacks that Jefferson had expressed in his *Notes on the State of Virginia.* Although Banneker's scientific accomplishments alone refuted Jefferson's racist theories, he wrote the letter to expose the hypocrisy of racism practiced by those who also professed beliefs in Christian morality, equality, and freedom.

David Walker's *Appeal* (1829) and Martin R. Delany's *The Condition, Elevation, and Destiny of the Colored People* (1852) also dissect American racism in the pre–Civil War years. Significantly, both writers called for black activism, hoping to inspire blacks to fight collectively for freedom from slavery.

With Freedom, New Responsibilities and Dreams

In the years following Emancipation, as the first generation of manumitted blacks structured new lives throughout the country, African American nonfiction emphasized the goals and values blacks needed to become successful free citizens. At the same time, pioneering black intellectuals presented studies demonstrating the value of blacks to American society, including George Washington Williams's *History of the Negro Race in America* (1883), William T. Alexander's *History of the Colored Race in America* (1888), and W. E. B. Du Bois's *The Philadelphia Negro: A Social Study* (1899).

Integral to the late nineteenth- and early twentieth-century efforts to improve and "uplift" the condition of African Americans was the activism of black women in numerous women's clubs. Many black women who spearheaded local clubs and national organizations argued their viewpoints on race relations in speeches, journals, newspaper articles, and pamphlets, often outlining the appropriate roles for black women in the public and private spheres. Charlotte Forten Grimké, Josephine St. Pierre Ruffin, Margaret Murray Washington, Fannie Barrier Williams, Ida B. Wells-Barnett, Anna Julia Cooper, and Charlotte Hawkins Brown were among the women educators and writers who guided blacks in challenging the color line. In particular, the work of Mary Church Terrell, whose "What Role Is the Educated Negro Woman to Play in the Uplifting of Her Race?" (1902) is reprinted here, exemplifies the thinking among black women at the time in regard to racial improvement.

Twentieth-Century Essayists as Political Leaders

Twentieth-century African American writers continued to write essays, articles, and books exploring economic, social, political, and educational issues. Historian Carter Woodson's intellectual investigations supplemented the cultural and historical works of W. E. B. Du Bois. During the Harlem Renaissance of the 1920s, A. Phillip Randolph, Chandler Owen, and Hubert H. Harrison used the presses to reach into the black urban communities and raise political awareness. Known for their captivating speaking abilities, Du Bois, Randolph, and Harrison capitalized on the power of the spoken word to influence their audiences. Du Bois couched his orations in standard English for his integrated audiences, appropriately respecting black vernacular but choosing to stress his command of formal language. Randolph and Harrison both sought to reach working-class African Americans, recognizing that black vernacular would be as effective as the written word.

Two other noted authors of the 1920s were both executive officers in the NAACP: James Weldon Johnson, a poet, novelist, editorialist, lyricist, and anthologist, and Walter White, a novelist and writer of nonfiction. Their writings merged with their political activism and philosophical leadership to further the advancement of African Americans.

In opposition to the NAACP and other integrationist groups, Marcus Garvey's leadership proposed the more radical goals of black nationalism and emigration, echoing the separatist sentiments expressed by Delany and other nineteenth-century writers. Admired also as an orator, Garvey used his persuasive verbal skills to popularize black nationalism among millions of African Americans. He coined such slogans as "Black Is Beautiful" that demonstrated his awareness of the power of words and of images that could inspire black cultural pride and unity. In the essay appearing here, "An Appeal to the Conscience of the Black Race to See Itself" (circa 1923), Garvey urges racial independence for African Americans and strikes out against black leaders who advise blacks to imitate whites as the way to achieve "progress."

Contemporary scholar David Levering Lewis has furnished perceptive viewpoints on the Harlem Renaissance in his book *When Harlem Was in Vogue* (1981) and in his introduction to *The Portable Harlem Renaissance Reader* (1994), which appears in this part. In it Lewis assesses the Harlem Renaissance as "artificial and overreaching" yet invaluable for the legacy it bequeathed African Americans and American society.

Twentieth-Century Essayists as Artists

During the decades following the Harlem Renaissance, many notable African American nonfiction writers had already gained prominence for their work in other literary genres. The authors of the Depression and civil rights eras maintained the battle cry for racial equality in all areas of society. Among those figures were Sterling Brown, a poet and educator; Pauli Murray, a poet and lawyer; Richard Wright, a novelist and poet; John Oliver Killens, a novelist, educator, and critic; and James Baldwin, a novelist and playwright.

In addition, the novelist and critic Ralph Ellison was as important to black culture for his acclaimed novel, *Invisible Man* (1952), as for his cultural essays. In the selection included here, "What America Would Be Like without Blacks" (1986), Ellison dismantles the racist fantasy of a "blackless" America, providing a provocative contrast to the selections by Delany and Garvey. Pointing out the contributions of black culture to society, Ellison argues that blacks are Americans despite their history of oppression and that their integration into a pluralistic American society is a necessity.

The 1960s and 1970s: Black Power and the Black Arts Movement

The views of Ellison and other integrationists were vociferously challenged by many African American essayists of the late 1960s and 1970s. The new Black Power philosophy forced a close examination of the meaning of "Negro" versus "black" and of the value of integration versus separation. In "Black Power: Its Need and Substance" (1967), Kwame Toure and Charles V. Hamilton discussed the economic and political need for an autonomous black community. Advocating black nationalism, Toure and Hamilton envision an inextricable relationship among cultural survival, self-determination, and the "ethnic basis for American politics."

The Black Power doctrines prompted debates and influenced the Black Arts Movement of the 1960s and 1970s (see Larry Neal's essay in Part Six, p. 925). Amiri Baraka, a revered black nationalist and dramatist, examines the cultural and political significance of the life of Malcolm X in "Malcolm as Ideology" (1992). Baraka condemns the numerous public figures, both black and white, who have exploited the image of Malcolm X since his death.

Feminist and Gay Writers and Other Culture Critics

As happened across all the literary genres, many prose writers who had espoused the ethnocentrism of the Black Arts Movement began in the mid-1970s to broaden their social criticism and challenge traditional attitudes.

Some of these authors exhorted the African American community to recognize how sexual politics impeded the progress of the race. Cultural feminist critic bell hooks, in "Revolutionary Black Women: Making Ourselves Subject" (1992), underscores the importance of feminism in validating both the collective rage of black women and the struggles and triumphs of individuals. Angela Davis's "We Do Not Consent: Violence against Women in a Racist Society" (1989) argues that the sexual abuse of women is directly connected to American racial, gender, and class biases.

In addition, definitions and notions of sexuality within African American culture are examined in two other selections. Audre Lorde's "Age, Race, Class, and Sex: Women Redefining Difference" (1984) criticizes the narrow definitions of the "norm" in American society and the failure of society to appreciate women of color. Lorde asserts that mainstream society's rejection of difference also exists in the black community, particularly as it pertains to black lesbians. Ron Simmons, in "Some Thoughts on the Challenges Facing Black Gay Intellectuals" (1991), confronts homophobia in the African American community. He counters arguments made by black writers, intellectuals, and religious leaders that homosexuality destroys black culture and black families, while he details the accomplishments of black gay intellectuals and organizations.

The relationship between the oral tradition and pop music is discussed in Michael Eric Dyson's "The Culture of Hip-Hop" (1993). In an assessment of the overall impact of rap music, Dyson points to the connections between rap music and the experiences of young inner-city blacks. His commentary also includes an examination of the patriarchal attitudes that permeate both rap music and the U.S. music business, as well as criticism of the sexism in some rap lyrics.

In This Part

Part Five begins with a Focused Study of W. E. B. Du Bois, featuring three prose pieces. Also a writer of fiction and poetry, Du Bois gained prominence as a spokesperson for African Americans through his prose. Achieving the highest educational goals of mainstream America, Du Bois appropriated tools acquired at white educational institutions for the political ends and cultural awareness of his people. Sometimes limited in his perspectives and intolerant of other black leaders' views, Du Bois nonetheless guided the black community through the racial oppression of the 1900s to the early 1960s. The Critical Perspective offered by Marcus Bruce in "Black and Blue: W. E. B. Du Bois and the Meaning of Blackness" investigates the ways in which Du Bois gives form to black experiences in his writings.

The nonfiction selections that follow include numerous autobiographical pieces as well as cultural and philosophical essays. In each of these two sections, the selections are organized by the author's birth years to emphasize the historical progression of African American nonfiction.

Work Cited

Early, Gerald, ed. *Lure and Loathing: Essays on Race, Identity, and the Ambivalence of Assimilation.* New York: Penguin, 1993.

Suggested Readings

Published slave narratives include Sojourner Truth's *Narrative of Sojourner Truth, Northern Slave* (1850); Elizabeth Keckley's *Behind the Scenes; or Thirty Years a Slave, and Four Years in the White House* (1868); Charles H. Nichols's *Many Thousand Gone: The Ex-Slaves' Account of Their Bondage and Freedom* (1963); and Gilbert Osofsky's *Puttin On Ole Massa* (1969).

For autobiographical writing by African American leaders in such areas as politics, education, entertainment, athletics, religion, and the military, see Mary Church Terrell's *A Colored Woman in a White World* (1940); W. E. B. Du Bois's *Dusk of Dawn* (1940); Walter White's *A Man Called White* (1948); Pauli Murray's *Proud Shoes* (1956); Paul Robeson's *Here I Stand* (1958); Claude Brown's *Manchild in the Promised Land* (1965); Anne Moody's *Coming of Age in Mississippi* (1968); Angela Davis's *Angela Davis: An Autobiography* (1974); Marita Golden's *Migration of the Heart: A Personal Odyssey* (1983); Amiri Baraka's *The Autobiography of LeRoi Jones* (1984); Bebe Moore Campbell's *Sweet Summer: Growing Up with and without My Dad* (1989); Lorene Cary's *Black Ice* (1991); Jake Lamar's *Bourgeois Blues: An American Memoir* (1992); Arthur Ashe's *Days of Grace* (1993); Brent Staples's *Parallel Time: A Memoir* (1994); Nathan McCall's *Makes Me Wanna Holler* (1994); and Lawrence Otis Graham's *Member of the Club: Reflections on Life in a Racially Polarized World* (1995).

Memorable autobiographies of literary figures include Langston Hughes's *The Big Sea* (1940); Zora Neale Hurston's *Dust Tracks on the Road* (1942); Richard Wright's *Black Boy* (1945); Gwendolyn Brooks's *Report from Part One* (1972); Chester Himes's *The Quality of Hurt: The Autobiography of Chester Himes* (1972); Addison Gayle's *Wayward Child: A Personal Odyssey* (1977); and Adrienne Kennedy's *People Who Led to My Plays* (1987).

Related critical and historical accounts of African Americans are numerous. Some sources examine black autobiography: *Where I'm Bound: Patterns of Slavery and Freedom in Black American Autobiography* (1974) by Sidonie Smith and *To Tell a Free Story: The First Century of Afro-American Autobiography, 1760–1865* (1986) by William Andrews. Other texts combine autobiography and criticism: *Bearing Witness: Selections from African-American Autobiography in the Twentieth Century* (1991) edited by Henry

Louis Gates, Jr., and *Lure and Loathing: Race, Identity, and the Ambivalence of Assimilation* (1993) edited by Gerald Early. For works that focus on black women by combining autobiography, history, criticism, and even fiction, see Hallie Q. Brown's *Homespun Heroines and Other Women of Distinction* (1926); Mari Evans's collection *Black Women Writers, 1950–1980* (1984); Paula Giddings's *When and Where I Enter: The Impact of Black Women on Race and Sex in America* (1984); and Mary Helen Washington's collection *Invented Lives: Narratives of Black Women, 1860–1960* (1987).

In addition to the volumes already identified, collections of essays and cultural criticism include Margaret Just Butcher's *The Negro in American Culture* (1956); Arnold Rampersad's *The Art and Imagination of W. E. B. Du Bois* (1976); Arnold Rampersad and Deborah McDowell's collection *Slavery and the Literary Imagination* (1989); Arna Bontemps's *One Hundred Years of Freedom* (1961); James Baldwin's *The Fire Next Time* (1963); Albert L. Murray's *The Omni Americans: New Perspectives on Black Experience and American Culture* (1970); Gloria T. Hull, Patricia Bell Scott, and Barbara Smith's collection *All the Women Are White, All the Blacks Are Men, but Some of Us Are Brave* (1982); Patricia Hill Collins's *Black Feminist Thought: Knowledge, Consciousness, and the Politics of Empowerment* (1990); Essex Hemphill's *Brother to Brother: New Writings by Gay Black Men* (1991); and Cornel West's *Race Matters* (1993) and *Keeping Faith: Philosophy and Race in America* (1993).

A FOCUSED STUDY:
W. E. B. DU BOIS (1868-1963)

William Edward Burghardt Du Bois emerged as the most outstanding and most influential black intellectual during the first half of the twentieth century. Born in the small town of Great Barrington, Massachusetts, Du Bois, an only child, was reared in an environment with a minimum of racial conflicts. His parents separated when he was small, and his mother died shortly after his high school graduation.

Du Bois graduated from Fisk University in 1880; he entered Harvard University, earning a second bachelor's in 1890 and his master's in 1891. After attending the University of Berlin, he returned to Harvard and, in 1896, became the first African American to receive a doctorate from that institution. His doctoral dissertation, *The Suppression of the African Slave-Trade to the United States of America, 1638–1870,* was honored by being published in 1896 as the first volume in a series of Harvard historical studies.

Before receiving his doctorate, Du Bois was a professor of Greek and Latin at Wilberforce College, but his stormy relationship with the college prompted him to accept an invitation from the University of Pennsylvania to launch a sociological study of African Americans living in Philadelphia. That study of racial and urban history, *The Philadelphia Negro* (1899), won Du Bois respect for his scholarly approach to race in America. In 1897, he became professor of economics and history at Atlanta University, while continuing his exploration of the status of blacks. Following a series of conferences at that university, Du Bois spearheaded the publication of eighteen significant studies of African American issues, including "The Negro in Business" and "The Negro American Family."

As is evident in the first selection appearing here, "Of Mr. Booker T. Washington and Others," Du Bois rejected the then-prevalent philosophy of Washington, who advocated industrial training, racial segregation, and accommodation to the political status quo for improving the conditions of African Americans. Du Bois's *The Souls of Black Folk* (1903) outlines his own cultural, philosophical, and political critique of the black experience in America, calling for higher education, civil rights, and racial integration. In 1905, commenting on an incident involving black journalist-activist Monroe Trotter, who was arrested for speaking out in opposition during a speech by Booker T. Washington, Du Bois concluded: "When Trotter went to jail my indignation overflowed. I did not always agree with Trotter. . . . But he was an honest, brilliant, unselfish man, and to treat as a crime that which was at worst mistaken judgment was an outrage. I sent out from Atlanta in June 1905 a call to a few selected persons for organized determination and aggressive action on the part of men who believe in Negro freedom and growth." His call led to the Niagara Movement, an all-black coalition that sought to obtain voting rights and higher education for African Americans. In 1909, the coalition, joined by supportive whites, established the National

Association for the Advancement of Colored People (NAACP) to mount a battle for civil rights in all forms. Du Bois, a founding officer of the NAACP, developed and edited *Crisis,* the organization's literary magazine.

Among Du Bois's many activities in the 1920s, he published a book of essays—*Darkwater: Voices from within the Veil* (1920)—and a novel—*Dark Princess: A Romance* (1928)—and championed the Harlem Renaissance celebration of black culture and expression. Yet he vehemently opposed another black leader of his time—Marcus Garvey, whose "back to Africa" movement was supported by many African Americans. Viewing Garvey as a threat to his integrationist endeavors, Du Bois denounced Garvey's Black Nationalism and the activities of Garvey's United Negro Improvement Association (UNIA).

By the 1930s, Du Bois found himself in conflict with NAACP leaders, partly as a result of his growing Pan-Africanism and his respect for communism. He moved back into academic life, returning to Atlanta University to serve as chairperson of the sociology department. Also in the 1930s, he published *Black Reconstruction* (1935), a historical study of blacks during the post–Civil War period, and *Black Folk, Then and Now* (1939), which considered the cultural connection between Africa and black Americans. In the following decade, his *Dusk of Dawn: An Essay toward an Autobiography of a Race Concept* (1940) appeared. In 1944, Du Bois founded *Phylon,* a scholarly journal investigating problems of race relations.

Returning to the NAACP between 1944 and 1948 to serve as research director, by 1945 Du Bois was guiding the fifth Pan-African Congress and seeking effective methods to liberate black Africa from colonialism. He became increasingly caught up in the international struggle for liberation and peace, as well as becoming more sympathetic with communism. His political activities, which included running for the U.S. Senate on the American Labor Party roster, were cited by the federal government when it indicted Du Bois as a foreign agent in 1951. Although he was acquitted, Du Bois's passport was taken away, preventing him from overseas travel until his appeal in 1958. At that time, Du Bois went to Europe, China, and the Soviet Union, where he was awarded the International Lenin Prize.

The attention and support Du Bois received during the 1950s and early 1960s from communists, as well as his lack of support from leaders of the civil rights movement due to his age and political beliefs, moved him closer to more radical ranks of politics. In 1961, he joined the Communist Party and left the United States for Ghana, where he remained until his death in 1963.

In addition to the publications already noted, Du Bois's writings include several works of fiction: *The Quest of the Silver Fleece* (1911), *The Ordeal of Mansart* (1957), *Mansart Builds a School* (1959), *The Worlds of Color* (1961), and *Prayers for a Dark People* (1980), which was edited by Herbert Aptheker and published posthumously. His only volume of poetry, *Selected Poems by W. E. B. Du Bois* (1965), was also released after his death. Among Du Bois's other essays and scholarly works are *The Negro* (1915), *The Gift of Black Folk: The Negroes in the Making of America* (1924), *Africa: Its Place in Modern History* (1930), *Color and Democracy: Colonies and Peace* (1945), and *The World and Africa: An Inquiry into the Part Which Africa Has Played in World History* (1947). Dozens of texts containing Du Bois's writings have been edited by other scholars, and numerous critical studies about his writings and philosophies have appeared.

The first two essays in the Focused Study of Du Bois—"Of Mr. Booker T. Washington and Others" (1903) and "The Talented Tenth" (1903)—convey the essense of his philosophy. The first essay outlines the programs needed for racial advancement, while the second discusses the nature of black leadership in the future. In "The Souls of White Folk" (1920), Du Bois's harsh criticism of white colonialism combines with an indictment of a moral weakness among whites.

Of Mr. Booker T. Washington and Others

> From birth till death enslaved; in word, in deed, unmanned! . . .
>
> Hereditary bondsmen! Know ye not
> Who would be free themselves must strike the blow?
>
> —Byron

Easily the most striking thing in the history of the American Negro since 1876 is the ascendancy of Mr. Booker T. Washington. It began at the time when war memories and ideals were rapidly passing; a day of astonishing commercial development was dawning; a sense of doubt and hesitation overtook the freedmen's sons,—then it was that his leading began. Mr. Washington came, with a single definite programme, at the psychological moment when the nation was a little ashamed of having bestowed so much sentiment on Negroes, and was concentrating its energies on Dollars. His programme of industrial education, conciliation of the South, and submission and silence as to civil and political rights, was not wholly original; the Free Negroes from 1830 up to war-time had striven to build industrial schools, and the American Missionary Association had from the first taught various trades; and Price and others had sought a way of honorable alliance with the best of the Southerners. But Mr. Washington first indissolubly linked these things; he put enthusiasm, unlimited energy, and perfect faith into this programme, and changed it from a by-path into a veritable Way of Life. And the tale of the methods by which he did this is a fascinating study of human life.

It startled the nation to hear a Negro advocating such a programme after many decades of bitter complaint; it startled and won the applause of the South, it interested and won the admiration of the North; and after a confused murmur of protest, it silenced if it did not convert the Negroes themselves.

To gain the sympathy and coöperation of the various elements comprising the white South was Mr. Washington's first task; and this, at the time Tuskegee was founded, seemed, for a black man, well-nigh impossible. And yet ten years later it was done in the word spoken at Atlanta: "In all things purely social we can be as separate as the five fingers, and yet one as the hand in all things essential to mutual progress." This "Atlanta Compromise" is by all odds the most notable thing in Mr. Washington's career. The South interpreted it in different ways: the radicals received it as a complete surrender of the demand for civil and political equality; the conservatives, as a generously conceived working basis for mutual understanding. So both approved it, and to-day its author is certainly the most distinguished Southerner since Jefferson Davis, and the one with the largest personal following.

Next to this achievement comes Mr. Washington's work in gaining place and consideration in the North. Others less shrewd and tactful had formerly essayed to sit on these two stools and had fallen between them; but as Mr. Washington knew the heart of the South from birth and training, so by singular insight he intuitively grasped the spirit of the age which was dominating the North. And so thoroughly did he learn the speech and thought of triumphant commercialism, and the ideals of material prosperity, that the picture of a lone black boy poring over a French grammar amid the weeds and dirt of a neglected home soon seemed to him the acme of absurdities. One wonders what Socrates and St. Francis of Assisi would say to this.

And yet this very singleness of vision and thorough oneness with his age is a mark of the successful man. It is as though Nature must needs make men narrow in order to give them force. So Mr. Washington's cult has gained unquestioning followers, his work has wonderfully prospered, his friends are legion, and his enemies are confounded. To-day he stands as the one recognized spokesman of his ten million fellows, and one of the most notable figures in a nation of seventy millions. One hesitates, therefore, to criticize a life which, beginning with so little, has done so much. And yet the time is come when one may speak in all sincerity and utter courtesy of the mistakes and shortcomings of Mr. Washington's career, as well as of his triumphs, without being thought captious or envious, and without forgetting that it is easier to do ill than well in the world.

The criticism that has hitherto met Mr. Washington has not always been of this broad character. In the South especially has he had to walk warily to avoid the harshest judgments,—and naturally so, for he is dealing with the one subject of deepest sensitiveness to that section. Twice—once when at the Chicago celebration of the Spanish-American War he alluded to the color-prejudice that is "eating away the vitals of the South," and once when he dined with President Roosevelt—has the resulting Southern criticism been violent enough to threaten seriously his popularity. In the North the feeling has several times forced itself into words, that Mr. Washington's counsels of submission overlooked certain elements of true manhood, and that his educational programme was unnecessarily narrow. Usually, however, such criticism has not found open expression, although, too, the spiritual sons of the Abolitionists have not been prepared to acknowledge that the schools founded before Tuskegee, by men of broad ideals and self-sacrificing spirit, were wholly failures or worthy of ridicule. While, then, criticism has not failed to follow Mr. Washington, yet the prevailing public opinion of the land has been but too willing to deliver the solution of a wearisome problem into his hands, and say, "If that is all you and your race ask, take it."

Among his own people, however, Mr. Washington has encountered the strongest and most lasting opposition, amounting at times to bitterness, and even to-day continuing strong and insistent even though largely silenced in outward expression by the public opinion of the nation. Some of this opposition is, of course, mere envy; the disappointment of displaced demagogues and the spite of narrow minds. But aside from this, there is among educated and thoughtful colored men in all parts of the land a feeling of deep regret, sorrow, and apprehension at the wide currency and ascendancy which some of Mr. Washington's theories have gained. These same men admire his sincerity of purpose, and are willing to forgive much to honest endeavor which is doing something worth the doing. They coöperate with Mr. Washington as far as they conscientiously can; and, indeed, it is no ordinary tribute to this man's tact and power that, steering as he must between so many diverse interests and opinions, he so largely retains the respect of all.

But the hushing of the criticism of honest opponents is a dangerous thing. It leads some of the best of the critics to unfortunate silence and paralysis of effort, and others to burst into speech so passionately and intemperately as to lose listeners. Honest and earnest criticism from those whose interests are most nearly touched,—criticism of writers by readers, of government by those governed, of leaders by those led,—this is the soul of democracy and the safeguard of modern society. If the best of the American Negroes receive by outer pressure a leader whom they had not recognized before, manifestly there is here a certain palpable gain. Yet there is also irreparable loss,—a loss of that peculiarly valuable education which a group receives when by search and criticism it finds and commissions its own leaders. The way in which this is done is at once the most elementary and the nicest problem of social growth. History is but the record of such group-leadership; and yet how infinitely changeful is its type and character! And of all types and kinds, what can be more instructive than the leadership of a group within a group?—that curious double movement where real progress may be negative and actual advance be relative retrogression. All this is the social student's inspiration and despair.

Now in the past the American Negro has had instructive experience in the choosing of group leaders, founding thus a peculiar dynasty which in the light of present conditions is worth while studying. When sticks and stones and beasts form the sole environment of a people, their attitude is largely one of determined opposition to and conquest of natural forces. But when to earth and brute is added an environment of men and ideas, then the attitude of the imprisoned group may take three main forms,—a feeling of revolt and revenge; an attempt to adjust all thought and action to the will of the greater group; or, finally, a determined effort at self-realization and self-development despite environing opinion. The influence of all of these attitudes at various times can be traced in the history of the American Negro, and in the evolution of his successive leaders.

Before 1750, while the fire of African freedom still burned in the veins of the slaves, there was in all leadership or attempted leadership but the one motive of revolt and revenge,—typified in the terrible Maroons, the Danish blacks, and Cato of Stono, and veiling all the Americans in fear of insurrection. The liberalizing tendencies of the latter half of the eighteenth century brought, along with kindlier relations between black and white, thoughts of ultimate adjustment and assimilation. Such aspiration was especially voiced in the earnest songs of Phillis, in the martyrdom of Attucks, the fighting of Salem and Poor, the intellectual accomplishments of Banneker and Derham, and the political demands of the Cuffes.

Stern financial and social stress after the war cooled much of the previous humanitarian ardor. The disappointment and impatience of the Negroes at the persistence of slavery and serfdom voiced itself in two movements. The slaves in the South, aroused undoubtedly by vague rumors of the Haytian revolt, made three fierce attempts at insurrection,—in 1800 under Gabriel in Virginia, in 1822 under Vesey in Carolina, and in 1831 again in Virginia under the terrible Nat Turner. In the Free States, on the other hand, a new and curious attempt at self-development was made. In Philadelphia and New York color-prescription led to a withdrawal of Negro communicants from white churches and the formation of a peculiar socio-religious institution among the Negroes known as the African Church,—an organization still living and controlling in its various branches over a million of men.

Walker's wild appeal against the trend of the times showed how the world was changing after the coming of the cotton-gin. By 1830 slavery seemed hopelessly fastened on the South, and the slaves thoroughly cowed into submission. The free Negroes of the North, inspired by the mulatto immigrants from the West Indies, began to change the basis of their demands; they recognized the slavery of slaves, but insisted that they themselves were freemen, and sought assimilation and amalgamation with the nation on the same terms with other men. Thus, Forten and Purvis of Philadelphia, Shad of Wilmington, Du Bois of New Haven, Barbadoes of Boston, and others, strove singly and together as men, they said, not as slaves; as "people of color," not as "Negroes." The trend of the times, however, refused them recognition save in individual and exceptional cases, considered them as one with all the despised blacks, and they soon found themselves striving to keep even the rights they formerly had of voting and working and moving as freemen. Schemes of migration and colonization arose among them; but these they refused to entertain, and they eventually turned to the Abolition movement as a final refuge.

Here, led by Remond, Nell, Wells-Brown, and Douglass, a new period of self-assertion and self-development dawned. To be sure, ultimate freedom and assimilation was the ideal before the leaders, but the assertion of the manhood rights of the Negro by himself was the main reliance, and John Brown's raid was the extreme of its logic. After the war and emancipation, the great form of Frederick Douglass, the greatest of American Negro leaders, still led the host. Self-assertion, especially in political lines, was the main programme, and behind Douglass came Elliot, Bruce, and Langston, and the Reconstruction politicians, and, less conspicuous but of greater social significance Alexander Crummell and Bishop Daniel Payne.

Then came the Revolution of 1876, the suppression of the Negro votes, the changing and shifting of ideals, and the seeking of new lights in the great night. Douglass, in his old age, still bravely stood for the ideals of his early manhood,—ultimate assimilation *through* self-assertion, and on no other terms. For a time Price arose as a new leader, destined, it seemed, not to give up, but to re-state the old ideals in a form less repugnant to the white South. But he passed away in his prime. Then came the new leader. Nearly all the former ones had become leaders by the silent suffrage of their fellows, had sought to lead their own people alone, and were usually, save Douglass, little known outside their race. But Booker T. Washington arose as essentially the leader not of one race but of two,—a compromiser between the South, the North, and the Negro. Naturally the Negroes resented, at first bitterly, signs of compromise which surrendered their civil and political rights, even though this was to be exchanged for larger chances of economic development. The rich and dominating North, however, was not only weary of the race problem, but was investing largely in Southern enterprises, and welcomed any method of peaceful coöperation. Thus, by national opinion, the Negroes began to recognize Mr. Washington's leadership; and the voice of criticism was hushed.

Mr. Washington represents in Negro thought the old attitude of adjustment and submission; but adjustment at such a peculiar time as to make his programme unique. This is an age of unusual economic development, and Mr. Washington's programme naturally takes an economic cast, becoming a gospel of Work and Money to such an extent as apparently almost completely to overshadow the higher aims of life. Moreover, this is an age when the more advanced races are coming in closer contact with the less developed races, and the race-feeling is therefore intensified; and Mr. Washington's programme practically accepts the alleged inferiority of the Negro races. Again, in our own land, the reaction from the sentiment of war time has given impetus to race-prejudice against Negroes, and Mr. Washington withdraws many of the high demands of Negroes as men and American citizens. In other periods of intensified prejudice all the Negro's tendency to self-assertion has been called forth; at this period a policy of submission is advocated. In the history of nearly all other races and peoples the doctrine preached at such crises has been that manly self-respect is worth more than lands and houses, and that a people who voluntarily surrender such respect, or cease striving for it, are not worth civilizing.

In answer to this, it has been claimed that the Negro can survive only through submission. Mr. Washington distinctly asks that black people give up, at least for the present, three things,—

First, political power,

Second, insistence on civil rights,

Third, higher education of Negro youth,—

and concentrate all their energies on industrial education, the accumulation of wealth, and the conciliation of the South. This policy has been courageously and insistently advocated for over fifteen years, and has been triumphant for perhaps ten years. As a result of this tender of the palm-branch, what has been the return? In these years there have occurred:

1. The disfranchisement of the Negro.
2. The legal creation of a distinct status of civil inferiority for the Negro.
3. The steady withdrawal of aid from institutions for the higher training of the Negro.

These movements are not, to be sure, direct results of Mr. Washington's teachings; but his propaganda has, without a shadow of doubt, helped their speedier accomplishment. The question then comes: Is it possible, and probable, that nine millions of men can make effective progress in economic lines if they are deprived of political rights, made a servile caste, and allowed only the most meagre chance for developing their exceptional men? If history and reason give any distinct answer to these questions, it is an emphatic *No.* And Mr. Washington thus faces the triple paradox of his career:

1. He is striving nobly to make Negro artisans business men and property-owners; but it is utterly impossible, under modern competitive methods, for workingmen and property-owners to defend their rights and exist without the right of suffrage.

2. He insists on thrift and self-respect, but at the same time counsels a silent submission to civic inferiority such as is bound to sap the manhood of any race in the long run.

3. He advocates common-school and industrial training, and depreciates institutions of higher learning; but neither the Negro common-schools, nor Tuskegee itself, could remain open a day were it not for teachers trained in Negro colleges, or trained by their graduates.

This triple paradox in Mr. Washington's position is the object of criticism by two classes of colored Americans. One class is spiritually descended from Toussaint the Savior, through Gabriel, Vesey, and Turner, and they represent the attitude of revolt and revenge; they hate the white South blindly and distrust the white race generally, and so far as they agree on definite action, think that the Negro's only hope lies in emigration beyond the borders of the United States. And yet, by the irony of fate, nothing has more effectually made this programme seem hopeless than the recent course of the United States toward weaker and darker peoples in the West Indies, Hawaii, and the Philippines—for where in the world may we go and be safe from lying and brute force?

The other class of Negroes who cannot agree with Mr. Washington has hitherto said little aloud. They deprecate the sight of scattered counsels, of internal disagreement; and especially they dislike making their just criticism of a useful and earnest man an excuse for a general discharge of venom from small-minded opponents. Nevertheless, the questions involved are so fundamental and serious that it is difficult to see how men like the Grimkes, Kelly Miller, J. W. E. Bowen, and other representatives of this group, can much longer be silent. Such men feel in conscience bound to ask of this nation three things:

1. The right to vote.
2. Civic equality.
3. The education of youth according to ability.

They acknowledge Mr. Washington's invaluable service in counselling patience and courtesy in such demands; they do not ask that ignorant black men vote when ignorant whites are debarred, or that any reasonable restrictions in the suffrage should not be applied; they know that the low social level of the mass of the race is responsible for much discrimination against it, but they also know, and the nation knows, that relentless color-prejudice is more often a cause than a result of the Negro's degradation; they seek the abatement of this relic of barbarism, and not its systematic encouragement and pampering by all agencies of social power from the Associated Press to the Church of Christ. They advocate, with Mr. Washington, a broad system of Negro common schools supplemented by thorough industrial training; but they are surprised that a man of Mr. Washington's insight cannot see that no such educational system ever has rested or can rest on any other basis than that of the well-equipped college and university, and they insist that there is a demand for a few such institutions throughout the South to train the best of the Negro youth as teachers, professional men, and leaders.

This group of men honor Mr. Washington for his attitude of conciliation toward the white South; they accept the "Atlanta Compromise" in its broadest interpretation; they recognize, with him, many signs of promise, many men of high purpose and fair judgment, in this section; they know that no easy task has been laid upon a region already tottering under heavy burdens. But, nevertheless, they insist that the way to truth and right lies in straightforward honesty, not in indiscriminate flattery; in praising those of the South who do well and criticising uncompromisingly those who do ill; in taking advantage of the opportunities at hand and urging their fellows to do the same, but at the same time in remembering that only a firm adherence to their higher ideals and aspirations will ever keep those ideals within the realm of possibility. They do not expect that the free right to vote, to enjoy civic rights, and to be educated, will come in a moment; they do not expect to see the bias and prejudices of years disappear at the blast of a trumpet; but they are absolutely certain that the way for a people to gain their reasonable rights is not by voluntarily throwing them away and insisting that they do not want them; that the way for a people to gain respect is not by continually belittling and ridiculing themselves; that, on the contrary, Negroes must insist continually, in season and out of season, that voting is necessary to modern manhood, that color discrimination is barbarism, and that black boys need education as well as white boys.

In failing thus to state plainly and unequivocally the legitimate demands of their people, even at the cost of opposing an honored leader, the thinking classes of American Negroes would shirk a heavy responsibility,—a responsibility to themselves, a responsibility to the struggling masses, a responsibility to the darker races of men whose future depends so largely on this American experiment, but especially a responsibility to this nation,—this common Fatherland. It is wrong to aid and abet a national crime simply because it is unpopular not to do so. The growing spirit of kindliness and reconciliation between the North and South after the frightful difference of a generation ago ought to be a source of deep congratulation to all, and especially those whose mistreatment caused the war; but if that reconciliation is to be marked by the industrial slavery and civic death of those same black men, with permanent legislation into a position of inferiority, then those black men, if they are really men, are called upon by every consideration of patriotism and loyalty to oppose such a course by all civilized methods, even though such opposition involves disagreement with Mr. Booker T. Washington. We have no right to sit silently by while the inevitable seeds are sown for a harvest of disaster to our children, black and white.

First, it is the duty of black men to judge the South discriminatingly. The present generation of Southerners are not responsible for the past, and they should not be blindly hated or blamed for it. Furthermore, to no class is the indiscriminate endorsement of the recent course of the South toward Negroes more nauseating than to the best thought of the South. The South is not "solid"; it is a land in the ferment of social change, wherein forces of all kinds are fighting for supremacy; and to praise the ill the South is to-day perpetrating is just as wrong as to condemn the good. Discriminating and broad-minded criticism is what the South needs,—needs it for the sake of her own white sons and daughters, and for the insurance of robust, healthy mental and moral development.

To-day even the attitude of the Southern whites toward the blacks is not, as so many assume, in all cases the same; the ignorant Southerner hates the Negro, the workingmen fear his competition, the money-makers wish to use him as a laborer, some of the educated see a menace in his upward development, while others—usually the sons of the masters—wish to help him to rise. National opinion has enabled this last class to maintain the Negro common schools, and to protect the Negro partially in property, life, and limb. Through the pressure of the money-makers, the Negro is in danger of being reduced to semi-slavery, especially in the country districts; the workingmen, and those of the educated who fear the Negro, have united to disfranchise him, and some have urged his deportation; while the passions of the ignorant are easily aroused to lynch and abuse any black man. To praise this intricate whirl of thought and prejudice is nonsense; to inveigh indiscriminately against "the South" is unjust; but to use the same breath in praising Governor Aycock, exposing Senator Morgan, arguing with Mr. Thomas Nelson Page, and denouncing Senator Ben Tillman, is not only sane, but the imperative duty of thinking black men.

It would be unjust to Mr. Washington not to acknowledge that in several instances he has opposed movements in the South which were unjust to the Negro; he sent memorials to the Louisiana and Alabama constitutional conventions, he has spoken against lynching, and in other ways has openly or silently set his influence against sinister schemes and unfortunate happenings. Notwithstanding this, it is equally true to assert that on the whole the distinct impression left by Mr. Washington's propaganda is, first, that the South is justified in its present attitude toward the Negro because of the Negro's degradation; secondly, that the prime cause of the Negro's failure to rise more quickly is his wrong education in the past; and, thirdly, that his future rise depends primarily on his own efforts. Each of these propositions is a dangerous half-truth. The supplementary truths must never be lost sight of: first, slavery and race-prejudice are potent if not sufficient causes of the Negro's position; second, industrial and common-school training were necessarily slow in planting because they had to await the black teachers trained by higher institutions,—it being extremely doubtful if any essentially different development was possible, and certainly a Tuskegee was unthinkable before 1880; and, third, while it is a great truth to say that the Negro must strive and strive mightily to help himself, it is equally true that unless his striving be not simply seconded, but rather aroused and encouraged by the initiative of the richer and wiser environing group, he cannot hope for great success.

In his failure to realize and impress this last point, Mr. Washington is especially to be criticised. His doctrine has tended to make the whites, North and South, shift the burden of the Negro problem to the Negro's shoulders and stand aside as critical and rather pessimistic spectators; when in fact the burden belongs to the nation, and the hands of none of us are clean if we bend not our energies to righting these great wrongs.

The South ought to be led, by candid and honest criticism, to assert her better self and do her full duty to the race she has cruelly wronged and is still wronging. The North—her co-partner in guilt—cannot salve her conscience by plastering it with gold. We cannot settle this problem by diplomacy and suaveness, by "policy" alone. If worse come to worst, can the moral fibre of this country survive the slow throttling and murder of nine millions of men?

The black men of America have a duty to perform, a duty stern and delicate,—a forward movement to oppose a part of the work of their greatest leader. So far as Mr. Washington preaches Thrift, Patience, and Industrial Training for the masses, we must hold up his hands and strive with him, rejoicing in his honors and glorying in the strength of this Joshua called of God and of man to lead the headless host. But so far as Mr. Washington apologizes for injustice, North or South, does not rightly value the privilege and duty of voting, belittles the emasculating effects of caste distinctions, and opposes the higher training and ambition of our brighter minds,—so far as he, the South, or the Nation, does this,—we must unceasingly and firmly oppose them. By every civilized and peaceful method we must strive for the rights which the world accords to men, clinging unwaveringly to those great words which the sons of the Fathers would fain forget: "We hold these truths to be self-evident: That all men are created equal; that they are endowed by their Creator with certain unalienable rights; that among these are life, liberty, and the pursuit of happiness."

The Talented Tenth

The Negro race, like all races, is going to be saved by its exceptional men. The problem of education, then, among Negroes must first of all deal with the Talented Tenth; it is the problem of developing the Best of this race that they may guide the Mass away from the contamination and death of the Worst, in their own and other races. Now the training of men is a difficult and intricate task. Its technique is a matter for educational experts, but its object is for the vision of seers. If we make money the object of man-training, we shall develop money-makers but not necessarily men; if we make technical skill the object of education, we may possess artisans but not, in nature, men. Men we shall have only as we make manhood the object of the work of the schools—intelligence, broad sympathy, knowledge of the world that was and is, and of the relation of men to it—this is the curriculum of that Higher Education, which must underlie true life. On this foundation we may build bread winning, skill of hand and quickness of brain, with never a fear lest the child and man mistake the means of living for the object of life.

If this be true—and who can deny it—three tasks lay before me; first to show from the past that the Talented Tenth as they have arisen among American Negroes have been worthy of leadership; secondly, to show how these men may be educated and developed; and thirdly, to show their relation to the Negro problem.

You misjudge us because you do not know us. From the very first it has been the educated and intelligent of the Negro people that have led and elevated the mass, and the sole obstacles that nullified and retarded their efforts were slavery and race prejudice; for what is slavery but the legalized survival of the unfit and the nullification of the work of natural internal leadership? Negro leadership, therefore, sought from the first to rid the race of this awful incubus that it might make way for natural selection and the survival of the fittest. In colonial days came Phillis Wheatley and Paul Cuffe striving against the bars of prejudice; and Benjamin Banneker, the almanac maker, voiced their longings when he said to Thomas Jefferson,

> I freely and cheerfully acknowledge that I am of the African race, and in colour which is natural to them, of the deepest dye; and it is under a sense of the most profound gratitude to the Supreme Ruler of the Universe, that I now confess to you that I am not under that state of tyrannical thraldom and inhuman captivity to which too many of my brethren are doomed, but that I have abundantly tasted of the fruition of those blessings which proceed from that free and unequalled liberty with which you are favored, and which I hope you will willingly allow, you have mercifully received from the immediate hand of that Being from whom proceedeth every good and perfect gift.
>
> Suffer me to recall to your mind that time, in which the arms of the British crown were exerted with every powerful effort, in order to reduce you to a state of servitude; look back, I entreat you, on the variety of dangers to which you were exposed; reflect on that period in which every human aid appeared unavailable, and in which even hope and fortitude wore the aspect of inability to the conflict, and you cannot but be led to a serious and grateful sense of your miraculous and providential preservation, you cannot but acknowledge, that the present freedom

> and tranquility which you enjoy, you have mercifully received, and that a peculiar blessing of heaven.
>
> This, sir, was a time when you clearly saw into the injustice of a state of Slavery, and in which you had just apprehensions of the horrors of its condition. It was then that your abhorrence thereof was so excited, that you publicly held forth this true and invaluable doctrine, which is worthy to be recorded and remembered in all succeeding ages: "We hold these truths to be self-evident, that all men are created equal; that they are endowed with certain inalienable rights, and that among these are life, liberty and the pursuit of happiness."

Then came Dr. James Derham, who could tell even the learned Dr. Rush something of medicine, and Lemuel Haynes, to whom Middlebury College gave an honorary A.M. in 1804. These and others we may call the Revolutionary group of distinguished Negroes—they were persons of marked ability, leaders of a Talented Tenth, standing conspicuously among the best of their time. They strove by word and deed to save the color line from becoming the line between the bond and free, but all they could do was nullified by Eli Whitney and the Curse of Gold. So they passed into forgetfulness.

But their spirit did not wholly die; here and there in the early part of the century came other exceptional men. Some were natural sons of unnatural fathers and were given often a liberal training and thus a race of educated mulattoes sprang up to plead for black men's rights. There was Ira Aldridge, whom all Europe loved to honor; there was that Voice crying in the Wilderness, David Walker, and saying:

> I declare it does appear to me as though some nations think God is asleep, or that he made the Africans for nothing else but to dig their mines and work their farms, or they cannot believe history, sacred or profane. I ask every man who has a heart, and is blessed with the privilege of believing—Is not God a God of justice to all his creatures? Do you say he is? Then if he gives peace and tranquility to tyrants and permits them to keep our fathers, our mothers, ourselves and our children in eternal ignorance and wretchedness to support them and their families, would he be to us a God of Justice? I ask, O, ye Christians, who hold us and our children in the most abject ignorance and degradation that ever a people were afflicted with since the world began—I say if God gives you peace and tranquility, and suffers you thus to go on afflicting us, and our children, who have never given you the least provocation—would He be to us a God of Justice? If you will allow that we are men, who feel for each other, does not the blood of our fathers and of us, their children, cry aloud to the Lord of Sabaoth against you for the cruelties and murders with which you have and do continue to afflict us?

This was the wild voice that first aroused Southern legislators in 1829 to the terrors of abolitionism.

In 1831 there met that first Negro convention in Philadelphia, at which the world gaped curiously but which bravely attacked the problems of race and slavery, crying out against persecution and declaring that "Laws as cruel in themselves as they were unconstitutional and unjust, have in many places been enacted against our poor, unfriended and unoffending Brethren (without a shadow of provocation on our part), at whose bare recital the very savage draws himself up for fear of contagion—looks noble and prides himself because he bears not the name of Christian." Side by side this free Negro movement, and the movement for abolition, strove until they merged into one strong stream. Too little notice has been taken of the work which the Talented Tenth among Negroes took in the great abolition crusade. From the very day that a Philadelphia colored man became the first subscriber to Garrison's *Liberator,* to the day when Negro soldiers made the Emancipation Proclamation possible, black leaders worked shoulder to shoulder with white men in a movement, the success of which would have been impossible without them. There was Purvis and Remond, Pennington and Highland Garnett, Sojourner Truth and Alexander Crummel, and above all, Frederick Douglass—what would the abolition movement have been without them? They stood as living examples of the possibilities of the Negro race, their own hard experiences and well wrought culture said silently more than all the drawn periods of orators—they were the men who made American slavery impossible. As Maria Weston Chapman once said, from the school of anti-slavery agitation:

> a throng of authors, editors, lawyers, orators and accomplished gentlemen of color have taken their degree! It has equally implanted hopes and aspirations, noble thoughts, and sublime purposes, in the hearts of both races. It has prepared the white man for the freedom of the black man, and it has made the black man scorn the thought of enslavement, as does a white man, as far as its influence has extended. Strengthen that noble influence! Before its organization, the country only saw here and there in slavery some faithful Cudjoe or Dinah, whose strong natures blossomed even in bondage, like a fine plant beneath a heavy stone. Now, under the elevating and cherishing influence of the American Anti-slavery Society, the colored race, like the white, furnishes Corinthian capitals for the noblest temples.

Where were these black abolitionists trained? Some, like Frederick Douglass, were self-trained, but yet trained liberally; others, like Alexander Crummell and McCune Smith, graduated from famous foreign universities. Most of them rose up through the colored schools of New York and Philadelphia and Boston, taught by college-bred men like Russworm, of Dartmouth, and college-bred white men like Neau and Benezet.

After emancipation came a new group of educated and gifted leaders: Langston, Bruce and Elliot, Greener, Williams and Payne. Through political organization, historical and polemic writing and moral regeneration, these men strove to uplift their people. It is the fashion of to-day to sneer at them and to say that with freedom Negro leadership should have begun at the plow and not in the Senate—a foolish and mischievous lie; two hundred and fifty years that black serf toiled at the plow and yet that toiling was in vain till the Senate passed the war amendments; and two hundred and fifty years more the half-free serf of to-day may toil at his plow, but unless he have political rights and righteously guarded civic status, he will still remain the poverty-stricken and ignorant plaything of rascals, that he now is. This all sane men know even if they dare not say it.

And so we come to the present—a day of cowardice and vacillation, of strident wide-voiced wrong and faint hearted compromise; of double-faced dallying with Truth and Right. Who are to-day guiding the work of the Negro people? The "exceptions" of course. And yet so sure as this Talented Tenth is pointed out, the blind worshippers of the Average cry out in alarm: "These are exceptions, look here at death, disease and crime—these are the happy rule." Of course they are the rule, because a silly nation made them the rule: Because for three long centuries this people lynched Negroes who dared to be brave, raped black women who dared to be virtuous, crushed dark-hued youth who dared to be ambitious, and encouraged and made to flourish servility and lewdness and apathy. But not even this was able to crush all manhood and chastity and aspiration from black folk. A saving remnant continually survives and persists, continually aspires, continually shows itself in thrift and ability and character. Exceptional it is to be sure, but this is its chiefest promise; it shows the capability of Negro blood, the promise of black men. Do Americans ever stop to reflect that there are in this land a million men of Negro blood, well-educated, owners of homes, against the honor of whose womanhood no breath was ever raised, whose men occupy positions of trust and usefulness, and who, judged by any standard, have reached the full measure of the best type of modern European culture? Is it fair, is it decent, is it Christian to ignore these facts of the Negro problem, to belittle such aspiration, to nullify such leadership and seek to crush these people back into the mass out of which by toil and travail, they and their fathers have raised themselves?

Can the masses of the Negro people be in any possible way more quickly raised than by the effort and example of this aristocracy of talent and character? Was there ever a nation on God's fair earth civilized from the bottom upward? Never; it is, ever was and ever will be from the top downward that culture filters. The Talented Tenth rises and pulls all that are worth the saving up to their vantage ground. This is the history of human progress; and the two historic mistakes which have hindered that progress were the thinking first that no more could ever rise save the few already risen; or second, that it would better the unrisen to pull the risen down.

How then shall the leaders of a struggling people be trained and the hands of the risen few strengthened? There can be but one answer: The best and most capable of their youth must be schooled in the colleges and universities of the land. We will not quarrel as to just what the university of the Negro should teach or how it should teach it—I willingly admit that each soul and each race-soul needs its own peculiar curriculum. But this is true: A university is a human invention for the transmission of knowledge and culture from generation to generation, through the training of quick minds and pure hearts, and for this work no other human invention will suffice, not even trade and industrial schools.

All men cannot go to college but some men must; every isolated group or nation must have its yeast, must have for the talented few centers of training where men are not so mystified and befuddled by the hard and necessary toil of earning a living, as to have no aims higher than their bellies, and no God greater than Gold. This is true training, and thus in the beginning were the favored sons of the freedmen trained. Out of the colleges of the North came, after the blood of war, Ware, Cravath, Chase, Andrews, Bumstead and Spence to build the foundations of knowledge and civilization in the black South. Where ought they to have begun to build? At the bottom, of course, quibbles the mole with his eyes in the earth. Aye! truly at the bottom, at the very bottom; at the bottom of knowledge, down in the very depths of knowledge there where the roots of justice strike into the lowest soil of Truth. And so they did begin; they founded colleges, and up from the normal schools went teachers, and around the normal teachers clustered other teachers to teach the public schools; the college trained in Greek and Latin and mathematics, 2,000 men; and these men trained full 50,000 others in morals and manners, and they in turn taught thrift and the alphabet to nine millions of men, who to-day hold $300,000,000 of property. It was a miracle—the most wonderful peace-battle of the 19th century, and yet to-day men smile at it, and in fine superiority tell us that it was a strange mistake; that a proper way to found a system of education is first to gather the children and buy them spelling books and hoes; afterward men may look about for teachers, if haply they may find them; or again they would teach men Work, but as for Life—why, what has Work to do with Life, they ask vacantly.

Was the work of these college founders successful; did it stand the test of time? Did the college graduates, with all their fine theories of life, really live? Are they useful men helping to civilize and elevate their less fortunate fellows? Let us see. Omitting all institutions which have not actually graduated students from a college course, there are to-day in the United States thirty-four institutions giving something above high school training for Negroes and designed especially for this race.

Three of these were established in border States before the War; thirteen were planted by the Freedmen's Bureau in the years 1864–1869; nine were established between 1870 and 1880 by various church bodies; five were established after 1881 by Negro churches, and four are state institutions supported by United States' agricultural funds. In most cases the college departments are small adjuncts to high and common school work. As a matter of fact six institutions—Atlanta, Fisk, Howard, Shaw, Wilberforce and Leland—are the important Negro colleges so far as actual work and number of students are concerned. In all these institutions, seven hundred and fifty Negro college students are enrolled. In grade the best of these colleges are about a year behind the smaller New England colleges and a typical curriculum is that of Atlanta University. Here students from the grammar grades, after a three years' high school course, take a college course of 136 weeks. One-fourth of this time is given to Latin and Greek; one-fifth, to English and modern languages; one-sixth, to history and social science; one-seventh, to natural science; one-eighth to mathematics, and one-eighth to philosophy and pedagogy.

In addition to these students in the South, Negroes have attended Northern colleges for many years. As early as 1826 one was graduated from Bowdoin College, and from that time till to-day nearly every year has seen elsewhere, other such graduates. They have, of course, met much color prejudice. Fifty years ago very few colleges would admit them at all. Even to-day no Negro has ever been admitted to Princeton, and at some other leading institutions they are rather endured than encouraged. Oberlin was the great pioneer in the work of blotting out the color line in colleges, and has more Negro graduates by far than any other Northern college.

The total number of Negro college graduates up to 1899, (several of the graduates of that year not being reported), was as [shown in the accompanying table]:

	Negro Colleges	White Colleges
Before 1876	137	75
1875–80	143	22
1880–85	250	31
1885–90	413	43
1890–95	465	66
1895–99	475	88
Class Unknown	57	64
Total	1,914	390

Of these graduates 2,079 were men and 252 were women; 50 per cent of Northern-born college men come South to work among the masses of their people, at a sacrifice which few people realize; nearly 90 per cent of the Southern-born graduates instead of seeking that personal freedom and broader intellectual atmosphere which their training has led them, in some degree, to conceive, stay and labor and wait in the midst of their black neighbors and relatives.

The most interesting question, and in many respects the crucial question, to be asked concerning college-bred Negroes, is: Do they earn a living? It has been intimated more than once that the higher training of Negroes has resulted in sending into the world of work, men who could find nothing to do suitable to their talents. Now and then there comes a rumor of a colored college man working at menial service, etc. Fortunately, returns as to occupations of college-bred Negroes, gathered by the Atlanta conference, are quite full—nearly 60 per cent of the total number of graduates.

This enables us to reach fairly certain conclusions as to the occupations of all college-bred Negroes. Of 1,312 persons reported, [occupations were as shown in the accompanying table]:

	Per Cent
Teachers	53.4
Clergymen	16.8
Physicians, etc.	6.3
Students	5.6
Lawyers	4.7
In Govt. Service	4.0
In Business	3.6
Farmers and Artisans	2.7
Editors, Secretaries and Clerks	2.4
Miscellaneous	0.5

Over half are teachers, a sixth are preachers, another sixth are students and professional men; over 6 per cent are farmers, artisans and merchants, and 4 per cent are in government service. In detail the occupations are as follows:

Occupations of College-Bred Men

Teachers:	
Presidents and Deans	19
Teachers of Music	7

Professors, Principals and Teachers	675	Total 701
Clergymen:		
Bishop	1	
Chaplains U.S. Army	2	
Missionaries	9	
Presiding Elders	12	
Preachers	197	Total 221
Physicians:		
Doctors of Medicine	76	
Druggists	4	
Dentists	3	Total 83
Students	74	
Lawyers	62	
Civil Service:		
U.S. Minister Plenipotentiary	1	
U.S. Consul	1	
U.S. Deputy Collector	1	
U.S. Gauger	1	
U.S. Postmasters	2	
U.S. Clerks	44	
State Civil Service	2	
City Civil Service	1	Total 53
Business Men:		
Merchants, etc.	30	
Managers	13	
Real Estate Dealers	4	Total 47
Farmers	26	
Clerks and Secretaries:		
Secretary of National Societies	7	
Clerks, etc.	15	Total 22
Artisans	9	
Editors	9	
Miscellaneous	5	

These figures illustrate vividly the function of the college-bred Negro. He is, as he ought to be, the group leader, the man who sets the ideals of the community where he lives, directs its thoughts and heads its social movements. It need hardly be argued that the Negro people need social leadership more than most groups: that they have no traditions to fall back upon, no long established customs, no strong family ties, no well defined social classes. All these things must be slowly and painfully evolved. The preacher was, even before the war, the group leader of the Negroes, and the church their greatest social institution. Naturally this preacher was ignorant and often immoral, and the problem of replacing the older type by better educated men has been a difficult one. Both by direct work and by direct influence on other preachers, and on congregations, the college-bred preacher has an opportunity for reformatory work and moral inspiration, the value of which cannot be overestimated.

It has, however, been in the furnishing of teachers that the Negro college has found its peculiar function. Few persons realize how vast a work, how mighty a revolution has been thus accomplished. To furnish five millions and more of ignorant people with teachers of their own race and blood, in one generation, was not only a very difficult undertaking, but a very important one, in that, it placed before the eyes of almost every Negro child an attainable ideal. It brought the masses of the blacks in contact with modern civilization, made black men the leaders of their communities and trainers of the new generation. In this work college-bred Negroes were first teachers, and then teachers of teachers. And here it is that the broad culture of college work has been of peculiar value. Knowledge of life and its wider meaning, has been the point of the Negro's deepest ignorance, and the sending out of teachers whose training has not been simply for bread winning, but also for human culture, has been of inestimable value in the training of these men.

In earlier years the two occupations of preacher and teacher were practically the only ones open to the black college graduate. Of later years a larger diversity of life among his people, has opened new avenues of employment. Nor have these college men been paupers and spendthrifts; 557 college-bred Negroes owned in 1899, $1,342,862.50 worth of real estate, (assessed value) or $2,411 per family. The real value of the total accumulations of the whole group is perhaps about $10,000,000, or $5,000 a piece. Pitiful, is it not, beside the fortunes of oil kings and steel trusts, but after all is the fortune of the millionaire the only stamp of true and successful living? Alas! it is, with many, and there's the rub.

The problem of training the Negro is to-day immensely complicated by the fact that the whole question of the efficiency and appropriateness of our present systems of education, for any kind of child, is a matter of active debate, in which final settlement seems still afar off. Consequently it often happens that persons arguing for or against certain systems of education for Negroes, have these controversies in mind and miss the real question at issue. The main question, so far as the Southern Negro is concerned, is: What under the present circumstance, must a system of education do in order to raise the Negro as quickly as possible in the scale of civilization? The answer to this question seems to me clear: It must strengthen the Negro's character, increase his knowledge and teach him to earn a living. Now it goes without saying, that it is hard to do all these things simultaneously or suddenly, and that at the same time it will not do to give all the attention to one and neglect the others: we could give the black boys trades, but that alone will not civilize a race of ex-slaves; we might simply increase their knowledge of the world, but this would not necessarily make them wish to use this knowledge honestly; we might seek to strengthen character and purpose, but to what end if this people have nothing to eat or to wear? A system of education is not one thing, nor does it have a single definite object, nor is it a mere matter of schools. Education is that whole system of human training within and without the school house walls, which molds and develops men. If then we start out to train an ignorant and unskilled people with a heritage of bad habits, our system of training must set before itself two great aims—the one dealing with knowledge and character, the other part seeking to give the child the technical knowledge necessary for him to earn a living under the present circumstances. These objects are accomplished in part by the opening of the common schools on the one, and of industrial schools on the other. But only in part, for there must also be trained those who are to teach these schools—men and women of knowledge and culture and technical skill who understand modern civilization, and have the training and aptitude to impart it to the children under them. There must be teachers, and teachers of teachers, and to attempt to establish any sort of a system of common and industrial school training, without *first* (and I say *first* advisedly) without *first* providing for the higher training of the very best teachers, is simply throwing your money to the winds. School houses do not teach themselves—piles of brick and mortar and machinery do not send out *men*. It is the trained, living human soul, cultivated and strengthened by long study and thought, that breathes the real breath of life into boys and girls and makes them human, whether they be black or white, Greek, Russian or American. Nothing, in these latter days, has so dampened the faith of thinking Negroes in recent educational movements, as the fact that such movements have been accompanied by ridicule and denouncement and decrying of those very institutions of higher training which made the Negro public school possible, and make Negro industrial schools thinkable. It was Fisk, Atlanta, Howard and Straight, those colleges born of the faith and sacrifice of the abolitionists, that placed in the black schools of the South the 30,000 teachers and more, which some, who depreciate the work of these higher schools, are using to teach their own new experiments. If Hampton, Tuskegee and the hundred other industrial schools prove in the future to be as successful as they deserve to be, then their success in training black artisans for the South, will be due primarily to the white colleges of the North and the black colleges of the South, which trained the teachers who to-day conduct these institutions. There was a time when the American people believed pretty devoutly that a log of wood with a boy at one end and Mark Hopkins at the other, represented the highest ideal of human training. But in these eager days it would seem that we have changed all that and think it necessary to add a couple of saw-mills and a hammer to this outfit, and, at a pinch, to dispense with the services of Mark Hopkins.

I would not deny, or for a moment seem to deny, the paramount necessity of teaching the Negro to work, and to work steadily and skillfully; or seem to depreciate in the slightest degree the important part industrial schools must play in the accomplishment of these ends, but I do say, and insist upon it, that it is industrialism drunk with its vision of success, to imagine that its own work can be accomplished without providing for the training of broadly cultured men and women to teach its own teachers, and to teach the teachers of the public schools.

But I have already said that human education is not simply a matter of schools; it is much more a matter of family and group life—the training of one's home, of one's daily companions, of one's social class. Now the black boy of the South moves in a black world—a world with its own leaders, its own thoughts, its own ideals. In this world he gets by far the larger part of his life training, and through the eyes of this dark world he peers into the veiled world beyond. Who guides and determines the education which he receives in his world? His teachers here are the group-leaders of the Negro people—the physicians and clergymen, the trained fathers and mothers, the influential and forceful men about him of all kinds; here it is, if at all, that the culture of the surrounding world trickles through and is handed on by the graduates of the higher schools. Can such culture training of group leaders be neglected? Can we afford to ignore it? Do you think that if the leaders of thought among Negroes are not trained and educated thinkers, that they will have no leaders? On the contrary a hundred half-trained demagogues will still hold the places they so largely occupy now, and hundreds of vociferous busy-bodies will multiply. You have no choice; either you must help furnish this race from within its own ranks with thoughtful men of trained leadership, or you must suffer the evil consequences of a headless misguided rabble.

I am an earnest advocate of manual training and trade teaching for black boys, and for white boys, too. I believe that next to the founding of Negro colleges the most valuable addition to Negro education since the war, has been industrial training for black boys. Nevertheless, I insist that the object of all true education is not to make men carpenters, it is to make carpenters men; there are two means of making the carpenter a man, each equally important: the first is to give the group and community in which he works, liberally trained teachers and leaders to teach him and his family what life means: the second is to give him sufficient intelligence and technical skill to make him an efficient workman; the first object demands the Negro college and college-bred men—not a quantity of such colleges, but a few of excellent quality; not too many college-bred men, but enough to leaven the lump, to inspire the masses, to raise the Talented Tenth to leadership; the second object demands a good system of common schools, well-taught, conveniently located and properly equipped.

The Sixth Atlanta Conference truly said in 1901:

> We call the attention of the Nation to the fact that less than one million of the three million Negro children of school age, are at present regularly attending school, and these attend a session which lasts only a few months.
>
> We are to-day deliberately rearing millions of our citizens in ignorance, and at the same time limiting the rights of citizenship by educational qualifications. This is unjust. Half the black youth of the land have no opportunities open to them for learning to read, write and cipher. In the discussion as to the proper training of Negro children after they leave the public schools, we have forgotten that they are not yet decently provided with public schools.
>
> Propositions are beginning to be made in the South to reduce the already meagre school facilities of Negroes. We congratulate the South on resisting, as much as it has, this pressure, and on the many millions it has spent on Negro education. But it is only fair to point out that Negro taxes and the Negroes' share of the income from indirect taxes and endowments have fully repaid this expenditure, so that the Negro public school system has not in all probability cost the white taxpayers a single cent since the war.
>
> This is not fair. Negro schools should be a public burden, since they are a public benefit. The Negro has a right to demand good common school training at the hands of the States and the Nation since by their fault he is not in position to pay for this himself.

What is the chief need for the building up of the Negro public school in the South? The Negro race in the South needs teachers to-day above all else. This is the concurrent testimony of all who know the situation. For the supply of this great demand two things are needed—institutions of higher education and money for school houses and salaries. It is usually assumed that a hundred or more institutions for Negro training are to-day turning out so many teachers and college-bred men that the race is threatened with an over-supply. This is sheer nonsense. There are to-day less than 3,000 living Negro college graduates in the United States, and less than 1,000 Negroes in college. Moreover, in the 164 schools for Negroes, 95 per cent of their students are doing elementary and secondary work, work which should be done in the public schools. Over half the remaining 2,157 students are taking high school studies. The mass of so-called "normal" schools for the Negro, are simply doing elementary common school work, or, at most, high school work, with a little instruction in methods. The Negro colleges and the post-graduate courses at other institutions are the only agencies for the broader and more careful training of teachers. The work of these institutions is hampered for lack of funds. It is getting increasingly difficult to get funds for training teachers in the best modern methods, and yet all over the South, from State Superintendents, county officials, city boards and school principals comes the wail, "We need TEACHERS!" and teachers must be trained. As the fairest minded of all white Southerners, Atticus G. Haygood, once said:

> The defects of colored teachers are so great as to create an urgent necessity for training better ones. Their excellencies and their successes are sufficient to justify the best hopes of success in the effort, and to vindicate the judgment of those who make large investments of money and service, to give to colored students opportunity for thoroughly preparing themselves for the work of teaching children of their people.

The truth of this has been strikingly shown in the marked improvement of white teachers in the South. Twenty years ago the rank and file of white public school teachers were not as good as the Negro teachers. But they, by scholarships and good salaries, have been encouraged to thorough normal and collegiate preparation, while the Negro teachers have been discouraged by starvation wages and the idea that any training will do for a black teacher. If carpenters are needed it is well and good to train men as carpenters. But to train men as carpenters, and then set them to teaching is wasteful and criminal; and to train men as teachers and then refuse them living wages, unless they become carpenters, is rank nonsense.

The United States Commissioner of Education says in his report for 1900:

> For comparison between the white and colored enrollment in secondary and higher education, I have added together the enrollment in high schools and secondary schools, with the attendance on colleges and universities, not being sure of the actual grade of work done in the colleges and universities. The work done in the secondary schools is reported in such detail in this office, that there can be no doubt of its grade.

He then makes the following comparisons of persons in every million enrolled in secondary and higher education:

	Whole Country	Negroes
1880	4,362	1,289
1900	10,743	2,061

And he concludes:

> While the number in colored high schools and colleges had increased somewhat faster than the population, it had not kept pace with the average of the whole country, for it had fallen from 30 per cent to 24 per cent of the average quota. Of all colored pupils, one (1) in one hundred was engaged in secondary and higher work, and that ratio has continued substantially for the past twenty years. If the ratio of colored population in secondary and higher education is to be equal to the average for the whole country, it must be increased to five times its present average.

And if this be true of the secondary and higher education, it is safe to say that the Negro has not one-tenth his quota in college studies. How baseless, therefore, is the charge of too much training! We need Negro teachers for the Negro common schools and colleges to train them. This is the work of higher Negro education and it must be done.

Further than this, after being provided with group leaders of civilization, and a foundation of intelligence in the public schools, the carpenter, in order to be a man, needs technical skill. This calls for trade schools. Now trade schools are not nearly such simple things as people once thought. The original idea was that the "Industrial" school was to furnish education, practically free, to those willing to work for it; it was to "do" things—i.e.: become a center of productive industry, it was to be partially, if not wholly, self-supporting, and it was to teach trades. Admirable as were some of the ideas underlying this scheme, the whole thing simply would not work in practice; it was found that if you were to use time and material to teach trades thoroughly, you could not at the same time keep the industries on a commercial basis and make them pay. Many schools started out to do this on a large scale and went into virtual bankruptcy. Moreover, it was found also that it was possible to teach a boy a trade mechanically, without giving him the full educative benefit of the process, and, vice versa, that there was a distinctive educative value in teaching a boy to use his hands and eyes in carrying out certain physical processes, even though he did not actually learn a trade. It has happened, therefore, in the last decade, that a noticeable change has come over the industrial schools. In the first place the idea of commercially remunerative industry in a school is being pushed rapidly to the background. There are still schools with shops and farms that bring an income, and schools that use student labor partially for the erection of their buildings and the furnishing of equipment. It is coming to be seen, however, in the education of the youths the world over, that it is the *boy* and not the material product, that is the true object of education. Consequently the object of the industrial school came to be the thorough training of boys regardless of the cost of the training, so long as it was thoroughly well done.

Even at this point, however, the difficulties were not surmounted. In the first place modern industry has taken great strides since the war, and the teaching of trades is no longer a simple matter. Machinery and long processes of work have greatly changed the work of the carpenter, the ironworker and the shoemaker. A really efficient workman must be to-day an intelligent man who has had good technical training in addition to thorough common school, and perhaps even higher training. To meet this situation the industrial schools began a further development; they established distinct Trade Schools for the thorough training of better class artisans, and at the same time they sought to preserve for the purposes of general education, such of the simpler processes of elementary trade learning as were best suited therefor. In this differentiation of the Trade School and manual training, the best of the industrial schools simply followed the plain trend of the present educational epoch. A prominent educator tells us that, in Sweden,

> In the beginning the economic conception was generally adopted, and everywhere manual training was looked upon as a means of preparing the children of the common people to earn their living. But gradually it came to be recognized that manual training has a more elevated purpose, and one, indeed, more useful in the deeper meaning of the term. It came to be considered as an educative process for the complete moral, physical and intellectual development of the child.

Thus, again, in the manning of trade schools and manual training schools we are thrown back upon the higher training as its source and chief support. There was a time when any aged and wornout carpenter could teach in a trade school. But not so to-day. Indeed the demand for college-bred men by a school like Tuskegee, ought to make Mr. Booker T. Washington the firmest friend of higher training. Here he has as helpers the son of a Negro senator, trained in Greek and the humanities, and graduated at Harvard; the son of a Negro congressman and lawyer, trained in Latin and mathematics, and graduated at Oberlin; he has as his wife, a woman who read Virgil and Homer in the same class room with me; he has as college chaplain, a classical graduate of Atlanta University; as teacher of science, a graduate of Fisk; as teacher of history, a graduate of Smith,—indeed some thirty of his chief teachers are college graduates, and instead of studying French grammars in the midst of weeds, or buying pianos for dirty cabins, they are at Mr. Washington's right hand helping him in a noble work. And yet one of the effects of Mr. Washington's propaganda has been to throw doubt upon the expediency of such training for Negroes, as these persons have had.

Men of America, the problem is plain before you. Here is a race transplanted through the criminal foolishness of your fathers. Whether you like it or not the millions are here, and here they will remain. If you do not lift them up, they will pull you down. Education and work are the levers to uplift a people. Work alone will not do it unless inspired by the right ideals and guided by intelligence. Education must not simply teach work—it must teach Life. The Talented Tenth of the Negro race must be made leaders of thought and missionaries of culture among their people. No others can do this work and Negro colleges must train men for it. The Negro race, like all other races, is going to be saved by its exceptional men.

The Souls of White Folk

High in the tower, where I sit above the loud complaining of the human sea, I know many souls that toss and whirl and pass, but none there are that intrigue me more than the Souls of White Folk.

Of them I am singularly clairvoyant. I see in and through them. I view them from unusual points of vantage. Not as a foreigner do I come, for I am native, not foreign, bone of their thought and flesh of their language. Mine is not the knowledge of the traveler or the colonial composite of dear memories, words and wonder. Nor yet is my knowledge that which servants have of masters, or mass of class, or capitalist of artisan. Rather I see these souls undressed and from the back and side. I see the working of their entrails. I know their thoughts and they know that I know. This knowledge makes them now embarrassed, now furious! They deny my right to live and be and call me misbirth! My word is to them mere bitterness and my soul, pessimism. And yet as they preach and strut and shout and threaten, crouching as they clutch at rags of facts and fancies to hide their nakedness, they go twisting, flying by my tired eyes and I see them ever stripped,—ugly, human.

The discovery of personal whiteness among the world's peoples is a very modern thing,—a nineteenth and twentieth century matter, indeed. The ancient world would have laughed at such a distinction. The Middle Age regarded skin color with mild curiosity; and even up into the eighteenth century we were hammering our national manikins into one, great, Universal Man, with fine frenzy which ignored color and race even more than birth. Today we have changed all that, and the world in a sudden, emotional conversion has discovered that it is white and by that token, wonderful!

This assumption that of all the hues of God whiteness alone is inherently and obviously better than brownness or tan leads to curious acts; even the sweeter souls of the dominant world as they discourse with me on weather, weal, and woe are continually playing above their actual words an obligato of tune and tone, saying:

"My poor, un-white thing! Weep not nor rage. I know, too well, that the curse of God lies heavy on you. Why? That is not for me to say, but be brave! Do your work in your lowly sphere, praying the good Lord that into heaven above, where all is love, you may, one day, be born—white!"

I do not laugh. I am quite straight-faced as I ask soberly:

"But what on earth is whiteness that one should so desire it?" Then always, somehow, some way, silently but clearly, I am given to understand that whiteness is the ownership of the earth forever and ever, Amen!

Now what is the effect on a man or a nation when it comes passionately to believe such an extraordinary dictum as this? That nations are coming to believe it is manifest daily. Wave on wave, each with increasing virulence, is dashing this new religion of whiteness on the shores of our time. Its first effects are funny: the strut of the Southerner, the arrogance of the Englishman amuck, the whoop of the hoodlum who vicariously leads your mob. Next it appears dampening generous enthusiasm in what we once counted glorious; to free the slave is discovered to be tolerable only in so far as it freed his master! Do we sense somnolent writhings in black Africa or angry groans in India or triumphant banzais in Japan? "To your tents, O Israel!" These nations are not white!

After the more cosmic manifestations and the chilling of generous enthusiasm come subtler, darker deeds. Everything considered, the title to the universe claimed by White Folk is faulty. It ought, at least, to look plausible. How easy, then, by emphasis and omission to make children believe that every great soul the world ever saw was a white man's soul; that every great thought the world ever knew was a white man's thought; that every great deed the world ever did was a white man's deed; that every great dream the world ever sang was a white man's dream. In fine, that if from the world were dropped everything that could not fairly be attributed to White Folk, the world would, if anything, be even greater, truer, better than now. And if all this be a lie, is it not a lie in a great cause?

Here it is that the comedy verges to tragedy. The first minor note is struck, all unconsciously, by those worthy souls in whom consciousness of high descent brings burning desire to spread the gift abroad,—the obligation of nobility to the ignoble. Such sense of duty assumes two things: a real possession of the heritage and its frank appreciation by the humble-born. So long, then, as humble black folk, voluble with thanks, receive barrels of old clothes from lordly and generous whites, there is much mental peace and moral satisfaction. But when the black man begins to dispute the white man's title to certain alleged bequests of the Fathers in wage and position, authority and training; and when his attitude toward charity is sullen anger rather than humble jollity; when he insists on his human right to swagger and swear and waste,—then the spell is suddenly broken and the philanthropist is ready to believe that Negroes are impudent, that the South is right, and that Japan wants to fight America.

After this the descent to Hell is easy. On the pale, white faces which the great billows whirl upward to my tower I see again and again, often and still more often, a writing of human hatred, a deep and passionate hatred, vast by the very vagueness of its expressions. Down through the green waters, on the bottom of the world, where men move to and fro, I have seen a man—an educated gentleman—grow livid with anger because a little, silent, black woman was sitting by herself in a Pullman car. He was a white man. I have seen a great, grown man curse a little child, who had wandered into the wrong waiting-room, searching for its mother: "Here, you damned black——" He was white. In Central Park I have seen the upper lip of a quiet, peaceful man curl back in a tigerish snarl of rage because black folk rode by in a motor car. He was a white man. We have seen, you and I, city after city drunk and furious with ungovernable lust of blood; mad with murder, destroying, killing, and cursing; torturing human victims because somebody accused of crime happened to be of the same color as the mob's innocent victims and because that color was not white! We have seen,—Merciful God! in these wild days and in the name of Civilization, Justice, and Motherhood,—what have we not seen, right here in America, of orgy, cruelty, barbarism, and murder done to men and women of Negro descent.

Up through the foam of green and weltering waters wells this great mass of hatred, in wilder, fiercer violence, until I look down and know that today to the millions of my people no misfortune could happen,—of death and pestilence, failure and defeat—that would not make the hearts of millions of their fellows beat with fierce, vindictive joy! Do you doubt it? Ask your own soul what it would say if the next census were to report that half of black America was dead and the other half dying.

Unfortunate? Unfortunate. But where is the misfortune? Mine? Am I, in my blackness, the sole sufferer? I suffer. And yet, somehow, above the suffering, above the shackled anger that beats the bars, above the hurt that crazes there surges in me a vast pity,—pity for a people imprisoned and enthralled, hampered and made miserable for such a cause, for such a phantasy!

Conceive this nation, of all human peoples, engaged in a crusade to make the "World Safe for Democracy"! Can you imagine the United States protesting against Turkish atrocities in Armenia, while the Turks are silent about mobs in

Chicago and St. Louis; what is Louvain compared with Memphis, Waco, Washington, Dyersburg, and Estill Springs? In short, what is the black man but America's Belgium, and how could America condemn in Germany that which she commits, just as brutally, within her own borders?

A true and worthy ideal frees and uplifts a people; a false ideal imprisons and lowers. Say to men, earnestly and repeatedly: "Honesty is best, knowledge is power; do unto others as you would be done by." Say this and act it and the nation must move toward it, if not to it. But say to a people: "The one virtue is to be white," and the people rush to the inevitable conclusion, "Kill the 'nigger'!"

Is not this the record of present America? Is not this its headlong progress? Are we not coming more and more, day by day, to making the statement "I am white," the one fundamental tenet of our practical morality? Only when this basic, iron rule is involved is our defense of right nation-wide and prompt. Murder may swagger, theft may rule and prostitution may flourish and the nation gives but spasmodic, intermittent and luke-warm attention. But let the murderer be black or the thief brown or the violator of womanhood have a drop of Negro blood, and the righteousness of the indignation sweeps the world. Nor would this fact make the indignation less justifiable did not we all know that it was blackness that was condemned and not crime.

In the awful cataclysm of World War, where from beating, slandering, and murdering us the white world turned temporarily aside to kill each other, we of the Darker Peoples looked on in mild amaze.

Among some of us, I doubt not, this sudden descent of Europe into hell brought unbounded surprise; to others, over wide area, it brought the *Schaden Freude* of the bitterly hurt; but most of us, I judge, looked on silently and sorrowfully, in sober thought, seeing sadly the prophecy of our own souls.

Here is a civilization that has boasted much. Neither Roman nor Arab, Greek nor Egyptian, Persian nor Mongol ever took himself and his own perfectness with such disconcerting seriousness as the modern white man. We whose shame, humiliation, and deep insult his aggrandizement so often involved were never deceived. We looked at him clearly, with world-old eyes, and saw simply a human thing, weak and pitiable and cruel, even as we are and were.

These super-men and world-mastering demi-gods listened, however, to no low tongues of ours, even when we pointed silently to their feet of clay. Perhaps we, as folk of simpler soul and more primitive type, have been most struck in the welter of recent years by the utter failure of white religion. We have curled our lips in something like contempt as we have witnessed glib apology and weary explanation. Nothing of the sort deceived us. A nation's religion is its life, and as such white Christianity is a miserable failure.

Nor would we be unfair in this criticism: We know that we, too, have failed, as you have, and have rejected many a Buddha, even as you have denied Christ; but we acknowledge our human frailty, while you, claiming super-humanity, scoff endlessly at our shortcomings.

The number of white individuals who are practising with even reasonable approximation the democracy and unselfishness of Jesus Christ is so small and unimportant as to be fit subject for jest in Sunday supplements and in *Punch, Life, Le Rire,* and *Fliegende Blätter*. In her foreign mission work the extraordinary self-deception of white religion is epitomized: solemnly the white world sends five million dollars worth of missionary propaganda to Africa each year and in the same twelve months adds twenty-five million dollars worth of the vilest gin manufactured. Peace to the augurs of Rome!

We may, however, grant without argument that religious ideals have always far outrun their very human devotees. Let us, then, turn to more mundane matters of honor and fairness. The world today is trade. The world has turned shopkeeper; history is economic history; living is earning a living. Is it necessary to ask how much of high emprise and honorable conduct has been found here? Something, to be sure. The establishment of world credit systems is built on splendid and realizable faith in fellow-men. But it is, after all, so low and elementary a step that sometimes it looks merely like honor among thieves, for the revelations of highway robbery and low cheating in the business world and in all its great modern centers have raised in the hearts of all true men in our day an exceeding great cry for revolution in our basic methods and conceptions of industry and commerce.

We do not, for a moment, forget the robbery of other times and races when trade was a most uncertain gamble; but was there not a certain honesty and frankness in the evil that argued a saner morality? There are more merchants today, surer deliveries, and wider well-being, but are there not, also, bigger thieves, deeper injustice, and more calloused selfishness in well-being? Be that as it may,—certainly the nicer sense of honor that has risen ever and again in groups of forward-thinking men has been curiously and broadly blunted. Consider our chiefest industry,—fighting. Laboriously the Middle Ages built its rules of fairness—equal armament, equal notice, equal conditions. What do we see today? Machine-guns against assegais; conquest sugared with religion; mutilation and rape masquerading as culture,—all this, with vast applause at the superiority of white over black soldiers!

War is horrible! This the dark world knows to its awful cost. But has it just become horrible, in these last days, when under essentially equal conditions, equal armament, and equal waste of wealth white men are fighting white men, with surgeons and nurses hovering near?

Think of the wars through which we have lived in the last decade: in German Africa, in British Nigeria, in French and Spanish Morocco, in China, in Persia, in the Balkans, in Tripoli, in Mexico, and in a dozen lesser places—were not these horrible, too? Mind you, there were for the most of these wars no Red Cross funds.

Behold little Belgium and her pitiable plight, but has the world forgotten Congo? What Belgium now suffers is not half, not even a tenth, of what she has done to black Congo since Stanley's great dream of 1880. Down the dark forests of inmost Africa sailed this modern Sir Galahad, in the name of "the noble-minded men of several nations," to introduce commerce and civilization. What came of it? "Rubber and murder, slavery in its worst form," wrote Glave in 1895.

Harris declares that King Leopold's régime meant the death of twelve million natives,

> but what we who were behind the scenes felt most keenly was the fact that the real catastrophe in the Congo was desolation and murder in the larger sense. The invasion of family life, the ruthless destruction of every social barrier, the shattering of every tribal law, the introduction of criminal practices which struck the chiefs of the people dumb with horror—in a word, a veritable avalanche of filth and immorality overwhelmed the Congo tribes.

Yet the fields of Belgium laughed, the cities were gay, art and science flourished; the groans that helped to nourish this civilization fell on deaf ears because the world round about was doing the same sort of thing elsewhere on its own account.

As we saw the dead dimly through rifts of battle-smoke and heard faintly the cursings and accusations of blood brothers, we darker men said: This is not Europe gone mad; this is not aberration nor insanity; this *is* Europe; this seeming Terrible is the real soul of white culture—back of all culture,—stripped and visible today. This is where the world has arrived,—these dark and awful depths and not the shining and ineffable heights of which it boasted. Here is whither the might and energy of modern humanity has really gone.

But may not the world cry back at us and ask: "What better thing have you to show? What have you done or would do better than this if you had today the world rule? Paint with all riot of hateful colors the thin skin of European culture,—is it not better than any culture that arose in Africa or Asia?"

It is. Of this there is no doubt and never has been; but why is it better? Is it better because Europeans are better, nobler, greater, and more gifted than other folk? It is not. Europe has never produced and never will in our day bring forth a single human soul who cannot be matched and over-matched in every line of human endeavor by Asia and Africa. Run the gamut, if you will, and let us have the Europeans who in sober truth over-match Nefertari, Mohammed, Rameses and Askia, Confucius, Buddha, and Jesus Christ. If we could scan the calendar of thousands of lesser men, in like comparison, the result would be the same; but we cannot do this because of the deliberately educated ignorance of white schools by which they remember Napoleon and forget Sonni Ali.

The greatness of Europe has lain in the width of the stage on which she has played her part, the strength of the foundations on which she has builded, and a natural, human ability no whit greater (if as great) than that of other days and races. In other words, the deeper reasons for the triumph of European civilization lie quite outside and beyond Europe,—back in the universal struggles of all mankind.

Why, then, is Europe great? Because of the foundations which the mighty past have furnished her to build upon: the iron trade of ancient, black Africa, the religion and empire-building of yellow Asia, the art and science of the "dago" Mediterranean shore, east, south, and west, as well as north. And where she has builded securely upon this great past and learned from it she has gone forward to greater and more splendid human triumph; but where she has ignored this past and forgotten and sneered at it, she has shown the cloven hoof of poor, crucified humanity,—she has played, like other empires gone, the world fool!

If, then, European triumphs in culture have been greater, so, too, may her failures have been greater. How great a failure and a failure in what does the World War betoken? Was it national jealousy of the sort of the seventeenth century? But Europe has done more to break down national barriers than any preceding culture. Was it fear of the balance of power in Europe? Hardly, save in the half-Asiatic problems of the Balkans. What, then, does Hauptmann mean when he says: "Our jealous enemies forged an iron ring about our breasts and we knew our breasts had to expand,—that we had to split asunder this ring or else we had to cease breathing. But Germany will not cease to breathe and so it came to pass that the iron ring was forced apart."

Whither is this expansion? What is that breath of life, thought to be so indispensable to a great European nation? Manifestly it is expansion overseas; it is colonial aggrandizement which explains, and alone adequately explains, the World War. How many of us today fully realize the current theory of colonial expansion, of the relation of Europe which is white, to the world which is black and brown and yellow? Bluntly put, that theory is this: It is the duty of white Europe to divide up the darker world and administer it for Europe's good.

This Europe has largely done. The European world is using black and brown men for all the uses which men know. Slowly but surely white culture is evolving the theory that "darkies" are born beasts of burden for white folk. It were silly to think otherwise, cries the cultured world, with stronger and shriller accord. The supporting arguments grow and twist themselves in the mouths of merchant, scientist, soldier, traveler, writer, and missionary: Darker peoples are dark in mind as well as in body; of dark, uncertain, and imperfect descent; of frailer, cheaper stuff; they are cowards in the face of mausers and maxims; they have no feelings, aspirations, and loves; they are fools, illogical idiots,—"half-devil and half-child."

Such as they are civilization must, naturally, raise them, but soberly and in limited ways. They are not simply dark white men. They are not "men" in the sense that Europeans are men. To the very limited extent of their shallow capacities lift them to be useful to whites, to raise cotton, gather rubber, fetch ivory, dig diamonds,—and let them be paid what men think they are worth—white men who know them to be well-nigh worthless.

Such degrading of men by men is as old as mankind and the invention of no one race or people. Ever have men striven to conceive of their victims as different from the victors, endlessly different, in soul and blood, strength and cunning, race and lineage. It has been left, however, to Europe and to modern days to discover the eternal world-wide mark of meanness,—color!

Such is the silent revolution that has gripped modern European culture in the later nineteenth and twentieth centuries. Its zenith came in Boxer times: White supremacy was all but world-wide, Africa was dead, India conquered, Japan isolated, and China prostrate, while white America whetted her sword for mongrel Mexico and mulatto South America, lynching her own Negroes the while. Temporary halt in this program was made by little Japan and the white world immediately sensed the peril of such "yellow" presumption! What sort of a world would this be if yellow men must be treated "white"? Immediately the eventual overthrow of Japan became a subject of deep thought and intrigue, from St. Petersburg to San Francisco, from the Key of Heaven to the Little Brother of the Poor.

The using of men for the benefit of masters is no new invention of modern Europe. It is quite as old as the world. But Europe proposed to apply it on a scale and with an elaborateness of detail of which no former world ever dreamed. The imperial width of the thing,—the heaven-defying audacity—makes its modern newness.

The scheme of Europe was no sudden invention, but a way out of long-pressing difficulties. It is plain to modern white civilization that the subjection of the white working classes cannot much longer be maintained. Education, political power, and increased knowledge of the technique and meaning of the industrial process are destined to make a more and more equitable distribution of wealth in the near future. The day of the very rich is drawing to a close, so far as individual white nations are concerned. But there is a loophole. There is a chance for exploitation on an immense scale for inordinate profit, not simply to the very rich, but to the middle class and to the laborers. This chance lies in the exploitation of darker peoples. It is here that the golden hand beckons. Here are no labor unions or votes or questioning onlookers or inconvenient consciences. These men may be used down to the very bone, and shot and maimed in "punitive" expeditions when they revolt. In these dark lands "industrial development" may repeat in exaggerated form every horror of the industrial history of Europe, from slavery and rape to disease and maiming, with only one test of success,—dividends!

This theory of human culture and its aims has worked itself through warp and woof of our daily thought with a thoroughness that few realize. Everything great, good, efficient, fair, and honorable is "white"; everything mean, bad, blundering, cheating, and dishonorable is "yellow"; a bad taste is "brown"; and the devil is "black." The changes of this theme are continually rung in picture and story, in newspaper heading and moving-picture, in sermon and school book, until, of course, the King can do no wrong,—a White Man is always right and a Black Man has no rights which a white man is bound to respect.

There must come the necessary despisings and hatreds of these savage half-men, this unclean *canaille* of the world—these dogs of men. All through the world this gospel is preaching. It has its literature, it has its priests, it has its secret propaganda and above all—it pays!

There's the rub,—it pays. Rubber, ivory, and palm-oil; tea, coffee, and cocoa; bananas, oranges, and other fruit; cotton, gold, and copper—they, and a hundred other things which dark and sweating bodies hand up to the white world from their pits of slime, pay and pay well, but of all that the world gets the black world gets only the pittance that the white world throws it disdainfully.

Small wonder, then, that in the practical world of things-that-be there is jealousy and strife for the possession of the labor of dark millions, for the right to bleed and exploit the colonies of the world where this golden stream may be had, not always for the asking, but surely for the whipping and shooting. It was this competition for the labor of yellow, brown, and black folks that was the cause of the World War. Other causes have been glibly given and other contributing causes there doubtless were, but they were subsidiary and subordinate to this vast quest of the dark world's wealth and toil.

Colonies, we call them, these places where "niggers" are cheap and the earth is rich; they are those outlands where like a swarm of hungry locusts white masters may settle to be served as kings, wield the lash of slave-drivers, rape girls and wives, grow as rich as Croesus and send homeward a golden stream. They belt the earth, these places, but they cluster in the tropics, with its darkened peoples: in Hong Kong and Anam, in Borneo and Rhodesia, in Sierra Leone and Nigeria, in Panama and Havana—these are the El Dorados toward which the world powers stretch itching palms.

Germany, at last one and united and secure on land, looked across the seas and seeing England with sources of wealth insuring a luxury and power which Germany could not hope to rival by the slower processes of exploiting her own peasants and workingmen, especially with these workers half in revolt, immediately built her navy and entered into a desperate competition for possession of colonies of darker peoples. To South America, to China, to Africa, to Asia Minor, she turned like a hound quivering on the leash, impatient, suspicious, irritable, with blood-shot eyes and dripping fangs, ready for the awful word. England and France crouched watchfully over their bones, growling and wary, but gnawing industriously, while the blood of the dark world whetted their greedy appetites. In the background, shut out from the highway to the seven seas, sat Russia and Austria, snarling and snapping at each other and at the last Mediterranean gate to the El Dorado, where the Sick Man enjoyed bad health, and where millions of serfs in the Balkans, Russia, and Asia offered a feast to greed well-nigh as great as Africa.

The fateful day came. It had to come. The cause of war is preparation for war; and of all that Europe has done in a century there is nothing that has equaled in energy, thought, and time her preparation for wholesale murder. The only adequate cause of this preparation was conquest and conquest, not in Europe, but primarily among the darker peoples of Asia and Africa; conquest, not for assimilation and uplift, but for commerce and degradation. For this, and this mainly, did Europe gird herself at frightful cost for war.

The red day dawned when the tinder was lighted in the Balkans and Austro-Hungary seized a bit which brought her a step nearer to the world's highway; she seized one bit and poised herself for another. Then came that curious chorus of challenges, those leaping suspicions, raking all causes for distrust and rivalry and hatred, but saying little of the real and greatest cause.

Each nation felt its deep interests involved. But how? Not, surely, in the death of Ferdinand the Warlike; not, surely, in the old, half-forgotten *revanche* for Alsace-Lorraine; not even in the neutrality of Belgium. No! But in the possession of land overseas, in the right to colonies, the chance to levy endless tribute on the darker world,—on coolies in China, on starving peasants in India, on black savages in Africa, on dying South Seas Islanders, on Indians of the Amazon—all this and nothing more.

Even the broken reed on which we had rested high hopes of eternal peace,—the guilt of the laborers—the front of that very important movement for human justice on which we had builded most, even this flew like a straw before the breath of king and kaiser. Indeed, the flying had been foreshadowed when in Germany and America "international" Socialists had all but read yellow and black men out of the kingdom of industrial justice. Subtly had they been bribed, but effectively: Were they not lordly whites and should they not share in the spoils of rape? High wages in the United States and England might be the skilfully manipulated result of slavery in Africa and of peonage in Asia.

With the dog-in-the-manger theory of trade, with the determination to reap inordinate profits and to exploit the weakest to the utmost there came a new imperialism,—the rage for one's own nation to own the earth or, at least, a large enough portion of it to insure as big profits as the next nation. Where sections could not be owned by one dominant nation there came a policy of "open door," but the "door" was open to "white people only." As to the darkest and weakest of peoples there was but one unanimity in Europe,—that which Herr Dernberg of the German Colonial Office called the agreement with England to maintain white "prestige" in Africa,—the doctrine of the divine right of white people to steal.

Thus the world market most widely and desperately sought today is the market where labor is cheapest and most helpless and profit is most abundant. This labor is kept cheap and helpless because the white world despises "darkies." If one has the temerity to suggest that these workingmen may walk the way of white workingmen and climb by votes and self-assertion and education to the rank of men, he is howled out of court. They cannot do it and if they could, they shall not, for they are the enemies of the white race and the whites shall rule forever and forever and everywhere. Thus the hatred and despising of human beings from whom Europe wishes to extort her luxuries has led to such jealousy and bickering between European nations that they have fallen afoul of each other and have fought like crazed beasts. Such is the fruit of human hatred.

But what of the darker world that watches? Most men belong to this world. With Negro and Negroid, East Indian, Chinese, and Japanese they form two thirds of the population of the world. A belief in humanity is a belief in colored men. If the uplift of mankind must be done by men, then the destinies of this world will rest ultimately in the hands of darker nations.

What, then, is this dark world thinking? It is thinking that as wild and awful as this shameful war was, *it is nothing to compare with that fight for freedom which black and brown and yellow men must and will make unless their oppression and humiliation and insult at the hands of the White World cease. The Dark World is going to submit to its present treatment just as long as it must and not one moment longer.*

Let me say this again and emphasize it and leave no room for mistaken meaning: The World War was primarily the jealous and avaricious struggle for the largest share in exploiting darker races. As such it is and must be but the prelude to the armed and indignant protest of these despised and raped peoples. To-day Japan is hammering on the door of justice, China is raising her half-manacled hands to knock next, India is writhing for the freedom to knock, Egypt is sullenly muttering, the Negroes of South and West Africa, of the West Indies, and of the United States are just awakening to their shameful slavery. Is, then, this war the end of wars? Can it be the end, so long as sits enthroned, even in the souls of those who cry peace, the despising and robbing of darker peoples? If Europe hugs this delusion, then this is not the end of world war,—it is but the beginning!

We see Europe's greatest sin precisely where we found Africa's and Asia's,—in human hatred, the despising of men; with this difference, however: Europe has the awful lesson of the past before her, has the splendid results of widened areas of tolerance, sympathy, and love among men, and she faces a greater, an infinitely greater, world of men than any preceding civilization ever faced.

It is curious to see America, the United States, looking on herself, first, as a sort of natural peacemaker, then as a moral protagonist in this terrible time. No nation is less fitted for this rôle. For two or more centuries America has marched proudly in the van of human hatred,—making bonfires of human flesh and laughing at them hideously, and making the insulting of millions more than a matter of dislike,—rather a great religion, a world war-cry: Up white, down black; to your tents,. O white folk, and world war with black and parti-colored mongrel beasts!

Instead of standing as a great example of the success of democracy and the possibility of human brotherhood America has taken her place as an awful example of its pitfalls and failures, so far as black and brown and yellow peoples are concerned. And this, too, in spite of the fact that there has been no actual failure; the Indian is not dying out, the Japanese and Chinese have not menaced the land, and the experiment of Negro suffrage has resulted in the uplift of twelve million people at a rate probably unparalleled in history. But what of this? America, Land of Democracy, wanted to believe in the failure of democracy so far as darker peoples were concerned. Absolutely without excuse she established a caste system, rushed into preparation for war, and conquered tropical colonies. She stands today shoulder to shoulder with Europe in Europe's worst sin against civilization. She aspires to sit among the great nations who arbitrate the fate of "lesser breeds without the law" and she is at times heartily ashamed even of the large number of "new" white people whom her democracy has admitted to place and power. Against this surging forward of Irish and German, of Russian Jew, Slav and "dago" her social bars have not availed, but against Negroes she can and does take her unflinching and immovable stand, backed by this new public policy of Europe. She trains her immigrants to this despising of "niggers" from the day of their landing, and they carry and send the news back to the submerged classes in the fatherlands.

All this I see and hear up in my tower, above the thunder of the seven seas. From my narrowed windows I stare into the night that looms beneath the cloud-swept stars. Eastward and westward storms are breaking,—great, ugly whirlwinds of hatred and blood and cruelty. I will not believe them inevitable. I will not believe that all that was must be, that all the shameful drama of the past must be done again today before the sunlight sweeps the silver seas.

If I cry amid this roar of elemental forces, must my cry be in vain, because it is but a cry,—a small and human cry amid Promethean gloom?

Back beyond the world and swept by these wild, white faces of the awful dead, why will this Soul of White Folk,—this modern Prometheus,—hang bound by his own binding, tethered by a fable of the past? I hear his mighty cry reverberating through the world, "I am white!" Well and good, O Prometheus, divine thief! Is not the world wide enough for two colors, for many little shinings of the sun? Why, then, devour your own vitals if I answer even as proudly, "I am black!"

A Critical Perspective
Marcus Bruce (1955–)

Cultural critic and theologian Marcus Bruce has written about and taught African American culture, American intellectual history, religion, and philosophy during his distinguished academic career. He earned a bachelor's from Bates College in 1977 and a master's and doctorate from Yale University in 1986 and 1990, respectively. In addition, he received a master of divinity in 1982 from Yale's Divinity School.

Born in San Antonio, Texas, Bruce grew up in New England, where he excelled as an athlete in high school and college. However, it was the intellectual challenge that most inspired him as a college student, and after serving as an apprentice minister for several years, he committed himself to research and teaching on the university level. Since 1982, Bruce has taught at Southern Connecticut State University, Yale University, and Bates College. He has also studied Christian theology at the L'Abri Fellowship Foundation in Switzerland, attended the Aspen Institute Wye Faculty Seminar, and received teaching fellowships and research grants from Yale and Bates.

In addition to publishing numerous articles in scholarly journals, Bruce, a popular speaker, has presented his papers at various conferences and seminars. He has served as a consultant to such organizations as the Maine State Board of Education, New England Foundation for the Humanities, Maine Public Broadcasting Network, and Northeast Historic Film Society. In 1991, he was a visiting scholar at the W. E. B. Du Bois Institute at Harvard, and in 1992, he was a guest speaker at the International Conference on African Americans and Europe at the Université de la Sorbonne Nouvelle in Paris.

The following essay, "Black and Blue: W. E. B. Du Bois and the Meaning of Blackness," appears here in print for the first time. In it Bruce evaluates Du Bois and his critics in their exploration of the symbolic and practical significance of racial identity.

Black and Blue: W. E. B. Du Bois and the Meaning of Blackness

> Perhaps I like Louis Armstrong because he's made poetry out of being invisible.[1]

> What did they ever think of us transitory ones . . . birds of passage who were too obscure for learned classifications, too silent for the most sensitive recorders of sound; of natures too ambiguous for the most ambiguous words, and too distant from the centers of historical decision to sign or even to applaud the signers of historical documents? . . . Who knew but that [we] were the saviors, the true leaders, the bearers of something precious? The stewards of something uncomfortable, burdensome, which [we] hated because, living outside of the realm of history, there was no one to applaud [our] value and [we ourselves] failed to understand it.[2]

In two of his most notable autobiographies, W. E. B. Du Bois poses two questions that continue to challenge critics of African-American and American culture. The first, "How does it feel to be a problem?"[3] serves as the guiding question of his now classic work, *The Souls of Black Folk,* a book in which Du Bois attempted to "translate the finer feelings" of black folk "into words."[4] The second question, implicit in the first and surely a concern to Du Bois during the composition of *The Souls of Black Folk,* came much later and presented a different challenge. In *Dusk of Dawn: An Essay toward an Autobiography of a Race Concept* Du Bois asked, "How shall I explain and clarify its meaning for a soul?"[5]

Du Bois considered both questions, one dealing with the experience of African Americans, the other with the appropriate form or forms for expressing that experience, important for understanding African-American culture. Yet the two questions were not entirely separate; in fact, they were linked together. This was particularly true in *The Souls of Black Folk.* As Du Bois so skillfully demonstrates throughout the work, being labeled and considered a "problem" had profoundly shaped the experience of people of African descent. It made them poignantly aware of what others perceived as their "difference." Furthermore, the status of African Americans as a "problem" denied them "souls," consciousness, and a complexity of which the entire book was a testament. How, Du Bois seemed to ask, was one to describe something that, heretofore, had been thought not to exist? How was one to describe something for which there were no words, someone for whom, as James Baldwin so eloquently put it, "the universe had evolved no terms"?[6] Or even more troubling, what other alternatives were available to one who would "translate the finer feelings" of black folk into words when the very language seemed to allow them "no true self-consciousness"? These questions—and others—posed a challenging dilemma for a man who sought "to sketch . . . the spiritual world in which ten thousand Americans live and strive."[7] Still he had high hopes that his work might provide some answers or at least some insight.

Du Bois's awareness of this dilemma, of what Ralph Ellison has referred to as "the process of making artistic forms out of one's experience,"[8] is evident in a little known, and rarely read, 1904 review of *The Souls of Black Folk,* written by the author himself. In this brief essay, Du Bois reveals that he had tried to "speak from within—to depict a world as we see it who dwell therein" yet he acknowledges that "the style and workmanship of the book" might not make this world or "meaning altogether clear."[9] Comprised of "fourteen essays written under various circumstances and for different purposes," the book, writes Du Bois,

> has considerable, perhaps too great diversity. There are bits of history and biography, some description of scenes and persons, something of controversy and criticism, some statistics and a bit of story-telling. All this leads to rather abrupt transitions of style, tone, and viewpoint and, too, without doubt, to a distinct sense of incompleteness and sketchiness.[10]

Though he considered his book a work of translation, the act of making accessible to the larger world the varied and complex feelings of black folk, he confessed—in what seemed a neo-Kantian moment—that "the thing itself" eluded his conceptual and literary grasp.[11] And once he had "dressed it out in periods," given it a literary form, it seemed vague, uncouth, and inchoate. Yet he was confident of one thing: that there was unity in the book, a unity provided by the "subjective note" that ran through each and every essay.[12]

For Du Bois, the question of the form or manner in which to convey his subject was paramount and would profoundly affect the way in which others viewed the experience of African Americans. Yet the form could also shape the experience of African Americans. The experience of being a problem, and the added dilemma of how to make its meaning clear, seemed to dictate its own form. This was especially true when Du Bois confronted the concept of race with all its social, political, economic, cultural, and psychological implications. How could he challenge race, "not so much scientific race, as that deep conviction of myriads of men that congenital differences among the main masses of human beings absolutely condition the individual destiny of every member of a group"?[13] How should he convey the manner in which a belief in races, one into which he was born, had "guided, embittered, illuminated, and enshrouded" his life? How should he "explain and clarify its meaning for a soul"?[14]

More often than not, critics of Du Bois's work have tended to focus more on the inadequacies of what he produced, the shortcomings of his journalism, historical works, and sociological studies, than on the experiences which he sought so valiantly to convey. It is this process which deserves our attention and yields the greatest insight. For throughout his career, yet especially in works regarding the concept of race, Du Bois sought a means by which he could convey his sense of life as an African American. What ensued then, and is manifest in many of his writings, is a "struggle with form."[15]

While the two questions are well nigh inseparable in the work of Du Bois, scholars have often neglected the former for the latter, opting to critique, with the confidence of hindsight, the manner in which Du Bois expressed his experience as a black man. To critique the style and the manner in which a work is written is the work of the critic, yet to criticize the formal aspects of the work and neglect the author's sense of life is to overlook something significant in the work of Du Bois. A number of scholars have critiqued Du Bois's success at articulating the finer feelings of black folk. Of note are three brief yet thought-provoking essays by Arnold Rampersad, Kwame Anthony Appiah, and Houston Baker.

Throughout his life, Du Bois experimented with a variety of literary forms. In addition to his more widely publicized works in sociology, history, and journalism, Du Bois chose the genres of poetry and fiction to convey the strange meaning of being black. Herein lies the insight of Arnold Rampersad's essay, "W. E. B. Du Bois as a Man of Literature." Rampersad observes that in *The Souls of Black Folk* Du Bois developed "a dazzling variety of metaphoric, ironic, pietistic, and sentimental rhetorical strategies."[16] This work, which in some ways marks the beginning of Du Bois's experimentation with poetry and fiction, has even greater import when we consider the kind of questions that motivated him in the first place. For it appears that whenever Du Bois reached what he considered to be the limits of his ability to describe the plight of African Americans in a sociological, historical, or journalistic fashion, he would turn to poetry, fiction, or music. Consequently, as late as the 1940 work *Dusk of Dawn,* Du Bois would turn to another form, fiction, when a detailed explanation or even popular notions of race failed to do justice to what he was experiencing as a black man or to convey the strange meaning of being black. Yet he would make the following remark concerning the concept of race and the difficulty of explaining its import for his life and its meaning to his reader.

> With the best will the factual outline of a life misses the essence of its spirit. Thus in my life the chief fact has been race—not so much scientific race, as that deep conviction of myriads of men that congenital differences among the main masses of human beings absolutely condition the individual destiny of every member of a group. Into the spiritual provincialism of this belief I have been born and this fact has guided, embittered, illuminated, and enshrouded my life. Yet, how can I explain and clarify its meaning for a soul?[17]

Rampersad concludes that Du Bois's neglected poems and novels are the "awkward side" of his fame, the expressive yet technically flawed portions of his work. He insists that Du Bois's efforts "extend our understanding of the history and character of his people and, indeed, of humanism itself."[18] Still readers are left wondering how Du Bois has extended their knowledge of the writer, his people, and humanity.

Du Bois's success or failure as a man of literature or culture must always be judged in light of what he was trying to convey: the souls or spiritual world of black folk. Neither science nor popular culture could provide satisfactory terms for his existence as an African American. And what terms did exist—that is, nineteenth-century notions of race—relegated him to an inferior status.

In an essay entitled "The Uncompleted Argument: Du Bois and the Illusion of Race," and a subsequent revision of the same essay in the collection *In My Father's House: Africa in the Philosophy of Culture,* Kwame Anthony Appiah offers new insight into the very heated discussion over Du Bois's struggle with the concept of race. Appiah observes that Du Bois never actually abandoned the troublesome concept. Though mindful of the numerous problems connected with using "race" as an organizing concept for defining the cultural experience of African Americans, Du Bois, Appiah argues, still felt that the concept could be revised and put to good use. Reviewing an early essay by Du Bois entitled "The Conservation of Race" and a later autobiographical work, *Dusk of Dawn: An Essay toward an Autobiography of a Race Concept,* Appiah shows the evolution of Du Bois's thinking about the concept of race and his growing sense of its inadequacies and the difficulties surrounding its use.

In "The Conservation of Races" Du Bois acknowledges, like Appiah, that science has failed to provide any conclusive evidence that races actually exist. Yet while there are the "gross physical differences of blood, color, hair, and cranial measurements" that have come to define the differences between one group of human beings and another, one "race" and another, Du Bois thinks that these do not "define or explain the (still) deeper differences—the cohesiveness and continuity of these groups. The deeper differences are spiritual, psychical, differences—undoubtedly based on the physical, but infinitely transcending them."[19] Appiah notes that whereas Du Bois challenges the scientific arguments for the concept of race, he began to view race from a sociohistorical perspective, that is, from the belief that there are distinct racial groups, each with its own common history, common destiny, and special message for the world.

Turning to *Dusk of Dawn,* Appiah reveals that Du Bois, with hindsight, had been consciously aware of the challenges posed by using the concept of race yet had sought to rehabilitate it for use by African Americans, especially by those like the very mission-conscious members of the American Negro Academy. Du Bois's formulation of a pragmatic agenda and even a creed for the Academy is further evidence that he felt, at least initially, that a new spin, a new interpretation, could be put on an old, oppressive concept like race. (Perhaps Du Bois, like so many other African Americans, had hoped that in redefining the concept of race he could "change the joke and slip the yoke"—modify racism and rise above the burden of race. This is evident in a very revealing line near the end of "The Conservation of Races" where he argues that a new definition of race, one which would outline a new mission and message for black people, would enable African Americans to "justify our existence.")[20]

Appiah's critical examination of the way in which Du Bois used the concept of race argues that Du Bois was never able to "transcend" a nineteenth-century concept of race. Instead, what Appiah discovers by tracing Du Bois's use of the concept of race from early essays such as "The Conservation of Races" to the more substantial work *Dusk of Dawn* is Du Bois's struggle with the concept of what Appiah calls a "classic dialectic." Appiah writes:

> I call this pattern a classic dialectic, and indeed, we find it in feminism also. On the one hand, a simple claim to equality, a denial of substantial difference; on the other, a claim to a special message, revaluing the feminine "Other" not as the "helpmeet" of sexism but as the New Woman.[21]

Yet what Appiah calls a classical dialectic—Du Bois's denial of substantial differences between himself and others, his group and others, and his assertion that he and his group are the bearers of some special message—might also be viewed as an instance of a classic dilemma: double-consciousness. "One ever feels his two-ness," writes Du Bois in *The Souls of Black Folk*—"an American, a Negro: two souls, two thoughts, two unreconciled strivings: two warring ideals in one dark body, whose dogged strength alone keeps it from being torn asunder."[22] The dilemma faced by Du Bois was how to write about his particular experience without using the very language which had not only defined the terms for the debate (and none for his existence) but also played such a profound role in shaping his experience.

In this instance, Appiah notes that Du Bois's continued use of the concept of race makes it difficult for him to both deny the existence of "races" *and* claim that African Americans have "a special message" (the strange meaning of being black) for the world. Yet Du Bois's experience of the world was so inextricably tied to the language of race—"this belief . . . has guided, embittered, illuminated, and enshrouded my life"—that it was almost impossible to talk about one without talking about the other, to convey what Du Bois believed was the "special message" of African Americans without implying that there were "substantial differences" between people, and to express his experience of being a "problem" without using the concept of race.

Appiah correctly concludes that Du Bois never abandoned the use of the concept of race as a means of describing his experience or that of other African Americans. Du Bois admits as much himself in *Dusk of Dawn;* he never provides the kind of philosophical justification for the existence of African Americans that he had set out to. Appiah's essay deftly demonstrates the numerous machinations that Du Bois underwent as he struggled with the concept. Yet it is precisely here that Du Bois achieves, in some measure, what he set out to do in his later works, *The Souls of Black Folk* and *Dusk of Dawn:* to explain, clarify, and give expression to "the strange meaning of being black." As evidenced by the style in which both books were written and his continued engagement with the concept of race, Du Bois's struggle with form and his confessed "longing to . . . merge his double self into a better and truer self" were illustrations of the strange meaning of being black. In fact, Du Bois argues that "the history of the American Negro is the history of this strife."[23]

Houston Baker, in response to Appiah's essay, sees this last point quite clearly. In "Caliban's Triple Play," a general response to a collection of essays written for *Critical Inquiry* entitled *"Race," Writing, and Difference,* and a pointed criticism of Appiah's "The Uncompleted Argument: Du Bois and the Illusion of Race," Baker uses Shakespearean figure Caliban to illustrate the peculiar dilemma implicit in Du Bois's two questions and faced by Du Bois and critics of African-American culture. Baker considers Caliban's famous lament to Prospero—"You taught me language; and my profit on't is I know how to curse"—a "metacurse," a sorrowful acknowledgment that the displacement, and one might even say the erasure, of his native tongue by a new language has left him nearly speechless, aware of "the impossibility of feeling anything other than cursed by language."[24] Caliban's utterance is a sign of "vernacular speech" struggling to express itself within the boundaries of a language which makes no allowances for its existence or presence. Consequently, Caliban's triple play is that of "a maroon or guerilla action carried out *within* linguistic territories of the erstwhile masters, bringing forth *sounds* that have been taken for crude hooting, but which are, in reality, racial poetry."[25]

Baker criticizes Appiah and other critics of African-American culture for their inattentiveness to "Caliban's sound" and the "vernacular dimensions of an ongoing black liberation struggle in America."[26] This oversight leads Appiah and others to invoke "philosophical criteria of 'racial' identity and difference in order to reduce Du Bois's assertions of a 'common' Afro-American racial history and identity to affective wishes."[27] Thus Appiah, argues Baker, is trapped in the same duality, the same dilemma, as the characters from Shakespeare's *The Tempest* who represent "self-and-other, the West and the Rest of Us, the rationalist and the debunker, the colonizer and the indigenous people." More importantly, according to Baker, Appiah overlooks Caliban's and even Du Bois's triple play "that changes a dualistic Western joke and opens space for the *sui generis* and liberating sound of the formerly yoked."[28] Baker finds Caliban's sound and the vernacular speech of black life most audible in Du Bois's *The Souls of Black Folk.*

Two earlier works by Baker develop this insight in more detail. In "The Black Man of Culture: W. E. B. Du Bois and *The Souls of Black Folk,*" Baker argues that it is Du Bois's "synthesis" of the ideals of black folk experience with "the arts of the Western world" that distinguishes him as a "black man of culture" and a "transcriber of folk values," not the "invidious distinctions" made throughout *The Souls of Black Folk* between the cultured individual and the black masses, the high and the low, the leaders and the laborers. Du Bois's achievement in *The Souls of Black Folk* is in his ability to both broaden Western definitions of culture to include black experience and illustrate how black folk experience, especially as evident in the spirituals, can be used as a paradigm for the process by which a people "create beauty from wretchedness, intellectuals from victims of slavery, and viable institutions from rigidly proscribed patterns of action."[29]

In the seventh chapter of *Modernism and the Harlem Renaissance,* Baker discusses at length Du Bois's use of the spirituals as an alternative, and perhaps more authentic, means of expressing the meaning of blackness. He concludes that the central place of the spirituals in *The Souls of Black Folk* transforms the text into both a kind of "cultural performance," where "the drama of RACE in the modern world dances before our eyes," and a "singing book" in which Du Bois "offers a bright, sounding spiritual display of men, women, institutions, doctrines, debates, follies, tragedies, hopes, expectations, and policies that combine to form a 'problem.' "[30] For Du Bois, the spirituals were the evidence of the souls of black folks, the literal *sounds* of blackness. Yet for Baker, the spirituals, or what he refers to as vernacular speech, stand for this and much more. Du Bois's use of the spirituals as medium for expressing his experience, argues Baker, serves as both an implicit critique of, and challenge to, the pervasive discourse of race and a moment when the strange meaning of being black, the struggle to give to expression to one's experience in spite of the concept of race, is made audibly clear.

Throughout his career, Du Bois sought to convey the experience and meaning of being black, yet his efforts were often frustrated by a host of popular opinions and scientific theories regarding the existence of races. Du Bois was compelled to acknowledge that race was more than a theoretical construct, a mere fiction to be critiqued and quickly brushed aside; it was also a deeply held conviction on the part of many Americans, one that served to reinforce the social, political, economic, and cultural realities that had profoundly shaped the lives of African Americans. Thus while Du Bois could admit that there was no scientific evidence to justify a belief in races, he had to acknowledge that such a belief had been used to justify the oppression of African Americans; and while he could celebrate the spirituals as the unique contribution of African-American culture to America and the world, he realized that in the conceptual order of race this gift counted for little, if anything at all. Consequently, Du Bois's early work is distinguished by its search for a way to express this complex situation, one that results from the desire to speak of the finer feelings of black folks where none were thought to exist and to celebrate a culture without reinscribing a fictitious racial hierarchy. And though Du Bois could never fully answer the questions that continue to challenge critics of African-American culture, he did reveal the strange meaning of being black in the "painful self-consciousness" that resulted from this complex fate.

> From the double life every American Negro must live, as a Negro and as an American . . . —from this must arise a painful self-consciousness, an almost morbid sense of personality and moral hesitancy which is fatal to self-confidence. The worlds within and without the Veil of Color are changing, and changing rapidly, but not at the same rate, not in the same way; and this must produce a peculiar sense of doubt and bewilderment. Such a double life, with double thoughts, double duties, and double social classes, must give rise to double words and double ideals, and tempt the mind to pretence or to revolt, to hypocrisy or to radicalism.[31]

These sentiments, and the experience of double-consciousness that produced them, have been expressed by many African Americans. Yet they find poignant expression in a verse from Louis Armstrong's socially and politically provocative rendition of the Fats Waller, Andy Razaf, and Harry Brooks composition, "(What Did I Do to Be So) Black and Blue," a song that conveys both the physical and psychological meanings in the double-entendre of its title:

> How will it end
> I ain't got a friend
> my only sin
> is in my skin
> What did I do
> to be so black and blue.[32]

ENDNOTES

1. Ralph Ellison, *The Invisible Man* (New York: Vintage Books, 1990), 8.
2. Ibid., 439–41.
3. W. E. B. Du Bois, *The Souls of Black Folk* (New York: Vintage Books, 1990), 7.

4. W. E. B. Du Bois, "The Independent," November 17, 1904, 57:1152.
5. W. E. B. Du Bois, *Dusk of Dawn: An Essay toward an Autobiography of a Race Concept* (New York: Harcourt Brace, 1940), 140.
6. James Baldwin, *The Fire Next Time* (New York: Dell Publishing Co., Inc., 1962), 46.
7. Du Bois, "The Independent," 1152.
8. Ralph Ellison, *Shadow and Act* (New York: Random House, 1964), 146.
9. Du Bois, "Independent," 1152.
10. Ibid.
11. Ibid.
12. Ibid.
13. Du Bois, *Dusk of Dawn,* 140.
14. Ibid.
15. Ellison, *Shadow and Act,* 145.
16. Arnold Rampersad, "W. E. B. Du Bois as a Man of Literature," in *Critical Essays on W. E. B. Du Bois,* ed. William L. Andrews (Boston: Hall, 1985), 63–64.
17. Du Bois, *Dusk of Dawn,* 140.
18. Rampersad, "W. E. B. Du Bois," 71.
19. W. E. B. Du Bois, "The Conservation of Races," in *W. E. B. Du Bois: Speeches and Addresses, 1890–1919,* ed. Philip S. Foner (New York: Pathfinder Press, 1970), 77.
20. Ibid., 83.
21. Kwame Anthony Appiah, *In My Father's House: Africa in the Philosophy of Culture* (New York: Oxford University Press, 1992), 30.
22. Du Bois, *The Souls of Black Folk,* 8–9.
23. Ibid., 9.
24. Houston Baker, "Caliban's Triple Play," in *"Race," Writing, and Difference* (Chicago: University of Chicago Press, 1985), 391.
25. Ibid., 394.
26. Ibid., 389, 394.
27. Ibid., 384.
28. Ibid., 382.
29. Houston A. Baker, Jr., "The Black Man of Culture: W. E. B. Du Bois and *The Souls of Black Folk,*" in *Critical Essays on W. E. B. Du Bois,* ed. William L. Andrews (Boston: Hall, 1985), 137.
30. Houston Baker, *Modernism and the Harlem Renaissance* (Chicago: University of Chicago Press, 1987), 58.
31. Du Bois, *The Souls of Black Folk,* 146.
32. Thomas "Fats" Waller, Andy Razaf, and Harry Brooks, "(What Did I Do to Be So) Black and Blue," *Souvenirs of Hot Chocolates,* cond. Louis Armstrong and his Orchestra, Columbia, P14587, 1978.

AUTOBIOGRAPHY

Olaudah Equiano (c. 1745–97)

After having endured the experiences common to black Africans ensnared within the slave trade, Olaudah Equiano nonetheless went on to lead a distinguished life—writing, traveling, and speaking for the abolitionist cause.

First captured at about age eleven in Nigeria by black slave hunters, Equiano found himself a slave in Africa for a time before being transported to the coast and sold to slavers heading for the West Indies. He was then sold in Virginia to Captain Pascal, a naval officer who gave his new slave a new name: Gustavus Vassa. As Pascal's slave, Equiano journeyed to Canada and England, observing different settings and learning maritime procedures. After Pascal sent Equiano back to the West Indies, he was sold to the Philadelphia Quaker Robert King, who worked in the rum and sugar trade. The three years he spent with King, traveling between the West Indies and the American colonies, exposed Equiano to the slave system of both locales and gave him the opportunity to accumulate money of his own. In 1766, Equiano, about twenty-one, bought his freedom and worked as a sailor until he moved to England in 1777.

He continued to travel, sometimes orating against slavery as his interests took him to the diverse environments of Central America, Turkey, Italy, and Spain. He became a Methodist and applied to the bishop of London to become a missionary to Africa. His request was denied, but in 1786, Equiano was given the position of commissary of provisions and stores for the Black Poor Going to Sierra Leone colonization project. However, the project was plagued by administrative problems, and Equiano's open criticism of white officials resulted in his termination from the project.

Following that disappointment, he went on to write his autobiography, The Interesting Narrative of the Life of Olaudah Equiano, or Gustavus Vassa, the African *(1789), which enjoyed huge popularity. In 1792, he married Susan Cullen, an English woman, and the couple had at least one child before Equiano died in 1797.*

Following are two chapters from Equiano's autobiography, which critic Mason Lowance, Jr., described as a "masterpiece among the early accounts. . . . Equiano clearly established the model for the slave narrative genre. His first-person, retrospective recapitulation of the past leads the reader along a purposeful journey. The language of this account is erudite and polished, obviously the work of an educated, even learned writer." In Chapter 2, Equiano describes his African family, his capture, and his introduction to the horrors of slavery. Chapter 5 covers the time he spent as a slave with Robert King, during which he observed the cruelty of slavery in the West Indies and the efforts of blacks to escape the system.

from The Interesting Narrative of the Life of Olaudah Equiano, or Gustavus Vassa, the African

CHAPTER 2

The author's birth and parentage—His being kidnapped with his sister—Their separation—Surprise at meeting again—Are finally separated—Account of the different places and incidents the author met with till his arrival on the coast—The effect the sight of a slave-ship had on him—He sails for the West Indies—Horrors of a slave-ship—Arrives at Barbadoes, where the cargo is sold and dispersed.

I hope the reader will not think I have trespassed on his patience in introducing myself to him, with some account of the manners and customs of my country. They had been implanted in me with great care, and made an impression on my mind, which time could not erase, and which all the adversity and variety of fortune I have since experienced, served only to rivet and record: for, whether the love of one's country be real or imaginary, or a lesson of reason, or an instinct of nature, I still look back with pleasure on the first scenes of my life, though that pleasure has been for the most part mingled with sorrow.

I have already acquainted the reader with the time and place of my birth. My father, besides many slaves, had a numerous family, of which seven lived to grow up, including myself and sister, who was the only daughter. As I was the youngest of the sons, I became, of course, the greatest favorite with my mother, and was always with her; and she used to take particular pains to form my mind. I was trained up from my earliest years in the art of war: my daily exercise was shooting and throwing javelins, and my mother adorned me with emblems, after the manner of our greatest warriors. In this way I grew up till I had turned the age of eleven, when an end was put to my happiness in the following manner: Generally, when the grown people in the neighborhood were gone far in the fields to labor, the children assembled together in some of the neighboring premises to play; and commonly some of us used to get up a tree to look out for any assailant, or kidnapper, that might come upon us—for they sometimes took those opportunities of our parents' absence, to attack and carry off as many as they could seize. One day as I was watching at the top of a tree in our yard, I saw one of those people come into the yard of our next neighbor but one, to kidnap, there being many stout young people in it. Immediately on this I gave the alarm of the rogue, and he was surrounded by the stoutest of them, who entangled him with cords, so that he could not escape, till some of the grown people came and secured him. But, alas! ere long it was my fate to be thus attacked, and to be carried off, when none of the grown people were nigh. One day, when all our people were gone out to their works as usual, and only I and my dear sister were left to mind the house, two men and a woman got over our walls, and in a moment seized us both, and, without giving us time to cry out, or make resistance, they stopped our mouths, and ran off with us into the nearest wood. Here they tied our hands, and continued to carry us as far as they could, till night came on, when we reached a small house, where the robbers halted for refreshment, and spent the night. We were then unbound, but were unable to take any food;

and, being quite overpowered by fatigue and grief, our only relief was some sleep, which allayed our misfortune for a short time. The next morning we left the house, and continued travelling all the day. For a long time we had kept the woods, but at last we came into a road which I believed I knew. I had now some hopes of being delivered; for we had advanced but a little way before I discovered some people at a distance, on which I began to cry out for their assistance; but my cries had no other effect than to make them tie me faster and stop my mouth, and then they put me into a large sack. They also stopped my sister's mouth, and tied her hands; and in this manner we proceeded till we were out of sight of these people. When we went to rest the following night, they offered us some victuals, but we refused it; and the only comfort we had was in being in one another's arms all that night, and bathing each other with our tears. But alas! we were soon deprived of even the small comfort of weeping together. The next day proved a day of greater sorrow than I had yet experienced; for my sister and I were then separated, while we lay clasped in each other's arms. It was in vain that we besought them not to part us; she was torn from me, and immediately carried away, while I was left in a state of distraction not to be described. I cried and grieved continually; and for several days did not eat anything but what they forced into my mouth. At length, after many days' travelling, during which I had often changed masters, I got into the hands of a chieftain, in a very pleasant country. This man had two wives and some children, and they all used me extremely well, and did all they could do to comfort me; particularly the first wife, who was something like my mother. Although I was a great many days' journey from my father's house, yet these people spoke exactly the same language with us. This first master of mine, as I may call him, was a smith, and my principal employment was working his bellows, which were the same kind as I had seen in my vicinity. They were in some respects not unlike the stoves here in gentlemen's kitchens, and were covered over with leather; and in the middle of that leather a stick was fixed, and a person stood up, and worked it in the same manner as is done to pump water out of a cask with a hand pump. I believe it was gold he worked, for it was of a lovely bright yellow color, and was worn by the women on their wrists and ankles. I was there I suppose about a month, and they at last used to trust me some little distance from the house. This liberty I used in embracing every opportunity to inquire the way to my own home; and I also sometimes, for the same purpose, went with the maidens, in the cool of the evenings, to bring pitchers of water from the springs for the use of the house. I had also remarked where the sun rose in the morning, and set in the evening, as I had travelled along; and I had observed that my father's house was towards the rising of the sun. I therefore determined to seize the first opportunity of making my escape, and to shape my course for that quarter; for I was quite oppressed and weighed down by grief after my mother and friends; and my love of liberty, ever great, was strengthened by the mortifying circumstance of not daring to eat with the freeborn children, although I was mostly their companion. While I was projecting my escape one day, an unlucky event happened, which quite disconcerted my plan, and put an end to my hopes. I used to be sometimes employed in assisting an elderly slave to cook and take care of the poultry; and one morning, while I was feeding some chickens, I happened to toss a small pebble at one of them, which hit it on the middle, and directly killed it. The old slave, having soon after missed the chicken, inquired after it; and on my relating the accident (for I told her the truth, for my mother would never suffer me to tell a lie), she flew into a violent passion, and threatened that I should suffer for it; and, my master being out, she immediately went and told her mistress what I had done. This alarmed me very much, and I expected an instant flogging, which to me was uncommonly dreadful, for I had seldom been beaten at home. I therefore resolved to fly; and accordingly I ran into a thicket that was hard by, and hid myself in the bushes. Soon afterwards my mistress and the slave returned, and, not seeing me, they searched all the house, but not finding me, and I not making answer when they called to me, they thought I had run away, and the whole neighborhood was raised in the pursuit of me. In that part of the country, as in ours, the houses and villages were skirted with woods, or shrubberies, and the bushes were so thick that a man could readily conceal himself in them, so as to elude the strictest search. The neighbors continued the whole day looking for me, and several times many of them came within a few yards of the place where I lay hid. I expected every moment, when I heard a rustling among the tree, to be found out, and punished by my master; but they never discovered me, though they were often so near that I even heard their conjectures as they were looking about for me; and I now learned from them that any attempts to return home would be hopeless. Most of them supposed I had fled towards home; but the distance was so great, and the way so intricate, that they thought I could never reach it, and that I should be lost in the woods. When I heard this I was seized with a violent panic, and abandoned myself to despair. Night, too, began to approach, and aggravated all my fears. I had before entertained hopes of getting home, and had determined when it should be dark to make the attempt; but I was now convinced it was fruitless, and began to consider that, if possibly I could escape all other animals, I could not those of the human kind; and that, not knowing the way, I must perish in the woods. Thus was I like the hunted deer—

> Every leaf and every whisp'ring breath,
> Convey'd a foe, and every foe a death.

I heard frequent rustlings among the leaves, and being pretty sure they were snakes, I expected every instant to be stung by them. This increased my anguish, and the horror of my situation became now quite insupportable. I at length quitted the thicket, very faint and hungry, for I had not eaten or drank anything all the day, and crept to my master's kitchen, from whence I set out at first, which was an open shed, and laid myself down in the ashes with an anxious wish for death, to relieve me from all my pains. I was scarcely awake in the morning, when the old woman slave, who was the first up, came to light the fire, and saw me in the fireplace. She was very much surprised to see me, and could scarcely believe her own eyes. She now promised to intercede for me, and went for her master, who soon after came, and, having slightly reprimanded me, ordered me to be taken care of, and not ill treated.

Soon after this, my master's only daughter, and child by his first wife, sickened and died, which affected him so much that for sometime he was almost frantic, and really would have killed himself, had he not been watched and prevented. However, in a short time afterwards he recovered, and I was again sold. I was now carried to the left of the sun's rising, through many dreary wastes and dismal woods, amidst the hideous roarings of wild beasts. The people I was sold to used to carry me very often, when I was tired, either on their shoulders or on their backs. I saw many convenient well-built sheds along the road, at proper distances, to accommodate the merchants and travellers, who lay in those buildings along with their wives, who often accompany them; and they always go well armed.

From the time I left my own nation, I always found somebody that understood me till I came to the sea coast. The languages of different nations did not totally differ, nor were they so copious as those of the Europeans, particularly the English. They were therefore, easily learned; and, while I was journeying thus through Africa, I acquired two or three different tongues. In this manner I had been travelling for a considerable time, when, one evening, to my great surprise, whom should I see brought to the house where I was but my dear sister! As soon as she saw me, she gave a loud shriek, and ran into my arms—I was quite overpowered; neither of us could speak, but, for a considerable time, clung to each other in mutual embraces, unable to do anything but weep. Our meeting affected all who saw us; and, indeed, I must acknowledge, in honor of those sable destroyers of human rights, that I never met with any ill treatment, or saw any offered to their slaves, except tying them, when necessary, to keep them from running away. When these people knew we were brother and sister, they indulged us to be together; and the man, to whom I supposed we belonged, lay with us, he in the middle, while she and I held one another by the hands across his breast all night; and thus for a while we forgot our misfortunes, in the joy of being together; but even this small comfort was soon to have an end; for scarcely had the fatal morning appeared when she was again torn from me forever! I was now more miserable, if possible, than before. The small relief which her presence gave me from pain, was gone, and the wretchedness of my situation was redoubled by my anxiety after her fate, and my apprehensions lest her sufferings should be greater than mine, when I could not be with her to alleviate them. Yes, thou dear partner of all my childish sports! thou sharer of my joys and sorrows! happy should I have ever esteemed myself to encounter every misery for you and to procure your freedom by the sacrifice of my own. Though you were early forced from my arms, your image has been always riveted in my heart, from which neither time nor fortune have been able to remove it; so that, while the thoughts of your sufferings have damped my prosperity, they have mingled with adversity and increased its bitterness. To that Heaven which protects the weak from the strong, I commit the care of your innocence and virtues, if they have not already received their full reward, and if your youth and delicacy have not long since fallen victims to the violence of the African trader, the pestilential stench of a Guinea ship, the seasoning in the European colonies, or the lash and lust of a brutal and unrelenting overseer.

I did not long remain after my sister. I was again sold, and carried through a number of places, till after travelling a considerable time, I came to a town called Tinmah, in the most beautiful country I had yet seen in Africa. It was extremely rich, and there were many rivulets which flowed through it, and supplied a large pond in the centre of the town, where the people washed. Here I first saw and tasted cocoanuts, which I thought superior to any nuts I had ever tasted before; and the trees, which were loaded, were also interspersed among the houses, which had commodious shades adjoining, and were in the same manner as ours, the insides being neatly plastered and whitewashed. Here I also saw and tasted for the first time, sugar-cane. Their money consisted of little white shells, the size of the finger nail. I was sold here for one hundred and seventy-two of them, by a merchant who lived and brought me there. I had been about two or three days at his house, when a wealthy widow, a neighbor of his, came there one evening, and brought with her an only son, a young gentleman about my own age and size. Here they saw me; and, having taken a fancy to me, I was bought of the merchant, and went home with them. Her house and premises were situated close to one of those rivulets I have mentioned, and were the finest I ever saw in Africa: they were very extensive, and she had a number of slaves to attend her. The next day I was washed and perfumed, and when meal time came, I was led into the presence of my mistress, and ate and drank before her with her son. This filled me with astonishment; and I could scarce help expressing my surprise that the young gentleman should suffer me, who was bound, to eat with him who was free; and not only so, but that he would not at any time either eat or drink till I had taken first, because I was the eldest, which was agreeable to our custom. Indeed, every thing here, and all their treatment of me, made me forget that I was a slave. The language of these people resembled ours so nearly, that we understood each other perfectly. They had also the very same customs as we. There were likewise slaves daily to attend us, while my young master and I, with other boys, sported with our darts and bows and arrows, as I had been used to do at home. In this resemblance to my former happy state, I passed about two months; and I now began to think I was to be adopted into the family, and was beginning to be reconciled to my situation, and to forget by degrees my misfortunes, when all at once the delusion vanished; for, without the least previous knowledge, one morning early, while my dear master and companion was still asleep, I was awakened out of my reverie to fresh sorrow, and hurried away even amongst the uncircumcised.

Thus, at the very moment I dreamed of the greatest happiness, I found myself most miserable; and it seemed as if fortune wished to give me this taste of joy only to render the reverse more poignant. The change I now experienced was as painful as it was sudden and unexpected. It was a change indeed, from a state of bliss to a scene which is inexpressible by me, as it discovered to me an element I had never before beheld, and till then had no idea of, and wherein such instances of hardship and cruelty continually occurred, as I can never reflect on but with horror.

All the nations and people I had hitherto passed through, resembled our own in their manners, customs, and language; but I came at length to a country, the inhabitants of which differed from us in all those particulars. I was very much struck with this difference, especially when I came among a people who did not circumcise, and ate without washing their hands. They cooked also in iron pots, and had European cutlasses and cross bows, which were unknown to us, and fought with their fists among themselves. Their women were not so modest as ours, for they ate, and drank, and slept with their men. But above all, I was amazed to see no sacrifices or offerings among them. In some of those places the people ornamented themselves with scars, and likewise filed their teeth very sharp. They wanted sometimes to ornament me in the same manner, but I would not suffer them; hoping that I might some time be among a people who did not thus disfigure themselves, as I thought they did. At last I came to the banks of a large river which was covered with canoes, in which the people appeared to live with their household utensils, and provisions of all kinds. I was beyond measure astonished at this, as I had never before seen any water larger than a pond or a rivulet; and my surprise was mingled with no small fear when I was put into one of these canoes, and we began to paddle and move along the river. We continued going on thus till night, and when we came to land, and made fires on the banks, each family by themselves; some dragged their canoes on shore, others stayed and cooked in theirs, and laid in them all night. Those on the land had mats, of which they made tents, some in the shape of little houses; in these we slept; and after the morning meal, we embarked again and proceeded as before. I was often very much astonished to see some of the women, as well as the men, jumping into the water, dive to the bottom, come up again, and swim about. Thus I continued to travel, sometimes by land, sometimes by water, through different countries and various nations, till, at the end of six or seven months after I had been kidnapped, I arrived at the sea coast. It would be tedious and uninteresting to relate all the incidents which befell me during this journey, and which I have not yet forgotten; of the various hands I passed through, and the manners and customs of all the different people among whom I lived—I shall therefore only observe, that in all the places where I was, the soil was exceedingly rich; the pumpkins, eadas, plantains, yams, &c. &c., were in great abundance, and of incredible size. There were also vast quantities of different gums, though not used for any purpose, and everywhere a great deal of tobacco. The cotton even grew quite wild, and there was plenty of red-wood. I saw no mechanics whatever in all the way, except such as I have mentioned. The chief employment in all these countries was agriculture, and both the males and females, as with us, were brought up to it, and trained in the arts of war.

The first object which saluted my eyes when I arrived on the coast, was the sea, and a slave ship, which was then riding at anchor, and waiting for its cargo. These filled me with astonishment, which was soon converted into terror, when I was carried on board. I was immediately handled, and tossed up to see if I were sound, by some of the crew; and I was now persuaded that I had gotten into a world of bad spirits, and that they were going to kill me. Their complexions, too, differing so much from ours, their long hair, and the language they spoke (which was very different from any I had ever heard), united to confirm me in this belief. Indeed, such were the horrors of my views and fears at the moment, that, if ten thousand worlds had been my own, I would have freely parted with them all to have exchanged my condition with that of the meanest slave in my own country. When I looked round the ship too, and saw a large furnace of copper boiling, and a multitude of black people of every description chained together, every one of their countenances expressing dejection and sorrow, I no longer doubted of my fate; and, quite overpowered with horror and anguish, I fell motionless on the deck and fainted. When I recovered a little, I found some black people about me, who I believed were some of those who had brought me on board, and had been receiving their pay; they talked to me in order to cheer me, but all in vain. I asked them if we were not to be eaten by those white men with horrible looks, red faces, and long hair. They told me I was not, and one of the crew brought me a small portion of spirituous liquor in a wine glass; but, being afraid of him, I would not take it out of his hand. One of the blacks, therefore, took it from him and gave it to me, and I took a little down my palate, which, instead of reviving me, as they thought it would, threw me into the greatest consternation at the strange feeling it produced, having never tasted any such liquor before. Soon after this, the blacks who brought me on board went off, and left me abandoned to despair.

I now saw myself deprived of all chance of returning to my native country, or even the least glimpse of hope of gaining the shore, which I now considered as friendly; and I even wished for my former slavery in preference to my present situation, which was filled with horrors of every kind, still heightened by my ignorance of what I was to undergo. I was not long suffered to indulge my grief; I was soon put down under the decks, and there I received such a salutation in my nostrils as I had never experienced in my life: so that, with the loathsomeness of the stench, and crying together, I became so sick and low that I was not able to eat, nor had I the least desire to taste anything. I now wished for the last friend, death, to relieve me; but soon, to my grief, two of the white men offered me eatables; and, on my refusing to eat, one of them held me fast by the hands, and laid me across, I think, the windlass, and tied my feet, while the other flogged me severely. I had never experienced anything of this kind before, and, although not being used to the water, I naturally feared that element the first time I saw it, yet, nevertheless, could I have got over the nettings, I would have jumped over the side, but I could not; and besides, the crew used to watch us very closely who were not chained down to the decks, lest we should leap into the water; and I have seen some of these poor African prisoners most severely cut, for attempting to do so, and hourly whipped for not eating. This indeed was often the case with myself. In a little time after, amongst the poor chained men, I found some of my own nation, which in a small degree gave ease to my mind. I inquired of these what was to be done with us? They gave me to understand, we were to be carried to these white people's country to work for them. I then was a little revived, and thought, if it were no worse than working, my situation was not so desperate; but still I feared I should be put to death, the white people looked and acted, as I thought, in so savage a manner; for I had never seen among any people such instances of brutal cruelty; and this not only shown towards us blacks, but also to some of the whites themselves. One white man in particular I saw, when we were permitted to be on deck, flogged so unmercifully with a large rope near the foremast, that he died in consequence of it; and they tossed him over the side as they would have done a brute. This made me fear these people the more; and I expected nothing less than to be treated in the same manner. I could not help expressing my fears and apprehensions to some of my countrymen; I asked them if these people had no country, but lived in this hollow place (the ship)? They told me they did not, but came from a distant one. "Then," said I, "how comes it in all our country we never heard of them?" They told me because they lived so very far off. I then asked where were their women? had they any like themselves? I was told they had. "And why," said I, "do we not see them?" They answered, because they were left behind. I asked how the vessel could go? They told me they could not tell; but that there was cloth put upon the masts by the help of the ropes I saw, and then the vessel went on; and the white men had some spell or magic they put in the water when they liked, in order to stop the vessel. I was exceedingly amazed at this account, and really thought they were spirits. I therefore wished much to be from amongst them, for I expected they would sacrifice me; but my wishes were vain—for we were so quartered that it was impossible for any of us to make our escape.

While we stayed on the coast I was mostly on deck; and one day, to my great astonishment, I saw one of these vessels coming in with the sails up. As soon as the whites saw it, they gave a great shout, at which we were amazed; and the more so, as the vessel appeared larger by approaching nearer. At last, she came to an anchor in my sight, and when the anchor was let go, I and my countrymen who saw it, were lost in astonishment to observe the vessel stop—and were now convinced it was done by magic. Soon after this the other ship got her boats out, and they came on board of us, and the people of both ships seemed very glad to see each other. Several of the strangers also shook hands with us black people, and made motions with their hands, signifying I suppose, we were to go to their country, but we did not understand them.

At last, when the ship we were in, had got in all her cargo, they made ready with many fearful noises, and we were all put under deck, so that we could not see how they managed the vessel. But this disappointment was the least of my sorrow. The stench of the hold while we were on the coast was so intolerably loathsome, that it was dangerous to remain there for any time, and some of us had been permitted to stay on the deck for the fresh air; but now that the whole ship's cargo was confined together, it became absolutely pestilential. The closeness of the place, and the heat of the climate, added to the number in the ship, which was so crowded that each had scarcely room to turn himself, almost suffocated us. This produced copious perspirations, so that the air soon became unfit for respiration, from a variety of loathsome smells, and brought on a sickness among the slaves, of which many died—thus falling victims to the improvident avarice, as I may call it, of their purchasers. This wretched situation was again aggravated by the galling of the chains, now become insupportable, and the filth of the necessary tubs, into which the children often fell, and were almost suffocated. The shrieks of the women, and the groans of the dying, rendered the whole a scene of horror almost inconceivable. Happily perhaps, for myself, I was soon reduced so low here that it was thought necessary to keep me almost always on deck; and from my extreme youth I was not put in fetters. In this situation I expected every hour to share the fate of my companions, some of whom were almost daily brought upon deck at the point of death, which I began to hope would soon put an end to my miseries. Often did I think many of the inhabitants of the deep much more happy than myself. I envied them the freedom they enjoyed, and as often wished I could change my condition for theirs. Every circumstance I met with, served only to render my state more painful, and heightened my apprehensions, and my opinion of the cruelty of the whites.

One day they had taken a number of fishes; and when they had killed and satisfied themselves with as many as they thought fit, to our astonishment who were on deck, rather than give any of them to us to eat, as we expected, they tossed the remaining fish into the sea again, although we begged and prayed for some as well as we could, but in vain; and some of my countrymen, being pressed by hunger, took an opportunity, when they thought no one saw them, of trying to get a little privately; but they were discovered, and the attempt procured them some very severe floggings. One day, when we had a smooth sea and moderate wind, two of my wearied countrymen who were chained together (I was near them at the time), preferring death to such a life of misery, somehow made through the nettings and jumped into the sea; immediately, another quite dejected fellow, who, on account of his illness, was suffered to be out of irons, also followed their example; and I believe many more would very soon have done the same, if they had not been prevented by the ship's crew, who were instantly alarmed. Those of us that were the most active, were in a moment put down under the deck; and there was such a noise and confusion amongst the people of the ship as I never heard before, to stop her, and get the boat out to go after the slaves. However, two of the wretches were drowned, but they got the other, and afterwards flogged him unmercifully, for thus attempting to prefer death to slavery. In this manner we continued to undergo more hardships than I can now relate, hardships which are inseparable from this accursed trade. Many a time we were near suffocation from the want of fresh air, which we were often without for whole days together. This, and the stench of the necessary tubs, carried off many.

During our passage, I first saw flying fishes, which surprised me very much; they used frequently to fly across the ship, and many of them fell on the deck. I also now first saw the use of the quadrant; I had often with astonishment seen the mariners make observations with it, and I could not think what it meant. They at last took notice of my surprise; and one of them, willing to increase it, as well as to gratify my curiosity, made me one day look through it. The clouds appeared to me to be land, which disappeared as they passed along. This heightened my wonder; and I was now more persuaded than ever, that I was in another world, and that every thing about me was magic. At last, we came in sight of the island of Barbadoes, at which the whites on board gave a great shout, and made many signs of joy to us. We did not know what to think of this; but as the vessel drew nearer, we plainly saw the harbor, and other ships of different kinds and sizes, and we soon anchored amongst them, off Bridgetown. Many merchants and planters now came on board, though it was in the evening. They put us in separate parcels, and examined us attentively. They also made us jump, and pointed to the land, signifying we were to go there. We thought by this, we should be eaten by these ugly men, as they appeared to us; and, when soon after we were all put down under the deck again, there was much dread and trembling among us, and nothing but bitter cries to be heard all the night from these apprehensions, insomuch, that at last the white people got some old slaves from the land to pacify us. They told us we were not to be eaten, but to work, and were soon to go on land, where we should see many of our country people. This report eased us much. And sure enough, soon after we were landed, there came to us Africans of all languages.

We were conducted immediately to the merchant's yard, where we were all pent up together, like so many sheep in a fold, without regard to sex or age. As every object was new to me, everything I saw filled me with surprise. What struck me first, was, that the houses were built with bricks and stories, and in every other respect different from those I had seen in Africa; but I was still more astonished on seeing people on horseback. I did not know what this could mean; and, indeed, I thought these people were full of nothing but magical arts. While I was in this astonishment, one of my fellow prisoners spoke to a countryman of his, about the horses, who said they were the same kind they had in their country. I understood them, though they were from a distant part of Africa; and I thought it odd I had not seen any horses there; but afterwards, when I came to converse with different Africans, I found they had many horses amongst them, and much larger than those I then saw.

We were not many days in the merchant's custody, before we were sold after their usual manner, which is this: On a signal given (as the beat of a drum), the buyers rush at once into the yard where the slaves are confined, and make choice of that parcel they like best. The noise and clamor with which this is attended, and the eagerness visible in the countenances of the buyers, serve not a little to increase the apprehension of terrified Africans, who may well be supposed to consider them as the ministers of that destruction to which they think themselves devoted. In this manner, without scruple, are relations and friends separated, most of them never to see each other again. I remember, in the vessel in which I was brought over, in the men's apartment, there were several brothers, who, in the sale, were sold in different lots; and it was very moving on this occasion, to see and hear their cries at parting. O, ye nominal Christians! might not an African ask you—Learned you this from your God, who says unto you, Do unto all men as you would men should do unto you? Is it not enough that we are torn from our country and friends, to toil for your luxury and lust of gain? Must every tender feeling be likewise sacrificed to your avarice? Are the dearest friends and relations, now rendered more dear by their separation from their kindred, still to be parted from each other, and thus prevented from cheering the gloom of slavery, with the small comfort of being together, and mingling their sufferings and sorrows? Why are parents to lose their children, brothers their sisters, or husbands their wives? Surely, this is a new refinement in cruelty, which, while it has no advantage to atone for it, thus aggravates distress, and adds horrors even to the wretchedness of slavery.

CHAPTER 5

The author's reflections on his situation—Is deceived by a promise of being delivered—His despair at sailing for the West Indies—Arrives at Montserrat, where he is sold to Mr. King—Various interesting instances of oppression, cruelty, and extortion, which the author saw practised upon the slaves in the West Indies, during his captivity from the year 1763 to 1766—Address on it to the planters.

Thus, at the moment I expected all my toils to end, was I plunged, as I supposed, in a new slavery; in comparison of which, all my service hitherto had been perfect freedom; and whose horrors, always present to my mind, now rushed on it with tenfold aggravation. I wept very bitterly for some time, and began to think I must have done something to displease the Lord, that he thus punished me so severely. This filled me with painful reflections on my past conduct; I recollected that on the morning of our arrival at Deptford, I had rashly sworn that as soon as we reached London, I would spend the day in rambling and sport. My conscience smote me for this unguarded expression. I felt that the Lord was able to disappoint me in all things, and immediately considered my present situation as a judgment of Heaven, on account of my presumption in swearing. I therefore, with contrition of heart, acknowledged my transgression to God, and poured out my soul before him with unfeigned repentance, and with earnest supplications. I besought him not to abandon me in my distress, nor cast me from his mercy forever. In a little time, my grief, spent with its own violence, began to subside, and after the first confusion of my thoughts was over, I reflected with more calmness on my present condition. I considered that trials and disappointments are sometimes for our good, and I thought God might perhaps have permitted this, in order to teach me wisdom and resignation; for he had hitherto shadowed me with the wings of his mercy, and by his invisible but powerful hand brought me the way I knew not. These reflections gave me a little comfort, and I rose at last from the deck with dejection and sorrow in my countenance, yet mixed with some faint hope that the Lord would appear for my deliverance.

Soon afterwards, as my new master was going on shore, he called me to him, and told me to behave myself well, and do the business of the ship the same as any of the rest of the boys, and that I should fare the better for it; but I made him no answer. I was then asked if I could swim, and I said, No. However, I was made to go under the deck, and was well watched. The next tide the ship got under way, and soon after arrived at the Mother Bank, Portsmouth, where she waited a few days for some of the West India convoy. While I was here I tried every means I could devise, amongst the people of the ship, to get me a boat from the shore, as there was none suffered to come alongside of the ship; and their own, whenever it was used, was hoisted in again immediately. A sailor on board took a guinea from me on pretence of getting me a boat, and promised me, time after time, that it was hourly to come off. When he had the watch upon deck, I watched also, and looked long enough, but all in vain; I could never see either the boat or my guinea again. And what I thought was still the worst of all, the fellow gave information, as I afterwards found, all the while to the mates, of my intention to go off, if I could in any way do it; but, rogue-like, he never told them he had got a guinea from me to procure my escape. However, after we had sailed, and his trick was made known to the ship's crew, I had some satisfaction in seeing him detested and despised by them all, for his behavior to me. I was still in hopes that my old shipmates would not forget their promise to come for me at Portsmouth. And, indeed, at last, but not till the day before we sailed, some of them did come there, and sent me off some oranges, and other tokens of their regard. They also sent me word they would come off to me themselves the next day, or the day after; and a lady also, who lived in Gosport, wrote to me that she would come and take me out of the ship at the same time. This lady had been once very intimate with my former master. I used to sell and take care of a great deal of property for her, in different ships; and in return, she always showed great friendship for me, and used to tell my master that she would take me away to live with her. But, unfortunately for me, a disagreement soon afterwards took place between them; and she was succeeded in my master's good graces by another lady, who appeared sole mistress of the *Etna*, and mostly lodged on board. I was not so great a favorite with this lady as with the former; she had conceived a pique against me on some occasion when she was on board, and she did not fail to instigate my master to treat me in the manner he did.[1]

However, the next morning, the 30th of December, the wind being brisk and

[1]Thus was I sacrificed to the envy and resentment of this woman for knowing that the lady whom she had succeeded in my master's good graces, designed to take me into her service; which, had I once got on shore, she would not have been able to prevent. She felt her pride alarmed at the superiority of her rival, in being attended by a black servant. It was not less to prevent this, than to be revenged on me, that she caused the captain to treat me thus cruelly.

easterly, the *Eolus* frigate, which was to escort the convoy, made a signal for sailing. All the ships then got up their anchors; and, before any of my friends had an opportunity to come off to my relief, to my inexpressible anguish, our ship had got under way. What tumultuous emotions agitated my soul when the convoy got under sail, and I a prisoner on board, not without hope! I kept my swimming eyes upon the land in a state of unutterable grief; not knowing what to do, and despairing how to help myself. While my mind was in this situation, the fleet sailed on, and in one day's time I lost sight of the wished-for land. In the first expression of my grief I reproached my fate, and wished I had never been born. I was ready to curse the tide that bore us, the gale that wafted my prison, and even the ship that conducted us. And I called on death to relieve me from the horrors I felt and dreaded, that I might be in that place

> Where slaves are free, and men oppress no more.
> Fool that I was, inur'd so long to pain,
> To trust to hope, or dream of joy again. . . .
>
> Now dragg'd once more beyond the western main,
> To groan beneath some dastard planter's chain;
> Where my poor countrymen in bondage wait
> The long enfranchisement of a ling'ring fate.
> Hard ling'ring fate! while, ere the dawn of day,
> Rous'd by the lash they go their cheerless way;
> And as their souls with shame and anguish burn,
> Salute with groans unwelcome morn's return;
> And, chiding ev'ry hour the slow pac'd sun,
> Pursue their toils till all his race is run.
> No eye to mark their suff'rings with a tear,
> No friend to comfort, and no hope to cheer;
> Then, like the dull unpity'd brutes, repair
> To stalls as wretched, and as coarse a fare;
> Thank heaven one day of misery was o'er,
> Then sink to sleep, and wish to wake no more.[2]

The turbulence of my emotions, however, naturally gave way to calmer thoughts, and I soon perceived what fate had decreed no mortal on earth could prevent. The convoy sailed on without any accident, with a pleasant gale and smooth sea, for six weeks, till February, when one morning the *Eolus* ran down a brig, one of the convoy, and she instantly went down, and was engulfed in the dark recesses of the ocean. The convoy was immediately thrown into great confusion till it was day-light; and the *Eolus* was illumined with lights, to prevent any further mischief. On the 13th of February, 1763, from the mast-head, we descried our destined island, Montserrat; and soon after I beheld those

[2] "The Dying Negro," a poem originally published in 1733. Perhaps it may not be deemed impertinent here to add, that this elegant and pathetic little poem was occasioned, as appears by the advertisement prefixed to it, by the following incident. "A black, who, a few days before had run away from his master, and got himself christened, with intent to marry a white woman, his fellow-servant, being taken and sent on board a ship in the Thames, took an opportunity of shooting himself through the head."

> Regions of sorrow, doleful shades, where peace
> And rest can rarely dwell. Hope never comes
> That comes to all, but torture without end
> Still urges.

At the sight of this land of bondage, a fresh horror ran through all my frame, and chilled me to the heart. My former slavery now rose in dreadful review to my mind, and displayed nothing but misery, stripes, and chains; and, in the first paroxysm of my grief, I called upon God's thunder, and his avenging power, to direct the stroke of death to me, rather than permit me to become a slave, and be sold from lord to lord.

In this state of my mind our ship came to anchor, and soon after discharged her cargo. I now knew what it was to work hard; I was made to help unload and load the ship. And, to comfort me in my distress in that time, two of the sailors robbed me of all my money, and ran away from the ship. I had been so long used to a European climate, that at first I felt the scorching West India sun very painful, while the dashing surf would toss the boat and the people in it, frequently above high water mark. Sometimes our limbs were broken with this, or even attended with instant death, and I was day by day mangled and torn.

About the middle of May, when the ship was got ready to sail for England, I all the time believing that fate's blackest clouds were gathering over my head, and expecting their bursting would mix me with the dead, Captain Doran sent for me ashore one morning, and I was told by the messenger that my fate was then determined. With trembling steps and fluttering heart, I came to the captain, and found with him one Mr. Robert King, a Quaker, and the first merchant in the place. The captain then told me my former master had sent me there to be sold; but that he had desired him to get me the best master he could, as he told him I was a very deserving boy, which Captain Doran said he found to be true; and if he were to stay in the West Indies, he would be glad to keep me himself; but he could not venture to take me to London, for he was very sure that when I came there I would leave him. I at that instant burst out a crying, and begged much of him to take me to England with him, but all to no purpose. He told me he had got me the very best master in the whole island, with whom I should be as happy as if I were in England, and for that reason he chose to let him have me, though he could sell me to his own brother-in-law for a great deal more money than what he got from this gentleman. Mr. King, my new master, then made a reply, and said the reason he had bought me was on account of my good character; and as he had not the least doubt of my good behavior, I should be very well off with him. He also told me he did not live in the West Indies, but at Philadelphia, where he was going soon; and, as I understood something of the rules of arithmetic, when we got there he would put me to school, and fit me for a clerk. This conversation relieved my mind a little, and I left those gentlemen considerably more at ease in myself than when I came to them; and I was very thankful to Captain Doran, and even to my old master, for the character they had given me. A character which I afterwards found of infinite service to me. I went on board again, and took leave of all my ship-mates, and the next day the ship sailed. When she weighed anchor, I went to the waterside and looked at her with a very wishful and aching heart, and followed her with my eyes until she was totally out of sight. I was so bowed down with grief, that I could not hold up my head for many months; and if my new master had not been kind to me, I believe I should have died under it at last. And, indeed, I soon found that he fully deserved the good character which Captain Doran gave me of him, for he possessed a most amiable disposition and temper, and was very charitable and humane. If any of his slaves behaved amiss he did not beat or use them ill, but parted with them. This made them afraid of disobliging him; and as he treated his slaves better than any other man on the island, so he was better and more faithfully served by them in return. By this kind treatment I did at last endeavor to compose myself; and with fortitude, though moneyless, determined to face whatever fate had decreed for me. Mr. King soon asked me what I could do; and at the same time said he did not mean to treat me as a common slave. I told him I knew something of seamanship, and could shave and dress hair pretty well; and I could refine wines, which I had learned on shipboard, where I had often done it; and that I could write, and understood arithmetic tolerably well, as far as the Rule of Three. He then asked me if I knew anything of gauging; and, on my answering that I did not, he said one of his clerks should teach me to gauge.

Mr. King dealt in all manner of merchandise, and kept from one to six clerks. He loaded many vessels in a year; particularly to Philadelphia, where he was born; and was connected with a great mercantile house in that city. He had, besides, many vessels and droggers, of different sizes, which used to go about the island; and others, to collect rum, sugar, and other goods. I understood pulling and managing those boats very well. And this hard work, which was the first that he set me to, in the sugar seasons used to be my constant employment. I have rowed the boat, and slaved at the oars, from one hour to sixteen in the twenty-four, during which I had fifteen pence sterling per day to live on, though sometimes only ten pence. However, this was considerably more than was allowed to other slaves that used to work often with me, and belonged to other gentlemen on the island. Those poor souls had never more than nine pence per day, and seldom more than six pence, from their masters or owners, though they earned them three or four pistareens.[3] For it is a common practice in the West Indies for men to purchase slaves, though they have not plantations themselves, in order to let them out to planters and merchants at so much a piece by the day, and they give what allowance they choose out of this product of their daily work to their slaves, for subsistence; this allowance is often very scanty. My master often gave the owners of the slaves two and a half of these pieces per day, and found the poor fellows in victuals himself, because he thought their owners did not feed them well enough according to the work they did. The slaves used to like this very well; and, as they knew my master to be a man of feeling, they were always glad to work for him, in preference to any other gentleman; some of whom, after they had been paid for these poor people's labors, would not give them their allowance out of it. Many times have I even seen these unfortunate wretches beaten for asking for their pay; and often severely flogged by their owners if they did not bring them their daily or weekly money exactly to the time; though the poor creatures were obliged to wait on the gentlemen they had worked for, sometimes more than half the day before they could get their pay; and this generally on Sundays, when they wanted the time for themselves. In particular, I knew a countryman of mine who once did not bring the weekly

[3]These pistareens are of the value of a shilling.

money directly that it was earned; and, though he brought it the same day to his master, yet he was staked to the ground for his pretended negligence, and was just going to receive a hundred lashes, but for a gentleman who begged him off with fifty. This poor man was very industrious; and by his frugality, had saved so much money by working on ship-board, that he had got a white man to buy him a boat, unknown to his master. Some time after he had this little estate, the governor wanted a boat to bring his sugar from different parts of the island; and, knowing this to be a Negro man's boat, he seized upon it for himself, and would not pay the owner a farthing. The man, on this, went to his master, and complained to him of this act of the governor; but the only satisfaction he received was to be damned very heartily by his master, who asked him how dared any of his Negroes to have a boat. If the justly merited ruin of the governor's fortune could be any gratification to the poor man he had thus robbed, he was not without consolation. Extortion and rapine are poor providers; and some time after this the governor died in the King's Bench in England, as I was told, in great poverty. The last war favored this poor Negro man, and he found some means to escape from his Christian master. He came to England, where I saw him afterwards several times. Such treatment as this often drives these miserable wretches to despair, and they run away from their masters at the hazard of their lives. Many of them, in this place, unable to get their pay when they have earned it, and fearing to be flogged, as usual, if they return home without it, run away where they can for shelter, and a reward is often offered to bring them in dead or alive. My master used sometimes, in these cases, to agree with their owners, and to settle with them himself; and thereby he saved many of them a flogging.

Once, for a few days, I was let out to fit a vessel, and I had no victuals allowed me by either party; at last I told my master of this treatment, and he took me away from it. In many of the estates, on the different islands where I used to be sent for rum or sugar, they would not deliver it to me, or any other Negro; he was therefore obliged to send a white man along with me to those places; and then he used to pay him from six to ten pistareens a day. From being thus employed, during the time I served Mr. King, in going about the different estates on the island, I had all the opportunity I could wish for, to see the dreadful usage of the poor men; usage that reconciled me to my situation, and made me bless God for the hands into which I had fallen.

I had the good fortune to please my master in every department in which he employed me; and there was scarcely any part of his business, or household affairs, in which I was not occasionally engaged. I often supplied the place of a clerk, in receiving and delivering cargoes to the ships, in tending stores, and delivering goods. And besides this, I used to shave and dress my master when convenient, and take care of his horse; and when it was necessary, which was very often, I worked likewise on board of different vessels of his. By these means I became very useful to my master, and saved him, as he used to acknowledge, above a hundred pounds a year. Nor did he scruple to say I was of more advantage to him than any of his clerks; though their usual wages in the West Indies are from sixty to a hundred pounds current a year.

I have sometimes heard it asserted that a Negro cannot earn his master the first cost; but nothing can be further from the truth. I suppose nine-tenths of the mechanics throughout the West Indies are Negro slaves; and I well know the coopers among them earn two dollars a day, the carpenters the same, and oftentimes more; as also the masons, smiths, and fishermen, &c. And I have known many slaves whose masters would not take a thousand pounds current for them. But surely this assertion refutes itself; for, if it be true, why do the planters and merchants pay such a price for slaves? And, above all, why do those who make this assertion exclaim the most loudly against the abolition of the slave trade? So much are men blinded, and to such inconsistent arguments are they driven by mistaken interest! I grant, indeed, that slaves are sometimes, by half-feeding, half-clothing, over-working, and stripes, reduced so low, that they are turned out as unfit for service, and let to perish in the woods, or expire on the dung-hill.

My master was several times offered, by different gentlemen, one hundred guineas for me, but he always told them he would not sell me, to my great joy. And I used to double my diligence and care, for fear of getting into the hands of those men who did not allow a valuable slave the common support of life. Many of them even used to find fault with my master for feeding his slaves so well as he did, although I often went hungry, and an Englishman might think my fare very indifferent; but he used to tell them he always would do it, because the slaves thereby looked better and did more work.

While I was thus employed by my master, I was often a witness to cruelties of every kind, which were exercised on my unhappy fellow slaves. I used frequently to have different cargoes of new Negroes in my care for sale; and it was almost a constant practice with our clerks, and other whites, to commit violent depredations on the chastity of the female slaves; and these I was, though with reluctance, obliged to submit to at all times, being unable to help them. When we have had some of these slaves on board my master's vessels, to carry them to other islands, or to America, I have known our mates to commit these acts most shamefully, to the disgrace, not of Christians only, but of men. I have even known them to gratify their brutal passion with females not ten years old; and these abominations, some of them practised to such scandalous excess, that one of our captains discharged the mate and others on that account. And yet in Montserrat I have seen a Negro man staked to the ground, and cut most shockingly, and then his ears cut off bit by bit, because he had been connected with a white woman, who was a common prostitute. As if it were no crime in the whites to rob an innocent African girl of her virtue, but most heinous in a black man only to gratify a passion of nature, where the temptation was offered by one of a different color, though the most abandoned woman of her species.

One Mr. D—— told me that he had sold 41,000 Negroes, and that he once cut off a Negro man's leg for running away. I asked him if the man had died in the operation, how he, as a Christian, could answer for the horrid act before God? and he told me, answering was a thing of another world, what he thought and did were policy. I told him that the Christian doctrine taught us to do unto others as we would that others should do unto us. He then said that his scheme had the desired affect—it cured that man and some others of running away.

Another Negro man was half hanged, and then burnt, for attempting to poison a cruel overseer. Thus, by repeated cruelties, are the wretched first urged to despair, and then murdered, because they still retain so much of human nature about them as to wish to put an end to their misery, and retaliate on their tyrants! These overseers are indeed for the most part persons of the worst character of any denomination of men in the West Indies. Unfortunately, many humane gentlemen, but not residing on their estates, are obliged to leave the management of them in the hands of these human butchers, who cut and mangle the slaves in a shocking manner on the most trifling occasions, and altogether treat them in every respect like brutes. They pay no regard to the situation of pregnant women, nor the least attention to the lodging of the field Negroes. Their huts, which ought to be well covered, and the place dry where they take their little repose, are often open sheds, built in damp places; so that when the poor creatures returned tired from the toils of the field, they contract many disorders, from being exposed to the damp air in this uncomfortable state, while they are heated, and their pores are open. This neglect certainly conspires with many others to cause a decrease in the births as well as in the lives of the grown Negroes. I can quote many instances of gentlemen who reside on their estates in the West Indies, and then the scene is quite changed; the Negroes are treated with lenity and proper care, by which their lives are prolonged, and their masters profited. To the honor of humanity, I knew several gentlemen who managed their estates in this manner, and they found that benevolence was their true interest. And, among many I could mention in several of the islands, I knew one in Montserrat[4] whose slaves looked remarkably well, and never needed any fresh supplies of Negroes; and there are many other estates, especially in Barbadoes, which, from such judicious treatment, need no fresh stock of Negroes at any time. I have the honor of knowing a most worthy and humane gentleman, who is a native of Barbadoes, and has estates there.[5] This gentleman has written a treatise on the usage of his own slaves. He allows them two hours of refreshment at mid-day, and many other indulgencies and comforts, particularly in their lodging; and, besides this, he raises more provisions on his estate than they can destroy; so that by these attentions he saves the lives of his Negroes, and keeps them healthy, and as happy as the condition of slavery can admit. I myself . . . managed an estate, where, by those attentions, the Negroes were uncommonly cheerful and healthy, and did more work by half than by the common mode of treatment they usually do. For want, therefore, of such care and attention to the poor Negroes, and otherwise oppressed as they are, it is no wonder that the decrease should require 20,000 new Negroes annually, to fill up the vacant places of the dead.

Even in Barbadoes, notwithstanding those humane exceptions which I have mentioned, and others I am acquainted with, which justly make it quoted as a place where slaves meet with the best treatment, and need fewest recruits of any in the West Indies, yet this island requires 1,000 Negroes annually to keep up the original stock, which is only 80,000. So that the whole term of a Negro's life may be said to be there but sixteen years![6] And yet the climate here in every respect is the same as that from which they are taken, except in being more wholesome. Do the British colonies decrease in this manner? And yet what prodigious difference is there between an English and West India climate?

While I was in Montserrat I knew a Negro man, named Emanuel Sankey, who endeavored to escape from his miserable bondage, by concealing himself on board of a London ship, but fate did not favor the poor oppressed man; for, being discovered when the vessel was under sail, he was delivered up again to

---

[4]Mr. Dubury, and many others, Montserrat.

[5]Sir Phillip Gibbes, Baronet, Barbadoes.

[6]Benezet's "Account of Guinea," p. 16.

his master. This *Christian master* immediately pinned the wretch down to the ground at each wrist and ankle, and then took some sticks of sealing wax, and lighted them, and dropped it all over his back. There was another master who was noted for cruelty; and I believe he had not a slave but what had been cut, and had pieces fairly taken out of the flesh. And after they had been punished thus, he used to make them get into a long wooden box or case he had for that purpose, in which he shut them up during pleasure. It was just about the height and breadth of a man; and the poor wretches had no room, when in the case, to move.

It was very common in several of the islands, particularly in St. Kitts, for the slaves to be branded with the initial letters of their master's name; and a load of heavy iron hooks hung about their necks. Indeed, on the most trifling occasions, they were loaded with chains; and often instruments of torture were added. The iron muzzle, thumb-screws, &c., are so well known as not to need a description, and were sometimes applied for the slightest faults. I have seen a Negro beaten till some of his bones were broken, for only letting a pot boil over. Is it surprising that usage like this should drive the poor creatures to despair, and make them seek a refuge in death from those evils which render their lives intolerable?—while,

> With shudd'ring horror pale, and eyes aghast,
> They view their lamentable lot, and find
> No rest!

This they frequently do. A Negro man, on board a vessel of my master, while I belonged to her, having been put in irons for some trifling misdemeanor, and kept in that state for some days, being weary of life, took an opportunity of jumping overboard into the sea; however, he was picked up without being drowned. Another, whose life was also a burden to him, resolved to starve himself to death, and refused to eat any victuals. This procured him a severe flogging; and he also, on the first occasion which offered, jumped overboard at Charleston, but was saved.

Nor is there any greater regard shown to the little property than there is to the persons and lives of the Negroes. I have already related an instance or two of particular oppression out of many which I have witnessed; but the following is frequent in all the islands. The wretched field slaves, after toiling all the day for an unfeeling owner, who gives them but little victuals, steal sometimes a few moments from rest or refreshment to gather some small portion of grass, according as their time will admit. This they commonly tie up in a parcel; either a bit's worth (six pence) or half a bit's worth, and bring it to town, or to the market, to sell. Nothing is more common than for the white people on this occasion to take the grass from them without paying for it; and not only so, but too often also, to my knowledge, our clerks, and many others, at the same time have committed acts of violence on the poor, wretched, and helpless females; whom I have seen for hours stand crying to no purpose, and get no redress or pay of any kind. Is not this one common and crying sin enough to bring down God's judgment on the islands? He tells us the oppressor and the oppressed are both in his hands; and if these are not the poor, the broken-hearted, the blind, the captive, the bruised, which our Saviour speaks of, who are they? One of these depredators once, in St. Eustatius, came on board of our vessel, and bought some fowls and pigs of me; and a whole day after his departure with the things, he returned again and wanted his money back. I refused to give it, and, not seeing my captain on board, he began the common pranks with me; and swore he would even break open my chest and take my money. I therefore expected, as my captain was absent, that he would be as good as his word. And was just proceeding to strike me, when fortunately a British seaman on board, whose heart had not been debauched by a West India climate, interposed and prevented him. But had the cruel man struck me I certainly should have defended myself at the hazard of my life; for what is life to a man thus oppressed? He went away, however, swearing, and threatened that whenever he caught me on shore, he would shoot me, and pay for me afterwards.

The small account in which the life of a Negro is held in the West Indies is so universally known that it might seem impertinent to quote the following extract, if some people had not been hardy enough of late to assert that Negroes are on the same footing in that respect as Europeans. By the 329th Act, page 125, of the Assembly of Barbadoes, it is enacted "That if any Negro, or other slave, under punishment by his master, or his order, for running away, or any other crime or misdemeanor towards his said master, unfortunately shall suffer in life or member, no person whatsoever shall be liable to a fine; but if any person shall, out of wantonness, or only of bloody-mindedness, or cruel intention, willfully kill a Negro, or other slave, of his own, he shall pay into the public treasury fifteen pounds sterling." And it is the same in most, if not all of the West India islands. Is not this one of the many acts of the islands which call loudly for redress? And do not the assembly which enacted it deserve the appellation of savages and brutes, rather than of Christians and men? It is an act at once unmerciful, unjust, and unwise; which for cruelty would disgrace an assembly of those who are called barbarians; and for its injustice and insanity would shock the morality and common sense of a Samaide or Hottentot.

Shocking as this and many other acts of the bloody West India code at first view appear, how is the iniquity of it heightened when we consider to whom it may be extended! Mr. James Tobin, a zealous laborer in the vineyard of slavery, gives an account of a French planter of his acquaintance, in the island of Martinique, who showed him many mulattoes working in the field like beasts of burden; and he told Mr. Tobin these were all the produce of his own loins! And I myself have known similar instances. Pray, reader, are these sons and daughters of the French planter less his children by being the progeny of black women? And what must be the virtue of those legislators, and the feelings of those fathers, who estimate the lives of their sons, however begotten, at no more than fifteen pounds; though they should be murdered, as the act says, out of wantonness and bloody-mindedness! But is not the slave trade entirely at war with the heart of man? And surely that which is begun by breaking down the barriers of virtue, involves in its continuance destruction to every principle, and buries all sentiment in ruin!

I have often seen slaves, particularly those who were meagre, in different islands, put into scales and weighed, and then sold for three pence to six pence or nine pence a pound. My master, however, whose humanity was shocked at this mode, used to sell such by the lump. And at or after a sale, it was not uncommon to see Negroes taken from their wives, wives taken from their husbands, and children from their parents, and sent off to other islands, and wherever else their merciless lords choose; and probably never more during life see each other! Oftentimes my heart has bled at these partings, when the friends of the departed have been at the waterside, and with sighs and tears, have kept their eyes fixed on the vessel, till it went out of sight.

A poor Creole Negro, I knew well, who, after having been often thus transported from island to island, at last resided in Montserrat. This man used to tell me many melancholy tales of himself. Generally, after he had done working for his master, he used to employ his few leisure moments to go a fishing. When he had caught any fish, his master would frequently take them from him without paying him; and at other times some other white people would serve him in the same manner. One day he said to me, very movingly, "Sometimes when a white man take away my fish, I go to my maser, and he get me my right; and when my maser by strength take away my fishes, what me must do? I can't go to any body to be righted; then," said the poor man, looking up above, "I must look up to God Mighty, in the top, for right." This artless tale moved me much, and I could not help feeling the just cause Moses had in redressing his brother against the Egyptian. I exhorted the man to look up still to the God on the top, since there was no redress below. Though I little thought then that I myself should more than once experience such imposition, and need the same exhortation hereafter, in my own transactions in the islands, and that even this poor man and I should some time after suffer together in the same manner. . . .

Nor was such usage as this confined to particular places or individuals, for in all the different islands in which I have been (and I have visited no less than fifteen) the treatment of the slaves was nearly the same; so nearly, indeed, that the history of an island, or even a plantation, with a few such exceptions as I have mentioned, might serve for a history of the whole. Such a tendency has the slave trade to debauch men's minds, and harden them to every feeling of humanity! For I will not suppose that the dealers in slaves are born worse than other men—No; such is the fatality of this mistaken avarice that it corrupts the milk of human kindness and turns it into gall. And, had the pursuits of those men been different, they might have been as generous, as tender-hearted and just, as they are unfeeling, rapacious, and cruel. Surely this traffic cannot be good, which spreads like a pestilence, and taints what it touches! which violates that first natural right of mankind, equality and independency, and gives one man a dominion over his fellows which God could never intend! For it raises the owner to a state as far above man as it depresses the slave below it; and, with all the presumption of human pride, sets a distinction between them, immeasurable in extent, and endless in duration! Yet how mistaken is the avarice even of the planters. Are slaves more useful by being thus humbled to the condition of brutes than they would be if suffered to enjoy the privileges of men? The freedom which diffuses health and prosperity throughout Britain answers you—No. When you make men slaves, you deprive them of half their virtue; you set them, in your own conduct, an example of fraud, rapine, and cruelty, and compel them to live with you in a state of war; and yet you complain that they are not honest or faithful! You stupify them with stripes, and think it necessary to keep them in a state of ignorance. And yet you assert that they are incapable of learning; that their minds are such a barren soil or moor that culture would be lost on them; and that they come from a climate where nature, though prodigal of her bounties in a degree unknown to yourselves, has left man alone scant and unfinished, and incapable of enjoying the treasures she has poured out for him! An assertion at once impious and absurd. Why do you use those instruments of torture? Are they fit to be applied by one rational being to another? And are ye not struck with shame and mortification, to see the partakers of your nature reduced so low? But, above all, are there no dangers attending this mode of treatment? Are you not hourly in dread of an insurrection? Nor would it be surprising; for when

> No peace is given
> To us enslav'd, but custody severe,
> And stripes and arbitrary punishment
> Inflicted—What peace can we return?
> But to our power, hostility and hate;
> Untam'd reluctance, and revenge, though slow.
> Yet ever plotting how the conqueror least
> May reap his conquest, and may least rejoice
> In doing what we most in suffering feel.

But by changing your conduct, and treating your slaves as men, every cause of fear would be banished. They would be faithful, honest, intelligent, and vigorous; and peace, prosperity, and happiness would attend you. . . .

Harriet Jacobs (1813–97)

S*lave narratives by black women, critic Mary Helen Washington observes, let us "hear the voices of slave women; they show women as active agents rather than objects of pity, capable of interpreting their experiences and, like men, able to turn their victimization into triumph." In* Incidents in the Life of a Slave Girl *(1860), Harriet Jacobs takes the reader beyond formulaic studies of slavery into the particular dynamics that black women slaves had to face. Despite its sentimental and fictional qualities, the narrative paints a vivid picture of a slave woman's daily struggles against male domination while also proclaiming the writer's resourcefulness and courage in taking control of her life and destiny.*

Born into slavery in North Carolina, Jacobs learned to read and write from her white mistress. Beginning at about age fifteen, however, Jacobs found herself a target of sexual abuse by her white master, Dr. Flint. Rather than succumb to a life of sexual domination, Jacobs became involved with a white man of her choosing, with whom she had two children. But when Dr. Flint refused to sell her and her children, Jacobs designed a plan to escape slavery. Dressed in men's clothing, she made it to her grandmother's home, where she hid for years in the attic.

In 1842, she continued her escape by going north and working there as a nursemaid for white employers. Her children finally joined her, and in 1852, her abolitionist friends bought her freedom for several hundred dollars.

A white abolitionist journalist, Amy Post, encouraged Jacobs to write her story. To do so, however, would mean exposing events that the white reading public would deem disgraceful, promiscuous, and a validation of the then-prevalent assumption that black women did not possess the virtues presumably intrinsic to white women. In a letter to Post, Jacobs explained: "Your proposal to me has been thought over and over again, but not without some most painful remembrance. Dear Amy . . . I never would consent to give my past life to anyone without giving the whole truth. If it could help save another from my fate it would be selfish and unchristian in me to keep it back."

In 1860, Jacobs published her narrative Incidents in the Life of a Slave Girl *under the pseudonym Linda Brent. Concerned about its reception by her intended audience—white northern women—Jacobs expressed throughout her narrative her anxiety about revealing her intimate experiences. Nevertheless, her commitment to exposing the truth in the hope of influencing the end of slavery ultimately outweighed all other concerns.*

In the following excerpt, "The Perils of a Slave Woman's Life," Jacobs relates her anxious determination to control her fate and that of her children.

The Perils of a Slave Woman's Life

The Trials of Girlhood

During the first years of my service in Dr. Flint's family, I was accustomed to share some indulgences with the children of my mistress. Though this seemed to me no more than right, I was grateful for it, and tried to merit the kindness by the faithful discharge of my duties. But I now entered on my fifteenth year—a sad epoch in the life of a slave girl. My master began to whisper foul words in my ear. Young as I was, I could not remain ignorant of their import. I tried to treat them with indifference or contempt. The master's age, my extreme youth, and the fear that his conduct would be reported to my grandmother, made him bear this treatment for many months. He was a crafty man, and resorted to many means to accomplish his purposes. Sometimes he had stormy, terrific ways, that made his victims tremble; sometimes he assumed a gentleness that he thought must surely subdue. Of the two, I preferred his stormy moods, although they left me trembling. He tried his utmost to corrupt the pure principles my grandmother had instilled. He peopled my young mind with unclean images, such as only a vile monster could think of. I turned from him with disgust and hatred. But he was my master. I was compelled to live under the same roof with him—where I saw a man forty years my senior daily violating the most sacred commandments of nature. He told me I was his property; that I must be subject to his will in all things. My soul revolted against the mean tyranny. But where could I turn for protection? No matter whether the slave girl be as black as ebony or as fair as her mistress. In either case, there is no shadow of law to protect her from insult, from violence, or even from death; all these are inflicted by fiends who bear the shape of men. The mistress, who ought to protect the helpless victim, has no other feelings towards her but those of jealousy and rage. The degradation, the wrongs, the vices, that grow out of slavery, are more than I can describe. They are greater than you would willingly believe. Surely, if you credited one half the truths that are told you concerning the helpless millions suffering in this cruel bondage, you at the north would not help to tighten the yoke. You surely would refuse to do for the master, on your own soil, the mean and cruel work which trained bloodhounds and the lowest class of whites do for him at the south.

Every where the years bring to all enough of sin and sorrow; but in slavery the very dawn of life is darkened by these shadows. Even the little child, who is accustomed to wait on her mistress and her children, will learn, before she is twelve years old, why it is that her mistress hates such and such a one among the slaves. Perhaps the child's own mother is among those hated ones. She listens to violent outbreaks of jealous passion, and cannot help understanding what is the cause. She will become prematurely knowing in evil things. Soon she will learn to tremble when she hears her master's footfall. She will be compelled to realize that she is no longer a child. If God has bestowed beauty upon her, it will prove her greatest curse. That which commands admiration in the white woman only hastens the degradation of the female slave. I know that some are too much brutalized by slavery to feel the humiliation of their position; but many slaves feel it most acutely, and shrink from the memory of it. I cannot tell how much I suffered in the presence of these wrongs, nor how I am still pained by the retrospect. My master met me at every turn, reminding me that I belonged to him, and swearing by heaven and earth that he would compel me to submit to him. If I went out for a breath of fresh air, after a day of unwearied toil, his footsteps dogged me. If I knelt by my mother's grave, his dark shadow fell on me even there. The light heart which nature had given me became heavy with sad fore-bodings. The other slaves in my master's house noticed the change. Many of them pitied me; but none dared to ask the cause. They had no need to inquire. They knew too well the guilty practices under that roof; and they were aware that to speak of them was an offence that never went unpunished.

I longed for some one to confide in. I would have given the world to have laid my head on my grandmother's faithful bosom, and told her all my troubles. But Dr. Flint swore he would kill me, if I was not as silent as the grave. Then, although my grandmother was all in all to me, I feared her as well as loved her. I had been accustomed to look up to her with a respect bordering upon awe. I was very young, and felt shamefaced about telling her such impure things, especially as I knew her to be very strict on such subjects. Moreover, she was a woman of a high spirit. She was usually very quiet in her demeanor; but if her indignation was once roused, it was not very easily quelled. I had been told that she once chased a white gentleman with a loaded pistol, because he insulted one of her daughters. I dreaded the consequences of a violent outbreak; and both pride and fear kept me silent. But though I did not confide in my grandmother, and even evaded her vigilant watchfulness and inquiry, her presence in the neighborhood was some protection to me. Though she had been a slave, Dr. Flint was afraid of her. He dreaded her scorching rebukes. Moreover, she was known and patronized by many people; and he did not wish to have his villainy made public. It was lucky for me that I did not live on a distant plantation, but in a town not so large that the inhabitants were ignorant of each other's affairs. Bad as are the laws and customs in a slaveholding community, the doctor, as a professional man, deemed it prudent to keep up some outward show of decency.

O, what days and nights of fear and sorrow that man caused me! Reader, it is not to awaken sympathy for myself that I am telling you truthfully what I suffered in slavery. I do it to kindle a flame of compassion in your hearts for my sisters who are still in bondage, suffering as I once suffered.

I once saw two beautiful children playing together. One was a fair white child; the other was her slave, and also her sister. When I saw them embracing each other, and heard their joyous laughter, I turned sadly away from the lovely sight. I foresaw the inevitable blight that would fall on the little slave's heart. I knew how soon her laughter would be changed to sighs. The fair child grew up to be a still fairer woman. From childhood to womanhood her pathway was blooming with flowers, and overarched by a sunny sky. Scarcely one day of her life had been clouded when the sun rose on her happy bridal morning.

How had those years dealt with her slave sister, the little playmate of her childhood? She, also, was very beautiful; but the flowers and sunshine of love were not for her. She drank the cup of sin, and shame, and misery, whereof her persecuted race are compelled to drink.

In view of these things, why are ye silent, ye free men and women of the north? Why do your tongues falter in maintenance of the right? Would that I had more ability! But my heart is so full, and my pen is so weak! There are noble men and women who plead for us, striving to help those who cannot help themselves. God bless them! God give them strength and courage to go on! God bless those, every where, who are laboring to advance the cause of humanity!

The Jealous Mistress

I would ten thousand times rather that my children should be the half-starved paupers of Ireland than to be the most pampered among the slaves of America. I would rather drudge out my life on a cotton plantation, till the grave opened to give me rest, than to live with an unprincipled master and a jealous mistress. The felon's home in a penitentiary is preferable. He may repent, and turn from the error of his ways, and so find peace; but it is not so with a favorite slave. She is not allowed to have any pride of character. It is deemed a crime in her to wish to be virtuous.

Mrs. Flint possessed the key to her husband's character before I was born. She might have used this knowledge to counsel and to screen the young and the innocent among her slaves; but for them she had no sympathy. They were the objects of her constant suspicion and malevolence. She watched her husband with unceasing vigilance; but he was well practised in means to evade it. What he could not find opportunity to say in words he manifested in signs. He invented more than were ever thought of in a deaf and dumb asylum. I let them pass, as if I did not understand what he meant; and many were the curses and threats bestowed on me for my stupidity. One day he caught me teaching myself to write. He frowned, as if he was not well pleased; but I suppose he came to the conclusion that such an accomplishment might help to advance his favorite scheme. Before long, notes were often slipped into my hand. I would return them, saying, "I can't read them, sir." "Can't you?" he replied; "then I must read them to you." He always finished the reading by asking, "Do you understand?" Sometimes he would complain of the heat of the tea room, and order his supper to be placed on a small table in the piazza. He would seat himself there with a well-satisfied smile, and tell me to stand by and brush away the flies. He would eat very slowly, pausing between the mouthfuls. These intervals were employed in describing the happiness I was so foolishly throwing away, and in threatening me with the penalty that finally awaited my stubborn disobedience. He boasted much of the forbearance he had exercised towards me, and reminded me that there was a limit to his patience. When I succeeded in avoiding opportunities for him to talk to me at home, I was ordered to come to his office, to do some errand. When there, I was obliged to stand and listen to such language as he saw fit to address to me. Sometimes I so openly expressed my contempt for him that he would become violently enraged, and I wondered why he did not strike me. Circumstanced as he was, he probably thought it was better policy to be forbearing. But the state of things grew worse and worse daily. In desperation I told him that I must and would apply to my grandmother for protection. He threatened me with death, and worse than death, if I made any complaint to her. Strange to say, I did not despair. I was naturally of a buoyant disposition, and always I had a hope of somehow getting out of his clutches. Like many a poor, simple slave before me, I trusted that some threads of joy would yet be woven into my dark destiny.

I had entered my sixteenth year, and every day it became more apparent that my presence was intolerable to Mrs. Flint. Angry words frequently passed between her and her husband. He had never punished me himself, and he would not allow any body else to punish me. In that respect, she was never satisfied; but, in her angry moods, no terms were too vile for her to bestow upon me. Yet I, whom she detested so bitterly, had far more pity for her than he had, whose duty it was to make her life happy. I never wronged her, or wished to wrong her; and one word of kindness from her would have brought me to her feet.

After repeated quarrels between the doctor and his wife, he announced his intention to take his youngest daughter, then four years old, to sleep in his apartment. It was necessary that a servant should sleep in the same room, to be on hand if the child stirred. I was selected for that office, and informed for what purpose that arrangement had been made. By managing to keep within sight of people, as much as possible, during the day time, I had hitherto succeeded in eluding my master, though a razor was often held to my throat to force me to change this line of policy. At night I slept by the side of my great aunt, where I felt safe. He was too prudent to come into her room. She was an old woman, and had been in the family many years. Moreover, as a married man, and a professional man, he deemed it necessary to save appearances in some degree. But he resolved to remove the obstacle in the way of his scheme; and he thought he had planned it so that he should evade suspicion. He was well aware how much I prized my refuge by the side of my old aunt, and he determined to dispossess me of it. The first night the doctor had the little child in his room alone. The next morning, I was ordered to take my station as nurse the following night. A kind Providence interposed in my favor. During the day Mrs. Flint heard of this new arrangement, and a storm followed. I rejoiced to hear it rage.

After a while my mistress sent for me to come to her room. Her first question was, "Did you know you were to sleep in the doctor's room?"

"Yes, ma'am."

"Who told you?"

"My master."

"Will you answer truly all the questions I ask?"

"Yes, ma'am."

"Tell me, then, as you hope to be forgiven, are you innocent of what I have accused you?"

"I am."

She handed me a Bible, and said, "Lay your hand on your heart, kiss this holy book, and swear before God that you tell me the truth."

I took the oath she required, and I did it with a clear conscience.

"You have taken God's holy word to testify your innocence," she said. "If you have deceived me, beware! Now take this stool, sit down, look me directly in the face, and tell me all that has passed between your master and you."

I did as she ordered. As I went on with my account her color changed frequently, she wept, and sometimes groaned. She spoke in tones so sad, that I was touched by her grief. The tears came to my eyes; but I was soon convinced that her emotions arose from anger and wounded pride. She felt that her marriage vows were desecrated, her dignity insulted; but she had no compassion for the poor victim of her husband's perfidy. She pitied herself as a martyr; but she was incapable of feeling for the condition of shame and misery in which her unfortunate, helpless slave was placed.

Yet perhaps she had some touch of feeling for me; for when the conference was ended, she spoke kindly, and promised to protect me. I should have been much comforted by this assurance if I could have had confidence in it; but my experiences in slavery had filled me with distrust. She was not a very refined woman, and had not much control over her passions. I was an object of her jealousy, and, consequently, of her hatred; and I knew I could not expect kindness or confidence from her under the circumstances in which I was placed. I could not blame her. Slaveholders' wives feel as other women would under similar circumstances. The fire of her temper kindled from small sparks, and now the flame became so intense that the doctor was obliged to give up his intended arrangement.

I knew I had ignited the torch, and I expected to suffer for it afterwards; but I felt too thankful to my mistress for the timely aid she rendered me to care much about that. She now took me to sleep in a room adjoining her own. There I was an object of her especial care, though not of her especial comfort, for she spent many a sleepless night to watch over me. Sometimes I woke up, and found her bending over me. At other times she whispered in my ear, as though it was her husband who was speaking to me, and listened to hear what I would answer. If she startled me, on such occasions, she would glide stealthily away; and the next morning she would tell me I had been talking in my sleep, and ask who I was talking to. At last, I began to be fearful for my life. It had been often threatened; and you can imagine, better than I can describe, what an unpleasant sensation it must produce to wake up in the dead of night and find a jealous woman bending over you. Terrible as this experience was, I had fears that it would give place to one more terrible.

My mistress grew weary of her vigils; they did not prove satisfactory. She changed her tactics. She now tried the trick of accusing my master of crime, in my presence, and gave my name as the author of the accusation. To my utter astonishment, he replied, "I don't believe it; but if she did acknowledge it, you tortured her into exposing me." Tortured into exposing him! Truly, Satan had no difficulty in distinguishing the color of his soul! I understood his object in making this false representation. It was to show me that I gained nothing by seeking the protection of my mistress; that the power was still all in his own hands. I pitied Mrs. Flint. She was a second wife, many years the junior of her husband; and the hoary-headed miscreant was enough to try the patience of a wiser and better woman. She was completely foiled, and knew not how to proceed. She would gladly have had me flogged for my supposed false oath; but, as I have already stated, the doctor never allowed any one to whip me. The old sinner was politic. The application of the lash might have led to remarks that would have exposed him in the eyes of his children and grandchildren. How often did I rejoice that I lived in a town where all the inhabitants knew each other! If I had been on a remote plantation, or lost among the multitude of a crowded city, I should not be a living woman at this day.

The secrets of slavery are concealed like those of the Inquisition. My master was, to my knowledge, the father of eleven slaves. But did the mothers dare to tell who was the father of their children? Did the other slaves dare to allude to it, except in whispers among themselves? No, indeed! They knew too well the terrible consequences.

My grandmother could not avoid seeing things which excited her suspicions. She was uneasy about me, and tried various ways to buy me; but the never-changing answer was always repeated: "Linda does not belong to *me*. She is my daughter's property, and I have no legal right to sell her." The conscientious man! He was too scrupulous to *sell* me; but he had no scruples whatever about committing a much greater wrong against the helpless young girl placed under his guardianship, as his daughter's property. Sometimes my persecutor would ask me whether I would like to be sold. I told him I would rather be sold to any body than to lead such a life as I did. On such occasions he would assume the air of a very injured individual, and reproach me for my ingratitude. "Did I not take you into the house, and make you the companion of my own children?" he would say. "Have I ever treated you like a negro? I have never allowed you to be punished, not even to please your mistress. And this is the recompense I get, you ungrateful girl!" I answered that he had reasons of his own for screening me from punishment, and that the course he pursued made my mistress hate me and persecute me. If I wept, he would say, "Poor child! Don't cry! don't cry! I will make peace for you with your mistress. Only let me arrange matters in my own way. Poor, foolish girl! you don't know what is for your own good. I would cherish you. I would make a lady of you. Now go, and think of all I have promised you."

I did think of it.

Reader, I draw no imaginary pictures of southern homes. I am telling you the plain truth. Yet when victims make their escape from this wild beast of Slavery, northerners consent to act the part of bloodhounds, and hunt the poor fugitive back into his den, "full of dead men's bones, and all uncleanness." Nay, more, they are not only willing, but proud, to give their daughters in marriage to slaveholders. The poor girls have romantic notions of a sunny clime, and of the flowering vines that all the year round shade a happy home. To what disappointments are they destined! The young wife soon learns that the husband in whose hands she has placed her happiness pays no regard to his marriage vows. Children of every shade of complexion play with her own fair babies, and too well she knows that they are born unto him of his own household. Jealousy and hatred enter the flowery home, and it is ravaged of its loveliness.

Southern women often marry a man knowing that he is the father of many little slaves. They do not trouble themselves about it. They regard such children as property, as marketable as the pigs on the plantation; and it is seldom that they do not make them aware of this by passing them into the slave-trader's hands as soon as possible, and thus getting them out of their sight. I am glad to say there are some honorable exceptions.

I have myself known two southern wives who exhorted their husbands to free those slaves towards whom they stood in a "parental relation;" and their request was granted. These husbands blushed before the superior nobleness of their wives' natures. Though they had only counselled them to do that which it was their duty to do, it commanded their respect, and rendered their conduct more exemplary. Concealment was at an end, and confidence took the place of distrust.

Though this bad institution deadens the moral sense, even in white women, to a fearful extent, it is not altogether extinct. I have heard southern ladies say of Mr. Such a one, "He not only thinks it no disgrace to be the father of those little niggers, but he is not ashamed to call himself their master. I declare, such things ought not to be tolerated in any decent society!"

The Lover

Why does the slave ever love? Why allow the tendrils of the heart to twine around objects which may at any moment be wrenched away by the hand of violence? When separations come by the hand of death, the pious soul can bow in resignation, and say, "Not my will, but thine be done, O Lord!" But when the ruthless hand of man strikes the blow, regardless of the misery he causes, it is hard to be submissive. I did not reason thus when I was a young girl. Youth will be youth. I loved, and I indulged the hope that the dark clouds around me would turn out a bright lining. I forgot that in the land of my birth the shadows are too dense for light to penetrate. A land

> Where laughter is not mirth; nor thought the mind;
> Nor words a language; nor e'en men mankind.
> Where cries reply to curses, shrieks to blows,
> And each is tortured in his separate hell.

There was in the neighborhood a young colored carpenter; a free-born man. We had been well acquainted in childhood, and frequently met together afterwards. We became mutually attached, and he proposed to marry me. I loved him with all the ardor of a young girl's first love. But when I reflected that I was a slave, and that the laws gave no sanction to the marriage of such, my heart sank within me. My lover wanted to buy me; but I knew that Dr. Flint was too wilful and arbitrary a man to consent to that arrangement. From him, I was sure of experiencing all sorts of opposition, and I had nothing to hope from my mistress. She would have been delighted to have got rid of me, but not in that way. It would have relieved her mind of a burden if she could have seen me sold to some distant state, but if I was married near home I should be just as much in her husband's power as I had previously been,—for the husband of a slave has no power to protect her. Moreover, my mistress, like many others, seemed to think that slaves had no right to any family ties of their own; that they were created merely to wait upon the family of the mistress. I once heard her abuse a young slave girl, who told her that a colored man wanted to make her his wife. "I will have you peeled and pickled, my lady," said she, "if I ever hear you mention that subject again. Do you suppose that I will have you tending *my* children with the children of that nigger?" The girl to whom she said this had a mulatto child, of course not acknowledged by its father. The poor black man who loved her would have been proud to acknowledge his helpless offspring.

Many and anxious were the thoughts I revolved in my mind. I was at a loss what to do. Above all things, I was desirous to spare my lover the insults that had cut so deeply into my own soul. I talked with my grandmother about it, and partly told her my fears. I did not dare to tell her the worst. She had long suspected all was not right, and if I confirmed her suspicions I knew a storm would rise that would prove the overthrow of all my hopes.

This love-dream had been my support through many trials; and I could not bear to run the risk of having it suddenly dissipated. There was a lady in the neighborhood, a particular friend of Dr. Flint's, who often visited the house. I had a great respect for her, and she had always manifested a friendly interest in me. Grandmother thought she would have great influence with the doctor. I went to this lady, and told her my story. I told her I was aware that my lover's being a free-born man would prove a great objection; but he wanted to buy me; and if Dr. Flint would consent to that arrangement, I felt sure he would be willing to pay any reasonable price. She knew that Mrs. Flint disliked me; therefore, I ventured to suggest that perhaps my mistress would approve of my being sold, as that would rid her of me. The lady listened with kindly sympathy, and promised to do her utmost to promote my wishes. She had an interview with the doctor, and I believe she pleaded my cause earnestly; but it was all to no purpose.

How I dreaded my master now! Every minute I expected to be summoned to his presence; but the day passed, and I heard nothing from him. The next morning, a message was brought to me: "Master wants you in his study." I found the door ajar, and I stood a moment gazing at the hateful man who claimed a right to rule me, body and soul. I entered, and tried to appear calm. I did not want him to know how my heart was bleeding. He looked fixedly at me, with an expression which seemed to say, "I have half a mind to kill you on the spot." At last he broke the silence, and that was a relief to both of us.

"So you want to be married, do you?" he said, "and to a free nigger."

"Yes, sir."

"Well, I'll soon convince you whether I am your master, or the nigger fellow you honor so highly. If you *must* have a husband, you may take up with one of my slaves."

What a situation I should be in, as the wife of one of *his* slaves, even if my heart had been interested!

I replied, "Don't you suppose, sir, that a slave can have some preference about marrying? Do you suppose that all men are alike to her?"

"Do you love this nigger?" said he, abruptly.

"Yes, sir."

"How dare you tell me so!" he exclaimed, in great wrath. After a slight pause, he added, "I suppose you thought more of yourself; that you felt above the insults of such puppies."

I replied, "If he is a puppy I am a puppy, for we are both of the negro race. It is right and honorable for us to love each other. The man you call a puppy never insulted me, sir; and he would not love me if he did not believe me to be a virtuous woman."

He sprang upon me like a tiger, and gave me a stunning blow. It was the first time he had ever struck me; and fear did not enable me to control my anger. When I had recovered a little from the effects, I exclaimed, "You have struck me for answering you honestly. How I despise you!"

There was silence for some minutes. Perhaps he was deciding what should be my punishment; or, perhaps, he wanted to give me time to reflect on what I had said, and to whom I had said it. Finally, he asked, "Do you know what you have said?"

"Yes sir; but your treatment drove me to it."

"Do you know that I have a right to do as I like with you,—that I can kill you, if I please?"

"You have tried to kill me, and I wish you had; but you have no right to do as you like with me."

"Silence!" he exclaimed, in a thundering voice. "By heavens, girl, you forget yourself too far! Are you mad? If you are, I will soon bring you to your senses. Do you think any other master would bear what I have borne from you this morning? Many masters would have killed you on the spot. How would you like to be sent to jail for your insolence?"

"I know I have been disrespectful, sir," I replied; "but you drove me to it; I couldn't help it. As for the jail, there would be more peace for me there than there is here."

"You deserve to go there," said he, "and to be under such treatment, that you would forget the meaning of the word *peace*. It would do you good. It would take some of your high notions out of you. But I am not ready to send you there yet, notwithstanding your ingratitude for all my kindness and forbearance. You have been the plague of my life. I have wanted to make you happy, and I have been repaid with the basest ingratitude; but though you have proved yourself incapable of appreciating my kindness, I will be lenient towards you, Linda. I will give you one more chance to redeem your character. If you behave yourself and do as I require, I will forgive you and treat you as I always have done; but if you disobey me, I will punish you as I would the meanest slave on my plantation. Never let me hear that fellow's name mentioned again. If I ever know of your speaking to him, I will cowhide you both; and if I catch him lurking about my premises, I will shoot him as soon as I would a dog. Do you hear what I say? I'll teach you a lesson about marriage and free niggers! Now go, and let this be the last time I have occasion to speak to you on this subject."

Reader, did you ever hate? I hope not. I never did but once; and I trust I never shall again. Somebody has called it "the atmosphere of hell;" and I believe it is so.

For a fortnight the doctor did not speak to me. He thought to mortify me; to make me feel that I had disgraced myself by receiving the honorable addresses of a respectable colored man, in preference to the base proposals of a white man. But though his lips disdained to address me, his eyes were very loquacious. No animal ever watched its prey more narrowly than he watched me. He knew that I could write, though he had failed to make me read his letters; and he was now troubled lest I should exchange letters with another man. After a while he became weary of silence; and I was sorry for it. One morning, as he passed through the hall, to leave the house, he contrived to thrust a note into my hand. I thought I had better read it, and spare myself the vexation of having him read it to me. It expressed regret for the blow he had given me, and reminded me that I myself was wholly to blame for it. He hoped I had become convinced of the injury I was doing myself by incurring his displeasure. He wrote that he had made up his mind to go to Louisiana; that he should take several slaves with him, and intended I should be one of the number. My mistress would remain where she was; therefore I should have nothing to fear from that quarter. If I merited kindness from him, he assured me that it would be lavishly bestowed. He begged me to think over the matter, and answer the following day.

The next morning I was called to carry a pair of scissors to his room. I laid them on the table, with the letter beside them. He thought it was my answer, and did not call me back. I went as usual to attend my young mistress to and from school. He met me in the street, and ordered me to stop at his office on my way back. When I entered, he showed me his letter, and asked me why I had not answered it. I replied, "I am your daughter's property, and it is in your power to send me, or take me, wherever you please." He said he was very glad to find me so willing to go, and that we should start early in the autumn. He had a large practice in the town, and I rather thought he had made up the story merely to frighten me. However that might be, I was determined that I would never go to Louisiana with him.

Summer passed away, and early in the autumn Dr. Flint's eldest son was sent to Louisiana to examine the country, with a view to emigrating. That news did not disturb me. I knew very well that I should not be sent with *him*. That I had not been taken to the plantation before this time, was owing to the fact that his son was there. He was jealous of his son; and jealousy of the overseer had kept him from punishing me by sending me into the fields to work. Is it strange that I was not proud of these protectors? As for the overseer, he was a man for whom I had less respect than I had for a bloodhound.

Young Mr. Flint did not bring back a favorable report of Louisiana, and I heard no more of that scheme. Soon after this, my lover met me at the corner of the street, and I stopped to speak to him. Looking up, I saw my master watching us from his window. I hurried home, trembling with fear. I was sent for, immediately, to go to his room. He met me with a blow. "When is mistress to be married?" said he, in a sneering tone. A shower of oaths and imprecations followed. How thankful I was that my lover was a free man! that my tyrant had no power to flog him for speaking to me in the street!

Again and again I revolved in my mind how all this would end. There was no hope that the doctor would consent to sell me on any terms. He had an iron will, and was determined to keep me, and to conquer me. My lover was an intelligent and religious man. Even if he could have obtained permission to marry me while I was a slave, the marriage would give him no power to protect me from my master. It would have made him miserable to witness the insults I should have been subjected to. And then, if we had children, I knew they must "follow the condition of the mother." What a terrible blight that would be on the heart of a free, intelligent father! For *his* sake, I felt that I ought not to link his fate with my own unhappy destiny. He was going to Savannah to see about a little property left him by an uncle; and hard as it was to bring my feelings to it, I earnestly entreated him not to come back. I advised him to go to the Free States, where his tongue would not be tied, and where his intelligence would be of more avail to him. He left me, still hoping the day would come when I could be bought. With me the lamp of hope had gone out. The dream of my girlhood was over. I felt lonely and desolate.

Still I was not stripped of all. I still had my good grandmother, and my affectionate brother. When he put his arms round my neck, and looked into my eyes, as if to read there the troubles I dared not tell, I felt that I still had something to love. But even that pleasant emotion was chilled by the reflection that he might be torn from me at any moment, by some sudden freak of my master. If he had known how we loved each other, I think he would have exulted in separating us. We often planned together how we could get to the north. But, as William remarked, such things are easier said than done. My movements were very closely watched, and we had no means of getting any money to defray our expenses. As for grandmother, she was strongly opposed to her children's undertaking any such project. She had not forgotten poor Benjamin's sufferings, and she was afraid that if another child tried to escape, he would have a similar or a worse fate. To me, nothing seemed more dreadful than my present life. I said to myself, "William *must* be free. He shall go to the north, and I will follow him." Many a slave sister has formed the same plans.

A Perilous Passage in the Slave Girl's Life

After my lover went away, Dr. Flint contrived a new plan. He seemed to have an idea that my fear of my mistress was his greatest obstacle. In the blandest tones, he told me that he was going to build a small house for me, in a secluded place, four miles away from the town. I shuddered; but I was constrained to listen, while he talked of his intention to give me a home of my own, and to make a lady of me. Hitherto, I had escaped my dreaded fate, by being in the midst of people. My grandmother had already had high words with my master about me. She had told him pretty plainly what she thought of his character, and there was considerable gossip in the neighborhood about our affairs, to which the open-mouthed jealousy of Mrs. Flint contributed not a little. When my master said he was going to build a house for me, and that he could do it with little trouble and expense, I was in hopes something would happen to frustrate his scheme; but I soon heard that the house was actually begun. I vowed before my Maker that I would never enter it. I had rather toil on the plantation from dawn till dark; I had rather live and die in jail, than drag on, from day to day, through such a living death. I was determined that the master, whom I so hated and loathed, who had blighted the prospects of my youth, and made my life a desert, should not, after my long struggle with him, succeed at last in trampling his victim under his feet. I would do any thing, every thing, for the sake of defeating him. What *could* I do? I thought and thought, till I became desperate, and made a plunge into the abyss.

And now, reader, I come to a period in my unhappy life, which I would gladly forget if I could. The remembrance fills me with sorrow and shame. It pains me to tell you of it; but I have promised to tell you the truth, and I will do it honestly, let it cost me what it may. I will not try to screen myself behind the plea of compulsion from a master; for it was not so. Neither can I plead ignorance or thoughtlessness. For years, my master had done his utmost to pollute my mind with foul images, and to destroy the pure principles inculcated by my grandmother, and the good mistress of my childhood. The influences of slavery had had the same effect on me that they had on other young girls; they had made me prematurely knowing, concerning the evil ways of the world. I knew what I did, and I did it with deliberate calculation.

But, O, ye happy women, whose purity has been sheltered from childhood, who have been free to choose the objects of your affection, whose homes are protected by law, do not judge the poor desolate slave girl too severely! If slavery had been abolished, I, also, could have married the man of my choice; I could have had a home shielded by the laws; and I should have been spared the painful task of confessing what I am now about to relate; but all my prospects had been blighted by slavery. I wanted to keep myself pure; and, under the most adverse circumstances, I tried hard to preserve my self-respect; but I was struggling alone in the powerful grasp of the demon Slavery; and the monster proved too strong for me. I felt as if I was forsaken by God and man; as if all my efforts must be frustrated; and I became reckless in my despair.

I have told you that Dr. Flint's persecutions and his wife's jealousy had given rise to some gossip in the neighborhood. Among others, it chanced that a white unmarried gentleman had obtained some knowledge of the circumstances in which I was placed. He knew my grandmother, and often spoke to me in the street. He became interested for me, and asked questions about my master, which I answered in part. He expressed a great deal of sympathy, and a wish to aid me. He constantly sought opportunities to see me, and wrote to me frequently. I was a poor slave girl, only fifteen years old.

So much attention from a superior person was, of course, flattering; for human nature is the same in all. I also felt grateful for his sympathy, and encouraged by his kind words. It seemed to me a great thing to have such a friend. By degrees, a more tender feeling crept into my heart. He was an educated and eloquent gentleman; too eloquent, alas, for the poor slave girl who trusted in him. Of course I saw whither all this was tending. I knew the impassable gulf between us; but to be an object of interest to a man who is not married, and who is not her master, is agreeable to the pride and feelings of a slave, if her miserable situation has left her any pride or sentiment. It seemed less degrading to give one's self, than to submit to compulsion. There is something akin to freedom in having a lover who has no control over you, except that which he gains by kindness and attachment. A master may treat you as rudely as he pleases, and you dare not speak; moreover, the wrong does not seem so great with an unmarried man, as with one who has a wife to be made unhappy. There may be sophistry in all this; but the condition of a slave confuses all principles of morality, and, in fact, renders the practice of them impossible.

When I found that my master had actually begun to build the lonely cottage, other feelings mixed with those I have described. Revenge, and calculations of interest, were added to flattered vanity and sincere gratitude for kindness. I knew nothing would enrage Dr. Flint so much as to know that I favored another; and it was something to triumph over my tyrant even in that small way. I thought he would revenge himself by selling me, and I was sure my friend, Mr. Sands, would buy me. He was a man of more generosity and feeling than my master, and I thought my freedom could be easily obtained from him. The crisis of my fate now came so near that I was desperate. I shuddered to think of being the mother of children that should be owned by my old tyrant. I knew that as soon as a new fancy took him, his victims were sold far off to get rid of them; especially if they had children. I had seen several women sold, with his babies at the breast. He never allowed his offspring by slaves to remain long in sight of himself and his wife. Of a man who was not my master I could ask to have my children well supported; and in this case, I felt confident I should obtain the boon. I also felt quite sure that they would be made free. With all these thoughts revolving in my mind, and seeing no other way of escaping the doom I so much dreaded, I made a headlong plunge. Pity me, and pardon me, O virtuous reader! You never knew what it is to be a slave; to be entirely unprotected by law or custom; to have the laws reduce you to the condition of a chattel, entirely subject to the will of another. You never exhausted your ingenuity in avoiding the snares, and eluding the power of a hated tyrant; you never shuddered at the sound of his footsteps, and trembled within hearing of his voice. I know I did wrong. No one can feel it more sensibly than I do. The painful and humiliating memory will haunt me to my dying day. Still, in looking back, calmly, on the events of my life, I feel that the slave woman ought not to be judged by the same standard as others.

The months passed on. I had many unhappy hours. I secretly mourned over the sorrow I was bringing on my grandmother, who had so tried to shield me from harm. I knew that I was the greatest comfort of her old age, and that it was a source of pride to her that I had not degraded myself, like most of the slaves. I wanted to confess to her that I was no longer worthy of her love; but could not utter the dreaded words.

As for Dr. Flint, I had a feeling of satisfaction and triumph in the thought of telling *him*. From time to time he told me of his intended arrangements, and I was silent. At last, he came and told me the cottage was completed, and ordered me to go to it. I told him I would never enter it. He said, "I have heard enough of such talk as that. You shall go, if you are carried by force; and you shall remain there."

I replied, "I will never go there. In a few months I shall be a mother."

He stood and looked at me in dumb amazement, and left the house without a word. I thought I should be happy in my triumph over him. But now that the truth was out, and my relatives would hear of it, I felt wretched. Humble as were their circumstances, they had pride in my good character. Now, how could I look them in the face? My self-respect was gone! I had resolved that I would be virtuous, though I was a slave. I had said, "Let the storm beat! I will brave it till I die." And now, how humiliated I felt!

I went to my grandmother. My lips moved to make confession, but the words stuck in my throat. I sat down in the shade of a tree at her door and began to sew. I think she saw something unusual was the matter with me. The mother of slaves is very watchful. She knows there is no security for her children. After they have entered their teens she lives in daily expectation of trouble. This leads to many questions. If the girl is of a sensitive nature, timidity keeps her from answering truthfully, and this well-meant course has a tendency to drive her from maternal counsels. Presently, in came my mistress, like a mad woman, and accused me concerning her husband. My grandmother, whose suspicions had been previously awakened, believed what she said. She exclaimed, "O Linda! has it come to this? I had rather see you dead than to see you as you now are. You are a disgrace to your dead mother." She tore from my fingers my mother's wedding ring and her silver thimble. "Go away!" she exclaimed, "and never come to my house, again." Her reproaches fell so hot and heavy, that they left me no chance to answer. Bitter tears, such as the eyes never shed but once, were my only answer. I rose from my seat, but fell back again, sobbing. She did not speak to me; but the tears were running down her furrowed cheeks, and they scorched me like fire. She had always been so kind to me! *So* kind! How I longed to throw myself at her feet, and tell her all the truth! But she had ordered me to go, and never to come there again. After a few minutes, I mustered strength, and started to obey her. With what feelings did I now close that little gate, which I used to open with such an eager hand in my childhood! It closed upon me with a sound I never heard before.

Where could I go? I was afraid to return to my master's. I walked on recklessly, not caring where I went, or what would become of me. When I had gone four or five miles, fatigue compelled me to stop. I sat down on the stump of an old tree. The stars were shining through the boughs above me. How they mocked me, with their bright, calm light! The hours passed by, and as I sat there alone a chilliness and deadly sickness came over me. I sank on the ground. My mind was full of horrid thoughts. I prayed to die; but the prayer was not answered. At last, with great effort I roused myself, and walked some distance further, to the house of a woman who had been a friend of my mother. When I told her why I was there, she spoke soothingly to me; but I could not be comforted. I thought I could bear my shame if I could only be reconciled to my grandmother. I longed to open my heart to her. I thought if she could know the real state of the case, and all I had been bearing for years, she would perhaps judge me less harshly. My friend advised me to send for her. I did so; but days of agonizing suspense passed before she came. Had she utterly forsaken me? No. She came at last. I knelt before her, and told her things that had poisoned my life; how long I had been persecuted; that I saw no way of escape; and in an hour of extremity I had become desperate. She listened in silence. I told her I would bear any thing and do any thing, if in time I had hopes of obtaining her forgiveness. I begged of her to pity me, for my dead mother's sake. And she did pity me. She did not say, "I forgive you;" but she looked at me lovingly, with her eyes full of tears. She laid her old hand gently on my head, and murmured, "Poor child! Poor child!"

Booker T. Washington (1856–1915)

An inspiration to many black leaders—including Marcus Garvey—and an embarrassment to others, Booker Taliaferro Washington assumed an unparalleled position of popularity and authority in late nineteenth-century America. He bore many labels—Negro cultural leader, accommodationist, educator, businessman, pragmatist—but irrespective of how favorably or unfavorably he was regarded, Washington played a primary role in shaping the relationship between the African American community and mainstream America.

Washington was born into slavery on a Virginia plantation. His father was a white man whom he never knew, and his mother was a slave. In his autobiography, he praised his mother's strength, service, and nurturance, asserting: "She, to me, will always remain the noblest embodiment of womanhood. . . . The lessons in virtue and thrift which she instilled into me during the short period of my life that she lived will never leave me."

Washington and his mother, two siblings, and stepfather agonized through the Reconstruction era, living and working in West Virginia. In his mid-teens, Washington's hunger for education urged him to walk hundreds of miles to attend Hampton Institute. His work ethic and persistence got him through his schooling by 1875 and into his calling as a teacher. In 1881, he founded Tuskegee Institute in Alabama, developed around his belief in the importance of trade education and in preparing African Americans for marketable, practical jobs. In his famous 1895 address to the Atlanta Exposition, included here, Wash-

ington advocated racial segregation as a way of fostering a positive economic relationship between blacks and whites in America.

Among many other activities, Washington helped organize the National Negro Business League, became an active public speaker, served as the Negro adviser to the Roosevelt and Taft administrations, and received an honorary master's degree from Harvard University. He also wrote numerous books, including The Future of the American Negro *(1899),* Sowing and Reaping *(1900),* Working with the Hands *(1904),* Tuskegee and Its People *(1905),* Life of Frederick Douglass *(1907),* My Larger Education *(1911), and* The Man Farthest Down *(1912).*

The following chapters from Washington's autobiography, Up from Slavery *(1901), highlight aspects of his success story—a story that celebrates the individual spirit, racial progress, and the possibilities of American capitalism.*

from Up from Slavery

CHAPTER 1
A Slave among Slaves

I was born a slave on a plantation in Franklin County, Virginia. I am not quite sure of the exact place or exact date of my birth, but at any rate I suspect I must have been born somewhere and at some time. As nearly as I have been able to learn, I was born near a cross-roads post-office called Hale's Ford, and the year was 1858 or 1859.* I do not know the month or the day. The earliest impressions I can now recall are of the plantation and the slave quarters—the latter being the part of the plantation where the slaves had their cabins.

My life had its beginning in the midst of the most miserable, desolate, and discouraging surroundings. This was so, however, not because my owners were especially cruel, for they were not, as compared with many others. I was born in a typical log cabin, about fourteen by sixteen feet square. In this cabin I lived with my mother and a brother and sister till after the Civil War, when we were all declared free.

Of my ancestry I know almost nothing. In the slave quarters, and even later, I heard whispered conversations among the colored people of the tortures which the slaves, including, no doubt, my ancestors on my mother's side, suffered in the middle passage of the slave ship while being conveyed from Africa to America. I have been unsuccessful in securing any information that would throw any accurate light upon the history of my family beyond my mother. She, I remember, had a half-brother and a half-sister. In the days of slavery not very much attention was given to family history and family records—that is, black family records. My mother, I suppose, attracted the attention of a purchaser who was afterward my owner and hers. Her addition to the slave family attracted about as much attention as the purchase of a new horse or cow. Of my father I know even less than of my mother. I do not even know his name. I have heard reports to the effect that he was a white man who lived on one of the near-by plantations. Whoever he was, I never heard of his taking the least interest in me or providing

* Now generally believed to be 1856.

in any way for my rearing. But I do not find especial fault with him. He was simply another unfortunate victim of the institution which the Nation unhappily had engrafted upon it at that time.

The cabin was not only our living-place, but was also used as the kitchen for the plantation. My mother was the plantation cook. The cabin was without glass windows; it had only openings in the side which let in the light, and also the cold, chilly air of winter. There was a door to the cabin—that is, something that was called a door—but the uncertain hinges by which it was hung, and the large cracks in it, to say nothing of the fact that it was too small, made the room a very uncomfortable one. In addition to these openings there was, in the lower right-hand corner of the room, the "cat-hole,"—a contrivance which almost every mansion or cabin in Virginia possessed during the ante-bellum period. The "cat-hole" was a square opening, about seven by eight inches, provided for the purpose of letting the cat pass in and out of the house at will during the night. In the case of our particular cabin I could never understand the necessity for this convenience, since there were at least a half-dozen other places in the cabin that would have accommodated the cats. There was no wooden floor in our cabin, the naked earth being used as a floor. In the centre of the earthen floor there was a large, deep opening covered with boards, which was used as a place in which to store sweet potatoes during the winter. An impression of this potato-hole is very distinctly engraved upon my memory, because I recall that during the process of putting the potatoes in or taking them out I would often come into possession of one or two, which I roasted and thoroughly enjoyed. There was no cooking-stove on our plantation, and all the cooking for the whites and slaves my mother had to do over an open fireplace, mostly in pots and "skillets." While the poorly built cabin caused us to suffer with cold in the winter, the heat from the open fireplace in summer was equally trying.

The early years of my life, which were spent in the little cabin, were not very different from those of thousands of other slaves. My mother, of course, had little time in which to give attention to the training of her children during the day. She snatched a few moments for our care in the early morning before her work began, and at night after the day's work was done. One of my earliest recollections is that of my mother cooking a chicken late at night, and awakening her children for the purpose of feeding them. How or where she got it I do not know. I presume, however, it was procured from our owner's farm. Some people may call this theft. If such a thing were to happen now, I should condemn it as theft myself. But taking place at the time it did, and for the reason that it did, no one could ever make me believe that my mother was guilty of thieving. She was simply a victim of the system of slavery. I cannot remember having slept in a bed until after our family was declared free by the Emancipation Proclamation. Three children—John, my older brother, Amanda, my sister, and myself—had a pallet on the dirt floor, or, to be more correct, we slept in and on a bundle of filthy rags laid upon the dirt floor.

I was asked not long ago to tell something about the sports and pastimes that I engaged in during my youth. Until that question was asked it had never occurred to me that there was no period of my life that was devoted to play. From the time that I can remember anything, almost every day of my life has been occupied in some kind of labour; though I think I would now be a more useful man if I had had time for sports. During the period that I spent in slavery

I was not large enough to be of much service, still I was occupied most of the time in cleaning the yards, carrying water to the men in the fields, or going to the mill, to which I used to take the corn, once a week, to be ground. The mill was about three miles from the plantation. This work I always dreaded. The heavy bag of corn would be thrown across the back of the horse, and the corn divided about evenly on each side; but in some way, almost without exception, on these trips, the corn would shift as to become unbalanced and would fall off the horse, and often I would fall with it. As I was not strong enough to reload the corn upon the horse, I would have to wait, sometimes for many hours, till a chance passer-by came along who would help me out of my trouble. The hours while waiting for some one were usually spent in crying. The time consumed in this way made me late in reaching the mill, and by the time I got my corn ground and reached home it would be far into the night. The road was a lonely one, and often led through dense forests. I was always frightened. The woods were said to be full of soldiers who had deserted from the army, and I had been told that the first thing a deserter did to a Negro boy when he found him alone was to cut off his ears. Besides, when I was late in getting home I knew I would always get a severe scolding or a flogging.

I had no schooling whatever while I was a slave, though I remember on several occasions I went as far as the schoolhouse door with one of my young mistresses to carry her books. The picture of several dozen boys and girls in a schoolroom engaged in study made a deep impression upon me, and I had the feeling that to get into a schoolhouse and study in this way would be about the same as getting into paradise.

So far as I can now recall, the first knowledge that I got of the fact that we were slaves, and that freedom of the slaves was being discussed, was early one morning before day, when I was awakened by my mother kneeling over her children and fervently praying that Lincoln and his armies might be successful, and that one day she and her children might be free. In this connection I have never been able to understand how the slaves throughout the South, completely ignorant as were the masses so far as books or newspapers were concerned, were able to keep themselves so accurately and completely informed about the great National questions that were agitating the country. From the time that Garrison, Lovejoy, and others began to agitate for freedom, the slaves throughout the South kept in close touch with the progress of the movement. Though I was a mere child during the preparation for the Civil War and during the war itself, I now recall the many late-at-night whispered discussions that I heard my mother and the other slaves on the plantation indulge in. These discussions showed that they understood the situation, and that they kept themselves informed of events by what was termed the "grape-vine" telegraph.

During the campaign when Lincoln was first a candidate for the Presidency, the slaves on our far-off plantation, miles from any railroad or large city or daily newspaper, knew what the issues involved were. When war was begun between the North and the South, every slave on our plantation felt and knew that, though other issues were discussed, the primal one was that of slavery. Even the most ignorant members of my race on the remote plantations felt in their hearts, with a certainty that admitted of no doubt, that the freedom of the slaves would be the one great result of the war, if the Northern armies conquered. Every success of the Federal armies and every defeat of the Confederate forces was watched with the keenest and most intense interest. Often the slaves got knowledge of the results of great battles before the white people received it. This news was usually gotten from the coloured man who was sent to the post-office for the mail. In our case the post-office was about three miles from the plantation and the mail came once or twice a week. The man who was sent to the office would linger about the place long enough to get the drift of the conversation from the group of white people who naturally congregated there, after receiving their mail, to discuss the latest news. The mail-carrier on his way back to our master's house would as naturally retail the news that he had secured among the slaves, and in this way they often heard of important events before the white people at the "big house," as the master's house was called.

I cannot remember a single instance during my childhood or early boyhood when our entire family sat down to the table together, and God's blessing was asked, and the family ate a meal in a civilized manner. On the plantation in Virginia, and even later, meals were gotten by the children very much as dumb animals get theirs. It was a piece of bread here and a scrap of meat there. It was a cup of milk at one time and some potatoes at another. Sometimes a portion of our family would eat out of the skillet or pot, while some one would eat from a tin plate held on the knees, and often using nothing but the hands with which to hold the food. When I had grown to sufficient size, I was required to go to the "big house" at meal-times to fan the flies from the table by means of a large set of paper fans operated by a pulley. Naturally much of the conversation of the white people turned upon the subject of freedom and the war, and I absorbed a good deal of it. I remember that at one time I saw two of my young mistresses and some lady visitors eating ginger-cakes, in the yard. At that time those cakes seemed to me to be absolutely the most tempting and desirable things that I had ever seen; and I then and there resolved that, if I ever got free, the height of my ambition would be reached if I could get to the point where I could secure and eat ginger-cakes in the way that I saw those ladies doing.

Of course as the war was prolonged the white people, in many cases, often found it difficult to secure food for themselves. I think the slaves felt the deprivation less than the whites, because the usual diet for the slaves was corn bread and pork, and these could be raised on the plantation; but coffee, tea, sugar, and other articles which the whites had been accustomed to use could not be raised on the plantation, and the conditions brought about by the war frequently made it impossible to secure these things. The whites were often in great straits. Parched corn was used for coffee, and a kind of black molasses was used instead of sugar. Many times nothing was used to sweeten the so-called tea and coffee.

The first pair of shoes that I recall wearing were wooden ones. They had rough leather on the top, but the bottoms, which were about an inch thick, were of wood. When I walked they made a fearful noise, and besides this they were very inconvenient, since there was no yielding to the natural pressure of the foot. In wearing them one presented an exceedingly awkward appearance. The most trying ordeal that I was forced to endure as a slave boy, however, was the wearing of a flax shirt. In the portion of Virginia where I lived it was common to use flax as part of the clothing for the slaves. That part of the flax from which our clothing was made was largely the refuse, which of course was the cheapest and roughest part. I can scarcely imagine any torture, except, perhaps, the pulling of a tooth, that is equal to that caused by putting on a new flax shirt for the first time. It is almost equal to the feeling that one would experience if he had a dozen or more chestnut burrs, or a hundred small pinpoints, in contact with his flesh. Even to this day I can recall accurately the tortures that I underwent when putting on one of these garments. The fact that my flesh was soft and tender added to the pain. But I had no choice. I had to wear the flax shirt or none; and had it been left to me to choose, I should have chosen to wear no covering. In connection with the flax shirt, my brother John, who is several years older than I am, performed one of the most generous acts that I ever heard of one slave relative doing for another. On several occasions when I was being forced to wear a new flax shirt, he generously agreed to put it on in my stead and wear it for several days, till it was "broken in." Until I had grown to be quite a youth this single garment was all that I wore.

One may get the idea from what I have said, that there was bitter feeling toward the white people on the part of my race, because of the fact that most of the white population was away fighting in a war which would result in keeping the Negro in slavery if the South was successful. In the case of the slaves on our place this was not true, and it was not true of any large portions of the slave population in the South where the Negro was treated with anything like decency. During the Civil War one of my young masters was killed, and two were severely wounded. I recall the feeling of sorrow which existed among the slaves when they heard of the death of "Mars' Billy." It was no sham sorrow but real. Some of the slaves had nursed "Mars' Billy"; others had played with him when he was a child. "Mars' Billy" had begged for mercy in the case of others when the overseer or master was thrashing them. The sorrow in the slave quarter was only second to that in the "big house." When the two young masters were brought home wounded, the sympathy of the slaves was shown in many ways. They were just as anxious to assist in the nursing as the family relatives of the wounded. Some of the slaves would even beg for the privilege of sitting up at night to nurse their wounded masters. This tenderness and sympathy on the part of those held in bondage was a result of their kindly and generous nature. In order to defend and protect the women and children who were left on the plantations when the white males went to war, the slaves would have laid down their lives. The slave who was selected to sleep in the "big house" during the absence of the males was considered to have the place of honour. Any one attempting to harm "young Mistress" or "old Mistress" during the night would have had to cross the dead body of the slave to do so. I do not know how many have noticed it, but I think that it will be found to be true that there are few instances, either in slavery or freedom, in which a member of my race has been known to betray a specific trust.

As a rule, not only did the members of my race entertain no feelings of bitterness against the whites before and during the war, but there are many instances of Negroes tenderly caring for their former masters and mistresses who for some reason have become poor and dependent since the war. I know of instances where the former masters of slaves have for years been supplied with money by their former slaves to keep them from suffering. I have known of still other cases in which the former slaves have assisted in the education of the descendants of their former owners. I know of a case on a large plantation in the South in which a young white man, the son of the former owner of the estate, has become so reduced in purse and self-control by reason of drink that he is a pitiable creature; and yet, notwithstanding the poverty of the colored people themselves on this plantation, they have for years supplied this young white man with the necessities of life. One sends him a little coffee or sugar, another a little meat, and so on. Nothing that the colored people possess is too good for the son of "old Mars' Tom," who will perhaps never be permitted to suffer while any remain on the place who knew directly or indirectly of "old Mars' Tom."

I have said that there are few instances of a member of my race betraying a specific trust. One of the best illustrations of this which I know of is in the case of an ex-slave from Virginia whom I met not long ago in a little town in the state of Ohio. I found that this man had made a contract with his master, two or three years previous to the Emancipation Proclamation, to the effect that the slave was to be permitted to buy himself, by paying so much per year for his body; and while he was paying for himself, he was to be permitted to labor where and for whom he pleased. Finding that he could secure better wages in Ohio, he went there. When freedom came, he was still in debt to his master some three hundred dollars. Notwithstanding that the Emancipation Proclamation freed him from any obligation to his master, this black man walked the greater portion of the distance back to where his old master lived in Virginia, and placed the last dollar, with interest, in his hands. In talking to me about this, the man told me that he knew that he did not have to pay the debt, but that he had given his word to his master, and his word he had never broken. He felt that he could not enjoy his freedom till he had fulfilled his promise.

From some things that I have said one may get the idea that some of the slaves did not want freedom. This is not true. I have never seen one who did not want to be free, or who would return to slavery.

I pity from the bottom of my heart any nation or body of people that is so unfortunate as to get entangled in the net of slavery. I have long since ceased to cherish any spirit of bitterness against the Southern white people on account of the enslavement of my race. No one section of our country was wholly responsible for its introduction, and, besides, it was recognized and protected for years by the General Government. Having once got its tentacles fastened on to the economic and social life of the Republic, it was no easy matter for the country to relieve itself of the institution. Then, when we rid ourselves of prejudice, or racial feeling, and look facts in the face, we must acknowledge that, notwithstanding the cruelty and moral wrong of slavery, the ten million Negroes inhabiting this country, who themselves or whose ancestors went through the school of American slavery, are in a stronger and more hopeful condition, materially, intellectually, morally, and religiously, than is true of an equal number of black people in any other portion of the globe. This is so to such an extent that Negroes in this country, who themselves or whose forefathers went through the school of slavery, are constantly returning to Africa as missionaries to enlighten those who remained in the fatherland. This I say, not to justify slavery—on the other hand, I condemn it as an institution, as we all know that in America it was established for selfish and financial reasons, and not from a missionary motive—but to call attention to a fact, and to show how Providence so often uses men and institutions to accomplish a purpose. When persons ask me in these days how, in the midst of what sometimes seem hopelessly discouraging conditions, I can have such faith in the future of my race in this country, I remind them of the wilderness through which and out of which, a good Providence has already led us.

Ever since I have been old enough to think for myself, I have entertained the idea that, notwithstanding the cruel wrongs inflicted upon us, the black man got nearly as much out of slavery as the white man did. The hurtful influences of the institution were not by any means confined to the Negro. This was fully illustrated by the life upon our own plantation. The whole machinery of slavery was so constructed as to cause labor, as a rule, to be looked upon as a badge of degradation, of inferiority. Hence labor was something that both races on the slave plantation sought to escape. The slave system on our place, in a large measure, took the spirit of self-reliance and self-help out of the white people. My old master had many boys and girls, but not one, so far as I know, ever mastered a single trade or special line of productive industry. The girls were not taught to cook, sew or to take care of the house. All of this was left to the slaves. The slaves, of course, had little personal interest in the life of the plantation, and their ignorance prevented them from learning how to do things in the most improved and thorough manner. As a result of the system, fences were out of repair, gates were hanging half off the hinges. doors creaked, window-panes were out, plastering had fallen but was not replaced, weeds grew in the yard. As a rule, there was food for whites and blacks, but inside the house, and on the dining-room table, there was wanting that delicacy and refinement of touch and finish which can make a home the most convenient, comfortable, and attractive place in the world. Withal there was a waste of food and other materials which was sad. When freedom came, the slaves were almost as well fitted to begin life anew as the master, except in the matter of book-learning and ownership of property. The slave owner and his sons had mastered no special industry. They unconsciously had imbibed the feeling that manual labor was not the proper thing for them. On the other hand, the slaves, in many cases, had mastered some handicraft, and none were ashamed, and few unwilling, to labor.

Finally the war closed, and the day of freedom came. It was a momentous and eventful day to all upon our plantation. We had been expecting it. Freedom was in the air, and had been for months. Deserting soldiers returning to their homes were to be seen every day. Others who had been discharged, or whose regiments had been paroled, were constantly passing near our place. The "grapevine telegraph" was kept busy night and day. The news and mutterings of great events were swiftly carried from one plantation to another. In the fear of "Yankee" invasions, the silverware and other valuables were taken from the "big house," buried in the woods, and guarded by trusted slaves. Woe be to any one who would have attempted to disturb the buried treasure. The slaves would give the Yankee soldiers food, drink, clothing—anything but that which had been specifically intrusted to their care and honor. As the great day drew nearer, there was more singing in the slave quarters than usual. It was bolder, had more ring, and lasted later into the night. Most of the verses of the plantation songs had some reference to freedom. True, they had sung those same verses before, but they had been careful to explain that the "freedom" in these songs referred to the next world, and had no connection with life in this world. Now they gradually threw off the mask; and were not afraid to let it be known that the "freedom" in their songs meant freedom of the body in this world. The night before the eventful day, word was sent to the slave quarters to the effect that something unusual was going to take place at the "big house" the next morning. There was little, if any, sleep that night. All was excitement and expectancy. Early the next morning word was sent to all the slaves, old and young, to gather at the house. In company with my mother, brother, and sister, and a large number of other slaves, I went to the master's house. All of our master's family were either standing or seated on the veranda of the house, where they could see what was to take place and hear what was said. There was a feeling of deep interest, or perhaps sadness, on their faces, but not bitterness. As I now recall the impression they made upon me, they did not at the moment seem to be sad because of the loss of property, but rather because of parting with those whom they had reared and who were in many ways very close to them. The most distinct thing that I now recall in connection with the scene was that some man who seemed to be a stranger (a United States officer, I presume) made a little speech and then read a rather long paper—the Emancipation Proclamation, I think. After the reading we were told that we were all free, and could go when and where we pleased. My mother, who was standing by my side, leaned over and kissed her children, while tears of joy ran down her cheeks. She explained to us what it all meant, that this was the day for which she had been so long praying, but fearing that she would never live to see.

For some minutes there was great rejoicing, and thanksgiving, and wild scenes of ecstasy. But there was no feeling of bitterness. In fact, there was pity among the slaves for our former owners. The wild rejoicing on the part of the emancipated colored people lasted but for a brief period, for I noticed that by the time they returned to their cabins there was a change in their feelings. The great responsibility of being free, of having charge of themselves, of having to think and plan for themselves and their children, seemed to take possession of them. It was very much like suddenly turning a youth of ten or twelve years out into the world to provide for himself. In a few hours the great questions with which the Anglo-Saxon race had been grappling for centuries had been thrown upon these people to be solved. These were the questions of a home, a living, the rearing of children, education, citizenship, and the establishment and support of churches. Was it any wonder that within a few hours the wild rejoicing ceased and a feeling of deep gloom seemed to pervade the slave quarters? To some it seemed that, now that they were in actual possession of it, freedom was a more serious thing than they had expected to find it. Some of the slaves were seventy or eighty years old; their best days were gone. They had no strength with which to earn a living in a strange place and among strange people, even if they had been sure where to find a new place of abode. To this class the problem seemed especially hard. Besides, deep down in their hearts there was a strange and peculiar attachment to "old Marster" and "old Missus," and to their children, which they found it hard to think of breaking off. With these they had spent in some cases nearly a half-century, and it was no light thing to think of parting. Gradually, one by one, stealthily at first, the older slaves began to wander from the slave quarters back to the "big house" to have a whispered conversation with their former owners as to the future.

CHAPTER 14
The Atlanta Exposition Address

The Atlanta Exposition, at which I had been asked to make an address as a representative of the Negro race . . . was opened with a short address from Governor Bullock. After other interesting exercises, including an invocation from

Bishop Nelson, of Georgia, a dedicatory ode by Albert Howell, Jr., and addresses by the President of the Exposition and Mrs. Joseph Thompson, the President of the Woman's Board, Governor Bullock introduced me with the words, "We have with us to-day a representative of Negro enterprise and Negro civilization."

When I arose to speak, there was considerable cheering, especially from the colored people. As I remember it now, the thing that was uppermost in my mind was the desire to say something that would cement the friendship of the races and bring about hearty coöperation between them. So far as my outward surroundings were concerned, the only thing that I recall distinctly now is that when I got up, I saw thousands of eyes looking intently into my face. The following is the address which I delivered:—

MR. PRESIDENT AND GENTLEMEN OF THE BOARD OF DIRECTORS AND CITIZENS:

One-third of the population of the South is of the Negro race. No enterprise seeking the material, civil, or moral welfare of this section can disregard this element of our population and reach the highest success. I but convey to you, Mr. President and Directors, the sentiment of the masses of my race when I say that in no way have the value and manhood of the American Negro been more fittingly and generously recognized than by the managers of this magnificent Exposition at every stage of its progress. It is a recognition that will do more to cement the friendship of the two races than any occurrence since the dawn of our freedom.

Not only this, but the opportunity here afforded will awaken among us a new era of industrial progress. Ignorant and inexperienced, it is not strange that in the first years of our new life we began at the top instead of at the bottom; that a seat in Congress or the state legislature was more sought than real estate or industrial skill; that the political convention of stump speaking had more attractions than starting a dairy farm or truck garden.

A ship lost at sea for many days suddenly sighted a friendly vessel. From the mast of the unfortunate vessel was seen a signal, "Water, water; we die of thirst!" The answer from the friendly vessel at once came back, "Cast down your bucket where you are." A second time the signal, "Water, water; send us water!" ran up from the distressed vessel, and was answered, "Cast down your bucket where you are." And a third and fourth signal for water was answered, "Cast down your bucket where you are." The captain of the distressed vessel, at last heeding the injunction, cast down his bucket, and it came up full of fresh, sparkling water from the mouth of the Amazon River. To those of my race who depend on bettering their condition in a foreign land or who underestimate the importance of cultivating friendly relations with the Southern white man, who is their next-door neighbor, I would say: "Cast down your bucket where you are"—cast it down in making friends in every manly way of the people of all races by whom we are surrounded.

Cast it down in agriculture, mechanics, in commerce, in domestic service, and in the professions. And in this connection it is well to bear in mind that whatever other sins the South may be called to bear, when it comes to business, pure and simple, it is in the South that the Negro is given a man's chance in the commercial world, and in nothing is this Exposition more eloquent than in emphasizing this chance. Our greatest danger is that in the great leap from slavery to freedom we may overlook the fact that the masses of us are to live by the productions of our hands, and fail to keep in mind that we shall prosper in proportion as we learn to dignify and glorify common labor and put brains and skill into the common occupations of life; shall prosper in proportion as we learn to draw the line between the superficial and the substantial, the ornamental gewgaws of life and the useful. No race can prosper till it learns that there is as much dignity in tilling a field as in writing a poem. It is at the bottom of life we must begin, and not at the top. Nor should we permit our grievances to overshadow our opportunities.

To those of the white race who look to the incoming of those of foreign birth and strange tongue and habits for the prosperity of the South, were I permitted I would repeat what I say to my own race, "Cast down your bucket where you are." Cast it down among the eight millions of Negroes whose habits you know, whose fidelity and love you have tested in days when to have proved treacherous meant the ruin of your firesides. Cast down your bucket among these people who have, without strikes and labor wars, tilled your fields, cleared your forests, builded your railroads and cities, and brought forth treasures from the bowels of the earth, and helped make possible this magnificent representation of the progress of the South. Casting down your bucket among my people, helping and encouraging them as you are doing on these grounds, and to education of head, hand, and heart, you will find that they will buy your surplus land, make blossom the waste places in your fields, and run your factories. While doing this, you can be sure in the future, as in the past, that you and your families will be surrounded by the most patient, faithful, law-abiding, and unresentful people that the world has seen. As we have proved our loyalty to you in the past, in nursing your children, watching by the sick-bed of your mothers and fathers, and often following them with tear-dimmed eyes to their graves, so in the future, in our humble way, we shall stand by you with a devotion that no foreigner can approach, ready to lay down our lives, if need be, in defense of yours, interlacing our industrial, commercial, civil, and religious life with yours in a way that shall make the interests of both races one. In all things that are purely social we can be as separate as the fingers, yet one as the hand in all things essential to mutual progress.

There is no defense or security for any of us except in the highest intelligence and development of all. If anywhere there are efforts tending to curtail the fullest growth of the Negro, let these efforts be turned into stimulating, encouraging, and making him the most useful and intelligent citizen. Effort or means so invested will pay a thousand per cent interest. These efforts will be twice blessed—"blessing him that gives and him that takes."

There is no escape through law of man or God from the inevitable:—

The laws of changeless justice bind
  Oppressor with oppressed;
And close as sin and suffering joined
  We march to fate abreast.

Nearly sixteen millions of hands will aid you in pulling the load upward, or they will pull against you the load downward. We shall constitute one-third and more of the ignorance and crime of the South, or one-third its intelligence and progress; we shall contribute one-third to the business and industrial prosperity of the South, or we shall prove a veritable body of death, stagnating, depressing, retarding every effort to advance the body politic.

Gentlemen of the Exposition, as we present to you our humble effort at an exhibition of our progress, you must not expect overmuch. Starting thirty years ago with ownership here and there in a few quilts and pumpkins and chickens (gathered from miscellaneous sources), remember the path that has led from these to the inventions and production of agricultural implements, buggies, steam-engines, newspapers, books, statuary, carving, paintings, the management of drug-stores and banks, has not been trodden without contact with thorns and thistles. While we take pride in what we exhibit as a result of our independent efforts, we do not for a moment forget that our part in this exhibition would fall far short of your expectations but for the constant help that has come to our educational life, not only from the Southern states, but especially from Northern philanthropists, who have made their gifts a constant stream of blessing and encouragement.

The wisest among my race understand that the agitation of questions of social equality is the extremest folly, and that progress in the enjoyment of all the privileges that will come to us must be the result of severe and constant struggle rather than of artificial forcing. No race that has anything to contribute to the markets of the world is long in any degree ostracized. It is important and right that all privileges of the law be ours, but it is vastly more important that we be prepared for the exercises of these privileges. The opportunity to earn a dollar in a factory just now is worth infinitely more than the opportunity to spend a dollar in an opera-house.

In conclusion, may I repeat that nothing in thirty years has given us more hope and encouragement, and drawn us so near to you of the white race, as this opportunity offered by the Exposition; and here bending, as it were, over the altar that represents the results of the struggles of your race and mine, both starting practically empty-handed three decades ago. I pledged that in your effort to work out the great and intricate problem which God has laid at the doors of the South, you shall have at all times the patient, sympathetic help of my race; only let this be constantly in mind, that, while from representations in these buildings of the product of field, of forest, of mine, of factory, letters, and art, much good will come, yet far above and beyond material benefits will be that higher good, that, let us pray God, will come, in a blotting out of sectional differences and racial animosities and suspicions, in a determination to administer absolute justice, in a willing obedience among all classes to the mandates of law. This, then, coupled with our material prosperity, will bring into our beloved South a new heaven and a new earth.

The first thing that I remember, after I had finished speaking, was that Governor Bullock rushed across the platform and took me by the hand, and that others did the same. I received so many and such hearty congratulations that I found it difficult to get out of the building. I did not appreciate to any degree, however, the impression which my address seemed to have made, until the next morning, when I went into the business part of the city. As soon as I was recognized, I was surprised to find myself pointed out and surrounded by a crowd of men who wished to shake hands with me. This was kept up on every street on to which I went, to an extent which embarrassed me so much that I went back to my boarding-place. The next morning I returned to Tuskegee. At the station in Atlanta, and at almost all of the stations at which the train stopped between that city and Tuskegee, I found a crowd of people anxious to shake hands with me.

The papers in all parts of the United States published the address in full, and for months afterward there were complimentary editorial references to it. Mr. Clark Howell, the editor of the Atlanta *Constitution,* telegraphed to a New York paper, among other words, the following, "I do not exaggerate when I say that Professor Booker T. Washington's address yesterday was one of the most notable speeches, both as to character and as to the warmth of its reception, ever delivered to a Southern audience. The address was a revelation. The whole speech is a platform upon which blacks and whites can stand with full justice to each other."

The Boston *Transcript* said editorially: "The speech of Booker T. Washington at the Atlanta Exposition, this week, seems to have dwarfed all the other proceedings and the Exposition itself. The sensation that it has caused in the press has never been equalled."

I very soon began receiving all kinds of propositions from lecture bureaus, and editors of magazines and papers, to take the lecture platform, and to write articles. One lecture bureau offered me fifty thousand dollars, or two hundred dollars a night and expenses, if I would place my services at its disposal for a given period. To all these communications I replied that my life-work was at Tuskegee; and that whenever I spoke it must be in the interests of the Tuskegee school and my race, and that I would enter into no arrangements that seemed to place a mere commercial value upon my services.

Some days after its delivery I sent a copy of my address to the President of the United States, the Hon. Grover Cleveland. I received from him the following autograph reply:—

GRAY GABLES, BUZZARD'S BAY, MASS.,
OCTOBER 6, 1895

BOOKER T. WASHINGTON, ESQ.:

MY DEAR SIR: I thank you for sending me a copy of your address delivered at the Atlanta Exposition.

I thank you with much enthusiasm for making the address. I have read it with intense interest, and I think the Exposition would be fully justified if it did not do more than furnish the opportunity for its delivery. Your words cannot fail to delight and encourage all who wish well for your race; and if our colored fellow-citizens do not from your utterances gather new hope and form new determinations to gain every valuable advantage offered them by their citizenship, it will be strange indeed.

Yours very truly,
GROVER CLEVELAND

Later I met Mr. Cleveland, for the first time, when, as President, he visited the Atlanta Exposition. At the request of myself and others he consented to spend an hour in the Negro Building, for the purpose of inspecting the Negro exhibit and of giving the colored people in attendance an opportunity to shake hands with him. As soon as I met Mr. Cleveland I became impressed with his simplicity, greatness, and rugged honesty. I have met him many times since then, both at public functions and at his private residence in Princeton, and the more I see of him the more I admire him. When he visited the Negro Building in Atlanta he seemed to give himself up wholly, for that hour, to the colored people. He seemed to be as careful to shake hands with some old colored "auntie" clad partially in rags, and to take as much pleasure in doing so, as if he were greeting some millionaire. Many of the colored people took advantage of the occasion to get him to write his name in a book or on a slip of paper. He was as careful and patient in doing this as if he were putting his signature to some great state document.

Mr. Cleveland has not only shown his friendship for me in many personal ways, but has always consented to do anything I have asked of him for our school. This he has done, whether it was to make a personal donation or to use his influence in securing the donations of others. Judging from my personal acquaintance with Mr. Cleveland, I do not believe that he is conscious of possessing any color prejudice. He is too great for that. In my contact with people I find that, as a rule, it is only the little, narrow people who live for themselves, who never read good books, who do not travel, who never open up their souls in a way to permit them to come into contact with other souls—with the great outside world. No man whose vision is bounded by color can come into contact with what is highest and best in the world. In meeting men, in many places, I have found that the happiest people are those who do the most for others; the most miserable are those who do the least. I have also found that few things, if any, are capable of making one so blind and narrow as race prejudice. I often say to our students, in the course of my talks to them on Sunday evenings in the chapel, that the longer I live and the more experience I have of the world, the more I am convinced that, after all, the one thing that is most worth living for—and dying for, if need be—is the opportunity of making some one else more happy and more useful.

The colored people and the colored newspapers at first seemed to be greatly pleased with the character of my Atlanta address, as well as with its reception. But after the first burst of enthusiasm began to die away, and the colored people began reading the speech in cold type, some of them seemed to feel that they had been hypnotized. They seemed to feel that I have been too liberal in my remarks toward the Southern whites, and that I had not spoken out strongly enough for what they termed the "rights" of the race. For a while there was a reaction, so far as a certain element of my own race was concerned, but later these reactionary ones seemed to have been won over to my way of believing and acting.

While speaking of changes in public sentiment, I recall that about ten years after the school at Tuskegee was established, I had an experience that I shall never forget. Dr. Lyman Abbott, then the pastor of Plymouth Church, and also editor of the *Outlook* (then the *Christian Union*), asked me to write a letter for his paper giving my opinion of the exact condition, mental and moral, of the colored ministers in the South, as based upon my observations. I wrote the letter, giving the exact facts as I conceived them to be. The picture painted was a rather black one—or, since I am black, shall I say "white"? It could not be otherwise with a race but a few years out of slavery, a race which had not had time or opportunity to produce a competent ministry.

What I said soon reached every Negro minister in the country, I think, and the letters of condemnation which I received from them were not few. I think that for a year after the publication of this article every association and every conference or religious body of any kind, of my race, that met, did not fail before adjourning to pass a resolution condemning me, or calling upon me to retract or modify what I had said. Many of these organizations went so far in their resolutions as to advise parents to cease sending their children to Tuskegee. One association even appointed a "missionary" whose duty it was to warn the people against sending their children to Tuskegee. This missionary had a son in the school, and I noticed that, whatever the "missionary" might have said or done with regard to others, he was careful not to take his son away from the institution. Many of the colored papers, especially those that were the organs of religious bodies, joined in the general chorus of condemnation or demands for retraction.

During the whole time of the excitement, and through all the criticism, I did not utter a word of explanation or retraction. I knew that I was right, and that time and the sober second thought of the people would vindicate me. It was not long before the bishops and other church leaders began to make a careful investigation of the conditions of the ministry, and they found out that I was right. In fact, the oldest and most influential bishop in one branch of the Methodist Church said that my words were far too mild. Very soon public sentiment began making itself felt, in demanding a purifying of the ministry. While this is not yet complete by any means, I think I may say, without egotism, and I have been told by many of our most influential ministers, that my words had much to do with starting a demand for the placing of a higher type of men in the pulpit. I have had the satisfaction of having many who once condemned me thank me heartily for my frank words.

The change of the attitude of the Negro ministry, so far as regards myself, is so complete that at the present time I have no warmer friends among any class than I have among the clergymen. The improvement in the character and life of the Negro ministers is one of the most gratifying evidences of the progress of the race. My experience with them, as well as other events in my life, convince me that the thing to do, when one feels sure that he has said or done the right thing, and is condemned, is to stand still and keep quiet. If he is right, time will show it.

In the midst of the discussion which was going on concerning my Atlanta speech, I received the letter which I give below, from Dr. Gilman, the President of Johns Hopkins University, who had been made chairman of the judges of award in connection with the Atlanta Exposition:—

JOHNS HOPKINS UNIVERSITY, BALTIMORE,
President's Office, September 30, 1895

DEAR MR. WASHINGTON: Would it be agreeable to you to be one of the Judges of Award in the Department of Education at Atlanta? If so, I shall be glad to place your name upon the list. A line by telegraph will be welcomed.

Yours very truly,
D. C. GILMAN

I think I was even more surprised to receive this invitation than I had been to receive the invitation to speak at the opening of the Exposition. It was to be a part of my duty, as one of the jurors, to pass not only upon the exhibits of the colored schools, but also upon those of the white schools. I accepted the position, and spent a month in Atlanta in performance of the duties which it entailed. The board of jurors was a large one, consisting in all of sixty members. It was about equally divided between Southern white people and Northern white people. Among them were college presidents, leading scientists and men of letters, and specialists in many subjects. When the group of jurors to which I was assigned met for organization, Mr. Thomas Nelson Page, who was one of the number, moved that I be made secretary of that division, and the motion was unanimously adopted. Nearly half of our division were Southern people. In performing my duties in the inspection of the exhibits of white schools I was in every case treated with respect, and at the close of our labors I parted from my associates with regret.

I am often asked to express myself more freely than I do upon the political condition and the political future of my race. These recollections of my experience in Atlanta give me the opportunity to do so briefly. My own belief is, although I have never before said so in so many words, that the time will come when the Negro in the South will be accorded all the political rights which his ability, character, and material possessions entitle him to. I think, though, that the opportunity to freely exercise such political rights will not come in any large degree through outside or artificial forcing, but will be accorded to the Negro by the Southern white people themselves, and that they will protect him in the exercise of those rights. Just as soon as the South gets over the old feeling that it is being forced by "foreigners," or "aliens," to do something which it does not want to do, I believe that the change in the direction that I have indicated is going to begin. In fact, there are indications that it is already beginning in a slight degree.

Let me illustrate my meaning. Suppose that some months before the opening of the Atlanta Exposition there had been a general demand from the press and public platform outside the South that a Negro be given a place on the opening program, and that a Negro be placed upon the board of jurors of award. Would any such recognition of the race have taken place? I do not think so. The Atlanta officials went as far as they did because they felt it to be a pleasure, as well as a duty, to reward what they considered merit in the Negro race. Say what we will, there is something in human nature which we cannot blot out, which makes one man, in the end, recognize and reward merit in another, regardless of color or race.

I believe it is the duty of the Negro—as the greater part of the race is already doing—to deport himself modestly in regard to political claims, depending upon the slow but sure influences that proceed from the possession of property, intelligence, and high character for the full recognition of his political rights. I think that the according of the full exercise of political rights is going to be a matter of natural, slow growth, not an over-night, gourd-vine affair. I do not believe that the Negro should cease voting, for a man cannot learn the exercise of self-government by ceasing to vote any more than a boy can learn to swim by keeping out of the water, but I do believe that in his voting he should more and more be influenced by those of intelligence and character who are his next-door neighbors.

I know colored men who, through the encouragement, help, and advice of Southern white people, have accumulated thousands of dollars' worth of property, but who, at the same time, would never think of going to those same persons for advice concerning the casting of their ballots. This, it seems to me, is unwise and unreasonable, and should cease. In saying this I do not mean that the Negro should truckle, or not vote from principle, for the instant he ceases to vote from principle he loses the confidence and respect of the Southern white man even.

I do not believe that any state should make a law that permits an ignorant and poverty-stricken white man to vote, and prevents a black man in the same condition from voting. Such a law is not only unjust, but it will react, as all unjust laws do, in time; for the effect of such a law is to encourage the Negro to secure education and property, and at the same time it encourages the white man to remain in ignorance and poverty. I believe that in time, through the operation of intelligence and friendly race relations, all cheating at the ballot box in the South will cease. It will become apparent that the white man who begins by cheating a Negro out of his ballot soon learns to cheat a white man out of his, and that the man who does this ends his career of dishonesty by the theft of property or by some equally serious crime. In my opinion, the time will come when the South will encourage all of its citizens to vote. It will see that it pays better, from every standpoint, to have healthy, vigorous life than to have that political stagnation which always results when one-half of the population has no share and no interest in the Government.

As a rule, I believe in universal, free suffrage, but I believe that in the South we are confronted with peculiar conditions that justify the protection of the ballot in many of the states, for a while at least, either by an educational test, a property test, or by both combined; but whatever tests are required, they should be made to apply with equal and exact justice to both races.

Malcolm X (1925–65)

Even before his assassination in 1965, civil rights leader Malcolm X had become a cultural and political legend, his philosophies inspiring many African American artists, educators, and students who revered his life—and his ultimate sacrifice. In 1992, the biographical feature film Malcolm X *by director Spike Lee turned the legendary figure into an American popular icon; his face and name appeared on T-shirts, bookcovers, jackets, and caps in a commercial rebirth of his legacy. Although the omnipresent image of Malcolm X in the early 1990s was merely a trendy fashion for mainstream America, the black community accorded Malcolm X an honor and acclaim that had been intensifying over the decades since his death.*

Born Malcolm Little in Omaha, Nebraska, the youngest of seven children, Malcolm X endured an unsettled childhood that took him from Nebraska to Milwaukee, Wisconsin, and then to Lansing, Michigan. In Lansing, a white supremacist group burned down his family's house and was later suspected of killing Malcolm's father, an outspoken minister who supported the separatist ideas of Marcus Garvey (see p. 733). Malcolm's mother could not support her family due to her psychological instability after her husband's death. When she was placed in a psychiatric institution, Malcolm and his siblings were separated into various detention homes. Malcolm remained in the custody of the state until he completed the eighth grade. He then moved to the Roxbury section of Boston to live with his half-sister. In this urban environment, the young Malcolm turned to criminal activities, and from 1946 to 1952, he served time for burglary in Charlestown State Prison.

Malcolm's imprisonment became a turning point in his life. During those six years, he educated himself by reading extensively, developing special interests in the history of racism in America and of the Nation of Islam (the Black Muslims). Encouraged by his sister, Ella, to become a Muslim, he left prison in 1952 to work with Elijah Muhammad, leader of the Nation of Islam. With his charismatic leadership skills and fervent, insistent voice, Malcolm went to Detroit and New York to convey the Muslims' message of black separation and black chauvinism to the urban masses. He subsequently changed his name to Malcolm X in repudiation of his family name, Little, which he considered a slave name.

In the early 1960s, following conflicts with Elijah Muhammad and the Black Muslim organization and a visit to the holy city of Mecca, Malcolm X sought to develop his own organization, one that would emphasize international alliances and work for human rights. His journey to Mecca also led Malcolm to adopt a new name, El-Hajj Malik El-Shabazz, and a new openness toward working with other activists regardless of their race or religion. In the year before his death, Malcolm founded the Organization of Afro-American Unity (OAAU), dedicated to exposing the political oppression of all people of color and the systematic destruction of their human rights. The promise of OAAU died young, like its founder, when in 1965 Malcolm X was gunned down while giving a speech in Harlem.

The following chapters from The Autobiography of Malcolm X *(1965), coauthored with Alex Haley just before Malcolm's death, tell much about his early and later life. In Chapter 2, which covers 1937 to 1940, Malcolm tells about his experiences in a Lansing detention home, including his discovery that racism could be fostered even by well-intentioned white Americans. Malcolm's letter from Chapter 17 details the changes in his attitude toward race brought about by his visit to Mecca. Finally, Chapter 19 clarifies Malcolm's positions in 1965 on such issues as the use of violence, interracial cooperation, and the future of racial politics in America. The chapter ends prophetically with Malcolm's expectation of assassination.*

from The Autobiography of Malcolm X

CHAPTER 2
Mascot

On June twenty-seventh of that year, nineteen thirty-seven, Joe Louis knocked out James J. Braddock to become the heavyweight champion of the world. And all the Negroes in Lansing, like Negroes everywhere, went wildly happy with the greatest celebration of race pride our generation had ever known. Every Negro boy old enough to walk wanted to be the next Brown Bomber. My brother Philbert, who had already become a pretty good boxer in school, was no exception. (I was trying to play basketball. I was gangling and tall, but I wasn't very good at it—too awkward.) In the fall of that year, Philbert entered the amateur bouts that were held in Lansing's Prudden Auditorium.

He did well, surviving the increasingly tough eliminations. I would go down to the gym and watch him train. It was very exciting. Perhaps without realizing it I became secretly envious; for one thing, I know I could not help seeing some of my younger brother Reginald's lifelong admiration for me getting siphoned off to Philbert.

People praised Philbert as a natural boxer. I figured that since we belonged to the same family, maybe I would become one, too. So I put myself in the ring. I think I was thirteen when I signed up for my first bout, but my height and raw-boned frame let me get away with claiming that I was sixteen, the minimum age—and my weight of about 128 pounds got me classified as a bantamweight.

They matched me with a white boy, a novice like myself, named Bill Peterson. I'll never forget him. When our turn in the next amateur bouts came up, all of my brothers and sisters were there watching, along with just about everyone else I knew in town. They were there not so much because of me but because of Philbert, who had begun to build up a pretty good following, and they wanted to see how his brother would do.

I walked down the aisle between the people thronging the rows of seats, and climbed in the ring. Bill Peterson and I were introduced, and then the referee called us together and mumbled all of that stuff about fighting fair and breaking clean. Then the bell rang and we came out of our corners. I knew I was scared, but I didn't know, as Bill Peterson told me later on, that he was scared of me, too. He was so scared I was going to hurt him that he knocked me down fifty times if he did once.

He did such a job on my reputation in the Negro neighborhood that I practically went into hiding. A Negro just can't be whipped by somebody white and return with his head up to the neighborhood, especially in those days, when sports and, to a lesser extent show business, were the only fields open to Negroes, and when the ring was the only place a Negro could whip a white man and not be lynched. When I did show my face again, the Negroes I knew rode me so badly I knew I had to do something.

But the worst of my humiliations was my younger brother Reginald's attitude: he simply never mentioned the fight. It was the way he looked at me—and avoided looking at me. So I went back to the gym, and I trained—hard. I beat bags and skipped rope and grunted and sweated all over the place. And finally I signed up to fight Bill Peterson again. This time, the bouts were held in his hometown of Alma, Michigan.

The only thing better about the rematch was that hardly anyone I knew was there to see it; I was particularly grateful for Reginald's absence. The moment the bell rang, I saw a fist, then the canvas coming up, and ten seconds later the referee was saying *"Ten!"* over me. It was probably the shortest "fight" in history. I lay there listening to the full count, but I couldn't move. To tell the truth, I'm not sure I wanted to move.

That white boy was the beginning and the end of my fight career. A lot of times in these later years since I became a Muslim, I've thought back to that fight and reflected that it was Allah's work to stop me: I might have wound up punchy.

Not long after this, I came into a classroom with my hat on. I did it deliberately. The teacher, who was white, ordered me to keep the hat on, and to walk around and around the room until he told me to stop. "That way," he said, "everyone can see you. Meanwhile, we'll go on with class for those who are here to learn something."

I was still walking around when he got up from his desk and turned to the blackboard to write something on it. Everyone in the classroom was looking when, at this moment, I passed behind his desk, snatched up a thumbtack and deposited it in his chair. When he turned to sit back down, I was far from the scene of the crime, circling around the rear of the room. Then he hit the tack, and I heard him holler and caught a glimpse of him spraddling up as I disappeared through the door.

With my deportment record, I wasn't really shocked when the decision came that I had been expelled.

I guess I must have had some vague idea that if I didn't have to go to school, I'd be allowed to stay on with the Gohannas' and wander around town, or maybe get a job if I wanted one for pocket money. But I got rocked on my heels when a state man whom I hadn't seen before came and got me at the Gohannas' and took me down to court.

They told me I was going to go to a reform school. I was still thirteen years old.

But first I was going to the detention home. It was in Mason, Michigan, about twelve miles from Lansing. The detention home was where all the "bad" boys and girls from Ingham County were held, on their way to reform school—waiting for their hearings.

The white state man was a Mr. Maynard Allen. He was nicer to me than most of the state Welfare people had been. He even had consoling words for the Gohannas' and Mrs. Adcock and Big Boy; all of them were crying. But I wasn't. With the few clothes I owned stuffed into a box, we rode in his car to Mason. He talked as he drove along, saying that my school marks showed that if I would just straighten up, I could make something of myself. He said that reform school had the wrong reputation; he talked about what the word "reform" meant—to change and become better. He said the school was really a place where boys like me could have time to see their mistakes and start a new life and become somebody everyone would be proud of. And he told me that the lady in charge of the detention home, a Mrs. Swerlin, and her husband were very good people.

They were good people. Mrs. Swerlin was bigger than her husband, I remember, a big, buxom, robust, laughing woman, and Mr. Swerlin was thin, with black hair, and a black mustache and a red face, quiet and polite, even to me.

They liked me right away, too. Mrs. Swerlin showed me to my room, my own room—the first in my life. It was in one of those huge dormitory-like buildings where kids in detention were kept in those days—and still are in most places. I discovered next, with surprise, that I was allowed to eat with the Swerlins. It was the first time I'd eaten with white people—at least with grown white people—since the Seventh Day Adventist country meetings. It wasn't my own exclusive privilege, of course. Except for the very troublesome boys and girls at the detention home, who were kept locked up—those who had run away and been caught and brought back, or something like that—all of us ate with the Swerlins sitting at the head of the long tables.

They had a white cook-helper, I recall—Lucille Lathrop. (It amazes me how these names come back, from a time I haven't thought about for more than twenty years.) Lucille treated me well, too. Her husband's name was Duane Lathrop. He worked somewhere else, but he stayed there at the detention home on the weekends with Lucille.

I noticed again how white people smelled different from us, and how their food tasted different, not seasoned like Negro cooking. I began to sweep and mop and dust around in the Swerlins' house, as I had done with Big Boy at the Gohannas'.

They all liked my attitude, and it was out of their liking for me that I soon became accepted by them—as a mascot, I know now. They would talk about anything and everything with me standing right there hearing them, the same way people would talk freely in front of a pet canary. They would even talk about me, or about "niggers," as though I wasn't there, as if I wouldn't understand what the word meant. A hundred times a day, they used the word "nigger." I suppose that in their own minds, they meant no harm; in fact they probably meant well. It was the same with the cook, Lucille, and her husband, Duane. I remember one day when Mr. Swerlin, as nice as he was, came in from Lansing, where he had been through the Negro section, and said to Mrs. Swerlin right in front of me, "I just can't see how those niggers can be so happy and be so poor." He talked about how they lived in shacks, but had those big, shining cars out front.

And Mrs. Swerlin said, me standing right there, "Niggers are just that way. . . ." That scene always stayed with me.

It was the same with the other white people, most of them local politicians, when they would come visiting the Swerlins. One of their favorite parlor topics was "niggers." One of them was the judge who was in charge of me in Lansing. He was a close friend of the Swerlins. He would ask about me when he came, and they would call me in, and he would look me up and down, his expression approving, like he was examining a fine colt, or a pedigreed pup. I knew they must have told him how I acted and how I worked.

What I am trying to say is that it just never dawned upon them that I could understand, that I wasn't a pet, but a human being. They didn't give me credit for having the same sensitivity, intellect, and understanding that they would have been ready and willing to recognize in a white boy in my position. But it has historically been the case with white people, in their regard for black people, that even though we might be *with* them, we weren't considered *of* them. Even though they appeared to have opened the door, it was still closed. Thus they never did really see *me.*

This is the sort of kindly condescension which I try to clarify today, to these integration-hungry Negroes, about their "liberal" white friends, these so-called "good white people"—most of them anyway. I don't care how nice one is to you; the thing you must always remember is that almost never does he really see you as he sees himself, as he sees his own kind. He may stand with you through thin, but not thick; when the chips are down, you'll find that as fixed in him as his bone structure is his sometimes subconscious conviction that he's better than anybody black.

But I was no more than vaguely aware of anything like that in my detention-home years. I did my little chores around the house, and everything was fine. And each weekend, they didn't mind my catching a ride over to Lansing for the afternoon or evening. If I wasn't old enough, I sure was big enough by then, and nobody ever questioned my hanging out, even at night, in the streets of the Negro section.

I was growing up to be even bigger than Wilfred and Philbert, who had begun to meet girls at the school dances, and other places, and introduced me to a few. But the ones who seemed to like me, I didn't go for—and vice versa. I couldn't dance a lick, anyway, and I couldn't see squandering my few dimes on girls. So mostly I pleasured myself these Saturday nights by gawking around the Negro bars and restaurants. The jukeboxes were wailing Erskine Hawkins' "Tuxedo Junction," Slim and Slam's "Flatfoot Floogie," things like that. Sometimes, big bands from New York, out touring the one-night stands in the sticks, would play for big dances in Lansing. Everybody with legs would come out to see any performer who bore the magic name "New York." Which is how I first heard Lucky Thompson and Milt Jackson, both of whom I later got to know well in Harlem.

Many youngsters from the detention home, when their dates came up, went off to the reform school. But when mine came up—two or three times—it was always ignored. I saw new youngsters arrive and leave. I was glad and grateful. I knew it was Mrs. Swerlin's doing. I didn't want to leave.

She finally told me one day that I was going to be entered in Mason Junior High School. It was the only school in town. No ward of the detention home had ever gone to school there, at least while still a ward. So I entered their seventh grade. The only other Negroes there were some of the Lyons children, younger than I was, in the lower grades. The Lyons and I, as it happened, were the town's only Negroes. They were, as Negroes, very much respected. Mr. Lyons was a smart, hardworking man, and Mrs. Lyons was a very good woman. She and my mother, I had heard my mother say, were two of the four West Indians in that whole section of Michigan.

Some of the white kids at school, I found, were even friendlier than some of those in Lansing had been. Though some, including the teachers, called me "nigger," it was easy to see that they didn't mean any more harm by it than the Swerlins. As the "nigger" of my class, I was in fact extremely popular—I suppose partly because I was kind of a novelty. I was in demand, I had top priority. But I also benefited from the special prestige of having the seal of approval from that Very Important Woman about the town of Mason, Mrs. Swerlin. Nobody in Mason would have dreamed of getting on the wrong side of her. It became hard for me to get through a school day without someone after me to join this or head up that—the debating society, the Junior High basketball team, or some other extracurricular activity. I never turned them down.

And I hadn't been in the school long when Mrs. Swerlin, knowing I could use spending money of my own, got me a job after school washing the dishes of a local restaurant. My boss there was the father of a white classmate whom I spent a lot of time with. His family lived over the restaurant. It was fine working there. Every Friday night when I got paid, I'd feel at least ten feet tall. I forget how much I made, but it seemed like a lot. It was the first time I'd ever had any money to speak of, all my own, in my whole life. As soon as I could afford it, I bought a green suit and some shoes, and at school I'd buy treats for the others in my class—at least as much as any of them did for me.

English and history were the subjects I liked most. My English teacher, I recall—a Mr. Ostrowski—was always giving advice about how to become something in life. The one thing I didn't like about history class was that the teacher, Mr. Williams, was a great one for "nigger" jokes. One day during my first week at school, I walked into the room and he started singing to the class, as a joke,

" 'Way down yonder in the cotton field, some folks say that a nigger won't steal." Very funny. I liked history, but I never thereafter had much liking for Mr. Williams. Later, I remember, we came to the textbook section on Negro history. It was exactly one paragraph long. Mr. Williams laughed through it practically in a single breath, reading aloud how the Negroes had been slaves and then were freed, and how they were usually lazy and dumb and shiftless. He added, I remember, an anthropological footnote on his own, telling us between laughs how Negroes' feet were "so big that when they walk, they don't leave tracks, they leave a hole in the ground."

I'm sorry to say that the subject I most disliked was mathematics. I have thought about it. I think the reason was that mathematics leaves no room for argument. If you made a mistake, that was all there was to it.

Basketball was a big thing in my life, though. I was on the team; we traveled to neighboring towns such as Howell and Charlotte, and wherever I showed my face, the audiences in the gymnasiums "niggered" and "cooned" me to death. Or called me "Rastus." It didn't bother my teammates or my coach at all, and to tell the truth, it bothered me only vaguely. Mine was the same psychology that makes Negroes even today, though it bothers them down inside, keep letting the white man tell them how much "progress" they are making. They've heard it so much they've almost gotten brainwashed into believing it—or at least accepting it.

After the basketball games, there would usually be a school dance. Whenever our team walked into another school's gym for the dance, with me among them, I could feel the freeze. It would start to ease as they saw that I didn't try to mix, but stuck close to someone on our team, or kept to myself. I think I developed ways to do it without making it obvious. Even at our own school, I could sense it almost as a physical barrier, that despite all the beaming and smiling, the mascot wasn't supposed to dance with any of the white girls.

It was some kind of psychic message—not just from them, but also from within myself. I am proud to be able to say that much for myself, at least. I would just stand around and smile and talk and drink punch and eat sandwiches, and then I would make some excuse and get away early.

They were typical small-town school dances. Sometimes a little white band from Lansing would be brought in to play. But most often, the music was a phonograph set up on a table, with the volume turned up high, and the records scratchy, blaring things like Glenn Miller's "Moonlight Serenade"—his band was riding high then—or the Ink Spots, who were also very popular, singing "If I Didn't Care."

I used to spend a lot of time thinking about a peculiar thing. Many of these Mason white boys, like the ones at the Lansing school—especially if they knew me well, and if we hung out together—would get me off in a corner somewhere and push me to proposition certain white girls, sometimes their own sisters. They would tell me that they'd already had the girls themselves—including their sisters—or that they were trying to and couldn't. Later on, I came to understand what was going on: If they could get the girls into the position of having broken the terrible taboo by slipping off with me somewhere, they would have that hammer over the girls' heads, to make them give in to them.

It seemed that the white boys felt that I, being a Negro, just naturally knew more about "romance," or sex, than they did—that I instinctively knew more about what to do and say with their own girls. I never did tell anybody that I really went for some of the white girls, and some of them went for me, too. They let me know in many ways. But anytime we found ourselves in any close conversations or potential intimate situations, always there would come up between us some kind of a wall. The girls I really wanted to have were a couple of Negro girls whom Wilfred or Philbert had introduced me to in Lansing. But with these girls, somehow, I lacked the nerve.

From what I heard and saw on the Saturday nights I spent hanging around in the Negro district I knew that race-mixing went on in Lansing. But strangely enough, this didn't have any kind of effect on me. Every Negro in Lansing, I guess, knew how white men would drive along certain streets in the black neighborhoods and pick up Negro streetwalkers who patrolled the area. And, on the other hand, there was a bridge that separated the Negro and Polish neighborhoods, where white women would drive or walk across and pick up Negro men, who would hang around in certain places close to the bridge, waiting for them. Lansing's white women, even in those days, were famous for chasing Negro men. I didn't yet appreciate how most whites accord to the Negro this reputation for prodigious sexual prowess. There in Lansing, I never heard of any trouble about this mixing, from either side. I imagine that everyone simply took it for granted, as I did.

Anyway, from my experience as a little boy at the Lansing school, I had become fairly adept at avoiding the white-girl issue—at least for a couple of years yet.

Then, in the second semester of the seventh grade, I was elected class president. It surprised me even more than other people. But I can see now why the class might have done it. My grades were among the highest in the school. I was unique in my class, like a pink poodle. And I was proud; I'm not going to say I wasn't. In fact, by then, I didn't really have much feeling about being a Negro, because I was trying so hard, in every way I could, to be white. Which is why I am spending much of my life today telling the American black man that he's wasting his time straining to "integrate." I know from personal experience. I tried hard enough.

"Malcolm, we're just so *proud* of you!" Mrs. Swerlin exclaimed when she heard about my election. It was all over the restaurant where I worked. Even the state man, Maynard Allen, who still dropped by to see me once in a while, had a word of praise. He said he never saw anybody prove better exactly what "reform" meant. I really liked him—except for one thing: he now and then would drop something that hinted my mother had let us down somehow.

Fairly often, I would go and visit the Lyons, and they acted as happy as though I was one of their children. And it was the same warm feeling when I went into Lansing to visit my brothers and sisters, and the Gohannas'.

I remember one thing that marred this time for me: the movie *Gone with the Wind*. When it played in Mason, I was the only Negro in the theater, and when Butterfly McQueen went into her act, I felt like crawling under the rug.

Every Saturday, just about, I would go into Lansing. I was going on fourteen, now. Wilfred and Hilda still lived out by themselves at the old family home. Hilda kept the house very clean. It was easier than my mother's plight, with eight of us always under foot or running around. Wilfred worked wherever he could, and he still read every book he could get his hands on. Philbert was getting a reputation as one of the better amateur fighters in this part of the state; everyone really expected that he was going to become a professional.

Reginald and I, after my fighting fiasco, had finally gotten back on good terms. It made me feel great to visit him and Wesley over at Mrs. Williams'. I'd offhandedly give them each a couple of dollars to just stick in their pockets, to have something to spend. And little Yvonne and Robert were doing okay, too, over at the home of the West Indian lady, Mrs. McGuire. I'd give them about a quarter apiece; it made me feel good to see how they were coming along.

None of us talked much about our mother. And we never mentioned our father. I guess none of us knew what to say. We didn't want anybody else to mention our mother either, I think. From time to time, though, we would all go over to Kalamazoo to visit her. Most often we older ones went singly, for it was something you didn't want to have to experience with anyone else present, even your brother or sister.

During this period, the visit to my mother that I most remember was toward the end of that seventh-grade year, when our father's grown daughter by his first marriage, Ella, came from Boston to visit us. Wilfred and Hilda had exchanged some letters with Ella, and I, at Hilda's suggestion, had written to her from the Swerlins'. We were all excited and happy when her letter told us that she was coming to Lansing.

I think the major impact of Ella's arrival, at least upon me, was that she was the first really proud black woman I had ever seen in my life. She was plainly proud of her very dark skin. This was unheard of among Negroes in those days, especially in Lansing.

I hadn't been sure just what day she would come. And then one afternoon I got home from school and there she was. She hugged me, stood me away, looked me up and down. A commanding woman, maybe even bigger than Mrs. Swerlin, Ella wasn't just black, but like our father, she was jet black. The way she sat, moved, talked, did everything, bespoke somebody who did and got exactly what she wanted. This was the woman my father had boasted of so often for having brought so many of their family out of Georgia to Boston. She owned some property, he would say, and she was "in society." She had come North with nothing, and she had worked and saved and had invested in property that she built up in value, and then she started sending money to Georgia for another sister, brother, cousin, niece or nephew to come north to Boston. All that I had heard was reflected in Ella's appearance and bearing. I had never been so impressed with anybody. She was in her second marriage; her first husband had been a doctor.

Ella asked all kinds of questions about how I was doing; she had already heard from Wilfred and Hilda about my election as class president. She asked especially about my grades, and I ran and got my report cards. I was then one of the three highest in the class. Ella praised me. I asked her about her brother, Earl, and her sister, Mary. She had the exciting news that Earl was a singer with a band in Boston. He was singing under the name of Jimmy Carleton. Mary was also doing well.

Ella told me about other relatives from that branch of the family. A number of them I'd never heard of; she had helped them up from Georgia. They, in their turn, had helped up others. "We Littles have to stick together," Ella said. It thrilled me to hear her say that, and even more, the way she said it. I had become a mascot; our branch of the family was split to pieces; I had just about forgotten about being a Little in any family sense. She said that different members of the family were working in good jobs, and some even had small businesses going. Most of them were homeowners.

When Ella suggested that all of us Littles in Lansing accompany her on a visit to our mother, we all were grateful. We all felt that if anyone could do anything that could help our mother, that might help her get well and come back, it would be Ella. Anyway, all of us, for the first time together, went with Ella to Kalamazoo.

Our mother was smiling when they brought her out. She was extremely surprised when she saw Ella. They made a striking contrast, the thin near-white woman and the big black one hugging each other. I don't remember much about the rest of the visit, except that there was a lot of talking, and Ella had everything in hand, and we left with all of us feeling better than we ever had about the circumstances. I know that for the first time, I felt as though I had visited with someone who had some kind of physical illness that had just lingered on.

A few days later, after visiting the homes where each of us were staying, Ella left Lansing and returned to Boston. But before leaving, she told me to write to her regularly. And she had suggested that I might like to spend my summer holiday visiting her in Boston. I jumped at that chance.

That summer of 1940, in Lansing, I caught the Greyhound bus for Boston with my cardboard suitcase, and wearing my green suit. If someone had hung a sign, "HICK," around my neck, I couldn't have looked much more obvious. They didn't have the turnpikes then; the bus stopped at what seemed every corner and cowpatch. From my seat in—you guessed it—the back of the bus, I gawked out of the window at white man's America rolling past for what seemed a month, but must have been only a day and a half.

When we finally arrived, Ella met me at the terminal and took me home. The house was on Waumbeck Street in the Sugar Hill section of Roxbury, the Harlem of Boston. I met Ella's second husband, Frank, who was now a soldier; and her brother Earl, the singer who called himself Jimmy Carleton; and Mary, who was very different from her older sister. It's funny how I seemed to think of Mary as Ella's sister, instead of her being, just as Ella is, my own half-sister. It's probably because Ella and I always were much closer as basic types; we're dominant people, and Mary has always been mild and quiet, almost shy.

Ella was busily involved in dozens of things. She belonged to I don't know how many different clubs; she was a leading light of local so-called "black society." I saw and met a hundred black people there whose big-city talk and ways left my mouth hanging open.

I couldn't have feigned indifference if I had tried to. People talked casually about Chicago, Detroit, New York. I didn't know the world contained as many Negroes as I saw thronging downtown Roxbury at night, especially on Saturdays. Neon lights, nightclubs, poolhalls, bars, the cars they drove! Restaurants made the streets smell—rich, greasy, down-home black cooking! Jukeboxes blared Erskine Hawkins, Duke Ellington, Cootie Williams, dozens of others. If somebody had told me then that some day I'd know them all personally, I'd have found it hard to believe. The biggest bands, like these, played at the Roseland State Ballroom, on Boston's Massachusetts Avenue—one night for Negroes, the next night for whites.

I saw for the first time occasional black-white couples strolling around arm in arm. And on Sundays, when Ella, Mary, or somebody took me to church, I saw churches for black people such as I had never seen. They were many times finer than the white church I had attended back in Mason, Michigan. There, the white people just sat and worshiped with words; but the Boston Negroes, like all other Negroes I had ever seen at church, threw their souls and bodies wholly into worship.

Two or three times, I wrote letters to Wilfred intended for everybody back in Lansing. I said I'd try to describe it when I got back.

But I found I couldn't.

My restlessness with Mason—and for the first time in my life a restlessness with being around white people—began as soon as I got back home and entered eighth grade.

I continued to think constantly about all that I had seen in Boston, and about the way I had felt there. I know now that it was the sense of being a real part of a mass of my own kind, for the first time.

The white people—classmates, the Swerlins, the people at the restaurant where I worked—noticed the change. They said, "You're acting so strange. You don't seem like yourself, Malcolm. What's the matter?"

I kept close to the top of the class, though. The top-most scholastic standing, I remember, kept shifting between me, a girl named Audrey Slaugh, and a boy named Jimmy Cotton.

It went on that way, as I became increasingly restless and disturbed through the first semester. And then one day, just about when those of us who had passed were about to move up to 8-A, from which we would enter high school the next year, something happened which was to become the first major turning point of my life.

Somehow, I happened to be alone in the classroom with Mr. Ostrowski, my English teacher. He was a tall, rather reddish white man and he had a thick mustache. I had gotten some of my best marks under him, and he had always made me feel that he liked me. He was, as I have mentioned, a natural-born "advisor," about what you ought to read, to do, or think—about any and everything. We used to make unkind jokes about him: why was he teaching in Mason instead of somewhere else, getting for himself some of the "success in life" that he kept telling us how to get?

I know that he probably meant well in what he happened to advise me that day. I doubt that he meant any harm. It was just in his nature as an American white man. I was one of his top students, one of the school's top students—but all he could see for me was the kind of future "in your place" that almost all white people see for black people.

He told me, "Malcolm, you ought to be thinking about a career. Have you been giving it thought?"

The truth is, I hadn't. I never have figured out why I told him, "Well, yes, sir, I've been thinking I'd like to be a lawyer." Lansing certainly had no Negro lawyers—or doctors either—in those days, to hold up an image I might have aspired to. All I really knew for certain was that a lawyer didn't wash dishes, as I was doing.

Mr. Ostrowski looked surprised, I remember, and leaned back in his chair and clasped his hands behind his head. He kind of half-smiled and said, "Malcolm, one of life's first needs is for us to be realistic. Don't misunderstand me, now. We all here like you, you know that. But you've got to be realistic about being a nigger. A lawyer—that's no realistic goal for a nigger. You need to think about something you *can* be. You're good with your hands—making things. Everybody admires your carpentry shop work. Why don't you plan on carpentry? People like you as a person—you'd get all kinds of work."

The more I thought afterwards about what he said, the more uneasy it made me. It just kept treading around in my mind.

What made it really begin to disturb me was Mr. Ostrowski's advice to others in my class—all of them white. Most of them had told him they were planning to become farmers. But those who wanted to strike out on their own, to try something new, he had encouraged. Some, mostly girls, wanted to be teachers. A few wanted other professions, such as one boy who wanted to become a county agent; another, a veterinarian; and one girl wanted to be a nurse. They all reported that Mr. Ostrowski had encouraged what they had wanted. Yet nearly none of them had earned marks equal to mine.

It was a surprising thing that I had never thought of it that way before, but I realized that whatever I wasn't, I *was* smarter than nearly all of those white kids. But apparently I was still not intelligent enough, in their eyes, to become whatever *I* wanted to be.

It was then that I began to change—inside.

I drew away from white people. I came to class, and I answered when called upon. It became a physical strain simply to sit in Mr. Ostrowski's class.

Where "nigger" had slipped off my back before, wherever I heard it now, I stopped and looked at whoever said it. And they looked surprised that I did.

I quit hearing so much "nigger" and "What's wrong?"—which was the way I wanted it. Nobody, including the teachers, could decide what had come over me. I knew I was being discussed.

In a few more weeks, it was that way, too, at the restaurant where I worked washing dishes, and at the Swerlins'.

One day soon after, Mrs. Swerlin called me into the living room, and there was the state man, Maynard Allen. I knew from their faces that something was about to happen. She told me that none of them could understand why—after I had done so well in school, and on my job, and living with them, and after everyone in Mason had come to like me—I had lately begun to make them all feel that I wasn't happy there anymore.

She said she felt there was no need for me to stay at the detention home any longer, and that arrangements had been made for me to go and live with the Lyons family, who liked me so much.

She stood up and put out her hand. "I guess I've asked you a hundred times, Malcolm—do you want to tell me what's wrong?"

I shook her hand, and said, "Nothing, Mrs. Swerlin." Then I went and got my things, and came back down. At the living room door I saw her wiping her eyes. I felt very bad. I thanked her and went out in front to Mr. Allen, who took me over to the Lyons'.

Mr. and Mrs. Lyons, and their children, during the two months I lived with them—while finishing eighth grade—also tried to get me to tell them what was wrong. But somehow I couldn't tell them, either.

I went every Saturday to see my brothers and sisters in Lansing, and almost every other day I wrote to Ella in Boston. Not saying why, I told Ella that I wanted to come there and live.

I don't know how she did it, but she arranged for official custody of me to be transferred from Michigan to Massachusetts, and the very week I finished the eighth grade, I again boarded the Greyhound bus for Boston.

I've thought about that time a lot since then. No physical move in my life has been more pivotal or profound in its repercussions.

If I had stayed on in Michigan, I would probably have married one of those Negro girls I knew and liked in Lansing. I might have become one of those state capitol building shoeshine boys, or a Lansing Country Club waiter, or gotten one of the other menial jobs which, in those days, among Lansing Negroes, would have been considered "successful"—or even become a carpenter.

Whatever I have done since then, I have driven myself to become a success at it. I've often thought that if Mr. Ostrowski had encouraged me to become a lawyer, I would today probably be among some city's professional black bourgeoisie, sipping cocktails and palming myself off as a community spokesman for and leader of the suffering black masses, while my primary concern would be to grab a few more crumbs from the groaning board of the two-faced whites with whom they're begging to "integrate."

All praise is due to Allah that I went to Boston when I did. If I hadn't, I'd probably still be a brainwashed black Christian.

from CHAPTER 17
Mecca

I knew that when my letter* became public knowledge back in America, many would be astounded—loved ones, friends, and enemies alike. And no less astounded would be millions whom I did not know—who had gained during my twelve years with Elijah Muhammad a "hate" image of Malcolm X.

Even I was myself astounded. But there was a precedent in my life for this letter. My whole life had been a chronology of—*changes*.

Here is what I wrote . . . from my heart:

"Never have I witnessed such sincere hospitality and the overwhelming spirit of true brotherhood as is practiced by people of all colors and races here in this Ancient Holy Land, the home of Abraham, Muhammad, and all the other prophets of the Holy Scriptures. For the past week, I have been utterly speechless and spellbound by the graciousness I see displayed all around me by people *of all colors*.

"I have been blessed to visit the Holy City of Mecca. I have made my seven circuits around the Ka'ba, led by a young *Mutawaf* named Muhammad. I drank water from the well of Zem Zem. I ran seven times back and forth between the hills of Mt. Al-Safa and Al-Marwah. I have prayed in the ancient city of Mina, and I have prayed on Mt. Arafat.

"There were tens of thousands of pilgrims, from all over the world. They were

* Malcolm X wrote that he mailed copies of this letter to his wife, his sister Ella, and "others who were very close to me."

of all colors, from blue-eyed blonds to black-skinned Africans. But we were all participating in the same ritual, displaying a spirit of unity and brotherhood that my experiences in America had led me to believe never could exist between the white and the non-white.

"America needs to understand Islam, because this is the one religion that erases from its society the race problem. Throughout my travels in the Muslim world, I have met, talked to, and even eaten with people who in America would have been considered 'white'—but the 'white' attitude was removed from their minds by the religion of Islam. I have never before seen *sincere* and *true* brotherhood practiced by all colors together, irrespective of their color.

"You may be shocked by these words coming from me. But on this pilgrimage, what I have seen, and experienced, has forced me to *re-arrange* much of my thought-patterns previously held, and to *toss aside* some of my previous conclusions. This was not too difficult for me. Despite my firm convictions, I have been always a man who tries to face facts, and to accept the reality of life as new experience and new knowledge unfolds it. I have always kept an open mind, which is necessary to the flexibility that must go hand in hand with every form of intelligent search for truth.

"During the past eleven days here in the Muslim world, I have eaten from the same plate, drunk from the same glass, and slept in the same bed (or on the same rug)—while praying to the *same God*—with fellow Muslims, whose eyes were the bluest of blue, whose hair was the blondest of blond, and whose skin was the whitest of white. And in the *words* and in the *actions* and in the *deeds* of the 'white' Muslims, I felt the same sincerity that I felt among the black African Muslims of Nigeria, Sudan, and Ghana.

"We were *truly* all the same (brothers)—because their belief in one God had removed the 'white' from their *minds,* the 'white' from their *behavior,* and the 'white' from their *attitude.*

"I could see from this, that perhaps if white Americans could accept the Oneness of God, then perhaps, too, they could accept *in reality* the Oneness of Man—and cease to measure, and hinder, and harm others in terms of their 'differences' in color.

"With racism plaguing America like an incurable cancer, the so-called 'Christian' white American heart should be more receptive to a proven solution to such a destructive problem. Perhaps it could be in time to save America from imminent disaster—the same destruction brought upon Germany by racism that eventually destroyed the Germans themselves.

"Each hour here in the Holy Land enables me to have greater spiritual insights into what is happening in America between black and white. The American Negro never can be blamed for his racial animosities—he is only reacting to four hundred years of the conscious racism of the American whites. But as racism leads America up the suicide path, I do believe, from the experiences that I have had with them, that the whites of the younger generation, in the colleges and universities, will see the handwriting on the wall and many of them will turn to the *spiritual* path of *truth*—the *only* way left to America to ward off the disaster that racism inevitably must lead to.

"Never have I been so highly honored. Never have I been made to feel more humble and unworthy. Who would believe the blessings that have been heaped upon an *American Negro?* A few nights ago, a man who would be called in

America a 'white' man, a United Nations diplomat, an ambassador, a companion of kings, gave me *his* hotel suite, *his* bed. By this man, His Excellency Prince Faisal, who rules this Holy Land, was made aware of my presence here in Jedda. The very next morning, Prince Faisal's son, in person, informed me that by the will and decree of his esteemed father, I was to be a State Guest.

"The Deputy Chief of Protocol himself took me before the Hajj Court. His Holiness Sheikh Muhammad Harkon himself okayed my visit to Mecca. His Holiness gave me two books on Islam, with his personal seal and autograph, and he told me that he prayed that I would be a successful preacher of Islam in America. A car, a driver, and a guide, have been placed at my disposal, making it possible for me to travel about this Holy Land almost at will. The government provides air-conditioned quarters and servants in each city that I visit. Never would I have even thought of dreaming that I would ever be a recipient of such honors—honors that in America would be bestowed upon a King—not a Negro.

"All praise is due to Allah, the Lord of all the Worlds.

"Sincerely,

"El-Hajj Malik El-Shabazz
"(Malcolm X)"

CHAPTER 19
1965

I must be honest. Negroes—Afro-Americans—showed no inclination to rush to the United Nations and demand justice for themselves here in America. I really had known in advance that they wouldn't. The American white man has so thoroughly brainwashed the black man to see himself as only a domestic "civil rights" problem that it will probably take longer than I live before the Negro sees that the struggle of the American black man is international.

And I had known, too, that Negroes would not rush to follow me into the orthodox Islam which had given me the insight and perspective to see that the black men and white men truly could be brothers. America's Negroes—especially older Negroes—are too indelibly soaked in Christianity's double standard of oppression.

So, in the "public invited" meetings which I began holding each Sunday afternoon or evening in Harlem's well-known Audubon Ballroom, as I addressed predominantly non-Muslim Negro audiences, I did not immediately attempt to press the Islamic religion, but instead to embrace all who sat before me:

"—not Muslim, nor Christian, Catholic, nor Protestant . . . Baptist nor Methodist, Democrat nor Republican, Mason nor Elk! I mean the black people of America—and the black people all over this earth! Because it is as this collective mass of black people that we have been deprived not only of our civil rights, but even of our human rights, the right to human dignity. . . ."

On the streets, after my speeches, in the faces and the voices of the people I met—even those who would pump my hands and want my autograph—I would feel the wait-and-see attitude. I would feel—and I understood—their uncertainty about where I stood. Since the Civil War's "freedom," the black man has gone down so many fruitless paths. His leaders, very largely, had failed him. The religion of Christianity had failed him. The black man was scarred, he was cautious, he was apprehensive.

I understood it better now than I had before. In the Holy World, away from America's race problem, was the first time I ever had been able to think clearly about the basic divisions of white people in America, and how their attitudes and their motives related to, and affected Negroes. In my thirty-nine years on this earth, the Holy City of Mecca had been the first time I had ever stood before the Creator of All and felt like a complete human being.

In that peace of the Holy World—in fact, the very night . . . when I lay awake surrounded by snoring brother pilgrims—my mind took me back to personal memories I would have thought were gone forever . . . as far back, even, as when I was just a little boy, eight or nine years old. Out behind our house, out in the country from Lansing, Michigan, there was an old, grassy "Hector's Hill," we called it—which may still be there. I remembered there in the Holy World how I used to lie on the top of Hector's Hill, and look up at the sky, at the clouds moving over me, and daydream, all kinds of things. And then, in a funny contrast of recollections, I remembered how years later, when I was in prison, I used to lie on my cell bunk—this would be especially when I was in solitary: what we convicts called "The Hole"—and I would picture myself talking to large crowds. I don't have any idea why such previsions came to me. But they did. To tell that to anyone then would have sounded crazy. Even I didn't have, myself, the slightest inkling. . . .

In Mecca, too, I had played back for myself the twelve years I had spent with Elijah Muhammad as if it were a motion picture. I guess it would be impossible for anyone ever to realize fully how complete was my belief in Elijah Muhammad. I believed in him not only as a leader in the ordinary *human* sense, but also I believed in him as a *divine* leader. I believed he had no human weaknesses or faults, and that, therefore, he could make no mistakes and that he could do no wrong. There on a Holy World hilltop, I realized how very dangerous it is for people to hold any human being in such esteem, especially to consider anyone some sort of "divinely guided" and "protected" person.

My thinking had been opened up wide in Mecca. In the long letters I wrote to friends, I tried to convey to them my new insights into the American black man's struggle and his problems, as well as the depths of my search for truth and justice.

"I've had enough of someone else's propaganda," I had written to these friends. "I'm for truth, no matter who tells it. I'm for justice, no matter who it is for or against. I'm a human being first and foremost, and as such I'm for whoever and whatever benefits humanity *as a whole*."

Largely, the American white man's press refused to convey that I was now attempting to teach Negroes a new direction. With the 1964 "long, hot summer" steadily producing new incidents, I was constantly accused of "stirring up Negroes." Every time I had another radio or television microphone at my mouth, when I was asked about "stirring up Negroes" or "inciting violence," I'd get hot.

"It takes no one to stir up the sociological dynamite that stems from the unemployment, bad housing, and inferior education already in the ghettoes. This explosively criminal condition has existed for so long, it needs no fuse; it fuses itself; it spontaneously combusts from within itself. . . ."

They called me "the angriest Negro in America." I wouldn't deny that charge. I spoke exactly as I felt. "I *believe* in anger. The Bible says there is a *time* for anger." They called me "a teacher, a fomentor of violence." I would say point blank, "That is a lie. I'm not for wanton violence, I'm for justice. I feel that if white people were attacked by Negroes—if the forces of law prove unable, or inadequate, or reluctant to protect those whites from those Negroes—then those white people should protect and defend themselves from those Negroes, using arms if necessary. And I feel that when the law fails to protect Negroes from whites' attack, then those Negroes should use arms, if necessary, to defend themselves."

"Malcolm X Advocates Armed Negroes!"

What was wrong with that? I'll tell you what was wrong. I was a black man talking about physical defense against the white man. The white man can lynch and burn and bomb and beat Negroes—that's all right. "Have patience" . . . "The customs are entrenched" . . . "Things are getting better."

Well, I believe it's a crime for anyone who is being brutalized to continue to accept that brutality without doing something to defend himself. If that's how "Christian" philosophy is interpreted, if that's what Gandhian philosophy teaches, well, then, I will call them criminal philosophies.

I tried in every speech I made to clarify my new position regarding white people—"I don't speak against the sincere, well-meaning, good white people. I have learned that there *are* some. I have learned that not all white people are racists. I am speaking against and my fight is against the white *racists*. I firmly believe that Negroes have the right to fight against these racists, by any means that are necessary."

But the white reporters kept wanting me linked with that word "violence." I doubt if I had one interview without having to deal with that accusation.

"I *am* for violence if non-violence means we continue postponing a solution to the American black man's problem—just to *avoid* violence. I don't go for non-violence if it also means a delayed solution. To me a delayed solution is a non-solution. Or I'll say it another way. If it must take violence to get the black man his human rights in this country, I'm *for* violence exactly as you know the Irish, the Poles, or Jews would be if they were flagrantly discriminated against. I am just as they would be in that case, and they would be for violence—no matter what the consequences, no matter who was hurt by the violence."

White society *hates* to hear anybody, especially a black man, talk about the crime the white man has perpetrated on the black man. I have always understood that's why I have been so frequently called "a revolutionist." It sounds as if *I* have done some crime! Well, it may be the American black man does need to become involved in a *real* revolution. The word for "revolution" in German is *Umwälzung*. What it means is a complete overturn—a complete change. The overthrow of King Farouk in Egypt and the succession of President Nasser is an example of a true revolution. It means the destroying of an old system, and its replacement with a new system. Another example is the Algerian revolution, led by Ben Bella; they threw out the French who had been there over 100 years. So how does anybody sound talking about the Negro in America waging some "revolution"? Yes, he is condemning a system—but he's not trying to overturn the system, or to destroy it. The Negro's so-called "revolt" is merely an asking to be *accepted* into the existing system! A *true* Negro revolt might entail, for instance, fighting for separate black states within this country—which several groups and individuals have advocated, long before Elijah Muhammad came along.

When the white man came into this country, he certainly wasn't demonstrating any "non-violence." In fact, the very man whose name symbolizes non-violence here today has stated:

"Our nation was born in genocide when it embraced the doctrine that the original American, the Indian, was an inferior race. Even before there were large numbers of Negroes on our shores, the scar of racial hatred had already disfigured colonial society. From the sixteenth century forward, blood flowed in battles over racial supremacy. We are perhaps the only nation which tried as a matter of national policy to wipe out its indigenous population. Moreover, we elevated that tragic experience into a noble crusade. Indeed, even today we have not permitted ourselves to reject or to feel remorse for this shameful episode. Our literature, our films, our drama, our folklore all exalt it. Our children are still taught to respect the violence which reduced a red-skinned people of an earlier culture into a few fragmented groups herded into impoverished reservations."

"Peaceful coexistence!" That's another one the white man has always been quick to cry. Fine! But what have been the deeds of the white man? During his entire advance through history, he has been waving the banner of Christianity . . . and carrying in his other hand the sword and the flintlock.

You can go right back to the very beginning of Christianity. Catholicism, the genesis of Christianity as we know it to be presently constituted, with its hierarchy, was conceived in Africa—by those whom the Christian church calls "The Desert Fathers." The Christian church became infected with racism when it entered white Europe. The Christian church returned to Africa under the banner of the Cross—conquering, killing, exploiting, pillaging, raping, bullying, beating—and teaching white supremacy. This is how the white man thrust himself into the position of leadership of the world—through the use of naked physical power. And he was totally inadequate spiritually. Mankind's history has proved from one era to another that the true criterion of leadership is spiritual. Men are attracted by spirit. By power, men are *forced.* Love is engendered by spirit. By power, anxieties are created.

I am in agreement one hundred per cent with those racists who say that no government laws ever can *force* brotherhood. The only true world solution today is governments guided by true religion—of the spirit. Here in race-torn America, I am convinced that the Islam religion is desperately needed, particularly by the American black man. The black man needs to reflect that he has been America's most fervent Christian—and where has it gotten him? In fact, in the white man's hands, in the white man's interpretation . . . where has Christianity brought this *world?*

It has brought the non-white two-thirds of the human population to rebellion. Two-thirds of the human population today is telling the one-third minority white man, "Get out!" And the white man is leaving. And as he leaves, we see the non-white peoples returning in a rush to their original religions, which had been labeled "pagan" by the conquering white man. Only one religion—Islam—had the power to stand and fight the white man's Christianity for a *thousand years!* Only Islam could keep white Christianity at bay.

The Africans are returning to Islam and other indigenous religions. The Asians are returning to being Hindus, Buddhists and Muslims.

As the Christian Crusade once went East, now the Islamic Crusade is going West. With the East—Asia—closed to Christianity, with Africa rapidly being converted to Islam, with Europe rapidly becoming un-Christian, generally today it is accepted that the "Christian" civilization of America—which is propping up the white race around the world—is Christianity's remaining strongest bastion.

Well, if *this* is so—if the so-called "Christianity" now being practiced in America displays the best that world Christianity has left to offer—no one in his right mind should need any much greater proof that very close at hand is the *end* of Christianity.

Are you aware that some Protestant theologians, in their writings, are using the phrase "post-Christian era"—and they mean *now?*

And what is the greatest single reason for this Christian church's failure? It is its failure to combat racism. It is the old "You sow, you reap" story. The Christian church sowed racism—blasphemously; now it reaps racism.

Sunday mornings in this year of grace 1965, imagine the "Christian conscience" of congregations guarded by deacons barring the door to black would-be worshipers, telling them "You can't enter *this* House of God!"

Tell me, if you can, a sadder irony than that St. Augustine, Florida—a city named for the black African saint who saved Catholicism from heresy—was recently the scene of bloody race riots.

I believe that God now is giving the world's so-called "Christian" white society its last opportunity to repent and atone for the crimes of exploiting and enslaving the world's non-white peoples. It is exactly as when God gave Pharaoh a chance to repent. But Pharaoh persisted in his refusal to give justice to those whom he oppressed. And, we know, God finally destroyed Pharaoh.

Is white America really sorry for her crimes against the black people? Does white America have the capacity to repent—and to atone? Does the capacity to repent, to atone, exist in a majority, in one-half, in even one-third of American white society?

Many black men, the victims—in fact most black men—would like to be able to forgive, to forget, the crimes.

But most American white people seem not to have it in them to make any serious atonement—to do justice to the black man.

Indeed, how *can* white society atone for enslaving, for raping, for unmanning, for otherwise brutalizing *millions* of human beings, for centuries? What atonement would the God of Justice demand for the robbery of the black people's labor, their lives, their true identities, their culture, their history—and even their human dignity?

A desegregated cup of coffee, a theater, public toilets—the whole range of hypocritical "integration"—these are not atonement.

After a while in America, I returned abroad—and this time, I spent eighteen weeks in the Middle East and Africa.

The world leaders with whom I had private audiences this time included President Gamal Abdel Nasser, of Egypt; President Julius K. Nyerere, of Tanzania; President Nnamoi Azikiwe, of Nigeria; Osagyefo Dr. Kwame Nkrumah, of Ghana; President Sekou Touré, of Guinea; President Jomo Kenyatta, of Kenya; and Prime Minister Dr. Milton Obote, of Uganda.

I also met with religious leaders—African, Arab, Asian, Muslim, and non-Muslim. And in all of these countries, I talked with Afro-Americans and whites of many professions and backgrounds.

An American white ambassador in one African country was Africa's most respected American ambassador: I'm glad to say that this was told to me by one ranking African leader. We talked for an entire afternoon. Based on what I had heard of him, I had to believe him when he told me that as long as he was on the African continent, he never thought in terms of race, that he dealt with human beings, never noticing their color. He said he was more aware of language differences than of color differences. He said that only when he returned to America would he become aware of color differences.

I told him, "What you are telling me is that it isn't the American white *man* who is a racist, but it's the American political, economic, and social *atmosphere* that automatically nourishes a racist psychology in the white man." He agreed.

We both agreed that American society makes it next to impossible for humans to meet in America and not be conscious of their color differences. And we both agreed that if racism could be removed, America could offer a society where rich and poor could truly live like human beings.

That discussion with the ambassador gave me a new insight—one which I like: that the white man is *not* inherently evil, but America's racist society influences him to act evilly. The society has produced and nourishes a psychology which brings out the lowest, most base part of human beings.

I had a totally different kind of talk with another white man I met in Africa—who, to me, personified exactly what the ambassador and I had discussed. Throughout my trip, I was of course aware that I was under constant surveillance. The agent was a particularly obvious and obnoxious one; I am not sure for what agency, as he never identified it, or I would say it. Anyway, this one finally got under my skin when I found I couldn't seem to eat a meal in the hotel without seeing him somewhere around watching me. You would have thought I was John Dillinger or somebody.

I just got up from my breakfast one morning and walked over to where he was and I told him I knew he was following me, and if he wanted to know anything, why didn't he ask me. He started to give me one of those too-lofty-to-descend-to-you attitudes. I told him then right to his face he was a fool, that he didn't know me, or what I stood for, so that made him one of those people who let somebody else do their thinking; and that no matter what job a man had, at least he ought to be able to think for himself. That stung him; he let me have it.

I was, to hear him tell it, anti-American, un-American, seditious, subversive, and probably Communist. I told him that what he said only proved how little he understood about me. I told him that the only thing the FBI, the CIA, or anybody else could ever find me guilty of, was being open-minded. I said I was seeking for the truth, and I was trying to weigh—objectively—everything on its own merit. I said what I was against was strait-jacketed thinking, and strait-jacketed societies. I said I respected every man's right to believe whatever his intelligence tells him is intellectually sound, and I expect everyone else to respect my right to believe likewise.

This super-sleuth then got off on my "Black Muslim" religious beliefs. I asked him hadn't his headquarters bothered to brief him—that my attitudes and beliefs were changed? I told him that the Islam I believed in now was the Islam which was taught in Mecca—that there was no God but Allah, and that Muhammad ibn Abdullah who lived in the Holy City of Mecca fourteen hundred years ago was the Last Messenger of Allah.

Almost from the first I had been guessing about something; and I took a chance—and I really shook up that "super-sleuth." From the consistent subjectivity in just about every thing he asked and said, I had deduced something, and I told him, "You know, I think you're a Jew with an Anglicized name." His involuntary expression told me I'd hit the button. He asked me how I knew. I told him I'd had so much experience with how Jews would attack me that I usually could identify them. I told him all I held against the Jew was that so many Jews actually were hypocrites in their claim to be friends of the American black man, and it burned me up to be so often called "anti-Semitic" when I spoke things I knew to be the absolute truth about Jews. I told him that, yes, I gave the Jew credit for being among all other whites the most active, and the most vocal, financier, "leader" and "liberal" in the Negro civil rights movement. But I said at the same time I knew that the Jew played these roles for a very careful strategic reason: the more prejudice in America could be focused upon the Negro, then the more the white Gentiles' prejudice would keep diverted off the Jew. I said that to me, one proof that all the civil rights posturing of so many Jews wasn't sincere was that so often in the North the quickest segregationists were Jews themselves. Look at practically everything the black man is trying to "integrate" into for instance; if Jews are not the actual owners, or are not in controlling positions, then they have major stockholdings or they are otherwise in powerful leverage positions—and do they really sincerely exert these influences? No!

And an even clearer proof for me of how Jews truly regard Negroes, I said, was what invariably happened wherever a Negro moved into any white residential neighborhood that was thickly Jewish. Who would always lead the whites' exodus? The Jews! Generally in these situations, some whites stay put—you just notice who they are: they're Irish Catholics, they're Italians; they're rarely ever any Jews. And, ironically, the Jews themselves often still have trouble being "accepted."

Saying this, I know I'll hear "anti-Semitic" from every direction again. Oh, yes! But truth is truth.

Politics dominated the American scene while I was traveling abroad this time. In Cairo and again in Accra, the American press wire services reached me with trans-Atlantic calls, asking whom did I favor, Johnson—or Goldwater?

I said I felt that as far as the American black man was concerned they were both just about the same. I felt that it was for the black man only a question of Johnson, the fox, or Goldwater, the wolf.

"Conservatism" in America's politics means "Let's keep the niggers in their place." And "liberalism" means "Let's keep the *knee*-grows in their place—but tell them we'll treat them a little better; let's fool them more, with more promises." With these choices, I felt that the American black man only needed to choose which one to be eaten by, the "liberal" fox or the "conservative" wolf—because both of them would eat him.

I didn't go for Goldwater any more than for Johnson—except that in a wolf's den, I'd always know exactly where I stood; I'd watch the dangerous wolf closer than I would the smooth, sly fox. The wolf's very growling would keep me alert and fighting him to survive, whereas I *might* be lulled and fooled by the tricky fox. I'll give you an illustration of the fox. When the assassination in Dallas made Johnson President, who was the first person he called for? It was for his best friend, "Dicky"—Richard Russell of Georgia. Civil rights was "a moral issue,"

Johnson was declaring to everybody—while his best friend was the Southern racist who *led* the civil rights opposition. How would some sheriff sound, declaring himself so against bank robbery—and Jesse James his best friend?

Goldwater as a man, I respected for speaking out his true convictions—something rarely done in politics today. He wasn't whispering to racists and smiling at integrationists. I felt Goldwater wouldn't have risked his unpopular stand without conviction. He flatly told black men he wasn't for them—and there is this to consider: always, the black people have advanced further when they have seen they had to rise up against a system that they clearly saw was outright against them. Under the steady lullabys sung by foxy liberals, the Northern Negro became a beggar. But the Southern Negro, facing the honestly snarling white man, rose up to battle that white man for his freedom—long before it happened in the North.

Anyway, I didn't feel that Goldwater was any better for black men than Johnson, or vice-versa. I wasn't in the United States at election time, but if I had been, I wouldn't have put myself in the position of voting for either candidate for the Presidency, or of recommending to any black man to do so. It has turned out that it's Johnson in the White House—and black votes were a major factor in his winning as decisively as he wanted to. If it had been Goldwater, all I am saying is that the black people would at least have known they were dealing with an honestly growling wolf, rather than a fox who could have them half-digested before they even knew what was happening.

I kept having all kinds of troubles trying to develop the kind of Black Nationalist organization I wanted to build for the American Negro. Why Black Nationalism? Well, in the competitive American society, how can there ever be any white-black solidarity before there is first some black solidarity? . . . In my childhood I had been exposed to the Black Nationalist teachings of Marcus Garvey—which, in fact, I had been told had led to my father's murder. Even when I was a follower of Elijah Muhammad, I had been strongly aware of how the Black Nationalist political, economic and social philosophies had the ability to instill within black men the racial dignity, the incentive, and the confidence that the black race needs today to get up off its knees, and to get on its feet, and get rid of its scars, and to take a stand for itself.

One of the major troubles that I was having in building the organization that I wanted—an all-black organization whose ultimate objective was to help create a society in which there could exist honest white-black brotherhood—was that my earlier public image, my old so-called "Black Muslim" image, kept blocking me. I was trying to gradually reshape that image. I was trying to turn a corner, into a new regard by the public, especially Negroes; I was no less angry than I had been, but at the same time the true brotherhood I had seen in the Holy World had influenced me to recognize that anger can blind human vision.

Every free moment I could find, I did a lot of talking to key people whom I knew around Harlem, and I made a lot of speeches, saying: "True Islam taught me that it takes *all* of the religious, political, economic, psychological, and racial ingredients, or characteristics, to make the Human Family and the Human Society complete.

"Since I learned the *truth* in Mecca, my dearest friends have come to include *all* kinds—some Christians, Jews, Buddhists, Hindus, agnostics, and even atheists! I have friends who are called capitalists, Socialists, and Communists! Some of my friends are moderates, conservatives, extremists—some are even Uncle Toms! My friends today are black, brown, red, yellow and *white!*"

I said to Harlem street audiences that only when mankind would submit to the One God who created all—only then would mankind even approach the "peace" of which so much *talk* could be heard . . . but toward which so little *action* was seen.

I said that on the American racial level, we had to approach the black man's struggle against the white man's racism as a human problem, that we had to forget hypocritical politics and propaganda. I said that both races, as human beings, had the obligation, the responsibility, of helping to correct America's human problem. The well-meaning white people, I said, had to combat, actively and directly, the racism in other white people. And the black people had to build within themselves much greater awareness that along with equal rights there had to be the bearing of equal responsibilities.

I knew, better than most Negroes, how many white people truly wanted to see American racial problems solved. I knew that many whites were as frustrated as Negroes. I'll bet I got fifty letters some days from white people. The white people in meeting audiences would throng around me, asking me, after I had addressed them somewhere, "What *can* a sincere white person do?"

When I say that here now, it makes me think about [a] . . . co-ed . . . who flew from her New England college down to New York and came up to me in the Nation of Islam's restaurant in Harlem, and I told her that there was "nothing" she could do. I regret that I told her that. I wish that now I knew her name, or where I could telephone her, or write to her, and tell her what I tell white people now when they present themselves as being sincere, and ask me, one way or another, the same thing she asked.

The first thing I tell them is that at least where my own particular Black Nationalist organization, the Organization of Afro-American Unity, is concerned, they can't *join* us. I have these very deep feelings that white people who want to join black organizations are really just taking the escapist way to salve their consciences. By visibly hovering near us, they are "proving" that they are "with us." But the hard truth is this *isn't* helping to solve America's racist problem. The Negroes aren't the racists. Where the really sincere white people have got to do their "proving" of themselves is not among the black *victims,* but out on the battle lines of where America's racism really *is*—and that's in their own home communities; America's racism is among their own fellow whites. That's where the sincere whites who really mean to accomplish something have got to work.

Aside from that, I mean nothing against any sincere whites when I say that as members of black organizations, generally whites' very presence subtly renders the black organization automatically less effective. Even the best white members will slow down the Negroes' discovery of what they need to do, and particularly of what they can do—for themselves, working by themselves, among their own kind, in their own communities.

I sure don't want to hurt anybody's feelings, but in fact I'll even go so far as to say that I never really trust the kind of white people who are always so anxious to hang around Negroes, or to hang around in Negro communities. I don't trust the kind of whites who love having Negroes always hanging around them. I don't know—this feeling may be a throwback to the years when I was hustling in Harlem and all of those red-faced, drunk whites in the afterhours clubs were always grabbing hold of some Negroes and talking about "I just want you to know you're just as good as I am—." And then they got back in their taxicabs and black limousines and went back downtown to the places where they lived and worked, where no blacks except servants had better get caught. But, anyway, I know that every time that whites join a black organization, you watch, pretty soon the blacks will be leaning on the whites to support it, and before you know it a black may be up front with a title, but the whites, because of their money, are the real controllers.

I tell sincere white people, "Work in conjunction with us—each of us working among our own kind." Let sincere white individuals find all other white people they can who feel as they do—and let them form their own all-white groups, to work trying to convert other white people who are thinking and acting so racist. Let sincere whites go and teach non-violence to white people!

We will completely respect our white co-workers. They will deserve every credit. We will give them every credit. We will meanwhile be working among our own kind, in our own black communities—showing and teaching black men in ways that only other black men can—that the black man has got to help himself. Working separately, the sincere white people and sincere black people actually will be working together.

In our mutual sincerity we might be able to show a road to the salvation of America's very soul. It can only be salvaged if human rights and dignity, in full, are extended to black men. Only such real, meaningful actions as those which are sincerely motivated from a deep sense of humanism and moral responsibility can get at the basic causes that produce the racial explosions in America today. Otherwise, the racial explosions are only going to grow worse. Certainly nothing is ever going to be solved by throwing upon me and other so-called black "extremists" and "demagogues" the blame for the racism that is in America.

Sometimes, I have dared to dream to myself that one day, history may even say that my voice—which disturbed the white man's smugness, and his arrogance, and his complacency—that my voice helped to save America from a grave, possibly even a fatal catastrophe.

The goal has always been the same, with the approaches to it as different as mine and Dr. Martin Luther King's non-violent marching, that dramatizes the brutality and the evil of the white man against defenseless blacks. And in the racial climate of this country today, it is anybody's guess which of the "extremes" in approach to the black man's problems might *personally* meet a fatal catastrophe first—"non-violent" Dr. King, or so-called "violent" me.

Anything I do today, I regard as urgent. No man is given but so much time to accomplish whatever is his life's work. My life in particular never has stayed fixed in one position for very long. You have seen how throughout my life, I have often known unexpected drastic changes.

I am only facing the facts when I know that any moment of any day, or any night, could bring me death. This is particularly true since the last trip that I made abroad. I have seen the nature of things that are happening, and I have heard things from sources which are reliable.

To speculate about dying doesn't disturb me as it might some people. I never have felt that I would live to become an old man. Even before I was a Muslim—when I was a hustler in the ghetto jungle, and then a criminal in prison, it always stayed on my mind that I would die a violent death. In fact, it runs in my family. My father and most of his brothers died by violence—my father because of what he believed in. To come right down to it, if I take the kind of things in which I believe, then add to that the kind of temperament that I have, plus the one hundred per cent dedication I have to whatever I believe in—these are ingredients which make it just about impossible for me to die of old age.

I have given to this [autobiography] so much of whatever time I have because I feel, and I hope, that if I honestly and fully tell my life's account, read objectively it might prove to be a testimony of some social value.

I think that an objective reader may see how in the society to which I was exposed as a black youth here in America, for me to wind up in a prison was really just about inevitable. It happens to so many thousands of black youth.

I think that an objective reader may see how when I heard "The white man is the devil," when I played back what had been my own experiences, it was inevitable that I would respond positively; then the next twelve years of my life were devoted and dedicated to propagating that phrase among the black people.

I think, I hope, that the objective reader, in following my life—the life of only one ghetto-created Negro—may gain a better picture and understanding than he has previously had of the black ghettoes which are shaping the lives and the thinking of almost all of the 22 million Negroes who live in America.

Thicker each year in these ghettoes is the kind of teen-ager that I was—with the wrong kinds of heroes, and the wrong kinds of influences. I am not saying that all of them become the kind of parasite that I was. Fortunately, by far most do not. But still, the small fraction who do add up to an annual total of more and more costly, dangerous youthful criminals. The FBI not long ago released a report of a shocking rise in crime each successive year since the end of World War II—ten to twelve per cent each year. The report did not say so in so many words, but I am saying that the majority of that crime increase is annually spawned in the black ghettoes which the American racist society permits to exist. In the 1964 "long, hot summer" riots in major cities across the United States, the socially disinherited black ghetto youth were always at the forefront.

In this year, 1965, I am certain that more—and worse—riots are going to erupt, in yet more cities, in spite of the conscience-salving Civil Rights Bill. The reason is that the *cause* of these riots, the racist malignancy in America, has been too long unattended.

I believe that it would be almost impossible to find anywhere in America a black man who has lived further down in the mud of human society than I have; or a black man who has been any more ignorant than I have been; or a black man who has suffered more anguish during his life than I have. But it is only after the deepest darkness that the greatest joy can come; it is only after slavery and prison that the sweetest appreciation of freedom can come.

For the freedom of my 22 million black brothers and sisters here in America, I do believe that I have fought the best that I knew how, and the best that I could, with the shortcomings that I have had. I know that my shortcomings are many.

My greatest lack has been, I believe, that I don't have the kind of academic education I wish I had been able to get—to have been a lawyer, perhaps. I do believe that I might have made a good lawyer. I have always loved verbal battle, and challenge. You can believe me that if I had the time right now, I would not be one bit ashamed to go back into any New York City public school and start where I left off at the ninth grade, and go on through a degree. Because I don't begin to be academically equipped for so many of the interests that I have. For instance, I love languages. I wish I were an accomplished linguist. I don't know anything more frustrating than to be around people talking something you can't understand. Especially when they are people who look just like you. In Africa, I heard original mother tongues, such as Hausa, and Swahili, being spoken, and there I was standing like some little boy, waiting for someone to tell me what had been said; I never will forget how ignorant I felt.

Aside from the basic African dialects, I would try to learn Chinese, because it looks as if Chinese will be the most powerful political language of the future. And already I have begun studying Arabic, which I think is going to be the most powerful spiritual language of the future.

I would just like to *study.* I mean ranging study, because I have a wide-open mind. I'm interested in almost any subject you can mention. I know this is the reason I have come to really like, as individuals, some of the hosts of radio or television panel programs I have been on, and to respect their minds—because even if they have been almost steadily in disagreement with me on the race issue, they still have kept their minds open and objective about the truths of things happening in this world. Irv Kupcinet in Chicago, and Barry Farber, Barry Gray and Mike Wallace in New York—people like them. They also let me see that they respected my mind—in a way I know they never realized. The way I knew was that often they would invite my opinion on subjects off the race issue. Sometimes, after the programs, we would sit around and talk about all kinds of things, current events and other things, for an hour or more. You see, most whites, even when they credit a Negro with some intelligence, will still feel that all he can talk about is the race issue; most whites never feel that Negroes can contribute anything to other areas of thought, and ideas. You just notice how rarely you will ever hear whites asking any Negroes what they think about the problem of world health, or the space race to land men on the moon.

Every morning when I wake up, now, I regard it as having another borrowed day. In any city, wherever I go, making speeches, holding meetings of my organization, or attending to other business, black men are watching every move I make, awaiting their chance to kill me. I have said publicly many times that I know that they have their orders. Anyone who chooses not to believe what I am saying doesn't know the Muslims in the Nation of Islam.

But I am also blessed with faithful followers who are, I believe, as dedicated to me as I once was to Mr. Elijah Muhammad. Those who would hunt a man need to remember that a jungle also contains those who hunt the hunters.

I know, too, that I could suddenly die at the hands of some white racists. Or I could die at the hands of some Negro hired by the white man. Or it could be some brainwashed Negro acting on his own idea that by eliminating me he would be helping out the white man, because I talk about the white man the way I do.

Anyway, now, each day I live as if I am already dead, and I tell you what I would like for you to do. When I *am* dead—I say it that way because from the things I *know,* I do not expect to live long enough to read this [autobiography] in its finished form—I want you just to watch and see if I'm not right in what I say: that the white man, in his press, is going to identify me with "hate."

He will make use of me dead, as he has made use of me alive, as a convenient symbol of "hatred"—and that will help him to escape facing the truth that all I have been doing is holding up a mirror to reflect, to show, the history of unspeakable crimes that his race has committed against my race.

You watch. I will be labeled as, at best, an "irresponsible" black man. I have always felt about this accusation that the black "leader" whom white men consider to be "'responsible" is invariably the black "leader" who never gets any results. You only get action as a black man if you are regarded by the white man as "irresponsible." In fact, this much I had learned when I was just a little boy. And since I have been some kind of a "leader" of black people here in the racist society of America, I have been more reassured each time the white man resisted me, or attacked me harder—because each time made me more certain that I was on the right track in the American black man's best interests. The racist white man's opposition automatically made me know that I did offer the black man something worthwhile.

Yes, I have cherished my "demagogue" role. I know that societies often have killed the people who have helped to change those societies. And if I can die having brought any light, having exposed any meaningful truth that will help to destroy the racist cancer that is malignant in the body of America—then, all of the credit is due to Allah. Only the mistakes have been mine.

Maya Angelou (1928–)

A*n author of poetry, screenplays, children's books, and autobiography, Maya Angelou says she writes "for the Black voice and any ear which can hear it. As a composer writes for musical instruments and a choreographer creates for the body, I search for sound, tempos, and rhythms to ride through the vocal cord over the tongue and out the lips of Black people. . . . I write because I am a Black woman, listening attentively to her talking people." Angelou made history on January 20, 1993, when she became the first African American poet to write and read for the inauguration ceremonies of a U.S. president. Americans nationwide listened to her reading of "On the Pulse of Morning," the poem she wrote for the occasion, and to her call to the nation to celebrate and respect voices from different ethnic groups, social classes, and generations.*

Born Marguerite Johnson in St. Louis, Missouri, Angelou lived her early life in Stamps, Arkansas, where she was raised by a religious grandmother. At the age of eight, while visiting her mother in St. Louis, Angelou was raped by her mother's male friend, and the experience sent the child into a traumatic five-year silence. By sixteen, Angelou was living with her mother in California and discovering the responsibilities of motherhood herself.

Angelou went on to become an actress, dancer, and singer. She joined the civil rights movement, serving as a coordinator in the Southern Christian Leadership Conference (SCLC). She also worked as a reporter, editor, and administrator in Cairo and as an administrative assistant at the University of Ghana. She has taught in the California State University system, at Wichita State University, and at Wake Forest University.

Although the multitalented Angelou has written and directed theatrical plays and written television scripts and poetry, she made her initial impact as a writer with the five volumes of her autobiography: I Know Why the Caged Bird Sings

(1970), Gather Together in My Name *(1974),* Swingin' and Singin' and Gettin' Merry like Christmas *(1976),* The Heart of a Woman *(1981), and* All God's Children Need Travelin' Shoes *(1986).*

Her other publications include two children's books, Life Doesn't Frighten Me *(1993) and* Souls Look Back in Wonder *(1994), and several collections of poems:* Just Give Me a Cool Drink of Water 'fore I Die *(1971),* Oh Pray My Wings Are Gonna Fit Me Well *(1975),* And Still I Rise *(1978),* Shaker, Why Don't You Sing *(1983),* Now Sheba Sings the Song *(1987),* I Shall Not Be Moved *(1990), and* Wouldn't Take Nothing for My Journey Now *(1993). Her screenplay,* Georgia, Georgia *(1972), was followed by the television movie scripts for* I Know Why the Caged Bird Sings *(1978),* Sister, Sister *(1982), and* Blacks, Blues, Blacks *(1979), a public television miniseries.*

The following selection comes from I Know Why the Caged Bird Sings, *which documents the first sixteen years of Angelou's life, including her experiences with racism in the South, the trauma of sexual assault, and sexual awakening and motherhood as an adolescent.*

from I Know Why the Caged Bird Sings

CHAPTER 1

When I was three and Bailey four, we had arrived in the musty little town, wearing tags on our wrists which instructed—"To Whom It May Concern"—that we were Marguerite and Bailey Johnson Jr., from Long Beach, California, en route to Stamps, Arkansas, c/o Mrs. Annie Henderson.

Our parents had decided to put an end to their calamitous marriage, and Father shipped us home to his mother. A porter had been charged with our welfare—he got off the train the next day in Arizona—and our tickets were pinned to my brother's inside coat pocket.

I don't remember much of the trip, but after we reached the segregated southern part of the journey, things must have looked up. Negro passengers, who always traveled with loaded lunch boxes, felt sorry for "the poor little motherless darlings" and plied us with cold fried chicken and potato salad.

Years later I discovered that the United States had been crossed thousands of times by frightened Black children traveling alone to their newly affluent parents in Northern cities, or back to grandmothers in Southern towns when the urban Negro reneged on its economic promises.

The town reacted to us as its inhabitants had reacted to all things new before our coming. It regarded us a while without curiosity but with caution, and after we were seen to be harmless (and children) it closed in around us, as a real mother embraces a stranger's child. Warmly, but not too familiarly.

We lived with our grandmother and uncle in the rear of the Store (it was always spoken of with a capital *s*), which she had owned some twenty-five years.

Early in the century, Momma (we soon stopped calling her Grandmother) sold lunches to the sawmen in the lumberyard (east Stamps) and the seedmen at the cotton gins (west Stamps). Her crisp meat pies and cool lemonade, when joined to her miraculous ability to be in two places at the same time, assured her business success. From being a mobile lunch counter, she set up a stand between the two points of fiscal interest and supplied the workers' needs for a few years. Then she had the Store built in the heart of the Negro area. Over the years it became the lay center of activities in town. On Saturdays, barbers sat their customers in the shade on the porch of the Store, and troubadours on their ceaseless crawlings through the South leaned across its benches and sang their sad songs of The Brazos while they played juice harps and cigar-box guitars.

The formal name of the Store was the Wm. Johnson General Merchandise Store. Customers could find food staples, a good variety of colored thread, mash for hogs, corn for chickens, coal oil for lamps, light bulbs for the wealthy, shoestrings, hair dressing, balloons, and flower seeds. Anything not visible had only to be ordered. . . .

CHAPTER 6

Reverend Howard Thomas was the presiding elder over a district in Arkansas that included Stamps. Every three months he visited our church, stayed at Momma's over the Saturday night and preached a loud passionate sermon on Sunday. He collected the money that had been taken in over the preceding months, heard reports from all the church groups and shook hands with the adults and kissed all small children. Then he went away. (I used to think that he went west to heaven, but Momma straightened me out. He just went to Texarkana.)

Bailey and I hated him unreservedly. He was ugly, fat, and he laughed like a hog with the colic. We were able to make each other burst with giggling when we did imitations of the thick-skinned preacher. Bailey was especially good at it. He could imitate Reverend Thomas right in front of Uncle Willie and never get caught because he did it soundlessly. He puffed out his cheeks until they looked like wet brown stones, and wobbled his head from side to side. Only he and I knew it, but that was old Reverend Thomas to a tee.

His obesity, while disgusting, was not enough to incur the intense hate that we felt for him. The fact that he never bothered to remember our names was insulting, but neither was that slight, alone, enough to make us despise him. But the crime that tipped the scale and made our hate not only just but imperative was his actions at the dinner table. He ate the biggest, brownest and best parts of the chicken at every Sunday meal.

The only good thing about his visits was the fact that he always arrived late on Saturday nights, after we had had dinner. I often wondered if he tried to catch us at the table. I believe so, for when he reached the front porch his little eyes would glitter toward the empty dining room and his face would fall with disappointment. Then immediately, a thin curtain would fall over his features and he'd laugh a few barks, "Uh, huh, uh, huh, Sister Henderson, just like a penny with a hole in it, I always turn up."

Right on cue every time, Momma would answer, "That's right, Elder Thomas, thank the blessed Jesus, come right in."

He'd step in the front door and put down his Gladstone (that's what he called it) and look around for Bailey and me. Then he opened his awful arms and groaned, "Suffer little children to come unto me, for such is the Kingdom of Heaven."

Bailey went to him each time with his hand stretched out, ready for a manly handshake, but Reverend Thomas would push away the hand and encircle my brother for a few seconds. "You still a boy, buddy. Remember that. They tell me the Good Book say, 'When I was a child I spake as a child, I thought as a child, but when I became a man, I put away childish things.' " Only then would he open his arms and release Bailey.

I never had the nerve to go up to him. I was quite afraid that if I tried to say, "Hello, Reverend Thomas," I would choke on the sin of mocking him. After all, the Bible did say, "God is not mocked," and the man was God's representative. He used to say to me, "Come on, little sister. Come and get this blessing." But I was so afraid and I also hated him so much that my emotions mixed themselves up and it was enough to start me crying. Momma told him time after time, "Don't pay her no mind, Elder Thomas, you know how tender-hearted she is."

He ate the leftovers from our dinner and he and Uncle Willie discussed the developments of the church programs. They talked about how the present minister was attending to his flock, who got married, who died and how many children had been born since his last visit.

Bailey and I stood like shadows in the rear of the Store near the coal-oil tank, waiting for the juicy parts. But when they were ready to talk about the latest scandal, Momma sent us to her bedroom with warnings to have our Sunday School lesson perfectly memorized or we knew what we could expect.

We had a system that never failed. I would sit in the big rocking chair by the stove and rock occasionally and stamp my feet. I changed voices, now soft and girlish, then a little deeper like Bailey's. Meanwhile, he would creep back into the Store. Many times he came flying back to sit on the bed and to hold the open lesson book just before Momma suddenly filled the doorway.

"You children get your lesson good, now. You know all the other children looks up to you all." Then, as she turned back into the Store Bailey followed right on her footsteps to crouch in the shadows and listen for the forbidden gossip.

Once, he heard how Mr. Coley Washington had a girl from Lewisville staying in his house. I didn't think that was so bad, but Bailey explained that Mr. Washington was probably "doing it" to her. He said that although "it" was bad just about everybody in the world did it to somebody, but no one else was supposed to know that. And once, we found out about a man who had been killed by whitefolks and thrown into the pond. Bailey said the man's things had been cut off and put in his pocket and he had been shot in the head, all because the whitefolks said he did "it" to a white woman.

Because of the kinds of news we filched from those hushed conversations, I was convinced that whenever Reverend Thomas came and Momma sent us to the back room they were going to discuss whitefolks and "doing it." Two subjects about which I was very dim.

On Sunday mornings Momma served a breakfast that was geared to hold us quiet from 9:30 A.M. to 3 P.M. She fried thick pink slabs of home-cured ham and poured the grease over sliced red tomatoes. Eggs over easy, fried potatoes and onions, yellow hominy and crisp perch fried so hard we would pop them in our mouths and chew bones, fins and all. Her cathead biscuits were at least three inches in diameter and two inches thick. The trick to eating catheads was to get the butter on them before they got cold—then they were delicious. When, unluckily, they were allowed to get cold, they tended to a gooeyness, not unlike a wad of tired gum.

We were able to reaffirm our findings on the catheads each Sunday that

Reverend Thomas spent with us. Naturally enough, he was asked to bless the table. We would all stand; my uncle, leaning his walking stick against the wall, would lean his weight on the table. Then Reverend Thomas would begin. "Blessed Father, we thank you this morning . . ." and on and on and on. I'd stop listening after a while until Bailey kicked me and then I cracked my lids to see what had promised to be a meal that would make any Sunday proud. But as the Reverend droned on and on and on to a God who I thought must be bored to hear the same things over and over again, I saw that the ham grease had turned white on the tomatoes. The eggs had withdrawn from the edge of the platter to bunch in the center like children left out in the cold. And the catheads had sat down on themselves with the conclusiveness of a fat woman sitting in an easy chair. And still he talked on. When he finally stopped, our appetites were gone, but he feasted on the cold food with a non-talking but still noisy relish.

In the Christian Methodist Episcopal Church the children's section was on the right, cater-cornered from the pew that held those ominous women called the Mothers of the Church. In the young people's section the benches were placed close together, and when a child's legs no longer comfortably fitted in the narrow space, it was an indication to the elders that that person could now move into the intermediate area (center church). Bailey and I were allowed to sit with the other children only when there were informal meetings, church socials or the like. But on the Sundays when Reverend Thomas preached, it was ordained that we occupy the first row, called the mourners' bench. I thought we were placed in front because Momma was proud of us, but Bailey assured me that she just wanted to keep her grandchildren under her thumb and eye.

Reverend Thomas took his text from Deuteronomy. And I was stretched between loathing his voice and wanting to listen to the sermon. Deuteronomy was my favorite book in the Bible. The laws were so absolute, so clearly set down, that I knew if a person truly wanted to avoid hell and brimstone, and being roasted forever in the devil's fire, all she had to do was memorize Deuteronomy and follow its teaching, word for word. I also liked the way the word rolled off the tongue.

Bailey and I sat alone on the front bench, the wooden slats pressing hard on our behinds and the backs of our thighs. I would have wriggled just a bit, but each time I looked over at Momma, she seemed to threaten, "Move and I'll tear you up," so, obedient to the unvoiced command, I sat still. The church ladies were warming up behind me with a few hallelujahs and Praise the Lords and Amens, and the preacher hadn't really moved into the meat of the sermon.

It was going to be a hot service.

On my way into church, I saw Sister Monroe, her open-faced gold crown glinting when she opened her mouth to return a neighborly greeting. She lived in the country and couldn't get to church every Sunday, so she made up for her absences by shouting so hard when she did make it that she shook the whole church. As soon as she took her seat, all the ushers would move to her side of the church because it took three women and sometimes a man or two to hold her.

Once when she hadn't been to church for a few months (she had taken off to have a child), she got the spirit and started shouting, throwing her arms around and jerking her body, so that the ushers went over to hold her down, but she tore herself away from them and ran up to the pulpit. She stood in front of the altar, shaking like a freshly caught trout. She screamed at Reverend Taylor. "Preach it. I say, preach it." Naturally he kept on preaching as if she wasn't standing there telling him what to do. Then she screamed an extremely fierce, "I said, preach it" and stepped up on the altar. The Reverend kept on throwing out phrases like home-run balls and Sister Monroe made a quick break and grasped for him. For just a second, everything and everyone in the church except Reverend Taylor and Sister Monroe hung loose like stockings on a washline. Then she caught the minister by the sleeve of his jacket and his coattail, then she rocked him from side to side.

I have to say this for our minister, he never stopped giving us the lesson. The usher board made its way to the pulpit, going up both aisles with a little more haste than is customarily seen in church. Truth to tell, they fairly ran to the minister's aid. Then two of the deacons, in their shiny Sunday suits, joined the ladies in white on the pulpit, and each time they pried Sister Monroe loose from the preacher he took another deep breath and kept on preaching, and Sister Monroe grabbed him in another place, and more firmly. Reverend Taylor was helping his rescuers as much as possible by jumping around when he got a chance. His voice at one point got so low it sounded like a roll of thunder, then Sister Monroe's "Preach it" cut through the roar, and we all wondered (I did, in any case) if it would ever end. Would they go on forever, or get tired out at last like a game of blindman's bluff that lasted too long, with nobody caring who was "it"?

I'll never know what might have happened, because magically the pandemonium spread. The spirit infused Deacon Jackson and Sister Willson, the chairman of the usher board, at the same time. Deacon Jackson, a tall, thin, quiet man, who was also a part-time Sunday school teacher, gave a scream like a falling tree, leaned back on thin air and punched Reverend Taylor on the arm. It must have hurt as much as it caught the Reverend unawares. There was a moment's break in the rolling sounds and Reverend Taylor jerked around surprised, and hauled off and punched Deacon Jackson. In the same second Sister Willson caught his tie, looped it over her fist a few times, and pressed down on him. There wasn't time to laugh or cry before all three of them were down on the floor behind the altar. Their legs spiked out like kindling wood.

Sister Monroe, who had been the cause of all the excitement, walked off the dais, cool and spent, and raised her flinty voice in the hymn, "I came to Jesus, as I was, worried, wound, and sad, I found in Him a resting place and He has made me glad."

The minister took advantage of already being on the floor and asked in a choky little voice if the church would kneel with him to offer a prayer of thanksgiving. He said we had been visited with a mighty spirit, and let the whole church say Amen.

On the next Sunday, he took his text from the eighteenth chapter of the Gospel according to St. Luke, and talked quietly but seriously about the Pharisees, who prayed in the streets so that the public would be impressed with their religious devotion. I doubt that anyone got the message—certainly not those to whom it was directed. The deacon board, however, did appropriate funds for him to buy a new suit. The other was a total loss.

Our presiding elder had heard the story of Reverend Taylor and Sister Monroe, but I was sure he didn't know her by sight. So my interest in the service's potential and my aversion to Reverend Thomas caused me to turn him off. Turning off or tuning out people was my highly developed art. The custom of letting obedient children be seen but heard was so agreeable to me that I went one step further: Obedient children should not see or hear if they chose not to do so. I laid a handful of attention on my face and tuned up the sounds in the church.

Sister Monroe's fuse was already lit, and she sizzled somewhere to the right behind me. Elder Thomas jumped into the sermon, determined, I suppose, to give the members what they came for. I saw the ushers from the left side of the church near the big windows begin to move discreetly, like pallbearers, toward Sister Monroe's bench. Bailey jogged my knee. When the incident with Sister Monroe, which we always called simply "the incident," had taken place, we had been too astounded to laugh. But for weeks after, all we needed to send us into violent outbursts of laughter was a whispered "Preach it." Anyway, he pushed my knee, covered his mouth and whispered, "I say, preach it."

I looked toward Momma, across that square of stained boards, over the collection table, hoping that a look from her would root me safely to my sanity. But for the first time in memory Momma was staring behind me at Sister Monroe. I supposed that she was counting on bringing that emotional lady up short with a severe look or two. But Sister Monroe's voice had already reached the danger point. "Preach it!"

There were a few smothered giggles from the children's section, and Bailey nudged me again. "I say, preach it"—in a whisper. Sister Monroe echoed him loudly, "I say, preach it!"

Two deacons wedged themselves around Brother Jackson as a preventive measure and two large determined-looking men walked down the aisle toward Sister Monroe.

While the sounds in the church were increasing, Elder Thomas made the regrettable mistake of increasing his volume too. Then suddenly, like a summer rain, Sister Monroe broke through the cloud of people trying to hem her in, and flooded up to the pulpit. She didn't stop this time but continued immediately to the altar, bound for Elder Thomas, crying "I say, preach it."

Bailey said out loud, "Hot dog" and "Damn" and "She's going to beat his butt."

But Reverend Thomas didn't intend to wait for that eventuality, so as Sister Monroe approached the pulpit from the right he started descending from the left. He was not intimidated by his change of venue. He continued preaching and moving. He finally stopped right in front of the collection table, which put him almost in our laps, and Sister Monroe rounded the altar on his heels, followed by the deacons, ushers, some unofficial members and a few of the bigger children.

Just as the elder opened his mouth, pink tongue waving, and said, "Great God of Mount Nebo," Sister Monroe hit him on the back of his head with her purse. Twice. Before he could bring his lips together, his teeth fell, no, actually his teeth jumped, out of his mouth.

The grinning uppers and lowers lay by my right shoe, looking empty and at the same time appearing to contain all the emptiness in the world. I could have stretched out a foot and kicked them under the bench or behind the collection table.

Sister Monroe was struggling with his coat, and the men had all but picked her up to remove her from the building. Bailey pinched me and said without moving his lips, "I'd like to see him eat dinner now."

I looked at Reverend Thomas desperately. If he appeared just a little sad or embarrassed, I could feel sorry for him and wouldn't be able to laugh. My sympathy for him would keep me from laughing. I dreaded laughing in church. If I lost control, two things were certain to happen. I would surely pee, and just as surely get a whipping. And this time I would probably die because everything was funny—Sister Monroe, and Momma trying to keep her quiet with those threatening looks, and Bailey whispering "Preach it" and Elder Thomas with his lips flapping loose like tired elastic.

But Reverend Thomas shrugged off Sister Monroe's weakening clutch, pulled out an extra-large white handkerchief and spread it over his nasty little teeth. Putting them in his pocket, he gummed, "Naked I came into the world, and naked I shall go out."

Bailey's laugh had worked its way up through his body and was escaping through his nose in short hoarse snorts. I didn't try any longer to hold back the laugh, I just opened my mouth and released sound. I heard the first titter jump up in the air over my head, over the pulpit and out the window. Momma said out loud, "Sister!" but the bench was greasy and I slid off onto the floor. There was more laughter in me trying to get out. I didn't know there was that much in the whole world. It pressed at all my body openings, forcing everything in its path. I cried and hollered, passed gas and urine. I didn't see Bailey descend to the floor, but I rolled over once and he was kicking and screaming too. Each time we looked at each other we howled louder than before, and though he tried to say something, the laughter attacked him and he was only able to get out "I say, preach." And then I rolled over onto Uncle Willie's rubber-tipped cane. My eyes followed the cane up to his good brown hand on the curve and up the long, long white sleeve to his face. The one side pulled down as it usually did when he cried (it also pulled down when he laughed). He stuttered, "I'm gonna whip you this time myself."

I have no memory of how we got out of church and into the parsonage next door, but in that overstuffed parlor, Bailey and I received the whipping of our lives. Uncle Willie ordered us between licks to stop crying. I tried to, but Bailey refused to cooperate. Later he explained that when a person is beating you you should scream as loud as possible; maybe the whipper will become embarrassed or else some sympathetic soul might come to your rescue. Our savior came for neither of these reasons, but because Bailey yelled so loud and disturbed what was left of the service, the minister's wife came out and asked Uncle Willie to quiet us down.

Laughter so easily turns to hysteria for imaginative children. I felt for weeks after that I had been very, very sick, and until I completely recovered my strength I stood on laughter's cliff and any funny thing could hurl me off to my death far below.

Each time Bailey said "Preach it" to me, I hit him as hard as I could and cried.

CHAPTER 35

The Well of Loneliness was my introduction to lesbianism and what I thought of as pornography. For months the book was both a treat and a threat. It allowed me to see a little of the mysterious world of the pervert. It stimulated my libido and I told myself that it was educational because it informed me of the difficulties in the secret of the pervert. I was certain that I didn't know any perverts. Of course I ruled out the jolly sissies who sometimes stayed at our house and cooked whopping eight-course dinners while the perspiration made paths down their made-up faces. Since everyone accepted them, and more particularly since they accepted themselves, I knew that their laughter was real and that their lives were cheerful comedies, interrupted only by costume changes and freshening of make-up.

But true freaks, the "women lovers," captured yet strained my imagination. They were, according to the book, disowned by their families, snubbed by their friends and ostracized from every society. This bitter punishment was inflicted upon them because of a physical condition over which they had no control.

After my third reading of *The Well of Loneliness* I became a bleeding heart for the downtrodden misunderstood lesbians. I thought "lesbian" was synonymous with hermaphrodite, and when I wasn't actively aching over their pitiful state, I was wondering how they managed simpler body functions. Did they have a choice of organs to use, and if so, did they alternate or play favorite? Or I tried to imagine how two hemaphrodites made love, and the more I pondered the more confused I became. It seemed that having two of everything other people had, and four where ordinary people just had two, would complicate matters to the point of giving up the idea of making love at all.

It was during this reflective time that I noticed how heavy my own voice had become. It droned and drummed two or three whole tones lower than my schoolmates' voices. My hands and feet were also far from being feminine and dainty. In front of the mirror I detachedly examined my body. For a sixteen-year-old my breasts were sadly undeveloped. They could only be called skin swellings, even by the kindest critic. The line from my rib cage to my knees fell straight without even a ridge to disturb its direction. Younger girls than I boasted of having to shave under their arms, but my armpits were as smooth as my face. There was also a mysterious growth developing on my body that defied explanation. It looked totally useless.

Then the question began to live under my blankets: How did lesbianism begin? What were the symptoms? The public library gave information on the finished lesbian—and that woefully sketchy—but on the growth of a lesbian, there was nothing. I did discover that the difference between hermaphrodites and lesbians was that hermaphrodites were "born that way." It was impossible to determine whether lesbians budded gradually, or burst into being with a suddenness that dismayed them as much as it repelled society.

I had gnawed into the unsatisfying books and into my own unstocked mind without finding a morsel of peace or understanding. And meantime, my voice refused to stay up in the higher registers where I consciously pitched it, and I had to buy my shoes in the "old lady's comfort" section of the shoe stores.

I asked Mother.

Daddy Clidell was at the club one evening, so I sat down on the side of Mother's bed. As usual she woke completely and at once. (There is never any yawning or stretching with Vivian Baxter. She's either awake or asleep.)

"Mother, I've got to talk to you . . ." It was going to kill me to have to ask her, for in the asking wouldn't it be possible that suspicion would fall on my own normality? I knew her well enough to know that if I committed almost any crime and told her the truth about it she not only wouldn't disown me but would give me her protection. But just suppose I was developing into a lesbian, how would she react? And then there was Bailey to worry about too.

"Ask me, and pass me a cigarette." Her calmness didn't fool me for a minute. She used to say that her secret to life was that she "hoped for the best, was prepared for the worst, so anything in between didn't come as a surprise." That was all well and good for most things but if her only daughter was developing into a . . .

She moved over and patted the bed, "Come on, baby, get in the bed. You'll freeze before you get your question out."

It was better to remain where I was for the time being.

"Mother . . . my pocketbook . . ."

"Ritie, do you mean your vagina? Don't use those Southern terms. There's nothing wrong with the word 'vagina.' It's a clinical description. Now, what's wrong with it?"

The smoke collected under the bed lamp, then floated out to be free in the room. I was deathly sorry that I had begun to ask her anything.

"Well . . . Well? Have you got crabs?"

Since I didn't know what they were, that puzzled me. I thought I might have them and it wouldn't go well for my side if I said I didn't. On the other hand, I just might not have them, and suppose I lied and said I did?

"I don't know, Mother."

"Do you itch? Does your vagina itch?" She leaned on one elbow and jabbed out her cigarette.

"No, Mother."

"Then you don't have crabs. If you had them, you'd tell the world."

I wasn't sorry or glad not to have them, but made a mental note to look up "crabs" in the library on my next trip.

She looked at me closely, and only a person who knew her face well could have perceived the muscles relaxing and interpreted this as an indication of concern.

"You don't have a venereal disease, do you?"

The question wasn't asked seriously, but knowing Mother I was shocked at the idea. "Why, Mother, of course not. That's a terrible question." I was ready to go back to my room and wrestle alone with my worries.

"Sit down, Ritie. Pass me another cigarette." For a second it looked as if she was thinking about laughing. That would really do it. If she laughed, I'd never tell her anything else. Her laughter would make it easier to accept my social isolation and human freakishness. But she wasn't even smiling. Just slowly pulling in the smoke and holding it in puffed cheeks before blowing it out.

"Mother, something is growing on my vagina."

There, it was out. I'd soon know whether I was to be her ex-daughter or if she'd put me in the hospital for an operation.

"Where on your vagina, Marguerite?"

Uh-huh. It was bad all right. Not "Ritie" or "Maya" or "Baby." "Marguerite."

"On both sides. Inside." I couldn't add that they were fleshy skin flaps that had been growing for months down there. She'd have to pull that out of me.

"Ritie, go get me that big *Webster's* and then bring me a bottle of beer."

Suddenly, it wasn't all that serious. I was "Ritie" again, and she just asked for beer. If it had been as awful as I anticipated, she'd have ordered Scotch and water. I took her the huge dictionary that she had bought as a birthday gift for Daddy Clidell and laid it on the bed. The weight forced a side of the mattress down and Mother twisted her bed lamp to beam on the book.

When I returned from the kitchen and poured her beer, as she had taught Bailey and me beer should be poured, she patted the bed.

"Sit down, baby. Read this." Her fingers guided my eyes to VULVA. I began to read. She said, "Read it out loud."

It was all very clear and normal-sounding. She drank the beer as I read, and when I had finished she explained it in every-day terms. My relief melted the fears and they liquidly stole down my face.

Mother shot up and put her arms around me.

"There's nothing to worry about, baby. It happens to every woman. It's just human nature."

It was all right then to unburden my heavy, heavy heart. I cried into the crook of my arm. "I thought maybe I was turning into a lesbian."

Her patting of my shoulder slowed to a still and she leaned away from me.

"A lesbian? Where the hell did you get that idea?"

"Those things growing on my . . . vagina, and my voice is too deep and my feet are big, and I have no hips or breasts or anything. And my legs are so skinny."

Then she did laugh. I knew immediately that she wasn't laughing at me. Or rather that she was laughing at me, but it was something about me that pleased her. The laugh choked a little on the smoke in its way, but finally broke through cleanly. I had to give a small laugh too, although I wasn't tickled at all. But it's mean to watch someone enjoy something and not show your understanding of their enjoyment.

When she finished with the laughter, she laid it down a peal at a time and turned to me, wiping her eyes.

"I made arrangements, a long time ago, to have a boy and a girl. Bailey is my boy and you are my girl. The Man upstairs, He don't make mistakes. He gave you to me to be my girl and that's just what you are. Now, go wash your face, have a glass of milk and go back to bed."

I did as she said but I soon discovered my new assurance wasn't large enough to fill the gap left by my old uneasiness. It rattled around in my mind like a dime in a tin cup. I hoarded it preciously, but less than two weeks later it became totally worthless.

A classmate of mine, whose mother had rooms for herself and her daughter in a ladies' residence, had stayed out beyond closing time. She telephoned me to ask if she could sleep at my house. Mother gave her permission, providing my friend telephoned her mother from our house.

When she arrived, I got out of bed and we went to the upstairs kitchen to make hot chocolate. In my room we shared mean gossip about our friends, giggled over boys and whined about school and the tedium of life. The unusualness of having someone sleep in my bed (I'd never slept with anyone except my grandmothers) and the frivolous laughter in the middle of the night made me forget simple courtesies. My friend had to remind me that she had nothing to sleep in. I gave her one of my gowns, and without curiosity or interest I watched her pull off her clothes. At none of the early stages of undressing was I in the least conscious of her body. And then suddenly, for the briefest eye span, I saw her breasts. I was stunned.

They were shaped like light-brown falsies in the five-and-ten-cent store, but they were real. They made all the nude paintings I had seen in museums come to life. In a word they were beautiful. A universe divided what she had from what I had. She was a woman.

My gown was too snug for her and much too long, and when she wanted to laugh at her ridiculous image I found that humor had left me without a promise to return.

Had I been older I might have thought that I was moved by both an esthetic sense of beauty and the pure emotion of envy. But those possibilities did not occur to me when I needed them. All I knew was that I had been moved by looking at a woman's breasts. So all the calm and casual words of Mother's explanation a few weeks earlier and the clinical terms of Noah Webster did not alter the fact that in a fundamental way there was something queer about me.

I somersaulted deeper into my snuggery of misery. After a thorough self-examination, in the light of all I had read and heard about dykes and bulldaggers, I reasoned that I had none of the obvious traits—I didn't wear trousers, or have big shoulders or go in for sports, or walk like a man or even want to touch a woman. I wanted to be a woman, but that seemed to me to be a world to which I was to be eternally refused entrance.

What I needed was a boyfriend. A boyfriend would clarify my position to the world and, even more important, to myself. A boyfriend's acceptance of me would guide me into that strange and exotic land of frills and femininity.

Among my associates, there were no takers. Understandably the boys of my age and social group were captivated by the yellow- or light-brown-skinned girls, with hairy legs and smooth little lips, and whose hair "hung down like horses' manes." And even those sought-after girls were asked to "give it up or tell where it is." They were reminded in a popular song of the times, "If you can't smile and say yes, please don't cry and say no." If the pretties were expected to make the supreme sacrifice in order to "belong," what could the unattractive female do? She who had been skimming along on life's turning but never-changing periphery had to be ready to be a "buddy" by day and maybe by night. She was called upon to be generous only if the pretty girls were unavailable.

I believe most plain girls are virtuous because of the scarcity of opportunity to be otherwise. They shield themselves with an aura of unavailableness (for which after a time they begin to take credit) largely as a defense tactic.

In my particular case, I could not hide behind the curtain of voluntary goodness. I was being crushed by two unrelenting forces: the uneasy suspicion that I might not be a normal female and my newly awakening sexual appetite.

I decided to take matters into my own hands. (An unfortunate but apt phrase.)

Up the hill from our house, and on the same side of the street, lived two handsome brothers. They were easily the most eligible young men in the neighborhood. If I was going to venture into sex, I saw no reason why I shouldn't make my experiment with the best of the lot. I didn't really expect to capture either brother on a permanent basis, but I thought if I could hook one temporarily I might be able to work the relationship into something more lasting.

I planned a chart for seduction with surprise as my opening ploy. One evening as I walked up the hill suffering from youth's vague malaise (there was simply nothing to do), the brother I had chosen came walking directly into my trap.

"Hello, Marguerite." He nearly passed me.

I put the plan into action. "Hey." I plunged, "Would you like to have a sexual intercourse with me?" Things were going according to the chart. His mouth hung open like a garden gate. I had the advantage and so I pressed it.

"Take me somewhere."

His response lacked dignity, but in fairness to him I admit that I had left him little chance to be suave.

He asked, "You mean, you're going to give me some trim?"

I assured him that that was exactly what I was about to give him. Even as the scene was being enacted I realized the imbalance in his values. He thought I was giving him something, and the fact of the matter was that it was my intention to take something from him. His good looks and popularity had made him so inordinately conceited that they blinded him to that possibility.

We went to a furnished room occupied by one of his friends, who understood the situation immediately and got his coat and left us alone. The seductee quickly turned off the lights. I would have preferred them left on, but didn't want to appear more aggressive than I had been already. If that was possible.

I was excited rather than nervous, and hopeful instead of frightened. I had not considered how physical an act of seduction would be. I had anticipated long soulful tongued kisses and gentle caresses. But there was no romance in the knee which forced my legs, nor in the rub of hairy skin on my chest.

Unredeemed by shared tenderness, the time was spent in laborious gropings, pulling, yankings and jerkings.

Not one word was spoken.

My partner showed that our experience had reached its climax by getting up abruptly, and my main concern was how to get home quickly. He may have sensed that he had been used, or his disinterest may have been an indication that I was less than gratifying. Neither possibility bothered me.

Outside on the street we left each other with little more than "Okay, see you around."

Thanks to Mr. Freeman nine years before, I had had no pain of entry to endure, and because of the absence of romantic involvement neither of us felt much had happened.

At home I reviewed the failure and tried to evaluate my new position. I had had a man. I had been had. I not only didn't enjoy it, but my normalcy was still a question.

What happened to the moonlight-on-the-prairie feeling? Was there something so wrong with me that I couldn't share a sensation that made poets gush out rhyme after rhyme, that made Richard Arlen brave the Arctic wastes and Veronica Lake betray the entire free world?

There seemed to be no explanation for my private infirmity, but being a product (is "victim" a better word?) of the Southern Negro upbringing, I decided that I "would understand it all better by-and-by." I went to sleep.

Three weeks later, having thought very little of the strange and strangely empty night, I found myself pregnant.

CHAPTER 36

The world had ended, and I was the only person who knew it. People walked along the streets as if the pavements hadn't all crumbled beneath their feet. They pretended to breathe in and out while all the time I knew the air had been sucked away in a monstrous inhalation from God Himself. I alone was suffocating in the nightmare.

The little pleasure I was able to take from the fact that if I could have a baby I obviously wasn't a lesbian was crowded into my mind's tiniest corner by the massive pushing in of fear, guilt, and self-revulsion.

For eons, it seemed, I had accepted my plight as the hapless, put-upon victim of fate and the Furies, but this time I had to face the fact that I had brought my new catastrophe upon myself. How was I to blame the innocent man whom I had lured into making love to me? In order to be profoundly dishonest, a person must have one of two qualities: either he is unscrupulously ambitious, or he is unswervingly egocentric. He must believe that for his ends to be served all things and people can justifiably be shifted about, or that he is the center not only of his own world but of the worlds which others inhabit. I had neither element in my personality, so I hefted the burden of pregnancy at sixteen onto my own shoulders where it belonged. Admittedly, I staggered under the weight.

I finally sent a letter to Bailey, who was at sea within the merchant marine. He wrote back, and he cautioned me against telling Mother of my condition. We both knew her to be violently opposed to abortions, and she would very likely order me to quit school. Bailey suggested that if I quit school before getting my high school diploma I'd find it nearly impossible to return.

The first three months, while I was adapting myself to the fact of pregnancy (I didn't really link pregnancy to the possibility of my having a baby until weeks before my confinement), were a hazy period in which days seemed to lie just below the water level, never emerging fully.

Fortunately, Mother was tied up tighter than Dick's hatband in the weave of her own life. She noticed me, as usual, out of the corner of her existence. As long as I was healthy, clothed and smiling she felt no need to focus her attention on me. As always, her major concern was to live the life given to her, and her children were expected to do the same. And to do it without too much brouhaha.

Under her loose scrutiny I grew more buxom, and my brown skin smoothed and tight-pored, like pancakes fried on an unoiled skillet. And still she didn't suspect. Some years before, I had established a code which never varied. I didn't lie. It was understood that I didn't lie because I was too proud to be caught and forced to admit that I was capable of a less than Olympian action. Mother must have concluded that since I was above out-and-out lying I was also beyond deceit. She was deceived.

All my motions focalized on pretending to be that guileless schoolgirl who had nothing more wearying to think about than mid-term exams. Strangely enough, I very nearly caught the essence of teenage capriciousness as I played the role. Except that there were times when physically I couldn't deny to myself that something very important was taking place in my body.

Mornings, I never knew if I would have to jump off the streetcar one step ahead of the warm sea of nausea that threatened to sweep me away. On solid ground, away from the ship-motioned vehicle and the smell of hands coated with recent breakfasts, I regained my balance and waited for the next trolley.

School recovered its lost magic. For the first time since Stamps, information was exciting for itself alone. I burrowed myself into caves of facts, and found delight in the logical resolutions of mathematics.

I credit my new reactions (although I didn't know at the time that I had learned anything from them) to the fact that during what surely must have been a critical period I was not dragged down by hopelessness. Life had a conveyor-belt quality. It went on unpursued and unpursuing, and my only thought was to remain erect, and keep my secret along with my balance.

Midway along to delivery, Bailey came home and brought me a spun-silver bracelet from South America, Thomas Wolfe's *Look Homeward, Angel,* and a slew of new dirty jokes.

As my sixth month approached, Mother left San Francisco for Alaska. She was to open a night club and planned to stay three or four months until it got on its feet. Daddy Clidell was to look after me but I was more or less left on my own recognizance and under the unsteady gaze of our lady roomers.

Mother left the city amid a happy and cheerful send-off party (after all how many Negroes were in Alaska?), and I felt treacherous allowing her to go without informing her that she was soon to be a grandmother.

Two days after V-Day, I stood with the San Francisco Summer School class at Mission High School and received my diploma. That evening, in the bosom of the now-dear family home I uncoiled my fearful secret and in a brave gesture left a note on Daddy Clidell's bed. It read: *Dear Parents, I am sorry to bring this disgrace on the family, but I am pregnant. Marguerite.*

The confusion that ensued when I explained to my stepfather that I expected to deliver the baby in three weeks, more or less, was reminiscent of a Molière comedy. Except that it was funny only years later. Daddy Clidell told Mother that I was "three weeks gone." Mother, regarding me as a woman for the first time, said indignantly, "She's more than any three weeks." They both accepted the fact that I was further along than they had first been told but found it nearly impossible to believe that I had carried a baby, eight months and one week, without their being any the wiser.

Mother asked, "Who is the boy?" I told her. She recalled him, faintly.

"Do you want to marry him?"

"No."

"Does he want to marry you?" The father had stopped speaking to me during my fourth month.

"No."

"Well, that's that. No use ruining three lives." There was no overt or subtle condemnation. She was Vivian Baxter Jackson. Hoping for the best, prepared for the worst, and unsurprised by anything in between.

Daddy Clidell assured me that I had nothing to worry about. That "women been gittin' pregnant ever since Eve ate that apple." He sent one of his waitresses to I. Magnin's to buy maternity dresses for me. For the next two weeks I whirled around the city going to doctors, taking vitamin shots and pills, buying clothes for the baby, and except for the rare moments alone, enjoying the imminent blessed event.

After a short labor, and without too much pain (I decided that the pain of delivery was overrated), my son was born. Just as gratefulness was confused in my mind with love, so possession became mixed up with motherhood. I had a baby. He was beautiful and mine. Totally mine. No one had bought him for me. No one had helped me endure the sickly gray months. I had had help in the child's conception, but no one could deny that I had had an immaculate pregnancy.

Totally my possession, and I was afraid to touch him. Home from the hospital, I sat for hours by his bassinet and absorbed his mysterious perfection. His extremities were so dainty they appeared unfinished. Mother handled him easily with the casual confidence of a baby nurse, but I dreaded being forced to change his diapers. Wasn't I famous for awkwardness? Suppose I let him slip, or put my fingers on that throbbing pulse on the top of his head?

Mother came to my bed one night bringing my three-week-old baby. She pulled the cover back and told me to get up and hold him while she put rubber sheets on my bed. She explained that he was going to sleep with me.

I begged in vain. I was sure to roll over and crush out his life or break those fragile bones. She wouldn't hear of it, and within minutes the pretty golden baby was lying on his back in the center of my bed, laughing at me.

I lay on the edge of the bed, stiff with fear, and vowed not to sleep all night long. But the eat-sleep routine I had begun in the hospital, and kept up under Mother's dictatorial command, got the better of me. I dropped off.

My shoulder was shaken gently. Mother whispered, "Maya, wake up. But don't move."

I knew immediately that the awakening had to do with the baby. I tensed. "I'm awake."

She turned the light on and said, "Look at the baby." My fears were so powerful I couldn't move to look at the center of the bed. She said again, "Look at the baby." I didn't hear sadness in her voice, and that helped me to break the bonds of terror. The baby was no longer in the center of the bed. At first I thought he had moved. But after closer investigation I found that I was lying on my stomach with my arm bent at a right angle. Under the tent of blanket, which was poled by my elbow and forearm, the baby slept touching my side.

Mother whispered, "See, you don't have to think about doing the right thing. If you're for the right thing, then you do it without thinking."

She turned out the light, and I patted my son's body lightly and went back to sleep. . . .

Itabari Njeri (1953–)

Considering herself a salient example of the African diaspora, Itabari Njeri recognizes that with her African, Indian, English, and French bloodlines, she is a New World black, a person with a complex identity who has been neglected by contemporary racial nomenclature and racist ideas. In a provocative essay on multiethnic identity and colorism, Njeri argues that African Americans should be free to acknowledge all components of their ethnic heritage: "Clearly, African Americans are not just the descendants of enslaved Americans in the United States. . . . Every black person with white ancestry should, no matter how they came by it, own it. That is not a rejection of African American identity, but an affirmation to the complex ancestry that defines us as an ethnic group. . . . Further, the acknowledgement of our ties by blood and culture puts the lie to the official silence on America's historically miscegenated identity."

With a life as varied as her ethnic makeup, Njeri was born Jill Stacey Moreland in Brooklyn, New York. Raised by a supportive mother and an intellectual but abusive father, Njeri initially sought a career as a singer—first in opera and then in popular music. She studied singing at the High School of Music and Art in New York and went on to earn a B.S. from the Boston University School of Public Communications and an M.S. from the Columbia University School of Journalism.

Among many other notable events in her life as a teen, Njeri joined the Congress of African People, a Pan-African nationalist group under the leadership of Amiri Baraka. As she explains in the selection that follows, it was under Baraka's influence that she changed her name to Itabari, which "means an esteemed person or one in whom you can place your trust or faith." Within a few years, however, she left the group over differences in perspective.

Despite her talents in singing and acting, Njeri shifted her professional interests to journalism in order to bypass the racist and sexist barriers that confront black women seeking performing arts careers. In 1972 and 1973, she worked as a reporter for National Public Radio in Boston, eventually hosting and producing radio programs. Since the 1970s, she has been a staff writer at various newspapers, including the Greenville News, *the* Miami Herald, *and the* Los Angeles Times.

Njeri has won several awards for her feature writing, including a South Carolina Associated Press Award (1980), a University of Missouri Journalism Prize (1983), and a National Association of Black Journalism Award (1990). She has also received a National Endowment for the Humanities Fellowship (1983) and an American Book Award for her autobiography, Every Good-Bye Ain't Gone: Family Portraits and Personal Escapades *(1990). Her other books include* Sushi and Grits: The Challenge of Diversity *(1993), a collection of essays, and* The Last Plantation *(1994), a book of social and cultural criticism. She is currently working on her first novel,* The Secret Life of Fred Astaire.

The following selection, "Has-beens Who Never Were," is taken from Every Good-bye Ain't Gone, *Njeri's autobiographical account of her personal and professional experiences as well as the triumphs and tragedies of her family.*

Has-beens Who Never Were

A man I have not seen for fifteen years is telling a room full of strangers about my past.

I suppose many among the crowd already know me in an impersonal way. They have seen my byline in the *Miami Herald* and paused out of curiosity at the double consonants—even if they did not go on to read what was under it: offbeat feature stories, unusual first-person tales of my dysfunctional family, and reviews and essays about the arts. I have never, except to my employers, made known my credentials for assuming the role of critic. But this man, whom I've not seen since my adolescence, is, unexpectedly, about to expose bits of my curriculum vitae. And I don't like it.

"You shouldn't fear," he tells them, "that your children's future will be limited if they go to a school for the arts." This man, with the *Fame* logo pinned to his lapel, possesses the same gentle, soft-spoken manner I remember as a teenager; though my classmates and I at the High School of Music and Art gave Richard Klein lots of cause to lose his cool. The painter and administrator began his tenure as principal of the school that inspired the movie *Fame* as a man under siege.

Virtually every college campus in America in the late sixties and early seventies was lit by the fire of revolutionary rhetoric and defiant, nonconformist behavior. I was only in high school, but it was a school full of congenital nonconformists. Janice Ian ("Society's Child" and "At Seventeen") epitomized it. The image of her haunting the corridors between the school's Gothic walls has never left me: silent, her eyes cast down, her body bending in on itself, the retracting form intent on reclaiming its fetal posture.

But as soon as one passed that portrait of near catatonia, Liz Abzug (Bella-the-hat's daughter) would appear, lecture me in animated tones on leftist politics, then pronounce me a "Negro" because of my button-down-collar blouses, straightened hair, disdain for pot and support for liberal Republican John Lindsay in the upcoming mayoral election.

Across the street from our high school campus, Black Panthers at City College were protesting, with others, U.S. racism at home and imperialism abroad: Get out of Vietnam. End U.S. support for South Africa. And a few blocks farther away, more of the same was going on at Columbia University.

It did not take long to get caught up in the political fervor. I was sixteen. I wanted the approval of my peers and, appropriate to the age, was breaking out of the world defined for me by my parents, both of whom were essentially Victorian. No matter that my father was a proclaimed Marxist whose library helped to fuel my natural intellectual curiosity and filled me, early in life, with ideas that challenged the political status quo. Or that my mother was fundamentally liberal in her style of parenting.

My father, after all, was born at the beginning of the twentieth century, went to the "Oxford" of Canada, the University of Toronto, and before that the bastion of Negro middle-class elitism, Morehouse. Further, true to the Victorian tradition, he believed that a patriarch was to be respected and served without challenge by the women and children in his household.

My mother's sensibilities were shaped by parents born in the British colonial empire *during* Victoria's reign. She's a product of Catholic schools, as well. While she received a fine education in these schools, she also learned from the nuns the dreaded Mother Superior pose, which she still assumes—lips pursed, shoulders back, spine stiff, crossed hands on her abdomen—when confronted with anything she finds distasteful. Bessie Smith, for instance. Having discovered her at sixteen, I dragged my mother into the living room to hear one of Bessie's blues and was frozen by my mother's contempt: "Why would you bring me in here to listen to anything as vulgar as a woman singing about her jelly roll?"

I watched my mother press her lips into oblivion, then walk away with a stiff back. I didn't get it. I just loved Bessie's voice. I didn't know there was anything bad about jelly or a roll.

Culturally—like most middle-class non-WASPs of their generation who sought any degree of mainstream acceptance—one assimilated the cultural assumptions of Euro-America no matter how destructive to colored people's psyche. And the image of mainstream society most assimilationist blacks held was usually the most conservative—the safest, most proper conduct. After all, you're black, don't do anything else to stand out.

I was getting ready to stand out.

Richard Klein was present at the metamorphosis, mine and thousands of others'. That he didn't confuse me with all the rest, fifteen years later, is partly happenstance. He has come to Miami to tout the New World School of the Arts to parents and community leaders several months before he assumes the job of provost of the new school. I am covering the story for the paper. Interviewing this figure from my past turns out to be my last assignment for the *Herald*. In a few weeks, I will join the staff of the *Los Angeles Times* and begin a new phase in my career as a writer.

That I am now Itabari and not Jill should add all the more to his confusion about who I am, out of the thousands who swarmed through the six-story school that housed so much teenage energy, creativity and despair.

But he claims particular recall where I am concerned.

"An arts education," Klein tells the crowd, "increases your child's options in the world. It doesn't narrow them." Most of the students from Music and Art and Performing Arts (two different divisions of the same school, now called the LaGuardia School of the Arts) "do not become performers. They are doctors, teachers, lawyers, architects, writers. They receive both an arts education and a rigorous college preparatory education," he assures them.

"Right here, you have an outstanding journalist who could have had a great career in opera if she chose. She had one of the most beautiful voices of any student who ever came to the school. . . ."

I am an obvious blusher. Usually it's just my cheeks. But now I feel my earlobes turn hot. All who know me understand that I've never suffered from false modesty. But what sense is there in talking about a gift one failed to use as one might have, could have, should have? What is there to say about a "great" voice heard only by a limited public audience and a small circle of academics and professional musicians? The biggest crowds that heard me sing really came to hear the Ohio Players or the Spinners, for whom Major Harris was the opening act and I one of his mediocre background singers.

I stare at my reporter's pad as Klein speaks and gestures toward me. I hear the murmurs of surprise and know what will come.

"With a voice like that why didn't you do something with it?" one woman asks after Klein's speech.

I'm working the crowd, trying to get a few quotes for my story. But people are trying to pry into the particulars of my past and I am ticked.

"Why would anybody in their right mind" give up the chance of an operatic career "for this?" says some other woman, who points her long nose at my reporter's notebook.

The cynical journalist in me doubts that Klein really remembers me all that well. A day earlier when we talked, I told him I had graduated from Music and Art and that my name had been Jill Moreland. I think he called the school, asked them to check my records and talked to some of my former teachers who told him about me. I was a good example for his speech. And a few compliments to pump up the ego of a reporter covering him couldn't hurt.

"I hope I didn't embarrass you?" he says after the woman with the long nose departs.

"No," I say, and smile. I feel bad. When I feel this bad I want to slip into silk pajamas, eat chocolate brownies, drink champagne and watch Fred Astaire.

At home, after Klein's speech, I bite into a brownie and think: He might not have used me as a convenient anecdote if he knew how much I mourned the state of my gift.

My voice is now a lover that comes and goes. I am euphoric in its presence.

And even when it fades—because of misuse at a young age, chronic throat problems since infancy, fatigue at an older age from the daily strain of being a reporter, and just age—I can induce the euphoria through memory. The exhilaration of a beautiful and powerful sound, self-created, produces a high . . . leaves one light-headed . . . touches the same pleasure center as sex and cocaine. . . . Recall is enough to induce the sensations.

And when that self-induced high generates a response—applause—it is the ultimate drug. I was never so adored, I believed, as when I sang. When I sang, even my father looked at me with love. When I sang, people who said I had "personality" saw me onstage and told me I was beautiful, too.

I don't sing anymore.

When I think I know why, I realize I am still not sure.

There is no Fred Astaire on TV. I am a low-tech person, so I don't own a VCR and can't rent him. So I put on Verdi. His was the first music I heard floating from the tower of the building that housed Music and Art.

The school was on Convent Avenue then, a few blocks north of our Harlem apartment, a few streets past the Church of the Annunciation, where my mother had tried in vain to have me baptized. I don't know how I'd missed the building before, with its Gothic spires and gargoyles. I had combed the neighborhood since moving there more than a year before, often venturing up Convent Avenue with my bag of barbecue potato chips and a dill pickle, the sound of Motown in my head. Perhaps there had been silence when I passed the building before. But as I approached it that day, my brain drenched with Stevie Wonder's "Fingertips," I heard thunderous music:

> Dies irae, dies illa,
> solvet saeclum in favilla
> teste David cum Sibylla
> Quantus tremor est futurus,
> quando judex est venturus,
> cuncta stricte discussurus!
>
> Day of wrath and doom impending,
> David's word with Sibyl's blending:
> Heaven and earth in ashes ending.
> Oh, what fear man's bosom rendeth,
> When from heaven the judge descendeth,
> On whose sentence all dependeth!

I had never heard so powerful a chorus singing live before. I stood on the corner with my mouth open. Then they stopped . . . began again. . . . And I heard her . . . a disembodied soprano voice whose sound fell to my skin as silk would. *Requiem aeternam dona eis, Domine, et lux perpetua luceat eis.* ("Eternal rest grant unto them, O Lord, and let perpetual light shine upon them.") I would learn one day that I was hearing the end of Verdi's *Requiem*.

I walked home slowly. What was that place? I wondered. No one was home when I got there. I pulled out some 78 recordings that were stored in the cabinet of an old combination radio and phonograph that stood in our long apartment hallway. There was another, modern, phonograph in the living room—my father's part of the house—but I liked the relic better. It was broken. It had a short. But if you spun the turntable manually to get it going, it played well for a while. I put on the first Sarah Vaughan record I ever heard, "The Lord's Prayer." I think "Sometimes I Feel Like a Motherless Child" was on the flip side.

Nat King Cole and Louis Armstrong were among the 78s too. But I kept playing Sarah. Her voice had the same ethereal quality I'd heard floating from the Gothic tower.

That night, I lay in bed singing to myself. It must have been an Indian summer, or an unusual mid-September in New York, because school had just started but it was very hot. The air conditioner in my room was on. No one, I thought, could hear me above its rumble.

My mother knocked on my door and came in. "Sweetheart," she said; she was smiling, her voice was gentle. I could tell she didn't want to say the words. "Your father says it's late. You should be asleep. Please stop singing."

The next day I asked Mrs. Johnson, my fifth-grade music teacher, "What is that place? What do they do in there?" When she told me it was a special high school for the arts, I wanted to know how I could get in it. She told me I had to audition, and to "work on your vibrato." I had too much of it, she insisted. From that moment, I spent every day till I was fifteen preparing to enter Music and Art.

My first year in the school was fine. But the second year, I lost my voice. I am still not certain why it happened. But my voice was so weak, I couldn't pass the audition to enter New York's All City Chorus. The director, John Motley, could not understand it. Just months before, I'd been the soloist in a concert at Columbia University's McMillin Hall, singing music arranged by him. The piece was a German folk song demanding a lyric soprano with perfect control and a stratospheric vocal reach. The concert had been recorded, probably the only recording of me in perfect voice. Despite the rigors of that performance, I couldn't get through a simple song for the choral audition.

"What happened?" asked a girl I had gone to junior high school with. Hers was not a sympathetic inquiry. She had been my musical rival in school, always placing second to me.

"I don't know," I said. "I've been having vocal problems for months." My father had been back for months, too. My parents had separated, but my mother, always seeking Ozzie and Harriet heaven, let him move into our Flatbush brownstone. I never considered the connections between him and my failing vocal powers at the time. Perhaps there were none. But every now and then, when the fog lifts about those years, I glimpse the child and her father standing in a shaft of light surrounded by the dark: He is seated on the bed in his boxer shorts, awestruck and speaking tenderly after I have sung. "My girl, you have the celestial vibration." Then he stands and touches the top of my head with the flat of his palm. I am nine and cannot see his face because he is standing so close, and my head doesn't reach beyond his bare chest. But I do not need to see him. I feel what is welling inside him and walk away self-satisfied.

But then I am thirteen. My father walks to the front of the auditorium where I have just performed. I remember the song, "Summertime." The aisles are filled with the departing crowd. Both my father and mother are standing nearby. But in my mind, my daddy and I are again alone, standing in that single column of light. He is speaking to me, but seems as physically distant as it is possible to be and still talk without shouting. "Very good, indeed," he says, then reaches into his pocket and pulls out a ten-dollar bill. The infinite distance is only imagined and immediately I feel the cash pressed into my palm. That was the night of my first paying gig.

I had no pockets, I had no purse, and I clutched the ten until my hand felt numb. But I could feel, even at that age, how lonely my father must have been, unable to find a suitable expression of his love for me or anyone else.

The weight I ultimately attached to my ability to sing well—no, perform perfectly—is tied to the love and appreciation my father articulated only when he heard me sing.

Even in recent years, when I have resumed voice lessons, the fear of failing at something that once defined me so totally paralyzed my voice—either that or some virus would take hold of me and provide a clinical reason for my disabled sound.

In my early adolescence I made no connection between my psyche and my throat. I suffered from the usual case of nerves before a performance until I was sixteen. But after that, it was torture for me to control my stage fright.

One afternoon, while taping a concert for National Public Radio, I had an anxiety attack and lost control of my voice, even though I'd already sung two art songs perfectly. I had been chosen by Music and Art to represent the school in a special series of radio recitals. But I suddenly choked. I went on with the taping, but it was a lost cause. I sounded breathy and amateurish. I pleaded with the school to scrap the broadcast. They did.

I couldn't comprehend what was happening to me. But the voice hides nothing; the instrument and the artist are indivisible.

Anna Ext, one of the school's most venerated voice teachers (she was featured on *60 Minutes* once in a segment about her former star pupil, mezzo-soprano Julia Migenes), told me flatly one day, "You are emotionally unstable." She could have said "Your hair is brown" in the same tone. She didn't bother to ask what was going on in my life. She just left me to think I was crazy. Perhaps she didn't mean to be unkind. Perhaps she held the romantic notion that great talent and madness frequently cohabit. I certainly felt crazy back then. And she certainly felt I had a great instrument.

To affirm her confidence in my gift, if not my sanity, Madame Ext recommended I be placed in the school's solo voice class, Music and Art's singing elite. It bolstered my confidence.

Unlike the television and movie versions of the school, there was little dancing in the hallways and few sudden bursts into pop songs by members of the student body. Jazz and popular music were not forbidden in the school—great jazz artists were occasional guest performers. But our formal training was strictly in the European classical tradition. Students indulged in pop, rock, soul and jazz after school. In my early teens, I still had my sights set on the Metropolitan Opera's stage. (No, that's not quite true. The New York City Opera had endeared itself to me because I could afford their tickets, and I never missed a Saturday afternoon performance during the City Opera's season.) Nonetheless, I decided to take a break from the classical world.

I entered New York's 1969 equivalent of *Star Search*. It was called "New Groove '69," a talent show sponsored by M-G-M Records and WNEW-TV. The show toured through New York City giving performances in schools and hospitals, then culminated in a contest on the stage of the Brooklyn Academy of Music, judged by music industry executives, performers and disc jockeys.

I belted a torchy version of "You're Gonna Hear from Me," accompanied by a wonderful big band. I won. I got the title of M-G-M Records' "Best New Pop Vocalist of 1969." After the show, a man claiming to be a Motown representative asked me to audition for the label. I demurely told him I had plans to be an opera singer and wasn't interested. I don't think I blew anything. I remember the little-girl-would-you-like-some-candy look in his watery eyes.

Nonetheless, I was willing to take the winner's prize: an audition with the late Joe Raposo for the Skitch Henderson show.

Relying on my own counsel, I thought it wise to sing something drastically different from the showstopper I'd won with. I wanted to show my versatility, my vocal range. I sang "It Might as Well Be Spring." I sang it as unembellished as Rodgers and Hammerstein had written it.

Raposo, who had been one of the "New Groove '69" judges, told me my voice was beautiful. But my style was not commercial enough.

I rarely react to anything immediately. As with other setbacks, I absorbed that one and took it as a lesson. I had to find my own style.

One afternoon in solo voice class I decided to try out "You're Gonna Hear from Me." Mrs. Mandel, our teacher and head of the voice department at the time, didn't mind if we occasionally went outside of the classical repertoire. Many students in the school were already professionals, singing in Broadway shows. Mandel was as interested in our perfecting our skills as interpreters of songs—becoming actors—as she was in teaching us the basic repertoire.

I gave her the music to "You're Gonna Hear from Me." Like most of my classmates, she'd never heard me sing a popular song.

"Fascinating," she said when I finished. "Very good, the voice is quite different." She meant that the character of my voice was totally different when I used my lower register. I sounded like a different singer. I had nearly a five-octave range; I could make my voice do almost anything.

And my classmates, especially the black ones, looked at me with new respect. "I didn't think you could sing anything but that bel canto stuff," one girl teased.

It was all beautiful singing. But until very recently, anybody with a voice who chose to study music formally had to do so in the European classical tradition—this is the basis of good vocal technique for any singer. But performing anything outside of the classical repertoire was viewed with contempt by most of the musical establishment. There was no such thing as a jazz vocal music major at American schools when I was a student. But it was becoming clear to me, as I sat in our Flatbush living room—lights out at 2:00 A.M., sipping vodka on the sly, listening to Miles play "My Funny Valentine," Sarah sing "You Go to My Head," Bird blow "Embraceable You"—that I wanted to stand on a stage in a strapless blue gown and sing beside a man with a horn.

I loved the peer approval I received when I sang jazz, pop and gospel. I was more relaxed when I wasn't singing classical music, too. But it had been drummed into my head that if one was going to be an "artist," one had to perform within the realm of "high" culture.

All this added to my adolescent confusion. About this time, I started popping the Thorazine samples I found in the doctor's office I worked in after school. I was so drugged some days, I walked into the walls at Music and Art. I fell off the stage one day in solo voice class. My suicidal impulses increased, and I finally sought therapy.

After months in therapy, my acute depression subsided, my anxiety attacks abated and my simmering sexuality erupted. I spent the last year and a half of high school in most perfect voice. I ran for class president braless, sporting an Afro, wearing big, round dark glasses and a micro-mini dress and offering a platform based on nothing that interested my classmates. (I don't even remember what it was.) I lost.

No matter, I was on a roll. I decided to use the school's vast talent to entertain patients in hospitals. With the help of students who'd go on to be award-winning performers (like Ben Harney, a Tony winner for *Dreamgirls*), we organized the best show then running in New York.

People who'd mistaken my insecurity and depression for snobbery were suddenly friendly. Especially several male teachers, one of whom was fired for making sexual overtures to me.

At rehearsals for my high school graduation, it was announced that I'd won the school's vocal music award. I would have been devastated, I think, if I hadn't. But I was shocked when they called me to the stage to receive something called the Simon Simeon Award from the mayor's office for social service to the city of New York—just because I wanted to entertain sick people. How, as I became older, could I have forgotten that one needn't abandon art for social activism?

The day I graduated with my class at Carnegie Hall—dressed in an African gown—guess who helped lead the Black Power chant from the audience as a contingent of blacks walked across the stage with the African liberation flag? Richard Klein had been warned: Allow the red, black and green flag of the Black Liberation Movement onstage or we'll disrupt the ceremony.

From the balcony of Carnegie Hall, white parents were shouting, "Nazis, Nazis."

A black parent looked toward the balcony wearily and said, "Oh, shut up." Then looked at me just as disgustedly.

Ten rows directly behind me, I heard my mother gasp each time I punched the air with the Black Power salute. After the ceremony she grabbed me by the neck and lifted me out of Carnegie Hall. "That was very nice," she growled as she dragged me down the aisle.

After that, my mother reluctantly realized she'd have to steel herself in preparation for my full metamorphosis.

Two years after my high school graduation, I am rushing to my cousin Karen's wedding in a big Brooklyn Catholic church. It is a blustery day in late autumn. I am in full African regalia, with a wool coat over it, and I am wearing sandals in the snow.

"No," I tell my mother, my big toe a brighter red than my nose as we meet in the church vestibule. "I'm not cold." Hell no. I'm an African.

During the summers and holidays of my college years, I lived in Newark, the headquarters for the Congress of African People [CAP]. Its chairman was the major literary figure of the Black Arts Movement of the sixties and seventies and a major force in the Pan-African political movement, Amiri Baraka.

The rest of the year, I was a student at Boston University. I decided in my senior year of high school that I did not want to go to a conservatory. I was tired of being around people whose sole preoccupation was music. I wanted to be as intellectually challenged as I was artistically. Boston University wasn't my first choice of schools. I wanted to go to Montreal and study at McGill University. But Canada was overrun with Americans during the Vietnam War era and the school refused to accept any more U.S. citizens.

BU seemed an acceptable alternative: it was close to New York but got me away from home; it was in a city I was familiar with from childhood stays with my aunt Rae and it had a good music department—but, it turned out, an extremely conservative one. I don't think anyone in that school uttered the name of a twentieth-century composer without fear.

The first day I walked into the building, however, a group of students were performing in what they considered the modern mode. A half dozen kids surrounded a black upright piano and sang the corniest interpretation of Broadway show tunes I'd ever heard.

My "It Might as Well Be Spring" days were over. After all, during my last year at Music and Art I'd studied theory with the great jazz flautist Yusef Lateef. And I'd spent most of my summer in Greenwich Village hanging out in jazz clubs. Within a year of entering college, I heard, at a birthday party for Baraka, the greatest pure jazz singer on the planet: Betty Carter. There was no turning back.

My sophomore year, I wrote a new curriculum for the school that, I thought, brought it into the twentieth century. Among other things, it called for a recognition of non-Western music and the establishment of a division of ethnomusicology.

When I completed my proposed curriculum, I demanded a meeting with the university's new president, John Silber—the tough, conservative Texan intent on ridding the campus of radical students and professors, as well as making the academically uneven school uniformly first-rate.

He received me cordially. He was surprised that a teenager had made so sound and thorough a proposal. He was never condescending. It was clear he respected intelligent people who presented their case rationally—even if he disagreed. At least that was his manner behind closed doors with a student, back then.

More recently, I have interviewed him for the *Los Angeles Times* on the issue of expanding the traditional Western civilization curriculum to include ethnic studies. He agreed that the classical literature of other cultures—Confucian philosophy, for example—should be studied in addition to the Western classics. But he generally ranted and raved like a rabid animal over the phone, spouting the right-wing intellectual line on the sanctity of a traditional Western education, and our Greek and Roman heritage, and so on.

No matter how attentive he was to my concerns when I was a student, he didn't go for the cultural pluralism line back then, either. My proposal had no impact on the music curriculum.

But the music school was having an impact on me, despite its conservatism. There, I found the best voice teacher I ever had, Ruth Thompson. I'd been studying voice privately while at Music and Art, but neither the group instruction I received at Music and Art nor my private teacher had taught me proper vocal technique.

Thompson made me start at the beginning, none of the big Verdi and Puccini arias I'd been singing. I learned again, but with proper technique, the Italian and German art songs I'd been taught at Music and Art. Then we moved on to Mozart.

I was a quick study. In master classes, older students and Thompson told me I had more than a fine instrument. I had the electricity found in great voices.

One afternoon, after my lesson, I turned to Thompson. It was the end of the first semester of my sophomore year. Her studio was always dimly lit, I remember, and the Boston sky was a dirty gray.

"I'm leaving," I told her. I'd been watching the formation of my mouth in the mirror for weeks as I practiced "Musetta's Waltz" from *La Bohème*. How was singing "Quando me'n vo" going to change the world, improve the lot of poor people and people of color across the planet? I had asked myself between Puccini's lyrics.

If I was going to sing, I told her, I was going to sing jazz. And since I couldn't study that at BU, I might as well get my degree in something more useful.

Thompson looked up from the piano keyboard. Her eyes were full of contempt. "You would give up the chance of an opera career to sing jazz, that junk that anybody off the street can do?"

If I had any doubts about my decision at that moment, her cultural chauvinism was precisely the provocation I needed to stand my ground.

I had decided to get my undergraduate degree in journalism. I didn't just want to write, though; I wanted to own a newspaper one day, or a radio or television station. I wanted to help revolutionize the way people viewed the world and their place in it. And though I'd always taken my writing skills for granted—it was just something that I could do—I was now enamored with the beauty and power of language. I'd read and heard Baraka. Talk about black magic poetry. This was music, too. And its message shot down all the cultural imperialists like my voice teacher. It took aim at the psyche of black people gagging on a diet of self-hate for generations, and preached the worth of our own aesthetic and intellectual values.

But while I was reaching some valid conclusions about the world, I was doing so without the tempering insight of life experience. (That may be as good a definition of youth as any.)

Arrogantly and ignorantly, I presumed myself the most rational assessor of the world around me. I knew what was best. And my will has always been such that no one seriously tried to dissuade me when I made my decision. I abandoned the blueprint I'd created for my life from the age of three. In doing so, I'd forgotten the intimate power of a song to change a heart. This was the era of the soapbox.

The message from the nationalist soapbox was collective self-esteem, but based on a cultural chauvinism that became indistinguishable from the racist mentality we claimed to be fighting. Self-love, self-respect predicated on hating other people—white people in general and the vicious scapegoating of Jews in particular—was the ultimate contradiction of the cultural nationalist movement. That contradiction—among many others—would compel me to leave CAP. But that was years away.

In the summer of 1971, Baraka named me Itabari, a Swahili corruption of the Arabic Itibari. It means an esteemed person or one in whom you can place your trust or faith. Several years later, my mother provided my last name, Njeri, which is Kikuyu and means "worthy of a warrior." (Sexist, Ma, but I get your drift. Later, she claimed the sentiment was sincere but she didn't know I'd really use the name.)

I spent my college years as a political organizer for CAP, probably the most sophisticated Pan-African nationalist organization of the era, due to Baraka's intellectual leadership, as well as that of his wife, Amina Baraka. But like most nationalist organizations, it was a bastion of sexism—women bowing and scrapping before men. It was puritanical—no sex outside of marriage, which I think nobody but me followed. But I took everything literally in those days. I gave up my birth control pills when I entered the organization and halted a very active sex life begun at seventeen. (Remember those posters with different sexual positions for every astrological sign—you know, the one that glowed under a black light? Well, I met an Indian graduate student, who looked like Zubin Mehta in his prime, at an orgy my freshman year. We became great friends, mastering every pose on the poster and adding some new ones. This man was the walking Kamasutra. I was really committed to the revolution to give him up.)

Baraka, I realize now, was a father figure to me. I was a teenager when I met him and joined the organization, just beginning to assert my individuality. Suddenly, I had to suppress my personality to conform to the organization. It was a hard fit. At heart, I was a rebellious, angry child who'd repressed her feelings to survive in an alcoholic family. I was making a similar adaption while in CAP because I felt the organization was the key to revolutionizing black people's self-image and gaining political empowerment. And if I had to relinquish all my bourgeois tendencies—as I was told—to achieve that goal, I was ready to purge myself. There was a lot to purge. I was light-skinned, so it was assumed that I thought myself better than darker-skinned black people. My only religious background was Catholic—when they found that out they knew I was near hopeless. And I'd been singing the devil's unadulterated music—opera. No one in the organization liked my voice, except when they heard me sing jazz. But I did win some respect because I could act. I was a natural comic. Baraka put me in his plays. During rehearsals, I'd catch him falling out of his chair laughing at me. He'd look at me with the kind of delight I'd seen in my father's eyes when I sang.

But after three years in the organization, I decided to leave. It was stifling. Baraka, a cosmopolite and intellectual renegade, had seen firsthand the world I wanted to experience. Members of the organization—we all lived together but in various locations—were told that the world outside was racist and bourgeois. That's why we didn't need to read the *New York Times*. We should live vicariously, through Baraka.

Leaving the organization was like leaving the convent. I tried to do it in person, but didn't have the guts. Several months after my first attempt, I mailed back my uniform—my black orthopedic-styled shoes, my long black jacket, my long black skirt.

Though I'd left BU's School of Fine and Applied Arts for its School of Public Communications, I hadn't abandoned performing.

When I wasn't acting with Baraka's theater company, the Spirit House Movers, I was performing with a group called Blakluv in Boston. We did a lot of university concerts, prison gigs, local TV and radio concerts throughout New England.

At the same time, I'd gotten my first paying job as a journalist while still in school. I was a reporter for National Public Radio [NPR] in Boston, then a producer and host of my own syndicated show, *The Pan-African News Report,* as well as a reporter and co-producer for several other news programs.

I was carrying a double load at school, too, because I had switched majors and needed additional credits to graduate on time. Despite my schedule, I was an A student and a University Trustee Scholar.

I had a lot of energy.

I was doing a lot of sublimating.

Several months after I finished college, I collapsed from exhaustion.

I was out of a job, too. WBUR-FM, the NPR station for which I worked, had its budget cut. Last hired, first canned.

I spent the rest of the year singing part-time, doing secretarial work part-time and deprogramming myself from the CAP experience. The latter meant that I could show my legs and cleavage again. But I couldn't expect everybody to speak to me in Swahili when we met. Nor could I expect everybody to share the same code of conduct, as we did in CAP: cooperative effort for a shared goal, trustworthiness, honesty and a genuine love and understanding of black people and culture.

My major post–CAP cultural experience came when I toured with Mr. "Love Won't Let Me Wait" in the land of the doo-wops. That, of course, contributed to my decision to go to graduate school and write instead of sing for my living.

I do not know if I made the right decision. I do find a balance as a writer I never had as a musician—perhaps because I meant the singing to serve me in ways it could not. It was an escape. It was an act of self-healing. Richard Klein might have trod more gently had he known that.

But singing never satisfied me intellectually. Writing feeds both my creative and intellectual cravings. And there is some solace in thinking that, if I'm good enough, what I create as a writer could last forever. I look on the shelf where two copies of my father's book, *The Tolono Station and Beyond,* sit side by side. It is palpable evidence that he created something of value in the world. A song is such an ephemeral thing.

Yet, beside my father's book is one he gave me when I graduated from Music and Art, Gustav Kobbe's *Complete Opera Book.* Inside it he wrote: "To Jill the Pill—A song is but a little thing, but what a joy it is to sing."

The decade was about to end when I started my first newspaper job. The seventies might have been the disco generation for some, but it was a continuation of the Black Power, post–Civil Rights era for me. Of course in some parts of America if was still the pre–Civil Rights era. And that was the part of America I wanted to explore. As a good reporter I needed a sense of the whole country, not just the provincial Northeast Corridor in which I was raised.

I headed for Greenville ("Pearl of the Piedmont"), South Carolina.

"*Wheeere,*" some people snarled, their nostrils twitching, their mouths twisted so their top lips went slightly to the right, the bottom ones way down and to the left, "did you get *that* name from?"

Itabiddy. Etabeedy. Etabeeree. Eat a berry. Mata Hari. Theda Bara. And one secretary in the office of the Greenville Urban League told her employer: "It's Ms. Idi Amin."

Then, and now, there are a whole bunch of people who greet me with: "Hi,

Ita." They think "Bari" is my last name. Even when they don't, they still want to call me "Ita." When I tell them my first name is Itabari, they say, "Well, what do people call you for short?"

"They don't call me anything for short," I say. "The name is Itabari."

Sophisticated white people, upon hearing my name, approach me as would a cultural anthropologist finding a piece of exotica right in his own living room. This happens a lot, still, at cocktail parties.

"Oh, what an unusual and beautiful name. Where are you from?"

"Brooklyn," I say. I can see the disappointment in their eyes. Just another homegrown Negro.

Then there are other white people who, having heard my decidedly north-eastern accent, will simply say, "What a lovely name," and smile knowingly, indicating that they saw *Roots* and understand.

Then there are others, black and white, who for different reasons take me through this number.

"What's your *real* name?"

"Itabari Njeri is my real, legal name," I explain.

"Okay, what's your original name?" they ask, often with eyes rolling, exasperation in their voices.

After Malcolm X, Muhammad Ali, Kareem Abdul-Jabaar, Ntozake Shange and Kunta Kinte, who, I ask, should be exasperated by this question-and-answer game?

Nevertheless, I explain, "Because of slavery, black people in the Western world don't usually know their original names. What you really want to know is what my slave name was."

Now this is where things get tense. Four hundred years of bitter history, culture and politics between blacks and whites in America is evoked by this one term, "slave name."

Some white people wince when they hear the phrase, pained and embarrassed by this reminder of their ancestors' inhumanity. Further, they quickly scrutinize me and conclude that mine was a post–Emancipation Proclamation birth. "You were never a slave."

I used to be reluctant to tell people my slave name unless I surmised that they wouldn't impose their cultural values on me and refuse to use my African name. I don't care anymore. When I changed my name, I changed my life, and I've been Itabari for more years now than I was Jill. Nonetheless, people will say: "Well, that's your *real* name, you were born in America and that's what I am going to call you." My mother tried a variation of this on me when I legalized my traditional African name. I respectfully made it clear to her that I would not tolerate it. Her behavior, and subsequently her attitude, changed.

But many black folks remain just as skeptical of my name as my mother was.

"You're one of those black people who changed their name, huh," they are likely to begin. "Well, I still got the old slave master's Irish name," said one man named O'Hare at a party. This man's defensive tone was a reaction to what I call the "blacker than thou" syndrome perpetrated by many black nationalists in the sixties and seventies. Those who reclaimed their African names made blacks who didn't do the same thing feel like Uncle Toms.

These so-called Uncle Toms couldn't figure out why they should use an African name when they didn't know a thing about Africa. Besides, many of them were proud of their names, no matter how they had come by them. And it should be noted that after the Emancipation Proclamation in 1863, four million black people changed their names, adopting surnames such as Freeman, Freedman and Liberty. They eagerly gave up names that slave masters had imposed upon them as a way of identifying their human chattel.

Besides names that indicated their newly won freedom, blacks chose common English names such as Jones, Scott and Johnson. English was their language, America was their home, and they wanted names that would allow them to assimilate as easily as possible.

Of course, many of our European surnames belong to us by birthright. We are the legal as well as "illegitimate" heirs to the names Jefferson, Franklin, Washington, et al; and in my own family, Lord.

Still, I consider most of these names to be by-products of slavery, if not actual slave names. Had we not been enslaved, we would not have been cut off from our culture, lost our indigenous languages and been compelled to use European names.

The loss of our African culture is a tragic fact of history, and the conflict it poses is a profound one that has divided blacks many times since Emancipation: Do we accept the loss and assimilate totally or do we try to reclaim our culture and synthesize it with our present reality?

A new generation of black people in America is reexamining the issues raised by the cultural nationalists and Pan-Africanists of the sixties and seventies: What are the cultural images that appropriately convey the "new" black aesthetic in literature and art?

The young Afro-American novelist Trey Ellis has asserted that the "New Black Aesthetic shamelessly borrows and reassembles across both race and class lines." It is not afraid to embrace the full implications of our hundreds of years in the New World. We are a new people who need not be tied to externally imposed or self-inflicted cultural parochialism. Had I understood that as a teenager, I might still be singing today.

Even the fundamental issue of identity and nomenclature, raised by Baraka and others twenty years ago, is back on the agenda: Are we to call ourselves blacks or African-Americans?

In reality, it's an old debate. "Only with the founding of the American Colonization Society in 1816 did blacks recoil from using the term African in referring to themselves and their institutions," the noted historian and author Sterling Stuckey pointed out in an interview with me. They feared that using the term "African" would fuel white efforts to send them back to Africa. But they felt no white person had the right to send them back when they had slaved to build America.

Many black institutions retained their African identification, most notably the African Methodist Episcopal Church. Changes in black self-identification in America have come in cycles, usually reflecting the larger dynamics of domestic and international politics.

The period after World War II, said Stuckey, "culminating in the Cold War years of Roy Wilkins's leadership of the NAACP," was a time of "frenzied integrationism." And there was "no respectable black leader on the scene evincing any sort of interest in Africa—neither the NAACP or the Urban League."

This, he said, "was an example of historical discontinuity, the likes of which we, as a people, had not seen before." Prior to that, for more than a century and a half, black leaders were Pan-Africanists, including Frederick Douglass. "He recognized," said Stuckey, "that Africa was important and that somehow one had to redeem the motherland in order to be genuinely respected in the New World."

The Reverend Jesse Jackson has, of course, placed on the national agenda the importance of blacks in America restoring their cultural, historical and political links with Africa.

But what does it really mean to be called an African-American?

"Black" can be viewed as a more encompassing term, referring to all people of African descent. "Afro-American" and "African-American" refer to a specific ethnic group. I use the terms interchangeably, depending on the context and the point I want to emphasize.

But I wonder: As the twenty-first century breathes down our necks—prodding us to wake up to the expanding mélange of ethnic groups immigrating in record numbers to the United States, inevitably intermarrying, and to realize the eventual reshaping of the nation's political imperatives in a newly multicultural society—will the term "African-American" be as much of a racial and cultural obfuscation as the term "black"? In other words, will we be the only people, in a society moving toward cultural pluralism, viewed to have no history and no culture? Will we just be a color with a new name: African-American?

Or will the term be—as I think it should—an ethnic label describing people with a shared culture who descended from Africans, were transformed in (as well as transformed) America and are genetically intertwined with myriad other groups in the United States?

Such a definition reflects the historical reality and distances us from the fallacious, unscientific concept of separate races when there is only one: *Homo sapiens.*

But to comprehend what should be an obvious definition requires knowledge and a willingness to accept history.

When James Baldwin wrote *Nobody Knows My Name,* the title was a metaphor—at the deepest level of the collective African-American psyche—for the blighting of black history and culture before the nadir of slavery and since.

The eradication or distortion of our place in world history and culture is most obvious in the popular media. Liz Taylor—and, for an earlier generation, Claudette Colbert—still represent what Cleopatra—a woman of color in a multiethnic society, dominated at various times by blacks—looks like.

And in American homes, thanks to reruns and cable, a new generation of black kids grow up believing that a simpleton shouting "Dy-no-mite!" is a genuine reflection of Afro-American culture, rather than a white Hollywood writer's stereotype.

More recently, *Coming to America,* starring Eddie Murphy as an African prince seeking a bride in the United States, depicted traditional African dancers in what amounted to a Las Vegas stage show, totally distorting the nature and beauty of real African dance. But with every burlesque-style pelvic thrust on the screen, I saw blacks in the audience burst into applause. They think that's African culture, too.

And what do Africans know of us, since blacks don't control the organs of communication that disseminate information about us?

"No!" screamed the mother of a Kenyan man when he announced his engagement to an African-American woman who was a friend of mine. The mother said marry a European, marry a white American. But please, not one of those low-down, ignorant, drug-dealing, murderous black people she had seen in American movies. Ultimately, the mother prevailed.

In Tanzania, the travel agent looked at me indignantly. "Njeri, that's Kikuyu. What are you doing with an African name?" he demanded.

I'd been in Dar es Salaam about a month and had learned that Africans assess in a glance the ethnic origins of the people they meet.

Without a greeting, strangers on the street in Tanzania's capital would comment, "Oh, you're an Afro-American or West Indian."

"Both."

"I knew it," they'd respond, sometimes politely, sometimes not.

Or, people I got to know while in Africa would mention, "I know another half-caste like you." Then they would call in the "mixed-race" person and say, "Please meet Itabari Njeri." The darker-complected African, presumably of unmixed ancestry, would then smile and stare at us like we were animals in the zoo.

Of course, this "half-caste" (which I suppose is a term preferable to "mulatto," which I hate, and which every person who understands its derogatory meaning—"mule"—should never use) was usually the product of a mixed marriage, not generations of ethnic intermingling. And it was clear from most "half-castes" I met that they did not like being compared to so mongrelized and stigmatized a group as Afro-Americans.

I had minored in African studies in college, worked for years with Africans in the United States and had no romantic illusions as to how I would be received in the motherland. I wasn't going back to find my roots. The only thing that shocked me in Tanzania was being called, with great disdain, a "white woman" by an African waiter. Even if the rest of the world didn't follow the practice, I then assumed everyone understood that any known or perceptible degree of African ancestry made one "black" in America by law and social custom.

But I was pleasantly surprised by the telephone call I received two minutes after I walked into my Dar es Salaam hotel room. It was the hotel operator. "Sister, welcome to Tanzania. . . . Please tell everyone in Harlem hello for us." The year was 1978, and people in Tanzania were wearing half-foot-high platform shoes and dancing to James Brown wherever I went.

Shortly before I left, I stood on a hill surrounded by a field of endless flowers in Arusha, near the border of Tanzania and Kenya. A toothless woman with a wide smile, a staff in her hand and two young girls at her side, came toward me on a winding path. I spoke to her in fractured Swahili and she to me in broken English.

"I know you," she said smiling. "Wa-Negro." "Wa" is a prefix in Bantu language meaning people. "You are from the lost tribe," she told me. "Welcome," she said, touching me, then walked down a hill that lay in the shadow of Mount Kilimanjaro.

I never told her my name, but when I told other Africans, they'd say: "*Emmmm,* Itabari. Too long. How about I just call you Ita."

CULTURAL AND PHILOSOPHICAL ESSAYS

Benjamin Banneker (1731–1806)

Perceived as an anomaly by some eighteenth-century white Americans, scholar and inventor Benjamin Banneker was among the great intellectuals of his time. Born free in Maryland of "thrifty and industrious parents," Banneker attended a private school in Baltimore that provided education to both whites and blacks. His precocious command of mathematics and science impressed his family and friends, particularly Andrew Ellicott, a socially prominent Quaker. Exchanging books and ideas about mathematics and astronomy, Banneker and Ellicott developed a friendship that later led to Banneker's association with other white socialites and politicians.

Banneker's skills in astronomy led him to write and publish a series of almanacs between 1791 and 1797. He is also credited with constructing one of the first clocks to be made of wooden components in America. He served as a member of the commission that planned the boundaries and streets for Washington, D.C. The Georgetown Weekly Ledger *referred to Banneker as "an Ethiopian whose abilities as surveyor and astronomer already prove that Mr. [Thomas] Jefferson's concluding that that race of men were void of mental endowment was without foundation." Banneker's brilliance thus repudiated eighteenth-century racist notions regarding the supposed inabilities of blacks. Although he remained aloof from the two traditional institutions of his day—marriage and the church—Banneker dedicated his life to his work. According to critic Ruth Miller, he "lived quietly near his sisters," but "two days after his death all his papers were consumed by fire."*

Reprinted here is Banneker's 1791 letter to then-Secretary of State Thomas Jefferson. In it Banneker addresses Jefferson's denial of the intellectual potential of African Americans.

Letter to Thomas Jefferson

Maryland, Baltimore County
Near Ellicotts' Lower Mills, August 19th, 1791

Thomas Jefferson, Secretary of State.

Sir:—I am fully sensible of the greatness of that freedom, which I take with you on the present occasion, a liberty which seemed to me scarcely allowable, when I reflected on that distinguished and dignified station in which you stand, and the almost general prejudice and prepossession which is so prevalent in the world against those of my complexion.

I suppose it is a truth too well attested to you, to need a proof here, that we are a race of beings who have long laboured under the abuse and censure of the world, that we have long been considered rather as brutish than human, and scarcely capable of mental endowments.

Sir, I hope I may safely admit, in consequence of that report which hath reached me, that you are a man far less inflexible in sentiments of this nature than many others, that you are measurably friendly and well disposed towards us, and that you are willing and ready to lend your aid and assistance to our relief, from those many distresses and numerous calamities, to which we are reduced.

Now, sir, if this is founded in truth, I apprehend you will readily embrace every opportunity to eradicate that train of absurd and false ideas and opinions, which so generally prevails with respect to us, and that your sentiments are concurrent with mine, which are that one universal Father hath given Being to us all, and that he hath not only made us all of one flesh, but that he hath also without partiality afforded us all the same sensations, and endued us all with the same faculties, and that however variable we may be in society or religion, however diversified in situation or colour, we are all of the same family, and stand in the same relation to him.

Sir, if these are sentiments of which you are fully persuaded, I hope you cannot but acknowledge, that it is the indispensable duty of those who maintain for themselves the rights of human nature, and who profess the obligations of Christianity, to extend their power and influence to the relief of every part of the human race, from whatever burden or oppression they may unjustly labour under, and this I apprehend a full conviction of the truth and obligation of these principles should lead all to.

Sir, I have long been convinced that if your love for yourselves and for those inesteemable laws, which preserve to you the rights of human nature, was found on sincerity, you could not but be solicitous that every individual of whatever rank or distinction, might with you equally enjoy the blessings thereof, neither could you rest satisfied, short of the most active diffusion of your exertions in order to their promotions from any state of degradation to which the unjustifiable cruelty and barbarism of men have reduced them.

Sir, I freely and cheerfully acknowledge that I am of the African race, and in that colour which is natural to them of the deepest dye, and it is under a sense of the most profound gratitude to the Supreme Ruler of the universe that I now confess to you that I am not under that state of tyrannical thraldom and inhuman captivity to which too many of my brethren are doomed; but that I have abundantly tasted of the fruition of those blessings which proceed from that free and unequalled liberty with which you are favoured and which, I hope you will willingly allow you have received from the immediate hand of that Being, from whom proceedeth every good and perfect gift.

Sir, suffer me to recall to your mind that time in which the arms and tyranny of the British Crown were exerted with every powerful effort in order to reduce you to a State of Servitude, look back I entreat you on the variety of dangers to which you were exposed; reflect on that time in which every human aid appeared unavailable, and in which even hope and fortitude wore the aspect of inability to the conflict and you cannot but be led to a serious and grateful sense of your miraculous and providential preservation; you cannot but acknowledge that the present freedom and tranquility which you enjoy you have mercifully received and that it is the peculiar blessing of Heaven.

This sir, was a time in which you clearly saw into the injustice of a state of slavery and in which you had just apprehensions of the horrors of its condition, it is now, sir, that your abhorrence thereof was so excited, that you publickly held forth this true and valuable doctrine, which is worthy to be recorded and remembered in all succeeding ages. "We hold these truths to be self-evident, that all men are created equal, and that they are endowed by their creator with certain unalienable rights, that among these are life, liberty and the pursuit of happiness."

Here, sir, was a time in which your tender feelings for yourselves had engaged you thus to declare, you were then impressed with proper ideas of the great valuation of liberty and the free possession of those blessings to which you were entitled by nature; but, sir, how pitiable is it to reflect that although you were so fully convinced of the benevolence of the Father of mankind and of his equal and impartial distribution of those rights and privileges which he had conferred upon them, that you should at the same time counteract his mercies in detaining by fraud and violence so numerous a part of my brethren under groaning captivity and cruel oppression, that you should at the same time be found guilty of that most criminal act which you professedly detested in others with respect to yourselves.

Sir, I suppose that your knowledge of the situation of my brethren is too extensive to need a recital here; neither shall I presume to prescribe methods by which they may be relieved, otherwise than by recommending to you and all others to wean yourselves from those narrow prejudices which you have imbibed with respect to them and as Job proposed to his friends, "put your souls in their souls stead," thus shall your hearts be enlarged with kindness and benevolence towards them, and thus shall you need neither the direction of myself or others, in what manner to proceed herein.

And now, sir, although my sympathy and affection for my brethren hath caused my enlargement thus far, I ardently hope that your candour and generosity will plead with you in my behalf when I make known to you that it was not originally my design; but that having taken up my pen in order to direct to you as a present, a copy of an almanac, which I have calculated for the succeeding year, I was unexpectedly and unavoidably led thereto.

This calculation, sir, is the production of my arduous study in this my advanced stage of life; acquainted with the secrets of nature, I have had to gratify my curiosity herein through my own assiduous application to astronomical study, in which I need not to recount to you the many difficulties and disadvantages which I have had to encounter.

And although I had almost declined to make my calculation for the ensuing year, in consequence of that time which I had allotted therefor being taken up at the Federal Territory by the request of Mr. Andrew Ellicott, yet finding myself under several engagements to printers of this state, to whom I had communicated my design, on my return to my place of residence I industriously applied myself thereto which I hope I have accomplished with correctness and accuracy, a copy of which I have taken the liberty to direct to you and which I humbly request you will favorably receive. Although you may have the opportunity of perusing it after its publication yet I chose to send it to you in manuscript previous thereto that you might not only have an earlier inspection but that you might also view it in my own handwriting.

And now, sir, I shall conclude and subscribe myself, with the most profound respect, your most obedient humble servant,

B. BANNEKER

David Walker (1785–1830)

David Walker was born a free Negro in North Carolina. His father was a slave, but his mother was free. Later he moved north to Boston, where he married and became a businessman.

It was not in business, however, where Walker made his strongest mark. He turned to writing, and in the year before his death he published Walker's Appeal in Four Articles Together with a Preamble to the Colored Citizens of the World, but in Particular and Very Expressly to Those of the United States *(1829). Unlike Old Testament and European renditions of oppression and slavery,* Walker's Appeal *used the Jewish-Egyptian biblical story as a paradigm for American slavery. Writing before the Civil War, Walker presented American whites as cruel and corrupt barbarians and exhorts black slaves to grasp their freedom and destiny by fighting against the institution of slavery.*

The reaction to Walker's publication was immediate. Copies of the book were found in the South, where laws had been passed to prohibit the writing and distribution of incendiary material. A reward was put out for the writer's capture, dead or alive. Months after publication of his Appeal, *Walker was found dead on the doorsteps of his home in Boston.*

In the following excerpt from Walker's Appeal, *the author evaluates the effects of slavery and racism on blacks, particularly the fostering of ignorance in matters of religion and culture.*

from Walker's Appeal in Four Articles Together with a Preamble to the Colored Citizens of the World, but in Particular and Very Expressly to Those of the United States

Our Wretchedness in Consequence of Ignorance

Ignorance, my brethren, is a mist, low down into the very dark and almost impenetrable abyss in which, our fathers for many centuries had been plunged. The Christians, and enlightened of Europe, and some of Asia, seeing the ignorance and consequent degradation of our fathers, instead of trying to enlighten them, by teaching them that religion and light with which God had blessed them, they have plunged them into wretchedness ten thousand times more intolerable, than if they had left them entirely to the Lord, and to add to their miseries, deep down into which they have plunged them tell them, that they are an *inferior* and *distinct race* of beings, which they will be glad enough to recall and swallow by and by. Fortune and misfortune, two inseparable companions, lay rolled up in the wheel of events, which have from the creation of the world, and will continue to take place among men until God shall dash worlds together.

When we take a retrospective view of the arts and sciences—the wise legislators—the Pyramids, and other magnificent buildings—the turning of the channel of the river Nile, by the sons of Africa or of Ham, among whom learning originated, and was carried thence into Greece, where it was improved upon and refined. Thence among the Romans, and all over the then enlightened parts of the world, and it has been enlightening the dark and benighted minds of men from then, down to this day. I say, when I view retrospectively, the renown of that once mighty people, the children of our great progenitor I am indeed cheered. Yea further, when I view that mighty son of Africa, Hannibal, one of the greatest generals of antiquity, who defeated and cut off so many thousands of the white Romans or murderers, and who carried his victorious arms, to the very gate of Rome, and I give it as my candid opinion, that had Carthage been well united and had given him good support, he would have carried that cruel and barbarous city by storm. But they were dis-united, as the colored people are now, in the United States of America, the reason our natural enemies are enabled to keep their feet on our throats.

Beloved brethren—here let me tell you, and believe it, that the Lord our God, as true as he sits on his throne in heaven, and as true as our Savior died to redeem the world, will give you a Hannibal, and when the Lord shall have raised him up, and given him to you for your possession, O my suffering brethren! remember the divisions and consequent sufferings of *Carthage* and of *Hayti*. Read the history particularly of Hayti, and see how they were butchered by the whites, and do you take warning. The person whom God shall give you, give him your support and let him go his length, and behold in him the salvation of your God. God will indeed, deliver you through him from your deplorable and wretched condition under the Christians of America. I charge you this day before my God to lay no obstacle in his way, but let him go.

The whites want slaves, and want us for their slaves, but some of them will curse the day they ever saw us. As true as the sun ever shone in its meridian splendor, my color will root some of them out of the very face of the earth. They shall have enough of making slaves of, and butchering, and murdering us in the manner which they have. No doubt some may say that I write with a bad spirit, and that I being a black, wish these things to occur. Whether I write with a bad or a good spirit, I say if these things do not occur in their proper time, it is because the world in which we live does not exist, and we are deceived with regard to its existence.—It is immaterial however to me, who believe, or who refuse—though I should like to see the whites repent peradventure God may have mercy on them, some however, have gone so far that their cup must be filled.

But what need have I to refer to antiquity, when Hayti, the glory of the blacks and terror of tyrants, is enough to convince the most avaricious and stupid of wretches—which is at this time, and I am sorry to say it, plagued with that scourge of nations, the Catholic religion; but I hope and pray God that she may yet rid herself of it, and adopt in its stead the Protestant faith; also, I hope that she may keep peace within her borders and be united, keeping a strict look out for tyrants, for if they get the least chance to injure her, they will avail themselves of it, as true as the Lord lives in heaven. But one thing which gives me joy is, that they are men who would cut off to a man, before they would yield to the combined forces of the whole world—in fact, if the whole world was combined against them, it could not do any thing with them, unless the Lord delivers them up.

Ignorance and treachery one against the other—a grovelling servile and abject submission to the lash of tyrants, we see plainly, my brethren, are not the natural elements of the blacks, as the Americans try to make us believe; but these are misfortunes which God has suffered our fathers to be enveloped in for many ages, no doubt in consequence of their disobedience to their Maker, and which do, indeed, reign at this time among us, almost to the destruction of all other principles: for I must truly say, that ignorance, the mother of treachery and deceit, gnaws into our very vitals. Ignorance, as it now exists among us, produces a state of things, Oh my Lord! too horrible to present to the world. Any man who is curious to see the full force of ignorance developed among the colored people of the United States of America, has only to go into the southern and western states of this confederacy, where, if he is not a tyrant, but has the feelings of a human being, who can feel for a fellow creature, he may see enough to make his very heart bleed! He may see there, a son take his mother, who bore almost the pains of death to give him birth, and by the command of a tyrant, strip her as naked as she came into the world, and apply the cow-hide to her, until she falls a victim to death in the road! He may see a husband take his dear wife, not unfrequented in a pregnant state, and perhaps far advanced, and beat her for an unmerciful wretch, until his infant falls a lifeless lump at her feet! Can the Americans escape God Almighty? If they do, can he be to us a God of Justice? God is just, and I know it—for he has convinced me to my satisfaction—I cannot doubt him. My observer may see fathers beating their sons, mothers their daughters, and children their parents, all to pacify the passions of unrelenting tyrants. He may also, see them telling news and lies, making mischief one upon another. These are some of the productions of ignorance, which he will see practiced among my dear brethren, who are held in unjust slavery and wretchedness, by avaricious and unmerciful tyrants, to whom, and their hellish deeds, I would suffer my life to be taken before I would submit. And when my curious observer comes to take notice of those who are said to be free, (which assertion I deny) and who are making some frivolous pretentions to common sense, he will see that branch of ignorance among the slaves assuming a more cunning and deceitful course of procedure.—He may see some of my breathren in league with tyrants, selling their own brethren into *hell upon earth,* not dissimilar to the exhibitions in Africa, but in a more secret, servile and abject manner. Oh Heaven! I am full!!! I can hardly move my pen!!!! and as I expect some will try to put me to death, to strike terror into others, and to obliterate from their minds the notion of freedom, so as to keep my brethren the more secure in wretchedness, where they will be permitted to stay but a short time (whether tyrants believe it or not)—I shall give the world a development of facts, which are already witnessed in the courts of heaven. My observer may see some of those ignorant and treacherous creatures (colored people) sneaking about the large cities, endeavoring to find out all strange colored people, where they work and where they reside, asking them questions, and trying to ascertain whether they are runaways or not, telling them, at the same time, that they always have been, are, and always will be, friends to their brethren; and, perhaps, that they themselves are absconders, and a thousand such treacherous lies to get the better information of the more ignorant!!! There have been and are at this day in Boston, New-York, Philadelphia, and Baltimore, colored men, who are in league with tyrants, and who receive a great portion of their daily bread, of the moneys which they acquire from the blood and tears of their more miserable brethren, whom they scandalously delivered into the hands of our *natural enemies!!!!!* . . .

Our Wretchedness in Consequence of the Preachers of the Religion of Jesus Christ

Religion, my brethren, is a substance of deep consideration among all nations of the earth. The Pagans have a kind, as well as the Mahometans, the Jews and the Christians. But pure and undefiled religion, such as was preached by Jesus Christ and his apostles, is hard to be found in all the earth. God, through his instrument, Moses, handed a dispensation of his Divine will, to the children of Israel after they had left Egypt for the land of Canaan or of Promise, who through hypocrisy, oppression and unbelief, departed from the faith.—He then, by his apostles, handed a dispensation of his, together with the will of Jesus Christ, to the Europeans in Europe, who, in open violation of which, have made *merchandise* of us, and it does appear as though they take this very dispensation to aid them in their *infernal* depredations upon us. Indeed, the way in which religion was and is conducted by the Europeans and their descendants, one might believe it was a plan fabricated by themselves and the *devils* to oppress us. But hark! My master has taught me better than to believe it—he has taught me that his gospel as it was preached by himself and his apostles remains the same, notwithstanding Europe has tried to mingle blood and oppression with it.

It is well known to the Christian world, that Bartholomew Las Casas, that very notoriously avaricious Catholic priest or preacher, and adventurer with Columbus, in his second voyage, proposed to his countrymen, the Spaniards in Hispaniola to import the Africans from the Portuguese settlement in Africa, to dig up gold and silver, and work their plantations for them, to effect which, he made a voyage thence to Spain, and opened the subject to his master, Ferdinand then in declining health, who listened to the plan: but who died soon after, and left it in the hand of his successor, Charles V. This wretch, ("Las Casas, the Preacher,") succeeded so well in his plans of oppression, that in 1503, the first blacks had been imported into the new world. Elated with this success, and stimulated by sordid avarice only, he importuned Charles V in 1511, to grant permission to a Flemish merchant, to import 4000 blacks at one time. Thus we see, through the instrumentality of a pretended preacher of the gospel of Jesus Christ our common master, our wretchedness first commenced in America—where it has been continued from 1503, to this day, 1829. A period of three hundred and twenty-six years. But two hundred and nine, from 1620 [1619]—when twenty of our fathers were brought into Jamestown, Virginia, by a Dutch man of war, and sold off like brutes to the highest bidders; and there is not a doubt in my mind, but that tyrants are in hope to perpetuate our miseries under them and their children until the final consummation of all things—But if they do not get dreadfully deceived, it will be because God has forgotten them.

The Pagans, Jews and Mahometans try to make proselytes to their religions, and whatever human beings adopt their religions they extend to them their protection. But Christian Americans not only hinder their fellow creatures, the Africans, but thousands of them *will absolutely beat a colored person nearly to death, if they catch him on his knees, supplicating the throne of grace.* This barbarous cruelty was by all the heathen nations of antiquity, and is by the Pagans, Jews and Mahometans of the present day, left entirely to Christian Americans to inflict on the Africans and their descendants, that their cup which is nearly full may be completed. I have known tyrants or usurpers of human liberty in different parts of this country to take their fellow creatures, the colored people, and beat them until they would scarcely leave life in them; what for? Why they say "The black devils had the audacity to be found *making prayers and supplications to the God who made them!!!*" Yes, I have known small collections of colored people to have convened together, for no other purpose than to worship God Almighty, in spirit and in truth, to the best of their knowledge; when tyrants, calling themselves *patrols,* would also convene and wait almost in breathless silence for the poor colored people to commence singing and praying to the Lord our God, as soon as they had commenced, the wretches would burst in upon them and drag them out and commence beating them as they would rattle-snakes—many of whom, they would beat so unmercifully, that they would hardly be able to crawl for weeks and sometimes for months. Yet the American ministers send out missionaries to convert the heathen, while they keep us and our children sunk at their feet in the most abject ignorance and wretchedness that ever a people was afflicted with since the world began. Will the Lord suffer this people to proceed much longer? Will he not stop them in their career? Does he regard the heathens abroad, more than the heathens among the Americans? Surely the Americans must believe that God is partial, notwithstanding his Apostle Peter, declared before Cornelius and others that he has no respect to persons, but in every nation he that feareth God and worketh righteousness is accepted with him.—"The word," said he, "which God sent unto the children of Israel, preaching peace, by Jesus Christ (he is Lord of all)." Have not the Americans the Bible in their hands? Do they believe it? Surely they do not. See how they treat us in open violation of the Bible!! They no doubt will be greatly offended with me, but if God does not awaken them, it will be, because they are superior to other men, as they have represented themselves to be. Our divine Lord and Master said, "all things whatsoever ye would that men should do unto you, do ye even so unto them." But an American minister, with the Bible in his hand, holds us and our children in the most abject slavery and wretchedness. Now I ask them, would they like for us to hold them and their children in abject slavery and wretchedness? No, says one, that never can be done—you are too abject and ignorant to do it—you are not men—you were made to be slaves to us, to dig up gold and silver for us and our children. Know this, my dear sirs, that although you treat us and our children now, as you do your domestic beast—yet the final result of all future events are known but to God Almighty alone, who rules in the armies of heaven and among the inhabitants of the earth, and who dethrones one earthly king and sits up another, as it seemeth good in his holy sight. We may attribute these vicissitudes to what we please, but the God of armies and of justice rules in heaven and earth, and the whole American people shall see and know it yet, to their satisfaction. I have known pretended preachers of the gospel of my Master, who not only held us as their natural inheritance, but treated us with as much rigor as any Infidel or Deist in the world—just as though they were intent only on taking our blood and groans to glorify the Lord Jesus Christ. The wicked and ungodly, seeing their preachers treat us with so much cruelty, they say: our preachers, who must be right, if any body are, treat them like brutes, and why cannot we?—They think it is no harm to keep them in slavery and put the whip to them, and why cannot we do the same!—They being preachers of the gospel of Jesus Christ, if it were any harm, they would surely preach against their oppression and do their utmost to erase it from the country; not only in one or two cities, but one continual cry would be raised in all parts of this confederacy, and would cease only with the complete overthrow of the system of slavery, in every part of the country. But how far the American preachers are from preaching against slavery and oppression, which have carried their country to the brink of a precipice; to save them from plunging down the side of which, will hardly be affected, will appear in the sequel of this paragraph, which I shall narrate just as it transpired. I remember a Camp Meeting in South Carolina, for which I embarked in a Steam Boat at Charleston, and having been five or six hours on the water, we at last arrived at the place of hearing, where was a very good concourse of people, who were no doubt, collected together to hear the word of God (that some had collected barely as spectators to the scene, I will not here pretend to doubt, however, that is left to themselves and their God). Myself and boat companions, having been there, a little while, we were all called up to hear; I among the rest went up and took my seat—being seated, I fixed myself in a complete position to hear the word of my Savior and to receive such as I thought was authenticated by the Holy Scriptures; but to my no ordinary astonishment, our Reverend gentleman got up and told us (colored people) that slaves must be obedient to their masters—must do their duty to their masters or be whipped—the whip was made for the backs of fools, &c. Here I pause for a moment, to give the world time to consider what was my surprise, to hear such preaching from a minister of my Master, whose very gospel is that of peace and not of blood and whips, as this pretended preacher tried to make us believe. What the American preachers can think of us, I aver this day before my God, I have never been able to define. They have newspapers and monthly periodicals, which they receive in continual succession, but on the pages of which, you will scarcely ever find a paragraph respecting slavery, which is ten thousand times more injurious to this country than all the other evils put together; and which will be the final overthrow of its government, unless something is very speedily done; for their cup is nearly full.—Perhaps they will laugh at or make light of this; but I tell you Americans that unless you speedily alter your course, *you* and your *Country are gone!!!!!!* For God Almighty will tear up the very face of the earth!!! Will not that very remarkable passage of Scripture be fulfilled on Christian Americans? Hear it Americans!! "He that is unjust, let him be unjust still:—and he which is filthy, let him be filthy still: and he that is righteous, let him be righteous still: and he that is holy, let him be holy still." I hope that the Americans may hear, but I am afraid that they have done us so much injury, and are so firm in the belief that our Creator made us to be an inheritance to them for ever, that their hearts will be hardened, so that their destruction may be sure. This language, perhaps is too harsh for the American's delicate ears. But Oh Americans! Americans!! I warn you in the name of the Lord, (whether you will hear, or forbear,) to repent and reform, or you are ruined!!! Do you think that our blood is hidden from the Lord, because you can hide it from the rest of the world, by sending out missionaries, and by your charitable deeds to the Greeks, Irish, &c.? Will he not publish your secret crimes on the house top? Even here in Boston, pride and prejudice have got to such a pitch, that in the very houses erected to the Lord, they have built little places for the reception of colored people, where they must sit during meeting, or keep away from the house of God, and the preachers say nothing about it—much less go into the hedges, and highways seeking the lost sheep of the house of Israel, and try to bring them in to their Lord and Master. There are not a more wretched, ignorant, miserable, and abject set of beings in all the world, than the blacks in the Southern and Western sections of this country, under tyrants and devils. The preachers of America cannot see them, but they can send out missionaries to convert the heathens, notwithstanding. Americans! unless you speedily alter your course of proceeding, if God Almighty does not stop you, I say it in his name, that you may go on and do as you please for ever, both in time and eternity—never fear any evil at all!!!!!!!

Martin R. Delany (1812–85)

A *physician, abolitionist, scholar, and politician, Martin R. Delany defied America's racism throughout his adult life. In a public address delivered just after the Fugitive Slave Law (1850) was passed, he stated: "If any man approaches the house in search of a slave—I care not who he may be . . . if he crosses the threshold of my door, and I do not lay him a lifeless corpse at my feet, I hope the grave may refuse my body a resting place, and righteous Heaven my spirit a home."*

Born of parents who were free Negroes, Delany was raised in his birth state of Virginia. In 1822, he moved with his family to Pennsylvania and began attending school. While still a young man, in 1831 he spent time at the Thebon Literary Society in Pittsburgh—an organization for Negro men—developing his political awareness. Later, he went to New York to attend the African Free School and the Oneida Institute. Marrying and eventually fathering eleven children, Delany published his newspaper the Mystery, *from 1843 to 1847, and he worked with Frederick Douglass on the* North Star *newspaper from 1847 to 1849.*

However, journalism was by no means Delany's sole interest. In 1849, he entered Harvard Medical School. Despite protests from white students, Delany received his medical degree in 1852. He served as a doctor during the 1854 cholera epidemic in Philadelphia, and in 1856, he opened his own practice in Ohio.

Throughout his work as a physician, Delany found time for ardent political activities, particularly in support of relocating American blacks out of the country. In 1852, he wrote The Condition, Elevation, and Destiny of the Colored People of the United States, Politically Considered. *The publication evaluated the future of blacks in the mid-nineteenth-century United States, advocating their emigration to Central America. Delany was one of the 1854 organizers of the National Emigration of Colored Men, eventually becoming chief commissioner of a group that journeyed to Nigeria in 1859 to investigate that country's potential as a relocation site for American blacks. In 1855, Delany traveled to London to attend, without official status, the International Statistical Congress presided over by Prince Albert. When the prince acknowledged him among the official American delegates at the Congress, Delany stated: "I rise, your Regal Highness, to thank his lordship, the unflinching friend of the Negro, for the remarks he has made in reference to myself, and to assure your Regal Highness and his lordship that I am a man."*

In 1861, Delany published his Official Report of the Niger Valley Exploring Party. *With the outbreak of the Civil War, he became involved in recruiting Negro soldiers for the Union Army, serving as an examining surgeon in Chicago.*

Toward the end of the war, before retiring, Delany was granted the rank of major by President Abraham Lincoln, making him the first black man to be so commissioned. After the war, Delany worked in Charleston at the Freedman's Bureau and served as a trial judge for the city. He was an unsuccessful candidate for lieutenant governor of South Carolina in 1874. Delany's other publications include serialized chapters from his novel, Blake, or the Huts of America *(1859), and* Principles of Ethnology: The Origin of Race and Color *(1879).*

The following chapters from The Condition, Elevation, and Destiny of the Colored People of the United States, Politically Considered *reveal Delany's intense resolve regarding the relocation of blacks outside of the United States.*

from The Condition, Elevation and Destiny of the Colored People of the United States, Politically Considered

CHAPTER 2
Comparative Condition of the Colored People of the United States

The United States, untrue to her trust and unfaithful to her professed principles of republican equality, has also pursued a policy of political degradation to a large portion of her native born countrymen, and that class is the Colored People. Denied an equality not only of political, but of natural rights, in common with the rest of our fellow citizens, there is no species of degradation to which we are not subject.

Reduced to abject slavery is not enough, the very thought of which should awaken every sensibility of our common nature; but those of their descendants who are freemen even in the non-slaveholding States, occupy the very same position politically, religiously, civilly and socially, (with but few exceptions,) as the bondman occupies in the slave States.

In those States, the bondman is disfranchised, and for the most part so are we. He is denied all civil, religious, and social privileges, except such as he gets by mere sufferance, and so are we. They have no part nor lot in the government of the country, neither have we. They are ruled and governed without representation, existing as mere nonentities among the citizens, and excrescences on the body politic—a mere dreg in community, and so are we. Where then is our political superiority to the enslaved? none, neither are we superior in any other relation to society, except that we are defacto masters of ourselves and joint rulers of our own domestic household, while the bondman's self is claimed by another, and his relation to his family denied him. What the unfortunate classes are in Europe, such are we in the United States, which is folly to deny, insanity not to understand, blindness not to see, and surely now full time that our eyes were opened to these startling truths, which for ages have stared us full in the face.

It is time that we had become politicians, we mean, to understand the political economy and domestic policy of nations; that we had become as well as moral theorists, also the practical demonstrators of equal rights and self-government. Except we do, it is idle to talk about rights, it is mere chattering for the sake of being seen and heard—like the slave, saying something because his so called "master" said it, and saying just what he told him to say. Have we not now sufficient intelligence among us to understand our true position, to realize our actual condition, and determine for ourselves what is best to be done? If we have not now, we never shall have, and should at once cease prating about our equality, capacity, and all that.

Twenty years ago, when the writer was a youth, his young and yet uncultivated mind was aroused, and his tender heart made to leap with anxiety in anticipation of the promises then held out by the prime movers in the cause of our elevation.

In 1830 the most intelligent and leading spirits among the colored men in the United States, such as James Forten, Robert Douglass, I. Bowers, A. D. Shadd, John Peck, Joseph Cassey, and John B. Vashon of Pennsylvania; John T. Hilton, Nathaniel and Thomas Paul, and James G. Barbodoes of Massachusetts; Henry Sipkins, Thomas Hamilton, Thomas L. Jennings, Thomas Downing, Samuel E. Cornish, and others of New York; R. Cooley and others of Maryland, and representatives from other States which cannot now be recollected, the data not being at hand, assembled in the city of Philadelphia, in the capacity of a National Convention, to "devise ways and means for the bettering of our condition." These Conventions determined to assemble annually, much talent, ability, and energy of character being displayed; when in 1831 at a sitting of the Convention in September, from their previous pamphlet reports, much interest having been created throughout the country, they were favored by the presence of a number of whites, some of whom were able and distinguished men, such as Rev. R. R. Gurley, Arthur Tappan, Elliot Cresson, John Rankin, Simeon Jocelyn and others, among them William Lloyd Garrison, then quite a young man, all of whom were staunch and ardent Colonizationists, young Garrison at that time, doing his mightiest in his favorite work.

Among other great projects of interest brought before the convention at a previous sitting, was that of the expediency of a general emigration, as far as it was practicable, of the colored people to the British Provinces of North America. Another was that of raising sufficient means for the establishment and erection of a College for the proper education of the colored youth. These gentlemen long accustomed to observation and reflection on the condition of their people, saw at once, that there must necessarily be means used adequate to the end to be attained—that end being an unqualified equality with the ruling class of their fellow citizens. He saw that as a class, the colored people of the country were ignorant, degraded and oppressed, by far the greater portion of them being abject slaves in the South, the very condition of whom was almost enough, under the circumstances, to blast the remotest hope of success, and those who were freemen, whether in the South or North, occupied a subservient, servile, and menial position, considering it a favor to get into the service of the whites, and do their degrading offices. That the difference between the whites and themselves, consisted in the superior advantages of the one over the other, in point of attainments. That if a knowledge of the arts and sciences, the mechanical occupations, the industrial occupations, as farming, commerce, and all the various business enterprises, and learned professionals were necessary for the superior position occupied by their rulers, it was also necessary for them. And very reasonably too, the first suggestion which occurred to them was, the advantages of a location, then the necessity of a qualification. They reasoned with themselves, that all distinctive differences made among men on account of their origin, is wicked, unrighteous, and cruel, and never shall receive countenance in any shape from us, therefore, the first acts of the measures entered into by them, was to protest, solemnly protest, against every unjust measure and policy in the country, having for its object the proscription of the colored people, whether state, national, municipal, social, civil, or religious.

But being far-sighted, reflecting, discerning men, they took a political view of the subject, and determined for the good of their people to be governed in their policy according to the facts as they presented themselves. In taking a glance at Europe, they discovered there, however unjustly, . . . that there are and have been numerous classes proscribed and oppressed, and it was not for them to cut short their wise deliberations, and arrest their proceedings in contention, as to the cause, whether on account of language, the color of eyes, hair, skin, or their origin of country—because all this is contrary to reason, a contradiction to common sense, at war with nature herself and at variance with facts as they stare us every day in the face, among all nations, in every country—this being made the pretext as a matter of *policy* alone—a fact worthy of observation, that wherever the objects of oppression are the most easily distinguished by any peculiar or general characteristics, these people are the more easily oppressed, because the war of oppression is the more easily waged against them. This is the case with the modern Jews and many other people who have strongly-marked, peculiar, or distinguishing characteristics. This arises in this wise. The policy of all those who proscribe any people, induces them to select as the objects of proscription, those who differed as much as possible, in some particulars, for themselves. This is to ensure the greater success, because it engenders the greater prejudice, or in other words, elicits less interest on the part of the oppressing class, in their favor. This fact is well understood in national conflicts, as the soldier or civilian, who is distinguished by his dress, mustache, or any other peculiar appendage, would certainly prove himself a madman, if he did not take the precaution to change his dress, remove his mustache, and conceal as much as possible his peculiar characteristics, to give him access among the repelling party. This is mere policy, nature having nothing to do with it. Still, it is a fact, a great truth well worthy of remark, and as such we adduce it for the benefit of those of our readers, unaccustomed to an enquiry into the policy of nations.

In view of these truths, our fathers and leaders in our elevation, discovered that as a policy, we the colored people were selected as the subordinate class in this country, not on account of any actual or supposed inferiority on their part, but simply because, in view of all the circumstances of the case, they were the very best class that could be selected. They would have as readily had any other class as subordinates in the country, as the colored people, but the condition of society *at the time,* would not admit of it. In the struggle for American Independence, there were among those who performed the most distinguished parts, the most common-place peasantry of the Provinces. English, Danish, Irish, Scotch, and others, were among those whose names blazoned forth as heroes in the American Revolution. But a single reflection will convince us, that no course of policy could have induced the proscription of the parentage and relatives of such men as Benjamin Franklin the printer, Roger Sherman the cobbler, the tinkers, and others of the signers of the Declaration of Independence. But as they were determined to have a subservient class, it will readily be conceived, that according to the state of society at the time, the better policy on their part was, to select some class, who from their political position—however much they may have contributed their aid as we certainly did, in the general struggle for liberty by force of arms—who had the least claims upon them, or who had the *least chance,* or was the *least potent* in urging their claims. This class of course was the colored people and Indians.

The Indians who in the early settlement of the continent, before an African captive had ever been introduced thereon, were reduced to the most abject slavery, toiling day and night in the mines, under the relentless hands of heartless Spanish taskmasters, but being a race of people raised to the sports of fishing, the chase, and of war, were wholly unaccustomed to labor, and therefore sunk under the insupportable weight, two millions and a half having fallen victims to the cruelty of oppression and toil suddenly placed upon their shoulders. And it was only this that prevented their farther enslavement as a class, after the provinces were absolved from the British Crown. It is true that their general enslavement took place on the islands and in the mining districts of south America, where indeed, the Europeans continued to enslave them, until a comparatively recent period; still, the design, the feeling, and inclination from policy, was the same to do so here, in this section of the continent.

Nor was it until their influence became too great, by the political position occupied by their brethren in the new republic, that the German and Irish peasantry ceased to be sold as slaves for a term of years fixed by law, for the repayment of their passage-money, the descendants of these classes of people for a long time being held as inferiors, in the estimation of the ruling class, and it was not until they assumed the rights and privileges guaranteed to them by the established policy of the country, among the leading spirits of whom were their relatives, that the policy towards them was discovered to be a bad one, and accordingly changed. Nor was it, as is frequently very erroneously asserted, by colored as well as white persons, that it was on account of hatred to the African, or in other words, on account of hatred to his color, that the African was selected as the subject of oppression in this country. This is sheer nonsense; being based on policy and nothing else, as shown in another place. The Indians, who being the most foreign to the sympathies of the Europeans on this continent, were selected in the first place, who, being unable to withstand the hardships, gave way before them.

But the African race had long been known to Europeans, in all ages of the world's history, as a long-lived, hardy race, subject to toil and labor of various kinds, subsisting mainly by traffic, trade, and industry, and consequently being as foreign to the sympathies of the invaders of the continent as the Indians, they were selected, captured, brought here as a laboring class, and as a matter of policy held as such. Nor was the absurd idea of natural inferiority of the African ever dreamed of, until recently adduced by the slave-holders and their abettors, in justification of their policy. This, with contemptuous indignation, we fling back into their face, as a scorpion to a vulture. And so did our patriots and leaders in the cause of regeneration know better, and never for a moment yielded to the base doctrine. But they had discovered the great fact, that a cruel policy was pursued towards our people, and that they possessed distinctive characteristics which made them the objects of proscription. These characteristics being strongly marked in the colored people, as in the Indians, by color, character of hair and so on, made them the more easily distinguished from other

Americans, and the policies more effectually urged against us. For this reason they introduced the subject of emigration to Canada, and a proper institution for the education of the youth.

At this important juncture of their proceedings, the afore named white gentlemen were introduced to the notice of the Convention, and after gaining permission to speak, expressed their gratification and surprise at the qualification and talent manifested by different members of the Convention, all expressing their determination to give the cause of the colored people more serious reflection. Mr. Garrison, the youngest of them all, and none the less honest on account of his youthfulness, being but 26 years of age at the time, (1831) expressed his determination to change his course of policy at once, and espouse the cause of the elevation of the colored people here in their own country. We are not at present well advised upon this point, it now having escaped our memory, but we are under the impression that Mr. Jocelyn also, at once changed his policy.

During the winter of 1832, Mr. Garrison issued his *Thoughts on African Colonization,* and near about the same time or shortly after, issued the first number of the *Liberator,* in both of which, his full convictions of the enormity of American slavery, and the wickedness of their policy towards the colored people, were fully expressed. At the sitting of the Convention in this year, a number, perhaps all of these gentlemen were present, and those who had denounced the Colonization scheme, and espoused the cause of the elevation of the colored people in this country, or the Anti-Slavery cause, as it was not termed, expressed themselves openly and without reserve.

Sensible of the high-handed injustice done to the colored people in the United States, and the mischief likely to emanate from the unchristian proceedings of the deceptious Colonization scheme, like all honest hearted penitents, with the ardor only known to new converts, they entreated the Convention, whatever they did, not to entertain for a moment, the idea of recommending emigration to their people, nor the establishment of separate institutions of learning. They earnestly contended and doubtless honestly meaning what they said, that they (the whites) had been our oppressors and injurers, they had obstructed our progress to the high positions of civilization, and now, it was their bounden duty to make full amends for the injuries thus inflicted on an unoffending people. They exhorted the Convention to cease; as they had laid on the burden, they would also take it off; as they had obstructed our pathway, they would remove the hindrance. In a word, as they had oppressed and trampled down the colored people, they would now elevate them. These suggestions and promises, good enough to be sure, after they were made, were accepted by the convention—though some gentlemen were still in favor of the first project as the best policy, Mr. A. D. Shadd of West Chester, Pa., as we learn from himself, being one among that number—ran through the country like wild-fire, no one thinking, and if he thought, daring to speak above his breath of going any where out of certain prescribed limits, or of sending a child to school, if it should but have the name of "colored" attached to it, without the risk of being termed a "traitor" to the cause of his people, or an enemy to the Anti-Slavery cause.

At this important point in the history of our efforts, the colored men stopped suddenly, and with their hands thrust deep in their breeches-pockets, and their mouths gaping open, stood gazing with astonishment, wonder, and surprise, at the stupendous moral colossal statues of our Anti-Slavery friends and brethren, who in the heat and zeal of honest hearts, from a desire to make atonement for the many wrongs inflicted, promised a great deal more than they have ever been able half to fulfill, in thrice the period in which they expected it. And in this, we have no fault to find with our Anti-Slavery friends, and here wish it to be understood, that we are not laying any thing to their charge as blame, neither do we desire for a moment to reflect on them, because we heartily believe that all that they did at the time, they did with the purest and best of motives, and further believe that they now are, as they then were, the truest friends we have among the whites in this country. And hope, and desire, and request, that our people should always look upon *true* anti-slavery people, Abolitionists we mean, as their friends, until they have just cause for acting otherwise. It is true, that the Anti-Slavery, like all good causes, has produced some recreants, but the cause itself is no more to be blamed for that, than Christianity is for the malconduct of any professing hypocrite, nor the society of Friends, for the conduct of a broad-brimmed hat and shad-belly coated horse-thief, because he spoke *thee* and *thou* before stealing the horse. But what is our condition even amidst our Anti-Slavery friends? And here, as our sole intention is to contribute to the elevation of our people, we must be permitted to express our opinion freely, without being thought uncharitable.

In the first place, we should look at the objects for which the Anti-Slavery cause was commenced, and the promises or inducements it held out at the commencement. It should be borne in mind, that Anti-Slavery took its rise among *colored men,* just at the time they were introducing their greatest projects for their own elevation, and that our Anti-Slavery brethren were converts of the colored men, in behalf of their elevation. Of course, it would be expected that being baptized into the new doctrines, their faith would induce them to embrace the principles therein contained, with the strictest possible adherence.

The cause of dissatisfaction with our former condition, was, that we were proscribed, debarred, and shut out from every respectable position, occupying the places of inferiors and menials.

It was expected that Anti-Slavery, according to its professions, would extend to colored persons, as far as in the power of its adherents, those advantages nowhere else to be obtained among white men. That colored boys would get situations in their shops and stores, and every other advantage tending to elevate them as far as possible, would be extended to them. At least, it was expected, that in Anti-Slavery establishments, colored men would have the preference. Because, there was no other ostensible object in view, in the commencement of the Anti-Slavery enterprise, than the *elevation* of the *colored man,* by facilitating his efforts in attaining to equality with the white man. It was urged, and it was true, that the colored people were susceptible of all that the whites were, and all that was required was to give them a fair opportunity, and they would prove their capacity. That it was unjust, wicked, and cruel, the result of an unnatural prejudice, that debarred them from places of respectability, and that public opinion could and should be corrected upon this subject. That it was only necessary to make a sacrifice of feeling, and an innovation on the customs of society, to establish a different order of things,—that as Anti-Slavery men, they were willing to make these sacrifices, and determined to take the colored man by the hand, making common cause with him in affliction, and bear a part of the odium heaped upon him. That his cause was the cause of God—that "In as much as ye did it not unto the least of these my little ones, ye did it not unto me," and that as Anti-Slavery men, they would "do right if the heavens fell." Thus, was the cause espoused, and thus did we expect much. But in all this, we were doomed to disappointment, sad, sad disappointment. Instead of realizing what we had hoped for, we find ourselves occupying the very same position in relation to our Anti-Slavery friends, as we do in relation to the pro-slavery part of the community—a mere secondary, underlying position, in all our relations to them, and any thing more than this, is not a matter of course affair—it comes not by established anti-slavery custom or right, but like that which emanates from the proslavery portion of the community, by mere sufferance.

It is true, that the *Liberator* office, in Boston, has got Elijah Smith, a colored youth, at the cases—the *Standard,* in New York, a young colored man, and the *Freeman,* in Philadelphia, William Still, another, in the publication office, as "packing clerk;" yet these are but three out of the hosts that fill these offices in their various departments, all occupying places that could have been, and as we once thought, would have been, easily enough, occupied by colored men. Indeed, we can have no idea about anti-slavery in this country, than that the legitimate persons to fill any and every position about an anti-slavery establishment are colored persons. Nor will it do to argue in extenuation, that white men are as justly entitled to them as colored men; because white men do not from *necessity* become anti-salvery men in order to get situations; they being white men, may occupy any position they are capable of filling—in a word, their chances are endless, every avenue in the country being opened to them. They do not therefore become abolitionists, for the sake of employment—at least, it is not the song that anti-slavery sung, in the first love of the new faith, proclaimed by its disciples.

And if it be urged that colored men are incapable as yet to fill these positions, all that we have to say is, that the cause has fallen far short; almost equivalent to a failure, of a tithe, of what it promised to do in half the period of its existence, to this time, if it have not as yet, now a period of twenty years, raised up colored men enough, to fill the offices within its patronage. We think it is not unkind to say, if it had been half as faithful to itself, as it should have been—its professed principles we mean; it could have reared and tutored from childhood, colored men enough by this time, for its own especial purpose. These we know could have been easily obtained, because colored people in general, are favorable to the anti-slavery cause, and wherever there is an adverse manifestation, it arises from sheer ignorance; and we have now but comparatively few such among us. There is one thing certain, that no colored person, except such as would reject education altogether, would be adverse to putting their child with an anti-slavery person, for educational advantages. This then, could have been done. But it has not been done, and let the cause of it be whatever it may, and let whoever may be to blame, we are willing to let all that pass, and extend to our anti-slavery brethren the right-hand of fellowship, bidding them God-speed in the propagation of good and wholesome sentiments—for whether they are practically carried out or not, the professions are in themselves all right and good. Like Christianity, the principles are holy and of divine origin. And we believe, if ever a man started right, with pure and holy motives, Mr. Garrison did; and that, had he the power of making the cause what it should be, it would all be right, and there never would have been any cause for the remarks we have made, though in kindness, and with the purest of motives. We are nevertheless, still occupying a miserable position in the community, wherever we live; and what we most desire is, to draw the attention of our people to this fact, and point out what, in our opinion, we conceive to be a proper remedy.

CHAPTER 4
Our Elevation in the United States

That very little comparatively as yet has been done, to attain a respectable position as a class in this country, will not be denied, and that the successful accomplishment to this end is also possible, must also be admitted; but in what manner, and by what means, has long been, and is even now, by the best thinking minds among the colored people themselves, a matter of difference of opinion.

We believe in the universal equality of man, and believe in that declaration of God's word, in which it is there positively said, that "God has made of one blood all the nations that dwell on the face of the earth." Now of "the nations that dwell on the face of the earth," that is, all the people—there are one thousand millions of souls, and of this vast number of human beings, two-thirds are colored, from black, tending in complexion to the olive or that of the Chinese, with all the intermediate and admixtures of black and white, with the various "crosses" as they are physiologically, but erroneously termed, to white. We are thus explicit in stating these points, because we are determined to be understood by all. We have then, two colored to one white person throughout the earth, and yet, singular as it may appear, according to the present geographical and political history of the world, the white race predominates over the colored; or in other words, wherever there is one white person, that one rules and governs two colored persons. This is a living undeniable truth, to which we call the especial attention of the colored reader in particular. Now there is a cause for this, as there is no effect without a cause, a comprehensible remediable cause. We all believe in the justice of God, that he is impartial, "looking upon his children with an eye of care," dealing out to them all, the measure of his goodness; yet, how can we reconcile ourselves to the difference that exists between the colored and the white races, as they truthfully present themselves before our eyes? To solve this problem, is to know the remedy; and to know it, is but necessary, in order successfully to apply it. And we shall but take the colored people of the United States, as a fair sample of the colored races everywhere of the present age, as the arguments that apply to the one, will apply to the other, whether Christians, Mahomedans, or pagans.

The colored races are highly susceptible of religion; it is a constituent principle of their nature, and an excellent trait in their character. But unfortunately for them, they carry it too far. Their hope is largely developed, and consequently, they usually stand still—hope in God, and really expect Him to do that for them, which it is necessary they should do themselves. This is their great mistake, and arises from a misconception of the character and ways of Deity. We must know God, that is understand His nature and purposes, in order to serve Him; and to serve Him well, is but to know him rightly. To depend for assistance upon God, is a *duty* and right; but to know when, how, and in what manner to obtain it, is the key to this great Bulwark of Strength, and Depository of Aid.

God himself is perfect; perfect in all his works and ways. He has means for every end; and every means used must be adequate to the end to be gained. God's means are laws—fixed laws of nature, a part of His own being, and as immutable, as unchangeable as Himself. Nothing can be accomplished but through the medium of, and comformable to these laws.

They are *three*—and like God himself, represented in the three persons in the God-head—the *Spiritual, Moral* and *Physical* Laws.

That which is Spiritual, can only be accomplished through the medium of the Spiritual law; that which is Moral, through the medium of the Moral law; and that which is Physical, through the medium of the Physical law. Otherwise than this, it is useless to expect anything. Does a person want a spiritual blessing, he must apply through the medium of the spiritual law—*pray* for it in order to obtain it. If they desire to do a moral good, they must apply through the medium of the moral law—exercise their sense and feeling of *right* and *justice,* in order to effect it. Do they want to attain a physical end, they can only do so through the medium of the physical law—go to *work* with muscles, hands, limbs, might and strength, and this, and nothing else will attain it.

The argument that man must pray for what he receives, is a mistake, and one that is doing the colored people especially, incalculable injury. That man must pray in order to get to Heaven, every Christian will admit—but a great truth we have yet got to learn, that he can live on earth whether he is religious or not, so that he conforms to the great law of God, regulating the things of earth; the great physical laws. It is only necessary, in order to convince our people of their error and palpable mistake in this matter, to call their attention to the fact, that there are no people more religious in this Country, than the colored people, and none so poor and miserable as they. That prosperity and wealth, smiles upon the efforts of wicked white men, whom we know to utter the name of God with curses, instead of praises. That among the slaves, there are thousands of them religious, continually raising their voices, sending up their prayers to God, invoking His aid in their behalf, asking for a speedy deliverance; but they are still in chains, although they have thrice suffered out their three score years and ten. That "God sendeth rain upon the just and unjust," should be sufficient to convince us that our success in life, does not depend upon our religious character, but that the physical laws governing all earthly and temporary affairs, benefit equally the just and the unjust. Any other doctrine than this, is downright delusion, unworthy of a free people, and only intended for slaves. That all men and women, should be moral, upright, good and religious—we mean *Christians*—we would not utter a word against, and could only wish that it were so; but, what we here desire to do is, to correct the long standing error among a large body of the colored people in this country, that the cause of our oppression and degradation, is the displeasure of God towards us, because of our unfaithfulness to Him. This is not true; because if God is just—and he is—there could be no justice in prospering white men with his fostering care, for more than two thousand years, in all their wickedness, while dealing out to the colored people, the measure of his displeasure, for not half the wickedness as that of the whites. Here then is our mistake, and let it forever henceforth be corrected. We are no longer slaves, believing any interpretation that our oppressors may give the word of God, for the purpose of deluding us to the more easy subjugation; but freemen, comprising some of the first minds of intelligence and rudimental qualifications, in the country. What then is the remedy, for our degradation and oppression? This appears now to be the only remaining question—the means of successful elevation in this our own native land? This depends entirely upon the application of the means of Elevation.

CHAPTER 23
Things as They Are

And if thou boast TRUTH to utter,
SPEAK, and leave the rest to God.

In presenting this work, we have but a single object in view, and that is, to inform the minds of the colored people at large, upon many things pertaining to their elevation, that but few among us are acquainted with. Unfortunately for us, as a body, we have been taught to believe, that we must have some person to think for us, instead of thinking for ourselves. So accustomed are we to submission and this kind of training, that it is with difficulty, even among the most intelligent of the colored people, an audience may be elicited for any purpose whatever, if the expounder is to be a colored person; and the introduction of any subject is treated with indifference, if not contempt, when the originator is a colored person. Indeed, the most ordinary white person, is almost revered, while the most qualified colored person is totally neglected. Nothing from them is appreciated.

We have been standing comparatively still for years, following in the footsteps of our friends, believing that what they promise us can be accomplished, just because they say so, although our own knowledge should long since, have satisfied us to the contrary. Because even were it possible, with the present hate and jealousy that the whites have towards us in this country, for us to gain equality of rights with them; we never could have an equality of the exercise and enjoyment of these rights—because the great odds of numbers are against us. We might indeed, as some at present, have the right of the elective franchise—nay, it is not the elective franchise, because the *elective franchise* makes the enfranchised, *eligible* to any position attainable; but we may exercise the right of *voting* only, which to us, is but poor satisfaction; and we by no means care to cherish the privilege of voting somebody into office, to help to make laws to degrade us.

In religion—because they are both *translators* and *commentators,* we must believe nothing, however absurd, but what our oppressors tell us. In Politics, nothing but such as they promulge; in Anti-Slavery, nothing but what our white brethren and friends say we must; in the mode and manner of our elevation, we must do nothing, but that which may be laid down to be done by our white brethren from some quarter or other; and now, even on the subject of emigration, there are some colored people to be found, so lost to their own interest and self-respect, as to be gulled by slave owners and colonizationists, who are led to believe there is no other place in which they can become elevated, but Liberia, a government of American slave-holders, as we have shown—simply, because white men have told them so.

Upon the possibility, means, mode and manner, of our Elevation in the United States—Our Original Rights and Claims as Citizens—Our Determination not to be Driven from our Native Country—the Difficulties in the Way of our Elevation—Our Position in Relation to our Anti-Slavery Brethren—the Wicked Design and Injurious Tendency of the American Colonization Society—Objections to Liberia—Objections to Canada—Preferences to South America, &c., &c., all of which we have treated without reserve; expressing our mind freely, and with candor, as we are determined that as far as we can at present do so, the minds of our readers shall be enlightened. The custom of concealing information upon vital and important subjects, in which the interest of the people is involved, we do not agree with, nor favor in the least; we have therefore, laid this cursory treatise before our readers, with the hope that it may prove instrumental in directing the attention of our people in the right way, that leads to their Elevation. Go or stay—of course each is free to do as he pleases—one thing is certain; our Elevation is the work of our own hands. And Mexico, Central America, the West Indies, and South America, all present now, opportunities for the individual enterprise of our young men, who prefer to remain in the United States, in preference to going where they can enjoy real freedom, and equality of rights. Freedom of Religion, as well as of politics, being tolerated in all of these places.

Let our young men and women, prepare themselves for usefulness and business; that the men may enter into merchandise, trading, and other things of importance; the young women may become teachers of various kinds, and otherwise fill places of usefulness. Parents must turn their attention more to the education of their children. We mean, to educate them for useful practical business purposes. Educate them for the Store and the Counting House—to do every-day practical business. Consult the children's propensities, and direct their education according to their inclinations. It may be, that there is too great a desire on the part of parents, to give their children a professional education, before the body of the people, are ready for it. A people must be a business people, and have more to depend upon than mere help in people's houses and Hotels, before they are either able to support, or capable of properly appreciating the services of professional men among them. This has been one of our great mistakes—we have gone in advance of ourselves. We have commenced at the superstructure of the building, instead of the foundation—at the top instead of the bottom. We should first be mechanics and common tradesmen, and professions as a matter of course would grow out of the wealth made thereby. Young men and women, must now prepare for usefulness—the day of our Elevation is at hand—all the world now gazes at us—and Central and South America, and the West Indies, bid us come and be men and women, protected, secure, beloved and Free.

The branches of Education most desirable for the preparation of youth, for practical useful every-day life, are Arithmetic and good Penmanship, in order to be Accountants; and a good rudimental knowledge of Geography—which has ever been neglected, and under estimated—and of Political Economy; which without the knowledge of the first, no people can ever become adventurous—nor of the second, never will be an enterprising people. Geography, teaches a knowledge of the world, and Political Economy, a knowledge of the wealth of nations or how to make money. These are not abstruse sciences, or learning not easily acquired or understood; but simply, common School Primer learning, that every body may get. And, although it is the very Key to prosperity and success in common life, but few know any thing about it. Unfortunately for our people, so soon as their children learn to read a Chapter in the New Testament, and scribble a miserable hand, they are pronounced to have "Learning enough"; and taken away from School, no use to themselves, nor community. This is apparent in our Public Meetings, and Official Church Meetings; of the great number of men present, there are but few capable of filling a Secretaryship. Some of the large cities may be an exception to this. Of the multitudes of Merchants, and Business men throughout this country, Europe, and the world, few are qualified, beyond the branches here laid down by us as necessary for business. What did John Jacob Astor, Stephen Girard, or do the millionaires and the greater part of the merchant princes, and mariners, know about Latin and Greek, and the Classics? Precious few of them know any thing. In proof of this, in 1841, during the Administration of President Tyler, when the mutiny was detected on board of the American Man of War Brig Somers, the names of the Mutineers, were recorded by young S—a Midshipman in Greek. Captain Alexander Slidell McKenzie, Commanding, was unable to read them; and in his despatches to the Government, in justification of his policy in executing the criminals, said that he "discovered some curious characters which he was unable to read," &c.; showing thereby, that that high functionary, did not understand even the Greek Alphabet, which was only necessary, to have been able to read proper names written in Greek.

What we most need then, is a good business practical Education; because, the Classical and Professional education of so many of our young men, before their parents are able to support them, and community ready to patronize them, only serves to lull their energy, and cripple the otherwise, praiseworthy efforts they would make in life. A Classical education, is only suited to the wealthy, or those who have a prospect of gaining a livelihood by it. The writer does not wish to be understood, as underrating a Classical and Professional education; that is not his intention; he fully appreciates them, having had some such advantages himself; but he desires to give a proper guide, and put a check to the extravagant idea that is fast obtaining, among our people especially, that a Classical, or as it is termed, a "finished education," is necessary to prepare one for usefulness in life. Let us have an education, that shall practically develope our thinking faculties and manhood; and then, and not until then, shall we be able to vie with our oppressors, go where we may. We as heretofore, have been on the extreme; either no qualification at all, or a Collegiate education. We jumped too far; taking a leap from the deepest abyss to the highest summit; rising from the ridiculous to the sublime; without medium or intermission.

Let our young women have an education; let their minds be well informed; well stored with useful information and practical proficiency, rather than the light superficial acquirements, popularly and fashionably called accomplishments. We desire accomplishments, but they must be *useful.*

Our females must be qualified, because they are to be the mothers of our children. As mothers are the first nurses and instructors of children; from them children consequently, get their first impressions, which being always the most lasting, should be the most correct. Raise the mothers above the level of degradation, and the offspring is elevated with them. In a word, instead of our young men, transcribing in their blank books, recipes for *Cooking;* we desire to see them making the transfer of *Invoices of Merchandise.* Come to our aid then; the *morning* of our *Redemption* from degradation, adorns the horizon.

In our selection of individuals, it will be observed, that we have confined ourself entirely to those who occupy or have occupied positions among the whites, consequently having a more general bearing as useful contributors to society at large. While we do not pretend to give all such worthy cases, we gave such as possessed information of, and desire it to be understood, that a large number of our most intelligent and worthy men and women, have not been named, because from their more private position in community, it was foreign to the object and design of this work. If we have said aught to offend, "take the will for the deed," and be assured, that it was given with the purest of motives, and best intention, from a true hearted man and brother; deeply lamenting the sad fate of his race in this country, and sincerely desiring the elevation of man, and submitted to the serious consideration of all, who favor the promotion of the cause of God and humanity.

Mary Church Terrell (1863–1954)

Coming from a relatively privileged background for her time, Mary Church Terrell was nonetheless aware of prejudice in America and actively crusaded against racism and sexism. At the 1890 convention of the National Woman Suffrage Association in Washington, D.C., she commented: "A White Woman has only one handicap to overcome—a great one, true, her sex; a colored woman faces two—her sex and race."

Terrell's parents, former slaves, were able to structure a stable livelihood by the time their daughter was born in Memphis. Hoping to provide her with a solid education, they sent the six-year-old Terrell to live with a black family while attending Antioch College Model School in Yellow Springs, Ohio. Later, Terrell attended Oberlin College, where she earned a bachelor's in 1884, after four years of classical studies. She returned to Memphis to live with her wealthy, divorced father, whose home had become a notable location for social gatherings.

Later on, Terrell taught at Wilberforce College in Ohio and at a high school in Washington, D.C., where she met Robert Terrell, the black Harvard graduate who would become her husband. While teaching in Washington, D.C., Mary Church Terrell completed her master's at Oberlin in 1884 and then traveled for two years in Europe. When she returned to the United States, she settled for a time into her role as a homemaker. But in 1892, when a Memphis friend was lynched, Terrell's public activism intensified. She and Frederick Douglass, a family friend, conferred with President Benjamin Harrison about the lynchings of black Americans. In 1892, she helped establish the Colored Women's League of the District of Columbia, which joined with the Boston-based league led by black activist Josephine St. Pierre Ruffin. That union resulted in the 1896 establishment of the National Association of Colored Women (NACW), which elected Terrell as its first president. Among its other goals, the NACW sought to improve civil rights and employment opportunities for African Americans and to promote suffrage for black women.

By the early years of the twentieth century, Terrell had gained international respect as a leader of the women's suffrage movement. She was invited to speak at white women's suffrage conventions as well as at the Berlin International Congress of Women and the International League for Peace and Freedom in Zurich. Although at the turn of the century her accommodationist position was supportive of Booker T. Washington's approach to race relations, by 1909 Terrell had moved toward W. E. B. Du Bois's philosophies, accepting his invitation to become a founding member of the NAACP.

At age seventy-seven, Terrell published her autobiography, A Colored Woman in a White World *(1940). In 1949, she served as chairperson of the Coordinating Committee for the Enforcement of District of Columbia Anti-Discrimination Laws, one of the primary groups that led the fight for desegregation in Washington, D.C.*

In "What Role Is the Educated Negro Woman to Play in the Uplifting of Her Race?" (1902), Terrell outlines the NACW's goals for improving living conditions of African Americans at the turn of the twentieth century.

What Role Is the Educated Negro Woman to Play in the Uplifting of Her Race?

Should any one ask what special phase of the Negro's development makes me most hopeful of his ultimate triumph over present obstacles, I should answer unhesitatingly, it is the magnificent work the women are doing to regenerate and uplift the race. Judge the future of colored women by the past since their emancipation, and neither they nor their friends have any cause for anxiety.

For years, either banding themselves into small companies or struggling alone, colored women have worked with might and main to improve the condition of their people. The necessity of systematizing their efforts and working on a larger scale became apparent not many years ago and they decided to unite their forces. Thus it happened that in the summer of 1896 the National Association of Colored Women was formed by the union of two large organizations, each of which has done much to show our women the advantage of concerted action. So tenderly has this daughter of the organized womanhood of the race been nurtured and so wisely ministered unto, that it has grown to be a child hale, hearty and strong, of which its fond mothers have every reason to be proud. Handicapped though its members have been, because they lacked both money and experience, their efforts have, for the most part, been crowned with success in the twenty-six States where it has been represented.

Kindergartens have been established by some of our organizations, from which encouraging reports have come. A sanitarium with a training school for nurses has been set on such a firm foundation by the Phyllis Wheatley Club of New Orleans, Louisiana, and has proved itself to be such a blessing to the entire community that the municipal government has voted it an annual appropriation of several hundred dollars. By the Tuskegee, Alabama, branch of the association the work of bringing the light of knowledge and the gospel of cleanliness to their poor benighted sisters on the plantations has been conducted with signal success. Their efforts have thus far been confined to four estates, comprising thousands of acres of land, on which live hundreds of colored people, yet in the darkness of ignorance and the grip of sin, miles away from churches and schools.

Plans for aiding the indigent, orphaned and aged have been projected and in some instances have been carried into successful execution. One club in Memphis, Tennessee, has purchased a large tract of land, on which it intends to erect an old folks' home, part of the money for which has already been raised. Splendid service has been rendered by the Illinois Federation of Colored Women's Clubs, through whose instrumentality schools have been visited, truant children looked after, parents and teachers urged to cooperate with each other, rescue and reform work engaged in, so as to reclaim unfortunate women and tempted girls, public institutions investigated, garments cut, made and distributed to the needy poor.

Questions affecting our legal status as a race are sometimes agitated by our women. In Tennessee and Louisiana colored women have several times petitioned the legislature of their respective States to repeal the obnoxious Jim Crow car laws. In every way possible we are calling attention to the barbarity of the convict lease system, of which Negroes and especially the female prisoners are the principal victims, with the hope that the conscience of the country may be touched and this stain on its escutcheon be forever wiped away. Against the one room cabin we have inaugurated a vigorous crusade. When families of eight or ten men, women and children are all huddled promiscuously together in a single apartment, a condition common among our poor all over the land, there is little hope of inculcating morality and modesty. And yet in spite of the fateful heritage of slavery, in spite of the manifold pitfalls and peculiar temptations to which our girls are subjected, and though the safeguards usually thrown around maidenly youth and innocence are in some sections entirely withheld from colored girls, statistics compiled by men not inclined to falsify in favor of my race show that immorality among colored women is not so great as among women in some foreign countries who are equally ignorant, poor and oppressed.

Believing that it is only through the home that a people can become really good and truly great the National Association has entered that sacred domain. Homes, more homes, better homes, purer homes is the text upon which sermons have been and will be preached. There has been a determined effort to have heart to heart talks with our women that we may strike at the root of evils, many of which lie at the fireside. If the women of the dominant race, with all the centuries of education, culture and refinement back of them, with all the wealth and opportunity ever present with them, feel the need of a mother's congress, that they may be enlightened upon the best methods of rearing their children and conducting their homes, how much more do our women, from whom shackles have but yesterday been stricken, need information on the same vital subjects. And so the association is working vigorously to establish mothers' congresses on a small scale, wherever our women can be reached.

From this brief and meager account of the work which has been and is still being accomplished by colored women through the medium of their clubs, it is easy to observe how earnest and effective have been their efforts to elevate the race. No people need ever despair whose women are fully roused to the duties which rest upon them and are willing to shoulder responsibilities which they alone can successfully assume. The scope of our endeavors is constantly widening. Into the various channels of generosity and beneficence we are entering more and more every day.

Some of our women are now urging their clubs to establish day nurseries, a charity of which there is an imperative need. Thousands of our wage-earning mothers with large families dependent almost entirely upon them for support are obliged to leave their children all day, entrusted to the care of small brothers and sisters, or some good-natured neighbor who promises much, but who does little.

Some of these infants are locked alone in the room from the time the mother leaves in the morning, until she returns at night. Not long ago I read in a Southern newspaper that an infant thus locked alone in a room all day, while its mother went out to wash, had cried itself to death. When one reflects upon the slaughter of the innocents which is occurring with pitiless persistency every day and thinks of the multitudes who are maimed for life or are rendered imbecile because of the treatment received during their helpless infancy, it is evident that by establishing day nurseries colored women will render one of the greatest services possible to humanity and to the race.

Nothing lies nearer the heart of colored women than the children. We feel keenly the need of kindergartens and are putting forth earnest efforts to honeycomb this country with them from one extremity to the other. The more unfavorable the environments of children the more necessary it is that steps be taken to counteract baleful influences upon innocent victims. How imperative is it then that as colored women we inculcate correct principles and set good examples for our own youth whose little feet will have so many thorny paths of temptation, injustice and prejudice to tread. So keenly alive is the National Association to the necessity of rescuing our little ones whose evil nature alone is encouraged to develop and whose noble qualities are deadened and dwarfed by the very atmosphere which they breathe, that its officers are trying to raise money with which to send out a kindergarten organizer, whose duty it shall be to arouse the conscience of our women and to establish kindergartens wherever means therefor can be secured.

Through the children of today we believe we can build the foundation of the next generation upon such a rock of morality, intelligence and strength, that the floods of proscription, prejudice and persecution may descend upon it in torrents and yet it will not be moved. We hear a great deal about the race problem and how to solve it. The real solution of the race problem lies in the children, both so far as we who are oppressed and those who oppress us are concerned. Some of our women who have consecrated their lives to the elevation of their race feel that neither individuals nor organizations working toward this end should be entirely satisfied with their efforts unless some of their energy, money or brain is used in the name and for the sake of the children.

The National Association has chosen as its motto: Lifting as We Climb. In order to live strictly up to this sentiment, its members have determined to come into the closest possible touch with the masses of our women, through whom the womanhood of our people is always judged. It is unfortunate, but it is true, that the dominant race in this country insists upon gauging the Negro's worth by his most illiterate and vicious representatives than by the more intelligent and worthy classes. Colored women of education and culture know that they cannot escape altogether the consequences of the acts of their most depraved sisters. They see that even if they were wicked enough to turn a deaf ear to the call of duty, both policy and self-preservation demand that they go down among the lowly, the illiterate and even the vicious, to whom they are bound by the ties of race and sex, and put forth every possible effort to reclaim them. By coming into close touch with the masses of our women it is possible to correct many of the evils which militate so seriously against us and inaugurate the reforms, without which, as a race, we cannot hope to succeed.

Through the clubs we are studying the labor question and are calling the attention of our women to the alarming rapidity with which the Negro is losing ground in the world of labor. If this movement to withhold employment from him continues to grow, the race will soon be confronted by a condition of things disastrous and serious, indeed. We are preaching in season and out that it is the duty of every wage-earning colored woman to become thoroughly proficient in whatever work she engages, so that she may render the best service of which she is capable, and thus do her part toward establishing a reputation for excellent workmanship among colored women.

Our clubs all over the country are being urged to establish schools of domestic science. It is believed that by founding schools in which colored girls could be trained to be skilled domestics, we should do more toward solving the labor question as it affects our women, than by using any other means it is in our power to employ. We intend to lay the Negro's side of the labor question clearly before our large-hearted, broad-minded sisters of the dominant race and appeal to them to throw their influence on the right side. We shall ask that they train their children to be broad and just enough to judge men and women by their intrinsic merit rather than by the adventitious circumstances of race or color or creed. Colored women are asking the white mothers of the land to teach their children that when they grow to be men and women, if they deliberately prevent their fellow creatures from earning an honest living by closing their doors of trade against them, the Father of all men will hold them responsible for the crimes which are the result of their injustice and for the human wrecks which the ruthless crushing of hope and ambition always makes.

Through our clubs colored women hope to improve the social atmosphere by showing the enormity of the double standard of morals, which teaches that we should turn the cold shoulder upon a fallen sister, but greet her destroyer with open arms and a gracious smile. The duty of setting a high moral standard and living up to it devolves upon colored women in a peculiar way. False accusations and malicious slanders are circulated against them constantly, both by the press and by the direct descendants of those who in years past were responsible for the moral degradation of their female slaves.

Carefully and conscientiously we shall study the questions which affect the race most deeply and directly. Against the convict lease system, the Jim Crow car laws, lynchings and all other barbarities which degrade us, we shall protest with such force of logic and intensity of soul that those who oppress us will either cease to disavow the inalienability and equality of human rights, or be ashamed to openly violate the very principles upon which this government was founded. By discharging our obligation to the children, by coming into the closest possible touch with the masses of our people, by studying the labor question as it affects the race, by establishing schools of domestic science, by setting a high moral standard and living up to it, by purifying the home, colored women will render their race a service whose value it is not in my power to estimate or express. The National Association is being cherished with such loyalty and zeal by our women that there is every reason to hope it will soon become the power for good, the tower of strength and the source of inspiration to which it is destined.

And so lifting as we climb, onward and upward we go, struggling and striving and hoping that the buds and blossoms of our desires will burst into glorious fruition ere long. With courage born of success achieved in the past, with a keen sense of the responsibility which we must continue to assume we look forward to the future, large with promise and hope. Seeking no favors because of our color or patronage because of our needs, we knock at the bar of justice and ask for an equal chance.

Marcus Garvey (1887–1940)

Dreamer and prophet, Marcus Garvey has been an inspiration to many African Americans—both during and after his life. Contributing to the black cultural awakening of the Harlem Renaissance of the 1920s, Garvey's speeches, writings, and leadership offered a pathway to pride in black history, black culture and the beauty of Africa itself. Although not the first to express the idealistic longing of blacks to reclaim their black pride by reclaiming Africa, Garvey was unequaled in his influence, persuading millions of black people to support that vision.

Born in Jamaica, Garvey was already politically active when he came to the United States in his late twenties. He had earlier studied law in London and traveled and worked in Central and South America, returning to Jamaica to establish a political organization that attempted to curtail the exploitation of blacks. Not obtaining the success he wanted, Garvey sailed for the United States in 1916, organizing the Universal Negro Improvement and Conservation Association (UNIA) in the following year.

Having missed the chance to meet the late Booker T. Washington, one of his inspirations, Garvey began rallying people in Harlem. In 1918, UNIA began printing the Negro World, *its official newspaper. As Garvey's followers grew in number, his principles, plans, and even his appearance—his dark complexion and black African features—antagonized some other black leaders, who denounced and challenged Garvey's rejection of integration. At the same time, financial problems with UNIA's Black Star Line (the ships purchased and overhauled to carry blacks to Africa), along with continued scrutiny by the Department of Justice, began to erode the foundation of Garvey's vision. In 1925, he was convicted of mail fraud and sentenced to a five-year prison term. However, in 1927, the term was commuted, and Garvey was deported. Outside the United States, Garvey continued to travel and make public appearances, but he was unable to maintain a cohesive organization. He finally settled in London in the mid-1930s, living there until his death in 1940.*

In 1923 and 1926, two volumes of Garvey's speeches and writings, The Philosophy and Opinions of Marcus Garvey, *were collected and edited by his wife, Amy Jacques Garvey. The volumes were reprinted in 1967 as one book by the same title, from which the following selection is taken. In "An Appeal to the Conscience of the Black Race to See Itself," Garvey calls for black unity and pride.*

An Appeal to the Conscience of the Black Race to See Itself

It is said to be a hard and difficult task to organize and keep together large numbers of the Negro race for the common good. Many have tried to congregate us, but have failed, the reason being that our characteristics are such as to keep us more apart than together.

The evil of internal division is wrecking our existence as a people, and if we do not seriously and quickly move in the direction of a readjustment it simply means that our doom becomes imminently conclusive.

For years the Universal Negro Improvement Association has been working for the unification of our race, not on domestic-national lines only, but universally. The success which we have met in the course of our effort is rather encouraging, considering the time consumed and the environment surrounding the object of our concern.

It seems that the whole world of sentiment is against the Negro, and the difficulty of our generation is to extricate ourselves from the prejudice that hides itself beneath, as well as above, the action of an international environment.

Prejudice is conditional on many reasons, and it is apparent that the Negro supplies, consciously or unconsciously, all the reasons by which the world seems to ignore and avoid him. No one cares for a leper, for lepers are infectious persons, and all are afraid of the disease, so, because the Negro keeps himself poor, helpless and undemonstrative, it is natural also that no one wants to be of him or with him.

Progress and Humanity

Progress is the attraction that moves humanity, and to whatever people or race this "modern virtue," attaches itself, there will you find the splendor of pride and self-esteem that never fail to win the respect and admiration of all.

It is the progress of the Anglo-Saxons that singles them out for the respect of all the world. When their race had no progress or achievement to its credit, then, like all other inferior peoples, they paid the price in slavery, bondage, as well as through prejudice. We cannot forget the time when even the ancient Briton was regarded as being too dull to make a good Roman slave, yet today the influence of the race rules the world.

It is the industrial and commercial progress of America that causes Europe and the rest of the world to think appreciatively of the Anglo-American race. It is not because one hundred and ten million people live in the United States that the world is attracted to the republic with so much reverence and respect—a reverence and respect now shown to India with its three hundred millions, or to China with its four hundred millions. Progress of and among any people will advance them in the respect and appreciation of the rest of their fellows. It is such a progress that the Negro must attach to himself if he is to rise above the prejudice of the world.

The reliance of our race upon the progress and achievements of others for a consideration in sympathy, justice and rights is like a dependence upon a broken stick, resting upon which will eventually consign you to the ground.

Self-Reliance and Respect

The Universal Negro Improvement Association teaches our race self-help and self-reliance, not only in one essential, but in all those things that contribute to human happiness and well-being. The disposition of the many to depend upon the other races for a kindly and sympathetic consideration of their needs, without making the effort to do for themselves, has been the race's standing disgrace by which we have been judged and through which we have created the strongest prejudice against ourselves.

There is no force like success, and that is why the individual makes all efforts to surround himself throughout life with the evidence of it. As of the individual, so should it be of the race and nation. The glittering success of Rockefeller makes him a power in the American nation; the success of Henry Ford suggests him as an object of universal respect, but no one knows and cares about the bum or hobo who is Rockefeller's or Ford's neighbor. So, also, is the world attracted by the glittering success of races and nations, and pays absolutely no attention to the bum or hobo race that lingers by the wayside.

The Negro must be up and doing if he will break down the prejudice of the rest of the world. Prayer alone is not going to improve our condition, nor the policy of watchful waiting. We must strike out for ourselves in the course of material achievement, and by our own effort and energy present to the world those forces by which the progress of man is judged.

A Nation and Country

The Negro needs a nation and a country of his own, where he can best show evidence of his own ability in the art of human progress. Scattered as an unmixed and unrecognized part of alien nations and civilizations is but to demonstrate his imbecility, and point him out as an unworthy derelict, fit neither for the society of Greek, Jew nor Gentile.

It is unfortunate that we should so drift apart, as a race, as not to see that we are but perpetuating our own sorrow and disgrace in failing to appreciate the first great requisite of all peoples—organization.

Organization is a great power in directing the affairs of a race or nation toward a given goal. To properly develop the desires that are uppermost, we must first concentrate through some system or method, and there is none better than organization. Hence, the Universal Negro Improvement Association appeals to each and every Negro to throw in his lot with those of us who, through organization, are working for the universal emancipation of our race and the redemption of our common country, Africa.

No Negro, let him be American, European, West Indian or African, shall be truly respected until the race as a whole has emancipated itself, through self-achievement and progress, from universal prejudice. The Negro will have to build his own government, industry, art, science, literature and culture, before the world will stop to consider him. Until then, we are but wards of a superior race and civilization, and the outcasts of a standard social system.

The race needs workers at this time, not plagiarists, copyists and mere imitators; but men and women who are able to create, to originate and improve, and thus make an independent racial contribution to the world and civilization.

Monkey Apings of "Leaders"

The unfortunate thing about us is that we take the monkey apings of our "so-called leading men" for progress. There is no progress in Negroes aping white people and telling us that they represent the best in the race, for in that respect any dressed monkey would represent the best of its species, irrespective of the creative matter of the monkey instinct. The best in a race is not reflected through or by the action of its apes, but by its ability to create of and by itself. It is such a creation that the Universal Negro Improvement Association seeks.

Let us not try to be the best or worst of others, but let us make the effort to be the best of ourselves. Our own racial critics criticize us as dreamers and "fanatics," and call us "benighted" and "ignorant," because they lack racial backbone. They are unable to see themselves creators of their own needs. The slave instinct has not yet departed from them. They still believe that they can only live or exist through the good graces of their "masters." The good slaves have not yet thrown off their shackles; thus, to them, the Universal Negro Improvement Association is an "impossibility."

It is the slave spirit of dependence that causes our "so-called leading men" (apes) to seek the shelter, leadership, protection and patronage of the "master" in their organization and so-called advancement work. It is the spirit of feeling secured as good servants of the master, rather than as independents, why our modern Uncle Toms take pride in laboring under alien leadership and becoming surprised at the audacity of the Universal Negro Improvement Association in proclaiming for racial liberty and independence.

But the world of white and other men, deep down in their hearts, have much more respect for those of us who work for our racial salvation under the banner of the Universal Negro Improvement Association, than they could ever have, in all eternity, for a group of helpless apes and beggars who make a monopoly of undermining their own race and belittling themselves in the eyes of self-respecting people, by being "good boys" rather than able men.

Surely there can be no good will between apes, seasoned beggars and independent minded Negroes who will at least make an effort to do for themselves. Surely, the "dependents" and "wards" (and may I not say racial imbeciles?) will rave against and plan the destruction of movements like the Universal Negro Improvement Association that expose them to the liberal white minds of the world as not being representative of the best in the Negro, but, to the contrary, the worst. The best of a race does not live on the patronage and philanthropy of others, but makes an effort to do for itself. The best of the great white race doesn't fawn before and beg black, brown or yellow men; they go out, create for self and thus demonstrate the fitness of the race to survive; and so the white race of America and the world will be informed that the best in the Negro race is not the class of beggars who send out to other races piteous appeals annually for donations to maintain their coterie, but the groups within us that are honestly striving to do for themselves with the voluntary help and appreciation of that class of other races that is reasonable, just and liberal enough to give to each and every one a fair chance in the promotion of those ideals that tend to greater human progress and human love.

The work of the Universal Negro Improvement Association is clear and clean-cut. It is that of inspiring an unfortunate race with pride in self and with the determination of going ahead in the creation of those ideals that will lift them to the unprejudiced company of races and nations. There is no desire for hate or malice, but every wish to see all mankind linked into a common fraternity of progress and achievement that will wipe away the odor of prejudice, and elevate the human race to the height of real godly love and satisfaction.

Ralph Ellison (1914–94)

Ralph Ellison is regarded as one of the most distinguished twentieth-century writers of fiction and nonfiction. His one novel, Invisible Man *(1952), is considered a milestone in American literature by critics and educators, serving as a focal point for discussing opposing views about the African American experience—particularly integration versus black nationalism and the individual versus collective identity.*

Born in Oklahoma City, Oklahoma, Ellison and his brother were raised by their mother after their father died when Ellison was three. Exposed to books at an early age, Ellison at age eight also developed an interest in music. In high school, he studied music theory and played the trumpet and saxophone. Ellison received a scholarship to study music at Tuskegee Institute, aspiring to become a symphonic composer despite his earlier interest in jazz. At the end of his junior year, however, he moved to New York to study sculpture. While still in New York, Ellison drifted back to music; he also met Richard Wright, in 1936, with whom he shared a respect for leftist politics. During the New Deal era, Ellison worked with the Works Progress Administration (WPA) and published essays in New Masses. *In the 1940s, he continued to write articles, literary and political criticism, and short fiction. Honored with a Rosenwald Grant in 1945, he was able to support his writing of* Invisible Man, *which won a National Book Award in 1952.*

In his essays and fiction, Ellison expresses himself as artist, philosopher, intellectual, or humanist, but always as a black writer rooted within a culture marked by distinctive experiences, musical forms, humor, and ethos. Commenting on Ellison's first collection of essays, Shadow and Act *(1964), black critic Robert G. O'Meally observes that the writer "sometimes gently punctures, sometimes wields an ax against, inadequate definitions of black experience. In place of what he detects as false prophecy, usually uttered by social scientists, he chooses as broad a frame of reference as possible to interpret black experience in richly optimistic terms." Ellison's other works include a number of uncollected short stories; published excerpts from a second, unfinished novel; and* Going to the Territory *(1986), a collection of interviews, essays, and lectures from which the following selection is taken.*

In "What America Would Be Like without Blacks," Ellison dismisses racist notions about a thriving "blackless America" while praising the contributions made to American culture and society by blacks.

What America Would Be Like without Blacks

The fantasy of an America free of blacks is at least as old as the dream of creating a truly democratic society. While we are aware that there is something inescapably tragic about the cost of achieving our democratic ideals, we keep such tragic awareness segregated to the rear of our minds. We allow it to come to the fore only during moments of great national crisis.

On the other hand, there is something so embarrassingly absurd about the notion of purging the nation of blacks that it seems hardly a product of thought at all. It is more like a primitive reflex, a throwback to the dim past of tribal experience, which we rationalize and try to make respectable by dressing it up in the gaudy and highly questionable trappings of what we call the "concept of race." Yet, despite its absurdity, the fantasy of a blackless America continues to turn up. It is a fantasy born not merely of racism but of petulance, of exasperation, of moral fatigue. It is like a boil bursting forth from impurities in the bloodstream of democracy.

In its benign manifestations, it can be outrageously comic—as in the picaresque adventures of Percival Brownlee who appears in William Faulkner's story "The Bear." Exasperating to his white masters because his aspirations and talents are for preaching and conducting choirs rather than for farming, Brownlee is "freed" after much resistance and ends up as the prosperous proprietor of a New Orleans brothel. In Faulkner's hands, the uncomprehending drive of Brownlee's owners to "get shut" of him is comically instructive. Indeed, the story resonates certain abiding, tragic themes of American history with which it is interwoven, and which are causing great turbulence in the social atmosphere today. I refer to the exasperation and bemusement of the white American with the black, the black American's ceaseless (and swiftly accelerating) struggle to escape the misconceptions of whites, and the continual confusing of the black American's racial background with his individual culture. Most of all, I refer to the recurring fantasy of solving one basic problem of American democracy by "getting shut" of the blacks through various wishful schemes that would banish them from the nation's bloodstream, from its social structure, and from its conscience and historical consciousness.

This fantastic vision of a lily-white America appeared as early as 1713, with the suggestion of a white "native American," thought to be from New Jersey, that all the Negroes be given their freedom and returned to Africa. In 1777, Thomas Jefferson, while serving in the Virginia legislature, began drafting a plan for the gradual emancipation and exportation of the slaves. Nor were Negroes themselves immune to the fantasy. In 1815, Paul Cuffe, a wealthy merchant, shipbuilder, and landowner from the New Bedford area, shipped and settled at his own expense thirty-eight of his fellow Negroes in Africa. It was perhaps his example that led in the following year to the creation of the American Colonization Society, which was to establish in 1821 the colony of Liberia. Great amounts of cash and a perplexing mixture of motives went into the venture. The slaveowners and many Border-state politicians wanted to use it as a scheme to rid the country not of slaves but of the militant free Negroes who were agitating against the "peculiar institution." The abolitionists, until they took a lead from free Negro leaders and began attacking the scheme, also participated as a means of righting a great historical injustice. Many blacks went along with it simply because they were sick of the black and white American mess and hoped to prosper in the quiet peace of the old ancestral home.

Such conflicting motives doomed the Colonization Society to failure, but what amazes one even more than the notion that anyone could have believed in its success is the fact that it was attempted during a period when the blacks, slave and free, made up eighteen percent of the total population. When we consider how long blacks had been in the New World and had been transforming it and being Americanized by it, the scheme appears not only fantastic, but the product of a free-floating irrationality. Indeed, a national pathology.

Nevertheless, some of the noblest of Americans were bemused. Not only Jefferson but later Abraham Lincoln was to give the scheme credence. According to historian John Hope Franklin, Negro colonization seemed as important to Lincoln as emancipation. In 1862, Franklin notes, Lincoln called a group of prominent free Negroes to the White House and urged them to support colonization, telling them, "Your race suffers greatly, many of them by living among us, while ours suffers from your presence. If this is admitted, it affords a reason why we should be separated."

In spite of his unquestioned greatness, Abraham Lincoln was a man of his times and limited by some of the less worthy thinking of his times. This is demonstrated both by his reliance upon the concept of race in his analysis of the American dilemma and by his involvement in a plan of purging the nation of blacks as a means of healing the badly shattered ideals of democratic federalism. Although benign, his motive was no less a product of fantasy. It envisaged an attempt to relieve an inevitable suffering that marked the growing pains of the youthful body politic by an operation which would have amounted to the severing of a healthy and indispensable member.

Yet, like its twin, the illusion of secession, the fantasy of a benign amputation that would rid the country of black men to the benefit of a nation's health not only persists; today, in the form of neo-Garveyism, it fascinates black men no less than it once hypnotized whites. Both fantasies become operative whenever the nation grows weary of the struggle toward the ideal of American democratic equality. Both would use the black man as a scapegoat to achieve a national catharsis, and both would, by way of curing the patient, destroy him.

What is ultimately intriguing about the fantasy of "getting shut" of the Negro American is the fact that no one who entertains it seems ever to have considered what the nation would have become had Africans *not* been brought to the New World, and had their descendants not played such a complex and confounding role in the creation of American history and culture. Nor do they appear to have considered with any seriousness the effect upon the nation of having any of the schemes for exporting blacks succeed beyond settling some fifteen thousand or so in Liberia.

We are reminded that Daniel Patrick Moynihan, who has recently aggravated our social confusion over the racial issue while allegedly attempting to clarify it, is co-author of a work which insists that the American melting pot didn't melt because our white ethnic groups have resisted all assimilative forces that appear to threaten their identities. The problem here is that few Americans know who and what they really are. That is why few of these groups—or at least few of the children of these groups—have been able to resist the movies, television, baseball, jazz, football, drum-majoretting, rock, comic strips, radio commercials, soap operas, book clubs, slang, or any of a thousand other expressions and carriers of our pluralistic and easily available popular culture. And it is here precisely that ethnic resistance is least effective. On this level the melting pot did indeed melt, creating such deceptive metamorphoses and blending of identities, values, and life-styles that most American whites are culturally part Negro American without even realizing it.

If we can resist for a moment the temptation to view everything having to do with Negro Americans in terms of their racially imposed status, we become aware of the fact that for all the harsh reality of the social and economic injustices visited upon them, these injustices have failed to keep Negroes clear of the cultural mainstream; Negro Americans are in fact one of its major tributaries. If we can cease approaching American social reality in terms of such false concepts as white and nonwhite, black culture and white culture, and think of these apparently unthinkable matters in the realistic manner of Western pioneers confronting the unknown prairie, perhaps we can begin to imagine what the United States would have been, or not been, had there been no blacks to give it—if I may be so bold as to say—color.

For one thing, the American nation is in a sense the product of the American language, a colloquial speech that began emerging long before the British colonials and Africans were transformed into Americans. It is a language that evolved from the king's English but, basing itself upon the realities of the American land and colonial institutions—or lack of institutions, began quite early as a vernacular revolt against the signs, symbols, manners, and authority of the mother country. It is a language that began by merging the sounds of many tongues, brought together in the struggle of diverse regions. And whether it is admitted or not, much of the sound of that language is derived from the timbre of the African voice and the listening habits of the African ear. So there is a *de'z* and *do'z* of slave speech sounding beneath our most polished Harvard accents, and if there is such a thing as a Yale accent, there is a Negro wail in it—doubtlessly introduced there by Old Yalie John C. Calhoun, who probably got it from his mammy.

Whitman viewed the spoken idiom of Negro Americans as a source of a native grand opera. Its flexibility, its musicality, its rhythms, freewheeling diction, and metaphors, as projected in Negro American folklore, were absorbed by the creators of our great nineteenth-century literature even when the majority of blacks were still enslaved. Mark Twain celebrated it in the prose of *Huckleberry Finn;* without the presence of blacks, the book could not have been written. No Huck and Jim, no American novel as we know it. For not only is the black man a co-creator of the language that Mark Twain raised to the level of literary eloquence, but Jim's condition as American and Huck's commitment to freedom are at the moral center of the novel.

In other words, had there been no blacks, certain creative tensions arising from the cross-purposes of whites and blacks would also not have existed. Not only would there have been no Faulkner; there would have been no Stephen Crane, who found certain basic themes of his writing in the Civil War. Thus, also, there would have been no Hemingway, who took Crane as a source and guide. Without the presence of Negro American style, our jokes, our tall tales, even our sports would be lacking in the sudden turns, the shocks, the swift changes of pace (all jazz-shaped) that served to remind us that the world is ever unexplored, and that while a complete mastery of life is mere illusion, the real secret of the game is to make life swing. It is its ability to articulate this tragic-comic attitude toward life that explains much of the mysterious power and attractiveness of that quality of Negro American style known as "soul." An expression of American diversity within unity, of blackness with whiteness, soul announces the presence of a creative struggle against the realities of existence.

Without the presence of blacks, our political history would have been otherwise. No slave economy, no Civil War; no violent destruction of the Reconstruction; no K.K.K. and no Jim Crow system. And without the disenfranchisement of black Americans and the manipulation of racial fears and prejudices, the disproportionate impact of white Southern politicians upon our domestic and foreign policies would have been impossible. Indeed, it is almost impossible to conceive of what our political system would have become without the snarl of forces—cultural, racial, religious—that make our nation what it is today.

Absent, too, would be the need for that tragic knowledge which we try ceaselessly to evade: that the true subject of democracy is not simply material well-being but the extension of the democratic process in the direction of perfecting itself. And that the most obvious test and clue to that perfection is the inclusion—*not* assimilation—of the black man.

Since the beginning of the nation, white Americans have suffered from a deep inner uncertainty as to who they really are. One of the ways that has been used to simplify the answer has been to seize upon the presence of black Americans and use them as a marker, a symbol of limits, a metaphor for the "outsider." Many whites could look at the social position of blacks and feel that color formed an easy and reliable gauge for determining to what extent one was or was not American. Perhaps that is why one of the first epithets that many European immigrants learned when they got off the boat was the term "nigger"—it made them feel instantly American. But this is tricky magic. Despite his racial difference and social status, something indisputably American about Negroes not only raised doubts about the white man's value system but aroused the troubling suspicion that whatever else the true American is, he is also somehow black.

Materially, psychologically, and culturally, part of the nation's heritage is Negro American, and whatever it becomes will be shaped in part by the Negro's presence. Which is fortunate, for today it is the black American who puts pressure upon the nation to live up to its ideals. It is he who gives creative tension to our struggle for justice and for the elimination of those factors, social and psychological, which make for slums and shaky suburban communities. It is he who insists that we purify the American language by demanding that there be a closer correlation between the meaning of words and reality, between ideal and conduct, our assertions and our actions. Without the black American, something irrepressibly hopeful and creative would go out of the American spirit, and the nation might well succumb to the moral slobbism that has ever threatened its existence from within.

When we look objectively at how the dry bones of the nation were hung together, it seems obvious that some one of the many groups that compose the United States had to suffer the fate of being allowed no easy escape from experiencing the harsh realities of the human condition as they were to exist under even so fortunate a democracy as ours. It would seem that some one group had to be stripped of the possibility of escaping such tragic knowledge by taking sanctuary in moral equivocation, racial chauvinism, or the advantage of superior social status. There is no point in complaining over the past or apologizing for one's fate. But for blacks, there are no hiding places down there, not in suburbia or in penthouse, neither in country nor in city. They are an American people who are geared to what *is* and who yet are driven by a sense of what it is possible for human life to be in this society. The nation could not survive being deprived of their presence because, by the irony implicit in the dynamics of American democracy, they symbolize both its most stringent testing and the possibility of its greatest human freedom.

Amiri Baraka (1934–)

Writer of more than thirty books of poetry, fiction, essays, and drama, Amiri Baraka has served as a black cultural icon since the 1960s. His personal and public lives intersect as a symbol of the cultural consciousness and racial affirmation of African American artists and intellectuals. As black critic William J. Harris notes, "Baraka . . . addresse[s] his audience as both a singularly powerful advocate of individual expression and as an outraged spokesman for all black artists."

Born Everett LeRoy Jones in Newark, New Jersey, and raised by middle-class parents, Baraka graduated from high school at age fifteen and went on to attend Howard University. However, in his senior year he failed his classes and left college to join the air force. Reading extensively, writing poetry, and traveling to Africa and Europe during his military years, Baraka settled in New York's Greenwich Village after a dishonorable discharge from the service. He interacted with a number of "beat generation" writers in the Village, as he wrote poetry and critical essays and edited literary magazines. During these New York years, Baraka also studied at Columbia University and married Hettie Roberta Cohen, a white writer.

From 1960 to 1965, a number of experiences combined to transform Baraka's personal and literary lives, moving him toward the revolutionary posture that would make him a highly visible spokesperson for the Black Arts Movement by mid-decade. In 1960, a trip to Cuba influenced his new perception of art as a political tool and reshaped his purpose in his writing. He also severed his connections with white beat generation writers, decrying the passiveness he perceived in their work. He thus infused his own writings with a racial consciousness and political tone, as seen in a collection of poems, The Dead Lecturer *(1964), and four remarkable plays, all appearing in 1964:* Dutchman, The Slave, The Baptism, *and* The Toilet. *In addition, he left Greenwich Village and his white wife to live in Harlem, where he founded the Black Arts Repertory Theater School.*

Moving back to Newark in 1966, Baraka married a black woman, with whom he had five children. He also organized the Spirit House, a theatrical group and community center, and was a founder of the Black Community Development of Newark, an organization committed to shaping an independent and self-sustaining black Newark. At this time, he changed his name to Imamu Amiri Baraka, becoming a Black Muslim and donning an African-designed wardrobe. By the late 1960s, the black cultural nationalist had gained both mainstream publication and wide popularity among black artists, readers, and critics. Shortening his name to Amiri Baraka in the early 1970s, his political ideology grew to embrace Marxism and denounce global oppression. In the early 1980s, he received tenure at the State University of New York at Stony Brook, teaching African Studies and African American literature. Still a vital intellectual voice in the United States today, Baraka continues to write poetry and cultural criticism and to address the nature of political exploitation within and outside the country.

In addition to the works already mentioned, Baraka has produced a host of books in various genres. His poetry collections include Preface to a Twenty-Volume Suicide Note *(1961),* Black Magic *(1969),* Hard Facts *(1975), and* Selected Poetry *(1979). Two major works of his fiction have been issued:* The

System of Dante's Hell *(1965), a novel, and* Tales *(1967), a collection of short stories. Baraka wrote numerous short dramas that were produced in the late 1960s, including* Experimental Death Unit 1, Jello, A Black Mass, The Slave Ship, Arm Yrself or Harm Yrself, Great Goodness of Life, Madheart, The Eighth Ditch, *and* Home on the Range. *In 1978 he published* The Motion of History, *a collection of Marxist plays.*

In addition to numerous essays and articles, Baraka has published several books of cultural essays and criticism: Blues People *(1963),* Home: Social Essays *(1966),* Black Music *(1967),* Black Value System *(1970),* In Our Terribleness *(coauthored with Billy Abernathy, 1970),* Raise Race Rays Raze: Essays since 1965 *(1971), and* Daggers and Javelins *(1984). He also wrote his memoir,* The Autobiography of LeRoi Jones/Amiri Baraka *(1984), and edited two anthologies,* Black Fire *(1968) and* Confirmation: An Anthology of African-American Women *(coedited with Amina Baraka, 1983).*

The following essay, "Malcolm as Ideology" (1992), was originally published in Malcolm X: In Our Own Image *(1992) edited by Joe Wood. In it, Baraka criticizes filmmaker Spike Lee, middle-class blacks, and white politicians for creating superficial images of Malcolm X to suit their own agendas and thereby distorting the political meaning of the man's life and leadership.*

Malcolm as Ideology

Malcolm X continues today, twenty-seven years after his murder, to be at the center of ideological development and discussion in the Black Liberation Movement, the Black national community—and to some still broadening extent, America, the general.

There is, of course, the syndrome that Lenin spoke about when he said that once opponents of the bourgeoisie are dead, the rulers transform these class enemies into ciphers or agreeable sycophants of Imperialism (however "askew" they might have "seemed" in life) who are now "rehabilitated" all the way into being represented as the very opposite ideologically of what they actually were in life.

But Malcolm is also, himself, a figure of ideological development and change. So that it is easier to focus on some particular period or aspect of his life and make that the entire substance of who he was.

Because Malcolm's life was shaped by such continuous ideological development, if we take the whole of that development into consideration, analyze and explicate each period—what it was, why that was, given time, place, and condition, and why it changed, and what it changed to—then we will get a deeper biographical portrait of Malcolm, one that is not static and "ideal" but in motion.

The portrait Spike Lee had drawn, in his "fourth-draft script," is an instance of absolutizing the middle portion of Malcolm's life and trying to use that as a defining spine of the entire life.

Spike begins his proposed film of Malcolm with himself, apparently, as "Shorty" (a sidekick of Detroit Red's) running up the street, arms full of "Congolene" supplies. Shorty is about to "Konk" a big country boy's head, Malcolm Little, so that he can become "Detroit Red."

This is Spike's point of departure, as well as the perspective through which he shreds piecemeal the earlier aspects of Malcolm's life. In other words, Malcolm's young life is seen mainly as a memory in Detroit Red's mind.

In fact, Detroit Red holds center stage in Spike's screenplay. Even the character Shorty appears more than Malcolm's father or mother. So Spike sees the Detroit Red years as "real time" while the early years are just disparate flashes of memory.

This is because, to Spike, Detroit Red is the *real* Malcolm, and flashbacks are all that is required of the formative years.

This perception is further elaborated upon by Spike's treatment of the later "political" years. They are shuffled toward us, almost like cards, coming at us face down, so superficial is their use to us as drama or politics, which at their most powerful would be a single composite!

Each of us sees a thing or event according to our own experiences and interests and ideological stance. Malcolm's life itself was also an ideological statement, one that is ironically consolidated, made more explicit, by its specific changes.

But to understand the *overall statement* Malcolm's life makes, one must make a *material* analysis, an evaluation of concrete conditions, but one that is also dialectical, i.e., sensitive to the point and cause and dimension of change.

The Bruce Perry calumny (*Malcolm: The Life of a Man Who Changed Black America*)[1] seems to me the action of one of George Bush's CIA "proprietaries" (subcontractors contracted to do a specific job) whose mission is to cover Malcolm's real life with a barrage of psychopathic untruths. So that Malcolm's life becomes simply the disoriented thrashings of schizophrenia.

Perry's "research," which consists of disconnected "interviews," half by telephone, dredges up irrelevant and fragmented "events" and strings them together as the proof of his "theory"—that Malcolm was "white" and that his "problem," the real cause of his "militancy," was his dissatisfaction with his false "Blackness" and the hatred of his mother and father. That, plus his continuing "cowardice" and pathological "criminality."

Malcolm's father, mother, Aunt Ella, etc., were likewise pathological criminals. Indeed, the whole of the Black Liberation Movement was (is) pathological.

It is significant that Pathfinder Press, the cat's paw of the Socialist Workers Party (Trot), had Perry edit and write the introduction to its edition of Malcolm's *Last Speeches!*

Why not? The Trots have never supported Afro-American self-determination. Their suit against Abdul Al Kalimat and the Black-owned Readers and Writers Press for publishing a Malcolm Reader for Beginners is simply base capitalist business practice.

The irony is that here another white corporation is fighting Black people for control of their lives. The SWP is historically and actively opposed to Malcolm as ideology, yet it would go into the bourgeois court to sue Black people to franchise Malcolm as property!

I was recently summoned to a Malcolm celebration in D.C. at Howard University by Betty Shabazz. The gathering featured middle-class Negroes of mostly backward persuasions. What was stunning is how this assembly of Negro bureaucrats, academics, middle-class "conscientious objectors" to Black struggle were furiously, if stiffly, rubbing up against Malcolm like self-manipulated "firesticks" trying to make at least a little smoke.

Sharon Pratt Dixon, D.C.'s outspokenly pro-capitalist mayor, led a motley crew of small businessmen and half-hip promoters of "Black," the product, using Malcolm as if to sanctify and legitimatize their own lives, and paths, as somehow, any way, connected to Malcolm.

It is like the paradox of "Blackness" as an ideology, in that it is the most superficial i.d. of the nation, classless and ultimately deceptive. Both Buthelezi and Mandela are "Black." Like Roy Innis and Malcolm X.

It is the ideology, the class stance, their acts, that define persons, exclusive of nationality. So, now, to confirm Lenin's teaching, these Negroes were serving the big bourgeoisie and themselves as apprentice torturers, by distorting and hiding Malcolm's life to enhance their own and U.S. imperialisms.

It made me remember 1965 when I returned to Newark and went with Ben Caldwell and another brother up to Montclair to a gathering of the Howard U. alumni where I had been asked to speak. When I mentioned Malcolm X the Negroes actually booed! They even wanted to throw Ben out because he had no tie. I gave him mine and talked bad to these Negroes for thirty minutes.

These are the same kinds of Negroes who sat in the Howard student center rubbing up against Malcolm X because he had become not safe but clearly usable.

That is why Spike's "use" is so obvious and painful, since it is in neon. Spike's films reveal him as the apologist for this same sector of the Black petty bourgeoisie that holds Black life a caricature, Black struggle a ridiculous hypocrisy, whose incomes "prove" this, whose "Blackness" is only a job description.

Since this is a period of reaction, like the bottom of the downward stroke of the Sisyphus Syndrome of Black life in America, there is a retrograde trend, a specific sociopolitical tendency in U.S. society, expressed in all aspects of the society, with part of its social base a reactionary sector of the Black petty bourgeoisie, comprising a comprador class (that part of the Black bourgeoisie and petty bourgeoisie whose *market* is imperialism, not other Black people). Negroes serving imperialism and white supremacy as a sector of "black opinion."

For these, Black struggle is mainly *commercial,* economic as a pay raise. The "Civil Rights Movement" is passé, hypocrisy or delusion. It has *been* over! (Remember that, and you can make some money!)

African Kings and Queens can be put to work for Budweiser. Martin Luther King for McDonald's and Malcolm X for Warner Brothers. ABC makes millions from our *Roots.*

The Sowells, Walter Williams, Crouches, Playtoy Beenyesmen, Glenn Lourys, Roy Innises, Melvin Williams, Juan Williams, and Tom Ass Clarences tell us the same things white racists told us earlier. Their employment is how the bourgeoisie adapts to our past victories. These racists camouflage themselves as backward Negroes, who during the '60s upsurge of the Black Liberation Movement were pods growing in the cellars of our politics.

Skip Gates and the Negro deconstructionists actually re-raise the reaction of the backward white Southern agrarian so-called "New Critics" of the '40s and '50s. The attempted disconnection of literature from real life. To render beauty and intelligence neuter and abstract. To make truth mysterious and an individual perception; and society metaphor and metaphysical.

So we begin to understand if we analyze this retrograde trend, these bought-and-paid-for Negro white supremacist "intellectuals" and academics, these petty surrogate racist Negro politicians, as mayors, Congress or councilpersons, corporate figureheads, institutional jigaboos, these eurocentricoon "happen-to-be-Negro" artists whose notoriety is that now their confessions of submission can be included in the curricula.

After any social-political upsurge by the people, it is necessary for the rulers to, as quickly as possible, cover, obscure, distort, reverse, outlaw any trace of the entire epoch, its meaning, its victims, its ideas, its victories, and its material human life.

Just as the two other previous epochs of Black American social-political upsurges are now obscured: the nineteenth-century antislavery movement including the Civil War and Reconstruction, and the early twentieth-century social insurgency, including the sharpened Afro-American and international Black democratic struggle, Pan Africanism and its Anti-Colonialism, the Harlem Renaissance and Garvey movement. These were initially resisted by the continuing slave society, then obstructed, then distorted, then "deconstructed" and made obscure. So the most recent upsurge of the '60s has likewise suffered the same overall attack. The Black retrograde trend of diverse new and long-in-the-tooth "buppie" spokespersons is one leading edge of this attack. Confirming not only a pattern of slave master to imperialist repression and suppression of African Americans, but of the post–'60s consolidation of an expanded Black petty bourgeoisie with an expanded and more powerful conservative sector, including a more powerful comprador sector.

It is a bitter irony that this expansion of the Black petty bourgeois was created by the struggle, victories, and impact of the '50s and '60s Black national democratic civil rights and liberation movement. The expansion of the Black petty bourgeoisie was an expression, supposedly, of the expanded power (socio-pol-eco) of the Afro-American people and the fruits of their victory over formal American apartheid.

But within the movement, the objective Black United Front, like the whole people, is divided into classes whose internal class struggle is only obscured by the struggle of the whole people against white supremacy and imperialism.

Since the '50s–60s upsurge, the Afro-American people's movement has been co-opted by the Black bourgeoisie. But since they only "represent" Black people but are not organically or ideologically connected to the people, they do not *actually* have power. So they become expressions of betrayal, collaboration, co-optation, of the need for actual power, democracy, and self-determination.

Jesse Jackson, one of the best-known and articulate spokespersons for what purports to be a progressive sector of the Black petty bourgeoisie, demonstrated the final sterility of even these "well-meaning" folks, viz., Jesse's open capitulation to the Democratic party, even after the insulting Dukakis lie about offering the VP nomination to him.

The question of self-determination, once the mainstream of the Black petty bourgeoisie feels they are in a position to compete for or contest "space in America," becomes more or less irrelevant. They see it as "separatism" or, from farther right, the very reason for our "failing to make progress."

They see the historical struggle for Afro-American Self-Determination useful only to pimp, as a cosmetic political device, hence the publicly "powerful" Blacks in society who should by their own declarations be leading Black struggle for self-determination, who betray and disclaim it hourly.

They tell us, "Our struggle is best handled by the electoral system, by electing Black elected officials, so that Black Power becomes a reality. Didn't Malcolm say 'The ballot or the bullet'?"

But these officials in most cases become colored "public servants" controlled by big business and big politics. Like the Black police we struggled for in the '50s and '60s. Now they become mercenaries of white supremacy and Black national oppression. They keep it manageable under imperialism!

In too many of the schools, Black teachers are entirely part of the racist superstructure. Poison Negroes poisoning our children with submission and self-hate. We see the more known of these backward academics. Along with them, the retrograde Negro body-snatchers who cavort as critics, journalists, media personalities, spokespersons, who are responsible to vilify, defame, and frame Black people, in order to work out their own opportunism and self-hate as profitably as possible.

Ngugi (*Petals of Blood*)[2] has told how in the neo-colonial development of Kenya, after the Mau Mau drove out the British, international imperialism raised up many traitor Negroes to assume the bureaucratic formalities of running the neo-colonial state to keep real power from the Kenyan people.

Many of the reactionary and conservative Negro voices now being pumped up by imperialism in the U.S. were on the defensive, under attack, obscure, in the '50s to '70s. Now they have become "prominent," inflated by white supremacy resurgent in the '90s.

There is even a sector of the newer generation of this backward Negro petty bourgeoisie that has never even lived with Black people, never lived in the ghetto. Children of Negroes the anti-us apartheid movement of the '50s and '60s allowed to move to the suburbs and be the token. Black people would not move forward, only a small sector of a class as "role models."

But now there are more Negroes for whom "Black culture" is abstract or theoretical or a *style*. These last are the pop-bup Negroes, whose soi disant "new Black aesthetic" or "blues aesthetic" seeks to disconnect Black culture and art from its material history and revolutionary essence.

Like Spike Lee's, their opportunistic use of Black culture is exploitative, a form of "economism" (as Lenin called it), replacing the political struggle for self-determination with a superficial rhetoric aimed at gaining economic concessions under imperialism. Some even put out the line that "racism will always exist."

In essence, this is ideological, in form, often a crass commercialism crossing many times over into straight-out mercenary comprador betrayal. Spike's cry of "independent" Black filmmaker has very quickly revealed itself as a marketing device, like the "Blackness" of his movies.

Also, there is another historically verifiable pattern of imperialist repression that mandates that after every period of Black militance, not only must this be "covered" (like Elvis P covered Big Mama Thornton, etc.) but also caricatured and distorted. One constant method has been minstrelsy, whether it is *Birth of a Nation,* Al Jolson, *Gone with the Wind,* Step 'n Fetchit, Elvis, Playtoy Beenyesman, or Vanilla Ice.

So that the militant post–Civil War folk must be replaced with Griffith's eye-rolling blackface whites. Consider the connection between ideology and social organization, when the white Rice Minstrels, performing a blackface skit called *Jim Crow,* should be used to title the continuation of the slave society as segregation and discrimination. Or the apparent self-mockery of the Black performers using blackface who continued the slander.

All this is necessary to understand not only the historical impact and significance of Malcolm X, but the need imperialism has now to cover, distort, and caricature his historical factual existence. Particularly as ideological.

Malcolm's real life, from his childhood, intersected American social reality and was shaped by it. Not only as a Black youth, whose life must invariably be formed by the American system of Black national oppression, but in its internal development, which is always principal; his father, a Garvey preacher and organizer, his mother, a Grenadan nationalist, gave the initial direction to his early growth.

It cannot be mere coincidence, for example, that Malcolm's father's Garveyism, so critical as an early twentieth-century expression of Black struggle for self-determination, should be renewed through the Black nationalist teaching of Elijah Muhammad.

His father's murder, and the subsequent destruction of his family by the white supremacist state organs, including the intense psychological terror that drove his mother to a nervous breakdown, directed Malcolm's life into America as a *conscious* victim.

The fact that Michigan presented a superficial integration to the American society Malcolm X grew in adds the ironic summation of Black rejection as the essence of U.S. social organization. The much-referenced rejection of Malcolm's dream to become a lawyer is met, even in the "integrated" classroom, with an enforced continuation of slave status that blocks Malcolm's youthful aspirations *to be* in America. Malcolm's reaction to this rejection, his eventual emergence in urban ghetto society as an "outlaw," is classic, even predictable.

Malcolm's father was a working-class Black whose "vocation" as preacher provided a lower-middle-class field of proposed social mobility for the family, but his father's murder quickly threw the family back into a constantly diminishing status as impoverished working class.

From here, racist social barriers and his own sense of rebellion threw Malcolm into the criminal world as he became partially "lumpenized," i.e., broken, by imperialism.

Spike's focus on the Detroit Red personality and social world as the basis of Malcolm's development is, for instance, a form of commercialism and ideological belittling of the personal, political, and social factors that helped create Detroit Red. Malcolm's early life is not just disconnected "memory," as Spike would have it, but a catalyst for his real life and ideological "Journey." Malcolm's life is consistently, in overview, a struggle for Self-Determination. A material base for his expressed consciousness.

It is his consciousness, and its meaning and development, that is the most critical to an understanding of Malcolm. Why and to what does it change? And how is it reflected in the masses of the Afro-American people?

When Malcolm goes to prison, a prisoner so opposed to the social life and philosophical "status quo" of U.S. society he is called SATAN, he is seen as opposed even to the American (Xtian) "God." He is insisting that he exists outside of "the given." That he is not the submissive Negro, the Black victim, or the nigger cipher.

His prison education, including Elijah Muhammad, gives him the form with which overtly to combine consciousness with his actual life. Or at least more so than ever before. As a function of experience and maturity, but also of philosophical revelation.

From his father's Garveyism to the revelations of Elijah Muhammad, Malcolm is still actually on a continuous line of *nationalist development* and expanding consciousness. The entrance into the Nation of Islam gives total expression to this historical ideological continuum!

But compare Malcolm's early tenure as the Messenger's messenger, the chief spokesman for the "Honorable Elijah Muhammad," and his last years when he had developed a clearly political nationalist line, in open contrast to the more metaphysical cultural and economic nationalism of Elijah Muhammad.

What changed is that as Malcolm gained more of an overview of American society and the forces at work within it, and the alignment of these forces, even internationally, he diminished his "White Devil-Mothership," "nonpolitical" metaphysical rhetoric and began to speak to the specific character of the Black Liberation Movement as a struggle for political self-determination.

The Civil Rights Movement has as one element of its total political thrust the struggle for democracy. Even in the "nonviolent" expression posited by Martin Luther King, there was an activist aspect that made Elijah Muhammad's "noninvolvement" in politics seem openly conservative. No matter the metaphysical rhetoric of white society's divine doom!

Malcolm was moved by the political force inherent in Elijah Muhammad's teaching, though his Detroit Red life had made the "religious atonement" and conversion aspect of it relevant, as if they were one and the same.

But his "conversion" was at base political, like his philosophically enhanced nationalism. Malcolm eventually saw that it was revolution that made change in the here and the now more directly than "Allah," that it was Black revolution that was needed, which was political, not metaphysical and religious.

Elijah Muhammad's call for Black separation from the U.S. and five Southern "Black belt" states as the landbase of the Black nation (also expressed, in various ways, by the old African Blood Brotherhood, late-1920s Communist Party USA, the '60s African Peoples' Party, and some of the organizations of the so-called New Left of that same period, including the still-existent Republic of New Africa) becomes more and more subsumed in Malcolm's "Message to the Grass Roots" and "Ballot or the Bullet" into a call for Black unity against white supremacy and Black national oppression. It becomes a call for Self-Determination, as a function of unified Black political struggle, rather than the "independence" Elijah Muhammad preached, which implied the existence of a Black state within the boundaries of an imperialist USA.

It was not a Bantustan Malcolm X called for but mobilization against national oppression. In the '60s we summed up Malcolm as calling for Self-Determination, Self-Respect, and Self-Defense. The act of struggle was itself an act of Self-Determination, expressing and the expression of Self-Respect, the "true Self-Consciousness" Du Bois called for.

Imperialism and its spokespersons always try to make Malcolm's call for "Self-Defense" a call for violence. But in reality it is a call for a force that will stop the wanton violence against the Afro-American people. In the backward corridors of today's political climate, where violent physical (and verbal) attacks on Black people have accelerated, Malcolm's call takes on an enhanced relevance.

"If the federal government won't protect us then we will do it ourselves." Against the Howard Beach, Yusef Hawkins, Tawana Brawley, Philip Pannel, new Klan attacks, this call reverberates in and reignites the Black consciousness.

Malcolm's "separatism" became the call for a Black national revolutionary unity to struggle for Self-Determination. Black people would be served by their own struggle, the catalyst being their own consciousness and historical will.

Malcolm's split with Elijah Muhammad and the Nation of Islam was another example of how "one splits into two." That is, how entities are transformed by the dialectical motion of their internal contradictions.

Malcolm's call for Self-Determination was revolutionary in the sense that it saw Black Self-Determination coming only as the result of the political confrontation with and destruction of the continuing slave society. Elijah Muhammad's "separate states" theoretically could be accomplished under existing U.S. imperialism. Not too different from Buthelezi's projection of a "cultural autonomy" for South African Blacks, postapartheid apartheid.

Malcolm's last years, the whole of his overtly political years, are a casebook of ideological change, of social cause and effect. From cultural and religious nationalism, he moves through expansion and clarification of the political dimension into a more politically defined Black nationalism.

The religious and metaphysical trappings of his nationalism were shredded by the real-life politics of the insurgent Black national united front as well as by the revelation of Elijah Muhammad's personal sexual corruption and the petty obstructions of his Nation of Islam theocrat "rivals."

What is so telling is that JFK's assassination, which is the context for the confirmation of Malcolm's call for black political Self-Determination, corresponds to Black perception that Kennedy's murder removes the "helping hand" of white liberalism from Black people, forcing them to go it alone!

It is now that Malcolm becomes the principal spokesman for the Black struggle for Self-Determination and so is doomed himself to assassination. At this point the Black Liberation Movement emerges as the raised voice of Black struggle. The Civil Rights Movement is transformed into the Black Liberation Movement. "Separation," Self-Defense, and Black Consciousness (Self-Respect) become the dynamic interior of Afro-American struggle.

For Malcolm, Self-Respect was a call to "Black consciousness." In the "true self-consciousness" that W. E. B. Du Bois called for, which opposed the "double consciousness" of the Black-hating, white-submitting schizophrenic "house Negro." This Self-Respect would best be served through organizational and institutional development.

SNCC (Student Non-Violent Coordinating Committee), at first shaped by SCLC (Southern Christian Leadership Conference) and its "Christian nonviolence" à la Dr. King, not only splits between "separatists" and "integrationists" but is changed by the exit of many of the white student activists, ultimately into the antiwar movement.

Jimmy Baldwin's *Blues for Mr. Charlie*[3] characterizes the class struggle for influence over the student movement. So that now the A. J. Muste pacifist type leadership, such as Bob Moses, gave way to the more militant Stokely Carmichaels, and H. Rap Browns. Where the struggle for democracy and self-determination is unified in Malcolm X's catalyzed militance.

Malcolm's trip to Mecca, and subsequently to Africa, was the further expansion and consolidation of an ideology of Black revolutionary self-determination, plus now with an added universalism—actually, internationalism. The recognition of "white Muslims" was, objectively, an expression of Malcolm's recognition of internationalism and the worldwide antiimperialist struggle.

Yet Malcolm's close-up on the Bandung conference of Third World nations, his exposure to the Organization of African Unity (OAU), his meetings with the great African (including Arab) leaders as a Black national (Pan-Africanist) front provided a practical clarification of the need for such a front in the U.S., the OAAU.

In my meeting with Malcolm in January 1965, in Muhammad Babu's hotel room at the Waldorf-Astoria, one month before his murder, Malcolm stressed the need for political activists, including myself, to animate and make politically viable a Black united front in the U.S. He insisted that we must move the whole people into a live revolutionary unity.

This is the opposite of the religious sectarianism of the Nation of Islam. It is an admission that Islam is not the only road to revolutionary consciousness and that Muslims, Christians, Nationalists, and Socialists can be joined together as an antiimperialist force in the U.S.

Malcolm had made the connection between Black struggle for democracy and Self-Determination, between white supremacy and its political economic base, imperialism.

Malcolm's Oxford speech (January '65), during the same period he was expelled from France, where he predicted white uprising as a collateral development to Black revolution, indicated an even more advanced internationalist rationale to substantiate a victorious struggle for Black Self-Determination.

The Nation of Islam justified Malcolm's murder, and the government even placed his assassins within the Nation of Islam. But the Nation of Islam and Elijah Muhammad were not the assassins, it was the U.S. government! The same murderers of JFK, RFK, and MLK. The same forces who currently inhabit the *white house*.

And even at the pit of current social backwardness in the U.S. and the world created by the elimination and co-optation of people's revolutionary forces, there is a visible rise in the reforming revolutionary movement. There is a "fight back," a resistance, especially among the young, and in some quarters of the Black "intelligentsia." Black people in Louisiana unified to spank David Duke. Howard students rejected Bush's Atwater. Political rap artists carry a sharp and aggressive attack on white supremacy. The Black studies and multicultural forces reflect Malcolm's call for Self-Determination, Self-Respect, and Self-Defense.

The ideological struggle and development of Black Self-Determination begins with Malcolm's OAAU and proceeds past the general United Front to a political party. A party created to struggle for total U.S. social transformation, based on the call and mobilization for Black Self-Determination. An independent U.S. party, probably formed and, in the main, led by Afro-Americans, but open to the whole of the U.S. people.

Malcolm X, in essence, is a figure representing struggle and Black Self-Determination. Attention to his life and teachings will show immediately how the co-optation of the Black Liberation Movement by the Black bourgeoisie must be resisted and exposed.

His "House Negro" vs. "Field Negro" example of class struggle among the

Afro-American people analyzes and exposes Black liberals and conservatives and describes the whole backward sector of the Black petty bourgeoisie.

Part of the Black bourgeoisie's attack on Malcolm X will be to make him their spokesperson. To render Malcolm's embrace of "internationalism" (i.e., the "revelation" that revolution is a worldwide process, in which Black people are not only included but required to make alliances and coalitions as confirmation of this fact and as the concrete furthering of their own struggle) as the abandoning of Elijah Muhammad's separatism and a militant and acceptable form of "integration," actually submission to U.S. imperialism and white supremacy.

Malcolm's fundamental ideological stance to white supremacy is opposition and an attempt to destroy it. Not coexistence as employment. Like Spike's waving of the red, black, and green in opposing a white director for the Malcolm film is the transparent nationalism of any bourgeoisie trying to secure its market. In effect, it's Spike saying "Only Black me truly can sell y'all these swine foots . . . no whitey can sell authentic swine foots." Hey, they still swine foots! Afro Sheen vs. Vaseline. Securing an economic concession under imperialism, not attempting to destroy it.

And even though the Black national bourgeoisie must be included in the broad Afro-American United Front against imperialism (national bourgeoisie, the sector that still does serve a Black market, as opposed to the compradors, that sector whose market is imperialism), we must still understand the essential *shallowness* of the Black bourgeoisie's commitment to actual Black Self-Determination. They are not there for the long haul, and ours is a protracted struggle.

So Spike's swine foot declaration is the narrowest (i.e., almost wholly economic) claiming of "Black." The removing of the political essence of such "independence" makes it more an attempt at inclusion in imperialism than a point of departure for Black Self-Determination. Indeed, Spike's much-touted call for Black "independence" has vanished quickly right before our eyes, and with 25 million Warner Brothers' dollars on the line, he has already moved to the point where he must answer to imperialism and he now publicly dismisses as "repression" any question of him "answering" to Black people.

Malcolm's last ideological disposition was, again, a movement toward internationalism. After the Mecca and Africa trips, Malcolm used orthodox (Sunni) Islam to disassociate himself from Elijah Muhammad and the Nation of Islam. The trips themselves better familiarized him with international third-world leadership and streams of revolutionary thought inside the third world.

His statement on forming the Organization of Afro-American Unity shows he still identified publicly as a "Black Nationalist" ("Black control of the politics and economics of the Black community . . .") for whom religion had become a "personal" matter.

The political faces of the Black movement must now be formed as a united front of the entire community. This was certainly the essence of what we discussed those several hours at the Waldorf a month before his murder.

But even earlier, Malcolm had said in a speech, "find a capitalist and you find a bloodsucker!" And then in that stunning bit of recorded history, during his Oxford speech, Malcolm chided the mostly white students that "when Black people make revolution, the majority of white folks will rise up with us."

The specter of Malcolm no longer limited by the ideological parameters of the

Nation of Islam, possibly giving leadership to a broad Black united front and able to make international alliances and coalitions (in the whole sense and meaning of that world) could not be tolerated by imperialism.

Recent and proposed attacks on Malcolm X by the bourgeoisie (including Spike's film) seem to indicate that they do not intend for Malcolm's image to survive either. No accurate historical portrait can be drawn of Malcolm without some ideological precision, rendering each of his changes, his stages, in exact dimension. But the bourgeoisie's intentions are not clarity of image, but the exact opposite.

To distort Malcolm so that, like most of Black history, there will be no trace of the actual Malcolm, no trace of his struggle for Self-Determination or our own.

Just as today Spike Lee and others lead a trend of *real* Black exploitation flicks, made by Black reactionaries, while any real analysis of those '60s films media "gofers" call "Black Exploitation films" (e.g., *The Education of Sonny Carson, Superfly, The Mack, Buck and the Preacher, Across 110th Street,* even *Shaft*) will find them much more progressive, even much more pro-Black Self-Determination than the "She's Gotta Have It," "In Living Color," "House Party" syndrome of neo-Step 'n Fetchit derogations and caricatures of Black life, which completely eliminate even the slightest discussion of Black Self-Determination. (Except, perhaps the twisted superficial backwardness of *Do the Right Thing* where Black struggle is perverted to mean photos in a pizza parlor.)

But since these pictures are made by Black reactionaries, as the expression of our domestic neo-colonialism—"imperialism ruling through native agents," Cabral called it—those of us unused to "close reading" of films (or anything else, for that matter) or educated analysis are "chumped off" by the color trick and absorb even larger doses of "double consciousness" Negro antiblackness than we would ever accept from white folks.

Spike Lee's general "dis" of the Black Liberation Movement [includes] his treatment of Elijah Muhammad in the film [and] his dismissal of Malcolm's political meaning. . . . Let us hope it will be understood for what it is and widely opposed.

The main focus of these attempts (with more sighted coming up every day) to distort Malcolm's life is the youth and the future generations more than those of us who lived through that period when he was alive and leading the Black Liberation Movement. The widespread signs that Black youth are not content to be set up as confused and essentially self-destructive targets of white supremacy, uninformed "public enemies" as a result of their miseducation by imperialism and the co-optation of the leadership of the Black Liberation Movement by the Black bourgeoisie, has made the twisting of Malcolm's image a priority in the official U.S. disinformation bureaus and businesses.

Du Bois not only said the problem of the twentieth century is the color line, but he also said that the twentieth century was the epoch of propaganda, since we (human beings) had already formally and legally obtained human rights and now the rulers had to convince us not to make use of them. Malcolm's life, in its real dimension, is a resource and an instrument to be used by all progressive people, but certainly the Afro-American and Pan-African peoples for Self-Determination.

Malcolm's very ideological movement, his groping and seeking, his stumbling and continuous rising from confusion to partial clarity and on, are something that should be taught and studied and widely understood by all of us who would make sweeping social transformation and revolution.

The very struggle for multicultural and Black studies courses in schools is part of that struggle for clarity, and against the masters of propaganda. This must be part of an even broader cultural revolution, where revolutionary politics are struggled for in the area of the superstructure, those ideas and institutions created to forward those ideas created by the economic base of the society. Since this is a society with an imperialist economic base, the main superstructural ideas and institutions that carry them are imperialist, which means economically exploitative, politically oppressive, socially racist, and male chauvinist.

It was Mao who pointed out the importance of Class Struggle, elaborating on what Lenin had said about the need to destroy the state apparatus of imperialism; otherwise it would retard the building of socialism even after the military victory of the proletariat. It is the need to continue the class struggle, the revolutionary struggle in the sphere of culture, the arts, education, otherwise even though we win a revolutionary battle by force of arms, our enemies will reverse that victory if they maintain control of the superstructure.

This has been shown to be viciously, tragically true in both the USSR and People's China, where now we see the Soviet Union itself overthrown and capitalism restored. In China, where Mao said if the people did not continue the Cultural Revolution, the party would "change colors" and become a party controlled by capitalist roaders, maybe even a fascist party. This is exactly what has happened. The grim events in Tiananmen Square a few years ago, where Deng (pronounced Dung) Tsiao Peng, a reactionary Mao once made to wear a dunce hat during the Cultural Revolution, has now killed more communists than Ronald Reagan.

In the U.S.—though we are not defending a socialist state—the gains that we made in the '50s, and '60s, not only the outright defeat of American apartheid, but the advance of the Afro American peoples' struggle for Self-Determination, must be protected at all costs.

In the dimensions of the Sisyphus Syndrome I . . . we are now at downward stroke. The whole host of progressive leaders that were murdered, the aggressive disruption of the movement by government counterinsurgency forces such as KAOS and Cointelpro, added to the principal negative, which was *inside* the Black Liberation Movement, i.e., the absence of a scientific revolutionary party, plus the co-optation of the movement by the Black bourgeoisie (principally through electoral politics, and more recently through the arts). These are the factors that left us open to the dogged and continuous decline in the focus and mobilized militancy of the movement.

The covering and distortion of Malcolm X is just another technique to disrupt the "orderly" passage of revolution from one generation to another. Now that the younger generation is looking for more profound reasons for our lives, naturally they turn to the most profound struggle in this society, the most profound confirmation of the nobility of their lives. So they must turn to the Black Liberation Movement, they must inevitably turn to Malcolm, who ultimately will be revealed as the most profound figure of the '50s–'60s black political upsurge.

Part of our cultural revolution must be to protect the reality of Malcolm's life, because that is the only way we will protect the reality of our own, and the actual historical gravity and meaning of our struggle. This is the reason we ourselves must take our struggle into the schools, into the movie studios, the theaters, the concert halls and nightclubs. It is why we must build cultural and educational and arts institutions to provide an alternative to the poisonous fruits of the American superstructure, even though we must not abandon our struggle for influence and control over those sectors of the superstructure where such relationship is possible.

This is why we are in contention about Malcolm's life and image and history. This is why imperialism and white supremacy and their little running dogs are too. . . .

Malcolm X, *objectively,* was a leading force of struggle for Afro-American Self-Determination. That this is a *fact,* whether it is praiseworthy or to be condemned, is a matter of ideology.

NOTES

1. Bruce Perry, *Malcolm: The Life of a Man Who Changed Black America* (New York: Station Hill Press, 1991).
2. Ngugi Wa Thiong 'O, *Petals of Blood* (New York: NAL, 1978).
3. James Baldwin, *Blues for Mr. Charlie* (New York: Dial Press, 1964).

Audre Lorde (1934–92)

A *poet, teacher, lecturer, and black lesbian feminist, Audre Lorde once explained the motivation behind her work as the "duty to speak the truth . . . and to share not just my triumphs, not just the things that felt good, but the pain, the intense, often unmitigating pain. . . . Art for art's sake doesn't really exist for me. . . . I loved poetry and I loved words. But what was beautiful had to serve the purpose of changing my life, or I would have died. If I cannot air this pain and alter it, I will surely die of it."*

Lorde was born in Harlem to parents who had emigrated from Grenada. At Hunter High School, she was literary editor of the art magazine, and in a now-famous incident, Seventeen *magazine published one of her poems after a high school teacher had dismissed the poem's merit. Lorde earned her bachelor's from Hunter College in 1959 and her master's in library science from Columbia University in 1961. In addition, she received honorary doctorates from Hunter College, Oberlin College, and Haverford College. A civil rights activist in the 1950s and 1960s, she also taught at various academic institutions, including the City College of New York, John Jay College of Criminal Justice, Lehman College, and Hunter College.*

In numerous volumes of poetry and prose, Lorde pursues themes that cut away at sexism, racism, and other prejudices. Although her writing reflects her personal experiences with marriage and divorce, motherhood, lesbianism, and cancer, the author's sensitivity to the loss of human dignity by other blacks is just as prominent in her works. She first gained critical notice as a writer in the late 1960s, when she was awarded a grant from the National Endowment for the Arts. A Creative Arts Public Service Award Grant followed in 1972. Her poetry volume From a Land Where Other People Live *(1973) was nominated for a National Book Award. A Broadside Poet's Award came in 1975, followed by a Creative Artists Public Service Award in 1980. She was also honored as the 1991 Poet Laureate of the State of New York.*

Lorde's extensive publications cover various genres, with an emphasis on poetry that includes several collections: The First Cities *(1970),* Cables of Rage *(1970),* The New York Head Shop and Museum *(1974),* Coal *(1976),* Between Ourselves *(1976),* The Black Unicorn *(1978),* Chosen Poems: Old and New *(1982),* Our Dead behind Us *(1986), and* The Marvelous Arithmetics of Distance *(1992). Her "biomythography"* Zami: A New Spelling of My Name *was issued in 1982. Her other books of nonfiction are* The Uses of Erotic: Erotic as Power *(1979),* The Cancer Journals *(1980),* Sister, Outsider *(1984),* I Am Your Sister: Black Women Organizing Across Sexualities *(1985),* A Burst of Light *(1988),* Hell under God's Orders *(1990),* Need: A Chorale for Black Woman Voices *(1990), and* Showing Our Colors: Afro-German Women Speak Out *(1991).*

In 1981, Lorde helped found Kitchen Table: Women of Color Press, a publishing entity intent on functioning as a conduit for the distinctive political, cultural, and personal voices of ethnic women writers.

The following essay, originally written for presentation by Lorde at the Copeland Colloquium at Amherst College in 1980, was later published in her Sister, Outsider *in 1984. "Age, Race, Class, and Sex: Women Redefining Difference," considers the positive and confirming values of that "difference" within society.*

Age, Race, Class, and Sex: Women Redefining Difference

Much of Western European history conditions us to see human differences in simplistic opposition to each other: dominant/subordinate, good/bad, up/down, superior/inferior. In a society where the good is defined in terms of profit rather than in terms of human need, there must always be some group of people who, through systematized oppression, can be made to feel surplus, to occupy the place of the dehumanized inferior. Within the society, that group is made up of Black and Third World people, working-class people, older people, and women.

As a forty-nine-year-old Black lesbian feminist socialist mother of two, including one boy, and a member of an interracial couple, I usually find myself a part of some group defined as other, deviant, inferior, or just plain wrong. Traditionally, in American society, it is the members of oppressed, objectified groups who are expected to stretch out and bridge the gap between the actualities of our lives and the consciousness of our oppressor. For in order to survive, those of use for whom oppression is as American as apple pie have always had to be watchers, to become familiar with the language and manners of the oppressor, even sometimes adopting them for some illusion of protection. Whenever the need for some pretense of communication arises, those who profit from our oppression call upon us to share our knowledge with them. In other words, it is the responsibility of the oppressed to teach the oppressors their mistakes. I am responsible for educating teachers who dismiss my children's culture in school. Black and Third World people are expected to educate white people as to our humanity. Women are expected to educate men. Lesbians and gay men are expected to educate the heterosexual world. The oppressors maintain their position and evade responsibility for their own actions. There is a constant drain of energy which might be better used in redefining ourselves and devising realistic scenarios for altering the present and constructing the future.

Institutionalized rejection of difference is an absolute necessity in a profit economy which needs outsiders as surplus people. As members of such an economy, we have *all* been programmed to respond to the human differences between us with fear and loathing and to handle that difference in one of three ways: ignore it, and if that is not possible, copy it if we think it is dominant, or destroy it if we think it is subordinate. But we have no patterns for relating across our human differences as equals. As a result, those differences have been misnamed and misused in the service of separation and confusion.

Certainly there are very real differences between us of race, age, and sex. But it is not those differences between us that are separating us. It is rather our refusal to recognize those differences, and to examine the distortions which result from our misnaming them and their effects upon human behavior and expectation.

Racism, the belief in the inherent superiority of one race over all others and thereby the right to dominance. Sexism, the belief in the inherent superiority of one sex over the other and thereby the right to dominance. Ageism. Heterosexism. Elitism. Classism.

It is a lifetime pursuit for each one of us to extract these distortions from our living at the same time as we recognize, reclaim, and define those differences upon which they are imposed. For we have all been raised in a society where those distortions were endemic within our living. Too often, we pour the energy needed for recognizing and exploring difference into pretending those differences are insurmountable barriers, or that they do not exist at all. This results in a voluntary isolation, or false and treacherous connections. Either way, we do not develop tools for using human difference as a springboard for creative change within our lives. We speak not of human difference, but of human deviance.

Somewhere, on the edge of consciousness, there is what I call a *mythical norm,* which each one of us within our hearts knows "that is not me." In america, this norm is usually defined as white, thin, male, young, heterosexual, christian, and financially secure. It is with this mythical norm that the trappings of power reside within this society. Those of us who stand outside that power often identify one way in which we are different, and we assume that to be the primary cause of all oppression, forgetting other distortions around difference, some of which we ourselves may be practicing. By and large within the women's movement today, white women focus upon their oppression as women and ignore differences of race, sexual preference, class, and age. There is a pretense to a homogeneity of experience covered by the word *sisterhood* that does not in fact exist.

Unacknowledged class differences rob women of each others' energy and creative insight. Recently a women's magazine collective made the decision for one issue to print only prose, saying poetry was a less "rigorous" or "serious" art form. Yet even the form our creativity takes is often a class issue. Of all the art forms, poetry is the most economical. It is the one which is the most secret, which requires the least physical labor, the least material, and the one which can be done between shifts, in the hospital pantry, on the subway, and on scraps of surplus paper. Over the last few years, writing a novel on tight finances, I came to appreciate the enormous differences in the material demands between poetry and prose. As we reclaim our literature, poetry has been the major voice of poor, working class, and Colored women. A room of one's own may be a necessity for writing prose, but so are reams of paper, a typewriter, and plenty of time. The actual requirements to produce the visual arts also help determine, along class lines, whose art is whose. In this day of inflated prices for material, who are our sculptors, our painters, our photographers? When we speak of a broadly based women's culture, we need to be aware of the effect of class and economic differences on the supplies available for producing art.

As we move toward creating a society within which we can each flourish, ageism is another distortion of relationship which interferes without vision. By ignoring the past, we are encouraged to repeat its mistakes. The "generation gap" is an important social tool for any repressive society. If the younger members of a community view the older members as contemptible or suspect or excess, they will never be able to join hands and examine the living memories of the community, nor ask the all important question, "Why?" This gives rise to a historical amnesia that keeps us working to invent the wheel every time we have to go to the store for bread.

We find ourselves having to repeat and relearn the same old lessons over and over that our mothers did because we do not pass on what we have learned, or because we are unable to listen. For instance, how many times has this all been said before? For another, who would have believed that once again our daughters are allowing their bodies to be hampered and purgatoried by girdles and high heels and hobble skirts?

Ignoring the differences of race between women and the implications of those differences presents the most serious threat to the mobilization of women's joint power.

As white women ignore their built-in privilege of whiteness and define *woman* in terms of their own experience alone, then women of Color become "other," the outsider whose experience and tradition is too "alien" to comprehend. An example of this is the signal absence of the experience of women of Color as a resource for women's studies courses. The literature of women of Color is seldom included in women's literature studies as a whole. All too often, the excuse given is that the literatures of women of Color can only be taught by Colored women, or that they are too difficult to understand, or that classes cannot "get into" them because they come out of experiences that are "too different." I have heard this argument presented by white women of otherwise quite clear intelligence, women who seem to have no trouble at all teaching and reviewing work that comes out of the vastly different experiences of Shakespeare, Molière, Dostoyefsky, and Aristophanes. Surely there must be some other explanation.

This is a very complex question, but I believe one of the reasons white women have such difficulty reading Black women's work is because of their reluctance to see Black women as women and different from themselves. To examine Black women's literature effectively requires that we be seen as whole people in our actual complexities—as individuals, as women, as human—rather than as one of those problematic but familiar stereotypes provided in this society in place of genuine images of Black women. And I believe this holds true for the literatures of other women of Color who are not Black.

The literatures of all women of Color re-create the textures of our lives, and many white women are heavily invested in ignoring the real differences. For as long as any difference between us means one of us must be inferior, then the recognition of any difference must be fraught with guilt. To allow women of Color to step out of stereotypes is too guilt provoking, for it threatens the complacency of those women who view oppression only in terms of sex.

Refusing to recognize difference makes it impossible to see the different problems and pitfalls facing us as women.

Thus, in a patriarchal power system where whiteskin privilege is a major prop, the entrapments used to neutralize Black women and white women are not the same. For example, it is easy for Black women to be used by the power structure against Black men, not because they are men, but because they are Black. Therefore, for Black women, it is necessary at all times to separate the needs of the oppressor from our own legitimate conflicts within our communities. This same problem does not exist for white women. Black women and men have shared racist oppression and still share it, although in different ways. Out of that shared oppression we have developed joint defenses and joint vulnerabilities to each other that are not duplicated in the white community, with the exception of the relationship between Jewish women and Jewish men.

On the other hand, white women face the pitfall of being seduced into joining the oppressor under the pretense of sharing power. This possibility does not exist in the same way for women of Color. The tokenism that is sometimes extended to us is not an invitation to join power; our racial "otherness" is a visible reality that makes that quite clear. For white women there is a wider range of pretended choices and rewards for identifying with patriarchal power and its tools.

Today, with the defeat of ERA, the tightening economy, and increased conservatism, it is easier once again for white women to believe the dangerous fantasy that if you are good enough, pretty enough, sweet enough, quiet enough, teach the children to behave, hate the right people, and marry the right men, then you will be allowed to co-exist with patriarchy in relative peace, at least until a man needs your job or the neighborhood rapist happens along. And true, unless one lives and loves in the trenches it is difficult to remember that the war against dehumanization is ceaseless.

But Black women and our children know the fabric of our lives is stitched with violence and with hatred, that there is no rest. We do not deal with it only on the picket lines, or in dark midnight alleys, or in the places where we dare to verbalize our resistance. For us, increasingly, violence weaves through the daily tissues of our living—in the supermarket, in the classroom, in the elevator, in the clinic and the schoolyard, from the plumber, the baker, the saleswoman, the bus driver, the bank teller, the waitress who does not serve us.

Some problems we share as women, some we do not. You fear your children will grow up to join the patriarchy and testify against you, we fear our children will be dragged from a car and shot down in the street, and you will turn your backs upon the reasons they are dying.

The threat of difference has been no less blinding to people of Color. Those of us who are Black must see that the reality of our lives and our struggle does not make us immune to the errors of ignoring and misnaming difference. Within Black communities where racism is a living reality, differences among us often seem dangerous and suspect. The need for unity is often misnamed as a need for homogeneity, and a Black feminist vision mistaken for betrayal of our common interests as a people. Because of the continuous battle against racial erasure that

Black women and Black men share, some Black women still refuse to recognize that we are also oppressed as women, and that sexual hostility against Black women is practiced not only by the white racist society, but implemented within our Black communities as well. It is a disease striking the heart of Black nationhood, and silence will not make it disappear. Exacerbated by racism and the pressures of powerlessness, violence against Black women and children often becomes a standard within our communities, one by which manliness can be measured. But these woman-hating acts are rarely discussed as crimes against Black women.

As a group, women of Color are the lowest paid wage earners in America. We are the primary targets of abortion and sterilization abuse, here and abroad. In certain parts of Africa, small girls are still being sewed shut between their legs to keep them docile and for men's pleasure. This is known as female circumcision, and it is not a cultural affair as the late Jomo Kenyatta insisted, it is a crime against Black women.

Black women's literature is full of the pain of frequent assault, not only by a racist patriarchy, but also by Black men. Yet the necessity for and history of shared battle have made us, Black women, particularly vulnerable to the false accusation that anti-sexist is anti-Black. Meanwhile, womanhating as a recourse of the powerless is sapping strength from Black communities, and our very lives. Rape is on the increase, reported and unreported, and rape is not aggressive sexuality, it is sexualized aggression. As Kalamu ya Salaam, a Black male writer points out, "As long as male domination exists, rape will exist. Only women revolting and men made conscious of their responsibility to fight sexism can collectively stop rape."*

Differences between ourselves as Black women are also being misnamed and used to separate us from one another. As a Black lesbian feminist comfortable with the many different ingredients of my identity, and a woman committed to racial and sexual freedom from oppression, I find I am constantly being encouraged to pluck out some one aspect of myself and present this as the meaningful whole, eclipsing or denying the other parts of self. But this is a destructive and fragmenting way to live. My fullest concentration of energy is available to me only when I integrate all the parts of who I am, openly, allowing power from particular sources of my living to flow back and forth freely through all my different selves, without the restrictions of externally imposed definition. Only then can I bring myself and my energies as a whole to the service of those struggles which I embrace as part of my living.

A fear of lesbians, or of being accused of being a lesbian, has led many Black women into testifying against themselves. It has led some of us into destructive alliances, and others into despair and isolation. In the white women's communities, heterosexism is sometimes a result of identifying with the white patriarchy, a rejection of that interdependence between women-identified women which allows the self to be, rather than to be used in the service of men. Sometimes it reflects a die-hard belief in the protective coloration of heterosexual relationships, sometimes a self-hate which all women have to fight against, taught us from birth.

---

* From Rape: "A Radical Analysis, An African-American Perspective" by Kalamu ya Salaam in *Black Books Bulletin,* vol. 6, no. 4 (1980).

Although elements of these attitudes exist for all women, there are particular resonances of heterosexism and homophobia among Black women. Despite the fact that woman-bonding has a long and honorable history in the African and African-American communities, and despite the knowledge and accomplishments of many strong and creative women-identified Black women in the political, social and cultural fields, heterosexual Black women often tend to ignore or discount the existence and work of Black lesbians. Part of this attitude has come from an understandable terror of Black male attack within the close confines of Black society, where the punishment for any female self-assertion is still to be accused of being a lesbian and therefore unworthy of the attention or support of the scarce Black male. But part of this need to misname and ignore Black lesbians comes from a very real fear that openly women-identified Black women who are no longer dependent upon men for their self-definition may well reorder our whole concept of social relationships.

Black women who once insisted that lesbianism was a white woman's problem now insist that Black lesbians are a threat to Black nationhood, are consorting with the enemy, are basically un-Black. These accusations, coming from the very women to whom we look for deep and real understanding, have served to keep many Black lesbians in hiding, caught between the racism of white women and the homophobia of their sisters. Often, their work has been ignored, trivialized, or misnamed, as with the work of Angelina Grimke, Alice Dunbar-Nelson, Lorraine Hansberry. Yet women-bonded women have always been some part of the power of Black communities, from our unmarried aunts to the amazons of Dahomey.

And it is certainly not Black lesbians who are assaulting women and raping children and grandmothers on the streets of our communities.

Across this country, as in Boston during the spring of 1979 following the unsolved murders of twelve Black women, Black lesbians are spearheading movements against violence against Black women.

What are the particular details within each of our lives that can be scrutinized and altered to help bring about change? How do we redefine difference for all women? Is it not our differences which separate women, but our reluctance to recognize those differences and to deal effectively with the distortions which have resulted from the ignoring and misnaming of those differences.

As a tool of social control, women have been encouraged to recognize only one area of human difference as legitimate, those differences which exist between women and men. And we have learned to deal across those differences with the urgency of all oppressed subordinates. All of us have had to learn to live or work or coexist with men, from our fathers on. We have recognized and negotiated these differences, even when this recognition only continued the old dominant/subordinate mode of human relationship, where the oppressed must recognize the masters' difference in order to survive.

But our future survival is predicated upon our ability to relate within equality. As women, we must root out internalized patterns of oppression within ourselves if we are to move beyond the most superficial aspects of social change. Now we must recognize differences among women who are our equals, neither inferior nor superior, and devise ways to use each others' difference to enrich our visions and our joint struggles.

The future of our earth may depend upon the ability of all women to identify and develop new definitions of power and new patterns of relating across difference. The old definitions have not served us, nor the earth that supports us. The old patterns, no matter how cleverly rearranged to imitate progress, still condemn us to cosmetically altered repetitions of the same old exchanges, the same old guilt, hatred, recrimination, lamentation, and suspicion.

For we have, built into all of us, old blueprints of expectation and response, old structures of oppression, and these must be altered at the same time as we alter the living conditions which are a result of those structures. For the master's tools will never dismantle the master's house.

As Paulo Freire shows so well in *The Pedagogy of the Oppressed,** the true focus of revolutionary change is never merely the oppressive situations which we seek to escape, but that piece of the oppressor which is planted deep within each of us, and, which knows only the oppressors' tactics, the oppressor's relationships.

Change means growth, and growth can be painful. But we sharpen self-definition by exposing the self in work and struggle together with those whom we define as different from ourselves, although sharing the same goals. For Black and white, old and young, lesbian and heterosexual women alike, this can mean new paths to our survival.

> We have chosen each other
> and the edge of each other's battles
> the war is the same
> if we lose
> someday women's blood will congeal
> upon a dead planet
> if we win
> there is no telling
> we seek beyond history
> for a new and more possible meeting.**

David Levering Lewis (1936–)

Born in Little Rock, Arkansas, David Levering Lewis earned his bachelor's from Fisk University in 1956 and his master's from Columbia University in 1958. He studied abroad for his doctorate, earning that degree from the London School of Economics and Political Science in 1962.

Lewis has taught history at the University of Ghana-Accra, Howard University, University of Notre Dame, Morgan State College, and University of the District of Columbia. Presently he is the Martin Luther King, Jr., chair in history at Rutgers University. He has won numerous awards and grants, including honors from the American Philosophical Society, the National Endowment for the Humanities, the Social Science Research Council, and the Woodrow Wilson International Center for Scholars.

Among his many books, which cover a range of historical, political, and ethnic themes, are Martin Luther King: A Critical Biography *(1971),* Prisoners of Honor: The Dreyfus Affair *(1973),* District of Columbia: A Bicentennial History

* Seabury Press, New York, 1970.

** From "Outlines," unpublished poem.

(1977), and When Harlem Was in Vogue: The Politics of the Arts in the Twenties and Thirties *(1981). In addition, he has edited two anthologies*—W. E. B. Du Bois: A Reader *(1994) and* The Portable Harlem Renaissance Reader *(1994)—and has written a Pulitzer Prize-winning work,* W. E. B. Du Bois: Biography of a Race *(1993), which also won a Francis Parkman Prize and a Bancroft Prize.*

"The Harlem Renaissance" was originally published as the introduction to The Portable Harlem Renaissance Reader. *Providing a historical background for the Harlem Renaissance, Lewis connects the literary, political, and social figures of that distinctive artistic movement.*

The Harlem Renaissance

The Harlem Renaissance was a somewhat forced phenomenon, a cultural nationalism of the parlor, institutionally encouraged and directed by leaders of the national civil rights establishment for the paramount purpose of improving race relations in a time of extreme national backlash, caused in large part by economic gains won by Afro-Americans during the Great War. W. E. B. Du Bois labeled this mobilizing elite the "Talented Tenth" in a seminal 1903 essay. He fleshed out the concept that same year in "The Advance Guard of the Race," a piece in *Booklover's* magazine in which he identified the poet Paul Lawrence Dunbar, the novelist Charles W. Chesnutt, and the painter Henry O. Tanner, among a small number of other well-educated professionals, as representatives of this class. The Talented Tenth formulated and propagated a new ideology of racial assertiveness that was to be embraced by the physicians, dentists, educators, preachers, businesspeople, lawyers, and morticians who comprised the bulk of the African American affluent and influential—some ten thousand men and women out of a total population in 1920 of more than ten million. (In 1917, traditionally cited as the natal year of the Harlem Renaissance, there were 2,132 African Americans in colleges and universities, probably no more than fifty of them attending "white" institutions.)

It was, then, the minuscule vanguard of a minority—a fraction of 0.1 percent of the racial total—that jump-started the New Negro Arts Movement, using as its vehicles the National Association for the Advancement of Colored People (NAACP) and the National Urban League (NUL), and their respective publications, the *Crisis* and *Opportunity* magazine. The Harlem Renaissance was not, as some students have maintained, all-inclusive of the early twentieth-century African American urban experience. Not everything that happened between 1917 and 1935 was a Renaissance happening. The potent mass movement founded and led by the charismatic Marcus Garvey was to the Renaissance what nineteenth-century populism was to progressive reform: a parallel but socially different force related primarily through dialectical confrontation. Equally different from the institutional ethos and purpose of the Renaissance was the Black Church. If the leading intellectual of the race, Du Bois, publicly denigrated the personnel and preachings of the Black Church, his animadversions were merely more forthright than those of other New Negro notables James Weldon Johnson, Charles S. Johnson, Jessie Redmon Fauset, Alain Locke, and Walter Francis White. An occasional minister (such as the father of poet Countee Cullen), or exceptional Garveyites (such as Yale-Harvard man William H. Ferris) might move in both worlds, but black evangelism and its cultist manifestations, such as Black Zionism, represented emotional and cultural retrogression in the eyes of the principal actors in the Renaissance.

When Du Bois wrote a few years after the beginning of the New Negro movement in arts and letters that "until the art of the black folk compels recognition they will not be rated as human," he, like most of his Renaissance peers, fully intended to exclude the blues of Bessie Smith and the jazz of "King" Oliver. Spirituals sung like *Lieder* by the disciplined Hall Johnson Choir—and, better yet, *Lieder* sung by conservatory-trained Roland Hayes, 1924 recipient of the NAACP's prestigious Spingarn Medal—were deemed appropriate musical forms to present to mainstream America. The deans of the Renaissance were entirely content to leave discovery and celebration of Bessie, Clara, Trixie, and various other blues-singing Smiths to white music critic Carl Van Vechten's effusions in *Vanity Fair*. When the visiting Russian film director Sergei Eisenstein enthused about new black musicals, Charles S. Johnson and Alain Locke expressed mild consternation in their interview in *Opportunity* magazine. As board members of the Pace Phonograph Company, Du Bois, James Weldon Johnson, and others banned "funky" artists from the Black Swan list of recordings, thereby contributing to the demise of the African American-owned firm. But the wild Broadway success of Miller and Lyles's musical *Shuffle Along* (which helped to popularize the Charleston) or Florence Mills's *Blackbirds* revue flouted such artistic fastidiousness. The very centrality of music in black life, as well as of black musical stereotypes in white minds, caused popular musical forms to impinge inescapably on Renaissance high culture. Eventually, the Renaissance deans made a virtue out of necessity; they applauded the concert-hall ragtime of "Big Jim" Europe and the "educated" jazz of Atlanta University graduate and big-band leader Fletcher Henderson, and took to hiring Duke Ellington or Cab Calloway as drawing cards for fund-raising socials. Still, their relationship to music remained beset by paradox. New York ragtime, with its "Jelly Roll" Morton strides and Joplinesque elegance, had as much in common with Chicago jazz as Mozart did with "Fats" Waller.

Although the emergence of the Harlem Renaissance seems much more sudden and dramatic in retrospect than the historic reality, its institutional elaboration was, in fact, relatively quick. Because so little fiction or poetry had been produced by African Americans in the years immediately prior to the Harlem Renaissance, the appearance of a dozen or more poets and novelists and essayists seemed all the more striking and improbable. Death from tuberculosis had silenced poet-novelist Dunbar in 1906, and poor royalties had done the same for novelist Chesnutt after publication the previous year of *The Colonel's Dream*. Since then, no more than five African Americans had published significant works of fiction and verse. There had been *Pointing the Way* in 1908, a flawed, fascinating civil rights novel by the Baptist preacher Sutton Griggs. Three years later, Du Bois's sweeping sociological allegory *The Quest of the Silver Fleece* appeared. The following year came James Weldon Johnson's well-crafted *The Autobiography of an Ex-Colored Man*, but the author felt compelled to disguise his racial identity. A ten-year silence fell afterward, finally to be broken in 1922 by Claude McKay's *Harlem Shadows*, the first book of poetry since Dunbar.

Altogether, the Harlem Renaissance evolved through three stages. The first phase, ending in 1923 with the publication of Jean Toomer's unique prose poem *Cane,* was deeply influenced by white artists and writers—Bohemians and Revolutionaries—fascinated for a variety of reasons with the life of black people. The second phase, from early 1924 to mid-1926, was presided over by the Civil Rights Establishment of the NUL and the NAACP, a period of interracial collaboration between Zora Neale Hurston's "Negrotarian" whites and the African American Talented Tenth. The last phase, from mid-1926 to the Harlem Riot of March 1935, was increasingly dominated by the African American artists themselves—the "Niggerati," in Hurston's pungent phrase. The movement, then, was above all literary and self-consciously an enterprise of high culture well into its middle years. When Charles S. Johnson, new editor of *Opportunity,* sent invitations to some dozen young and mostly unknown African American poets and writers to attend a celebration at Manhattan's Civil Club of the sudden outpouring of "Negro" writing, on March 21, 1924, the Renaissance shifted into high gear. "A group of the younger writers, which includes Eric Walrond, Jessie Fauset, Gwendolyn Bennett, Countee Cullen, Langston Hughes, Alain Locke, and some others," would be present, Johnson promised each invitee. All told, in addition to the "younger writers," some fifty persons were expected: "Eugene O'Neill, H. L. Mencken, Oswald Garrison Villard, Mary Johnston, Zona Gale, Robert Morss Lovett, Carl Van Doren, Ridgely Torrence, and about twenty more of this type. I think you might find this group interesting enough to draw you away for a few hours from your work on your next book," Johnson wrote almost coyly to the recently published Jean Toomer.

Although both Toomer and Langston Hughes were absent in Europe, approximately 110 celebrants and honorees assembled that evening; included among them were Du Bois, James Weldon Johnson, and the young NAACP officer Walter Francis White, whose energies as a literary entrepreneur would soon excel even Charles Johnson's. Locke, a professor of philosophy at Howard University and the first African American Rhodes scholar, served as Civil Club master of ceremonies. Fauset, the literary editor of the *Crisis* and a Phi Beta Kappa graduate of Cornell University, enjoyed the distinction of having written the second fictional work and first novel of the Renaissance, *There Is Confusion,* just released by Horace Liveright. Liveright, who was present, rose to praise Fauset as well as Toomer, whose prose poem *Cane* his firm had published in 1923. Speeches followed pell mell—Du Bois, James Weldon Johnson, Fauset. White called attention to the next Renaissance novel—his own, *The Fire in the Flint,* shortly forthcoming from Knopf. Albert Barnes, the crusty Philadelphia pharmaceutical millionaire and art collector, described the decisive impact of African art on modern art. Poets and poems were commended—Hughes, Cullen, and Georgia Douglas Johnson of Washington, D.C., with Gwendolyn Bennett's stilted yet appropriate "To Usward" punctuating the evening: "We claim no part with racial dearth, / We want to sing the songs of birth!" Charles Johnson wrote the vastly competent Ethel Ray Nance, his future secretary, of his enormous gratification that Paul Kellogg, editor of the influential *Survey Graphic,* had proposed that evening to place a special number of his magazine "at the service of representatives of the group."

Two compelling messages emerged from the Civic Club gathering: Du Bois's that the literature of apology and the denial to his generation of its authentic voice were now ending; Van Doren's that African American artists were developing at a uniquely propitious moment. They were "in a remarkable strategic position with reference to the new literary age which seems to be impending," Van Doren predicted. "What American literature decidedly needs at this moment," he continued, "is color, music, gusto, the free expression of gay or desperate moods. If the Negroes are not in a position to contribute these items," Van Doren could not imagine who else could. The African American had indisputably moved to the center of Mainstream imagination with the end of the Great War, a development nurtured in the chrysalis of the Lost Generation—Greenwich Village Bohemia. Ready conversance with the essentials of Freud and Marx became the measure of serious conversation in MacDougal Street coffeehouses, Albert Boni's Washington Square Book Shop, or the Hotel Brevoort's restaurant, where Floyd Dell, Robert Minor, Matthew Josephson, Max Eastman, and other *enragés* denounced the social system, the Great War to which it had ineluctably led, and the soul-dead world created in its aftermath, with McKay and Toomer, two of the Renaissance's first stars, participating. The first issue of Randolph Bourne's *Seven Arts* (November 1916)—which featured, among others of the "Lyrical Left," Waldo Frank, James Oppenheim, Robert Frost, Paul Rosenfeld, Van Wyck Brooks, and the French intellectual Romain Rolland—professed contempt for "the people who actually ran things" in America. Waldo Frank, Toomer's bosom friend and literary mentor, foresaw a revolutionary new America emerging "out of our terrifying welter or steel and scarlet." The Marxist radicals (John Reed, Floyd Dell, Helen Keller, Max Eastman) associated with *Masses* and its successor magazine, *Liberator,* edited by Max and Crystal Eastman, were theoretically much more oriented to politics. The inaugural March 1918 issue of *Liberator* announced that they would "fight for the ownership and control of industry by the workers."

Among the Lyrical Left writers gathered around *Broom, S4N,* and *Seven Arts* and the political radicals associated with *Liberator,* there was a shared reaction against the ruling Anglo-Saxon cultural paradigm. Bourne's concept of a "transnational" America, democratically respectful of its ethnic, racial, and religious constituents, complemented Du Bois's earlier concept of divided racial identity in *The Souls of Black Folk.* From such conceptions, the Village's discovery of Harlem followed both logically and, more compellingly, psychologically, for if the factory, campus, office, and corporation were dehumanizing, stultifying, or predatory, the African American, largely excluded because of race from all of the above, was a perfect symbol of cultural innocence and regeneration. He was perceived as an integral, indispensable part of the hoped-for design, somehow destined to aid in the reclamation of a diseased, desiccated civilization.

Public annunciation of the rediscovered Negro came in the fall of 1917 with Emily Hapgood's production at the old Garden Street Theatre of three one-act plays by her husband, Ridgely Torrence. *The Rider of Dreams, Simon the Cyrenian,* and *Granny Maumee* were considered daring because the casts were black and the parts were dignified. The drama critic from *Theatre* magazine enthused of one lead player that "nobody who saw Opal Cooper—and heard him as the dreamer, Madison Sparrow—will ever forget the lift his performance gave." Du Bois commended the playwright by letter, and James Weldon Johnson excitedly wrote his friend, the African American literary critic Benjamin Brawley, that *The Smart Set*'s Jean Nathan "spoke most highly about the work of these colored performers." From this watershed flowed a number of dramatic productions, musicals, and several successful novels by whites—yet also, with great significance, *Shuffle Along,* a cathartic musical by the African Americans Aubry Lyles and Flournoy Miller. Theodore Dreiser grappled with the explosive subject of lynching in his 1918 short story "Nigger Jeff." Two years later, the magnetic African American actor Charles Gilpin energized O'Neill's *Emperor Jones* in the 150-seat theater in a MacDougal Street brownstone taken over by the Provincetown Players.

The year 1921 brought *Shuffle Along* to the 63rd Street Theatre, with music, lyrics, choreography, cast, and production uniquely in African American hands, and composer Eubie Blake's "I'm Just Wild about Harry" and "Love Will Find a Way" entered the list of all-time favorites. Mary Hoyt Wiborg's *Taboo* was produced that year, with a green Paul Robeson making his theatrical debut. Clement Wood's 1922 sociological novel *Nigger* sympathetically tracked a beleaguered African American family from slavery through the Great War into urban adversity. *Emperor Jones* (revived in 1922 with Robeson in the lead part) showed civilization's pretentions being mocked by forces from the dark subconscious. That same year T. S. Stribling's *Birthright* appeared, a novel remarkable for its effort to portray an African American male protagonist of superior education (a Harvard-educated physician) martyred for his ideals after returning to the South. "Jean Le Negre," the black character in e. e. cummings's *The Enormous Room* (1922), was another Noble Savage paradigm observed through a Freudian prism.

But Village artists and intellectuals were aware and unhappy that they were theorizing about Afro-America and spinning out African American fictional characters in a vacuum—that they knew almost nothing firsthand about these subjects. Sherwood Anderson's June 1922 letter to H. L. Mencken spoke for much of the Lost Generation: "Damn it, man, if I could really get inside the niggers and write about them with some intelligence, I'd be willing to be hanged later and perhaps would be." Anderson's prayers were answered almost immediately when he chanced to read a Jean Toomer short story in *Double-Dealer* magazine. With the novelist's assistance, Toomer's stories began to appear in the magazines of the Lyrical Left and the Marxists, in *Dial, S4N, Broom,* and *Liberator.* Anderson's 1925 novel *Dark Laughter* bore unmistakable signs of indebtedness to Toomer, whose work, Anderson readily admitted, had given him a true insight into the cultural energies that could be harnessed to pull America back from the abyss of fatal materialism. Celebrity in the Village brought Toomer into Waldo Frank's circle, and with it criticism from Toomer about the omission of African Americans from Frank's sprawling work *Our America.* After a trip with Toomer to South Carolina in the fall of 1922, Frank published *Holiday* the following year, a somewhat overwrought treatment of the struggle between the two races in the South, "each of which . . . needs what the other possesses."

Claude McKay, whose volume of poetry *Harlem Shadows* (1922) made him a Village celebrity (he lived in Gay Street, then entirely inhabited by nonwhites), found his niche among the *Liberator* group, where he soon became co-editor of the magazine with Michael Gold. The Eastmans saw the Jamaican poet as the kind of writer who would deepen the magazine's proletarian voice. McKay increased the circulation of *Liberator* to sixty thousand, published the first poetry of e. e. cummings (over Gold's objections), introduced Garvey's Universal Negro Improvement Association (UNIA), and generally treated the readership to experimentation that had little to do with proletarian literature. "It was much easier to talk about real proletarians writing masterpieces than to find such masterpieces," McKay told the Eastmans and the exasperated hard-line Marxist Gold. Soon all manner of Harlem radicals began meeting, at McKay's invitation, in West 13th Street, while the Eastmans fretted about Justice Department surveillance. Richard B. Moore, Cyril Briggs, Otto Huiswood, Grace Campbell, W. A. Domingo, inter alia, represented Harlem movements ranging from Garvey's UNIA and Briggs's African Blood Brotherhood to the CPUSA with Huiswood and Campbell. McKay also attempted to bring the Village to Harlem, in one memorable sortie taking Eastman and another Villager to Ned's, his favorite Harlem cabaret. Ned, notoriously anti-white, expelled them.

This was part of the background to the Talented Tenth's abrupt, enthusiastic, and programmatic embrace of arts and letters after the First World War. With white Broadway audiences flocking to O'Neill plays and shrieking with delight at *Liza, Runnin' Wild,* and other imitations of *Shuffle Along,* Charles Johnson and James Weldon Johnson, Du Bois, Fauset, White, Locke, and others saw a unique opportunity to tap into the American mainstream. Harlem, the Negro Capital of the World, filled up with successful bootleggers and racketeers, political and religious charlatans, cults of exotic character ("Black Jews"), street-corner pundits and health practitioners (Hubert Harrison, "Black Herman"), beauty culturists and distinguished professionals (Madame C. J. Walker, Louis T. Wright), religious and civil rights notables (Reverends Cullen and Powell, Du Bois, Johnson, White), and hard-pressed, hard-working families determined to make decent lives for their children. Memories of the nightspots in "The Jungle" (133rd Street), of Bill "Bojangles" Robinson demonstrating his footwork on Lenox Avenue, of raucous shows at the Lafayette that gave Florenz Ziegfeld some of his ideas, of the Tree of Hope outside Connie's Inn where musicians gathered as at a labor exchange, have been vividly set down by Arthur P. Davis, Regina Andrews, Arna Bontemps, and Langston Hughes.

If they were adroit, African American civil rights officials and intellectuals believed they stood a fair chance of succeeding in reshaping the images and repackaging the messages out of which Mainstream racial behavior emerged. Bohemia and the Lost Generation suggested to the Talented Tenth the new approach to the old problem of race relations, but their shared premise about art and society obscured the diametrically opposite conclusions white and black intellectuals and artists drew from them. Harold Stearns's Lost Generation *revoltés* were lost in the sense that they professed to have no wish to find themselves in a materialistic, mammon-mad, homogenizing America. Locke's New Negroes very much wanted full acceptance by Mainstream America, even if some, like Du Bois, McKay, and the future *enfant terrible* of the Renaissance, Wallace Thurman, might have immediately exercised the privilege of rejecting it. For the whites, art was the means to change society before they would accept it. For the blacks, art was the means to change society in order to be accepted into it. For this reason, many of the Harlem intellectuals found the white vogue in Afro-Americana troubling, although they usually feigned enthusiasm about the new dramatic and literary themes. Despite the insensitivity, burlesquing, and calumny, however, the Talented Tenth convinced itself that the civil rights dividends were potentially greater than the liabilities. Benjamin Brawley put this potential straightforwardly to James Weldon Johnson: "We have a tremendous opportunity to boost the NAACP, letters, and art, and anything else that calls attention to our development along the higher lines."

Brawley knew that he was preaching to the converted. Johnson's preface to his best-selling anthology *The Book of American Negro Poetry* (1922) proclaimed that nothing could "do more to change the mental attitude and raise his status than a demonstration of intellectual parity by the Negro through his production of literature and art." Putting T. S. Stribling's *Birthright* down, an impressed Jessie Fauset nevertheless felt that she and her peers could do better. "We reasoned," she recalled later, " 'Here is an audience waiting to hear the truth about us. Let us who are better qualified to present that truth than any white writer, try to do so.' " The result was *There Is Confusion*, her novel about genteel life among Philadelphia's aristocrats of color. Similarly troubled by *Birthright* and other two-dimensional or symbolically gross representations of African American life, Walter White complained loudly to H. L. Mencken, who finally silenced him with the challenge "Why don't you do the right kind of novel? You could do it, and it would create a sensation." White did. And the sensation turned out to be *The Fire in the Flint* (1924), the second novel of the Renaissance, which he wrote in less than a month in a borrowed country house in the Berkshires. Meanwhile, Langston Hughes, whose genius (like that of Toomer's) had been immediately recognized by Fauset, published several poems in the *Crisis* that would later appear in the collection *The Weary Blues*. The euphonious "The Negro Speaks of Rivers" (dedicated to Du Bois) ran in the *Crisis* in 1921. With the appearance of McKay's *Harlem Shadows* and Toomer's *Cane* the next year, 1923, the African American officers of the NAACP and the NUL saw how a theory could be put into action. The young New York University prodigy Countee Cullen, already published in the *Crisis* and *Opportunity*, had his Mainstream breakthrough in 1923 in *Harper's* and *Century* magazines. Two years later, with Carl Sandburg as one of the three judges, Cullen won the prestigious Witter Bynner poetry prize. Meanwhile, Paul Kellogg's *Survey Graphic* project moved apace under the editorship of Locke.

Two preconditions made this unprecedented mobilization of talent and group support in the service of a racial arts-and-letters movement more than a conceit in the minds of a handful of leaders: demography and repression. The Great Black Migration from the rural South to the industrial North produced the metropolitan dynamism undergirding the Renaissance. The Red Summer of 1919, a period of socialist agitation and conservative backlash following the Russian Revolution, produced the trauma that led to the cultural sublimation of civil rights. In pressure-cooker fashion, the increase in its African American population caused Harlem to pulsate as it pushed its racial boundaries south below 135th Street to Central Park and north beyond 139th ("Strivers' Row"). In the first flush of Harlem's realization and of general African American exuberance, the Red Summer of 1919 had a cruelly decompressing impact upon Harlem and Afro-America in general. Charleston, South Carolina, erupted in riot in May, followed by Longview, Texas, in July, and Washington, D.C., later in the month. Chicago exploded on July 27. Lynchings of returning African American soldiers and expulsion of African American workers from unions abounded. In the North, the white working classes struck out against perceived and manipulated threats to job security and unionism from blacks streaming north. In Helena, Arkansas, where a pogrom was unleashed against black farmers organizing a cotton cooperative, and outside Atlanta, where the Ku Klux Klan was reconstituted, the message of the white South to African Americans was that the racial *status quo ante bellum* was on again with a vengeance. Twenty-six race riots in towns, cities, and counties swept across the nation all the way to Nebraska. The "race problem" became definitively an American dilemma in the summer of 1919, and no longer a remote complexity in the exotic South.

The term "New Negro" entered the vocabulary in reaction to the Red Summer, along with McKay's poetic catechism—"Like men we'll face the murderous, cowardly pack/Pressed to the wall, dying, but fighting back!" There was a groundswell of support for Marcus Garvey's UNIA. Until his 1924 imprisonment for mail fraud, the Jamaican immigrant's message of African Zionism, anti-integrationism, working-class assertiveness, and Bookerite business enterprise, increasingly threatened the hegemony of the Talented Tenth and its major organizations, the NAACP and NUL, among people of color in America (much of Garvey's support came from the West Indians). "Garvey," wrote Mary White Ovington, one of the NAACP's white founders,"was the first Negro in the United States to capture the imagination of the masses." The *Negro World,* Garvey's multilingual newspaper, circulated throughout Latin America and the African empires of Britain and France. Locke spoke for the alarmed "respectable" civil rights leadership when he wrote, in his introductory remarks to the special issue of *Survey Graphic,* that, although "the thinking Negro has shifted a little to the left with the world trend," black separatism (Locke clearly had Garveyism in mind) "cannot be—even if it were desirable." Although the movement was its own worst enemy, the Talented Tenth was pleased to help the Justice Department speed its demise.

No less an apostle of high culture than Du Bois, initially a Renaissance enthusiast, vividly expressed the farfetched nature of the arts-and-letters movement as early as 1926: "How is it that an organization of this kind [the NAACP] can turn aside to talk about art? After all, what have we who are slaves and black to do with art?" It was the brilliant insight of the men and women associated with the NAACP and NUL that, although the road to the ballot box, the union hall, the decent neighborhood, and the office was blocked, there were two untried paths that had not been barred, in large part because of their very implausibility, as well as irrelevancy to most Americans: arts and letters. They saw the small cracks in the wall of racism that could, they anticipated, be widened through the production of exemplary racial images in collaboration with liberal white philanthropy, the robust culture industry primarily located in New York, and artists from white Bohemia (like themselves marginal and in tension with the status quo). If, in retrospect, then, the New Negro Arts Movement has been interpreted as a natural phase in the cultural evolution of another American group, as a band in the literary continuum running from New England, Knickerbocker New York, Hoosier Indiana, to the Village's Bohemia, to East Side Yiddish drama and fiction, and then on to the Southern Agrarians, such an interpretation sacrifices causation to appearance. Instead, the Renaissance represented much less an evolutionary part of a common experience than it did a generation-skipping phenomenon in which a vanguard of the Talented Tenth elite recruited, organized, subventioned, and guided an unevenly endowed cohort of artists and writers to make statements that advanced a certain conception of the race, a cohort of men and women most of whom would never have imagined the possibility of artistic and literary careers.

Toomer, McKay, Hughes, and Cullen possessed the rare ability combined with personal eccentricity that defined the artist, but the Renaissance not only needed more like them but a large cast of supporters and extras. American dropouts heading for seminars in garrets and cafés in Paris were invariably white and descended from an older gentry displaced by new moneyed elites. Charles Johnson and his allies were able to make the critical Renaissance mass possible. Johnson assembled files on prospective recruits throughout the country, going so far as to cajole Aaron Douglas, the artist from Kansas, and others into coming to Harlem, where a network manned by his secretary, Ethel Ray Nance, and her friends Regina Anderson and Louella Tucker (assisted by gifted Trinidadian short-story writer Eric Walrond) looked after them until a salary or a fellowship was secured. White, the very self-important assistant secretary of the NAACP, urged Paul Robeson to abandon law for an acting career, encouraged Nella Larsen to follow his own example as a novelist, and passed the hat for artist Hale Woodruff. Fauset continued to discover and publish short stories and verse, such as those of Wallace Thurman and Arna Bontemps. Shortly after the Civil Club evening, both the NAACP and the NUL announced the creation of annual awards ceremonies bearing the titles of their respective publications, *Crisis* and *Opportunity*.

The award of the first *Opportunity* prizes came in May 1925 in an elaborate ceremony at the Fifth Avenue Restaurant with some three hundred participants. Twenty-four distinguished judges (among them Carl Van Doren, Zona Gale, Eugene O'Neill, James Weldon Johnson, and Van Wyck Brooks) had ruled on the worthiness of entries in five categories. The awards ceremony was interracial, but white capital and influence were crucial to success, and the white presence, in the beginning, was pervasive, setting the outer boundaries for what was creatively normative. Money to start the *Crisis* prizes had come from Amy Spingarn, an accomplished artist and poet, and wife of Joel Spingarn, chairman of the NAACP's board of directors. The wife of the influential attorney, Fisk University trustee, and Urban League Board chairman, L. Hollingsworth Wood, had made a similar contribution to initiate the *Opportunity* prizes. These were the whites Zora Neal Hurston, one of the first *Opportunity* prizewinners, memorably dubbed "Negrotarians." There were several categories: Political Negrotarians like progressive journalist Ray Stannard Baker, and maverick socialist types associated with *Modern Quarterly* (V. F. Calverton, Max Eastman, Lewis Mumford, Scott Nearing); salon Negrotarians like Robert Chanler, Charles Studin, Carl and Fania (Marinoff) Van Vechten, and Eleanor Wylie, for whom the Harlem artists were more exotics than talents. They were kindred spirits to Lost Generation Negrotarians, drawn to Harlem on their way to Paris by a need for personal nourishment and confirmation of a vision of cultural health, in which their romantic or revolutionary perceptions of African American vitality played a key role—Anderson, O'Neill, Georgia O'Keeffe, Zona Gale, Waldo Frank, Louise Bryant, Sinclair Lewis, Hart Crane. The commercial Negrotarians like the Knopfs, the Gershwins, Rowena Jelliffe, Horace Liveright, V. F. Calverton, and Sol Hurok scouted and mined Afro-American like prospectors.

The May 1925 *Opportunity* gala showcased the steadily augmenting talent in the Renaissance—what Hurston characterized as the "Niggerati." Two laureates, Cullen and Hughes, had already won notice beyond Harlem. The latter had engineered "discovery" as a Washington, D.C., bellhop by placing dinner and three poems on Vachel Lindsay's hotel table. Some prizewinners were barely to be heard from again: Joseph Cotter, G. D. Lipscomb, Warren MacDonald, Fidelia

Ripley. Others, like John Matheus (first prize in the short-story category) and Frank Horne (honorable mention in short-story writing), fell short of first-rank standing in the Renaissance. Most of those whose talent had staying power were introduced that night: E. Franklin Frazier, who won the first prize for an essay on social equality; Sterling Brown, who took second prize for an essay on the singer Roland Hayes; Hurston, awarded second prize for a short story, "Spunk"; and Eric Walrond, third-prize winner for his short story "Voodoo's Revenge." James Weldon Johnson read the poem that took first prize, "The Weary Blues," Langston Hughes's turning-point poem, combining the gift of a superior artist and the enduring, music-encased spirit of the black migrant. Comments from Negrotarian judges ranged from O'Neill's advice to "be yourselves," to novelist Edna Worthley Underwood's exultant anticipation of a "new epoch in American letters," and Clement Wood's judgment that the general standard "was higher than such contests usually bring out."

The measures of Charles S. Johnson's success were the announcement of a second *Opportunity* contest to be underwritten by Harlem "businessman" (and numbers king) Caspar Holstein, former *Times* music critic Carl Van Vechten's enthusiasm over Hughes and subsequent arranging of a contract with Knopf for Hughes's first volume of poetry, and, one week after the awards ceremony, a prediction by the New York *Herald Tribune* that the country was "on the edge, if not already in the midst of, what might not improperly be called a Negro renaissance"—thereby giving the movement its name. Priming the public for the Fifth Avenue Restaurant occasion, the special edition of *Survey Graphic,* "Harlem: Mecca of the New Negro," edited by Locke, had reached an unprecedented 42,000 readers in March 1926. The ideology of cultural nationalism at the heart of the Renaissance was crisply delineated in Locke's opening essay, "Harlem," stating that, "without pretense to their political significance, Harlem has the same role to play for the New Negro as Dublin has had for the New Ireland or Prague for the New Czechoslovakia." A vast racial formation was under way in the relocation of the peasant masses ("they stir, they move, they are more than physically restless"), the editor announced. "The challenge of the new intellectuals among them is clear enough." The migrating peasants from the South were the soil out of which all success must come, but soil must be tilled, and the Howard University philosopher reserved that task exclusively for the Talented Tenth in liaison with its Mainstream analogues—in the "carefully maintained contacts of the enlightened minorities of both race groups." There was little amiss about America that interracial elitism could not set right, Locke and the others believed. Despite historic discrimination and the Red Summer, the Rhodes scholar assured readers that the increasing radicalism among African Americans was superficial. At year's end, Albert and Charles Boni published Locke's *The New Negro,* an expanded and polished edition of the poetry and prose from the *Opportunity* contest and the special *Survey Graphic*.

The course of American letters was unchanged by the offerings in *The New Negro*. Still, it carried several memorable works, such as the short story "The South Lingers On" by Brown University and Howard Medical School graduate Rudolph Fisher; the acid poem "White House(s)" and the euphonic "The Tropics in New York" by McKay, now in European self-exile; and several poetic vignettes from Toomer's *Cane*. Hughes's "Jazzonia," previously published in the *Crisis,* was so poignant as to be almost tactile as it described "six long-headed jazzers" playing while a dancing woman "lifts high a dress of silken gold." In "Heritage," a poem previously unpublished, Cullen outdid himself in his grandest (if not his best) effort with its famous refrain, "What is Africa to me." The book carried the distinctive silhouette drawings and Egyptian-influenced motifs by Aaron Douglas, whose work was to become the artistic signature of the Renaissance. With thirty-four African American contributors (four were white), Locke's work included most of the Renaissance regulars. The notable omissions from *The New Negro* were Asa Randolph, George Schuyler, and Wallace Thurman. These were the gifted men and women who were to show by example what the potential of some African Americans could be and who proposed to lead their people into an era of opportunity and justice.

By virtue of their symbolic achievements and their adroit collaboration with the philanthropic and reform-minded Mainstream, their augmenting influence would ameliorate the socioeconomic conditions of their race over time and from the top downward. Slowly but surely, they would promote an era of opportunity and justice. It was a Talented Tenth conceit, Schuyler snorted in Asa Randolph's *Messenger* magazine, worthy of a "high priest of the intellectual snobbocracy," and he awarded Locke the magazine's "elegantly embossed and beautifully lacquered dill pickle." Yet it seemed to work, for although the objective conditions confronting most African Americans in Harlem and elsewhere were deteriorating, optimism remained high. Harlem recoiled from Garveyism and socialism to applaud Phi Beta Kappa poets, university-trained painters, concertizing musicians, and novel-writing officers of civil rights organizations. "Everywhere we heard the sighs of wonder, amazement and sometimes admiration when it was whispered or announced that here was one of the 'New Negroes,' " Bontemps recalled.

By summer of 1926, Renaissance titles included *Cane* (1923), *There Is Confusion* (1924), *Fire in the Flint* (1924), *Flight* (1926), McKay's *Harlem Shadows* (1922), Cullen's *Color* poetry volume (1924), and *The Weary Blues* volume of poetry (1926). The second *Opportunity* awards banquet, April 1926, was another artistic and interracial success. Playwright Joseph Cotter was honored again, as was Hurston, for a short story. Bontemps, a California-educated poet struggling in Harlem, won first prize for "Golgotha Is a Mountain," and Dorothy West, a Bostonian aspiring to make a name in fiction, made her debut, as did essayist Arthur Fauset, Jessie's able brother. The William E. Harmon Foundation transferred its attention at the beginning of 1926 from student loans and blind children to the Renaissance, announcing seven annual prizes for literature, music, fine arts, industry, science, education, and race relations, with George Edmund Haynes, African American official in the Federal Council of Churches, and Locke as chief advisors. That same year, the publishers Boni & Liveright offered a thousand-dollar prize for the "best novel on Negro life" by an African American. Caspar Holstein contributed one thousand dollars that year to endow *Opportunity* prizes. Van Vechten made a smaller contribution to the same cause. Amy Spingarn provided six hundred dollars toward the *Crisis* awards. Otto Kahn underwrote two years in France for the young artist Hale Woodruff. There were Louis Rodman Wanamaker prizes in music composition.

The third *Opportunity* awards dinner was a vintage one for poetry, with entries by Bontemps, Sterling Brown, Hughes, Helene Johnson, and Jonathan H. Brooks. In praising their general high quality, the white literary critic Robert T.

Kerlin added the revealing comment that their effect would be "hostile to lynching and to jim-crowing." Eric Walrond's lush, impressionistic collection of short stories *Tropic Death* appeared from Boni & Liveright at the end of 1926, the most probing exploration of the psychology of culture underdevelopment since Toomer's *Cane.* If *Cane* recaptured in a string of glowing vignettes (most of them about women) the sunset beauty and agony of a preindustrial culture, *Tropic Death* did much the same for the Antilles. Hughes's second volume of poetry, *Fine Clothes to the Jew* (1927), spiritedly portrayed the city life of ordinary men and women who had traded the hardscrabble of farming for the hardscrabble of domestic work and odd jobs. Hughes scanned the low-down pursuits of "Bad Man," "Ruby Brown," and "Beale Street" and shocked Brawley and other Talented Tenth elders with the bawdy "Red Silk Stockings." "Put on yo red silk stockings,/Black gal," it began, urging the protagonist to show herself to white boys. It ended wickedly with "An' tomorrow's chile'll/Be a high yaller."

A veritable Ministry of Culture now presided over Afro-America. McKay, viewing the scene from abroad, spoke derisively of the artistic and literary autocracy of "that NAACP crowd." The Ministry mounted a movable feast to which the anointed were invited, sometimes to Walter and Gladys White's apartment at 409 Edgecombe Avenue, where they might share cocktails with Sinclair Lewis or Mencken; often (after 1928) to the famous 136th Street "Dark Tower" salon maintained by beauty culture heiress A'Lelia Walker, where guests might include Sir Osbert Sitwell, the Crown Prince of Sweden, or Lady Mountbatten; and very frequently to the home of Carl and Fania Van Vechten, to imbibe the host's sidecars and listen to Robeson sing or Jim Johnson recite from "God's Trombones" or George Gershwin play the piano. Meanwhile, Harlem's appeal to white revellers inspired the young physician Rudolph Fisher to write "The Caucasian Storms Harlem," a satiric piece in the August 1927 *American Mercury.*

The third phase of the Harlem Renaissance began even as the second had only just gotten under way. The second phase (1924 to mid-1926) was dominated by the officialdom of the two major civil rights organizations, with its ideology of civil rights advancement of African Americans through the creation and mobilization of an artistic-literary movement. Its essence was summed up in blunt declarations by Du Bois that he didn't care "a damn for any art that is not used for propaganda" or in exalted formulations by Locke that the New Negro was "an augury of a new democracy in American culture." The third phase of the Renaissance, from mid-1926 to the end of 1934, was marked by rebellion against the Civil Rights Establishment on the part of many of the artists and writers whom that Establishment had assembled and promoted. Three publications during 1926 formed a watershed between the genteel and the demotic Renaissance. Hughes's "The Negro Artist and the Racial Mountain," which appeared in the June 1926 issue of the *Nation,* served as manifesto of the breakaway from the arts-and-letters party line. Van Vechten's *Nigger Heaven,* released by Knopf that August, drove much of literate Afro-America into a dichotomy of approval and apoplexy over "authentic" versus "proper" cultural expression. Wallace Thurman's *Fire!!,* available in November, assembled the rebels for a major assault against the Civil Rights Ministry of Culture.

Hughes's turning-point essay had been provoked by Schuyler's essay in the *Nation,* "The Negro-Art Hokum," ridiculing "eager apostles from Greenwich Village, Harlem, and environs" who made claims for a special African American artistic vision distinct from that of white Americans. "The Aframerican is merely a lamp-blacked Anglo-Saxon," Schuyler had sneered. In a famous peroration, Hughes answered that he and his fellow artists intended to express their "individual dark-skinned selves without fear or shame. If white people are pleased we are glad. . . . If colored people are pleased we are glad. If they are not, their displeasure doesn't matter either." There was considerable African American displeasure; and it was complex. Much of the condemnation of the license for expression Hughes, Thurman, Hurston, and other artists arrogated to themselves was generational or puritanical, and usually both. "Vulgarity has been mistaken for art," Brawley spluttered after leafing the pages of the new magazine *Fire!!*, which contained among other shockers Richard Bruce Nugent's extravagantly homoerotic short story "Smoke, Lillies and Jade!" Du Bois was said to be deeply aggrieved.

But much of the condemnation stemmed from racial sensitivity, from sheer mortification at seeing uneducated, crude, and scrappy black men and women depicted without tinsel and soap. Thurman and associate editors John Davis, Aaron Douglas, Gwendolyn Bennett, Arthur Huff Fauset, Hughes, Hurston, and Nugent took the Renaissance out of the parlor, the editorial office, and the banquet room. With African motifs by Douglas and Nordic-featured African Americans with exaggeratedly kinky hair by Nugent; poems to an elevator boy by Hughes; a taste for the jungle by Edward Silvera; short stories about prostitution ("Cordelia and Crude") by Thurman, gender conflict between black men and women at the bottom of the economy ("Sweat") by Hurston, and a burly boxer's hatred of white people ("Wedding Day") by Gwendolyn Bennett; a short play about pigment complexes within the race (*Color Struck*) by Hurston—the focus shifted to Locke's "peasant matrix," to the sorrows and joys of those outside the Talented Tenth. "Let the blare of Negro jazz bands and the bellowing voice of Bessie Smith . . . penetrate the closed ears of the colored near-intellectuals," Hughes exhorted in "The Negro Artists and the Racial Mountain."

Carl Van Vechten's influence decidedly complicated the reactions of otherwise worldly critics like Du Bois, Fauset, Locke, and Cullen. While the novel's title alone enraged many Harlemites who felt their trust and hospitality betrayed, the deeper objections of the sophisticated to *Nigger Heaven* lay in its message that the Talented Tenth's preoccupation with cultural improvement was a misguided affectation that would cost the race its vitality. It was the "archaic Negroes" who were at ease in their skins and capable of action, Van Vechten's characters demonstrated. Significantly, although Du Bois and Fauset found themselves in the majority among the Renaissance leadership (ordinary Harlemites burned Van Vechten in effigy at 135th Street and Lenox Avenue), Charles Johnson, James Weldon Johnson, Schuyler, White, and Hughes praised the novel's sociological verve and veracity and the service they believed it rendered to race relations.

The younger artists embraced Van Vechten's fiction as a worthy model because of its ribald iconoclasm and iteration that the future of African American arts and letters lay in the culture of the working poor and even of the underclass—in bottom-up drama, fiction, music, and poetry, the painting. Regularly convening at the notorious "267 House," the brownstone an indulgent landlady provided Thurman rent-free on 136th Street (alternately known as "Niggerati Manor"), the group that came to produce *Fire!!* saw art not as politics by other means—civil rights between covers or from a stage or an easel—but as an expression of the intrinsic conditions most men and women of African descent were experiencing. They spoke of the need "for a truly Negroid note," for empathy with "those elements within the race which are still too potent for easy assimilation," and they openly mocked the premise of the Civil Rights Establishment that (as a Hughes character says in *The Ways of White Folks*) "art would break down color lines, art would save the race and prevent lynchings! Bunk!" Finally, like creative agents in society from time immemorial, they were impelled to insult their patrons and to defy conventions.

To put the Renaissance back on track, Du Bois sponsored a symposium in late 1926, "The Criteria of Negro Art," inviting a spectrum of views about the appropriate course the arts should take. His unhappiness was readily apparent, both with the overly literary tendencies of Locke and with the bottom-up school of Hughes and Thurman. The great danger was that politics were dropping out of the Renaissance, that the movement was turning into an evasion, sedulously encouraged by certain whites. "They are whispering, 'Here is a way out. Here is the real solution to the color problem. The recognition accorded Cullen, Hughes, Fauset, White and others shows there is no real color line,' " Du Bois charged. He then announced that *Crisis* literary prizes would henceforth be reserved for works encouraging "general knowledge of banking and insurance in modern life and specific knowledge of what American Negroes are doing in these fields." Walter White's own effort to sustain the civil-rights-by-copyright strategy was the ambitious novel *Flight,* edited by his friend Sinclair Lewis and released by Knopf in 1926. Kind critics found White's novel (a tale of near-white African Americans of unusual culture and professional accomplishment who prove their moral superiority to their oppressors) somewhat flat. The reissue the following year of *The Autobiography of an Ex-Colored Man* (with Johnson's authorship finally acknowledged) and publication of a volume of Cullen poetry, *Copper Sun,* continued the tradition of genteel, exemplary letters. In a further effort to restore direction, Du Bois's *Dark Princess* appeared in 1928 from Harcourt Brace, a large, serious novel in which the "problem of the twentieth century" is taken in charge by a Talented Tenth International whose prime mover is a princess from India. But the momentum stayed firmly with the rebels.

Although Thurman's magazine died after one issue, respectable Afro-America was unable to ignore the novel that embodied the values of the Niggerati—the first Renaissance best-seller by a black author—McKay's *Home to Harlem,* released by Harper & Brothers in spring 1928. Its milieu is wholly plebeian. The protagonist, Jake, is a Lenox Avenue Noble Savage who demonstrates (in marked contrast to the book-reading Ray) the superiority of the Negro mind uncorrupted by European learning. *Home to Harlem* finally shattered the enforced literary code of the Civil Rights Establishment. Du Bois confessed to feeling "distinctly like needing a bath" after reading McKay's novel about the "debauched tenth." Rudolph Fisher's *The Walls of Jericho,* appearing that year from Knopf, was a brilliant, deftly executed satire which upset Du Bois as much as it heartened Thurman. Fisher, a successful Harlem physician with solid Talented Tenth family credentials, satirized the NAACP, the Negrotarians, Harlem high society, and easily recognized Renaissance notables, while entering convincingly into the world of the working classes, organized crime, and romance across classes.

Charles Johnson, preparing to leave the editorship of *Opportunity* for a professorship in sociology at Fisk University, now encouraged the young rebels. Renaissance artists were "now less self-conscious, less interested in proving that they are just like white people. . . . Relief from the stifling consciousness of being a problem has brought a certain superiority" to the Harlem Renaissance, Johnson asserted. Meanwhile, McKay's and Fisher's fiction inspired the Niggerati to publish an improved version of *Fire!!*. The magazine, *Harlem,* appeared in November 1928. Editor Thurman announced portentously, "The time has now come when the Negro artist can be his true self and pander to the stupidities of no one, either white or black." While Brawley, Du Bois, and Fauset continued to grimace, *Harlem* benefitted from significant defections. It won the collaboration of Locke and White, and lasted two issues. Roy de Coverly, George W. Little, and Schuyler signed on, and Hughes contributed one of the finest short stories, based on his travels down the West Coast of Africa—"Luani of the Jungles," a polished genre piece on the seductions of the civilized and the primitive.

The other Renaissance novel that year from Knopf, Nella Larsen's *Quicksand,* achieved the distinction of being praised by Du Bois, Locke, and Hughes. Larsen claimed to have been the daughter of a Danish mother and an African American father from the Danish Virgin Islands. In fact, her father was probably a chauffeur who lived in New York; and Larsen was probably born in New York, rather than in Chicago as she claimed. Trained in the sciences at Fisk, she never pursued further studies, as has been reported, at the University of Copenhagen. She would remain something of a mystery woman, helped in her career by Van Vechten and White but somehow always receding, and finally disappearing altogether from the Harlem scene. *Quicksand* was a triumph of vivid yet economic writing and rich allegory. Its very modern heroine experiences misfortunes and ultimate destruction from causes that are both racial and individual. She is not a tragic mulatto but a mulatto who is tragic for reasons that are both sociological and existential. Helga Crane, Larsen's protagonist, was the Virginia Slim of Renaissance fiction. If there were reviews (*Crisis, New Republic, New York Times*) that were as laudatory about Fauset's *Plum Bun,* also a 1928 release, they were primarily due to the novel's engrossing reconstruction of rarefied, upper-class African American life in Philadelphia, rather than to special literary merit. Angela Murray (Angele, in her white persona), the heroine of Fauset's second novel, was the Gibson Girl of Renaissance fiction. *Plum Bun* continued the second phase of the Renaissance, as did Cullen's second volume of poetry, published in 1929, *The Black Christ.* Ostensibly about a lynching, the lengthy title poem lost its way in mysticism, paganism, and religious remorse. The volume also lost the sympathies of most reviewers.

Thurman's *The Blacker the Berry,* published by Macaulay in early 1929, although talky and awkward in spots (Thurman had hoped to write the Great African American Novel), was a breakthrough novel. The reviewer for the Chicago *Defender* enthused, "Here at last is the book for which I have been waiting, and for which you have been waiting." Hughes praised it as a "gorgeous book," mischievously writing Thurman that it would embarrass those who bestowed the "seal-of-high-and-holy approval of Harmon awards." The Ministry of Culture found the novel distinctly distasteful, *Opportunity* judging *The Blacker the Berry* to be fatally flawed by "immaturity and gaucherie." For the first time in African American fiction, color prejudice within the race was the central theme of a novel. Emma Lou, its heroine (like the author very dark and conventionally unattractive), is obsessed with respectability as well as tortured by her pigment, for Thurman makes the point on every page that Afro-America's aesthetic and spiritual center resides in the unaffected, unblended, noisome common folk and the liberated, unconventional artists. With the unprecedented Broadway success of *Harlem,* Thurman's sensationalized romp through the underside of Harlem, the triumph of Niggerati aesthetics over Civil Rights arts and letters was impressively confirmed. Another equally sharp smell of reality irritated Establishment nostrils that same year, with the publication of McKay's second novel, *Banjo,* appearing only weeks after *The Blacker the Berry.* "The Negroes are writing against themselves," lamented the reviewer for the *Amsterdam News.* Set among the human flotsam and jetsam of Marseilles and West Africa, the message of McKay's novel was again that European civilization was inimical to Africans everywhere.

The stock market collapsed, but reverberations from the Harlem Renaissance seemed stronger than ever. Larsen's second novel, *Passing,* appeared. Its theme, like Fauset's, was the burden of mixed racial ancestry. But, although *Passing* was less successful than *Quicksand,* Larsen's novel again evaded the trap of writing another tragic-mulatto novel by opposing the richness of African American life to the material advantages afforded by the option of "passing." In February 1930, Marc Connelly's dramatization of Roark Bradford's book of short stories opened on Broadway as *The Green Pastures.* The Hall Johnson Choir sang in it, Richard Harrison played "De Lawd," and scores of Harlemites found parts during 557 performances at the Mansfield Theatre, and then on tour across the country. The demanding young critic and Howard University professor English Sterling Brown pronounced the play a "miracle." After *The Green Pastures* came *Not without Laughter,* Hughes's glowing novel from Knopf. Financed by Charlotte Osgood Mason (the often tyrannical bestower of artistic largesse nicknamed "Godmother") and Amy Spingarn, Hughes had resumed his college education at Lincoln University and completed *Not without Laughter* his senior year. The beleaguered family at the center of the novel represents Afro-America in transition in white America. Hughes's young male protagonist learns that proving his equality means affirming his distinctive racial qualities. Not only Locke admired *Not without Laughter;* the *New Masses* reviewer embraced it as "our novel." The Ministry of Culture decreed Hughes worthy of the Harmon gold medal for 1930. The year ended with Schuyler's ribald, sprawling satire *Black No More,* an unsparing demolition of every personality and institution in Afro-America. Little wonder that Locke titled his retrospective piece in the February 1931 *Opportunity* "The Year of Grace."

Depression notwithstanding, the health of the Renaissance appeared to be more robust than ever. The first Rosenwald fellowships for African Americans had been secured largely due to James Weldon Johnson's influence the previous year. Since 1928, advised by Locke, the Harmon Foundation had mounted an annual traveling exhibition of drawings, paintings, and sculpture by African Americans. The 1930 participants introduced the generally unsuspected talent and genius of Palmer Hayden, William H. Johnson, Archibald Motley, Jr., James A. Porter, and Laura Wheeler Waring in painting. Sargent Johnson, Elizabeth Prophet, and Augusta Savage were the outstanding sculptors of the show. Both Aaron Douglas and Romare Bearden came to feel that the standards of the foundation were somewhat indulgent and, therefore, injurious to many young artists, which was undoubtedly true even though the 1931 Harmon Travelling Exhibition of the Work of Negro Artists was seen by more than 150,000 people.

Superficially, Harlem itself appeared to be in fair health well into 1931. James Weldon Johnson's celebration of the community's strengths, *Black Manhattan,* was published near the end of 1930. "Harlem is still in the process of making," the book proclaimed, and the author's confidence in the power of the "recent literary and artistic emergence" to ameliorate race relations was unshaken. In Johnson's Harlem, redcaps and cooks cheered when Renaissance talents won Guggenheim and Rosenwald fellowships; they rushed to newstands whenever the *American Mercury* or *New Republic* mentioned activities above Central Park. It was much too easy for Talented Tenth notables like Johnson, White, and Locke not to notice in the second year of the Great Depression that, for the great majority of the population, Harlem was in the process of unmaking. Still, there was a definite prefiguration of Harlem's mortality when A'Lelia Walker suddenly died in August 1931, a doleful occurrence shortly followed by the sale of Villa Lewaro, her Hudson mansion, at public auction. By the end of 1929, African Americans lived in the five-hundred block of Edgecombe Avenue, known as "Sugar Hill." The famous "409" overlooking the Polo Grounds was home at one time or another to the Du Boises, the Fishers, and the Whites. Below Sugar Hill was the five-acre Rockefeller-financed Dunbar Apartments complex, its 511 units fully occupied in mid-1928. The Dunbar eventually became home for the Du Boises, E. Simms Campbell (illustrator and cartoonist), Fletcher Henderson, the A. Philip Randolphs, Leigh Whipper (actor), and (briefly) Paul and Essie Robeson. The complex published its own weekly bulletin, the *Dunbar News,* an even more valuable record of Talented Tenth activities during the Renaissance than the *Inter-State Tattler.*

The 1931 *Report on Negro Housing,* presented to President Hoover, was a document starkly in contrast to the optimism found in *Black Manhattan.* Nearly 50 percent of Harlem's families would be unemployed by the end of 1932. The syphilis rate was nine times higher than white Manhattan's; the tuberculosis rate was five times greater; pneumonia and typhoid were twice that of whites. Two African American mothers and two babies died for every white mother and child. Harlem General Hospital, the single public facility, served 200,000 African Americans with 273 beds. A Harlem family paid twice as much of their income for rent as a white family. Meanwhile, median family income in Harlem dropped 43.6 percent by 1932. The ending of Prohibition would devastate scores of marginal speakeasies, as well as prove fatal to theaters like the Lafayette. Connie's Inn would eventually migrate downtown. Until then, however, the clubs in "The Jungle" (133rd Street)—Bamville, Connor's, Clam House, Nest Club—and elsewhere (Pod's and Jerry's, Smalls' Paradise) continued to do a land-office business. With the repeal of the Eighteenth Amendment, honorary Harlemites like Van Vechten sobered up and turned to other pursuits. Locke's letters to Charlotte Osgood Mason turned increasingly pessimistic in the winter of 1931. In June 1932, he perked up a bit to praise the choral ballet presented at the Eastman School of Music—*Sahdji,* with music by William Grant Still and scenario by Nugent, but most of Locke's news was distinctly downbeat. The writing partnership of two of his protégés, Hughes and Hurston, their material needs underwritten in a New Jersey township by "Godmother" Charlotte Mason, collapsed in acrimonious dispute. Each claimed principal authorship of the only dramatic comedy written during the Renaissance, *Mule Bone,* a three-act folk play unperformed (as a result of the dispute) until 1991. Locke took the side of Hurston, undermining the tie of affection between Godmother and Hughes and effectively ending his relationship with the latter. The part played in this controversy by their brilliant secretary, Louise Thompson, the strong-willed, estranged wife of Wallace Thurman, remains murky, but it seems clear that Thompson's Marxism had a deep influence on Hughes in the aftermath of his painful breakup with Godmother, Locke, and Hurston.

In any case, beginning with "Advertisement for the Waldorf-Astoria" published in December 1931 *New Masses,* Hughes's poetry became markedly political. "Elderly Race Leaders" and "Goodbye Christ," as well as the play "Scottsboro, Limited," were irreverent, staccato offerings to the coming triumph of the proletariat. The poet's departure in June 1932 for Moscow, along with Louise Thompson, Mollie Lewis, Henry Moon, Loren Miller, Theodore Poston, and thirteen others, ostensibly to act in Soviet film about American race relations, *Black and White,* symbolized the shift in patronage and accompanying politicization of Renaissance artists. *One Way to Heaven,* Cullen's first novel, badly flawed and clearly influenced by *Nigger Heaven,* appeared in 1932, but it seemed already a baroque anachronism with its knife-wielding Lotharios and elaborately educated types. An impatient Du Bois, already deeply alienated from the Renaissance, called for a second Amenia Conference to radicalize the movement's ideology and renew its personnel. Jessie Fauset remained oblivious to the profound artistic and political changes under way. Her final novel, *Comedy: American Style* (1933), was technically much the same as *Plum Bun.* Her subject, once again, was skin pigment and the neuroses of those who had just enough of it to spend their lives obsessed by it. James Weldon Johnson's autobiography, *Along This Way,* an elegantly written review of his sui generis public career as archetypal renaissance man in both meanings of the word, was the publishing event of the year. McKay's final novel also appeared that year. He worried familiar themes, but *Banana Bottom* represented a philosophical advance over *Home to Harlem* and *Banjo* in its reconciliation through the protagonist, Bita Plant, of the previously destructive tension in McKay between the natural and the artificial—soul and civilization.

The publication at the beginning of 1932 of Thurman's last novel, *Infants of the Spring,* had already announced the end of the Harlem Renaissance. The action of Thurman's novel is in the ideas of the characters, in their incessant talk about themselves, Booker T. Washington, Du Bois, racism, and the destiny of the race. Its prose is generally disappointing, but the ending is conceptually poignant. Paul Arbian (Richard Bruce Nugent) commits suicide in a full tub of water, which splashes over and obliterates the pages of Arbian's unfinished novel on the bathroom floor. A still legible page, however, contains this paragraph, which was, in effect, an epitaph:

> He had drawn a distorted, inky black skyscraper, modeled after Niggerati Manor, and on which were focused an array of blindingly white beams of light. The foundation of this building was composed of crumbling stone. At first glance it

could be ascertained that the skyscraper
would soon crumple and fall, leaving the
dominating white lights in full possession
of the sky.

The literary energies of the Renaissance finally slumped. McKay returned to Harlem in February 1934 after a twelve-year sojourn abroad, but his creative powers were spent. The last novel of the movement, Hurston's beautifully written *Jonah's Gourd Vine,* went on sale in May 1934. Charles Johnson, James Weldon Johnson, and Locke applauded Hurston's allegorical story of her immediate family (especially her father) and the mores of an African American town in Florida called Eatonville. Fisher and Thurman could have been expected to continue to write, but their fates were sealed by professional carelessness. Thurman died a few days before Christmas 1934, soon after his return from an abortive Hollywood film project. Ignoring his physician's strictures, he hemorrhaged after drinking to excess while hosting a party in the infamous house at 267 West 136th Street. Four days later, Fisher expired from intestinal cancer caused by repeated exposure to his own X-ray equipment.

Locke's *New Negro* anthology had been crucial to the formation of the Renaissance. As the movement ran down, another anthology, English heiress Nancy Cunard's *Negro,* far more massive in scope, recharged the Renaissance for a brief period, enlisting the contributions of most of the principals (though McKay and Walrond refused, and Toomer no longer acknowledged his African American roots), and captured its essence in the manner of expert taxidermy. A grieving Locke wrote Charlotte Mason from Howard University, "It is hard to see the collapse of things you have labored to raise on a sound base."

Arthur Fauset, Jessie's perceptive brother, attempted to explain the collapse to Locke and the readers of *Opportunity* at the beginning of 1934. He foresaw "a socio-political-economic setback from which it may take decades to recover." The Renaissance had left the race unprepared, Fauset charged, because of its unrealistic belief "that social and economic recognition will be inevitable when once the race has produced a sufficiently large number of persons who have properly qualified themselves in the arts." Du Bois had not only turned his back on the movement, he had left the NAACP and Harlem for a university professorship in Atlanta after an enormous row over civil rights policy. Marxism had begun to exercise a decided appeal for him, but as the 1933 essay "Marxism and the Negro Problem" had made abundantly clear, Du Bois ruled out collaboration with American Marxists because they were much too racist. James Weldon Johnson's philosophical *tour d'horizon* appearing in 1934, *Negro Americans, What Now?,* asked precisely the question of the decade. Most Harlemites were certain that the riot exploding on the evening of March 19, 1935, taking three lives and costing two million dollars in property damage, was not an answer. By then, the Works Progress Administration (WPA) had become the major patron of African American artists and writers. Writers William Attaway, Ralph Ellison, Margaret Walker, Richard Wright, and Frank Yerby would emerge under its aegis, as would painters Romare Bearden, Jacob Lawrence, Charles Sebree, Lois Maillou Jones, and Charles White. The Communist Party was another patron, notably for Richard Wright, whose 1937 essay "Blueprint for Negro Writing" would materially contribute to the premise of Hughes's "The Negro Artist and the

Racial Mountain." For thousands of ordinary Harlemites who had looked to Garvey's UNIA for inspiration, then to the Renaissance, there was now Father Divine and his "heavens."

In the ensuing years, much was renounced, more was lost or forgotten, yet the Renaissance, however artificial and overreaching, left a positive mark. Locke's *New Negro* anthology featured thirty of the movement's thirty-five stars. They and a small number of less gifted collaborators generated twenty-six novels, ten volumes of poetry, five Broadway plays, countless essays and short stories, three performed ballets and concerti, and a considerable output of canvas and sculpture. If the achievement was less than the titanic expectations of the Ministry of Culture, it was an arts-and-letters legacy, nevertheless, of which a beleaguered and belittled Afro-American could be proud, and by which it could be sustained. If more by osmosis than conscious attention, Mainstream America was also richer for the color, emotion, humanity, and cautionary vision produced by Harlem during its Golden Age.

"If I had supposed that all Negroes were illiterate brutes, I might be astonished to discover that they can write good third rate poetry, readable and unreadable magazine fiction," wrote one contemporary white Marxist passing flinty judgment upon the Renaissance. Nevertheless there were many white Americans—perhaps the majority—who found the African American artistic and literary ferment of the period wholly unexpected and little short of incredible. If the judgment of the Marxist observer soon became a commonplace, it was because the Harlem Renaissance demonstrated—finally, irrefutably, during slightly more than a decade—the considerable creative capacities of the best and brightest of a disadvantaged racial minority.

Kwame Toure (1941–) and **Charles V. Hamilton** (1929–)

K*wame Toure symbolizes the manner in which political ideology changed for a young generation of African Americans in the mid-1960s. As the civil rights movement slowly edged toward legal goals under its "Negro" leadership, young people grew weary of its slow pace, its nonviolent philosophy, and the unfulfilled promises of mainstream society. Toure, among that young generation of blacks, espoused an aggressive "black" leadership that would not apologize to, beg from, or wait for white society to bestow human rights to blacks.*

Born Stokely Carmichael in Port-of-Spain, Trinidad, Toure came with his parents to the United States when he was two years old and was raised in the New York City area. His political awareness developed early. He was active in the civil rights movement during his first year at Howard University, participating in the southern freedom rides organized by the Congress of Racial Equality (CORE), an interracial activist group established in 1942. Although CORE took some direct action against racial segregation on interstate transportation, the young student activists were dissatisfied, and in 1960 established the Student Non-violent Coordinating Committee (SNCC [pronounced "snick"]). Made up primarily of black students, SNCC dedicated itself to direct action, such as sit-ins, freedom rides, and voter-registration drives in the South.

Toure became a member of SNCC in 1964, the same year he earned his bachelor's in philosophy from Howard. Working in Alabama, he helped to shape the Lowndes County Freedom Association, which labored to register black voters in the area. When in 1965 Toure became the head of SNCC, his political experience and his exposure to the violence directed against southern blacks had led him to develop a more combative philosophy. His suggestion that SNCC limit its membership to blacks only and his revolutionary agenda caused some observers to credit Toure as the source of the slogan "Black Power." Some blacks and whites reacted negatively to the tenets of the Black Power movement, whereas others embraced its philosophy. By the late 1960s, Toure had left SNCC to become a frequent speaker against American racism and imperialism, as well as against the U.S. involvement in Vietnam. As a result of an anti-America speech given in Cuba, Toure's passport was revoked in 1968. In the same year, he was designated honorary prime minister of the Black Panther Party.

In 1969, Toure relocated to the west African republic of Guinea, ostensibly to support Kwame Nkrumah in his efforts to return as ruler of Ghana. However, the move was also a symbol of Toure's severance from the United States and from what he perceived as American colonialism. While in Africa, he changed his name from Stokely Carmichael to Kwame Toure. In 1971, he published Stokely Speaks: Black Power Back to Pan-Africanism, *a collection of his essays and speeches that traces the development of his political philosophy and activism. Still living in west Africa today, Toure continues to write and occasionally speaks in the United States. When in 1993 he addressed an audience at Michigan State University, his politically charged speech condemned systematic exploitation and oppression as the ongoing nemesis to human rights.*

Charles V. Hamilton, born in Muskogee, Oklahoma, has taught at Lincoln University, Roosevelt University, Tuskegee University, and Rutgers University. Presently, he is a professor of political science at Columbia University. He has written a number of books, including Minority Politics in Black Belt Alabama *(1962) and* Adam Clayton Powell, Jr.: The Political Biography of an American Dilemma *(1991).*

"Black Power: Its Need and Substance" comes from Black Power: The Politics of Liberation *(1967), in which Toure and Hamilton voiced their revolutionary philosophy for uniting blacks and transforming the American system in new economic, educational, and political directions. In the excerpt appearing here, the writers define the goals of the Black Power philosophy as it was conceived in 1967.*

Black Power: Its Need and Substance

"To carve out a place for itself in the politico-social order," V. O. Key, Jr., wrote in *Politics, Parties and Pressure Groups,* "a new group may have to fight for reorientation of many of the values of the old order" (p. 57). This is especially true when that group is composed of black people in the American society—a society that has for centuries deliberately and systematically excluded them from political participation. Black people in the United States must raise hard questions, questions which challenge the very nature of the society itself: its long-standing values, beliefs and institutions.

To do this, we must first redefine ourselves. Our basic need is to reclaim our history and our identity from what must be called cultural terrorism, from the depredation of self-justifying white guilt. We shall have to struggle for the right to create our own terms through which to define ourselves and our relationship to the society, and to have these terms recognized. This is the first necessity of a free people, and the first right that any oppressor must suspend.

In *Politics among Nations,* Hans Morgenthau defined political power as "the psychological control over the minds of men" (p. 29). This control includes the attempt by the oppressor to have *his* definitions, *his* historical descriptions, *accepted* by the oppressed. This was true in Africa no less than in the United States. To black Africans, the word "Uhuru" means "freedom," but they had to fight the white colonizers for the right to use the term. The recorded history of this country's dealings with red and black men offers other examples. In the wars between the white settlers and the "Indians," a battle won by the Cavalry was described as a "victory." The "Indians' " triumphs, however, were "massacres." (The American colonists were not unaware of the need to define their acts in their own terms. They labeled their fight against England a "revolution"; the English attempted to demean it by calling it "insubordination" or "riotous.")

The historical period following Reconstruction in the South after the Civil War has been called by many historians the period of Redemption, implying that the bigoted southern slave societies were "redeemed" from the hands of "reckless and irresponsible" black rulers. Professor John Hope Franklin's *Reconstruction* or Dr. W. E. B. Dubois's *Black Reconstruction* should be sufficient to dispel inaccurate historical notions, but the larger society persists in its own self-serving accounts. Thus black people came to be depicted as "lazy," "apathetic," "dumb," "shiftless," "good-timers." Just as red men had to be recorded as "savages" to justify the white man's theft of their land, so black men had to be vilified in order to justify their continued oppression. Those who have the right to define are the masters of the situation. Lewis Carroll understood this:

> "When I use a word," Humpty Dumpty said in a rather scornful tone, "it means just what I choose it to mean—neither more nor less."
>
> "The question is," said Alice, "whether you *can* make words mean so many different things."
>
> "The question is," said Humpty Dumpty, "which is to be master—that's all."[1]

Today, the American educational system continues to reinforce the entrenched values of the society through the use of words. Few people in this country question that this is "the land of the free and the home of the brave." They have had these words drummed into them from childhood. Few people question that this is the "Great Society" or that this country is fighting "Communist aggression" around the world. We mouth these things over and over, and they become truisms not to be questioned. In a similar way, black people have been saddled with epithets.

"Integration" is another current example of a word which has been defined according to the way white Americans see it. To many of them, it means black men wanting to marry white daughters; it means "race mixing"—implying bed or dance partners. To black people, it has meant a way to improve their lives—economically and politically. But the predominant white definition has stuck in the minds of too many people.

Black people must redefine themselves, and only *they* can do that. Through-

[1] Lewis Carroll, *Through the Looking Glass*. New York: Doubleday Books, Inc., p. 196.

out this country, vast segments of the black communities are beginning to recognize the need to assert their own definitions, to reclaim their history, their culture; to create their own sense of community and togetherness. There is a growing resentment of the word "Negro," for example, because this term is the invention of our oppressor; it is *his* image of us that he describes. Many blacks are now calling themselves African-Americans, Afro-Americans or black people because that is *our* image of ourselves. When we begin to define our own image, the stereotypes—that is, lies—that our oppressor has developed will begin in the white community and end there. The black community will have a positive image of itself that *it* has created. This means we will no longer call ourselves lazy, apathetic, dumb, good-timers, shiftless, etc. Those are words used by white America to define us. If we accept these adjectives, as some of us have in the past, then we see ourselves only in a negative way, precisely the way white America wants us to see ourselves. Our incentive is broken and our will to fight is surrendered. From now on we shall view ourselves as African-Americans and as black people who are in fact energetic, determined, intelligent, beautiful and peace-loving.

There is a terminology and ethos peculiar to the black community of which black people are beginning to be no longer ashamed. Black communities are the only large segments of this society where people refer to each other as brother—soul-brother, soul-sister. Some people may look upon this as *ersatz,* as make-believe, but it is not that. It is real. It is a growing sense of community. It is a growing realization that black Americans have a common bond not only among themselves, but with their African brothers. In *Black Man's Burden,* John O. Killens described his trip to ten African countries as follows:

> Everywhere I went people called me brother. . . . "Welcome, American brother." It was a good feeling for me, to be in Africa. To walk in a land for the first time in your entire life knowing within yourself that your color would not be held against you. No black man ever knows this in America [p. 160].

More and more black Americans are developing this feeling. They are becoming aware that they have a history which pre-dates their forced introduction to this country. African-American history means a long history beginning on the continent of Africa, a history not taught in the standard textbooks of this country. It is absolutely essential that black people know this history, that they know their roots, that they develop an awareness of their cultural heritage. Too long have they been kept in submission by being told that they had no culture, no manifest heritage, before they landed on the slave auction blocks in this country. If black people are to know themselves as a vibrant, valiant people, they must know their roots. And they will soon learn that the Hollywood image of man-eating cannibals waiting for, and waiting on, the Great White Hunter is a lie.

With redefinition will come a clearer notion of the role black Americans can play in this world. This role will emerge clearly out of the unique, common experiences of Afro-Asians. Killens concludes:

> I believe furthermore that the American Negro can be the bridge between the West and Africa-Asia. We black Americans can serve as a bridge to mutual understanding. The one thing we black Americans have in common with the other

> colored peoples of the world is that we have all felt the cruel and ruthless heel of white supremacy. We have all been "niggerized" on one level or another. And all of us are determined to "deniggerize" the earth. To rid the world of "niggers" is the Black Man's Burden, human reconstruction is the grand objective [p. 176].

Only when black people fully develop this sense of community, of themselves, can they begin to deal effectively with the problems of racism in *this* country. This is what we mean by a new consciousness; this is the vital first step. . . .

The next step is what we shall call the process of political modernization—a process which must take place if the society is to be rid of racism. "Political modernization" includes many things, but we mean by it three major concepts: (1) questioning old values and institutions of the society; (2) searching for new and different forms of political structure to solve political and economic problems; and (3) broadening the base of political participation to include more people in the decision-making process. These notions (we shall take up each in turn) are central to our thinking [here] and to contemporary American history as a whole. As David Apter wrote in *The Politics of Modernization,* ". . . the struggle to modernize is what has given meaning to our generation. It tests our cherished institutions and our beliefs. . . . So compelling a force has it become that we are forced to ask new questions of our own institutions. Each country, whether modernized or modernizing, stands in both judgment and fear of the results. Our own society is no exception" (p. 2).

The values of this society support a racist system; we find it incongruous to ask black people to adopt and support most of those values. We also reject the assumption that the basic institutions of this society must be preserved. The goal of black people must *not* be to assimilate into middle-class America, for that class—as a whole—is without a viable conscience as regards humanity. The values of the middle class permit the perpetuation of the ravages of the black community. The values of that class are based on material aggrandizement, not the expansion of humanity. The values of that class ultimately support cloistered little closed societies tucked away neatly in tree-lined suburbia. The values of that class do *not* lead to the creation of an open society. That class *mouths* its preference for a free, competitive society, while at the same time forcefully and even viciously denying to black people as a group the opportunity to compete.

We are not unmindful of other descriptions of the social utility of the middle class. Banfield and Wilson, in *City Politics,* concluded:

> The departure of the middle class from the central city is important in other ways. . . . The middle class supplies a social and political leavening in the life of a city. Middle-class people demand good schools and integrity in government. They support churches, lodges, parent-teacher associations, scout troops, better-housing committees, art galleries, and operas. It is the middle class, in short, that asserts a conception of the public interest. Now its activity is increasingly concentrated in the suburbs [p. 14].

But this same middle class manifests a sense of superior group position in regard to race. This class wants "good government" *for themselves*; it wants good schools *for its children*. At the same time, many of its members sneak into the black community by day, exploit it, and take the money home to their middle-class communities at night to support their operas and art galleries and comfortable homes. When not actually robbing, they will fight off the handful of more affluent black people who seek to move in; when they approve or even seek token integration, it applies only to black people like themselves—as "white" as possible. *This class is the backbone of institutional racism in this country.*

Thus we reject the goal of assimilation into middle-class America because the values of that class are in themselves anti-humanist and because that class as a social force perpetuates racism. We must face the fact that, in the past, what we have called the movement has not really questioned the middle-class values and institutions of this country. If anything, it has accepted those values and institutions without fully realizing their racist nature. Reorientation means an emphasis on the dignity of man, not on the sanctity of property. It means the creation of a society where human misery and poverty are repugnant to that society, not an indication of laziness or lack of initiative. The creation of new values means the establishment of a society based, as Killens expresses it in *Black Man's Burden,* on "free people," not "free enterprise" (p. 167). To do this means to modernize—*indeed, to civilize*—this country.

Supporting the old values are old political and economic structures; these must also be "modernized." We should at this point distinguish between "structures" and "system." By system, we have in mind the entire American complex of basic institutions, values, beliefs, etc. By structures, we mean the specific institutions (political parties, interest groups, bureaucratic administrations) which exist to conduct the business of that system. Obviously, the first is broader than the second. Also, the second assumes the legitimacy of the first. Our view is that, given the illegitimacy of the system, we cannot then proceed to transform that system with existing structures.

The two major political parties in this country have become non-viable entities for the legitimate representation of the real needs of masses—especially blacks—in this country. Walter Lippmann raised the same point in his syndicated column of December 8, 1966. He pointed out that the party system in the United States developed before our society became as technologically complex as it is now. He says that the ways in which men live and define themselves are changing radically. Old ideological issues, once the subject of passionate controversy, Lippmann argues, are of little interest today. He asks whether the great urban complexes—which are rapidly becoming the centers of black population in the U.S.—can be run with the same systems and ideas that derive from a time when America was a country of small villages and farms. While not addressing himself directly to the question of race, Lippmann raises a major question about our political institutions; and the crisis of race in America may be its major symptom.

Black people have seen the city planning commissions, the urban renewal commissions, the boards of education and the police departments fail to speak to their needs in a meaningful way. We must devise new structures, new institutions to replace those forms or to make them responsive. There is nothing sacred or inevitable about old institutions; the focus must be on people, not forms.

Existing structures and established ways of doing things have a way of perpetuating themselves and for this reason, the modernizing process will be difficult. Therefore, timidity in calling into question the boards of education or the police departments will not do. They must be challenged forcefully and clearly. If this means the creation of parallel community institutions, then that must be the solution. If this means that black parents must gain control over the operation of the schools in the black community, then that must be the solution. The search for new forms means the search for institutions that will, for once, make decisions in the interest of black people. It means, for example, a building inspection department that neither winks at violations of building codes by absentee slumlords nor imposes meaningless fines which permit them to continue their exploitation of the black community.

Essential to the modernization of structures is a broadened base of political participation. More and more people must become politically sensitive and active (we have already seen this happening in some areas of the South). People must no longer be tied, by small incentives or handouts, to a corrupting and corruptible white machine. Black people will choose their own leaders and hold those leaders responsible to *them*. A broadened base means an end to the condition described by James Wilson in *Negro Politics,* whereby "Negroes tended to be the objects rather than the subjects of civic action. Things are often done for, or about, or to, or because of Negroes, but they are less frequently done *by* Negroes" (p. 133). Broadening the base of political participation, then, has as much to do with the quality of black participation as with the quantity. We are fully aware that the black vote, especially in the North, has been pulled out of white pockets and "delivered" whenever it was in the interest of white politicians to do so. That vote must no longer be controllable by those who have neither the interests nor the demonstrated concern of black people in mind.

As the base broadens, as more and more black people become activated, they will perceive more clearly the special disadvantages heaped upon them as a group. They will perceive that the larger society is growing more affluent while the black society is retrogressing, as daily life and mounting statistics clearly show. . . . V. O. Key describes what often happens next, in *Politics, Parties and Pressure Groups:* "A factor of great significance in the setting off of political movements is an abrupt change for the worse in the status of one group relative to that of other groups in society. . . . A rapid change for the worse . . . in the relative status of any group . . . is likely to precipitate political action" (p. 24). Black people will become increasingly active as they notice that their retrogressive status exists in large measure because of values and institutions arraigned against them. They will begin to stress and strain and call the entire system into question. Political modernization will be in motion. We believe that it is now in motion. One form of that motion is Black Power.

The adoption of the concept of Black Power is one of the most legitimate and healthy developments in American politics and race relations in our time. The concept of Black Power speaks to all the needs mentioned in this [essay]. It is a call for black people in this country to unite, to recognize their heritage, to build a sense of community. It is a call for black people to begin to define their own goals, to lead their own organizations and to support those organizations. It is a call to reject the racist institutions and values of this society.

The concept of Black Power rests on a fundamental premise: *Before a group can enter the open society, it must first close ranks.* By this we mean that group solidarity is necessary before a group can operate effectively from a bargaining position of strength in a pluralistic society. Traditionally, each new ethnic group in this society has found the route to social and political viability through the organization of its own institutions with which to represent its needs within the larger society. Studies in voting behavior specifically, and political behavior generally, have made it clear that politically the American pot has not melted. Italians vote for Rubino over O'Brien; Irish for Murphy over Goldberg, etc. This phenomenon may seem distasteful to some, but it has been and remains today a central fact of the American political system. There are other examples of ways in which groups in the society have remembered their roots and used this effectively in the political arena. Theodore Sorensen describes the politics of foreign aid during the Kennedy Administration in his book *Kennedy:*

> No powerful constituencies or interest groups backed foreign aid. The Marshall Plan at least had appealed to Americans who traced their roots to the Western European nations aided. But there were few voters who identified with India, Colombia or Tanganyika [p. 351].

The extent to which black Americans can and do "trace their roots" to Africa, to that extent will they be able to be more effective on the political scene.

A white reporter set forth this point in other terms when he made the following observation about white Mississippi's manipulation of the anti-poverty program:

> The war on poverty has been predicated on the notion that there is such a thing as a community which can be defined geographically and mobilized for a collective effort to help the poor. This theory has no relationship to reality in the deep South. In every Mississippi county there are two communities. Despite all the pious platitudes of the moderates on both sides, these two communities habitually see their interests in terms of conflict rather than cooperation. Only when the Negro community can muster enough political, economic and professional strength to compete on somewhat equal terms, will Negroes believe in the possibility of true cooperation and whites accept its necessity. En route to integration, the Negro community needs to develop a greater independence—a chance to run its own affairs and not cave in whenever "the man" barks—or so it seems to me, and to most of the knowledgeable people with whom I talked in Mississippi. To OEO [the Office of Equal Opportunity], this judgment may sound like black nationalism. . . .[2]

The point is obvious: black people must lead and run their own organizations. Only black people can convey the revolutionary idea—and it is a revolutionary idea—that black people are able to do things themselves. Only they can help create in the community an aroused and continuing black consciousness that will provide the basis for political strength. In the past, white allies have often furthered white supremacy without the whites involved realizing it, or even wanting to do so. Black people must come together and do things for themselves. They must achieve self-identity and self-determination in order to have their daily needs met.

[2] Christopher Jencks, "Accommodating Whites: A New Look at Mississippi," *The New Republic* (April 16, 1966).

Black Power means, for example, that in Lowndes County, Alabama, a black sheriff can end police brutality. A black tax assessor and tax collector and county board of revenue can lay, collect, and channel tax monies for the building of better roads and schools serving black people. In such areas as Lowndes, where black people have a majority, they will attempt to use power to exercise control. This is what they seek: control. When black people lack a majority, Black Power means proper representation and sharing of control. It means the creation of power bases, of strength, from which black people can press to change local or nation-wide patterns of oppression—instead of from weakness.

It does not mean *merely* putting black faces into office. Black visibility is not Black Power. Most of the black politicians around the country today are not examples of Black Power. The power must be that of a community, and emanate from there. The black politicians must start from there. The black politicians must stop being representatives of "downtown" machines, whatever the cost might be in terms of lost patronage and holiday handouts.

Black Power recognizes—it must recognize—the ethnic basis of American politics as well as the power-oriented nature of American politics. Black Power therefore calls for black people to consolidate behind their own, so that they can bargain from a position of strength. But while we endorse the *procedure* of group solidarity and identity for the purpose of attaining certain goals in the body politic, this does not mean that black people should strive for the same kind of rewards (i.e., end results) obtained by the white society. The ultimate values and goals are not domination or exploitation of other groups, but rather an effective share in the total power of the society.

Nevertheless, some observers have labeled those who advocate Black Power as racists; they have said that the call for self-identification and self-determination is "racism in reverse" or "black supremacy." This is a deliberate and absurd lie. There is no analogy—by any stretch of definition or imagination—between the advocates of Black Power and white racists. Racism is not merely exclusion on the basis of race but exclusion for the purpose of subjugating or maintaining subjugation. The goal of the racists is to keep black people on the bottom, arbitrarily and dictatorially, as they have done in this country for over three hundred years. The goal of black self-determination and black self-identity—Black Power—is full participation in the decision-making process affecting the lives of black people, and recognition of the virtues in themselves as black people. The black people of this country have not lynched whites, bombed their churches, murdered their children and manipulated laws and institutions to maintain oppression. White racists have. Congressional laws, one after the other, have not been necessary to stop black people from oppressing others and denying others the full enjoyment of their rights. White racists have made such laws necessary. The goal of Black Power is positive and functional to a free and viable society. No white racist can make this claim.

A great deal of public attention and press space was devoted to the hysterical accusation of "black racism" when the call for Black Power was first sounded. A national committee of influential black churchmen affiliated with the National Council of Churches, despite their obvious respectability and responsibility, had to resort to a paid advertisement to articulate their position, while anyone yapping "black racism" made front-page news. In their statement, published in the *New York Times* of July 31, 1966, the churchmen said:

> We, an informal group of Negro churchmen in America, are deeply disturbed about the crisis brought upon our country by historic distortions of important human realities in the controversy about "black power." What we see shining through the variety of rhetoric is not anything new but the same old problem of power and race which has faced our beloved country since 1619.
>
> . . . The conscience of black men is corrupted because having no power to implement the demands of conscience, the concern for justice in the absence of justice becomes a chaotic self-surrender. Powerlessness breeds a race of beggars. We are faced with a situation where powerless conscience meets conscienceless power, threatening the very foundations of our Nation.
>
> We deplore the overt violence of riots, but we feel it is more important to focus on the real sources of these eruptions. These sources may be abetted inside the Ghetto, but their basic cause lies in the silent and covert violence which white middle class America inflicts upon the victims of the inner city.
>
> . . . In short, the failure of American leaders to use American power to create equal opportunity *in life* as well as *law,* this is the real problem and not the anguished cry for black power.
>
> . . . Without the capacity to participate with power, i.e., to have some organized political and economic strength to really influence people with whom one interacts, integration is not meaningful.
>
> . . . America has asked its Negro citizens to fight for opportunity as *individuals,* whereas at certain points in our history what we have needed most has been opportunity for the *whole group,* not just for selected and approved Negroes.
>
> . . . We must not apologize for the existence of this form of group power, for we have been oppressed as a group and not as individuals. We will not find our way out of that oppression until both we and America accept the need for Negro Americans, as well as for Jews, Italians, Poles, and white Anglo-Saxon Protestants, among others, to have and to wield group power.

It is a commentary on the fundamentally racist nature of this society that the concept of group strength for black people must be articulated—not to mention defended. No other group would submit to being led by others. Italians do not run the Anti-Defamation League of B'nai B'rith. Irish do not chair Christopher Columbus Societies. Yet when black people call for black-run and all-black organizations, they are immediately classed in a category with the Ku Klux Klan. This is interesting and ironic, but by no means surprising: the society does not expect black people to be able to take care of their business, and there are many who prefer it precisely that way.

In the end, we cannot and shall not offer any guarantees that Black Power, if achieved, would be non-racist. No one can predict human behavior. Social change always has unanticipated consequences. If black racism is what the larger society fears, we cannot help them. We can only state what we hope will be the result, given the fact that the present situation is unacceptable and that we have no real alternative but to work for Black Power. The final truth is that the white society is not entitled to reassurances, even if it were possible to offer them.

We have outlined the meaning and goals of Black Power; we have also discussed one major thing which it is not. There are others of greater importance. The advocates of Black Power reject the old slogans and meaningless rhetoric of previous years in the civil rights struggle. The language of yesterday is indeed irrelevant: progress, non-violence, integration, fear of "white backlash," coalition. Let us look at the rhetoric and see why these terms must be set aside or redefined.

One of the tragedies of the struggle against racism is that up to this point there has been no national organization which could speak to the growing militancy of young black people in the urban ghettos and the black-belt South. There has been only a "civil rights" movement, whose tone of voice was adapted to an audience of middle-class whites. It served as a sort of buffer zone between that audience and angry young blacks. It claimed to speak for the needs of a community, but it did not speak in the tone of that community. None of its so-called leaders could go into a rioting community and be listened to. In a sense, the blame must be shared—along with the mass media—by those leaders for what happened in Watts, Harlem, Chicago, Cleveland and other places. Each time the black people in those cities saw Dr. Martin Luther King get slapped they became angry. When they saw little black girls bombed to death *in a church* and civil rights workers ambushed and murdered, they were angrier; and when nothing happened, they were steaming mad. We had nothing to offer that they could see, except to go out and be beaten again. We helped to build their frustration.

We had only the old language of love and suffering. And in most places—that is, from the liberals and middle class—we got back the old language of patience and progress. The civil rights leaders were saying to the country: "Look, you guys are supposed to be nice guys, and we are only going to do what we are supposed to do. Why do you beat us up? Why don't you give us what we ask? Why don't you straighten yourselves out?" For the masses of black people, this language resulted in virtually nothing. In fact, their objective day-to-day condition worsened. The unemployment rate among black people increased while that among whites declined. Housing conditions in the black communities deteriorated. Schools in the black ghettos continued to plod along on outmoded techniques, inadequate curricula, and with all too many tired and indifferent teachers. Meanwhile, the President picked up the refrain of "We Shall Overcome" while the Congress passed civil rights law after civil rights law, only to have them effectively nullified by deliberately weak enforcement. "Progress is being made," we were told.

Such language, along with admonitions to remain non-violent and fear the white backlash, convinced some that that course was the *only* course to follow. It misled some into believing that a black minority could bow its head and get whipped into a meaningful position of power. The very notion is absurd. The white society devised the language, adopted the rules and had the black community narcotized into believing that that language and those rules were, in fact, relevant. The black community was told time and again how *other* immigrants finally won *acceptance:* that is, by following the Protestant Ethic of Work and Achievement. They worked hard; therefore, they achieved. We were not told that it was by building Irish Power, Italian Power, Polish Power or Jewish Power that these groups got themselves together and operated from positions of strength. We were not told that "the American dream" wasn't designed for black people. That while today, to whites, the dream may *seem* to include black people, it cannot do so by the very nature of this nation's political and economic system, which imposes institutional racism on the black masses if not upon every individual black. A notable comment on that "dream" was made by Dr. Percy Julian, the black scientist and director of the Julian Research Institute in Chicago, a man for whom the dream seems to have come true. While not subscribing to "black power" as he understood it, Dr. Julian clearly understood the basis for it: "The false concept of basic Negro inferiority is one of the curses that still lingers. It is a problem created by the white man. Our children just no longer are going to accept the patience we were taught by our generation. We were taught a pretty little lie—excel and the whole world lies open before you. I *obeyed the injunction and found it to be wishful thinking*" (authors' italics).[3]

A key phrase in our buffer-zone days was non-violence. For years it has been thought that black people would not literally fight for their lives. Why this has been so is not entirely clear; neither the larger society nor black people are noted for passivity. The notion apparently stems from the years of marches and demonstrations and sit-ins where black people did not strike back and the violence always came from white mobs. There are many who still sincerely believe in that approach. From our viewpoint, rampaging white mobs and white night-riders must be made to understand that their days of free head-whipping are over. Black people should and must fight back. Nothing more quickly repels someone bent on destroying you than the unequivocal message: "O.K., fool, make your move, and run the same risk I run—of dying."

When the concept of Black Power is set forth, many people immediately conjure up notions of violence. The country's reaction to the Deacons for Defense and Justice, which originated in Louisiana, is instructive. Here is a group which realized that the "law" and law enforcement agencies would not protect people, so they had to do it themselves. If a nation fails to protect its citizens, then that nation cannot condemn those who take up the task themselves. The Deacons and all other blacks who resort to self-defense represent a simple answer to a simple question: what man would not defend his family and home from attack?

But this frightened some white people, because they knew that black people would now fight back. They knew that this was precisely what *they* would have long since done if *they* were subjected to the injustices and oppression heaped on blacks. Those of us who advocate Black Power are quite clear in our own minds that a "non-violent" approach to civil rights is an approach black people cannot afford and a luxury white people do not deserve. It is crystal clear to us—and it must become so with the white society—*that there can be no social order without social justice*. White people must be made to understand that they must stop messing with black people, or the blacks *will* fight back!

Next, we must deal with the term "integration." According to its advocates, social justice will be accomplished by "integrating the Negro into the mainstream institutions of the society from which he has been traditionally excluded." This concept is based on the assumption that there is nothing of value in the black community and that little of value could be created among black people. The thing to do is siphon off the "acceptable" black people into the surrounding middle-class white community.

The goals of integrationists are middle-class goals, articulated primarily by a small group of Negroes with middle-class aspirations or status. Their kind of

[3] *New York Times,* April 30, 1967, p. 30.

integration has meant that a few blacks "make it," leaving the black community, sapping it of leadership potential and know-how. . . . Those token Negroes—absorbed into a white mass—are of no value to the remaining black masses. They become meaningless show-pieces for a conscience-soothed white society. Such people will state that they would prefer to be treated "only as individuals, not as Negroes"; that they "are not and should not be preoccupied with race." This is a totally unrealistic position. In the first place, black people have not suffered as individuals but as members of a group; therefore, their liberation lies in group action. This is why SNCC—and the concept of Black Power—affirms that helping *individual* black people to solve their problems on an *individual* basis does little to alleviate the mass of black people. Secondly, while color blindness *may* be a sound goal ultimately, we must realize that race is an overwhelming fact of life in this historical period. There is no black man in this country who can live "simply as a man." His blackness is an ever-present fact of this racist society, whether he recognizes it or not. It is unlikely that this or the next generation will witness the time when race will no longer be relevant in the conduct of public affairs and in public policy decision-making. To realize this and to attempt to deal with it does not make one a racist or overly preoccupied with race; it puts one in the forefront of a significant *struggle*. If there is no intense struggle today, there will be no meaningful results tomorrow.

"Integration" as a goal today speaks to the problem of blackness not only in an unrealistic way but also in a despicable way. It is based on complete acceptance of the fact that in order to have a decent house or education, black people must move into a white neighborhood or send their children to a white school. This reinforces, among both black and white, the idea that "white" is automatically superior and "black" is by definition inferior. For this reason, "integration" is a subterfuge for the maintenance of white supremacy. It allows the nation to focus on a handful of Southern black children who get into white schools at a great price, and to ignore the ninety-four percent who are left in unimproved all-black schools. Such situations will not change until black people become equal in a way that means something, and integration ceases to be a one-way street. Then integration does not mean draining skills and energies from the black ghetto into white neighborhoods. To sprinkle black children among white pupils in outlying schools is at best a stop-gap measure. The goal is not to take black children out of the black community and expose them to white middle-class values; the goal is to build and strengthen the black community.

"Integration" also means that black people must give up their identity, deny their heritage. We recall the conclusion of Killian and Grigg: "At the present time, integration as a solution to the race problem demands that the Negro foreswear his identity as a Negro." The fact is that integration, as traditionally articulated, would abolish the black community. The fact is that what must be abolished is not the black community, but the dependent colonial status that has been inflicted upon it.

The racial and cultural personality of the black community must be preserved and that community must win its freedom while preserving its cultural integrity. Integrity includes a pride—in the sense of self-acceptance, not chauvinism—in being black, in the historical attainments and contributions of black people. No person can be healthy, complete and mature if he must deny a part of himself; this is what "integration" has required thus far. This is the essential difference between integration as it is currently practiced and the concept of Black Power.

The idea of cultural integrity is so obvious that it seems almost simple-minded to spell things out at this length. Yet millions of Americans resist such truths when they are applied to black people. Again, that resistance is a comment on the fundamental racism in the society. Irish Catholics took care of their own first without a lot of apology for doing so, without any dubious language from timid leadership about guarding against "backlash." Everyone understood it to be a perfectly legitimate procedure. Of course, there would be "backlash." Organization begets counterorganization, but this was no reason to defer.

The so-called white backlash against black people is something else: the embedded traditions of institutional racism being brought into the open and calling forth overt manifestations of individual racism. In the summer of 1966, when the protest marches into Cicero, Illinois, began, the black people knew they were not allowed to live in Cicero and the white people knew it. When blacks began to demand the right to live in homes in that town, the whites simply reminded them of the status quo. Some people called this "backlash." It was, in fact, racism defending itself. In the black community, this is called "White folks showing their color." It is ludicrous to blame black people for what is simply an overt manifestation of white racism. Dr. Martin Luther King stated clearly that the protest marches were not the cause of the racism but merely exposed a long-term cancerous condition in the society. . . .

WORKS CITED

Apter, David, *The Politics of Modernization,* Chicago, University of Chicago Press, 1965.

Banfield, Edward and Wilson, James Q., *City Politics,* New York, Random House (Vintage Books), 1966.

Du Bois, W. E. B., *Black Reconstruction in America,* New York, Meridian Books, 1964.

Franklin, John Hope, *From Slavery to Freedom,* New York, Alfred A. Knopf, 1957.

Key, V. O., Jr., *Politics, Parties and Pressure Groups,* New York, Thomas Y. Crowell, 1964.

Killens, John O., *Black Man's Burden,* New York, Trident Press, 1965.

Killian, Lewis and Grigg, Charles, *Racial Crises in America,* Englewood Cliffs, N.J., Prentice-Hall, 1964.

Morgenthau, Hans, *Politics among Nations,* New York, Alfred A. Knopf, 1966.

Sorensen, Theodore, *Kennedy,* New York, Harper & Row, 1965.

Wilson, James Q., *Negro Politics,* Glencoe, Ill., The Free Press, 1960.

Angela Davis (1944–)

"Revolutionary" is a term aptly assigned to Angela Davis, whose personal life and intellectual pursuits are a contemporary model of revolt against the American status quo. A decade after events that marked her as one of the leading radical figures of the 1970s, Davis offered this perspective on her life: "The same kinds of problems exist today as they did ten years ago. . . . I still attempt to participate in seeking solutions to these problems. . . . Hopefully, I can apply

some of the lessons that emerged from the struggles of the sixties and seventies to make a more substantial contribution today. But I still consider myself a revolutionary."

Born in Birmingham, Alabama, Davis grew up in a segregated neighborhood known as Dynamite Hill and went to segregated schools. At age fifteen, she moved to New York to attend a private high school in Greenwich Village on scholarship while living with a host family. But she was no typical scholarship student: as a teenager, she joined a Marxist-Leninist group called Advance. Later, at Brandeis University, she majored in French and studied with social and political philosopher Herbert Marcuse, who taught the doctrines of resistance and rebellion. After earning her bachelor's from Brandeis in 1965, Davis studied philosophy at Goethe University in Frankfurt, Germany, where she also became active in socialist student groups demonstrating against the Vietnam War. Returning to the United States in 1967, she studied again with Marcuse at the University of California in San Diego, receiving her master's in philosophy in 1969.

Davis's return to the United States also allowed her to participate in the struggle against racism. She met with activists in the Student Non-violent Coordinating Committee (SNCC), the Black Panthers, and the Communist Party, which she joined in 1968. In 1980 and 1984, she served as the party's candidate for vice president of the United States.

In 1969, administrator at the University of California at Los Angeles and then-Governor Ronald Reagan attempted to dismiss Davis from the UCLA faculty because of her Communist Party membership, but she legally won the right to remain on staff. However, by 1970, she found herself fired from UCLA after giving speeches in support of two Soledad Prison inmates—W. L. Nolen and George Jackson, also advocates of Marxism—whose killings by prison guards in separate incidents Davis denounced as conspiratorial. Then, in the summer of 1970, Davis was marked for arrest by the FBI for her alleged involvement in a failed attempt to rescue a San Quentin inmate from a Marin County courthouse that resulted in a violent confrontation and the deaths of four people, including a white judge and George Jackson's brother. Going underground to avoid arrest, Davis was placed on the FBI's Ten Most Wanted list until she was apprehended two months later in New York. At her trial, she was found not guilty of kidnapping, conspiracy, and murder.

Since the mid-1970s, Davis has taught at Claremont College, Stanford University, the California College of the Arts and Crafts, the University of California at Santa Cruz, and San Francisco State University. In 1979, she received the Lenin Peace Prize. She also has been awarded honorary doctorates from Lenin University and the University of Leipzig.

Along with her speeches, media appearances, and articles, Davis has published If They Come in the Morning: Voices of Resistance *(1971), a collection of essays;* Angela Davis *(1974), her autobiography;* Women, Race, and Class *(1983);* Violence against Women and the Ongoing Challenge to Racism *(1987), a pamphlet; and* Women, Culture, and Politics *(1989), from which the following selection is taken.*

In "We Do Not Consent: Violence against Women in a Racist Society," Davis investigates the link between sexual violence and "race, gender, and class oppression" within American society.

We Do Not Consent

Violence against Women in a Racist Society

Even tonight and I need to take a walk and clear
my head about this poem about why I can't
go out without changing my clothes my shoes
my body posture my gender identity my age
my status as a woman alone in the evening/
alone on the streets/alone not being the point/
the point being that I can't do what I want
to do with my own body because I am the wrong
sex the wrong age the wrong skin and
suppose it was not here in the city but down on the beach/
or far into the woods and I wanted to go
there by myself thinking about God/or thinking
about children or thinking about the world/all of it
disclosed by the stars and the silence:
I could not go and I could not think and I could not
stay there
alone
as I need to be
alone because I can't do what I want to with my own
body and
who in the hell set things up
like this
and in France they say if the guy penetrates
but does not ejaculate then he did not rape me
and if after stabbing him if after screams if
after begging the bastard and if even after smashing
a hammer to his head if even after that if he
and his buddies fuck me after that
then I consented and there was
no rape because finally you understand finally
they fucked me over because I was wrong I was
wrong again to be me being me where I was/wrong
to be who I am
which is exactly like South Africa
penetrating into Namibia penetrating into
Angola and does that mean I mean how do you know if
Pretoria ejaculates what will the evidence look like the
proof of the monster jackboot ejaculation on Blackland
and if
after Namibia and if after Angola and if after Zimbabwe
and if after all of my kinsmen and women resist even to
self-immolation of the villages and if after that
we lose nevertheless what will the big boys say will they
claim my consent:
Do You Follow Me: We are the wrong people of

> the wrong skin on the wrong continent and what
> in the hell is everybody being reasonable about . . .[1]

This excerpt from June Jordan's "Poem about My Rights" graphically reveals the parallels between sexual violence against individual women and neocolonial violence against peoples and nations. Her message deserves serious consideration: We cannot grasp the true nature of sexual assault without situating it within its larger sociopolitical context. If we wish to comprehend the nature of sexual violence as it is experienced by women as individuals, we must be cognizant of its social mediations. These include the imperialist violence imposed on the people of Nicaragua, the violence of South African apartheid, and the racist-inspired violence inflicted on Afro-Americans and other racially oppressed people here in the United States.

Rape, sexual extortion, battering, spousal rape, sexual abuse of children, and incest are among the many forms of overt sexual violence suffered by millions of women in this country. When we are prohibited from exercising our abortion rights by the terroristic tactics of so-called "right-to-lifers" who bomb abortion clinics, and the criminal actions of the government as it withdraws federal subsidies for abortion, we experience violence aimed at our reproductive choices and our sexuality. Poor women, and specifically women of color, continue to fall prey to the surgical violence of sterilization abuse. Innumerable women unwittingly injure their bodies with the Dalkon Shield and other potentially fatal methods of birth control, while physically and mentally disabled women are presumptuously defined as nonsexual and therefore as requiring no special attention with respect to their birth-control needs. Reproductive rights, however, entail more than access to abortions and safe birth-control methods. They encompass, for example, the right of lesbians to have children outside of the confines of heterosexual relationships, and they will require nonrepressive laws governing new reproductive technologies involving donor insemination, in vitro fertilization, and surrogate motherhood.

These particular manifestations of violence against women are situated on a larger continuum of socially inflicted violence, which includes concerted, systematic violations of women's economic and political rights. As has been the case throughout history, these attacks most gravely affect women of color and their white working-class sisters. The dreadful rape epidemic of our times, which has become so widespread that one out of every three women in this country can expect to be raped at some point during her life, grimly mirrors the deteriorating economic and social status of women today. Indeed, as domestic racist violence mounts—and as global imperialist aggression becomes more widespread—so women can expect that individual men will be more prone to commit acts of sexual violence against the women around them. Though the Reagan administration attempts to displace the responsibility for this fact, it cannot escape blame for this rising threat of violence in our society. It is not only the most sexist government—the only one, for example, to actively oppose the Equal Rights Amendment at the same time that it supports the sexist and homophobic Family Life Amendment—and it is not only the most racist government, persistently seeking to dismantle thirty years of gains by the civil rights movement, but it is by far the most fiercely warmongering government of this century. Indeed, for the first time in the history of human-kind, we face the very real threat of global nuclear omnicide.

Leaving aside this larger picture for the time being, let us focus more precisely on the recent history of our social consciousness regarding sexual violence against women. When the contemporary antirape movement began to take shape during the early 1970s, shortly after the emergence of the women's liberation movement, the antirape movement—along with the campaign to decriminalize abortion—proved to be the most dramatic activist mass movement associated with the fight for women's equality. In January of 1971, the New York Radical Feminists organized a Rape Speak-Out, which, for the first time in history, provided large numbers of women with a forum from which to relate publicly their often terrifying individual experiences of rape.[2] Also in 1971, women in Berkeley, California, responded to the painfully discriminatory treatment received by rape survivors in police departments, hospitals, and courts by organizing a community-based twenty-four-hour crisis line known as Bay Area Women against Rape. This crisis center became the model for countless similar institutions that arose throughout the country during the 1970s.

In 1971, Susan Griffin published a historic article in *Ramparts* magazine entitled "Rape: The All-American Crime." Her article opened with these words:

> I have never been free of the fear of rape. From a very early age I, like most women, have thought of rape as part of my natural environment—something to be feared and prayed against like fire or lightning. I never asked why men raped; I simply thought it one of the many mysteries of human nature.
>
> . . . At the age of eight . . . my grandmother took me to the back of the house where the men wouldn't hear, and told me that strange men wanted to do harm to little girls. I learned not to walk on dark streets, not to talk to strangers or get into strange cars, to lock doors, and to be modest. She never explained why a man would want to harm a little girl, and I never asked.
>
> If I thought for a while that my grandmother's fears were imaginary, the illusion was brief. That year, on the way home from school, a schoolmate a few years older than I tried to rape me. Later, in an obscure aisle of the local library (while I was reading *Freddy the Pig*), I turned to discover a man exposing himself. Then, the friendly man around the corner was arrested for child molesting.[3]

That virtually all of us can retrieve similar episodes from our childhood memories is proof of the extent to which misogynist violence conditions the female experience in societies such as ours. I recall that when I was an elementary-school student—I must have been about ten years old—a girlfriend of mine who lived around the corner suddenly disappeared for a week or so. During her absence from school, there were embarrassed whispers that she had been raped. When she returned, she never mentioned the reason for her absence, and no one dared attempt to break through her shroud of silence. I remember distinctly that all of the hushed conversations behind her back assumed that my friend had done something terribly wrong, and she walked around with a mysterious aura of immorality surrounding her for the rest of the time we spent in elementary school. More than any of the other girls, she was the target of the boys' sexual jeers. Assuming that she had transgressed the moral standards of our community, no one ventured to argue that she was the tragic victim of a crime that should never have gone uninvestigated or unpunished.

The antirape movement of the early seventies challenged many of the prevalent myths regarding rape. For example, women militantly refuted the myth that the rape victim is morally responsible for the crime committed against her—a myth that is based on the notion that women have control over whether or not their bodies are violated during the act of rape. It used to be the case that defense attorneys would unhesitatingly presume to demonstrate the impossibility of rape by asking witnesses to insert a phallic object into a receptacle that was rapidly moved from one place to another. Oleta Abrams, one of the co-founders of Bay Area Woman against Rape, has related an anecdote that clearly reveals the most probable power relations in an actual rape incident. When a policeman asked a woman to insert his billy club into a cup that he continually maneuvered around, the woman simply took the club and struck him on the shoulder, causing him to drop the cup, into which she easily inserted the billy club.[4]

Another widespread myth is that if a woman does not resist, she is implicitly inviting the violation of her body. Transfer this assumption to the context of a case involving the criminal violation of property. Is a businessman asked to resist the encroachment of a robber in order to guarantee that his property rights will be protected by the courts? Even today, the persisting mystification of rape causes it to be perceived as a victim-precipitated crime, as was the case in the ruling of a Wisconsin judge who, in 1977, found a fifteen-year-old male's rape of a teenager who was wearing a loose shirt, Levi's, and tennis shoes to be a "normal" reaction to the "provocative" dress of the young woman.

Although there is a pervasive fear among most women of being raped, at the same time, many women feel that it cannot really happen to them. Yet *one* out of *three* women will be sexually assaulted in her lifetime, and *one* out of *four* girls will be raped before she reaches the age of eighteen. Despite these startling statistics, there is only a 4 percent conviction rate of rapists—and these convictions reflect only the minute percentage of rapes that are actually reported.

Rape happens anytime, anywhere, to females of all ages. Infants of four months have been raped, and women over ninety years old have been raped, although the single largest group of rape survivors is composed of adolescent girls between the ages of sixteen and eighteen. Rape happens to women of all races and all classes, regardless of their sexual orientation.

Although most of us tend to visualize rape episodes as sudden, unanticipated attack by perverse strangers, most victims actually know their rapists and, in fact, more than half of all rapes occur in the home of either the survivor or the offender. Furthermore, it is often assumed that rape is an act of lust and that, consequently, rapists are simply men who cannot control their sexual urges. The truth is that most rapists do not impulsively rape in order to satisfy an uncontrollable sexual passion. Instead, men's motives for rape often arise from their socially imposed need to exercise power and control over women through the use of violence. Most rapists are not psychopaths, as we are led to believe by typical media portrayals of men who commit crimes of sexual violence. On the contrary, the overwhelming majority would be considered "normal" according to prevailing social standards of male normality.

Certainly the most insidious myth about rape is that it is most likely to be committed by a Black man. As a direct consequence of the persistent insinuation of racism into prevailing social attitudes, white women are socialized to harbor far more fear that they will be raped by a Black man than by a white man. In actuality, however, for the simple reason that white men compose a larger proportion of the population, many more rapes are committed by white men than by Black men. But as a consequence of this country's history of ubiquitous racism in law enforcement, there are a disproportionately large number of Black men in prison on rape convictions. The myth of the Black rapist renders people oblivious to the realities of rape and to the fact, for example, that over 90 percent of all rapes are intraracial rather than interracial. Moreover, as has been pointed out in studies on sexual assault—and as indeed was the case during the era of slavery—proportionately more white men rape Black women than Black men rape white women. Nonetheless, the average white woman in this country maintains a far greater suspicion of Black men than of white men as potential rapists. These distorted social attitudes, which are racist by their very nature, constitute an enormous obstacle to the development of a movement capable of winning substantive victories in the struggle against rape.

If we examine the reasons why laying the foundation for an effective multiracial antirape movement has been such an arduous process, we discover that the confounding influence of the myth of the Black rapist looms large. During the early 1970s, when the antirape campaign was in its infancy, the presence of Afro-American women in that movement was a rarity. This no doubt was in part attributable to the underdeveloped awareness regarding the interconnectedness of racism and sexism in general among the white women who pioneered the women's liberation movement. At the same time, antirape activists failed to develop an understanding of the degree to which rape and the racist use of the fraudulent rape charge are historically inseparable. If, throughout our history in this country, the rape of Black women by white men has constituted a political weapon of terror, then the flip side of the coin has been the frame-up rape charge directed at Black men. Thousands of terroristic lynchings have been justified by conjuring up the myth of the Black rapist.

Since much of the early activism against rape was focused on delivering rapists into the hands of the judicial system, Afro-American women were understandably reluctant to become involved with a movement that might well lead to further repressive assaults on their families and their communities. Yet, at the same time, Black women were and continue to be sorely in need of an antirape movement, since we compromise a disproportionately large number of rape survivors. It is all the more ironic that Black women were absent from the contemporary antirape movement during its early days, since antirape activism actually has a long history in the Black community. Probably the first progressive movement to launch a frontal challenge to sexual violence was the Black Women's Club Movement, which originated in the late 1890s based on the antilynching activities of women like Ida B. Wells.[5] Today, organizations such as the National Black Women's Health Project in Atlanta are conducting organizing and educational campaigns around such issues as rape and sterilization abuse.

Certainly any woman can understand the intense anger that characterized the first phase of the antirape campaign. Throughout all of history, the judicial system and society in general had not even acknowledged women as legitimate victims of a crime if the crime committed against them was rape. Much of women's cumulative rage about rape was understandably aimed at men. When a feminist theoretical foundation for the campaign began to develop, the theories tended to bolster and legitimize indiscriminate antimale anger by defining rape as an inevitable product of masculine nature. Masculinity was understood not so much in terms of its social determinations, especially under conditions of capitalism, but rather as an immutable biologically and psychologically determined product of men's inherent nature.

These theories most often did not take into account the class and racial components of many rapes suffered by working-class white women and women of color. In fact, the failure of the antirape movement of the early 1970s to develop an analysis of rape that acknowledged the social conditions that foster sexual violence as well as the centrality of racism in determining those social conditions, resulted in the initial reluctance of Black, Latina, and Native American women to involve themselves in that movement. Throughout Afro-American women's economic history in this country, for example, sexual abuse has been perceived as an occupational hazard. In slavery, Black women's bodies were considered to be accessible at all times to the slavemaster as well as to his surrogates. In "freedom," the jobs most frequently open to Black women were as domestic workers. This relegation of Black women to menial jobs did not begin to change until the late 1950s, and there is ample documentation that as maids and washerwomen, Black women have been repeatedly the victims of sexual assault committed by the white men in the families for which they worked.

Sexual harassment and sexual extortion are still occupational hazards for working women of *all* racial backgrounds. In a survey conducted by *Redbook,* in 1976, 90 percent of the nine thousand respondents reported that they had encountered sexual harassment on the job.[6] According to Julia Schwendinger, in her book entitled *Rape and Inequality,* one congresswoman discovered that a certain congressman was asking prospective women employees whether they engaged in oral sex, as though this were a requirement for the job.[7]

If we assume that rape is simply a by-product of maleness, a result of men's anatomical construction or of an immutable male psychological constitution, then how do we explain the fact that the countries that are now experiencing an epidemic of rape are precisely those advanced capitalist countries that face severe economic and social crises and are saturated with violence on all levels? Do men rape because they are men, or are they socialized by their own economic, social, and political oppression—as well as by the overall level of social violence in the country in which they live—to inflict sexual violence on women?

Sexual violence often flows directly from official policy. In Vietnam, as Arlene Eisen has pointed out in her book *Women in Vietnam,* U.S. soldiers often received instructions for their search and destroy missions that involved "searching" Vietnamese women's vaginas with their penises.[8] The following observation has been made about sexual violence under the conditions of fascist dictatorship in Chile:

> The tortures of women included the agony of scorching their nipples and genitals, the blind terror of applying shock treatments to all parts of their bodies, and, of course, gang rape. An unknown number of women have been raped; some of them pregnant after rape have been refused abortions. Women have had insects forced up their vaginas; pregnant women have been beaten with rifle butts until they have aborted.[9]

Indeed, rape is frequently a component of the torture inflicted on women political prisoners by fascist governments and counterrevolutionary forces. In the history of our own country, the Ku Klux Klan and other racist groups have used rape as a weapon of political terror.

Rape bears a direct relationship to all of the existing power structures in a given society. This relationship is not a simple, mechanical one, but rather involves complex structures reflecting the interconnectedness of the race, gender, and class oppression that characterize the society. If we do not comprehend the nature of sexual violence as it is mediated by racial, class, and governmental violence and power, we cannot hope to develop strategies that will allow us eventually to purge our society of oppressive misogynist violence.

In our attempt to understand the structure of rape, it would be a grievous mistake to limit our analysis to individual cases or even to conduct our analysis only in terms of male psychology. The only logical strategies for the elimination of rape that would follow from this type of analysis would be a reliance on repression to punish and deter rapists. But as the use of the repressive paraphernalia of the state has generally demonstrated, further crimes are seldom deterred by punishment meted out to those who have been caught committing them. Thus, for each punished rapist, how many more would be lurking in our neighborhoods—indeed, in our workplaces and even in our homes? This is not to argue that men who commit rape should go unpunished, but rather that punishment alone will not stem the rising tide of sexual violence in our country.

The experience of the 1970s demonstrates that antirape strategies that depend primarily on law-enforcement agencies will continue to alienate many women of color. Indeed, the experience of Black women has been that the very same white policemen who are charged with protecting them from rapists and other criminals will sometimes go so far as to rape Black women in their custody. Ann Braden, a veteran civil rights organizer, has referred to such conduct by southern white policemen who arrested Black women activists during the civil rights struggle and subsequently raped them. I recall an experience I had as a graduate student in San Diego when a friend and I found a young Black woman, beaten and bloody, on the shoulder of the freeway. She had been raped by several white men and dropped by the side of the road. When the police found her, they, too, raped her and left her on the freeway, barely conscious. Because these cases are by no means isolated, Black women have found it extremely difficult to accept policemen as enforcers of antirape measures.

Moreover, police forces often employ tactics ostensibly designed to capture rapists, but whose ulterior aim is to augment their arsenal of racist repression. During the 1970s, a rapist was terrorizing the Berkeley community. He initially attacked scores and scores of Black women. Hundreds of rapes in the area were attributed to "Stinky," as he was called. However, it was not until he began to rape white women, and specifically when he raped a well-known Black woman television newscaster, that the police began to turn their attention to the case. They released a description of him so general that it probably fit no less than a third of the Black men in the area, and countless men were arrested for no other reason than that they were Black. Moreover, Berkeley police proposed to the city council a strategy to capture Stinky that involved hiring more police officers, acquiring helicopters and other aircraft, and using tracking and attack dogs. The police department had been attempting to get approval for the use of dogs since the student movement of the 1960s, but had failed because of community opposition. In order to implement their repressive agenda, they seized a moment in which many of the women in the community felt utterly terror-stricken. Unfortunately, the antirape movement, which at that time was almost exclusively white, did not perceive the hidden agenda of the police force and agreed to cooperate with the proposed strategy. Thus, they unwittingly became collaborators in a plan that would inevitably result in increased police brutality in Berkeley's Black community.

The antirape movement today must remain cognizant of such potential pitfalls. It must beware of concentrating exclusively on strategies such as crisis centers, which, important as they may be, treat only the effects and leave the cause of the crime unremedied. The very same social conditions that spawn racist violence—the same social conditions that encourage attacks on workers, and the political posture that justifies U.S. intervention in Central America and aid to the apartheid government in South Africa—encourage sexual violence. Thus, sexual violence can never be completely eradicated until we have successfully effected a whole range of radical social transformations in our country.

We must strive to link our efforts to ensure the safety of women with our concern for the safety of this planet. It is no coincidence that the explosion of sexual violence in this country takes place at a time when the United States government has developed the means with which to annihilate human life itself. It is no accident that a government that spends $41 million an hour on the most devastating instruments of violence ever known in human history, also encourages the perpetuation of violence on all levels of society, including sexual attacks on women. It has been calculated that $200 million, just five hours of military spending, could provide annual support for sixteen hundred rape crisis centers and battered women's shelters.

We will never get past the first step in eliminating the horrendous violence done to women in our society if we do not recognize that rape is only one element in the complex structure of women's oppression. And the systematic oppression of women in our society cannot be accurately evaluated except as it is connected to racism and class exploitation at home and imperialist aggression and the potential nuclear holocaust that menace the entire globe.

The antirape movement should therefore attempt to establish closer ties to other campaigns for women's rights, as well as to labor struggles wherever they unfold. If we are militant activists challenging violence against women, we must also fulfill our duties as fearless fighters against police violence, and we must express our passionate solidarity with the racially and nationally oppressed people who are its main targets. We must defend, for example, the memory of Eleanor Bumpurs, the sixty-seven-year-old Black woman from the Bronx who was murdered in 1984 by New York Housing Authority policemen because she took a stand and attempted to resist eviction.

The banners and voices we raise against rape must also be raised against racist and anti-Semitic Ku Klux Klan and Nazi violence. They must be raised in defense of political prisoners like Leonard Peltier, the Native American Indian leader, and Johnny Imani Harris, the Black prison activist who, after twelve long years, was removed from Alabama's death row.

If we aspire to eradicate sexual violence, we must also call for the immediate freedom of Nelson and Winnie Mandela and all political prisoners in South

Africa. Our sisters and brothers in Nicaragua and El Salvador need our solidarity, as do our Palestinian friends who are fighting for their land and their dignity. And certainly, we cannot forget our Iranian sisters who are attempting to complete the democratic revolution that has been violently stifled by Khomeini's Islamic Republic.

To recognize the larger sociopolitical context of the contemporary epidemic of sexist violence does not, however, mean that we ignore the specific and concrete necessity for the ongoing campaign against rape. This battle must be waged quite concretely on all of its myriad fronts. As we further shape the theoretical foundation of the antirape movement and as we implement practical tasks, let us constantly remind ourselves that even as individual victories are claimed, the complete elimination of sexist violence will ultimately depend on our ability to forge a new and revolutionary global order, in which every form of oppression and violence against humankind is obliterated.

NOTES

1. June Jordan, *Passion* (Boston: Beacon Press, 1980).
2. cf. Noreen Connell and Cassandra Wilson, ed., *Rape: The First Sourcebook for Women by New York Radical Feminists* (New York: New American Library, 1974).
3. Jo Freeman, ed., *Women: A Feminist Perspective* (Palo Alto: Mayfield Publishing Co., 1975).
4. Julia and Herman Schwendinger, *Rape and Inequality* (Beverly Hills: Sage Library of Social Research, 1983), p. 23.
5. cf. Paula Giddings, *When and Where I Enter* (New York: William Morrow, 1984), chap. 6.
6. Schwendinger, op. cit., p. 50.
7. Ibid.
8. Arlene Eisen, *Women in Vietnam* (San Francisco: People's Press, 1975), p. 62.
9. Schwendinger, op. cit., p. 203.

Ron Simmons (1950–)

Since his undergraduate days, when he wrote weekly columns on gay and lesbian issues for the campus newspaper at the State University of New York at Albany, Ron Simmons has published numerous articles and made films that contemplate the nature of gay life-styles and homophobia. He earned his bachelor's and master's from SUNY-Albany and his doctorate in mass communications from Howard University.

Simmons is a filmmaker, professor, and community activist in addition to a writer. He has written, produced, and directed over a dozen video and film productions. Most notably, he served as the still photographer and the Washington, D.C., field producer on Tongues Untied *(1989), an award-winning black gay documentary film. He has also taught in the department of radio, TV, and film at Howard University. As a community activist, Simmons has served as the coordinator of public relations in the Newark Public Schools (1973–76) and as executive director of the Institute for the Preservation and Study of African American Writing in Washington, D.C. (1985–86). Presently, he is executive director of Us Helping Us, People into Living, a nonprofit organization committed to teaching people with HIV/AIDS the various ways of treating the disease through natural, holistic therapies.*

"Some Thoughts on the Challenges Facing Black Gay Intellectuals" was originally published in the anthology Brother to Brother: New Writings by Black Gay

Men *(1991), edited by Essex Hemphill. As a companion piece to Charles I. Nero's "Toward a Black Gay Aesthetic" (**see p. 971 in Part Six**), Simmons argues that the African American community brands homosexuals as enemies of black progress and thereby negates the contributions that Black gay intellectuals make to that community.*

Some Thoughts on the Challenges Facing Black Gay Intellectuals

One of the most serious challenges facing black gay intellectuals is the development of a progressive view of homosexuality in the African American community. Such a perspective is needed to assist the larger African American community's struggle for self-determination by freeing it from the limitations of homophobia, as well as to liberate and self-actualize black gay genius. Unfortunately, the black gay scholar is faced with a unique burden when intellectualizing with his or her racial peers.[1] Because we are gay, they believe our lives are invalid and our knowledge irrelevant. The insight black gay scholars may provide on the critical problems confronting the African American community is ignored by our heterosexual brothers and sisters who are attempting to solve those problems. Indeed, they often think of homosexuality as one more problem caused by white oppression.

In the African American community, "homophobia" is not so much a fear of "homosexuals" but a fear that homosexuality will become pervasive in the community. Thus, a homophobic person can accept a homosexual as an individual friend or family member, yet not accept homosexuality. This is the attitude that predominates in the African American community. The motivation for homophobia is "heterosexism"—the belief that heterosexual sex is good and proper, and homosexual sex is bad and immoral.

Historically, discussions and theories on homosexuality in the African American community have been offered by scholars who have little, if any, understanding of the homosexual experience. Homophobic and heterosexist viewpoints are espoused by some of our most respected leaders, writers, and scholars, such as Nathan Hare, Jawanza Kunjufu, Robert Staples, Louis Farrakhan, Molefi Asante, Haki Madhubuti, Amiri Baraka, and Yosuf Ben-Jochannan.

There are three basic challenges facing black gay intellectuals. First, we must develop an analysis and understanding of homosexuality in the African American community that is affirming and constructive. Second, we must correct the bias and misinformation put forth by black homophobic and heterosexist scholars. Third, we must not allow the hurt and anger we may feel toward such scholars to cause us to dismiss them or their ideas on other issues that we may agree on.

Black Homophobic Literature

In reviewing African American literature, one finds that black homophobic and heterosexist scholars believe homosexuality in the African American community is the result of (1) the emasculation of black men by white oppression (e.g., Staples, Madhubuti, Asante, Farrakhan, and Baraka); (2) the breakdown of the family structure and the loss of male role models (e.g., Kunjufu, Madhubuti,

Farrakhan, and Hare); (3) a sinister plot perpetuated by diabolical racists who want to destroy the black race (e.g., Hare); and (4) immorality as defined in biblical scriptures, Koranic suras, or Egyptian "Books of the Dead" (e.g., Farrakhan and Ben-Jochannan).

In their 1984 book, *The Endangered Black Family: Coping with the Unisexualization and Coming Extinction of the Black Race,* Nathan Hare and his wife, Julia, cite ancient Greece and the modern Western world as examples of societies in a "state of decay" where norms and values are confused, and

> people are alienated and set apart from their natural origins. [In such societies] there emerges a breakdown in childrearing and socialization. . . . Without a solid core to their personalities, children—grow up confused—develop[ing] problems of identity, most notably that of gender confusion. Homosexuality accordingly will proliferate.[2]

The Hares' view of black homosexuality is a simple one in which "homosexuality," "gender confusion," and "sex-change operations" are synonymous. To them, homosexuality, along with "unisexualization," "feminism," and "birth control," are all part of a genocidal plot masterminded by the "white liberal-radical-moderate-establishment coalition." The Hares feel "no need to engage in endless debates about the pros and cons of homosexuality. . . . Homosexuality does not promote black family stability and—historically has been a product largely of European society."[3]

The Hares are what Jawanza Kunjufu calls "traditionalists."[4] They long for a primal past in which the male role was "protection [and] providing" while the female attended to "nurturing and gathering."[5] They lament, "Where once there were pretty women and working men, there now are pretty men and working women."[6]

Both the Hares and Kunjufu believe that black boys become homosexuals because of the preponderance of white female schoolteachers; the Hares, in particular, claim that "white teachers infiltrate black child centers, nurseries and primary schools, compelling black boys to play with blonde dolls in the name of progress."[7]

Nathan and Julia Hare's homophobic raving does not negate the fact that there may be racist genocidal plots against the black community, or that black men are systematically destroyed. Our homosexuality, however, is not a part of such plots and our love is not genocidal. It is their divisive homophobic and heterosexist reactions to our natural sexual expression that play into the plot of divide and conquer.

Robert Staples, in his book *Black Masculinity,* asserts that the "nation's prisons are the main places where homosexual preferences are evident—because of the unavailability of women."[8] He goes on to allege that some black men continue the "homosexual lifestyle" after being released for various reasons, "ranging from a desire to escape family responsibilities to acquiring money through prostitution." The increasing visibility of black lesbians, according to Staples, is a result of "the shortage of Black men or—the conflict in male/female relationships." He also contends that black homosexuals are "deeply involved in the white homosexual community."[9]

In a 1983 speech at Morgan State University, Minister Louis Farrakhan cited incarceration and the lack of positive male role models as causes of homosexuality among black men, stating:

> Those of you—who are homosexual—you weren't born [that] way brother—You never had a strong male image. . . . [These] are conditions that are forced on black men. You're filling up the jails and they're turning [you] into freaks in the jails.[10]

In his book *Afrocentricity,* Molefi Asante also blames "prison breeding" for the "outburst of homosexuality among black men." He is particularly outraged that "black gays are often put in front of white or integrated organizations to show the liberalism of the group." To Asante, homosexuality is a "white decadence" that cannot be condoned or accepted. It can, however, be "tolerated until such time as our families and schools are engaged in Afrocentric instruction for males."[11]

Asante suggests that gay brothers and submerge their homosexuality to satisfy what he terms the "collective will," stating:

> Afrocentric relationships are based upon . . . what is best for the collective imperative of the people. . . . All brothers who are homosexuals should know that they too can become committed to the collective will. It means the submergence of their own wills into the collective will of our people.[12]

Haki Madhubuti claims in his book *Enemies: The Clash of Races* that there is a preponderance of black homosexuals in the higher socio-economic groups. He believes that homosexuality is backward, abnormal, and "rampant in significant parts of the black community":

> It is a profound comment on the power of the system that [it] is able to transform black men into sexual lovers of each other. . . . On many black college campuses [and in] the black church, homosexuality and bisexuality [have become] an accepted norm. And far too often these homosexual Black men, because of their *sensitivity, talent and connections* are found in the most sensitive positions of responsibility in the . . . working world . . . actually directing many community, political and educational programs [emphasis added].[13]

Ironically, in a footnote, Madhubuti presents a voice of reason about the "human complexity of homosexuality." Calling for understanding and dialogue, he states that:

> Black homosexuality is on the rise and the question becomes do we enlist them into our struggle, or do we continue to alienate and make enemies of them? . . . If we are truly conscious adults we have to show a sensitivity to their personal differences as well as the political and cultural differences of our people.[14]

That such logic and compassion would be relegated to a footnote might indicate a fear on Madhubuti's part of appearing soft on homosexuality. In the black community, a male is often forced to denounce homosexuality in order to avoid suspicion. Calls for understanding and dialogue must be posed as tactical maneuvers, not strategic goals. Nathan and Julia Hare present a similar stance in

The Endangered Black Family. After claiming that homosexuality does not promote black family stability, they state:

> On the other hand—and this is crucial—we will refuse to embark on one more tangent of displaced contempt and misdirected scorn for the homosexualized [*sic*] black brothers or sisters and drive them over to the camp of the white liberal-radical-moderate-establishment coalition. What we must do is offer the homosexual brother or sister a proper compassion and acceptance without advocacy. . . . Some of them may yet be saved. And yet, we must declare open warfare upon the sources of [their] confusion.[15]

Haki Madhubuti published *Enemies* in 1978. Twelve years later, he published another book titled *Black Men: Obsolete, Single, Dangerous? The Afrikan American Family in Transition: Essays in Discovery, Solution, and Hope.* Despite the intriguing title, Madhubuti is hopeless in discovering or understanding black men who are gay. In fact, he regresses on the gay issue. Whereas a footnote in *Enemies* called for "dialogue" and "sensitivity," in *Black Men,* Madhubuti offers no insight whatsoever on homosexuality. He does not even categorize gays as black men, stating, "Much of the current Black studies have focused on either the Black family, Black women, Afrika, the Black homosexual community or Europe's and America's influence on the Black world. Few Black scholars or activists have given serious attention to the condition of Black men."[16]

In analyzing homosexuality, Madhubuti returns to the "white oppression" model. In a listing of the "most prevalent tactics [used by the] U.S. white supremacy system to disrupt black families and neutralize black men," he states that one tactic is to make black men into "so-called 'women,' in which case homosexual and bisexual activity becomes the norm rather than the exception. Men of other cultures do not fear the so-called 'woman-like' men of any race."[17]

Madhubuti seems incapable of envisioning black gay men as anything other than effeminate men who pretend to be women. He doesn't realize that black men who are soft and feminine are still a threat to the system if they are politically conscious. Loving each other as men does not make black gays any less dangerous to the racist status quo. As a group, black gays can only be accused of being as politically "unconscious" as our heterosexual peers.

The lack of insight about African American homosexuality displayed by some of our heterosexual intellectuals is tragic. Their simplistic and shortsighted analyses promote ignorance and confusion in the African American community, and the oppression of black gays and lesbians. This oppression cripples the vital resources of the community insomuch as it requires a tremendous amount of energy to hate one another, as opposed to utilizing our differences constructively toward empowerment of the African American community.

Respond with Love, Not Anger

Confronted by racial oppression in the larger society and sexual oppression in our own community, black gay intellectuals face formidable challenges. As stated earlier, we must not allow ourselves to be paralyzed by the hurt, anger, and rage we may feel toward homophobic and heterosexist scholars. Rejecting us is their loss—and it comes back to haunt us *all.* We have the right to criticize their erroneous ideas and to help build a better world for everyone. We know the reality of our lives. We know that we are not gay because of "prison." The vast majority of black gay men have never been near a prison. For Staples, Farrakhan, and Asante to suggest that most black gay men are gay because of prison shows a serious lack of competent insight and scholarship.

We know we are not gay because of "white oppression." Too many of us realized we were "different" during preadolescence before we knew what racism was or who white people were. Our feelings for other males were not taught by white schoolteachers or white dolls. America has done everything in its power to make black men hate themselves. Black men have been taught for hundreds of years that they are worthless. Yet despite this, black gay men love each other. We have protected, comforted, and cared for ourselves, and for thousands of our brothers, in a white society that despises our "blackness" and in a black community that condemns our love. When black men love each other in an environment that negates them, it is not a sign of sickness. It is a sign of health.

As gay men, we know that our desire to love each other is not wrong. There is a sacredness in the act of men loving men. We have experienced the exultation of brothers bonding together. Countless precious moments we have shared with friends and lovers validate the value of our lives. The sacredness of our love is our strength. It gives us the courage to challenge the homophobia and heterosexism of our brothers and sisters, and sustains us in the face of their rejection and ridicule.

It is our task to provide an understanding and a vision of homosexuality motivated by our love and not our anger. Anger eats within. It destroys the person who is angry more often than the subject of the anger. Love nurtures and strengthens us to challenge our brothers and sisters because we love them too much to allow their ignorance to continue.

We must help Haki Madhubuti see that his homophobia and heterosexism kept him separated from Max Robinson, his "friend and brother in the struggle." Robinson's death had a great impact on Madhubuti's feelings about AIDS. Before Robinson's death, Madhubuti was "convinced that AIDS was a white middle-class homosexual disease that, at worse, would only touch Black homosexuals." The first time he saw Robinson in the hospital, Madhubuti was "inwardly crushed" by Robinson's emaciated look and found it difficult to "keep back the tears." He states:

> Max did not tell me that he had AIDS. . . . According to him, he was improving quickly and would be able to go home soon. I let it go at that, and two months later—without my seeing him again—Max was dead. It was his wish that people know he died of AIDS and did not contract it through the *assumed avenues* of drug use or homosexual activity. Max was a woman's man to the bone (one of his problems), and he did drink a great deal.[18]

Madhubuti's tale of Max Robinson's death is tragic in so many ways. It is a tragedy that on his deathbed Max Robinson had to lie to his friend. He did not tell Madhubuti the nature and extent of his illness, nor the nature and extent of his sexuality because he probably knew that Madhubuti viewed AIDS as something that "at worse, would only touch black homosexuals." Members of the black gay community knew that Robinson was more complex than simply being a "woman's man to the bone," and perhaps this pretense, that people like Madhubuti forced upon him, contributed to Robinson's three divorces and his drinking problem.

Baraka's Dilemma: To Be or Not to Be?

Too often the homophobia and heterosexism within the African American community forces men to be the "hardest hard." They must nullify any feelings and emotions others may consider unmanly. To prove their manhood, they will often attack that which they fear in themselves. Amiri Baraka (born Everett Leroy Jones) constantly denounces homosexuality in his writings. He despises "faggots" and believes being called one is the worst insult a man can suffer. In "A Poem for Black Hearts," Baraka praises the late Malcolm X as a "black god" whose death black men must avenge or be called "faggots till the end of the earth."[19]

Faggots are the epitome of what Baraka opposes. "Faggot" is the description he uses to insult black leaders he disagrees with. In the poem "Black Art," he speaks of the "negro leader on the steps of the white house—kneeling between the sheriff's thighs negotiating coolly for his people."[20] In "Civil Rights Poem," Baraka begins by stating, "Roywilkins is an eternal faggot. His spirit is a faggot."[21] In the poem "The Black Man Is Making New Gods," he refers to the crucifixion of Christ as "The Fag's Death they give us on a cross."[22] For Baraka, faggots have no redeeming qualities and should be persecuted as a matter of principle. In the poem "Hegel," he states, "I am not saying 'Let the State fuck its faggots,' only that no fag go unfucked, for purely impersonal reasons."[23]

In plays such as *The Baptism* and *The Toilet,* Baraka portrays homosexuals as degenerates and cowards.[24] They are weak, soft, and unmanly. Gay men are the antithesis of what he idealizes as the "Black man," and they become synonymous with his image of white men. In an essay titled "American Sexual Reference: Black Male," he writes "Most American white men are trained to be fags. . . . [T]heir faces are weak and blank . . . that red flush, those silk blue faggot eyes."[25]

According to Baraka, since white men have black men doing their manual labor, white men have become "estranged from . . . actual physical work." As a consequence, white men are alienated from reality and nature. They have no real "claim to manhood." He states:

> [A] people who lose their self-sufficiency because they depend on their "subjects" to do the world's work become effeminate and perverted. . . . Do you understand the softness of the white man, the weakness . . . the estrangement from reality? Can you for a second imagine the average middle-class white man able to do somebody harm? Alone? Without the technology that at this moment [allows] him [to] rule the world.[26]

Baraka characterizes white men as spineless, middle-class bureaucrats, and black men as natural super-strong studs. To support his position, he points with pride to the fact that blacks dominate the "manly art" of boxing.[27]

Amiri Baraka is a fascinating study of the homosexual-heterosexual conflict among African American males, for the tragic irony is that the "faggot" Baraka attacks so viciously is in reality himself. He has never reconciled his homosexual past with his persona as the clenched-fist black militant leading mass movements, the perfect example of the black warrior. This conflict is alluded to in "Tone Poem" in which he writes:

> Read this line young colored or white and know I felt the twist of dividing memory. Blood spoiled in the air, caked and anonymous. Arms opening, opened last night, we sat up howling and kissing. Men who loved each other. Will that be understood? That we could, and still move under cold nights with clenched-fists.[28]

Perhaps it is the homosexual desires Baraka had as an adolescent and young adult that motivate his homophobia. His homosexual desires are not revealed in *The Autobiography of LeRoi Jones.* No, to truly understand the paradox of Baraka's need to denounce faggots while at the same time suppressing his attraction, one must read an autobiographical novel he wrote twenty years earlier, *The System of Dante's Hell.*[29] It is a story many gay brothers can relate to. After reading it, one's anger toward Baraka's homophobia is replaced with sympathy. We understand the pain and the fear.

Before he deemed himself Imamu Amiri Baraka, before he divorced his white wife, before he changed the spelling of his name from Leroy, to LeRoi, Baraka was a "short . . . skinny . . . runt [with] big bulbous eyes." He felt inadequate because of his size and was obsessed with growing taller. In grade school, his peers told him about "dicks and pussies and fags and bulldaggers." He saw how people reacted to "cocksuckers," and he grew to understand "what fucking was and what it had to do with sucking."[30]

As a teenager Baraka pretended to have only heterosexual desires, for he understood the penalty of being a faggot. "We did a lot of things, [those] years. . . . We [told] lies to keep from getting belted, and [watched] a faggot take a beating in the snow from our lie. Our fear."[31]

As an undergraduate at Howard University, Baraka saw gay men harassed and ridiculed.[32] He felt alienated. It was at Howard that he changed his name to LeRoi, and began to read Gertrude Stein.[33] Poor grades, however, forced him to leave Howard in his junior year. He joined the Air Force and was stationed at various bases, including one in Rantoul, Illinois, near Chicago. It was in Chicago, that he again engaged in homosexuality. In *The System of Dante's Hell,* he writes:

> In Chicago I kept making the queer scene. Under the "El" with a preacher. . . . [He] held my head under the quilt. The first guy . . . spoke to me grinning and I said my name was Stephen Dedalus. . . . One more guy and it was over. On the train, I wrote all this down. A journal now sitting in a tray on top the closet. . . . The journal says "Am I like that?"[34]

Once more, Baraka found himself disconnected and alienated.[35] His homosexual desires would not cease. He felt guilty and frightened of himself. "My cold sin in the cities," he writes; "My fear of my own death's insanity, and an actual longing for men that brooked in each finger of my memory."[36]

One night in the "Bottom," a poor black ghetto in Shreveport, Louisiana, the shame Baraka feels as a homosexual reaches a climax when he finds himself drunk in a whorehouse, dancing with a prostitute named Peaches. He becomes ill and attempts to leave, but she prevents him.

> She came around and rubbed my tiny pecker with her fingers. And still I moved away. I saw the look she gave me and wanted somehow to protest, say, "I'm sorry. I'm fucked up. My mind, is screwy, I don't know why. I can't think. I'm sick. I've been fucked in the ass. I love books. . . . You don't want me. Please, Please, don't want me."[37]

Outside, Peaches and her friends tease Baraka like some "fag" by taking his cap and tossing it amongst themselves.[38] To get his hat back, Baraka agrees to buy Peaches another drink. He, too, has more to drink and becomes more intoxicated. Overwhelmed with shame, he longs to be "Some other soul, than the filth I feel. Have in me. Guilt like something of God's. Some separate suffering self."[39] Voices begin to haunt him. "You've got to like girls. Say something. . . . Move. Frightened bastard. Frightened scared sissy motherfucker."[40]

Delirious, Baraka reminisces about his cold sin in the cities.

> It was Chicago. The fags and the winter. Sick thin boy, comes out of those els. . . . To go back. To sit lonely. Need to be used, touched. . . . I hate it. . . . To feel myself go soft and want some person not myself. . . . That I walked the streets hunting for warmth. To be pushed under a quilt, and call it love. To shit water for days and say I've been loved. Been warm.[41]

After dragging Baraka back to her house, Peaches strips him and grabs his penis. He is unable to get an erection. She chastises him and becomes violent.

> She pulled, breathing spit on my chest. "Comeon, Baby, Comeon. . . . Get hard. . . . Get hard." And she slapped me now, with her hand. A short hard punch. . . . She cursed and pulled as hard as she could. [She said] "You don't like women, huh? . . . No wonder you so pretty . . . ol bigeye faggot. . . . God-dam punk, you gonna fuck me tonight or I'm gonna pull your fuckin dick aloose."
>
> I was crying now. Hot hot tears and trying to . . . say to Peaches, "Please, you don't know me. Not what's in my head. I'm beautiful. Stephen Dedalus. . . . Feel my face, how tender. My eyes. . . ."
>
> And I [thought] of a black man under the el who took me home. . . . I remembered telling him all these things. . . . And [crawling] out of bed in the morning. . . . Loved. Afraid.
>
> [Peaches] started yelling. Faggot. Faggot. Sissy. Motherfucker. And I pumped myself. Straining. Threw my hips at her. And she yelled, for me to fuck her. Fuck her. Fuck me, you lousy fag. And I twisted, spitting tears, and hitting my hips on hers, pounding my flesh in her, hearing myself weep.[42]

After fucking Peaches, Baraka dresses and leaves. He stumbles through the streets, lost and intoxicated. A gay man approaches him in the darkness saying, "Lemme suck yo dick, honey. . . ." Once again Baraka is confronted with homosexual desire. The man begs him, but Baraka won't give in. Peaches has freed him of his past. He walks away as the gay man screams behind him like "some hurt ugly thing dying alone."[43]

Baraka returns to Peaches's house to sleep. He awakes a new man, a heterosexual man.

> I woke up. . . . And I felt myself smiling. . . . [It] seemed that things had come to order. . . . It seemed settled. . . . I thought of black men sitting on their beds this Saturday of my life listening quietly to their wives' soft talk. And felt the world grow together as I hadn't known it. All lies before, I thought. All fraud and sickness. This was the world. . . . I cursed Chicago, and softened at the world. "You look so sweet," [Peaches] was saying. "Like you're real rested."[44]

Understanding Baraka's life turns our anger toward him to sympathy; indeed, pity. That he would feel so much guilt and shame for desiring male love is the lesser tragedy. The greater tragedy is that once he claims "heterosexuality," perhaps as a disguise, he then denounces and ridicules "faggots" so vehemently. How could a factor of life affording him the opportunity to be understanding and compassionate become one of pathetic hypocrisy? Baraka is not the first man to become a homophobe after experiencing homosexuality or repressing homosexual desire. We have encountered his kind before. Have taken them to our beds and soothed their fears. Made them feel whole in our arms. Our anger will not help these brothers to understand that they fear themselves. We must show them through compassion and understanding that one can be gay and be a socially, culturally and politically useful man. We can be gay and committed to "Blackness," committed to the liberation of black people. We can be clenched-fist militants no matter what gender we love.

Clap If You Believe

We can specifically reject the homophobia and heterosexism of writers and scholars such as Madhubuti, Asante, and others, but we should not allow our rejection of their ideas and opinions in regard to those issues to prevent us from supporting them on issues we agree on. We cannot totally reject them. Our common problems as African Americans are too immense and our common resources too scarce. We may all agree with Madhubuti when he observes that:

> [M]any Black men have defined their lives as Black duplicates of the white male ethos. . . . Black men, acting out of frustration and *ignorance,* adopt attitudes that are not productive or progressive. . . . The political and sexual games that . . . are demeaning and disrespectful . . . become, due to a lack of *self-definition,* Black men's games also.[45]

We should also include homophobia as another attitude that black males have adopted largely from the white culture.

If Madhubuti is sincere in his call for "sensitivity [to the] personal differences as well as the political and cultural differences" of black people, we can indeed achieve understanding and dialogue. We can work with him if he truly believes that:

> *The search for truth* should always be our guiding force. . . . Always be willing to question past actions as well as accept constructive criticism. Advocating an Afrikan American cultural movement doesn't mean being dogmatic and insensitive to other positions. Good is good, no matter where it comes from.[46]

If we, as African American people, join together in a "search for truth" that is mutually respectful of our differences, we will all benefit from the insights uncovered and the constructive criticism offered by each other. As black gays and lesbians, we must develop alliances with progressive black groups, organizations, and individuals to work together for the common good of the black community.

Developing an alliance with an organization such as the Nation of Islam, however, may not be as simple. Minister Farrakhan is undoubtedly becoming one of the great African American orators of this century in the tradition of Dr. King, Malcolm X, Du Bois, and others. Millions of people listen to his speeches and respect what he says. He has an ability to communicate ideas that is exciting to behold. Unfortunately, Farrakhan's homophobic and heterosexist comments contribute to the oppression of black gays, lesbians, and women.

In 1990, members of the Nation of Islam began to run for political office in Washington, D.C., and in Maryland. If Farrakhan or his followers were to gain political power in the community, to what extent would their policies be secular rather than religious? Would they advocate that all issues in the black community be decided by the Koran?

Why should Africa's descendants base their lives and their future on the Koran, or the Bible? With all due respect, the Koran is not an artifact of African culture, it is Arabian. And the Bible in its present form was given to us by white slavemasters. Indeed, both books were introduced to Africa by people more interested in increasing their wealth than in Africa's well-being. Europeans and Arabs enslaved Africans. We don't owe them anything, so why should we be subservient to their books?

On May 20, 1990, Minister Farrakhan gave a speech in Oakland entitled, "The Time and What Must Be Done," in which he stated that African Americans are "polluted" by the decadence of white society. He advocated the strict enforcement of Old Testament and Koranic laws to force black people out of their wickedness and degeneracy. As the audience cheered, Farrakhan proclaimed that to save the nation, "the punishment for sleeping with your daughter—is death" and "the punishment for rape is death." He also included adultery and homosexuality as crimes that should be punished by death, stating:

> God is no respector of persons—[Y]our mother is not above the law. Your brother, your sister, your friend—nobody is above God's law.
>
> Do you know why [in biblical times] they [stoned you to death] for adultery? Because there is nothing more sacred than marriage and family. Nothing . . . [applause]. And every time you stone [an adulterer] you're killing the thought in your own mind. . . . You make an example [by stoning someone] because the individual is not more important than the community [or the] nation. So you sacrifice the individual for the preservation of a nation. [applause]
>
> Now brothers, in the Holy world you can't switch. [Farrakhan walks across the stage like an effeminate man] No, no, no . . . in the Holy world you better hide that stuff 'cause see if God made you for a woman, you can't go with a man. . . . You know what the penalty of that is in the Holy land? Death. . . . They don't play with that . . . [he laughs] Sister get to going with another sister—Both women [are decapitated.][47]

It is dangerous and unwise for Farrakhan to equate homosexuality and adultery with rape and child molestation. The former are victimless activities between consenting adults. The latter are acts of victimization using force and coercion. Has Farrakhan forgotten the dilemma he and Malcolm X faced when they discovered that the Honorable Elijah Muhammad was a *repeated* adulterer? On page 295 of his autobiography, Malcolm states:

> As far back as 1955, I had heard hints. . . . [My] mind simply refused to accept anything so grotesque as adultery mentioned in the same breath with Mr. Muhammad's name. . . .
>
> [In April 1963,] I told Mr. Muhammad what was being said. . . . Elijah Muhammad [replied,] "When you read about how David took another man's wife, I'm that David. You read about Noah, who got drunk—that's me. You read about Lot, who went and laid up with his own daughters. I have to fulfill all of those things."
>
> I found—some [Muslim officials] had already heard [the rumors]. One of them, Minister Louis [Farrakhan] of Boston, as much as seven months before. They had been living with the dilemma themselves.[48]

Farrakhan did not call for the death penalty to punish the Honorable Elijah Muhammad's adultery. No, he remained silent. And after Malcolm X left the Nation of Islam, Farrakhan was given Malcolm's former position as the head of the New York City Mosque.

It is a mistake, tactically and strategically, to advocate the killing of black gays and lesbians. Why encourage more death in the African American community? Too many black men are being killed daily. Farrakhan's statements against homosexuality give the men who follow him a license to harass black men and women who they think are gay. Persecuting gays reinforces a false sense of manhood. Rather than confront the real enemy—those who actually cause and control the oppression—their frustrations caused by powerlessness are soothed by intimidating those who they consider weak. It's easy to prove your manhood by putting down "faggots." Baraka did it for years.

The Bible and the Koran are not the only holy books used to defend heterosexism and homophobia. Egyptologists and African historians, such as Yosef Ben-Jochannan, refer to the *Book of Coming Forth by Day and by Night* (better known as the Egyptian Book of the Dead) as an Egyptian spiritual text that condemns homosexuality. Ben-Jochannan is clearly one of the foremost African scholars of the twentieth century. Thus, his claims that the ancient Egyptians forbade homosexuality must be investigated seriously by black gay scholars.

In his book *The Black Man's Religion,* Ben-Jochannan lists twenty-nine of the forty-two "Negative Confessions" that a departed Egyptian soul had to affirm on the Day of Judgment. The Negative Confessions are rules to live by, similar to the Ten Commandments. Two of the confessions he cites refer to sexual activity: number 19—"I have not defiled the wife of a man"—and number 27—"I have not committed acts of impurity or sodomy."[49]

For a reference, Ben-Jochannan cites E. A. Wallis Budge's *The Egyptian Book of the Dead.* Budge, however, does not use the word "sodomy." According to Budge, three of the forty-two Negative Confessions stated in the hieroglyphic text refer to sexual activity: number 11—"I have not committed fornication"; number 21—"I have not defiled the wife of a man"; and number 22—"I have not polluted, or defiled, myself."[50] It is the latter confession that Ben-Jochannan misinterpreted as forbidding homosexuality. A study of the actual hieroglyph with the assistance of a hieroglyphic dictionary reveals that the Negative Confession of "polluting or defiling" oneself actually refers to "masturbation [or the] irregular emission of semen," not sodomy.[51] Within the dictionary, there is a hieroglyphics symbol that means "sodomy" and it is not used anywhere in the Negative Confessions.

Redefining Ourselves and Our Future

While it is critically important to rebut homophobia and heterosexism, the most crucial challenge facing black gay scholars is to develop an affirming and liberating philosophical understanding of homosexuality that will self-actualize black gay genius. Such a task requires a new epistemology, a new way of "knowing," that incorporates the views our African ancestors had about the material and the metaphysical world. We can no longer accept American society's views of us and the purpose of our lives. We should see ourselves as "geniuses" in the root sense of the world, i.e., *genii*—divine spirits that have a higher purpose to manifest on the physical plane.

In some African cultures, gays were considered blessed because the Creator had endowed them with both male and female principles. Often they served as the spiritual advisors for the community.[52] In light of this should we be surprised that so many gay men are active in the black church?

Another important issue we must address is the role that gay men will play in the socialization of black males. Our younger brothers desperately need an outlook on life that goes beyond the world of Hollywood or Madison Avenue. They need role models and rituals that symbolize rites of passage from childhood to adulthood. Young gay males, in particular, and black males generally, need a definition of "manhood" radically different from the one adopted through assimilation. Such a definition must liberate and empower us, enhance our self-esteem and stimulate the manifestation of creative potential. Black male youth need to know that the measure of a man should be based not on the gender of his sex partner, but on his contribution to the community.

The argument that homosexuality threatens black male-female relationships and the black family lacks credibility. Homosexual love does not destabilize true heterosexual love relationships, the black family, or the black community. If a man is sexually attracted to other men, but community homophobia forces him to hide his feelings, he might marry a woman who then bears their children. Should that man one day be unable to sustain the psychic pain of ignoring his true sexual feelings and leave his family, the fault lies not in his homosexuality but in the community's homophobia that forced him to live a lie.

Our straight brothers and sisters need to be more honest and to admit that their relationships are falling apart even when both parties are staunch heterosexuals. The sisters are constantly complaining about "niggers," while the brothers complain about "bitches." Between them there's an abundance of blame, anger, distrust, and hatred, but little love.

Gay men *do* contribute to the black family. A significant number of us are fathers who support our children. Many of us have nieces and nephews whom we advise, guide, and watch out for. We send money to our parents and give shelter to cousins. Unfortunately, homophobia in the black community forces many of us into "closets." We don't say we're gay, thus our families and the community do not realize the significant contributions we make as gay and lesbian members of the family and the community.

The freeing of black gay genius requires that we develop institutions to secure the foundation of the black gay community. Madhubuti's call for "dialogue" notwithstanding, homophobic statements such as his, and those of Molefi Asante and Nathan Hare, indicate that their tolerance for homosexuality is one of expediency. The reality of our situation dictates that we negotiate with them, and others like them, from a position of cultural, economic, and political strength in the mutual understanding of needing each other.

To achieve the goals outlined herein, the political consciousness of black gay men will have to be raised. Too often, we are narrowly focused on fabulous parties, fierce clubs, fashion, face, and fun. There is a desperate need for organizations to provide social activities that are culturally, educationally, and politically constructive. Organizations such as Gay Men of African Descent (GMAD) in New York City, and Adodi and Unity, Inc., in Philadelphia, should be commended for their efforts in this area.

The tasks faced by black gay intellectuals are formidable. The problems we confront are complex and intertwined. To the extent that our people are homophobic and heterosexist, our tasks become more difficult. We should acknowledge the "sensitivities" and "talents" within us, the root of which is black gay genius. We have been blessed with gifts to share in a society that views love and tenderness between men as a weakness. As we balance and synthesize the male and female energy within our souls, we come closer to the Supreme Being. The inner Voice tells us that our feelings of love are righteous. Black men loving black men is indeed a sacred act.

NOTES

1. This essay focuses on black gay males. It does not address the experiences of black lesbians. Thus, the masculine pronoun and possessive will be used in most cases.
2. Nathan Hare and Julia Hare, *The Endangered Black Family: Coping with the Unisexualization and Coming Extinction of the Black Race* (San Francisco: Black Think Tank, 1984), p. 64.
3. Ibid., p. 65.
4. See Jawanza Kunjufu, "Not Allowed to Be Friends and/or Lovers," in *Crisis Black Sexual Politics,* ed. Nathan Hare and Julia Hare (San Francisco: Black Think Tank, 1989), p. 110.
5. Hare and Hare, *The Endangered Black Family,* p. 151.
6. Nathan Hare and Julia Hare, eds., *Crisis in Black Sexual Politics* (San Francisco: Black Think Tank), p. 2.
7. Hare and Hare, *The Endangered Black Family,* p. 66.
8. Robert Staples, *Black Masculinity: The Black Man's Role in American Society* (San Francisco: Black Scholar Press, 1982), p. 88.
9. Ibid., p. 90.
10. Joseph Eure and Richard Jerome, eds., *Back Where We Belong: Selected Speeches by Minister Louis Farrakhan* (Philadelphia: PC International Press, 1989), p. 138.
11. Molefi Keke Asante, *Afrocentricity: The Theory of Social Change* (Buffalo: Amulefi, 1980), p. 65. Apparently, Asante is so homophobic that he uses "Homosexuality" as a section heading, yet he doesn't list the section in the table of contents.
12. Ibid.
13. Haki R. Madhubuti (Don L. Lee), *Enemies: The Clash of Races* (Chicago: Third World Press, 1979), p. 148.
14. Ibid.
15. Hare and Hare, *The Endangered Black Family,* p. 65.
16. Haki R. Madhubuti, *Black Men: Obsolete, Single, Dangerous? The Afrikan American Family*

in Transition: Essays in Discovery, Solution, and Hope (Chicago: Third World Press, 1990), p. 60.
17. Ibid., pp. 73–74.
18. Ibid., p. 52.
19. LeRoi Jones (Amiri Baraka), *Black Magic* (New York: Bobbs-Merrill, 1969), p. 112.
20. LeRoi Jones (Amiri Baraka) and Larry Neal, *Black Fire* (New York: Morrow, 1968), p. 302.
21. Jones (Baraka), *Black Magic,* p. 140.
22. Ibid., pp. 205–206.
23. Ibid., pp. 23–24.
24. LeRoi Jones (Amiri Baraka), *The Baptism* and *The Toilet* (New York: Grove Press, 1966).
25. LeRoi Jones (Amiri Baraka), *Home: Social Essays* (New York: Morrow, 1966), p. 216.
26. Ibid., pp. 217 and 220.
27. Ibid., p. 217.
28. Jones (Baraka), *Black Magic,* p. 28.
29. LeRoi Jones (Amiri Baraka), *The System of Dante's Hell* (London: MacGibbon & Kee, 1966). The thesis of this essay regarding Baraka's former homosexuality rests primarily on the premise that *The System of Dante's Hell* is an autobiographical novel. This researcher believes such a premise to be correct for several reasons. First, *The System of Dante's Hell* is written in the first person. It is set in Newark, New Jersey, and many of the names of characters and places, as well as sequences of events, in *The System of Dante's Hell* parallels Baraka's own life as stated in his autobiography. See Imamu Amiri Baraka, *The Autobiography of LeRoi Jones* (New York: Freundlich Books, 1984). Second, Baraka has cited *The System of Dante's Hell* in an autobiographical context. In his *Autobiography,* Baraka refers the reader to *The System of Dante's Hell* and the incident involving Peaches for details about his once being AWOL while in the military. On page 12 of the *Autobiography,* he states: "In Shreveport . . . I ended up two days AWOL. I had gotten lost and laid up with a sister down in the Bottom (one black community of Shreveport—see *The System of Dante's Hell*) and finally came back rumpled and hung over and absolutely broke." Third, Baraka's homosexuality is referred to by his first wife, Hettie Jones, in *How I Became Hettie Jones* (New York: Dutton, 1990), p. 86. She states: "[Roi] once confessed to me some homosexual feelings, though never any specific experiences."
30. Baraka, *The Autobiography of LeRoi Jones,* pp. 1 and 12.
31. Jones (Baraka), *The System of Dante's Hell,* p. 65. In his play *The Toilet,* Baraka writes of a similar incident in high school where one boy, "Karolis," is beaten by a boy named Ray and his friends. Ray is described as "short, intelligent," and "popeyed." Karolis is attacked for writing Ray a love letter. Ray watches silently as his friends beat Karolis unconscious, but at the end of the play it is clear that Ray lied about not having had a homosexual encounter with Karolis.
32. See LeRoi Jones (Baraka), "The Alternative," in *Tales* (New York: Grove Press, 1967).
33. Baraka, *The Autobiography of LeRoi Jones,* pp. 87–88.
34. Jones (Baraka), *The System of Dante's Hell,* pp. 57–58.
35. Baraka, *The Autobiography of LeRoi Jones,* p. 100.
36. Jones (Baraka), *The System of Dante's Hell,* pp. 125 and 127.
37. Ibid., p. 131.
38. Ibid., p. 132.
39. Ibid., p. 134.
40. Ibid., pp. 134 and 135.
41. Ibid., pp. 138–139.
42. Ibid., pp. 139–141.
43. Ibid., p. 142.
44. Ibid., pp. 147–148.
45. Madhubuti, *Black Men,* p. 61.
46. Ibid., p. 111.
47. Louis Farrakhan, *The Time and What Must Be Done,* a videotape of a speech delivered in Oakland, California, May 20, 1990. The videotape was produced by the Final Call, Inc., Chicago, Illinois.
48. Malcolm X and Alex Haley, *The Autobiography of Malcolm X* (New York: Grove Press, 1966), pp. 295–299.

49. Yosef Ben-Jochannan, *The Black Man's Religion and Extracts and Comments from the Holy Black Bible* (New York: Alkebu-lan Books Associates, 1974), p. 46.
50. E. A. Wallis Budge, *The Egyptian Book of the Dead* (New York: Dover, 1967), pp. 196–201. It's interesting to note that Ben-Jochannan did not include in his list the Negative Confession, "I have not committed fornication." To have done so would have implied that the Egyptians forbade sexual activity between unmarried persons—a commandment few heterosexual cultural nationalists would ever consider obeying.
51. E. A. Wallis Budge, *An Egyptian Hieroglyphic Dictionary,* vol. 2. (New York: Dover, 1978), p. 818.
52. See Judy Grahn, *Another Mother Tongue* (Boston: Beacon Press, 1984), pp. 120–126; Arthur Evans, *Witchcraft and the Gay Counterculture* (Boston: Fag Rag Books, 1978), pp. 106–107; Esther Newton, "Of Yams, Grinders, and Gays," *Outlook: National Lesbian and Gay Quarterly* 1 (Summer 1988): 28–37; and Cary Alan Johnson, "Inside Gay Africa," *Black/Out: The Magazine of the National Coalition of Black Lesbians and Gays* 1, no. 2 (Fall 1986): 18–21, 30–31.

bell hooks (1952–)

B*orn Gloria Jean Watkins, bell hooks says she took her adult name from her "sharp-tongued" grandmother "who spoke her mind" and "was not afraid to talk back." One of six children in a cohesive, loving family, hooks was reared in Hopkinsville, Kentucky. Writing poetry as well as reciting the poems of James Weldon Johnson, Langston Hughes, and Gwendolyn Brooks for her family at age ten, hooks laid the foundation for a creative career. Her family supported her efforts to gain an education and to keep her creative vision alive in a segregated environment.*

At Stanford University in the early 1970s, hooks became interested in women's studies, while recognizing the unacknowledged racism that pervaded feminist classes and writings. Her graduate studies underscored her experiences with institutional racism and sexism; nevertheless, she earned a master's from the University of Wisconsin in 1976 and a doctorate from the University of California at Santa Cruz in 1983. Since then she has taught black studies, women's studies, and American literature at the University of Southern California, Yale University, Oberlin College, and City College of New York, among other institutions.

Although hooks's first publication was the book of poems And There We Went *(1978), it was her prose of the 1980s and 1990s that made her a widely read feminist and cultural critic. She sounded her first trumpet against the walls of racism and sexism in* Ain't I a Woman: Black Women and Feminism *(1981). It was followed by* Feminist Theory: From Margin to Center *(1984) and* Talking Back: Thinking Feminist, Thinking Black *(1989). Her remarkable productivity has increased in the 1990s. In several recent books, hooks's focus on racism and sexism expands into areas of popular culture:* Yearning: Race, Gender and Cultural Politics *(1990);* Breaking Bread: Insurgent Black Intellectual Life *(1991), coauthored with Cornel West;* Black Looks: Race and Representation *(1992);* A Woman's Mourning Song *(1992);* Sisters of the Yam: Black Women and Self-Recovery *(1993);* Outlaw Culture: Resisting Representations *(1994); and* Art on My Mind: Visual Politics *(1995).*

In "Revolutionary Black Women: Making Ourselves Subject," taken from Black Looks, *the writer explores African American women's literature to emphasize the need for contemporary black women to develop a "critical feminist consciousness" of their own.*

Revolutionary Black Women

Making Ourselves Subject

Sitting in a circle with several black women and one black man, children running in and out, on a hot Saturday evening at the office of the Council on Battered Women, after working all day, my spirits are renewed sharing with this group aspects of my development as a feminist thinker and writer. I listen intently as a sister comrade talks about her responses to my work. Initially she was disturbed by it. "I didn't want to hear it," she says. "I resented it." The talk in the group is about black women and violence, not just the violence inflicted by black men, but the violence black women do to children, and the violence we do to one another. Particularly challenged by the essay in *Talking Back,* "Violence in Intimate Relationships: A Feminist Perspective," because of its focus on a continuum of dominating violence that begins not with male violence against women but with the violence parents do to children, individual black women in the group felt they had to interrogate their parental practice.

There is little feminist work focusing on violence against children from a black perspective. Sharing our stories, we talked about the ways styles of parenting in diverse black communities support and perpetuate the use of violence as a means of domestic social control. We connected common acceptance of violence against children with community acceptance of male violence against women. Indeed, I suggested many of us were raised in families where we completely accepted the notion that violence was an appropriate response to crisis. In such settings it was not rare for black women to be verbally abusive and physically violent with one another. Our most vivid memories (in the group) of black women fighting one another took place in public settings where folks struggled over men or over gossip. There was no one in the group who had not witnessed an incident of black women doing violence to one another.

I shared with the group the declaration from Nikki Giovanni's "Woman Poem": "I ain't shit. You must be lower than that to care." This quote speaks directly to the rage and hostility oppressed/exploited people can turn inward on themselves and outward towards those who care about them. This has often been the case in black female encounters with one another. A vast majority of black women in this society receive sustained care only from other black women. That care does not always mediate or alter rage, or the desire to inflict pain; it may provoke it. Hostile responses to care echo the truth of Giovanni's words. When I first puzzled over them, I could hear voices in the background questioning, "How can you be worth anything if you care about me, who is worth nothing?" Among black women, such deeply internalized pain and self-rejection informs the aggression inflicted on the mirror image—other black women. It is this reality Audre Lorde courageously describes in her essay "Eye to Eye: Black Women, Hatred, and Anger." Critically interrogating, Lorde asks:

> why does that anger unleash itself most tellingly against another Black woman at the least excuse? Why do I judge her in a more critical light than any other, becoming enraged when she does not measure up? And if behind the object of my attack should lie the face of my own self, unaccepted, then what could possibly quench a fire fueled by such reciprocating passions?

I was reminded of Lorde's essay while seated among black women, listening to them talk about the intensity of their initial "anger" at my work. Retrospectively, that anger was vividly evoked so that I would know that individual black women present had grappled with it, moved beyond it, and come to a place of political awareness that allowed us to openly acknowledge it as part of their process of coming to consciousness and go on to critically affirm one another. They wanted me to understand the process of transformation, the movement of their passions from rage to care and recognition. It is this empowering process that enables us to meet face to face, to greet one another with solidarity, sisterhood, and love. In this space we talk about our different experiences of black womanhood, informed by class, geographical location, religious backgrounds, etc. We do not assume that all black women are violent or have internalized rage and hostility.

In contrast, Lorde writes in "Eye to Eye":

> We do not love ourselves, therefore we cannot love each other. Because we see in each other's face our own face, the face we never stopped wanting. Because we survived and survival breeds desire for more self. A face we never stopped wanting at the same time as we try to obliterate it. Why don't we meet each other's eyes? Do we expect betrayal in each other's gaze, or recognition?

Lorde's essay chronicles an understanding of ways "wounded" black women, who are not in recovery, interact with one another, helping us to see the way in which sexism and racism as systems of domination can shape and determine how we regard one another. Deeply moved by her portrait of the way internalized racism and sexism informs the formation of black female social identity, the way it can and often does affect us, I was simultaneously disturbed by the presumption, expressed by her continual use of collective "we," that she was speaking to an experience all black women share. The experience her essay suggests black women share is one of passively receiving and absorbing messages of self-hate, then directing rage and hostility most intensely at one another. While I wholeheartedly agree with Lorde that many black women feel and act as she describes, I am interested in the reality of those black women, however few, who even if they have been the targets of black female rage do not direct hostility or rage toward other black women.

Throughout "Eye to Eye," Lorde constructs a monolithic paradigm of black female experience that does not engage our differences. Even as her essay urges black women to openly examine the harshness and cruelty that may be present in black female interaction so that we can regard one another differently, an expression of that regard would be recognition, without hatred or envy, that not all black women share the experience she describes. To some extent Lorde's essay acts to shut down, close off, erase, and deny those black female experiences that do not fit the norm she constructs from the location of her experience. Never in Lorde's essay does she address the issue of whether or not black women from different cultural backgrounds (Caribbean, Latina, etc.) construct diverse identities. Do we all feel the same about black womanhood? What about regional differences? What about those black women who have had the good fortune to be raised in a politicized context where their identities were constructed by resistance and not passive acceptance? By evoking this negative experience of black womanhood as "commonly" shared, Lorde presents it in a way that suggests it represents "authentic" black female reality. To not share the critique she posits is to be made an "outsider" yet again. In Donna Haraway's essay "A Manifesto for Cyborgs," she warns feminist thinkers against assuming positions that "appear to be the telos of the whole," so that we do not "produce epistemologies to police deviation from official women's experience." Though Haraway is speaking about mainstream feminist practice, her warning is applicable to marginalized groups who are in the process of making and remaking critical texts that name our politics and experience.

Years ago I attended a small gathering of black women who were meeting to plan a national conference on black feminism. As we sat in a circle talking about our experiences, those individuals who were most listened to all told stories of how brutally they had been treated by "the" black community. Speaking against the construction of a monolithic experience, I talked about the way my experience of black community differed, sharing that I had been raised in a segregated rural black community that was very supportive. Our segregated church and schools were places where we were affirmed. I was continually told that I was "special" in those settings, that I would be "somebody" someday and do important work to "uplift" the race. I felt loved and cared about in the segregated black community of my growing up. It gave me the grounding in a positive experience of "blackness" that sustained me when I left that community to enter racially integrated settings, where racism informed most social interactions. Before I could finish speaking, I was interrupted by one of the "famous" black women present, who chastised me for trying to erase another black woman's pain by bringing up a different experience. Her voice was hostile and angry. She began by saying she was "sick of people like me." I felt both silenced and misunderstood. It seemed that the cathartic expression of collective pain wiped out any chance that my insistence on the diversity of black experience would be heard.

My story was reduced to a competing narrative, one that was seen as trying to divert attention from the "true" telling of black female experience. In this gathering, black female identity was made synonymous again and again with "victimization." The black female voice that was deemed "authentic" was the voice in pain; only the sound of hurting could be heard. No narrative of resistance was voiced and respected in this setting. I came away wondering why it was these black women could only feel bonded to each other if our narratives echoed, only if we were telling the same story of shared pain and victimization. Why was it impossible to speak an identity emerging from a different location?

A particular brand of black feminist "essentialism" had been constructed in that place. It would not allow for difference. And individual present who was seen as having inappropriate thoughts or lingering traces of politically incorrect ideas was the target for unmediated hostility. Not surprisingly, those who had the most to say about victimization were also the ones who judged others harshly, who silenced others. Individual black women who were not a part of that inner circle learned that if they did not know the "right" thing to say, it was best to be silent. To speak against the grain was to risk punishment. One's speech might be interrupted or one might be subjected to humiliating verbal abuse.

At the close of this gathering, many black women gave testimony about how this had been a wonderful experience of sisterhood and black woman-bonding.

There was no space for those individuals whose spirits had been assaulted and attacked to name their experience. Ironically, they were leaving this gathering with a sense of estrangement, carrying with them remembered pain. Some of them felt that this was the first time in their lives that they had been so cruelly treated by other black women. The oldest black woman present, an academic intellectual who had often been the target for verbal assault, who often wept in her room at night, vowed never again to attend such a gathering. The memory of her pain has lingered in my mind. I have not forgotten this collective black female "rage" in the face of difference, the anger directed at individual black women who dared to speak as though we were more than our pain, more than the collective pain black females have historically experienced.

Sitting at the offices of the Council on Battered Women was different. After many years of feminist movement, it seems to me that black women can now come together in ways that allow for difference. At the Council, women could speak openly and honestly about their experience, describe their negative and positive responses to my work without fear or rebuke. They could name their rage, annoyance, frustration, and simultaneously critique it. In a similar setting where black women had talked openly about the way my work "enraged" them, I had asked a sister if she would talk about the roots of her hostility. She responded by telling me that I was "daring to be different, to have a different response to the shit black women were faced with every day." She said, "It's like you were saying, this is what the real deal is and this what we can do about it. When most of us have just been going along with the program and telling ourselves that's all we could do. You were saying that it don't have to be that way." The rage she articulated was in response to the demand that black women acknowledge the impact of sexism on our lives and engage in [the] feminist movement. That was a demand for transformation. At the offices of the Council, I was among black comrades who were engaged in a process of transformation. Collectively, we were working to problematize our notions of black female subjectivity. None of us assumed a fixed essential identity. It was so evident that we did not all share a common understanding of being black and female, even though some of our experiences were similar. We did share the understanding that it is difficult for black women to construct radical subjectivity within white supremacist capitalist patriarchy, that our struggle to be "subject," though similar, also differs from that of black men, and that the politics of gender create that difference.

Much creative writing by contemporary black women authors highlights gender politics, specifically black male sexism, poverty, black female labor, and the struggle for creativity. Celebrating the "power" of black women's writing in her essay "Women Warriors: Black Women Writers Load the Canon" in the *Voice Literary Supplement,* dated May 1990, Michelle Cliff asserts:

> There is continuity in the written work of many African-American women, whether writer is their primary identity or not. You can draw a line from the slave narrative of Linda Brent to Elizabeth Keckley's life to *Their Eyes Were Watching God* to *Coming of Age in Mississippi* to *Sula* to *The Salteaters* to *Praisesong for the Widow.* All of these define a response to power. All structure that response as a quest, a journey to complete, to realize the self; all involve the attempt to break out of expectations imposed on black and female identity. All work against the odds to claim the *I.*

Passionate declarations like this one, though seductive, lump all black female writing together in a manner that suggests there is indeed a totalizing *telos* that determines black female subjectivity. This narrative constructs a homogeneous black female subject whose subjectivity is most radically defined by those experiences she shares with other black women. In this declaration, as in the entire essay, Cliff glorifies black women writers even though she warns against the kind of glorification (particularly that accorded a writer that is expressed by sustained academic literary critique of their work) that has the potential to repress and contain.

Cliff's piece also contains. Defining black women's collective work as a critical project that problematizes the quest for "identity," she subsumes that quest solely by focusing on rites of passages wherein black women journey to find themselves. She does not talk about whether that journeying is fruitful. By focusing attention primarily on the journey, she offers paradigms for reading and understanding black women writers that invite readers (critics included) to stop there, to romanticize the journey without questioning the location of that journey's end. Sadly, in much of the fiction by contemporary black women writers, the struggle by black female characters for subjectivity, though forged in radical resistance to the *status quo* (opposition to racist oppression, less frequently to class and gender) usually takes the form of black women breaking free from boundaries imposed by others, only to practice their newfound "freedom" by setting limits and boundaries for themselves. Hence though black women may make themselves "subject" they do not become radical subjects. Often they simply conform to existing norms, even ones they once resisted.

Despite all the "radical" shifts in thought, location, class position, etc., that Celie undergoes in Alice Walker's novel *The Color Purple,* from her movement from object to subject to her success as a capitalist entrepreneur, Celie is reinscribed within the context of family and domestic relations by the novel's end. The primary change is that those relations are no longer abusive. Celie has not become a "feminist," a civil rights activist, or a political being in any way. Breaking free from the patriarchal prison that is her "home" when the novel begins, she creates her own household, yet radical politics of collective struggle against racism or sexism do not inform her struggle for self-actualization.

Earlier writing by black women, Linda Brent's slave narrative for example, records resistance struggles where black women confront and overcome incredible barriers in the quest to be self-defining. Often after those barriers have been passed, the heroines settle down into conventional gender roles. No tale of woman's struggle to be self-defining is as powerful as the Brent narrative. She is ever conscious of the way in which being female makes slavery "far more grievous." Her narrative creates powerful groundwork for the construction of radical black female subjectivity. She engages in a process of critical thinking that enables her to rebel against the notion that her body can be sold and insists on placing the sanctity of black ontological being outside modes of exchange. Yet this radical, visionary "take" on subjectivity does not inform who she becomes once she makes her way to freedom. After breaking the bonds of slavery, Harriet Jacobs takes on the pseudonym Linda Brent when she writes about the past and falls into the clutches of conventional notions of womanhood. Does the radical invented self "Linda Brent" have no place in the life of Harriet Jacobs? Freed, descriptions of her life indicate no use of the incredible oppositional imagination that has been a major resource enabling her to transgress boundaries, to take risks, and dare to survive. Does Jacobs's suppression of the radical self chart the journey that black women will follow, both in real life and in their fictions?

More than any other novel by a contemporary black woman writer, Toni Morrison's *Sula* chronicles the attempt by a black female to constitute radical black female subjectivity. Sula challenges every restriction imposed upon her, transgressing all boundaries. Defying conventional notions of passive female sexuality, she asserts herself as desiring subject. Rebelling against enforced domesticity, she chooses to roam the world, to remain childless and unmarried. Refusing standard sexist notions of the exchange of female bodies, she engages in the exchange of male bodies as part of a defiant effort to displace their importance. Asserting the primacy of female friendship, she attempts to break with patriarchal male identification and loses the friendship of her "conservative" buddy Nel, who has indeed capitulated to convention.

Even though readers of *Sula* witness her self-assertion and celebration of autonomy, which Sula revels in even as she is dying, we also know that she is not self-actualized enough to stay alive. Her awareness of what it means to be a radical subject does not cross the boundaries of public and private; hers is a privatized self-discovery. Sula's death at an early age does not leave the reader with a sense of her "power," instead she seems powerless to assert agency in a world that has no interest in radical black female subjectivity, one that seeks to repress, contain, and annihilate it. Sula is annihilated. The reader never knows what force is killing her, eating her from the inside out. Since her journey has been about the struggle to invent herself, the narrative implies that it is the longing for "selfhood" that leads to destruction. Those black women who survive, who live to tell the tale, so to speak, are the "good girls," the ones who have been self-sacrificing, hardworking black women. Sula's fate suggests that charting the journey of radical black female subjectivity is too dangerous, too risky. And while Sula is glad to have broken the rules, she is not a triumphant figure. Sula, like so many other black female characters in contemporary fiction, has no conscious politics, never links her struggle to be self-defining with the collective plight of black women. Yet this novel was written at the peak of contemporary feminist movement. Given the "power" of Sula's black female author/creator, Toni Morrison, why does she appear on the page as an "artist without an art form"? Is it too much like "treason"—like disloyalty to black womanhood—to question this portrait of (dare I say it) "victimization," to refuse to be seduced by Sula's exploits or ignore their outcome?

There are black female characters in contemporary fictions who are engaged in political work. Velma, the radical activist in Toni Cade Bambara's *The Salt-eaters,* has grounded her struggle for meaning within activist work for black liberation. Overwhelmed by responsibility, by the sense of having to bear too much, too great a weight, she attempts suicide. This novel begins with older radical black women problematizing the question of black female subjectivity. Confronting Velma's attempt at self-destruction and self-erasure, they want to know, "are you sure, sweetheart, that you want to be well?" Wellness here is synonymous with radical subjectivity. Indeed, the elders will go on to emphasize that Velma's plight, and that of other black women like her, reflects the loss of "maps" that will chart the journey for black females. They suggest that it is the younger generation's attempt to assimilate, to follow alien maps, that leads to the loss of perspective. Velma only came back to life (for though she fails to kill herself, she is spiritually dead) when she testifies to herself that she indeed will choose wellness, will claim herself and nurture that radical subjectivity. Like Paule Marshall's *Praisesong for the Widow* and Gloria Naylor's *Mama Day,* the "radical" black women elders with fresh memories of the slavery holocaust, of the anguish of reconstruction, who sustain their courage in resistance, live fruitfully outside conventional gender roles. They either do not conform or they acknowledge the way conformity rarely enables black female self-actualization.

Representing a new generation of "modern " black women, Velma, even as she is in the process of recovery, critiques her desire to make a self against the grain, and questions "what good did wild do you, since there was always some low-life gruesome gang-bang raping lawless careless petty last straw nasty thing ready to pounce—put your shit under total arrest and crack your back?" Wild is the metaphoric expression of that inner will to rebel, to move against the grain, to be out of one's place. It is the expression of radical black female subjectivity. Law professor Regina Austin calls black women to cultivate this "wildness" as a survival strategy in her piece "Sapphire Bound." Significantly, she begins the essay by calling attention to the fact that folks seem to be more eager to read about wild black women in fictions than to make way for us in real life. Reclaiming that wildness, she declares:

> Well, I think the time has come for us to get truly hysterical, to take on the role of "professional Sapphires" in a forthright way, to declare that we are serious about ourselves, and to capture some of the intellectual power and resources that are necessary to combat the systematic denigration of minority women. It is time for Sapphire to testify on her own behalf, *in writing,* complete with footnotes.

If the writers of black women's fiction are not able to express the wilder, more radical dimensions of themselves, in sustained and fruitful ways, it is unlikely that they will create characters who "act up" and flourish. They may doubt that there is an audience for fictions where black women are not first portrayed as victims. Though fictions portray black women being wild in resistance, confronting barriers that impede self-actualization, rarely is the new "self" defined. Though Bambara includes passages that let the reader know Velma lives, there are no clues that indicate how her radical subjectivity will emerge in the context of "wildness."

Consistently, contemporary black women writers link the struggle to become subject with a concern with emotional and spiritual well-being. Most often the narcissistic-based individual pursuit of self and identity subsumes the possibility of sustained commitment to radical politics. This tension is played out again and again in Alice Walker's *The Third Life of Grange Copeland.* While the heroine, Ruth, is schooled by her grandfather to think critically, to develop radical political consciousness, in the end he fights against whites alone. It is not clear what path Ruth will take in the future. Will she be a militant warrior for the revolution or be kept in her place by "strong" black male lovers/patriarchs who, like her grandfather, will be convinced that they can best determine what conditions are conducive to producing black female well-being? Ironically, *Meridian* takes up where Ruth's story ends, yet the older black woman activist, like Ruth, remains confined and contained by a self-imposed domesticity. Is Meridian in hiding because there is no place where her radical black subjectivity can be expressed without punishment? Is the non-patriarchal home the only safe place?

Contemporary fiction by black women focusing on the construction of self and identity breaks new ground in that it clearly names the ways structures of domination, racism, sexism, and class exploitation, oppress and make it practically impossible for black women to survive if they do not engage in meaningful resistance on some level. Defiantly naming the condition of oppression and personal strategies of opposition, such writing enables the individual black woman reader who has not yet done so to question and/or critically affirms the efforts of those readers who are already involved in resistance. Yet these writings often fail to depict any location for the construction of new identities. It is this textual gap that leads critic Sondra O'Neale to ask in her essay "Inhibiting Midwives, Usurping Creators: The Struggling Emergence of Black Women in American Fiction":

> For instance, where are the Angela Davises, Ida B. Wellses, and Daisy Bateses of black feminist literatures? Where are the portraits of those women who fostered their own action to liberate themselves, other black women, and black men as well? We see a sketch of such a character in *Meridian,* but she is never developed to a social and political success.

In an earlier essay, "The Politics of Radical Black Subjectivity," I emphasized that opposition and resistance cannot be made synonymous with self-actualization on an individual or collective level: "Opposition is not enough. In that vacant space after one has resisted there is still the necessity to become—to make oneself anew." While contemporary writing by black women has brought into sharp focus the idea that black females must "invent" selves, the question—what kind of self?—usually remains unanswered. The vision of selfhood that does emerge now and then is one that is in complete concordance with conventional western notions of a "unitary" self. Again it's worth restating Donna Haraway's challenge to feminist thinkers to resist making "one's own political tendencies to be the telos of the whole" so we can accept different accounts of female experience and also face ourselves as complex subjects who embody multiple locations. In "A Manifesto for Cyborgs," she urges us to remember that, "The issue is dispersion. The task is to survive in diaspora."

Certainly, collective black female experience has been about the struggle to survive in diaspora. It is the intensity of that struggle, the fear of failure (as we face daily the reality that many black people do not and are not surviving) that has led many black women thinkers, especially within [the] feminist movement, to wrongly assume that strength in unity can only exist if difference is suppressed and shared experience is highlighted. Though feminist writing by black women is usually critical of the racism that has shaped and defined the parameters of much contemporary feminist movement, it usually reiterates, in an uncritical manner, major tenets of dominant feminist thought. Admonishing black women for wasting time critiquing white female racism, Sheila Radford-Hill, in "Considering Feminism as a Model for Social Change," urges black feminists:

> to build an agenda that meets the needs of black women by helping black women to mobilize around issues that they perceive to have a direct impact on the overall

> quality of their lives. Such is the challenge that defined our struggle and constitutes our legacy. . . . Thus, black women need to develop their own leadership and their own agenda based on the needs of their primary constituent base; that is, based around black women, their families, and their communities. This task cannot be furthered by dialoging with white women about their inherent racism.

While I strongly agree with Radford-Hill's insistence that black critical thinkers engaged in feminist movement develop strategies that directly address the concerns of our diverse black communities, she constructs an either/or proposition that obscures the diversity of our experiences and locations. For those black women who live and work in predominantly white settings (and of course the reality is that most black women who work jobs where their supervisors are white women and men), it is an appropriate and necessary political project for them to work at critical interrogations and interventions that address white racism. Such efforts do not preclude simultaneous work in black communities. Evocations of an "essentialist" notion of black identity seek to deny the extent to which all black folk must engage with whites as well as exclude individuals from "blackness" whose perspectives, values, or lifestyles may differ from a totalizing notion of black experience that sees only those folk who live in segregated communities or have little contact with whites as "authentically" black.

Radford-Hill's essay is most insightful when she addresses "the crisis of black womanhood," stating that "the extent to which black feminists can articulate and solve the crisis of black womanhood is the extent to which black women will undergo a feminist transformation." The crisis Radford-Hill describes is a crisis of identity and subjectivity. When the major struggle black women addressed was opposition to racism and the goal of that struggle was equality in the existing social structures, when most black folks were poor and lived in racially segregated neighborhoods, gender roles for black women were more clearly defined. We had a place in the "struggle" as well as a place in the social institutions of our communities. It was easier for black women to chart the journey of selfhood. With few job options in the segregated labor force, most black women knew that they would be engaged in service work or become teachers. Today's black woman has more options even though most of the barriers that would keep her from exercising those options are still in place. Racial integration, economic changes in black class relations, the impact of consumer capitalism, as well as a male-centered contemporary black liberation struggle (which devalued the contributions of black females) and a feminist movement which called into question idealized notions of womanhood have radically altered black female reality. For many black women, especially the underclass, the dream of racial equality was intimately linked with the fantasy that once the struggle was over, black women would be able to assume conventional sexist gender roles. To some extent there is a crisis in black womanhood because most black women have not responded to these changes by radically reinventing themselves, by developing new maps to chart future journeys. And more crucially, most black women have not responded to this crisis by developing critical consciousness, by becoming engaged in radical movements for social change.

When we examine the lives of individual black women who did indeed respond to contemporary changes, we see just how difficult it is for black women to construct radical subjectivity. Two powerful autobiographies of radical black women were published in the early 1970s. In 1970, Shirley Chisholm published *Unbought and Unbossed,* chronicling the events that led to her becoming the first black congresswoman. In 1974, *Angela Davis: An Autobiography* was published. Both accounts demonstrate that the construction of radical black female subjectivity is rooted in a willingness to go against the grain. Though many folks may not see Chisholm as "radical," she was one of the first black female leaders to speak against sexism, stressing in the introduction to her book: "Of my two 'handicaps,' being female put many more obstacles in my path than being black." An outspoken advocate of reproductive and abortion rights for women, Chisholm responded to black males who were not opposed to compulsory pregnancy for black women by arguing: "Which is more like genocide, I have asked some of my black brothers—this, the way things are, or the conditions I am fighting for in which the full range of family planning service is fully available to women of all classes and colors; starting with effective contraception and extending to safe, legal termination of undesired pregnancies, at a price they can afford?"

Militant in her response to racism, Chisholm also stressed the need for education for critical consciousness to help eradicate internalized racism:

> It is necessary for our generation to repudiate Carver and all the lesser-known black leaders who cooperated with the white design to keep their people down. We need none of their kind today. Someday, when, God willing, the struggle is over and its bitterness has faded, those men and women may be rediscovered and given their just due for working as best they could see to do in their time and place, for their brothers and sisters. But at present their influence is pernicious, and where they still control education in the North or the South, they must be replaced with educators who are ready to demand full equality for the oppressed races and fight for it at any cost.

As a radical black female subject who would not allow herself to be the puppet of any group, Chisholm was often harassed, mocked, and ridiculed by colleagues. Psychological terrorism was often the weapon used to try and coerce her into silence, to convince her she knew nothing about politics, or worse yet that she was "crazy." Often her colleagues described her as mad if she took positions they could not understand or would not have taken. Radical black female subjects are constantly labeled crazy by those who hope to undermine our personal power and our ability to influence others. Fear of being seen as insane may be a major factor keeping black women from expressing their most radical selves. Just recently, when I spoke against the omnipresent racism and sexism at a conference, calling it terroristic, the organizers told folks I was "crazy." While this hurt and angered, it would have wounded me more had I not understood the ways this appellation is used by those in power to keep the powerless in their place. Remembering Chisholm's experience, I knew that I was not alone in confronting racist, sexist attacks that are meant to silence. Knowing that Chisholm claimed her right to subjectivity without apology inspires me to maintain courage.

Recently rereading the autobiography of Angela Davis, I was awed by her courage. I could appreciate the obstacles she confronted and her capacity to endure and persevere in a new way. Reading this work in my teens, her courage seemed like "no big deal." At the beginning of the work, Davis eschews any attempt to see herself as exceptional. Framing the narrative in this way, it is easy for readers to ignore the specificity of her experience. In fact, very few black females at the time had gone to radical high schools where they learned about socialism or traveled to Europe and studied at the Sorbonne. Yet Davis insists that her situation is like that of all black people. This gesture of solidarity, though important, at times obscures the reality that Davis' radical understanding of politics was learned as was her critical consciousness. Had she voiced her solidarity with underclass black people, while simultaneously stressing the importance of learning, of broadening one's perspective, she would have shared with black females tools that enable one to be a radical subject.

Like Chisholm, Davis confronted sexism when she fully committed herself to working for political change.

> I became acquainted very early with the widespread presence of an unfortunate syndrome among some Black male activists—namely to confuse their political activity with an assertion of their maleness. They saw—and some continue to see—Black manhood as something separate from Black womanhood. These men view Black women as a threat to their attainment of manhood—especially those Black women who take initiative and work to become leaders in their own right.

Working in the radical black liberation movement, Davis constantly confronted and challenged sexism even as she critiqued the pervasive racism in mainstream feminist movement. Reading her autobiography, it is clear that reading and studying played a tremendous role in shaping her radical political consciousness. Yet Davis understood that one needed to go beyond books and work collectively with comrades for social change. She critiqued self-focused work to emphasize the value of working in solidarity:

> Floating from activity to activity was no revolutionary anything. Individual activity—sporadic and disconnected—is not revolutionary work. Serious revolutionary work consists of persistent and methodical efforts through a collective of other revolutionaries to organize the masses for action. Since I had long considered myself a Marxist, the alternatives open to me were very limited.

Despite limited options, Davis' decision to advocate communism was an uncommon and radical choice.

When the Davis autobiography was written, she was thirty years old; her most militant expression of subjectivity erupted in her twenties. Made into a cultural icon, a gesture that was not in line with her insistence on the importance of collectivity and fellowship, she came to be represented in mass media as an "exceptional" black woman. Her experience was not seen as a model young black women could learn from. Many parents pointed to the prison sentence she served as reason enough for black women not to follow in her footsteps. Black males who wanted the movement to be male-centered were not trying to encourage other black women to be on the Left, to fully commit themselves to a revolutionary black liberation struggle. At public appearances, Angela Davis was not and is not flanked by other black women on the Left. Constantly projected as an "isolated" figure, her presence, her continued commitment to critical thinking and critical pedagogy, has not had the galvanizing impact on black females that it could have. Black women "worship" Davis from a distance, see her as exceptional. Though young black women adore Davis, they do not often read her work nor seek to follow her example. Yet learning about those black women who have dared to assert radical subjectivity, is a necessary part of black female self-actualization. Coming to power, to selfhood, to radical subjectivity cannot happen in isolation. Black women need to study the writings, both critical and autobiographical, of those women who have developed their potential and chosen to be radical subjects.

Critical pedagogy, the sharing of information and knowledge by black women with black women, is crucial for the development of radical black female subjectivity (not because black women can only learn from one another, but because the circumstances of racism, sexism, and class exploitation ensure that other groups will not necessarily seek to further our self-determination). This process requires of us a greater honesty about how we live. Black females (especially students) who are searching for answers about the social formation of identity want to know how radical black women think but they also want to know about our habits of being. Willingness to share openly one's personal experience ensures that one will not be made into a deified icon. When black females learn about my life, they also learn about the mistakes I make, the contradictions. They come to know my limitations as well as my strengths. They cannot dehumanize me by placing me on a pedestal. Sharing the contradictions of our lives, we help each other learn how to grapple with contradictions as part of the process of becoming a critical thinker, a radical subject.

The lives of Ella Baker, Fannie Lou Hamer, Septima Clark, Lucy Parson, Ruby Doris Smith Robinson, Angela Davis, Bernice Reagon, Alice Walker, Audre Lorde, and countless others bear witness to the difficulty of developing radical black female subjectivity even as they attest to the joy and triumph of living with a decolonized mind and participating in [an] ongoing resistance struggle. The narratives of black women who have militantly emerged in radical struggles for change offer insights. They let us know the conditions that enable the construction of radical black female subjectivity as well as the obstacles that impede its development. In most cases, radical black female subjects have willingly challenged the *status quo* and gone against the grain. Despite the popularity of Angela Davis as a cultural icon, most black women are "punished" and "suffer" when they make choices that go against the prevailing societal sense of what a black woman should be and do. Most radical black female subjects are not caught up in consumer capitalism. Living simply is often the price one pays for choosing to be different. It was no accident that Zora Neale Hurston died poor. [We] radical black female subjects have had to educate ourselves for critical consciousness, reading, studying, engaging in critical pedagogy, transgressing boundaries to acquire the knowledge we need. Those rare radical black women who have started organizations and groups are attempting to build a collective base that will support and enable their work. Many of these black women create sites of resistance that are far removed from conservatizing institutions in order to sustain their radical commitments. Those of us who remain in institutions that do not support our efforts to be radical subjects are daily assaulted. We persevere because we believe our presence is needed, is important.

Developing a feminist consciousness is a crucial part of the process by which one asserts radical black female subjectivity. Whether she has called herself a feminist or not, there is no radical black woman subject who has not been forced to confront and challenge sexism. If, however, that individual struggle is not connected to a larger feminist movement, then every black woman finds herself reinventing strategies to cope when we should be leaving a legacy of feminist resistance that can nourish, sustain, and guide other black women and men. Those black women who valiantly advocate feminism often bear the brunt of severe critique from other black folks. As a radical subject, the young Michele Wallace wrote one of the first book length, polemical works on feminism that focused on black folks. She did not become a cultural icon; to a great extent she was made a pariah. Writing about her experience in "The Politics of Location: Cinema/Theory/Literature/Ethnicity/Sexuality/Me," she remembers the pain:

> I still ponder the book I wrote, *Black Macho and the Myth of the Superwoman,* and the disturbance it caused: how black women are not allowed to establish their own intellectual terrain, to make their own mistakes, to invent their own birthplace in writing. I still ponder my book's rightness and wrongness, and how its reception almost destroyed me so that I vowed never to write political and/or theoretical statements about feminism again.

Wallace suffered in isolation, with no group of radical black women rallying to her defense, or creating a context where critique would not lead to trashing.

Without a context of critical affirmation, radical black female subjectivity cannot sustain itself. Often black women turn away from the radicalism of their younger days as they age because the isolation, the sense of estrangement from community, becomes too difficult to bear. Critical affirmation is a concept that embraces both the need to affirm one another and to have a space for critique. Significantly, that critique is not rooted in [a] negative desire to compete, to wound, to trash. Though I began this piece with critical statements about Audre Lorde's essay, I affirm the value of her work. The "Eye to Eye" essay remains one of the most insightful discussions of black female interaction. Throughout the essay, Lorde emphasizes the importance of affirmation, encouraging black women to be gentle and affectionate with one another. Tenderness should not simply be a form of care extended to those black women who think as we do. Many of us have been in situations where black females are sweet to the folks in their clique and completely hostile to anyone deemed an outsider.

In "Eye to Eye," Lorde names this problem. Offering strategies black women might use to promote greater regard and respect, she says that "black women must love ourselves." Loving ourselves begins with understanding the forces that have produced whatever hostility toward blackness and femaleness that is felt, but it also means learning new ways to think about ourselves. Often the black women who speak the most about love and sisterhood are deeply attached to essentialist notions of black female identity that promote a "policing" of anyone who does not conform. Ironically, of course, the only way black women can construct radical subjectivity is by resisting set norms and challenging the politics of domination based on race, class, and sex. Essentialist perspectives on black womanhood often perpetuate the false assumption that black females, simply by living in white supremacist/capitalist/patriarchy, are radicalized. They do not encourage black women to develop their critical thinking. Individual black women on the Left often find their desire to read or write "theory," to be engaged in critical dialogues with diverse groups, mocked and ridiculed. Often, I am criticized for studying feminist theory, especially writing by white women. And I am seen as especially "naive" when I suggest that even though a white woman theorist may be "racist," she may also have valuable information that I can learn from. Until black women fully recognize that we must collectively examine and study our experience from a feminist standpoint, there will always be lags and gaps in the structure of our epistemologies. Where are our feminist books on mothering, on sexuality, on feminist film criticism? Where are our autobiographies that do not falsely represent our reality in the interest of promoting monolithic notions of black female experience or celebrating how wonderfully we have managed to overcome oppression?

Though autobiography or any type of confessional narrative is often devalued in North American letters, this genre has always had a privileged place in African American literary history. As a literature of resistance, confessional narratives by black folks were didactic. More than any other genre of writing, the production of honest confessional narratives by black women who are struggling to be self-actualized and to become radical subjects are needed as guides, as texts that affirm our fellowship with one another. (I need not feel isolated if I know that there are other comrades with similar experiences. I learn from their strategies of resistance and from their recording of mistakes.) Even as the number of novels published by black women increase, this writing cannot be either a substitute for theory or for autobiographical narrative. Radical black women need to tell our stories; we cannot document our experience enough. Works like *Lemon Swamp, Balm in Gilead, Ready from Within,* and *Every Good-bye Ain't Gone,* though very different, and certainly not all narratives of radical black female subjectivity, enable readers to understand the complexity and diversity of black female experience.

There are few contemporary autobiographies by black women on the Left. We need to hear more from courageous black women who have gone against the grain to assert nonconformist politics and habits of being, folks like Toni Cade Bambara, Gloria Joseph, Faye Harrison, June Jordan, and so many others. These voices can give testimony and share the process of transformation black women undergo to emerge as radical subjects. We black females need to know who our revolutionary comrades are. Speaking about her commitment to revolution, Angela Davis notes:

> For me revolution was never an interim "thing-to-do" before settling down: it was no fashionable club with newly minted jargon, or a new kind of social life—made thrilling by risk and confrontation, made glamorous by costume. Revolution is a serious thing, the most serious thing about a revolutionary's life. When one commits oneself to the struggle, it must be for a lifetime.

The crisis of black womanhood can only be addressed by the development of resistance struggles that emphasize the importance of decolonizing our minds, developing critical consciousness. Feminist politics can be an integral part of a renewed black liberation struggle. Black women, particularly those of us who have chosen radical subjectivity, can move toward revolutionary social change that will address the diversity of our experiences and our needs. Collectively bringing our knowledge, resources, skills, and wisdom to one another, we make the site where radical black female subjectivity can be nurtured and sustained.

Michael Eric Dyson (1958–)

Scholar, writer, and critic Michael Eric Dyson is known for expressing his perspectives with candor and eloquence. In an assessment of America's racial tensions, he argues that the "nation's claims of racial peace are haunted by the hypocrisy of hidden white power and concealed bigotry. . . . A great deal of discourse about race is trapped in abstraction and avoidance as we ingeniously seek to deflect the link between past injustices and present injuries."

Born and raised in a Detroit ghetto, Dyson went to work in his family's nursery business at the age of twelve. At sixteen, he won a scholarship to Cranbrook, a Michigan boarding school attended by wealthy Caucasian students. After only two years at Cranbrook, however, he returned to Detroit, earning his high school diploma by attending evening classes while working at various day jobs.

Dyson traveled south to attend Knoxville College, a black institution, but later transferred to Carson-Newman College, a predominantly white Southern Baptist school. After earning his bachelor's from that institution, he entered Princeton University to study religion. He then taught ethics, philosophy, and cultural criticism at Hartford Theological Seminary and Chicago Theological Seminary, later joining the faculty at Brown University to teach American civilization and Afro-American studies. Presently, he is director of the Institute of African American Research and professor of communication studies at the University of North Carolina at Chapel Hill.

Dyson won the 1992 National Magazine Award for Black Journalists. In addition to numerous articles and reviews, he has published two books: Reflecting Black: African American Cultural Criticism *(1993) and* Making Malcolm: The Myth and Meaning of Malcolm X *(1995).*

Taken from Reflecting Black, *"The Culture of Hip-Hop" evaluates the history and impact of rap music.*

The Culture of Hip-Hop

From the very beginning of its recent history, hip-hop music—or rap, as it has come to be known—has faced various obstacles. Initially rap was deemed a passing fad, a playful and ephemeral black cultural form that steamed off the musical energies of urban black teens. As it became obvious that rap was here to stay, a permanent fixture in black ghetto youths' musical landscape, the reactions changed from dismissal to denigration, and rap music came under attack from both black and white quarters. Is rap really as dangerous as many critics argue? Or are there redeeming characteristics to rap music that warrant our critical attention: I will attempt to answer these and other questions as I explore the culture of hip-hop.

Trying to pinpoint the exact origin of rap is a tricky process that depends on when one acknowledges a particular cultural expression or product as rap. Rap can be traced back to the revolutionary verse of Gil Scott-Heron and the Last Poets, to Pigmeat Markham's "Here Come de Judge," and even to Bessie Smith's rapping to a beat in some of her blues. We can also cite ancient African oral traditions as the antecedents to various contemporary African-American cultural practices. In any case, the modern history of rap probably begins in 1979 with the rap song "Rapper's Delight," by the Sugarhill Gang. Although there were other (mostly underground) examples of rap, this record is regarded as the signal barrier breaker, birthing hip-hop and consolidating the infant art form's popularity. This first stage in a rap record production was characterized by rappers placing their rhythmic, repetitive speech over well-known (mostly R & B) black music hits. "Rapper's Delight" was rapped over the music to a song made by the popular seventies R & B group Chic, titled "Good Times." Although rap would later enhance its technical virtuosity through instrumentation, drum machines, and "sampling" existing records—thus making it creatively symbiotic—the first stage was benignly parasitic upon existing black music.

As rap grew, it was still limited to mostly inner-city neighborhoods and particularly its place of origin, New York City. Rap artists like Funky 4 Plus 1, Kool Moe Dee, Busy Bee, Afrika Bambaata, Cold Rush Brothers, Kurtis Blow, DJ Kool Hurk, and Grandmaster Melle Mel were experimenting with this developing musical genre. As it evolved, rap began to describe and analyze the social, economic, and political factors that led to its emergence and development: drug addiction, police brutality, teen pregnancy, and various forms of material deprivation. This new development was both expressed and precipitated by Kurtis Blow's "Those Are the Breaks" and by the most influential and important rap song to emerge in rap's early history, "The Message," by Grandmaster Flash and The Furious Five. The picture this song painted of inner-city life for black Americans—the hues of dark social misery and stains of profound urban catastrophe—screeched against the canvas of most suburban sensibilities:

> You'll grow up in the ghetto living second rate / And your eyes will sing a song of deep hate / The places you play and where you stay, / Looks like one great big alleyway / You'll admire all the number book takers / Thugs, pimps, and pushers, and the big money makers / Drivin' big cars, spendin' twenties and tens, And you want to grow up to be just like them / . . . It's like a jungle sometimes / It makes me wonder how I keep from goin' under.

"The Message," along with Flash's "New York, New York," pioneered the social awakening of rap into a form combining social protest, musical creation, and cultural expression.

As its fortunes slowly grew, rap was still viewed by the music industry as an epiphenomenal cultural activity that would cease as black youth became bored and moved on to another diversion, as they did with break-dancing and graffiti art. But the successes of the rap group Run-D.M.C. moved rap into a different sphere of artistic expression that signaled its increasing control of its own destiny. Run-D.M.C. is widely recognized as the progenitor of modern rap's creative integration of social commentary, diverse musical elements, and uncompromising cultural identification—an integration that pushed the music into the mainstream and secured its future as an American musical genre with an identifiable tradition. Run-D.M.C.'s stunning commercial and critical success almost single-handedly landed rap in the homes of many black and nonblack youths across America by producing the first rap album to be certified gold (five hundred thousand copies sold), the first rap song to be featured on the twenty-four-hour music video channel MTV, and the first rap album (1987's *Raising Hell*) to go triple platinum (3 million copies sold).

On *Raising Hell,* Run-D.M.C. showcased the sophisticated technical virtuosity of its DJ Jam Master Jay—the raw shrieks, scratches, glitches, and language of the street, plus the innovative and ingenious appropriation of hard-rock guitar riffs. In doing this, Run-D.M.C. symbolically and substantively wedded two traditions—the waning subversion of rock music and the rising, incendiary aesthetic of hip-hop music—to produce a provocative musical hybrid of fiery lyricism and potent critique. *Raising Hell* ended with the rap anthem, "Proud to Be Black," intoning its unabashed racial pride:

> Ya know I'm proud to be black ya'll, And that's a fact ya'll / . . . Now Harriet Tubman was born a slave, She was a tiny black woman when she was raised / She was livin' to be givin', There's a lot that she gave / There's not a slave in this day and age, I'm proud to be black.

At the same time, rap, propelled by Run-D.M.C.'s epochal success, found an arena in which to concentrate its subversive cultural didacticism aimed at addressing racism, classism, social neglect, and urban pain: the rap concert, where rappers are allowed to engage in ritualistic refusals of censored speech. The rap concert also creates space for cultural resistance and personal agency, loosing the strictures of the tyrannizing surveillance and demoralizing condemnation of mainstream society and encouraging relatively autonomous, often enabling, forms of self-expression and cultural creativity.

However, Run-D.M.C.'s success, which greatly increased the visibility and commercial appeal of rap music through record sales and rap concerts, brought along another charge that has had a negative impact on rap's perception by the general public: the claim that rap expresses and causes violence. Tipper Gore has repeatedly said that rap music appeals to "angry, disillusioned, unloved kids" and that it tells them it is "okay to beat people up." Violent incidents at rap concerts in Los Angeles, Pittsburgh, Cleveland, Atlanta, Cincinnati, and New York City have only reinforced the popular perception that rap is intimately linked to violent social behavior by mostly black and Latino inner-city youth. Countless black parents, too, have had negative reactions to rap, and the black radio and media establishment, although not as vocal as Gore, have voted on her side with their allocation of much less airplay and print coverage to rap than is warranted by its impressive record sales.

Such reactions betray a shallow understanding of rap, which in many cases results from people's unwillingness to listen to rap lyrics, many of which counsel antiviolent and antidrug behavior among the youths who are their avid audience. Many rappers have spoken directly against violence, such as KRS-One in his "Stop the Violence." Another rap record produced by KRS-One in 1989, the top-selling *Self-Destruction,* insists that violence predates rap and speaks against escalating black-on-black crime, which erodes the social and communal fabric of already debased black inner cities across America:

> Well, today's topic is self-destruction, It really ain't the rap audience that's buggin' / It's one or two suckers, ignorant brothers, Tryin' to rob and steal from one

> another / . . . 'Cause the way we live is positive. We don't kill our relatives / . . . Back in the sixties our brothers and sisters were hanged. How could you gang-bang? / I never, ever ran from the Ku Klux Klan, and I shouldn't have to run from a black man, 'Cause that's / Self-destruction, ya headed for self-destruction.

Despite such potent messages, many mainstream blacks and whites persist in categorically negative appraisals of rap, refusing to distinguish between enabling, productive rap messages and the social violence that exists in many inner-city communities and that is often reflected in rap songs. Of course, it is difficult for a culture that is serious about the maintenance of social arrangements, economic conditions, and political choices that create and reproduce poverty, racism, sexism, classism, and violence to display a significant appreciation for musical expressions that contest the existence of such problems in black and Latino communities. Also disappointing is the continued complicity of black radio stations in denying rap its rightful place of prominence on their playlists. The conspiracy of silence and invisibility has affected the black print media, as well. Although rapper M. C. Shan believes that most antirap bias arises from outside the black community, he faults black radio for depriving rap of adequate airplay and laments the fact that "if a white rock 'n' roll magazine like *Rolling Stone* or *Spin* can put a rapper on the cover and *Ebony* and *Jet* won't, that means there's really something wrong."

In this regard, rap music is emblematic of the glacial shift in aesthetic sensibilities between blacks of different generations, and it draws attention to the severe economic barriers that increasingly divide ghetto poor blacks from middle- and upper-middle-class blacks. Rap reflects the intraracial class division that has plagued African-American communities for the last thirty years. The increasing social isolation, economic hardship, political demoralization, and cultural exploitation endured by most ghetto poor communities in the past few decades have given rise to a form of musical expression that captures the terms of ghetto poor existence. I am not suggesting that rap has been limited to the ghetto poor, but only that its major themes and styles continue to be drawn from the conflicts and contradictions of black urban life. One of the later trends in rap music is the development of "pop" rap by groups like JJ Fad, The Fat Boys, DJ Jazzy Jeff and The Fresh Prince, and Tone Loc. DJ Jazzy Jeff and The Fresh Prince, for example, are two suburbanites from South West Philadelphia and Winfield. (For that matter, members of the most radical rap group, Public Enemy, are suburbanites from Long Island.) DJ Jazzy Jeff and The Fresh Prince's album, *He's the DJ, I'm the Rapper,* sold over 3 million copies, boosted by the enormously successful single "Parents Just Don't Understand." This record, which rapped humorously about various crises associated with being a teen, struck a chord with teenagers across the racial and class spectra, signaling the exploration of rap's populist terrain. The Fresh Prince's present success as the star of his own Quincy Jones–produced television series is further testimony to his popular appeal.

Tone Loc's success also expresses rap's division between "hardcore" (social consciousness and racial pride backed by driving rhythms) and "pop" (exploration of common territory between races and classes, usually devoid of social message). This division, while expressing the commercial expansion of rap, also means that companies and willing radio executives have increasingly chosen pop rap as more acceptable than its more realistic, politically conscious counterpart. (This bias is also evident in the selection of award recipients in the newly created rap category at the annual Grammy Awards.) Tone Loc is an L.A. rapper whose first single, "Wild Thing," sold over 2 million copies, topping *Billboard's* "Hot Single's Chart," the first rap song to achieve this height. Tone Loc's success was sparked by his video's placement in heavy rotation on MTV, which devotes an hour on Saturdays to *Yo! MTV Raps,* a show that became so popular that a daily hour segment was added.

The success of such artists as Tone Loc and DJ Jazzy Jeff and The Fresh Prince inevitably raises the specter of mainstream dilution, the threat to every emergent form of cultural production in American society, particularly the fecund musical tradition that comes from black America. For many, this means the sanitizing of rap's expression of urban realities, resulting in sterile hip-hop that, devoid of its original fire, will offend no one. This scenario, of course, is a familiar denouement to the story of most formerly subversive musical genres. Also, MTV's avid acceptance of rap and the staging of rap concerts run by white promoters willing to take a chance on rap artists add further commentary to the sad state of cultural affairs in many black communities: the continued refusal to acknowledge authentic (not to mention desirable) forms of rap artistry ensures rap's existence on the margins of many black communities.

Perhaps the example of another neglected and devalued black musical tradition, the blues, can be helpful for understanding what is occurring among rap, segments of the black community, and mainstream American society. The blues now has a mostly young white audience. Blacks do not largely support the blues through concert patronage or record buying, thus neglecting a musical genre that was once closely identified with devalued and despised people: poor southern agrarian blacks and the northern urban black poor, the first stratum of the developing underclass. The blues functioned for another generation of blacks much as rap functions for young blacks today: as a source of racial identity, permitting forms of boasting and asserting machismo for devalued black men suffering from social degradation, allowing commentary on social and personal conditions in uncensored language, and fostering the ability to transform hurt and anguish into art and commerce. Even in its heyday, however, the blues existed as a secular musical genre over against the religious traditions that saw the blues as "devil's music" and the conservative black cultural perspectives of the blues as barbaric. These feelings, along with the direction of southern agrarian musical energies into a more accessible and populist soul music, ensured the contraction of the economic and cultural basis for expressing life experience in the blues idiom.

Robert Cray's recent success in mainstreaming the blues perhaps completes the cycle of survival for devalued forms of black music: it originates in a context of anguish and pain and joy and happiness, it expresses those emotions and ideas in a musical language and idiom peculiar to its view of life, it is altered as a result of cultural sensibilities and economic factors, and it undergoes distribution, packaging, and consumption for leisurely or cathartic pleasure through concert attendance or record buying. Also, in the process, artists are sometimes removed from the immediate context and original site of their artistic production. Moreover, besides the everyday ways in which the music is used for a variety of entertainment functions, it may occasionally be employed in contexts that undermine its critique of the status quo, and it may be used to legitimize a cultural or social setting that, in negative ways, has partially given rise to its expression. A recent example of this is the late Lee Atwater's positioning of himself as a privileged patron of the blues and soul music traditions in the 1989 Bush inauguration festivities, which was preceded by his racist use of the Willie Horton case. Atwater's use of Willie Horton viciously played on the very prejudice against black men that has often led blues musicians to express the psychic, personal, and social pain occasioned by racism in American (political) culture. Rap's visibility may alter this pattern as it continues to grow, but its self-defined and continuing challenge is to maintain its aesthetic, cultural, and political proximity to its side of original expression: the ghetto poor.

Interestingly, a new wave of rap artists may be accomplishing this goal, but with foreboding consequences. For example, N.W.A. (Niggaz with Attitudes) reflects the brutal circumstances that define the boundaries within which most ghetto poor black youth in Los Angeles must live. For the most part they—unlike their socially conscientious counterparts Public Enemy, Boogie Down Productions, and Stetsasonic—have no ethical remove from the violence, gang-bangin', and drugs in L.A.'s inner city. In their song "—— Tha Police," N.W.A. gives a sample of their reality:

> Fuck the police, comin' straight from the underground. A young nigger got it bad 'cause I'm brown / And not the other color, so police think, / They have the authority to kill a minority / . . . Searchin' my car looking for the product, / Thinkin' every nigger is sellin' narcotic / . . . But don't let it be a black and a white one, / 'Cause they'll slam ya down to the street top, / Black police showin' out for the white cop.

Such expressions of violence certainly reflect the actual life circumstances of many black and Latino youth caught in the desperate cycle of drugs and gangs involved in L.A. ghetto living. N.W.A. celebrates a lethal mix of civil terrorism and personal cynicism. Their attitude is both one answer to, and the logical outcome of, the violence, racism, and oppression in American culture. On the other hand, their vision must be criticized, for the stakes are too high for the luxury of moral neutrality. Having at least partially lived the life they rap about, N.W.A. understands the viciousness of police brutality. However, they must also be challenged to develop an ethical perspective on the drug gangs that duplicate police violence in black-on-black crime. While rappers like N.W.A. perform an invaluable service by rapping in poignant and realistic terms about urban underclass existence, they must be challenged to expand their moral vocabulary and be more sophisticated in their understanding that description alone is insufficient to address the crisis of black urban life. Groups like N.W.A. should be critically aware that blacks are victims of the violence of both state repression *and* gang violence, that one form of violence is often the response to the other, and that blacks continue to be held captive to disenabling lifestyles (gang-bangin', drug dealing) that cripple the life of black communities.

Also problematic is the sexist sentiment that pervades so much of rap music. It is a rampant sexism that continues to mediate the relations within the younger black generation with lamentable intensity. While it is true that rap's sexism is indeed a barometer of the general tenor and mood that mediates black male-female relations, it is not the role of women alone to challenge it. Reproach must flow from women *and* men who are sensitive to the ongoing sexist attitudes and behavior that dominate black male-female relationships. Because women by and large do not run record companies, or even head independent labels that have their records distributed by larger corporations, it is naive to assume that protest by women alone will arrest the spread of sexism in rap. Female rappers are certainly a potential resource for challenging existing sexist attitudes, but given the sexist barriers that patrol rap's borders, male rappers must be challenged by antisexist men, especially male rappers who contest the portrayal of women in most rap music. The constant reference to women as "skeezers," "bitches," and "ho's" only reinforces the perverted expression of male dominance and patriarchy and reasserts the stereotyping of women as sexual objects intended exclusively for male pleasure.

Fortunately, many of the problems related to rap—particularly with black radio, media, and community acceptance—have only fostered a sense of camaraderie that transcends in crucial ways the fierce competitive streak in rap (which, at its best moment, urges rappers on to creative musical heights). While the "dis" rap (which humorously musicalizes "the dozens") is alive and well, the overall feeling among rap artists that rap must flourish outside the sanctions of traditional means of garnering high visibility or securing record sales has directed a communal energy into the production of their music. The current state of affairs has also precipitated cooperative entrepreneurial activity among young black persons. The rap industry has spawned a number of independent labels, providing young blacks (mostly men) with experience as heads of their own businesses and with exposure as managers of talent, positions that might otherwise be unavailable to them. Until recently, rap flourished, for the most part, outside of the tight artistic and economic constraints imposed by major music corporations. Although many independent companies have struck distribution deals with major labels—such as Atlantic, MCA, Columbia, and Warner Brothers—it has usually been the case, until the late 1980s, that the inexperience of major labels with rap, coupled with their relatively conservative musical tastes, has enabled the independent labels to control their destinies by teaching the major music corporations invaluable lessons about street sales, the necessity of having a fast rate of delivery from the production of a record to its date of distribution, and remaining close to the sensibilities of the street, while experimenting with their marketing approach in ways that reflect the diversification of styles in rap.

Rap expresses the ongoing preoccupation with literacy and orality that has characterized African-American communities since the inception of legally coerced illiteracy during slavery. Rap artists explore grammatical creativity, verbal wizardry, and linguistic innovation in refining the art of oral communication. The rap artist, as Cornel West has indicated, is a bridge figure who combines the two potent traditions in black culture: preaching and music. The rap artist appeals to the rhetorical practices eloquently honed in African-American religious experiences and the cultural potency of black singing/musical traditions to produce an engaging hybrid. They are truly urban griots dispensing social and cultural critique, verbal shamans exorcising the demons of cultural amnesia. The culture of hip-hop has generated a lexicon of life that expresses rap's B-boy/B-girl worldview, a perspective that takes delight in undermining "correct" English usage while celebrating the culturally encoded phrases that communicate in rap's idiom.

Rap has also retrieved historic black ideas, movements, and figures in combating the racial amnesia that threatens to relegate the achievements of the black past to the ash heap of dismemory. Such actions have brought a renewed sense of historical pride to young black minds that provides a solid base for racial self-esteem. Rap music has also focused renewed attention on black nationalist and black radical thought. This revival has been best symbolized by the rap group Public Enemy. Public Enemy announced its black nationalism in embryonic form on their first album, *Yo! Bum Rush the Show,* but their vision sprang forward full-blown in their important *It Takes a Nation of Millions to Hold Us Back.* The album's explicit black nationalist language and cultural sensibilities were joined with a powerful mix of music, beats, screams, noise, and rhythms from the streets. Its message is provocative, even jarring, a précis of the contained chaos and channeled rage that informs the most politically astute rappers. On the cut "Bring the Noise," they intone:

> We got to demonstrate, come on now, they're gonna have to wait / Till we get it right / Radio stations I question their blackness /They call themselves black, but we'll see if they'll play this / Turn it up! Bring the noise!

Public Enemy also speaks of the criminality of prison conditions and how dope dealers fail the black community. Their historical revivalism is noteworthy, for instance, as they rap on "Party for Your Right to Fight":

> Power Equality / And we're out to get it / I know some of you ain't wit' it / This party started right in '66 / With a pro-Black radical mix / Then at the hour of twelve / . . . J. Edgar Hoover, and he coulda' proved to 'ya / He had King and X set up / Also the party with Newton, Cleaver, and Seale / . . . Word from the honorable Elijah Muhummad / Know who you are to be Black / . . . the original Black Asiatic man.

Public Enemy troubled even more sociocultural waters with their Nation of Islam views, saying in "Don't Believe the Hype":

> The follower of Farrakhan / Don't tell me that you understand / Until you hear the man.

Such rap displays the power and pitfalls associated with the revival of earlier forms of black radicalism, nationalism, and cultural expression. The salutary aspect of the historical revival is that it raises consciousness about important figures, movements, and ideas, prompting rappers to express their visions of life in American culture. This renewed historicism permits young blacks to discern links between the past and their own present circumstances, using the past as a fertile source of social reflection, cultural creation, and political resistance.

On the other hand, it has also led to perspectives that do not provide *critical* reflection on the past. Rather, many rappers attempt to duplicate the past without challenging or expanding it. Thus, their historical sight fails to illumine our current cultural problems as powerfully as it might, and the present generation of black youth fails to benefit as fully from the lessons that it so powerfully revives. This is an unfortunate result of the lack of understanding and communication among various segments of the black community, particularly along generational and class lines, problems symbolized in the black community's response to rap. Historical revival cries out for contexts that render the past understandable and usable. This cannot occur if large segments of the black community continue to be segregated from one of the most exciting cultural transformations occurring in contemporary American life: the artistic expression, cultural exploration, political activity, and historical revival of hip-hop artists.

An issue in rap that is closely related to the acknowledgment of history and sources is sampling, or the grafting of music, voices, and beats from another sonic source onto a rap record. The practice of sampling expresses the impulse to collage that characterizes the best of black musical traditions, particularly jazz and gospel. Sampling is also [a] postmodernist activity that merges disparate musical and cultural forms to communicate an artistic message. Sampling is a transgressive activity because rappers employ it to interrupt the narrative flow and musical stability of other musical texts, producing a new and often radically different creation. But rap may potentially take back in its technical appropriation what it has given in its substantive, lyrical achievements: a recognition of history. While sampling permits a rap creator to reconfigure voices and rhythms in creating an alternate code of cultural exchange, the practice may also deprive other artists of recognition or even financial remuneration. The classic case in point is James Brown, who, along with George Clinton, is the most sampled man in rap and the primal progenitor of the beats and rhythms in hip-hop music. Although his voice, rhythms, and beats are often easily identifiable and rap's debt to him is obvious, Brown's benefit has been limited. Recent legal woes connected to the status of rap's practice of creative borrowing may hasten rap's codification of appropriate acknowledgment, particularly in an economic practice similar to the royalty that distinguishes between small bites of music and significant borrowing and quotation.

Rap is a form of profound musical, cultural, and social creativity. It expresses the desire of young black people to reclaim their history, reactivate forms of black radicalism, and contest the powers of despair and economic depression that presently besiege the black community. Besides being the most powerful form of black musical expression today, rap projects a style of self into the world that generates forms of cultural resistance and transforms the ugly terrain of ghetto existence into a searing portrait of life as it must be lived by millions of voiceless people. For that reason alone, rap deserves attention and should be taken seriously; and for its productive and healthy moments, it should be promoted as a worthy form of artistic expression and cultural projection and an enabling source of black juvenile and communal solidarity.

PART SIX

LITERARY CRITICISM AND THEORY

OVERVIEW

African American literary criticism has developed into a distinct genre; that is, the critical writing itself is often a topic of literary critics. Like poems, plays, and stories, essays of literary criticism are scrutinized for their imaginative use of language and cultural references, as well as for their research, in-depth analyses, and theoretical frameworks. In addition, a number of African American literary critics, like other black creative writers, have fashioned recognizable styles of writing.

The Importance of the Critic to African American Literature

Why are critics important to black literature? After all, a critic is a person often despised by artists, dismissed by readers, and begrudgingly tolerated by other critics. In the critic lurks a certain cannibalistic creativity that sustains itself on the works of others. Fiction writer Toni Morrison argues that literary criticism is a form of knowledge "capable of robbing literature not only of its own implicit and explicit ideology but of its ideas as well" (5). However, in a 1992 essay, black critic Hortense J. Spillers describes the relationship among critic, author, audience, and creative work in this way: "The critic's task . . . is to speak or explain where the work does not, to supply the right questions for a proffered riddle. . . . It is unnecessary for both writer and audience to agree that the process of writing is a distinctive act of consciousness. It teaches us something about being alive and asks riddles in a way that is peculiar to itself, and perhaps that really is enough" (612).

Although the jungle of jargon that characterizes some reviews and other critical works can hinder the general reader's understanding, literary criticism is important for its illuminating ideas about literature. The significance of African American critics includes their roles in explicating and unifying the literature and in making its meaning accessible to a wide readership. This relatively new area of African American writing is thus worth exploring, both for its own sake and for the light it sheds on works in other genres as well.

The recent growth of African American criticism has been promoted by two related factors: first, black scholars have gained university positions that encourage research, and second, university presses have been publishing books and journals that showcase these scholars. Because so many black literary critics come from academia, some of these critics are sometimes faulted for using terminology deemed cryptic and even impenetrable.

A History of Literary Criticism

Because many contemporary African American critics come from academia, it is not surprising that their approaches to evaluating literature are influenced by centuries of European and Anglo-American writings. Many literary trends in American literature are also influenced by other factors, such as movements in philosophy, linguistics, architecture, painting, music, theater, and film. A brief description of some of the best-known literary movements and techniques follows.

- *Neo-Classicism:* late eighteenth-century literature characterized by didactic and moralistic prose, incorporating lofty, eloquent language and religious and mythological allusions
- *Romanticism:* early nineteenth-century literature that celebrated the beauty and mystery of nature both literally and symbolically
- *Naturalism:* late nineteenth-century literature with a fatalistic tone and emphasis on the power of large forces, such as the control of nature and society over human behavior
- *Realism:* late nineteenth- and early twentieth-century literature that rendered the details of common experience in terms that attempted to mirror human behavior, especially as it related to psychological conditions
- *Expressionism:* early twentieth-century literature characterized by exaggerations and distortions of reality meant to emphasize emotions
- *Surrealism:* early twentieth-century literature that stressed the role of the unconscious by depicting experiences in dreamlike terms
- *Modernism:* literature written between the two world wars in which the alienated artist commented on the irrationality of the world by experimenting with language and elevating form over content
- *Existentialism:* post–World War II literature characterized by a belief in the individual's right to fashion his or her life, despite situations imposed by the outside world, and in the individual's responsibility for creating meaning in his or her own life
- *Post-Modernism:* literature of the 1950s marked by eclecticism and parody and aimed at deflating the self-importance seen in modernist writing

African American scholars continue to debate the relevance of these (and other) literary movements and approaches to black literature. Some critics point to the influence of these trends on African American writers—for example, neo-classicism on Phillis Wheatley, naturalism on Richard Wright and Ann Petry, modernism on Jean Toomer, surrealism and expressionism on Ralph Ellison, and post-modernism on Ishmael Reed and Ntozake Shange. Other critics argue that such evaluations fail to provide insight into the writers as African Americans, beyond allowing judgments about their individual tastes. Moreover, whereas black authors are undoubtedly shaped by the literary movements of their time, many are also equally inspired by ethnic and cultural elements. Hence literary critics debate whether, in African American literature, literary trends obscure or clarify the significance of the black experience—including black vernacular, musical forms, and other cultural expression. Some analysts even ask whether political elements in literary trends from the past might render evaluations of black literature meaningless. Black critics continue to debate these questions.

Early Concern with the "Universal"

African American literature has been analyzed by both black and white critics since the nineteenth century. Some African American authors have asserted that nonblack critics unfairly apply their own ethnic rubric to black literature and thereby fail to recognize its inherent merits. Other black writers counter that their creative writing possesses the depth, beauty, and relevance to stand up to any ethnic or cultural standards and that their art is as universal as the art of any other group.

Among the earliest African American critics was Benjamin Brawley, whose *The Negro in Literature and Art in the United States* (1930) and *Early Negro American Writers* (1935) examined and appraised the works of numerous writers and artists from the eighteenth century to the early twentieth. In the former work, Brawley explained his views on the importance of literature: "Literature is supposed to be [a] reflection of the national life. . . . The Negro's one request of literature so far as he is concerned, is that it be fearlessly and absolutely honest. Let it portray life, realistically . . . but let it cease to exploit outworn theories or be the vehicle . . . of burlesque. A new age—a new world—is upon us, with new men, new vision, new desires" (204).

Maintaining the interrelationship of literature and other cultural elements, such critics as W. E. B. Du Bois, Alaine Locke, James Weldon Johnson, Arna Bontemps, Sterling Brown, Margaret Just Butcher, J. Saunders Redding, Hugh M. Gloster, and Arthur P. Davis sought during the early to mid-twentieth century to determine the value of African American literature within the context of both black culture and mainstream society. Although sometimes deferring to white authorship as the only standard of excellence, these early critics nonetheless acknowledged the talents and contributions of African American authors. Margaret Just Butcher captured the sentiment of the times in *The Negro in American Culture* (1956) when she wrote: "There are various schools of thought among Negro critics as to the direction Negro writers should take in employing subject matter. Should Negro writers deal with Negro themes? Or 'universal themes'? Or should there be a synthesis of the two? Or should it matter?" (183).

The questions raised by Butcher illustrate the predicament that some black critics and writers faced during the first half of the century. African American literature was deemed too limited because of its focus on black experiences, which, by assumption, were not "universal." Yet white writers were not reproved for creating works based on their own experiences; white experiences were simply assumed to be "universal." The black critics and writers of the time should have argued that *all* writing is universal because it flows from human experience. But, some early black critics were reluctant to point to the connections between black literature and black cultural expressions, such as songs, idioms, and folktales. Instead, these black critics apologized for the presumed inability of black writers to imitate what was considered American literature at the time.

Post-World War II Critics and the Black Experience

In the decades following World War II, African American literary criticism blossomed with the writings of Ralph Ellison, John Oliver Killens, James Baldwin, George Kent, Albert Murray, Charles T. Davis, Dudley Randall, John Henrik Clarke, Nathan Scott, Richard Barksdale, and Darwin T. Turner, to name a few. Collectively, they helped to generate an appreciation for and interest in African American literature and to strengthen the reputations of black writers. Also during this time, black critics began to recognize African American experiences as valid subject matter. Writing in 1982, Charles T. Davis made this observation: "Awareness of being black is the most powerful and the most fertile single inspiration for black writers in America. . . . But for most, blackness was the spur, the barb, or the shirt of pain that moved the artist to achieve distinction" (3).

Since the late 1960s, a number of new critical schools of thought have emerged as a result of the Black Arts Movement, feminism, and gay and lesbian perspectives. Many prominent critics of these eras—including Amiri Baraka, Addison Gayle, Bernard W. Bell, Mary Helen Washington, Robert B. Stepto, Hortense Spillers, Houston A. Baker, Jr., bell hooks, Henry Louis Gates, Jr., Barbara Christian, Charles Johnson, Deborah McDowell, Arnold Rampersad, Hazel V. Carby, Cornel West, and Valerie Smith—were in academic settings that supported their research as well as the integration of their theories into university curricula and classrooms.

Subjective versus Objective Theories: Formalism, Marxism, and Feminism

Although some black critics debate the relevance of current mainstream approaches to evaluating the body of African American expression, others affirm the value of these theories, often by invoking the names of nonblack literary theoreticians such as John Crowe Ranson, Northrop Frye, Michel Foucault, Jacques Derrida, and Harold Bloom. In general, most current critical approaches to literature operate under one of two basic theories: subjective or objective. *Subjective critical theories*—including the Freudian, Marxist, feminist, and reader-response forms of criticism—suggest that meanings in a literary work are shaped by factors beyond the work itself. In contrast, *objective critical theories,* which include formalism, structuralism, post-structuralism, and deconstructionism, hold that meanings in a work of literature are not influenced by outside forces.

Three critical theories in particular have gained favor among today's black critics: formalism, Marxism, and feminism. *Formalism* (sometimes called the "new criticism") is an objective theory that assumes that the meaning of a creative work is self-contained and therefore that any critical examination should focus on the work's form—its rhythmic patterns, images, tone, and so on—rather than on the author's life and times. According to scholar Michael Meyer, this type of critical analysis involves a close reading and "pays special attention to what are often described as intrinsic matters in a literary work, such as diction, irony, paradox, metaphor, and symbol, as well as larger elements, such as plots, characterization, and narrative technique" (1999).

Unlike formalism, the subjective theory on which *Marxism* is based turns the critical emphasis to matters of content rather than form. Thus the social, economic, and political issues that speak directly to the realities of race and class fall within the realm of Marxist criticism and its focus on content. For African American literary critic Amiri Baraka, Marxist criticism was the next logical step beyond black nationalism. William J. Harris reports him as saying, "I came to my Marxist view as a result of having struggled as a Nationalist and found certain dead-ends theoretically and ideologically, as far as Nationalism was concerned, and had to reach out for a communist ideology" (23).

Also a subjective-based critical approach, *feminism* seeks to assess the manner in which the politics of gender have influenced literary images of women and diminished their significance. Feminist criticism seeks to restore women's views within the literary tradition. Taken a step further by black women critics, this criticism must speak to the dynamics of ethnicity and culture as well. According to one African American critic, Patricia Hills Collins, "Black feminist thought consists of specialized knowledge created by African-American women. . . . In other words, Black feminist thought encompasses theoretical interpretations of Black women's reality by those who live it" (22).

Alternative Critical Approaches

In opposition to the subjective and objective theories, which originated among white critics, several black critics and artists have insisted on the need to define and develop alternative approaches centered entirely within African American culture. At the heart of this opposition is the belief that methodology based outside of black culture is steeped in racist suppositions that intend to defame and even destroy that culture.

One prominent theory centered in African American culture has been the Black Aesthetic, fueled by the Black Arts Movement of the late 1960s and 1970s. The Black Aesthetic defines the perimeters of African American literature as writing by, about, and for blacks. In its rejection of literary traditions from outside black culture and its view of literature as a political weapon, the Black Aesthetic narrows the boundaries of what it means to be a black writer by demanding that the literature not stray from its main purpose of raising racial, political, and social consciousness. It consequently relegates artistic concerns to the background. For some critics, the Black Aesthetic goes beyond Black Nationalism to include Black Elitism and Black Essentialism, carrying with it a denial of difference among African Americans.

The *Womanist* perspective of literary criticism grew out of the philosophy introduced by Alice Walker in her collection of essays *In Search of Our Mothers' Gardens* (1983). (See the Focused Study of Walker's fiction in Part Three.) While endorsing feminism, Womanism seeks to shed light on issues not often explored by feminist critics, such as those affecting women of color and lesbians. In the introduction to her 1983 book, Walker describes a Womanist as a person who avoids defining people on the basis of differences and who is "committed to the survival and wholeness of entire people, male and female" (xi). Inclusive rather than exclusive, the Womanist approach to literary criticism usually focuses on a broad range of writings within African American culture.

Also emerging in the early 1980s, Henry Louis Gates, Jr. fashioned a linguistic model of criticism known as *signifyin*. This approach looks at elements of language, behavior, and psyche in evaluating the figurative, ambiguous, and polysemic nature of African American writing. It envisions black expression as a survival mechanism used by African American authors to conceal their intentions from a hostile white culture. By maintaining a rubric whose meaning is rooted in the language of black culture, signifyin emphasizes a cultural analysis of literature.

Most recently, author and critic Toni Morrison posed an approach to literature called *Africanism*. It seeks to recognize the influence of African American experience and culture on the body of American literature, including the works of white writers such as Henry James, Gertrude Stein, Willa Cather, Ernest Hemingway, and Flannery O'Connor. According to Morrison, this form of criticism focuses on the "denotative and connotative blackness that African people have come to signify, as well as the entire range of views, assumptions, readings, and misreadings that accompany Eurocentric learning about these people" (2–3). Given that centuries of American racial principles have influenced the literary works of African Americans, so, too, Morrison argues, have those principles molded the writings of white Americans. Morrison's observations imply that no American literature is free of racial ideology and that assessing a work's "Africanism" identifies connections between black and nonblack literature.

In This Part

Against the background of this history of literary techniques and critical theories, how is African American literature to be evaluated? Is there one strategy that works best to judge the merit and nature of any given poem, short story, or play? Can one approach be applied to appraise the entire body of African American literature? Black critics and scholars continue to wrestle with these and other questions. In the eight essays featured here, several of the black critics apply a methodology to specific works, while others analyze particular literary movements and theories. Unlike the selections in previous parts of this anthology, the selections that follow are organized thematically rather than by the birthdates of the authors.

In the excerpt of "There Is No More Beautiful Way" (1989), Houston A. Baker, Jr., defines and defends critical theory, arguing that black literature benefits from theories that explore a "metalevel of explanation." For Baker, applying critical theory to African American literature discourages simplistic evaluations and emphasizes the interaction of personal and cultural aspects within a work.

Valerie Smith's "Form and Ideology in . . . Slave Narratives" (1987)—edited to give focus to her commentary on the narratives of Olaudah Equiano and Harriet Jacobs (see Part Five)—examines the limitations of the slave narrative form. The writer asserts that the slave narrative fails to disclose both the artistic talent and thematic concerns of the black person who is its main subject.

The critical essays by Henry Louis Gates, Jr., and Michael Thelwell are included here as companion pieces. Gates's "The Blackness of Blackness: A Critique of the Sign and the Signifying Monkey" (1983) proposes a paradigm for investigating black literature: signifyin, the use of oral language by blacks to convey meaning on multiple levels. Thelwell's "Toward a Collective Vision: Issues in International Literary Criticism" (1990) challenges Gates's theory. Thelwell argues that Gates and other black critics encumber the critiquing of black literature with Eurocentric terminology and unnecessary abstraction.

Larry Neal's "The Black Arts Movement" (1968) offers a provocative contrast to Charles Johnson's "Being and Race" (1988). Neal defines African American literature in terms of the criteria and purpose of the Black Aesthetic, a literary movement rooted in politics and cultural awareness of the 1960s. In contrast, Johnson takes a metaphysical view of art in his history of black literature, suggesting that creativity comes from within the individual and from personal experience. Consequently, Johnson refutes Neal's premise by arguing that cultural movements such as the Black Arts Movement attempt to structure a rigid group identity and thereby restrict individual expression.

In "Rethinking Black Feminist Theory" (1987), Hazel V. Carby links contemporary and late nineteenth-century black feminist critics. Pointing out the different concerns of white and black feminists, Carby explores the imperatives of black feminists and their contributions to the development of black feminist politics.

Charles I. Nero's "Toward a Black Gay Aesthetic: Signifying in Contemporary Black Gay Literature" (1991) elaborates on some of the ideas expressed by Gates, Neal, and Johnson. Utilizing Gates's theory of signifyin to place black gay literature within the larger context of African American literature, Nero examines numerous literary and religious examples of homophobia to underscore its presence in literary images and definitions of black manhood.

The perspectives developed in these eight essays do not represent all of the current critical models. Nor do they lead to a consensus that might bring the debate about criticism to a harmonious resolution. Rather, the essays in this part demonstrate black critics' ongoing intellectual tug-of-war to define an African American literary tradition that continues to grow in breadth and eminence.

Works Cited

Brawley, Benjamin. *The Negro in Literature and Art in the United States.* New York: Duffield, 1930.

Butcher, Margaret Just. *The Negro in American Culture.* New York: Knopf, 1956.

Collins, Patricia Hill. *Black Feminist Thought.* New York: Routledge, 1990.

Davis, Charles T. *Black Is the Color of the Cosmos: Essays on Afro-American Literature and Culture, 1942–1981.* New York: Garland, 1982.

Harris, William J. "Amiri Baraka." *African American Writers.* Ed. Valerie Smith, Lea Baechler, and A. Walton Litz. New York: Scribner's, 1993. 15–27.

Meyer, Michael, ed. *The Bedford Introduction to Literature.* 3rd ed. Boston: Bedford, 1993.

Morrison, Toni. *Playing in the Dark: Whiteness and the Literary Imagination.* Cambridge, MA: Harvard UP, 1992.

Spillers, Hortense J. "Formalism Comes to Harlem." *The New Cavalcade.* Ed. Arthur P. Davis, J. Saunders Redding, and Joyce Ann Joyce. Vol. 2. Washington, DC: Howard UP, 1992. 608–20.

Walker, Alice. *In Search of Our Mothers' Gardens.* New York: Harcourt, 1983.

Suggested Readings

Some of the essential critical writing about African American literature has been mentioned in this text in the various chapter Overviews, as well as in the biographical headnotes for the authors in Chapters Five and Six.

Additional information can be found in the following: *To Make a Poet Black* (1939), by J. Saunders Redding; *Negro Voices in American Fiction* (1948) by Hugh M. Gloster; *The Black Aesthetic* (1971) edited by Addison Gayle, Jr.; *Harlem Renaissance* (1971) by Nathan Huggins; *In a Minor Chord: Three Afro-American Writers and Their Search for Identity* (1971) by

Darwin T. Turner; *Understanding the New Black Poetry: Black Speech and Black Music as Poetic References* (1972) edited by Stephen Henderson; *The Dark and Feeling: Black American Writers and Their Work* (1974) by Clarence Major; *The Omni-Americans* (1979) by Albert Murray; *From behind the Veil: A Study of Afro-American Narrative* (1979) by Robert B. Stepto; *The Craft of Ralph Ellison* (1980) by Robert O'Meally; *Black American Literature and Humanism* (1981) by R. Baxter Miller; *Black Is the Color of the Cosmos: Essays on Afro-American Literature and Culture, 1942–1981* (1982) by Charles T. Davis; *The Art of Slave Narratives: Original Essays in Criticism and Theory* (1982) edited by Darwin T. Turner and John Sekora; *Home Girls: A Black Feminist Anthology* (1983) edited by Barbara Smith; *The Poetry and Poetics of Amiri Baraka* (1985) by William J. Harris; *Conjuring: Black Women, Fiction, and the Literary Tradition* (1985) edited by Hortense J. Spillers and Marjorie Pryse; *Slavery and the Literary Imagination* (1988) by Arnold Rampersad and Deborah McDowell; *Specifying: Black Women Writing the American Experience* (1987) by Susan Willis; *A History of Afro-American Literature* (1989) by Blyden Jackson; *Choosing Our Own Words: Essays on Criticism, Theory, and Writing by Black Women* (1989) edited by Cheryl Wall; *Invisibility Blues: From Pop to Theory* (1990) by Michelle Wallace; *Comparative American Identities: Race, Sex, and Nationality in the Modern Text* (1991) by Hortense J. Spillers; and *Playing in the Dark: Whiteness and the Literary Imagination* (1992) by Toni Morrison.

Houston A. Baker, Jr. (1943–)

Among the most respected contemporary African American critics, Houston Baker is professor of English as well as Albert M. Greenfield Professor of Human Relations at the University of Pennsylvania, where he also directs the Center for the Study of Black Literature and Culture.

Born in Louisville, Kentucky, Baker was raised in the Washington, D.C., area. He earned his bachelor's from Howard University in 1965 and his masters's and doctorate from the University of California at Los Angeles in 1966 and 1968, respectively. Baker returned to Howard University as an instructor, later accepting a position at Yale University. In the early 1970s, he taught at the University of Virginia, then joined the University of Pennsylvania as director of Afro-American studies in 1974, a post he filled until 1981, when he assumed his present position.

Baker's professional affiliations, awards, and honors are extensive. Equally impressive is his astounding number of publications within the past twenty years. In addition to a volume of poetry, No Matter Where You Travel, You Still Be Black *(1979), Baker has written a half-dozen books of criticism:* Singers of Daybreak: Studies in Black American Literature *(1975),* The Journey Back: Issues in Black Literature and Criticism *(1980),* Blues, Ideology, and Afro-American Literature: A Vernacular Theory *(1984),* Modernism and the Harlem Renaissance *(1987),* Afro-American Poetics: Revision of Harlem and the Black Aesthetic *(1988), and* Black Studies, Rap, and the Academy *(1993). In addition to his many essays and books about African American writers, Baker has edited several notable anthologies, including* Black Literature in America *(1971),* Reading Black: Essays in the Criticism of African, Caribbean, and Black American Literature *(1976),* A Dark and Sudden Beauty: Two Essays in Black American Poetry *(1977),* Three American Literatures: Essays in Chicano, Native American, and Asian American Literature *(1982), and* Afro-American Literary Study in the 1990s *(1989), coedited with Patricia Redmond.*

"There Is No More Beautiful Way" was originally published in Afro-American Literary Study in the 1990s. *In the abridged version appearing here, Baker weighs the value and significance of literary criticism for African American literature. His examination of several other critics' antagonistic approaches leads him to conclude that even opposing theoretical inquiries contribute to a deeper appreciation of black literature.*

There Is No More Beautiful Way

I

A theory is an explanation. Successful theories offer global description and predictive adequacy. Their goal is an order of understanding different from intuitive knowledge, common sense, or appreciation. They begin where such modes of thought end, or at least where they fail to address questions that require for their answers more than enumeration, cataloguing, impressionistic summaries, selected lists, or nonce critical formulations.

Proposed responses to the question "What is Afro-American literature?" might include anthologies, literary histories, bibliographies, survey courses, or reading lists. These responses—as useful as they might be—are not theory. For theory is occupied preeminently with assumptions, presuppositions, and principles of production rather than with the orderly handling of material products represented by anthologies and survey courses. Theory's relentless tendency is to go beyond the tangible in search of a *metalevel* of explanation. A concern for metalevels, rather than tangible products, is also a founding condition of Afro-American intellectual history.

Africans uprooted from ancestral soil, stripped of material culture, and victimized by brutal contact with various European nations were compelled not only to maintain their cultural heritage at a *meta* (as opposed to a material) level, but also to apprehend the operative metaphysics of various alien cultures.

The primacy of nonmaterial transactions in the African's initial negotiations of the New World led to a privileging of the roles and figures of medicine men, griots, conjurers, priests, or priestesses.[1] This emphasis on spiritual leadership (and leadings of the spirit) was embodied in at least one form as the founding institution of Afro-American group life—the church, which in its very name sometimes bodies forth the spiritual syncretism of its founding: "African Methodist Episcopal."

The generative conditions of African life in the New World that privilege spiritual negotiation also make autobiography the premiere genre of Afro-American discourse. Bereft of material, geographical, or political inscriptions of a state and a common mind, New World Africans were compelled to seek a personal, spiritual assurance of worth. Their quest was analogous to Puritan religious meditations in the mainland British colonies of North America such as Jonathan Edwards's *Personal Narrative*.[2] For, like their Puritan fellows in deracination and sometimes forced immigration, Africans were compelled to verify a self's being-in-the-world. They were forced to construct and inscribe unique personhood in what appeared to be a blank and uncertain environment. Afro-American intellectual history, therefore, is keenly theoretical because it pays a compulsory attention both to metalevels of cultural negotiation and to autobiographical inscription. Our intellectual history privileges the unseen and the intangibly personal. The trajectory of this history is from what might be called the workings of a distinctively syncretic spirit to autobiographical incorporation or expressive embodiment of such spirit-work. Two images suggest themselves as illustrations of this trajectory.

One image is the frontispiece of Phillis Wheatley's *Poems on Various Subjects Religious and Moral* (1773).[3] Clad in servant's clothing, the young and distinctively African-featured poet Phillis holds pen in hand and looks meditatively ahead, concentrating on something that remains invisible for viewers of her portrait. But the quill pen in her hand has obviously been at work. There are visible lines written on the parchment that we see in the portrait. Perhaps the lines are the following ones:

> The happier *Terence* all the choir inspir'd,
> His soul replenish'd, and his bosom fir'd;
> But say, ye *Muses,* why this partial grace,
> To one alone of *Afric's* sable race:
> From age to age transmitting thus his name
> With the first glory in the rolls of fame?
> (p. 4)

We do know that Phillis inscribed these lines in her poem "To Maecenas." In doing so, she wrote her male precursor's African name (Terence) and body into the discourse of eighteenth-century heroics. Further, she comes to us in these lines as African embodiment of Terence's precursorial spirit. She calls the question on the muses, as it were—with her pen. That question, finally, is one of metalevels and canonicity. What is it, Phillis queries, that privileges Terence's presence and why is there a situation of "partial grace" and perpetual exclusion?

The second image reads as follows:

> The hearing of those wild notes always depressed my spirit, and filled me with ineffable sadness. I have frequently found myself in tears while hearing them. The mere recurrence to those songs, even now, afflicts me; and while I am writing these lines, an expression of feeling has already found its way down my cheek. To those songs I trace my first glimmering conception of the dehumanizing character of slavery. I can never get rid of that conception. Those songs still follow me, to deepen my hatred of slavery, and quicken my sympathies for my brethren in bonds.[4] (p. 58)

Here the precursors are legion, but it is their embodied *sound* that marks an expressive lineage. A self-conscious narrator of African ancestry can be envisioned staring straight ahead in the manner of Wheatley, hearing again from a position analytically outside the circle of song an informing sound. The tear on "these lines" is the unifying affective bonding between a spirited and singing text and the written autobiography of Frederick Douglass. Theory's intangible province is embodied in the image of the narrator writing black, lyrical, first principles that he has extrapolated from his meditations on song. "Slaves sing most when they are most unhappy." The tear, unhappiness, a soul-killing institutionalization of the African body, bring the narrator's present writing and the songs' past sounding together under the controlled pen of African autobiographical genius. We might say the spirit comes through; the vernacular resounds in brilliant coalescence with the formally literary. The metalevel prompting the African, slave impulse (an expressive impulse) to song is made readable.

The conflation of past and present, ineffable and readable, marked by Douglass's passage prepares the way for an entirely self-conscious translation of "unhappiness" in a soul-killing institution that brings the narrator into portrayed, pen-in-hand harmony with the Wheatley of *Poems on Various Subjects:*

> I had no bed. I must have perished with cold, but that, the coldest nights, I used to steal a bag which was used for carrying corn to mill. I would crawl into this bag, and there sleep on the cold, damp, clay floor, with my head in and feet out. My feet have been so cracked with the frost, that the pen with which I am writing might be laid in the gashes. (p. 72)

Deprivation, theft, commodification, the burlap (wool?) pulled over the slave's eyes, a sleep of reason that produces wounds ("cracked . . . gashes")—all of these merge in the meditation of a present narrator who has pen-in-hand. The spiritual bankruptcy of American slavery embodies itself as the wounded and commodified ("a bag which was used for carrying corn to the mill") body of the

African. The spiritual significance of such a scene emerges only through the pen laid, as poultice and portrayal, on the wound. A single fissure gives rise to written signification of immense proportions as Douglass, like his precursor Wheatley, calls the question.

These images of Wheatley and Douglass are images of Afro-American theory in its self-embodying resonance. They could be multiplied tenfold through a survey of Afro-American literary critical history. One thinks of W. E. B. Du Bois's autobiographical situation at the close of his "Forethought" to *The Souls of Black Folk* as well as his lyrical autobiographical situation at the conclusion of that collection. One can summon to mind the autobiographical situation of the writer in Richard Wright's "The Literature of the Negro in the United States," or James Baldwin's narrator in the "Autobiographical Notes" that opens his collection *Notes of a Native Son*. One thinks, as well, of Ralph Ellison's autobiographical introduction to *Shadow and Act* and of Amiri Baraka's opening autobiographical essay "Cuba Libre" in his collection entitled *Home*.

Such enumerations, however, are not theory. They are certainly metatheoretical, though, in a way that will helpfully clarify the project in Afro-American intellectual history that is at work here. For they serve to adumbrate the lineage of what I have designated as an "autobiographical negotiation of metalevels" that constitutes black discourse in its most cogent form.

II

At present in the United States there seems to have occurred a quite remarkable reversal of this form. Imagistically, this reversal displays itself in the person and voice of Afro-American critics, with pen in hand, suggesting that theory is *alien* to a founding Afro-American discourse. Such critics claim that black discourse is most aptly characterized as humanistic and unambiguously moral. Critics such as R. Baxter Miller and Joyce Joyce want, in fact, to suggest that Afro-American discourse *must* be taken as a palpable and simon-pure output of a loving, moral creature known as Man, or, more charitably and inclusively, Humankind.[5] Implicit in the claims of Miller and Joyce is the notion that Homo Africanus is somehow comprehensible by standards of scholarship and fields of rhetoric that are not implicated in the sphere of metalevels, or "theory."

That is, for Joyce, Miller, and their ilk, an adequate picture of Afro-American discourse can be achieved only via assumptions of a traditional humanism and methods of standard disciplines such as social history, philosophy, and group psychology. Claims of writers such as Miller and Joyce situate them with debunkers of a project in literary and expressive cultural theory that has been disruptively influential for, at least, the past two decades in American, French, and British universities. It also situates them, I believe, at some remove from discernible contours of Afro-American intellectual history. . . .

What I want to suggest is that the Afro-American's negotiation of metalevels, in combination with his or her propensity for autobiography as a form of African embodiment, enabled him or her to control a variety of levels of discourse in the United States. Such control has placed African Americans in a position that refutes, it seems to me, any claims for a simplistic humanity, humanism, or affective purity of black discourse.

The most forceful expressive cultural spokespersons of Afro-America have traditionally been those who have first mastered a master discourse—at its most rarefied metalevels as well as its quotidian performative levels—and then, autobiographically, written themselves and their *own* metalevels palimpsestically on the scroll of this mastery. The act of such mastery has sometimes moved hostilely *against* claims of a traditional humanism and has seldom been characterized by any sentiment that might unambiguously or simply be designated "love."

A case in point from black discourse is resonantly before us at this moment of celebration of the Constitution of the United States of America. When the black writer David Walker issued his *Appeal* in 1829, in the form of a revolutionarily African document containing a "preamble" and four "articles" and maintained throughout that document an autobiographical voice, he accomplished the type of founding, black, theoretical, discursive negotiation I have in mind.

As a document that, in a sense, writes itself on the enslaved body of the African, the Constitution of the United States contains both a foregrounded story of freedom and a variety of backgrounded narratives of suppression and enslavement. David Walker, like all theoretically adept Afro-American spokespeople, had absolute knowledge of one set of suppressions, and he took as his task an appealing writing (or re-righting) of the African body in the very foreground of the Constitution.

Walker, in Henry Louis Gates's sense of the word,[6] *signifies* with, on, and in the very face of the *meta* and performative levels of the founding discourse of Euroamerican culture. He knew, of course, that such discourse as the Constitution had to be survived and syncretically refigured if African freedom and community were to become American realities.

Now, whether Walker was more loving, humanistic, convivial, or inherently humane than, say, the average *white* Boston citizen of his day, is a stunningly irrelevant point where Afro-American expressive cultural theory is concerned. What is important is that he was both autobiographically astute and strikingly brilliant with respect to the foregrounded stories of such white citizenry. (His very title, in its long form, refers to colored *citizens*—a truly African, heretical invocation in 1829.) He was, in short, a successful Afro-American theorist who knew that simplistic assertions of a distinguishable African American cultural and discursive practice would yield nothing. He knew that he had to master the very forms of enslavement in order to write the African body in empowering terms. Walker's act, thus, constitutes an autobiographical revolution, an explosive superliteracy that writes the self not in terms of the other but in lines that adumbrate the suppressed story of *another*. The *Appeal* emerges as a new covenant, a new constitution embodied in the African. It repudiates a hypocritical constitutional humanism and urges a robust hatred of slavery. Theory understood in terms of David Walker's *Appeal* is, I believe, of the essence of Afro-American intellectual history.

What most discourages readers about "theory" in another form—specifically, as it has manifested itself in the academy in recent years—is its seeming self-absorption, its refusal to supply material examples and enumerations that make for general recognition and reading. Theory seems, perhaps to those like Miller and Joyce, merely self-indulgent, an endless spinning of personal webs, or the ceaseless construction of what Elizabeth Bruss calls "beautiful theories."[7] Not only do such efforts fail to yield material examples or general reading, they may seem, finally, to have no practical consequences whatsoever, refusing to translate complex expressive cultural texts into enumerative, catalogued, or syllabused forms.

There is much to be said in support of the suspicion and charges of theory's detractors. There exist, for example, forceful, comprehensive, and usable accounts of expressive texts that derive from such seemingly "theory-free" accountings as psychological and sociohistorical explanatory narratives. Still, the disparagement of theory by Afro-Americans who claim somehow to be nonobscurantist geniuses of racial love and/or knights of the order of humanism might be considered slightly bizarre. For it is, surely, theoretical discourse—conceived as autobiographical cultural commentary—that is the very foundation of Afro-American intellectual history. The incendiary deconstruction, defamiliarization, and signifying within the master discourse represented by Walker's *Appeal* or Du Bois's *Souls* or Baraka's *Home* (full as that text is of Wittgensteinian analytic philosophy) constitutes, indeed, the writing and informed ritualization of the African body in the New World.

Finally it is not theory, I think, that Afro-American detractors mean when they attack the Afro-American literary theoretical project, but rather *the politics of theory* as they have manifested themselves in recent years. Afro-Americans were the very first radically to call the question on the traditional exclusiveness of the American academy in recent years, and they called this question in traditionally Afro-American theoretical terms. At Yale, Cornell, and San Francisco State, for example, such workers as Armstead Robinson, Roy Bryce Laporte, Michael Thelwell, James Turner, Sonia Sanchez, and Nathan Hare astutely, personally (writing, talking, and thinking out of their own lives) adduced a different idea of the *real* story of higher education in the United States. The embodiment—the very African embodiment—of their endeavors was *black* or *Afro-American* studies. We might say that where the founding of Afro-American studies was concerned, the personal was the theoretical. Such theoretically adduced studies have been for the past two decades the visible sign of African American spirit-work on university campuses. The results of black studies initiatives have included: revised and refigured admissions policies, new courses, revised canons of study, and the creation of an atmosphere where myriad formerly suppressed or backgrounded discourses have taken to the open air in their unique significations.

From activist autobiography, or metalevel negotiation as it were, in the example of black studies, the academy has, on the one hand, moved to various other "studies," such as women's, Chicano, gay, Asian-American, etc. On the other hand, the actional character of theory that produced black studies has been recuperated by disciplines such as "English" as an occasion for sometimes esoteric and leisurely "readings" (for the eleven millionth time) of the same books by the same white, male authors who have marked syllabuses for decades. Theory, in this conservative manifestation, has been entirely adjectival—a project in which a mere *renaming* suffices for recuperation. Its work is held to be different or new because it is, say, "deconstructive." It goes by a different name, and a nominal modishness replaces metalevels' driving force. The traditionally privileged maintain their exclusive access to and control of scholarly rhetoric through perpetual renomination. And advancement is secured through rhetoric approved by these designers of the avant-garde. Today, a "new" generation in its forties and fifties looks just as white—if not as male—as its forefathers and foremothers. And the new generation remains just as uncommitted to actional theory as its forebears. Scarcely a socially active cohort, it represents itself as a coterie of white academicians traveling from place to place dropping deconstructive words.

Represented in the manner I have just described, theory does seem useless, and those Afro-American scholars and critics who are academicians must appear as traitors to fervid commentators such as Miller and Joyce. Further, Afro-American scholars who are adherents of an academic theoretical enterprise must seem resolutely to have turned away from some not-too-long-past clarity of purpose and prose. Who, after all, would deny that such a turning toward the adjectival groves of theory is a profitable—yes, even an entrepreneurially canny—gesture for an Afro-American intellectual?

Still, neither the remissness of white academicians—whether men or women—nor the entrepreneurial or careerist cunning of black academicians—whether men or women—should compel us to desert the most active traditions of theory in our own intellectual history in the name of a *return* to humanism or affectional moralism. Rather we should simply seek, in our own newly possible negotiation of metalevels to extrapolate what is actionally and autobiographically necessary and useful for us in order to move the founding and always resonantly in-action theoretical project of *our own* culture.

In short, the task seems to me one of negotiating the unseen and presuppositional domains of current popular white theorizing in much the same way that Walker, Douglass, Wheatley, Du Bois, or Baraka negotiated the heroics and analytics of their respective eras—pen in hand, listening to African sounds of precursors and mastering (both intellectually and rhetorically) the discursive forces and stories that suppress an African body. Like such spokespersons of our cultural past, we must be fully informed, indeed brilliant strategists of metalevels who trust our autobiographical impulses.

The most theoretically sophisticated act for the Afro-American scholar in our era is an autobiographical one—on the metalevels. For he or she is currently situated—by the very term "scholar" and the beneficence of Black Studies—within the very worlds of mastery. This *withinness* vis-à-vis the world of the masters is signified by Douglass and Wheatley with quill pens and by Walker's formal troping on the very Constitution of the United States. The autobiographical orientation of our past spokespersons is signified by their personal account of the *sound* of precursors, whether it is an African Terence or a plantation sorrow song. Douglass and Wheatley, like Walker and Baldwin, look toward the *unseen* and body it forth as rewriting, rereading, or, in some regard, the founding textuality of an African story in its syncretic primacy. Today, the Afro-American scholar's turn and eternal return is surely most usefully toward the type of founding theoretical project suggested by such traditional black, discursive efforts as those. The general goal is, finally, I believe, a family identity—a black, national script of empowerment.

NOTES

1. For a discussion of the expressive cultural, or ritual, responses of Africans to the trade, see Sterling Stuckey, *Slave Culture* (New York: Oxford University Press, 1987). See also Lawrence W. Levine, *Black Culture and Black Consciousness* (New York: Oxford University Press, 1977).
2. For a discussion of Afro-American autobiography, see Houston A. Baker, Jr., "Autobiographical Acts and the Voice of the Southern Slave," in his *The Journey Back* (Chicago: University of Chicago Press, 1980). See also William Andrews, *To Tell a Free Story* (Urbana: University of Illinois Press, 1986).
3. *The Poems of Phillis Wheatley,* ed. Julian Mason (Chapel Hill: University of North Carolina Press, 1986). All citations refer to this edition.

4. *Narrative of the Life of Frederick Douglass,* ed. Houston A. Baker, Jr. (New York: Penguin, 1982), p. 58. All citations are to this edition.
5. See *New Literary History* 18 (1986–87) for Joyce Joyce; see also R. Baxter Miller, ed., *Afro-American Literature and Humanism* (Lexington: University of Kentucky Press, 1978).
6. "The Blackness of Blackness: A Critique of the Sign and the Signifying Monkey," in *Black Literature and Literary Theory,* ed. Henry Louis Gates (New York: Methuen, 1984), pp. 285–321. [Gates's essay is reprinted in this anthology; see p. 880.]
7. *Beautiful Theories* (Baltimore: Johns Hopkins University Press, 1979).

Valerie Smith (1956–)

Valerie Smith is one of today's most productive and active African American scholars. Her work includes assessments of African American literature as well as critical studies of film, black independent filmmakers, and images of women in commercial cinema.

Smith earned her bachelor's from Bates College in 1975 and her master's and doctorate from the University of Virginia in 1978 and 1981, respectively. She has taught African American studies and women's studies at Princeton University, Columbia University, and the University of California at Los Angeles, where she is currently an associate professor of English. She received a National Endowment for the Humanities Fellowship for University Teachers. In addition, Smith has served as a research fellow at Harvard's W. E. B. Du Bois Institute for Afro-American Research, as convener for the Minority Discourse Project at the University of California Humanities Research Institute, as academic specialist for the U.S. Information Agency in Brazil in 1988, as co-organizer of the Conference on Black Independent Film at the Whitney Museum of American Art in 1990, and as curator for the Program of African American Films and Videos at the Los Angeles Festival in 1993.

In addition to her many published essays in the areas of African American, women's, and film studies, Smith has edited several significant books of literary criticism, including Self-Discovery and Authority in Afro-American Narratives *(1987),* The Columbia History of the American Novel *(1991),* African American Writers *(1991), and* Toni Morrison: A Collection of Critical Essays *(1994). She has been a member of the editorial boards of the* African American Review *since 1986, the* Quarterly Review of Film and Video, *and* Woman: A Cultural Review. *Smith is currently working on a book tentatively titled* Black Feminist Thought.

"Form and Ideology in . . . Slave Narratives" originally appeared in Self-Discovery and Authority in Afro-American Narrative. *In the abbreviated version reprinted here, Smith evaluates the dynamics influencing the content and structure of the slave narratives of Olaudah Equiano and Harriet Jacobs. (For selections by Equiano and Jacobs, see Part Five, pp. 597 and 618.)*

Form and Ideology in . . . Slave Narratives

The way in which the narratives of freed and fugitive slaves were produced has been largely responsible for their uncertain status as subjects of critical inquiry. In form they most closely resemble autobiographies. But if we expect autobiographies to present us with rhetorical figures and thematic explorations that reveal the author's sense of what his or her life means, then these stories disappoint. In each stage of their history, the presence of an intermediary renders the majority of the narratives not artistic constructions of personal experience but illustrations of someone else's view of slavery.

In the earliest examples of the genre, as William L. Andrews has shown, the relationship between narrator and text was triangulated through the ordering intelligence of a white amanuensis or editor. Relying on a model of slavery as a fundamentally benevolent institution, the early narratives portray the slave as either an outlaw or a wayfarer in need of the protection that only white paternal authority could provide.[1] Most of the middle-period accounts, published from the 1830s through the 1860s, claim to be written by the narrators themselves, yet these cases too serve an outside interest: the stories are shaped according to the requirements of the abolitionists who published them and provided them with readers. And as Marion Wilson Starling and Dorothy Sterling have acknowledged, even the narratives transcribed in the twentieth century by the Federal Writers' Project of the Works Progress Administration (WPA) bear more than their share of the interviewers' influence.[2] As Sterling remarks:

> Few of the interviewers were linguists. They transcribed the ex-slaves' speech as they heard it, as they thought they heard it, or as they thought it should have been said—and sometimes, the whiter the interviewer's skin, the heavier the dialect and the more erratic the spelling. A number of the interviews also went through an editorial process in which dialect was cleaned up or exaggerated, depending on the editors' judgment. To attempt to make the language of the interviews consistent or to "translate" them into standard English would add still another change.[3]

It is not surprising that a scholarly tradition that values the achievements of the classically educated, middle-class white male has dismissed the transcriptions of former slaves' oral accounts. Nor is it surprising that even those narratives that purport to be written by slaves themselves have come into disrepute: when three popular narratives were exposed as inauthentic between 1836 and 1838, serious doubts arose about authorship in the genre as a whole.[4] But the intrusive abolitionist influence has interfered with the critical reception of even those narratives that are demonstrably genuine. The former slaves may have seized upon the writing of their life stories as an opportunity to celebrate their escape and to reveal the coherence and meaning of their lives. These personal motives notwithstanding, the narratives were also (if not primarily) literary productions that documented the antislavery crusade. Their status as both popular art and propaganda imposed upon them a repetitiveness of structure, tone, and content that obscured individual achievements and artistic merit.[5]

As Henry Louis Gates, Jr., has shown, apologists and detractors alike have failed to attend to the formal dimensions of black texts:

> For all sorts of complex historical reasons, the very act of writing has been a "political" act for the black author. Even our most solipsistic texts, at least since the Enlightenment in Europe, have been treated as political evidence of one sort or another both implicitly and explicitly. And because our life in the West has been one struggle after another, our literature has been defined from without, and rather often from within, as primarily just one more polemic in those struggles.[6]

The formulaic and hybrid quality of the narratives has rendered their status as critical subjects even more elusive than that of other examples of Afro-American literary expression. Combining elements of history, autobiography, and fiction, they raise unique questions of interpretation. To study them as, for example, sustained images of an author's experience ignores the fact that they conform rather programmatically to a conventional pattern. Or to talk about the unity of an individual narrative is to ignore the fact that the texts as we read them contain numerous authenticating documents that create a panoply of other voices. Only by beginning from a clear sense of the narratives' generic properties does one capture the subtlety and achievement of the most compelling accounts.[7]

The narratives discussed here elude the domination of received generic structures and conventions. . . . I . . . include in this category Equiano's account, *The Interesting Narrative of the Life of Olaudah Equiano, or Gustavus Vassa, the African, Written by Himself* (1789), and Harriet Jacobs's *Incidents in the Life of a Slave Girl* (1861). As my formulation implies, my interest is both aesthetic and political. The narratives that test the limits of the formula tell us most about what those conventions signify. Furthermore, the narrators who transform the conventions into an image of what they believe their lives mean most closely resemble autobiographers; they leave the impress of their personal experience on the structure in which they tell their story. Perhaps most important, these narratives are of interest because in their variations on the formula they provide a figure for the author's liberation from slavery, the central act of the accounts themselves. In these places of difference, the narrators of these stories of freedom reveal their resistance even to the domination of their white allies.

Equiano's *Life* shares with other early narratives a relatively mild vision of slavery. As several critics have noted, the earliest accounts are essentially records of the authors' lives and experiences as slaves that include descriptions of the structure and practices of slavery.[8] Only with the rise of the antislavery influence and the passage of increasingly stringent legislation that rendered the institution even more inhumane did the narratives begin to stress its brutality and demand its abolition.

As Andrews has shown, the early narrators tended to choose one of two ways to represent the meaning of slavery in their lives.[9] Some, like Joseph Mountain, Arthur, Edmund Fortis, and Stephen Smith, followed the model of the popular criminal-confession narratives; others, like James Gronniosaw, George White, and Equiano, imitated the structure of the conversion narrative. The black criminal confessions identify the slaves' misfortune with their yearning for autonomy and feature slavery as a set of benevolent controls: "The average black criminal narrative is the story of a young man whose break with the authority figures in his life is presented as a symbol of his willful contempt for all systems of ordering and restraining the self."[10] The black conversion narratives likewise appropriated a rhetoric that denies the value of independence of mind and will. Moreover, their view of human existence as a drama of suffering that earns one a heavenly reward forestalled any questioning of slavery's injustices. The two forms thus either extol or deemphasize the impact of slavery in the life of the individual and minimize the writer-protagonist's significance and power.

In part because of his allegiance to both the Africa of his birth and the Europe and North America of his enslavement and choice, Equiano resists the ideological implications of the form of the conversion narrative in which he writes. Inscribed throughout his narrative, in his juxtapositions and in the modulations of his voice, is a simultaneous adoption of and withdrawal from the assumptions that inform the conventions of his genre. Equiano's narrative retains a quality of doubleness that correlates with the complex interrelation between his origins and socialization. That duplicity makes possible his authority over his form and its implicit ideology.

In his "Dedication," Equiano prepares his reader for the story of a life indebted to God's grace, an account that owes much to the structure and rhetoric of the conversion narrative. He writes: "By the horrors of [the slave trade] was I first torn away from all the tender connections that were naturally dear to my heart; but these, through the mysterious ways of Providence, I ought to regard as infinitely more than compensated by the introduction I have thence obtained to the knowledge of the Christian religion, and of a nation which . . . has exalted the dignity of human nature."[11] The passage features Providence as both the source of meaning and the central figure in the narrator's life, for it juxtaposes his naive misperceptions with the insights he attributes to God's grace. What he once saw as "horrors" and sufferings have been revealed as blessings in the course of time.

The ensuing narrative elaborates on this early allusion to the providential influence. Repeatedly Equiano invokes the presence of God's controlling hand in even the most insignificant circumstances. When, for example, his captain forbids him to bring aboard ship a set of bullocks he hopes to sell in foreign markets, Equiano is disappointed that he will have to settle for turkeys, less valuable lifestock. On this voyage, however, all the bullocks and the captain himself die, while Equiano's turkeys survive and bring him a considerable price. What might appear coincidental to another imagination provides Equiano with evidence of God's benevolence. Of the captain's death he remarks, "Had it pleased Providence that [the captain] had died but five months before, I verily believed I should not have obtained my freedom when I did, and . . . I might not have been able to get it . . . afterwards" (p. 135). Of the episode generally he writes, "I could not help looking upon this . . . circumstance, as a particular providence of God; and was accordingly thankful" (p. 135).

Equiano shares with other spiritual autobiographers this tendency to view the quotidian symbolically. More important, his treatment of his own conversion resembles the way this event is presented elsewhere in the genre. The process of his conversion follows the stages other narrators describe; it occupies as theirs do the thematic center of his account. He describes first an early transformation that initiates him into "easy self-righteousness" but not "the new birth of saving grace."[12] His authentic conversion, however, possesses like theirs a transcendent quality: the Lord appears to him in visions and voices and answers his supplications with specific instructions. Immediately after this transformation occurs, he endures a period of discouragement, a sense of his own inadequacy, from which he learns that grace, not works, is responsible for his salvation. This realization brings him profound joy and peace such as had been unknown to him previously. It provides the lens through which he reassesses past experiences and appreciates those to come, and it is the source of the tone, rhetoric, and imagery of his narration.[13]

But if Equiano's debt to the plot of the conversion narrative is clear, that is not his only story; his second story is the one told by the other voice in the text, the voice that jars during even a superficial reading of the account and that has been the focus of critical commentary.[14] Most of the narrative is told from Equiano's reasoned, equable, and worldly wise adult point of view. This tone, however, is interrupted on several occasions in the first third of the book by his uninitiated, naive point of view as a young African boy, as in the following excerpt:

> The first object that saluted my eyes when I arrived on the coast was the sea, and a slave ship. . . . These filled me with astonishment, that was soon converted into terror, which I am yet at a loss to describe. . . . I was immediately handled and tossed up to see if I was sound, by some of the crew; and I was now persuaded that I had got into a world of bad spirits, and that they were going to kill me. Their complexions too, differing so much from ours, their long hair, and the language they spoke, which was very different from any I had ever heard, united to confirm me in this belief. (p. 31)

In the first sentence he speaks from an adult perspective, the point of view of a man with sufficient experience to call a slave ship by name. But immediately thereafter he envelops his readers in his innocent perspective so that we witness his terror at seeing for the first time the sea, a ship, a race of men who look and sound nothing like him. His use of this technique operates at several levels and allows him to manipulate his relationship to his reader and to the form in which he writes.

At the most superficial level Equiano seems in this passage to ridicule his own ignorance and ally himself with his more sophisticated reader. But this interpretation assumes a capacity for self-loathing, a sense of distance from his African past, that belies the immediacy of his opening description of his beloved homeland. Not only does he describe the Africa of his childhood in utopian terms, as the following passage suggests, but he also clearly considers himself still an African: "We are almost a nation of dancers, musicians, and poets. Every great event, such as a triumphant return from battle . . . is celebrated in public dances" (p. 5). Rather than ridiculing his own naiveté, then, Equiano might be said to be introducing his youthful voice at least in part to underscore the process of his remarkable development. By showing his progress from childhood timidity to adult wisdom and courage, he dramatizes his exceptional nature and, alternatively, the miraculous workings of Providence.

At yet another level Equiano uses this technique as a means of commenting ironically on the ostensibly civilized nature of his European captors (and, by extension, readers). On the one hand he encourages us to consider his unjustified terror at the sight of the ship and of white men. But on the other hand, after he describes the conditions on the slave ship, he reminds us that in fact the vessel and those who operate it are the repository and the perpetrators, respectively, of inexpressible savageries: "When I looked round the ship too, and saw a large furnace or copper boiling, and a multitude of black people, of every description, chained together, every one of their countenances expressing dejection and sorrow, I no longer doubted of my fate" (p. 32). This juxtaposition suggests that Equiano manipulates the mask of naiveté to cover a scathing denunciation of European inhumanity. Precisely at the moment when he appears to embrace the reader, he issues a subtle indictment.

Most important, however, by introducing the voice of his youth and naiveté, Equiano gives credibility to his African origins, his pre-European consciousness. His commentary—reminding the reader of the influence of Providence—suggests that his conversion bestows upon his life its true meaning. But finally that voice does not fully usurp the emphasis from his prior perceptions. Rather, by showing that his imagination and perspective bear the indelible impress of his African origins, he demonstrates as well that only as an African does he understand and value Christianity, seizing upon it as the single feature of European society that restores the metaphysical certainty he lost when he was enslaved.[15]

To Equiano, Benin, the province in which he was born, represents an Edenic civilization, a world rich in natural resources and inhabited by industrious, reverent, contented people. He attributes the quality of life there to its orderliness: age-old, straightforward, consistent, and reasonable economic, legal, and religious customs prevail; unencumbered by superfluity of any kind, they guarantee a continued correspondence between part and whole, past and present, cause and effect. Throughout his description he emphasizes the efficiency of cultural practice in his homeland, remarking, for example, that "the history of what passes in one family or village, may serve as a specimen of the whole nation" (p. 3). Perhaps the most striking correspondence exists between word and deed. A person's name commemorates an event that marks his or her birth in some way; and people dare not blaspheme for fear of invoking their God's presence and wrath. In such a stable community an individual's status is determined by his or her place in the family and the family's social position; Equiano therefore knew even as a child that he, like his father and brother, was destined to wear the "Embrenche," or mark of distinction.

Given his idyllic representation of Benin, his abduction into slavery seems to be his introduction into temporality and human fallibility. Indeed, his points of emphasis throughout the narrative suggest that he considers slavery's greatest injustice to be the fact that it renders the slave's fate capricious, a matter entirely of his or her master's whim. Not only does he associate his first experience of suffering with his captivity, but it also precipitates his initial awareness that neither word and deed nor cause and effect need correspond according to his expectations. The Europeans' casual use of language thus disturbs him: he resists his masters' cavalier efforts to change his name, and is distressed by the freedom with which people blaspheme. He repeatedly remarks upon the discrepancy between his expectations of a situation and its actual outcome. Even when he describes specific sorrows, he emphasizes not the intensity of his sufferings but rather the fact that they are unexpected.

Just before he embarks on the dread Middle Passage, for example, he spends two months in the service of a wealthy widow and her son. He is only nominally enslaved by this family, who treat him as an equal, providing him with his own slaves. Just as Equiano has settled into his comfortable life, however, he is sold to slave traders. It is clear that his experience on the ship is devastating, but he is disturbed as much by its unexpectedness as by the experience itself: "Without the least previous knowledge, one morning early . . . I was awakened out of my reverie to fresh sorrow, and was hurried away even among the uncircumcised. *Thus, at the very moment I dreamed of the greatest happiness, I found myself most miserable;* and it seemed as if fortune wished to give me this taste of joy only to render the reverse more poignant" (pp. 28–29; emphasis mine).

Equiano appears to value the certainty of order in his life and laments its disruption. It is thus little wonder that he celebrates the ability of Christianity to offer him a context that attributes each event in his life to a First Cause. As he remarks during the account of his conversion: "Now every leading providential circumstance that happened to me, from the day that I was taken from my parents to that hour, was then in my view, as if it had just then occurred. I was sensible of the invisible hand of God, which guided and protected me, when in truth I knew it not" (p. 189). Events that seemed most inexplicable, such as his initial abduction, he can now interpret as a step in a divine plan whose meaningfulness he can trust even when it appears inscrutable.

What is remarkable about this formulation is that it constitutes a subtle revision of the conversion plot. Like other spiritual autobiographers, Equiano is quite willing to count as nothing his early life of self-righteousness. But the fact that he preserves the voice of his personal innocence and insightfulness and the image of an African paradise suggests his unwillingness to yield himself entirely to the religion and practices of his adopted country. No doubt he reveres the European's Christianity, but he presents it as his way of recovering a lost ideal and shows how it suits a system of values and priorities conditioned by African cultural practice.

His use of the double narrative voice, then, both unites him with and differentiates him from his reader. The prevailing mature voice articulates his acceptance of the values of his adoptive nation. The voice of his African boyhood remains, however, reminding his reader always that he filters, understands, and appropriates his new religion and culture from the point of view of an outsider.

If the double voice of Equiano's narrative symbolizes his allegiance to both his African heritage and his European acculturation, it allows him as well to adopt a critical stance toward the capacity for savagery of a society he otherwise admires. In other words, his ability to celebrate Western scientific advances does not prevent him from denouncing the brutality of the slave trade and its casual treatment of human life. Likewise, his love of Christianity does not blind him to the fact that self-professed Christians are capable of greater abuses than anyone he knew in his putatively heathen homeland. This indictment prefigures the distinction between the slaveholders' religion and the true religion drawn by countless later slave narrators. . . .

Like that of her male counterparts, Harriet Jacobs's freedom to reconstruct her life was limited by a genre that suppressed subjective experience in favor of abolitionist polemics. But if slave narrators in general were restricted by the antislavery agenda, she was doubly bound by the form in which she wrote, for it contained a plot more compatible with received notions of masculinity than with those of womanhood. As Niemtzow has suggested, Jacobs incorporated the rhetoric of the sentimental novel into her account, at least in part because it provided her with a way of talking about her vulnerability to the constant threat of rape. This form imposed upon her restrictions of its own.[16] Yet she seized authority over her literary restraints in much the same way that she seized power in life. From within her ellipses and ironies—equivalents of the garret in which she concealed herself for seven years—she expresses the complexity of her experience as a black woman.

In *Incidents in the Life of a Slave Girl,* the account of her life as a slave and her escape to freedom, Harriet Jacobs refers to the crawl space in which she concealed herself for seven years as a "loophole of retreat."[17] The phrase calls attention both to the closeness of her hiding place—three feet high, nine feet long, and seven feet wide—and the passivity that even voluntary confinement imposes. For if the combined weight of racism and sexism have already placed inexorable restrictions upon her as a black female slave in the antebellum South, her options seem even narrower after she conceals herself in the garret, where just to speak to her loved ones jeopardizes her own and her family's welfare.

And yet Jacobs's phrase "the loophole of retreat" possesses an ambiguity of meaning that extends to the literal loophole as well. For if a loophole signifies for Jacobs a place of withdrawal, it signifies in common parlance an avenue of escape. Likewise, and perhaps more important, the garret, a place of confinement, also renders the narrator spiritually independent of her master, and makes possible her ultimate escape to freedom. It is thus hardly surprising that Jacobs finds her imprisonment, however uncomfortable, an improvement over her "lot as a slave" (p. 117). As her statement implies, she dates her emancipation from the time she entered her loophole, even though she did not cross into the free states until seven years later. Given the constraints that framed her life, even the act of choosing her own mode of confinement constitutes an exercise of will, an indirect assault against her master's domination.[18]

The plot of Jacobs's narrative, her journey from slavery to freedom, is punctuated by a series of similar structures of confinement, both literal and figurative. Not only does she spend much of her time in tiny rooms (her grandmother's garret, closets in the homes of two friends), but she seems as well to have been penned in by the importunities of Dr. Flint, her master: "My master met me at every turn, reminding me that I belonged to him, and swearing by heaven and earth that he would compel me to submit to him. If I went out for a breath of fresh air after a day of unwearied toil, his footsteps dogged me. If I knelt by my mother's grave, his dark shadow fell on me even there" (p. 27). Repeatedly she escapes overwhelming persecutions only by choosing her own space of confinement: the stigma of unwed motherhood over sexual submission to her master; concealment in one friend's home, another friend's closet, and her grandmother's garret over her own and her children's enslavement on a plantation; Jim Crowism and the threat of the Fugitive Slave Law in the North over institutionalized slavery at home. Yet each moment of her apparent enclosure actually empowers Jacobs to redirect her own and her children's destiny. To borrow Elaine Showalter's formulation, she inscribes a subversive plot of empowerment beneath a more orthodox, public plot of weakness and vulnerability.[19]

It is not surprising that both literal and figurative enclosures proliferate in Jacobs's narrative. As a nineteenth-century black woman, former slave, and writer, she labored under myriad social and literary restrictions that shaped the art she produced.[20] Feminist scholarship has shown that, in general, women's writing in the nineteenth and twentieth centuries has been strongly marked by imagery of confinement, a pattern of imagery that reflects the limited cultural options available to the authors because of their gender and chosen profession.

Sandra Gilbert and Susan Gubar, for instance, describe the prodigious restraints historically imposed upon women that led to the recurrence of structures of concealment and evasion in their literature.[21] Not only were they denied access to the professions, civic responsibilities, and higher education, but also their secular and religious instruction encouraged them from childhood to adopt the "feminine," passive virtues of "submissiveness, modesty, self-lessness."[22] Taken to its extreme, such an idealization of female weakness and self-effacement contributed to what Ann Douglas has called a "domestication of death," characterized by the prevalence in literature of a hagiography of dying women and children, and the predilection in life for dietary, sartorial, and medical practices that led to actual or illusory weakness and illness.[23]

Literary women confronted additional restraints, given the widespread cultural identification of creativity with maleness. As Gubar argues elsewhere, our "culture is steeped in . . . myths of male primacy in theological, artistic, and scientific creativity," myths that present women as art objects, perhaps, but never as creators.[24] These ideological restraints, made concrete by inhospitable editors, publishers, and reviewers and disapproving relatives and friends have, as Gilbert and Gubar demonstrate, traditionally invaded women's literary undertakings with all manner of tensions. The most obvious sign of nineteenth-century women writers' anxiety about their vocation (but one that might also be attributed to the demands of the literary marketplace) is the frequency with which they published either anonymously or under a male pseudonym. Their sense of engaging in an improper enterprise is evidenced as well by their tendency both to disparage their own accomplishments in autobiographical remarks and to inscribe deprecations of women's creativity within their fictions. Moreover, they found themselves in a curious relation to the implements of their own craft. The literary conventions they received from genres dominated by male authors perpetuated reductive, destructive images of women that cried out to be revised. Yet the nature of women writers' socialization precluded their confronting problematic stereotypes directly. Instead, as Patricia Meyer Spacks, Carolyn Heilbrun, and Catharine Stimpson, as well as Showalter and Gilbert and Gubar have shown, the most significant women writers secreted revisions of received plots and assumptions either within or behind the more accessible content of their work.[25]

Jacobs's *Incidents* reveals just such a tension between the manifest and the concealed plot. Jacobs explicitly describes her escape as a progression from one small space to another. As if to underscore her helplessness and vulnerability, she indicates that although she ran alone to her first friend's home, she left each of her hiding places only with the aid of someone else. In fact, when she goes to her second and third hiding places, she is entirely at the mercy of her companion, for she is kept ignorant of her destination. Yet each closet, while at one level a prison, may be seen as well as a station on her journey to freedom. Moreover, from the garret of her seven-year imprisonment she uses to her advantage all the power of the voyeur—the person who sees but remains herself unseen. When she learns that Sands, her white lover and the father of her children, is about to leave town, she descends from her hiding place and, partly because she catches him unawares, is able to secure his promise to help free her children. In addition, she prevents her own capture not merely by remaining concealed but, more important, by embroiling her master, Dr. Flint, in an elaborate plot that deflects his attention. Fearing that he suspects her whereabouts, she writes him letters that she then has postmarked in Boston and New York to send him off in hot pursuit in the wrong direction. Despite her grandmother's trepidation, Jacobs clearly delights in exerting some influence over the man who has tried to control her.

Indeed, if the architectural close places are at once prisons and exits, then her relationship to Sands is both as well. She suggests that when she decides to take him as her lover, she is caught between Scylla and Charybdis. Forbidden to marry the free black man she loves, she knows that by becoming Sands's mistress she will compromise her virtue and reputation. But, she remarks, since her alternative is to yield to the master she loathes, she has no choice but to have sexual relations with Sands. As she writes: "It seems less degrading to give one's self, than to submit to compulsion. There is something akin to freedom in having a lover who has no control over you, except that which he gains by kindness and attachment" (p. 55).

One might argue that Jacobs's dilemma encapsulates the slave woman's sexual victimization and vulnerability. I do not mean to impugn that reading, but I would suggest that her relationship with Sands provides her with a measure of power. Out of his consideration for her, he purchases her children and her brother from Flint. William, her brother, eventually escapes from slavery on his own, but Sands frees the children in accordance with their mother's wishes. In a system that allowed the buying and selling of people as if they were animals, Jacobs's influence was clearly minimal. Yet even at the moments when she seems most vulnerable, she exercises some degree of control.

As the example of Equiano . . . reveal[s], the representative hero of the slave narrative, like the archetypal hero of the *Bildungsroman,* moves from the idyllic life of childhood ignorance in the country into a metaphoric wilderness, in this case the recognition of his status as a slave. His struggle for survival requires him to overcome numerous obstacles, but through his own talents (and some providential assistance) he finds the Promised Land of a responsible social position, a job, and a wife. The slave narrative typically extols the hero's stalwart individuality. And the narratives of male slaves often link the escape to freedom to the act of physically subduing the master. [Similarly, Frederick] Douglass writes [in *Narrative of the Life of Frederick Douglass, an American Slave* (1845)] that once he had overpowered the man whose job it was to break him, then he knew that he would soon be free.

Like the prototypical *Bildungsroman* plot, however, the plot of the slave narrative does not adequately accommodate differences in male and female development.[26] Jacobs's tale is not the classic story of the triumph of the individual will; rather it is more a story of a triumphant self-in-relation.[27] With the notable exception of the narrative of William and Ellen Craft, most of the narratives by men represent the life in slavery and the escape as essentially solitary journeys. This is not to suggest that male slaves were more isolated than their female counterparts, but it does suggest that they were attempting to prove their equality, their manhood, in terms acceptable to their white, middle-class readers.

Under different, equally restrictive injunctions, Jacobs readily acknowledges the support and assistance she received, as the description of her escape makes clear. Not only does she diminish her own role in her escape, but she is also quick to recognize the care and generosity of her family in the South and her friends in the North. The opening chapter of her account focuses not on the solitary "I" of so many narratives but on Jacobs's relatives. And she associates her desire for freedom with her desire to provide opportunities for her children.

By mythologizing rugged individuality, physical strength, and geographical mobility, the narratives enshrine cultural definitions of masculinity.[28] The plot of the standard narrative may thus be seen as not only the journey from slavery to freedom but also the journey from slavehood to manhood. Indeed, that rhetoric explicitly informs some of the best-known and most influential narratives. In the key scene in William Wells Brown's account, for example, a Quaker friend and supporter renames the protagonist, saying, "Since thee has got out of slavery, thee has become a man, and men always have two names."[29] [In his *Narrative,* Frederick] Douglass . . . explicitly contrasts slavehood with manhood, for he argues that learning to read made him a man but being beaten made him a slave. Only by overpowering his overseer was he able to become a man—thus free—again.

Simply by underscoring her reliance on other people, Jacobs reveals another way in which the story of slavery and escape might be written. But in at least one place in the narrative she makes obvious her problematic relation to the rhetoric she uses. The fourth chapter, "The Slave Who Dared to Feel like a Man," bears a title reminiscent of one of the most familiar lines from Douglass's 1845 *Narrative.* Here Jacobs links three anecdotes that illustrate the fact that independence of mind is incompatible with the demands of life as a slave. She begins with a scene in which her grandmother urges her family to content themselves with their lot as slaves; her son and grandchildren, however, cannot help resenting her admonitions. The chapter then centers on the story of her Uncle Ben, a slave who retaliates when his master tries to beat him and eventually escapes to the North.

The chapter title thus refers explicitly to Ben, the slave who, by defending himself, dares to feel like a man. And yet it might also refer to the other two stories included in the chapter. In the first, Jacobs's brother, William, refuses to capitulate to his master's authority. In the second, Jacobs describes her own earliest resolution to resist her master's advances. Although the situation does not yet require her to fight back, she does say that her young arm never felt half so strong. Like her uncle and brother, she determines to remain unconquered.

The chapter focuses on Ben's story, then, but it indicates also that his niece and nephew can resist authority. Its title might therefore refer to either of them as well. As Jacobs suggests by indirection, as long as the rhetoric of the genre identifies freedom and independence of thought with manhood, it lacks a category for describing the achievements of the tenacious black woman.

As L. Maria Child's introduction, Jacobs's own preface, and the numerous asides in the narrative make clear, Jacobs was writing for an audience of northern white women, a readership that by midcentury had grown increasingly leisured, middle class, and accustomed to the conventions of the novel of domestic sentiment. Under the auspices of Child, herself an editor and writer of sentimental fiction, Jacobs constructed the story of her life in terms that her reader would find familiar. Certainly Jacobs's *Incidents* contains conventional apostrophes that call attention to the interests she shares with her readers. But as an additional strategy for enlisting their sympathy, she couches her story in the rhetoric and structures of popular fiction.

The details of the narrator's life that made her experience as a slave more comfortable than most are precisely those that render her story particularly amenable to the conventions and assumptions of the sentimental novel. Like Douglass's [*Narrative*], slave narratives often begin with an absence, the narrator announcing from the first that he has no idea where or when he was born or who his parents were. But Jacobs was fortunate enough to have been born into a stable family at once nuclear and extended. Although both of her parents died young, she nurtured vivid, pleasant memories of them. Moreover, she remained close to her grandmother, an emancipated, self-supporting, property-owning black woman, and to her uncles and aunts, until she escaped to the North.

Jacobs's class affiliation, and the fact that she was subjected to relatively minor forms of abuse as a slave, enabled her to locate a point of identification both with her readers and with the protagonists of sentimental fiction. Like them, she aspired to chastity and piety as consummate feminine virtues and hoped that marriage and family would be her earthly reward. Her master, for some reason reluctant to force her to submit sexually, harassed her, pleaded with her, and tried to bribe her into capitulating in the manner of an importunate suitor like Richardson's seducer.* He tells her, for example, that he would be within his rights to kill her or have her imprisoned for resisting his advances, but he wishes to make her happy and thus will be lenient toward her. She likens his behavior to that of a jealous lover on one occasion when he becomes violent with her son. And he repeatedly offers to make a lady of her if she will grant him her favors, volunteering to set her up in a cottage of her own where she can raise her children.

By pointing up the similarities between her own story and those plots with which her readers would have been familiar, Jacobs could thus expect her readers to identify with her suffering. Moreover, this technique would enable them to appreciate the ways in which slavery converts into liabilities the very qualities of virtue and beauty that women were taught to cultivate. This tactic has serious limitations, however. As is always the case when one attempts to universalize a specific political point, Jacobs here trivializes the complexity of her situation when she likens it to a familar paradigm. Like Richardson's Pamela, Jacobs is her pursuer's servant. But Pamela is free to escape, if she chooses, to the refuge of her parents' home, while as Dr. Flint's property, Jacobs has severely limited options. Moreover, Mr. B., in the terms the novel constructs, can redeem his importunities by marrying Pamela and elevating her and their progeny to his position. No such possibility exists for Jacobs and her master. Indeed, the system of slavery, conflating as it does the categories of property and sexual relationships, ensures that her posterity will become his material possessions.

For other reasons as well, the genre seems inappropriate for Jacobs's purposes. [Her] . . . readers were accustomed to a certain degree of propriety and circumlocution in fiction. In keeping with cultural injunctions against women's assertiveness and directness in speech, the literature they wrote and read tended to be "exercises in euphemism" that excluded certain subjects from the purview of fiction.[30] But Jacobs's purpose was to celebrate her freedom to express what she had undergone, and to engender additional abolitionist support. Child and Jacobs both recognized that Jacobs's story might well violate the rules of decorum in the genre. Their opening statements express the tension between the content of the narrative and the form in which it appears.

Child's introduction performs the function conventional to the slave narrative

* In Samuel Richardson's 1740 novel *Pamela*.

of establishing the narrator's veracity and the reliability of the account. What is unusual about her introduction, however, is the basis of her authenticating statement: she establishes her faith in Jacobs's story on the correctness and delicacy of the author's manner.

> The author of the following autobiography is personally known to me, and her conversation and manners inspire me with confidence. During the last seventeen years, she has lived the greater part of the time with a distinguished family in New York, and has so deported herself as to be highly esteemed by them. This fact is sufficient, without further credentials of her character. I believe those who know her will not be disposed to doubt her veracity, though some incidents in her story are more romantic than fiction. (p. xi)

This paragraph attempts to equate contradictory notions; Child implies not only that Jacobs is both truthful and a model of decorous behavior but also that her propriety ensures her veracity. Child's assumption is troublesome, since ordinarily decorousness connotes the opposite of candor: one equates propriety not with openness but with concealment in the interest of taste.

Indeed, later in her introduction Child seems to recognize that an explicit political imperative may well be completely incompatible with bourgeois notions of propriety. While in the first paragraph she suggests that Jacobs's manner guarantees her veracity, by the last she has begun to ask if questions of delicacy have any place at all in discussions of human injustice. In the last paragraph, for example, she writes, "I am well aware that many will accuse me of indecorum for presenting these pages to the public." Here, rather than equating truthfulness with propriety, she acknowledges somewhat apologetically that candor about her chosen subject may well violate common rules of decorum. From this point she proceeds tactfully but firmly to dismantle the usefulness of delicacy as a category where subjects of urgency are concerned. She remarks, for instance, that "the experiences of this intelligent and much-injured woman belong to a class which some call delicate subjects, and others indelicate." By pointing to the fact that one might identify Jacobs's story as either delicate or its opposite, she acknowledges the superfluity of this particular label.

In the third and fourth sentences of this paragraph, Child offers her most substantive critique of delicacy, for she suggests that it allows the reader an excuse for insensitivity and self-involvement. The third sentence reads as follows: "This peculiar phase of slavery has generally been kept veiled; but the public ought to be made acquainted with its monstrous features, and I willingly take the responsibility of presenting them with the veil withdrawn." Here she invokes and reverses the traditional symbol of feminine modesty. A veil (read: euphemism) is ordinarily understood to protect the wearer (read: reader) from the ravages of a threatening world. Child suggests, however, that a veil (or euphemism) may also work the other way, concealing the hideous countenance of truth from those who choose ignorance above discomfort.

In the fourth sentence she pursues further the implication that considerations of decorum may well excuse the reader's self-involvement. She writes, "I do this for the sake of my sisters in bondage, who are suffering wrongs so foul, that our ears are too delicate to listen to them." The structure of this sentence is especially revealing, for it provides a figure for the narcissism of which she implicitly accuses the reader. A sentence that begins, as Child's does, "I do this for the sake of my sisters in bondage, who are suffering wrongs so foul that . . ." would ordinarily conclude with some reference to the "sisters" or the wrongs they endure. We would thus expect the sentence to read something like: "I do this for the sake of my sisters in bondage, who are suffering wrongs so foul that they must soon take up arms against their master," or "that they no longer believe in a moral order." Instead, Child's sentence rather awkwardly imposes the reader in the precise grammatical location where the slave woman ought to be. This usurpation of linguistic space parallels the potential for narcissism of which Child suggests her reader is guilty.

Child, the editor, the voice of form and convention in the narrative—the one who revised, condensed, and ordered the manuscript and "pruned [its] excrescences" (p. xi)—thus prepares the reader for its straightforwardness. Jacobs, whose life provides the narrative subject, in apparent contradiction to Child calls attention in her preface to her book's silences. Rather conventionally she admits to concealing the names of places and people to protect those who aided in her escape. And, one might again be tempted to say conventionally, she apologizes for the inadequacy of her literary skills. But in fact, when Jacobs asserts that her narrative is no fiction, that her adventures may seem incredible but are nevertheless true, and that only experience can reveal the abomination of slavery, she underscores the inability of her form adequately to capture her experience.

Although Child and Jacobs are aware of the limitations of the genre, the account often rings false. Characters speak like figures out of a romance. Moreover, the form allows Jacobs to talk about her sexual experiences only when they are the result of her victimization. She becomes curiously silent about the fact that her relationship with Sands continued even after Flint no longer seemed a threat.

Its ideological assumptions are the most serious problem the form presents. Jacobs invokes a plot initiated by Richardson's *Pamela,* and recapitulated in nineteenth-century American sentimental novels, in which a persistent male of elevated social rank seeks to seduce a woman of a lower class. Through her resistance and piety, she educates her would-be seducer into an awareness of his own depravity and his capacity for true, honorable love. In the manner of Pamela's Mr. B, the reformed villain rewards the heroine's virtue by marrying her.

As is true with popular literature generally, this paradigm affirms the dominant ideology, in this instance (as in Douglass's case) the power of patriarchy.[31] As Tania Modleski and Janice Radway have shown, the seduction plot typically represents pursuit of harassment as love, allowing the protagonist and reader alike to interpret the male's abusiveness as a sign of his inability to express his profound love for the heroine.[32] The problem is one that Ann Douglas attributes to sentimentalism as a mode of discourse, in that it never challenges fundamental assumptions and structures: "Sentimentalism is a complex phenomenon. It asserts that the values a society's activity denies are precisely the ones it cherishes; it attempts to deal with the phenomenon of cultural bifurcation by the manipulation of nostalgia. Sentimentalism provides a way to protest a power to which one has already in part capitulated."[33] Like Douglass, Jacobs does not intend to capitulate, especially since patriarchy is for her synonymous with slavocracy. But to invoke that plot is to invoke the clusters of associations and assumptions that surround it.

As Jacobs exercises authority over the limits of the male narrative, however, she triumphs as well over the limits of the sentimental novel, a genre more suited to the experience of her white, middle-class reader than to her own. From at least three narrative spaces, analogs to the garret in which she concealed herself, she displays her power over the forms at her disposal.

In a much-quoted line from the last paragraph of her account she writes: "Reader, my story ends with freedom, not in the usual way, with marriage" (p. 207). In this sentence she calls attention to the space between the traditional happy ending of the novel of domestic sentiment and the ending of her story. She acknowledges that however much her story may resemble superficially the story of the sentimental heroine, as a black woman she plays for different stakes; marriage is not the ultimate reward she seeks.

Another gap occurs at the point where she announces her second pregnancy. She describes her initial involvement with Sands as a conundrum. The brutality of neighboring masters, the indifference of the legal system, and her own master's harassment have forced her to take a white man as her lover. Both in the way she leads up to this revelation and in the apostrophes to the reader, she presents it as a situation in which she had no choice. Her explanation for taking Sands as her lover is accompanied by expressions of the appropriate regret and chagrin and then followed by two general chapters about slave religion and the local response to the Nat Turner rebellion. When we return to Jacobs's story, she remarks that Flint's harassment has persisted, and she announces her second pregnancy by saying simply, "When Dr. Flint learned that I was again to be a mother, he was exasperated beyond measure" (p. 79). Her continued relationship with Sands and her own response to her second pregnancy are submerged in the subtext of the two previous chapters and in the space between paragraphs. By consigning to the narrative silences those aspects of her own sexuality for which the genre does not allow, Jacobs points to an inadequacy in the form.

The third such gap occurs a bit later, just before she leaves the plantation. Her master's great aunt, Miss Fanny, a kind-hearted elderly woman who is a great favorite with Jacobs's grandmother, comes to visit. Jacobs is clearly fond of this woman, but as she tells the story, she admits that she resents Miss Fanny's attempts to sentimentalize her situation. As Jacobs tells it, Miss Fanny remarks at one point that she "wished that I and all my grandmother's family were at rest in our graves, for not until then should she feel any peace about us" (p. 91). Jacobs then reflects privately that "the good old soul did not dream that I was planning to bestow peace upon her, with regard to myself and my children; not by death, but by securing our freedom." Here, Jacobs resists becoming the object of someone else's sentimentality and calls attention to the inappropriateness of this response. Although she certainly draws on the conventions of sentimentalism when they suit her purposes, she is also capable of replacing the self-indulgent mythicization of death with the more practical solution of freedom.

The complex experience of the black woman has eluded analyses and theories that focus on any one of the variables of race, class, and gender alone. As Barbara Smith has remarked, the effect of the multiple oppression of race, class, and gender is not merely arithmetic.[34] That is, one cannot say only that in addition to racism, black women have had to confront the problem of sexism. Rather, issues of class and race alter one's experience of gender, just as gender alters the experience of class and race. Whatever the limitations of her narrative, Jacobs anticipates recent developments in class, race, and gender analysis. Her account indicates that this story of a black woman does not emerge from the superimposition of a slave narrative on a sentimental novel. Rather, in the ironies and silences and spaces of her book, she makes not quite adequate forms more truly her own.

NOTES

1. William L. Andrews, "The First Fifty Years of the Slave Narrative, 1760–1810," in *The Art of Slave Narrative: Original Essays in Criticism and Theory,* ed. John Sekora and Darwin T. Turner (Macomb, Ill.: Western Illinois University Press, 1982), p. 7.
2. Marion Wilson Starling, *The Slave Narrative: Its Place in American History* (Boston: G. K. Hall, 1981), pp. xvii–xviii; Dorothy Sterling, ed., *We Are Your Sisters: Black Women in the Nineteenth Century* (New York: W. W. Norton, 1984), pp. 3–4.
3. Sterling, *We Are Your Sisters,* p. 4. For a compelling discussion of ways in which the WPA narratives might be used, see Paul D. Escott, "The Art and Science of Reading WPA Slave Narratives," in *The Slave's Narrative,* ed. Charles T. Davis and Henry Louis Gates, Jr. (New York: Oxford University Press, 1985), pp. 40–48.
4. Starling, *The Slave Narrative,* pp. 226–232.
5. See James Olney's provocative discussion of this tension in " 'I Was Born': The Slave Narratives, Their Status as Autobiography and as Literature," *Callaloo,* 20 (Winter 1984), 46–73.
6. Henry Louis Gates, Jr., "Criticism in the Jungle," in *Black Literature and Literary Theory* (New York: Methuen, 1984), p. 5.
7. The narratives first emerge as a subject in critical literature in the 1970s. The nature of the commentary bespeaks their troublesomeness as a literary category more precisely than does their omission from earlier studies. Two seminal books, Stephen Butterfield's *Black Autobiography in America* (Amherst: University of Massachusetts Press, 1974) and Sidonie Ann Smith's *Where I'm Bound: Patterns of Slavery and Freedom in Black American Autobiography* (Westport, Conn.: Greenwood Press, 1974) explore the connections between the narratives and modern black autobiography. Neither acknowledges the characteristics of the narratives that distinguish them from either history or autobiography; both present an image of the narratives as a monolithic body of work.

   More recent studies seek to establish the relationship of the accounts to the conditions out of which they arose. Frances Smith Foster's *Witnessing Slavery* (Westport, Conn.: Greenwood Press, 1979) and Starling's *The Slave Narrative: Its Place in American History* contribute immeasurably to our understanding of the narratives in their political, cultural, and literary context. Both provide detailed summaries of the themes and plots of the narratives, but neither discusses the common rhetorical structures that bind the texts as a genre.

   H. Bruce Franklin in *The Victim as Criminal and Artist: Literature from the American Prison* (New York: Oxford University Press, 1978) and Houston A. Baker, Jr., in *The Journey Back: Issues in Black Literature and Criticism* (Chicago: University of Chicago Press, 1980), in contrast, demonstrate ways in which the texts respond to the ideological context in which they were produced. By analyzing the resonance and textual strategies of the Douglass and Jacobs narratives in the one case and of the Equiano and Douglass narratives in the other, they offer the most persuasive evidence of their literariness. To borrow Franklin's formulation (p. 7), by using methods that ordinarily illuminate our readings of classic texts, they make a strong argument for the narratives' subtlety and complexity.
8. See Starling, *The Slave Narrative,* p. 50; Andrews, "The First Fifty Years," pp. 9–10; and Foster, *Witnessing Slavery,* pp. 44–52. Paul Edwards locates Equiano's account in the context of contemporaneous works by Ignatius Sancho and Ottobah Cugoano. See his "Three West African Writers of the 1780s," in Davis and Gates, *The Slave's Narrative,* pp. 175–198.
9. Andrews, "The First Fifty Years," p. 8.
10. Ibid., p. 10.
11. Olaudah Equiano [Gustavus Vassa], *The Interesting Narrative of the Life of Olaudah Equiano, or Gustavus Vassa, the African, Written by Himself* (Leeds: James Nichols, 1814), p. iii. Subsequent references are to this edition and will be given in the text.

12. Daniel B. Shea, Jr., *Spiritual Autobiography in America* (Princeton: Princeton University Press, 1968), p. 87.
13. For a general discussion of patterns in spiritual autobiography, see ibid., pp. 87–110; and G. A. Starr, *Defoe and Spiritual Autobiography* (Princeton: Princeton University Press, 1965), pp. 3–50.
14. See Chinosole, " 'Tryin' to Get Over': Narrative Posture in Equiano's Autobiography," in Sekora and Turner, *The Art of Slave Narrative,* pp. 45–54; Andrews, "The First Fifty Years," pp. 19–22; and Baker, *The Journey Back,* pp. 15–22.
15. Susan Willis argues that slave narratives generally feature narrators who only partly comprehend their situation. See her essay "Crushed Geraniums: Juan Francisco Manzano and the Language of Slavery," in Davis and Gates, *The Slave's Narrative,* pp. 199–224.
16. Annette Niemtzow, "The Problematic of Self in Autobiography: The Example of the Slave Narrative," in Sekora and Turner, *The Art of Slave Narrative,* pp. 105–108.
17. Linda Brent [Harriet Jacobs], *Incidents in the Life of a Slave Girl* (New York: Harcourt Brace Jovanovich, 1973), p. 117. Subsequent references will be given in the text.
18. As I completed revisions of this discussion, I read Houston A. Baker, Jr.'s, *Blues, Ideology, and Afro-American Literature: A Vernacular Theory* (Chicago: University of Chicago Press, 1984). He too considers the significance of this image to Jacobs's account, but he focuses on Jacobs's ability to transform the economics of her oppression, whereas I concentrate on her use of received literary conventions.
19. Elaine Showalter, "Review Essay," *Signs,* 1 (1975), 435.
20. Only recently have scholars accepted the authenticity of Jacobs's account, thanks largely to Jean Fagan Yellin's meticulous and illuminating documentation of Jacobs's life and writing. See her essay "Texts and Contexts of Harriet Jacobs's *Incidents in the Life of a Slave Girl: Written by Herself,*" in Davis and Gates, *The Slave's Narrative,* pp. 262–282. See also Yellin's edition of this text (Cambridge, Mass.: Harvard University Press, 1987).
21. Sandra M. Gilbert and Susan Gubar, *The Madwoman in the Attic* (New Haven: Yale University Press, 1979), pp. 3–104 passim.
22. Ibid., p. 23.
23. Ann Douglas, *The Feminization of American Culture* (New York: Avon Books, 1977), pp. 240–273 passim.
24. Susan Gubar, " 'The Blank Page' and the Issues of Female Creativity," in *Writing and Sexual Difference,* ed. Elizabeth Abel (Chicago: University of Chicago Press, 1982), p. 74.
25. See Showalter, "Review Essay," and Gilbert and Gubar, *The Madwoman in the Attic.* See also Patricia Meyer Spacks, *The Female Imagination* (New York: Knopf, 1975), p. 317, and Carolyn Heilbrun and Catharine Stimpson, "Theories of Feminist Criticism: A Dialogue," in *Feminist Literary Criticism,* ed. Josephine Donovan (Lexington, Ky.: University Press of Kentucky, 1975), p. 62.
26. See Elizabeth Abel, Marianne Hirsch, and Elizabeth Langland, eds., *The Voyage In: Fictions of Female Development* (Hanover, N.H.: University Press of New England, 1983), pp. 3–19.
27. I draw here on the vocabulary of recent feminist psychoanalytic theory, which revises traditional accounts of female psychosexual development. See Jean Baker Miller, *Toward a New Psychology of Women* (Boston: Beacon Press, 1976); Nancy Chodorow, *The Reproduction of Mothering: Psychoanalysis and the Sociology of Gender* (Berkeley: University of California Press, 1978); and Carol Gilligan, *In a Different Voice* (Cambridge, Mass.: Harvard University Press, 1982).
28. I acknowledge here my gratitude to Mary Helen Washington for pointing out to me this characteristic of the narratives.
29. William Wells Brown, *Narrative of William W. Brown* (Boston: The Anti-Slavery Office, 1847; rpt. New York: Arno Press, 1968), p. 105.
30. Niemtzow, "The Problematic of Self," pp. 105–106.
31. See Douglas, *The Feminization of American Culture,* p. 72.
32. See Tania Modleski, *Loving with a Vengeance: Mass-Produced Fantasies for Women* (New York: Archon Books, 1982), p. 17, and Janice Radway, *Reading the Romance: Women, Patriarchy, and Popular Literature* (Chapel Hill: University of North Carolina Press, 1984), p. 75.
33. See Douglas, *The Feminization of American Culture,* p. 12.
34. See Barbara Smith, "Notes for Yet Another Paper on Black Feminism, or Will the Real Enemy Please Stand Up," *Conditions: Five,* 3 (October 1978), 123–132. For further discussion of this

issue see Paula Giddings, *When and Where I Enter: The Impact of Black Women on Race and Sex in America* (New York: William Morrow, 1984); Angela Davis, *Women, Race, and Class* (New York: Vintage Books, 1983); and Elizabeth V. Spelman, "Theories of Race and Gender: The Erasure of Black Women," *Quest,* 5 (1979), 36–62.

Henry Louis Gates, Jr. (1950–)

The influential and ubiquitous literary scholar Henry Louis Gates, Jr., had already distinguished himself before winning acclaim in 1983 for helping to confirm Harriet Wilson's Our Nig *(1859) as the first African American novel to be published in the United States. In addition, Gates was among the first critics to identify black language as a theoretical framework for assessing the merits of African American literature.*

Born in Keyser, West Virginia, Gates had originally planned to become a physician, even working in a hospital in Kenya as a college student. He graduated in 1973 from Yale University with a bachelor's in history. He then studied at Cambridge University in England, where he earned his master's in 1974 and his doctorate in 1979. His work with eminent black critic Charles T. Davis at Yale and Nigerian writer Wole Soyinka at Cambridge gave Gates exposure to diverse viewpoints regarding black literary and cultural expressions. The recipient of numerous awards and fellowships, Gates has taught English and literature at a host of academic institutions, including Yale University, Cornell University, and Duke University. Currently, he is W. E. B. Du Bois Professor of humanities and chair of African American studies at Harvard University.

It was in the 1980s that Gates emerged as a noted authority on African American literature and culture. He was awarded a MacArthur Foundation Award in 1981. In Figures in Black: Words, Signs, and the Racial Self *(1987), Gates assesses the nature of black literary criticism in this way: "The content of a black work of art has . . . assumed primacy in normative analysis, at the expense of the judgement of form. . . . Black literacy [has become] far more preoccupied with the literal representation of social content than with literary form, with ethics and thematics rather than poetics and aesthetics. Art, therefore, [is] argued implicitly and explicitly to be essentially referential." Given that customary focus on the content rather than the form of black literature, Gates has attempted to develop a methodology for assessing black literature that would attend to both content and form. In his critical study* The Signifying Monkey: A Theory of Afro-American Literary Criticism *(1988), which won an American Book Award, Gates, according to one critic, "identifies signifyin(g) [wordplay] as the leading characteristic of black American literature. . . . Signifyin(g) occurs not only as individual examples, but also as a rhetorical strategy and standard principle in black American literature. . . . Intertextuality and something akin to signifyin(g) exist in all literary traditions; Gates' point is not that these features are exclusive to black American literature, but that they are its distinguishing characteristics."*

In addition to publishing dozens of articles in scholarly journals and popular magazines, Gates has written his autobiography Colored People *(1994), and has edited a number of books and series on African American literature and culture, including* Black Is the Color of the Cosmos: Charles T. Davis's Essays on Black Literature and Culture *(1982);* The Slave's Narrative: Texts and Contexts

(1983), coedited with Charles T. Davis; Black Literature and Literary Theory *(1984);* The Classic Slave Narrative *(1987);* In the House of Oshugbo: A Collection of Essays on Wole Soyinka *(1985);* Reading Black, Reading Feminist: A Literary Critical Anthology *(1990);* Three Classic African American Novels *(1990); and* Bearing Witness: Selections from 150 Years of African American Autobiography *(1991). He has also served as general editor of the* Schomburg Library of Nineteenth-Century Black Women Writers *(1988). And in a highly productive collaboration, Gates and Kwame Anthony Appiah developed the groundbreaking series* Critical Perspectives Past and Present, *which includes numerous volumes on African American authors, including Alice Walker, Gloria Naylor, Langston Hughes, Richard Wright, Toni Morrison, Zora Neale Hurston, Chinua Achebe, Frederick Douglass, Harriet Jacobs, Ralph Ellison, and Wole Soyinka. Most recently, Gates and Appiah coedited* The Dictionary of Global Culture *(1995).*

In "The Blackness of Blackness: A Critique of the Sign and the Signifying Monkey," originally published in 1983 in the journal Critical Inquiry, *Gates explores the distinct dimensions of wordplay and speech patterns in African American literature.*

The Blackness of Blackness

A Critique of the Sign and the Signifying Monkey

Signification is the nigger's occupation.
—Traditional[1]

Be careful what you do,
Or Mumbo-Jumbo, God of the Congo
And all of the other
Gods of the Congo,
Mumbo-Jumbo will hoo-doo you,
Mumbo-Jumbo will hoo-doo you,
Mumbo-Jumbo will hoo-doo you.
—Vachel Lindsay, "The Congo"

I need not trace here the history of the concept of signification. Since Ferdinand de Saussure, at least, signification has become a crucial aspect of contemporary theory. It is curious to me that this neologism in the Western tradition is a homonym of a term in the black vernacular tradition that is approximately two centuries old. Tales of the Signifying Monkey had their origins in slavery; hundreds of these tales have been recorded since the nineteenth century. In black music, Jazz Gillum, Count Basie, Oscar Peterson, Oscar Brown, Jr., Little Willie Dixon, Nat King Cole, Otis Redding, Wilson Pickett and Johnny Otis—among others—have recorded songs called either "The Signifying Monkey" or, simply, "Signifyin(g)." My theory of interpretation, arrived at from within the black cultural matrix, is a theory of formal revision; it is tropological; it is often characterized by pastiche; and, most crucially, it turns on repetition of formal structures, and their difference. Signification is a theory of reading that arises from Afro-American culture; learning how "to signify" is often part of our adolescent education. I had to step outside my culture, had to defamiliarize the concept by translating it into a new mode of discourse, before I could see its potential in critical theory.[2]

Signifyin(g): Definitions

Perhaps only Tar Baby is as enigmatic and compelling a figure from Afro-American mythic discourse as is that oxymoron, the Signifying Monkey.[3] The ironic reversal of a received racist image of the black as simianlike, the Signifying Monkey—he who dwells at the margins of discourse, ever punning, ever troping, ever embodying the ambiguities of language—is our trope for repetition and revision, indeed, is our trope of chiasmus itself, repeating and simultaneously reversing in one deft, discursive act. If Vico and Burke, or Nietzsche, Paul de Man and Harold Bloom, are correct in identifying "master tropes," then we might think of these as the "master's tropes," and of *signifying* as the slave's trope, the trope of tropes, as Bloom characterizes metalepsis, "a trope-reversing trope, a figure of a figure." Signifying is a trope that subsumes other rhetorical tropes, including metaphor, metonymy, synecdoche and irony (the "master" tropes), and also hyperbole, litotes and metalepsis (Bloom's supplement to Burke). To this list, we could easily add aporia, chiasmus and catachresis, all of which are used in the ritual of signifying.

The black tradition has its own subdivisions of signifying, which we could readily identify with the typology of figures received from classical and medieval rhetoric, as Bloom has done with his "map of misprision." In black discourse "signifying" means modes of figuration itself. When one signifies, as Kimberly W. Bentson puns, one "tropes-a-dope." The black rhetorical tropes subsumed under signifying would include "marking," "loud-talking," "specifying," "testifying," "calling out" (of one's name), "sounding," "rapping," and "playing the dozens."[4]

Let us consider received definitions of the act of signifying and of black mythology's archetypal signifier, the Signifying Monkey. The Signifying Monkey is a trickster figure, of the order of the trickster figure of Yoruba mythology, Ẹ̀sù-Elẹ́gbára in Nigeria, and Legba among the Fon in Dahomey, whose New World figurations—Exú in Brazil, Echu-Elegua in Cuba, Papa Legba in the pantheon of the *loa* of *Vaudou* in Haiti, and Papa La Bas in the *loa* of Hoodoo in the United States—speak eloquently of the unbroken arc of metaphysical presuppositions and patterns of figuration shared through space and time among black cultures in West Africa, South America, the Caribbean and the United States. These trickster figures, aspects of Ẹ̀sù, are primarily *mediators:* as tricksters they are mediators and their mediations are tricks.[5]

The versions of Ẹ̀sù are all messengers of the gods: he interprets the will of the gods to human beings; he carries the desires of human beings to the gods. He is known as the divine linguist, the keeper of *àṣẹ* ("logos") with which Olódùmarè created the universe. Ẹ̀sù is guardian of the crossroads, master of style and the stylus, phallic god of generation and fecundity, master of the mystical barrier that separates the divine from the profane world. In Yoruba mythology, Ẹ̀sù always limps, because his legs are of different lengths: one is anchored in the realm of the gods, the other rests in the human world. The closest Western relative of Ẹ̀sù is Hermes, of course; and, just as Hermes' role as interpreter lent his name readily to "hermeneutics," the study of the process of interpretation, so too the figure of Èṣù can stand, for the critic of comparative black literature, as our metaphor for the act of interpretation itself. In African and Latin American mythologies, Èṣù is said to have taught Ifa how to read the signs formed by the sixteen sacred palm nuts which, when manipulated, configure into "the signature of an Odù," 256 of which comprise the corpus of *Ifá divination. The Ọpọ́n Ifá,* the carved wooden divination tray used in the art of interpretation, is said to contain at the center of its upper perimeter a carved image of Èṣù, meant to signify his relation to the act of interpretation, which we can translate either as *ìtúmò* ("to untie or unknot knowledge") or as *iyípadà* ("to turn around" or "to translate"). That which we call "close reading" the Yoruba call *Ọ̀da fá* ("reading the signs"). Above all else, Èṣù is the Black Interpreter, the Yoruba god of indeterminacy, the sheer plurality of meaning, or *àriyèmuyè* ("that which no sooner is held than slips through one's fingers"). As Hermes is to hermeneutics, Èṣù is to *Èṣù-'túfunààlò* ("bringing out the interstices of the riddle.")[6]

The Èṣù figures, among the Yoruba systems of thought in Dahomey and Nigeria, in Brazil and in Cuba, in Haiti and in New Orleans, are divine: they are gods who function in sacred myths as do characters in a narrative. Èṣù's functional equivalent in Afro-American profane discourse is the Signifying Monkey, a figure who seems to be distinctly Afro-American, probably derived from Cuban mythology which generally depicts Echu-Elegua with a monkey at his side.[7] Unlike his Pan-African Èṣù cousins, the Signifying Monkey exists in the discourse of mythology not primarily as a character in a narrative but rather as a vehicle for narration itself. It is from this corpus of mythological narratives that signifying derives. The Afro-American rhetorical strategy of signifying is a rhetorical practice unengaged in information-giving. Signifying turns on the play and chain of signifiers, and not on some supposedly transcendent signified. Alan Dundes suggests that the origins of signifying could "lie in African rhetoric." As anthropologists demonstrate, the Signifying Monkey is often called "the signifier," he who wreaks havoc upon "the signified." One is "signified upon" by the signifier. The Signifying Monkey is indeed the "signifier as such," in Julia Kristeva's phrase, "a presence that precedes the signification of object or emotion."[8]

Scholars have for some time commented upon the peculiar use of the word "signifying" in black discourse. Though sharing some connotations with the standard English-language word, "signifying" has its own definitions in black discourse. Roger D. Abrahams defines it this way:

> Signifying seems to be a Negro term, in use if not in origin. It can mean any of a number of things; in the case of the toast about the signifying monkey, it certainly refers to the trickster's ability to talk with great innuendo, to carp, cajole, needle, and lie. It can mean in other instances the propensity to talk around a subject, never quite coming to the point. It can mean making fun of a person or situation. Also it can denote speaking with the hands and eyes, and in this respect encompasses a whole complex of expressions and gestures. Thus it is signifying to stir up a fight between neighbors by telling stories; it is signifying to make fun of a policeman by parodying his motions behind his back; it is signifying to ask for a piece of cake by saying, "My brother needs a piece of cake."[9]

Essentially, Abrahams concludes, signifying is a "*technique* of indirect argument or persuasion," "a language of implication," "to imply, goad, beg, boast, by *indirect* verbal or gestural means." "The name 'signifying,' " he concludes, "shows the monkey to be a trickster, signifying being the language of trickery, that set of words or gestures achieving Hamlet's 'direction through indirection.' " The Monkey, in short, is not only "a master of technique," as Abrahams concludes; he is technique, or style, or the *literariness* of literary language; he is the great Signifier. In this sense, one does not signify something; rather, one signifies in *some way*.[10]

There are thousands of "toasts" of the Signifying Monkey, most of which commence with a variant of the following formulaic lines:

> Deep down in the jungle so they say
> There's a signifying monkey down the way.
> There hadn't been no disturbin' in the jungle for quite a bit,
> For up jumped the monkey in the tree one day and laughed,
> "I guess I'll start some shit."[11]

Endings, too, tend toward the formulaic, as in

> Monkey, said the Lion,
> Beat to his unbooted knees,
> You and all your signifying children
> Better stay up in them trees.
> Which is why today
> Monkey does his signifying
> *A-way-up* out of the way.[12]

In the narrative poems, the Signifying Monkey invariably "repeats" to his friend, the Lion, some insult purportedly generated by their mutual friend, the Elephant. The Lion, indignant and outraged, demands an apology from the Elephant, who refuses and then trounces the Lion. The Lion, realizing that his mistake was to take the Monkey literally, returns to trounce the Monkey. Although anthropologists and socio-linguists have succeeded in establishing a fair sample of texts featuring the Signifying Monkey, they have been less successful at establishing a consensus of definitions of black "signifying."

In addition to Abraham's definitions of "signifying," those by Thomas Kochman, Claudia Mitchell-Kernan, Geneva Smitherman, Zora Neale Hurston and Ralph Ellison are of particular interest here for what they reveal about the nature of Afro-American narrative parody.[13] I shall attempt to explicate Afro-American narrative parody and then to employ it in reading Ishmael Reed's third novel, *Mumbo Jumbo,* as a signifying pastiche of the Afro-American narrative tradition itself. Kochman argues that signifying depends upon the signifier *repeating* what someone else has said about a third person in order to *reverse* the status of a relationship heretofore harmonious; signifying can also be employed to *reverse* or *undermine* pretense or even one's opinion about one's own status. The use of repetition and reversal (chiasmus) constitutes an implicit parody of a subject's own complicity in illusion. Mitchell-Kernan, in perhaps the most thorough study of the concept, compares the etymology of "signifying" in black usage with usages from standard English:

> What is unique in Black English usage is the way in which signifying is extended to cover a range of meanings and events which are not covered in its Standard English usage. In the Black community it is possible to say, "He is signifying" and "Stop signifying"—sentences which would be anomalous elsewhere.[14]

Mitchell-Kernan points to the ironic, or dialectic, relation between "identical" terms in standard and black English which have vastly different meanings:

> The Black concept of *signifying* incorporates essentially a folk notion that dictionary entries for words are not always sufficient for interpreting meanings or messages, or that meaning goes beyond such interpretations. Complimentary remarks may be delivered in a left-handed fashion. A particular utterance may be an insult in one context and not another. What pretends to be informative may intend to be persuasive. The hearer is thus constrained to attend to all potential meaning carrying symbolic systems in speech events—the total universe of discourse. ("Sig.," p. 314)

This is an excellent instance of the nature of signifying. Mitchell-Kernan refines these definitions somewhat by suggesting that the Signifying Monkey is able to signify upon the Lion only because the Lion does not understand the nature of the Monkey's discourse: "There seems something of symbolic relevance from the perspective of language in this poem. The monkey and the lion do not speak the same language; the lion is not able to interpret the monkey's use of language" ("Sig.," p. 323). The Monkey speaks *figuratively,* in a symbolic code; the Lion interprets or "reads" *literally* and suffers the consequences of his folly, which is a reversal of his status as King of the Jungle. The Monkey rarely acts in these narrative poems; he simply speaks. As the signifier, he determines the actions of the signified—the hapless Lion and the puzzled Elephant.

As Mitchell-Kernan and Hurston attest, signifying is not a gender-specific rhetorical game, despite the frequent use, in the "masculine" versions, of expletives that connote intimate relations with one's mother. Hurston, in *Mules and Men* (1935), and Mitchell-Kernan, in her perceptive "Signifying, Loud-talking, and Marking," are the first scholars to record and explicate female signifying rituals. Hurston is the first author of the tradition to represent signifying itself as a vehicle of liberation for an oppressed woman, and as a rhetorical strategy in the narration of fiction.[15]

Hurston, whose definitions of the term in *Mules and Men* is one of the earliest in the linguistic literature, has made *Their Eyes Were Watching God* (1937) into a paradigmatic signifying text, for this novel resolves that implicit tension between the literal and the figurative contained in standard English usages of the term "signifying." *Their Eyes* represents the black trope of signifying both as thematic matter and as a rhetorical strategy of the novel itself. Janie, the protagonist, gains her voice, as it were, in her husband's store not only by engaging with the assembled men in the ritual of signifying (which her husband had expressly forbidden her to do) but also by openly *signifying upon* her husband's impotency. His image wounded fatally, he soon dies of a displaced "kidney" failure. Janie "kills" her husband, rhetorically. Moreover, Hurston's masterful use of free indirect discourse (*style indirect libre*) allows her to signify upon the tension between the two voices of Jean Toomer's *Cane* (1923) by adding to direct and indirect speech a strategy through which she can privilege the black oral tradition, which Toomer had found to be problematic, and dying. The text of *Their Eyes,* therefore, is itself a signifying structure, a structure of intertextual revision, because it revises key tropes and rhetorical strategies received from such precursory texts as Toomer's *Cane* and W. E. B. Du Bois's *The Quest of the Silver Fleece* (1911).

Afro-American literary history is characterized by such *tertiary* formal revision, by which I mean its authors seem to revise at least two antecedent texts, often taken from different generations or periods within the tradition. Hurston's opening of *Their Eyes* is a revision of *Narrative of the Life* (1845), Frederick Douglass's apostrophe to the ships at Chesapeake Bay; *Their Eyes* also revises the trope of the swamp in Du Bois's *Quest,* as well as the relation of character to setting in Toomer's *Cane*. The example of Ellison is even richer: *Invisible Man* (1952) revises Richard Wright's *Native Son* (1940) and *Black Boy* (1945), along with Du Bois's *The Souls of Black Folk* (1903) and Toomer's *Cane* (but it also revises Melville's *Confidence-Man* and Joyce's *Portrait of the Artist as a Young Man,* among others). Reed, in *Mumbo Jumbo* (1972), revises Hurston, Wright and Ellison.[16] It is clear that black writers read and critique other black texts as an act of rhetorical self-definition. Our literary tradition exists because of these precisely chartable formal literary relationships, relationships of signifying.

The key aspect of signifying for Mitchell-Kernan is "its indirect intent or metaphorical reference," a rhetorical indirection which she says is "almost purely stylistic": its art characteristics remain foregrounded. By "indirection," Mitchell-Kernan means that

> the correct semantic (referential interpretation) or signification of the utterance cannot be arrived at by a consideration of the dictionary meaning of the lexical items involved and the syntactic rules for their combination alone. The apparent significance of the message differs from its real significance. The apparent meaning of the sentence signifies its actual meaning. ("Sig.," p. 325)

This rhetorical naming by indirection is, of course, central to our notions of figuration, troping and parody. This parody of forms, or pastiche, is in evidence when one writer repeats another's structure by one of several means, including a fairly exact repetition of a given narrative or rhetorical structure, filled incongruously with a ludicrous or incongruent content. T. Thomas Fortune's "The Black Man's Burden" is an excellent example of this form of pastiche, signifying as it does upon Rudyard Kipling's "The White Man's Burden":

> What is the Black Man's Burden,
> Ye hypocrites and vile,
> Ye whited sepulchres
> From th' Amazon to the Nile?
> What is the Black Man's Burden,
> Ye Gentile parasites,
> Who crush and rob your brother
> Of his manhood and his rights?

Dante Gabriel Rossetti's "Uncle Ned," a dialect verse parody of Harriet Beecher Stowe's *Uncle Tom's Cabin,* provides a second example:

Him tale dribble on and on widout a break,
Till you hab no eyes for to see;
When I reach Chapter 4 I had got a headache;
So I had to let Chapter 4 be.

Another kind of formal parody suggests a given structure precisely by failing to coincide with it—that is, suggests it by dissemblance. Repeating a form and then inverting it through a process of variation is central to jazz—a stellar example is John Coltrane's rendition of "My Favorite Things," compared to Julie Andrews's vapid version. Resemblance thus can be evoked cleverly by dissemblance. Aristophanes' *Frogs,* which parodies the styles of both Aeschylus and Euripides; Cervantes' relationship to the fiction of knight-errantry; Fielding's parody, in *Joseph Andrews,* of the Richardsonian novel of sentiment; and Lewis Carroll's double parody in "Hiawatha's Photographing," which draws upon Longfellow's rhythms to parody the convention of the family photograph, all come readily to mind.

Ellison defines the parody aspect of signifying in several ways which I shall bring to bear on my discussion below of the formal parody strategies at work in Reed's *Mumbo Jumbo.* In his complex short story, "And Hickman Arrives" (1960), Ellison's narrator defines "signifying":

> And the two men [Daddy Hickman and Deacon Wilhite] standing side by side, the one large and dark, the other slim and light brown; the other reverends rowed behind them, their faces staring grim with engrossed attention to the reading of the Word; like judges in their carved, high-backed chairs. And the two voices beginning their call and countercall as Daddy Hickman began spelling out the text which Deacon Wilhite read, playing variations on the verses just as he did with his trombone when he really felt like signifying on a tune the choir was singing.[17]

Following this introduction, the two ministers demonstrate this "signifying," which in turn signifies upon the antiphonal structure of the Afro-American sermon. Ellison's parody of form here is of the same order as Richard Pryor's parody of that sermonic structure *and* Stevie Wonder's "Living for the City," which he effects by speaking the lyrics of Wonder's song in the form of and with the intonation peculiar to the Afro-American sermon in his "reading" of "The Book of Wonder." Pryor's parody is a signification of the second order, revealing simultaneously the received structure of the sermon (by its presence, demystified here by its incongruous content), the structure of Wonder's music (by the absence of its form and the presence of its lyrics) and the complex, yet direct, formal relationship between both the black sermon and Wonder's music specifically, and black sacred and secular narrative forms generally.

Ellison defines "signifying" in other ways as well. In his essay on Charlie Parker, "On Bird, Bird-Watching, and Jazz" (1962), Ellison defines the satirical aspect of signifying as one aspect of riffing in jazz.

> But what kind of bird was Parker? Back during the thirties members of the old Blue Devils Orchestra celebrated a certain robin by playing a lugubrious little tune called "They Picked Poor Robin." It was a jazz community joke, musically an extended "signifying riff" or melodic naming of a recurrent human situation, and

> was played to satirize some betrayal of faith or loss of love observed from the bandstand.[18]

Here again, the parody is twofold, involving a formal parody of the melody of "They Picked Poor Robin" as well as a ritual naming, and therefore a troping, of an action "observed from the bandstand."

Ellison, of course, is our Great Signifier, naming things by indirection and troping throughout his works. In his well-known review of LeRoi Jones's *Blues People,* Ellison defines "signifying" in yet a third sense, then signifies upon Jones's reading of Afro-American cultural history, which he argues is misdirected and wrongheaded: "The tremendous burden of sociology which Jones would place upon this body of music," writes Ellison, "is enough to give even the blues the blues." Ellison writes that Lydia Maria Child's title, *An Appeal in Favor of that Class of Americans Called Africans,*

> sounds like a fine bit of contemporary ironic *signifying*—"signifying" here meaning, in the unwritten dictionary of American Negro usage, "rhetorical understatements." It tells us much of the thinking of her opposition, and it reminds us that as late as the 1890s, a time when Negro composers, singers, dancers and comedians dominated the American musical stage, popular Negro songs (including James Weldon Johnson's "Under the Bamboo Tree," now immortalized by T. S. Eliot) were commonly referred to as "Ethiopian Airs."[19]

Ellison's stress upon "the unwritten dictionary of American Negro usage" reminds us of the problem of definitions, of signification itself, when one is translating between two languages. The Signifying Monkey, perhaps appropriately, seems to dwell in this space between two linguistic domains. One wonders, incidentally, about this Afro-American figure and a possible French connection between *signe* ("sign") and *singe* ("monkey").

Ellison's definition of the relation that his works bear to those of Wright constitutes a definition of "narrative signification," "pastiche" or "critical parody," although Ellison employs none of these terms. His explanation of what might be called "implicit formal criticism," however, comprises what is sometimes called "troping" and offers a profound definition of "critical signification" itself:

> I felt no need to attack what I considered the limitations of [Wright's] vision because I was quite impressed by what he had achieved. And in this, although I saw with the black vision of Ham, I was, I suppose, as pious as Shem and Japheth. Still I would write my own books and they would be in themselves, implicitly, criticisms of Wright's; just as all novels of a given historical moment form an argument over the nature of reality and are, to an extent, criticisms each of the other.[20]

Ellison in his fictions signifies upon Wright by parodying Wright's literary structures through repetition and difference. The complexities of the parodying I can readily suggest. The play of language, the signifying, starts with the titles: Wright's *Native Son* and *Black Boy,* titles connoting race, self and presence, Ellison tropes with *Invisible Man,* invisibility an ironic response, of absence, to the would-be presence of "blacks" and "natives," while "man" suggests a more mature and stronger status than either "son" or "boy." Wright's distinctive version of naturalism Ellison signifies upon with a complex rendering of modernism; Wright's reacting protagonist, voiceless to the last, Ellison signifies upon with a nameless protagonist. Ellison's protagonist is nothing but voice, since it is he who shapes, edits and narrates his own tale, thereby combining action with the representation of action to define "reality" by its representation. This unity of presence and representation is perhaps Ellison's most subtle reversal of Wright's theory of the novel as exemplified in *Native Son*. Bigger's voicelessness and powerlessness to act (as opposed to react) signify an absence, despite the metaphor of presence found in the novel's title; the reverse obtains in *Invisible Man,* where the absence implied by invisibility is undermined by the presence of the narrator as the narrator of his own text.

There are other aspects of critical parody at play here, too, one of the funniest being Jack's glass eye plopping into his water glass before him. This is functionally equivalent to the action of Wright's protagonist in "The Man Who Lived Underground" as he stumbles over the body of a dead baby, deep down in the sewer. It is precisely at this point in the narrative that we know Fred Daniels to be "dead, baby," in the heavy-handed way that Wright's naturalism was self-consciously "symbolic." If Daniels's fate is signified by the objects over which he stumbles in the darkness of the sewer, Ellison signifies upon Wright's novella by repeating this underground scene of discovery, but having his protagonist burn the bits of paper through which he had allowed himself to be defined by others. By explicitly repeating and reversing key figures of Wright's fictions, and by implicitly defining in the process of narration a sophisticated form more akin to Hurston's *Their Eyes Were Watching God,* Ellison exposed naturalism as merely a hardened conventional representation of "the Negro problem," and perhaps part of "the Negro problem" itself. I cannot emphasize enough the major import of this narrative gesture to the subsequent development of black narrative forms. Ellison recorded a new way of seeing and defined both a new manner of representation and its relation to the concept of presence.

The formal relationship that Ellison bears to Wright, Reed bears to both, though principally to Ellison. Not surprisingly, Ellison has formulated this type of complex and inherently polemical intertextual relationship of formal signifying. In a refutation of Irving Howe's critique of his work Ellison states:

> I agree with Howe that protest is an element of all art, though it does not necessarily take the form of speaking for a political or social program. It might appear in a novel as a *technical assault against the styles* which have gone before.[21]

This form of critical parody, of repetition and inversion, is what I define to be "critical signification," or "formal signifying," and is my metaphor for literary history.

I intend here to elicit the tertiary relationship in *Mumbo Jumbo* of Reed's signifying post-modernism to Wright's naturalism and Ellison's modernism. The set of intertextual relations that I chart through formal signification is related to what Mikhail Bakhtin labels "double-voiced" discourse, which he subdivides into parodic narration and the hidden or internal polemic. These two types of double-voiced discourse can merge, as they do in *Mumbo Jumbo*. In hidden polemic

> the other speech act remains outside the bounds of the author's speech, but is implied or alluded to in that speech. The other speech act is not reproduced with a new intention, but shapes the author's speech while remaining outside its boundaries. Such is the nature of discourse in hidden polemic. . . .
>
> In hidden polemic the author's discourse is oriented toward its referential object, as is any other discourse, but at the same time each assertion about that object is constructed in such a way that, besides its referential meaning, the author's discourse brings a polemical attack to bear against another speech act, another assertion, on the same topic. Here one utterance focused on its referential object clashes with another utterance on the grounds of the referent itself. That other utterance is not reproduced; it is understood only in its import.[22]

Ellison's definition of the formal relationship his works bear to Wright's is a salient example of the hidden polemic: Ellison's texts clash with Wright's "on the grounds of the referent itself." "As a result," Bakhtin continues, "the latter begins to influence the author's speech from within." In this double-voiced relationship, one speech act determines the internal structure of another, the second effecting the "voice" of the first by absence, by difference.

Much of the Afro-American literary tradition can, in a real sense, be read as successive attempts to create a new narrative space for representing the recurring referent of Afro-American literature—the so-called black experience. Certainly, this is the way we read the relation of Sterling Brown's regionalism to Toomer's lyricism, Hurston's lyricism to Wright's naturalism and, equally, Ellison's modernism to Wright's naturalism. This set of relationships can be illustrated by the schematic representation in Figure 1, which I intend only to be suggestive.[23]

These relationships are reciprocal because we are free to read in critical time machines, to read backwards. The direct relation most important to my own theory of reading is that solid black line connecting Reed with Hurston. While Reed and Hurston seem to relish the play of the tradition, Reed's work seems to be a magnificently conceived play *on* the tradition. Both Hurston and Reed have written myths of Moses, both draw upon black sacred and secular mythic discourse as metaphorical and metaphysical systems, both write self-reflexive texts which comment upon the nature of writing itself, both make use of the frame to bracket their narratives-within-a-narrative, and both are authors of fictions which

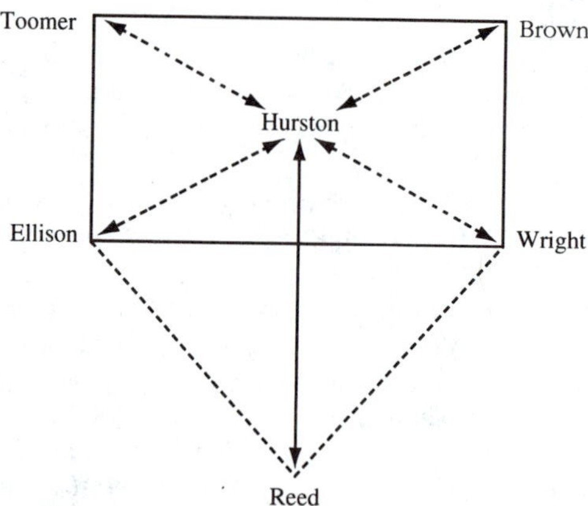

Figure 1

I characterize as "speakerly texts." Speakerly texts privilege the representation of the speaking black voice, of what the Russian Formalists called *skaz* and which Hurston and Reed have called "an oral book, a talking book" (a figure which occurs, remarkably enough, in five of the first six slave narratives in the black tradition).[24]

Reed's relation to these authors in the tradition is double-voiced at all points, since he seems to be especially concerned with employing satire to utilize literature in what Northrop Frye calls "a special function of analysis, of breaking up the lumber of stereotypes, fossilized beliefs, superstitious terrors, crank theories, pedantic dogmatisms, oppressive fashions, and all other things that impede the free movement . . . of society."[25] Reed, of course, seems to be most concerned with the "free movement" of writing itself. In his work, parody and hidden polemic overlap, in a process Bakhtin describes as follows:

> When parody becomes aware of substantial resistance, a certain forcefulness and profundity in the speech act it parodies, it takes on a new dimension of complexity via the tones of the hidden polemic. . . . A process of inner dialogization takes place within the parodic speech act.[26]

This "inner dialogization" can have curious implications, the most interesting, perhaps, being what Bakhtin describes as "the splitting of double-voiced discourse into two speech acts, into the two entirely separate and autonomous voices." The clearest evidence that Reed is signifying in *Mumbo Jumbo* through parody-as-hidden-polemic is his use of these two autonomous narrative voices. Reed employs these two voices in the manner of, and renders them through, foregrounding, to parody the two simultaneous stories of detective narration (that of the present and that of the past) in a narrative flow that moves hurriedly from cause to effect. In *Mumbo Jumbo,* however, the narrative of the past bears an ironic relation to the narrative of the present, because it comments not only upon the other narrative but upon the nature of *its writing itself.* Frye describes this, in another context, as "the constant tendency to self-parody in satiric rhetoric which prevents even the process of writing itself from becoming an oversimplified convention or ideal."[27] Reed's rhetorical strategy assumes the form of the relation between the text and the criticism of that text, which serves as discourse upon that text.

Talking Texts: Signifying Revisions

> Consult the text!
> —Ralph Ellison[28]

With these definitions of narrative parody and critical signification as a frame, let me turn directly to Reed's *Mumbo Jumbo.* A close reading of Reed's works strongly suggests his concerns with the received form of the novel, with the precise rhetorical shape of the Afro-American literary tradition, and with the relation that the Afro-American tradition bears to the Western tradition.[29] Reed's concerns, as exemplified in his narrative forms, seem to be twofold: (1) the relation his own art bears to his black literary precursors, including Hurston, Wright, Ellison and James Baldwin; and (2) the process of willing-into-being a rhetorical structure, a literary language, replete with its own figures and tropes, but one that allows the black writer to posit a structure of feeling that simultaneously critiques both the metaphysical presuppositions inherent in Western ideas and forms of writing and the metaphorical system in which the "blackness" of the writer and his experience have been valorized as a "natural" absence. In six demanding novels, Reed has criticized, through signifying, what he perceives to be the conventional structures of feeling that he has received from the Afro-American tradition. He has proceeded almost as if the sheer process of the analysis can clear a narrative space for the next generation of writers as decidedly as Ellison's narrative response to Wright and naturalism cleared a space for Leon Forrest, Toni Morrison, Alice Walker, James Alan McPherson and especially for Reed himself.

By undertaking the difficult and subtle art of pastiche, Reed criticizes the Afro-American idealism of a transcendent black subject, integral and whole, self-sufficient and plentiful, the "always already" black signified, available for literary representation in received Western forms as would be the water dippered from a deep and dark well. Water can be poured into glasses or cups or canisters, but it remains water just the same. Put simply, Reed's fictions argue that the so-called black experience cannot be thought of as a fluid content to be poured into received and static containers. For Reed, it is the signifier that both shapes and defines any discrete signified—and it is the signifiers of the Afro-American tradition with whom Reed is concerned.

Reed's first novel lends credence to this sort of reading and also serves to create a set of generic expectations for reading the rest of his works. *The Free-Lance Pallbearers* is, above all else, a parody of the confessional mode which is the fundamental, undergirding convention of Afro-American narrative, received, elaborated upon and transmitted in a chartable heritage from Briton Hammon's captivity narrative of 1760, through the ante-bellum slave narratives, to black autobiography, and into black fiction, especially the fictions of Hurston, Wright, Baldwin and Ellison.[30] The narrative of Reed's Bukka Doopeyduk is a pastiche of the classic black narrative of the questing protagonist's "journey into the heart of whiteness"; but it parodies that narrative form by turning it inside out, exposing the character of the originals and thereby defining their formulaic closures and disclosures. Doopeyduk's tale ends with his own crucifixion; as the narrator of his own story, therefore, Doopeyduk articulates, literally, from among the dead, an irony implicit in all confessional and autobiographical modes, in which any author is forced by definition to imagine him- or herself to be dead. More specifically, Reed signifies upon *Black Boy* and *Go Tell It on the Mountain* in a foregrounded critique which can be read as an epigraph to the novel: "read growing up in soulsville first of three installments—or what it means to be a backstage darky."[31] Reed foregrounds the "scat-singing voice" that introduces the novel against the "other" voice of Doopeyduk, whose "second" voice narrates the novel's plot. Here, Reed parodies both Hurston's use of free indirect discourse in *Their Eyes Were Watching God* and Ellison's use in *Invisible Man* of the foregrounded voice in the prologue and epilogue that frame his nameless protagonist's picaresque account of his own narrative. In his second novel, *Yellow Back Radio Broke-Down,* Reed more fully, and successfully, critiques both realism and modernism. The exchange between Bo Shmo and the Loop Garoo Kid is telling:

> It was Bo Shmo and the neo-social realist gang. They rode to this spot from their hideout in the hills. Bo Shmo leaned in his saddle and scowled at Loop, whom he considered a deliberate attempt to be obscure. A buffoon an outsider and frequenter of sideshows. . . .
>
> The trouble with you Loop is that you're too abstract, the part time autocrat monarchist and guru finally said. Crazy dada nigger that's what you are. You are given to fantasy and are off in matters of detail. Far out esoteric bullshit is where you're at. Why in those suffering books that I write about my old neighborhood and how hard it was every gumdrop machine is in place while your work is a blur and a doodle. I'll bet you can't create the difference between a German and a redskin.
>
> What's your beef with me Bo Shmo, what if I write circuses? No one says a novel has to be one thing. It can be anything it wants to be, a vaudeville show, the six o'clock news, the mumblings of wild men saddled by demons.
>
> All art must be for the end of liberating the masses. A landscape is only good when it shows the oppressor hanging from a tree.
>
> Right on! Right on, Bo, the henchmen chorused.
>
> Did you receive that in a vision or was it revealed to you?[32]

At several points in his first two novels, then, Reed deliberately reflects upon the history of the black tradition's debate over the nature and purpose of art.

Reed's third novel, *Mumbo Jumbo,* is a novel about writing itself—not only in the figurative sense of the post-modern, self-reflexive text but also in a literal sense: "So Jes Grew is seeking its words. Its text. For what good is a liturgy without a text?"[33] *Mumbo Jumbo* is both a book about texts and a book of texts, a composite narrative composed of sub-texts, pre-texts, post-texts and narratives-within-narratives. It is both a definition of Afro-American culture and its deflation. "The Big Lie concerning Afro-American culture," *Mumbo Jumbo*'s dust jacket states, "is that it lacks a tradition." The "Big Truth" of the novel, on the other hand, is that this very tradition is as rife with hardened convention and presupposition as is the rest of the Western tradition. Even this cryptic riddle of Jes Grew and its Text parodies Ellison: *Invisible Man*'s plot is set in motion with a riddle, while the themes of the relation between words and texts echo a key passage from Ellison's short story "And Hickman Arrives": "Good. Don't talk like I talk; talk like I *say* talk. Words are your business, boy. Not just *the* Word. Words are everything. The key to the Rock, the answer to the Question."[34]

Reed's signifying on tradition begins with his book's title. "Mumbo jumbo" is the received and ethnocentric Western designation for the rituals of black religions as well as for all black languages themselves. A vulgarized Western "translation" of a Swahili phrase, *mambo, jambo,* "mumbo jumbo," according to *Webster's Third New International Dictionary,* connotes "language that is unnecessarily involved and difficult to understand: GIBBERISH." The *Oxford English Dictionary* cites its etymology as "of unknown origin," implicitly serving here as the signified on which Reed's title signifies, recalling the myth of Topsy in *Uncle*

Tom's Cabin who, with no antecedents, "jes' grew"—a phrase with which James Weldon Johnson characterizes the creative process of black sacred music. *Mumbo Jumbo,* then, signifies upon Western etymology, abusive Western practices of deflation through misnaming, and Johnson's specious, albeit persistent, designation of black creativity as anonymous.

But there is even more parody in this title. Whereas Ellison tropes the myth of presence in Wright's titles of *Native Son* and *Black Boy* through his title of *Invisible Man,* Reed parodies all three titles by employing as his title the English-language parody of *black language itself.* Although the etymology of "mumbo jumbo" has been problematic for Western lexicographers, any Swahili speaker knows that the phrase derives from the common greeting *jambo* and its plural, *mambo,* which loosely translated mean "What's happening?" Reed is also echoing, and signifying upon, Vachel Lindsay's ironic poem, "The Congo," which so (fatally) influenced the Harlem Renaissance poets, as Charles T. Davis has shown.[35] From its title on, *Mumbo Jumbo* serves as a critique of black and Western literary forms and conventions, and of the complex relations between the two.

On the book's cover, which Reed designed (with Allen Weinberg), repeated and reversed images of a crouching, sensuous Josephine Baker are superimposed upon a rose.[36] Counterposed to this image is a medallion depicting a horse with two riders. These signs, the rose and the medallion, adumbrate the two central oppositions of the novel's complicated plot. The rose and the double image of Baker together form a cryptic *vé vé.* A *vé vé* is a key sign in Haitian *Vaudou,* a sign drawn on the ground with sand, cornmeal, flour and coffee to represent the *loas.* The *loas* are the deities comprising the pantheon of *Vaudou* gods. The rose is a sign of Erzulie, goddess of love, as are the images of Baker, who became the French goddess of love in the late 1920s, in the Parisian version of the Jazz Age. The doubled image, as if mirrored, is meant to suggest the divine crossroads, where human beings meet their fate. At its center presides the *loa* Legba (Èṣù), guardian of the divine crossroads, messenger of the gods, the figure representing the interpreter and interpretation itself, the muse or *loa* of the critic. Legba is master of that mystical barrier separating the divine from the profane world. This complex yet cryptic *vé vé* is meant both to placate Legba himself and to summon his attention and integrity in a double act of criticism and interpretation: that of Reed in the process of his representation of the tradition, to be found between the covers of the book, and of the critic's interpretation of Reed's figured interpretation.

Located outside of the *vé vé,* as counterpoint, placed almost off the cover itself, is the medallion, the sign of the Knights Templar, representing the heart of the Western tradition. The opposition between the *vé vé* and the medallion represents two distinct warring forces, two mutually exclusive modes of reading. Already we are in the realm of doubles, but not the binary realm; rather, we are in the realm of doubled doubles. ("Doubled doubles" are central figures in Yoruba mythology, as is Èṣù.) Not only are two distinct and conflicting metaphysical systems here represented and invoked, but Reed's cover also serves as an overture to the critique of dualism and binary opposition which gives a major thrust to the text of *Mumbo Jumbo.* Reed parodies this dualism—which he thinks is exemplified in Ellison's *Invisible Man*—not just in *Mumbo Jumbo* but also in another text, his poem "Dualism: in ralph ellison's invisible man."

This critique of dualism is implicit in *Mumbo Jumbo*'s central *speaking* character, PaPa LaBas. I emphasize "speaking" here because the novel's central character, of course, is Jes Grew itself, which never speaks and is never seen in its "abstract essence," only in discrete manifestations, or "outbreaks." Jes Grew is the supraforce which sets the text of *Mumbo Jumbo* in motion, as Jes Grew and Reed seek their texts, as all characters and events define themselves against this omnipresent, compelling force. Jes Grew, here, is a clever and subtle parody of similar forces invoked in the black novel of naturalism, most notably in Wright's *Native Son*.

Unlike Jes Grew, PaPa LaBas does indeed speak. He is the chief detective in hard-and-fast pursuit of both Jes Grew and its Text. PaPa LaBas's name is a conflation of two of the several names of Èṣù, the Pan-African trickster. Called "Papa Legba" as his Haitian honorific and invoked through the phrase "eh là-bas" in New Orleans jazz recordings of the 1920s and 1930s, PaPa LaBas is the Afro-American trickster figure from black sacred tradition. His surname, of course, is French for "over there," and his presence unites "over there" (Africa) with "right here." He is indeed the messenger of the gods, the divine Pan-African interpreter, pursuing, in the language of the text, "The Work," which is not only *Vaudou* but also the very work (and play) of art itself. PaPa LaBas is the figure of the critic, in search of the text, decoding its telltale signs in the process. Even the four syllables of his name recall *Mumbo Jumbo*'s play of doubles. Chief sign reader, LaBas also in a sense is a sign himself. Indeed, PaPa LaBas's incessant and ingenious search for the Text of Jes Grew, culminating as it does in his recitation and revision of the myth of Thoth's gift of writing to civilization, constitutes an argument against the privileging in black discourse of what Reed elsewhere terms "the so-called oral tradition" in favor of the primacy and priority of the written text. It is a brief for the permanence of the written text, for the need of criticism, for which LaBas's myth of origins also accounts ("Guides were initiated into the Book of Thoth, the 1st anthology written by the 1st choreographer"; *MJ,* p. 164).

Let us examine the text of *Mumbo Jumbo* as a textbook, complete with illustrations, footnotes and a bibliography. A prologue, an epilogue and an appended "Partial Bibliography" frame the text proper, again in a parody of Ellison's framing devices in *Invisible Man*. (Reed supplements Ellison's epilogue with the bibliography, parodying the device both by its repeated presence and by the subsequent asymmetry of *Mumbo Jumbo*.) This documentary scheme of notes, illustrations and bibliography parodies the documentary conventions of black realism and naturalism, as does Reed's recurrent use of lists and catalogs. These "separate" items Reed fails to separate with any sort of punctuation, thereby directing attention to their presence as literary conventions rather than as sources of information, particularly about the "black experience." Reed's text also includes dictionary definitions, epigraphs, epigrams, anagrams, photo-duplicated type from other texts, newspaper clips and headlines, signs (such as those that hang on doors), invitations to parties, telegrams, "Situation Reports" (which come "from the 8-tubed Radio"; *MJ,* p. 32), yin–yang symbols, quotations from other texts, poems, cartoons, drawings of mythic beasts, handbills, photographs, book-jacket copy, charts and graphs, playing cards, a representation of a Greek vase, and a four-page handwritten letter, among even other items. Just as our word "satire" derives from *satura,* "hash," so Reed's form of satire is a version of "gumbo," a parody of form itself.[37]

Reed here parodies and underscores our notions of intertextuality, present in all texts. *Mumbo Jumbo* is the great black inter-text, replete with intra-texts referring to one another within the text of *Mumbo Jumbo* and also referring outside themselves to all those other named texts, as well as to those texts unnamed but invoked through concealed reference, repetition and reversal. The "Partial Bibliography" is Reed's most brilliant stroke, since its unconcealed presence (along with the text's other undigested texts) parodies both the scholar's appeal to authority and all studied attempts to conceal literary antecedents and influence. All texts, claims *Mumbo Jumbo,* are inter-texts, full of intra-texts. Our notions of originality, Reed's critique suggests, are more related to convention and material relationships than to some supposedly transcendent truth. Reed lays bare that mode of concealment and the illusion of unity which characterize modernist texts. Coming as it does after the epilogue, Reed's "Partial Bibliography" is an implicit parody of Ellison's ideas of craft and technique in the novel and suggests an image of Ellison's nameless protagonist, buried in his well-lighted hole, eating vanilla ice cream smothered by sloe gin, making annotations for his sequel to *Invisible Man*. The device, moreover, mimics the fictions of documentation and history which claim to order the ways societies live. The presence of the bibliography also recalls Ellison's remarks about the complex relationship between the "writer's experience" and the writer's experiences with books.

Reed's parodic use of intertextuality demonstrates that *Mumbo Jumbo* is a post-modern text. But what is its parody of the Jazz Age and the Harlem Renaissance about, and for whom do the characters stand? Reed's novel is situated in the 1920s because, as the text explains, the Harlem Renaissance was the first full-scale, patronized attempt to capture the essence of Jes Grew in discrete *literary* texts. Jes Grew had made its first appearance in the 1890s, when "the Dance" swept the country. Indeed, James Weldon Johnson appropriated the phrase "jes' grew" to refer to the composition of the musical texts of Ragtime, which depended upon signifying riffs to transform black secular, and often vulgar, songs into formal, repeatable compositions. Ellison makes essentially the same statement about the 1890s by suggesting that signifying is implicit in the common designation of this music as "Ethiopian Airs." Ellison's pun could well serve as still another signified upon which *Mumbo Jumbo* signifies. The power of Jes Grew was allowed to peter out in the 1890s, Reed argues, because it found no literary texts to contain, define, interpret and thereby will it to subsequent black cultures.

Although the Harlem Renaissance did succeed in the creation of numerous texts of art and criticism, most critics agree that it failed to find its voice, which lay muffled beneath the dead weight of Romantic convention, which most black writers seemed not to question but to adopt eagerly. This is essentially the same critique rendered by Wallace Thurman in his *Infants of the Spring* (1932), a satirical novel about the Harlem Renaissance, written by one of its most thoughtful literary critics. Few of Reed's characters stand for historical personages; most are figures for types. Hinckle Von Vampton, however, suggests Carl Van Vechten, but his first name, from the German *hinken* ("to limp"), could suggest the German engraver Hermann Knackfuss, whose name translates as "a person with a clubfoot."[38] Abdul Sufi Hamid recalls a host of Black Muslims, most notably Duse Mohamed Ali, editor of the *African Times and Orient Review,* as well as

Elijah Muhammad's shadowy mentor, W. D. Fard. The key figures in the action of the plot, however, are the Atonist Path and its military wing, the Wallflower Order, on one hand, and the Neo-HooDoo detectives, headed by PaPa LaBas, and its "military" wing, the *Mu'tafikah,* on the other. "Wallflower Order" is a two-term pun on "Ivy League," while *Mu'tafikah* puns on a twelve-letter word which signifies chaos. Also, "mu" is the twelfth letter of the Greek alphabet, suggesting "the dozens," which forms a subdivision of the black ritual of signifying; the *Mu'tafikah* play the dozens on Western art museums. The painter Knackfuss created a heliogravure from Wilhelm II's allegorical drawing of the European authority to go to war against the Chinese. This heliogravure, *Völker Europas, wahrt eure heiligsten Güter* ("People of Europe, protect that which is most holy to you"), was completed in 1895. It appears in *Mumbo Jumbo* as part of a chapter in which members of the Wallflower Order plot against the *Mu'tafikah* (see *MJ,* p. 155). The pun on "Knackfuss" and *hinken* is wonderfully consistent with Reed's multiple puns on the "Wallflower Order" and "Atonist."

"Atonist" signifies multiply here. "One who atones" is an Atonist; a follower of Aton, Pharaoh Akhnaton's Supreme Being who "reappears" as Jehovah, is an Atonist; but also one who lacks physiological tone, especially of a contractile organ, is an Atonist. On a wall at Atonist headquarters are the Order's symbols, "the Flaming Disc, the #1 and the creed":

> *Look at them! Just look at them! throwing their hips this way, that way* while I, my muscles, stone, the marrow of my spine, plaster, *my back supported by decorated paper, stand here as goofy as a Dumb Dora. Lord, if I can't dance, no one shall* (*MJ,* p. 65; original in italics, emphasis mine).

The Atonists and the Jes Grew Carriers ("JGC's") re-enact allegorically a primal, recurring battle between the forces of light and the forces of darkness, between forces of the Left Hand and forces of the Right Hand, between the descendants of Set and the descendants of Osiris, all symbolized in Knackfuss's heliogravure.

We learn of this war in *Mumbo Jumbo*'s marvelous parody of the scene of recognition so fundamental to the structure of detective fiction, which occurs in the library of a black-owned villa at Irvington-on-Hudson, called Villa Lewaro, "an anagram," the text tells us, "upon the Hostess' name, by famed tenor Enrico Caruso" (*MJ,* p. 156). Actually, "Lewaro" is an anagram for "we oral." This recognition scene in which PaPa LaBas and his sidekick, Black Herman, arrest Hinckle Von Vampton and his sidekick, Hubert "Safecracker" Gould, parodies its counterpart in the detective novel by its exaggerated frame. When forced to explain the charges against Von Vampton and Gould, LaBas replies, "Well if you must know, it all began 1000s of years ago in Egypt, according to a high up member in the Haitian aristocracy" (*MJ,* p. 160). He then proceeds to narrate, before an assembled company of hundreds, the myth of Set and Osiris and its key subtext, the myth of the introduction of writing in Egypt by the god Thoth. The parody involved here is the length of the recapitulation of facts—of the decoded signs—which LaBas narrates in a thirty-one-page chapter, the longest in the book (see *MJ,* pp. 161–91). The myth, of course, recapitulates the action of the novel up to this point of the narrative, but by an *allegorical* representation through mythic discourse. By fits and turns, we realize that Von Vampton and the Wallflower Order are the descendants of Set, by way of the story of Moses and

Jethro and the birth of the Knights Templar in AD 1118. Von Vampton, we learn, was the Templar librarian, who found the sacred Book of Thoth, "the 1st anthology written by the 1st choreographer," which is Jes Grew's sacred Text (*MJ,* p. 164). In the twentieth century, Von Vampton subdivided the Book of Thoth into fourteen sections, just as Set had dismembered his brother Osiris' body into fourteen segments. The fourteen sections of the anthology he mailed anonymously to fourteen black people, who are manipulated into mailing its parts to each other in a repeating circle, in the manner of a "chain book" (*MJ,* p. 69). Abdul Sufi Hamid, one of these fourteen who, we learn, are unwitting Jes Grew Carriers, calls in the other thirteen chapters of the anthology, reassembles the Text, and even translates the Book of Thoth from the hieroglyphics. Sensing its restored Text, Jes Grew surfaces in New Orleans, as it had in the 1890s with the birth of Ragtime, and heads toward New York. Ignorant of the existence or nature of Jes Grew and of the true nature of the sacred Text, Abdul destroys the Book, and then, when he refuses to reveal its location, is murdered by the Wallflower Order. LaBas, Von Vampton's arch-foe, master of HooDoo, devout follower of Jes Grew ("PaPa LaBas carries Jes Grew in him like most other folk carry genes"; *MJ,* p. 23), chief decoder of signs, recapitulates this complex story, in elaborate detail, to the assembled guests at Villa Lewaro, thereby repeating, through the recited myth, the figures of *Mumbo Jumbo*'s own plot, functioning as what Reed calls "the shimmering Etheric Double of the 1920s. The thing that gives it its summary" (*MJ,* p. 20). Despite numerous murders and even the arrests of Von Vampton and Gould and their repatriation to Haiti for trial by the *loas* of *Vaudou,* neither the mystery of the nature of Jes Grew nor the identity of its Text is ever resolved. The epilogue presents PaPa LaBas in the 1960s, delivering his annual lecture to a college audience on the Harlem Renaissance and its unconsummated Jes Grew passion.

But just as we can define orders of multiple substitution and signification for Reed's types and caricatures, as is true of allegory generally (e.g. Von Vampton/Van Vechten, *hinken*/Knackfuss), so too we can find many levels of meaning which could provide a closure to the text. The first decade of readers of *Mumbo Jumbo* have attempted, with great energy, to find one-to-one correlations, decoding its allegorical structure by finding analogues between, for example, the Harlem Renaissance and the Black Arts Movement. As interesting as such parallel universes are, however, I am more concerned here with *Mumbo Jumbo*'s status as a rhetorical structure, as a mode of narration, and with relating this mode of narration to a critique of traditional notions of closure in interpretation. Reed's most subtle achievement in *Mumbo Jumbo* is to parody, to signify upon, the notions of closure implicit in the key texts of the Afro-American canon. *Mumbo Jumbo,* in contrast to that canon, is a novel that figures and glorifies *indeterminacy.* In this sense, *Mumbo Jumbo* stands as a profound critique and elaboration upon the convention of closure, and its metaphysical implications, in the black novel. In its stead, Reed posits the notion of aesthetic *play:* the play of the tradition, the play on the tradition, the sheer play of indeterminacy itself.

Indeterminacy and the Text of Blackness

The text of *Mumbo Jumbo* is framed by devices characteristic of film narration. The prologue, situated in New Orleans, functions as a "false start" of the action: five pages of narration are followed by a second title page, a second copyright and acknowledgment page, and a second set of epigraphs, the first of which concludes the prologue. This prologue functions like the prologue of a film, with the title and credits appearing next, before the action continues. The novel's final words are "Freeze frame" (*MJ,* p. 218). The relative fluidity of the narrative structure of film, compared with that of conventional prose narrative, announces here an emphasis upon figural multiplicity rather than singular referential correspondence, an emphasis that Reed recapitulates throughout the text by an imaginative play of doubles. The play of doubles extends from the title and the double-Erzulie image of Baker on the novel's cover ("Erzulie" means "love of mirrors"; *MJ,* p. 162) to the double beginning implicit in every prologue, through all sorts of double images scattered in the text (such as the "two heads" of PaPa LaBas [see *MJ,* pp. 24, 45] and the frequently repeated arabic numerals 4 and 22), all the way to the double ending of the novel implied by its epilogue and "Partial Bibliography." The double beginning and double ending frame the text of *Mumbo Jumbo,* a book of doubles, from its title on.

These thematic aspects of doubleness represent only its most obvious form of doubling; the novel's narrative structure, a brilliant elaboration upon that of the detective novel, is itself a rather complex doubling. Reed refers to this principle of "structuration" as "a doubleness, not just of language, but the idea of a double-image on form. A mystery-mystery, *Erzulie-Erzulie.*"[39] In *Mumbo Jumbo,* form and content, theme and structure, all are ordered upon this figure of the double; doubling is Reed's "figure in the carpet." The form the narration takes in *Mumbo Jumbo* replicates the tension of the two stories which grounds the form of the detective novel, defined by Tzvetan Todorov as "the missing story of the crime, and the presented story of the investigation, the role justification of which is to make us discover the first story." Todorov describes three forms of detective fiction—the whodunit, the *série noire* (the thriller, exemplified by Chester Himes's *For Love of Imabelle*) and the suspense novel, which combines the narrative features of the first two.[40] Let us consider Todorov's typology in relation to the narrative structure of *Mumbo Jumbo.*

The whodunit comprises two stories: the story of the crime and the story of the investigation. The first story, that of the crime, has ended by the time the second story, that of the investigation of the crime, begins. In the story of the investigation, the characters "do not act, they learn." The whodunit's structure, as in Agatha Christie's *Murder on the Orient Express,* is often framed by a prologue and an epilogue, "that is, the discovery of the crime and the discovery of the killer" (*PP,* p. 45). The second story functions as an explanation not just of the investigation but also of how the book came to be written; indeed, "it is precisely the story of that very book" (*PP,* p. 45). As Todorov concludes, these two stories are the same as those which the Russian Formalists isolated in every narrative, that of the *fable* (story) and that of the *subject* (or plot): "The story is what has happened in life, the plot is the way the author presents it to us" (*PP,* p. 45). "Story," here, describes the reality represented, while "plot" describes the mode of narration, the literary convention and devices, used to represent. A detective novel merely renders these two principles of narrative *present* simultaneously. The story of the crime is a story of an absence, since the crime of the whodunit has occurred before the narrative begins; the second story, therefore, "serves only as mediator between the reader and the story of the crime" (*PP,* p. 46). This second story, the plot, generally depends upon temporal inversions and subjective, shifting points of view. These two conventions figure prominently in the narrative structure of *Mumbo Jumbo.*

Todorov's second type of detective fiction, the *série noire,* or thriller, combines the two stories into one, suppressing the first and vitalizing the second. Whereas the whodunit proceeds from effect to cause, the thriller proceeds from cause to effect: the novel reveals at its outset the causes of the crime, the *données* (in *Mumbo Jumbo,* the Wallflower Order, the dialogue of whose members occupies 60 per cent of the prologue), and the narration sustains itself through sheer suspense, through the reader's expectation of what will happen next. Although *Mumbo Jumbo*'s narrative strategy proceeds through the use of suspense, its two stories, as it were, are not fused; accordingly, neither of these categories fully describes it.

Mumbo Jumbo imitates and signifies upon the narrative strategy of the third type of detective novel, the suspense novel. According to Todorov, its defining principles are these: "it keeps the mystery of the whodunit and also the two stories, that of the past and that of the present; but it refuses to reduce the second to a simple detection of the truth" (*PP,* p. 50). What *has* happened is only just as important to sustaining interest as what *shall* happen; the second story, then, the story of the present, is the focus of interest. Reed draws upon this type of narrative as his rhetorical structure in *Mumbo Jumbo,* with one important exception. We do find the two-stories structure intact. What's more, the mystery presented at the outset of the text, the double mystery of the suppression of both Jes Grew *and* its Text (neither of which is ever revealed nor their mysteries solved in the standard sense of the genre), is relayed through the dialogue of the *données.* This means that the movement of the narration is from cause to effect, from the New Orleans branch of the Wallflower Order and their plans to "decode this coon mumbo jumbo" (*MJ,* p. 4) through their attempts to kill its Text and thereby dissipate its force. The detective of the tale, PaPa LaBas, moreover, is integrated solidly into the action and universe of the other characters, risking his life and systematically discovering the murdered corpses of his friends and colleagues as he proceeds to decode the signs of the mystery's solution, in the manner of "the vulnerable detective," which Todorov identifies as a subtype of the suspense novel (*PP,* p. 51).

In these ways, the structure of *Mumbo Jumbo* conforms to that of the suspense novel. The crucial exception to the typology, however, whereby Reed is able to parody even the mode of the two stories themselves and transform the structure into a self-reflecting text or allegory upon the nature of writing itself, is *Mumbo Jumbo*'s device of drawing upon the story of the past *to reflect upon, analyze and philosophize about* the story of the present. The story of the present is narrated from the limited but multiple points of view of the characters who people its subplots and sub-mysteries; the story of the past, however, is narrated in an omniscient voice, which "reads" the story of the present, in the manner of a literary critic close reading a primary text. *Mumbo Jumbo*'s double narrative, then, its narrative-within-a-narrative, is an allegory of the act of reading itself. Reed uses this second mode of ironic omniscient narration to signify upon the nature of the novel in general but especially upon Afro-American naturalism and modernism.

The mystery type of narrative discourse is characterized by plot inversions, which, of course, function as temporal inversions. Before discussing Reed's use of the narrative-within-a-narrative and its relation to the sort of indeterminacy the text seems to be upholding, it would be useful to chart his use of inversion as impediment. The summary of the *fable,* the essential causal-temporal relationships of the work which I have sketched above, is somewhat misleading, for the novel can be related in summary fashion only *after* we have read it. In the reading process we confront a collection of mysteries, mysteries-within-mysteries, all of which are resolved eventually except for the first two. We can list the following mysteries which unfold in this order as the *subject,* or the plot:[41]

1 The mystery of Jes Grew ("the Thing").	These are basic mysteries.
2 The mystery of its Text.	They frame the plot and remain unresolved.
3 The mystery of the Wallflower Order's history and its relation to that of the Knights Templar.	The mystery of the identity of these medieval orders, Jes Grew's antagonists, runs the length of the novel and is resolved only in the recognition scene at Villa Lewaro. Figures as antithetical dance metaphors.
4 The *Mu'tafikah*'s raids on American art museums, especially the North Wing of the Center of Art Detention.	This partial mystery is resolved, but disastrously for LaBas's forces. It creates a series of imbalances between Earline and Berbelang, and between Berbelang and PaPa LaBas, which function as structural parts to the tension between the Wallflower Order and the Knights Templar.
5 Installation of the anti–Jes Grew President Warren Harding and mystery of his complex racial heritage.	Plot impediments.
6 The mystery of the Talking Android.	
7 Gang wars between Buddy Jackson and Schlitz, "the Sarge of Yorktown."	
8 Mystery of the U.S. Marine invasion of Haiti.	Resolved midway; allows for ironic denouncement.
9 Mystery of PaPa LaBas's identity and Mumbo Jumbo Kathedral.	Resolved in epilogue.
10 Woodrow Wilson Jefferson and the mystery of the Talking Android.	Plot impediments; resolved, but ambiguously. Explanations resort to fantastic element.
11 Staged mystery of "Charlotte's (Isis) Pick" (Doctor Peter Pick).	
12 Hinckle Von Vampton's identity.	This mystery is resolved and in the process resolves the mysteries of the Wallflower Order and the Atonist Path.

13 Mystery of the fourteen JGCs and the sacred anthology.	This resolves mystery 2, but only partially, superficially.
14 The mystery of Abdul Sufi Hamid's murder and his riddle, "Epigram on American-Egyptian Cotton."	These mysteries function in a curious way, seemingly to resolve the mystery of Jes Grew's Text.
15 Berbelang's murder and betrayal of the *Mu'tafikah* by Thor Wintergreen. Charlotte's murder.	Plot impediments.
16 Earline's possession by Erzulie and Yemanjá *loas;* Doctor Peter Pick's disappearance.	
17 Mystery of *The Black Plume* and Benoit Battraville, and the ring of the Dark Tower.	VooDoo/HooDoo exposition. Resolves Knights Templar mystery. Leads to capture of Von Vampton.

Most of these interwoven mysteries impede the plot in the manner of detective fiction by depicting, as does jazz, several simultaneous actions whose relationship is not apparent. These mysteries run parallel throughout the novel, only to be resolved in the scene of recognition in the library at the Villa Lewaro, where PaPa LaBas presents his decoded evidence through his elaborate recasting of the myth of Osiris and Set. This allegory recapitulates, combines and decodes the novel's several simultaneous sub-plots and also traces the novel's complex character interrelationships from ancient Egypt up to the very moment of LaBas's narration. The narration leads to the arrest of Gould and Von Vampton, but also to the antidiscovery of the sacred Book of Thoth, the would-be Text of Jes Grew. Recast myths serve the same function of plot impediment for the purpose of repeating the novel's events through metaphorical substitution in two other places: these are the allegories of Faust and of the *houngan,* Ti Bouton (see *MJ,* pp. 90–2, 132–9). These recast myths serve as the play of doubles, consistent with the "double-image on form," which Reed sought to realize, and are implicit in the nature of allegory itself.

Plot impediment can be created in ways other than through temporal inversion; local-color description does as well. Local color, of course, came to be a standard feature in the social novel; in the Afro-American narrative, realism-as-local-color is perhaps the most consistent aspect of black rhetorical strategy from the slave narratives to *Invisible Man*. Reed uses and simultaneously parodies the convention of local color as plot impediment by employing unpunctuated lists and categories throughout the text. Local color is provided in the novel's first paragraph:

> A True Sport, the Mayor of New Orleans, spiffy in his patent-leather brown and white shoes, his plaid suit, the Rudolph Valentino parted-down-the-middle hair style, sits in his office. Sprawled upon his knees is Zuzu, local doo-wack-a-doo and voo-do-dee-odo-fizgig. A slatternly floozy, her green, sequined dress quivers. (*MJ,* p. 3)

The following sentence exemplifies Reed's undifferentiated catalogs: "The dazzling parodying punning mischievous pre-Joycean style-play of your Cakewalking your Calinda your Minstrelsy give-and-take of the ultra-absurd" (*MJ,* p. 152). Viktor Šklovskij says that the mystery novel was drawn upon formally by the social novel; Reed's use of devices from the detective novel to parody the black social novel, then, reverses this process, appropriately and ironically enough.[42]

I have discussed how the tension of the two stories generally operates in the types of detective fiction. Reed's play of doubles assumes its most subtle form in his clever rhetorical strategy of using these two narratives, the story of the past and the story of the present. It is useful to think of these two as the narrative of *understanding* and the narrative of *truth*. The narrative of understanding is the presented narrative of the investigation of a mystery, in which a detective (reader) interprets or decodes "clues." Once these signs are sufficiently decoded, this narrative of understanding reconstitutes the missing story of the crime, which we can think of as the narrative of truth. The presented narrative, then, is implicitly a story of another, absent story and hence functions as an internal allegory.

The nature of this narrative of the investigation in *Mumbo Jumbo* can be easily characterized: the narrative remains close to the action with local-color description and dialogue as its two central aspects; character-as-description and extensive catalogs propel the narrative forward; the narrative remains essentially in the present tense, and the point of view is both in the third person and limited, as it must be if the reader's understanding of the nature of the mystery is to remain impeded until the novel's detective decodes all the clues, assembles all the suspects, interprets the signs and reveals the truth of the mystery. The detective makes his arrests, and then everyone left eats dinner.

Mumbo Jumbo's prologue opens in this narrative mode of the story of the present. Near the end of the prologue, however, a second narrative mode intrudes. It is separated from the first narrative by spacing and is further foregrounded by italic type (see *MJ,* p. 6). It not only interprets and comments upon characters and actions in the first story but does so in a third-person omniscient mode. In other words, it *reads* its counterpart narrative, of which it is a negation. Following its italic type are three other sorts of subtexts which comprise crucial aspects of this second, antithetical narration of past, present and future: a black-and-white photograph of people dancing; an epigraph on the nature of the "second line," written by Louis Armstrong; and an etymology of the phrase "mumbo jumbo," taken from the *American Heritage Dictionary*. That which the characters ponder or "misunderstand," this foregrounded antithetical narration reads "correctly" for the reader.

> *But they did not understand that the Jes Grew epidemic was unlike physical plagues. Actually Jes Grew was an anti-plague. Some plagues caused the body to waste away; Jes Grew enlivened the host. . . . So Jes Grew is seeking its words. Its text. For what good is a liturgy without a text? In the 1890s the text was not available and Jes Grew was out there all alone. Perhaps the 1920s will also be a false alarm and Jes Grew will evaporate as quickly as it appeared again broken-hearted and double-crossed* (+ +). (*MJ,* p. 6)

This second, anti-, narration consists of all of *Mumbo Jumbo*'s motley subtexts which are not included in its first narration. Whereas the first story adheres to the present, the second roams remarkably freely through space and time, between myth and "history," humorously employing the device of anachronism. It is discontinuous and fragmentary, not linear like its counterpart; it never contains dialogue; it contains all of the text's abstractions.

All of the novel's subtexts (illustrations, excerpts from other texts, Situation Reports, etc.) are parts of this second narration, which we might think of as an extended discourse on the history of Jes Grew. The only mysteries this antithetical narration does not address are the text's first two mysteries—what exactly Jes Grew is and what precisely its Text is. After chapter 8, the foregrounding of italics tends to disappear, for the narration manages to bracket or frame itself, functioning almost as the interior monologue of the first narrative mode. While the first story remains firmly in the tradition of the presented detective story, the second turns that convention inside out, functioning as an ironic double, a reversed mirror image like the cryptic *vé vé* on the novel's cover.

This second mode of narration allows for the "allegorical double" of *Mumbo Jumbo*. As many critics have gone to great lenghs to demonstrate, *Mumbo Jumbo* is a thematic allegory of the Black Arts Movement of the 1960s rendered through causal connections with the Harlem Renaissance of the 1920s. A more interesting allegory, however, is that found in the antithetical narrative, which is a discourse on the history and nature of writing itself, especially that of the Afro-American literary tradition. *Mumbo Jumbo,* then, is a text that directs attention to its own writing, to its status as a text, related to other texts which it signifies upon. Its second narration reads its first, as does discourse upon a text. It is Reed reading Reed and the tradition. A formal metaphor for Reed's mode of writing is perhaps the bebop mode of jazz, as exemplified in that great reedist, Charlie Parker, who sometimes played a chord on the alto saxophone, then repeated and reversed the same chord to hear, if I understand him correctly, what he had just played. Parker is a recurring figure in Reed's works: "Parker, the houngan (a word derived from *n'gana gana*) for whom there was no master adept enough to award him the Asson, is born" (*MJ,* p. 16).[43] Just as Jes Grew, the novel's central "character," in searching for its Text is seeking to actualize a desire, to "find its Speaking or strangle upon its own ineloquence," so too is the search for a text replicated and referred to throughout the second, signifying narration (*MJ,* p. 34).

What is the status of this desired Text? How are we to read Reed? Jes Grew's desire would be actualized only by finding its Text. *Mumbo Jumbo*'s parodic use of the presented story of the detective novel states this desire; the solution of the novel's central mystery would be for Jes Grew to find its Text. This Text, PaPa LaBas's allegorical narrative at the Villa Lewaro tells us, is in fact the vast and terrible Text of Blackness itself, "always already" there:

> the Book of Thoth, the sacred Work . . . of the Black Birdman, an assistant to Osiris. (If anyone thinks this is "mystifying the past" [the narrative intrudes] kindly check out your local bird book and you will find the sacred Ibis' Ornithological name to be *Threskiornis aethiopicus*). (*MJ,* p. 188)

The irony of the mystery structure evident in *Mumbo Jumbo* is that this Text, Jes Grew's object of desire, is "defined" only by its absence; it is never seen or found. At the climax of LaBas's amusingly detailed and long recapitulation of his process of reading the signs of the mystery (as well as the history of the dissemination of the Text itself), LaBas instructs his assistant, T Malice, to unveil the Text:

> Go get the Book T!
>
> T Malice goes out to the car and returns with a huge gleaming box covered with snakes and scorpions shaped of sparkling gems.
>
> The ladies intake their breath at such a gorgeous display. On the top can be seen the Knights Templar seal; 2 Knights riding Beaseauh, the Templars' piebald horse. T Malice places the box down in the center of the floor and removes the 1st box, an iron box, and the 2nd box, which is bronze and shines so that they have to turn the ceiling lights down. And within this box is a sycamore box and under the sycamore, ebony, and under this ivory, then silver and finally gold and then . . . empty!! (*MJ,* p. 196)

The nature of the Text remains undetermined and, indeed, indeterminate, as it was at the novel's beginning. Once the signs of its presence have been read, the Text disappears, in what must be the most humorous anticlimax in the whole of Afro-American fiction.

We can read this anticlimax against the notion of indeterminacy. Geoffrey H. Hartman defines the function of indeterminacy as "a bar separating understanding and truth."[44] The "bar" in *Mumbo Jumbo* is signified by that unbridgeable white space that separates the first narrative mode from the second, the narrative of truth. *Mumbo Jumbo* is a novel about indeterminacy in interpretation itself. The text repeats this theme again and again. In addition to the two narrative voices, the Atonist Path and its Wallflower Order are criticized severely for a foolish emphasis upon unity, upon the number 1, upon what the novel calls "point." One of the three symbols of the Atonist Order is "the #1" (*MJ,* p. 65). Their leader is called "Hierophant 1" (*MJ,* p. 63). A "hierophant," of course, is an expositor. The Atonists are defined in the antithetical narrative as they who seek to interpret the world through one interpretation:

> To some if you owned your own mind you were indeed sick but when you possessed an Atonist mind you were healthy. A mind which sought to interpret the world by using a single loa. Somewhat like filling a milk bottle with an ocean. (*MJ,* p. 24)

The novel defines the nature of this urge for the reduction of unity:

> 1st they intimidate the intellectuals by condemning work arising out of their own experience as being 1-dimensional, enraged, non-objective, preoccupied with hate and not universal, universal being a word co-opted by the Catholic Church when the Atonists took over Rome, as a way of measuring every 1 by their deals. (*MJ,* p. 133)

One is an Atonist, the novel maintains consistently, who attempts to tie the sheer plurality of signification to one, determinate meaning.

In contrast is the spirit of Jes Grew and PaPa LaBas. As I have shown, the name "LaBas" is derived from Èṣù-Ẹlẹ́gbára. The Yoruba call Èṣù the god of indeterminacy (*àriyẹ̀muyẹ̀*) and of uncertainty. PaPa LaBas, in contradistinction to Hierophant 1, has not one but two heads, like the face of the sign: "PaPa LaBas, noonday HooDoo, fugitive-hermit, obeah-man, botanist, animal impersonator, 2-headed man, You-Name-It" (*MJ,* p. 45). Moreover, he functions, as the detective of Jes Grew, as a decoder, as a sign reader, the man who cracked *de* code, by using his two heads: "Evidence? Woman, I dream about it, I feel it, I use my 2 heads. My Knockings" (*MJ,* p. 25). LaBas is the critic, engaged in The Work, the work of art, refusing to reduce it to a "point":

> People in the 60s said they couldn't follow him. (In Santa Cruz the students walked out.) What's your point? they asked in Seattle whose central point, the Space Needle, is invisible from time to time. What are you driving at? they would say in Detroit in the 1950s. In the 40s he haunted the stacks of a ghost library. (*MJ,* p. 218)

While arguing ironically with Abdul Sufi Hamid, the Black Muslim who subsequently burns the Book of Thoth, LaBas critiques Abdul's "black aesthetic" in terms identical to his critique of the Atonists:

> Where does that leave the ancient Vodun aesthetic: pantheistic, becoming, 1 which bountifully permits 1000s of spirits, as many as the imagination can hold. Infinite Spirits and Gods. So many that it would take a book larger than the Koran and the Bible, the Tibetan Book of the Dead and all of the holy books in the world to list, and still room would have to be made for more. (*MJ,* p. 35; see also Abdul's letter to LaBas, *MJ,* pp. 200–3)

It is indeterminacy, the sheer plurality of meaning, the very play of the signifier itself, which *Mumbo Jumbo* celebrates. *Mumbo Jumbo* addresses the *play* of the black literary tradition and, as a parody, is a *play* upon that same tradition. Its central character, Jes Grew, cannot be reduced by the Atonists, as they complain: "It's nothing we can bring into focus or categorize; once we call it 1 thing it forms into something else" (*MJ,* p. 4). Just as LaBas the detective is the text's figure for indeterminacy (paradoxically because he is a detective), so too is Jes Grew's "nature" indeterminate: its Text is never a presence, and it disappears when its Text disappears, as surely as does Charlotte when Doctor Peter Pick recites, during his reverse-minstrel plantation routine, an incantation from PaPa LaBas's *Blue Back: A Speller* (see *MJ,* pp. 104–5, 199).

Even the idea of one transcendent subject, Jes Grew's Text, the Text of Blackness itself, *Mumbo Jumbo* criticizes. When the poet, Nathan Brown, asks the Haitian *houngan* Benoit Battraville how to catch Jes Grew, Benoit replies: "don't ask me how to catch Jes Grew. Ask Louis Armstrong, Bessie Smith, your poets, your painters, your musicians, ask them how to catch it" (*MJ,* p. 152). Jes Grew also manifests itself in more curious forms:

> The Rhyming Fool who sits in Rē'-mote Mississippi and talks "crazy" for hours. The dazzling parodying punning mischievous pre-Joycean style-play of your Cakewalking your Calinda your Minstrelsy give-and-take of the ultra-absurd. Ask the people who put wax paper over combs and breathe through them. In other words, Nathan, I am saying Open-up-to-Right-Here and then you will have something coming from your experience that the whole world will admire and need. (*MJ,* p. 152)

Jes Grew's Text, in other words, is not a transcendent signified but must be *produced* in a dynamic process and manifested in discrete forms, as in black music and black speech acts: "The Blues is a Jes Grew, as James Weldon Johnson surmised. Jazz was a Jes Grew which followed the Jes Grew of Ragtime. Slang is Jes Grew too," PaPa LaBas tells his 1960s audience in his annual lecture on the Harlem Renaissance (*MJ,* p. 214).

"Is this the end of Jes Grew?" the narrative questions when we learn that its Text does not exist. "Jes Grew has no end and no beginning," the text replies (*MJ,* p. 204). The echoes here are intentional: Reed echoes Ellison or, rather, Ellison's echo of T. S. Eliot. "In my end is my beginning," writes Eliot in "East Coker," "In my beginning is my end." The "end," writes Ellison, "is in the beginning and lies far ahead."[45] Reed signifies upon Ellison's gesture of closure here, and that of the entire Afro-American literary tradition, by positing an open-endedness of interpretation, of the play of signifiers, just as his and Ellison's works both signify upon the idea of the transcendent signified of the black tradition, the Text of Blackness itself.

The tradition's classic text on the "blackness of blackness" is found in the prologue of *Invisible Man:*

> "Brothers and sisters, my text this morning is the 'Blackness of Blackness.' "
> And a congregation of voices answered: "That blackness is most black, brother, most black . . ."
> "In the beginning . . ."
> "At the very start," they cried.
> ". . . there was blackness . . ."
> "Preach it . . ."
> ". . . and the sun . . ."
> "The sun, Lawd . . ."
> ". . . was bloody red . . ."
> "Red . . ."
> "Now black is . . ." the preacher shouted.
> "Bloody . . ."
> "I said black is . . ."
> "Preach it, brother . . ."
> ". . . an' black ain't . . ."
> "Red, Lawd, red: He said it's red!"
> "Amen, brother . . ."
> "Black will git you . . ."
> "Yes, it will . . ."
> ". . . an' black won't . . ."
> "Naw, it won't!"
> "It do . . ."
> "It do, Lawd . . ."
> ". . . an' it don't"
> "Halleluiah . . ."
> ". . . It'll put you, glory, glory, Oh my Lawd, in the WHALE'S BELLY."
> "Preach it, dear brother . . ."
> ". . . an' make you tempt . . ."
> "Good God a-mighty!"

"Old Aunt Nelly!"
"Black will make you . . ."
"Black . . ."
". . . or black will un-make you."
"Ain't it the truth, Lawd?" (*IM*, pp. 12–13)

This sermon signifies on Melville's passage in *Moby-Dick* on "the blackness of darkness" and on the sign of blackness, as represented by the algorithm $\frac{\text{signified}}{\text{signifier}}$.[46] As Ellison's text states, "black is" and "black ain't," "It do, Lawd," "an' it don't." Ellison parodies here the notion of essence, of the supposedly natural relation between the symbol and the symbolized. The vast and terrible Text of Blackness, we realize, has no essence; rather, it is signified into being by a signifier. The trope of blackness in Western discourse has signified absence at least since Plato. Plato, in the *Phaedrus,* recounts the myth of Theuth (*Mumbo Jumbo*'s "Thoth") and the introduction of writing into Egypt. Along the way, Plato has Socrates draw upon the figure of blackness as a metaphor for one of the three divisions of the soul, that of "badness":

> The other is crooked of frame, a massive jumble of a creature, with thick short neck, snub nose, black skin, and gray eyes; hot-blooded, consorting with wantonness and vainglory; shaggy of ear, deaf, and hard to control with whip and goad.[47]

Reed's use of the myth of Thoth is, of course, not accidental or arbitrary: he repeats and inverts Plato's dialogue, salient point for salient point, even down to Socrates' discourse on the excesses of the dance, which is a theme of *Mumbo Jumbo*.[48] It is not too much to say that *Mumbo Jumbo* is one grand signifying riff on the *Phaedrus,* parodying it through the hidden polemic.

Both Ellison and Reed, then, critique the received idea of blackness as a negative essence, as a natural, transcendent signified; but implicit in such a critique is an equally thorough critique of blackness as a *presence,* which is merely another transcendent signified. Such a critique, therefore, is a critique of the structure of the sign itself and constitutes a profound critique. The Black Arts Movement's grand gesture was to make of the trope of blackness a trope of presence. That movement willed it to be, however, a transcendent presence. Ellison's "text for today," "the 'Blackness of Blackness' " (*IM,* p. 12), analyzes this gesture, just as surely as does Reed's Text of Blackness, the "sacred Book of Thoth." In literature, blackness is *produced* in the text only through a complex process of signification. There can be no transcendent blackness, for it cannot and does not exist beyond manifestations of it in specific figures. Put simply, Jes Grew cannot conjure its texts; "texts," in the broadest sense of this term (Parker's music, Ellison's fictions, Romare Bearden's collages, etc.), conjure Jes Grew.

Reed had, in *Mumbo Jumbo,* signified upon Ellison's critique of the central presupposition of the Afro-American literary tradition, by drawing upon Ellison's trope as a central theme of the plot of *Mumbo Jumbo* and by making explicit Ellison's implicit critique of the nature of the sign itself, of a transcendent signified, an essence, which supposedly exists prior to its figuration. Their formal relationship can only be suggested by the relation of modernism to postmodernism, two overworked terms. Blackness exists, but "only" as a function of its signifiers. Reed's open-ended structure, and his stress on the indeterminacy of the text, demands that we, as critics, in the act of reading, *produce* a text's signifying structure. For Reed, as for his great precursor, Ellison, figuration is indeed the "nigger's occupation."

Coda: The Warp and the Woof

Reed's signifying relation to Ellison is exemplified in his poem, "Dualism: in ralph ellison's invisible man":

> i am outside of
> history. i wish
> i had some peanuts, it
> looks hungry there in
> its cage.
> i am inside of
> history. its
> hungrier than i
> thot.[49]

The figure of history, here, is the Signifying Monkey; the poem signifies upon that repeated trope of dualism figured initially in black discourse in Du Bois's essay "Of Our Spiritual Strivings," which forms the first chapter of *The Souls of Black Folk*. The dualism parodied by Reed's poem is that represented in the epilogue of *Invisible Man:* "Now I know men are different and that all life is divided and that only in division is there true health" (*IM,* p. 499). For Reed, this belief in the "reality" of dualism spells death. Ellison, here, had refigured Du Bois's trope:

> After the Egyptian and Indian, the Greek and Roman, the Teuton and Mongolian, the Negro is a sort of seventh son, born with a veil, and gifted with second-sight in this American world,—a world which yields him no true self-consciousness, but only lets him see himself through the revelation of the other world. It is a peculiar sensation, this double-consciousness, this sense of always looking at one's self through the eyes of others, of measuring one's soul by the tape of a world that looks on in amused contempt and pity. One ever feels his two-ness,—an American, a Negro; two souls, two thoughts, two unreconciled strivings; two warring ideals in one dark body, whose dogged strength alone keeps it from being torn asunder.
>
> The history of the American Negro is the history of this strife,—this longing to attain self-conscious manhood, to merge his double self into a better and truer self. In this merging he wishes neither of the older selves to be lost.[50]

Reed's poem parodies, profoundly, both the figure of the black as outsider and the figure of the divided self. For, he tells us, even these are only tropes, figures of speech, rhetorical constructs like "double-consciousness," and not some pre-ordained reality or thing. To read these figures literally, Reed tells us, is to be duped by figuration, just like the signified Lion. Reed has secured his place in the canon precisely by his critique of the received, repeated tropes peculiar to that very canon. His works are the grand works of critical signification.

NOTES

1. Quoted in Roger D. Abrahams, *Deep Down in the Jungle . . .: Negro Narrative Folklore from the Streets of Philadelphia* (Chicago, Ill.: Aldine, 1970), p. 53.
2. The present essay is extracted from my larger work, *The Signifying Monkey: Towards a Theory of Literary History* (New York: Oxford University Press, 1985).
3. On Tar Baby, see Ralph Ellison, "Hidden Name and Complex Fate: A Writer's Experience in the United States," *Shadow and Act* (New York: Vintage Books, 1964), p. 147, and Toni Morrison, *Tar Baby* (New York: Knopf, 1981). On the black as quasi-simian, see Jean Bodin, *Method for the Easy Comprehension of History,* trans. Beatrice Reynolds (1945; New York: Octagon Books, 1966), p. 105; Aristotle, *Historia animalium,* 606b; Thomas Herbert, *Some Years Travels* (London, 1677), pp. 16–17; and John Locke, *An Essay Concerning Human Understanding,* 8th edn, 2 vols (London, 1721), vol. 2, p. 53.
4. Geneva Smitherman defines these and other black tropes and then traces their use in several black texts. Smitherman's work, like that of Claudia Mitchell-Kernan and Abrahams, is especially significant for literary theory. See Smitherman, *Talkin' and Testifyin': The Language of Black America* (Boston, Mass.: Houghton Mifflin, 1977), pp. 101–66. See also notes 13 and 14 below.
5. On versions of Èṣù, see Robert Farris Thompson, *Black Gods and Kings* (1971; Bloomington, Ind.: Indiana University Press, 1976), ch. 4, pp. 1–12, and *Flash of the Spirit* (New York: Random House, 1983); Pierre Verger, *Notes sur le culte des Orisa et Vodun* (Dakar: IFAN, 1957); Joan Westcott, "The Sculpture and Myths of Eshu-Elegba, the Yoruba Trickster," *Africa,* 32 (October 1962), pp. 336–54; Leo Frobenius, *The Voice of Africa,* 2 vols (London, 1913); J. Melville and Frances Herskovits, *Dahomean Narrative* (Evanston, Ill.: Northwestern University Press, 1958); Wande Abimbola, *Sixteen Great Poems of Ifa* (New York: Unesco, 1975); William R. Bascom, *Ifa Divination: Communication between Gods and Men in West Africa* (Bloomington, Ind.: Indiana University Press, 1969); Ayodele Ogundipe, "Esu Elegbara: The Yoruba God of Chance and Uncertainty," 2 vols (PhD dissertation, Indiana University, 1978); E. Bolaji Idowu, *Olódùmaré, God in Yoruba Belief* (London: Longman, 1962), pp. 80–5; and Robert Pelton, *The Trickster in West Africa* (Los Angeles, Calif.: University of California Press, 1980).
6. On Èṣù and indeterminacy, see Robert Plant Armstrong, *The Powers of Presence: Consciousness, Myth, and Affecting Presence* (Philadelphia, Pa.: University of Pennsylvania Press, 1981), p. 4. See ibid., p. 43, for a drawing of the *Ọpọ́n Ifá,* and Thompson, *Black Gods and Kings,* ch. 5.
7. On Èṣù and the Monkey, see Lydia Cabrerra, *El Monte: Notes sobre las religiones, la magia, las supersticiones y el folklore de los negros criollos y el pueblo de Cuba* (Miami, Fla.: Ediciones Universal, 1975), p. 84, and Alberto de Pozo, *Oricha* (Miami, Fla.: Oricha, 1982), p. 1. On the Signifying Monkey, see Abrahams, op. cit., pp. 51–3, 66, 113–19, 142–7, 153–6 and esp. 264; Bruce Jackson (comp.), *"Get Your Ass in the Water and Swim Like Me": Narrative Poetry from Black Oral Tradition* (Cambridge, Mass.: Harvard University Press, 1974), pp. 161–80; Daryl Cumber Dance, *Shuckin' and Jivin': Folklore from Contemporary Black Americans* (Bloomington, Ind.: Indiana University Press, 1978), pp. 197–9; Dennis Wepman, Ronald B. Newman and Murray B. Binderman (comps), *The Life: The Lore and Folk Poetry of the Black Hustler* (Philadelphia, Pa.: University of Pennsylvania Press, 1976), pp. 21–9; Lawrence W. Levine, *Black Culture and Black Consciousness: Afro-American Folk Thought from Slavery to Freedom* (New York: Oxford University Press, 1977), pp. 346, 378–80, 438; and Richard M. Dorson (comp.), *American Negro Folktales* (New York: Fawcett, 1967), pp. 98–9.
8. Julia Kristeva, *Desire in Language: A Semiotic Approach to Literature and Art,* ed. Leon S. Roudiez, trans. Thomas Gora, Alice Jardine and Leon S. Roudiez (New York: Columbia University Press, 1980), p. 31.
9. Abrahams, op. cit., pp. 51–2. See also Roger D. Abrahams, "Playing the Dozens," *Journal of American Folklore,* 75 (July–September 1962), pp. 209–20; "The Changing Concept of the Negro Hero," in Mody C. Boatright, Wilson H. Hudson and Allen Maxwell (eds), *The Golden Log,* Publications of the Texas Folklore Society, no. 31 (Dallas, Tex., 1962), pp. 125–34; and *Talking Black* (Rowley, Mass.: Newbury House, 1976).
10. Abrahams, *Deep Down in the Jungle,* pp. 52, 264, 66, 67; my emphasis. Abrahams's awareness of the need to define uniquely black significations is exemplary; as early as 1964, when

he published the first edition of *Deep Down in the Jungle,* he saw fit to add a glossary, as an appendix of "Unusual Terms and Expressions," a title that unfortunately suggests the social scientist's apologia.

11. Ibid., p. 113. In the second line of the stanza, "motherfucker" is often substituted for "monkey."
12. "The Signifying Monkey," in *The Book of Negro Folklore,* ed. Langston Hughes and Arna Bontemps (New York: Dodd, Mead, 1958), pp. 365–6.
13. On signifying as a rhetorical trope, see Thomas Kochman (ed.), *Rappin' and Stylin' Out: Communication in Urban Black America* (Urbana, Ill.: University of Illinois Press, 1972) and " 'Rappin' in the Black Ghetto," *Trans-action,* 6 (February 1969), p. 32; Smitherman, op. cit., pp. 101–67; Alan Dundes (ed.), *Mother Wit from the Laughing Barrel* (Englewood Cliffs, NJ: Prentice-Hall, 1973), p. 310; and Ethel M. Albert, " 'Rhetoric,' 'Logic,' and 'Poetics' in Burundi: Culture Patterning of Speech Behavior," in John J. Gumperz and Dell Hymes (eds), *The Ethnography of Communication, American Anthropologist,* 66, pt 2 (December 1964), pp. 35–54.

    One example of signifying can be gleaned from an anecdote. While writing this essay, I asked a colleague, Dwight Andrews, if as a child he had heard of the Signifying Monkey. "Why, no," he replied intently, "I never heard of the Signifying Monkey until I came to Yale and read about him in a book." I had been signified upon. If I had responded to Dwight Andrews, "I know what you mean; your Momma read to me from that same book the last time I was in Detroit," I would have signified upon him in return.
14. Claudia Mitchell-Kernan, "Signifying," in Dundes (ed.), op. cit., p. 313; all further references to this work, abbreviated "Sig.," will be included parenthetically in the text. See also her "Signifying, Loud-talking, and Marking," in Kochman (ed.), op. cit., pp. 315–35.
15. See Mitchell-Kernan, "Signifying, Loud-talking, and Marking," pp. 315–35. For Zora Neale Hurston's definition of "signifying," see *Mules and Men: Negro Folktales and Voodoo Practices in the South* (1935; New York: Harper & Row, 1970), p. 161.
16. For a definitive study of revision and its relation to ideas of modernism, see Kimberly W. Bentson, *Afro-American Modernism.* Benston's reading of Hurston's revision of Frederick Douglass has heavily informed my own.
17. Ralph Ellison, "And Hickman Arrives," in *Black Writers of America: A Comprehensive Anthology,* ed. Richard Barksdale and Keneth Kinnamon (New York: Macmillan, 1972), p. 704.
18. Ellison, "On Bird, Bird-Watching, and Jazz," *Shadow and Act,* p. 231.
19. Ellison, "Blues People," *Shadow and Act,* pp. 249–50.
20. Ellison, "The World and the Jug," *Shadow and Act,* p. 117.
21. Ibid., p. 137; my emphasis.
22. Mixhail Baxtin (Mikhail Bakhtin), "Discourse Typology in Prose," in Ladislav Matejka and Krystyna Pomorska (eds), *Readings in Russian Poetics: Formalist and Structuralist Views* (Cambridge, Mass.: MIT Press, 1971), p. 187; see also pp. 176–96.
23. The use of interlocking triangles as a metaphor for the intertextual relationships of the tradition is not meant to suggest any form of concrete, inflexible reality. On the contrary, it is a systematic metaphor, as René Girard puts it, "systematically pursued":

    > The triangle is no *Gestalt.* The real structures are intersubjective. They cannot be localized anywhere; *the triangle has no reality whatever; it is a systematic metaphor, systematically pursued.* Because changes in size and shape do not destroy the identity of this figure . . . the diversity as well as the unity of the works can be simultaneously illustrated. The purpose and limitations of this structural geometry may become clearer through a reference to "structural models." The triangle is a model of a sort, or rather a whole family of models. But these models are not "mechanical" like those of Claude Lévi-Strauss. They always allude to the mystery, transparent yet opaque, of human relations. All types of structural thinking assume that human reality is intelligible; it is a *logos* and, as such, *it is an incipient logic, or it degrades itself into a logic.* It can thus be systematized, at least up to a point, however unsystematic, irrational, and chaotic it may appear even to those, or rather especially to those who operate the system. [René Girard, *Deceit, Desire, and the Novel: Self and Other in Literary Structure,* trans. Yvonne Freccero (Baltimore, Md: Johns Hopkins University Press, 1965), pp. 2–3; my emphasis]

24. For Ishmael Reed on a "talking book," see "Ishmael Reed: A Self Interview," *Black World,* 23 (June 1974), p. 25. For the slave narratives in which this figure appears, see James Albert

Ukawsaw Gronniosaw, *A Narrative of the Most Remarkable Particulars of the Life of James Albert Ukawsaw Gronniosaw, An African Prince* (Bath, 1770); John Marrant, *Narrative of the Lord's Wonderful Dealings with John Marrant, A Black* (London, 1785); Ottabah Cugoano, *Thoughts and Sentiments on the Evil and Wicked Traffic of the Slavery and Commerce of the Human Species* (London, 1787); Olaudah Equiano, *The Interesting Narrative of the Life of Olaudah Equiano, or Gustavus Vassa, the African, Written by Himself* (London, 1789); and John Jea, *The Life and Sufferings of John Jea, an African Preacher* (Swansea, 1806).

25. Northrop Frye, *Anatomy of Criticism: Four Essays* (Princeton, NJ: Princeton University Press, 1957), p. 233.
26. Baxtin (Bakhtin), op. cit., p. 190.
27. Frye, op. cit., p. 234.
28. Ellison, "The World and the Jug," *Shadow and Act,* p. 140.
29. See Ishmael Reed, *The Free-Lance Pallbearers* (Garden City, NY: Doubleday, 1967), *Yellow Back Radio Broke-Down* (Garden City, NY: Doubleday, 1969), *Mumbo Jumbo* (Garden City, NY: Doubleday, 1972), *The Last Days of Louisiana Red* (New York: Random House, 1974), *Flight to Canada* (New York: Random House, 1976) and *The Terrible Twos* (New York: St. Martin's/Marek, 1982).
30. See Neil Schmitz, "Neo-HooDoo: The Experimental Fiction of Ishmael Reed," *Twentieth Century Literature,* 20 (April 1974), pp. 126–8. Schmitz's splendid reading is, I believe, the first to discuss the salient aspect of Reed's rhetorical strategy. This paragraph is heavily indebted to Schmitz's essay.
31. Reed, *The Free-Lance Pallbearers,* p. 107.
32. Reed, *Yellow Back Radio Broke-Down,* pp. 34–6. For an excellent close reading of *Yellow Back Radio Broke-Down,* see Michel Fabre, "Postmodern Rhetoric in Ishmael Reed's *Yellow Back Radio Broke-Down,*" in Peter Bruck and Wolfgang Karrer (eds). *The Afro-American Novel since 1960* (Amsterdam: B. R. Gruner, 1982), pp. 167–88.
33. Reed, *Mumbo Jumbo,* p. 6; all further references to this work, abbreviated *MJ,* will be included parenthetically in the text.
34. Ellison, "And Hickman Arrives," p. 701.
35. See Charles T. Davis, *Black Is the Color of the Cosmos: Essays on Black Literature and Culture, 1942–1981,* ed. Henry Louis Gates, Jr (New York: Garland, 1982), pp. 167–233.
36. My reading of the imagery on Reed's cover was inspired by a conversation with Robert Farris Thompson.
37. On Reed's definition of "gombo" (gumbo), see his "The Neo-HooDoo Aesthetic," *Conjure: Selected Poems, 1963–1970* (Amherst, Mass.: University of Massachusetts Press, 1972), p. 26.
38. This clever observation is James A. Snead's, for whose Yale seminar on parody I wrote the first draft of this essay.
39. Reed, interview by Calvin Curtis, 29 January 1979.
40. Tzvetan Todorov, "The Two Principles of Narrative," trans. Philip E. Lewis, *Diacritics,* 1 (Fall 1979), p. 41. See his *The Poetics of Prose,* trans. Richard Howard (Ithaca, NY: Cornell University Press, 1977), pp. 42–52; all further references to this work, abbreviated *PP,* will be included parenthetically in the text.
41. For a wonderfully useful discussion of *fabula* ("fable") and *sjužet* ("subject"), see Victor Šklovskij, "The Mystery Novel: Dickens's *Little Dorrit,*" in Matejka and Pomorska (eds), op. cit., pp. 220–6. On use of typology, see p. 222.
42. See ibid., pp. 222, 226.
43. A *houngan* is a priest of *Vaudou*. On *Vaudou,* see Jean Price-Mars, *Ainsi parla l'Oncle* (Port-au-Prince: Imprimerie de Campiègne, 1928), and Alfred Métraux, *Le Vodou haitien* (Paris: Gallimard, 1958).
44. Geoffrey H. Hartman, *Criticism in the Wilderness: The Study of Literature Today* (New Haven, Conn.: Yale University Press, 1980), p. 272.
45. Ralph Ellison, *Invisible Man* (New York: Random House, 1952), p. 9; all further references to this work, abbreviated *IM,* will be included parenthetically in the text.
46. Melville's passage from *Moby-Dick* reads:

> It seemed the great Black Parliament sitting in Tophet. A hundred black faces turned round in their rows to peer; and beyond, a black Angel of Doom was beating a book in a pulpit. It was a negro church; and the preacher's text was about the blackness of darkness, and the weeping and wailing and teeth-gnashing there. Ha, Ishmael, muttered

I, backing out, Wretched entertainment at the sign of "The Trap." [*Moby-Dick* (1851; New York: W. W. Norton, 1967), p. 18]

This curious figure also appears in James Pike's *The Prostrate State: South Carolina under Negro Government* (New York: 1874), p. 62.

47. Plato, *Phaedrus,* 253d–254a. For the myth of Theuth, see 274c–275b.
48. See ibid., 259b–259e.
49. Ishmael Reed, "Dualism: in ralph ellison's invisible man," *Conjure,* p. 50.
50. W. E. B. Du Bois, *The Souls of Black Folk: Essays and Sketches* (1903; New York: Fawcett, 1961), pp. 16–17.

Michael Thelwell (1939–)

In an autobiographical essay, Michael Thelwell identifies the honor he values most in his career as "the warm friendship of my two heroes, James Baldwin and Chinua Achebe. I am humbled and deeply moved that . . . Baldwin [wrote the] introduction to my collection and that Chinua Achebe saw fit to dedicate [a] book of essays—a massive giant of a book—to me." Many other honors have been bestowed on Thelwell—for his teaching, his research, and his novel, The Harder They Come *(1980). Called a minor classic, Thelwell's fictional account of a Jamaican singer-turned-criminal who becomes a heroic figure to working-class Jamaicans has been praised as "the most authentic and evocative portrait of the Jamaican poor—the rich and sustaining vernaculars of their culture, the sheer heroism of their economic existence."*

Born in Ulster Spring, Jamaica, Thelwell came to the United States in the late 1950s. He earned his bachelor's from Howard University in 1964 and his master's from the University of Massachusetts at Amherst in 1969. Active in the civil rights movement in the mid-1960s, he worked as director of the Washington, D.C.–based offices of the Student Non-violent Coordinating Committee (SNCC) and with the Mississippi Freedom Democratic Party. Accepting a position at the University of Massachusetts at Amherst in 1969, Thelwell took on the task of constructing a department of Afro-American studies. During the ensuing six years, he guided the development of the department's curriculum and its acquisition of a distinguished faculty, including teaching appointments for Chinua Achebe, James Baldwin, Johnetta B. Cole, William Julius Wilson, and Julius Lester.

Thelwell has won a National Foundation for the Arts and Humanities Award, a Rockefeller Foundation Literary Award, and a Cornell University Society for the Humanities Fellowship. In addition to his novel, he has written filmscripts and contributed critical essays to numerous anthologies. A book of his essays, Duties, Pleasures, and Conflicts, *appeared in 1987.*

The following selection was originally presented as a speech by Thelwell to an international panel of African American writers at the 1990 National Festival of Black Arts in Atlanta. Commenting on "Toward a Collective Vision: Issues in International Literary Criticism," Thelwell says it "is a most seriously intended *discussion of certain contemporary academic critical methods, about which the author is highly skeptical; its closing section is high parody, a* 'wickedly funny' *application of those critical methods to one of its prominent black practitioners." (The "prominent" critic that Thelwell quotes here is Henry Louis Gates.) Despite its sarcastic tone, the selection thoughtfully examines the value of using Eurocentric language and critical models to assess African American literature.*

Toward a Collective Vision

Issues in International Literary Criticism

Good morning. We have a choice of titles, either

> "Cap'n Dey Done Stole de Canon, Best We Bring Up Our Howitzer!"

or, not necessarily more precisely, but in the fashion of the day:

> "The problematique of de-situating the re-marginalization of Afro-centric tropistic significations, intertextually, against the ambience of a phallo- and Euro-centric, post-Derridian canonical discourse, mediated by a post-Freudian, pre-coital detumescence and seminal exhaustion, other-ality, and the influential anxieties of race and gender."

[AUDIENCE: *laughter, somewhat tentative.*]

As you may well have guessed, considerable care and thought went into the composition of that title. [*Laughter*] I wanted to ensure that it "privileged" and "valorized" every one of the issues which so currently engage the concerns and energies of our influential critics. Even so, I'm terrified that there may be some that I forgot. Are there?

[AUDIENCE: *laughter. "Hegemonistic." "Post-structuralist, peripheralizations!"* A BOOMING VOICE: *"Foccou you, an yo' mamma too."*]

Well, thank you too. I was certain I must have missed some. One simply can't remember them all. For, as they say in this part of the world, "The one thang you ain't never goin' to see is no one-legged man win no ass-kicking contest." Well, I do feel a little like that one-legged man today. But, with your help, I shall try.

The remarks of the preceding speakers [at this National Festival of Black Arts are] examples of literary criticism in the traditional sense. That is, they discussed—as I thought, with admirable insight and seriousness—aspects of contemporary black literature. Which is what criticism is, or ought be: reasoned, informed, serious analysis or explication, either of individual works and authors, or of more general tendencies and developments within our literary tradition. And, this always, *always* in service to enhanced understanding, appreciation, and clarity of shared and communicated meaning. At its best, such criticism can be of inestimable value—a tripartite communion between our critics, our writers and our readers while we, as a people, sharpen our shared perceptions of our historical circumstance with its effect on our literary and cultural necessities. The subject of criticism is literature and through literature, reality itself. As Richard Wright once observed after receiving a letter of thinly disguised instruction from his fellow Mississippian William Faulkner, "Literature is a struggle over the nature of reality."

However, I had understood this panel's charge somewhat differently, and so will not be exercising that usual critical function today. That is, my subject will not be our literature, but our criticism: what today the critical enterprise has become, or seems in grave and eminent danger of becoming.

Permit me to begin with the obvious: the fundamental relationship between "us" and "them." The dynamic of the engagement between the African world—

whether at home or in diaspora—and Europe—has been, and continues to be, in every important area of human concern and activity, a contentious one. This conflict was not of our making nor of our choice. But for all of modern history it has been a constant, defining element of our experience, whether at home or in diaspora.

Historically, the expression of this antagonism has changed. But whether it can be said to have *evolved* is quite another question. At times it has been blatant and brutal; at others, as at present, it is more subtle or, if you will, insidious. It is at its most overt in its economic, political and military manifestations. But it is no less present and effective in those allegedly less stridently confrontational matters of culture. For culture is precisely the arena in which human beings define and express—to themselves and others—the values and meanings of their presence in the world.

In the last decade of this perverse century, the lines of European cultural imposition appear to have moderated, to be less crudely drawn than previously. But to imagine that they have ceased to exist is a dangerous delusion. This is no less true in literary and cultural discourses than it is for economic arrangements; for the politics of culture no less than for the more obviously predatory politics of the marketplace. Which is why in our time, we of the Black World, seeking to control the articulation of our presence and experience in the world, of the meaning of our history and culture, and the forms and integrity of their expression, urgently need a focused and disciplined criticism which is both purposeful and consequential to these ends.

This is so because Europe and her progeny imagine the province of literature to be their special property by virtue—they assert—of invention, of inheritance and by birthright. It is, as they suggest in numerous ways, terrain on which we only trespass, or may, by special invitation, visit briefly; rude interlopers tolerated by permission and binding and inflexible instruction, only so long as we scrupulously continue to observe native law, institution, and practice.

You are a literate audience, so there is no need to recapitulate the inhospitable treatment our ancestors have endured; nor the debasement that our cultural patrimony has received under those laws and traditional practices. It is this historical inhospitality that accounts for the on-going tension in the dialogue—more accurately confrontation—between Africa and Europe in the world of modern culture. Which is also why, in the dust, smoke, and confusion of this heated engagement, the informing and clarifying role of the critic takes on an enhanced importance.

The situation could indeed be quite accurately formulated in terms of an Old Testament metaphor evoking images of Joshua and the Promised Land. In this case, the Hebrew Children are us, and literature (in their formulation) is the promised land.

Our advanced parties have broached the terrain, and firmly established outposts and beachheads. But what exactly is the character and purpose of this presence? Do we seek permission? Embrace whatever terms the "native owners" care to impose, pay their rents and tributes, and beg assimilation and acceptance under whatever terms may occur to them? Are we refugees, hoping to be tenants, or are we invaders, an army of potential liberation?

Do we boldly claim territories on which to raise edifices of our own design, suited to our purposes, and in service only to the visions and interests of our own logic and necessity? Independent yes, but where convenient and appropriate, to annex the ruinate forms of an exhausted culture and invigorate and fortify them with a new spirit and vitality: the proverbial new wine in old skins? How, indeed—as the mystic Revelations of Ras Tafari ask—do we sing our Fathers' songs in a strange land?

Like the spies sent by Joshua into the Promised Land, our critics, God bless 'em, should have by now mapped and surveyed the literary terrain. They should by now be ready with accurate readings, clear strategic reports, informed advice, and cautionary intelligences as to where advantage lies or dangers lurk.

OK, let me concede that the image may be somewhat overwrought and "fevered." But even so, the point is clear: that black critics should in these times be about the creation, from our own literary experience, of a critical vocabulary appropriate to, and illuminating of, this historically critical stage of our cultural and literary development. A language organic to our cultural experience and which advances our understanding of the price and goals of struggle, the implications of defeat, and the rewards of success.

At the very least, our critics should represent one element within an ongoing conversation between our writers, our readers and our critics in the black world. A discourse whose primary purpose is to clarify and advance generally shared perceptions of our literary circumstance and cultural necessities during this stage of our history. I shall, with your permission, return later to further belabor this question.

But for now I would like to read from some remarks I made earlier this year at the University of Nigeria in Nsukka. The occasion was an international symposium poetically called, "Eagle on Iroko," in recognition of the work and contribution of Chinua Achebe, one of the black world's greatest writers. Then, it seemed both natural and instructive for me to begin by considering Achebe's extraordinary contribution in conjunction with that of James Baldwin. I think that the relevance of those remarks to this discussion of international issues and collective visions will be clear:

> For me, if any hint of possibie sadness could conceivably attend this occasion, it is the absence of the luminous presence of James Arthur Baldwin. What a fellowship and a joy Jimmy would have taken in this gathering, in this place, and for this purpose. Even perhaps, and much more appropriately, standing here, in my place this morning. For Jimmy and Chinua were truly brothers of the spirit. It is not usual to meet two writers of such towering stature who were so pure and so eloquent in the mutuality of their affection, admiration and respect, each for the other.
>
> But this warm and powerful affinity was not accidental. The mutual respect and affection between the two men who from the twin poles of our diaspora—Africa and America—simultaneously emerged in our generation to define new terms of our existence in literature and therefore in our own, and the world's, imagination, was natural and inevitable. For Achebe and Baldwin were twins in much more than an obvious literary virtuosity, or in their prodigious endowment of mind and craft. Beneath surface differences of style in their work, there lay between them a fundamental bedrock of shared vision and intention.
>
> Out of the idiom of our experience, the vocabulary and values of our cultures, the styles of our sensibilities, these two brothers fashioned prose instruments of an uncommon precision and compelling poetry. Deployed always in service to en-

lightenment and struggle, both commanded, however grudgingly, the respectful attention of an indifferent world. The similarities are in one sense remarkable, in another deeper sense, not so remarkable at all, being entirely organic to our cultural circumstances, and therefore quite logical.

Baldwin, whose uncompromisingly clear vision and magnificent prose was firmly anchored in the rich cultural traditions and bitter historical experience of Black America, never subsumed those gifts—and the responsibility that attended them—into any morally smug and complacent consensus of the white American literary establishment. A commitment to principle for which a terrible price was, of course, exacted. But, in the textures, the resonances, the righteous witness of Baldwin's prose, all the elements of the African-American cultural heritage found the most perfect literary expression that we have yet seen. This was a prose voice informed by, and fashioned out of, the blues' rough-edged poetry, the gospel's soaring rhythms, the prophetic fires of the Old Testament, the mournful affirmation of the sorrow songs, the preacher's shout, the field hand's holler, the blues man's growl, and the disciplined freedom of the jazz improvisation. On the smithy of his art, all these elements were forged and transmuted into an imperishable prose instrument of black—which is to say universal—struggle and moral affirmation.

And in that mission, and accomplishment, Baldwin gladly recognized in Achebe—he said so to me often and movingly—his truest kindred of the spirit.

I know that Jimmy derived immense and continuing satisfaction—a writer's satisfaction—from Chinua's work, in the clean lines and effortless elegance of his prose, as from Chinua's unfailing clarity of cultural purpose. I shall always remember one winter evening in Pelham finding him by a fire reading the Achebe essay, "Named for Victoria."

"Isn't the language a pleasure?" I asked. Jimmy raised his extraordinary eyes over the top of the book, peered at me over the rims of his reading glasses with his brow furrowed. Always the preacher.

"A pleasure?" he repeated. "Michael, this language is not a mere pleasure, it is a benefaction." As I said, a recognition—two masked, ancestral spirits finding and greeting one another.

For across the sea, a similar magic was being performed. Out of the vast resources of African linguistic tradition and values, the poetic styles and idiom of proverbial expression, riddle, parable and song, sacred and secular myth and ritual, Chinua Achebe, appropriating to his purposes the medium of the English language, was forging a prose universal in its reach while remaining uniquely African in image, reference, and tonality. It is a language appropriate to the experience and organic to the sensibilities of the culture it presents. A prose of the most extraordinary lyrical lucidity, gracefully masking in its deceptive simplicity, undercurrents of the utmost profundity and originality of craft and purpose. Entirely natural and consonant with its subject, its universality lies in the integrity of its particularity.

Having been graced by the instruction of these examples, our generation can have no excuse.

Now, there can be no possible justification for those of our kinfolk who can seem to find no language of our own, with terms of our fashioning which are sufficient to our cultural concerns. Those kinsmen and women who appear not to see any fundamental—indeed demeaning—contradiction; no self-condemning admission to a poverty of language and imagination, in having to recourse for the explication of our own literary and cultural realities to graceless and obscuring vocabularies of alien, mostly Gallic, ancestry and questionable applicability.

Why indeed? And for what possible reason, should writers and thinkers of the Black World, now well and, one hopes, truly embarked on a vibrant literary renaissance and a necessary cultural regeneration, gratuitously encumber this effort with this alien language? Particularly a language of such unsurpassed ugliness and evasiveness? A language bespeaking, under [the] color of "theory," the spiritual exhaustion and intellectual anxieties of another literary culture which is both in profound crisis and childishly arrogant—bumptiously projecting its disabilities and insecurities to the center of universal cultural concern, and against which they assume, we should all be measured?

Because, let us be quite clear, it is a language which at the very least betrays a cynical nihilism—a profound confusion of direction and purpose, a crisis of confidence disfiguring what in the West they call "the humanities." What Baldwin and Achebe have demonstrated by their rooted purity of language and concern is that we need not wander through these particular gates to deform our birthright with this newest dispensation of the white man's burden.

For, my brothers and sisters, it is indeed a burden. To sheepishly and unthinkingly encumber our work with these fetters of middle-class European disaffection is a cultural and historical stupidity that beggars belief and strains tolerance. . . . This language seems to admit of only two categories of statement; stripped of the obscuring preciosity, they emerge as either quite obvious or plain foolish.

Forget the foolish—"texts talking to texts"—or the denial of the very possibility of meaning in literature, which, of course, our critics, rather than challenge, tend to accept and advance as [if] . . . liberating discoveries. And, to our great sorrow and the impoverishment of our literature, so do some . . . misguided [black] writers. Not so, however, for Achebe. As I said about his work in Nsukka:

> Coming at a period of extended crisis for the western modernist novel, Achebe's work affirms the viability of the form as an instrument of serious moral and cultural discourse. In the modernist mode the emphasis is on fragmentation rather than coherence. Elements of experience never coalesce into meaning. The part frequently is greater than and unrelated to the whole. It is a style of pastiche and collage, of shattered mirrors and refracted images, of willful and capricious distortion. Ultimately, it is a mockery of purposeful intelligence, a denial of causality [and] therefore, of moral or political consequence, and an assault on the concept and possibility of meaning itself.
>
> One variant of this dispensation is a genre highly praised and encouraged in Third World writers, the name of which is itself a logical contradiction—"Magical Realism." Significantly enough, this tendency does not seem to apply to the representation of the texture of experience in western societies. It would appear to be appropriate only to those "areas of darkness," those "crippled cultures" which we are seen to inhabit.
>
> This is so, presumably because in the moral darkness and intellectual chaos represented by our cultures, the very nature of reality, or reason itself, is at risk. Ours is the domain of the distorted, the phantasmagoric, the irrational, the

superstitious, the fantastic and, of course, the primitive. This suspension—indeed, denial—of cause, effect and consequence, of the very concept of meaning and reality, is a denial of the possibility of intelligent action and moral responsibility.

In the midst of this hysterical nihilism, Achebe's masterly controlled fictions stand as an enduring rebuke and an affirmation of purposeful intelligence. They are novels of illumining coherence, of serious historical explanation and purpose, of moral and political consequence, rooted in recognizable national experience, informed by the styles and resources of indigenous popular and literary culture. In them our experience has meaning restored. And in its own terms!

Then, too, among these other critics, there is the belaboring of the obvious, the tedious . . . elaborate, obscure restatements of what black folks have always understood: that the white man's canon represents a narrow monopoly of definition, values, meaning and interpretation in which we either are absent or have had our presence and meaning in the world debased. Charles Chesnutt's remarkable career was a struggle to subvert that. Sterling Brown described it in clear language nearly 50 years ago. In 1940, Richard Wright summarized the argument declaring, "Literature is a struggle over the nature of reality." Did we therefore need Derrida or Foucault to retell us this in terms of such Gallic preciosity and capricious obscurantism?

Let me demonstrate two of the most obvious ways in which a slavish recapitulation of European intellectual trendiness and literary fashion is harmful to the health of our literature.

Few of us here today are too young to remember a unitary, vibrant tradition of Black (or Negro, as it was once called) literature in this country. As I recall, a rich tradition—folk and formal—varied, many-toned and textured, but inclusive. So that in it Black folk—men and women—could explore our people's condition—social, psychic, and moral—from a set of intellectual perspectives, cultural sensibilities, and political understandings that were generally shared . . . in . . . what might broadly . . . be called "the Black experience."

Damn, but weren't we naive? We certainly were, if we now accept the assertions of certain of our scholar-hucksters; those expedient brothers and sisters so quick to accommodate their work (or maybe only their careers) to every capricious wind of intellectual fashion blowing out of Europe. According to them, we must now subdivide our literature into its male and female manifestations; two distinct, mutually exclusive, if not implicitly antagonistic versions of experience. And in service to what end? Is this even necessary, much less progress?

I think our critics and theoreticians need to explain to us exactly why the literary fall-out from a strident and rancorous family squabble over social status and control between white American women and their men should even affect us. And worse, why it should necessarily result in the balkanization by gender of our literature. *Baa, Baa Black Sheep. Or, as the Jack-legs Preacher said, "If the Lord had not wanted them shorn, he would not have made them sheep."*

Then, too, there is the evident seductions of what some academics are pleased to call "literary theory," a thoroughly aberrant development which has very little to do with literature as, over the centuries, humanity has known it.

By now, it is hardly possible to have missed one of the most tedious and distressing tendencies in Euro-modernist literature: that in which the literary undertaking is its own subject. In it, literature becomes the subject of literature. Novels are no longer concerned with human experience in all its complex moral, political, psychological, and erotic dimensions, but with the process of literature itself. *"This important new novel explores the nature of fiction and the workings of the imagination."* "Gimme a break," as my students say. That this turning inward, this precious self-consciousness with its cannibalizing of earlier works, reflects the kind of creative exhaustion sometimes called "decadence" in a literary tradition is quite clear.

But, not to be outdone in point of fashion, critical theoreticians follow suit with long, indecipherable, rarefied "theoretical discourses and significations" which [have] no meaningful reference to any work of literature, but only to earlier, equally disconnected, self-referential theoretical texts. *"Explicating,"* as our brother Chinweizu so aptly put it, *"the already quite sufficiently obscure by means of the even more obscure."* So just as the literature is no longer primarily about experience, but about "art," the criticism is not about literature but about itself—theory talking to theory, intertextually, of course.

Since this activity can have no applicability to literary cultures seeking to formulate usable approaches to history and struggle—to culture and political reality—what possible meaning can it have for black writers and for our literature? Why should black thinkers labor so foolishly to embroider their discussions of *our* cultural inheritance with this alienating, borrowed language? Do our cultural and literary traditions only become consequential when expressed in and reduced to terms of European reference? That this tendency is . . . detrimental . . . to the necessary and honorable intellectual struggle which is this generation's historical duty, will be clear from the following story. No more abstractions; let us in the time remaining [here] consider a concrete experience.

When Alex Haley published *Roots* in this country it evoked much commentary among our white countrymen, not all of which was well informed or even intelligent. No less a cultural luminary than James A. Michener was moved to dismiss the book as fanciful and inaccurate, . . . pathetic, ahistorical consequence of the need on the part of Black Americans to invent for themselves a "glorious past."

What disturbed Michener, it turns out, was Kunta Kinte's religion. Haley, against all historical evidence, he huffed, "made" Kinte a Muslim, out of a transparent need to invest his ancestor with a cultural dignity that the slaves could not possibly have had. There was no evidence, Michener asserted, that any followers of Islam were, or could possibly have been, among the Africans brought to these shores. "Oh Lawd," as my Jack-leg friend would say in similar circumstances, "Everah time ah leaves mah Bible at home, ah meets a soul that ah could save."

A curious combination of ignorance *and* arrogance asserted with such magisterial finality. Clearly, [Michener] had not a clue about the historical presence of Islam in West Africa or the presence on the slave ships of thousands of Hausa, Mandingo, Fulani and other of the Islamic peoples of the western Sudan, at least twenty percent of the total cargo.

More significant even than the ignorance was the crude cultural chauvinism which attended it, the curious notion that *any* African Muslim, by virtue of conversion to a religion of which Michener had previously heard, was culturally more advanced than, say, a queen mother from the Dahomey Royal Court, an Ifa priest from Oyo or Benin, or an Ashanti general from the capital city of Kumasi, all of which *we know to* have met the misfortune of deportation to enslavement in the Americas.

Michener's assertions and the prominence accorded them in the media so amazed and incensed my colleague Professor Allen Austin that he immediately began a definitive work of refutation. The result of which was the excellent book, *African Muslims in Ante-Bellum America,* published in 1983. It is a nice irony that *this* splendid scholarly restoration of historical truth to the "official" record almost certainly would not have happened had it not been for Michener's provocations.

In the book, Professor Austin does a number of things very well. He outlines the presence and scope of the Islamic faith in the western Sudan, and relates this cultural and geographic area to the slave trade. Allen goes even further; he recounts the stories of a *number of Muslims in the American slave community, and includes translations of thirteen biographical narratives written in Arabic by slaves or former slaves*. This is not only a concrete refutation of Michener. . . . It [also] presents in commendable detail and clarity, early African perspectives on American society—which unlike the more generally known Christian "slave narratives," are the product of cultures and references utterly independent of European languages, traditions, or sensibilities.

Austin's book appeared in 1983. Published in a small edition by a specialized, scholarly house, it, as one might expect, was accorded nothing like the media prominence given Michener's original remarks. In fact, there was hardly any critical notice taken of its publication. Yet it is a very important work in our ongoing mission of reclaiming our past from the meat grinder of white historical interpretation and one that merits wide popular attention in our community. Particularly because it is not only scrupulously careful in its scholarship, but is [also] written with a commendable clarity and purposefulness. But it languished in relative obscurity until 1988.

Surely, if ever there were one, this would be a job for Super-critic: the bringing of important but neglected works to the people to whom the work is addressed and about whose history it has significant information to contribute. And sure enough, into the vacuum steps a journal called, encouragingly, *Black American Literature Forum,* in a special volume guest edited by one Professor Henry Louis Gates, Jr. There is, after all, justice in the world—the mills of God *may* grind slowly but they grind exceeding fine. This neglected, but important book, will at last receive extended and detailed discussion to a length of some four thousand words.

But the regrettable truth is that, as a result of my brief description, you now have a much clearer idea of the book, its contents, and significance than the readers of those four thousand words.

[AUDIENCE: *No. Lie. Impossible.*]

You think not? Let me quote a more or less representative passage from the review, being charitable enough not to identify the writer.

[AUDIENCE: *Name him. Name him.*]

Paraphrasing Foucault . . .

[A BOOMING VOICE: *You an' you mamma!*]

Paraphrasing Foucault then, I ask "What is modernity?" And, pursuant with the paraphrasing, hence being bound by, but not to, the verbatim, I might respond like Foucault with an echo: Modernity is the attempting to answer the question raised (imprudently) in 1784 by the paper *Berlinische Monatschrift: Was ist Aufklarung?* ("What is Enlightenment?"). This inflation of Foucault's well-known inquiry about modern philosophy in order to consider Kant's response to the question of Enlightenment is aimed towards the foreclosure of any diachronically integral story.

[AUDIENCE: *Naturally!*]

The modernity against which (in both the dependent as well as antagonistic sense of the word) the slave narratives are situated does not derive from a neat teleological telling driven by a merely material event or circumstance, nor a neatly isolatable idea.

[AUDIENCE: *True, true, preach.*]

The event, if there is one, is thematic. [*Whuh!*] That is to say, that which is evidenced is a belief in a certain self-apprehension fueled by historically lived experiences which articulate in myriad ways, one of which was Kant's response to *Berlinische:* "Enlightenment is man's emergence from his self-incurred immaturity" (its motto being *Sapere aude,* "Dare to be wise"!).

[AUDIENCE: *Well, Hoodoo, to you too.*]

While this possibility of risk neither begins nor ends with Kant, it is coextensive with the emergence of the promise of a comprehensive apprehension resulting from the splitting off of cognition from lived experience, with the isolation of the cognating subject of a man (as isolated substance, differentiated attribute, autonomous calculus, and so on and so on).

[AUDIENCE: *Of course! Nice! Get it.*]

The promise is that the distance will be bridged, and the cogito will comprehend the world of things. This is not an immediate achievement; at work here is a tale, a narrative with a tremendous expansive energy. And as Spinoza realized in his dictum, *"Ordo et connexio idearum idem est, ac ordo et connexio rerum"* [mistranslated as "The order and connection of ideas are the same as the order and connection of the thing"], it is the expansivity of narrative that is a hallmark of the modern.

[AUDIENCE: *"Expansivity of narrative, Ahmen! Praise his holy name." Loud laughter.*]

Please! Please! I know it is impossible not to laugh, but it is also and regrettably much more than simply funny. As I read I kept thinking that I was hearing a voice. Perhaps it is because we are here in Spelman's hallowed halls, but did anyone else hear an earnest, sad echoing voice insistent with lamentation? It said quite clearly, *"A mind is a terrible thing to waste."*

Two minds, actually. First is the perpetrator's who committed this prose, who may in fact also be a victim. . . . There is obviously, beneath this torrent of European reference and obligatory erudition, a very resourceful mind yearning to breathe free. For there are ideas here, even important ideas, but cruelly imprisoned within this flatulence of language. As the only fully innocent victim—Professor Allen—remarked on the review with an admirable forbearance, "Most regrettable is that another intelligent and industrious young scholar has been misdirected into this abstract, pseudo-philosophical . . . jargon-encrusted netherworld."

You know, our Ashanti ancestors observed that "a log may lie in a river for ten years, but it will never become a crocodile." That proverbial wisdom is true, even self-evident. But our ancestors had no way to anticipate what could happen to intelligent young black minds subjected to five years of American graduate education in the "humanities" in the closing decades of this century. Given a choice, the poor sacrifices would do better as crocodiles or even logs. Can we, without lethal prejudice to the possibilities of our culture, continue to inflict this fate on our brightest young minds?

But there is one greater culprit, the editor who accepted and published this prose apparently without thought or remorse. What can we make of this figure, the protean and prolific Henry Louis Gates, Jr., the noted peripatetic?

[A BOOMING VOICE: *Not only peripatetic . . . he don't seem to have no fixed address neither.*]

What, indeed, are we to make of this mysterious yet so everlastingly present figure, who not unlike the enigmatic Eshu of Yoruba religious cosmology, demands some little explication. But the appropriate terms [with] which to do this [are] elusive, a puzzlement.

Has anyone here actually seen this Brother? Let's see hands. Not a glimpse now, a positive identification, something confirmed. I see. Thank you. Can't say I really am surprised. But . . . you have read him. No? Shame on y'awl. That must undoubtedly be because like most of your race, you are "resistant to theory."

But that does suggest an approach. It should perhaps be theoretical, if only because having been cavalierly dismissive of it thus far, one should in fairness allow the method to demonstrate its usefulness. But we can't merely employ "pure" theory. Since we are a "signifying people," that being, according to Professor Gates, the highest form of our cultural expression, we will add a measure of black signifying to white theoretics. What follows now could be called "A Theoretical Deconstruction (in a Signifying Mode) of the Henry Louis Gates Problematique."

The first theoretical framework that we shall deploy is the newest to enjoy a sudden currency within the academy. It is variously called entrepeneutics or supply-side mercantilosophy. To scholars of this persuasion, all writers—scholarly or profane—being producers, must be located in an economic context, a commercial environment controlled by market forces. Their discourses fairly ring with an arsenal of inventive critical terms including but not limited to: literary currency (and its devaluation), intellectual capital, venture criticism, literary name recognition, critical interest rates, canonical monopoly, rhetorical inflation, teleological take over and, of course, *profitability*.

Subjected to this approach our subject emerges as a successful profit-making enterprise. A flexible, multi-institutional individual (in the corporate sense) with off-shore registration located for tax purposes in Panama. It is no respecter of institutional boundaries, relocating operations frequently, the better to avail itself of favorable business opportunities, and through the manipulation of an ingenious tax shelter structure [it] is fully, even overcapitalized. Though not entirely successful in its struggle over market share with the Baker Corporation of Houston, it has rebounded in recent years with a strong Nigerian portfolio and a shrewd marketing strategy geared to consumer gullibility in the academic sector. Modest growth is projected, but some analysts project a severe decline in intellectual interest rates forcing a devaluation of the firm's literary currency and intellectual capital reserves. This is compounded by rumors of an SCC [Sophistry Control Commission] investigation of HLG's intellectual short selling (particularly of Black culture stocks) and the utterance of critical junk-bond issues.

A high-level commission spokesman said that they are investigating the most imaginative junk issued by HLG to date. HLG tried to sell, under oath, the garbage issuing from 2 Live Crew as blue-chip black cultural stock "in the tradition of Ralph Ellison." The commissioner said, "Bet on it, you can expect indictments. This is a real scandal. In a more just world or a more rational intellectual climate, someone would do time for this. Hard time too, no community service crap either." Let the church say, "Ahmen."

But without a smoking gun it appears that the company motto may not be entirely fanciful: "When H. L. Gates Speaks, Pedants Listen."

That was fun. At last I understand, cried he, the consolidations of theoretics. It is so liberating: imagination and inventiveness hold sway, and evidence means, to paraphrase Humpty Dumpty, exactly what one wants it to mean. Shall we indulge ourselves some more?

According to the information-age theoreticians of artificial intelligence, Professor Gates is considerably less (or perhaps more) than would appear. These baby-boomers who cut their methodological eyeteeth on videogames maintain that Gates is really a computer program, a fiendish simulation constructed secretly by night in a hidden room in the basement of Bloom Hall at Yale by two purple-haired semioticians and a crazed German deconstructionist. If one reads the English Department faculty list, they say, you will find three professors whose middle names are, respectively, Gates, Louis and Henry. Names which, in a surfeit of creative hubris, they could not resist bestowing upon their creation. The "Jr." was added for verisimilitude, an Afro-American cultural dimension. For as they reasoned, "Those people are fascinated by patrilineal dynasties."

Since its introduction into the computer memory of a black literary journal some 15 years ago, the HLG virus has reproduced itself prodigiously in numerous other journals. It has, as programmed to do, amended texts, debased language, edited special issues of numbing obscurity, issued discrete texts and otherwise made its presence felt, even going so far as to "discover," to great self-generated fanfare, texts which were never lost.

At a celebratory dinner last fall, the three collaborators are reported to have exulted, "In thirty hours on the computer we have accomplished what twenty years in the classroom . . . could not. We have created the perfect black theoretician, as it were, 'Our Nig.' " And they chortled in their glee. Towards morning, the semiotician, now quite drunk, is said to have bellowed, "So Junebug Jones, tell us how that Yale University has ruint more good niggers than whisky? Why don't you? Eat your uppity heart out, you ingrate."

Persuasive. A lovely theory, illumining so much that is otherwise murky. If he hadn't existed, Yale would have had to invent him. But now, many of you claim to have actually seen him. Alas, we must then retreat back to the drawing board. That is the great weakness of "theory," brute reality does tend to intrude. . . .

Our last excursion into the rarefied elevations of theory is my favorite. It owes allegiance to no movement, sect, cult or dispensation. It is entirely original to my friend the great Afro-American autodidact Benjamin. He describes his methodology as Afro-centric inductive eclecticism and calls this particular expression the "Doppel-ganger Syndrome of literary signification."

As you might be aware, your vice-president, Mr. J. Danforth Quayle, at a recent meeting of the United Negro College Fund, uttered the following enlightening variation on a familiar theme: "What a waste it is to lose one's mind," lamented Mr. Quayle, speaking, one assumes, from experience, "or not to have a mind at all as being very wasteful." Which suggested to Benjamin that J. Danforth Quayle is arguably a closet deconstructionist of language and thought. As is the mysterious Professor Gates. They hold in common, so Benjamin observes, a shared felicity of expression and plangency of thought. Their political positions are impossible to determine from their utterances; they unpredictably appear in unlikely settings, yet have never been reported together in the same place.

Benjamin, enabled by a handsome NEH grant, has spent two years in a close and (so he says) rewarding computer-aided, word-by-word analysis of the public utterances of the two. He has generated elaborate graphs tracking and dating the public appearances of both men. The results, which I have not seen, he claims to be conclusive. He maintains that the odds against the American population's producing *at the same time* two separate and distinct minds of such close conceptual and linguistic affinity is mathematically prohibitive, and can be ignored only at our grave peril. The only tenable, indeed, inescapable, conclusion, says Benjamin, one which must be faced in all its awful implications, is that J. Danforth Quayle and Henry Louis Gates, Jr., are one and the same being—a conceptual breakthrough which explains much which otherwise, as our young critic wrote, "defies neat teleological telling."

So much for theory. If I may resort for a minute to seriousness. Without, I hope, undue sanctimony, I have to say that there is an aspect of all this which borders on the moral. In what sense moral? Certainly not in the manner that Jerry Fallwell and his associates are accustomed to abusing that term.

But moral in a different sense. It is our misfortune to live in an age in which the systematic debasement of language and thought is endemic. We understand that bureaucracies of all kinds—Madison Avenue, the information media, the military, lawyers, politicians, sociologists, philosophers, street-corner rappers and other representatives of the learned professions—routinely inflict great violence on the language, usually—if not always—to obscure shameful deeds or intentions.

But for writers and students of literature, whose special responsibility must be the conservation of whatever purity and clarity of language survives, to abandon themselves so promiscuously to this orgy of rhetorical vandalism is surely a species of sacrilege, a cynical corruption of vocation not unlike that of renegade priests leading mobs in desecration of the sacred hosts and icons entrusted to their care. Whatever the case may be among the "others," this is an intellectual debauchery which the black world can ill afford. And not merely because its consequences are, ultimately and inevitably, political.

Larry Neal (1937–81)

One of the best-known cultural theorists of the late 1960s, Larry Neal was born in Atlanta, Georgia, and raised in Philadelphia. He earned his bachelor's from Lincoln University in Pennsylvania in 1961 and his master's from the University of Pennsylvania in 1963. He taught at the City College of New York, Yale University, and Wesleyan University.

Recognized for his work as a poet, playwright, filmmaker, folklorist, and essayist, Neal made his greatest impact on African American culture as a leader of the Black Arts Movement, which sought to blend politics and black art into an indivisible entity. One-time education director of the Black Panther Party, Neal espoused black aesthetic perspectives on the purpose of black creative expression—namely, that African American literature should function as a political weapon created by and for blacks. Along with Amiri Baraka and others, Neal helped to establish the Black Arts Repertory Theater in Harlem in 1964. He also served as a contributing writer and arts editor for Liberator, *a magazine known for its focus on the radical political and cultural issues of the time.*

Showcasing the literature of the Black Arts Movement, Black Fire: An Anthology of Afro-American Writing *(1968) was coedited by Neal and Baraka. In another collaboration, Neal, Baraka, and A. B. Spellman coauthored* Trippin: A Need for Change *(1969). In addition to numerous critical essays asserting his views on African American literature and art as political weapons, Neal wrote poetry and drama.*

His first volume of poetry, Black Boogaloo *(1969), explores his "fascination with discovering the historical moment when Africans lost their connection with their gods and ancestors, thereby losing themselves." It was followed by* Hoodoo Hollerin Bebop Ghosts *(1971), a collection of poems about black folk culture and cultural politics. Neal's two plays were produced in New York:* The Glorious Monster in the Bell of the Horn *(1976) is "a poetic interpretation of the hopes and aspirations of black artists and the middle class on the eve of the dropping of the A-Bomb on Hiroshima," while* In an Upstate Motel *(1981) is an existential work exploring the "circular and therefore hopeless quality" of life. In the late 1960s, Neal also worked on the small screen, as both a host for black talk shows and a scriptwriter.* Visions of a Liberated Future, *a collection of Neal's poetry and prose, was published posthumously in 1989.*

In "The Black Arts Movement," originally published in The Drama Review *in 1968, Neal presents his blueprint for a Black Aesthetic and the Black Arts Movement, as he critiques the value of specific literary pieces by African American authors.*

The Black Arts Movement

1

The Black Arts Movement is radically opposed to any concept of the artist that alienates him from his community. Black Art is the aesthetic and spiritual sister of the Black Power concept. As such, it envisions an art that speaks directly to the needs and aspirations of Black America. In order to perform this task, the Black Arts Movement proposes a radical reordering of the western cultural aesthetic. It proposes a separate symbolism, mythology, critique, and iconology. The Black Arts and the Black Power concept both relate broadly to the Afro-American's desire for self-determination and nationhood. Both concepts are nationalistic. One is concerned with the relationship between art and politics; the other with the art of politics.

Recently, these two movements have begun to merge: the political values inherent in the Black Power concept are now finding concrete expression in the aesthetics of Afro-American dramatists, poets, choreographers, musicians, and novelists. A main tenet of Black Power is the necessity for Black people to define the world in their own terms. The Black artist has made the same point in the context of aesthetics. The two movements postulate that there are in fact and in spirit two Americas—one black, one white. The Black artist takes this to mean that his primary duty is to speak to the spiritual and cultural needs of Black people. Therefore, the main thrust of this new breed of contemporary writers is to confront the contradictions arising out of the Black man's experience in the racist West. Currently, these writers are re-evaluating western aesthetics, the traditional role of the writer, and the social function of art. Implicit in this re-evaluation is the need to develop a "black aesthetic." It is the opinion of many Black writers, I among them, that the Western aesthetic has run its course: it is impossible to construct anything meaningful within its decaying structure. We advocate a cultural revolution in art and ideas. The cultural values inherent in western history must either be radicalized or destroyed, and we will probably find that even radicalization is impossible. In fact, what is needed is a whole new system of ideas. Poet Don L. Lee expresses it:

> . . . We must destroy Faulkner, dick, jane, and other perpetrators of evil. It's time for Du Bois, Nat Turner, and Kwame Nkrumah. As Frantz Fanon points out: destroy the culture and you destroy the people. This must not happen. Black artists are culture stabilizers; bringing back old values, and introducing new ones. Black Art will talk to the people and with the will of the people stop impending "protective custody."

The Black Arts Movement eschews "protest" literature. It speaks directly to Black people. Implicit in the concept of "protest" literature, as Brother Knight has made clear, is an appeal to white morality:

> Now any Black man who masters the technique of his particular art form, who adheres to the white aesthetic, and who directs his work toward a white audience is, in one sense, protesting. And implicit in the act of protest is the belief that a change will be forthcoming once the masters are aware of the protestor's "grievance" (the very word connotes begging, supplications to the gods). Only when that belief has faded and protestings end, will Black art begin.

Brother Knight also has some interesting statements about the development of a "Black aesthetic":

> Unless the Black artist establishes a "Black aesthetic" he will have no future at all. To accept the white aesthetic is to accept and validate a society that will not allow him to live. The Black artist must create new forms and new values, sing new songs (or purify old ones); and along with other Black authorities, he must create a new history, new symbols, myths and legends (and purify old ones by fire). And the Black artist, in creating his own aesthetic, must be accountable for it only to the Black people. Further, he must hasten his own dissolution as an individual (in the Western sense)—painful though the process may be, having been breast-fed the poison of "individual experience."

When we speak of a "Black aesthetic" several things are meant. First, we assume that there is already in existence the basis for such an aesthetic. Essentially, it consists of an African-American cultural tradition. But this aesthetic is finally, by implication, broader than that tradition. It encompasses most of the useable elements of Third World culture. The motive behind the Black aesthetic is the destruction of the white thing, the destruction of white ideas, and white ways of looking at the world. The new aesthetic is mostly predicated on an Ethics which asks the question: whose vision of the world is finally more meaningful, ours or the white oppressors? What is truth? Or more precisely, whose truth shall we express, that of the oppressed or of the oppressors? These are basic questions. Black intellectuals of previous decades failed to ask them. Further, national and international affairs demand that we appraise the world in terms of our own interests. It is clear that the question of human survival is at the core of contemporary experience. The Black artist must address himself to this reality in the strongest terms possible. In a context of world upheaval, ethics and aesthetics must interact positively and be consistent with the demands for a more spiritual world. Consequently, the Black Arts Movement is an ethical movement. Ethical, that is, from the viewpoint of the oppressed. And much of the oppression confronting the Third World and Black America is directly traceable to the Euro-American cultural sensibility. This sensibility, anti-human in nature, has, until recently, dominated the psyches of most Black artists and intellectuals; it must be destroyed before the Black creative artist can have a meaningful role in the transformation of society.

It is this natural reaction to an alien sensibility that informs the cultural attitudes of the Black Arts and the Black Power movement. It is a profound ethical sense that makes a Black artist question a society in which art is one thing and the actions of men another. The Black Arts Movement believes that your ethics and your aesthetics are one. That the contradictions between ethics and aesthetics in western society is symptomatic of a dying culture.

The term "Black Arts" is of ancient origin, but it was first used in a positive sense by LeRoi Jones [Amiri Baraka]:

> We are unfair
> And unfair
> We are black magicians
> Black arts we make
> in black labs of the heart
>
> The fair are fair
> and deathly white
>
> The day will not save them
> And we own the night

There is also a section of the poem "Black Dada Nihilismus" that carries the same motif. But a fuller amplification of the nature of the new aesthetics appear in the poem "Black Art":

> Poems are bullshit unless they are
> teeth or trees or lemons piled
> on a step. Or black ladies dying
> of men leaving nickel hearts
> beating them down. Fuck poems

and they are useful, would they shoot
come at you, love what you are,
breathe like wrestlers, or shudder
strangely after peeing. We want live
words of the hip world, live flesh &
coursing blood. Hearts and Brains
Souls splintering fire. We want poems
like fists beating niggers out of Jocks
or dagger poems in the slimy bellies
of the owner-jews . . .

Poetry is a concrete function, an action. No more abstractions. Poems are physical entities: fists, daggers, airplane poems, and poems that shoot guns. Poems are transformed from physical objects into personal forces:

. . . Put it on him poem. Strip him naked
to the world. Another bad poem cracking
steel knuckles in a jewlady's mouth
Poem scream poison gas on breasts in green berets . . .

Then the poem affirms the integral relationship between Black Art and Black people:

. . . Let Black people understand
that they are the lovers and the sons
of lovers and warriors and sons
of warriors Are poems & poets &
all the loveliness here in the world

It ends with the following lines, a central assertion in both the Black Arts Movement and the philosophy of Black Power:

We want a black poem. And a
Black World.
Let the world be a Black Poem
And let All Black People Speak This Poem
Silently
Or LOUD

The poem comes to stand for the collective conscious and unconscious of Black America—the real impulse in back of the Black Power movement, which is the will toward self-determination and nationhood, a radical reordering of the nature and function of both art and the artist.

2

In the spring of 1964, LeRoi Jones, Charles Patterson, William Patterson, Clarence Reed, Johnny Moore, and a number of other Black artists opened the Black Arts Repertoire Theatre School. They produced a number of plays including Jones's *Experimental Death Unit # One, Black Mass, Jello,* and *Dutchman*. They also initiated a series of poetry readings and concerts. These activities represented the most advanced tendencies in the movement and were of excellent artistic quality. The Black Arts School came under immediate attack by the New York power structure. The Establishment, fearing Black creativity, did exactly what it was expected to do—it attacked the theatre and all of its values. In the meantime, the school was granted funds by OEO [Office of Economic Opportunity] through HARYOU-ACT. Lacking a cultural program itself, HARYOU turned to the only organization which addressed itself to the needs of the community. In keeping with its "revolutionary" cultural ideas, the Black Arts Theatre took its programs into the streets of Harlem. For three months, the theatre presented plays, concerts, and poetry readings to the people of the community. Plays that shattered the illusions of the American body politic, and awakened Black people to the meaning of their lives.

Then the hawks from the OEO moved in and chopped off the funds. Again, this should have been expected. The Black Arts Theatre stood in radical opposition to the feeble attitudes about culture of the "War on Poverty" bureaucrats. And later, because of internal problems, the theatre was forced to close. But the Black Arts group proved that the community could be served by a valid and dynamic art. It also proved that there was a definite need for a cultural revolution in the Black community.

With the closing of the Black Arts Theatre, the implications of what Brother Jones and his colleagues were trying to do took on even more significance. Black Art groups sprang up on the West Coast and the idea spread to Detroit, Philadelphia, Jersey City, New Orleans, and Washington, D.C. Black Arts movements began on the campuses of San Francisco State College, Fisk University, Lincoln University, Hunter College in the Bronx, Columbia University, and Oberlin College. In Watts, after the rebellion, Maulana Karenga welded the Black Arts Movement into a cohesive cultural ideology which owed much to the work of LeRoi Jones. Karenga sees culture as the most important element in the struggle for self-determination:

> Culture is the basis of all ideas, images and actions. To move is to move culturally, i.e. by a set of values given to you by your culture.
>
> Without a culture Negroes are only a set of reactions to white people.
>
> The seven criteria for culture are:
>
> 1. Mythology
> 2. History
> 3. Social Organization
> 4. Political Organization
> 5. Economic Organization
> 6. Creative Motif
> 7. Ethos

In drama, LeRoi Jones represents the most advanced aspects of the movement. He is its prime mover and chief designer. In a poetic essay entitled "The Revolutionary Theatre," he outlines the iconology of the movement:

> The Revolutionary Theatre should force change: it should be change. (All their faces turned into the lights and you work on them black nigger magic, and cleanse

> them at having seen the ugliness. And if the beautiful see themselves, they will love themselves.) We are preaching virtue again, but by that to mean NOW, toward what seems the most constructive use of the word.

The theatre that Jones proposes is inextricably linked to the Afro-American political dynamic. And such a link is perfectly consistent with Black America's contemporary demands. For theatre is potentially the most social of all of the arts. It is an integral part of the socializing process. It exists in direct relationship to the audience it claims to serve. The decadence and inanity of the contemporary American theatre is an accurate reflection of the state of American society. Albee's *Who's Afraid of Virginia Woolf?* is very American: sick white lives in a homosexual hell hole. The theatre of white America is escapist, refusing to confront concrete reality. Into this cultural emptiness come the musicals, an up-tempo version of the same stale lives. And the use of Negroes in such plays as *Hello Dolly* and *Hallelujah Baby* does not alert their nature; it compounds the problem. These plays are simply hipper versions of the minstrel show. They present Negroes acting out the hang-ups of middle-class white America. Consequently, the American theatre is a palliative prescribed to bourgeois patients who refuse to see the world as it is. Or, more crucially, as the world sees them. It is no accident, therefore, that the most "important" plays come from Europe—Brecht, Weiss, and Ghelderode. And even these have begun to run dry.

The Black Arts theatre, the theatre of LeRoi Jones, is a radical alternative to the sterility of the American theatre. It is primarily a theatre of the Spirit, confronting the Black man in his interaction with his brothers and with the white thing.

> Our theatre will show victims so that their brothers in the audience will be better able to understand that they are the brothers of victims, and that they themselves are blood brothers. And what we show must cause the blood to rush, so that pre-revolutionary temperaments will be bathed in this blood, and it will cause their deepest souls to move, and they will find themselves tensed and clenched, even ready to die, at what the soul has been taught. We will scream and cry, murder, run through the streets in agony, if it means some soul will be moved, moved to actual life understanding of what the world is, and what it ought to be. We are preaching virtue and feeling, and a natural sense of the self in the world. All men live in the world, and the world ought to be a place for them to live.

The victims in the world of Jones' early plays are Clay, murdered by the white bitch-goddess in *Dutchman,* and Walker Vessels, the revolutionary in *The Slave.* Both of these plays present Black men in transition. Clay, the middle-class Negro trying to get himself a little action from Lula, digs himself and his own truth only to get murdered after telling her like it really is:

> Just let me bleed you, you loud whore, and one poem vanished. A whole people neurotics, struggling to keep from being sane. And the only thing that would cure the neurosis would be your murder. Simple as that. I mean if I murdered you, then other white people would understand me. You understand? No. I guess not. If Bessie Smith had killed some white people she wouldn't needed that music. She could have talked very straight and plain about the world. Just straight two and

two are four. Money. Power. Luxury. Like that. All of them. Crazy niggers turning their back on sanity. When all it needs is that simple act. Just murder. Would make us all sane.

But Lula understands, and she kills Clay first. In a perverse way it is Clay's nascent knowledge of himself that threatens the existence of Lula's idea of the world. Symbolically, and in fact, the relationship between Clay (Black America) and Lula (white America) is rooted in the historical castration of black manhood. And in the twisted psyche of white America, the Black man is both an object of love and hate. Analogous attitudes exist in most Black Americans, but for decidedly different reasons. Clay is doomed when he allows himself to participate in Lula's "fantasy" in the first place. It is the fantasy to which Frantz Fanon alludes in *The Wretched of the Earth* and *Black Skins, White Mask:* the native's belief that he can acquire the oppressor's power by acquiring his symbols, one of which is the white woman. When Clay finally digs himself it is too late.

Walker Vessels, in *The Slave,* is Clay reincarnated as the revolutionary confronting problems inherited from his contact with white culture. He returns to the home of his ex-wife, a white woman, and her husband, a literary critic. The play is essentially about Walker's attempt to destroy his white past. For it is the past, with all of its painful memories, that is really the enemy of the revolutionary. It is impossible to move until history is either recreated or comprehended. Unlike Todd, in Ralph Ellison's *Invisible Man,* Walker cannot fall outside history. Instead, Walker demands a confrontation with history, a final shattering of bullshit illusions. His only salvation lies in confronting the physical and psychological forces that have made him and his people powerless. Therefore, he comes to understand that the world must be restructured along spiritual imperatives. But in the interim it is basically a question of *who* has power:

EASLEY: You're so wrong about everything. So terribly, sickeningly wrong. What can you change? What do you hope to change? Do you think Negroes are better people than whites . . . that they can govern a society *better* than whites? That they'll be more judicious or more tolerant? Do you think they'll make fewer mistakes? I mean really, if the Western white man has proved one thing . . . it's the futility of modern society. So the have-not peoples become the haves. Even so, will that change the essential functions of the world? Will there be more love or beauty in the world . . . more knowledge . . . because of it?

WALKER: Probably. Probably there will be more . . . if more people have a chance to understand what it is. But that's not even the point. It comes down to baser human endeavor than any social-political thinking. What does it matter if there's more love or beauty? Who the fuck cares? Is that what the Western ofay thought while he was ruling . . . that his rule somehow brought more love and beauty into the world? Oh, he might have thought that concomitantly, while sipping a gin rickey and scratching his ass . . . but that was not ever the point. Not even on the Crusades. The point is that you had your chance, darling, now these other folks have theirs. [*Quietly.*] Now they have theirs.

EASLEY: God, what an ugly idea.

This confrontation between the black radical and the white liberal is symbolic of larger confrontations occurring between the Third World and Western society.

It is a confrontation between the colonizer and the colonized, the slavemaster and the slave. Implicit in Easley's remarks is the belief that the white man is culturally and politically superior to the Black Man. Even though Western society has been traditionally violent in its relation with the Third World, it sanctimoniously deplores violence or self-assertion on the part of the enslaved. And the Western mind, with clever rationalizations, equates the violence of the oppressed with the violence of the oppressor. So that when the native preaches self-determination, the Western white man cleverly misconstrues it to mean hate of *all* white men. When the Black political radical warns his people not to trust white politicians of the left and the right, but instead to organize separately on the basis of power, the white man cries: "racism in reverse." Or he will say, as many of them do today: "We deplore both white and black racism." As if the two could be equated.

There is a minor element in *The Slave* which assumes great importance in a later play entitled *Jello*. Here I refer to the emblem of Walker's army: a red-mouthed grinning field slave. The revolutionary army has taken one of the most hated symbols of the Afro-American past and radically altered its meaning.* This is the supreme act of freedom, available only to those who have liberated themselves psychically. Jones amplifies this inversion of emblem and symbol in *Jello* by making Rochester (Ratfester) of the old Jack Benny (Penny) program into a revolutionary nationalist. Ratfester, ordinarily the supreme embodiment of the Uncle Tom Clown, surprises Jack Penny by turning on the other side of the nature of the Black man. He skillfully, and with an evasive black humor, robs Penny of all of his money. But Ratfester's actions are "moral." That is to say, Ratfester is getting his back pay; payment of a long over-due debt to the Black man. Ratfester's sensibilities are different from Walker's. He is *blues people* smiling and shuffling while trying to figure out how to destroy the white thing. And like the blues man, he is the master of the understatement. Or in the Afro-American folk tradition, he is the signifying Monkey, Shine, and Stagolee all rolled into one. There are no stereotypes any more. History has killed Uncle Tom. Because even Uncle Tom has a breaking point beyond which he will not be pushed. Cut deeply enough into the most docile Negro, and you will find a conscious murderer. Behind the lyrics of the blues and the shuffling porter loom visions of white throats being cut and cities burning.

Jones' particular power as a playwright does not rest solely on his revolutionary vision, but is instead derived from his deep lyricism and spiritual outlook. In many ways, he is fundamentally more a poet than a playwright. And it is his lyricism that gives body to his plays. Two important plays in this regard are *Black Mass* and *Slave Ship*. *Black Mass* is based on the Muslim myth of Yacub. According to this myth, Yacub, a Black scientist, developed the means of grafting different colors of the Original Black Nation until a White Devil was created. In

* In Jones' study of Afro-American music, *Blues People*, we find the following observation: "Even the adjective *funky*, which once meant to many Negroes merely a stink (usually associated with sex), was used to qualify the music as meaningful (the word became fashionable and is now almost useless). The social implication, then, was that even the old stereotype of a distinctive Negro smell that white America subscribed to could be turned against white America. For this smell now, real or not, was made a valuable characteristic of 'Negro-ness.' And 'Negro-ness,' by the fifties, for many Negroes (and whites) was the only strength left to American culture."

Black Mass, Yacub's experiments produce a raving White Beast who is condemned to the coldest regions of the North. The other magicians implore Yacub to cease his experiments. But he insists on claiming the primacy of scientific knowledge over spiritual knowledge. The sensibility of the White Devil is alien, informed by lust and sensuality. The Beast is the consummate embodiment of evil, the beginning of the historical subjugation of the spiritual world.

Black Mass takes place in some pre-historical time. In fact, the concept of time, we learn, is the creation of an alien sensibility, that of the Beast. This is a deeply weighted play, a colloquy on the nature of man, and the relationship between legitimate spiritual knowledge and scientific knowledge. It is LeRoi Jones' most important play mainly because it is informed by a mythology that is wholly the creation of the Afro-American sensibility.

Further, Yacub's creation is not merely a scientific exercise. More fundamentally, it is the aesthetic impulse gone astray. The Beast is created merely for the sake of creation. Some artists assert a similar claim about the nature of art. They argue that art need not have a function. It is against this decadent attitude toward art—ramified throughout most of Western society—that the play militates. Yacub's real crime, therefore, is the introduction of a meaningless evil into a harmonious universe. The evil of the Beast is pervasive, corrupting everything and everyone it touches. The play ends with destruction of the holy place of the Black Magicians. Now the Beast and his descendants roam the earth. An off-stage voice chants a call for the Jihan to begin. It is then that myth merges into legitimate history, and we, the audience, come to understand that all history is merely someone's version of mythology.

Slave Ship presents a more immediate confrontation with history. In a series of expressionistic tableaux it depicts the horrors and the madness of the Middle Passage. It then moves through the period of slavery, early attempts at revolt, tendencies toward Uncle Tom-like reconciliation and betrayal, and the final act of liberation. There is no definite plot (LeRoi calls it a pageant), just a continuous rush of sound, groans, screams, and souls wailing for freedom and relief from suffering. This work has special affinities with the New Music of Sun Ra, John Coltrane, Albert Ayler, and Ornette Coleman. Events are blurred, rising and falling in a stream of sound. Almost cinematically, the images flicker and fade against a heavy back-drop of rhythm. The language is spare, stripped to the essential. It is a play which almost totally eliminates the need for a text. It functions on the basis of movements and energy—the dramatic equivalent of the New Music.

Slave Ship's energy is, at base, ritualistic. As a matter of fact, to see the play any other way is to miss the point. All the New York reviewers, with the possible exception of John Lahr, were completely cut off from this central aspect of the play when it was performed at the Brooklyn Academy under the brilliant direction of Gilbert Moses. One of the prime motivations behind the work is to suck the audience into a unique and very precise universe. The episodes of this "pageant" do not appear as strict interpretations of history. Rather, what we are digging is ritualized history. That is, history that allows emotional and religious participation on the part of the audience. And, like all good ritual, its purpose is to make the audience stronger, more sensitive to the historical realities that have shaped our lives and the lives of our ancestors. The play acts to extend memory. For black people to forget the realities posed by *Slave Ship* is to fall prey to an existential paralysis. History, like the blues, demands that we witness the painful events of our prior lives; and that we either confront these painful events or be destroyed by them.

3

LeRoi Jones is the best known and the most advanced playwright of the movement, but he is not alone. There are other excellent playwrights who express the general mood of the Black Arts ideology. Among them are Ron Milner, Ed Bullins, Ben Caldwell, Jimmy Stewart, Joe White, Charles Patterson, Charles Fuller, Aisha Hughes, Carol Freeman, and Jimmy Garrett.

Ron Milner's *Who's Got His Own* is of particular importance. It strips bare the clashing attitudes of a contemporary Afro-American family. Milner's concern is with legitimate manhood and morality. The family in *Who's Got His Own* is in search of its conscience, or more precisely its own definition of life. On the day of his father's death, Tim and his family are forced to examine the inner fabric of their lives: the lies, self-deceits, and sense of powerlessness in a white world. The basic conflict, however, is internal. It is rooted in the historical search for black manhood. Tim's mother is representative of a generation of Christian Black women who have implicitly understood the brooding violence lurking in their men. And with this understanding, they have interposed themselves between their men and the object of that violence—the white man. Thus unable to direct his violence against the oppressor, the Black man becomes more frustrated and the sense of powerlessness deepens. Lacking the strength to be a man in the white world, he turns against his family. So the oppressed, as Fanon explains, constantly dreams violence against his oppressor, while killing his brother on fast weekends.

Tim's sister represents the Negro woman's attempt to acquire what Eldridge Cleaver calls "ultrafemininity." That is, the attributes of her white upper-class counterpart. Involved here is a rejection of the body-oriented life of the working class Black man, symbolized by the mother's traditional religion. The sister has an affair with a white upper-class liberal, ending in abortion. There are hints of lesbianism, i.e., a further rejection of the body. The sister's life is a pivotal factor in the play. Much of the stripping away of falsehood initiated by Tim is directed at her life, which they have carefully kept hidden from the mother.

Tim is the product of the new Afro-American sensibility, informed by the psychological revolution now operative within Black America. He is a combination ghetto soul brother and militant intellectual, very hip and slightly flawed himself. He would change the world, but without comprehending the particular history that produced his "tyrannical" father. And he cannot be the man his father was—not until he truly understands his father. He must understand why his father allowed himself to be insulted daily by the "honky" types on the job; why he took a demeaning job in the "shit-house"; and why he spent on his family the violence that he should have directed against the white man. In short, Tim must confront the history of his family. And that is exactly what happens. Each character tells his story, exposing his falsehood to the other until a balance is reached.

Who's Got His Own is not the work of an alienated mind. Milner's main thrust is directed toward unifying the family around basic moral principles, toward bridging the "generation gap." Other Black playwrights, Jimmy Garrett for example, see the gap as unbridgeable.

Garrett's *We Own the Night*. . . takes place during an armed insurrection. As the play opens we see the central characters defending a section of the city against attacks by white police. Johnny, the protagonist, is wounded. Some of his Brothers intermittently fire at attacking forces, while others look for medical help. A doctor arrives, forced at gun point. The wounded boy's mother also comes. She is a female Uncle Tom who berates the Brothers and their cause. She tries to get Johnny to leave. She is hysterical. The whole idea of Black people fighting white people is totally outside of her orientation. Johnny begins a vicious attack on his mother, accusing her of emasculating his father—a recurring theme in the sociology of the Black community. In Afro-American literature of previous decades the strong Black mother was the object of awe and respect. But in the new literature her status is ambivalent and laced with tension. Historically, Afro-American women have had to be the economic mainstays of the family. The oppressor allowed them to have jobs while at the same time limiting the economic mobility of the Black man. Very often, therefore, the woman's aspirations and values are closely tied to those of the white power structure and not to those of her man. Since he cannot provide for his family the way white men do, she despises his weakness, tearing into him at every opportunity until, very often, there is nothing left but a shell.

The only way out of this dilemma is through revolution. It either must be an actual blood revolution, or one that psychically redirects the energy of the oppressed. Milner is fundamentally concerned with the latter and Garrett with the former. Communication between Johnny and his mother breaks down. The revolutionary imperative demands that men step outside the legal framework. It is a question of erecting *another* morality. The old constructs do not hold up, because adhering to them means consigning oneself to the oppressive reality. Johnny's mother is involved in the old constructs. Manliness is equated with white morality. And even though she claims to love her family (her men), the overall design of her ideas are against black manhood. In Garrett's play the mother's morality manifests itself in a deep-seated hatred of Black men; while in Milner's work the mother understands, but holds her men back.

The mothers that Garrett and Milner see represent the Old Spirituality—the Faith of the Fathers of which Du Bois spoke. Johnny and Tim represent the New Spirituality. They appear to be a type produced by the upheavals of the colonial world of which Black America is a part. Johnny's assertion that he is a criminal is remarkably similar to the rebel's comments in Aimé Césaire's play, *Les Armes Miraculeuses* (*"The Miraculous Weapons"*). In that play the rebel, speaking to his mother, proclaims: "My name—an offense; my Christian name—humiliation; my status—a rebel; my age—the stone age." To which the mother replies: "My race—the human race. My religion—brotherhood." The Old Spirituality is generalized. It seeks to recognize Universal Humanity. The New Spirituality is specific. It begins by seeing the world from the concise point-of-view of the colonialized. Where the Old Spirituality would live with oppression while ascribing to the oppressors an innate goodness, the New Spirituality demands a radical shift in point-of-view. The colonialized native, the oppressed must, of necessity, subscribe to a *separate* morality. One that will liberate him and his people.

The assault against the Old Spirituality can sometimes be humorous. In Ben Caldwell's play, *The Militant Preacher,* a burglar is seen slipping into the home of a wealthy minister. The preacher comes in and the burglar ducks behind a large chair. The preacher, acting out the role of the supplicant minister begins to moan, praying to De Lawd for understanding.

In the context of today's politics, the minister is an Uncle Tom, mouthing platitudes against self-defense. The preacher drones in a self-pitying monologue about the folly of protecting oneself against brutal policemen. Then the burglar begins to speak. The preacher is startled, taking the burglar's voice for the voice of God. The burglar begins to play on the preacher's old time religion. He *becomes* the voice of God insulting and goading the preacher on until the preacher's attitudes about protective violence change. The next day the preacher emerges militant, gun in hand, sounding like Reverend Cleage in Detroit. He now preaches a new gospel—the gospel of the gun, an eye for an eye. The gospel is preached in the rhythmic cadences of the old Black church. But the content is radical. Just as Jones inverted the symbols in *Jello,* Caldwell twists the rhythms of the Uncle Tom preacher into the language of the new militancy.

These plays are directed at problems within Black America. They begin with the premise that there is a well defined Afro-American audience. An audience that must see itself and the world in terms of its own interests. These plays, along with many others, constitute the basis for a viable movement in the theatre—a movement which takes as its task a profound re-evaluation of the Black man's presence in America. The Black Arts Movement represents the flowering of a cultural nationalism that has been suppressed since the 1920s. I mean the "Harlem Renaissance"—which was essentially a failure. It did not address itself to the mythology and the life-styles of the Black community. It failed to take roots, to link itself concretely to the struggles of that community, to become its voice and spirit. Implicit in the Black Arts Movement is the idea that Black people, however dispersed, constitute a *nation* within the belly of white America. This is not a new idea. Garvey said it and the Honorable Elijah Muhammad says it now. And it is on this idea that the concept of Black Power is predicated.

Afro-American life and history [are] full of creative possibilities, and the movement is just beginning to perceive them. Just beginning to understand that the most meaningful statements about the nature of Western society must come from the Third World of which Black America is a part. The thematic material is broad, ranging from folk heroes like Shine and Stagolee to historical figures like Marcus Garvey and Malcolm X. And then there is the struggle for Black survival, the coming confrontation between white America and Black America. If art is the harbinger of future possibilities, what does the future of Black America portend?

Charles Johnson (1948–)

The multitalented Charles Johnson is an established fiction writer, essayist, scriptwriter, and newspaper cartoonist. His versatility is bolstered by his strong academic background. Born in Evanston, Illinois, Johnson studied literature at Southern Illinois University, earning his bachelor's in 1971 and his master's in 1973. He went on to complete a doctorate in phenomenology and literary aesthetics at the State University of New York at Stony Brook.

Johnson had already emerged as a cartoonist by the time he was seventeen, seeing his work published in periodicals and later collected into two books: Black Humor *(1970) and* Half-Past Nation-Time *(1972). With his experience as a cartoonist and reporter at various newspapers in the late 1960s and 1970s, including the* Chicago Tribune, *Johnson made the transition into television scriptwriting. While still in his early twenties, Johnson wrote, co-produced, and hosted the PBS television show* Charlie's Pad *(1971), a fifty-two-part series on cartooning. His relationship with PBS continued as he wrote scripts for other shows, including* Charlie Smith and the Fritter-Tree *(1978),* For Me and Myself *(1982),* Booker *(1984), and* A Place for Myself *(1992). For* Booker, *Johnson won a Writers Guild Award for Best Children's Show in 1986.*

While working as a cartoonist and television scriptwriter, Johnson methodically studied the craft of fiction, completing six novels before he believed himself ready to seek publication. Faith and the Good Thing *(1974), his first published novel, was followed by three other works of fiction:* Oxherding Tale *(1982), a novel about a mulatto slave;* The Sorcerer's Apprentice *(1986), a short-story collection; and* Middle Passage *(1990), a National Book Award–winning novel. The author assesses his writing in this way: "As a writer, I am committed to the development of what one might call a genuinely systematic philosophical black American literature, a body of work that explores classical problems and metaphysical questions against the background of black American life. . . . I attempt to interface Eastern and Western philosophical traditions, always with the hope that some new perception of experience—especially 'black experience'—will emerge from these meditations."*

The following selection comes from Johnson's book of essays, Being and Race: Black Writing since 1970 *(1988). In "Being and Race," the writer analyzes the relationship between black literary creativity and the ongoing pursuit to define race and ethnicity in a pluralistic society.*

Being and Race

A novelist blundering into the field of literary criticism should first apologize to his colleagues who analyze fiction for a living and then make some effort to explain why he has briefly left the business of writing stories to talk about them. My credentials for this chore are modest, but my curiosity about how fiction "works" is great. It has been so from the first day I took up writing. Life is baffling enough for every novelist, and for writers of Afro-American fiction it presents even more artistic and philosophical questions than for writers who are white. Few writers, black or white, bother with such questions, and in the long run they may have importance only to a few people who wonder, as I have for twenty years, about the forms our stories have taken, what they say about the world, and what they don't say. These are not idle questions. Our faith in fiction comes from an ancient belief that language and literary art—all speaking and showing—clarify our experience. Our most sacred cliché in contemporary criticism, and also in creative-writing courses, is that writers should "write about what they know," and for the Afro-American author that inevitably means the "black" experience. This idea is doubtlessly true, or at least half-true in some narrow sense we have yet to determine. But it leads, I believe, from loose, casual talk about "experience" to esthetic and epistemological questions difficult to answer. . . .

It might be helpful to digress a moment to dwell on the artistic impulse itself. Do we *begin* at the same place, writers black and white? In his study of painting, *The Voices of Silence,* André Malraux says, "What makes the artist is that in his youth he was more deeply moved by his visual experience of works of art than by that of the things they represent—and perhaps of Nature as a whole."[1] He adds, "We have no means of knowing how a great artist, who had never seen a work of art, but only the forms of nature, would develop." In other words, we *encounter* art in some form, blunder onto it—or have it placed before us by teachers or parents—as a being different from others in the world. Many black authors confess in interviews that the origin of their artistic journey began when, as children, they heard folktales or ghost stories in the South from elders; and one young American novelist, whom I won't name, is known to say he decided to write when, after passing an auditorium where a distinguished author was reading, he thought to himself, "I can do *that.*" It helps, clearly, if a novice writer has a healthy sense of contempt for his predecessors, or if one's first exposure is, let us say, to easy art rather than to something as intimidating as *Hamlet* or Thomas Mann's *Doktor Faustus.* My own students and friends, once polled, reported an array of first impressions or seductions—Nancy Drew novels, picture books of Bible stories, "Twilight Zone" episodes, Marvel comic books, science fiction, "The Little Engine That Could," or stories they were assigned to read from *Scholastic* magazine. For American kids, it seems to matter little whether they cut their teeth on Louis L'Amour's westerns or Aesop's fables before moving on to more complex novels. Novelist John Gardner often cited his primary influences as Walt Disney and Jean-Paul Sartre, and his best-known book, *Grendel,* seems to bear this out. It's important to remember that this early seduction of the artist by some artwork, vulgar or distinguished, is experienced as delightful—thrilling *as* a story of novel or poem, an encounter that pleases one that such a thing as this can be. Now, delight need not be joyful. I daresay we take pleasure in encounters that shake us to the core, terrorize us, or contradict our most cherished beliefs as well as in those that leave us feeling smug. But in many of these earliest encounters we discover we have been changed. More precisely, our perception—or way of seeing—has been shaken, if one is talking about great art, which is all I care to consider here. In a word, writers begin their lifelong odyssey in art with expression or experience *interpreted* by others, not with, as popular wisdom sometimes has it, an ensemble of events that already mean something.

Going even further, Malraux tells us that "artists do not stem from their childhood, but from their conflicts with the achievements of their predecessors; not from their formless world, but from their struggle with the forms which others have imposed on life." Some of this curious idea can be seen in, for example, figure-drawing classes, where you stand with the canvas to your side and with brush poised as you study the model at the front of the room, and then, miraculously, something happens in the flickerish moment between shifting your gaze from the model, with all his concrete, specific, individual features, to the canvas. You have drawn, you discover, not *his* hand but instead your *idea* of how a hand should look, an idea built up doubtlessly from viewing, not hundreds of individual models, but rather other artists' renditions of the hand. It is precisely this heavily conditioned seeing, this calcification of perception, that figure-drawing classes seek to liberate—we might well call this retraining of the eye, the artist's equivalent to the phenomenological *epoché,* or "bracketing" of all presuppositions in order to seize a fresh, original vision.

Malraux's point is that often the apprentice artist, thinking about the world of experience transfigured in the text—a novel, painting, poem, or film—says, "That's not so." Or, "He didn't get it quite right." He might also say, "How perfectly done. Let *me* reply with a composition of my own." Whatever the case, fiction—indeed, all art—points to others with whom the writer argues about what *is*. He cannot begin *ex nihilo*. He must have models with which to agree, partly agree, or outright oppose, and these can come only from the tradition of literature itself, for Nature seems to remain silent, providing no final text or court of judgment. If any of these ruminations sound reasonable, does it seem possible that the "black experience" in literature truly exists only there—*in* literature—and therefore must vary from one author's viewpoint to the next, with nothing invariant in the "experience" that we can agree on as final?

As a young novelist, I found the problem of what is or is not the "black" experience staring at me more steadily than I could stare at it, particularly after I'd written six bad, apprentice novels, three that aped the style of James Baldwin, Richard Wright, and John A. Williams, all fine writers whom I admire, and three that were heavily influenced by what a few critics now call the "Black Aesthetic." The first three of the six were misery-filled protest stories about the sorry condition of being black in America and might be called "naturalistic." I couldn't read them after they were done. Something was wrong, but I couldn't jump the problem until years later when I realized how uncritical I'd been about nearly every aspect of fiction, each element in this discipline being somewhat like a thread, which, if pulled, leads on to the unraveling of an entire garment. Surely naturalism in its various strains is suitable for certain kinds of stories, and for a certain social message, but lost in it for a time I ran into artistic restrictions I couldn't resolve, never realizing that writing doesn't so much record an experience—or even imitate or represent it—as it *creates* that experience, and that each literary form, style, or genre is a different, distinct method of reasoning, of shaping what is to body it forth intelligibly.

In hindsight, naturalism seemed to conceal profound prejudices about Being, what a person is, the nature of society, causation, and a worm can of metaphysical questions about what could and could not logically occur in our "experience" and conscious life. Its implied physics was dated—or at best only provisional—and, even worse, it concealed a reductionistic model of human psychology, of what motivates men and women (and had no theory of the self at all), that made my characters dull and predictable in their inner lives and perceptions of the world. Like gravity, it held the imagination close to the ground by creating the camera-like illusion of objectivity, of events unmediated—or untampered with—by any narrative presence. Although easy to imitate as a style, it scaled down experiential possibilities and put curious limits on narrative voice and language, as well as on such poetic devices as simile and metaphor, those inherently existential strategies that allow a writer to pluck similarities from our experiences or to illuminate one object by reference to another by saying A *is* B. . . . Naturalism gained its power, its punch, by strictly controlling what could be said, seen, and shown.

Adopting such means uncritically, I discovered by error what novelist Linsey Abrams seemed to know by instinct, that "style is never simply technical choice, but evolves from how a writer sees the world." In her brilliant essay "A Maximalist Novelist Looks at Some Minimalist Fiction" (1985), she says that to embrace a "readily identifiable prose style without being aware of its tyranny and inevitability of voice" is to embrace "a ready-made point-of-view." In short, naturalism is clearly a massaging and kneading of life, a style as full of tricks and false bottoms as any other. Of course, none of these observations is new. Philosopher Edmund Husserl (and also Albert Schweitzer) said as much seventy years ago in his criticism of the "Natural Attitude." And so, like the editors who read those three early efforts of mine, I had no interest in revisiting their fictional worlds ever again.

Not much later I foundered again, this time with three novels created under the spell of the Black Arts Movement, the "cultural wing" of the Black Power Movement, which was inescapable in the late 1960s and which is more or less alive today as a quasi-philosophical position with its roots deep in Pan-Africanism and race pride. In order to understand black fiction, its problems and promise, and why these last novels I've mentioned were artistic failures, you must appreciate some of the pitfalls to be found in the history of black American literature and what confronts a young writer when he considers his place in this still relatively young tradition.

The political and social status of the work of art has been a point of interest since the earliest philosophical reflections on poetry. "It is phantoms, not realities that they produce," Plato's Socrates says of the artist in the tenth book of *The Republic*.[2] If a preestablished model is assumed for our experience, or for *any* experience—if meaning is seen as fixed rather than as evolving, changing, and historical, if reality is reified for political or social or even moral reasons—the independent writer who departs from the "forms" can only be seen as one who "sets up in each individual soul a vicious constitution by fashioning phantoms far removed from reality," or what is taken to be the "objective" model for the Real. And so Socrates banishes all but a few poets from the republic, retaining only those who write hymns and praises. Although twenty-five centuries separate us from *The Republic,* the problems raised by black fiction return us to Plato's musings, for nowhere are the questions of social and political relevance in literature more pronounced than in this body of American literature.

From its beginnings in the poetry of Phillis Wheatley and the narrative of Gustavus Vassa, black fiction comprises, one must confess, an overwhelmingly tragic literature. It is full of failures. A catalogue of man's inhumanity to man and woman. Book after book discloses the desperate struggle of a people first to survive against stupendous odds and then to secure the most basic rights in a perpetually hostile environment. Whites in this history act; blacks can only *re*act.

The black American novel begins with *Clotelle, or the Colored Heroine* (1853) by William Wells Brown. *Clotelle* has always been regarded as a pivotal book in black letters insofar as many critics have used it as a departure point for two directions in nineteenth century black writing—the tradition of black social criticism and the novel. Always, and forever, these forms must be understood in terms of the catastrophe of American slavery, detailed fully by Frederick Douglass and others in slave narratives that are the ancestral roots of black fiction. It is a bloody history of atrocity, of stripping a people of cultural identity, then grotesquely caricaturing them in the national (white) imagination. The burden on the free, literate black population was staggering—to lead the antislavery effort, counteract the ideology of racism, and prove themselves worthy of equality. Two tendencies—a clear dialectic—surely exist here at the beginning of black fiction, as critic Addison Gayle, Jr., argues in his study *The Way of the New World* (1975). In the writings of Martin Delany, a man of many literary and political accomplishments, and in those of Sutton Griggs, we find the first glimmerings of black separatism in their call for blacks to consider migrating to other lands to escape oppression (an idea also entertained by Abraham Lincoln), while Douglass, W. E. B. Du Bois, and others developed writings that were integrationist—indeed, for Du Bois (who probably studied Hegel during his days at Harvard), integration was not simply a way of social organization but the dialectical process of evolution itself, a movement that as it pushed society forward would preserve the essential elements in such polarities as black and white. Historically, the black novel appears close to the hour that post–Civil War gains in the South toppled, as Reconstruction's advances were rolled back—one of the most violent periods of black history when, between 1885 and 1900, 2,500 blacks were lynched: an average of about one murder every third day. This was the time of Douglass's death; of Booker T. Washington's ascension; and of repression: white southern reaction in the form of Jim Crow legislation, "black codes," and revivified racial stereotypes.

Here we can only sketch that history, but it is, on the whole and in general, a nightmare. The black American writer begins his or her career with—and continues to exhibit—a crisis of identity. If anything, black fiction is *about* the troubled quest for identity and liberty, the agony of social alienation, the longing for a real and at times a mythical home. Something similar, of course, can be said of early American writers in respect to their struggle to break with European culture and to carve out an "American" sense of selfhood. In his literary manifesto, "Blueprint for Negro Writing" (1937), Richard Wright suggests that eighteenth- and nineteenth-century black writers composed fiction and poetry to impress whites with their humanity and thereby to win for themselves a more comfortable place in the racial world. If Wright is even half-correct about this, then we must say, tentatively, that a serious question for early black fiction was audience. For whom did one write? In the language of the time—neoclassical verse larded with sentiment if one were a Wheatley—and not in black folk idioms, at least not until Paul Lawrence Dunbar produced dialect verse about plantation life (humorously portrayed) that tragically became both a showcase and a trap for his poetic talents. His white sponsors and audience would accept nothing else, though some of Dunbar's standard-English poems are outstanding. But this was not the only artistic problem that faced early black authors.

In *The Negro Novel in America* (1958), critic Robert Bone points out a more serious problem, the necessity of developing well-rounded black characters (and I would add white ones as well) to balance the degrading stereotypes created by whites in the post-Reconstruction period, a problem that still shadows all black fiction today. . . . The black novel, Bone says, began at the tail end of the romantic tradition, opting for the then-fading strategy of melodrama, but still retained a strong abolitionist flavor from its origins in the slave narrative. According to Bone, melodrama deals primarily with issues of Right and Wrong. His evaluation of early black novels bears much truth, but we should not blink away the beauty, the charm, and the artistic interest to be found in such pivotal writers as Charles Chesnutt, who achieved in imaginative short stories such as "The

Goophered Grapevine" and "The Passing of Grandison" levels of irony, ingenuity, and invention that are, even by today's standards, pretty satisfying. More, Chesnutt's work reveals a great deal about the genesis of the modern American short story, for it is during his time that writers were wrestling with definitions of this form, trying to distinguish it from the tale and the novella. His tales published in *The Conjure Woman* (1899) are just that—tales that recall the work of Washington Irving and Nathaniel Hawthorne. Yet they are structurally informed by the story form of the late 1800s. It is Edgar Allan Poe who first clarified the form in his crucial essay, "The Philosophy of Composition" (1842); here he gives primacy to brevity and emotional effect in the short story. Those elements are later formularized by O. Henry in such stories as "The Gift of the Magi" and held up as models for effective storytelling in writing handbooks published around the turn of the century: the brisk, tightly plotted magazine story that emphasizes a twist or reversal and that contains a touch of fantasy (Rod Serling's better "Twilight Zone" tales are a modern-day descendant of this nineteenth-century form). And does this kind of story have drawbacks? Yes, if you place great value on character in fiction, for this form generally only permits types, people given only the slightest brush strokes for development so that the forward motion of events can proceed steadily and unhampered to a denouement. For all these faults, Chesnutt manages in such stories as "The Wife of His Youth" the at times remarkable feat of transforming elements of the slave experience into light yet serious entertainment and never minimalizes the pathos of bondage. They are stories rich in humor, which always means that a writer has distance from his material, and equally rich in suspense, a charming Jamesian narrative voice, and gentle but effective social criticism. In these tales, love of unusual characters and life's surprises replace the grind and grim predictability of melodrama, which as a strategy does not so much probe values as it exhorts, indicts, accuses. Bone argues, and rightly I think, that but for one or two exceptions the universe of early black fiction did little to expand beyond this less than complex treatment of racial affairs.

The Harlem Renaissance, which spanned the 1920s, has been much discussed, most interestingly by historian Nathan Huggins. It is usually explained in terms of large-scale developments in black history such as the black migrations from southern repression to the northern factory cities; the development of Harlem as a black cultural center in the East; the rise of a black middle class, heir to the social ethic of Booker T. Washington and his program for self-help; and the cultural impact when West Indians, Africans, and American blacks found themselves side-by-side in Harlem. Also, it was the time of Marcus Garvey's United Negro Improvement Association (predecessor first to the Nation of Islam, then to Louis Farrakhan), a back-to-Africa movement inspired by Washington's separatist philosophy and led by a theatrical little man who envisioned universal black liberation and the shoring up of Africa as a modern nation-state styled on the culture of England, complete with black kings and queens and the Black Star Shipping Line. For whites, it was the period when the Negro became . . . well, "interesting." But for all the wrong reasons. In the period of national exhaustion following World War I, a somewhat weary America grew interested in Sigmund Freud's idea that civilization is based on the repression of eros and became suspicious of tight-sphinctered Victorian values, which many Negroes shared nevertheless, Du Bois probably and Countee Cullen among them. For some, it was easy to perceive blacks as exotic, sexually liberated creatures free of white men's cares. This dubious interest won many white patrons for a few black writers, who might not have seen publication without such tainted support, though many were at work trying to destroy this vicious black stereotype and others. In "A Century of Negro Portraiture in America" (1966), Sterling Brown isolated a few such damaging images current at the time: the Comic Negro (who cannot talk, or talks funny), the Exotic Primitive, the Contented Slave of Joel Chandler Harris's stories. To them we can add the most frightening of all, the Negro Beast described by Joseph Gobineau and portrayed in such films as *Birth of a Nation,* a creature of fierce appetites and lust, usually guided by northern whites (or Reds). In his essay "The New Negro" (1925), which promoted the idea of a new Negro race consciousness, as well as Pan-Africanism, scholar Alain Locke wrote, half to present this change and half to inspire it, that "the day of 'aunties,' 'uncles,' and 'mammies' is equally gone. Uncle Tom and Sambo have passed on. . . . In the very process of being transplanted, the Negro is being transformed."

Looking back, we see that Locke's pronouncement was at least half-right. The 1920s were a time of creating images aimed at achieving new racial understanding. Several reasons are often cited for the failure of this ambitious project: the Great Depression; the inability of black writers in the 1920s to understand fully the nature of the changes they were calling for; their inability (according to Harold Cruse) to formulate a black cultural ideology, as later happened in the 1960s; and the appropriation of black material and talent by well-meaning white authors such as Carl Van Vechten, who, despite his encouragement of black writers, still saw blacks as most true to themselves when they were most unlike white men. These are historical reasons for the failure of the Harlem Renaissance; I would submit a philosophical one: namely, the inherent difficulty in trying to control the image—meaning—in the first place. Except in the case of mathematical objects, or experiences known *a priori,* we find meaning in flux, on the side of Heraclitus (change) and not Parmenides (stasis); we find, I am saying, the black world *overflowing* with meaning, so rich and multisided that literally anything—and everything—can be found there, good and bad, and one of the first chores of the writer is to be immersed in this embarrassment of rich, contradictory material. . . .

Although brief, the Harlem Renaissance is notable for the frequent return of some of its writers to black folk sources, a wellspring of creativity and perhaps the only truly indigenous American folklore that reached full flower in Jean Toomer's highly sophisticated, perennially hypnotic book, *Cane* (1923), a montage of poetry and short fiction. And in Zora Neale Hurston's *Their Eyes Were Watching God* (1937), a book remarkable for its beautiful use of southern folk material and its emphasis on the complex relation between black men and women—clearly, this novel and Hurston's ground-breaking anthropological work in *Mules and Men* (1935) provide the platform and the framework for black feminist writing in the 1980s. In them we see prefigured the work of Toni Morrison, Alice Walker, and such younger talents as Amirh Bahari; yet one walks away from Hurston amazed by how thoroughly she treated this (now) popular subject almost fifty years ago, using the most interesting Harlem Renaissance ideas—the importance of the common folk—to explore the "New Negro" female on subtler levels than her contemporaries did. In short, Hurston was not only a brilliant writer but also a prophetic one, a full half-century ahead of her time on questions of sexual politics. With George Schuyler's wonderful (in idea, not execution) science-fiction novel *Black No More* (1931) and Wallace Thurman's *The Blacker the Berry* (1929), the Harlem Renaissance closed with novels of black satire, books that foreshadow the barbed fiction of Ishmael Reed.

The depression, though it saw this remarkable output dwindle, gave birth to the Federal Writers' Project, which offered creative outlets to a younger generation that would become major writers in the 1940s and 1950s—Richard Wright, Ralph Ellison, Frank Yerby, William Motley. The role of the Communist party figures largely in this period. Earlier, Locke suggested that smarter blacks of the 1920s were leaning left with other progressive elements in America, but the thematization of blacks in American labor had been present in the late 1800s in the writings of T. Thomas Fortune, and for Du Bois, early in his career. Nevertheless, as one old organizer once told me, joining the Party was simply "something everybody did." Wright and such celebrities as Paul Robeson attracted others to the Party, but blacks were largely interested, if I'm not mistaken, in communism's promise of racial equality rather than in wholeheartedly embracing dialectical materialism and abolishing private property. On black literature, Wright's *Native Son,* an overnight bestseller in 1940, left a large artistic impression. Probably it is one of the two or three best-known novels by black American writers, and it produced many imitators but also a reaction against the brutal "realism" (if we may call it that) of his fiction during and after the depression years, a realism that gained its visceral power at the expense of portraying positive cultural features in black life—in other words, much that is affirmative and joyful in black culture is lost in the literary Lifeworld of Richard Wright.

But it *is* with Wright that something of a watershed is reached in black fiction. Nearly fifty years after its publication, *Native Son* still remains one of our most phenomenologically successful novels, a nightmare as frightening, in its own way, as George Orwell's *1984.* I am at a loss to number all the black authors who were inspired by this work: James Baldwin, Chester Himes, John A. Williams—a full generation of writers, we are forced to say, because as Baldwin once remarked, Wright's "great forte . . . was an ability to convey inward states by means of externals." What I take him to mean by this—or what he should be saying—is that for the first time in black American literature we are presented with a masterfully drawn *Lebenswelt;* we are made to see and experience meaning—the world—from the distorted perspective of a petty thief so mangled by oppression in its many forms that his only possibility for creative action is murder. Like any fully orchestrated, over-rich work of art, *Native Son* resists easy description. It is multileveled, exhaustive in detail, layered with existentialist, Marxist, and even religious themes; it echoes Dostoyevsky's *Crime and Punishment* and Dreiser's *An American Tragedy,* conjures the image of Nat Turner, and anticipates the thesis of Frantz Fanon in *The Wretched of the Earth* (1961) as Bigger Thomas finds release from fear and self-hatred through murder. It achieves, in the end, a dimension bordering on racial mythology (the hunt for the killer-slave), yet *Native Son* remains more than anything else a phenomenological description of the black urban experience. Wright forces us to ask, "What is it like to be thoroughly manipulated by others?" He shifts from historical details of black poverty in Chicago to a startling use of poetry and metaphor—the white world, the racial Other, is presented to Bigger's ravaged consciousness as a natural force like snow, or a blizzard, or a storm; he projects himself into innumerable objects littering the black wasteland of his family—for example, the rat killed in the opening scene—and sees his guilt in the red-hot furnace where he has placed Mary Dalton's decapitated body. Page after page, we are forced to *interpret* everyday phenomena from Bigger's unsteady position in the world, a position of powerlessness, of Pavlovian reactions to whites who are godlike but "blind" to his inner life and humanity, a position where black life is experienced as being predestined for tragedy. On yet another level, the "world" of *Native Son* is that of Greek tragedy, and for this I use John M. Anderson's definition: "The hero [of tragedy] symbolizes participation in a process dominated by what is alien to him";[3] all one must do is replace the gods of Sophocles with modern gods who hide behind such names as "social forces" and "conditioning."

What Wright achieved in *Native Son,* and what no American writer has done quite so well since (including Wright), was the construction of a consistent, coherent, and complete racial universe—Southside Chicago—that is fully shaped by a sensitive if seared black subjectivity. Every prop on the stage of this sustained, brutal thriller refers *back* to Bigger's mind, to his special, twisted way of seeing. Nothing is neutral. Everything is charged by the broken heart and broken mind of a black boy reduced to a state of thinghood. Everything *means* something; every physical, historical object is a metaphor for feeling. Notice the ontology of Bigger's world. It is Manichean. To *be* is to be white. The Daltons' world is pure Being, a plenum, filled to overflowing with its own whiteness, while Bigger's world has a weedlike contingency—is, in fact, relative being. (Yet the alien white world's ways of seeing are *within* Bigger, like a knot in his belly.) This is Plato's world of the Divided Line and the Cave. Furthermore, Bigger is *stained* (sin) by a black body the coloration of which suggests defilement. And his world before the murder is strangely ahistorical, a shadow realm outside time. If *Native Son* is about anything, it is about the drama of consciousness itself, the effort of this boy to come fully aware of the meaning of his life and those around him. We see the "facts" of black Chicago life for the poor in the 1930s: Wright is meticulous with sociological details; he absorbs the information provided by other authors about political and economic disenfranchisement. The book "teaches." But more important than all this reportage is the fact that Wright reminds us through his method here—eidetic description, or presenting things in their lived essence (meaning) for a historical subject—that the world we live in is, first and foremost, one shaped by the mind. A writer reads him with awe. Nowhere does he cheat by resorting to narrative summary, or "telling," when a full, dramatic scene is required to show Bigger's character in and through action. Indeed, the relentless pace of *Native Son* is fueled precisely because most of the book is unmediated scene, as in a play. We see everything. We are forced to be witnesses to every thought and emotion of a national tragedy two centuries in the making. More: it is *we* whom Wright turns into murderers. Wright is shrewd, very cunning as a craftsman, using various forms of repetition (we are forced to review uneasily the details of Mary's murder at least twenty times as that awful event resurfaces in Bigger's mind) to reinforce the novel's dominant impression in a welter of details about race, class, and sexuality. Every writer dreams of achieving this, I believe—a fictional world so fully rendered that even a single glove, as Prosper Mérimée once said, has its theory and reinforces the unifying vision, the truth, of the novel as a whole.

The completeness of Wright's *Native Son* left black writers with the alternatives of repeating that vision in their fiction or grappling again with the perceptual flux of experience that characterizes the black world—and all worlds—to originate new meaning. This, indeed, was the direction taken, and grandly realized, in Ralph Ellison's *Invisible Man* (1952), which has become something of the modern Ur-text for black fiction. Ellison is indebted to Wright for certain themes (blindness, invisibility) and even, I suspect, for certain characters (his Vet greatly resembles the madman in Bigger's cell in book three of *Native Son*); but Ellison conceives his novel in an exuberant Hegelian spirit that traces a nameless black student from one "posture" of twentieth-century black life to another in prose both bewitching and (at times) prolix. And, as if this were not enough, he gives our age a new metaphor for alienation. Every chapter is structured according to the principle of "rising conflict to resolution." The book brims with stylish set pieces: the eviction scene in which every object reveals black history; Ras's monologue to Todd Clifton, which captures the essential thought of Black Nationalism; and allusions to James Joyce's *Portrait of the Artist as a Young Man,* Sigmund Freud, Booker T. Washington, and concerns spanning the Harlem Renaissance and the years following it. Almost everything one could want in a novel or vision is here: humor, suspense, black history from which Ellison's vivid imagination teases forth truth beneath mere facts, and a rogues' gallery of grotesques—Ellison is, one must admit, a sort of intellectual cartoonist when it comes to characterization; his people are, for the most part, principles.

If one must find faults with Ellison's masterpiece, they would be the artistic flaws often found in first novels. His many characters lack individual psychological realism and depth. Their vividness derives from what they represent. Nevertheless, one cannot feel terribly much, for example, about the police slaying of Todd Clifton because really no *one* has died, only the idea of "slipping outside history," which Clifton represents. Like Ellison's people in general, including his protagonist, he is a caricature without a biographical sketch, without background, without the dimensionality we expect in "rounded" characters, and Ellison admits this when he writes, "The blood ran like blood in a comic-book day in a comic-book world." At times, *Invisible Man*'s allegorical level weighs a bit heavily on the story, which becomes top-heavy with symbols (all heaped into the narrator's briefcase, which is itself a symbol from the "Battle Royal" sequence). And Ellison pads out many chapters, milks them, really, with lyricism as a way of marking time when the action slows down or when connections between episodes are tenuous. An example of this would be the moment when his protagonist is released from the factory hospital and the novel structurally breaks in half. Hitherto, his protagonist has been propelled from incident to incident, from Norton to Bledso to Emerson to Liberty Paints, but now he stands directionless on a Harlem street until Mary Rambo, out of the goodness of her heart, takes him in. Or, put differently, the missing chapter called "Out of the Hospital and Under the Bar," if Ellison's editor had included it, would have provided a smoother, energetic flow between chapters eleven and twelve. Also, one must say that *Invisible Man* is a one-idea book that works its magic by carefully unpacking its central idea that meaning cannot be fixed, that Being is formless, a field of imagination and possibility that defies intellectual systemization; and by using Freudian references to the subconscious to demolish first the nineteenth-century bourgeois myths created by Booker T.

Washington, then other naive optimisms of the Industrial Age, and at last the twentieth-century belief in collective action (the Brotherhood, I mean, though Ellison does seem faintly sympathetic to Pan-Africanism as symbolized by Ras) as a panacea for social ills. In this dramatized thesis, Ellison is playing with philosophical fire. But as startling as this faintly existential idea is when powerfully presented in the Rinehart section, Ellison gets the point wrong, or backward: it is not reality or the world that is formless and fluid but human perception—consciousness itself that allows us infinitely to perceive meaning as a phenomenon of change, transformation, and process; it is Mind (the subject pole of experience), not Matter (the object pole), that gives the perceived world a polymorphous character.

At bottom, *Invisible Man* is an outstanding rebellion against all forms of "authority," all "fathers"; against anything that limits Ellison's idea of freedom as equaling the lack of restraints. It is, in a way, the ultimate protest novel. Sadly, though, it leaves his protagonist nowhere to go except outside the lives of others, below the social world, which he lives off parasitically. Even sadder, this primary metaphor—invisibility—seems to force Ellison into a corner where our links to predecessors and contemporaries have been shattered. True, in the epilogue Ellison reaffirms the "principles" of *The Republic,* or plays with such reaffirmation for a paragraph, but the idea hasn't been dramatically earned. Yet, having said all this, I must add that *Invisible Man* is, as critic Roger Sale puts it, one of those rare books that cannot be ignored, and which, I believe, provided an artistic direction for black writing in the 1970s.

The other direction was offered by the Black Arts Movement, a child of Negritude (or at least its first cousin) and Cultural Nationalism.

In her article "The Black Writer and His Role," which appeared in the anthology *The Black Aesthetic* (1972), Carolyn F. Gerald writes:

> I can hold a rose before you; the image of that rose is mirrored in your eyes; it is a real image. Or I can describe a rose for you, and my words will create an image which you can visualize mentally. Perhaps you will even imagine the smell and the feel; the words I choose and the way I build them into the image are evoked, until well-defined patterns of associations based upon sensory perceptions pervade in a very vague way the whole of a man's experience.

Gerald argues that blacks, surrounded by works created by the racial Other, encounter a zero image of themselves and that a program for black cultural reconstruction is required to create positive images. Her article points out important questions of morality and value, for the image as part of our store of knowledge gives form to present perceptual experience and guides anticipation, projection into the future, plans, actions. "The artist, then, is the guardian of image: the writer is the myth-maker of his people." Gerald's insight is fine as far as it goes. It provides an interesting phenomenological foundation for a literary program, but such a program is by no means new. Image control has been the aim of black fiction—and perhaps its problem—from the very beginning of black literary production and was sounded as a specific goal, as noted earlier, during the Harlem Renaissance. Correctly, the Harlem Renaissance writers understood the image to be a workshop of meaning and prehaps even understood that the first step in treating social corruption is treating the corruption of consciousness.

Their original concern with reenvisioning the lived black world touches on the dogged, very noble belief that black people, by virtue of their position in society, are somehow privy to perceptions valuable, even crucial, for fully understanding the structures of the social world. But, after critiquing the images created by the racial Other, after posing the question of black being and language, how do we "guard" the image (or meaning)? Looking back, we see the Harlem Renaissance as a tremendously productive period, and from it emerged such truly important talents as Claude McKay, whose poem "If We Must Die" is a lasting expression of man's determination to endure, one quite as good as, say, William Ernest Henley's "Invictus." But the Harlem Renaissance writers did not so much promote the efflorescence of meaning in black literature and life as they replaced old stereotypes with new ones. In order to consider a more methodological attempt at controlling meaning, it might be helpful to give a furtive glance at the esthetic "philosophy" called Negritude.

The concept of Negritude was developed in the years between 1934 and 1948 by Léopold Sédar Senghor and Aimé Césaire, who were, as it turned out, admirers of Claude McKay. With Leon Damas they founded the journal *L'Étudiant Noir* and nurtured a literary movement memorable for its attempt to give authenticity to a unique African personality. Writing in "The Psychology of the African Negro" (1959), Senghor asserted that "Negro reason . . . is not, as one might guess, the discursive reason of Europe, *reason through sight,* but *reason through touch. . . .*" He added, "European reason is analytic through utilization; Negro reason is intuitive through participation." Finally, he stated that "the African Negro reacts more easily to excitements; he espouses naturally the rhythm of the object. This sensual feeling of *rhythm* is one of his specific characteristics."

For Senghor, "Emotion was Negroid," and by emotion he meant a sympathetic, even magical grasp of the world. Generally speaking, this is the spirit, or *élan,* of Negritude. According to Janheinz Jahn in *Neo-African Literature* (1966), the term "Negritude" broadly covered several meanings: (1) It was to be an instrument for liberation. (2) It was an incantatory approach to poetry that called forth the essence of things. (3) It was more often the style, feeling, and vision of a poetical work than its content. (4) It was rhythm sprung from deep emotion and feeling states, and from humor. (5) It was sympathy in contrast to understanding. (6) It was the self-affirmation of blackness. (7) It was also skin coloration and the shared experience of oppression. And finally, (8) it was the *élan* of African civilization. Obviously, these ideas presuppose what they are supposed to explain. Africa, for example, is not a homogeneous culture, and it has its own history of oppression; it is, rather, a diverse ensemble of cultures. Oppression is shared across racial lines, involving, among others, the Jews of Europe and native Americans. Skin coloration cannot be regarded as a criterion, for among Indians, both American and Hindu, and Orientals, dark pigmentation is also found. Sympathetic feeling, far from distinguishing the African personality from that of the European (equated with reason, analysis), is noetic—that is, feeling states, as Heidegger demonstrates in *Being and Time,* are not easily counterpoised to reason, which also bears an affective tone (*Begriffsgefühl*).[4] What we have in Negritude, I suspect, is an inversion of black typifications derived from earlier white stereotypes. What is interesting in Senghor's explanation is that his dualism is almost Cartesian at times. He equates consciousness, *res cogitantes,* with Europe and the disembodied mind while he equates the body and its vegetable and mineral processes with Africa. He assumes racial essences that are timeless and ahistorical; in fact, for Senghor, black people seem to be less historical beings than metaphysical types.

Yet if Negritude is found wanting, it was nevertheless a well-intended effort to correct destructive racial images. The primary aim was to profile the African personality as spiritual. The African universe, according to Negritude, is full of "forces," one of which is man. A hierarchy exists, laddering forces such that at the apex is a supreme force, and below this supreme force are others of lesser efficacy that serve as intermediaries between man and God. Comparing the Afro-American concept of "soul" to Negritude, Stephen Henderson, in *The Militant Black Writer in Africa and the United States* (1969), says that both emphasize intuition, dance, the power of words, wholeness, and harmony. However, that emphasis on communalism and anti-individualism, if we look hard enough at it, trivializes the role of the very person Negritude wishes to elevate. Negritude's theory of "forces" is fairly close to the doctrine of Neoplatonism, such that the African Lifeworld is vibrant with divinity. There's really nothing wrong with this. But it is not philosophy. We have a doctrine, not analysis. My own feeling leads me to believe that Negritude's failure is the failure of all Kitsch. In *The Meaning of Modern Art,* philosopher Karsten Harries defines Kitsch this way: "In dread of freedom man pretends that the meanings with which he has endowed the world transcend their creator."[5] Surely everyone can see that the situation most characterizing our age is the fact that everything, even God, has been reduced since the Cartesian revolution to an *object* for the ego. Nothing can *be* an object unless it be for consciousness, a perceiving subject, which means the world and everything in it bears our own face, our limits, dreams, hopes. Yet Harries writes, "Unlike most modern art, which betrays the precariousness of its project, Kitsch seems to be sure of itself. Kitsch pretends to be in possession of an adequate image of man. Most modern art is too self-conscious to be that confident. . . ." Harries argues that it is precisely a lack of clarity about the world's meaning that grounds one's freedom. "To be free," he says, "is to be capable of determining, at least to some extent, what one is to be." Like fascist art in Germany during the 1930s, Negritude—all Kitsch—is a retreat from ambiguity, the complexity of Being occasioned by the conflict of interpretations, and a flight by the black artist from the agony of facing a universe silent as to its sense, where even black history (or all history) must be seen as an ensemble of experiences and documents difficult to read, indeed, as an experience capable of inexhaustible readings. But Negritude, in one incarnation or another, as one answer to the problem of controlling meaning, still exerts in the 1980s a strong influence on contemporary black literary production.

Amiri Baraka (LeRoi Jones) is perhaps the most important single figure in contemporary black arts and letters for the theoretical development of Negritude after Césaire and Senghor. It is this remarkably talented man who in "black writing," an article among his social essays in *Home* (1966), says:

> I think though that there are now a great many young black writers in America who do realize that their customary isolation from the mainstream is a valuable way into any description they might make of America. In fact, it is just this alienation that should serve to make a very powerful American literature, since its hypothetical writers function in many senses within the main structure of the

American society as well. The Negro, as he exists in America now, and has always existed in this place (certainly after formal slavery), is a natural nonconformist. Being black in a society where such a state is an extreme liability is the most extreme form of nonconformity available. The point is, of course, that nonconformity should be put to use. The vantage point is classically perfect—outside and inside at the same time. Think of the great Irish writers—Wilde, Yeats, Shaw, Synge, Joyce, O'Casey, Beckett, etc.—and their clear and powerful understanding (social as well as aesthetic) of where they were and how they could function inside and outside the imaginary English society, even going so far as teaching the mainstreamers their own language, and revitalizing it in the doing.

Baraka placed his finger perfectly on the role all "outsiders" have played in respect to a host society: "outside and inside at the same time," and thereby capable of the observations and omniscience neither group—black or white—can generate from its center. And, as Baraka knew in his earlier days, Caliban is ironically empowered to revitalize Prospero's tongue, teaching perhaps whites the secrets of their own speech and way of seeing. Yes, this is fine indeed, but this essay is early Baraka. Like many other talented writers, he was destined to endure many changes over the years that followed its publication. By 1968, in a decade full of political assassinations, an unpopular war, and a new militancy, Baraka, like many others, was thrust completely "outside" the mainstream. In the weird, self-flagellating days of the 1960s, the dominant themes in black arts and letters were paranoia and genocide. The "evidence" for a black American holocaust seemed irrefutable. On the historical side, three centuries' worth of grim documentation, new histories such as those of Stanley M. Elkins and Eugene Genovese drove home the sense that black history was, and might always be, a slaughterhouse—a form of being characterized by stasis, denial, humiliation, dehumanization, and "relative being." Toomer had died in anonymity, an underpublished writer living out his last years in a rest home. Ellison was silent. Both Wright, in self-exile in France, and Du Bois, who became a citizen of Ghana after almost a century of struggling for civil rights, had given up on America. It isn't difficult to see why. Children were dynamited in black churches, militants and pacifists both were murdered in their sleep, or blown off balconies, or set up by the FBI. It was a period when John A. Williams, in *The Man Who Cried I Am,* could write powerfully of the secret "King Alfred plan" to contain blacks during riots; when in Chicago the Black People's Topographical Library held back-room lectures (no whites allowed) on how in most cities blacks were concentrated in ghettos alongside broad freeways and through which ran railroad lines that would be used by government troops and tanks to seal us off during the "long, hot summers"; when Sam Greenlee's clumsily written *The Spook Who Sat by the Door* (1969) became the most unexpected bestseller of the early 1970s because, as one friend told me, young blacks read it to gain recipes for insurrection. (That same friend's leg was blown up—so the story was related to me—when he attempted to plant a homemade bomb in the administration building at the college we attended.) Every new incident, every experience reinforced the idea that if we stayed in America, if the old order of oppression could not be changed, we would one day again be in chains. My African friends, I learned, lived (and still live) in fear that recolonization of the African continent was just around the corner. For a young writer, these political and literary changes, which were often more symbolic than substantive, produced vertigo: that old standby periodical, *Negro Digest,* a forum for fiction and essays, transmogrified into *Black World,* and hardly an issue passed that did not feature a proponent of either Black or Cultural Nationalism. If one had even the slightest concern, or sensitivity, or distaste for injustice, one could not help being caught up in this confusion, the polarization of black and white, young and old, middle class and poor. The pressure to write "politically" was (and still is) tremendous, though little of this fiction survives today, its character—I know from experience—being less that of enduring art than that of journalism hastily written at the front, hammered out in reaction to fast-breaking (bad) news. The age produced, if you will, a new racial melodrama, or recycled the old ones of the nineteenth century with a new cast: racist spider-bellied cops, noble revolutionaries. You know this crew. No question that some black authors held fast during those trying years to produce balanced, responsible, well-crafted fiction that revealed both life's failures and its triumphs, but the air we breathed was too thick with pain for careful fiction to move center stage—as philosopher William Earle once wrote in *Public Sorrows and Private Pleasures,* "Who has the wind to shout a *qualified* thought?"[6] And one of the most powerful literary voices that reached our constantly ringing ears was Amiri Baraka's.

Theodore R. Hudson explains in *From LeRoi Jones to Amiri Baraka* (1973) that in Harlem, Baraka was instrumental in founding the Black Arts Repertory Theatre and School. Earlier, in 1927, Alain Locke had argued in "The Negro and the American Theatre" that the future of black theater was in the folk play, which expressed the beauty and colorful aspects of black life. But the essay, "The Black Arts Movement" (1968) by Larry Neal, one of the most highly respected theoreticians of the 1960s, indicates some forty years later that the perception of the Negro had changed, and so had his drama. Neal identified Baraka as the prime mover behind this new theater, a theater obligated above all else to *teach.* Baraka's theater was to be owned and operated only by black people. Although the theater later failed, Baraka was well on his way to immersing himself in the Black Power struggle of the late 1960s and formulating key ideas for the Black Arts Movement, its literary sister.

Baraka moved into Newark politics, established Spirit House, and developed a close relationship with Ron Karenga, then head of the militant, nationalist, self-defense organization called US. (They were brought together as early as 1967 at San Francisco State College.) For Karenga, in his essay "Black Cultural Nationalism" (1968), black art was part of the revolutionary machinery of change. It was to be judged on two levels—the social and the artistic—and for Karenga the social was primary. Technical innovation and linguistic inventiveness he considered superfluous. He argued that black art must be (1) functional, (2) collective, and (3) committed. It must "expose the enemy, praise the people, and support the revolution." Clearly, Karenga's art is agitprop and Kitsch. There are enormous problems with the apparently deathless idea that art must be "useful," especially useful to some passing social or political trend, and that it is only, as Karenga once said, "everyday life given more form and color." This is wrong. This is patently false, and I repeat these embarrassing ideas not to hold Karenga up to ridicule but only to trace to its source—or run into the ground—a form of silliness that spoils too many discussions of black fiction. Art is not *useful* in the sense that a commodity is useful (though publishers and movie producers are inclined, as they must be, to treat it as such), and art has no business begging for approval or acceptance on these terms. Although Sartre claims in *What Is Literature?* that words can be picked up by desperate men and used as a neutral tool or weapon, which is the thought behind Karenga's idea, and behind all nationalist art, the truth is otherwise: we live in language. It works upon us as we upon it—like the presence of another person before us, which in fact it, as a work of consciousness, indirectly is. The work of art raises around itself a special esthetic attitude, or intention of listening in which we momentarily leave the Natural Attitude of utility.

Nevertheless, throughout the late 1960s and the 1970s Baraka seemed indefatigable, the busiest black lecturer, teacher, and organizer in memory, and more will undoubtedly have been added to his unique story by the time you read this. My own contact with Baraka has, regrettably, been limited to the auditorium, but I must admit that no other speaker has moved me quite so thoroughly. Flanked by guards wearing dashikis (this in 1969), Baraka read poetry—sang it, really—that was intended to indict, arouse, and incite his audience, which it did; he answered no questions from whites; he urged young black artists to bring their talent back to the black community and, leaving, carried away the breath of the young, impressionable audience with him. He acquired dozens of black imitators. In Newark he organized the Black Community Development and Defense Organization, and his efforts eventually aided the election of black mayor Kenneth Gibson.

Baraka's ever-evolving work includes numerous plays; collections of poems and essays and stories; a novel, *The System of Dante's Hell* (1966); political tracts and essays such as "A Black Value System" (1970); and propaganda plays such as *A Black Mass* (1969), in which he uses the Nation of Islam's myth of Yacub to explain the origin of the white race and describes time as a European invention. With Larry Neal he coedited the controversial 1968 anthology *Black Fire* (recalling the Harlem Renaissance magazine *Fire*), which profiled the new black esthetics. It is Baraka, I believe, who for the most part established the style of Cultural Nationalist poetics in the period between 1960 and 1970—for an entire generation of writers, though his thought moves some distance from Negritude, drawing heavily at times on the Marxist critique of culture and economics, and occasionally from Wittgenstein in a few of his esthetic arguments. By *some* standard, Baraka is a genius. There is from the very beginning a tension in his thought between modern leftist intellectualism and race politics, between international Marxism and black nationalism—a classic conflict described by Cruse, by Wright in his autobiographical *American Hunger* (1977), and by Ellison; it is Du Bois's famous problem of the Negro who "ever feels his twoness—an American, a Negro; two souls, two thoughts, two unreconciled strivings; two warring ideals in one dark body, whose dogged strength alone keeps it from being torn asunder." The sense of black literature since the 1960s, what it means for a literary work to be socially relevant, owes much to Baraka and his followers, and we shall not be free of this art-as-weapon conception for some time. Thousands of black writers breathed the politico-esthetic atmosphere of the 1960s, a field in which Baraka was very visible as one of the angriest, most charismatic black writers; and elements of that field are still discernible in the work of younger poets and writers—male and female—working toward control of images and meaning in the 1970s and even into the 1980s. We see the influence of its odd anti-intellectualism in the late, gifted poet Henry Dumas, who eschews thought and reflection for the immediacy of feeling:

> I flew into the country of the mind
> And there my wings froze.
> I fell.
> Thought sculpted me in stone.

Dumas was, or worked at being, a mythologist. He embraced, as Carolyn Rodgers wished, African values as interpreted by Western blacks and used them to evoke a world in which everything is an essence, not existence. Objects and others, as in medieval allegorical art, *are* their names and meanings. Poet Michael Harper's views are related to Negritude's emphasis on spirituality as well, but for Harper, in his interview in *Interviews with Black Writers* (1973), the term "modality" (made to function in both a musical and a metaphysical way) best describes the Real:

> Modality assumes many things which society has not fully understood, although there are singular members of the society who do accept them. Number one is that man is basically spiritual. Second is that one has a "holistic" concept of the universe. This means that the universe is not fragmented, that man has a place in it, that man is a reflection of the environment, and that the environment is a reflection of man. John Coltrane was a modal musician.

For many of the post-1960s writers, the black musician is, possibly, closer to the Real than the writer is. In Dumas's story "Will the Circle Be Unbroken?" (1966), the musician Probe plays music so indigenous to the black world that it kills white members of the audience. Improvisation and spontaneity, which supposedly express feelings as they occur, are taken to be fundamental to African music and the African personality.

Black music, these thinkers argued, developed improvisation, encouraged audience participation (call-response patterns), and remained linked to functional and religious occasions. Where music was a "thing" in the West, fixed and made permanent by a text, in the black world it is short-lived deliberately, unrepeatable, and the product of spontaneity. (See, for example, Ishmael Reed's *Mumbo Jumbo,* where a search occurs for what is called "The Text," which is destroyed at the novel's end, thereby liberating man. One must also mention here James Baldwin's short story "Sonny's Blues" [1957], with its triumphant conclusion that fuses jazz, character, and racial as well as spiritual redemption in a single, masterfully evoked scene when the narrator's brother, Sonny, plays in a Harlem nightclub.) Such modern jazz musicians as Ornette Coleman, Cecil Taylor, John Coltrane, Sonny Rollins, and Sun Ra were paradigmatic artists for the cultural-nationalist writers. In this connection, one black writer even argued for the "destruction of text" in poetry. By this was meant that, although a poem was written on the page, it was not to be permanently fixed; from one reading to the next, the poem was to be deliberately altered, changed to accommodate the poet's shifting moods and those of the audience, which "participated" in the poem's spontaneous creation.

To sum up, black writers are concerned with the meaning of the black world, and this concern in literature and life has led to the creation of various racial ideologies for the African experience. In a strange way, these esthetics are seamless. They are founded on what seems at first blush a non-European theory of man, Nature, and social life, although this soon shows itself to be deceptive, insofar as European philosophies are diverse, some involving process (Whitehead) and a nonfragmentary sense of Being. There is an almost point-by-point correspondence among esthetics, social theory, and the conception of humanity here; but let us come down to cases: the problem with all this is that it is ideology. While ideology may create a fascinating vision of the universe, and also fascinating literary movements, it closes off the free investigation of phenomena. The many elements in the mix of any ideology (for example, the notion of communalism) are often unanalyzed or rest on appeals to faith or authority or one of the several logical fallacies, and the meanings of such crucial terms are seldom defined with precision. Such esthetics are beyond critical analysis, for they are, if nothing else, fervently held forms of belief. Finally, while philosophical inquiry is devoted to understanding, a process that may or may not lead to political change, ideology must ever be geared toward action, making the reader *do* something.

And from a phenomenological perspective something very peculiar happens to consciousness with Cultural Nationalism. In his essay "The Primeval Mitosis" (1968), Eldridge Cleaver broached the stereotype of black American physicality by checking his own feelings against this myth and concluded, "The gulf between the Mind and Body will be seen to coincide with the gulf between the two races." Cleaver, focusing on one aspect of our lived experience of the body, the psychophysical, claimed the blacks were stripped of a mental life, leaving them only a bodily existence in the West—the *way* blacks are culturally intended by whites—though this bodily existence is a superior one. He assigns blacks the name "The Supermasculine Menial." And he writes, "The body is tropical, warm, hot; Fire! It is soft, pleasing to the touch, luscious to the kiss. The blood is hot. Muscles are strength." Alienated from this sensuous profile of the body, whites are characterized by Cleaver as "The Omnipotent Administrator." Weakness, frailty, cowardice, effeminacy, decay, and impotency are profiles associated with the white man's situation of abstraction from the body. Obviously, these are crude, broadly drawn outlines of our experience of the body, but Cleaver's remarks are often echoed in many black folktales that present the sexual or physical prowess of black males and in Fanon's statement in *The Wretched of the Earth* that "there are times when the black man is locked into his body," or the physical.

In my own essay "The Primeval Mitosis: A Phenomenology of the Black Body" (1976), I attempt to develop Cleaver's idea by tracing its origins to the Cartesian bifurcation of *res cogitantes* and *res extensae,* and of course to the more primordial Platonic dualism, indicating how Western ontological divisions between higher (spirit) and lower (body) coupled with Christian symbologies for light and dark develop the black body as being in a state of "stain." "The Negro suffers in his body quite differently from the white man," Fanon wrote, and this is so insofar as we have attributed to blacks the contents that white consciousness itself fears to contain and confront: bestiality, uncleanliness, criminality, all the purported "dark things." In R. W. Shufeldt's *The Negro, a Menace to Civilization* (1907) and Thomas Dixon, Jr.'s *The Leopard's Spots* (1902), the idea is extended to include black blood, which carries the germ of the underworld and the traits of lower orders of animals; one drop of black blood, for example, will cause a white family to revert to Negroid characteristics even after a full century; the mulatto, though possessing white blood, is depicted as dangerous precisely because his "outside," not being stained, betrays the criminality and animality of his interior.

And consider the concern black people of earlier generations had with body complexion, "brightening the race" through careful marriage, the terrible importance of fair skin, curly hair, and "yellah women." They were not fools, those old folks; they knew what they experienced—and understood skin-bleaching creams and straightening combs as important because these changed their stained "outsides," by which, in this social system, the depth of their "insides" would be gauged by others. (Indeed, Robert Bone has called Christianity in James Baldwin's *Go Tell It on the Mountain* [1953] a "spiritual bleaching cream.") Stain recalls defilement, symbols of guilt, sin, corpses that contaminate, menstruating women; and with them come the theological meanings of punishment, ostracism, and the need to be "cleansed."

Black literature abounds with faintly Hegelian variations on the phenomenon of the black body as stained. Once you are so one-sidedly seen by the white Other, you have the option of (a) accepting this being seen from the outside and craftily using the "invisibility" of your interior to deceive, and thus to win survival as the folk hero Trickster John does in the "Old Marster and John" cycle. In this case, stain is like the heavy makeup of a clown; it conceals you completely. The motto of this useful opacity is the rhyme "Got one mind for whitefolks to see/Got another one that's really me"—that is, not being acknowledged as a subject is your strength, your chance for cunning and masquerade, for guerrilla warfare; you are a spy, so to speak, in the Big House. You cynically play with the frozen intentions of whites, their presuppositions and stereotypes; you shuffle or appear lazy to avoid work, or—if you are modern—you manipulate their basic fear of you as Darkness and Brute Power to win concessions. It is what Ellison calls "Rinehartism" in *Invisible Man*. It is the tactic taken by Cross Damon in Wright's *The Outsider* (1953) when Damon, after he is freed from his former life by a train wreck and begins to construct a new identity for himself, must secure a false birth certificate and thinks, "He would have to present to the officials a Negro so scared and ignorant that no white man would ever dream that he was up to anything deceptive."

Or you may (b) seize this situation at its roots by reversing the negative meaning of the black body. "It is beautiful," you might say, "I am a child of the Sun." The situation of the black-as-body possessing noncognitive traits is not here—in Cultural Nationalism—rejected, but rather stood on its head: the meaning still issues, of course, from the white Other. You applaud your athletic, amorous, and dancing abilities, your street wisdom and *savoir faire*, your "soul," the food your body eats; you speak of the communal (single-body) social life of your African ancestors before the fifteenth-century slave trade, their bodily closeness to the earth. You are Antaeus in this persuasion of the alienated black self's phenomenological pilgrimage to itself, and the whites—flesh-starved invaders, freebooters, buccaneers, seamen who bring syphilis to ancient Alkebu-lan—are alienated physically from the earth. They see their lost humanity in you. They steal you to take it home. If you are a member of the early Nation of Islam and believe in the mythology of Yacub, the black scientist who created a "white Beast" from the black community, you intend whites as quasi men "grafted" from the original black-as-body until, by degrees, the Caucasian appears as a pale and pitiful abstraction from yourself, ontologically removed several stages from the basic reality you represent.

This control and reconstitution of images, which arises out of the noble work of counteracting cultural lies, easily slips toward dogma that ends the process of literary discovery. In short, toward Kitsch. The Black Aesthetic culminated, curiously, in a devotedness to God and Country. The god, however, is plural, manifested in all beings; and the country, regrettably, refers to a black nation-state that exists only in the minds of the nationalists. It must be said, however, that the Cultural Nationalists and image controllers wished to be—and many are—moral men and women. In his essay "Richard Wright's Blues" (1945), Ellison borrows the term "pre-individual" from critic Edward Bland to describe the black community. Bland is quoted:

> In the pre-individualistic thinking of the Negro stress is on the group. Instead of seeing in terms of the individual, the Negro sees in terms of "races," masses of people separated from other masses of people according to color. Hence, an act bears intent against him as a Negro individual. He is singled out not as a person but as a specimen of an ostracized group. He knows that he never exists in his own right but only to the extent that others hope to make the race suffer vicariously through him.

Throughout the control-of-images argument, Negritude, and Cultural Nationalism, this "pre-individualistic" tendency emerges again and again. "The pre-individualistic black," writes Ellison, "discourages individuality out of self-defense. Having learned through experience that the whole group is punished for the actions of the single member, it has worked out efficient techniques for behavior control." Obviously, it cannot be through such ideologies that genuine creative work is achieved. Rather, all presuppositions, all theories, must be suspended before experience and meaning can be brought forth in black literary art.

NOTES

1. André Malraux, *The Voices of Silence*, trans. Stuart Gilbert (New York: Doubleday, 1953), p. 281.
2. *The Collected Dialogues of Plato*, ed. Edith Hamilton and Huntington Cairns (Princeton: Princeton University Press, 1961), p. 284.
3. John M. Anderson, "The Source of Tragedy," in *An Invitation to Phenomenology*, ed. James Edie (Chicago: Quadrangle, 1965).
4. Martin Heidegger, *Being and Time*, trans. John Macquarrie and Edward Robinson (New York: Harper and Row, 1963), p. 179. I refer the interested reader to the entirety of section 30 in chapter five, where "fear" as a phenomenon-disclosing intention is discussed.
5. Karsten Harries, *The Meaning of Modern Art* (Evanston: Northwestern University Press, 1968), p. 158.
6. William Earle, *Public Sorrows and Private Pleasures* (Bloomington: Indiana University Press, 1976), p. 66. In his first section, "Ideology," Earle provides an extensive, eloquent, and, one might add, hilarious critique of philosophical errors in the rhetoric of the 1960s.

Hazel V. Carby (1948–)

A *respected contemporary critic and professor of English and Afro-American studies at Yale University, Hazel V. Carby received her master's in 1979 and her doctorate in cultural studies in 1984 from Birmingham University in the United Kingdom.*

Carby has published many articles on black culture, African American literature, and gender politics. She edited The Empire Strikes Back: Race and Racism in Seventies Britain *(1982) and wrote* Reconstructing Womanhood: The Emergence of the Afro-American Woman Novelist *(1987). Presently, she is working on two other books*—Race Men: Genealogies of Race, Nation, and Manhood *and* Black Women, Migration, and the Formation of a Blues Culture. *Her scholarly papers have been presented at various institutions in the United States, Italy, Australia, and England. Between 1988 and 1993, she was honored as a fellow and lecturer at Wesleyan University, University of Chicago, Washington State University, and Harvard University. She also serves on the editorial boards of* Differences: A Journal of Gender and Culture, Diaspora: A Journal of Transnational Studies, *and the* Yale Journal of Criticism, *among others.*

The following selection is the opening chapter to Reconstructing Womanhood. *In "Rethinking Black Feminist Theory," Carby considers contributions of such critical thinkers as Frances Harper, Anna Julia Cooper, Barbara Smith, Mary Helen Washington, Alice Walker, Barbara Christian, and Deborah McDowell to evaluate the evolution of African American feminist theory in literature and criticism.*

Rethinking Black Feminist Theory

On May 20, 1893, Frances Harper addressed the World's Congress of Representative Women assembled as part of the Columbian Exposition in Chicago. She encouraged her audience to see themselves standing "on the threshold of woman's era" and urged that they be prepared to receive the "responsibility of political power."[1] Harper was the last of six black women to address the delegates; on the previous two days Fannie Barrier Williams, Anna Julia Cooper, Fannie Jackson Coppin, Sarah J. Early, and Hallie Quinn Brown had been the black spokeswomen at this international but overwhelmingly white women's forum. Williams spoke of the women "for whom real ability, virtue, and special talents count for nothing when they become applicants for respectable employment" and asserted that black women were increasingly "a part of the social forces that must help to determine the questions that so concern women generally."[2] Anna Julia Cooper described the black woman's struggle for sexual autonomy as "a struggle against fearful and overwhelming odds, that often ended in a horrible death. . . . The painful, patient, and silent toil of mothers to gain a fee simple title to the bodies of their daughters, the despairing fight . . . to keep hallow their own persons." She contrasted the white woman who "could at least plead for her own emancipation" to the black women of the South who have to "suffer and struggle and be silent" and made her concluding appeal to "the solidarity of humanity, the oneness of life, and the unnaturalness and injustice of all special favoritisms, whether of sex, race, country, or condition."[3] Fannie

Jackson Coppin declared that the conference should not be "indifferent to the history of the colored women of America," for their fight could only aid all women in their struggle against oppression," and Sarah J. Early and Hallie Quinn Brown gave detailed accounts of the organizations that black women had established.[4]

It appeared that the Columbian Exposition had provided the occasion for women in general and black women in particular to gain a space for themselves in which they could exert a political presence. However, for black women the preparations for the World's Congress had been a disheartening experience, and the World's Congress itself proved to be a significant moment in the history of the uneasy relations between organized black and white women. Since emancipation black women had been active within the black community in the formation of mutual-aid societies, benevolent associations, local literary societies, and the many organizations of the various black churches, but they had also looked toward the nationally organized suffrage and temperance movements, dominated by white women, to provide an avenue for the expression of their particular concerns as women and as feminists. The struggle of black women to achieve adequate representation within the women's suffrage and temperance movements had been continually undermined by a pernicious and persistent racism, and the World's Congress was no exception. While Harper, Williams, Cooper, Coppin, Early, and Brown were on the women's platform, Ida B. Wells was in the Haitian pavilion protesting the virtual exclusion of Afro-Americans from the exposition, circulating the pamphlet she had edited, *The Reason Why: The Colored American Is Not in the World's Columbian Exposition*.[5]

The fight for black representation had begun at the presidential level with an attempt to persuade Benjamin Harrison to appoint a black member to the National Board of Commissioners for the exposition. The president's intransigent refusal to act led the black community to focus their hopes on the Board of Lady Managers appointed to be "the channel of communication through which all women may be brought into relation with the exposition, and through which all applications for space for the use of women or their exhibits in the buildings shall be made."[6] Two organizations of black women were formed, the Woman's Columbian Association and the Women's Columbian Auxiliary Association, and both unsuccessfully petitioned the Board of Lady Managers to establish mechanisms of representation for black Americans. Sympathetic sentiments were expressed by a few members of the board, but no appointment was made, and some members of the board threatened to resign rather than work with a black representative. Indeed, the general belief of the board members was that black women were incapable of any organized critique of their committee and that a white woman must be behind such "articulate and sustained protests."[7] The fact that six black women eventually addressed the World's Congress was not the result of a practice of sisterhood or evidence of a concern to provide a black political presence but part of a discourse of exoticism that pervaded the fair. Black Americans were included in a highly selective manner as part of exhibits with other ethnic groups which reinforced conventional racist attitudes of the American imagination. The accommodation of racial diversity in ethnic villages at the fair was an attempt to scientifically legitimate racist assumptions, and, as one historian notes, "the results were devastating not only for American blacks, Native Americans, and the Chinese, but also for other non-white peoples of the world."[8]

The Columbian Exposition was widely regarded as "the greatest fair in history."[9] The "White City," symbol of American progress, was built to house the exposition in Jackson Park on the shores of Lake Michigan in Chicago. It has been characterized by a contemporary cultural critic as simultaneously "a fitting conclusion of an age" and the inauguration of another. "It lays bare a plan for a future. Like the Gilded Age, White City straddles a divide: a consummation and a new beginning."[10] For black Americans it was "literally and figuratively a White City" which symbolized "not the material progress of America, but a moral regression—the reconciliation of the North and South at the expense of Negroes."[11] At the time, black visitors expressed their resentment at their virtual exclusion by renaming the fair "the great American white elephant" and "the white American's World's Fair"; Frederick Douglass, attending the fair as commissioner from Haiti, called the exposition "a whited sepulcher."[12] The Columbian Exposition embodied the definitive failure of the hopes of emancipation and reconstruction and inaugurated an age that was to be dominated by "the problem of the color-line."[13]

To appear as a black woman on the platform of the Congress of Representative Women was to be placed in a highly contradictory position, at once part of and excluded from the dominant discourse of white women's politics. Contradictions . . . were experienced by these women and other black women who tried to establish a public presence in the nineteenth century. . . . The arguments are theoretical and political, responding to contemporary black and white feminist cultural politics. The historical and literary analyses are materialist, interpreting individual texts in relation to the dominant ideological and social formations in which they were produced. [There are] four major concerns.

First, in order to gain a public voice as orators or published writers, black women had to confront the dominant domestic ideologies and literary conventions of womanhood which excluded them from the definition "woman." . . . These ideologies of womanhood . . . were adopted, adapted, and transformed to effectively represent the material conditions of black women, and . . . black women intellectuals reconstructed the sexual ideologies of the nineteenth century to produce an alternative discourse of black womanhood.

Second, [there are] questions [surrounding] those strands of contemporary feminist historiography and literary criticism which seek to establish the existence of an American sisterhood between black and white women. Considering the history of the failure of any significant political alliances between black and white women in the nineteenth century, I challenge the impulse in the contemporary women's movement to discover a lost sisterhood and to reestablish feminist solidarity. Individual white women helped publish and promote individual black women, but the texts of black women from ex-slave Harriet Jacobs to educator Anna Julia Cooper are testaments to the racist practices of the suffrage and temperance movements and indictments of the ways in which white women allied themselves not with black women but with a racist patriarchal order against all black people. Only by confronting this history of difference can we hope to understand the boundaries that separate white feminists from all women of color.[14]

Third, though Afro-American cultural and literary history commonly regards the late nineteenth and early twentieth centuries in terms of great men, as the Age of Washington and Du Bois, marginalizing the political contributions of black women, these were the years of the first flowering of black women's autonomous organizations and a period of intense intellectual activity and productivity. . . . The literary contributions of Frances Harper and Pauline Hopkins and the political writings of Anna Julia Cooper and Ida B. Wells . . . reconstruct our view of this period. Writing in the midst of a new "black women's renaissance," the contemporary world of academia, publishing, and Hollywood—marked by the celebrity of Alice Walker and Toni Morrison— . . . [establishes] the existence of an earlier and perhaps more politically resonant renaissance [for rethinking] the cultural politics of black women.

Fourth . . . is [the] literary history of the emergence of black women as novelists. To understand the first novels which were written at the end of the nineteenth century, one has to understand not only the discourse and context in which they were produced but also the intellectual forms and practices of black women that preceded them: . . . narratives of slave and free women, the relation of political lecturing to the politics of fiction, and a variety of essay, journalistic, and magazine writing. Consequently, [my concern here] is not [with] conventional literary history, nor is it limited to drawing on feminist or black feminist literary theories, but it is [the] cultural history and critique of the forms in which black women intellectuals made political as well as literary interventions in the social formations in which they lived.

Two fields of academic inquiry [have recently] emerged: black feminist literary criticism and black women's history. As a first step toward assessing what has come to be called black feminist theory, I want to consider its history and to analyze its major tendencies.

It is now a decade since Barbara Smith published "Toward a Black Feminist Criticism" (1977), addressing the conditions of both politics and literature that she felt could provide the necessary basis for an adequate consideration of black women's literature.[15] Smith argued that since the "feminist movement was an essential precondition to the growth of feminist literature, criticism, and women's studies," the lack of an autonomous black feminist movement contributed to the neglect of black women writers and artists, there being no "political movement to give power or support to those who want to examine Black women's experience." Hence, without a political movement there was no black feminist political theory to form a basis for a critical approach to the art of black women. Smith argued for the development of both the political movement and the political theory so that a black feminist literary criticism would embody "the realization that the politics of sex as well as the politics of race and class are crucially interlocking factors in the works of Black women writers" (170). To support her argument, Smith indicted a variety of male critics and white feminist critics for their sexist and racist assumptions which prevented the critical recognition of the importance of the work of black women writers.

In many ways, "Toward a Black Feminist Criticism" acted as a manifesto for black feminist critics, stating both the principles and the conditions of their work. Smith argued that a black feminist approach should have a primary commitment to the exploration of the interrelation of sexual and racial politics and that black and female identities were "inextricable elements in Black women's writings." Smith also asserted that a black feminist critic should "work from the assumption that Black women writers constitute an identifiable literary tradition" (174).

Smith was convinced that it was possible to reveal a verifiable literary tradition because of the common experience of the writers and the shared use of a black female language.

> The use of Black women's language and cultural experience in books *by* Black women *about* Black women results in a miraculously rich coalescing of form and content and also takes their writing far beyond the confines of white/male literary structures. The Black feminist critic would find innumerable commonalities in works by Black women. (174)

A second principle that Smith proposed to govern black feminist critical practice was the establishment of precedents and insights in interpretation within the works of other black women. The critic should write and think "out of her own identity," asserted Smith, the implication being that the identity of the critic would be synonymous with that of the author under scrutiny. The identities that most concerned Smith were those of a black feminist and a black lesbian. The principles of interpretation that she employed, she hoped, would combine to produce a new methodology, a criticism that was innovative and constantly self-conscious of the relationship between its own perspective and the political situation of all black women. Black feminist criticism, in Smith's terms was defined as being both dependent on and contributing to a black feminist political movement (175). Convinced of the possibilities for radical change, Smith concluded that it was possible to undertake a "total reassessment of Black literature and literary history needed to reveal the Black woman-identified woman" (182–83).

Smith's essay was an important statement that made visible the intense repression of the black female and lesbian voice. As a critical manifesto it represented a radical departure from the earlier work of Mary Helen Washington, who had edited the first contemporary anthology of black women's fiction, *Black-Eyed Susans,* two years earlier.[16] Washington did not attempt to define, explicitly, a black feminist critical perspective but concentrated on recovering and situating the neglected fiction of black women writers and establishing the major themes and images for use in a teaching situation.[17] However, there are major problems with Smith's essay as a critical manifesto, particularly in its assertion of the existence of an essential black female experience and an exclusive black female language in which this experience is embodied. Smith's essay assumes a very simple one-to-one correspondence between fiction and reality, and her model of a black feminist critical perspective is undermined as a political practice by being dependent on those who are, biologically, black and female. For Smith, her reliance on common experiences confines black feminist criticism to black women critics of black women artists depicting black women. This position can lead to the political cul de sac identified by Alice Walker as a problem of white feminist criticism in her essay "One Child of One's Own."[18] Walker criticized the position taken by Patricia Meyer Spacks, in the introduction to her book *The Female Imagination,* where she justified her concentration on the lives of white middle-class women by reiterating Phyllis Chesler's comment: "I have no theory to offer of Third World female psychology in America. . . . As a white woman, I'm reluctant and unable to construct theories about experiences I haven't had." To which Spacks added, "So am I." Walker challenged Spack's exclusive concentration on white middle-class writers by asking:

> Why only these? Because they are white, and middle class, and because, to Spacks, female imagination is only that. Perhaps, however, this *is* the white female imagination, one that is "reluctant *and unable* to construct theories about experiences I haven't had." (Yet Spacks never lived in nineteenth-century Yorkshire, so why theorize about the Brontës?)[19]

Walker's point should be seriously considered, for a black feminist criticism cannot afford to be essentialist and ahistorical, reducing the experience of all black women to a common denominator and limiting black feminist critics to an exposition of an equivalent black "female imagination."

In 1982, Smith's manifesto was reprinted in a text which attempted to realize its project.[20] *All the Women Are White, All the Blacks Are Men, But Some of Us Are Brave,* edited by Gloria T. Hull, Patricia Bell Scott, and Barbara Smith, was a text dedicated to the establishment of black women's studies in the academy.

> Merely to use the term "Black women's studies" is an act charged with political significance. At the very least, the combining of these words to name a discipline means taking the stance that Black women exist—and exist positively—a stance that is in direct opposition to most of what passes for culture and thought on the North American continent. To use the term and to act on it in a white-male world is an act of political courage.[21]

To state unequivocally, as the editors do, that black women's studies is a discipline is a culminating act of the strand of black feminist theory committed to autonomy. The four issues that the editors see as being most important in relation to black women's studies acknowledge no allies or alliances:

> (1) the general political situation of Afro-American women and the bearing this has had upon the implementation of Black women's studies; (2) the relationship of Black women's studies to Black feminist politics and the Black feminist movement; (3) the necessity for Black women's studies to be feminist, radical, and analytical; and (4) the need for teachers of Black women's studies to be aware of our problematic political positions in the academy and of the potentially antagonistic conditions under which we must work.[22]

However, in the foreword to the book, Mary Berry, while criticizing women's studies for not focusing on black women, recognized that women's studies exists on the "periphery of academic life, like Black Studies."[23] Where, then, we can ask, lie black women's studies? On the periphery of the already marginalized, we could assume, a very precarious and dangerous position from which to assert total independence. For, as Berry acknowledged, pioneering work on black women was undertaken by white as well as black women historians, and black women's studies has a crucial contribution to make to the understanding of the oppression of the whole of the black community. Berry, then, implicitly understood that work on black women should be engaged with women's studies and Afro-American studies. The editors acknowledged the contributions to the volume made by white female scholars but were unclear about the relation of their work to a black feminism. They constantly engaged, as teachers and writers, with women's studies and Afro-American studies, yet it is unclear how or whether black women's studies should transform either or both of the former.[24] The editors acknowledged with dismay that "much of the current teaching and writing about Black women is not feminist, is not radical, and unfortunately is not always even analytical" and were aggressively aware of the pitfalls of mimicking a male-centered canonical structure of "great black women." In opposition to teaching about exceptional black women, the editors were committed to teaching as an act that furthered liberation in its exploration of "the experience of supposedly 'ordinary' Black women whose 'unexceptional' actions enabled us and the race to survive."[25] *But Some of Us Are Brave* was a collective attempt to produce a book that could be a pedagogical tool in this process.

An alternative approach to black feminist politics is embodied in Deborah McDowell's 1980 essay, "New Directions for Black Feminist Criticism," and in Barbara Christian's *Black Feminist Criticism: Perspectives on Black Women Writers*.[26] McDowell, like Smith, showed that white female critics continued to perpetrate against black women the exclusive practices they condemned in white-male scholarship by establishing the experience of white middle-class women as normative within the feminist arena. She also attacked male critics for the way in which their masculine-centered values dominated their criticism of the work of black women writers (186–87). However, the main concern of McDowell's essay was to look back at "Toward a Black Feminist Criticism" in order to assess the development of black feminist scholarship.

While acknowledging the lack of a concrete definition for or substantial body of black feminist criticism, McDowell argued that "the theories developed thus far have often lacked sophistication and have been marred by slogans, rhetoric, and idealism" (188). Two very important critiques of Smith's position were made by McDowell. She questioned the existence of a monolithic black female language (189) and problematized what she saw to be Smith's oversimplification and obscuring of the issue of lesbianism. McDowell called for a firmer definition of what constituted lesbianism and lesbian literature and questioned "whether a lesbian aesthetic is not finally a reductive approach to the study of Black women's literature" (190).

Moreover, unlike Smith's asserting the close and necessary links between a black feminist political framework and a black feminist criticism, McDowell was concerned to warn feminist critics of "the dangers of political ideology yoked with aesthetic judgment" and worried that Smith's "innovative analysis is pressed to the service of an individual political persuasion" (190). McDowell made more complex the relationship between fiction and criticism on the one hand and the possibilities of social change in the lives of the masses of black women on the other and also doubted the feasibility of a productive relationship between the academy and political activism.

McDowell's project was to establish the parameters for a clearer definition of black feminist criticism. Like Smith, McDowell applied the term to "Black female critics who analyze the works of Black female writers from a feminist or political perspective" but also departed from Smith's definitions when she extended her argument to state that

> the term can also apply to any criticism written by a Black woman regardless of her subject or perspective—a book written by a male from a feminist or political perspective, a book written by a Black woman or about Black women authors in general, or any writings by women. (191)

Thus, McDowell identified the need for a specific methodology while at the same time producing a very mystifying definition of her own. The semantic confusion of the statement gives cause to wonder at the possibility that an antifeminist celebration of a racist tract could be called black feminist as long as it was written by a black woman! Surely black feminist theory is emptied of its feminist content if the perspective of the critic doesn't matter.

Nevertheless, McDowell posed very pertinent questions that have yet to be adequately answered regarding the extent to which black and white feminist critics have intersecting interests and the necessity for being able to discern culturally specific analytic strategies that may distinguish black from white feminist criticism. McDowell also argued for a contextual awareness of the conditions under which black women's literature was produced, published, and reviewed, accompanied by a rigorous textual analysis which revealed any stylistic and linguistic commonalities across the texts of black women. She regarded the parameters of a tradition as an issue to be argued and established, not assumed, and warned against an easy reliance on generalities, especially in relation to the existence of a black female "consciousness" or "vision" (196). Like Washington, McDowell stressed that the "immediate concern of Black feminist critics must be to develop a fuller understanding of Black women writers" but did not support a "separatist position" as a long-term strategy and argued for an exploration of parallels between the texts of black women and those of black men. However, McDowell did not include the possibility of a black feminist reading of literature written by either white male or female authors, and while she called for black feminist criticism to ultimately "expand to embrace other modes of critical inquiry," these modes remain unspecified. In an attack against "critical absolutism," McDowell concluded by making an analogy between Marxism as dogma and black feminist criticism as a separatist enterprise, an analogy which did not clarify her political or theoretical position and confused her appeal for a "sound, thorough articulation of the Black feminist aesthetic" (196–97).

As opposed to the collective act of *But Some of Us Are Brave,* Christian has collected together her own essays written between 1975 and 1984. The introduction, "Black Feminist Process: In the Midst of . . . ," reflects the structure of the collection as a whole as the essays cover the period of the development of contemporary black feminist criticism. However, the book does not exemplify the history of the development of contemporary black feminist criticism but rather concentrates on situating the contributions of an individual critic over the period of a decade. Christian's work has been concerned with establishing a literary history of black women's writing and has depended very heavily on the conceptual apparatus of stereotypes and images.[27] However, it is necessary to confront Christian's assertions that the prime motivation for nineteenth- and early twentieth-century black writers was to confront the negative images of blacks held by whites and to dispute the simplistic model of the literary development of black women writers indicated by such titles as "From Stereotype to Character."[28] Christian's work represents a significant strand of black feminist criticism that has concentrated on the explication of stereotypes at the expense of engaging in the theoretical and historical questions raised by the construction of a tradition of black women writing. Indeed, in the introduction to *Black Feminist Criticism,* Christian herself raises some of the questions that are left unanswered in the body of her work so far but which are crucial to understanding or defining a black feminist critical practice:

> What is a literary critic, a black woman critic, a black feminist literary critic, a black feminist social literary critic? The adjectives mount up, defining, qualifying, the activity. How does one distinguish them? The need to articulate a theory, to categorize the activities is a good part of the activity itself to the point where I wonder how we ever get around to doing anything else. What do these categories tell anyone about my method? Do I do formalist criticism, operative or expressive criticism, mimetic or structuralist criticism? . . . Can one theorize effectively about an evolving process? Are the labels informative or primarily a way of nipping questions in the bud? What are the philosophical questions behind my praxis? (x–xi)

Christian, unlike many feminist critics, divorces what she considers to be sound critical practice from political practice when she states that what irks her about "much literary criticism today" is that "so often the text is but an occasion for espousing [the critic's] philosophical point of view—revolutionary black, feminist, or socialist program."[29] Thus, ten years after the term *black feminist criticism* was coined, it is used as the title of a book as if a readership would recognize and identify its parameters; yet, in the very attempt to define itself, even in the work of one individual critic, the contradictory impulses of black feminist criticism are clear. In a review of Christian's book, Hortense Spillers points to the ideological nature of the apparent separation between the critical project and its political dimensions:

> The critical projects that relate to the African-American community point to a crucial aspect of the entire theme of liberation. The same might be said for the career of feminist inquiry and its impact on the community: in other words, the various critical projects that intersect with African-American life and thought in the United States complement the actualities of an objective and historic situation, even if, in the name of the dominant ruling discourses, and in the interests of the ruling cultural and political apparatus, the convergence between intellectual and political life remains masked.[30]

What I want to advocate is that black feminist criticism be regarded critically as a problem, not a solution, as a sign that should be interrogated, a locus of contradictions. Black feminist criticism has its source and its primary motivation in academic legitimation, placement within a framework of bourgeois humanistic discourse. But, as Cornel West has argued in a wider context, the dilemmas of black intellectuals seeking legitimation through the academy is that

> it is existentially and intellectually stultifying for black intellectuals. It is existentially debilitating because it not only generates anxieties of defensiveness on the part of black intellectuals; it also thrives on them. The need for hierarchical ranking and the deep-seated racism shot through bourgeois humanistic scholarship cannot provide black intellectuals with either the proper ethos or conceptual framework to overcome a defensive posture. And charges of intellectual inferiority can never be met upon the opponent's terrain—to try to do so only intensifies one's anxieties. Rather the terrain itself must be viewed as part and parcel of an antiquated form of life unworthy of setting the terms of contemporary discourse.[31]

This critique is applicable for a number of reasons. Black feminist criticism for the main part accepts the prevailing paradigms predominant in the academy, as have women's studies and Afro-American studies, and seeks to organize itself as a discipline in the same way. Also, it is overwhelmingly defensive in its posture, attempting to discover, prove, and legitimate the intellectual worthiness of black women so that they may claim their rightful placement as both subjects and creators of the curriculum.

Black feminist theory continues to be shaped by the tensions apparent in feminist theory in general that have been characterized by Elaine Showalter as three phases of development. To paraphrase and adapt her model, these would be (1) the concentration on the mysogyny (and racism) of literary practice; (2) the discovery that (black) women writers had a literature of their own (previously hidden by patriarchal [and racist] values) and the development of a (black) female aesthetic; and (3) a challenge to and rethinking of the conceptual grounds of literary study and an increased concern with theory.[32] Though it is not possible to argue that these different approaches appear chronologically over the last ten years in black feminist work, it is important to recognize that in addition to the specific concerns of black feminist theory it shares a structural and conceptual pattern of questions and issues with other modes of feminist inquiry.

Black feminist criticism has too frequently been reduced to an experiential relationship that exists between black women as critics and black women as writers who represent black women's reality. Theoretically this reliance on a common, or shared, experience is essentialist and ahistorical. Following the methodologies of mainstream literary criticism and feminist literary criticism, black feminist criticism presupposes the existence of a tradition and has concentrated on establishing a narrative of that tradition. This narrative constitutes a canon from these essentialist views of experience which is then placed alongside, though unrelated to, traditional and feminist canons. [We should not] assume the existence of a tradition or traditions of black women writing and [should be] critical of traditions of Afro-American intellectual thought that have been constructed as paradigmatic of Afro-American history.

One other essentialist aspect of black feminist criticism should be considered: the search for or assumption of the existence of a black female language. [My] theoretical perspective . . . is that no language or experience is divorced from the shared context in which different groups that share a language express their differing group interests. Language is accented differently by competing groups, and therefore the terrain of language is a terrain of power relations.[33] This struggle within and over language reveals the nature of the structure of social relations and the hierarchy of power, not the nature of one particular group. The sign, then, is an arena of struggle and a construct between socially organized persons in the process of their interaction; the forms that signs take are conditioned by the social organization of the participants involved and also by the immediate conditions of their interactions. Hence, [it is argued] that we must be historically specific and aware of the differently oriented social interests within one and the same sign community. In these terms, black and feminist cannot be absolute, transhistorical forms (or form) of identity.

Reconstructing Womanhood embodies a feminist critical practice that pays particular attention to the articulation of gender, race, and class.[34] Social, political, and economic analyses that use class as a fundamental category often assert the necessity for white and black to sink their differences and unite in a common and general class struggle. The call for class solidarity is paralleled within contemporary feminist practice by the concept of sisterhood. This appeal to sisterhood has two political consequences that should be questioned. First, in order to establish the common grounds for a unified women's movement, material differences in the lives of working-class and middle-class women or white and black women [should be] dismissed. The search to establish that these bonds of sisterhood have always existed has led to a feminist historiography and criticism which denies the hierarchical structuring of the relations between black and white women and often takes the concerns of middle-class, articulate white women as a norm.

[*Reconstructing Womanhood*] works within the theoretical premises of societies "structured in dominance" by class, by race, and by gender and is a materialist account of the cultural production of black women intellectuals within the social relations that inscribed them.[35] It delineates the sexual ideologies that defined the ways in which white and black women "lived" their relation to their material conditions of existence. Ideologies of white womanhood were the sites of racial and class struggle which enabled white women to negotiate their subordinate role in relation to patriarchy and at the same time to ally their class interests with men and against establishing an alliance with black women. We need more feminist work that interrogates sexual ideologies for their racial specificity and acknowledges whiteness, not just blackness, as a racial categorization. Work that uses race as a central category does not necessarily need to be about black women.

An emphasis on the importance of establishing historically specific forms of racism should also apply to gender oppression. It is not enough to use the feminist theoretical back door to assert that because racism and sexism predate capitalism there is no further need to specify their particular articulation with economic systems of oppression. On the contrary, racisms and sexisms need to be regarded as particular historical practices articulated with each other and with other practices in a social formation. For example, the institutionalized rape of black women as slaves needs to be distinguished from the institutionalized rape of black women as an instrument of political terror, alongside lynching, in the South. Rape itself should not be regarded as a transhistorical mechanism of women's oppression but as one that acquires specific political or economic meanings at different moments in history.

For feminist historiography and critical practice the inclusion of the analytic categories of race and class means having to acknowledge that women were not only the subjects but also the perpetrators of oppression. The hegemonic control of dominant classes has been secured at the expense of sisterhood. Hegemony is never finally and utterly won but needs to be continually worked on and reconstructed, and sexual and racial ideologies are crucial mechanisms in the maintenance of power. For women this has meant that many of their representative organizations have been disabled by strategies and struggles which have been race-specific, leading to racially divided movements like the temperance and suffrage campaigns. No history should blandly label these organizations "women's movements," for we have to understand the importance of the different issues around which white and black women organized and how this related to their differing material circumstances. A revision of contemporary feminist historiography should investigate the different ways in which racist ideologies have been constructed and made operative under different historical conditions. But, like sexual ideologies, racism, in its appeal to the natural order of things, appears as a transhistorical, essentialist category, and critiques of racism can imitate this appearance.

[*Reconstructing Womanhood*] is a contribution to such a revision, a revision that examines the boundaries of sisterhood, for the contradictions faced by the black women intellectuals at the Columbian Exposition continue to haunt the contemporary women's movement.

NOTES

1. Frances Harper, "Woman's Political Future," in May Wright Sewell, ed., *World's Congress of Representative Women* (Chicago: Rand McNally, 1894), pp. 433–37.
2. Fannie Barrier Williams, "The Intellectual Progress of the Colored Women of the United States since the Emancipation Proclamation," in Sewell, *World's Congress,* pp. 696–711.
3. Anna Julia Cooper, "The Intellectual Progress of the Colored Women of the United States since the Emancipation Proclamation," in Sewell, *World's Congress,* pp. 711–15.
4. Fannie Jackson Coppin, and Sarah J. Early and Hallie Quinn Brown, "The Organized Efforts of the Colored Women of the South to Improve Their Condition," in Sewell, *World's Congress,* pp. 715–17, 718–29.
5. Ida B. Wells, ed., *The Reason Why: The Colored American Is Not in the World's Columbian Exposition* (Chicago: by the author, 1893).
6. Report of Mrs. Potter Palmer, President, to the Board of Lady Managers, September 2, 1891 (Chicago), cited in Ann Massa, "Black Women in the 'White City,' " *Journal of American Studies* 8 (December 1974): 320.
7. Ibid., p. 329.
8. Robert W. Rydell, "The World's Columbian Exposition of 1893: Racist Underpinnings of a Utopian Artifact," *Journal of American Culture* 1 (Summer 1978): 253–75.
9. David F. Burg, *Chicago's White City of 1893* (Lexington: University of Kentucky Press, 1976), p. 75.
10. Alan Trachtenberg, *The Incorporation of America: Culture and Society in the Gilded Age* (New York: Hill and Wang, 1982), p. 209.
11. F. L. Barnett, "The Reason Why," in Wells, *The Reason Why,* p. 79; Elliot M. Rudwick and August Meier, "Black Man in the 'White City': Negroes and the Columbian Exposition, 1893," *Phylon* 26 (Winter 1965): 361.
12. Rudwick and Meier, "Black Man in the 'White City,' " p. 354; Frederick Douglass, "Introduction," in Wells, *The Reason Why,* p. 4.
13. W. E. B. Du Bois, *The Souls of Black Folk* (1903; reprint New York: Fawcett World Library, 1961), p. 23.
14. Hazel V. Carby, "White Woman Listen: Black Feminism and the Boundaries of Sisterhood," in Centre for Contemporary Cultural Studies, *The Empire Strikes Back: Race and Racism in Seventies Britain* (London: Hutchinson, 1982), pp. 212–35.
15. Barbara Smith, "Toward a Black Feminist Criticism," *Conditions: Two* 1 (October 1977), reprinted in Elaine Showalter, ed., *The New Feminist Criticism: Essays on Women, Literature, and Theory* (New York: Pantheon, 1985), pp. 168–85. References are to this edition; page numbers will be given parenthetically in the text.
16. Mary Helen Washington, ed. *Black-Eyed Susans* (New York: Anchor Press, 1975). The first contemporary anthology of black women's writings, fiction and nonfiction, was Toni Cade, ed., *The Black Woman* (New York: New American Library, 1970).
17. See also Mary Helen Washington, "Teaching Black-Eyed Susans: An Approach to the Study of Black Women Writers," in Gloria T. Hull, Patricia Bell Scott, and Barbara Smith, eds., *All the Women Are White, All the Blacks Are Men, But Some of Us Are Brave* (Old Westbury, N.Y.: Feminist Press, 1982), pp. 208–17.
18. Alice Walker, "One Child of One's Own: A Meaningful Digression within the Work(s)," *In Search of Our Mothers' Gardens* (New York: Harcourt Brace Jovanovich, 1983), pp. 361–83.
19. Ibid., p. 372.
20. See also the introduction to Barbara Smith, ed., *Home Girls: A Black Feminist Anthology* (New York: Kitchen Table Women of Color Press, 1983).

21. Hull et al., "The Politics of Black Women's Studies," in *But Some of Us Are Brave,* p. xvii.
22. Ibid.
23. Mary Berry, "Foreword," Hull et al., *But Some of Us Are Brave,* p. xv.
24. My position is that cultural studies is not disciplinary, nor does it seek to be a discipline even in the sense that American studies, Afro-American studies, or women's studies are interdisciplinary; rather it is a critical position which interrogates the assumptions of and principles of critical practice of all three modes of inquiry. As a practitioner of cultural studies notes: "The relation of cultural studies to the other disciplines is rather one of critique: of their historical construction, of their claims, of their omissions, and particularly of the forms of their separation. At the same time, a critical relationship to the disciplines is also a critical stance to their forms of knowledge production—to the prevalent social relations of research, the labor process of higher education." Michael Green, "The Centre for Contemporary Cultural Studies," in Peter Widdowson, ed., *Rereading English* (London: Methuen, 1982), p. 84.
25. Hull et al., "Politics of Black Women's Studies," *But Some of Us Are Brave,* pp. xxi–xxii.
26. Deborah McDowell, "New Directions for Black Feminist Criticism," *Black American Literature Forum* 14 (1980), reprinted in Showalter, *The New Feminist Criticism,* pp. 186–99. References are to this edition; page numbers will be given parenthetically in the text. Barbara Christian, *Black Feminist Criticism: Perspectives on Black Women Writers* (New York: Pergamon Press, 1985).
27. See also Barbara Christian, *Black Women Novelists: The Development of a Tradition, 1892–1976* (Westport, Conn.: Greenwood Press, 1980).
28. Christian, *Black Feminist Criticism,* pp. 1–30.
29. Ibid., pp. x–xi.
30. Hortense Spillers, "Black/Female/Critic," *Women's Review of Books* 2 (September 1985): 9–10.
31. Cornel West, "The Dilemma of the Black Intellectual," *Cultural Critique* 1 (Fall 1985): 116–17.
32. Showalter, "The Feminist Critical Revolution," in *The New Feminist Criticism,* pp. 3–17.
33. This argument is drawn from V. N. Volosinov, *Marxism and the Philosophy of Language* (New York: Seminar Press, 1973). Volosinov was a Soviet theorist associated with the circle of Mikhail Bakhtin.
34. I am particularly drawing on that aspect of cultural studies which has analyzed issues of race and the study of black culture. A key figure is Stuart Hall. For many years the director of the Centre for Contemporary Cultural Studies, he has written a number of major theoretical essays on culture and ideology, including: "Cultural Studies: Two Paradigms," *Media, Culture, and Society* 2 (1980): 57–72; "The Rediscovery of 'Ideology': Return of the Repressed in Media Studies," in Michael Gurevitch, Tony Bennett, James Curran, and Janet Woolacott, eds., *Culture, Society, and the Media* (New York: Methuen, 1982), pp. 56–90; "Culture, the Media, and the 'Ideological' Effect," in James Curran, Michael Gurevitch, and Janet Woolacott, eds., *Mass Communications and Society* (London: Edward Arnold, 1977), pp. 315–48; "Notes on Deconstructing 'The Popular,'" in Ralph Samuel, ed., *People's History and Socialist Theory,* History Workshop Series (London: Routledge and Kegan Paul, 1981); "A 'Reading' of Marx's *1857* Introduction to the Grundrisse," *CCCS Stencilled Papers* 1 (1973); "Rethinking the Base/Superstructure Metaphor," in John Bloomfield, ed., *Class, Party, and Hegemony* (London: Lawrence and Wishart, 1977), pp. 43–72. Hall's work on race that has been particularly influential includes: *Policing the Crisis: Mugging, the State, and Law and Order* (London: Macmillan, 1978); "Pluralism, Race, and Class in Caribbean Society," in *Race and Class in Post-Colonial Society* (Paris: UNESCO, 1977), pp. 150–82; "Racism and Reaction," in *Five Views of Multi-Racial Britain* (London: Commission for Racial Equality, 1978), pp. 23–35; "Race, Articulation and Societies Structured in Dominance," in *Sociological Theories: Race and Colonialism* (Paris: UNESCO, 1980), pp. 305–45; "The Whites of Their Eyes: Racist Ideologies and the Media," in George Bridges and Rosalind Brunt, eds., *Silver Linings: Some Strategies for the Eighties* (London: Lawrence and Wishart, 1981), pp. 28–52. Younger scholars influenced by Hall and the work of C. L. R. James include the authors of *The Empire Strikes Back* (see note 14) and Paul Gilroy, "Managing the 'Underclass': A Further Note on the Sociology of Race Relations in Britain," *Race and Class* 22 (Summer 1980): 47–62; Paul Gilroy, "You Can't Fool the Youths: Race and Class Formation in the 1980s," *Race and Class* 23 (Autumn 1981/Winter 1982): 207–22; and Paul Gilroy, *There Ain't No Black in the Union*

Jack (London: Hutchinson, 1987). For collections of essays by C. L. R. James, see *The Future in the Present* (London: Allison and Busby, 1977); *Spheres of Existence* (London: Allison and Busby, 1980); *At the Rendezvous of Victory* (London: Allison and Busby, 1984); and his cultural history of cricket in the West Indies, *Beyond a Boundary* (1963; reprint London: Stanley Paul, 1980). In the United States there is the related work of Cedric J. Robinson, *Black Marxism: The Making of the Black Radical Tradition* (London: Zed Press, 1983); Cornel West, *Prophesy Deliverance! An Afro-American Revolutionary Christianity* (Philadelphia: Westminster Press, 1982); and Cornel West, "The Dilemma of the Black Intellectual" (see note 31); John Brown Childs, "Afro-American Intellectuals and the People's Culture," *Theory and Society* 13 (1984): 69–90; John Brown Childs, "Concepts of Culture in Afro-American Political Thought, 1890–1920," *Social Text* 4 (Fall 1981): 28–43; and Ronald Takaki, *Iron Cages: Race and Culture in 19th-Century America* (Seattle: University of Washington Press, 1979), which fuses black intellectual tradition, cultural studies, and western Marxism.

35. The phrase is taken from Hall, "Race, Articulation, and Societies Structured in Dominance."

Charles I. Nero (1956–)

A *frequent speaker at conferences and workshops, Charles I. Nero is presently director of African American studies at Bates College in Lewiston, Maine. Concurrently, with a Rockefeller Foundation Fellowship in the humanities, he conducts research at the Center for Lesbian and Gay Studies at the City University of New York.*

Nero graduated in 1978 from Xavier University, with a bachelor's in communication and theater education. He earned his master's from Wake Forest University in 1980 and his doctorate from Indiana University in 1990. His wide-ranging scholarly and teaching activities integrate cultural studies, speech communication, and gay and lesbian perspectives. Concerned with issues of race, gender, and sexual orientation, Nero fills what have long been gaps in both African American studies and academia at large.

Among numerous other articles and essays, Nero has written "Black Queer Identity, Imaginative Rationality, and the Language of Home" and "Social and Cultural Sensitivity in Group Specific HIV/AIDS Programming." He is currently working on a book tentatively titled Invisible Lives: Black Gay Men, the Family, and the Reconstruction of Manhood.

"Toward a Black Gay Aesthetic: Signifying in Contemporary Black Gay Literature" was originally published in the anthology Brother to Brother: New Writings by Black Gay Men *(1991), edited by Essex Hemphill. As a companion piece to Ron Simmons's "Some Thoughts on the Challenges Facing Black Gay Intellectuals" (see p. 805 in Part Five), Nero's essay employs signification theory to present a provocative and insightful overview of the biases depicted by African American authors in their literary representations of homosexuality.*

Toward a Black Gay Aesthetic

Signifying in Contemporary Black Gay Literature

> Western literature has often posited the heterosexual white male as hero, with Gays, Blacks and women as Other. . . . The development of Black literature, women's literature, Gay literature, and now Black Gay literature is not so much a rewriting of history as an additional writing of it; together

> these various literatures, like our various selves, produce history. . . . Our past as Black Gay men is only now being examined.
>
> —Daniel Garrett, "Other Countries: The Importance of Difference"[1]

> Much of the Afro-American literary tradition can be read as successive attempts to create a new narrative space for representing the recurring referent of Afro-American literature, the so-called Black Experience.
>
> —Henry Louis Gates, Jr., *The Signifying Monkey*[2]

> All I can say is—if this is my time in life . . . goodbye misery.
>
> —Lorraine Hansberry, *A Raisin in the Sun*[3]

Introduction

With only a few exceptions, the intellectual writings of black Americans have been dominated by heterosexual ideologies that have resulted in the gay male experience being either excluded, marginalized, or ridiculed.[4] Because of the heterosexism among African American intellectuals and the racism in the white gay community, black gay men have been an invisible population. However, the last five years have seen a movement characterized by political activism and literary production by openly gay black men. Given their invisibility by both black heterosexism and white gay racism, two questions emerge: How have black gay men created a positive identity for themselves and how have they constructed literary texts which would render their lives visible, and therefore valid? I propose in this essay to answer the former by answering the latter, i.e., I will focus on the strategies by black men who have either identified themselves as gay or who feature black gay characters prominently in their work. The writers I examine will be Samuel Delany, George Wolfe, Billi Gordon, Larry Duplechan, Craig G. Harris, and Essex Hemphill.

The critical framework that I use is strongly influenced by my reading of Mary Helen Washington's *Invented Lives* and Henry Louis Gates, Jr.'s critical method of signifying. In *Invented Lives,* Washington brilliantly analyzes the narrative strategies ten black women have used between 1860 and 1960 to bring themselves into visibility and power in a world dominated by racism and sexism.[5] Like Washington, Gates's concern is with the paradoxical relationship of African Americans with the printed text, i.e., since Eurocentric writing defines the black as "other," how does the "other" gain authority in the text? To resolve this, Gates proposes a theory of criticism based upon the African American oral tradition of signifying. Signifying is, for Gates, "the black term for what in classical European rhetoric are called the figures of signification," or stated differently, "the indirect use of words that changes the meaning of a word or words."[6] Signifying has numerous figures which include: capping, loud-talking, the dozens, reading, going off, talking smart, sounding, joaning (jonesing), dropping lugs, snapping, woofing, styling out, and calling out of one's name.

As a rhetorical strategy, signifying assumes that there is shared knowledge between communicators and, therefore, that information can be given indirectly.

Geneva Smitherman in *Talkin and Testifyin* gives the following examples of signifying:

- Stokely Carmichael, addressing a white audience at the University of California, Berkeley, 1966: "It's a privilege and an honor to be in the white intellectual ghetto of the West."
- Malcolm X on Martin Luther King, Jr.'s nonviolent revolution (referring to the common practice of singing "We Shall Overcome" at civil rights protests of the sixties): "In a revolution, you swinging, not singing."
- Reverend Jesse Jackson, merging sacred and secular siggin in a Breadbasket Saturday morning sermon: "Pimp, punk, prostitute, preacher, Ph.D.—all the P's—you still in slavery!"
- A black middle-class wife to her husband who had just arrived home several hours later than usual: "You sho got home early today for a change."[7]

Effective signifying is, Smitherman states, "to put somebody in check . . . to make them think about and, one hopes, correct their behavior."[8] Because signifying relies on indirection to give information, it requires that participants in any communicative encounter pay attention to, as Claudia Mitchell-Kernan states, "the total universe of discourse."[9]

Gates's theory of signifying focuses on black forms of talk. I believe that identifying these forms of talk in contemporary black gay literature is important for two reasons. First, the use of signifying by black gay men places their writing squarely within the African American literary tradition. Second, signifying permits black gay men to revise the "Black Experience" in African American literature and, thereby, to create a space for themselves.

The remainder of this essay is divided into two parts. The first part examines the heterosexist context in which black gay men write. Examined are heterosexism and homophobia in the writings of contemporary social scientists, scholars, and, in a longer passage, the novels of Toni Morrison. The last section discusses black gay men's attempts to revise the African American literary tradition. Specifically examined are the signifying on representations of desire, the black religious experience, and gender configurations.

Heterosexism and African American Intellectuals

Some social scientists have claimed that homosexuality is alien to the black community. Communication scholar Molefi Asante has argued in *Afrocentricity: A Theory of Social Change* that homosexual practices among black men were initially imposed on them by their white slave owners and that the practice is maintained by the American prison institution.[10] Asante has attributed homosexuality to Greco-Roman culture, with the added assertion that "homosexuality does not represent an Afrocentric way of life."[11] Likewise, in *Black Skin, White Masks,* Frantz Fanon, the widely read Martiniquois psychiatrist and freedom-fighter, declared that "Caribbean men never experience the Oedipus complex," and therefore, in the Caribbean, "there is no homosexuality, which is, rather, an attribute of the white race, Western civilization."[12]

Other scholars and writers have contended that homosexuality is a pathology stemming from the inability of black men to cope with the complexities of manhood in a racist society. Alvin Poussaint, the noted Harvard psychiatrist and adviser to the *Cosby Show,* stated in a 1978 *Ebony* article that some black men adopt homosexuality as a maneuver to help them avoid the increasing tension developing between black men and women.[13] "Homosexuality," according to black writer and liberationist Imamu Amiri Baraka, "is the most extreme form of alienation acknowledged within white society" and it occurs among "a people who lose their self-sufficiency because they depend on their subjects to do the world's work," thus rendering them "effeminate and perverted."[14] According to Eldridge Cleaver, homosexuality among black men is a "racial death wish," and a frustrating experience because "in their sickness [black men who practice homosexuality] are unable to have a baby by a white man."[15] In *The Endangered Black Family,* Nathan Hare and Julia Hare view homosexuals as confused but worthy of compassion because, they state, "Some of them may yet be saved."[16] The Hares seem to imply that black gay and lesbian people require treatment for either illness or brainwashing: "What we must do is offer the homosexual brother or sister a proper compassion and acceptance without advocacy. We might not advocate, for instance, the religion of Mormonism, or venereal disease, laziness or gross obesity. . . ."[17]

The acclaimed writer Toni Morrison has woven into her novels these ideas of homosexuality as alien to African cultures, as forced upon black men by racist European civilizations, and as the inability to acquire and sustain manhood. In her first novel, *The Bluest Eye,* she played on the stereotype of the "light-skinned" black man as weak, effeminate, and sexually impotent. Soaphead Church, "a cinnamon-eyed West Indian with lightly browned skin," limited his sexual interests to little girls because, Morrison wrote, "he was too diffident to confront homosexuality" and found "little boys insulting, scary, and stubborn."[18] In *Tar Baby,* black homosexual men were self-mutilating transvestites who had dumped their masculinity because they "found the whole business of being black and men at the same time too difficult."[19]

In her 1988 Pulitzer Prize–winning *Beloved,* Morrison surpassed her earlier efforts in using homophobia with the creation of the five heroic black men of the Sweet Home plantation. Sweet Home men were unlike slaves on nearby plantations, as their owner Mr. Garner bragged to other farmers: "Y'all got boys. Young boys, old boys, picky boys, stroppin boys. Now at Sweet Home, my niggers is men every one of em. Bought um thataway, raised em thataway. Men every one."[20] Although deprived of sex with women, Sweet Home men were capable of enormous restraint and for sexual relief they either masturbated or engaged in sex with farm animals. When Mr. Garner added to his plantation a new slave, the thirteen-year-old "iron-eyed" Sethe, the Sweet Home men "let the girl be" and allowed her to choose one of them despite the fact that they "were young and so sick with the absence of women they had taken to *calves*" (emphasis added).[21] Sethe took over a year to choose one of the Sweet Home men. Morrison described that year of waiting: "[It was] a long, tough year of thrashing on pallets eaten up with dreams of her. A year of yearning, when rape seemed the solitary gift of life. The restraint they had exercised possible only because they were Sweet Home men. . . ."[22]

Yet Morrison's description of the restrained Sweet Home men does a great disservice to the complexity of men's lives. Her description reinforces a false notion of a hierarchy of sexual practices in which masturbation is only a substitute for intercourse. Morrison's description is homophobic because it reveals her inability to imagine homosexual relationships among heroic characters. By implication, sex with farm animals is preferable to homoerotic sex, which is like a perverse reading of a spiritual: "Before I practice homosexuality, I'll practice bestiality, and go home to my Father and be free."

Morrison rejects from her fiction the idea that homosexual desire among slave men could actually lead to loving relationships. This, in fact, did happen. Autobiographical evidence exists that slave men in the Americas practiced and even institutionalized homosexuality. Esteban Montejo, the subject of *The Autobiography of a Runaway Slave,* twice discusses the prevalence of homosexuality among Cuban slave men in his comments on the sexual customs of the plantation. The first incident refers to physical abuse and possibly the rape of young black boys. Montejo states:

> If a boy was pretty and lively he was sent inside, to the master's house. And there they started softening him up . . . well, I don't know! They used to give the boy a long palm-leaf and make him stand at one end of the table while they ate. And they said, "Now see that no flies get in the food!" If a fly did, they scolded him severely and even whipped him.[23]

The second incident is discussed within the context of the scarcity of women on the plantation. "To have one [a woman] of your own," Montejo writes, "you had either to be over twenty-five or catch yourself one in the fields."[24] Some men, however, he states, "had sex among themselves and did not want to know anything of women."[25] Montejo's comments include observations about the economics of homosexual households. He notes that the division of labor in these households resembled male–female roles in which the "effeminate men washed the clothes and did the cooking too, if they had a husband."[26] The men in these relationships also benefited financially from the existence of the "provision grounds," lands allocated to slaves in the Caribbean to grow crops to sell in the local markets on Sunday. Montejo writes: "They [effeminate men] were good workers and occupied themselves with their plots of land, giving the produce to their husbands to sell to the white farmers."[27]

Most interesting in Montejo's narrative is the reaction of other slaves to their homosexual brethren. The older men hated homosexuality, he states, and they "would have nothing to do with queers."[28] Their hatred leads Montejo to speculate that the practice did not come from Africa. Unfortunately, Montejo limits his speculations on homosexuality to origins and not to prohibitions. Thus, another speculation could be that homosexuality was prohibited, but that the practice itself was neither unknown nor undreamt. Montejo's narrative suggests that the influence of the old men over the feelings and attitudes of other slaves about homosexuality was limited. The slaves did not have a pejorative name for those who practiced homosexuality and it was not until "after Abolition that the term [effeminate] came into use," Montejo states.[29] Montejo, himself, held the view that the practice of homosexuality was a private matter: "To tell the truth, it [homosexuality] never bothered me. I am of the opinion that a man can stick his arse where he wants."[30] Montejo's narrative challenges the heterosexist assumptions about the sexualities and the family life of blacks before abolition in the Americas. At least in Cuba, homoerotic sex and exclusively male families were not uncommon.

In the United States, accounts of homosexuality among blacks before abolition are scanty. This is because accounts of slaves' sexuality are sparse and, until recently, social customs in the United States and Great Britain proscribed public discussions of sexuality.[31] Homosexuality, however, did occur during the colonial period among black men because laws forbidding the practice were created and sentences were carried out. These laws and sentences are discussed in A. Leon Higginbotham, Jr.'s *In the Matter of Color: Race and the American Legal Process* and Jonathan Katz's two documentary works *Gay/Lesbian Almanac* and *Gay American History*. Katz documents the case of Jan Creoli, identified as a "negro," who in 1646 in New Netherland (Manhattan) was sentenced to be "choked to death, and then burnt to ashes" for committing the act of sodomy with ten-year-old Manuel Congo.[32] Congo, whose name suggests that he was black, was sentenced "to be carried to the place where Creoli is to be executed, tied to a stake, and faggots piled around him, for justice sake, and to be flogged. . . ."[33] In a second case, "Mingo alias Cocke Negro," a Massachusetts slave, was reportedly executed for "forcible Buggery," a term that Katz suggests is a male–male act, rather than bestiality.[34] Both Katz and Higginbotham discuss the development of sexual crime laws in Pennsylvania between 1700 and 1780 that carefully distinguished between blacks and whites: Life imprisonment was the penalty for whites and death was for blacks convicted of buggery which, Katz notes, probably meant bestiality and sodomy.[35]

Although the evidence for homosexual practices among black male slaves is small, it does suggest that we do not exclude homoeroticism from life on the plantation. The gay Jewish historian Martin Bauml Duberman's words are most appropriate here:

> After all, to date we've accumulated only a tiny collection of historical materials that record the existence of *heterosexual* behavior in the past. Yet no one claims that the minuscule amount of evidence is an accurate measure of the actual amount of heterosexual activity which took place.[36]

Duberman's words and the evidence we have suggest that, at best, our understanding of the sexuality of our slave ancestors is fragmentary. We need to uncover more and to reread diaries, letters, and narratives to gain a greater understanding of the sexuality of our forebears. At the very least, we need to revise our models of the black family and of homosexuality as alien to black culture.

Morrison's homophobia, [like] that of so many other black intellectuals, is perhaps more closely related to Judeo–Christian beliefs than to the beliefs of her ancestors. Male homosexuality is associated with biblical ideas of weakness as effeminacy.[37] Many of these intellectuals would also argue that the Judeo–Christian tradition is a major tool of the Western–Eurocentric view of reality that furthers the oppression of blacks. Paradoxically, by their condemnation of homosexuality and lesbianism, these intellectuals contribute to upholding an oppressive Eurocentric view of reality.

Enter Black Gay Men

It should be obvious that black gay men must look at other black intellectuals with great caution and skepticism because the dominant view of reality expressed is oppressively heterosexist. Black gay men must also be cautious of looking for an image of themselves in white gay men because the United States is still a racist society. For example, even though one in five homosexual or bisexual men with AIDS is black, it can be argued that Larry Kramer's searing AIDS polemic, *The Normal Heart,* is about gay people, *not* black people. The characters in the drama are from the "fabled 1970s Fire Island/*After Dark* crowd," which tended to be white, middle-class, and very exclusionary on the basis of race, unless one counts the occasional presence of the reigning "disco diva"—who was usually a black woman or the wonderful African American gender-blurring singer Sylvester. In addition, Kramer makes several remarks in *The Normal Heart* that imply that he accepts certain historically racist ideas about blacks.[38] With a critical eye, one can also find occurrences of racism in works ranging from literature to visual pornography created by or aimed at gay men that employ a racist vision of reality.[39]

Partly as a reaction to racism in gay culture, but mostly in response to the heterosexism of black intellectuals and writers, African American gay men signify on many aspects of the "Black Experience" in their literature. The areas discussed in this section are representations of sexual desire, the black religious experience, and gender configurations.

Representing Sexual Desire

Because of the historical and often virulent presence of racism, black literature has frequently had as its goal the elevation of "the race" by presenting the group in its "best light." The race's "best light" often has meant depicting blacks with those values and ways that mirrored white Americans and Europeans. For black writers this has usually meant tremendous anxiety over the representation of sexuality. An excellent example of this anxiety is W. E. B. Du Bois's reaction to Claude McKay's 1920 novel *Home to Harlem.* In the novel, McKay, gay and Jamaican, wrote about much of the night life in Harlem, including one of the first descriptions of a gay and lesbian bar in an African American work of fiction. Du Bois wrote:

> Claude McKay's *Home to Harlem* for the most part nauseates me, and after the dirtier parts of its filth I feel distinctly like taking a bath. . . . McKay has set out to cater for that prurient demand on the part of white folks for a portrayal in Negroes of that utter licentiousness . . . which a certain decadent section of the white world . . . wants to see written out in black and white and saddled on black Harlem. . . . He has used every art and emphasis to paint drunkenness, fighting, lascivious sexual promiscuity and utter absence of restraint in as bold and bright colors as he can. . . . As a picture of Harlem life or of Negro life anywhere, it is, of course, nonsense. Untrue, not so much as on account of its facts, but on account of its emphasis and glaring colors.[40]

The anxiety that Du Bois felt was as acute for black women. Mary Helen Washington comments that this anxiety about the representation of sexuality "goes back to the nineteenth century and the prescription for womanly 'virtues' which made slave women automatically immoral and less feminine than white women," as in the case of the slave woman Harriet Jacobs, who considered not publishing her 1860 narrative *Incidents in the Life of a Slave Girl* because she "bore two children as a single woman rather than submit to forced concubinage."[41] The representation of sexuality is even more problematic for black gay men than for heterosexual African Americans because of societal disapproval against impersonal sex, in which gay men frequently engage, and because gay sex is not connected in any way with the means of reproduction.

Black gay science fiction writer Samuel Delany, in his autobiography *The Motion of Light in Water,* takes particular delight in signifying on society's disapproval of impersonal homoerotic sex. His signifying is greatly aided by using the autobiographical form, a successful mode for black Americans, as Michael Cooke maintains, because "the self is the source of the system of which it is a part, creates what it discovers, and although it is nothing unto itself, it is the possibility of everything for itself."[42] By using himself as the source of the system, Delany is able to signify on ideas about impersonal sex. Delany imbues situations involving impersonal sex with social and political significance in the context of the repressive 1950s and early 1960s. Contrary to stereotypes that group sex is wild and out of control, the situation on the piers at the end of Christopher Street "with thirty-five, fifty, a hundred all-but-strangers is," Delany states, "hugely ordered, highly social, attentive, silent, and grounded in a certain care, if not community."[43] At the piers, when arrests of eight or nine men occurred and were reported in the newspapers without mentioning the hundreds who had escaped, it was a reassurance to the city fathers, the police, the men arrested, and even those who escaped "that the image of the homosexual as outside society—which is the myth that the outside of language, with all its articulation, is based on—was, somehow, despite the arrests, intact."[44] Delany's first visit to the St. Mark's Baths in 1963 produced a Foucault-like revelation that the legal and medical silences on homosexuality was "a huge and pervasive discourse" which prevented one from gaining "a clear, accurate, and extensive picture of extant public sexual institutions."[45] The result of Delany's signification is that his participation in impersonal sex in public places is given a political and social importance much like the significance given to ordinary, day-to-day acts of resistance recounted by the subjects of African American autobiographies from Frederick Douglass's *My Bondage and My Freedom* to Maya Angelou's *I Know Why the Caged Bird Sings.*

Just as Delany seeks to revise attitudes about impersonal sex, Larry Duplechan signifies on both black middle-class and gay stereotypes of interracial love and lust. On the one hand, the black middle class and the mental health professions have conspired together to label a black person's sexual attraction to a white as pathology.[46] On the other, gay men have created a host of terms to denigrate participants in black–white sexual relationships, e.g.: *dinge queen, chocolate lover,* and *snow queen.* In *Blackbird* and *Eight Days a Week,* we are introduced to Duplechan's protagonist, Johnnie Ray Rousseau, as a senior in high school in the former, and as a 22-year-old aspiring singer living in Los Angeles in the latter. In Duplechan's first novel, *Eight Days a Week,* he summarizes both the gay and the black middle-class stereotype: "I was once told by a black alto sax player named Zaz (we were in bed at the time, mind you) that my preference for white men (and blonds, the whitest of white, to boot) was the sad but understandable end result of 300 years of white male oppression."[47] Contrary to Zaz's opinion, Johnnie Ray's sexual attraction to white men is anything but the result of 300 years of white male oppression, and if it is, it allows

Duplechan a major moment of signifying in African American literature: the sexual objectification of white men by a black man.

Revising our culture's ideas about male–male sexual desire and love is a major concern in Essex Hemphill's collection of poems *Conditions*.[48] In particular, "Conditions XXIV" signifies on heterosexual culture's highly celebrated "rite of passage," the marriage ceremony. Hemphill signifies on the marriage ceremony in an excellent example of "capping," a figure of speech which revises an original statement by adding new terms. Hemphill honors the bonds created from desire by capping on the exchange of wedding bands. In the opening and closing sentences, fingers are not the received place for wedding rings:

In america
I place my ring
on your cock
where it belongs . . .

In america,
place your ring
on my cock
where it belongs.

Vows are also exchanged in the poem, but they do not restrict and confine. Instead, these vows are "What the rose whispers / before blooming. . . ." The vows are:

I give you my heart,
a safe house.
I give you promises other than
milk, honey, liberty.
I assume you will always
be a free man with a dream.

Implicitly, "Conditions XXIV" strips away the public pomp and spectacle of the wedding ceremony to reveal its most fundamental level: desire. By capping on the wedding ceremony, Hemphill places homoerotic desire on an equal plane with heterosexuality.

Signifying on the Church

Historically religion has served as a liberating force in the African American community. Black slaves publicly and politically declared that Christianity and the institution of slavery were incompatible as early as 1774, according to Albert Raboteau in *Slave Religion*. "In that year," Raboteau notes, "the governor of Massachusetts received 'The Petition of a Grate Number of Blacks in this Province who by divine permission are held in a state of slavery within the bowels of a free and Christian Country.' "[49] In the petition slaves argued for their freedom by combining the political rhetoric of the Revolution with an appeal to the claims of Christian fellowship. Christian churches were some of the first institutions blacks created and owned in the United States. From 1790 to 1830 ambitious northern free black men like Richard Allen and Absalom Jones circumvented racism by creating new Christian denominations, notably the African Methodist Episcopal and the African Methodist Episcopal Zion churches.

The organized black church, however, has not been free from oppressing its constituents. Historically, the black church has practiced sexism. In her 1849 narrative, Jarena Lee, a spiritual visionary and a free black woman, reported having her desire to preach thwarted by her husband and Rev. Richard Allen.[50] Lee, however, overcame the objections of men by claiming that her instructions came directly from God; thus, those instructions superseded the sexist prohibitions of men. Some contemporary black churches and their ministers have adopted heterosexist policies and have openly made homophobic remarks. In an essay which appeared in the gay anthology *Black Men/White Men,* Leonard Patterson, a black gay minister, movingly wrote about how he was forced to leave Ebenezer Baptist Church in Atlanta, Georgia. Patterson's troubles at Ebenezer began when Reverend Joseph Roberts replaced Reverend Martin L. King, Sr. Roberts objected to the fact that Patterson's white lover also attended Ebenezer. Moreover, Patterson was guilty of not playing the game: "I was told, in effect, that as long as I played the political game and went with a person who was more easily passed off as a 'cousin,' I would be able to go far in the ministry. Perhaps I should even marry and have someone on the side. Apparently these arrangements would make me more 'respectable.' "[51] For refusing to play the political game, Patterson states that he was "attacked verbally from the pulpit, forbidden to enter the study for prayer with the other associate ministers, and had seeds of animosity planted against [him] . . . in the minds of certain members so that in meetings with them the subject of homosexuality would inevitably be brought up."[52] Patterson recounts an extremely offensive remark made to him by a church member one Sunday: "If you lie down with dogs, you get up smelling like dirt."[53] Patterson and his lover finally left Ebenezer. Although disillusioned with organized religion, Patterson writes encouragingly that what he and his lover experienced at Ebenezer has "given us more strength to love each other and others."[54]

Exorcism is a practice used to oppress gays in the church. The late Pentecostal minister and professor, Reverend James Tinney, underwent an exorcism when he came out as a gay man. Tinney briefly mentions the experience in his essay "Struggles of a Black Pentecostal," which was originally published in a 1981 issue of *Insight.* Five years later in *Blackbird* Duplechan signifies on Tinney's reflections on exorcism. It should be noted that Duplechan was probably familiar with Tinney's essay. Both that essay and Duplechan's short story "Peanuts and the Old Spice Kid" appeared in Michael Smith's anthology *Black Men/White Men.*

The events which precipitate the exorcism are similar in *Blackbird* and in Tinney's essay. Both Tinney and Duplechan's protagonist, Johnnie Ray Rousseau, are aware of their sexual identity. Tinney writes that he was aware of his homoerotic feelings "even at the age of four."[55] Johnnie Ray's exorcism is preceded by an enjoyable first sexual experience with the older bi-ethnic Marshall Two Hawks McNeil, a college student. Publicly stating and affirming their sexual identity actually causes the exorcisms. Put another way, their exorcisms are punishments for stating that they practice "the love that dares not speak its name." Tinney announced to his wife of three years that he was gay. Her reaction set into motion the events that caused the exorcism: "She immediately called the pastor and his wife and other close confidants to pray for me."[56] Johnnie Ray's exorcism was set into motion by two events. First, his confidential confession to Daniel Levine, the youth minister, that he had gay feelings. Then, Levine's betrayal of the confidential confession to Johnnie Ray's parents provoked the second event: the teenager's affirmation of his sexual identity to his parents in the presence of the minister.

Tinney does not discuss the events of his exorcism. In fact, he limits the actions of his wife, minister, and church members to one sentence: "Pray and talk and counsel they did."[57] Tinney's description of the exorcism is brief, but the event left him traumatized. The exorcism, he wrote, "was extremely painful to my own sense of worth and well-being. It was an experience I would not wish upon anyone ever."[58]

Duplechan signifies explicitly and implicitly on Tinney's remark "Pray and talk and counsel they did." Explicitly Duplechan "reads" Tinney by giving a fuller narrative description of the praying, talking, and counseling of the church people. Implicitly, Duplechan's "reading" of Tinney is a critique of the clergy and the values of the middle class. Further, Duplechan's "reading" is an example of what Smitherman calls heavy signifying, "a way of teaching or driving home a cognitive message but . . . without preaching or lecturing."[59]

Let us consider Duplechan's "read" or "heavy signifying" of each of the three terms—pray, talk, and counsel—as they occur in the confrontation between Johnnie Ray and the church people—his parents and the youth minister. The confrontation about Johnnie Ray's homosexuality happens at his home. Duplechan shows that prayer is often a means of ensuring conformity. In an emotional outburst Johnnie Ray's mother asks the teen: "Have you asked him? Have you asked the savior to help you? . . . Have you prayed every day for help? Every day?"[60] When Johnnie Ray answers no, his mother incredulously asks him, "Don't you want to be normal?"[61] Normality, which is conforming to existing value structures, is believed by the middle classes to be what will guarantee them success in the world. Johnnie Ray's mother reveals that she is less concerned with his happiness than she is with his possibilities of success. To insure his success, she and her husband must use talk to force Johnnie Ray to become normal. Talk, thus, is a means of intimidation. When Johnnie Ray claims that he has accepted it as a fact that he is gay, his mother intimidates him by "loud talking":

> You probably think you're real cute . . . going to Daniel [the youth minister] with this "I think I'm a homosexual" crap, and now sittin' here and tellin' us you've *accepted* that you're gay. . . . Lord ha' mercy today! I don't know what I coulda done to give birth to a *pervert*.[62]

While Johnnie Ray's mother uses "loud talking" to intimidate her son, his father cries. When his father finally talks, it is a mixture of intimidation and compassion: "You're no pervert," he says. "No son of mine is gonna be a pervert. You're just a little confused."[63] Finally, there is the expert, Reverend Levine, who offers counsel. Levine, however, is a scoundrel. Although he has betrayed Johnnie Ray's confidence, he sits throughout the entire family crisis "looking as holy and righteous at having done so as my parents looked utterly devastated at the news."[64] Levine is able to sit "in beatific calm" because of the family's unhappiness.[65] In other words, the family crisis that Levine has provided proves that the ministry is necessary. Levine's expert counsel to the family, which they reluctantly agree upon, is an exorcism—"a deliverance from unclean spirits."[66]

By signifying on Tinney, Duplechan exposes an unholy alliance between the church and the middle classes. The church is eager to oppress gay people to prove its worth to the middle classes. For the sake of conformity which, with hope, leads to success, the middle class is willing to oppress its children. The middle class, thus, is denounced for its willingness to use the church to further its ambitions.

In the short story "Cut Off from among Their People," Craig G. Harris does a "heavy sig" on the black family which also signifies on strategies from slave narratives. The story takes place at the funeral of Jeff's lover, who has died of complications from AIDS. Both the family and the church, two major institutions in the heterosexual African American community, are allied against Jeff. The lover's biological family has "diplomatically" excluded Jeff from the decisions about the funeral. At the funeral Jeff is ignored by the family and humiliated by the church. The lover's mother stares at him contemptuously. Jeff is not allowed to sit with the family. The minister chosen by the family only adds to Jeff's humiliation. The minister is asked not to wear his ceremonial robes but instead to wear an ordinary suit.

The "heavy sig" is done by using irony. The minister is exposed as a scoundrel, similar to Levine in *Blackbird*. At the funeral he delivers a homophobic sermon from the book of Leviticus:

> In Leviticus, Chapter 20, the Lord tell [*sic*] us: If a man lie with mankind as he lieth with a woman, both of them have committed an abomination: they shall surely be put to death; their blood shall be upon them. There's no cause to wonder why medical science could not find a cure for this man's illness. How could medicine cure temptation? What drug can exorcise Satan from a young man's soul? The only cure is to be found in the Lord. The only cure is repentance, for Leviticus clearly tells us, ". . . whoever shall commit any of these abominations, even the souls that commit them shall be cut off from among their people."[67]

After the funeral Jeff is abandoned and left to his own devices to get to the burial site. His humiliation is relieved by a sympathetic undertaker who offers Jeff a ride to the burial site. Ironically, it is the undertaker, the caregiver to the dead—not the minister, who is the caregiver to the living—who offers Jeff the compassion he so desperately needs. Denouncing both the family and the church, the undertaker's remarks to Jeff become the authentic sermon in the story:

> I lost my lover to AIDS three months ago. It's been very difficult—living with these memories and secrets and hurt, and with no one to share them. These people won't allow themselves to understand. If it's not preached from a pulpit and kissed up to the Almighty, they don't want to know about it. So, I hold it in, and hold it in, and then I see us passing, one after another—tearless funerals, the widowed treated like nonentities, and these "another faggot burns in hell" sermons. My heart goes out to you brother. You gotta let your love for him keep you strong.[68]

As a result of Harris's use of ironic signifying, one is left to ponder the meaning of the story's title, "Cut Off from among Their People." Who is cut off from their people? The story immediately implies that black gays are oppressed because they are alienated from their families. The opposite, however, is also true: Black families are oppressors, are alienated from their gay children, and thus, suffer. Black families suffer because their oppression robs them of a crucial sign of humaneness: compassion. By their oppression, the family of Jeff's deceased lover has lost the ability to be compassionate.

Harris's strategy—the cost of oppression is the loss of humanity—signifies on slave narratives by authors such as Frederick Douglass. Slave owners' loss of compassion, the sign of humaneness, is a recurring theme in Frederick Douglass's 1845 narrative. Slavery, Douglass contended, placed in the hands of whites "the fatal poison of irresponsible power."[69] Douglass gives numerous grisly examples of his contention: murderous overseers, greedy urban craftsmen, and raping masters. But perhaps none of his examples is meant to be as moving as that of his slave mistress, Mrs. Auld. Originally a woman of independent means, Douglass describes her before "the fatal poison of irresponsible power" took full control of her:

> I was utterly astonished at her goodness. I scarcely knew how to behave towards her. She was entirely unlike any other white woman I had ever seen. I could not approach her as I was accustomed to approach other white ladies. My early instruction was all out of place. The crouching servility, usually so acceptable a quality in a slave, did not answer when manifested toward her. Her favor was not gained by it; she seemed to be disturbed by it. She did not deem it imprudent or unmannerly for a slave to look her in the face. The meanest slave was put fully at ease in her presence, and none left without feeling better for having seen her. Her face was made of heavenly smiles, and her voice of tranquil music.[70]

Mrs. Auld even disobeyed the law and taught Douglass some rudiments of spelling. However, Douglass states, "Slavery proved as injurious to her as it did to me. . . . Under its influence, the tender heart became stone, and the lamblike disposition gave way to one of tiger-like fierceness."[71]

"Cut Off from among Their People" is an extraordinary act of "heavy signifying." By using a strategy similar to Frederick Douglass's, Harris equates heterosexism and homophobia with slavery. For upholding heterosexism and homophobia, the church and the black family are oppressors. As rendered by Harris, they are like the Mrs. Auld of Douglass's narrative. They are kind to the black gay man when he is a child, and corrupted by intolerance years later. Their oppression has robbed them of compassion. The black family and their church, thus, have lost the sign of humanity.

Gender Configurations

The last section of this essay examines gay men and the problem of gender configurations. Specifically, in the black literary tradition gay men have been objects of ridicule for not possessing masculine-appearing behaviors. This ridicule was especially evident in the militant Black Power movement of the 1960s and 1970s. The militancy that characterized that movement placed an enormous emphasis on developing black "manhood." Manhood became a metaphor for the strength and potency necessary to overthrow the oppressive forces of a white racist society. Images of pathetic homosexuals were often used to show what black manhood was not or to what it could degenerate. For example, Haki Madhubuti (Don L. Lee) wrote in "Don't Cry Scream":

> swung on a faggot who politely
> scratched his ass in my presence.
> he smiled broken teeth stained from
> his over-used tongue, fisted-face.
> teeth dropped in tune with ray
> charles singing "yesterday."[72]

Concurrent with the Black Power movement's image of manhood was the development of the urban tough, loud, back-talking gay black man. This stereotype was seen on the Broadway stage in Melvin Van Peeble's *Ain't Supposed to Die a Natural Death,* but it was most clearly articulated by Antonio Fargas's character, Lindy, in the film *Car Wash*. When the black militant Abdullah accused Lindy of being another example of how the white man has corrupted the black man and robbed him of his masculinity, Lindy responded, "Honey, I'm more man than you'll ever be and more woman than you'll ever get." Lindy was a gratifying character because he was tough and articulate, yet his character was not revolutionary. Vito Russo comments in *The Celluloid Closet:* "Lindy is only a cartoon—[his] effect in the end was just that of the safe sissy who ruled the day in the topsy-turvy situations of Thirties comedies."[73] But the stereotype of the tough, loud, back-talking effeminate black gay man as an object of ridicule is revised in works by Samuel Delany, George Wolfe, and Billi Gordon.

Delany signifies on such a stereotype in a section of *The Motion of Light in Water* called "A black man. . . ? A gay man. . . ?" The section's title itself suggests the dilemma of a bifurcated identity that Julius Johnson discusses in his doctoral dissertation "Influence of Assimilation on the Psychosocial Adjustment of Black Homosexual Men."[74] Johnson documented the fact that some African American brothers become "black gay men" while others become "gay black men"; the designation often underscores painful decisions to have primary identities either in the black or in the gay community.

Delany's first memory of a gay black man was Herman, an outrageously effeminate musician who played the organ in his father's mortuary. As a child, Delany admits that he was as confused as he was amused by Herman's aggressive antics. When a casket delivery man asked Herman if he was "one of them faggots that likes men," Herman quickly signified on the man:

> "Me? Oh, chile', chile', you must be ill or something! . . . I swear, you must have been workin' out in the heat too long today. I do believe you must be sick!" Here he would feel the man's forehead, then removing his hand, look at the sweat that had come off on his own palm, touch his finger to his tongue, and declare, "Oh, my lord, you are tasty! . . . Imagine, honey! Thinkin' such nastiness like that about a woman like me! I mean, I just might faint right here, and you gonna have to carry me to a chair and fan me and bring me my smellin' salts!" Meanwhile he would be rubbing the man's chest and arms.[75]

Ultimately Delany's attitude toward Herman was one of ambivalence. Delany's sig on the stereotype was his recognition of its artifice. He recognized that there were many unanswered questions about Herman's sexual life: "Had he gone to bars? Had he gone to baths? . . . Had there been a long-term lover, waiting for him at home, unmet by, and unmentioned to, people like my father whom he worked for?"[76] Herman had played a role to survive in a heterosexist and homophobic world. In that role "Herman had a place in our social scheme," Delany wrote, "but by no means an acceptable place, and certainly not a place I wanted to fill."[77] Thus, as a teen, Delany remembered that he did not see Herman as a role model for a man. As an adult, however, Delany's opinion of Herman changed. He did not see Herman as a role model, but, he stated, "I always treasured the image of Herman's outrageous and defiant freedom to say absolutely anything. . . . Anything except, of course, I am queer, and I like men sexually better than women."[78]

In *The Colored Museum,* George Wolfe introduces Miss Roj, a black transvestite "dressed in striped patio pants, white go-go boots, a halter and cat-shaped sunglasses."[79] Wolfe makes it clear that Miss Roj is a subject most appropriate for African American literature by signifying, perhaps deliberately, on Ralph Ellison's *Invisible Man.* In particular, he signifies on its prologue, to create a powerful social comment on the alienation of the black urban poor. Wolfe's character, Miss Roj, comments that she "comes from another galaxy, as do all snap queens. That's right," she says, "I ain't just your regular oppressed American Negro. No-no-no! I am an extra-terrestrial, and I ain't talkin none of that shit you seen in the movies."[80] Compare that with the first two sentences in the prologue of *Invisible Man:* "I am an invisible man. No, I am not a spook like those who haunted Edgar Allan Poe; nor am I one of your Hollywood-movie ectoplasms."[81] Ellison's nameless protagonist lives in a hole lit by 1,369 bulbs; Miss Roj, whose real name the audience never learns, inhabits every Wednesday, Friday, and Saturday night a disco with blaring lights called the Bottomless Pit, "the watering hole for the wild and weary which asks the question, 'Is there life after Jherri-curl?' "[82] In Ellison's prologue the protagonist gets high on marijuana; Miss Roj gets drunk on Cuba libres [perhaps a veiled reference to popular drinks in the early 1950s, which is when *Invisible Man* was written] and proceeds *to snap,* that is, "when something strikes . . . [one's] fancy, when the truth comes piercing through the dark, well you just can't let it pass unnoticed. No darling. You must pronounce it with a snap [of the fingers]."[83]

Ellison's protagonist almost beats a man to death for calling him a nigger. Of course, one wonders how one can be beaten by invisibility. In a scene with a provocation and an outcome similar to Ellison's, Miss Roj "snaps" (signifies) on an assailant. She states:

> Like the time this asshole at Jones Beach decided to take issue with my culotte-sailor ensemble. This child, this muscle-bound Brooklyn thug in a skin-tight bikini, very skin-tight so the whole world can see that instead of a brain, God gave him an extra-thick piece of sausage. You know the kind who beat up on their wives for breakfast. Well he decided to blurt out while I walked by, "Hey look at da monkey coon in da faggit suit." Well, I walked up to the poor dear, very calmly lifted my hand and . . . (rapid snaps) A heart attack, right there on the beach. You don't believe it?[84]

Ellison's prologue ends with the protagonist listening to Louis Armstrong's "What Did I Do to Be So Black and Blue?"; the lights fade on Miss Roj dancing to Aretha Franklin's "Respect." As white Americans must have been puzzled, outraged, and even guilt-stricken after reading Ellison's *Invisible Man,* so too is the effect Miss Roj has had on the assimilated blacks Wolfe chose to confront. During performances of *The Colored Museum,* black audience members have verbally attacked the actor playing Miss Roj and African American intellectuals have lambasted Wolfe for either not portraying blacks in their "best light" or for demeaning women.[85]

One of the oddest works to appear in black gay culture is Billi Gordon's cookbook, *You've Had Worse Things in Your Mouth.* The title itself is an act of signifying. While one may think it odd to include a cookbook here, it is important to keep in mind that that mode of presentation has been used to create social history in two other books by Afro-Americans. National Public Radio commentator and self-styled writing griot Vertamae Smart Grosvenor came to public prominence [with] her 1970 *Vibration Cooking; or the Travel Notes of a Geechee Girl.* The format of the book itself was signifying on the published travel narratives of eighteenth- and nineteenth-century whites such as Frederick Law Olmsted, whose observations on slavery have been treated by some historians as more reliable than artifacts actually left by the slaves. Norma Jean and Carole Darden's 1978 *Spoonbread and Strawberry Wine* was as much a family history of North Carolina middle-class blacks as it was a compendium of recipes.

Like George Wolfe, Gordon signifies repeatedly on racial stereotypes and on middle-class culture. On the cover of his cookbook, Gordon, a three-hundred-pound-plus dark-skinned black man, appears in drag. But not just any drag. He is wearing a red kerchief, a red-and-white checkered blouse, and a white apron, calling to mind some combination of Aunt Jemima and Hattie McDaniel in *Gone with the Wind.* As if that were not enough, Gordon signifies in every way imaginable on the American cultural stereotype of mammies as sexless, loyal, no-nonsense creatures. Gordon's character is lusty, vengeful, and flirtatious. Gordon appears in pictures surrounded by adoring muscled, swimsuit-clad white men; she wears bikini swimsuits, tennis outfits, long blond wigs, huge rebellious Afro-wigs, and shocking lamé evening wear. As for recipes, one is quite reluctant to try any of them, particularly those from the section called "Revenge Cooking" in which the ingredients include laxatives, seaweed, and entire bottles of Tabasco sauce. Billi Gordon signifies on the American stereotype of the mammy by reversing it and turning it upside down: His depiction of a mammy with a sex life is far from loyal, and certainly his character cannot and/or does not want to cook.

Conclusion: Toward a Black Gay Aesthetic

Restricted by racism and heterosexism, writers such as Samuel Delany, Larry Duplechan, Essex Hemphill, Craig G. Harris, George Wolfe, and Billi Gordon have begun to create a literature that validates our lives as black and as gay. My critical reading of this literature relied upon techniques based in the African American tradition of signifying. The writers discussed in this essay are some of the newest members of the African American literary tradition. Clearly, they also seek to revise the aesthetics of that tradition. Homophobia and heterosexism are oppressive forces which must be eliminated from the social, scientific, critical, and imaginative writings within the African American literary tradition.

NOTES

1. Daniel Garrett, "Other Countries: The Importance of Difference," in *Other Countries: Black Gay Voices,* ed. Cary Alan Johnson, Colin Robinson, and Terence Taylor (New York: Other Countries, 1988), p. 27.
2. Henry Louis Gates, Jr., *The Signifying Monkey: A Theory of African American Literary Criticism* (New York: Oxford University Press, 1988), p. 111.
3. Lorraine Hansberry, *A Raisin in the Sun* (New York: New American Library, 1958), p. 79.
4. Cogent discussions of homophobia among Black American intellectuals can be found in Cheryl Clarke, "The Failure to Transform: Homophobia in the Black Community," in *Home Girls: A Black Feminist Perspective,* ed. Barbara Smith (New York: Kitchen Table Press, 1983), pp. 197–208; Ann Allen Shockley, "The Illegitimates of Afro-American Literature," *Lambda Rising Book Report,* 1, no. 4: 1+.
5. Mary Helen Washington, *Invented Lives* (Garden City, N.Y.: Doubleday, 1987).
6. Gates, *The Signifying Monkey,* p. 81.
7. Geneva Smitherman, *Talkin and Testifyin* (Boston: Houghton Mifflin, 1977), p. 120.
8. Smitherman, *Talkin and Testifying,* p. 121.
9. Claudia Mitchell-Kernan, "Signifying as a Form of Verbal Art," in *Mother Wit from the Laughing Barrel: Readings in the Interpretation of Afro-American Folklore,* ed. Alan Dundes (Englewood Cliffs, N.J.: Prentice-Hall, 1973), p. 314.
10. Molefi Kete Asante, *Afrocentricity: A Theory of Social Change* (Buffalo, N.Y.: Amulefi, 1980), p. 66.
11. Asante, *Afrocentricity,* p. 64.
12. Frantz Fanon, *Black Skin, White Masks,* trans. Constance Farrington (New York: Grove Press, 1963), p. 84.
13. Alvin Poussaint, "What Makes Them Tick," *Ebony,* October 1978, p. 79.
14. Quoted in Georges-Michel Sarotte, *Like a Brother, Like a Lover: Male Homosexuality in the American Novel and Theatre from Herman Melville to James Baldwin,* trans. Richard Miller (New York: Doubleday, 1978), p. 94.
15. Eldridge Cleaver, *Soul on Ice* (New York: Random House, 1969), p. 174.
16. Nathan Hare and Julia Hare, *The Endangered Black Family: Coping with the Unisexualization and Coming Extinction of the Black Race* (San Francisco: Black Think Tank, 1984), p. 65.
17. Hare and Hare, *The Endangered Black Family,* p. 65.
18. Toni Morrison, *The Bluest Eye* (New York: Holt, Rhinehart & Winston, 1970), p. 132.
19. Toni Morrison, *Tar Baby* (New York: Random House, 1981), p. 216.
20. Toni Morrison, *Beloved* (New York: Random House, 1988), p. 10.
21. Ibid.
22. Ibid.
23. Esteban Montejo, *The Autobiography of a Runaway Slave,* trans. Jocasta Innes, ed. Miguel Barnet (New York: Random House, 1968), p. 21.
24. Ibid., p. 41.
25. Ibid.
26. Ibid.
27. Ibid.
28. Ibid.
29. Ibid.
30. Ibid.
31. On the social practices surrounding the sexuality of slaves, see: John Blassingame, *The Slave Community: Plantation Life in the Antebellum South* (New York: Oxford University Press, 1979), pp. 154–191; Eugene Genovese, *Roll, Jordan, Roll: The World the Slaves Made* (New York: Random House, 1974), pp. 458–475; Mary Helen Washington, *Invented Lives: Narratives of Black Women: 1860–1960* (New York: Doubleday, 1987), pp. 4–8; Deborah Gray White, *Ar'n't I a Woman? Female Slaves in the Plantation South* (New York: Norton, 1985), pp. 142–160.
32. Jonathan Ned Katz, *Gay American History: Lesbians and Gay Men in the U.S.A.* (New York: Avon Books, 1976), p. 35; Jonathan Ned Katz, *Gay/Lesbian Almanac: A New Documentary* (New York: Harper & Row, 1983), p. 61.
33. Katz, *Gay American History,* pp. 35–3C.

34. Ibid., p. 61.
35. A. Leon Higginbotham, Jr., *In the Matter of Color: Race and the American Legal Process: The Colonial Period* (New York: Oxford University Press, 1978), pp. 281–282; Katz, *Gay/Lesbian Almanac,* p. 61.
36. Martin Bauml Duberman, "Writhing Bedfellows," in *About Time: Exploring the Gay Past* (New York: Gay Presses of New York, 1986), pp. 13–14.
37. Tom Horner, *Jonathan Loved David: Homosexuality in Biblical Times* (Philadelphia: Westminster Press, 1978), pp. 91–99.
38. For example, toward the end of *The Normal Heart,* one of the indignities that befall a deceased person with AIDS is to be cremated by a black undertaker "for a thousand dollars, no questions asked" (p. 106). The implication here is that the deceased was unable to have a decent or respectable burial, which would, of course, be by a white undertaker. This is significant because it is part of a tradition in Western aesthetics that associates blacks and Africans with indignity. This also reflects an instance of racism by the author.
39. An interesting case occurred in a serious article in the gay male pornography magazine *Stallion.* The author, Charles Jurrist, criticized the gay literary establishment for its exclusion of or, when included, stereotypical depiction of black men. However, the article perpetuated a stereotype by featuring a series of pictures of a spectacularly endowed Black man.
40. W. E. B. Du Bois, review of *Quicksand* by Nella Larson and *Home to Harlem* by Claude McKay, *Crisis* 35 (June 1928): 202; quoted in Lovie Gibson, "Du Bois's Propaganda Literature: An Outgrowth of His Sociological Studies," doctoral dissertation, State University of New York at Buffalo, 1977, p. 21.
41. Washington, *Invented Lives,* pp. xxiii–xxiv.
42. Michael G. Cooke, *Afro-American Literature in the Twentieth Century: The Achievement of Intimacy* (New Haven: Yale University Press, 1984), p. 95.
43. Samuel R. Delany, *The Motion of Light in Water* (New York: Morrow, 1988), p. 129.
44. Ibid., p. 175.
45. Ibid., p. 176.
46. William H. Grier and Price M. Cobbs, *Black Rage* (New York: Basic Books, 1968), pp. 91–100.
47. Larry Duplechan, *Eight Days a Week* (Boston: Alyson Publications, 1985), p. 28.
48. Essex Hemphill, *Conditions* (Washington, D.C.: Be Bop Books, 1986).
49. Albert Raboteau, *Slave Religion: The "Invisible Institution" in the Antebellum South* (New York: Oxford University Press, 1978), p. 290.
50. Jarena Lee, *Religious Experience and Journal of Mrs. Jarena Lee, Giving an Account of Her Call to Preach the Gospel* (Philadelphia, 1849); found in Ann Allen Shockley, *Afro-American Women Writers, 1746–1933* (New York: New American Library, 1988).
51. Leonard Patterson, "At Ebenezer Baptist Church," in *Black Men/White Men,* ed. Michael Smith (San Francisco: Gay Sunshine Press, 1983), p. 164.
52. Ibid., pp. 164–165.
53. Ibid., p. 165.
54. Ibid., p. 166.
55. James S. Tinney, "Struggles of a Black Pentecostal," in *Black Men/White Men,* ed. Michael Smith (San Francisco: Gay Sunshine Press, 1983), p. 167.
56. Ibid., p. 170.
57. Ibid.
58. Ibid., pp. 170–171.
59. Smitherman, *Talkin and Testifyin,* p. 120.
60. Larry Duplechan, *Blackbird* (New York: St. Martin's, 1986), p. 152.
61. Ibid., p. 153.
62. Ibid., p. 151.
63. Ibid., p. 153.
64. Ibid., p. 150.
65. Ibid., p. 152.
66. Ibid., p. 155.
67. Craig G. Harris, "Cut Off from among Their People," in *In the Life,* ed. Joseph Beam (Boston: Alyson Publications, 1986), p. 66.
68. Ibid., p. 67.

69. Frederick Douglass, *Narrative of the Life of Frederick Douglass: An American Slave* (1845; New York: New American Library, 1968), p. 48.
70. Ibid.
71. Ibid., pp. 52–53.
72. Haki Madhubuti, "Don't Cry Scream," quoted in Smitherman, *Talkin and Testifyin,* p. 142.
73. Vito Russo, *The Celluloid Closet: Homosexuality in the Movies* (New York: Harper & Row, 1981), p. 229.
74. Julius Marcus Johnson, "Influence of Assimilation on the Psychosocial Adjustment of Black Homosexual Men," doctoral dissertation, California School of Professional Psychology at Berkeley, 1981.
75. Delany, *Motion of Light,* p. 219.
76. Ibid., p. 221.
77. Ibid., p. 220.
78. Ibid., p. 223.
79. George Wolfe, *The Colored Museum,* in *American Theatre,* ed. James Leverett and M. Elizabeth Osborn, February 1987, p. 4.
80. Ibid.
81. Ralph Ellison, *Invisible Man* (New York: New American Library, 1952), p. 7.
82. Wolfe, *Colored Museum,* p. 4.
83. Ibid.
84. Ibid.
85. See Thulani Davis, "Sapphire Attire: A Review," *Village Voice,* Nov. 11, 1986, p. 91; Roger Fristoe, "George C. Wolfe," *Louisville Courier-Journal,* p. I1; Jack Kroll, "Zapping Black Stereotypes," *Newsweek,* Nov. 17, 1986, p. 85.

Acknowledgments (continued from copyright page)

Amiri Baraka. "Malcolm as Ideology." Copyright © 1992 from *Malcolm X: In His Own Image* by Joe Wood. Reprinted with permission of St. Martin's Press, Incorporated.

Mary McLeod Bethune. "A Century of Progress of Negro Women." From *Black Women in White America,* edited by Gerda Lerner, New York: Random House, 1973, pp. 579–584. Reprinted with permission of The Amistad Research Center, New Orleans, LA.

Gwendolyn Brooks. "A Bronzeville Mother Loiters in Mississippi. Meanwhile, a Mississippi Mother Burns Bacon," "The Bean Eaters," "The Children of the Poor." From *Selected Poems* by Gwendolyn Brooks. Reprinted by permission of Gwendolyn Brooks. "The Boy Died in My Alley." From *Beckonings* by Gwendolyn Brooks. Detroit: Broadside Press, 1975. Reprinted by permission of Broadside Press.

Sterling Brown. All lines from "Children of the Mississippi," "Return," and "Sharecroppers" from *The Collected Poems of Sterling A. Brown* by Michael S. Harper, Editor. Copyright © 1980 by Sterling A. Brown. Reprinted by permission of HarperCollins Publishers, Inc.

William Wells Brown. Excerpt from *Clotel, or, The President's Daughter.* Permission given by Ayer Company Publishers, Inc., N. Stratford, NH 03590.

Marcus Bruce. "Black and Blue: W. E. B. DuBois, Race, and the Meaning of Blackness." Reprinted by permission of the author.

Octavia Butler. "The River," excerpt from *Kindred.* Reprinted by permission of Writers House, Inc. Copyright © 1979 by Octavia Butler.

Hazel V. Carby. "Rethinking Black Feminist Theory," pp. 3–19. From *Reconstructing Womanhood: The Emergence of the Afro-American Woman Novelist* by Hazel V. Carby. Copyright © 1987 by Oxford University Press, Inc. Reprinted by permission.

Barbara Christian. "Alice Walker: The Black Woman Artist As Wayward" from *Black Women Writers (1950–1980)* by Mari Evans. Copyright © 1983 by Mari Evans. Used by permission of Doubleday, a division of Bantam Doubleday Dell Publishing Group, Inc.

Wanda Coleman. "Dear Mama (2)," "In This Waking," and "Shopping Bag Lady." Copyright © 1983 by Wanda Coleman. Reprinted from *Imagoes* with the permission of Black Sparrow Press.

Pearl Cleage. *Hospice.* Copyright © 1986 by Pearl Cleage. All inquiries concerning the play should be addressed to the Author's agent ROSENSTONE/WENDER, 3 E. 48th St., New York, NY 10017.

Suzan D. Johnson Cook. "God's Woman." From *Those Preachin Women,* Volume 1, edited by Ella Pearson Mitchell, Valley Forge: Judson Press, 1985, pp. 119–126. Used by permission of Judson Press.

J. California Cooper. "Happiness Does Not Come in Colors." From *Homemade Love* by J. California Cooper. Copyright © 1986 by J. California Cooper. Reprinted by permission of St. Martin's Press, Inc., New York, NY.

Countee Cullen. "Heritage," "Yet Do I Marvel," and "From the Dark Tower." Reprinted by permission of GRM Associates, Inc., Agents for the Estate of Ida M. Cullen from *Color* by Countee Cullen. Copyright © 1925 by Harper & Brothers; copyright renewed 1953 by Ida M. Cullen. "The Wise." Reprinted by permission of GRM Associates, Inc., Agents for the Estate of Ida M. Cullen from *Copper Sun* by Countee Cullen. Copyright © 1927 by Harper & Brothers; copyright renewed 1955 by Ida M. Cullen.

Angela Davis. "We Do Not Consent: Violence against Women in a Racist Society," from *Women, Culture and Politics* by Angela Davis. Copyright © 1984, 1985, 1986, 1987, 1988, 1989 by Angela Davis. Reprinted by permission of Random House, Inc.

Rita Dove, "Particulars," "After Reading *Mickey in the Night Kitchen* for the Third Time before Bed," and "Your Death." Reprinted from *Grace Notes, Poems* by Rita Dove, by permission of W. W. Norton & Company, Inc. Copyright © 1989 by Rita Dove.

W. E. B. Du Bois. "The Talented Tenth," taken from *The Negro Problem: A Series of Articles by Representative Negroes of Today,* pp. 33–75. Originally published by James Pott & Company, 1903. Reprinted by permission of Ayer Company Publishers, P.O. Box 958, Salem, NH 03079.

"The Souls of White Folk," originally from *Darkwater: Voices from within the Veil*. Published by Harcourt Brace, 1920; reprinted in 1975 by Kraus-Thomson. Reprinted with permission of Kraus International Publications.

Henry Dumas. Loretta Dumas and Eugene B. Redmond for "Afro-American" and "Black Star Line." Reprinted from *Knees of a Natural Man: The Selected Poetry of Henry Dumas*. Edited and with an Introduction by Eugene B. Redmond. New York: Thunder's Mouth Press, 1989. Copyright © 1989–1994 by the Henry Dumas Estate.

Paul Laurence Dunbar. "We Wear the Mask" and "Sympathy." From *The Negro Caravan*, edited by Sterling Brown, et. al., New York, Arno Press, 1970. Book available from Ayer Company Publishers, P.O. Box 958, Salem, NH 03079.

Michael Eric Dyson. "The Culture of Hip-Hop." Reprinted by permission of the author.

Ralph Ellison. "What America Would Be Like without Blacks," from *Going to the Territory* by Ralph Ellison. Copyright © 1986 by Ralph Ellison. Reprinted by permission of Random House, Inc.

Jessie Fauset. 7 pages from "Mary Elizabeth" by Jessie Fauset from *Calling the Wind* by Clarence Major. Copyright © 1993 by Clarence Major. Reprinted by permission of HarperCollins Publishers, Inc.

Siedah Garrett & Glen Ballard. "The Man in the Mirror." © 1987 Yellowbrick Road Music, MCA Music Publishing, a Division of MCA Inc. and Acrostation Corporation. All Rights on behalf of Yellowbrick Road Music administered by WB Music Corp. All Rights Reserved. Used by permission of Warner Bros. Publications U.S. Inc., Miami, Fl. 33014.

Marcus Garvey. "An Appeal to the Conscience of the Black Race to See Itself," from Amy Jacques Garvey, ed., *The Philosophy and Opinions of Marcus Garvey* (Dover, MA: The Majority Press, 1986), first pub. in 1923 and 1925.

Henry Louis Gates, Jr. "The Blackness of Blackness" by Henry Louis Gates, Jr. First appeared in *Critical Inquiry*. Copyright © 1987 by Henry Louis Gates, Jr. Reprinted by permission of Brandt & Brandt Literary Agents, Inc. and Methuen & Company.

Marvin Gaye. "What's Going On." Reprinted by permission of Jobete Music Company, Inc.

Nikki Giovanni. "True Import of Dialogue: Black versus Negro" from *Black Feeling, Black Talk, Black Judgment*, copyright © 1968, 1970. "Age" and "Adulthood II," from *Cotton Candy on a Rainy Day*, copyright © 1978. "Love: Is a Human Condition" from *Those Who Ride the Night Winds*, copyright © 1983 by Nikki Giovanni. By permission of William Morrow & Company, Inc.

Sutton Griggs. Excerpt from *Imperium in Imperio*. Copyright © Mnemosyne Publishing Company, University of Miami, PO Box 248008, Coral Gables, FL 33124. Reprinted with permission.

Robert Hayden. "Night, Death, Mississippi" and "El-Hajj Malik El-Shabazz (Malcolm X)." Reprinted from *Collected Poems of Robert Hayden*, edited by Frederick Glaysher, by permission of Liveright Publishing Corporation. Copyright © 1985 by Erma Hayden.

Chester Himes. "One More Way to Die." Reprinted by permission of Roslyn Targ Literary Agency, Inc. Copyright © 1973 by Chester Himes (*Black on Black*); Copyright © 1990 by Lesley Himes (*The Collected Stories of Chester Himes*).

bell hooks. "Revolutionary Black Women: Making Ourselves Subject." From *Black Looks* by bell hooks. Boston: South End Press, 1992. Reprinted by permission of the publisher.

Pauline Elizabeth Hopkins. "A Dash for Liberty" from *Short Fiction by Black Women, 1900–1920*, edited by Elizabeth Ammons, pp. 243–247. Copyright © 1991 by Oxford University Press, Inc. Reprinted by permission.

Langston Hughes. "As I Grew Older," "Afro-American Fragment," "Mother to Son," "Georgia Dusk," and "Democracy." From *Selected Poems* by Langston Hughes. Copyright 1926, 1927, 1948 by Alfred A. Knopf, Inc. Copyright © 1959 by Langston Hughes. Copyright © 1967 by Arna Bontemps and George Houston Bass. Copyright renewed 1954, 1955 by Langston Hughes. Reprinted by permission of Alfred A Knopf, Inc.

Zora Neale Hurston. "Sweat." Reprinted by permission of The Hurston Estate. "Why Negroes Are Black," "Why Women Always Take Advantage of Men," "Ole Massa and John Who

Wanted to Go to Heaven," and "What Smelled Worse." From *Mules and Men* by Zora Neale Hurston. Copyright 1935 by Zora Neale Hurston. Copyright renewed 1963 by John C. Hurston and Joel Hurston. Reprinted by permission of HarperCollins Publishers, Inc.

Jesse Jackson. "Common Ground and Common Sense" (Speech delivered at the Democratic National Convention, July 20, 1988), pp. 649–653. From *Vital Speeches of the Day,* Volume 54, August 15, 1988, Issue #21. Reprinted with permission.

Charles Johnson. "Being and Race," from *Being and Race* by Charles Johnson, Bloomingdale: Indiana University Press, 1988. Reprinted by permission of Indiana University Press.

Fenton Johnson. "The Ethiopian's Song" and "To an Afro-American Maiden." Reprinted from *A Little Dreaming* by Fenton Johnson. Published by McGrath Publishing Company, 1913 (reprinted 1969). Reprinted with permission of Ayer Company Publishers, Inc., N. Stratford, NH 03590.

Gayl Jones. "White Rat." From *White Rat: Short Stories* by Gayl Jones. Copyright © 1971, 1973, 1975, 1977 by Gayl Jones. Reprinted by permission of Random House, Inc.

Barbara Jordan. "Who Then Will Speak for the Common Good?" (Speech as keynote address to the Democratic National Convention, July 12, 1976), pp. 645–646. From *Vital Speeches of the Day,* Volume 42, August 15, 1976, Issue #21. Reprinted with permission.

George Kent. "Gwendolyn Brooks' Poetic Realism" from *Black Women Writers (1950–1980)* by Mari Evans. Copyright © 1983 by Mari Evans. Used by permission of Doubleday, a division of Bantam Doubleday Dell Publishing Group, Inc.

Martin Luther King, Jr. "Love, Law, and Civil Disobedience." From *The Oratory of Negro Leaders 1900–1968,* edited by Marcus H. Boulware, © 1969, pp. 258–270. Published by Negro Universities Press, an imprint of Greenwood Publishing Group, Inc., Westport, CT. Reprinted with permission.

Etheridge Knight. "For Freckle-Faced Gerald," "Dark Prophecy: I Sing of Shine," and "For Black Poets Who Think of Suicide" are reprinted from *The Essential Etheridge Knight,* by Etheridge Knight, by permission of the University of Pittsburgh Press. © 1986 by Etheridge Knight.

Nella Larsen. "Passing" excerpt from *Quicksand and Passing* (Nella Larsen), Deborah E. McDowell, ed., copyright © 1986 by Rutgers, The State University.

David Levering Lewis. "The Harlem Renaissance" (Introduction to *The Portable Harlem Renaissance Reader*). Reprinted by permission of Harold Ober Associated Incorporated. Copyright © 1994 by David Levering Lewis.

Audre Lorde. "Age, Race, Class, and Sex: Women Redefining Difference," Copyright © 1984 by Audre Lorde from *Sister Outsider* published by The Crossing Press, Freedom, CA 95019.

Haki Madhubuti. "But He Was Cool or: he even stopped for green lights." From *Don't Cry, Scream* by Haki Madhubuti, Third World Press. "Womenblack: We Begin with You" and "Black Manhood: Toward a Definition." From *Earthquake and Sunrise Missions* by Haki Madhubuti, Third World Press, 1984. Reprinted with permission.

Malcolm X. Excerpts from *The Autobiography of Malcolm X* by Malcolm X with Alex Haley. Copyright © 1964 by Alex Haley and Malcolm X. Copyright © 1965 by Alex Haley and Betty Shabazz. Reprinted by permission of Random House, Inc.

Claude McKay. "If We Must Die," "White House," and "America." Reprinted by permission of the Archives of Claude McKay, Carl Cowl, Administrator, from *Selected Poems* by Claude McKay, Harcourt Brace, 1979.

Terry McMillan. "Zora" from *Disappearing Acts* by Terry McMillan. Copyright © 1989 by Terry McMillan. Used by permission of Viking Penguin, a division of Penguin Books USA Inc.

Toni Morrison. "Recitatif." Copyright © 1983 by Toni Morrison. Reprinted by permission of Toni Morrison.

Walter Mosley. Excerpt from *Devil in a Blue Dress.* Reprinted from *Devil in a Blue Dress* by Walter Mosley, with the permission of W. W. Norton & Company, Inc. Copyright © 1990 by Walter Mosley.

Jess Mowry. "Crusader Rabbit." Copyright © 1992, Jess Mowry. All other rights reserved. Reprinted by permission of Jess Mowry.

Cecil L. Murray. "Making an Offer You Can't Refuse," May 1992. Courtesy of the Reverend Cecil L. Murray.

Gloria Naylor. "Lucielia Louise Turner," from *The Women of Brewster Place* by Gloria Naylor. Copyright © 1980, 1982 by Gloria Naylor. Used by permission of Viking Penguin, a division of Penguin Books USA Inc.

Larry Neal. "The Black Arts Movement," by Larry Neal from *The Black Aesthetic* (1971), edited by Addison Gayle, Jr. Reprinted by permission.

Charles I. Nero. "Toward a Black Gay Aesthetic: Signifying in Contemporary Black Gay Literature" was originally published in *Brother to Brother: New Writings by Black Gay Men,* ed. Essex Hemphill (Boston: Alyson, 1991). Copyright © 1991 by Charles I. Nero. Reprinted with permission of Charles I. Nero.

Itabari Njeri. Excerpts from *Every Goodbye Ain't Gone* by Itabari Njeri. Copyright © 1982, 1983, 1984, 1986, 1990 by Itabari Njeri. Reprinted by permission of Random House, Inc.

Dana Owens. "U.N.I.T.Y." © 1993 Queen Latifah Music, Inc., written by Dana Owens. Reprinted with permission of Flavor Unit Management.

Ann Petry. "The Witness." Reprinted by permission of Russell & Volkening as agents for the author. Copyright © 1971 by Ann Petry.

Public Enemy. "Fight the Power." Produced by The Bomb Squad, Hank Shocklee, Carl Ryder, Eric (Vietnam) Sadler and Keith Shocklee. © 1989, 1990 Def Jam Recordings. Manufactured and marketed by Def Jam Recordings, New York, N.Y. Distributed by Polygram Group Dist. Inc., N.Y., N.Y. All rights reserved. Reprinted by permission of Def Jam Recordings and Vernon Brown & Co.

Ishmael Reed. Excerpt from *Japanese by Spring*. Reprinted with the permission of Atheneum Publishers, an imprint of Macmillan Publishing Company from *Japanese by Spring* by Ishmael Reed. Copyright © 1993 by Ishmael Reed.

Sonia Sanchez. "Blk/Rhetoric" and "Summer Words of a Sistuh Addict" by Sonia Sanchez. From *I've Been a Woman,* Black Scholar Press, 1978. Reprinted by permission of Sonia Sanchez. "elegy," from *Under a Soprano Sky,* by Sonia Sanchez, 1987, is reprinted with permission from the publisher, Africa World Press, Inc. All rights reserved.

Gil Scott-Heron. "The Revolution Will Not Be Televised." Published by permission of Third World Press. P.O. Box 19730, Chicago, IL 60619. (312) 651–0700.

Ron Simmons. "Some Thoughts on the Challenges Facing Black Gay Intellectuals." Copyright Ron Simmons, Ph.D. Reprinted with permission of the author from *Brother to Brother: New Writings by Black Gay Men,* ed. Essex Hemphill (Boston: Alyson, 1991).

Valerie Smith. "Form and Ideology in Three Slave Narratives." For permission to photocopy this selection, please contact Harvard University Press. Reprinted by permission of the publishers from *Self Discovery and Authority in Afro-American Narrative* by Valerie Smith, Cambridge, Mass.: Harvard University Press, copyright © 1987 by the President and Fellows of Harvard College.

Anne Spencer. "White Things" and "Black Man O' Mine." Reprinted from J. Lee Greene, *Time's Unfading Garden: Anne Spencer's Life and Poetry,* with the permission of J. Lee Greene.

"St. Louis Blues," "Mamie's Blues," and **"Hard Times Blues,"** from *The Negro Caravan* edited by Sterling Brown, et. al., New York: Arno Press, 1970. Book available from Ayer Company Book Publishers, P.O. Box 958, Salem, NH, 03079.

Mary Church Terrell. "What Role Is the Educated Woman to Play in the Uplifting of Her Race?" pp. 151–156. From *Quest for Equality: The Life and Writings of Mary Eliza Church Terrell, 1863–1954,* volume 13, edited by Beverly Washington Jones, Brooklyn, New York: Carlson Publishing, Inc., 1990.

Michael Thelwell. "Toward Collective Visions: Issues in International Literary Criticism." Reprinted by permission of Michael Thelwell.

Wallace Thurman. Excerpt from "Emma Lou," from *The Blacker the Berry* by Wallace Thurman, pp. 9–15, 25–45. Published by Arno Press, New York, 1969. Book available from Ayer Company Publishers, PO Box 958, Salem, NH 03079.

Jean Toomer. Excerpt from "Theater." Reprinted from *Cane* by Jean Toomer, by permission of Liveright Publishing Corporation. Copyright 1923 by Boni & Liveright. Copyright renewed 1951 by Jean Toomer.

Kwame Toure [Stokely Carmichael] and Charles Hamilton. "Black Power: Its Need and Substance." From *Black Power* by Stokely Carmichael and Charles V. Hamilton. Copyright © 1967 by Stokely Carmichael and Charles Hamilton. Reprinted by permission of Random House, Inc.

Quincy Troupe. "South African Bloodstone" © 1972/1993 Quincy Troupe. "After Hearing a Radio Announcement" © 1991 Quincy Troupe, from *Weather Reports: New and Selected Poems,* Harlem River Press. Reprinted by permission of Quincy Troupe.

Derek Walcott. "Storm Figure" from *The Arkansas Testament* by Derek Walcott. Copyright © 1987 by Derek Walcott. Reprinted by permission of Farrar, Straus and Giroux, Inc. "Blues" from *The Gulf* by Derek Walcott. Copyright © 1970 by Derek Walcott. Reprinted by permission of Farrar, Straus and Giroux, Inc.

Alice Walker. "Her Sweet Jerome" from *In Love & Trouble: Stories of Black Women,* copyright © 1970 by Alice Walker, reprinted by permission of Harcourt, Brace & Company. "A Sudden Trip Home in the Spring" from *You Can't Keep a Good Woman Down,* copyright © 1971 by Alice Walker, reprinted with permission of Harcourt Brace & Company. Excerpt from *The Color Purple,* copyright © 1982 by Alice Walker, reprinted by permission of Harcourt Brace & Company.

Phillis Wheatley. "On the Death of a Young Gentleman," and "To S. M., A Young African Painter, on Seeing His Works." Reprinted from *The Poems of Phillis Wheatley.* Revised and Enlarged Edition. Edited with an Introduction by Julian D. Mason, Jr. Copyright © 1989 by The University of North Carolina Press. Used by permission.

John Edgar Wideman. "Doc's Story." From *Fever* by John Edgar Wideman. Copyright © 1989 by John Edgar Wideman. First Published in *Esquire,* 1986. Reprinted by permission of Henry Holt and Company, Inc.

August Wilson. "Fences" by August Wilson. Copyright © 1986 by August Wilson. Used by permission of Dutton Signet, a division of Penguin Books USA Inc.

John A. Williams. "Son in the Afternoon." From *Best Short Stories by Negro Writers,* edited by Langston Hughes, published by Little, Brown, and Company, 1967. Used by permission of the Author. © 1962, 1976.

Stevie Wonder. "Living for the City." Reprinted by permission of Jobete Music Company, Inc.

Jay Wright. "The Appearance of a Lost Goddess" and "Benjamin Banneker Helps to Build a City," from *Soothsayers and Omens,* published by Seven Woods Press, 1976. Copyright © 1976 by Jay Wright. "Journey to the Place of Ghosts," from *Elaine's Book,* published by the University Press of Virginia, 1988. Copyright © 1986 by Jay Wright. Reprinted with permission.

Richard Wright. "The Man Who Killed a Shadow." From *Eight Men* by Richard Wright. Copyright © 1987.

Index of Authors and Titles